DIARMAID MacCULLOCH

Thomas Cromwell
A Life

ALLEN LANE
an imprint of
PENGUIN BOOKS

ALLEN LANE

UK | USA | Canada | Ireland | Australia
India | New Zealand | South Africa

Allen Lane is part of the Penguin Random House group of companies
whose addresses can be found at global.penguinrandomhouse.com

First published 2018
004

Copyright © Diarmaid MacCulloch, 2018

The moral right of the author has been asserted

Set in 10.2/13.5 pt Sabon LT Std
Typeset by Jouve (UK), Milton Keynes
Printed and bound in Great Britain by Clays Ltd, Elcograf S.p.A.

A CIP catalogue record for this book is available from the British Library

ISBN: 978–1–846–14429–5

In Memoriam G. R. Elton

Contents

PART FOUR
Power and its Reward

PART FIVE
Nemesis

List of Illustrations

TEXT ILLUSTRATIONS

PLATES

Maps

Cromwell's Europe

SCOTLAND

• Edinburgh

North Sea

Ireland

Dublin •

• York

Wales

ENGLAND

London •

Calais •

Low Countries

Mü

• Bergen o

Antwerp

Cologne

Frankfurt ar

• Paris

Strassbur

ATLANTIC OCEAN

Blois •

Loire

Basel

Zü

• Genev

FRANCE

Rhône

Bilbao •

NAVARRE

PORTUGAL

SPAIN

ARAGON

CASTILE

Granada

M e d i t e r r a n e a n   S e

N

200 miles
400 km

LIVONIA

NMARK

Teutonic
Order

amburg
en

Vistula

OLY

•Wittenberg

n   Saxony

P O L A N D

MAN

•Prague

•Nuremberg

BOHEMIA

burg
•
ugsburg

PIRE

HUNGARY

Venice•

Bologna
•

PAPAL

Florence•

STATES

O T T O M A N

Danube

ome•

ITALY

Adriatic Sea

E M P I R E

Naples•

English Tudor Counties & Wales

N

25

Newcastle upon Tyne
Carlisle
7
11 • Durham
40
Lancaster •
• York 39
41 Humber
19
St Asaph
• Bangor
5
Chester
8 26
• Lincoln
21
• Beddgelert
Derby Nottingham
31
• Stafford
28
23
Shrewsbury
20
Oakham
• Norwich
29
Leicester
EAST
Ludlow
34
17 Huntingdon
Warwick 24
4 ANGLIA
37
• Northampton
Severn
• Worcester
• Cambridge 32
15
Bedford • 1
• Ipswich
Hereford •
Brecon •
27 Aylesbury
Hertford
• St David's
Lordship of Rhymney
Gloucester
16
12 • Chelmsford
Monmouth
13
Thames Oxford 3
22
Llanishen
Reading •
LONDON •
Llandaff •
36
2
38
• Maidstone
30
14
18
Salisbury
• Winchester
33
• Taunton
10
• Lewes
9
Dorchester
Exeter •
FRANCE
Bodmin •
6
English Channel
0   50 miles
0   50 km

1 Bedfordshire	10 Dorset	19 Lancashire	28 Rutland	37 Worcestershire
2 Berkshire	11 Durham	20 Leicestershire	29 Shropshire	38 Surrey
3 Buckinghamshire	12 Essex	21 Lincolnshire	30 Somerset	39 East Riding
4 Cambridgeshire	13 Gloucestershire	22 Middlesex	31 Staffordshire	40 North Riding } Yorkshire
5 Cheshire	14 Hampshire	23 Norfolk	32 Suffolk	41 West Riding
6 Cornwall	15 Herefordshire	24 Northamptonshire	33 Sussex	
7 Cumberland	16 Hertfordshire	25 Northumberland	34 Warwickshire	
8 Derbyshire	17 Huntingdonshire	26 Nottinghamshire	35 Westmorland	
9 Devon	18 Kent	27 Oxfordshire	36 Wiltshire	

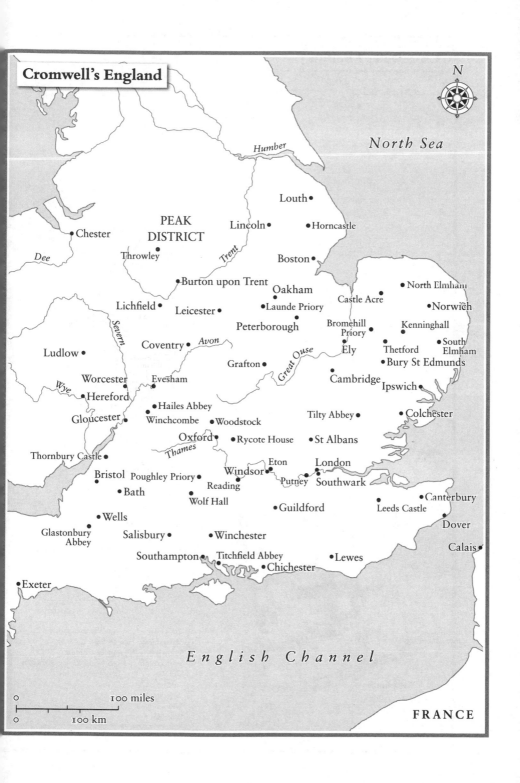

Cromwell's England

N

North Sea

Louth

PEAK
DISTRICT
Lincoln • Horncastle
Chester
Dee Throwley
Boston
• North Elmham
Burton upon Trent
Oakham
Lichfield Leicester • Laude Priory Castle Acre • Norwich
Peterborough Bromehill Kenninghall
Priory
Coventry • *Avon* Ely Thetford South
Ludlow Grafton Bury St Edmunds Elmham
Worcester Evesham Cambridge Ipswich
Hereford
Wye Hailes Abbey Tilty Abbey • Colchester
Gloucester Winchcombe Woodstock
Oxford • Rycote House • St Albans
Thornbury Castle *Thames* Eton London
Bristol Poughley Priory Windsor
Bath Reading Putney Southwark
Wolf Hall Canterbury
Wells Guildford Leeds Castle
Glastonbury Salisbury • Winchester Dover
Abbey
Southampton Titchfield Abbey Calais
Chichester Lewes
Exeter

Severn

Trent

Humber

Great Ouse

English Channel

0 100 miles
0 100 km

FRANCE

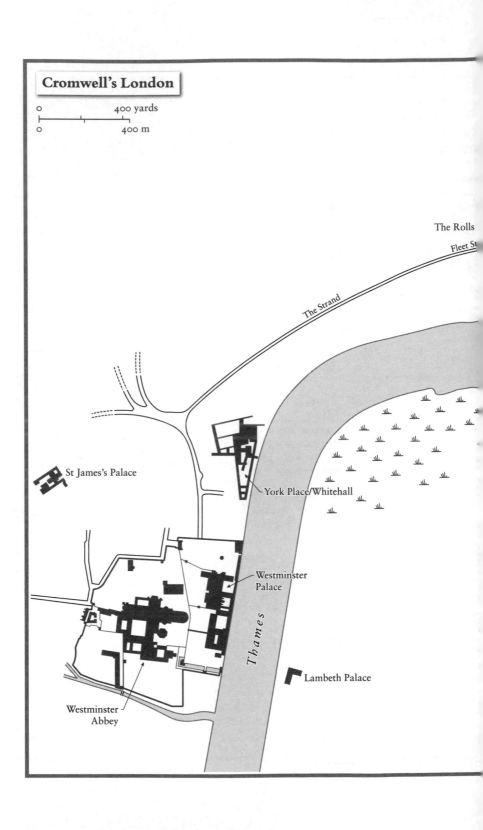

Cromwell's London

0   400 yards

0   400 m

The Rolls

Fleet St

The Strand

St James's Palace

York Place/Whitehall

Westminster
Palace

Thames

Lambeth Palace

Westminster
Abbey

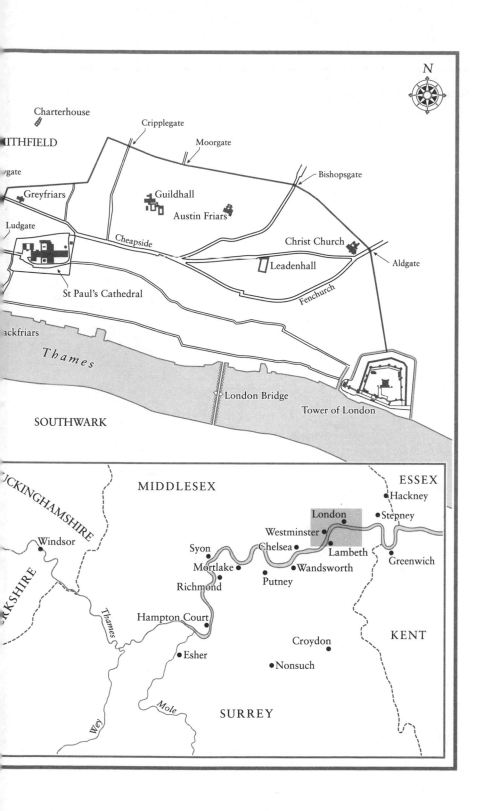

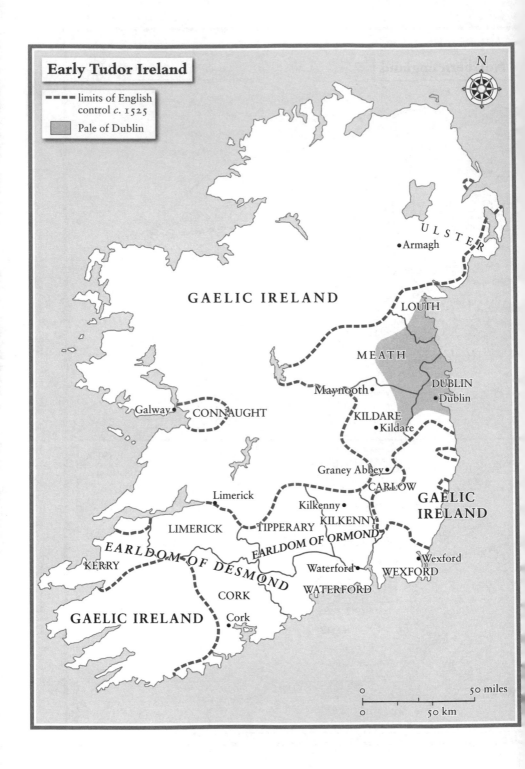

Early Tudor Ireland

- - - limits of English control *c.* 1525
Pale of Dublin

N

U L S T E R
•Armagh

GAELIC IRELAND

LOUTH

MEATH

Maynooth •
DUBLIN
•Dublin

Galway • CONNAUGHT
KILDARE
• Kildare

Graney Abbey •
CARLOW
GAELIC
IRELAND

Limerick •
Kilkenny •

LIMERICK
TIPPERARY
KILKENNY
EARLDOM OF ORMOND

EARLDOM OF DESMOND
Wexford •

KERRY
Waterford •
WEXFORD

CORK
WATERFORD

GAELIC IRELAND
• Cork

0   50 miles
0   50 km

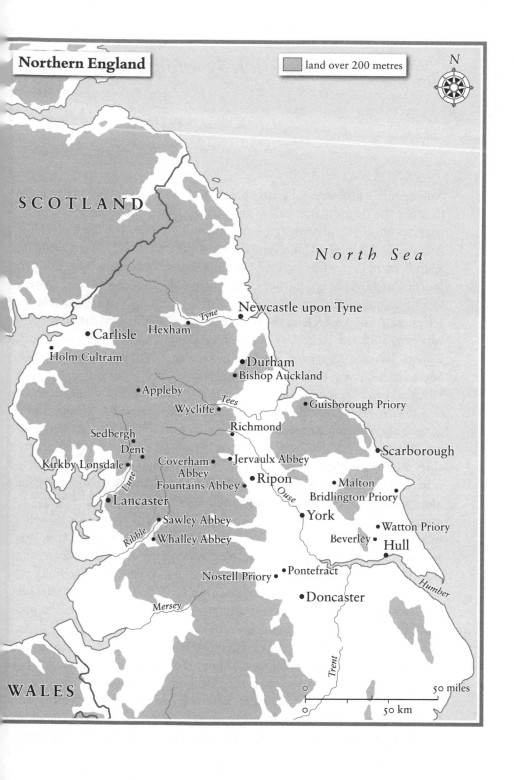

Northern England

land over 200 metres

N

SCOTLAND

North Sea

Tyne

Hexham   Newcastle upon Tyne

• Carlisle

• Holm Cultram

• Durham
• Bishop Auckland

• Appleby

Tees

Wycliffe •   • Guisborough Priory

Richmond •

Sedbergh •   • Scarborough
  Dent •
Kirkby Lonsdale •   Coverham • • Jervaulx Abbey
                    Abbey
  Lune   Fountains Abbey •   • Ripon   • Malton
                                    Ouse   Bridlington Priory •
• Lancaster

  • Sawley Abbey   • York
Ribble   • Whalley Abbey   • Watton Priory
              Beverley • • Hull

    Nostell Priory • • Pontefract

Mersey   • Doncaster   *Humber*

Trent

50 miles

WALES   50 km

Acknowledgements

Among many professional debts spread over many years (and I have more to say in the Introduction below and *passim* about one particular debt), I must mention the generosity of the following fellow-scholars: Caroline Adams, Rod Ambler, Colin Armstrong, Giulia Bartrum, Susan Brigden, Alan Brown, James Carley, Paul Cavill, Margaret Condon, John Cooper, Judith Curthoys, Mark Earngey, Teri Fitzgerald, Andrew Foster, Dorian Gerhold, Jeremy Goldsmith, Steven Gunn, John Guy, Jane Ingle, Henry Jefferies, Anik Laferrière, Rory McEntegart, Hilary Mantel, Martin Murphy, Richard Rex, David Skinner, David Starkey, Thomas Steel, Robert Swanson, Spencer Weinreich, Rowan Williams, Robert Yorke. Some, particularly Colin Armstrong, James Carley, John Cooper, Teri Fitzgerald and Steven Gunn, have heroically read some or all of the draft text, to its great advantage. Besides these, I am grateful to scholars who gave me permission to use unpublished dissertations listed at the end of my Bibliography, and to well-informed friends on Facebook who gave me clues on various queries I posted. In this hugely enjoyable if taxing adventure, Teri Fitzgerald and Hilary Mantel have been particularly stimulating and generous intellectual companions, and it was a pleasure to get to know Ben Miles, who lent to his stage portrayal of Thomas Cromwell a wonderful energy worthy of Till Eulenspiegel. Equally instructive, and equally informative about the complex personality of Master Secretary, was the introspection and unknowability presented by the television performance of Mark Rylance. It was a very kind thought of the late Jill, Duchess of Hamilton, to give me a portrait of Thomas Cromwell to preside over my writing in my study.

One magnificent project has made my own work not simply easier but possible: the website *State Papers Online, 1509–1714*, published by Cengage/Gale in collaboration with the National Archives and the British Library. This digital arrangement of hundreds of thousands of documents from the Tudor and Stuart era has involved many of our leading historians in its construction and maintenance. I remember refereeing it enthusiastically when financial backing was being canvassed for its creation, but I had little idea how accurate my words of praise would turn out to be. It is one of the great scholarly achievements of the modern age, and I salute those academics and technicians who steered it to fruition. I have looked at many other primary sources for this book, but *State Papers Online* has been indispensable. And it is thanks to the magnificent resources and generosity of the University of Oxford and the Bodleian Library under successive Bodley's Librarians Sarah Thomas and Richard Ovenden that I have been afforded the luxury of digital access to this, and much more.

Behind that work lies another monument of Victorian and Edwardian scholarship, *Letters and Papers Foreign and Domestic, Henry VIII*: a staggering intellectual achievement, whose many editors and researchers I salute with awe and gratitude. Frequently they made mistakes and misdated documents, but they fully acknowledged that this would be the case, and encouraged their readers to do better. It is a pity that subsequent historians have so often ignored their admonition and accepted many suggested dates without the critical eye that they recommended. I would like to couple with my gratitude for their work the products of three modern scholars who single-handed have produced astonishingly useful works of reference with heroism worthy of those great Victorians. I say something of Muriel St Clare Byrne below; Sir John Baker's *The Men of Court* and Professor David Smith's *Heads of Religious Houses 1377–1540* are both marvellous gifts to research.

My colleagues in the Faculty of Theology and Religion in the University of Oxford deserve my warm thanks for their constant forbearance in allowing me to get on with this book rather than asking me to assume more administrative burdens. I am especially grateful to the Hensley Henson Fund of the Faculty for making a generous contribution to the provision of its illustrations, after a version of part of the text became the University's Hensley Henson Lectures for 2017–18. As always, I must thank for their patience and encouragement my literary agent Felicity Bryan and my editors Stuart Proffitt and Joy de Menil. Additionally in this enterprise I am hugely grateful to Peter James for his masterly copy-editing, Cecilia Mackay for her zestful picture research and Ben Sinyor, Richard Duguid and Stephen Ryan for general efficiency and unflappability. And Sam Patel knows what I owe him.

Diarmaid MacCulloch
Advent 2017

Thomas Cromwell was a freak in English history, and that, perhaps, is why he has been so disliked: an iron-fisted bureaucrat who crammed into his brief reign the kind of process which in England, we like to maintain, is carried out insensibly, over centuries. He overhauled the machinery of government as it had never been overhauled since the reign of Henry II; and he overhauled it so drastically that much of it was not radically altered till the reign of Victoria. In six hundred years of history he stands out as the most radical of modernisers. Modern history, if it begins anywhere, begins, in England, with him.

Hugh Trevor-Roper, *Historical Essays*, 1957

Introduction

Thomas Cromwell's name has happily become much more familiar in the last decade, thanks principally to Hilary Mantel's inspired novel series beginning with *Wolf Hall*. To call them 'historical novels' does them an injustice; they are novels which happen to be set in the sixteenth century, and with a profound knowledge of how that era functioned. Novels they remain, as Mantel herself has frequently (and with mounting weariness) emphasized to would-be critics. This book is different. It invites you, the reader, to find the true Thomas Cromwell of history, by guiding you through the maze of his surviving papers – and a real maze they are, composed of thousands on thousands of individual documents. The journey is worth making, because this Thomas Cromwell shaped a great revolution in his own country's affairs, which has in turn shaped much of the modern world, not least that still-Protestant power, the United States of America.

Cromwell may have wished to remain an enigma, yet the main reason that we find him enigmatic is not personal choice, but a particular archival circumstance. His papers were confiscated by the Crown when he was arrested in 1540, and that is why we still have them, divided now between the National Archives (where the Victorians unhelpfully re-arranged them from the original bundles) and the British Library, papers filched from the main hoard in the seventeenth century. Elsewhere there is no more than the scattering in the correspondence of others that one would expect of a great man of the realm in the early Tudor age. The confiscation is a stroke of luck for us, albeit not for him at the time. But there is a problem: when sifting through the vast collection (not including his formidable traces in the general administrative papers of Tudor government), one thing becomes obvious. From his muniment room, we have virtually exclusively the in-tray. Where outgoing letters from Cromwell himself survive in this collection, with a little experience one can usually account for their presence: by and large they reappeared at home at times when he was away, and were therefore filed as incoming and not

outgoing correspondence, or were returned by some conscientious official, coupled with an answer to questions they contained. Otherwise the
pattern, the vast absence, is quite consistent.

We might come to the casual conclusion that it would be logical for
Cromwell's archive to consist of the letters he received. But this is not
how Tudor archives worked. The same febrile atmosphere in spring 1540
that brought Cromwell to the scaffold resulted in a further private archive passing into the hands of the King: that of Arthur Plantagenet Lord
Lisle, Deputy of Calais, imprisoned in the Tower of London for reasons
which will become apparent in due course. In Lisle's voluminous papers
(superbly published and edited by a single-minded benefactor of Tudor
scholarship, Muriel St Clare Byrne, with an endearing partisanship for
her subject) we have both in-tray and out-tray. The latter is normally
represented by the last draft of the letter before my Lord signed a fair
copy for dispatch, often interestingly covered in second thoughts. This is
almost universally missing from Cromwell's papers.

If so slapdash and unbusinesslike a nobleman as Lord Lisle could adhere
to best archival practice of the day (true, he had an excellent staff and a
strong-minded, efficient wife), how much more would that be the case with
the mastermind of the Tudor Revolution in Government? So meticulous and
orderly a mind as Cromwell's would have made sure that his letters were
there, ready for reference in case of need. In fact there is inferential evidence
that his archive was organized into categories of in-tray and out-tray, through
the survival of a third category of document, his 'remembrances', slips of
paper providing us with a marvellous if often cryptic guide to his current
concerns: we find lists of topics to be dealt with and ticked off as done. A
few survive from the 1520s, but once he had gained power under the Crown
in the early 1530s, they are there as a regular series, available as needed for
reference, and described in the systematic catalogue of his papers made by
one of his clerks in 1533 as 'a bundle of my master's remembrances etc,
signed by the King'. That latter note suggests that, at least at this early date,
the remembrances were designed to enable orderly discussion in Cromwell's
meetings with King Henry. In 1536 the brother of one of his employees
knew of this collection, asking Cromwell to enter a request 'in your book of
remembrance' – we should here understand 'book' in the Tudor sense of a
sheet or two of paper.[1]

Such a vast loss of the out-tray can only be the result of deliberate
destruction. I hazard that when Cromwell's household heard of his arrest
in June 1540, they began a systematic process of destroying the out-tray
of his principal archive, much aided by the fact that two of his own officers were left in charge of it for least another year. Their hope would have

been to save their master from destruction, for a man is much more easily convicted by his own writings than by the letters he has received. The royal confiscation team would not initially have noticed the character of the huge quantities of papers deferentially presented for their inspection when they arrived at the door.[2] It was a good try, although it did not succeed. The result is that amid the torrent of paperwork through which the conscientious biographer wades to recapture what is left of Thomas Cromwell, the man's own voice is largely missing. We hear more of it out of Lord Lisle's papers than in Cromwell's own.

Hilary Mantel has sensitively captured this quality in Thomas Cromwell's archive in her novels: her Cromwell is pre-eminently an observer, even of himself, not 'I' but 'he'. After a day spent with Cromwell's papers, I have often felt alarmingly like Master Secretary, listening with increasing exhaustion to the cacophony of voices crackling out of the pages, wheedling, complaining, flattering, decorously demanding; bringing news of crisis, catastrophe or sometimes even good fortune. It is thus not surprising that so few of the recent attempts at biography of the man (some opportunistically inspired by Mantel's success) have succeeded in capturing much of him.

The man who knew more of Thomas Cromwell than anyone since his execution was the dedicatee of this book, Sir Geoffrey Elton. Elton was not an admirer of the biographical genre, which he regarded as frivolous. He chose to channel his admiration of his hero into meticulous accounts of administrative, governmental and constitutional change (on his first promotion to a chair in Cambridge, he chose the unfashionable title of Professor of English Constitutional History).[3] What he could have done is evident from his brilliant if contestable sketch of Cromwell's final tragedy, 'Thomas Cromwell's decline and fall'. Late in his career he bluntly said, in words which instantly recall those deep and almost accented tones, 'one reason why I haven't done what I have always been asked to do, which is to write a biography of Cromwell, is that he is *not biographable*.'[4]

It is a mark of Elton's exceptional quality as a graduate supervisor that he formed historians with the independence of mind to take on their *Doktorvater*'s work and remould it: to name but a few, John Guy, Virginia Murphy, Graham Nicholson and David Starkey. Occasionally during our private conversations in his last years, he would acknowledge with grace how they had modified the most expansive propositions of his younger days on the role of Thomas Cromwell. There may be more of the same here, and his opinion on biography will be flatly contradicted. It is therefore in conscious tribute to this great historian, patron and friend that I make my own hubristic attempt to fill the gap in biography, though I know his moustache might bristle and his glasses gleam dangerously at some of my conclusions. Many of my endnotes are a ghostly conversation with him, albeit lacking the hospitable single malts which did not lessen my usual state of intimidation in his presence. He taught me to privilege on every occasion the message of primary sources over those who have sought to interpret them, and in this book I have tried to follow his admonition (which I have to say he did not always observe himself).

Delving into the archives, I have gained a new respect for the very early historians of these events – Alexander Alesius, George Cavendish, John Foxe, Thomas Fuller, Edward Hall, Nicholas Harpsfield, Edward Lord Herbert of Chirbury and assorted Roman Catholic hagiographers. They have often been patronized by later writers, who have not fully understood what they were trying to say. We have to remember that many of them were *there*. We need to respect their observations, and comprehend their limitations and concerns. I am especially impressed by George Cavendish, pioneer of biography in the English language, and his gentleman-usher's-eye view of his master Thomas Wolsey.[5]

My primary purpose is not to write a history of England in the early sixteenth century, but to place Thomas Cromwell on that stage. The leading actor in the 1530s was not Cromwell but his king, Henry VIII, whose welfare and kaleidoscopic changes of mood would have occupied the thoughts of his minister for much of any day for an entire decade. But still, standing apart from that inescapable presence is my subject. Cromwell had his own preoccupations. Not the least of them was that of any Tudor statesman not a priest (though there were some exceptions there too, as we will see): securing immortality by fathering a dynasty. We will discover Cromwell's dynastic ambitions as one leading cause of his fall, though we may also consider his disaster inevitable at the Court of a master who beyond a certain point was almost impossible to serve successfully.

We will also explore the religious agenda of a statesman who has often been seen as Machiavellian, secular-minded or 'modern' (in a sense which now sounds old-fashioned for a twenty-first century depressingly marred by religious fanaticism). I will demonstrate how important Cromwell's religious agenda was in his political actions, how great a part it played in his destruction and how much can be recovered from his often elaborate efforts to conceal his religious motivation from the imperceptive, both then and now. I will also deliberately give a much more detailed and extensive account than any previous biographer of Cromwell of his life up to 1532–3, when his power suddenly became very great. I have chosen do this partly because there has been so much confusion and misdating of events in the first forty-five years of his life, partly because his sudden rise was so remarkable and puzzled so many observers at the time, and finally because I am convinced that the later stages of any life are usually best understood by what can be gleaned of the earlier. That is not to fall into the trap of trying to turn history into an amateurish form of psycho-biography; it's just common sense.

I have modernized virtually all quotations, unless original spelling makes some useful particular point, and modernized place-names and surnames. It is always enjoyable to speculate on Tudor pronunciation of surnames, which we occasionally catch fossilized in unexpected places, like the small state of the United States of America known as Delaware, which gives us one venerable title from the Tudor peerage – De La Warr – in phonetic form. In the process, it tells us how to pronounce de la Pole – Dellapool. In a related pronunciation, Henry VIII's cousin and eventual enemy Cardinal Reginald Pole was 'one brain-sick Poole, or . . . one witless fool', as Crom-well himself lets us know in a particularly bitter letter.[6] It is often thought that the contemporary spelling of Anne Bullen is an attempt to put down Henry VIII's second consort by those who hated her, but it probably simply indicates how her surname was pronounced. Many people wrote St Leger at the time as Sellinger, and today most St Clares are written down as Sinclair, though one has to be a resident of these islands to know by oral tradition that St John is Sinjun.

Thomas Cromwell's surname was generally spelled Crumwell by his English correspondents, and that must have reflected how they thought the name sounded. It is harder work to pronounce the 'w' in his surname after a short 'u' sound than with a short 'o' sound; try it for yourself. The name was indeed increasingly written as 'Cromwell' in official documents, and it is not surprising therefore that non-native speakers, mostly reading rather than hearing the name, did their best with formulations such as 'Cromuello'. Yet I think that John Buchan was correct in his haunting historical fantasy *The Blanket of the Dark* (which I commend to the young at heart) in styling him Crummle. The famous insults to him from the great explosion of rebel-lion in 1536, the Pilgrimage of Grace, really only work with that pronunciation: 'Crim, Cram and Rich . . .'; 'we would Crum him and Crum him that he was never so Crumwed.'[7] The last word on the subject can go to the King who both made him and destroyed him, writing in the closing days of June 1540 when his hatred and resentment were greatest towards his fallen minister: Henry VIII stripped the Earl of Essex he had created back to his birth surname, and wrote it in his own hand as 'Cromell'.[8]

Some technical details are useful to negotiate the story. Tudor folk, shar-ing the general illogicality of the human race, made a great celebration of New Year's Day on 1 January, but the year itself then changed on 25 March. All dates here are cited in New Style, converting the beginning of the year to 1 January without further comment. Then there is the complex question of money, puzzling even to those in the United Kingdom who still use pounds and pence. Tudor currency added to the mix another unit, the shilling, so the pound was not divided as now into a hundred pennies, but into 240 pennies, twelve of which made up a shilling – thus there were twenty shillings in a pound. Multipliers of Tudor money to our economy are difficult to make, for their emphases in purchasing were different, concentrating on clothing and food, and many people survived on their own resources of food and shelter without much input from wages. A contemporary wage-labourer might then earn nine pounds a year; the average gentleman's yearly income from land was around seventeen pounds, and a knight's around two hundred pounds. Those are useful measures in putting into perspective Thomas Cromwell's income in fees, wages or lands, or his land purchases, and the sorts of winnings which King Henry VIII made from Cromwell's help in dissolving monasteries.

Draft in Henry VIII's hand of questions to be put to Cromwell about the Cleves marriage, c. 29/30 June 1540; he heads it 'Questions to be axid of Thomas Cromell'. This document was in the section of the Cottonian manuscript collection badly damaged by fire at Ashburnham House in 1731.

PART ONE

Journeys

He that forsaketh his father shall come to shame; and he that defieth his mother, is cursed of God.

Ecclesiasticus 3.16, in the translation of
Miles Coverdale, 1535

Over against Fulham, on the Bank of the River Thames, is situated Putney, a small village, and famous for little, but giving birth to that remarkable instance of the inconstancy of fortune, Thomas Cromwell, son of a blacksmith of this place, raised from the anvil and forge to the most beneficial places, and highest honours in the nation . . .

John Aubrey, *The natural history and antiquities of the county of Surrey,* 1718

I

Ruffian

A time there was when a son was born to humble parents in the Surrey village of Putney, a place of little account, at a ferry crossing on the bank of the Thames, 6 miles upstream from the King's Palace of Westminster. He was a bright boy, so he left this place and had a wild youth, doing shocking things. But he became a man of great account, to make his family proud, and rose very high in the affairs of the realm. His name was Nicholas West, and he became Bishop of Ely.

Growing up in Putney, Thomas Cromwell would have been familiar with tales of this prodigal son; on the best calculations we can make, and they are not perfect, he was born some quarter of a century after West, around 1485.[1] His later career interestingly shadowed that of Bishop West. Nicholas did not rise quite so high as Thomas, but compensated by chalking up a much worse outrage in his youth: a splendidly gossipy seventeenth-century historian, Thomas Fuller, records that as a Cambridge undergraduate West burned down the Provost's Lodging of King's College.[2] That was poor thanks for his parents' achievement in sending him to a great university. Only the cleverest boys from such a modest background would make it to Oxford or Cambridge, perhaps with backing from some influential local cleric or interested patron. Putney had many possibilities of both, close as it was to the King's palace at Richmond and to a fine house of the Archbishop of Canterbury at Mortlake.

The Cromwells and the Wests were classified in fifteenth-century England's intricately stratified society as yeomen: busy industrious folk who liked to see their promising boys get on in the world, and who valued schooling as the key to advancement. Thomas Cromwell never had the advantage of a university education, but he more than made up for it by efforts of self-help, which remain utterly hidden from us. He was proud of his transformation, and we should take him seriously when he ruefully described his turbulent younger self to later friends such as Archbishop Thomas Cranmer as a 'ruffian', in the mould of the young Nicholas West.[3]

As we will see, he came to understand and practise English law, busy himself in commerce, speak many languages, act like a gentleman and even, in the end, like one of the highest nobles in the land. Like West, he would have started off learning the basics of reading (and, a little later, writing) in some informal school in his or the next village: perhaps courtesy of some chantry priest at Putney parish church, supplementing his modest income from saying masses for the dead by dinning the ABC and scraps of liturgical Latin into some bored boys, while they sought diversion from waterfront noises off. Then there may have been some instruction in Latin grammar at a local school, but for most of his astonishing accomplishments, Cromwell would be his own tutor. (See Plate 1.)

A yeoman like Thomas Cromwell's father Walter found many ways of prospering, aiming to do well enough to break through social barriers to the esteem of being thought a gentleman. As we will see, Walter's family hovered on that boundary. Any respectable way of making money would do; he had some land to farm around Putney and later in nearby Wandsworth and Roehampton, and he brewed beer on a commercial scale. That meant tavern-keeping near the waterfront, a good living at a time when the Thames was the equivalent of a modern main highway. Walter moved from Putney to Wandsworth around 1501; his property there included a water-mill, which could have been for either grain or cloth-fulling. Later memories were that he was also a blacksmith, and while perfectly possible, the idea may simply have arisen because the Cromwells, like a great many Tudor families humble and landed alike, doubled their distinctive surname with the alias of Smith. English surnames were still not altogether stable in those years, at any social level.[4]

If Putney was a place of little note, the unkind among Europe's sophisticates might say the same of early Tudor England. It was the largest kingdom in an archipelago of islands on the western margins of the continent, facing the Atlantic. At various times over the previous five centuries, its monarchs had built successive empires that bound it to mainland Europe and episodically embraced the other parts of the archipelago as well. Its distinctive language, English, reflected a history of invasions both inwards and outwards: English was a complex hybrid of Anglo-Saxon and Norse, with a strong overlay of Norman-French, and was difficult for outsiders to learn fluently because of its consequent lack of linguistic logic. It was nevertheless spoken widely in the Atlantic archipelago beyond English frontiers. In a northern kingdom ruled by the Stewart dynasty whom English kings never succeeded in permanently defeating, the Stewart monarchs united English-speakers with Gaels in an alliance of the unconquered, who found it useful to share a common identity as 'Scotland'. It is significant how little Scotland will feature in Thomas Cromwell's story, even in his years in government.

Wherever the English kings held sway, it was prudent to learn their language, so the Welsh, Cornish and Manx acquired it if they wanted to make a successful career beyond their own lands. Even some Gaels in the neighbouring island of Ireland did the same, for dealings with the ancient English-speaking enclaves in their midst, especially with English government based in the city of Dublin. Since the twelfth century English monarchs had maintained a rather unstable 'Lordship of Ireland' from Dublin, claiming a grant from the Pope in Rome for this amorphous dignity. Dublin's administration for the Lordship was modelled on England's royal government, though very old-fashioned by the standards of early Tudor Westminster. Ireland had occasional meetings of its own Parliament, representing the comparatively Anglicized territory around Dublin called 'the Pale', together with a scattering of English-style boroughs around the coasts, and other parts of the island that Anglo-Norman noblemen had conquered long ago; their descendants still lived in aristocratic pomp alongside the territories of the Gaelic chieftains. If anything united the much fragmented island, it was the shared institutions of the Western Latin Church: archbishops, bishops and monastic orders for Anglo-Irish and Gaels alike.

No one in mainland Europe bothered to learn the English language unless they had regular business with the subjects of the king of England. The English did produce remarkably good cloth for export; otherwise, there was not much point in making the effort. English folk remembered fondly various past imperial glories they had enjoyed beyond their shores. In memory of particularly cheering moments in this chequered story, when Henry II, Edward I or Edward III had commanded allegiance from Galway to Berwick to the Pyrenees, English monarchs were generally called Henry or Edward. After an especially glorious and exceptionally futile King Richard I (the Crusader 'Lionheart') in the twelfth century, neither of the two subsequent Richards could be counted a success.

In the sequence of generally shortlived English territorial conquests in mainland Europe, a last effort crashed in ignominy fifty years before Thomas Cromwell's birth. The Plantagenet dynasty ruling from London spent a century from the 1330s trying to displace the Valois dynasty ruling from Paris, with no more long-term success than against the Stewarts in Scotland. The English still massage their egos with the memory of occasional military victories on the way – Crécy, Poitiers, Agincourt – but the reality was that by 1453 they had been roundly expelled from

France, retaining only a toehold with some islands off the French coast, plus a heavily guarded coastal town called Calais, which defended the shortest sea-route to England towards Dover.

That mid-fifteenth-century defeat was a terrible humiliation for the Plantagenets, and it was one of the reasons that the royal line descended into murderous quarrels which for a while made Plantagenet England into something of a failed state. Out of civil wars between Plantagenet factions, Lancastrians and Yorkists, the least likely winner emerged, the grandson of a personable Welshman called Owen Tudor (ap Tewdwr in his native language), who had married the widow of martial hero King Henry V. Henry Tudor, Earl of Richmond, possessed the most tenuous of hereditary claims to the crown when he arrived in London in 1485, having killed the last Plantagenet king, Richard III, in battle at Bosworth in the English Midlands. Henry, to whom remaining Lancastrians looked in default of any more convincing candidate, was aided by the King's general unpopularity among the English nobility, who probably rightly blamed Richard for the mysterious death of the previous boy-king, Edward V.

As Henry VII, the new King spent a troubled quarter-century on the throne convincing his subjects that the decision in 1485 had been God's, though well aware that he needed to exercise his considerable personal talents to sustain that notion. His victory at Bosworth did suggest divine favour to pious contemporaries, but Henry backed up God's choice by marrying Elizabeth of York, daughter of King Edward IV. The Tudor dynasty was henceforward slightly more plausible in terms of royal descent. Henry's surviving son, eighth Henry on the English throne, grew up with a profound sense of divine favour for his crown; in this he was much encouraged by the intense piety of Henry VII's extremely capable mother, Lady Margaret Beaufort, whose political skill had done much to aid Heaven in the rise of the Tudors.

The second Tudor king nevertheless remained keenly conscious that some members of the English nobility also enjoyed a high quotient of Plantagenet blood. Like his father, Henry VIII paid due deference to the Church, which gave its blessing to the change of monarchs in 1485 just as it had done for each previous change. Ecclesiastical power and wealth in his kingdom were formidable. Around 600 religious houses – monasteries, nunneries, friaries, colleges devoted to soul-prayer – dotted the landscape, the immense value of their estates and rents never so far totalled. There were twenty-three magnificent cathedral churches for some of the most richly endowed bishoprics in the whole of Western Christendom, and thousands of parish churches, each financed by the levy of a tenth of farm produce (the 'tithe'). Monarchs like Henry VII and the young Henry VIII might cast envious eyes at the Church's wealth, but they did not seriously challenge churchmen's right to enjoy possessions which, in many cases, had been given by devout Anglo-Saxon kings and aristocrats before ever there was a single kingdom of England.

The Tudor kings nevertheless remained resentfully conscious of the constraints on their ability to raise revenue from their subjects. They were constantly hobbled by the fact that England had become a central-ized polity much earlier than other European kingdoms, and so its tax system, sophisticated by fourteenth-century standards, was now creaky and incapable of doing justice to the riches represented by England's farms and fisheries. Customary lay taxation was also dependent on the consent of meetings of commons, nobility and leading clergy in Parlia-ment, together with agreement to taxation on churchmen by two clerical assemblies which met in parallel to Parliamentary sessions, called Con-vocations.* Both Tudor Henrys spent much of their energy finding ways round these obstacles, and it was to be a major theme of the reign of Henry VIII, particularly since he much enjoyed spending money in spec-tacular ways – on palaces, castles, soldiers, ships, works of art and even books and manuscripts.

Henry became heir to the Tudor throne on the death of his teenage elder brother Arthur in 1502. He was formidable in his own way: tall even by our standards, good-looking, possessed of boisterous charm, and more intelligence than the average product of hereditary rule. When he succeeded his father in 1509 (Thomas Cromwell then being in his mid-twenties), the new King married Catalina, a Spanish princess of impeccable royal lineage whom Henry VII had originally acquired for Prince Arthur and who was too much of a dynastic asset to be lost when Arthur died. Such marriages of a deceased brother's wife were tricky in the law of the Western Church, but the marriage went ahead, despite doubts expressed by the Archbishop of Canterbury, William Warham. Katherine of Aragon proved a capable and popular queen, despite a worrying record of miscarriages or infant death in her essential duty of providing heirs for this still fragile dynasty. Yet even in the early 1520s, there was biological time to spare, and mean-while King Henry did his best to stride the European stage as if he were one of its really important monarchs, doing his best to equal the Valois

---

* The Convocation of the Province of Canterbury, the larger of the two bodies which repre-sented the clergy of the realm, met in London during Parliamentary sessions, the smaller Convocation of the Northern Province in York at around the same time. They both had upper and lower houses of clergy, in the same manner as peers and commons in Parliament.

King of France, the Habsburg Holy Roman Emperor or the Jagiellon King
of Poland-Lithuania.

In the first year of his reign, the King began promoting a talented
churchman, a former Fellow of Magdalen College Oxford, to more and
more responsibilities in government. Thomas Wolsey started his public
career as a protégé of one of old King Henry's principal advisers, Bishop
Richard Fox of Winchester. His chief duty came to be the promotion
of Henry's mission of self-glorification in constant European-wide diplomacy, but his general busy competence and appetite for good
administration won him his master's gratitude and even affection. Basking in royal approval, Wolsey gathered wealth, estates and honours.
Henry prevailed on the Pope to appoint him as a cardinal, and even made
two attempts to get Wolsey himself elected pope. Since there had not
been an English pope since Nicholas Breakspear in the twelfth century,
this was characteristic over-assertion, but the King did secure Wolsey the
office of special papal representative in England: legate *a latere* (literally,
'on the side', bypassing the power of Archbishop Warham). Henry also
promoted the Cardinal to be Lord Chancellor, the highest legal office in
the land. Wolsey's power outstripped that of everyone in the kingdom
under the sovereign, sidelining both Warham and his old patron Fox.

Not only these veteran councillors but England's leading noblemen
were furious at Wolsey's triumph. Nobles saw themselves as born royal
advisers, and deeply resented an upstart whose father had been no more
than a prosperous butcher and livestock-dealer in the provincial port
town of Ipswich. England in Tudor times was a society obsessed with
gradations of hierarchy and status (some say it still is), but there was nothing that outraged nobility and gentry could do while Wolsey continued to
please the King, and of course many of them hastened to profit from his
spectacular good fortune. The busy folk of Putney would see the Cardinal's barge passing upstream on the Thames as his great new palace of
Hampton Court, a gift from the King, took shape. There was much traffic
of the powerful along their river: the King himself, moving between the
ancient castle of Windsor and his array of palaces reaching down-river
beyond London to Greenwich; Archbishop Warham's barge sailing
upstream from his chief palace at Lambeth to his country house at Mortlake, 3 miles beyond Putney; ambassadors, courtiers, hopefuls of all sorts.

In this story, Putney is nothing and everything. Cromwell's smartest
move was to flee it while still in his teens, to travel through mainland
Europe and thus refashion himself as much more than a Tudor Englishman. Yet once he could enjoy the reward for his travels and administrative

drudgery, he triumphantly reasserted his link to that ferry-side village on the Thames. In summer 1536, he vaulted up the social scale in a move whose chutzpah did much to destabilize politics and sparked a great upheaval of rebellion in northern parts of the realm, the Pilgrimage of Grace: he was made Lord Privy Seal and a peer of the realm. He took the title Baron Cromwell of Wimbledon. This was a very calculated gesture, deliberately provocative to the English nobility. As everybody knew, for half a millennium Putney had been a limb of the Archbishop of Canterbury's manor of Wimbledon. Now that great and ancient lordship, with its stately house at Mortlake, had fallen to the newly minted baron, born on its soil fifty years before.

Before 1536, Cromwell had not a scrap of land in the village of his birth, though he had by then built up handsome estates elsewhere. This assumption of a title from Wimbledon was a statement that the Putney boy had come a long way: a symbolic return of the native. How did a brewer's son from Putney become (late in his career) Cardinal Wolsey's trusted servant and then, in nine years serving Henry VIII, transform Tudor England? He was around forty-five when he became a royal councillor, and the King left him only one more decade to live before sending him to the executioner's block. His spectacular tightrope act in the 1530s can be properly understood only in light of his earlier life – about which we apparently know so little. Yet there are ways of penetrating it; sources from his years of greatness can be squeezed for meaning and reminiscence, and ranging forward into the 1530s restores precious glimpses of those early years from 1485.

The scrappy evidence about Walter Cromwell alias Smith has traditionally been taken to suggest that Thomas made a sensible choice in getting away from him as soon as possible. Yet most of this picture is Victorian fantasy, the work of an imaginative nineteenth-century local antiquary.[5] Even the arresting opening of Mantel's *Wolf Hall*, the boy staggering under his father's blows, is no more substantial than that. The few reliable elements are drawn from the court rolls of the Manor of Wimbledon, which do include charges against Walter of assault and falsifying deeds. However, court records are constructed to be records of offences, even when these are purely technical, aimed at triggering a judicial process to resolve a dispute: Walter was not the only Tudor yeoman to bear such a record. One consistent set of entries about him in the court rolls, no fewer than forty-eight instances between 1475 and 1501, are fines for breaking the assize of ale. Commentators on Cromwell's early life have assumed that this reveals Walter's consistent penchant for watering the ale he sold. The very frequency of the fines should have aroused doubts: what we are seeing here is a routine manorial system of licensing ale-selling, couched in terms easy to mistake for a fine in the modern sense.[6]

The one traceable mention of Walter in the thousands of letters in Cromwell's personal archive throws a completely positive light on the Putney yeoman. In October 1536, Anthony St Leger (or Sellinger), future Lord Deputy of Ireland and a protégé of Thomas Cromwell, was worried about his lack of promotion and his uncertain finances, so he appealed to the now Lord Privy Seal to remember him. He stressed how much he already owed not just to Thomas, but to Walter Cromwell before him: '[But] for the goodness that I found in your father, and also in you in my Lord Cardinal his days . . . I had been utterly undone, and so I shall pray for you and all your blood.'[7] St Leger was born about 1496 into an ancient gentry family from a village in central Kent called Ulcombe. Walter Cromwell's goodness to him would have come in his childhood and teenage years, for most of which time young Thomas Cromwell was overseas, before Thomas himself returned to carry on the favours in the 1520s.

The link of the Cromwells with St Leger came through Putney's ancient manorial relationship with the archbishops of Canterbury, because Anthony was a favourite nephew of William Warham, Archbishop from 1503. This kinship is likely to have brought him as a boy from his Kentish home scores of miles from Putney up to the Archbishop's house at Mortlake (it is possible that the Cromwell family already had a much humbler link there in domestic service to the Archbishop).[8] In another fulsome letter of around 1533, St Leger professed himself grateful for promotion in equal shares to Archbishop Warham and Thomas Cromwell. As the deceased Archbishop's shadow diminished a year or two later, a further letter revised St Leger's estimate of his gratitude to Cromwell up from half to 'all my living'.[9] Here is a glimpse of how the returned native in the 1510s already had one sure entry into the goodwill of Kentish gentry through a significant and well-connected family, the St Legers. Cromwell had much to do with their many relatives in Kent, in ways important not just for him but for the remoulding of Tudor politics after his death.

Walter Cromwell may actually have come from Ireland. That was the confident statement of an anonymous chronicler in early Tudor London who certainly knew the precise facts that Walter kept a brewhouse and lived in Wandsworth, and the story was repeated in bilious and probably bibulous remarks about Cromwell by the courtier George Paulet in 1537: he 'was so affectionate unto the same land because his ancestors were born there'.[10] Thomas's mother was, however, English. She remains so obscure that we do not know her Christian name for certain, though it is generally given as Katherine. Her maiden surname has rarely been noticed, which is puzzling because she came from an identifiable gentry family, a reminder that the lowliness of Cromwell's origins has often been exaggerated. In 1535 a correspondent of one of Cromwell's servants was trying to obtain the office of prior at the Staffordshire monastery of Tutbury for its Sub-Prior, Arthur Meverell, and he mentioned hopefully that Cromwell's mother had been one of the same family, the Meverells of Throwley, on the Staffordshire side of the Peak District. In fact Arthur Meverell did get the appointment.[11] A relationship with the Meverells gave Cromwell a different sprinkling of potential gentry contacts: around the Peak into Derbyshire, Yorkshire and Nottinghamshire.

In his years of prosperity, Cromwell became friendly with the head of the Throwley family, Francis Meverell, and did small favours for him and his close relatives in neighbouring Derbyshire, the Babingtons of Dethick. One of the latter, John Babington, actually became a servant of Cromwell's in the 1530s, after being a colleague in Cardinal Wolsey's service. He shared his reformist religious outlook, and championed vulnerable members of the minority in the northern Midlands who also sought religious reformation.[12] Another relative via Cromwell's mother was a young gentleman called Francis Bassett of Blore in Derbyshire, whose mother was also one of the Throwley Meverells. In 1538 he too proved a useful agent of Cromwell's iconoclastic policies in that same area. Bassett's reforming convictions are attested by the fact that he became a favourite servant of Nottinghamshire-born Archbishop Cranmer, who was not slow to invoke the young man's kinship to Cromwell when seeking to intimidate the Earl of Shrewsbury in a Staffordshire land dispute.[13]

Descending the social scale, various other needy relatives from the Peak badgered the rising politician and succeeded in embroiling him in their legal business, but it was a question of activating a fairly dormant relationship.[14] One correspondent of Cromwell at the beginning of the 1530s was an aged minor servant of the Bishop of Lincoln called Nicholas Glossop. Glossop introduced himself as the son of Cromwell's aunt, and mentioned another relative from the Derbyshire Peak town of Wirksworth, around 15 miles from Throwley, but it is significant that Glossop had to explain all this to Master Secretary in order to get the letter of recommendation he was after.[15] The maternal Staffordshire and Derbyshire side of Cromwell's family were not high in his priorities, even those who gave him some claim to straddle the contested border between yeoman and gentle status.

By contrast, people from Cromwell's Putney days reappeared in significant roles in his later life. The only other eminent escapee from Putney in his time was Nicholas West; West was already Bishop of Ely by the time that Putney's second-favourite son returned from his travels abroad. Their relationship tells us much about the period in which England entered the upheaval of the Protestant Reformation, springing out of the German friar Martin Luther's confrontation with the Church authorities after 1517. It will be one of the main arguments of this book that Thomas Cromwell's enthusiasm for the Reformation was a constant force in shaping his public career and policy, and that from early in the 1520s he was what a later generation would call Protestant. The term 'Protestant' is best put aside in dealing with the very early stage of the English Reformation which Cromwell did so much to advance. 'Evangelical' is a better description, for in Cromwell's lifetime 'Protestant' was not a term used to describe English adherents of the Reformation and is best reserved for its place of origin in Germany. By contrast, the terms 'evangelic' or 'evangelical' were used in England at the time, and that is the usage I will generally adopt throughout this story.[16]

Cromwell's eventual evangelical religious commitment makes the later dealings between the two Putney prodigal sons Nicholas West and Thomas Cromwell all the more interesting. It illustrates an important second strand in his outlook, which during his career often clashed with his religious conviction, yet was characteristic of his times. Place and family mattered profoundly to him, and might outweigh religion. When the relationship of West and Cromwell had utterly changed, and West found himself on the wrong side of Henry VIII's temper in 1533, he reminded Cromwell of their common origins (as you would): 'Thus I am bold to write unto you, desiring your favour, and the rather moved thereunto because of our native country [by which he meant 'county', Surrey], and that we be god-brothers.'[17] Maybe this was literally true, and Nicholas and Thomas shared a godfather, but West may simply have meant that they had both been baptized in the same font in Putney parish church.

In religious outlook, Bishop West and Cromwell proved not to be soulmates, given the royal minister's central role in religious change which was already all too apparent in 1533. The Bishop shared Cromwell's fixation with his childhood home, so we can still enjoy viewing his splendid if much altered chantry chapel as part of Putney parish church, and he made equally lavish traditional chantry provision for his soul in his cathedral church of Ely. He was among the foremost opponents of 'Lutheranism' from its first arrival in England in the 1520s.[18] Yet the Putney connection still proved potent despite the two men's religious differences. When Nicholas West died that same year of 1533, he was succeeded as Bishop of Ely by Thomas Goodricke, one of England's first unmistakably evangelical bishops, a boyhood friend of the most highly placed evangelical clergyman of all, Archbishop Thomas Cranmer.[19] One would have expected Cromwell the evangelical to have found a natural sympathy with Goodricke, but the reverse proved to be the case.*

When Cromwell began constructing a web of acquaintance across lowland England in the 1520s, Nicholas West's network of relatives in Cambridgeshire and the Isle of Ely provided him with one set of useful local contacts, and that did not change when West died. Alas for Bishop Goodricke, these family links continued to trump religious affiliation. Nicholas West had entrenched his nephew and employee Thomas Megges in an important diocesan Stewardship, and Goodricke could not get rid of him. The new Bishop found himself ranged against a Putney affinity in the Isle of Ely who owed their social position to Bishop West's clerical career, but who now sustained it through their link with another Putney lad. Thomas Cromwell was probably of much the same age as Thomas Megges, and it is not unlikely that they knew each other as boys. In any case, before his death West made a point of recommending Megges to Cromwell as his business agent, and the relationship blossomed.[20] Not only did Cromwell take a protégé of Megges into his own service a couple of years after West's death, but at much the same time he procured some minor royal office for Megges himself.[21] There is no doubt that it was also by his means that in 1538–9 Megges became Sheriff of Cambridgeshire and Huntingdonshire, in succession to Cromwell's own nephew Richard.

Bishop Goodricke's origins in a lesser gentry family of Lincolnshire gave him a more elevated start in Tudor society than either West or Cromwell, but now he was at a decided disadvantage in dealing with the legacy of his episcopal predecessor, in the malign shape of Thomas Megges. A long series of conflicts developed between the increasingly infuriated Bishop and his unwanted official, who drew on Cromwell's support with consistent success, despite a stream of letters from both parties vying for the minister's favour.[22] In 1537 Bishop Goodricke's frustration exploded after Richard Cromwell visited him to impart the appalling news that Megges had made over his Ely diocesan Stewardship jointly to Richard himself and to Cromwell's own son Gregory. This key

* Since writing my biography of Cranmer, I have been persuaded by present representatives of the family to adopt their preferred modern spelling, Goodricke.

episcopal office thus continued irretrievably beyond the Bishop's control. Richard enjoyed describing to his uncle the Bishop's impotent rage.[23]

There are other Putney straws in the wind. A delicate little reminiscence of Cromwell's familiarity with his childhood home and its manorial administration comes in a letter to him from his trusted old servant Henry Polstead, a Surrey man, advising him not to let a gentleman tenant of the Manor of Wimbledon get away with an easy deal on transferring a valuable copyhold property in Putney: 'I suppose your Lordship is not unremembered of the custom: ye must set a great fine, at the least forty pounds.'[24] We will find that, unlike Cromwell's parents, his two sisters and the families of his three brothers-in-law continued to play an important part in his career, and when Cromwell married (probably some time in the 1510s), it was to a local girl. His long-term household servant from the 1520s into the 1530s, Thomas Avery, likewise came from Putney.[25]

In 1534, looking far westwards to Cornwall, Cromwell dealt with the important but troublesome Augustinian priory at Bodmin by brusquely replacing a newly elected prior with his own man. This Augustinian canon not only had significantly evangelical associations in London, but also bore the particularly unCornish surname in religion of Wandsworth.[26]* Here sounded echoes of the village on the Surrey bank of the Thames where Walter Cromwell lived, and indeed the grateful carpet-bagger Thomas Mundy alias Wandsworth arrived from Merton Priory, one of the nearest religious houses to the village of Cromwell's birth. Prior Wandsworth came to be seen as a symbol of Cromwell's presence in Cornwall, not to the advantage of his local popularity, but at least Bodmin Priory lasted until as late as February 1539 under his leadership.[27] Perhaps the boy Mundy and Cromwell had been schoolfriends, along with Thomas Megges.

All these later illuminations of the early years are consistent with the judgement of one of the finest historians of the century after Cromwell's life, Edward Lord Herbert of Chirbury. Herbert wrote with a proper sense of his own exalted ancestry, his inheritance spreading from his fantasy-castle soaring above the rooftops of Montgomery to the furthest hills, but he admired the way Cromwell was at ease with the memory of his unglamorous childhood: 'He was noted in the exercise of his places of judicature, to have used much moderation; and in his greatest pomp, to have taken notice, and been thankful to mean persons of his old

---

* It was a common custom at the time for monks to leave behind their old surname when entering the monastery and take the name of the place where they came from. Wandsworth's family surname was Mundy.

acquaintance, and therein had a virtue which his master the Cardinal wanted.'[28] It is also noticeable that the young Cromwell had not apparently drawn on the obvious source of social advancement in the Wimbledon area, its feudal lord the Archbishop of Canterbury, despite various obvious connections of family and relatives to the Warham household. His career had other more unusual foundations, which took him a long way from Putney and indeed out of his native land as far as the Mediterranean Sea.

2

The Return of the Native

Around the turn of the sixteenth century, a teenaged Thomas shook off the constraints of Surrey and left for mainland Europe. Rather than a quarrel with his father, the impulse may simply have been the restlessness and original intelligence which characterized his public career, and which had made him a 'ruffian' in youth. The imperial ambassador Eustace Chapuys, writing a generally well-informed mini-biography of Cromwell in the 1530s, claimed that Cromwell had left England for Flanders and then Italy after a spell in prison; there is no reason to disbelieve him.[1] The spine of what happened when Cromwell eventually arrived in Mediterranean Europe is provided by the most unexpected of sources: an Italian novella by a prolific author and occasional bishop, Matteo Bandello, who in writing his concise little tales took more of an interest in England than most Italians did. Tudor England's prime Protestant historian John Foxe, author of the great *Acts and Monuments* ('Foxe's Book of Martyrs'), found Bandello's account so fascinating that he ignored the deeply negative view of Henry VIII's marital adventures evident in one or two of the other novellas. In 1570 Foxe inserted a specially translated abridgement of Bandello's Cromwell story in a newly crafted hagiography of his Protestant hero, a good while before the novelist's other tales were turned into English.[2]

Bandello is the best we can do for the obscurity of Cromwell's Italian years. He takes his hero far from Putney, fleeing his father for Italy: that is the tiny spark of the later idea about Walter Cromwell's violence towards his son. Interestingly, Foxe slightly modified Bandello's 'che fuggendo da mio padre' – 'fleeing from my father' – to the more neutral 'I am strayed from my country', which may reflect a warmer tradition about Walter Cromwell that he had heard from his English sources. The novelist records something so specific that it does not sound an invention: Thomas's presence with the French army at the battle of Garigliano just north of Naples on 29 December 1503, when he was probably not yet twenty.[3] This engagement was decisive for placing the future of Naples and Sicily in Spanish hands and ending French hopes in southern Italy.[4] Among the casualties on the French side at Garigliano was an exiled but exalted Florentine, Piero de' Medici, then the leading family representative of the former de facto rulers of Florence. In resonance with Piero's death, which postponed Medici hopes of regaining power in the city for a further decade, Cromwell's story now moved to Florence.[5]

Bandello's narrative is a picaresque tale of young Thomas rescued from destitution on the streets of Florence by Francesco Frescobaldi, out of sheer pity for the starving youth. Frescobaldi came from another great Florentine mercantile family, and there were long-term virtuous consequences for both in later years, when the tables were turned for the two protagonists, and Cromwell was able to help his former saviour. Just as in Bandello's novella, Francesco Frescobaldi did indeed find himself in financial difficulties in the years of Cromwell's greatness. In October 1533, he pledged his gratitude and continued service to Master Secretary, now in a position to return early favours.[6] Nevertheless Bandello has exercised the novelist's prerogative to create a fairy-tale around a real story. This Francesco Frescobaldi was born in 1495, so he is unlikely to have been responsible for rescuing a teenager about twice his age in the first decade of the sixteenth century.[7] Perhaps the charitable deed was performed by his father Girolamo, or his elder brother Leonardo.

Nor should we take literally the denouement for Bandello's story, in which a tearful Cromwell reveals his true identity to the astonished Frescobaldi, much as Joseph did to his brethren in Pharaoh's Egypt. This quasi-biblical enrichment belies the fact that Cromwell and Francesco Frescobaldi remained in contact in the intervening years, as Francesco took over the family business. During Cromwell's service with Cardinal Wolsey in the 1520s, it would have been impossible for him not to know of the enormous financial debt Frescobaldi, his brother Leonardo and other Italian partners owed to Henry VIII, about which Francesco wrote with anxiety to Wolsey when matters reached a malevolent level of complexity. Probably a later stage of these same financial headaches still concerned him in writing to Cromwell in 1533.[8] Frescobaldi's co-operation with Cromwell is evident in the early 1530s, when Cromwell used him to channel money to a financially demanding Italian friend and spy, Dr Agostino de Augustinis (in his English career, 'Dr Augustine'), during the doctor's travels in mainland Europe.[9]

Yet the likelihood of a continued connection between Cromwell and Frescobaldi has much greater implications than these fairly late encounters. The Frescobaldi were one of Florence's great mercantile families, involved in trade with England since the thirteenth century. When Cromwell was a boy and over the course of his time in Italy, their English business grew massively in clandestine co-operation with King Henry VII, to include a large-scale alum-smuggling industry to northern Europe via England: they imported this vital dyestuff for the cloth industry from Egypt and the Ottomans in the infidel eastern Mediterranean. This was despite the Papacy's determined efforts to maintain its monopoly of European supply from mines in the Papal States, backed up by the most solemn papal curses, which Henry VII acknowledged with due reverence and completely ignored. Their impudent bypassing of the papal monopoly netted both the Frescobaldi and the first Tudor king a fine profit, although the enterprise has only recently been discovered as accounting for a major component of Henry VII's notorious wealth.[10] More decorously and festively, the Frescobaldi of Florence are still involved today in the wine business they launched 700 years ago, which in the early Tudor age made them a leading supplier of wine to England.

The Frescobaldis' mixed interests in woollen cloth and wine are typical of high commerce in their age. Wine was a luxury trade, but cloth concerned everyone. We all have three basic needs: food, housing and clothing. Modern Western consumers will need to make an effort of imagination to enter a world where little else mattered in commerce: of those three priorities, clothing was the only one involving international trade. Treated carefully, cloth does not readily perish if transported long distances, and of the trio of basics it was the only one to be much subject to changes in fashion. Consequently, commerce across the whole continent was largely about cloth, and in the cold of Europe the basic fabric was woollen. England's complicated geology is a fine basis for intricate variation in breeding sheep, with local specialities of wool producing a rich variety of garments. The English were known for their cloth-weaving; their chief export had become half-finished cloth for others to work up into garments in current styles, via sophisticated markets run by their neighbours across the North Sea in the Low Countries – what are now Belgium and the Netherlands.

The towns and cities of the Low Countries staged great fairs at certain seasons of the year, to which merchants and manufacturers flocked from southern and northern Europe alike. Thomas Cromwell made his first way in the world amid such commerce. Out of this trade came huge profits for producers and entrepreneurs, and the English economy hinged on the relationship. That was ample reason for the English monarchy to seek the best of relations with whoever ruled the Low Countries. Currently that ruler was the Habsburg Holy Roman Emperor; since the 1490s the

Habsburgs had been locked in continent-wide military and diplomatic confrontation with the Valois dynasty of France. That made the relationship even more obviously desirable, since the default reaction of the English was always to see the French monarchy as their arch-enemy.

Apart from London, the chief port handling Italian wine and cloth business was Southampton, where Francesco Frescobaldi's brother Leonardo was sufficiently involved to purchase an expensive but clearly profitable licence to buy wool during 1512–14.[11] It is therefore fascinating to find that the earliest reference to any of the adult Thomas Cromwell's friendships is from a leading Southampton merchant. Henry Hotoft or Huttoft was a warm and frequent correspondent of his into the 1530s, and benefited in later years from Cromwell's favour, while his son John entered the minister's service.[12] Henry became extremely wealthy in Southampton's wine and cloth trade, rose to be Collector of Customs in the town, and even had an Italian son-in-law from the London expat community, Antonio Guidotti. In summer 1535 Guidotti went bankrupt and Huttoft was pulled into the disaster. In an emotional and very personal letter to his old friend, he expressed his shame and anger at the disgrace: 'Sir, your Mastership hath known me above 25 years for a poor man to have led, I trust, an honest life.'[13] So thanks to Huttoft's misfortune we have a fix on the length of their friendship, taking us back to 1509 or 1510, when Cromwell was in his early twenties.

The Frescobaldi commercial interests in wine, wool and alum-smuggling also necessarily involved the Low Countries, and it is in that connection that we find a less intimate acquaintance of Cromwell's helpfully prompting him to recall their first encounter, a couple of years or so after Cromwell and Huttoft had first met. An evangelically minded London mercer, George Elyot, wrote to Cromwell in 1535 with a proposal to redeploy Dover's Benedictine priory as a parish church, inspired, he said, for the honour of God 'and for the good love and true heart that have held unto you since the Syngsson [Whitsun] Mart at Middelburg in anno 1512'.[14] Middelburg becomes part of a skein of early Cromwell and Frescobaldi connections. Francesco and Leonardo Frescobaldi became the Habsburg lessees of tolls in the province of Zeeland, of which Middelburg is the capital – this nice little earner was the ideal counterpart for Frescobaldi export licences in Southampton for English wool. Not only that, but the family's executive officer in collecting these tolls in Zeeland was a Franco-Englishman from Calais, John Hacket, who took up residence in the Low Countries around 1505. Hacket spent the rest of his life there, and from the 1520s became a remarkably popular resident ambassador to the Habsburg Court in Brussels, the only such permanent representative Henry VIII maintained abroad apart from his diplomats at the papal Court.[15]

Hacket was Thomas Cromwell's intimate friend; in the 1530s he shows up as a frequent correspondent from Brussels. Cromwell served as executor of his will, a role which he performed for only a few people and which in this case proved a headache, principally because a former servant of the Frescobaldi obstinately stood out for what he claimed was Hacket's old debt.[16] The ambassador certainly earned his country's gratitude and Cromwell's pains in sorting out his affairs. His letters constituted a royal news service first for Cardinal Wolsey and then for Cromwell about politics in the Low Countries, and alongside his official dispatches to Henry VIII he frequently sent Cromwell a more unbuttoned letter.[17] He larded these letters to Cromwell with laddish jokes, latterly at the Pope's expense, and lapsed from time to time into French, a language which they clearly both spoke fluently.

Naturally Hacket also paid as much attention to Antwerp, England's most important commercial depot in mainland Europe, as he did to the imperial Court in Brussels. All this adds substance to John Foxe's rather vague remark about Cromwell, that 'being at Antwerp, he was there retained of the English merchants to be their Clerk or Secretary, or in some such like condition placed pertaining to their affairs.'[18] Indeed, in a petition of complaint to the Court of Chancery, Cromwell described his transactions in Antwerp with other English merchants in 1513–14 which had sparked a dispute on debt.[19] His memories of Antwerp remained warm, to judge by a bitter joke of his old servant and friend Stephen Vaughan, who in 1536 was not enjoying himself on a royal diplomatic mission there, and observed to Cromwell in characteristically self-pitying mood: 'You think I am in Paradise, and I think in Purgatory.'[20] How much did Cromwell know of the Frescobaldis' clandestine co-operation with Henry VII to defraud the Pope of alum revenues? No insider to the Antwerp/London/Southampton commercial world with personal connections to the Frescobaldi can have failed to hear the story. The young Cromwell would have learned some useful lessons in how to render unto Caesar that which belonged to the Vicar of Christ.

In the mid-teens of the century Cromwell was in his early thirties; his life had taken him from Putney to Italy and Antwerp, and back to England. What people remembered about those early years, particularly if inclined (as many were) to shape their memories with malicious snobbery, was his connection to the cloth trade. It was in fact an honourable achievement to be admitted to the great London trade gild of the Merchant Taylors.

When Cromwell pursued a routine plea of debt in the Court of Common Pleas in 1523, he was described as citizen and Merchant Taylor (*civis et mercator scissor*) of London.[21] This gave rise to the repeated sneer that he was a 'shearman', just as Archbishop Cranmer was habitually dismissed in widely separate parts of traditionalist England as an 'ostler' (stableman at an inn).[22] The 'shearman' jibe was so well known and so toxic that in the immediate aftermath of my Lord of Essex's fall in 1540, Henry VIII at the height of his vindictiveness against his fallen minister decreed that no one should call him Lord Privy Seal or by any other title of office or nobility, but only Thomas Cromwell, shearman.[23]

A more rounded perspective suggests that through Cromwell's own efforts over a decade and more he had become an exceptionally cosmopolitan Englishman, with a web of connections to northern Italy, the Low Countries and the ports of London and Southampton. Working in Antwerp, the entrepôt uniting these various commercial hubs, he knew well some of the most enterprising merchants of England's international trade, many of whom figure constantly in his later correspondence: William Lock and Richard Gresham, for instance, both on the way to becoming seriously wealthy, and like him enthusiasts for the European Reformation as it unfolded after 1517. Their influence in the City of London was soon to make its mercantile community into a power-base for England's developing Protestantism: a congenial partner for Cromwell's own religious programmes in the 1530s.[24] Unsurprisingly, John Hacket was by no means his only friend in Calais, and much later Lord Lisle (in a justified panic at finding a war on his doorstep) added a postscript to a letter to a man who was now the King's chief minister: 'there is no man living knoweth the open way between Arde [Ardres, in Picardy] and Calais better than you.'[25]

Judging from Cromwell's correspondence, he had a gift for learning languages, though there is no clue to how he acquired them. He spoke, read or wrote fluent Italian and French. He seems to have been at ease in Spanish, certainly in reading it: two people who had the measure of him in English politics, Queen Katherine of Aragon and her imperial nephew's long-term ambassador in England, Eustace Chapuys, both chose to write to him in Spanish on important occasions.[26] While he may have been able to read some German, one of his German correspondents habitually wrote to him in Italian, and in 1532 his Italian friend Dr Augustine suggested he get a merchant of the Steelyard to translate the German of an imperial decree against Albrecht of Prussia.[27]

Cromwell also understood the universal European language of power: the self-consciously elegant Latin written and spoken by Renaissance 'humanists', those ardent explorers of a re-emerging classical past. Over a thousand years after the fall of the Western Roman Empire, the Western Church used but also much adapted the Latin language for the purposes of Christian conversation and liturgy, transforming even its grammar and sentence construction. Humanist scholars, writers and poets modishly reached back across the centuries to classical Latin idioms, and tried to sound as much as possible like great orators of ancient Rome such as Cicero, or poets such as Virgil. They learned their Latin from a mass of ancient texts newly appearing in print. Cromwell loved and avidly collected books. He would recognize that humanism was a practical skill: good expression and forceful rhetoric were essential tools of effective politics. As a good humanist, he also had enough acquaintance with Greek for scholars occasionally to flatter him with a learned tag.

Of all these self-taught accomplishments, Cromwell's fluency in Italian mattered the most. A significant witness to that is one of the earliest dated items surviving from his archive, from summer 1522: his close friend the merchant John Creke prefaced a letter full of extravagantly expressed and intimate affection with the address 'Carissimo quanto homo in questo mondo!' – Italian, even though Creke was writing from Bilbao in Spain.[28] Fifteen years later, the seasoned traveller Richard Morison likewise repeatedly turned to Italian in personal letters to him, on one occasion to convey a particularly confidential final sentence, but elsewhere just to be agreeable.[29] Cromwell shared Italian books with like-minded friends and colleagues: in 1530 Edmund Bonner begged him to fulfil his promise to send Petrarch's *I Trionfi* and Castiglione's newly published *Il Cortegiano* up from London to Yorkshire, so Bonner could while away his Yorkshire exile improving his Italian.[30] An exceptionally cultured nobleman and enthusiast for translation, Henry Lord Morley, was Cromwell's friend and shared his love of things Italian.[31] It is therefore significant that some time in the late 1530s Morley could assume that Cromwell would be pleased by a gift of Niccolò Machiavelli's best-known works the *History of Florence* and *The Prince*, in Italian editions, for recreational and instructive reading. He accompanied the present with reminiscences about the many occasions he had heard Cromwell observe of the Florentines that he had 'been conversant with them, seen their factions and manners'.[32]

Much of Cromwell's early career rested on his ability to be the best Italian in all England. The first identifiable example of this comes from 1514, when he turned up in Rome, staying at the English Hospice while giving evidence in a tithe dispute concerning east London.[33] Thus began an acquaintance with Lancelot Collins, who was testifying in the same case; it ripened into a lasting friendship. Collins was a nephew and leading servant of England's resident Cardinal in Rome, Christopher Bainbridge, who among much empire-building for himself in the city had taken over the management of the Hospice.[34] Colourfully, Bainbridge was murdered that very summer, by another servant who was reputedly his male lover; after his master's death, Collins returned to England to the Treasurership of York Minster, to which Bainbridge (a necessarily absentee Archbishop of York) had appointed him. He held this office until his death in 1538, together with one of the Minster's prebends (an endowment providing a comfortable income).[35]

The Treasurer's frequent later letters to Cromwell, invariably written in his own endearingly individual italic hand, reveal him as a cheerful, whimsical and generous soul. Even Cromwell's cynical lieutenant Dr Thomas Lee gave Collins an admiring obituary: 'it is thought that that man was not rich . . . seeing he kept so honest hospitality, greatly commended in these parts.'[36] Collins came to look on Cardinal Bainbridge and Thomas Cromwell as equal patrons in his career, unlikely as the pairing might at first sight appear. Remarkably, he displayed their heraldry side by side on the façade of his house in York. That public statement brought Collins much trouble in 1536 during the Pilgrimage of Grace, the worst rebellion that Henry VIII ever faced, in which the rebels were intent on targeting any trace of the hated royal minister in northern England (see below, Chapter 16).[37]

All major elements in Cromwell's early career – Italy, Antwerp and London – are now linked. A further legal dispute places him securely back in London in January 1516, when he appealed to the sheriffs of London against his imprisonment for debt. One should not consider such debt disputes as anything more than oiling the wheels of credit in early Tudor commerce, and this was just a routine case on a minor sum of money.[38] The earliest evidence in his surviving papers for any of his own business transactions dates from 1519, when a London goldsmith accepted a bond from Cromwell and Thomas Allen, an Essex man with strong City connections. Thomas Allen's brother John was soon to be Cromwell's colleague under Cardinal Wolsey, and later his protégé as a singularly ill-fated Archbishop of Dublin. The Allen brothers were close kin to one of London's leading merchants, another John Allen, likewise one of Cromwell's close business partners. There was a strong set of connections here for the future.[39]*

---

* Both these John Allens must be distinguished from their relative John Allen who became Master of the Rolls in Ireland in 1533.

Cromwell was already being described in the litigation of 1516 as 'gentleman', rather than merely as merchant, suggesting that by then he was well advanced in the practice of English common law, alongside all his other sources of income. How much legal training he undertook is no clearer than any other aspect of his education. Tudor law and its tangle of exotically named courts of justice can now seem very intimidating, but a sharp-witted boy from Putney would have soon mastered as much as his modern equivalent determined to penetrate the arcane world of finance in Manhattan. Where Cromwell can be traced acting as a lawyer, it is in the relatively straightforward business of land conveyancing, the equity law on trusts and credit agreements practised in the Court of Chancery or the informal legal business brought before the royal Council when it turned itself into a court, sitting in the Palace of Westminster's Star Chamber.

As Cromwell's career developed, we rarely find him venturing into the more arcane tangles of the ancient royal courts of King's Bench or Common Pleas that also sat in the Palace of Westminster; when he chose high legal office in 1534, it was the Court of Chancery's Mastership of the Rolls. A multitude of interests suited him better than concentration on the law, and we should not think of him having a job in the modern sense: such a man was more like our conception of a freelance consultant. These early transactions, and a mass of evidence throughout Cromwell's archive in the 1520s, suggest a business built on moneylending and the law, particularly practice in the Court of Chancery, with London commerce at the heart of his prosperity.

Yet Italy consistently lurked in the background. In the early sixteenth century London's foreign trade was dominated by Italians to an extraordinary extent, until the Reformation and a changing dynamic in international commerce virtually wiped out this ancient and flourishing community within a few decades of Cromwell's death.[40] So every leading London merchant had much to do with Italians. What is striking about Cromwell is that he chose to make this relationship unusually close and personal. Few of his contemporaries bothered to learn Italian with anything approaching his own fluency.

His connections extended much further than Florence. His first known home lay in the parish of St Gabriel Fenchurch, the base for the Genoese mercantile colony in the City. London's Tudor historian John Stow notes this, and provides the information that these so-called 'galley men' 'brought up wines and other merchandises, which they landed in Thames Street, at a place called Galley Quay'.[41] As if on cue, we find in Thomas Cromwell's early papers a lawsuit of 1522–3 concerning a consignment of white soap shipped up from Southampton into Fenchurch parish by Niccolò and Antonio Duodo.[42] The Duodos were not Genoese but Venetians, and that fellow-Italianate Englishman Cardinal Reginald Pole asserted in an unfriendly but well-informed biographical sketch that Cromwell was at one stage an accountant to a Venetian merchant.[43] It is tempting to identify that merchant with their mutual friend Donato Rullo, who came from southern Italy to make his fortune in Venice. Rullo was personally acquainted with Cromwell before he knew Pole, and in the early 1530s was very happy to do him a favour by being agreeable to that polished young nonentity Thomas Winter, Cardinal Wolsey's son, then visiting Venice.[44]

One wonders whether papal alum had been used to manufacture the Duodos' shipment of soap. Italy of course meant not just commerce, but also the Bishop of Rome. England's elite needed middlemen like Cromwell to deal with the complexity of papal bureaucracy, and that has left many clues at this stage of his career. As well as the tithe case of 1514, there was another similar in 1524, when Cromwell acted as London-based attorney in a Hertfordshire tithe dispute which involved an appeal to Rome.[45] Cromwell as expert Italian fixer also took on a major assignment which left a considerable mark on his life and led him back to Italy. This was a consultancy for the extremely wealthy and expanding Gild of Our Lady at Boston in Lincolnshire.

Gilds were the bedrock of late medieval popular religion: voluntary associations with all sorts of purposes, some commercial, some social, but all with some religious dimension. Among the thousands of such institutions vastly varied in scale, Our Lady's Gild of Boston became a flagship. Originally a fairly modest body with a local focus, it hugely expanded its activities in the early 1500s. Its finances were boosted by the sale of indulgences, pardons granting a shortening of time in purgatory for the purchasers and their loved ones. The Gild systematically peddled its indulgences on regular circuits across the kingdom and on at least one occasion as far as Ireland; it may have become the largest such operation in the kingdom.[46] We still see its stately side-chapel in one of England's most prodigious parish churches, whose tower has no rivals in a Lincolnshire Fenland landscape not short of mighty towers.

If the 'Boston Stump' triumphantly sees off all competition among neighbouring belfries, the same could not be said of the Boston Gild's indulgence trade. Its profits needed constant defence against rival indulgence enterprises, particularly the equally expansionist salesmanship of the English Province of Austin Friars (known in the Germany of Martin

Luther as the Augustinian Eremites). In early 1517, a few months
before Friar Luther started his fateful campaign against indulgences far
away in Saxony, thus inadvertently launching the Protestant Reformation, a battle royal for control of the English indulgence market broke
out between his English confrères and the Boston Gild. Boston sent its
Gild clerk to Cardinal Wolsey to seek a suspension of the Austin Friars'
privileges.[47] Yet even Wolsey in his legatine splendour was only a local
representative of the Holy Father. More ambitiously, determined to
secure reaffirmation and authorization directly from Rome, the Gild
recruited Thomas Cromwell. As 'Master Cromwell', a form of address
which stands out in the Gild accounts as once more indicating gentleman's status, he first appears in the Boston Gild accounts for Whitsun
1517–18, travelling up to Boston and generally running up expenses and
fees to the tidy sum of £4 6s 8d.[48]

The following accounting year, Whitsun 1518–19, Cromwell undertook a much more ambitious task in the Boston Gild's campaign. He
accompanied Geoffrey Chamber, the Gild secretary, on an expedition to
Rome. John Foxe described Cromwell's special contribution with relish,
a perfect anecdote to illustrate papal worldliness and corruption. Cromwell followed the Pope on the hunting field, and secured renewal of
Boston's bulls by charming his Holiness with the aid of fine dishes of
English jelly, serenaded by a group of singers demonstrating English
three-part harmony. So Pope Leo, 'knowing of them what their suits
were, and requiring them to make known the making of that meat . . .
without any more ado, stamped both their pardons, as well the greater as
the lesser'.[49] The Boston accounts less picturesquely reveal Chamber as
main negotiator; it was in fact Chamber's second trip in two years, and
when Cromwell went home he left Chamber to spend another sixteen
weeks in Rome working out details of the deal with Pope Leo X's
officials.[50]

Nevertheless, Cromwell's contribution was still important, earning
him £47 12s 7d in expenses from the grateful Gild and a fee of £13 6s 8d.
He spent half a year (exactly twenty-six weeks) in Rome and getting there
and back via Calais. Given that Pope Leo was the younger brother of that
Piero de' Medici who had died at the battle of Garigliano, Cromwell's
Florentine links might have been of value oiling the bureaucratic wheels.
We also have one intriguing survival in the State Papers suggesting that
while in Rome he made himself useful in clearing up other bits of business with papal officials. This document is a fragmentary draft of court
pleadings by Richard Belamy, attorney for Joan Harte and John Turner,
to prove that they had fulfilled conditions of a bond dated 8 February

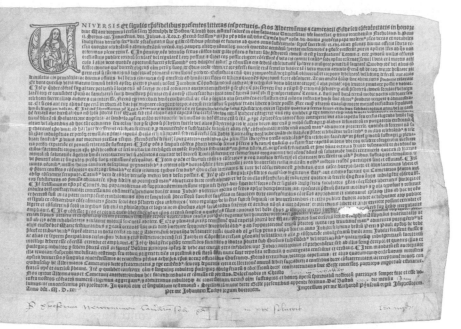

A specimen of English indulgence literature: a letter printed by Richard Pynson for the Gild of St Mary, Boston. The date is completed by hand for 16 June 1530, but this is the sort of material for which Cromwell was acting as agent in the early 1520s.

1519, concerning a dispensation from the Roman bureaucracy for the said Joan and Thomas Addington, a London skinner: each to be at liberty to marry any suitable person. Addington and his future wife Joan remained Cromwell's good friends, and the draft appears to be in Cromwell's hand.[51] Perhaps he set off to the Eternal City with that bond from February stuffed into his file of papers; if so, we could narrow down his travels to winter and spring 1519.

The whole three-year saga of the papal bull cost the Boston Gild the astonishing sum of £1,212 12s 8½d, but when we see that a year or two later the Gild's various revenue streams reached a peak of £1,550 in a single year, Our Lady's Gildsmen would think it money well spent.[52] The irony is obvious. Cromwell the future architect of English reformation was agent in advancing the indulgence trade in the very years when Martin Luther was denouncing it, though it was equally ironic that his employers' rivals in indulgence-peddling, the English Austin Friars, were actually part of Luther's order. John Foxe was himself born in Boston around a year before Cromwell's expedition to Rome; when he came to construct a glowing account of Cromwell's career in his classic Protestant narrative, he felt very uncomfortable about this story. As a conscientious historian he could hardly ignore it, for he had rich reminiscences from the ultimate primary source, Cromwell himself, talking to Archbishop Cranmer, who relayed it to his secretary Ralph Morice (another Boston boy).

Foxe punctiliously pointed out that his hero had told Archbishop Cranmer 'what a great doer he was with Geoffrey Chamber in publishing and setting forth the pardon of Boston everywhere in churches as he went'. Foxe's refuge was to treat the whole affair with clumsy satire, including the sneers at papal love for jellies, and a sarcastic marginal commentary alongside one of Boston Gild's bulls to which he had access (not actually the one Cromwell's expedition had obtained). Foxe did however take relief in a reminiscence which likewise came to him from Morice: Cromwell's remark to Cranmer that he spent his time on the Rome expedition getting acquainted with Desiderius Erasmus's newly published edition of the Greek and Latin New Testament, and that this reading first set off doubts in his mind about what he was doing. This cheering thought Foxe noted twice.[53]

Whatever immediate effect Erasmus had on Cromwell – and there is no reason to doubt the story in itself – his dealings with Boston Gild were not over. One letter in Cromwell's archive from the early 1520s shows him acting as agent for a new print-run of 4,000 indulgences and as many publicity letters from the Gild's customary London printer Richard Pynson (who, in a generously ecumenical spirit of entrepreneurship, also printed the Austin Friars' indulgence in 1517).[54] Cromwell's correspondent was the Gild's Alderman during this period, John Robinson, who thanked him for sending Pynson's previous batch of Gild printing, passed on warm greetings to his wife and mother-in-law, and said he expected to see him soon in Boston: this had become a personal relationship.[55] His last recorded legal business for the Gild was in the accounting year 1523–4, when he was among a consortium of London lawyers acting in the Gild's dispute with its West Country pardoner, but he remained in friendly contact with the town leadership for the rest of his life.[56] They regularly sent him substantial presents of North Sea fish or wildfowl from the Fens (a Boston speciality), either for his own enjoyment or to pass on to even more powerful folk, first Wolsey, then the King and Queen. From being a useful dogsbody, by the 1530s he had become a potent patron.[57]

Throughout this long relationship, Cromwell never took the opportunity of joining the extensive and distinguished membership of Our

Lady's Gild of Boston. His professional work for such an extrovert expression of traditional piety as the Gild is no bar to supposing he was becoming precociously involved in the Reformation. The recent rediscovery of a stray document from his archive provides an interesting parallel case from exactly this stage of his career. Among many contract negotiations he undertook for London merchants, there remains a draft agreement of 1522 to build a new aisle to house a chantry altar in the Bedfordshire parish church of Biddenham: the client was the local squire, contracting with a St Albans freemason in partnership with Cromwell's friend Thomas Somer, a London stockfish merchant.[58]* Despite Somer's financial involvement in this eminently traditional project to found a chantry for soul-prayer, his evangelical credentials proved impeccable, to the extent of what amounted to martyrdom for his faith: Somer was a member of the shadowy dissident group known as the Christian Brethren, was punished in 1530 for owning a copy of William Tyndale's pioneering evangelical translation of the New Testament and died in prison.[59] In the first stages of the English Reformation, religious boundaries were yet to be defined clearly, particularly when people balanced lucrative careers with sincerely held but evolving belief. We will find plenty of evidence of this in Cromwell's later life.

John Robinson's greeting to Cromwell's wife is the first positive evidence of his marriage to Elizabeth. Her birth surname was either Wykes or Prior (her mother Mercy appears in his correspondence as Mistress Prior, which could be thanks to a second marriage). About the time of Robinson's letter, Henry Wykes wrote to Cromwell from Thorpe, a village upstream from Putney on the Thames, with commendations to 'my sister and your good bedfellow', who could of course be either his actual sister, his stepsister or his sister-in-law.[60] Regardless, the Wykes connection suggests a local alliance, at much the same social level from which Cromwell started out: on the borders between yeomen and minor gentry.[61] Mistress Mercy Prior moved into the Cromwell household after the marriage, at some stage in the 1520s.[62] She seems to have inspired widespread affection – Cromwell's long-time associate Stephen Vaughan called her 'after you my most singular friend' – particularly for her skill in preparing medicines. In 1536, Cromwell's leading propagandist Richard Morison paid handsome tribute to her talents: 'I thank God and Mistress Prior, I may go well again.'[63] She remained an honoured fixture at Cromwell's private London home at Austin Friars, apparently a more than

---

* The aisle still survives at Biddenham.

adequate substitute for his own mother, and she was still living at New Year 1540 when he sent her a gift via her grandson Gregory. One wishes to spare her the catastrophe of six months later.[64]

We know of three children of the marriage: one son, Gregory, and two daughters, probably younger, though these two girls Anne and Grace both died in late 1529, leaving Gregory alone to go on to adulthood and in the end, despite everything, a peerage.[65] After Elizabeth's death, earlier in that same year of 1529, Thomas sent his son to live most of the time till adulthood with a variety of tutors and sympathetic mentors, but one should not regard this as a rejection of the boy, whom, as we shall see, he clearly adored. Perhaps it was more a way to shield him from his father's increasingly frenetic and sometimes dangerous life in government. It is also worth registering the single devastating fact that after Elizabeth's death Thomas never remarried, ignoring hard-headed but well-intentioned suggestions from friends to take another wife straight away.[66] Not even in his years as the King's all-powerful minister, when he could have had almost any bride he pleased, on any terms he liked, is there any hint of serious marriage negotiations.* There is more than one interpretation of that, but the most likely is that he could not bear the thought of marrying anyone else.

Thomas and Elizabeth's marriage must have been in the 1510s, since Gregory's age revealed throughout his father's papers places his birth at the earliest in 1519 and far more likely 1520 – not 1516, as many commentators have asserted since the early nineteenth century.[67] Much patronizing nonsense has been written about Gregory based on that persistent miscalculation of his age. He has frequently been denigrated for not having the educational attainments of a teenager at a time when he was in fact ten years old or less, while the progress of his handwriting through the 1530s, plus the carefully planned steps in his education, tells the real story: not scholarly, but not stupid or embarrassing.[68] In Thomas Cromwell's whirlwind decade of royal service, Gregory's exact age was to prove of very great significance.

The boy's Christian name is also worthy of note. The oddness of the name Gregory in early Tudor terms has not been the subject of much comment, and yet not only Thomas's son but in the same generation one of his nephews, who must be a younger son of his brother-in-law Morgan Williams, was also called Gregory.[69] Is it too fanciful to see the baby son born around 1520 as named after Cromwell's visit to Rome in 1518–19,

---

* The one exception to that is the rather extraordinary possibility that at the end of his career he was contemplating marriage to Princess Mary: see below, p. 352.

in honour of Pope Gregory the Great, who sent Augustine to the Anglo-Saxons and hence was known as 'the Apostle of the English'?[70] Once more, we have to remember the fluidity of the Reformation in its first half-decade; there is no reason to back-project a fully formed version of Cromwell's later anti-papal outlook on to the Boston Gild's legal consultant when Gregory was christened.

Cromwell's wife also brought a link to her brother-in-law John Williamson. As Cromwell's public and private life became a large and complex operation, Williamson developed into an increasingly crucial, discreet and trusted domestic steward. His tact comes through in his letters to Cromwell, as their common mother-in-law Mercy Prior changed from 'your mother' to 'my mother' once Thomas became Principal Secretary and Master of the Rolls.[71] That whole relationship might have seemed awkward, but since the Wykes, Prior and Williamson families were clearly situated on the same margins of gentility as the Cromwells, they were happy to enjoy the fruits of his success.[72] That was also the case with William Wellifed, who married Cromwell's sister Elizabeth, lived in Putney and must have been the same William who was chief cook and senior servant to William Warham, Archbishop of Canterbury in the 1520s; Chapuys later heard with some slight confusion that an uncle of Cromwell's had been Warham's cook.[73]

The two Wellifed boys from this marriage joined Gregory Cromwell in his boyhood studies at Cambridge at the end of the 1520s. The elder, Christopher, Gregory's senior by several years, was genuinely clever. Supported by funding from his uncle which was generous though sometimes extracted only by dint of silky epistolary Latin, Christopher Wellifed stayed on at Cambridge, eventually at the well-endowed King's Hall. He repeatedly appears in later correspondence as the Trollopian-sounding 'Parson Wellifed', usually indeed in connection with his considerable appetite for acquiring cathedral prebends which his uncle's consistent generosity largely satisfied.[74]

Cromwell's other sister Katherine made the one marriage in his generation which could be considered without qualification to be to a gentleman, albeit a Welsh gentleman: Morgan Williams. He appears in Cromwell's correspondence under the polite form of address for a Welshman as 'Master Morgan'; he was the son of William Morgan ap Howell of Newchurch or Whitchurch, Glamorgan, maybe the same as a William Morgan who was in minor Court service to Henry VII.[75] William Morgan acquired property in Putney, which was certainly common among Court officials with duties at Richmond Palace; his son Morgan Williams was sufficiently close to Thomas Cromwell's father to name his second son Walter, presumably as Walter's godson: maybe another hint that Walter Cromwell was not as dislikeable as posterity has painted him. Yet the omnivorous historical traveller John Leland, who was in a position to know, made it clear that the family kept their Welsh connection. He provides us with the precious nugget of information that Richard son of Morgan Williams and Katherine Cromwell was born in Llanishen, the Glamorgan parish adjacent to Newchurch.[76]*

Of all Cromwell's family, it was the Williams connection that meant most to him, not least in status. Theirs was the name most securely tied into the gentry, boasting for instance among their dispersal in England John Williams, sometime Sheriff of Oxfordshire, and father to a second John. In the 1530s, on a career path leading him to a peerage as Lord Williams of Thame, the younger John hosted Thomas Cromwell's now teenaged son Gregory for an exceptionally enjoyable summer. But there was also something especially close in the relationship. After Morgan's death at the end of the 1520s, Cromwell – his wife and two little girls now dead – effectively adopted his brother-in-law's son Richard to be an elder brother for Gregory, then less than ten years old. Richard took the surname Cromwell alongside his Welsh patronymic, as did his younger brother Walter; for understandable reasons, a third brother, Gregory Williams, retained his Williams surname alone.[77] Richard seems to have taken up his new surname in autumn 1529, for in mid-December he was already referred to as 'Richard Cromwell'.[78] By the mid-1530s Thomas Cromwell had set Richard up with his own satellite household in Stepney, part of Thomas's growing landed estate.[79]

Particularly indicative is the heraldry Cromwell chose for himself, probably in the late 1520s when his rising position in society began to require it.[80] A lesser man might have invented a gentrifying link for himself to the medieval Barons Cromwell; they had taken their title from a Nottinghamshire village which was presumably also the original home of other Cromwells, and the last Lord Cromwell had died long ago, in 1455, without male heirs to cause a fuss over any later appropriation. Yet that grandly simple heraldry from Plantagenet days, *or a chief gules, over all a bend azure* (a blue diagonal band superimposed on both a gold field and a headband of red), was nothing like the design for the coat-armour Thomas Cromwell suggested to the heralds for his own grant. Rather he took his cue from the even simpler coat Morgan Williams used (*sable, a lion rampant argent*: a silver lion on a black field). His coat was dominated by three gold lions (*lions rampant or*), to which when he officially

---

* Both Whitchurch and Llanishen are now in the northern suburbs of Cardiff.

matriculated arms in 1532/3 he added allusive borrowings from the coat of Cardinal Wolsey, a reference then both pointed and brave.[81]

Lions rampant or recur not only in Cromwell's arms but in the new coat adopted by Morgan Williams's son Richard, after he took his uncle Thomas's surname: an allusion both to his birth and to his second father.[82] Moreover, Cromwell's first acquisition of a major seigneurial title was not in Surrey or the environs of London but far away in Wales, the lordship of Romney or Rhymney, up the valleys north of that Glamorgan parish where Richard Williams had been born. Thomas received this grant from the Crown (jointly with his son Gregory) in 1532, at much the same time as his official grant of arms. These two scraps of evidence suggest that he was at that stage making his bid for upper-gentry status via his Welsh family connections.[83]

In the early 1520s, that move was as yet several steps ahead. Cromwell's social position remained uncertain, on the lower margins of gentility, but at least in his business transactions it proved irreversible and was reinforced by his growing prosperity, founded on his varied enterprises. That

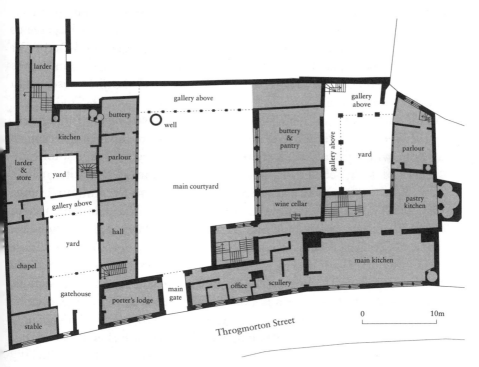

Nicholas Holder's reconstruction of the ground-plan of Cromwell's expanded Austin Friars house in the late 1530s.

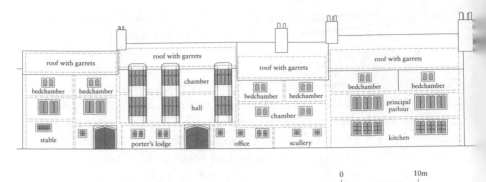

The Throgmorton Street façade of Cromwell's expanded Austin Friars house, in Holder's reconstruction.

inevitably meant acquiring a new house, and his choice (made, as far as the evidence goes, in 1523) was a property on the bounds of the Austin Friars, up in the north-east of the City (the familiar landmark of the area is now Liverpool Street Station). This was the chief English friary in the order that had so rivalled his recent employers at Boston in selling indulgences. Austin Friars became the nearest thing he had to a family home for the rest of his life. Even in the Act of Attainder that destroyed him seventeen years later, Cromwell was said to have committed his treason in the parish of St Peter-le-Poer, which embraced the precinct of the friary.[84]* Austin Friars properties were prime city real estate, and over a decade Cromwell here created a palatial house, devouring more and more of the friars' long-term leases to private occupants to form a freehold dwelling with garden space to match.[85]

Once more his choice of home brought him into close contact with Italy. Austin Friars was a particular favourite with the Italians of the City, who found it more congenial, or simply safer, to worship in a friary church than face xenophobia in a parish church. More prosaically, they might thus escape demands for tithe or other parish dues; Germans and Flemings worshipped at Austin Friars for the same reasons.[86] Cromwell added to his amoeba-like expanded estate in the late 1520s by buying up one of the most lavish Austin Friars houses from its rich Florentine occupants, the business partners Pier-Francesco de' Bardi and Giovanni Cavalcanti. Predictably, the Bardi and Cavalcanti were close allies of the

---

* The parish church of St Peter occupied part of the south-east fabric of the friary church, which it predated: an arrangement without parallel among medieval English friaries.

Cromwell's Throgmorton Street house (3), together with the parish church of
St Peter-le-Poer nestling beside the Austin Friars church (1) (assigned in Edward VI's
reign to the refugee 'Stranger Church'), is depicted in this section of London's
first detailed map, produced in Mary Tudor's reign; the friars' domestic buildings
(to the north) have been converted into a luxury mansion (2) and grounds for
William Paulet, by then Marquess of Winchester.

Frescobaldi. Cavalcanti, while still living at Austin Friars, became at one
stage in the early 1520s rather too intimately involved in the chaotic
administration of its Prior Edmund Bellond, a crisis which also drew in
Cromwell.[87] More positively, Cavalcanti demonstrated how important
the friary church was to the Italian community by donating an altarpiece
by the Florentine artist Antonio Toto del Nunziata to its chapel of St
John the Baptist, who happened to be patron saint of Florence.[88]

One of Cromwell's greatest Italian friends was Antonio Buonvisi, from
a great merchant-banking family of Lucca, with branch offices in Lyon,
Paris, Antwerp and Nuremberg as well as London. If anyone was the
doyen of London's Anglo-Italian community in the 1520s and 1530s, it
was Buonvisi. He was a few years older than Cromwell, and became

lessee of Crosby Hall, in the next parish to Austin Friars, one of the City's most magnificent houses.[89] Buonvisi was equally connected to that great humanist writer and lawyer Sir Thomas More: he had taken over the lease of Crosby Hall from More in 1523, and remained a loyal friend and sustainer right through More's imprisonment in the Tower and execution in 1535.* It is easy to forget, given those later dark events, that in earlier years there was no contradiction in being friends with both Cromwell and More.[90]

Naturally a stream of eminent visiting Italians came to the Bardi/ Cavalcanti in Austin Friars, several of them as long-term guests. In the year Cromwell moved next door, one of the visitors who stayed for six months or more was Gregorio Casali, sharing the house with the secretary of Cardinal Giulio de' Medici, soon to become Pope Clement VII.[91] Casali, an energetic young Italian with useful connections in the Vatican, was in the early stages of varied service for Henry VIII in Rome. Once he became Henry VIII's ambassador to the Papacy in the increasingly delicate diplomatic situation of the late 1520s, he would meet Cromwell again in royal service. For the time being, Casali was by any standards Cromwell's social superior, but in these earlier and happier days the two had plenty of time and every reason to get to know one another.[92]

Diplomacy was frequently work for senior clergy. Among the English episcopate was a series of absentee Italians, useful agents for the English Crown amid the complexities of the papal Court, but needing a handsome income for their trouble: a wealthy English bishopric was just what they needed. That offered further opportunities for those like Cromwell with a foothold in both England and Italy to oil the machinery of the dioceses back home and communicate with the absentee in Rome. Antonio Buonvisi, for instance, was a senior diocesan official for Silvestro Gigli, Bishop of Worcester, and likewise for his successor at Worcester from 1521, Hieronymo Ghinucci. Ghinucci, like Gigli a good servant of English interests in the Vatican, was at the time of acquiring Worcester also papal nuncio (ambassador) in London, and given this conjunction of acquaintance with Buonvisi he cannot have failed to have known Thomas Cromwell. He proved rather touchingly loyal to Henry VIII even after the break with Rome, and then he looked to Cromwell as the only man to secure him due financial recognition (again via Buonvisi) after he had eventually been deprived of his Bishopric. Dr Augustine, whom we shall meet frequently as Cromwell's friend and agent in the 1530s, was the Bishop's nephew.[93]

---

* The portion of Crosby Hall remaining in the nineteenth century has, with some appropriateness, been reconstructed next to Chelsea Old Parish Church, where More is buried.

Cromwell's correspondence in the early 1520s shows he had significant links also with Bristol, an even greater international port than Southampton, as well as chief city in the diocese of Worcester.[94] One of his Bristol friends, William Popley, who in the 1530s became one of his leading servants, developed a similar mixture of international diplomatic, ecclesiastical and commercial activity. In 1518 Popley acted as royal courier to the King's chaplain and diplomat William Knight, English ambassador in the Netherlands, while also acting as go-between with Cardinal Lang (a leading adviser to the Holy Roman Emperor), Knight's absentee predecessor in a Salisbury Cathedral prebend. Dr Knight was described in 1516 as a good Italian, a description equally applicable to Thomas Cromwell, who in the same years Knight had been studying law in Italy had been gaining a rather more eclectic education there.[95]

Now the Italians of Austin Friars brought Cromwell within one tantalizing remove of the English Court: much closer glimpses than the Putney boy in the 1490s would have seen of comings and goings at Richmond Palace. The Bardi/Cavalcanti firm ran the trade in luxury fabrics which meant so much to nobility and monarchy: silks, gold thread, Genoese black velvet. They frequently spent precious face-to-face time with King Henry VIII himself, tempting him with a range of splendid new outfits, presented with long-practised deference.[96] The nature of the occasion was likely to dispose Henry to the best of moods, and cheerfulness in that notoriously volatile monarch was a priceless opportunity for pressing advantage. These cultured and personable Italians were nothing if not versatile. One of the many opportunities for profit to come Giovanni Cavalcanti's way was a remarkable commission in 1521 from Pope Leo X, to arrange a mock-up of a magnificent tomb for Henry VIII to be paid for by the Pope, obviously in gratitude for Henry's recent repudiation of Martin Luther in his *Assertio Septem Sacramentorum*. Unlike the Pope's simultaneous grant of the honorific title 'Defender of the Faith', to which Henry clung with obstinate and illogical pride through all his religious adventures, this recipe for future embarrassment came to nothing. It was an astonishing might-have-been of history.[97]

While Italians went to Court to see the King, the King's courtiers also arrived as visitors to Cromwell's Bardi/Cavalcanti neighbours. Great men of the realm appeared for convivial evenings – no doubt some, like Charles Brandon Duke of Suffolk, were too socially exalted for Cromwell at that stage of his career to be included in the party, but others were well known to him from his old family connections with the Kentish gentry. Sir Henry Guildford was one, a leading gentleman of Kent and great courtier, in whose family affairs Cromwell became much entangled in the 1530s. Guildford was patron to another brilliant young man who shared Cromwell's enthusiasm for Italy, the budding poet Thomas Wyatt, a frequent and welcome visitor to the Bardi/Cavalcanti house in Austin Friars. The young Wyatt's talents, charm and immersion in Italian culture no doubt appealed to his Italian hosts, but they would not have been unaware that his father Sir Henry Wyatt, as Master of the King's Jewel House, was vital to their complex financial relationship with the Court.[98] Cromwell did much for Wyatt's survival and promotion through many troubles in the 1530s, and Wyatt was standing at the scaffold when he died.

Cromwell's arrival to live at the Austin Friars in 1523 had a further and darker resonance. Among the host of funeral monuments crowding the friars' church he would see a very recent grave: Edward Stafford Duke of Buckingham, hastily buried there after his execution for treason on 17 May 1521. The charges against Buckingham remain puzzling, but are unmistakably an early example of King Henry's ability to destroy members of the nobility with a penchant for boasting about their Plantagenet blood. The proceedings against the Duke show that there had been boasting enough. Over the previous century and more, the Austin Friars of London had come to render a specialist service to whoever was on the English throne, providing a last resting-place for those whom the regime deemed to be its enemies and beheaded as traitors. Treason was not quite so dire a crime as heresy, so such victims of politics deserved a decent Christian burial: only not too decent, nor as honourable as they and their families had no doubt planned.

A number of city friaries were drawn into this grisly post-mortem diplomacy (the best-known example now is from outside London, the Franciscan friary of Leicester which famously received the corpse of King Richard III after the battle of Bosworth, to lie eventually under a car park),[99] but the London Austin Friars were way ahead. The unfortunate Duke of Buckingham was in fact the last such 'traitor' whom the Austin Friars received into their mercy. The great advantage of their church was that its lay congregation was dominated by foreigners, thus going some way to quarantining such politically charged corpses from the wider Tudor public. A London burial also kept the graves of traitors away from provincial churches (some, indeed, friary churches) which were mausolea for the victims' families, where their presence amid the tombs of their ancestors might inflame seditious thoughts in relatives or former servants. For reasons that are not now clear, Buckingham had quite a following, and for a while even the church of Austin Friars was not immune from demonstrations of popular grief for him.[100]

There is no question that Thomas Cromwell came to some involvement in Buckingham's affairs around the Duke's last crisis of 1521; the problem is to gauge what it was. He was understandably not anxious later on to advertise any such toxic connection, and the most precise fragment of evidence is distorted by malice. A decade or so after the event, a relative of Cromwell's called John Gough, a member of the royal garrison in Calais (probably another Welshman, in his own language Ieuan Goch), wrote warning him in slightly impressionistic prose of wild but dangerous accusations by a Welsh colleague in the garrison, Robert ap Reynold, 'naughty words spoke behind your back ... such words ... that, an [if] company had not been, one of us had smarted':

> he saith that he sold you much stuff of the Duke of Buckingham, which he saith that you do owe him 47 angels [£18 16s 6d], with many rigorous words that he said he had done for you before any promotion that God did send you, and moreover he saith that he will come over into England and show it unto the King and the Duke of Norfolk of certain words that you should show him before the Duke [of Buckingham] died a month, as God knoweth, for I cannot tell what they be, but he spaketh like a naughty fellow.[101]

Ap Reynold's own contemporary letters to Cromwell about this debt or a smaller one are unsurprisingly less incendiary (and also interestingly emphasize his Welshness, in an effort to please his correspondent). Any repercussions Gough's revelation earned him from his increasingly intimidating debtor seem to have been fully expunged over the next few years.[102]

One might therefore be inclined to write off this incident as the result of an over-festive night out in Calais, were there not a cache of legal papers in Cromwell's archive, all directly concerning one of the chief accusers of the Duke of Buckingham in 1521, the senior ducal estate official Charles Knyvett. They are an extensive selection of drafts, some fifty-five folios, covering business in which Knyvett was involved, extensively annotated or prepared by Cromwell himself or his clerks, and they date from around 1521-2. Several are drafts of Knyvett's petitions to the King (plus one to Cardinal Wolsey) for restoration to estate offices from which the Duke had dismissed him, and they revisit Knyvett's recent accusations against Buckingham. The final item is a royal protection for Knyvett in travels between London and Calais as a member of the retinue of Lord Berners, Deputy of Calais in the 1520s, with a commencement date in April 1521, the very month when Buckingham was arrested.[103]

Calais; ap Reynold and Welshmen; Knyvett; Cromwell – if these are coincidences, they are remarkably suggestive, even if we cannot join the

dots any further than suggesting that he was drawn in some minor capacity into the Duke's destruction. The Duke of Buckingham was strongly
connected with south Wales, as greatest of the remaining Marcher lords
whose lands dominated the Welsh border with England; his last and in
the end unfinished headquarters, Thornbury Castle in Gloucestershire,
was in sight of the Welsh hills. Cromwell's first major acquisition of land
in 1532, the Welsh lordship of Rhymney, was a former Marcher lordship
of the Duke of Buckingham. Throughout the 1530s, Cromwell remained
a good and constant friend to two of the Duke's children in their continuing difficulties: his son and heir Henry Lord Stafford, struggling to
maintain his household on a fragment of his father's possessions in the
Midlands, and, even more consistently and demandingly, the Duke's
high-spirited daughter Elizabeth, victim of a dynastic marriage to
Thomas Howard Duke of Norfolk gone horribly wrong. These two
orphans remained close in their multiple misfortunes, as attested in a sad
little poem from Lord Stafford for Elizabeth, 'a mother, a sister, a friend
most dear', which he placed on her grave at Lambeth as late as 1558.[104] If
Cromwell's attention to the pair was intended to make amends to the
house of Stafford, then it was a creditable effort.

With Stafford fortunes in ruin after 1521, a different figure moved Cromwell's career in a new direction, with consequences for the whole realm
unfolding over decades. In 1523 he entered service with another of England's greatest men – yet it was not Cardinal Wolsey who first refocused
his interests from London and international legal work and commerce,
but a different Thomas: Thomas Grey, second Marquess of Dorset, England's only marquess at the time. It is likely that Cromwell's Welsh
gentleman cousin Morgan Williams, by then in Dorset's service, was the
means of introduction. In the later 1520s, when Cromwell was in the
household of that other Thomas (my Lord Cardinal), he still displayed
the Marquess's coat of arms in the hall of his house in Austin Friars.[105]
Not much correspondence survives from this phase of Cromwell's career,
and two crucial items have been misdated, causing commentators to
pass over his service with the Greys. What does remain extant confirms
that he was not merely some legal consultant to the Marquess, but actually in his household. He was go-between for private correspondence
between the Marquess and Marchioness and also with the Marquess's
younger brother Lord George Grey, and he acted at the beck and call of
their mother the Dowager Marchioness Cecily, to move household stuff
for her.[106]

Another reason why Cromwell's service to the Marquess has been ignored is that it lasted no longer than a year, which might lead us to suppose that the relationship cooled or at any rate ceased to be of significance – but not so. Morgan Williams continued to serve in the Marquess's household, and his son Richard, destined to be so important to Cromwell in his years of power, was also in the Marquess's service at the end of the 1520s.[107] Quite apart from that, a skein of connections runs between Cromwell himself and the Greys all through those years, including an extraordinarily cordial note from Lord George Grey of 1527 or 1528 addressed to 'my fellow and friend Master Thomas Cromwell' – a remarkable form of address to a former menial servant who had been moving his mother's wardrobe around only a few years before.[108] Even more remarkable is a letter from 1526 of a further brother of the Marquess, Lord John Grey, who calls Cromwell 'brother Cromwell'.[109]

The Greys were not slow to call on their former servant in his steadily increasing good fortune when he entered royal service. In 1532, the second Marquess of Dorset's brother Lord Leonard Grey enlisted Cromwell, newly appointed a royal councillor, in what turned out to be an unsuccessful quest to marry a rich Lincolnshire widow. Amid promises of handsome reward, Lord Leonard emphasized to his 'loving friend and fellow' that 'my whole trust next God and the King is in you.'[110] In the mid-1530s, this relationship became entangled in Cromwell's interventionist policies in Ireland, when he engineered Lord Leonard's appointment as the King's Lord Deputy in Dublin. Grey was meant to be Cromwell's deputy as well, equivalent to Master Secretary's friend Bishop Roland Lee in the Marches of Wales (though, it turned out, not nearly so effective).

Further members of the family, Lord Thomas and Lord Leonard Grey's sister Cecily Lady Dudley and her children, were also beneficiaries of Cromwell's kindness well beyond the call of duty. Cecily's fortunes were shipwrecked by the mental incapacity of her husband John Lord Dudley alias Sutton. In the mid-1530s Cromwell took her son Edward Dudley under his wing, and later even allowed the impoverished youth to dine regularly at his lodgings at St James's before getting him promoted to a military position in Ireland under his uncle Lord Leonard.[111] Touching if injudiciously overlong letters to Cromwell from young Edward survive, including repeated efforts to enlist the Lord Privy Seal, and through him the King himself, in his exceptionally callow pursuit of a wealthy young widow, the Dowager Lady Berkeley – she had more sense than to go beyond flirting with the boy. It was a similar story to Uncle Leonard's five years before, and although neither lovelorn (or predatory) swain won his desire, they evidently both had faith in Cromwell's ability to charm widows.[112]

Genealogy is all in the Tudor age, and the connections ramify. The second Marquess of Dorset married Margaret Wotton, from a distinguished family of Kent; they were part of that extensive Kentish gentry cousinage in which Cromwell became much involved. In 1525 the Marchioness's sister Mary Wotton married Sir Henry Guildford. A generation down in Sir Henry's family was his half-brother Edward's ward, a young man called John Dudley, who married Edward's daughter Jane, also in 1525. This same John Dudley much later became Duke of Northumberland, calling his youngest son Guildford (an ill-starred youth, it turned out). The tendrils go on extending beyond the Greys into Cromwell's expanding household. The Marquess of Dorset's chief house lay at Bradgate in Leicestershire; Cromwell's leading servants recruited from a family named Whalley came from Leicestershire, as did William Brabazon, whom Cromwell later made one of the most important royal officials in Ireland. Lord Leonard Grey reproachfully recalled his long acquaintance with Brabazon after the two fell out in Irish government.[113]

Cromwell's most troublesome inheritance from the Grey household turned out to be Anthony Budgegood, a veteran senior servant of the Marquess. Budgegood continued to serve the Marchioness in her widowhood, but also counted himself as servant to both Cromwell and Richard Cromwell (his former fellow-servant in Dorset service).[114] His story ended very messily: after Cromwell had sent Budgegood over to Lord Leonard on Irish business in 1537–8, the old man returned to England only to flee to Italy, intent on joining the exiled dissident group around Cardinal Pole, financing himself by purloining a sizeable hoard of Cromwell's cash. The last we hear of this servant of the Greys and the Lord Privy Seal is from a papal prison in Rome, trusted by neither side, desperately pouring out well-informed reminiscences about his English political acquaintance, and begging the Pope to lead an invasion of Henry VIII's realm.[115]

One important reason for the previous lack of attention to Cromwell's intimate relationship with the Grey family is an accident of history: Thomas Marquess of Dorset died on 10 October 1530, just too early to help Thomas Cromwell extract himself from the aftermath of Cardinal Wolsey's fall, or to become his ally at Court through the 1530s. His son Henry, third Marquess, was then a young teenager and so remained of no practical account in politics through the rest of Cromwell's career. Yet we should notice that this actually resulted in Cromwell taking on a crucial role in the affairs of the Greys. True to form, he got on very well with the second Marquess's widow Margaret, and sorted out for her the misgovernment of the Cistercian abbey of Tilty in Essex. This was her home, as the Greys as founder-family annexed its guest-house in the 1520s and 1530s.[116] Cromwell later arranged an early and discreet surrender of Tilty in 1536 before any general legislation on monastic dissolutions, using his nephew the Marchioness's former servant Richard Cromwell as agent (see below, pp. 308–9). The Greys' Steward at Tilty was one Henry Sadler, whose son was Ralph Sadler, one of Cromwell's most reliable and trusted servants. Henry Sadler was himself a good friend to Cromwell and Richard, who was probably much the same age as Ralph.[117]

Most remarkable of all was the Marchioness's tribute to Cromwell when the young Marquess was launched at Court in 1534. She begged her old servant to look after her son:

> Whenever you shall see in him any large playing [gambling] or great usual swearing, or any other demeanour unmeet for him to use, which I fear me shall be very often, then it may please you, good Master Cromwell, for my late Lord his good father's sake, whose soul God pardon, in some friendly fashion to rebuke him.[118]

So Cromwell, a long way now from Putney, was asked to step into the role of father for one of England's senior peers. This is not of mere anecdotal significance; for it needs to be remembered that this teenager in need of a firm paternal hand, at that time Marquess of Dorset by inheritance, later gained the even more exalted title Duke of Suffolk and in that capacity tried in 1553 to inaugurate a new royal dynasty through his ill-fated daughter Lady Jane Grey. That was important enough, but there were more profound results of Cromwell's relationship to the Grey family. They must await their proper place in his story (see below, Chapter 15).

This Grey connection suggests new answers for an old puzzle: when Thomas Cromwell became a member of Parliament for the first time, in 1523, for which borough did he sit? A borough constituency it would have to be; it was inconceivable at this stage of his career for such a nonentity to have been chosen as one of the pairs of knights representing a shire. It was too early for him to have looked to Wolsey for a place in Parliament, and in fact the long speech opposing military intervention in France which he may or may not have delivered to the Commons in that Parliament would have been decidedly unwelcome to the King and his chief minister.[119] The Marquess of Dorset was not as rich as his title implied (thanks partly to major estates held for the time being in dower by his mother), so there is little detectable long-standing Grey interest in the many constituencies for which we have no record of representation in the 1523 Parliament. All the more reason for the Marquess to get his man in.[120]

One fragment of evidence might lead us in that direction. It is part of a small bundle in Cromwell's papers dateable to 1523 that also contains his surviving draft note to Margaret Marchioness of Dorset forwarding her husband's and brother-in-law's letters. This memorandum in his own hand concerns an abortive private bill evidently intended for the 1523 Parliament, a petition for the Cistercian abbey of Holm Cultram in Cumberland for tax exemption because of its military importance on the borders.[121] The Marquess of Dorset's family had substantial estates in a more southerly part of Cumberland, and we find Cromwell doing legal work connected with them in 1523.[122] Yet, perhaps more significantly, in 1523 the Marquess of Dorset was on a major mission into Scotland and the Borders, as indeed Cromwell mentioned in his draft letter to the Marchioness. So it is possible that Holm Cultram Abbey lobbied Dorset while in the north, and so his servant sought to handle their request in Parliament. The draft bill for Holm Cultram might place Cromwell in the northern Parliamentary boroughs of Carlisle in Cumberland or Appleby in Westmorland: their MPs in the 1523 Parliament are presently unknown.[123] Otherwise, a natural borough for Cromwell to represent would be Southampton, where one burgess for the 1523 Parliament remains unnamed. The even greater port of Bristol, where neither name survives, would probably have been too big a prize for him at that stage.[124]

Cromwell's humorous reflections on his experience in this very turbulent Parliament have been the subject of much comment, not least because they occur in the very first letter of his we possess, from 17 August 1523, four days after the Commons had been sent home.[125] It is written with a careful though not especially successful attempt to make his undistinguished handwriting stylish, and its recipient was that same John Creke who had addressed him with such Italianate affection the previous year. Historians have rarely bothered to ask how we can still find within Cromwell's own archive an original letter of his written to a man in Bilbao: the answer probably appears if one fast-forwards Creke's life to the early 1530s. By then he was in deep financial trouble and made a series of characteristically impassioned appeals for help from his old friend (see below, pp. 131–2). It is plausible that having treasured this warm letter, worn from much folding and with pen-trials on the back, the stricken merchant then sent it back to its writer in 1531 to stimulate memories of the time when they were close.

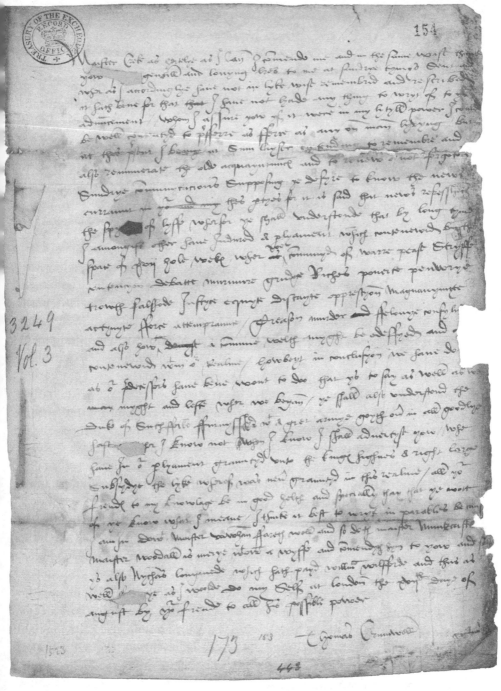

Cromwell writes to his friend John Creke, 17 August 1523; in later years, he rarely bothered to keep his hand this neat. In the middle is the famous satirical list of topics covered in the recent Parliamentary debates, ending, 'Howbeyt in conclusyon we have do[ne] as o'r p'decessors have bene wont to doo that ys to say as well as we myght and lefte wher we begann.'

Cromwell's letter rounds up London gossip for his friend in Spain, and demonstrates a relaxed satirical wit on the subject of Parliament, speaking volumes about his capacity for making friends:

> by long time I, amongst other, have endured a parliament, which continued by the space of seventeen whole weeks, where we communed of war, peace, strife, contention, debate, murmur, grudge, riches, poverty, penury, truth, falsehood, justice, equity, deceit, oppression, magnanimity, activity, force, attemperance [moderation] – treason, murder, felony [?]concealed – and also how a commonwealth might be edified and also continued within our realm. Howbeit, in conclusion, we have done as our predecessors have been wont to do, that is to say, as well as we might, and left where we began.

As Geoffrey Elton observed with justifiable tartness, 'it is a little difficult to understand why writer after writer has taken this amusing note to show contempt for Parliament': testimony that a sense of humour might be a useful tool of historical method.[126] Cromwell's voice resonates with the whimsical ruefulness of a man who could have organized things better if he had been in charge; anyone will recognize the tone if they have experienced the frustrations and incidental comic consolations of a committee meeting that could have been shorter. Windbaggery need not stop business getting done in the end. A good instance of Cromwell's combination of clubbability and efficiency survives from 1523, in a letter from a satisfied client and fellow-MP, Sir Richard Cornwall, from those same weeks following Parliament's end, 'for the great kindness that ye shewed unto me . . . in my time of business in the Parliament'.[127]

The presence in Cromwell's papers of a speech criticizing government plans to invade France has given this text a significance which is unwarranted. If it was in fact delivered, it is an echo from thousands of such frank contributions to Parliamentary debate, a great many of which would have been far more bilious and less well expressed than his. It is almost impossible to find a Parliament in early Tudor England not resounding with gritty opposition; King Henry VIII would have rolled his eyes in weary longing at modern historians' talk of 'Tudor despotism'. Parliament was a 'high court' of the realm, which meant that on many occasions, in conformity with the assumptions of the time, it showed due deference to the monarch's wishes, particularly when God's anointed ruler had properly explained the justification for what he wanted. At other times, it fulfilled the role of any good advisory council in remonstrating, but on a scale intimidating to any monarch: an assembly several hundred strong, ranging exuberantly from peers of the realm to borough burgesses, brimming with opinions and local knowledge, and many understandably grumpy at being uprooted from their families and businesses.

Parliament needed good managing if anything was to get done; often a great deal did not get done. Cromwell quickly learned how results might be achieved, and though as we will see on several occasions Parliament defeated even his capacities, he clearly loved the task. The Speaker of this Parliament, Sir Thomas More, with whom his acquaintance would both deepen and darken, may not have been so enthusiastic.[128] In Cromwell's meteoric career under the King in the 1530s, he amply demonstrated that he had acquired highly important lessons about the use of Parliament from those seventeen weeks back in 1523. This was in fact the main reason why the King raised him from the ranks of the merely useful among senior royal servants. He also made significant friendships from parts of the kingdom as yet beyond his experience, which in later manically busy years he never had a chance to visit. Now even more opportunities beckoned.

3

In the Cardinal's Service: 1524–1528

Early in 1524, towards the age of forty, Thomas Cromwell entered the service of Cardinal Wolsey. It was a plum job, as Gray's Inn recognized in admitting Cromwell to their number this year, and had the Cardinal lived and flourished for decades longer, it would no doubt have remained the basis of an honourable but unmemorable career.[1] No one has succeeded in pinning down exactly who launched him in Wolsey's employment. One relative, Robert Cromwell, Vicar of Battersea, had been Wolsey's Receiver-General, and might look promising, but Robert died in 1517 and he is probably irrelevant to Thomas's arrival in the Cardinal's service seven years later.[2]

Instead, there are connections aplenty among Cromwell's friends around the Greys, the Allens of London and Essex and the Dorsets' Essex abbey of Tilty – right up to Cromwell's previous employer the second Marquess of Dorset himself, who was a schoolboy when he first knew Wolsey in Oxford, and whose father the first Marquess had given Wolsey his first benefice in the Church.[3] Dr John Allen should be high on the list of candidates: a fellow Anglo-Italian with years of residence in Rome, who had been Commissary-General for Wolsey since 1518 – and strongly linked to the Greys.[4] The earliest piece of paperwork pulling Cromwell into Wolsey's business, from early March 1524, is a set of land conveyances involving Dr Allen's cousin, Alderman John Allen, apparently preliminary to the Cardinal's major acquisition of Yorkshire property. Cromwell's role, as 'gentleman of London' (in other words a lawyer), was in a routine service as nominal grantee of the property from its previous owners.[5]

Likewise, we do not have any explanation for why Cromwell left the service of the Greys; but that may not be the right question to ask, for the answer is provided by his entering Wolsey's employment. What Wolsey wanted, he got. What did he want from Thomas Cromwell, apart from a decent jobbing lawyer, when there were swarms of them to choose from? The answer is the Cardinal's legacy project: a monstrous tomb for himself, outclassing the tombs of kings, plus a pair of memorial colleges at Ipswich and Oxford. Wolsey may have been inspired by Pope Leo X's project for giving a tomb to Henry VIII in 1521 (see above, p. 43); certainly it followed soon after that eventually unfulfilled proposal. It is still not absolutely clear where Wolsey planned his tomb to end up, and perhaps he himself left the matter open, waiting to see what the most splendid setting might be, while the craftsmen busied themselves in Westminster. The twin Cardinal Colleges would in any case stand both as chantries for his soul and places of education – education was always a theme of great importance to the former Oxford don, and one of his solaces amid the crushing burden of his royal duties. A school textbook which adapted William Lily's grammar was published in Wolsey's name and branded with the name of Cardinal College Ipswich; it ran into multiple editions in England and Antwerp.[6]

Only a month after his first work on the Yorkshire conveyance, Cromwell was off on what became extensive travels. His brief was to close a considerable number of small monasteries and nunneries, one of the more dramatic proofs of Wolsey's willingness to exploit his powers as papal legate over the Church in England in the name of what he could claim was reform. There had been dissolutions of such small religious houses before, particularly during the long fourteenth- and fifteenth-century wars with France, when the Crown confiscated priories with mother houses across the Channel. Just as Wolsey did now, the monarchy had used the monastic estates for new religious purposes: Henry VI's colleges at King's Cambridge and Eton drew on such former monastic endowments, and the Cardinal's new colleges followed the lead of King Henry's lavish creations in this and in other respects, though always concerned to outdo the royal saint in fostering education and liturgical prayer. Such minor religious houses could be easily characterized by those concerned to reform the Church as being superfluous to ecclesiastical needs, too small-scale and poor to function properly.

It was a major administrative task to sort out the transfer of assets. All through his time in Wolsey's service, it was this 'legacy project' which was Cromwell's main work for the Cardinal, even when the Cardinal's power started disintegrating in 1528, and his servant moved in to cover duties deserted by men less loyal to Wolsey than himself. As the Cardinal said more than once amid the agony of disgrace and vanishing power, the Colleges had become 'in a manner, *opera manuum tuarum* [the work of your own hands]'.[7] Cromwell's first port of call was the small priory at Wallingford on the Thames in Berkshire.[8] He initially kept on his private legal practice in Chancery, and it is not always easy to distinguish between what came to him via his private office and what concerned Wolsey, whose administrative tentacles extended in many directions.[9]

Soon after his arrival in Wolsey's employment in 1524, Cromwell was drawn into disputes around a troublesome young protégé of the Cardinal's, Thomas Stanley Lord Monteagle, who had become the centre of a huge custody battle. His involvement in that particular tangle over several years may have been primarily on behalf of the royal servant Sir John Hussey; it was Hussey who had arranged for Monteagle's placement in Wolsey's household to keep other predators of the Stanley estates at bay, and who from 1526 paid Cromwell an annual pension, which must have been in connection with this prolonged affair. The Monteagle business was another way in which Cromwell's acquaintance with the nobility was widening beyond his early service to the Greys, since a great many noblemen took sides in this issue or were brought in to arbitrate. Among them were the Dukes of Suffolk and Norfolk and Thomas Lord Darcy of Templehurst, as well as Hussey and Cromwell's old patron Thomas Marquess of Dorset.[10]

Wolsey made Cromwell a member of his personal council in 1527, which might have given him some leeway to diversify his duties. Nevertheless, right up to Wolsey's last months in 1530, Cromwell's chief business remained helping the Cardinal to shepherd his soul into the next life, and it is likely that the promotion was intended to facilitate that intricate project.[11] Moreover, we have concentrated too much on the very large amount of archive material about Wolsey's dissolution of monasteries which funded the two Colleges, not paying enough attention to the centrality of Cardinal Wolsey's tomb in Cromwell's duties.[12] The vital clue is provided by two letters which survive not in the State Papers but in partial copies in an invaluable collection of notes made for Lord Herbert's life of Henry VIII by his secretary Thomas Master in the 1620s, now preserved in the archives of Jesus College Oxford.[13] Both letters were written at the moment when Wolsey's efforts to do King Henry's bidding in matters of high policy had finally failed and brought the Cardinal disaster.

The most important of the letters was written on 31 January 1530 to Wolsey, who was by that time ill and in disgrace at Esher, by the Florentine sculptor Benedetto Rovezzano. Rovezzano was the chief sculptor working on the Cardinal's tomb, as well as on a major altar for Cardinal College Oxford. He was seeking to get a final reckoning of his accounts on the tomb project, and return to his wife and children in Florence, from whom he claimed to have been separated for a decade. No doubt

Four bronze angels by Rovezzano topping Wolsey's tomb survived eventually
at Harrowden Hall (Northamptonshire), though their wings went missing as
late as the 1970s. The angels themselves are now safe in the Victoria and Albert
Museum.

Rovezzano's knowledge of the dire state of the Cardinal's affairs spurred
him on to this sudden rediscovery of family responsibilities and a re-
ignited sense of urgency on a project which, until then, he had been happy
to see drift serenely on its way.

What is noticeable is Cromwell's centrality to every aspect of the
tomb's creation. It had been Cromwell, said Rovezzano, who ordered the
contract with Antonio Cavallari, the King's agent for gilt work. Conspicuously, Rovezzano had received his first payment in June 1524, soon
after Cromwell had entered Wolsey's service. There had followed very
substantial further payments over five years, the regal scale of which he
pointedly commented was appropriate, since the project was 'of not less
workmanship, beauty or cost than the tomb of Henry VII' in Westminster Abbey. The money had come via Cavallari and his fellow-Lucchese
merchant Antonio Buonvisi, both of whom happened to be long-standing
friends of Cromwell.[14] Rovezzano had laid out his own money on bronze
and Florentine marble, and now he would appreciate Cromwell, Wolsey's
'consiliarius', rounding up matters so he could go home. A previous letter
from Cavallari to Wolsey made similar points, and also asked him to let
the gilder (a separate cost) return to Antwerp. There is no hint that either
of the Italians was dissatisfied with Cromwell's dealings with them;
indeed Rovezzano praised him as 'a man of great talent and exceptional
skill'.[15] Over the next decade, Cromwell, now risen to much greater
heights, continued to be good to Cavallari's widow in various troubles.[16]

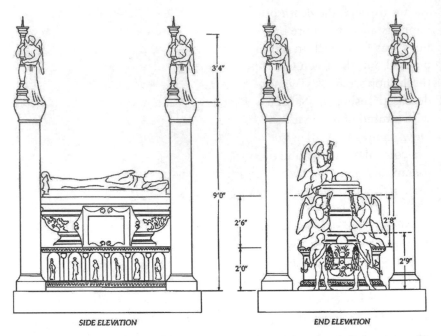

SIDE ELEVATION   *END ELEVATION*

Phillip Lindley's reconstruction of Wolsey's tomb, side and end elevations; unlike even the grandest of medieval English tombs, the footprint of this ultimate Renaissance monument was almost square.

All this suggests that the key to Cromwell's employment by Wolsey was his ability to deal with Italians. One more piece of evidence strengthens this idea, once we realize its significance: in 1525, Wolsey secured Cromwell's appointment as Town Clerk of Salisbury. This was Cromwell's very first appointment to public office anywhere, and actually it was more or less his only such appointment while Wolsey employed him, explaining perhaps his bitter remark to George Cavendish at the time of the Cardinal's fall that 'I never had any promotion by my lord to the increase of my living.'[17] So why Salisbury? It was not because Cromwell had any personal connection with the city, as became clear from the correspondence around his appointment. The Salisbury Cathedral prebendary John Bigges, who wrote Cromwell a letter of welcome, had not previously met him, and clearly also thought that it would be helpful to suggest a local deputy if the incumbent deputy died. Bigges even had to tell Cromwell the date of the next local 'law day' (the day for holding courts).[18]

Cromwell had become Town Clerk after a tip-off to Cardinal Wolsey from the diocesan Vicar-General, Dr Thomas Bennet, that the office was vacant through the death of the previous Clerk, Roger Twynhoe.[19] This happenstance was more important than it might seem. The city of Salisbury was very much in the hands of its bishop and cathedral; as Bigges pointed out, the Town Clerk's deputy customarily doubled as receiver of the bishop's rents.[20] Twynhoe had also been an executor of the lately deceased Bishop of Salisbury, Edmund Audley, a veteran churchman with a mind of his own, who had never been one of Wolsey's soulmates. Now, thanks to Audley's death, Wolsey had the chance to acquire effective control of the city and diocese, as its newly nominated Bishop was an Italian absentee, Lorenzo Campeggio, who left Wolsey to run the diocese, an opportunity of which the Cardinal took full advantage.

Twynhoe's death was a bonus. Within a month of Bennet's initial letter, Wolsey had shoehorned Cromwell into the office: who could be better than an officer of his own, familiar with Italy, to negotiate when necessary with the absentee Campeggio?[21] The Clerkship remained at a local level in the hands of a deputy supervised by Bennet. It did not personally involve Cromwell overmuch, sometimes to the vexation of the city fathers. He probably did a better job as Town Clerk than did Wolsey's talentless illegitimate son Thomas Winter as diocesan Chancellor; yet it may be significant that, when Cromwell was desperately looking for a Parliamentary seat in 1529, there is no evidence that he turned to Salisbury (see below, pp. 91–3).[22]

Dissolving small monasteries for the endowment of the new Cardinal Colleges sent Cromwell right across southern England and the Midlands as far north-west as Staffordshire. This brought several new dimensions to his life. The cosmopolitan European traveller had a fairly limited acquaintance with his own country: largely London, Surrey and Essex and the ports of Southampton and Bristol. Now he was given the chance to roam widely (on travel expenses) across the whole of lowland England, and used his considerable charm to make all sorts of interesting friendships. This meant that, just at the moment when the kingdom was beginning to divide on religious lines under the influence of the Reformation in mainland Europe, Cromwell came to the King's service on the fall of Wolsey equipped with a range of acquaintance on both sides of the gulf.

In East Anglia, for instance, Cromwell had previously known few people north of Essex (one exception was the Norwich merchant Reynold Littleprow, who may have got to know Cromwell in Antwerp, and through the 1530s exercised the prerogative of long friendship repeatedly to urge him to measures of social reform).[23] The plans for Cardinal College Ipswich changed all that. Cromwell's central role in creating the College there

threw him into the company of men in Wolsey's service who had come
from Suffolk or who were still important in the borough's affairs. What
started as business relationships blossomed into real friendships, especially
with the Suffolk gentleman Thomas Rush and his stepson Wolsey's servant
Thomas Alvard. Rush and Alvard were beneficiaries in Cromwell's never-
executed will of 1529, and it was to Rush that Cromwell first turned that
same year in trying to find a new seat in the House of Commons. What is
striking in this Rush/Alvard circle is that very few of its members went
on to show enthusiasm for the developing Reformation; on the contrary,
several were not afraid to be aggressively traditionalist. That did not stop
them from being numbered among Cromwell's friends who went on
expecting and getting favours: what bound them together was a shared
reverence for the memory of Cardinal Wolsey. This catholicity of friendships is a dimension of Cromwell's mastery of English government which
we will encounter again and again in the coming story.[24]

In his travels in west Sussex, Cromwell gained permanent gratitude from
a small Augustinian house called Shulbrede by securing it a reprieve from
dissolution. Here the threat came not from Wolsey's dissolution programme
but from parallel moves by the energetic and independent-minded Bishop of
Chichester, Robert Sherburne. Sherburne was evidently trying to use surplus monastic resources to help finance four brand-new prebends which he
had just founded for his cathedral.[25] In 1525 he got as far as demolishing
part of the church and domestic buildings at Shulbrede, no doubt intending
to create a feasible prebendal house there, but desperate pleas from the
monks to local gentry friends resulted in two of these gentlemen button-
holing Cromwell while on legal business in Westminster Hall. On their
suggestion, he lobbied the hereditary patron of the priory, the Earl of Northumberland, via his eldest son Henry Lord Percy. As a result, Shulbrede
Priory survived in its truncated premises another decade (not greatly to the
edification of the monastic life in England), and gratefully voted its saviour
an annuity. This was Cromwell's earliest pension from any monastery, no
doubt an eye-opener for him as a possible source of income.[26]

There is further evidence at exactly the same time of Cromwell's
involvement in a reprieve of one of Wolsey's intended dissolutions: another
small Augustinian priory called Bilsington, in Kent. Sir Henry Guildford
(as we have noted, brother-in-law of Cromwell's late employer the Marquess of Dorset) wrote in notably friendly terms asking him to call in on
him at Leeds Castle on his way back to London to continue their conversations about a lease of Bilsington from the Cardinal, since he understood
that Cromwell was supervising its dissolution alongside another Kentish
Augustinian house at Tonbridge.[27] In fact Bilsington remained undissolved

for another decade. It is difficult not to see its escape as connected to the fact that its Prior was Arthur St Leger, brother to another Kentish gentleman, Cromwell's friend Anthony St Leger. When Anthony reminisced in 1536 about 'the goodness that I found . . . in you in my Lord Cardinal his days', this may have been what he was thinking of. The community of Bilsington ceded Cardinal Wolsey the right to appoint a new prior to Bilsington in 1528, because Prior St Leger had moved on to head a slightly larger Augustinian house, Leeds Priory. It acted as chaplaincy to the neighbouring castle of Leeds, home to Sir Henry Guildford. This was a cosy set of arrangements.[28]

Cromwell the defender of monasteries is an unfamiliar figure. It must be pointed out that the Cardinal's programme of dissolutions triggered bitter opposition around some of the houses that he did indeed close. At the other end of Sussex, and over the border into Kent, there was serious trouble in summer 1525. Tenants of the Thames-side Augustinian abbey of Lesnes were downright obstructive when Cromwell's servant Stephen Vaughan turned up with a team to carry out surveys and hold courts.[29] Thirty miles south of Lesnes, the townsfolk of Tonbridge preferred the continuance of the Augustinian priory there to offers of scholarships at Cardinal College, while another 11 miles south in Wealden Sussex there was a full-scale riotous attempt to reopen Premonstratensian Bayham Abbey; in the two latter instances, there is a suspicion that Archbishop Warham had discreetly encouraged the resistance.[30] It is tempting to see Cromwell's lasting friendships with the Guildfords and Darrells, both local families of upper gentry with strong Court and government connections, as based on their common experience of riding out the storms at Bayham. Yet given that the Guildfords were so closely allied to the Marquess and Marchioness of Dorset, the chain of relationships may have worked the other way round, as Cromwell sought local backing in his work in difficult circumstances.

To these outbreaks of anger in Sussex and Kent, we might add evidence of trouble at Ipswich in early 1526. Cromwell and Thomas Rush obtained a legal order there that the Ipswich gentleman George Fastolf should keep the peace against Cromwell's friend and fellow-employee of Wolsey, John Smith.[31] Rather alarmingly for Cromwell, he and his friend and colleague John Allen were linked in 1527 in a worried report by the diplomat William Knight to Wolsey about gossip at Court, warning him not to use Allen as a messenger to Henry VIII: 'I have heard the King and noblemen speak things incredible of the acts of Master Allen and Cromwell, a great part whereof it shall be expedient that your Grace do know, as at your coming ye shall.' John Allen did indeed acquire a fearsome reputation in the monasteries he visited as inspector for Wolsey, as was recalled by a sarcastic remark a decade later about one of Vice-Gerent Cromwell's own monastic visitors: monks 'were never so much afraid of Dr Allen as they be of him, he uses such rough fashion with them'.[32] Unpopularity was the drawback of doing one's job efficiently. At least Wolsey appreciated the results, for this was the year that he promoted Cromwell to be styled one of his council.[33]

Despite understandable expressions of popular anger against Wolsey's agent in dissolution, it is clear that at the same time Cromwell became a welcome visitor in a widely dispersed range of monasteries beyond those which might be threatened. He appears (rather remarkably for a layperson in a cardinal's employ) to have taken on a general informal portfolio for monastic affairs. One is not surprised that he maintained a relationship with John Burton, former Prior of St Frideswide's Oxford, whose premises became Cardinal College; this was at the centre of his concerns in the legacy project. In April and May 1524 William Barton, the Augustinian Abbot of Osney outside Oxford, was induced to resign by Wolsey's officials, to make way for Prior Burton from St Frideswide's, now out of a job thanks to the creation of Cardinal College.[34] The newly promoted Abbot Burton of Osney remained a regular correspondent and dinner guest of Cromwell's into the 1530s, and made him the Abbey's High Steward.[35]

Other relationships with monasteries and friaries beyond Cromwell's explicit portfolio are particularly worthy of note. Some must be the result of simple proximity, so predictably he took an interest in the affairs of his landlords the Austin Friars, and surviving in his papers is a wonderfully colourful if semi-literate memorandum from an elderly member of the community, detailing the troubles there that contributed to the abrupt retirement of the aged Prior Bellond in the mid-1520s.[36] Richard Ingworth, a Dominican friar later to become Cromwell's main agent in destroying all friaries in the kingdom, dated their friendship to 1526, by which time Ingworth was probably already Prior of the important Dominican friary at King's Langley in Hertfordshire. That was close to Cardinal Wolsey's favourite country retreat, The More, as Ingworth, now promoted as Bishop of Dover, reminded his patron in a letter of 1538.[37]

Other lasting monastic friendships of Cromwell's reflect Wolsey's nationwide interventions which sprang from his legatine powers or his wider dominance of politics in the late 1520s. As late as 1538, the long-suffering Abbot Stonewell of the great Benedictine house of Pershore in Worcestershire expected Cromwell not only to remember straight away that Wolsey had placed him at Pershore after removing an unsatisfactory predecessor in 1526, but also to know something of the priory over which he had previously presided (and clearly much preferred), Tynemouth: 'I trust your lordship doth not forget now what I left when I came to this.' Stonewell did not even think it necessary to remind him of the name of Tynemouth.[38]

Cromwell developed a special relationship with an equally venerable Benedictine house south of Pershore on the edge of the Cotswolds, Winchcombe Abbey. This probably resulted from Cardinal Wolsey's tutelage after 1528 of the young heir of the extremely wealthy Sir William Compton, who had been one of Wolsey's chief rivals at Court up to an abrupt retirement from royal service, and whose death provided a chance too good to miss of completing a political triumph.[39] Wolsey made Cromwell a chief administrator of Compton's property, an example of a small widening of his duties now that he was the Cardinal's councillor. The connection with Winchcombe was that Compton's will had shown his deep affection for the Abbey (arising from local family connections) and he made it custodian of a fund to deal with any testamentary legal disputes.[40] Now Cromwell became Steward of Compton's chief London property at Tottenham, installed by Wolsey. He also saw to the technicalities of dealing with the royal Escheator for Compton's estates, and some of the drafts to do with this are in the hand of his clerk. Winchcombe would have been on his circuit of responsibilities.[41]

From this time onward, Cromwell became a recipient of warm letters from the retired Abbot of Winchcombe Richard Kidderminster, one of the most outstanding and respected churchmen of his age. As late as 1532 or 1533, the aged Kidderminster could write to Cromwell, now 'Councillor to the King', to affirm after many pious compliments, 'that I do daily hear of the increase of your honour and authority is more to my comfort in Jesu than I may express in writing'. Others of a traditional cast of mind in religion might not then have been so enthusiastic at Cromwell's rise into the King's favour.[42] Kidderminster's successor as Abbot was also a friendly correspondent, more than once expecting to see Cromwell at Winchcombe, and saying with mild reproach in one letter that the Abbey had thought to have entertained him over the Christmas season.[43] In forming friendships with such great figures of the Benedictine tradition, Cromwell was establishing links with English monasticism at its most scholarly and reform-minded: Winchcombe, Hailes and Evesham, near neighbours in the Cotswolds, enjoyed a lively and interconnected intellectual life, fully aware of humanist advances in learning, and also in close contact with the University of Oxford.[44] The intimate relationship between Winchcombe Abbey and the King's chief minister persisted until its belated dissolution on the eve of Christmas 1539, as we will discover.

Other relationships may have emerged out of Cromwell's continuing private legal practice or from his moneylending business. There were a good number of prominent abbeys and priories among his debtors when he rounded up his accounts in early 1529.[45] No later than that year, he was receiving an annual fee for legal services from one of the greatest and most politically significant monasteries in the North of England, St Mary's in York: this retainer was not a great sum at 40s per annum, but Abbot Whalley, who may have been a relative of servants of his, asked him to 'be good and friendly in all my causes as I shall stand need, which ye said ye would be at my last being in London, at what time I found you very loving and kind'. Before the Abbot died in 1530 he also made Cromwell a grant of the reversion of one of the abbey's Yorkshire parsonages.[46] Very many abbeys would be following suit with fees once Cromwell was prominent in the King's service, but such an early example as York deserves noting. St Mary's acted as depository for royal revenue in the North, so even more than in the case of Winchcombe there were good reasons for Cromwell's intimate contact with it to persist after Wolsey's fall.

One of the most charming examples of Cromwell's relationships with monasteries comes from the Augustinian priory of Launde in Leicestershire, for which Cromwell did several favours during his Wolsey years, and which after his execution was to become the chief home and indeed burial place of Gregory Cromwell. Thomas Frisby, a canon of Launde, wrote to Cromwell probably in 1531, presenting him with six cheeses and cheerfully reminding him of one of his visits to the priory when they were out together walking home from a neighbouring village, and Frisby fell over on his back in the snow.[47] None of these letters from Winchcombe, York or Launde were written at a time when Cromwell was the all-powerful statesman to be flattered and placated, unlike his depressingly voluminous pile of sycophantic monastic correspondence from 1532 onwards.

Altogether, Cromwell in his travels around monasteries gained an interest in and country-wide knowledge of monastic life which was very unusual among laypeople in his day, and which fatefully transmogrified with remarkable speed after he gained real power under King Henry in 1532. This distinctive set of relationships reflected his anomalous place among Wolsey's servants dealing with Church affairs. Most were clergy, as one would expect from the Pope's legate *a latere* in England, but Cromwell was not, because of his specialist role in preparing the Cardinal's plans for immortality in both this world and the next. In the typical style of his improvisatory genius, Cromwell was to develop this anomaly when as a layperson he revived Wolsey's legatine powers in the name of the King in the 1530s, eventually as Vice-Gerent.

There was also a very different and directly contradictory outcome of Wolsey's legacy project, which takes us deeper into Cromwell's religious outlook in the later 1520s. Drawing together a great deal of evidence will reveal his discreet but decisive and effective commitment to the forces of religious reform subverting traditional religion from various different directions.[48] At the centre of it all was the extraordinary circumstance that in 1528 Wolsey's new foundation of Cardinal College Oxford was revealed as a nest of England's leading clerical converts to evangelical religion. They were mostly imports from Cambridge, and their exposure was a national sensation. Dr John London, Warden of New College Oxford, wrote in frustration to John Longland, Bishop of Lincoln and University Chancellor, about one of the leading vipers in the bosom, John Clerk: 'Would God my Lord's Grace had never been motioned to call him or any other Cambridge man unto his most towardly [promising] College.'[49]

But who was doing this 'motioning'? It can only have been Cromwell. His involvement with Cardinal College Oxford did not end with setting it up, because from 1528 he was its Receiver-General and Surveyor, and he clearly went on spending a lot of time there: in March 1528, his friend the great humanist Thomas Elyot issued a standing invitation to his Oxfordshire home at Long Combe, but added self-deprecatingly, 'I cannot make you such cheer as you have in Oxford.'[50] The Sub-Dean of the College, Thomas Canner, wrote to thank him for securing the pleasant Oxfordshire benefice of East Hendred from the Cardinal, 'as I suppose by your special motion and procurement to my lord's Grace'.[51] At much the same time, a Suffolk gentleman wrote to Cromwell soliciting a place for a friend's son at Cardinal College Oxford; he evidently considered that a natural route to follow.[52] Most directly of all, the legal entanglements of William Cockes, a learned though troubled Dominican, have preserved a direct reference to Cromwell's central role in admissions to Cardinal College, for, as Cockes reminded the Lord Privy Seal eight years later, back in 1528 his wrongful arrest for debt and apostasy from his order had blocked his application to 'Your Goodness' and to Wolsey's other senior servant Thomas Arundell 'for a room in my Lord Cardinal's College'.[53]

At the very least, Cromwell was responsible for the costs of bringing the evangelical scholars over from Cambridge, but he could easily make informed choices in recruitment because he had so many personal contacts in Cambridge University, which as we will see, despite all these links with Cardinal College, he chose over Oxford to supervise his son Gregory's education.[54] The arrival of so many suspect men at Cardinal College was neither accident nor carelessness; there could have been quite different recruits from Cambridge. We know of at least one traditionalist-minded

Cambridge don who refused to accept the siren call to Oxford: his name was Thomas Cranmer.[55] Several strands of evidence reinforce this notion, and bear witness to Cromwell nurturing this evangelical group once they had arrived. First is the remarkable resonance of this Oxford scandal with an earlier phase of Cromwell's career: Boston, which provided some of the actors in the Oxford affair.

Boston was an odd place in the early Reformation, with much going on below the surface of its extrovert public religious life. The impressively long list of evangelical books from Germany and Switzerland rounded up in Oxford might usefully and unobtrusively have entered England via its quayside.[56] While, as we have seen, its Gild was a symbol of some of the most demonstrative late medieval devotion in all England, among the fleet of chaplains whom the Gild employed on a short-term basis to sing their round of masses in Michaelmas Term 1521 was one William Tyndale, surely the future biblical translator, while in 1525 the Gild accounts reveal a startling conjunction of later prominent evangelical names in the musical and clerical staff: Robert Testwood (with John Taverner just up the road at Tattershall College) and, among the clergy, Thomas Garrett, the master of Boston Grammar School, and Thomas Lawney.[57] Of these four, Testwood became master of the choristers at Cardinal College Ipswich, while Garrett, Lawney and Taverner appeared in the new foundation of Cardinal College Oxford; Garrett was in fact the leading actor in the 1528 scandal, though unlike most of the miscreants he had already been an Oxford man.[58]

But there is more. One of the small religious houses which Thomas Cromwell dissolved for Wolsey in 1525 was Poughley Priory, at the foot of the Berkshire Downs, 27 miles south of Oxford. Vivid snapshots of its dissolution and subsequent fate come from two discursive letters from Edward Fetyplace, a senior official of the Duke of Suffolk and a local gentleman with whom Cromwell was much engaged while winding up the priory's affairs. From Fetyplace's first letter in 1525, we glimpse furniture being removed from the priory for Oxford, presumably to help out in the chaotic first stages of setting up scholars at Cardinal College, but the residential buildings at Poughley remained habitable.[59] In Fetyplace's second letter, written just short of two years after Poughley's dissolution, he complained that the Cardinal scholars had thoughtlessly misused fittings while they stayed in the former priory in summer 1526.[60] The Dean and canons claimed that this transfer to Poughley was an attempt to escape the plague in Oxford – it was indeed a bad year for plague nationwide. Cardinal Wolsey was sceptical, and instituted enquiries into what he clearly suspected was a mere summer jaunt, but the visitors seem to have turned their time away from the building site that was Cardinal College into the equivalent of a long-vacation reading party.[61]

It is then clear from Dr London's letter of 1528 to Bishop Longland that there was a second summer stay in 1527, and now the Cardinal's suspicions were in one sense fully justified. On this second occasion, thanks to London, we know that the reading was on specifically evangelical texts and was led by John Clerk, canon of Cardinal College and a former colleague of Thomas Cranmer at Jesus College Cambridge. Clerk was a ringleader in the Oxford evangelical circle, fated to be one of those who sickened and died in August 1528 while imprisoned in the College cellars for his religious misdemeanours – an early martyr for the English Reformation. We have a letter from Clerk himself, written to Cromwell in August probably of 1527. In it he mentions a previous letter of his carried to Cromwell by one of the evangelical Fellows of Cardinal College, no less a figure than that better-known early Reformation martyr John Frith, another recruit from Cambridge.[62]

And there is still more about the Poughley adventures. A man Cromwell employed to collect the rents at Poughley Priory appears both in Cromwell's accounts for the priory and in the two letters from Edward Fetyplace, to whom he was consistently obstructive, nevertheless without earning dismissal from Cromwell.[63] He was a minor gentleman from nearby Hungerford who boasted two surnames, as was not uncommon at the time, though on this occasion both of them are rather frustratingly capable of major variation, and have been effective in concealing him from subsequent scrutiny by historians. He was called John Hidden or Eden alias Clydesdale, Glydesdale or Ledesdale – and he was a Lollard.[64] Although his surname 'Hidden' probably came from the Hungerford manor he held, it was appropriate for an activist in this discreet group of religious dissenters.

Lollardy was an irritant a century and a half old in early Tudor England's otherwise placid religious landscape: a native movement, taking its inspiration in the late fourteenth century from bitter critiques of the official Church developed by the Oxford philosopher John Wyclif. Official persecution by both Church and monarchy had rooted Lollards out of the universities and normally out of gentry society, but they clung on in their clandestine religious life, generally keeping a tepid outward conformity to their community's public worship. Not many made enough public fuss to attract examination by authority, though some suffered death at the stake as heretics, particularly if a bishop or Church official was unusually enthusiastic for ferreting them out. Lollards cherished increasingly tattered Bibles in English translation (banned by the Church)

and read aged handwritten pamphlets condemning the Church's power
and wealth. They had their own unofficial teachers helping them keep in
touch with one other across various regions of the country where they
had some strength; the Thames valley was one. When in 1517 Martin
Luther's dispute with the official Church erupted far away in Saxony, the
reverberations reached England in no more than a year or two; English
Lollards knew that they were no longer alone in their dissidence, and
they reached out to the first evangelicals, some of whom may have started
life in Lollard circles.

John Hidden's family were unusual among Lollards in having some
claim to gentry status, and his sister Alice in particular emerges from
documentation lovingly preserved by John Foxe as one of the most charismatic among them in the Oxfordshire/Berkshire area. After two marriages
and on the eve of a third to a local gentleman called Thomas Doyley, she
was exceptionally wealthy, worth well over a thousand pounds in money
and moveables, plus lands and tenements.[65] This rare example of a Lollard
gentlewoman had a galvanizing effect on her three successive husbands
and their families; in the last case, negatively. In 1527 the Court of Chancery had to be dragged in to shore up at least the legal side of the collapsing
marriage of Alice and Thomas Doyley. The lawyer responsible for the
paperwork in this enforced reconciliation between a Lollard wife and a
traditionalist husband, in the same year that Poughley had been sub-
verted by Oxford scholars on vacation, was none other than Cardinal
Wolsey's councillor Thomas Cromwell.[66] Those around him saw his partisanship for Alice as odd. A friend and colleague in Wolsey's service, a
friend of Thomas Doyley as well, reproached Cromwell in an otherwise
very cordial letter with being 'much friendly to the woman in obtaining
the same [settlement]'.[67]

Poughley was not the only setting for Cromwell's contacts with Cambridge evangelicals and their various connections among the Lollards.
During 1527–8, he was near neighbour at his home in Austin Friars to one
of the chief actors in the early English Reformation, the Augustinian friar
Robert Barnes. Barnes's dissidence was a sign that the divisions that a
decade earlier tore apart the Augustinian friars in Germany were now
spreading to the English Province. He was arrested and imprisoned in 1526
for a reformist sermon preached in Cambridge at Christmas 1525, while
Prior of the Austin Friars there. He bitterly denounced the Church's wealth;
clearly the English Austin Friars' own reckless pursuit of profits through
their indulgence sales (see above, pp. 31–4) was causing the order deep
heart-searching. After around six months in the Fleet Prison in London,
Barnes was transferred to a curiously open house arrest at the London

Austin Friars. He was active there in distributing copies of William Tyndale's New Testament, and received a steady procession of visitors from as far away as north Essex, fruitfully reconciling the two uneasily related streams of new evangelical and old Lollard dissent. Bishop Cuthbert Tunstall was well into a crackdown on Lollards in the London diocese before he recognized the folly of allowing Barnes's nominal confinement in the capital, and shipped him off to the Austin Friars at Northampton.[68]

It is inconceivable that Thomas Cromwell did not meet his extrovert evangelical neighbour at Austin Friars, and tempting to wonder if he had a hand in Barnes's move from the Fleet Prison to the friary. In the 1530s, unsurprisingly, Barnes became an eager client of Cromwell's. Yet if that early connection with Barnes remains clouded in discretion, there is nothing hidden about Cromwell's exactly contemporary relationship with Barnes's colleague and admirer at the Cambridge Austin Friars, Friar Miles Coverdale. Coverdale became one of the most important among those who created Tudor England's vernacular Bible; his psalm translations are still those sung by Anglican choirs from the Book of Common Prayer. Between 1525 and 1527, certainly before his abandonment of the regular life and flight from the kingdom in 1528, Coverdale wrote two letters to Cromwell remarkable for their fervently evangelical tone and deep gratitude to Cromwell for his encouragement.

Coverdale reminisced fondly in his first letter about his 'godly communication' with Cromwell on 'Easter even' and asked for financial help 'now I begin to taste of Holy Scriptures, and godly savour of holy and ancient doctors'.[69] The tone is both evangelical and humanist, fascinated by the biblical text and the early theologians of the Church now readily available in good editions, many by the great editor Erasmus. Cromwell is cast in the role of a humanist patron, whom Coverdale, 'your child and bedeman in Jesu Christ', can address in Latin without embarrassment to his correspondent, teasingly seeking a father's blessing like an unworthy son, as Jacob had done from the unsuspecting patriarch Isaac. A second letter is very similar in its warmth, its ready switching between Latin and English; it cheerfully conveys the latest scandal from Cambridge University.[70]

The Cromwell reflected in Coverdale's letters is a man versed in humanist culture, interested in goings-on at Cambridge and also happy to be addressed in the devotional rhetoric of the first generation of English evangelicals. Significantly both Coverdale and Barnes were currently active in establishing and widening communications between East Anglian Lollards and the developing Reformation in mainland Europe, distributing books and introducing religious dissidents to each other from these two different worlds, native dissent and university-based evangelicalism. This is the same pattern revealed through Cromwell's activities at Poughley Priory.[71]

Cromwell's careful plans for the education of his son Gregory are relevant here. He did not try to repeat his own triumphantly successful history of self-tutoring, but was concerned to do the best for his son. Over the years, as his own status rose, his priorities shifted from scholarly grounding to the moulding of a potential courtier (a move in any case encouraged by Gregory's manifest lack of enthusiasm for scholarly pursuits). What is significant is strong evidence of evangelical connections in the academic foundations of Gregory's programme of schooling. At the end of the 1520s, a year or two after Cromwell's correspondence with Coverdale and maybe before the death of Mistress Elizabeth Cromwell, he entrusted overall supervision of Gregory's education to Margaret Vernon, Prioress of the small Benedictine nunnery at Little Marlow on the Thames. They may have met during Cromwell's Oxford duties, though Prioress Vernon was clearly not a devotee of strict monastic enclosure, and had much acquaintance among Cromwell's friends in the City of London. She was a forceful and articulate lady, and her frequent holograph letters are written in a strong confident hand that her pupils would have done well to emulate. Even in later years she was not too intimidated by the Lord Privy Seal's power to refrain from haggling with him if necessary; significantly, while it was normal to send small boys to be educated by nuns, Cromwell was prepared to accept her insistence that her responsibility should extend as late as his son's twelfth birthday.[72]

Gregory's first academic tutor under the Prioress's regime was Cromwell's friend the internationally renowned exponent of language teaching John Palsgrave, prebendary of St Paul's Cathedral, but evidently this did not prove satisfactory, and in 1529, when Gregory was nine or ten, Vernon and Cromwell consulted about a replacement.[73] Her recommendation was William Englefield, a Fellow of Lincoln College Oxford, whom she had watched approvingly through his tutoring of another small boy at Little Marlow. To her annoyance, Cromwell overruled her and looked to the other university, despite her pointing out that his own friend 'Mr Somer' considered the Cambridge choice 'a man that will not take the pains which would be for my pleasure'. We have already encountered this London merchant Thomas Somer, involved in a Bedfordshire building contract, and with impeccable and precocious evangelical credentials (see above, p. 35).

Consequently, although Prioress Vernon retained her overall supervision of Gregory, Cromwell sent his son to be tutored in Cambridge in company with Gregory's older cousin Christopher Wellifed and a boy called Nicholas Sadler, who may have been a younger brother of Cromwell's talented young servant Ralph Sadler. The first chosen instructor who elbowed aside the Oxford don was a Fellow of Pembroke Hall, John Cheking, a fussy and assertive individual whose keen eye on his own interests nevertheless did not make him think it tactless to write to the vigilant parent in elegant humanist Latin, just as Coverdale had.[74] Pembroke Hall was already notable in the University for its group of Fellows who had an interest in evangelical reform, and Cheking was no exception: the reminiscences of the combative biblical translator George Joye place him squarely among the evangelical activists of Cambridge in the late 1520s. The inventory of his library at his death in March 1536 shows that it was bulging with avant-garde literature from across the spectrum of Reformations in mainland Europe: Bucer, Bugenhagen, Bullinger, François Lambert, Luther, Melanchthon, Oecolampadius, Zwingli.[75]

The evidence for Cromwell's involvement in England's networks of early evangelicals and even Lollards in the 1520s is thus inescapable. It is true that in his years of power under Henry VIII, while he steadily promoted his own dynamically evangelical agenda, he went on being capable of publicly making apparent gestures towards traditional religion. In 1517, at the dawn of the Reformation, Cromwell's service to the Gild of Boston promoted the very indulgence trade which in the same years sparked Martin Luther's wrath. Then he made his greatest career move so far on the basis of a spectacular project of soul-provision for England's papal legate.

Yet such apparently paradoxical employments were always on Cromwell's own terms, and ended up clandestinely promoting his private religious agenda. In his audacious manipulation of the new foundations of Cardinal College Oxford and Ipswich, he prefigured an equally ambitious and risky enterprise in 1536-40, when in effect he used Archbishop Cranmer as a front-man to create permanent links with Zürich (see below, Chapter 15). That Reformed city-state, leader of Swiss evangelical expansion, symbolized everything his master Henry VIII loathed most in the Reformations across the Channel, and yet Cromwell persisted in this project. Indeed, to this we can add Vice-Gerent Cromwell's steady official promotion in the 1530s of a vernacular Bible, the text of which was largely from William Tyndale, the man at whose murder the King had connived and whom he never forgave for heresy – ably supplemented by the work of Cromwell's early client the renegade friar Miles Coverdale.[76] In all these cases, Cromwell for a while got away with the sleight of hand.

How can we characterize this form of religion, already forged in Cromwell's career in the 1520s? It is deceitful, certainly, hypocritical perhaps: very different from the stentorian public proclamation which marked out the magisterial Reformations of Martin Luther, Huldrych Zwingli and John Calvin. At the time, Cromwell was often called a Lutheran, particularly by those who hated the Reformation. But the reality of his religion is anything but Lutheran. Ultimately, its nearest relative in mainland Europe is Italian. Frequently, beginning with diatribes from Cardinal Pole, Cromwell has been called a disciple of Machiavelli, not least by his most indefatigable and imperceptive of biographers, R. B. Merriman. Another Florentine might be just as relevant: the reformer Girolamo Savonarola, burned at the stake after his brief but dramatic dominance of Florence less than a decade before Cromwell knew the city. Savonarola's memory was still very much alive when he was there.

But there is yet another Italian speciality contemporary with Cromwell's public career: Nicodemism, that quiet decision to hide one's religious views and practice amid some degree of conformity to the surrounding official religion (as John Calvin pointed out sarcastically in coining the label, Nicodemus had dared come to see the Saviour only by night).[77] The Nicodemites of the Italian Reform demonstrate many features of Thomas Cromwell's mature religious creed: much that was outward did not reflect that which was inward. Perhaps we are looking at parallel Nicodemite developments in the two settings of Cromwell's early career, Italy and England, as we have found him in contact with Lollards since at least the mid-1520s. The life and practice of Lollards anticipated Nicodemism, and sustained them through more than a century of persecution, so that some of them held parish office in the Church from which they dissented.[78]

A consciously Nicodemite outlook might explain the apparently stark contradiction between Cromwell's developing evangelicalism and his loyal service to that most grandiose of late medieval English churchmen, Thomas Wolsey. In Italy, such conjunctions were not at all unusual while that paradoxical near-miss, an Italian Reformation, took shape in the 1530s. We have already met one of Cromwell's Italian friends, Donato Rullo of Venice, who became just such a Nicodemite radical. Rullo was well acquainted with Juan de Valdés, the unmistakably heterodox theologian, and refugee in Italy from the Spanish Inquisition. Valdés was the most distinguished and influential in the radical wing of those labelled 'Spirituali', clerics and laypeople of varied theological creativity and Nicodemite tendency who moved happily if discreetly amid the clientage of exalted Italian churchmen such as Gasparo Contarini and Giovanni

Morone. Among such clerical magnates in Italy was also eventually numbered Reginald Pole, and he was yet another friend of Donato Rullo.[79]
These leading clergy, despite their frequently lavish lifestyles, represented
hope for a renewed and evangelical Church, patrons to the most adventurous thinkers striving to create a renewed Catholic future.[80]

In the England of the 1520s, the best or speediest chance of reform
in Church and commonwealth alike was at the hands of a cardinal of
the Roman Church: the papal legate, Thomas Wolsey. Wolsey's general
concern for justice and reform was exemplified in his activity as Lord
Chancellor and in his galvanizing the King's Council to act more systematically as a court of law in Star Chamber. He spent a greater fraction
of his energy than was politically sensible in prosecuting enclosures of
arable land for pasture and extending existing legislation against it. It
may now seem surprising that this could be considered a moral issue, but
so it was for many people in Tudor England, concerned both for food
production and for social justice, protecting the weak against the strong.
Enclosures could be seen as disrupting the social fabric: greedy landowners maximized their profits from sheep and cattle by fencing in land for
their own purposes when it had previously produced grain under ancient
community arrangements. Wolsey's personal crusade to destroy such
enclosures infuriated some of the most powerful people in the land,
clerical and lay, and it may have contributed to the enthusiasm which
many felt about his fall from the King's favour in 1529.[81]

In the Church, the Cardinal had great plans for reorganization and
rationalization of the English diocesan system (not merely for the educational fruits of his monastic suppressions) and for wider intervention and
renewal in the orders of monks and friars – all of which made him detested
by his colleagues on the episcopal bench. It is remarkable how little support Wolsey had from the English episcopate, and curious how little he
was able to put his own men in among them; he had better success in
Ireland.[82] Relevant to Cromwell's present and future activities was that in
November 1528 the Cardinal secured two papal bulls for a radical renewal
of English monastic life by suppressing all religious houses with fewer
than six inmates, and uniting to greater houses all communities of fewer
than twelve.[83] If he had been given the time to do that, the regular life in
England would have been revolutionized – and what a feat of administration it would have taken, worthy of Master Cromwell himself.

Wolsey was consistently easy-going on heresy compared with his English episcopal confrères, never initiating the burning of a heretic. Indeed
after Bishop West of Ely had harassed the Cambridge don Hugh Latimer
in 1528 for what was already clearly outspoken evangelical preaching,

Wolsey examined the offender, and with open contempt for West granted Latimer a preaching licence, which that voluble reformer defiantly continued to use despite conservative harassment after Wolsey's fall from power. This significant clash over Latimer between Wolsey and a grand old man of the episcopal bench is preserved in a circumstantial reminiscence of Ralph Morice, which John Foxe found so difficult to fit into the architecture of his Reformation history that he decided not to publish it in his grand narrative of a classic Protestant martyr.[84] In 1529, Wolsey's reforming instincts also turned him to unprecedented if soon frustrated efforts at Church reform in the Lordship of Ireland, half a dozen monastic dissolutions included. This was spearheaded by his servant, Cromwell's friend and colleague in the contemporary English dissolution programme, Dr John Allen, newly arrived as Archbishop of Dublin, assisted by Edward Staples, another of Wolsey's servants and lately a canon of Cardinal College Oxford. Staples was appointed Bishop of Meath, the most senior diocese in Ireland apart from its four archbishoprics.[85] Why should an evangelical not have hopes of all this?

Yet Wolsey's handicap as Church reformer, apart from personal self-indulgence far outstripping any other late medieval English cleric, was the vast scope of his duties not simply as papal legate, but also as omni-competent royal minister and dispenser of justice in Star Chamber. It was just all too much.[86] Wolsey also had a personality defect deriving as much from his limited attention-span as from the burdens of his work. His old physician Dr Augustine reminded Cromwell of this after the Cardinal's death, when trying to wheedle some money out of a now much promoted former colleague: 'I wish you would always remember what you were so often accustomed to say to me and others, that our right reverend master was so universally detested for nothing but putting things off for so long, and for his many words, empty of deeds.'[87] A cheap rhetorical shot amid Augustine's pleas for cash, but not worth chancing if it had not reflected an old reality. It is clear that for Cromwell frustration long jostled with deep and lasting loyalty in his complex relationship with his master. While learning a great deal by observing Wolsey in government, and drawing on Wolsey's initiatives and schemes, he did his best not to make the same mistakes, once he had a chance to exploit his own power in the kingdom.

4
Managing Failure: 1528–1529

Ipswich has known many rain-sodden Septembers, but the good folk of that industrious borough have seldom enjoyed as festive a soaking as that on 7–8 September 1528. For one not present, Cardinal Wolsey, this was a milestone in his life, a ceremonial assertion of all he had achieved since he left his birthplace for Oxford. For one actually there – Master Cromwell – it was the fruit of much tedious planning and administration. The events had two foci: first the nascent Cardinal College itself, rapidly appearing out of the redundant buildings of St Peter's Priory, the smaller of two priories in the borough. The other was the celebrated shrine of Our Lady on the western edge of town, a holy place Wolsey had known since childhood; he had annexed it to his scheme with the same ruthlessness currently transforming St Peter's into his College of Our Lady.[1] The 8th of September was the feast of her Nativity, co-operatively falling at the beginning of a new academic year. This was the inauguration of a chief corporate festival for Cardinal College Ipswich: as it turned out, the perpetual annual celebrations scarcely survived another two years.[2]

The Monday vigil processing from the College to Our Lady's shrine was solemn enough, featuring the borough bailiffs and aldermen with Master Humphrey Wingfield, respected in both borough and county (he had his town house at the far end of the street from St Peter's Church). Then on the feast-day itself these worthies were jostled by a much greater crowd from further afield: two dozen other prominent county gentry, heads of religious houses, with representatives of the Bishop of Norwich and of the Duke of Norfolk, plus Cromwell and his clerical colleagues Dr Roland Lee and Dr Stephen Gardiner from the Cardinal's household. Torrential rain barred a repeat of the previous day's procession through town, so it had to take place in the former priory church: probably a relief to the guests, with ample compensation from splendid choral music and a lavish dinner to follow. Venison and other game were provided by the Dukes of Norfolk and Suffolk and other local magnates.

It was an auspicious beginning. The newly appointed Dean, William Capon (adding this promising office to his Mastership of Jesus College Cambridge) gave credit where it was due: 'Master Cromwell did take much pain and labour not only in surveying your Grace's stuff hither carried safely; but also in preparing and ordering of hangings, benches and other necessaries to the furniture of our Hall.' That was just the sort of detail in which Cromwell had come to excel as the Cardinal's legacy project had unfolded over four busy years. The legal niceties for handing over the Ipswich site to Wolsey had been narrowly finished in time, and Cromwell further advanced the programme of monastic dissolutions to complete the joint endowments of the Colleges during his East Anglian visit.[3] Back in London, the Italian craftsmen were at this point still taking care to show themselves busy on the Cardinal's tomb.

Other members of the cast assembled at Ipswich in September 1528 were deeply significant for Cromwell's future. Among the guests, Humphrey Wingfield was destined to be Speaker of the House of Commons, probably at Cromwell's behest, in 1533. Prominent in the home team were Roland Lee and Stephen Gardiner, his colleagues from Wolsey's staff, who when promoted to bishoprics became respectively his most reliable supporter and most reliable enemy. The senior staff of the College, the Dean and Sub-Dean, both look like Wolsey's own choices (like the Dean and Sub-Dean of Cardinal College Oxford, John Higden and Thomas Canner). Dean Capon, Wolsey's almoner, was a safe traditionalist clergyman, through whom, during business for both Cardinal and Jesus Colleges, Cromwell got to know another equally conventionally minded colleague of Capon's as Fellow of Jesus, Thomas Cranmer.[4] Dramatically promoted and with a changed religious outlook, Cranmer played a considerable part in Cromwell's later adventures.

We can probably credit Cromwell with the import from Boston to Ipswich of the future evangelical martyr Robert Testwood to be master of the College choristers; almost certainly he also secured Testwood's next appointment at St George's Chapel, Windsor, when the need arose.[5] The Sub-Dean at Ipswich was consistently referred to in its paperwork as 'Mr Ellis' or 'Ellice'. He has always seemed more elusive than Dean Capon, but the key to identifying him is to realize that he was being addressed by the polite Tudor convention of calling foreigners and Welshmen by their Christian name (presumably because the English scorned any ability to pronounce alien surnames). He was a young Cambridge don called Ellis ap Robert ap Rhys, an identification amusingly though obliquely confirmed by an administrative document generated in 1530 by the collapse of Wolsey's finances. Various London victuallers were trying to recoup money from the Cardinal's catering bills, and an internal household memorandum to Cromwell mentions various of Wolsey's officials answerable for the debts, among whom is twice named 'Mr Ellis the priest'. Evidently a clerk to whom this round-up was being irritably dictated misheard the name 'Mr Ellis ap Reece'.[6]

Ap Rhys, a talented exponent of civil law and a Cambridge don like Capon, was at the time only in his early twenties. He was son to Wolsey's chaplain and cross-bearer Robert ap Rhys (clerical celibacy did not greatly figure in the late medieval Welsh Church), and he himself became a chaplain to Wolsey, remaining loyal through the last few difficult months of the Cardinal's life.[7] Affectionately or sarcastically known in his native country as 'the Red Doctor' (y Doctor Coch), he later became an enthusiastic if raffish lieutenant of Cromwell's in promoting monastic dissolutions and Reformation in Wales, and he carried on a colourful career in Welsh administration as late as 1594, always sitting lightly to his clerical orders, despite much continuing involvement in ecclesiastical affairs. We will be meeting him again.[8] From such figures who stayed steadfast in Wolsey's last misfortunes was Cromwell's circle of particularly trustworthy assistants later constructed.

Wolsey must have regretted not savouring this collective act of homage from his native county at first hand, but he was at Court anticipating what appeared to be a still more momentous triumph: a solution to the matter of Anne Boleyn. For a year and more, the Cardinal had been troubled by the sudden emergence of King Henry's fateful passion for this high-spirited, articulate and fiercely intelligent young lady of the Court: what contemporaries with weary discretion called 'the King's Great Matter'. She was the younger daughter of Sir Thomas Boleyn, a leading Norfolk gentleman knighted in the course of a successful career as a royal diplomat. His service abroad had given Anne exceptional familiarity in childhood and teenage years with Europe's two greatest Courts, as attendant first on Archduchess Margaret of Austria in Brussels and then on the Queen of France; her French was fluent, her international sophistication rare among English ladies.

Both contemporary comment and the few depictions of her that have been allowed to survive show that Anne was not beautiful by the conventions of the day. That did not hold her back. When she returned home in 1521, now around twenty years old, she had many eager admirers, right up to Henry Percy, a nobleman of illustrious ancestry, heir to the Northumberland earldom, and the brilliant poet Thomas Wyatt. But they all had to fall away from her when a still more exalted passion became obvious during 1526: the King was smitten, as previously he had been at some length with her elder sister Mary, but this time to much more lasting effect. That year at the Shrovetide jousting (13 February), he took to the lists in a costume conveying the role of a lover in torment: 'Declare I dare not' was embroidered on it in French and English.[9]

Two factors turned Henry's amorous playfulness with Anne into a political and theological project to end his marriage to Katherine of Aragon, his wife of nearly two decades. First were the idiosyncratically pious King's long-standing doubts about the canonical validity of that marriage; Henry decided that he had breached biblical prohibitions on marrying one's deceased brother's wife, sparking the wrath of God. That seemed manifest in his lack of a male heir from all Katherine's pregnancies. If the King was right in his assessment of God's law, his marriage had never existed. For the good of his and Katherine's souls, as well as the kingdom's future, it must be publicly declared null.* Second, and subsequent to that existential disquiet, came Anne's unusual and unexpected insistence that she would not share Henry's bed unless she was his wife. Her charisma and sheer force of personality so captured the King that he accepted this audacious challenge.

It was the passionate nature of their relationship, so unusual in royal liaisons, that made Henry capable over the next few years of pursuing courses of action which a lesser man would have found too embarrassing or foolish to contemplate, against both common decency and the opposition of some of the most powerful people in the realm. Henry deeply resented such opposition, and was inclined to put the most sinister construction on it. Though he never admitted it for one moment, his father's claim to rule had been laughably feeble in hereditary terms, and throughout his reign he pursued to the death anyone who challenged his family's grasp on the crown, either by their actions or by merely existing.

Henry's first secret moves to secure a marriage annulment came in April 1527, and royal pressure on a reluctant Pope Clement VII began in the summer of that year.[10] The diplomatic and theological obstacles were huge, particularly because the understandably outraged Queen Katherine was aunt to the most powerful man in Europe, the Holy Roman Emperor Charles V, who was a good deal nearer and more practically menacing to the Pope than King Henry. Once Wolsey had realized that his initial gestures of resistance to the King's plans were getting nowhere,

---

* Divorce in the sense that we understand did not exist in the Western Church's canon law: only annulment, the judgment that a marriage had never existed.

he could not escape this uncongenial task becoming his main focus as both papal representative in England and royal chief minister.

Wolsey had built his spectacular career on smoothly and efficiently achieving Henry's wishes, but the King's confidence in him had already been severely shaken in 1525 by his humiliating failure to pull off a bold experiment in national taxation without consulting Parliament, the 'Amicable Grant'. Its innovative nature was uncomfortably advertised by this unprecedented name, and the tax-payers' reaction had been far from amicable, amounting to a tax strike. The Cardinal could not afford a defeat on an even more serious matter. His aristocratic enemies, who had always resented his power and intimacy with the King, would gleefully aid his destruction.[11] They were now encouraged in their malice by a queen-in-waiting, as they had not been in the Amicable Grant fiasco; Anne had decided that Wolsey was deliberately dragging his feet, and she was always quick to divide the world into friends and enemies.

At last in September 1528 a key to unlocking this impasse appeared imminent: the Pope had agreed to send a special representative to England to join Wolsey in deliberating on the annulment. That special legate was Cardinal Lorenzo Campeggio, Bishop of Salisbury (Thomas Cromwell's distant employer in his Town Clerkship there), who after a worryingly slow journey from Rome eventually reached London on 9 October, ostentatiously though no doubt accurately complaining about his gout.[12] On arrival, Campeggio did not unveil any dramatic initiative to solve the crisis, quite the reverse; but at least he was there, and Henry's unquenchable belief in the moral rightness of his cause fostered the illusion that something would turn up. Wolsey's problem remained Anne Boleyn, with her lifelong ability to polarize matters of policy and turn relationships into adversarial contests. She had decided that the Cardinal, and therefore all of his affinity, were her enemies to be destroyed. While Anne busily intrigued against Wolsey alongside courtiers who were her supporters either through family connections or through inclination to evangelical religion or through awareness of her inescapable power at Court, he could still draw on a considerable deposit account in his master's esteem and trust. All through the first half of 1529, her efforts came to little.[13]

Cromwell was for the moment remote from all this; that autumn of 1528 he still busied himself with the suppression of small monasteries to endow Cardinal College Ipswich. Beyond that preoccupation, we can find him involved in letters about overseas shipping needing Wolsey's signature, maybe because they concerned ships in which his own London merchant friends had an interest. That did not imply he had anything to do with the momentous business of foreign policy at the centre of Wolsey's concerns.[14] Yet, while still nowhere near high politics, his administrative role for Wolsey was widening a little, founded on matters which had already been his concern – chiefly, and of huge significance for the future, matters concerning monasteries, well beyond the programme of dissolutions rolling on into April 1529. He can be found acting as broker in the election of abbots and priors at fairly major houses right across the kingdom. One might expect him to be involved in a matter in the Ipswich area: the choice of Thomas Manning to be Prior of the flourishing Augustinian house of Butley in January 1529. Manning was a friend of his own friends and colleagues in business at Cardinal College Ipswich, Thomas Rush and Rush's stepson Thomas Alvard; the new Prior's continuing gratitude and usefulness eventually earned him the suffragan (assistant) Bishopric of Ipswich established in 1536.[15]

More significantly for the future, Cromwell can also be found intervening in two widely separated unholy rows which do not have such an obvious personal connection. One concerned the expelled Cistercian Abbot Chaffcombe of Bruerne (Oxfordshire), who wrote in March 1529 asking for his help to return from exile with the Cistercians at Rewley beside Oxford; Chaffcombe's career at Bruerne was prolonged till he was finally removed in 1533. That same summer, the serially troubled suffragan Bishop and commendatory Augustinian Abbot of Wigmore (Herefordshire) appealed for Cromwell's help in hanging on to his abbey. Bishop Smart proclaimed with the dramatic sincerity in which the disreputable specialize, 'Friendship in adversity is best proved; you did promise me one good turn – now you may with your worship [that is, given your influence] speak for me . . . Now is the time that you may evermore bind me, good Mr Cromwell; I pray you now to remember me as I shall never forget you.' Certainly by someone's means, most likely Cromwell's, the Bishop graced the Abbot's lodging at Wigmore for a decade more, until there was no abbey to mismanage.[16]

Besides this, Cromwell busied himself with tasks in one way or another concerning young men in the Cardinal's charge. We have already noted two jobs related to sons of magnates. Cromwell acted for the Cardinal following the death in summer 1528 of the immensely wealthy Sir William Compton, which placed his then six-year-old son Peter in wardship. It was at this time also that Cromwell's signature appears alongside an impressive tally of peers of the realm on what was hoped to be a final agreement in the affairs of Cardinal Wolsey's erstwhile youthful charge Thomas Lord Monteagle.[17] In an area of the kingdom which had so far been beyond his concerns, in 1528 Cromwell took up some financial business in Wolsey's diocese of Durham as the Cardinal prepared to resign it for the even richer see of Winchester.

This may sound like a non-sequitur, and one might explain the task by the fact that it involved securing a regular supply of coal and lead for Cardinal College Ipswich from the Bishop of Durham's mining operations. But more was involved: Cardinal (and Bishop) Wolsey had granted these mineral rights to his own illegitimate son Thomas Winter, by a lease Cromwell himself drafted just in time before Wolsey resigned Durham.[18] It was one of the first signs of Cromwell's long-term involvement in another important aspect of Wolsey's legacy project, on which we have not so far remarked: looking after Winter. To his great credit, Cromwell never relinquished this thankless task after the Cardinal's death, a mark of his continuing loyalty to his dead master.

Thomas Wolsey, a man whose appetite for enjoyment equalled his appetite for hard work, fathered at least two and maybe three illegitimate children, rather exceptionally for an English bishop in this self-consciously well-regulated region of the Western Church. A daughter was born in 1511, and quietly placed in the great West Country nunnery at Shaftesbury before Cromwell entered the Cardinal's service. Nevertheless another old servant of Wolsey belatedly brought her to Cromwell's attention when in 1535 she was caught up in his own bureaucracy as royal Vice-Gerent; she was still just young enough to fall under his new ban on people under twenty-four taking full monastic vows.[19] She clearly had no desire to leave Shaftesbury at that time, and it is interesting that this same autumn of 1535 a personal decision of Cromwell lowered the threshold for dismissal to twenty (see below, p. 307). After that, unnamed for posterity, she disappears from the record.

A hitherto unnoticed but likely third child of Thomas Wolsey is a young man called Thomas Minterne, who in 1529 entered Winchester College (Wolsey having just become Bishop of Winchester) as from the town of Sherborne, aged thirteen, so born around 1516. Minterne is a village 10 miles south of Sherborne, 20 miles from Wolsey's daughter at Shaftesbury Abbey: a notable Dorset coincidence. From Winchester, Minterne went on inevitably to New College Oxford, and in 1533 (aged seventeen!) became a Fellow, under Cromwell's complaisant friend Warden John London. His good fortune continued; by 1538 he was receiving five pounds a year as a royal scholar, and was off on foreign travels, writing stylish Latin letters of thanks in a fine mannered hand from Paris and Louvain to his 'Maecenas', Thomas Cromwell. A further begging letter to the King after Cromwell's fall significantly indicates that financial support had now dried up for his travels abroad, but he carried on some sort of clerical career as a canon of Salisbury Cathedral as late as the 1560s, not otherwise troubling the course of history.[20]

The most compelling argument for Minterne's paternity is that his career and Cromwell's part in it are amusingly reminiscent of Wolsey's undoubted son Thomas Winter, although Winter caused Cromwell much more work than Minterne. Born around 1510, and so the oldest of this trio, Thomas Winter gained an even more lavish education than Thomas Minterne: carefully chaperoned studies at Louvain, Padua and Paris, studies which left him with beautiful italic handwriting, an ability to turn a graceful phrase in humanist Latin and a breathtaking sense of entitlement. The best that one can say about Winter is that looking after him gave gainful employment in pleasant overseas surroundings to various of Wolsey's protégés and Cromwell's friends and acquaintances, notably that talented future Cromwellian propagandist Richard Morison, yet another evangelical finding his way on to the strength of Cardinal College Oxford in the 1520s.[21]

During Winter's various spells of residence in Italy, he was the unintentionally comic counterpoint to an equally cosseted protégé of Henry VIII, Reginald Pole, though unlike that high-minded cleric he would never have dreamed of biting the hand that fed him. In fact Winter wandered through the 1530s with the innocence of a Forrest Gump, sustained to the last by income from the Provostship of Beverley Minster which Cromwell saved for him from the stripping away of his other preferments, and whose regular disbursement he pursued with the nearest thing to energy he ever displayed. Cromwell must have blanched to read Winter's guileless account of his visit to Court while home in England, probably in 1534. The young man remarked sadly that the King did not really seem to be listening to him while he was recounting his Italian adventures, yet Queen Anne Boleyn made some (surprisingly) warm and encouraging remarks to him, asking him to consider her as among the number of his friends.[22] By then, Winter certainly needed friends, but his only consistent friendship came from Thomas Cromwell.

While the Cardinal was alive and in the fullness of his power, Winter's promotion in high Church office passed parody. Particularly offensive East Anglian deployments of the lad in the diocese of Norwich aroused the wrath of the venerable and conscientious Bishop, Richard Nix; Nix was one of that generation of elderly bishops like Audley of Salisbury (see above, p. 58) who thoroughly disapproved of Wolsey's general high-handedness, to say nothing of his progeny. Winter was high on Nix's list of grievances: appointed aged sixteen as Rector of the major benefice of St Matthew's Ipswich in succession to one of Suffolk's most respected secular clergy, in order to secure the shrine of Our Lady for Wolsey's plans for Cardinal College, and, worse still, in the same year becoming Archdeacon of Suffolk. Early in 1529, Winter added the Archdeaconry of Norfolk to his preferments, and this seems to have been the final straw for Nix. The Bishop took out his rage on the Archdeaconry scribe John Curatt for exercising probate jurisdiction on Winter's behalf, prompting that unfortunate official to write in terror to Cromwell twice in two days. Nix's own letter to Wolsey a month later in May 1529 was a not altogether coherent balance of abject pleas not to threaten his position combined with truculent demands for justification of the Cardinal's actions. Over the next few months, pleas disappeared and truculence increased.[23]

It is likely that already in spring 1529 the Duke of Norfolk was giving malicious hints to his diocesan that Wolsey's position was increasingly vulnerable to missteps in the royal annulment project. Wolsey's senior official Dr Stephen Gardiner, now part of a diplomatic mission to Rome to press the King's case, certainly drew that conclusion. In March 1529, quietly jettisoning his previous vigorous support for Queen Katherine, he prepared to leave Wolsey to whatever fate awaited him. Anne Boleyn warmly received Gardiner's unctuous overtures. She had spent the previous month or two cementing a covert alliance against Wolsey; she recruited such key figures as her courtier cousin and Gardiner's diplomatic colleague Sir Francis Bryan, plus the Dukes of Suffolk and Norfolk, heading a coterie of noblemen who had long resented being sidelined by a flamboyant and lowborn priest.[24]

In the middle of all this, Cromwell witnessed a significant moment of sourness in the otherwise rapid progress of Cardinal College Ipswich. He was at the College when the Duke of Norfolk paid it a visit on 11 April 1529. Norfolk arrived in a fury because he had heard that the small suppressed priory at Felixstowe, of which he counted himself founder, had been dismantled for building materials. It took some work to calm the Duke down and restore his good temper, and for the time being Norfolk said no more about Felixstowe.[25] The ambiguity of the encounter is reminiscent of Bishop Nix's challenge to the Cardinal at the same time. Still there was no outward sign that Wolsey was facing disaster.[26] Through that spring and early summer, events swayed uncertainly. Anne, now close at the King's side, and scheduled to accompany him on the summer progress once the legatine court had completed its work, was preparing the ground for further destructive action against Wolsey, with her group of assorted vengeful noblemen.[27] Documents drafted for this purpose by Thomas Lord Darcy of Templehurst sat unused in Darcy's archive until 1537, when the

sight of them (another royal confiscation of treasonous papers) further
sweetened Thomas Cromwell's own taste of revenge on behalf of his old
master after the Pilgrimage of Grace (see below, pp. 402–4).[28]

All depended on what the King was sure would be the successful culmination of his long campaign to have himself recognized as unmarried. On
31 May 1529, Campeggio and Wolsey opened the legatine court hearing
in the Dominican friary (Blackfriars) in London. Wolsey, desperately
juggling this vital task with supervising an important mission to canvass
support from King François of France, may at this point have shared the
King's optimism: Campeggio will not have confided to his fellow-judge
the fateful instructions from the Pope to make no decision at all. In the
end, after two months of legal deliberations at Blackfriars, on 30 July
1529 Cardinal Campeggio delivered the blow. He declared the legatine
court adjourned for the summer as if it were sitting in the city of Rome,
without any interim conclusion. The delay gave Queen Katherine ample
time to lodge an appeal to return the case to Rome, far beyond King
Henry's power to influence the result.

Campeggio had fooled and betrayed both the King and his Cardinal,
but Wolsey would feel the worst effects of the Blackfriars debacle. Anne
and her allies had among their other preparations drawn up thirty-four
charges against Wolsey, designed as a basis for that terrifyingly flexible
weapon of destruction in English law, a charge of *praemunire*: aiding
and abetting a foreign jurisdiction in the realm. That jurisdiction was the
Pope's. The Pope's agent was Wolsey himself – thanks of course to King
Henry's own insistence in getting him appointed as legate *a latere* eleven
years before. Ever since this species of indictment was formulated in a
Parliamentary statute of the late fourteenth century, it had been a weapon
the English Crown could wield against the Papacy at will, whenever there
was some issue of contention. There was thus nothing new about its
actual use, but over the next three years, this reassuringly traditional
procedure gained a new purpose: not merely to harass a pope in his English jurisdiction, or as instrument of Henry's anger at Wolsey's failure,
but to destroy papal jurisdiction altogether.

Amid the fury and recrimination following Campeggio's act of sabotage, Thomas Cromwell was drawn directly into the catastrophe. For the
first time he stepped beyond his allotted administrative duties on tomb,
colleges, monasteries and young gentlemen. One night, probably around
the time that Campeggio torpedoed the Blackfriars court, Cromwell
scribbled an urgent note to his colleague in Wolsey's service Dr William
Claybrook, 'as ever ye intend to do my lord pleasure or service', to find

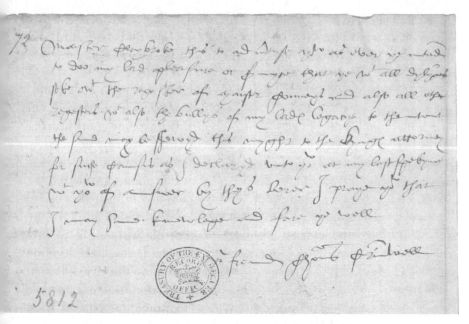

Cromwell's urgent note in late July 1529, begging William Claybrook 'as ever ye entend to doo my Lord pleasure or s'vyce' to search the archive for key documents defining Wolsey's legatine jurisdiction, in the wake of royal rage at the Blackfriars trial.

the registers in the legatine archives concerning the papal grant of Wolsey's powers, specifically with regard to his powers of dispensation (very relevant to the business at Blackfriars), 'that they may be shown this night to the King's attorney, for such causes as I declared to you at my last speaking with you'. This plea is a rare example of one of Cromwell's own letters, preserved only because it returned to his in-tray. Claybrook wrote an apologetic reply on the back of it, repeating that Wolsey's registers were in the care of other officials, but promising to do his best and arranging an early rendezvous with him at Blackfriars the following morning.[29]

The exchange is the first extant witness to Cromwell's errands between Cardinal and royal Court which came to dominate the next year of his life. He dutifully carried on with his normal tasks on Cardinal College estates and building work; they took him in August and September of 1529 back to East Anglia, where he arrived in time to represent the Cardinal's household at the second (and maybe subdued) College celebrations on the Nativity of Our Lady.[30] Yet the new direction is perceptible in a letter to Cromwell from his great friend and colleague Thomas Alvard on

23 September. Alvard meticulously described their master's present delicate but by no means hopeless situation as the Cardinal nervously tried to
keep close to the King during the royal progress to Grafton. Alvard noted
how the Cardinal eagerly and immediately read over a letter of Cromwell's to him (now of course lost), 'and so kept [it] always close to himself.
[I say this] unto you because I never saw him do the like [before].'[31]

Wolsey's relationship with his always efficient and trustworthy servant
was taking on a new dimension, reflected in a conversation concerning
King Henry's Great Matter, about which there has been unjustified scepticism.[32] It unites two main actors in the tragedy of the 1530s: Reginald
Pole and Cromwell. They were then mismatched: Cromwell the busy,
unspectacular servant of the Cardinal, and Pole the much promoted,
much travelled and favoured protégé of the King (a more talented version
of Thomas Winter, indeed). At some time between Pole's return from Italy
and his departure for Paris – in other words, in early autumn 1529, around
the time of Alvard's letter – they had a conversation. Cromwell asked Pole
'how a councillor of a Prince should conduct himself with that Prince,
if at any time the Prince's inclination turned away from what generally
seemed honourable, when he was not actually furnished with any authority in the matter that he sought'.[33] Shorn of Pole's obsessive later quest to
see Cromwell as the English Machiavelli, the question makes perfect sense
in autumn 1529. Pole does not suggest that Cromwell supplied any answer
at this juncture. His question merely echoed Wolsey's worries, about
which they may have frequently mused in their newfound intimacy.

By the end of July, the aristocratic conspirators against Wolsey thought
that they had him at their mercy, but the Cardinal diverted the King's
wrath for the time being with lavish quantities of money, to their great
disappointment and frustration. Their plans for Wolsey's arrest, the
confiscation of his papers and his indictment on a raft of charges came to
nothing.[34] Wolsey's situation took some time to deteriorate during August
and September, and when the King turned decisively against him, it was
not just because of the huge disappointment of the Blackfriars trial, but
also because of a second failure of Wolsey's policy: the simultaneous
negotiations with France yielded no new advantage for the King. That
snub from King François, with whom Henry always pursued a thoroughly adolescent rivalry, eroded Henry's confidence in the Cardinal to
the point where by October Anne could push home her advantage.

Wolsey's fall proceeded crabwise. The only part of the noblemen's earlier
plot against him which the King took up directly was to call a Parliament,
the first since 1523. Writs went out across England at the beginning of
October. Then matters accelerated. Wolsey was charged with *praemunire*

on 9 October, and on the 17th he was dismissed as Lord Chancellor. His conviction for *praemunire* made him 'attainted': an attainder in theory meant that he lost all legal existence. All his estates were at the King's mercy, notably York Place, Wolsey's archiepiscopal house alongside the Palace of Westminster – already in the middle of lavish rebuilding, it was soon to be rebranded and extended as a prime royal residence, Whitehall.[35] He was banished to Esher in Surrey, still not the worst fate in the world, for this rather stately house belonging to his diocese of Winchester was quite near the King's much used residence at Hampton Court. The future, that location suggested, was still open, but rumours swirled, and there was a settled conviction in the City of London as the Cardinal left York Place for the last time that his destination was not Esher but the Tower. The crowds of excited spectators in boats on the Thames must have been greatly disappointed as Wolsey's barge turned in the opposite direction towards Putney.[36] This is likely to have been the occasion when Reginald Pole, just before leaving for Paris, noted the widespread belief in London that Cromwell had been arrested for his part in the dissolution of monasteries, and might well be executed.[37]

As the worst crisis of his life so far moved towards this dire extremity, Thomas Cromwell put his affairs in order. Earlier this year, perhaps already in reaction to the growing atmosphere of uncertainty in high politics, he caused his clerks to draw up an elaborate catalogue of debts owing to him, augmented by his own memoranda extending up to June.[38] On 12 July 1529, as the Blackfriars trial meandered through its illusory progress, he began the even more solemn task of making his will, though circumstances dictated that neither this nor any other will of his was ever put into effect. Its text is a precious and remarkably meticulous snapshot of his affairs and status at this time, although he added alterations over the next year or two as circumstances changed and his finances blossomed, before the much altered document became too out of step with events even to act as a template.[39] Tragic new circumstances were the deaths of his two daughters, probably in late 1529, noted by his own erasures and substitutions. His wife was already dead by the time the neat and formal first text was first drawn up.

Two features of the will are worthy of comment: first what it says about his status in society, second about his religion. It is striking, despite the substantial sums of money that Cromwell felt confident of bestowing, how innocent the will is of reference to nobility, leading gentry or any character from high politics, despite the fact that for much of the previous decade his business had taken him to the edge of such circles. He did not even name Cardinal Wolsey as his supervisor, which may indicate that he was already wondering about his master's long-term future: the supervisor, normally a person of equal or superior status to the testator, was in this case an obscure individual called Roger More, then servant in the King's bakehouse and possibly a neighbour in Austin Friars, whom Cromwell did not even dignify with the honorific 'Mr'.[40] The most socially prominent person in the original will was another friend, John Croke, one of the Six Clerks of Chancery and also one of his colleagues in setting up Cardinal College Oxford for Wolsey.[41] Otherwise, it is noticeable that even the slightly later folio of bequests Cromwell himself added mentioned only two people of gentry status: both clients of Wolsey from Suffolk, his friends Thomas Rush and Thomas Alvard, whom it was natural to have added, since they played such a vital part in his life in autumn 1529. That appendix folio also brought in Cromwell's probable relative from Putney John Avery, but his office as Yeoman of the Bottle to the King does not trumpet courtly splendour. It all speaks of a man discreetly below stairs during this national crisis, and determined to stay there.

Second, there has been frequent remark on how traditional the religious reference of Cromwell's will appears: it opens with an unusually florid commendation of his soul to God, Our Lady and the other saints, stipulates in the end seven (substituted for three) years of chantry prayers for his soul, and makes the sort of bequests to London's five friaries and to poor prisoners in city gaols that one expects in the wills of particularly devout late medieval folk with plenty of spare cash. There are two feasible explanations. Was it a smokescreen for the benefit of London diocesan officials? When the future of Cromwell's son Gregory and his little daughters was at stake, amid stirrings in the City about heresy, many involving his friends, with his tolerant master perhaps not around for much longer to protect him, the last thing would be to step demonstratively out of line in matters of public religious profession. Yet it is also possible that the shock of his wife's death disposed Cromwell to think more kindly of traditional provision for souls: he remained a widower for life, rejecting friendly promptings for an immediate remarriage. Then followed the deaths of his daughters: his hopes of a family succession hung on the life of his son Gregory, who appears to have been physically small and maybe delicate as a boy. The prayers of priests and grateful recipients of charity might seem a reasonable investment.[42] At a dangerous time, outward traditional piety would do him no harm.

This trimming of his convictions, or genuine change of devotional mood, seems to have continued in the next few anxious months. In a well-known story, Wolsey's servant and biographer George Cavendish found his fellow-servant in the Great Chamber at Esher. It was All Hallows' Day (1 November 1529), and Cromwell was 'leaning in the great window, with a primer in his hand, saying of Our Lady Mattins, *which had been* [that is, would have been] *a strange sight in him afore*'.[43] This reading in various manuscripts of Cavendish's work was rejected by its nineteenth-century editor Samuel Singer as not making sense, and he preferred the alternative 'which had been since a very strange sight'. Nevertheless, it is likely to be the better reading. Cavendish knew his man, and a portrayal of Cromwell as a precocious evangelical before this moment fits the story of discreet backing for dissenting religion we have seen in his dealings at Oxford and Poughley, and with Miles Coverdale (to look no further), in the mid- to late 1520s.*

In any case, that All Hallows' Day Cromwell was in a highly emotional state, 'the tears upon his cheeks'. Lamenting that he was 'like to lose all that I have travailed for all the days of my life, for doing of my master true and diligent service' and that he was 'in disdain with most men for my master's sake', he told Cavendish of his resolve: 'I intend, God willing, this afternoon, when my Lord hath dined, to ride to London, and so to the Court, where I will either make or mar, ere I come again.' Cavendish goes on to record events later that same evening after dinner at Esher less frequently quoted than the story of the primer. Cromwell took his cue from Wolsey's commendations of his gentlemen and yeomen to suggest that 'he ought to consider their truth and loyal service.' As Wolsey replied sadly that his resources to reward them had gone, Cromwell pointedly contrasted the lack of reward for these layfolk with generous financial rewards in spiritual promotions enjoyed by Wolsey's fleet of chaplains: 'yet hath your poor servants taken much more pains for you in one day than all your idle chaplains hath done in a year.' Emotionally reacting to this challenge, the Cardinal summoned his houschold, clergy and layfolk and, on Cromwell's prompting, backed by an initial contribution of cash from Cromwell's own purse, forced his chaplains to hand over as much money as they could to his secular attendants. After this and prolonged 'private communication', Cromwell took his leave of his master and rode to London that night. Cavendish again repeated that vivid phrase (a favourite of Cromwell's, he said), 'to make or mar'.[44]

Cavendish, constructing a much more artful biographical narrative

---

* Interestingly the early versions of Cavendish's biography published in the Interregnum omitted the whole story; its suggestion that Cromwell was not a wholly consistent Protestant was inconvenient.

than is often acknowledged, would see the significance of the post-prandial confrontation at Esher that evening. It demonstrated both Cromwell's loyalty to Wolsey and his antipathy towards the generality of clergy: not just the chaplains surrounding the Cardinal (plus those, like Gardiner, who had already left him) but also clerics, mostly bastions of traditional religion, who deeply resented Wolsey's imperious ways and rejoiced as his power tottered – from old Bishop Nix of Norwich and Archbishop Warham of Canterbury downwards. This attitude shaped royal policy for a whole decade thereafter, as churchmen found them-selves relieved of unprecedented amounts of wealth for the benefit of laypeople. Cromwell combined that quiet resentment with his evangelical convictions to craft a decade-long programme of revolution for Henry VIII's kingdom.

Make or mar: Cromwell did not start out on All Hallows' Day Dick Whittington-like primarily to forge a new career for himself, but to save his master's. He was bound for London with a single purpose: to get him-self securely placed as a burgess of the House of Commons in the new Parliament. Though Henry might well choose to use its proceedings to launch Wolsey's legal destruction, summoning Parliament was a fairly obvious general move at this difficult time, and its purpose might change – indeed it did, for it began that momentous seven-year sequence of meetings which posterity has christened the 'Reformation Parliament' (not a term used in the Tudor period). Wolsey would feel it imperative to infiltrate representatives into the new assembly of the Commons, to have at least one or two voices to speak up for him against the weight of mal-ice and propaganda. The Cardinal's future is what his servant now set out to 'make or mar'.

All Hallows' Day 1529 came in the middle of Cromwell's efforts to find himself a seat in Parliament, an enterprise further illuminated by a letter of that clever young servant Ralph Sadler, telling his master what he done so far to sort this out. The letter provides a different perspective from Cavendish's account of that same day, but in fact they dovetail remarkably well. Commentators have thought that Sadler's letter, written from London, compromises Cavendish's vivid narrative of events on 1 November as he saw them, for Cavendish ends up by describing Sadler riding away with Cromwell from Esher for London. Actually there is no problem: Sadler obligingly told his reader the time of his letter – four o'clock in the afternoon – a most unusual specificity, showing how fast events were moving. That provided plenty of time for him to undertake (as he said he would) further negotiations to secure Cromwell's final berth in Parliament: a work in progress. Sadler could then still decide to bring his news in person to Cromwell and Wolsey, pursuing the messenger carrying the letter he had written, on the 18-mile ride down to Esher via Kingston upon Thames. The return trip to London with Cromwell would have been a long day for him, but not impossible, given the importance of what he had done and good-quality horses such as Wolsey could provide.[45] The intricacy and success of his day's work is a testimony to the qualities Sadler shared with his master: energy, diplomatic skill and charm.

Sadler's first meeting that day had been with Cromwell's friend the royal Vice-Chamberlain Sir John Gage, who was acting as go-between with the Duke of Norfolk on Cromwell's behalf. The mission here was to use the Duke himself as a go-between with the King, to secure royal permission for Cromwell's effort to enter Parliament. His approval was vital, since Cromwell was so publicly marked down as Wolsey's man ('in disdain with most men for my master's sake' as he said to Cavendish that same day). The Duke conveyed the King's approval, as long as 'ye would order yourself in the said room according to such instructions as the said Duke of Norfolk shall give you from the King'. Norfolk proposed to convey those instructions to Cromwell the following day, and as a token of favour and good faith he returned a ring with a turquoise which Cromwell had sent him: one of a considerable collection of jewelled rings kept at Austin Friars, no doubt for just such negotiations.[46*] At the same time Sadler was talking to Sir Thomas Rush (already elected as one of the burgesses for Ipswich), who had proposed his stepson Thomas Alvard's return for the much smaller Suffolk port of Orford. He was not yet certain whether Rush's local influence could get Cromwell a place at Orford as well, but in any case he had a second option with Sir William Paulet.[47]

In fact neither Rush nor Sadler could know (at least at four o'clock that Sunday) that Sir Thomas's plans at Orford had been completely foiled. Neither Alvard nor Cromwell was to be elected. For all that Orford might seem to be in sleepy decline, the little Suffolk borough was at the apex of a fierce property contest in the aristocratic Willoughby family which had already drawn in Wolsey and Queen Katherine, and was now exploited by the East Anglian magnate Sir William Paston to secure the election of his eldest son Erasmus to Parliament. Sir William used his advantage as current county Sheriff (and therefore returning officer) to return Erasmus alongside a worthy of the borough by the name of Richard Hunt, a local hero in the dispute.[48] The eventual answer to this hitch was to put into operation

---

* On the likelihood of this being the ring on his finger in the Holbein portrait, see below, p. 174.

Sadler's suggested Plan B: a seat in Wolsey's portfolio of Parliamentary boroughs dependent on his diocese of Winchester, brokered by Paulet, who among other offices was Steward of the Bishopric of Winchester.

Cromwell ended up as a burgess for one of the most significant of those Winchester episcopal boroughs, Taunton in Somerset. Alvard had to wait until an Ipswich by-election of 1533 returned him to sit alongside his stepfather, who just happened to be Sheriff of Norfolk and Suffolk that same year. It is unlikely that Cromwell had any previous acquaint-ance with Taunton, and remarkably the town is virtually absent from his correspondence both before and after his election there. One would have thought that in Cromwell's years of power the townsmen might have called on their former burgess for favours, but they did not, which suggests that they had not much appreciated his labours as their represen-tative. Indeed, he may not have been burgess at Taunton for any longer than necessary.[49] Still, for the time being here was at last a result: speed and diplomacy were still of the essence if mishap was not to follow. Sad-ler emphasized to his master at four o'clock that 'your friends would have you to tarry with my Lord there [that is, with Wolsey at Esher] as little as might be, for many considerations, as Mr Gage will show you, who desireth to speak with you.' As Cavendish tells us, Cromwell followed Sadler's suggestion that same night, in leaving for London.

Besides its information on the election, Sadler's letter usefully illumi-nates the line-up of those at Court who could bring him success in his quest. The King knew of him as Wolsey's servant, and could have been told by anyone of his previous Parliamentary experience. Over the years he might on some occasion have been admitted to the royal presence, but it was the Duke of Norfolk, personally familiar with Cromwell through the development of Cardinal College Ipswich, who approached the King about a Parliamentary seat. Norfolk's later relationship with this pres-ently obscure servant of the Cardinal cannot be described as friendship, but other courtiers were to remain vital in his path to power. Sir John Gage was there as adviser on the state of Court politics, only recently an agent in Cromwell's first major acquisition of rural property; they were to remain on warm terms through the next decade despite their marked difference in religious outlook.[50] Cromwell would have known Sir Wil-liam Paulet both through his recent diocesan connection to Wolsey in Winchester and through his dealings for Wolsey in the Court of Wards, of which Paulet had been joint Master since 1526. In the final part of his letter, rounding up what he had learned of Court gossip from Gage, Sad-ler listed those gentlemen of Wolsey's household whom the King had poached for his own service over the previous few days; they were headed by Thomas Alvard. Cromwell, by contrast, showed no sign yet of taking the road towards the King's Court which so many of his colleagues had chosen over the previous months.

Once Parliament was launched on 3 November, Cromwell could draw on all the valuable procedural experience and acquaintance gained in the Parliament of 1523. He would also be armed with the cheering knowledge that, the very same night that he left Esher to 'make or mar', the King in one of his frequent whims of favour had secretly pardoned the Cardinal by word of mouth, sending down Sir John Russell through pelting rain to Esher to convey the message; the promise of yet another turn in Wolsey's fortunes.[51] In any case, Cromwell had nothing to lose. As his old servant Stephen Vaughan had observed to him, writing from Antwerp the week before Parliament convened, 'You are more hated for your master's sake than for anything which I think you have wrongfully done against any man.'[52]

He was by no means totally isolated in the Commons. Among his fellow-MPs besides Thomas Rush was another on Sadler's list of royal servants newly recruited from the Cardinal's household, John Morris (or Mores; a burgess for Steyning in Sussex).[53] In the right circumstances other MPs might pluck up courage to join them, after years of service to Wolsey or friendship with Cromwell. Most prominent were Sir John Gage himself, knight of the shire for Sussex, and the Surrey-based courtier Sir William Fitzwilliam, knight of the shire for that county, whose correspondence likewise reveals particular friendship with Cromwell well into the 1530s. Lower down the social scale, but even closer friends, were Richard Page and Cromwell's relative George Lawson (both burgesses for York), Reynold Littleprow (Norwich), Paul Withipoll (London), Humphrey Wingfield (Yarmouth) and Wingfield's brother-in-law Francis Hall (Grantham), and there were other possibilities.[54] Maybe Cromwell could also be persuasive with the two burgesses for Salisbury, after years of dealings with the city as Town Clerk. Certainly one of them, Thomas Chaffyn, later reminded him of their business discussions in this session.[55] A variety of colleagues in the Commons might therefore be willing to join in speaking for the Cardinal.

Part of the King's preparations for Parliament had been to summon an informal assembly or Great Council of noblemen to Westminster on 1 October 1529, at which he instructed them to 'devise divers acts . . . for reformation of certain exactions, done by the clergy to the lay people': Wolsey was put through the ordeal of attending this event.[56] The King's aim in stirring up this activity, apart from his still equivocal response to

efforts to punish Wolsey, was to put pressure on the English Church hierarchy to make a decision for his annulment on theological grounds, to
match the support he had gathered among the secular peerage. The Commons eagerly responded to the anti-clerical cue from the Crown conveyed
through the Speaker, Thomas Audley. Once the whole House had had its
say in grievances against the Church hierarchy, Audley appointed a committee of lawyers to hammer out concrete proposals from the welter of
angry noise the King's move had released.[57]

Cromwell would have an obvious interest in sitting on this committee,
but disappointingly no list of its members survives to place him definitely
on it. The one committee from which definite evidence remains of his
membership concerns a minor piece of technical legislation on trade protection promoted by the London Mercers' Company, which was not even
enacted.[58] Given his mercantile connections, his membership of the Merchant Taylors' Company and a clutch of his London-based friends also
on that committee, his presence in that time-wasting group was more
or less inevitable, but the circumstances of 1529 equally present the logic
of his volunteering to deliberate on lay grievances against the Church.
Happily, one document does reveal him active in drafting a petition 'concerning an order to be taken and set in the spirituality'.[59] The body of this
petition is in a standard clerk's script, but it is punctuated by emendments in Cromwell's distinctive hand, the overall effect of which was to
tone down the broad-brush bitterness and make it more dignified, while
retaining the main thrust of curbing clerical excess. That sounds like All
Hallows' Day at Esher.

Straight away in the petition's third line, Cromwell subtly refined its
overall subject of complaint, adding the phrase 'having cure of souls' to
the phrase 'spiritual persons'. This may seem trivial, but there was an
important practical distinction between clergy who actually had pastoral
responsibilities ('cure of souls') for layfolk (such as parish priests or
bishops) and other clerical dignitaries such as cathedral canons who
might be supported in their careers by some particular piece of Church
revenue. Singing the praises of God in a great church does not count as
pastoral care, and there might be good and defensible reasons for such
clergy holding such income, as well as some unimpressive ones. Wolsey's
clerical employees, and Cromwell's friends among them, afforded examples of both; there was necessary pragmatism here. A similarly tiny
correction at folio 40v confined a denunciation of greedily excessive fee-
taking to 'divers' rather than 'any' spiritual persons presented to Church
office by the King or other patrons.

A concern for decorum of language is suggested when Cromwell altered a description of layfolk being 'extremely pilled and polled' to 'so very extremely handled' (f. 41r), and boiled down 'like a sort of ravenous wolves nothing else attending but their only private lucres' to 'coveting so much their private lucres' (f. 39v). Nevertheless, he did not tamper with a condemnation of clergy who gave benefices to 'certain young folks calling them their nephews being in their minority and within age' (f. 41r): any alteration of this on his part might have given rise to unkind comment about Thomas Winter. There was an incoherence in such anti-clerical vitriol which Cromwell the defender of Wolsey would have noted. If it was aimed at the Cardinal, it equally applied to his ultra-conservative enemies in the Church hierarchy who rejoiced at his humiliation, the foiling of his plans for radical restructuring in the Church and his infuriating lenience towards heretics.[60]

What were they after, the wide spectrum of those who raged at Wolsey? At one end were men frankly hostile to the power of the Church because they were enthusiasts for evangelical reformation, though that was still a dangerous cause to champion in public in 1529. At the other extreme were conservative secular peers like the aristocratic conspirator Thomas Lord Darcy of Templehurst, who included in his angry indictment of the Cardinal (intended for discussion in the forthcoming Parliament) 'whether the putting down of all the abbeys [that is, Wolsey's dissolutions to finance his Colleges] be lawful and good or no', along with 'all the surmises of the Cardinal for obtaining of his authorities and totquots [licences for holding plural church benefices]'. Darcy clearly regarded these as equal misuses of Wolsey's legatine powers which would justify *praemunire* charges against him.[61] He lined up in his fury beside traditionalist-minded monks like the anonymous chronicler at Butley Priory in Suffolk, a near observer of Wolsey's East Anglian monastic suppressions, who described them as being to the shame, scandal, destruction and ruin of all the monks and nuns of England.[62]

Anti-clerical rhetoric there certainly was in this Parliamentary session, but its main effect was to provoke a rejoinder in the House of Lords from Bishop John Fisher, grand old man of the episcopal bench, respected across Europe for his austere piety, humanist learning and closeness to the English royal family. He furiously denounced the Commons complaints against the clergy as likely to bring the Church 'into servile thraldom'. Fisher's further mention of Martin Luther and Jan Hus implied that elected members of the Lower House were heretics; this provoked a general row between the bishops in the Lords and secular peers in the Lords such as the Duke of Norfolk who aligned themselves with the Commons. The King himself had to intervene and force Fisher to make conciliatory noises. The chronicler Edward Hall reports that the Commons were still dissatisfied. The confrontation underlines the multiform and incoherent nature of anti-clericalism at this stage.[63]

The main statute on Church matters to survive debate, eventually agreed and passed through to royal assent, did not reflect the views of any anti-clerical hotheads in the Commons. It placed some carefully defined limits on clergy holding more than one benefice 'with cure of souls' – that same vital phrase which Cromwell had inserted in the Church committee's petition – and restricted clergy engaging in economic activities beyond their vocations. It was accompanied by two Acts of lesser significance regulating certain fees charged by clergy. This was hardly the most intimidating of assaults on the Church. The number of exceptions inserted into the Act on non-residence testified to how bitterly and relatively successfully the clergy in the Upper House contested it, maybe joined by traditionalist laypeople as well. Yet this Act, which was destined to remain the central regulatory legislation on the subject, was the first cautious step in a radical curtailing of clerical power: one of the great political themes of the 1530s under Cromwell's guidance.

Another important strand is worth exploring amid the general struggles over the Church which have to be reconstructed from the fragmentary evidence for this Parliamentary session. Modern historians have long doubted the authenticity of Bishop Fisher's speech: it is preserved only in hagiographical sources, and seems to contain one big anachronism, Fisher's emphasis on opposing proposed legislation to dissolve smaller monasteries. Surely that notion belonged to 1536, by which time Fisher had been dispatched to sainthood via the executioner's block. Henry VIII's biographer J. J. Scarisbrick first championed the basic accuracy of the text we have, and the only good reason for doubting the dissolution proposal is that no other source recorded it.[64]

If the Commons were enraged at Fisher's accusation of heresy, one reason is that in 1529 there was nothing necessarily heretical about dissolving monasteries. For who was then the arch-dissolver of monasteries? No anti-clerical radical, but Cardinal Wolsey. The most recent of his suppressions had taken place only seven months before the opening of Parliament, when on 1 April 1529, in the presence of Thomas Cromwell and Ralph Sadler, Dr Roland Lee took the surrender of the diminutive Augustinian priory of St Laurence Mountjoy in north Norfolk, to complete the endowment of Cardinal College Ipswich. Realistically, if any house deserved suppression as superfluous, it was Mountjoy.[65] Cromwell's activity in Cardinal Wolsey's dissolutions was the one thing most people knew about him that autumn (and hated him for it); that rebarbative pairing of Reginald Pole and John Foxe is in full agreement on this.[66]

A new proposal for dissolution would bridge the two matters currently on Cromwell's mind, which might otherwise seem incompatible: an attack on clerical wealth, and the defence of Thomas Wolsey's proceedings. The suggestion that more monasteries be dissolved was a red rag to Fisher, but would also have been of great interest and gratification to another keen observer of Parliamentary proceedings: King Henry VIII. The reason given to justify a dissolution programme, according to Fisher and his hagiographer, was to recompense the King for his great expenses in seeking an annulment of his supposed marriage. There is much resonance for the future here.

The confrontation provoked by Fisher's outspokenness in any case had lasting consequences. It began to shift the ground from a general attack on Wolsey to an increasingly polarized struggle between defenders and enemies of the Church hierarchy's centuries-old privileged status in the kingdom. The changing political configuration placed Sir Thomas More, who had only just replaced Wolsey as Lord Chancellor, in an increasingly awkward position at the moment of his greatest elevation in Tudor politics. More was in any case no natural enemy of Wolsey, and now found himself one of the chief defenders of traditional religion.[67] But for the moment there was still the matter of the Cardinal. More was prepared to join forces with the coalition of peers who had hoped to destroy Wolsey in the previous summer, but he did so probably only because the King had ordered him to.

On 1 December, the new Lord Chancellor (who by his office presided over the Lords like the Speaker in the Commons) put his signature to a petition against his predecessor. This substantially reproduced the aristocratic accusations against Wolsey drawn up in July, but, as is often the way in fast-moving political situations, appears to have changed its purpose and significance. More was not the only former friend of Wolsey in the list of signatories: alongside him was Sir William Fitzwilliam, one of Wolsey's most reliable allies at Court.[68] In fact, virtually all those signing it had attended an unusually high-profile meeting of the royal Council in Star Chamber on 19 October, designed to publicize Wolsey's fall. The fact that Edward Hall (a burgess for Wenlock) saw a copy of the petition bearing the Cardinal's signature suggests that the King had taken over the document, and that he was now using it to keep control of Wolsey's fate. Its public scrutiny in Parliament (Hall tells us that it was 'read in the common house', despite its considerable length) united leading politicians behind a document which Wolsey's signature had turned into a confession of guilt, without specifying what penalty that guilt deserved. The King could then use it in determining the Cardinal's fate as harshly or as leniently as he pleased.[69]

The Commons' consideration of this petition was surely the occasion when Cromwell openly defended his master. Cavendish gave his admiring praise to the performances of the burgess for Taunton, despite the fact that (like Gage) Cavendish can only have deplored Cromwell's later part in the English Reformation. He portrayed Cromwell as repeatedly making 'incontinent' ripostes to anything said against Wolsey, even speaking successfully against a bill to condemn him for treason. Cavendish probably meant a bill attempting to implement this set of articles, which were shot through with accusations of actions capable of being construed as treason, should the King wish to do so. There was irony here, considering that in 1523 Cromwell may have delivered a set-piece speech in the House against Wolsey's French war policy.[70]

To defend the Cardinal in open Parliament was a high-risk thing to do, but it would have got Cromwell noticed, and might not necessarily be contrary to the unstable inclinations of Henry VIII. Cavendish said it made a good impression on people, and interestingly gets contemporary support from an Essex parson who was a good friend of Cromwell's and became one of his chaplains. Thomas Shele wrote on 27 November, probably from the remote salt-marshes of Walton-le-Soken,

> I was informed that you were in great trouble for my lord Cardinal's causes and matters, which right sore did grieve me. Howbeit sithen I have had comfortable tidings that you be in favour highly with the King's Grace, Lords, and the Commonalty, as well spiritual as temporal, which to me is a comfort and pleasure as anything can be in this world, and so I beseech Our Lord continue you, as I have no doubt in you but you know what you have to do better than I can advise you.[71]

Lord Herbert a century later said something similar, in what sounds like an echo of Cavendish, and specifically referring to the petition of 1 December: 'upon this honest beginning, Cromwell obtained his first reputation.'[72] A reputation not, one notes, as an evangelical hothead, but as judicious defender of the stricken Cardinal against all comers, at a time when it was not necessarily in his own best interests, and when he was the public face of Wolsey's monastic dissolutions. Observers would and did decide whether this combination made him worthy of praise or hatred.

Sir Thomas More finally closed Parliament on 17 December. Cromwell had no doubt been commuting between Westminster and Esher to keep

Wolsey in his own neat hand begins his letter of 17 December 1529 with a desperate plea: 'Myn owne enterly belovyd Cromvel, I beseche yow as ye love me and wyl evyr do any thyng for me, repare hyther thys day as sonne as the Parlement ys brokyn up.' His second postscript says that Cromwell's warning about the Duke of Norfolk's visit went missing, and that he only knows of it via 'Mr Agusteyn', the Italian physician Dr Agostino de Augustinis.

the Cardinal informed; now Wolsey desperately sought him on the very day that Parliament broke up. In a note in his own hand he begged 'mine own entirely beloved Cromwell' to hasten down, as 'for my comfort and relief I would have your sad [judicious] and discreet advice' and 'commit certain things requiring expedition [speed] to you on my behalf to be solicited there' – 'there' being of course the Court. Cromwell had already been much engaged 'there', picking up what news he could. As the Cardinal noted in a postscript, Cromwell had tried to warn him about an impending visit of the Duke of Norfolk to Esher soon after the publication of the petition in Parliament.[73]

Since Wolsey now had a much reduced staff, Cromwell was tasked with managing gifts for courtiers who might help him. On 13 December, while Parliament was still in session, Thomas Winter (abruptly recalled in October from the pleasures of Parisian student life) was walked through a surrender of his only recently gained lead and coal leases in the Bishopric of Durham to one of the royal Knights for the Body, Sir Anthony Browne (who also happened to be son-in-law to Cromwell's friend Sir John Gage).[74] An even more strategic sweetener across the factional divide was a pair of grants of annuities from Wolsey's lands as Bishop of Winchester and commendatory Abbot of St Albans Abbey to Anne Boleyn's brother George, newly decked out as Viscount Rochford on their father's promotion to an earldom. Cromwell's corrections to the draft grants carefully upped the amount of honorific flummery.[75]

Ralph Sadler continued to act as Cromwell's agent at Court when he was not there. He heard gloomily from Gage that 'such as be my Lord's hinderers and enemies have had time with the King before his friends, nevertheless he trusteth that their purpose shall take small effect.' Sadler added his frank contempt for Stephen Gardiner, now royal Secretary, to whom he had also made overtures in person: 'in mine opinion the said Mr Secretary will do little or nothing that shall be to the avail or profit of my Lord his Grace, or any of his friends, more than he may not choose for very shame, considering the advancements and promotion that he hath had at my Lord his hand. I assure you I have in him small trust or affiance.'[76]

Several of the Cardinal's very personal letters to Cromwell survive from the next twelve months right through to his death, though some remain only in Thomas Master's seventeenth-century summaries. They reveal how dependent he became on his servant's loyalty and efficiency. Master made a judicious round-up of epithets from them: 'My only comfort'; 'My only help'; 'Mine own good Thomas'; 'My only refuge and aid'.[77] They are shot through with the miserable anxieties of a sick man, desperately concerned for his preferment and possessions in the face of ever-shifting signals from Court. 'For God be my judge,' he wrote to Cromwell probably in December,

> I never thought, and so I was assured at the making of my submission [of 22 October 1529], to depart from any of my promotions ... I hope his Grace will consider the same accordingly. I have had fair words, but little comfortable deeds, &c. Those noblemen did otherwise promise on their honours to me, upon trust whereof I made the frank gift of mine whole estate ... If it might be possible to retain Winchester, though the King had the most part of the profits, &c., or else there might be some good sum made for the retention of the same.[78]

It was just one more deathly blow when at the end of January 1530 Wolsey received that polite but businesslike letter from the chief sculptor of his tomb, centre of the whole legacy project (see above, pp. 56–8). Benedetto Rovezzano was in effect serving notice of his intention to settle his accounts and go home to Florence.[79]

Rovezzano was no doubt responding to what he had heard about the other components of the Cardinal's plans for immortality, Wolsey's Colleges and their ex-monastic endowments. Ever since the Cardinal's condemnation in October, East Anglian predators from the Duke of Norfolk downwards had been circling the hapless Dean Capon of Cardinal College Ipswich, waiting for the collapse of his institution and the disintegration of its estates. Cromwell continued to do his best to cope with this and other fallout from Wolsey's *praemunire* amid all his busyness in Parliament.[80] On 29 December, a month before Rovezzano's letter to Wolsey, Thomas Rush wrote to Cromwell from Ipswich, breaking bad news Speaker Audley had told him while they shared the journey back to their home country:

> [Audley] and Master Bonham had commandment to enter into Wix [Priory suppressed] by reason it was holden of the duchy [of Lancaster], and the licence of the King not obtained under the duchy seal, so that all is void. And over this, he said to me that he thought the King's Grace would take all the monasteries suppressed, by reason of the attainder of my Lord Cardinal, for the forfeiture of him had relation from the first time of his offence, and so that all is in the King's Grace, and that His Grace lawfully might set all the farms [leases] belonging to the said monasteries at his pleasure.[81]

One can catch authentic echoes of Audley's unmistakable lawyerly pedantry in this bombshell (which affected Rush's own leases). It cannot have been cheering either to read Rush's observation that 'to write to you the manifold tales and lies and slanderous words hath been spoken of me and you in these parts, ye would marvel.' That suggests the reason why Rush, Cromwell and Alvard had been rebuffed in the Orford election; they were too closely identified with the rise and now likely fall of Cardinal College Ipswich.[82]

Nevertheless Rush also made an interestingly positive comment beyond the normal simple polite finalities: 'I beseech you heartily: write to me of your affairs and estate at this presents, *which I doubt not but all is to your pleasure*; notwithstanding, I am much desirous to hear the good success of the same from time to time, which I pray God may long continue.' He may have heard via his stepson Alvard that their friend's transactions at Court for Wolsey were doing him no harm, putting him in a new position and moving him closer to the King than existing friendships had so far achieved. One could never predict the King's attitude in such tense situations: he valued authentic loyalty such as Cromwell was showing the Cardinal, and his attitude to his stricken minister was still remarkably volatile. Cromwell would soon graduate to serving two masters, and while he fought to preserve what he could of the legacy project which for half a decade had been his own great matter, he succeeded in making a far more graceful move into royal service than Stephen Gardiner had done. That in turn pitched him into far more momentous and dangerous business than any he had known in the Cardinal's service.

It may have been in these times of desperate uncertainty, with his wife and daughters dead and his future thrust back into his own hands, that Thomas Cromwell fathered an illegitimate daughter, Jane. Her chronological place in his story is a matter of back-projecting much later facts with the aid of a fairly generous dose of supposition, but the most likely conclusions place her birth at this juncture. One has to go as far forward as 1559 to find Cromwell's granddaughter by Jane as aged nine years old, which implies that the marriage of her mother to William Hough, a Cheshire and Oxfordshire gentleman, took place around a decade earlier: so 1549–50. If Jane was then around twenty or in her late teens, which is at least plausible since her husband had been born about 1527, we end up with Jane's birth at the beginning of the 1530s. The one glimpse of her in the Cromwell milieu is in 1539, by which time she was in the household of her half-brother Gregory, now himself a married man: Lord Cromwell paid Gregory's wife Lady Ughtred the very considerable sum of £12 14s 6d for 'apparel for mistress Jane'. It is to his credit that Jane had any place in the Cromwell circle at all; not all such children had such consideration.[83]

From the early 1530s, William Hough's father Richard was a servant of Cromwell's, particularly in his native Cheshire, but we must not ascribe to him the responsibility for William's match with Jane. It still rankled with Richard when he made his will as late as 1574, in which he commented sourly that William had 'married himself without his consent and goodwill to a stranger, not known who was her father'. Coming from Cromwell's former servant, this was a pointed, deliberate untruth.[84] The heralds were less tight-lipped about Jane Hough, making her 'base daughter of Thomas Cromwell, Earl of Essex'.[85] One likely reason for Richard's ill-will was that the younger Houghs, who acquired a home in Oxfordshire as well as Cheshire, were by then among the most pronounced and steadfast Catholic recusants in their countries. This was probably thanks to influence from a formidable pair of Catholic luminaries of Marian and Elizabethan England: their Oxfordshire landlord Sir Francis Englefield and William Hough's former master the Oxford don Nicholas Sander, who in his scathing accounts of the English Reformation had rather a lot to say about Jane Hough's putative father.[86]

One hopes that someone in this unexpected set of relationships found amusement in the paradoxical outcome of Cromwell's decades-old indiscretion. It would have been difficult in Elizabethan England to avoid brooding on how much difference a servant of Cardinal Wolsey with a fierce determination to escape consequences from his master's fall had made to the future of the realm.

5

Serving Two Masters: 1530

Some time in late January 1530, it became public knowledge that Thomas Cromwell's tottering fortunes had decisively changed for the better. He wrote as much to his servant and friend Stephen Vaughan, who on 3 February sent suitably mercantile congratulations from his Low Countries business in Bergen op Zoom that 'you now sail in a sure haven.' Vaughan swiftly moved, as was his wont, to extended monitory moralizing. Still, he was not wrong in ending his peroration with the sage observation that 'more threateneth them which enterprise difficult and urgent matters than those which only seeketh easy and light matters.'[1] Only three days later, another merchant friend, Reynold Littleprow, had the same story independently in Norwich (though he was more prosaic by temperament): 'I do hear you be the King's servant, and in his high favour.'[2]

Stephen Vaughan had heard a piece of gossip which he discounted, but which places Cromwell in a much more elevated room of the rumour factory than any he had known before. 'I hear of my Lord of Rochford's departure out of England towards the Emperor as ambassador for the King's Highness, and I heard also that you should go with him. If so it had been and as you desired, I would have been glad.' In fact Rochford's companions were John Stokesley, Edward Lee and Thomas Cranmer, by then all long-standing advocates of the royal annulment; yet the very fact that Cromwell was even seen as a possible candidate for this high-powered initiative in winning friends for the King's plans overseas shows how far he had travelled in a very short time. Wolsey's surviving correspondence with him is innocent of any discussion of the King's Great Matter – no doubt the stricken Cardinal was thankful to leave that particular worry behind – but it had never been Cromwell's business anyway.

Cromwell's rise into royal favour was so swift and unexpected that subsequent commentators were confused as to how it happened, and who constituted his chief champions. We have met some of the possible candidates in his correspondence: that nexus of courtiers including Vice-Chamberlain Sir John Gage, Treasurer Sir William Fitzwilliam and Sir Anthony Browne. Yet John Foxe has other names. Even when one discounts Foxe's misunderstandings or small slips about what he was told, his testimony should always be taken seriously, given his historical hot-line to Cromwell and Cranmer through that survivor of their turbulent times, Ralph Morice. Foxe's story maps on to the events already surveyed, beginning with Cromwell's efforts among Wolsey's household servants 'to be retained into the King's service':

> There was at that time one Sir Christopher Hales . . . who notwithstanding was then a mighty papist, yet bare he such favour and good liking to Cromwell, that he commended him to the King, as a man most fit for his purpose, having then to do against the Pope.[3]

Christopher Hales, then Attorney-General, was indeed a very good friend of Thomas Cromwell, quite apart from the fact that they had both been MPs in 1523. He married the sister of Nicholas Caunton, who became one of Cromwell's servants (although Hales's opinion of Nicholas was low).[4] His first surviving letter in Cromwell's archive dates back to 1526, in which Hales thanks him for 'all kindnesses shewed unto me' and asks him to use his influence with the City authorities to get a friend chosen as Common Serjeant.[5] Another note from the same period is full of New Year cheer, accompanying a piece of home-made brawn from Hales's wife in return for 'the pleasures which you gave her', a reference to some recent seasonal supper-party or Christmas hamper.[6]

Such friendly courtesies and offers of hospitality continued on into the 1530s. Equally significantly, as late as December 1533, by which time few would have dared cross the royal Secretary, Hales sent a really rude and frank letter about another young relative of his now in Cromwell's service, whom he regarded as a wastrel and whom he felt Cromwell was ridiculously indulging. Hales's aggression was tempered by a postscript with warm commendations to that other intimate mutual friend, Roland Lee, 'and to good Mr Bedell'. This was a relationship which could withstand such storms, and weather the two men's religious differences.[7] In fact, Hales was still associated with Cromwell in the popular mind in 1536, when the Lincolnshire insurgents included him in a wishlist of evil royal counsellors to be punished, otherwise dominated by evangelicals. Hales had then just then succeeded Cromwell as Master of the Rolls, a rare example of Cromwell relinquishing an office once he had been granted it.

Foxe continues his story equally circumstantially, describing the

resentment some courtiers felt at Cromwell's actions in dissolving monasteries for Wolsey, and revealing a second supporter at Court:

> But here before is to be understood, that Cromwell had greatly been com-
> plained of, and defamed by certain of authority about the King, for his rude
> manner and homely dealing in defacing the monks' houses, and in handling
> of their altars, etc. Wherefore the King hearing of the name of Cromwell,
> began to detest the mention of him: neither lacked there some standers-by,
> who with reviling words ceased not to increase and inflame the King's hat-
> red against him ... Among other there present at the same hearing, was the
> Lord Russell Earl of Bedford, whose life Cromwell before had preserved at
> Bononie [Bologna], through politic conveyance, at what time, the said Earl
> coming secretly in the King's affairs, was there espied, and therefore being
> in great danger to be taken, through the means and policy of Cromwell
> escaped. This Lord Russell therefore ... in a vehement boldness stood
> forth, to take upon him the defence of Thomas Cromwell ... declaring
> withal how by his singular device and policy, he had done for him at Bon-
> onie, being there in the King's affairs, in extreme peril. And forasmuch as
> now his Majesty had to do with the Pope, his great enemy, there was (he
> thought) in all England, none so apt for the King's purpose, which could
> say or do more in that matter than could Thomas Cromwell.

This account of Cromwell's public reputation as scourge of the monasteries matches events in autumn 1529, and Sir John Russell (as he actually
was in 1530, with a peerage still nine years off) is a very interesting
patron to have gained. Their early lives have curious similarities: mutual
obscurity for two decades after their births around 1485, including substantial foreign travel, which in the seventeenth century led that often
quirkily well-informed historian Thomas Fuller to assert that Russell was
'bred beyond the seas'. This gave Russell fluency in at least French and
Italian, maybe other languages too. He was another exotic in the provin-
ciality of early Tudor England – it is no coincidence that he and Cromwell
both became great friends with a further rare English cosmopolitan, Sir
Thomas Wyatt.[8]

Russell thus attributed a narrow escape in Bologna to his fellow-
'Italian', Cromwell, which has always made commentators doubt the reliability of Foxe's reminiscence, seeing that Cromwell was blamelessly busy
at home in Wolsey's service by late 1524–5 or 1527, the periods when
Russell was engaged on royal diplomatic missions in Italy. Foxe is, however, precise: Russell came to Bologna 'secretly in the King's affairs' – and
those later expeditions were high-profile embassies with little chance of a
royal ambassador passing incognito. Secret missions tend by their nature

not to leave traces in the records, and hence we should be thinking further back, to a moment in the first two decades of the century, when the young Russell was serving as a gentleman usher or in the English overseas garrisons at Calais or Tournai, and when Cromwell was indeed still in Italy. Maybe it was then that Russell undertook a clandestine and risky visit to Bologna for Henry VIII or even for Henry's father, during which young Cromwell had used his local knowledge to do some quick thinking.

It is also worth noting that John Russell was one of those at Court marked out for two causes that were unfashionable at the beginning of 1530. First, he was especially sympathetic to Wolsey. We have seen him as the royal emissary bringing Wolsey's pardon to Esher at the beginning of November. Around the time that Russell interceded with the King for Cromwell, as he told the imperial ambassador Eustace Chapuys in February, he earned himself the fury of both Anne Boleyn and her uncle the Duke of Norfolk by defending the Cardinal to the King; Anne would not speak to him for nearly a month after that.[9] In June 1530, with Wolsey now relegated to a new and circumscribed career as Archbishop of York, Russell wrote to Cromwell asking him to draft yet another diminution of Wolsey's revenues in the form of a grant from his diocese of Winchester to a courtier, Lord Chamberlain Sandys. Sandys, 'knowing the great familiarity *and also you my special friend*', was approaching Cromwell via Russell to smooth the administrative path of a concession that Wolsey would find distressing. Russell, aware of how regularly Cromwell was in touch with his old master, asked him to forward a note to Wolsey 'not for no great matter that is in it, but because I would His Grace should not think I had forgotten him'.[10]

Russell's affection for Wolsey was allied to the fact that he detested Anne Boleyn. He remained a partisan of Katherine of Aragon and her daughter, and during Anne's 'reign' that seriously slowed up his career. It was Russell who in 1536 after Anne's death made the ill-natured contrast between the fair and godly impression Jane Seymour made when richly dressed and Anne's appearance: 'the richlier *she* was apparelled, the worse she looked' – and at much the same time he commented even more dramatically, 'the King hath come out of hell into heaven for the gentleness in this, and the cursedness and unhappiness in the other.'[11] Russell's antipathy to Anne was shared by Cromwell's other friend at Court, Vice-Chamberlain Gage, who went so far as to resign his position there after her triumph, retiring to lodge with the Carthusians of Sheen (suitably austere, but near enough to the Court to overhear the gossip). Only when Anne was safely in the grave did Gage reappear from that

disapproving eyrie and his home in remote Sussex, to continue his political career.[12]

A pattern emerges from all this. Cromwell's supporters at Court were
those who owed Wolsey much and now felt sorry for the Cardinal and his
man. Not much surprise there. But it is also clear that generally they coupled that with a low opinion of Anne, and were complying with the drive
to annul the Aragon marriage only out of loyalty to the King. They were
by and large religious conservatives, but they shared or publicly professed
to share King Henry's fury with the Pope over his betrayal in the Blackfriars trial, and they were prepared to support a campaign of harassment
against the exercise of papal power in the kingdom.[13] Cromwell would
have felt the same anger, for Campeggio's adjournment at Blackfriars had
been a cynical abandonment by the Papacy of his own beloved master,
now struggling for survival. Attacking papal power and ecclesiastical
wealth was congenial to a man who had entered the evangelical camp
in the 1520s, and was a safe card to play in his delicate introduction to
royal favour.

And so he did, says Foxe, in the crucial meeting with the King which
after Russell's recommendation clinched his fortunes: 'providing beforehand for the matter, [he] had in readiness the copy of the [English]
bishops' oath, which they use commonly to make to the Pope at their
consecration, and so being called for, was brought to the King in his garden at Westminster.'[14] That last specification of the garden at Westminster
is a typical example of Foxe's capacity for artless detail that triangulates
with other sources, and narrows down the date of this interview to the
second half of January 1530. The King was at Greenwich until at least 9
January, and thereafter moved to Westminster, actually to sample the
considerable amenities of York Place so recently confiscated from the
Cardinal.[15]

Some eight or nine years later, in a characteristically interminable treatise addressed to Charles V, Reginald Pole wrote his own version of what
happened in the garden. Highly coloured and hostile, it represents the
'maximalist' view of what was transacted in that fateful meeting between
the King and his future chief minister.[16] Pole's account has to be treated
with some caution since at the time of these events he was in France. He
prefaced his narrative by conscientiously noting that he had been absent
from England (though he did not choose to remember that he had been
away as part of Henry's team seeking French approval for the annulment
of the royal marriage).[17] Although he could not affirm word for word what
Cromwell had said, Pole emphasized with some elaboration how he had

reconstructed it from various testimonies of those who were then at Court, and even subsequently from Cromwell himself.[18]

Pole would have had many opportunities to meet Cromwell while back in England over the next year. His approach to reconstructing the course of events is remarkably like that of John Foxe, and is not to be dismissed with undue cynicism.[19] In general terms, his account tallies with what we have learned so far, highlighting Cromwell's twin agenda of attacking the Papacy's power in the English Church and offering the King the benefit of lessons learned in dissolving monasteries. Pole's Cromwell, whom he named at this stage in his diatribe only as 'an ambassador of Satan', counselled the doleful King to ignore his councillors' indecision. Princes made and changed laws, so they were themselves above the law. All the universities had agreed with Henry's interpretation of the biblical prohibition on marrying one's deceased brother's wife. 'Indeed in this case, when the Prince had the law of God joined to his own resolve, what death would be cruel enough for the man who dared to oppose him?' That, it must be admitted, does sound like retrospective sarcasm, born out of the arrest and execution of so many of Pole's relatives and friends in 1538–9.

It would be worth making every effort, Cromwell continued, to get papal approval for the annulment, but if the Pope persisted in obstinacy he did not see why the Prince had any reason to fear that judgment. He might indeed seize this as the best of opportunities 'to deliver himself and his realm from slavery to the Roman pontiff', as the princes of Germany had realized that they could do:

> Two heads in one realm seemed a monstrosity in appearance. It was a priestly myth that clergy were exempt from royal jurisdiction. Just let him resume his right in what they had cunningly stolen; he would at a stroke honour, increase and enrich his royal power, in a manner never seen under any of his predecessors.

Pole now elevated his narrative to echo the Gospel stories of the Temptation in the Wilderness, brushing aside the rhetorical inconvenience that this cast Henry in the role of Jesus Christ:

> And when he had taken him, as it were, to a pinnacle of the Temple, or to a high mountain, from where all things subject to the Church might be viewed, he showed him all the numerous and wealthy monasteries of the Kingdom, the bishoprics and all the inheritance of the Church and concluded, 'All these are yours; only cause yourself to be styled what indeed you are, head of the Church, and cause yourself to be given this title with

the agreement of the Supreme Council of the Realm [Parliament] which
will not be difficult to accomplish, if you have the right servants who propose it in the right manner.'[20]

The only element in which Pole's narrative exceeds Foxe's is this account
of a very specific recommendation to use Parliament for a break with
Rome and a declaration of royal supremacy. Pole was writing with bitter
hindsight in 1539, and he was describing what had actually happened:
Cromwell's management of a break with Rome through innovative and
energetic use of Parliament. Yet that in itself does not render his reconstruction of Cromwell's words utterly implausible.

While it is perfectly possible that Thomas Cromwell made this suggestion now, it does not make him the man who brought King Henry VIII
the royal supremacy on a plate. The idea was already in the King's mind.
In a well-attested story, Anne Boleyn had introduced the King to an evangelical tract of 1528 forcefully advocating a royal resumption of power
from the Papacy: William Tyndale's *Obedience of a Christian Man*.[21]
The King was flailing around for any suggestion to resolve his marital
dilemma, and royal supremacy, while flattering his capacious ego, was
still only one potential way forward – as indeed Pole's rhetorical reconstruction of Cromwell's speech acknowledged. Even the most fervent
Boleyn supporters were still doing their best to win the Pope round, and
were happy to draw on papal bounty: this same year, Thomas Cranmer
profited from his time on embassy in Rome by becoming Penitentiary-
General for England and securing the grant of a plum benefice in
Worcestershire from one of England's absentee Italian bishops. Cromwell's advice, whether circumscribed or expansive, was one voice among
several on strategy and the matter of royal supremacy.[22]

One of the two men walking in the garden at Westminster remained
the servant of Wolsey most identified with a programme of monastic
dissolutions, offering a concrete and successful example of how Church
reform might be modelled with profit, if there was enough power in the
right hands. That would be enough to please a frustrated and perplexed
monarch, even if conversation turned additionally and expansively to
annulment strategy, royal supremacy and possible ways of securing it.
For Cromwell, royal service offered not only a way forward, but a chance
to manage the still open future of his old master, and save something
from what he now knew was the King's intention to confiscate Wolsey's
Colleges and their estates. Logically enough, the King now gave him
charge of them (or, more precisely, did not remove them from his charge),
since Cromwell was the person who knew them best.[23]

We need also to remember the linked project sitting at the heart of the Cardinal's plans for his legacy: his magnificent tomb, still being prepared by some of the Italian craftsmen with whom Cromwell had been liaising for six years, and by now nearly complete. Here was another logical use to which Wolsey's servant could be put: his fluency in Italian was as convenient for the King as for the Cardinal. It was not long before the King's eyes turned to Wolsey's tomb as well as his estates, seizing for himself the bronze and marble components still accumulating in the Italians' workshop in Westminster. Later in 1530, the Cardinal wrote in deep depression from Yorkshire to Cromwell in London, asking him to arrange to send up to York Minster 'mine image, with such part of the tomb as it shall please the King that I shall have, to the intent that now at my being at my church, I may order and dispose the same for my burial, which is like, by reason of my heaviness, to be shortly'.[24]

It was not to be. In the end Henry seized everything, and cannibalized for his own projected monument all the parts with no specific reference to Wolsey, discarding and no doubt melting down the other pieces such as the Cardinal's 'image', that is his bronze recumbent effigy (what an absorbing work of art that would have been). It was to Cromwell that a payment of twenty marks was made immediately after Wolsey's death 'for the King's tomb', and he went on liaising with Rovezzano, now back from Florence and doing the same job for the King.[25] After both Cromwell and Rovezzano had departed the scene for different reasons, the supervision went to Giovanni Portinari, an Italian engineer who had acquired good English and had been given much employment by Cromwell. The project puttered on indecisively into the 1560s. Time's whirligig has given Wolsey revenge, since none of the monument was eventually used for Henry VIII. Wolsey's central black marble casket now houses Lord Nelson in the crypt of St Paul's, bronze candlesticks from the monument survive at Ghent, and the recent startling recognition of Benedetto Rovezzano's four beautiful bronze angels also from the tomb, long reused as gatepost finials for a Midlands country house before being saved for the nation, has reminded the world once more of one of the great lost artistic commissions of the Renaissance.[26]

Cardinal College Oxford was not lost in the end, though its magnificence was curtailed, and it has traded in later years under two successive different names: first King Henry's College, and then, from the 1540s, Christ Church. We will be encountering it discreetly settling into its new identity over the next decade. Cardinal College Ipswich was gone for ever, but Cromwell did not forget it, helping the borough salve the wound of its loss by restoring the already ancient borough grammar school, which the town had been happy enough to see absorbed into the Cardinal's munificent new foundation. In 1531 Cromwell's Ipswich agent William Laurence reported on interim arrangements he had overseen with Thomas Rush and Thomas Alvard for paying the school staff, appropriately enough by raiding the offertory box of Wolsey's pet shrine, Our Lady of Ipswich. Cromwell went on taking a very personal interest in the shrine; his servants kept the key to that box right up to the moment he had the shrine and its wonder-working image destroyed in 1538.[27]

Matters settled down for the rescued borough school. In 1540 the bailiffs of Ipswich could look back with gratitude on Cromwell's care 'whereby the common school has been continued and maintained', now excellently housed in classic Reformation style in the dormitory of the town's former Dominican friary.[28] It may also have been at the fall of Ipswich College that no less a figure than Cromwell's friend and Wolsey's servant Sir Humphrey Wingfield, soon to be Speaker of the House of Commons in the Reformation Parliament, began a select little school for favoured bright young men, in his own palatial town house in Ipswich (as we noted, immediately beside the precinct of Cardinal College); it lasted probably for most of the 1530s. His pupils' destination was now not Cardinal College Oxford, but St John's College Cambridge.[29]

There were other reverberations from the College's fall. Around 1534, Cromwell had to deal with an accusation that its former Dean William Capon had been guilty of major embezzlement of its funds, plate and jewels, said to have been concealed with a servant of his at Ipswich. Since Capon was both a friend and brother to the recently appointed Bishop of Bangor, who had been very helpful with the King's Great Matter, it is likely that the matter was hushed up; Capon continued in his post as Master of Jesus College Cambridge.[30] The sad carcase of St Peter's Priory and parish church, its eastern parts already demolished, was another problem to solve. Its valuable parish plate was transferred to Cromwell's staff in London in 1535 on the death of his Ipswich colleague Sir Thomas Rush, and the parishioners had to petition the now Lord Privy Seal in 1538 to get the parish up and running again and their goods restored. They struggled with admirable persistence for another half-century to create a viable parish church out of the surviving fragment with its dominant west tower, and their efforts can still be admired by the Ipswich waterside.[31]

Through nearly all of 1530, Cromwell was thus servant of both King and Cardinal: acting, though he had no official title, as royal Secretary for Wolsey-Related Affairs. It was a sensible redeployment, parallel to duties assigned to his friend Thomas Alvard in his new charge of the

King's Privy Coffers, a private royal treasury which came to be housed in the Cardinal's former palace.[32] While complex negotiations and decisions on Wolsey's future proceeded that winter, with Cromwell as the line of communication between King and Cardinal, the new initiatives proceeding at that same time to get opinions from the Universities of Oxford and Cambridge on the King's Great Matter did not involve him at all. In fact right up to the end of 1530, it is difficult to find anything in his papers which concerns any official business but Wolsey.

A few apparent exceptions simply prove the rule. Through the year, Cromwell administered a good deal of royal building work, but the bulk of it concerned upgrading and expanding Wolsey's gargantuan former York Place into the even more gargantuan new royal palace of Whitehall. All the building drew on large resources of fine stone no doubt intended for Cardinal College Ipswich; so this really fell into the same category of responsibilities.[33] One pair of draft receipts for legal documents by royal messengers corrected by Cromwell, from August 1530, looks at first sight as if it might concern general royal business, so great is the number of leading men and lawyers named in them; but in fact this is precisely about the unravelling of Wolsey's estates, listing those commissioned by the King to inquire into them county by county.[34] George Cavendish, with his acute nose for the dynamics of Tudor Court politics, noted that Cromwell's duties during 1530 were the real foundation of his future success: by his diplomatic attention to satisfying the greed of those battening on Wolsey's estates, while constantly consulting with the Cardinal himself to keep the damage within bounds, 'now began matters to work to bring Master Cromwell into estimation in such sort as was afterwards much to his increase of dignity.'[35]

There was one serious possible obstruction to that 'increase of dignity': Anne Boleyn. We have excavated the views of those who did most to smooth Cromwell's path into the King's service. What was his own attitude to the character who had triggered the momentous events now preoccupying everyone at Court? In view of what was to happen in the next few years, and granted their shared enthusiasm for evangelical reform in religion, it has been natural to assume over the centuries that Cromwell and Anne were close allies. Such was the assumption of Anne's masterly modern biographer Eric Ives, following many commentators at the time from Ambassador Chapuys outwards, who loathed what Anne and Cromwell jointly represented in destroying the old Church.[36] In fact, however, Cromwell shows no sign of being Anne's enthusiastic partisan, in marked contrast to Thomas Cranmer, who was always grateful that his road into royal service had been paved by the Boleyns. Cromwell's surprisingly cool relationship with Cranmer's evangelical friend Bishop Thomas Goodricke may have arisen out of Goodricke's strong connection with the Boleyns.[37]

It is true that Cromwell behaved with decency to Anne's father in his miserable years of eclipse after her execution, but he had nothing to fear from the Earl of Wiltshire by then, and was subject in addition to much prompting from the kindly Cranmer. The evidence Ives marshals to suggest a more than formal nexus between Anne and Cromwell is surprisingly thin, and much of it ambiguous at best: for instance, Cromwell did indeed become High Steward of her lands, but at twenty pounds a year his fee for this fairly routine and nominal honour was not over-generous, and in any case he had to pay substantial cash to obtain it.[38] He seems to have kept his financial affairs carefully separate from the Queen's, unlike Cranmer, who was still considerably in debt to her at her fall.[39]

Anne's direct favours to Cromwell are certainly difficult to identify, and there are downright disfavours: for instance, her unreceptiveness to the overtures of his old servant Stephen Vaughan, who put forward his wife as her prospective silkwoman.[40] Particularly galling would have been Anne's failure to forward the marriage of Cromwell's favourite nephew Richard Williams alias Cromwell to the widowed daughter-in-law of Sir William Courtenay of Powderham. Courtenay was a Devon magnate with whom Cromwell had an especially warm friendship and apparently some already existing marital relationship; he was one of very few among Cromwell's correspondents who habitually signed off his letters as 'your brother'. He was very receptive to Cromwell's overtures for this match, but said that since the young lady was the Queen's close relative Anne would have ultimate veto on it. The marriage did not happen. Richard transferred his marital plans more successfully to the stepdaughter of Sir Thomas Denys, another great man of Devon, who was close to Courtenay and also happened to be an old servant of Wolsey.[41]

Very few letters from Anne survive in Cromwell's archive, mostly formal pieces of administration. The sole example soaked in the sort of evangelical jargon they both liked is Anne's rather peremptory command to Cromwell to help an evangelical client of hers in Antwerp, Richard Harman. It manages to refer to 'the late Cardinal' in a rather pointed manner as being responsible for Harman's troubles, and certainly does not bother with that customary politesse 'whose soul God pardon'.[42] Ives suggested that Anne 'normally communicated by messenger', but an argument from silence always has its risks. There is actually a remarkable contrast between this paucity of letters between Anne Boleyn and Cromwell and his considerable and increasingly warm and personal correspondence with another great lady, Princess Mary, to which we will return; there are friendly letters to Cromwell from her mother Queen Katherine as well.[43]

It is not surprising that any hostility between Anne and Cromwell did not receive publicity. Clashes were kept carefully out of sight until the final crisis of 1536, after which time it was in the interest of Protestant historians, particularly their doyen John Foxe, to smooth over this problematic relationship between the two heroes of the early Protestant Reformation. It is telling to see how few links Foxe makes between their two stories, which his *Acts and Monuments* narrates in growing and loving detail.[44] One domestic issue does obliquely surface from Cromwell's increasing interference in monastic affairs in summer 1533: an abbatial election for the great Benedictine house of Malmesbury. This contested election saw confident moves to secure the election of the abbey's 'cosiner' (domestic bursar), strongly backed by Anne's Vice-Chamberlain Sir Edward Baynton, but Cromwell's nominee won, after considerable trouble. Anne's own name did not appear in any of the extensive correspondence – the sort of silence that obscures the real situation.[45]

More fundamental, and more widely attested in the dispatches of the imperial ambassador Chapuys and in other sources, were the opposed alignments of Anne and Cromwell in England's balancing act between western Europe's real great powers, France and the Habsburg dominions. Anne, given her intimate knowledge of the French Court from her early years, was consistent in her enthusiasm for alliance with France, subject to her customary outbursts of bad temper. Cromwell was equally influenced as royal minister by his long-standing happy contacts in Antwerp and the imperial Low Countries towards alliance with the Holy Roman Emperor. This tension on one of the foremost issues of English policy became acute in 1535–6.[46]

Many were drawn into supporting King Henry's annulment campaign through natural loyalty to the monarch as well his undoubted personal charisma. They included notables of conservative temperament in religion, from Thomas Duke of Norfolk, George Earl of Shrewsbury and Reginald Pole through to Bishop Stephen Gardiner and indeed nearly all the English episcopate. Cromwell's equally conservative associates at Court would not regard Katherine as their enemy – far from it – and would realize that both the Cardinal and his servant were doing the bidding of the King, not of Anne Boleyn. That is easy to ignore, since over the next few years Cromwell on his own initiative turned busily to destroying the religious world which Mary and Katherine came to symbolize. The Queen and Princess were nevertheless casualties of political rather than religious logic, and during the 1530s Mary was not the Catholic rallying-point she eventually became. The King's wilfulness and disregard for decent conduct towards his first wife opened up a chasm amid the kingdom's traditionalist-minded leaders, with Bishop Fisher and Sir Thomas More ranged against the much larger number prepared, however reluctantly, to overlook the lack of decency.

By contrast, the small but growing evangelical group in high politics might seem united behind their revolutionary religious cause, driving towards the Reformation which Martin Luther had sparked in mainland Europe, and seeking to import it to King Henry's realm. But the greatest hindrance to a coherent evangelical bloc forming in England at the beginning of the 1530s was the fact and the personality of Anne Boleyn. Few will doubt that in religion she was a committed evangelical, a furtherer of the godly cause; the evidence is clear from the late 1520s, when she recommended the writings of William Tyndale to the King, and in her years of power she consistently saw to the promotion of clergy such as Thomas Cranmer, Hugh Latimer and Nicholas Shaxton who were already marked out as evangelical enemies of the old religion. No traditionalists similarly enjoyed her favour.[47]

The complication in understanding the relationship of Anne and Cromwell has always been the undoubted fact that together with her brother George, to whom she was very close, she was working in the same religious direction as the royal minister. Yet as far as Cromwell was concerned, the great fact which shaped their relations for the rest of her life, and which makes sense of the events which now played out at Court over more than half a decade, was that she was the person most responsible for destroying his dear master the Cardinal. Equally, for her, he was the Cardinal's man, promoted to the King's service by the Cardinal's friends, and Wolsey's right-hand man in the months when his fate was still in the balance; that outweighed his undoubted part in clearing her path to the throne. We will see that she was probably responsible for slowing Cromwell's further progress into royal service rather than furthering it, and his eventual lead in her destruction in 1536 is not surprising (see Chapter 14). Most evangelical leaders abroad, not least Martin Luther, regarded the King's campaign to marry Anne and discard Katherine as ridiculous, unjust and cruel. Anne's removal then solved a good deal of the problem for English evangelicals, and very soon after that the shock of conservative fury in the Pilgrimage of Grace suggested some excellent reasons why evangelicals should stand in solidarity to avoid destruction at the hands of traditionalists.[48]

*

For the moment, in winter 1530, the campaign against the Pope was a bipartisan cause, which in most politicians' minds had not taken on the ideological freight it gained in the next three years. It involved not so much religion as those other great Tudor preoccupations, honour and reputation. The Pope had offended the King's honour (and by extension God's) through his delays and subterfuges. Henry never forgot that, and we should take seriously the proposition that many of his ministers felt the same way. Meanwhile the fate of Wolsey was entirely detached from that question, and was as yet not at all finally decided. Cromwell's successful interview with the King in January 1530 was accompanied by a distinct upturn in the Cardinal's fortunes, as Henry took pity on the near-fatal illness he was now suffering. A procession of royal physicians was dispatched to help him, including Anne's cousin Dr William Butts. Even Anne was induced to send him a token to cheer him up, in the form of the little girdle-book of prayers which she habitually wore, a kindness that is unlikely to have been accompanied by much personal warmth.

It was thanks to Cromwell's mediation, significantly without the advice or even the knowledge of royal councillors, that soon after Candlemas (2 February) the King allowed Wolsey to move to the former royal palace at Richmond, which a few years before he had been given a long-term right to occupy.[49] The Cardinal was not expecting this concession any more than the King's Council, and in haste he expressed his fulsome thanks to his 'entirely beloved' servant – 'I cannot express how greatly your letters have comforted me, being in manner in extreme desperation.'[50] In fact, whether out of lack of provision at the Palace itself or from an unwonted political prudence, Wolsey moved only into a comfortable little lodge in Richmond Park, and a month later at the beginning of Lent (2 March) he transferred to the nearby Charterhouse of Sheen, occupying a not especially penitential guest wing built by Dean Colet of St Paul's some years before.[51*]

After Cromwell's no doubt tense negotiations with Stephen Gardiner and the Duke of Norfolk, Wolsey's formal pardon followed. It came on 10 February, elaborated by an agreement of 17 February whereby he kept the title of his Bishopric of Winchester and the abbey of St Albans, in return for losing control of their revenues to various interested parties. He was also granted full occupation of his archdiocese of York. It could have been much worse.[52] Wolsey's enemies would find the prospect of his resuming regal splendour and accessibility to the King at Richmond

---

* This would be the same lodging taken over by Sir John Gage in his retirement under Anne Boleyn (see above, pp. 107–8).

deeply alarming in its promise of a complete comeback. If they had to suffer him being in effect given a chance to launch a second clerical career, it ought to be well away from the River Thames, which provided a royal channel of communication from palace to palace for him to charm Henry further. The answer was to send him to his Archbishopric of York. Cromwell, now with 'daily access' to the Duke of Norfolk in his to-and-fro discussions about Wolsey's pardon, had to convey the Duke's angry insistence that the Cardinal's hope of retreating to his other diocese of Winchester would not do.[53] After all, Winchester's territory extended down the Thames as far as London Bridge; in asking for that, Wolsey was being either insincere or totally naive.

The Cardinal delayed his departure north as long as he could, but by Passiontide at the beginning of April he was reluctantly on the road, pausing nearly a fortnight at Peterborough Abbey from Palm Sunday (10 April) through Holy Week.[54] Thanks to Cromwell's soliciting Master Secretary Stephen Gardiner, Wolsey travelled armed with various royal letters of introduction. That to the Abbot of Peterborough simply enjoined a hearty welcome, but those to prominent people in the Province of York were more programmatic, stressing the long absence of a resident archbishop (true; it had been a quarter-century) and ordering them not merely to offer hospitality as Wolsey prepared his own houses but to give him every assistance in his administration. The letters were carefully revised by Cromwell and others to calibrate Wolsey's currently fragile status, reflecting the worries of his opponents at Court: the crucial point was whether the Cardinal should be described as 'our right trusty and entirely well-beloved councillor'. In the end he was just 'our right trusty and entirely well-beloved' – the loss of the title of Councillor presumably a last-minute victory for his opponents at Court.[55]

Cromwell never saw his master face to face again. Nevertheless, he played an even more vital part in the Cardinal's life once Wolsey was in the North, commuting along the Thames between Austin Friars and the Court. His frequent letters were a constant source of news, but also increasingly a voice of sense and realism against what he must soon have realized was the Cardinal's fatal lack of proportion. The Archbishop of York entered an unfamiliar northern world which far from intimidating him played to his worst instincts of self-aggrandizement and display. News quickly reached Court 'that he rode in such sumptuous fashion that some men thought he was of as good courage as in times past, and that there was no impediment but lack of authority'. In a now familiar chain of friendship, Vice-Chamberlain Gage abandoned his clerk and took up his pen to write confidentially in his own execrable hand to

Cromwell on Wednesday of Holy Week, while Wolsey was still at Peter-borough. Gage frankly told him to warn the Cardinal about display, and 'to have himself in good await what words pass him', particularly in making promises about payment of debts out of his resources.[56]

Many such warnings against indiscretion and ostentation would fol-low, and not just from Cromwell; none was heeded. There may have been calculation in what Wolsey was attempting. To judge not merely from George Cavendish's admiring account but also from a hostile and well-informed writer of a slightly later generation, the Archbishop of York adopted a new style calculated to build an image as a self-negating, gen-erous Father in God: feasting the nobility and gentry, but also showing himself open to the poor; distributing alms; abandoning his horses to go on foot and greet beggars; happy 'to say Mass many times among the common people'; and 'whilst he sat at meat ... well pleased to hear a chapter of the Old or New Testament read'. Here was the image of a prel-ate to equal any of the great episcopal names of that decade battling to promote Catholic reform, like Guillaume Briçonnet, Bishop of Meaux, or Christoph von Utenheim of Basel. Thomas Cromwell the evangelical would approve of the attempt, but he would also have noted that both Briçonnet's and von Utenheim's efforts had failed. Our anonymous com-mentator observed darkly of Wolsey that 'the more he travelled forward, the more was he cast behind, for albeit he distributed his money very liberally, yet could he get in the south parts little amity.'[57]

There are signs that Cromwell felt deeply (and understandably) inse-cure about his own future. Despite his royal service, he had not travelled any further up the social hierarchy, to be styled 'esquire' rather than just 'gentleman'. Thomas Donington, one of Wolsey's senior chaplains, did address a letter to him as esquire in 1530, but Donington (not a popular man among his fellow-servants or in the North generally) was sending extravagant thanks for favours, and one complimentary swallow does not make a summer, even during August.[58] Cromwell's archive still fea-tured legal business for private clients, which he may have regarded as an insurance policy if all else failed. As the Cardinal's fortunes finally crashed in the autumn, Cromwell showed a new interest in private com-merce overseas, using his old servant Stephen Vaughan as agent in his old haunts in the Low Countries. When Vaughan went over in November 1530, Cromwell asked him 'what things might be laden unto these parts', and Vaughan reported back on arriving that widespread flooding had sent grain prices rocketing, so 'you should no doubt take thereby right good advantage' by shipments from England.[59] Cromwell also made Vaughan try and sell a large consignment of whale oil ('spermaceti') which was a commercial flop and an increasingly exasperating liability for the unfortunate agent, until as late as February 1532 Vaughan bluntly told him that it would have to be sold off cheaply.[60] By then, it hardly mattered: Cromwell's upward progress in state affairs seemed unstoppable, and he confined his non-governmental enterprises to such undemanding and politically useful business as wine-importing licences (easy to sublet) and loans of money.[61]

Amid the remains of correspondence between Cardinal and servant seen and summarized by Thomas Master are two remarkable items. In one letter (which startled Master and remains startling) Cromwell told the Cardinal he had 'discovered lately some who favour Luther's sect, and read his books, and Tyndale; the books he hath taken are *The Revelation of Antichrist* and *Supplication of Beggars*, pestiferous books, and able if they be scattered among the common people, to destroy the whole obedience and policy of this realm. He exhorts the Cardinal to stay this Doctrine.' Actually only the first of these items (both published in 1529) was from Tyndale, largely a translation of a text by Luther; the second was by the anti-clerical pamphleteer Simon Fish. It might be tempting to think that Master had misattributed the letter, but a further letter to Wolsey, certainly from Cromwell and firmly dated a month later than Sir John Gage's cautionary letter, is equally strong. After further warnings about money and verbal indiscretions, Cromwell turned to supplying London news. He told him that the King had summoned bishops and learned men to purge the realm of heretical books, and in reporting what was in fact an inaccurate rumour 'that Luther is departed this life' added the emphatic comment 'I would he had never been born.'[62]

There are several ways of interpreting these sentiments. Cromwell may have been saying what Henry VIII ordered him to say or what the Cardinal would expect and want to hear. The correspondents would also be aware that the chief champion of Tyndale and Fish close to the King was Wolsey's nemesis, Anne Boleyn. We should avoid the hindsight that forces all evangelicals in these early confused days of the Reformation into a seamless web of solidarity. Cromwell's first encounter with the movement which swelled into the Reformation was on his own testimony (transmitted to John Foxe via Ralph Morice) not through Luther but through Erasmus, whom the world had seen bitterly clashing with Luther during the 1520s on the vital theological matter of human free will versus divine determinism. Cromwell remained a strong admirer of Erasmus, promoting translations and publications of his works by the various printers he favoured during his years of power in the 1530s, now unequivocally in the interests of evangelical reformation.[63]

Even for a reformer who enjoyed sneering at papal power, it was possible to blame Luther for splitting Christendom. Cromwell, writing again to Wolsey on 18 August 1530 and telling him of current affairs in Germany, used the phrase 'the Lutheran sect', and in the sixteenth century there were few greater put-downs than the word 'sect'. If again one argues that this is language tailored to the recipient, it is worth noting that Stephen Vaughan, much less inclined than his old master to dissembling his vigorously evangelical religious opinions, also commonly called Luther's associates in reports to Cromwell on his foreign travels 'the Lutheran sect'.[64] Moreover, no one scrabbling to do the King's will as desperately as Cromwell soon was in the annulment business would have any cause to love Luther, who was bitterly opposed to Henry's repudiation of Queen Katherine. If looking for evangelical soulmates over the water in that cause, it would be to the reformers of Switzerland, who proved much more amenable to Henry VIII's arguments that he had never so far been married.[65] In fact, as we will see, that was exactly the direction in which his eyes turned (see below, Chapter 15).

Putting together various fragments of evidence of the years 1529–30, it is nevertheless possible to suggest that this great crisis of Cromwell's fortunes did produce a serious jolt to his evangelical convictions, certainly as to how he was prepared to present himself to the world. First, those traditionalist provisions in his will; then his Lady Psalter clutched at Esher; now exclamations against Luther. Add to that, the group of Wolsey's friends and Anne's enemies who were happy to promote Cromwell into Henry VIII's service: no evangelical sympathizers there. There is also the one illegitimate child he is known to have fathered, if we think her birth came at this juncture. Collectively, there is the appearance of a real lurch in his behaviour, resembling nothing else in the record before or after these twelve months, that threatened to bring him down with his old master.

Wolsey's ongoing folly was not merely a matter of showing off in the North. About the time he left the Thames valley, he began putting out his own secret diplomatic feelers to Europe's two most powerful monarchs, King François of France and Charles V, then to King Henry's spurned Queen Katherine and Pope Clement VII.[66] Through the summer, as he brooded in his archiepiscopal country houses at Southwell and Scroby, his efforts redoubled, so that from August onwards he was in obsessively regular contact with Ambassador Chapuys, via his energetic Italian physician Dr Augustine. The Cardinal's aim now ran directly against Henry's plans: he tried to encourage the Pope explicitly to forbid the King to continue his liaison with Anne Boleyn. The French ambassador later claimed that the fallen minister hoped thereby to see the country plunged into such political chaos that he would be seen as the natural saviour of the situation, and would return to his old pre-eminence. It seems so crazy that one can only blame his continuing humiliation for his mental unbalance, furthered by the lack of anyone close at hand with the ability to recall him to a sense of proportion.[67]

The specific nudge into self-destruction for the Cardinal, moving him from vague plotting to something far more treasonous, may have been the news in the summer that the King was intent on dismantling his entire legacy project: tomb and Colleges together. Cardinal College Ipswich had puttered on unhappily through the first half of the year, trying to defend its interests against emboldened and obstreperous tenants and waiting for something to turn up. As we have seen, Cromwell continued to look after its affairs; although his new official dignity meant he was no longer the man to traipse the East Anglian roads holding manorial courts, he sent down his most trusted servant in financial matters, William Brabazon (Thomas Alvard also did his best for the College). Poor Dean Capon wrote gratefully to his 'own very singular good lover and friend' Cromwell on 15 May, 'you do shew yourself like a faithful friend unto us, which is well proved now in time of adversity.'[68] But there were limits to what Cromwell could achieve against the King's decision. Probably at the beginning of July he broke it to the Cardinal that the Colleges were to be dissolved. Wolsey was distraught. He wrote back (with forgivable hyperbole), 'I cannot write unto you, for weeping and sorrow,' while thanking him warmly 'for such great pains as ye have taken in all my causes'.[69]

It is unlikely that Wolsey hastened to reveal to his servant at Court the extent of his self-destructive intrigues with foreign powers. Cromwell did get angry and frustrated with him, but for other reasons: the Cardinal's bouts of mistrust of him, his continued reckless building plans in the North and the huge expenses accumulating in London in the clearing up of his affairs. Yet the letters contain no hint of warning on this other front, even while the servant passed on news of international affairs.[70] Out of all the correspondence, the most revealing of their relationship is the complete draft of a long letter from Cromwell to the Cardinal on 18 August 1530, a highly unusual stray from his lost out-tray archive. Maybe it survived because Cromwell surrendered it to the King for scrutiny at Wolsey's death, to demonstrate that he was not involved in the Cardinal's treasonous activities, and so already at the end of 1530 it would become lodged in the royal archive. In any case, it is precious for a rare

In Cromwell's long draft letter to Wolsey, 18 August 1530, Cromwell himself here begins to alter his secretary's text, opening 'Sir, I assure Your Grace that ye be moch bounde to o'r Lord God that in suche wise hathe suffered you so to behave and order yo'rself in thos p'rtyes to atteyne the good myndes and hertes of the people . . .' After that, his rewriting is extensive, prolonging the letter beyond its initial ending on the following page.

glimpse it gives of Cromwell's own thinking through his corrections and afterthoughts.[71]

He started by dictating to his clerk three pages of reassuring news about the legal status of Wolsey's archiepiscopal estates and the future of the Colleges, together with an update on various other legal business; all straightforward, if tiresome and partly unresolved. But then things became more difficult, and he started busily correcting the draft. There was unwelcome advice to convey. 'Sir, I assure Your Grace that ye be much bound to our Lord God that in such wise hath suffered you to attain the good minds and hearts of the people in the whole country there, the report whereof in the Court and elsewhere in these parts is and hath been to your great good,' ran the first version that the clerk took down. Cromwell looked at it, and felt that it was too sunny, because it was going to have to lead into a warning. Corrections (which I have italicized) made it more pointed:

> Sir, I assure Your Grace that ye be much bound to our Lord God that in such wise hath suffered you *so to behave and order yourself in those parts* to attain the good minds and hearts of the people there, the report whereof in the Court and elsewhere in these parts is and hath been to *the acquiring and augmenting the good opinions of many persons towards Your Grace . . .*

Now there was something really difficult to convey, which in the first draft ran, 'Notwithstanding your good, virtuous and charitable demeaning and using yourself there, I assure Your Grace you have enemies which do and will not let [hesitate] to interpret all your doings not in the best part, alleging that your only desires are continually building.' It needed to be less blunt, so:

> Notwithstanding your good, virtuous and charitable demeaning and using yourself *in those parts is not by your* enemies *interpreted after the best fashion, yet always follow and persevere ye attemperately in such things as (your worldly affections set apart) shall seem to stand best with the pleasure of God and the King. Sir, some there be that doth allege that Your Grace doth keep too great a house and family and that ye are continually building . . .*

and so 'eftsoons' (that is, once more – not the first time he had tried to get this message across) Cromwell launched into a further much corrected set of second and third thoughts, advising the Cardinal with increasing emphasis 'to refrain yourself for a season from all manner buildings more than necessity requireth'. After some thanks for sending a gift of two

horses south, the usual address, date and sign-off followed.[72] Then Cromwell thought better of finishing up, crossed them out, dismissed his clerk
and continued for another two and a half pages in his own hand: one of
the longest surviving examples we possess. First came some even more
straightforward moralizing worthy of Stephen Vaughan, once more seeking the best and kindest phrases to add to the text as he wrote:

> I do reckon Your Grace right happy that ye be now at liberty to serve God
> and to learn *to experiment how ye shall banish and exile* the vain desires
> of this unstable world, which undoubtedly doth nothing else but allure
> every person therein. And specially such as Our Lord hath most endued
> with his gifts, to desire the affections of their mind *to be satisfied* ...
> Wherefore in my opinion, Your Grace being as ye are, I suppose ye would
> not be as ye were, to win a hundred times as much as ye were possessed of.

Now the agonized drafting and redrafting was over, and the text of the
extended letter flowed smoothly to its end. There followed a solid dose of
international news – the first time in any surviving correspondence
between them that such matters were discussed – and apologies for not
coming up to Southwell to see the Cardinal in person; even the bearer
could be ill spared in London, 'but only that I perceived by your letters
that ye much desired to be put in quietation'.

No one reading the original of this letter can think of Cromwell simply
as a heartless bureaucrat. The repeated tinkering with the sections he
knew would wound Wolsey the most reveal a man trying to speak truth
to fading power. Wolsey must be made to realize that the glory days were
gone, and that there were worse fates than being Archbishop of York. If
only he had listened; but it was probably already too late. By October, the
evidence of his treasonous dealings was beginning to emerge at Court.
Anne eventually succeeded in badgering her indecisive royal lover to take
action.[73] Wolsey was arrested on 1 November, a week before his long-
postponed enthronement: in all his years as Archbishop, he never made it
to his own cathedral city.

Once more, the correspondence between Cromwell and Wolsey during
October has no hint of all this intrigue. It is preoccupied with a different
sort of tension: the Cardinal's continuing suspicion that his servant had
not pulled his weight in saving his Colleges and other possessions –
completely wide of the mark – followed by emotional declarations of his
trust when challenged.[74] Cromwell's last surviving letter to Wolsey, written
only ten days before the arrest, seems entirely innocent of any coming crisis; it not only conveyed important snippets of political and international
news, but also looked forward to a bounteous future by commending

various individuals to Wolsey's powers of patronage in the archdiocese: Cromwell's importunate clerical kinsman Henry Carbot, Wolsey's own servant Nicholas Gifford ('though young and somewhat wild, he is disposed to truth, honesty and hardiness') and 'my scholars in Cambridge', by whom Cromwell probably meant young Christopher Wellifed and Nicholas Sadler, then studying with his son at Pembroke Hall.[75]

Within a month of the Cardinal's arrest, he was dead, felled by some acute digestive illness on 29 November, while staying at Leicester Abbey on his melancholy way south. There he was buried, and it is unlikely that Cromwell was able to attend what would have been a quiet funeral. Wolsey's death at Leicester may have saved him from becoming the first victim of political execution in an increasingly bloodsoaked decade. If Cavendish is to be believed (and he usually is), the Cardinal had won real popularity, or at least widespread pity, during his months in the North, and that would not have been to his advantage at Court. Wolsey's fall left Cromwell desperately vulnerable, regardless of what he had actually known about the plotting. After all, he was a great friend of Dr Augustine, who was unquestionably entangled in the Cardinal's promiscuous intrigues; Augustine was arrested along with his master, unceremoniously called 'traitor' by Sir Walter Walsh the King's officer and ignominiously ridden to London with his feet tied under his horse's belly.[76]

Their joint asset in what happened next was the government's extreme embarrassment that Wolsey had (to a degree now probably irrecoverable) been in communication with the French. Henry and his advisers did not want to create too much fuss in protest, which would alienate their most important potential ally against any action the Emperor might take to support his aunt Katherine. Official reaction during November was to undertake a good deal of spin-doctoring around the events before issuing an economical public version of the truth, casting blame for Wolsey's misdemeanours on to the Pope and emphasizing that no blame attached to the French ambassador. One direct beneficiary of this policy was Dr Augustine himself. Far from ending up in a traitor's dungeon, he was now relaunched as a roving agent abroad for Anne Boleyn's uncle, the Duke of Norfolk. Soon he was acting in a similar capacity for a newly promoted Thomas Cromwell.[77]

Cromwell also escaped danger, maybe benefiting from the same official embarrassment. The story is told by Chapuys, as part of the well-informed and not unsympathetic mini-biography which the ambassador supplied five years later to Chancellor Granvelle in Brussels, a regular confidant:

At the said Cardinal's fall he was the only person who acquitted himself well towards him; and on the Cardinal's death, since Master Wallop (at present ambassador at the Court of France), pursued and threatened him in the worst possible manner, [Cromwell] saw no other refuge or remedy than to resort to the King. He did so much by entreaties and gifts that he gained a royal audience, at which he must have promised to make him the richest King that England had ever seen – and spoke so well and eloquently that the King from that moment made him of his Council, without consulting anyone else, and did not reveal this to any of his folk for four months.[78]

It is the precision of the account which impresses. Chapuys distinguishes this occasion after Wolsey's death in late 1530 from whatever had happened at the Cardinal's initial fall, a year before, and he makes no claim to know what was said at the meeting, beyond a sarcastic comment about it – that's what Cromwell must have said, he quipped. 'Four months' sounds implausibly specific, until one realizes that what Chapuys is conveying (or what has been conveyed to him) is that Cromwell was not given the outward position of a councillor until after the imminent next session of Parliament. That ended in the fourth month after Cromwell's interview with the King in early December 1530. A councillor would have stood out in a Commons session because of his distinctive clothing in red with gold trimmings, or the Tudor colours of green and white. Moreover, a councillor would sit in the front benches, unlike a 'back-bencher' such as a burgess for Taunton, which is what Cromwell remained while Parliament sat.[79] This gives confidence in the rest of what Chapuys said.

Sir John Wallop is an interesting enemy for Cromwell to have acquired. He was another unusual English cosmopolitan like Russell or Cromwell himself, and spent most of his life abroad on military or diplomatic missions.[80] At this stage, he had long-standing ties with the Duke of Norfolk's circle, and his wife was in Anne Boleyn's service. Though he had his own strong doubts about the King's annulment project, he was as hostile to Wolsey's servant as one would expect someone with those connections to have been. Later, in the clarified polarization at the end of the 1530s, Wallop's religious conservatism ranged him among the group which brought Cromwell down in 1540; it is unlikely he forgot this moment at the end of 1530 when he might just have nipped Cromwell's career in the bud.

The year ended as it began, in a productive interview with the King. Thomas Cromwell's service to the Cardinal was done. His seven years in Wolsey's employ had pulled him out of the ranks of London merchants and small-time lawyers to the point where this last summer the Cardinal came to call the Putney boy his 'special friend'.[81] Through 1530, the King watched Cromwell's work with evident approval, as George Cavendish noted: 'having a great occasion of access to the King for the disposition of divers lands, whereof he had the order and governance ... he grew continually into the King's favour.'[82] As usual, Cavendish's reliability can be triangulated from elsewhere. Cromwell's Court patron Sir John Russell reassured him that June from Hampton Court: 'After your departure from the King, His Grace had very good communication of you, which I shall advertise you at our next meeting.'[83] The fruits of this approval were enough to counter Wallop's malice.

Cromwell's preoccupation with saving Wolsey from himself and doing what he could to save Wolsey's plans for immortality had begun to constrain his further rise in the realm. Two of those problems were given decisive solutions by the King's fixed determination to obliterate Cardinal College Ipswich and his ruthless commandeering of Wolsey's tomb. That left substantial unfinished business in the triple shape of Thomas Winter, Cardinal College Oxford and the cannibalization of Wolsey's building projects. Yet those leftovers from the past now took their place in the in-tray of a new-minted councillor among a great deal else of much deeper importance and long-term significance. King Henry, on one of those personal and uncounselled impulses which were the wild card of politics in his reign, had abruptly thrown the tireless solver of Wolsey's problems into the centre of royal policy. There was much to solve. In the last month or so of 1530, Cromwell moved to tackle these new challenges with an energy and speed that launched a decade of revolution.

PART TWO

New Wine

Forsake not an old friend, for the new shall not be like him. A new friend is new wine: let him be old, and thou shalt drink him with pleasure.

Ecclesiasticus 9.10, in the translation
of Miles Coverdale, 1535

Ye say, it is new learning. Now I tell you it is the old learning. Yea, ye say, it is old heresy new scoured. Nay, I tell you, it is old truth, long rusted with your canker, and now new made bright and scoured.

Bishop Hugh Latimer, sermon 5 November 1536

6

Council and Parliament: 1531

As Chapuys has told us, at the beginning of 1531 Cromwell became a royal councillor, beginning open-ended responsibilities which never ceased expanding until the moment of his arrest in 1540. Even when his new status began to emerge from secrecy, as he gained the right to don a councillor's royal livery after the end of the Parliamentary session in March, the title of Councillor was a rather amorphous honour, which it could quite naturally remain, given that at the time the royal Council was about as amorphous a body as one could imagine.[1] As late as July 1531, Henry VIII merely called Cromwell 'our trusty and well-beloved servant' in a document relating to the former Cardinal College Oxford, and definite references by other people to him as Councillor only multiply from December.[2] Yet that spring of 1531 some people around the Court were in the know. One was his friend the merchant John Creke, desperate to find employment in royal service after bankruptcy: some time in April (around four months after the event, just as Chapuys suggested), Creke ingratiatingly addressed a letter to Cromwell as 'of the King's Council'.

Creke's plight is the historian's good fortune, as it provides perspective on Cromwell's place in politics at this vital moment in his rise to power. We first encountered John Creke back in 1522 on business in Bilbao (see above, pp. 28, 50), and most of his mercantile career had been spent in trade with Spain. By winter 1531 his business affairs and demands from his creditors had plunged him into such financial disaster that nothing short of flight to sanctuary in Westminster seemed a way out, as he lamented to Cromwell (Creke was clearly well aware that he would then find Cromwell occupied in royal or Parliamentary business at Westminster).[3] Grasping at his special expertise in all things Spanish as a marketable asset, Creke now turned to his Spanish friends in London to get himself a place in the service of Katherine of Aragon, and around Easter it looked as if he had succeeded.[4] Then politics intervened, as he dolefully told Cromwell:

By the labour of Sir John Russell unto my Lord Mountjoy [Katherine's Chamberlain], and also the Queen's almoner and the Queen's receiver, [it] was appointed amongst them that I should have been admitted her gentleman usher now at this feast of Easter past [9 April 1531], as they made promise unto Sir John Russell, where upon the following of the matter, Her Grace hath made answer that she will take no servants *till such time as she may be more in quietness than now she is.*[5]

It was only because of this gently regal rebuff that Creke turned to Cromwell (in this letter which first addressed him as 'Master Cromwell one of the King's Council') 'to accept and take me into anything in your service or office . . . also if at your Mastership's hand conveniently you at this present cannot help me then, if it please you . . . to prefer me to Mr Treasurer's service'. He wrote instead of coming to see him, 'for the great business that your Mastership have', but once more begged for a meeting at Westminster the following day.

What a snapshot of Court politics this provides! We hear two familiar names in Cromwell's circle: Sir John Russell and Sir William Fitzwilliam (Treasurer of the royal Household and Creke's third possible saviour). Creke, who clearly knew a good cross-section of people at Court and understood at least the outward balance of forces there, still regarded Queen Katherine as a player in the game that spring: her household, so far intact, was surely his best route out of his troubles. The Queen was more cautious about her future than her household officers had been in appointing him Gentleman Usher, though she still put a brave face on matters. Only after that door had closed did Creke consider Cromwell amid his busyness at Westminster. Cromwell was now several steps further up the Court ladder than in 1530, but there was some way to go before Creke judged him a better career prospect than Queen Katherine.

For the moment, the dominant figures among the King's advisers were those who had rejoiced in Wolsey's fall: Anne Boleyn's father the Earl of Wiltshire, her uncle the Duke of Norfolk and Principal Secretary Gardiner. The previous year Gardiner had been equipped with a fine Middlesex house at Hanworth on long lease from the royal estate, and by the end of 1531 he was Wolsey's successor as Bishop of Winchester.[6] Yet, although there were marked limits on Cromwell's position, the range of activities reflected in his surviving papers soon expanded out of all recognition. Much of what he did was in close concert with the regime's current leading figure the Duke of Norfolk, for instance their joint adjudication of a coastal trade dispute in Wales and the West Country or, in July,

Cromwell's preparation of an important proclamation regulating the export of coin and bullion.[7]

Cromwell's old expertise in Italian was useful in extending his joint work with Norfolk into foreign affairs, particularly since his Italian friend Dr Augustine, deftly avoiding disaster after the Wolsey debacle, was gathering intelligence abroad and reported back to both of them – that was no secret, for on one occasion, in June 1531, Augustine referred the Duke to the contents of a letter which he had just written to Cromwell. Pier-Francesco de' Bardi, an Italian friend and neighbour from Austin Friars (whom we have met before and will meet again), was part of the same circle of correspondence, passing on Augustine's letters to Cromwell and on at least one occasion obligingly translating the Italian text of Augustine's rather tiring small italic hand into Latin.[8]

Cromwell's smooth and untrumpeted move into a position of real power began at the end of summer. On 10 November 1531, the outgoing ambassador of the Venetian Republic, Lodovico Falier, arrived back home after a several weeks' journey across Europe. He sat down to write a full description of that remote kingdom of England after nearly three years' service, for the benefit of the Venetian Senate. It was a perceptive, sympathetic and generally well-informed account of some length. Towards the end, he listed the members of what he regarded as the King's inner Council at the time he left England in September.[9] He named eight – the Dukes of Norfolk and Suffolk, the Earl of Wiltshire, Treasurer Fitzwilliam, two veteran Household officers George Earl of Shrewsbury (Lord Steward) and Sir Henry Guildford (Comptroller), and finally Secretary Gardiner, but nestling amid these predictable names, without any mention of a particular office, was Thomas Cromwell.[10] It is interesting that the first mention of Cromwell as within the charmed circle of power came from an Italian; Falier may well have thought that the name would ring certain bells in Venice.

The list was in reality shorter than it looks. The Earls of Shrewsbury were a perennial honorific presence on royal councils throughout the sixteenth century, but that was thanks mostly to their rolling acres in the north Midlands, and although the elderly fourth Earl was destined to play a crucial role in blunting the force of the Pilgrimage of Grace in 1536, he was not a decisive presence at Court. Sir Henry Guildford was now compromised by his deep dislike of Anne Boleyn (like so many of Cromwell's friends) and by ill-health which would kill him in less than a year. Cromwell's new prominence among the remaining half-dozen must have been very recent. So far no one has identified any official document which calls Cromwell a royal councillor before September, in a memorandum from the King himself: a recital of Council business for Cromwell to prepare before Michaelmas Term began, including bills to be presented for a third session of the current Parliament planned for October. Henry ordered him to confer with royal lawyers on the Council over the entire gamut of domestic concerns, from royal exchanges of lands and debts through customs business and various Parliamentary bills.[11]

The inclusion of the bills is especially interesting. It is likely that after his vigorous performance in the previous sessions of Parliament, Cromwell owed his new position to the prospect of a Parliamentary recall, although the session was suddenly postponed to January 1532. Most bills mentioned were routine, but they included two measures of current political importance. One was the confiscation of goods of 'certain spiritual persons holding promotion and resident without the King's licence in the Court of Rome'. The main target here was Cardinal Campeggio, a belated subject of Henry's revenge for the Blackfriars debacle two summers before; the King had just stripped him of his title of Cardinal-Protector of England and he might well next lose his diocese of Salisbury.[12] The other was a measure with a dark significance for events over the next four years: 'The bill of Augmentation of Treasons to be made and engrossed against Parliament, with a clause about protection'. In the end this did not emerge as a piece of legislation until 1534.

The background to Cromwell's rise in 1531 was a significant change in the direction of royal policy and diplomacy in the King's Great Matter. English policy still seemed confused, because the King's strategy proceeded on two different tracks, one international and one internal to the realm. Cromwell's roles in the twin campaigns are best pursued separately. Henry continued in his efforts to persuade the rest of the world that he was morally in the right. His ultimate failure was to Thomas Cromwell's long-term advantage. While Henry was pursuing his aims mainly overseas, using a mixture of theological argument and diplomacy, the new Councillor could offer nothing obvious or exceptional: he had neither training in theology nor experience as an international diplomat. Indeed, as will become apparent, what interventions the King allowed him to make proved as fruitless as everybody else's.

During the previous year, embassies abroad had cost a lot and produced nothing. Their futility had been underlined in autumn 1530 by the revelation of Cardinal Wolsey's potentially treacherous contacts with the same foreign powers the King was trying to cultivate. Theologians and ambassadors had done their best – alternately bullying and wheedling the

Roman Curia, then jostling for friendship from the Emperor and the King of France. They invested inordinate time in seeking out top names in the great universities of Europe for endorsements of Henry's by no means contemptible theological case, encouraging their scholarship with cash sweeteners. This approach to overseas universities had been the policy suggested by Thomas Cranmer to Secretary Gardiner back in summer 1529, and although it proved vital in launching Cranmer's long career in public life, in reality it was a dead end in solving the Great Matter. No one could know this at the beginning of 1531, but it became increasingly obvious over the year. In those next few months, Cromwell finally came into his own.

The last months of 1530 saw the royal campaign abroad widen to include the various evangelical reformers of mainland Europe. No doubt frustration with the Catholic great powers and anger at Wolsey's clandestine diplomacy played their part in this; but, more hopefully for Henry's quest, for the first time a potentially powerful alternative political grouping was emerging in Germany, as various 'Protestant' princes and free cities of the Empire agreed to form a security alliance against any aggression from their overlord Charles V, secured by their combined military strength. Discussions successfully culminated in agreement in February 1531 at the small town of Schmalkalden, in the forests of Thuringia; hence the resulting coalition was known as the Schmalkaldic League.

The League remained a highly significant player in international politics through the remainder of Thomas Cromwell's career and beyond, up to a crushing military defeat at the hands of Charles V in 1547. Naturally it was a constant point of reference for those in English politics like Cromwell who wished to pull the kingdom into the orbit of the Reformation – but the League also came to fascinate King Henry, as his ecclesiastical adventures forced the King to rethink what Catholic Christianity might be, and to seek inspiration beyond his own bundle of increasingly contradictory theological opinions.[13] In 1531, therefore, English strategy went into reverse. In Rome, rather than the papal bureaucracy drawing out proceedings in the annulment business, the King's representatives were now told to hold up any further action while Henry looked elsewhere, and, as we have seen, during the summer the King openly humiliated Cardinal Campeggio; he had decided there was no point in pretending to be conciliatory.[14]

In August 1531, Henry sent a mission to Germany led by Stephen Gardiner's servant William Paget to discuss current manoeuvres within the Empire to weaken Habsburg power. Princes as varied in religion as the Protestant Elector of Saxony and the Catholic Duke of Bavaria were trying to revoke the Imperial Diet's election of Charles's brother Ferdinand as 'King of the Romans', heir-presumptive to the Empire.[15] Even though the English embassy and reciprocal missions from Germany involved both Catholic and Protestant rulers, there was something new, with major future implications: England's international diplomacy sought to embrace Rome's open enemies in the King's search for support in his marital troubles. Discussions even included the unpromising Martin Luther and his colleagues in Wittenberg and, more hopefully, reached out to the powerful and non-Lutheran evangelical city-states of Strassburg, Basel and Zürich, far south of Saxony.

Evangelicals were all greatly excited by Henry's overtures, and no fewer than five missions arrived in England in 1531 to explore possibilities.[16] On behalf of the Lutherans came feelers from the Schmalkaldic League even before the Schmalkalden agreement had been finalized in February, while at the end of the year the renegade English Austin Friar Robert Barnes appeared, armed with letters from Luther himself and from the leading prince of the League, Philipp of Hessen. He also brought a spare wardrobe of secular clothes which soon replaced his increasingly incongruous friar's habit.[17] Between these visits, the genial scholar of Greek Simon Grynaeus – friend not merely of Strassburg's chief pastor Martin Bucer, but also of the great Erasmus – arrived from Basel, sending his servants on further visits once he had left. Thomas Cranmer, returning from his mission to Italy in autumn 1530, was a particularly important go-between for the Court with this variety of envoys, the first officially received visitors from Europe's Reformations. He much impressed Grynaeus with his closeness to the King, and established a lasting friendship.[18]

Cranmer had probably not met any senior representative of continental evangelical Reformers before Grynaeus, and the same is probably true of Thomas Cromwell. It may only have been now, amid their frequent contacts at Court, that Cromwell and Cranmer turned their previous business contacts into the beginnings of friendship and close co-operation that fully blossomed after their joint elevation to high office in 1533. Cranmer's public career started almost as late as Cromwell's, and he was only slightly younger, born in 1489. His early life had lacked the colour of the Putney boy's adventures: this son of minor Nottinghamshire gentry spent a quarter-century in Cambridge University, the only unusual feature being an early marriage which ended with his wife's death in childbirth. That tragedy made possible his ordination to the priesthood, and a blamelessly useful scholarly career followed at Jesus College Cambridge.

Cranmer's life was transformed when in 1529 Stephen Gardiner, then a Cambridge colleague and friend, and much more used to the wider world, interested the Boleyns in him, as a man whose solid learning could promote the theology supporting the King's Great Matter. Cranmer suggested to Gardiner that universities across Europe could be systematically canvassed for favourable opinions; any new idea was worth trying at a desperate stage of the saga. Abruptly Cranmer left Cambridge behind for greater promotions, and blossomed amid the splendour of the royal Court. He was sent off abroad on missions which helped him catch up with Cromwell's old familiarity with the wider European world. The two men so newly prominent in the King's service in 1531 were renewing an acquaintance made at least as early as 1528, when William Capon, Master of Cranmer's Cambridge college, had been so briefly promoted to Cardinal College Ipswich.

I have argued elsewhere that it was in 1531 that Cranmer's religious conservatism began shifting to the evangelical convictions of his later career; it was also the moment when Cromwell's actions unmistakably moved back to the evangelical patterns we discerned in the 1520s.[19] This was a decisive year in forcing people to make choices in an increasingly obvious religious division, whatever they thought about the King's annulment plans – Stephen Gardiner, Thomas More and Reginald Pole would opt for the other side of the traditionalist/evangelical divide, though no one could ever accuse King Henry VIII of making the same sort of clearcut decision.

The continuing royal effort to win support across the Channel produced two important printed Latin statements of the King's case – that they were in Latin shows they were intended for international consumption, though they would also have had uses in Oxford and Cambridge and among English churchmen. They were presented so as to appeal across Europe's developing religious chasm. The judgements of universities gathered with such labour by Cranmer and his colleagues in 1530 were published in Latin in April 1531, but the *Academiarum Censurae* was a curious portmanteau work of two unequal halves. Despite the book's title, the 'judgements' were in fact a rather brief overture to the revised version of an entirely different, much longer document: a formal compilation of Henry's arguments in canon law for his annulment in 1529. This had already met its match in Cardinal Campeggio's duplicity when the King's lawyers presented it as the royal case at the Blackfriars trial, but it may subsequently have been hawked round the universities in the campaign for opinions, and now it was published for the international audience in a slightly more aggressive form.[20]

The *Censurae* is almost deliberately dull in order to establish the respectability of Henry's case. Rather more digestible was a much shorter tract, also at this stage in the learned language of Latin, entitled *Disputatio inter clericum et militem* ('A disputation between a cleric and a knight'). It had a long and peculiar back-story: a thirteenth-century French dialogue resurrected a century later by Lollards and turned into English. Now this new Latin version appeared, partly based on recent German editions, but also with new amplifications designed to point up its message and bolster it with scriptural texts. Its ancient message – clerical privilege must be curbed and royal power asserted – when suitably modernized, was as useful to Henry VIII as it had been to King Philippe le Bel of France in the 1290s, and its origins outside the realm of England might suggest to overseas readers that King Henry's grievances were not merely a piece of local selfishness. Chapuys, writing to the Emperor on 24 June 1531, noted its appearance in print, commenting sourly that it managed to combine being weak and colourless with offensively violent language against the Pope.[21] The *Disputatio* ran to two Latin editions. It was considered successful enough to merit an English translation a couple of years later, which again did well enough for a second edition.[22]

It is possible that we can link the publication of the *Disputatio* to Cromwell. On 26 January 1531 Stephen Vaughan wrote from Bergen op Zoom to Henry VIII. Apprehensive as to whether he was striking the right note to that unpredictable reader, he sent the letter first to his patron Cromwell with a covering letter asking him to vet it.[23] Vaughan mentioned that their mutual friend William Lock, prominent evangelical among London merchants, 'will bring you the *Dialogues* of Ockham which I gave him, in his male [that is, pack] within four days next'. This was the follow-up to a letter of mid-December 1530 in which Vaughan had apologized that 'Your books I labour to come by, but they will not as yet be had, but I will sure have them and send them in all haste possible.'[24]

The dialogic work Vaughan sent in January may well have been the late medieval printed version of the *Disputatio*, which probably because of its anti-papal content was then generally but mistakenly thought to be by William of Ockham, fourteenth-century Franciscan scourge of aberrant popes. The *Disputatio* text published in England during 1531 reflected both the edition likely to be available from booksellers in the Low Countries and the 150-year-old Lollard English translation of the original text. Even if Vaughan's book was one of certain other texts genuinely by Ockham and entitled 'dialogues', they too were employed in Henry VIII's construction of a case to defy Rome, and ended up in the King's library, covered in annotations added by his researchers.[25]

This letter of Vaughan's to Cromwell and Henry VIII is part of a correspondence between Vaughan and his old master attesting that Cromwell had been brought into the campaign for the royal annulment in the crucial last two months of 1530, just as Wolsey's career was ending. As Henry extended his charm offensive to the evangelical powers of northern Europe, the obvious intermediaries were English evangelicals who had fled from the country in the anti-Lutheran crackdown instituted by the English Church authorities from 1526, particularly if Henry could satisfy himself that their flight did not indicate irretrievable heresy. Most prominent among these exiles were William Tyndale and Robert Barnes, but there were also lesser figures like Miles Coverdale, George Joye and John Frith, all associates of Tyndale in clandestine English religious printing in the Low Countries.

All these men were already known to Cromwell, at the very least across a crowded room, and most of them in more familiar terms than that, as we have already observed. Tyndale may have put in a brief stint as a stipendiary priest at Boston parish church in 1521; Barnes had been an odd sort of prisoner next to Cromwell's house at Austin Friars in 1527–8; Coverdale was Cromwell's friend and correspondent.[26] Joye had been extensively examined both by Wolsey and by Cromwell's colleagues among his household officers; Frith was one of the evangelical recruits from Cambridge to Cardinal College Oxford, and had been the bearer of at least one message to Cromwell in 1526.[27] Out of those colleagues in exile, Tyndale was the King's first choice for attempted seduction, since his writings had already attracted favourable royal comment, thanks to Anne Boleyn.

While Wolsey made his miserable way south in November 1530, Henry was preparing overtures to secure Tyndale's return to England, believing he could be used as a propagandist in the Great Matter. On 1 December 1530, six days after arriving in Antwerp (ostensibly on legal business for the Merchant Venturers), Vaughan had written to Cromwell, apologizing that so far 'I have not greatly learned any assured knowledge concerning such matters as pleased your Mastership somewhat before my leave taken of you to common me of [that is, share with me].' He did not wish 'hastily to enterprise my intended purpose, lest thereby my policy might or should be in any wise prevented', but wanted to make sure that at the appropriate moment 'upon mine advertisement to you thereof, I may be provided for *their* safe-conducts'.[28]

All this is obviously phrased with great caution, but Vaughan's subsequent letter to the King on 26 January made it clear that Tyndale was the principal person being sought and promised safe passage, together with 'another', still nameless, who was in fact John Frith. Negotiations continued while Tyndale prepared the publication of his answer to the violent literary attack on him by Lord Chancellor Sir Thomas More, whom the King had chosen to replace Wolsey. Henry, by then at odds with More over the Aragon annulment, was interested to see what the Chancellor's opponent might say, until he read it in April 1531 and found it deeply unacceptable in its evangelical theology and forthright tone; Tyndale never chose to modify his message simply to please King Henry. Cromwell was then put to work to halt the courtship of Tyndale, which he did in a tone of severity designed to rein in Vaughan's evident enthusiasm for the task.

This letter to Vaughan ventriloquizing the King survives in a secretary's draft, much corrected and recorrected by Cromwell himself. In form, it is reminiscent of his letter of advice to Wolsey in the previous August, as an equally rare specimen from his out-tray. Just as with that much corrected draft, its freakish survival suggests it was retained in the King's archive to show what Cromwell had been made to say: severe and schoolmasterly criticism of the errant Bible translator. In fact it sounds distinctly as if Cromwell had done the redrafting in the King's presence: 'his Highness nothing liked the said book, being filled with seditious, slanderous lies and fantastical opinions.'[29] Certainly when Vaughan replied to the King on 20 May, he gingerly referred to the letter as 'certain instructions sent to me from my master Master Cromwell at the commandment of your Majesty'.[30]

Despite his obsequious words to his sovereign, Vaughan was not happy. He tried to make the best of things by commending a new work of Luther's and assuring the King that he would continue with the royal instructions to negotiate with John Frith. Nor did he leave the subject of Tyndale alone in his letters to his patron, constantly praising the translator's writings. By the autumn it was Robert Barnes whom Vaughan had moved to championing, on the eve of Barnes's mission to England. He repeatedly asked Cromwell to forward to the King a presentation copy of Barnes's major theological statement, his *Supplication*, a plea to Henry to embrace reformation of the Church. Cromwell's delay in doing so is eloquent.[31]

The whole year-long episode tells us much about both the King's international strategy and Cromwell's place in it. The Pope, Emperor and King of France had all failed Henry, so he turned to representatives of Europe's burgeoning Reformations and their English allies in exile to see what he might get from them. In the end, these discussions were as futile as all efforts in Rome, and the moment the theology of English evangelicals displeased his Majesty, he dropped them. As German and Swiss evangelicals steadily lost their faith in Henry's arguments for annulment, their hard-headed suggestion that he might solve his troubles by taking two wives like an Old Testament patriarch horrified that prudish monarch. Possibilities were exhausted by the end of 1531, the ignominious departure of Barnes from England in January 1532 forming the coda.[32]

Books feature a good deal in this saga. Cromwell loved books, and was regularly using contacts abroad to explore book outlets better stocked than those in provincial little England. Books were also one of his few obvious bonds with his King (apart from his sheer usefulness and competence), since he was still far from the social level where hunting alongside the King or displays of horsemanship in the tournament would be decorous or even conceivable. Henry, when not showing off his masculinity in sport and open-air pursuits, was similarly an addict of books, even though he often got other people to read them for him. The large accumulations of them in his various palaces were one of the most genuinely individual features among his displays of monarchical conspicuous expenditure. He spent laborious but clearly enjoyable hours annotating his collection, usually with some particular political or theological purpose in mind.[33]

Following Anne Boleyn's initial success in introducing King Henry to Tyndale's writings with *The Obedience of a Christian Man* three years earlier, it looks as if Cromwell and his evangelical sympathizers tried the same book-trick in 1531, but failed. Maybe he lacked the charismatic intervention of Anne, who had undoubtedly seeded the royal library with evangelical literature from mainland Europe, besides having her own discriminating private collection, particularly of French works.[34] Given his reaction to Tyndale and Barnes, it is unsurprising that Henry resisted one further literary overture at this time. Pier-Francesco de' Bardi, Cromwell's neighbour at Austin Friars, tried without success to interest the King in the visionary eloquence of the great Florentine reformer and martyr of the 1490s, Girolamo Savonarola. Bardi presented Henry with books from his own library, at least one covered in his own enthusiastic marginalia; they were probably New Year's gifts to the King in the same season that Barnes's mission failed so spectacularly. Bardi's agent in conveying the unappreciated present is likely to have been the King's servant whom he knew so well in the precinct of the Austin Friars.[35]

At this point Cromwell had no room for manoeuvre in the King's international transactions. He was a newly arrived and marginal royal councillor, no more than an agent, and his job was to make sure his over-enthusiastic evangelical assistant Vaughan remembered that. It should have been a lesson for the future: foreign policy was always going to be the King's prerogative. But Cromwell had no more intention of remaining passive there than in any other aspect of government. These events were an apprenticeship in deploying his considerable first-hand knowledge of mainland Europe to compensate for his lack of experience in formal diplomacy.

One straw in the wind for Cromwell's later adventuring in foreign alliances came in a small act of bureaucracy on 18 July 1531. On that day Henry VIII, holidaying at Chertsey Abbey in Surrey after his final furtive departure from Queen Katherine, signed a little clutch of documents, probably with Thomas Cromwell in personal attendance; one was that warrant to 'our trusty and well-beloved servant' on Cardinal College business which we have already encountered (see above, p. 131), but another was a grant of 'denization' (a Tudor version of permanent resident status) to a certain 'Christopher Montaborino', native of the Prince-Bishopric of Cologne in the Holy Roman Empire. The grant hung around in Cromwell's office throughout the summer, till Lord Chancellor More was prevailed on to finalize it at his home in Chelsea on 4 October.[36] This Christopher Mont or Mundt had on his own testimony been in service for England since 1527, suggesting either that Cromwell had met him around Wolsey's household or that Dr Augustine had drawn attention to him again while intelligence-gathering in 1531; it is even possible that an acquaintance with Mont stretched back to Cromwell's commercial days in Antwerp.

Mont was destined to be of major significance in English diplomacy in central Europe. As Cromwell furthered talks with the Schmalkaldic League through the 1530s, he was a member of all the English embassies – no fewer than seven – pursuing the negotiations. This was a congenial task, since Mont was an early and enthusiastic convert to Protestantism – drawn to its non-Lutheran ('Reformed'), variety, being particularly friendly with Heinrich Bullinger of Zürich and Martin Bucer of Strassburg. He was also that rare creature in sixteenth-century Europe, a thoroughgoing Anglophile who took the trouble to learn English so fluently that it occasionally distorted his German in letter-writing.[37] With extraordinary fidelity to his adopted country, throughout his long life he carried on being useful to successive English Protestant regimes (Mary's government would have nothing to do with him) right up to his death in 1572.

Maybe this enthusiasm came from warm memories of Thomas Cromwell, for whom Mont did so much; in 1533, writing with money and encouragement for royal errands in Germany, Cromwell called him 'Fellow Christopher'.[38] By then he was a familiar figure in Cromwell's household when in England: Stephen Vaughan, who had just accompanied him on the first of those embassies to the League, was now commissioned to buy yet more books in Antwerp, and reminded Cromwell of a clutch of German chronicles Mont had been busy translating into English at Austin Friars earlier in the year.[39] Appropriately, back in Germany that same month, Mont sent Cromwell a silver pen and inkhorn set.[40] He remained the epitome of 'Our Man in the Empire': busy, cultured, competent and anonymous, utterly reliable.

That royal signature at Chertsey thus cast a shadow across the future, but the fact remained that during the year 1531 diplomacy achieved little in any direction. For the moment, Cromwell found himself playing a much more productive part in the other strand of the King's policy: painfully slowly securing annulment of the marriage to Katherine by means which could be contained within the realm and could thus bypass the unhelpful bureaucracy in Rome. This was at the heart of the project Cromwell spearheaded in the next three years, resulting in a realignment of the kingdom of England in Western Christendom which has never been permanently reversed. Parliament was his forum, and the key to his new success.

When the English government published the *Censurae* in spring 1531, that weighty work represented the international aspect of the royal propaganda team's work begun in 1530. The other parallel enterprise was a compilation of historical texts found both abroad and in ancient manuscripts in English libraries, whose object was to prove the proposition that kings of England had always exercised supreme jurisdiction in their realms. If this was the case, any competition from other jurisdictions was an offence to God. England was an 'empire', which in the political jargon of the period meant a polity with no superior under God – in present circumstances, that would exclude the Bishop of Rome as an intermediary between Heaven and Westminster. Already in early autumn 1530, the King and his ministers were increasingly using this term 'empire', with its corollary that the King's Great Matter could be decided within the realm of England.

The work was never published, nor was meant to be in this form. Its original full compilation remains in a manuscript now in the British Library, on which is scrawled the name by which it has become known, the *Collectanea satis copiosa* ('Sufficiently abundant compilation'). It was the foundation for one of the most famous preambles to Parliamentary Reformation legislation written by Cromwell, the Act in Restraint of

Appeals of 1533: 'by divers sundry old authentic histories and chronicles it is manifestly declared and expressed that this realm of England is an empire.' Never mind that the prize exhibits of these 'histories and chronicles' were the twelfth-century Welsh lies of Geoffrey of Monmouth about King Arthur, augmented with various other mendacious specimens of medieval insular self-congratulation. The King, the main intended audience, perused and annotated the *Collectanea* with evident delight.[41]

The programme expressed in the *Collectanea* produced a new wave of political action from early October 1530.[42] That was when Henry consulted senior lawyers and clergy on the question whether Parliament might have enough power to grant him his annulment without any external reference: to his fury, a majority said that it did not. There was still a formidable group both at Court and in the wider political realm of England prepared to support Queen Katherine; they included the inconveniently thoughtful Lord Chancellor, Sir Thomas More, presiding over Parliamentary sessions by virtue of his office. Because of such obstructions, there was for the moment no point in calling the session of Parliament planned for October 1530, and the King decided not only to postpone it but to revise and augment the strategy of intimidating leading churchmen which had been building up since the summer.

Beginning in July 1530, Attorney-General Hales was instructed to issue indictments against selected individuals in the Church on *praemunire* charges of abetting Wolsey's jurisdiction (one should again remember the unfairness of this attack). The selection was a sample of senior members of the Church hierarchy, bishops including John Fisher, abbots and cathedral dignitaries; it stopped just short of including the Archbishop of Canterbury, who might be too useful to antagonize, and targeted instead a layman who was a senior official in church courts and may already have been working for Archbishop Warham, Anthony Hussey.[43] In late October these legal proceedings were abandoned for something much bolder, as Cromwell reported on 21 October in his last surviving letter to Cardinal Wolsey: 'The Parliament is prorogued until the 6 day of January [1531]. The prelates shall not appear in the *Praemunire*. There is another way devised in place thereof, as your Grace shall further know.'[44] The 'other way' was in fact to indict the entire clergy of the English Church on a charge of *praemunire*. They could be pardoned if they paid a fine for their crime: no less than £100,000, which was about the same as the entire annual income of the Tudor monarchy.[45]

Such a breathtaking assault on the largest corporate body in the realm apart from the Crown itself could hardly be digested by cumbersome *praemunire* procedures in royal courts such as had afflicted the smaller group of indicted clerics. The forum to lay the charges and negotiate the massive financial deal that rode on it would have to be those twelve-month-postponed parallel sessions of Parliament: more precisely, the two assemblies of the English clergy that customarily met at the same time as Parliament, the Convocations of the Provinces of Canterbury and York. It is tempting to connect the King's immense financial demand with Chapuys's sarcasm that in December 1530 Thomas Cromwell 'must have promised to make [Henry VIII] the richest King that England had ever seen' (see above, pp. 126–7), but to do so would pile our own speculation on the ambassador's. The change in strategy was so bold and assertive of royal power that its main author can hardly have been other than the greatest ego in the realm, the King himself. Cromwell may well have been one persuasive voice guiding Henry's choice from among available options to the one he found the most congenial, but his role now was what he did best: turning theory into practice at the King's bidding, using his genius for improvisation and command of detail to achieve a practical result, out of arguments and research gathered by Henry's tame Oxbridge academics.

Cromwell could do this in the setting in which he was by now very much at home, Parliament. He exploited what may in autumn 1530 simply have seemed the most obvious means of pursuing a *praemunire* indictment of the English Church, and turned it into a long-term strategy. After all the hesitations and uncertainties of 1529–30, the year 1531 saw audacious political moves and propaganda which culminated in the revolutionary programme of 1533–4; after much busy planning on Cromwell's part, Parliament was used to make a final break with the Papacy after nigh on a millennium, and to recognize the King as Supreme Head of the English Church. The message throughout this, gradually crowding out the increasingly unhappy and compromised efforts of English diplomats in Rome, was that England needed no external power to achieve the King's aim of obeying God's unalterable law in his marriage. From the beginning Cromwell was actively involved.

The immediate drama in January 1531 occurred not in Parliament itself but in the parallel session of the Convocation of Canterbury, for it was naturally there that the clergy faced the new royal demand for money. They were now far more on the defensive than in autumn 1529, when they had fairly effectively fought off the anti-clerical noise coming from the parallel session of Parliament. Although Convocation ceremonially opened in its normal meeting-place, St Paul's Cathedral in the City of London, after a week of stormy debate, its sessions were moved down to the chapter house of Westminster Abbey. That was just round the cloister walk from the abbey refectory, which had long been the normal meeting-place for the Commons, and a few minutes' stroll from the Lords' chamber. Bishop John Fisher revisited his role in the Parliament of 1529 and tried to rally opposition – this time unsuccessfully. On 24 January, three days after moving to Westminster, the clergy agreed to the King's financial demands in return for their pardon on the *praemunire* charge.[46] They also rather pointedly specified that the grant was in gratitude to the King for defending the Universal Church from its enemies, particularly Lutherans.[47]

Matters did not stop there. While the members of Convocation tried to make something positive of the situation by asking Henry to affirm clerical privileges and define for future reference what the crime of *praemunire* actually meant, on 7 February they found themselves confronted with startling new demands relating to royal powers in the Church: that they should recognize the King as 'protector and supreme head' of the English Church and clergy. Three days later, on 10 February 1531, 'Master Cromwell entered and had secret conference' with Archbishop Warham. That led to an agitated confabulation in which Convocation agreed that Warham should lead a small delegation of bishops to see the King. They found themselves rebuffed and fobbed off with the presiding judges of the common law courts, who were no more helpful.[48]

This is the first independent evidence of Cromwell performing any public representative function for the King. It was probably the most prominence the new royal Councillor had known in some forty-five years of life so far. A small indication that the scribe of Convocation did not quite know what to make of this new arrival is in his over-promoting description of the interloper as 'Dominus Cromewell'. That same afternoon, the next royal representative to impose himself on Convocation's anxious discussions was an undoubted peer of the realm, Anne Boleyn's brother Lord Rochford.[49] The conjunction of Cromwell and Rochford shows that the Boleyns had now decided that Wolsey's old man of affairs was worth enlisting, or at least that the King had decided this for them.

Convocation members were bewildered by these two unconventional emissaries, and tried once more unsuccessfully to bypass Rochford in dealing with the King. After the stalemate of 10 February, overnight Archbishop Warham arranged to see the King himself, and secured a significant modification to the royal demand: a clause added to the royal proposal on the supremacy explicitly stated that the clergy recognized him as 'singular protector, one and supreme Lord and supreme head of the English Church and clergy, as far as the law of Christ allows'. This grudging compromise Convocation accepted with an equally grudging silence.[50] It was an unsatisfactory tangle for both sides, and the King would have to unpick it at some later stage. At least he had his money.

Rochford had brought with him various position papers making clear what the King was now wanting his Parliament and Convocation to accept: at least two documents look like survivors of these tracts.[51] Their flavour can be gauged from the culminating flourish in one of them, which had none of the restraint which the compromise of 11 February imposed: the King's supreme authority, 'grounded on God's Word, ought in no case to be restrained by frustrate decrees of popish laws or void prescripts of human traditions, but . . . he may order and minister, yea and also execute the office of spiritual administration in the Church whereof he is Head'.[52] Both these extant pamphlets are in English. The King's case as enunciated within the realm was now escaping from the decorum of Latin, for if such assertions were to be made in Parliament, as well as Convocation, vernacular prose was essential. They correlate with an interesting reminiscence of the 1531 Parliamentary session from the following summer. An elderly Derbyshire yeoman found himself hauled off to gaol in London for indiscreet talk about Queen Katherine and boasting acquaintance with Anne Boleyn. In an attempt to prove his innocence, Roger Dycker of Kirk Hallam enlarged on the conversation which had caused his troubles: a report by his parish priest, Roger Page, returning from London around midsummer 1531, that 'the King was about to marry another wife, and that one Mr. Cromwell penned certain matters in the Parliament house, which no man a-gainsaid them.' This indicates how sharply the Queen's position had deteriorated since Easter, when John Creke had regarded her as his best hope of Court promotion, but gossip in the Derbyshire countryside about her humiliation was still enough to get a man arrested.

Parson Page implied in this rich snippet of intelligence that the first time that the King's new programme took public shape had been in the 1531 Parliament, and that for many observers Cromwell was the man most associated with it. It will not have been a coincidence that the man channelling the accusation against Dycker back to Westminster had been a genuine witness of the same events: one of the two knights of the shire for Derbyshire in that same Parliament, Sir Anthony Babington, who also happened to be a maternal cousin of Thomas Cromwell. Babington thus had two good reasons for acting on his irritation at a Derbyshire villager parading knowledge of Parliamentary proceedings and Lady Anne; Babington certainly took the case seriously, because Kirk Hallam is more than 20 miles from his home at Dethick.[53]

The interesting word in Roger Page's remark about Parliament is 'penned'. His understanding was that Cromwell was responsible for the literary propaganda offensive presented to MPs and peers (an offensive for the time being confined to the Parliamentary chambers). We may speculate that he pulled a stray copy of one of these manuscripts from his travelling pack as he chatted with his parishioners in the fields outside Kirk Hallam, which would make sense of the slight disjunction in chronology between his mention of Parliament and his previous remark about the Aragon marriage. The reality is probably that, rather than writing such material himself, Cromwell was its orchestrator and co-ordinator: that is the pattern which developed thereafter, as he identified the people with the right talents for the job.[54]

There is one remarkable possibility among various candidates for these documents: a fairly recent manuscript discovery in the archives of the Berkeley family at Berkeley Castle in Gloucestershire, presumably left from Thomas Lord Berkeley's attendance in early sessions of the Reformation Parliament, is explosive, indeed revolutionary. It is in an early Tudor hand, but its content was much older, for it is a petition presented to a Parliament in 1410 by a number of members of that Parliament who had Lollard sympathies. It suggested that the Crown should confiscate all temporal estates owned by the Church above the level of the parishes, and it was coupled with a brand-new petition which enlarged on the same themes of clerical corruption and greed with even more colourful and extended venom: 'now of late, most gracious sovereign, they have been dandled and made wantons as some delicate fathers make wanton their children and giveth them their own appetites until they fall to great inconvenience.'[55] A public rehabilitation of Lollardy was unprecedented in more than a century of their repression and persecution, yet here were freshly made copies of this venerable petition to a fifteenth-century Parliament, plus a suggestion for bringing it radically up to date.

A further piece of evidence clarifies this most surprising of developments. A reference to the same document is lodged in Thomas Cromwell's archive, in a list of Parliamentary bills which did not pass in the opening sessions of the Reformation Parliament. One item on the list is described as 'A bill put up to the King in his Parliament by his Commons in anno domini 1410, concerning the temporal possessions being in the hands of the Church'.[56] It seems oddly placed amid the newly failed bills (and the clerk itemizing it did a double-take on the date, first making it 1510, until he looked again at its heading), but then one sees from the Berkeley Castle document that the 1410 petition was paired with the new petition to

Parliament, which presumably had no separate heading for the clerk to note.[57] As propaganda, it sits well with Cromwell's actions in this Parliamentary session; in autumn 1529, his chief preoccupation and the source of his public reputation was the defence of his master Cardinal Wolsey. It might even be moved forward to the fresh wave of literary fireworks prepared for the 1532 session of Parliament. If the petition was given a Parliamentary airing now, it was at the same time as the government allowed publication in print of that other text embraced by the Lollards long ago, the *Disputatio inter clericum et militem*. But while the *Disputatio* was given the cachet of Latin, the resurrected 1410 petition was an English text for an English audience.

The price of winning hearts and minds for the King in a Tudor Parliament was eternal vigilance. The problem for official management was the constant difficulty of orchestrating three different arenas at the same time: Lords, Commons and Convocation (not to mention the fact that Convocation too had its upper and lower houses). That was shown when in late March a significantly large group in the House of Commons disrupted progress in the King's hard-fought deal with the clergy on the not unreasonable grounds that, if all the clergy of the realm were implicated in Wolsey's alarmingly open-ended violation of the *praemunire* statute, the layfolk of England might equally have sleep-walked into that crime. In the background was the Commons' alertness to the slightest hint that such an accusation might preface some new ingenious royal financial demand; after all, that had just been the case for the clergy. Accordingly in late March the MPs sent a deputation to the King himself, perforce led by their Speaker, a no doubt deeply embarrassed Thomas Audley, to demand their inclusion in the pardon.

This could have badly sabotaged the timing of a session rapidly drawing to its close. The King's response, even in the anodyne framing of it by the fervently loyal Edward Hall, was decidedly sharp, as is confirmed by a more detached summary presented by Chapuys to his imperial master. By now there was a readily identifiable scapegoat for Commons anger at this rebuff, according to Hall: 'some light persons said that Thomas Cromwell which was newly come to the favour of the King, had disclosed the secrets of the Commons, which thing caused the King to be so extreme.' They would, after all, have heard of Cromwell's part in the dramatic events in Convocation on 10 February. After a few days' delay for face-saving reasons, Henry did indeed grant them the pardon they wanted, drawn up by Sir Christopher Hales and published on 29 March (with loving thanks and praise from the MPs, said Hall – they would know how to play the theatre of a royal tactical retreat). It was only just in time, for there was still vital official business to complete in what had not been a trouble-free session.[58]

Over the following three days, 30 March–1 April, the sessions ended with an elaborate presentation of the King's reasons for considering his marriage a sham, rehearsed separately to Lords and Commons. Lord Chancellor More must have been sickened at having to make the principal speeches for this tedious performance, though Sir Brian Tuke, the Clerk of Parliament, was not by temperament likely to have felt similar agonies as he ploughed through the recitation of the European university judgements, twice. According to Ambassador Chapuys, never inclined to look for sweetness and light on such occasions, the Commons were not especially positive in their reaction.[59]

Altogether, apart from the King's huge financial gain from the clergy, the immediate results of the three-month sittings had not been impressive. Ecclesiastical recognition of his Supreme Headship was distinctly provisional. The other Convocation of the English Church, for the Province of York, continued its meetings in York into May; it did concede a grant of money proportionate to its resources and much smaller number of dioceses, but then took the gilt off this gift by recording a solemn protest from Cuthbert Tunstall (now Bishop of Durham) against the supremacy, even in the terms granted by Canterbury Province. Tunstall had been one of the chief counsel for Queen Katherine in the early stages of the annulment process, and he was prepared to extend his awkwardness to the royal attack on the Church. The King took his protest seriously enough to write an elaborate and for him rather temperate response to the points the Bishop had made.[60]

The King's moderation to Tunstall reflected his realization that, as yet, he was not in a strong legal position. The immediate danger that Parliament would be asked to make a decision on the King's marriage passed when the assembly was prorogued just before Easter 1531 till the following October. Chapuys reported back to the Emperor that Queen Katherine was 'in great spirits at having escaped the determination of Parliament on the divorce'.[61] Yet the Queen's mood did not long survive Easter, when as we have seen she reversed her officers' agreement to employ John Creke. The King anticipated formal settlement of his situation; on 14 July Katherine was excluded from accompanying the King on progress away from Windsor Castle, and she never saw her husband again.

Henry now started to behave as if he were betrothed to the Lady Anne, even taking her hunting with him, which made it clear to the general public that henceforth he would act as if the twenty-two years of his marriage had never enjoyed legal existence. Anne began forming her own household in preparation for greater things.[62] Although as late as November the Queen was taking her formal place on state occasions, it appears that husband and wife were never in the same room together; nor was Katherine ever allowed to see her daughter Mary. They were consigned to different great country houses in what was increasingly obviously house arrest, despite the punctilious ceremonial of their entourage, and right up to Katherine's death their only communication was by private letters carried by trustworthy servants.[63]

Through the year, Cromwell continued to promote the annulment case, chipping away at the opposition and recruiting useful helpers to the cause where he could. The proof comes from a reminiscence of Dr John Oliver, a canon and civil lawyer, and latterly Dean of King Henry's replacement for what had once been Cardinal College Oxford. In 1536 Oliver was devastated to learn in an interview with Cromwell that 'you had no sure argument that I had deposed [put away] those papistical dregs wherein I had been studied' – by which Cromwell meant Oliver's long studies at Oxford in the canon law of the Roman Church. The Dean wrote him an elaborate, pained and circumstantial refutation of that slur, reminding Cromwell of their very first meeting back in 1531. No doubt Oliver accentuated the positive in this, but there would be no point in outright lies to the only other person who had been present. It is worth quoting at length:

> I do not forget the first time that ever I spoke with your Lordship was in your law parlour in your old house at the Austin Friars concerning the Lady Dowager's matter, wherein I plainly declared unto you my opinion to be against her purpose, and how that I never did speak for her but as I was enforced by the old [Arch]Bishop of Canterbury [William Warham] which was then alive [until August 1532]. Upon the which communication, you of your mere goodness having pity and compassion upon me, were contented to restore me to the King's favour, and did indeed put me not only to be his Grace's chaplain, but also procured unto me all that living that I have, which is much better than I am worthy.[64]

The whole letter shows how Cromwell reeled in a canon lawyer to do his bidding. It tells us much about dating the process, beginning with Oliver's reference to being granted a royal chaplaincy as one of the consequences of his first meeting with Cromwell; he had this title by late February 1532 (by which time he was fully plunged into business for the King). He was already involved in notarial formalities before Warham's

official John Cockes concerning the 'determinations' of the overseas universities on the annulment in June 1531. So probably this incident in
Cromwell's book-lined study (his 'law parlour') at Austin Friars took
place that summer or autumn 1531 as Oliver was drawn into administration around the determinations, and at the very least no later than the
turn of the year 1531/2.[65] Oliver is also obliquely telling us of Cromwell's
continuing interest in the fate of Cardinal College Oxford and his success
in saving it from dissolution when the Ipswich College disappeared. After
the death of Dean Higden, reappointed as head of house on the College's
refoundation as King Henry's College, Oliver succeeded as second Dean
on 4 May 1533 and, as is apparent here, it was on Cromwell's personal
recommendation to the King.

Yet there is still more to learn of the atmosphere of Cromwell's household and his strategy from Oliver's letter:

> And then for my further comfort, you were contented to put me in some
> experiments of the King's civil causes, and to call me to your honourable
> board divers dinners and suppers, where in very deed, I heard such com-
> munication which were the very cause of the beginning of my conversion.
> For methought it were a stony heart and a blockish wit that could carry
> nothing away of such colloquy as was at your honourable board, and that
> made me to note them well, and when I came home to mete [compare]
> them with my English Bible. And I found always the conclusions which
> you maintained at your board to be consonant with the holy Word of God;
> and then I thought good to confer the English with the Latin through the
> whole Testament, and so I did . . . but for a further trial I went and con-
> ferred Erasmus's translation with the Vulgar which they call St Jerome's
> translation, and did interline Erasmus's translation through the whole Tes-
> tament in the other translation with my own hand . . . and then was I
> surely corroborate [strengthened as] an adversary to all papists at all com-
> munications and ever hath been since.

Oliver is giving us the nearest echo we have of Cromwell's 'Table Talk':
the King's Great Matter and his title to royal supremacy, presented over a
good dinner rich in biblical citations, which Oliver checked out against
what in the early 1530s can only have been William Tyndale's English New
Testament. Next in the hierarchy of Bibles in Oliver's library was the Erasmus Latin rendering, which had so impressed Cromwell back in his Boston
days, and then finally the Vulgate of Jerome. All this led to Oliver's 'conversion' – pure evangelical jargon – triggering a transformation in theological
outlook.[66] Behind this outcome was the politician who decided on defending King Henry's case with biblical arguments, and was eloquent in

presenting it in terms beyond crude English patriotism. Oliver's scholarly acceptance of its validity naturally cannot have been hindered by the fact that Cromwell held all the political cards, together with the key to preferments like the Deanery of an Oxford college – let alone the attractions of the cuisine in the house at Austin Friars. The Dean became one of Cromwell's leading assistants in unravelling the Aragon marriage.

From the end of 1531, another entirely different aspect of Cromwell's service to the King made an appearance, with momentous implications. For the first time, his horizons were widening beyond the obsession of the moment with the Great Matter. The mark of his next eight years of power was to be an omnicompetence as broad as Wolsey's, which would mean casting his sights across the seas. Among much else, he confronted the unceasing conundrum posed by the Tudor Crown's second greatest territory, the Lordship of Ireland: graveyard of English statesmanship over centuries. Even if his paternal ancestors really did come from Ireland, this distant lineage did not represent any useful present-day connection. He was going to have to learn about Irish complications the hard way.[67]

A sign of what was to come appears in a letter written to the new Councillor from an Irish castle the day after New Year 1532.[68] The writer thanked Cromwell for making sure his memoranda on Irish politics had been properly examined by the King and Council, and sent on more for their consideration. He was Piers Butler Earl of Ossory, one of the greatest men in that elite of formerly Norman nobility whose ancestors established themselves in parts of the island conquered by the English Crown in the twelfth and thirteenth centuries. A shrewd survivor who made loyalty to the Tudors his constant thread through the maze of Irish politics, Ossory knew England well. After a lifetime of struggle to establish his family's supremacy against their traditional Anglo-Norman rivals, the Fitzgerald earls of Kildare (the 'Geraldines'), he was looking for new allies at the English Court. He nursed a grievance at having to yield his long-standing claim to the family title of Earl of Ormond to Anne Boleyn's father the Earl of Wiltshire, and the Earldom of Ossory created for him was never adequate compensation. He clearly doubted how much he could trust to his old family alignments with Wiltshire and the Duke of Norfolk, who were forming an unwonted alliance with the hated Fitzgeralds.

The unfamiliar new name of Thomas Cromwell in the King's circle therefore suggested a promising alternative route for bringing Ossory's latest desires to royal attention. He had spent two rather unwilling years at the English Court from 1526 to 1528, developing a friendship with

Cardinal Wolsey, but even before that he had found the Cardinal's support extremely effective against the Geraldines and their followers. Now he acknowledged to Cromwell that 'the acquaintance is but new betwixt us.' So in all that time in England, despite Ossory's intimacy with the Cardinal, he and Cromwell had never met: additional proof of how remote from Court Cromwell's work for Wolsey had then been. Ossory's wooing of the new force in Court politics was evidently well under way during autumn 1531, so this letter of January 1532 was just one rather important stage in an existing correspondence.

There can be little doubt that the agent who alerted Ossory to Cromwell's potential importance was the recently appointed Archbishop of Dublin, John Allen, colleague in Wolsey's service whom we have met more than once. By the time Allen arrived to take up his new post in autumn 1529, the Cardinal was in deep trouble, but Allen persevered against great odds in the brief Wolsey had given him for reform in the Irish Church and Lordship, thereby incurring hatred from the Fitzgeralds and their allies.[69] Thomas Cromwell was Allen's only route to regaining favour in London against the malice of those who hated Wolsey, while in Ireland Ossory was Allen's main hope of keeping any sort of authority. Three interests therefore meshed together.

An Irish hawk arrived at Austin Friars from Kilkenny Castle soon afterwards as a small mark of gratitude for what Cromwell had done so far (had Allen told the Earl how fond his correspondent was of hawking?). It would serve as a gentle prompt for Cromwell to speak to the Earl of Wiltshire, to reinforce Ossory's urgent pleas not to break their natural alliance by favouring the Fitzgeralds. Ossory enclosed a copy of a memorandum on the state of Ireland as the Earl wanted the English Council to see it ('Instructions to my good friend Master Thomas Cromwell'), since 'ye wrote to me that the King's pleasure was that I should from time to time advertise his Highness of the affairs of this land.' This was too good an opportunity to miss. The Earl also sent Cromwell a copy of his frankly reproachful letter to Wiltshire; evidently he felt that the new Councillor was sufficiently influential and trustworthy for his purpose. From an English point of view, this was a familiar political alignment: Wolsey's former friends against the partisans of Anne Boleyn. From an Irish perspective, it would have seemed rather different: Butler versus Fitzgerald.

These links provided Cromwell with some of the connections he would need, in default of any personal acquaintance with that remote and baffling territory, whose wretchedly difficult communications meant that Westminster politicians made their decisions about it with all the finesse of knitting in boxing-gloves. Cromwell did his best to widen his contacts, aided by the fact that in 1520 Cardinal Wolsey had set up a new 'Privy Council' for English government in Dublin; this could act independently of whoever happened to be Lord Deputy at the time, and included experienced and competent administrators drawn from the Anglo-Irish elite. Wolsey's fall had not affected its work.[70] Not long before autumn 1531, for instance, Cromwell did an administrative favour for Thomas Cusack, a lawyer from County Meath with long-standing membership of the Inner Temple in London. Cusack became Irish Chancellor of the Exchequer a couple of years later, by which time he was emerging as one of the leaders among the native 'Old English' or Anglo-Irish, seeking a reformed Irish administration under the English Crown.[71]

Cromwell quickly learned that it was wise not to become too aligned with any one of the competing factions across the Irish Sea. Ossory's memorandum took its place among a number of such papers in his files. Much more followed, none of it predictable, as Cromwell began to view the King's dominions from end to end, Calais to Carlisle, Colchester to Cork. It was a year or two before Ireland came to rip through his careful memoranda of business into an urgent priority, but after that he would never be free of it.

7

New Year's Gifts: 1532

Cromwell's new position at the centre of government was not assuming a public face with any speed. It was only at New Year (1 January) 1532, as far as the evidence goes, that he was listed among those favoured enough to buy New Year's gifts for the King, a ring with a ruby and 'a box with the images of the French King's children' (five of them at the time: a handy number to decorate a box).[1] Maybe the presents, duly recorded amid a welter of other delights great and small, acted as a respectful prompt to his sovereign, because a week later Cromwell was reappointed to supervision of Wolsey's two former College estates.[2] This was his first formal office under the Crown, but it was simply the responsibility he had been carrying out anyway over the previous couple of years, by the King's fiat alone. Apart from the general title of Councillor he had been granted in such a curiously covert manner in December 1530, he still had nothing else.

It took three gruelling months in Parliament to make a difference. The previous sessions of Parliament and Convocation had been settings for his first appearances on the public political stage, and it was the imminent prospect of a Parliamentary session in October 1531 which provoked the first known official document to acknowledge him as Councillor; his further advancement was a reward for his achievements in the House of Commons in winter and spring 1532. There had been a very last-minute decision in autumn 1531 to postpone Parliament: the Convocation of Canterbury did in fact convene on 16 October, and quickly slipped in some business against an evangelical heretic before being told to observe a prorogation to early November.[3] That November meeting was in turn put off to January 1532, waiting on various royal diplomatic moves abroad. Partly the King wanted to see what might come of the ongoing negotiations with various evangelical emissaries from abroad (in the end, nothing). Equally, ever hopeful, he had suddenly made a decision in September to launch a last-ditch embassy to the Low Countries, to persuade

Charles V to see what Henry viewed as sense on his Great Matter. It was of course a failure, and the attempt must have been a terrible strain on the chosen English ambassador Sir Thomas Elyot, a friend of Cromwell who was rapidly developing a deep loathing for the annulment proceedings, and who turned to literary satire of some of those involved to cheer himself up.[4]

As news began to spread in December 1531 that Parliament really was reconvening, there was one striking difference from the previous session: those summoned were told they would have to refer to Thomas Cromwell if they wanted leave of absence. He was now openly a councillor, not merely a back-bench burgess for Taunton. His friend Christopher Hales consulted him from home in Canterbury on New Year's Eve, to learn whether Parliament would indeed go ahead in mid-January or once more be deferred. One would have thought that Hales as Attorney-General would have known the answer to that himself, but it is an indication of how indecisive the King was being about this renewed session of a Parliament which was now bordering on the unusual in duration, two years since its first summons.[5]

Cromwell had thus become Parliamentary manager. This was not a function with an office attached to it, but for the first time he was given an identifiable role with a public profile. Both Lords spiritual and temporal and members of the House of Commons have left evidence that they regarded him as formal agent for channelling requests for absence to the King and registering them with the Clerk of Parliament; in some cases peers gave him blank proxies so the government could make its own choices for substitutes.[6] As so often in his public career, once Cromwell had taken over a piece of administration, he did not let it go, using it to promote both royal control and his own intentions. So in March 1534 Sir Piers Edgecombe, a friend of his as well as a knight of the shire for Cornwall, applied to him (not to Speaker Wingfield, as formally he should have done) for leave to stay away from the Commons, since one of his household in London had measles.[7]

There were convenient absences from Parliament and Convocation in this session apart from those succeeding in their excuses to Cromwell. The King's cousin Reginald Pole was granted permission to leave the country that January: a relief for both him and King Henry, but also a way of ensuring he did not exercise his right as Dean of Exeter Cathedral to speak in Convocation.[8] He left England with searing memories of Cromwell's part in turning his world upside down, and would not return until the kingdom had righted itself, with his cousin Mary Tudor safely on a Catholic English throne, twenty-three years later. Among absent bishops,

Cuthbert Tunstall of Durham judged that the winter journey south had too many perils for a man who strongly disapproved of the King's current policy aims, and he stayed up at Bishop Auckland Castle; after his forceful protest against the royal supremacy in the Convocation of York in May 1531, that may have been with official encouragement.[9] Bishop Fisher of Rochester, who had no such inhibitions of either geography or prudence, was quickly felled by illness, a great advantage for the King.

And so on 15 January 1532 Parliament opened once more. By the time it was prorogued four months later, Cromwell had been prominent in drafting and seeing through to royal assent a good many pieces of worthy and useful legislation from both government and local interests, ranging from a long-lasting new framework for 'commissions of sewers' to administer flood defences and waterways through to a prohibition on selling horses to Scotsmen.[10] Yet any management he attempted of the most politically important and contentious proceedings was largely ineffective. In an inept fashion which reeks of King Henry's high-handedness, the first month was consumed by two bills both calculated to infuriate MPs and peers alike with threats to their purses. The first was a royal demand for a subsidy, on the premise that the King needed to defend his northern frontier against the Scots. The other was a revival of so far abortive legislation on primer seisin (the Crown's rights over feudal inheritance) which was designed to combat widespread evasion of royal feudal rights through setting up family trusts, 'feoffees to uses'. Both efforts had to be laid aside. Nor were efforts to rally support for a decision on the annulment within the realm any more successful; drafts of proposals with Cromwell's and Thomas Audley's corrections remain from this latest failure.[11]

One initiative the government did successfully pursue to the finish was a block (a 'Conditional Restraint') on payments to the Pope of 'annates', the first year of income sent to Rome by newly appointed bishops and archbishops. Yet, once more, neither House of Parliament was easily led. Opposition in the Lords was reinforced by a formal protest by Archbishop Warham, who until then had been grimly toeing an uncongenial line in relation to the King's policies, although he discreetly made this gesture in an instrument signed in his own palace across the Thames, rather than in the Lords' chamber.[12]* Cromwell wrote tensely to Secretary Gardiner, at that stage prevented by his embassy to France from exercising his episcopal vote in the Lords, 'this day was read in the Higher

---

* Could it be that the surrender of Christ Church Priory Aldgate, made that same day (see below, pp. 196–7), influenced his gesture of defiance?

House a bill touching the annates of bishoprics, for what end or effect it will succeed, surely I know not.' His letter obliquely reveals that these two members of the King's central team of advisers were not exactly operating hand in glove: 'news from hence I assure you that here be none but such as undoubtedly by a multitude of your friends . . . be to your Lordship already related.'[13]

In fact this legislation against annates did pass, with the help of what was then a very recent innovation in Parliamentary procedure. It has become known as a 'division', and is the method by which Lords and Commons vote at Westminster right up to the present day: separating out ayes and noes into their respective groups. Until the 1520s, decisions in Parliament were customarily taken by the same ancient procedure which elected knights and burgesses to the Commons: acclamation, or, to put it another way, shouting very loudly. The louder shout won. This procedure worked best when (as in well-regulated committees throughout history) there was already general agreement and the heat had been taken out of the issue in question. In circumstances of bitter disagreement, it became clumsy and contestable. The first recorded instance of a division was in contention over a royal tax demand in the 1523 Parliament, described in such detail by the chronicler Edward Hall that it was clearly a new way of doing things.* It is possible that the King's advisers had used the division as a way of flushing out and making visible the core of the opposition (in that case, the overwhelming majority of burgesses present in the Commons), and it would have the same usefulness again in 1532 for a new government purpose.[14]

Hall had not been an MP in 1523, but his fellow-member of Gray's Inn Thomas Cromwell had been – possibly one of those obstreperous burgesses. Although Chapuys gave King Henry the credit for thinking up this procedural device in 1532, the ambassador was not aware it had happened before; it looks like an instance of Cromwell seizing on a recent precedent to win back some advantage for a struggling royal administration.[15] It worked, just as Henry had eventually haggled his way to a grant of tax in 1523: the measure passed before the end of March. From then on, divisions became increasingly familiar in Parliamentary procedure. That is not surprising, for this division secured something remarkable: it was the first occasion on which Parliament had been asked to declare that it could interfere with a right belonging to the Pope. Despite strenuous

---

* Alasdair Hawkyard suggests that Sir Thomas More may have been responsible for the innovation of divisions in 1523, which would possess a certain irony.

opposition – clearly plenty of people could see the implications – the division did its job.

In parallel with this move, Cromwell was preparing another Parliamentary statement to push the Church hierarchy even further into a corner and, once more, this was launched in the arena where he had maximum control: the House of Commons. The measure was a Supplication of the House to the King 'against the Ordinaries', part of the revived assault on the Western Latin Church within the realm – one cannot of course as yet call it the Church of England. The importance of the Supplication in the religious changes of the next decade cannot be over-estimated. The 'Ordinaries' under attack were the bishops and their senior officials, controlling the entire system of Church courts, whose procedures were those of the Western Church's international system of canon law. Their activities ran in parallel with the business transacted in an intricate variety of temporal law courts which made up the King's judicial jurisdiction, and which operated England's unique legal system of royal writ and precedent dating back to the twelfth century – the common law.

If things were going well, Church courts complemented common law courts. If things were going badly, the two systems became rivals, with little parallel elsewhere in Europe. All medieval legal jurisdictions were liable to clash and try to steal each other's business, but nowhere else was there a contest of two such giants. English common law was unique because no other kingdom or sizeable principality in Europe had such a long tradition of centralized administration as England. Over four centuries, English monarchs had created royal courts whose practices in turn fostered a brotherhood of lawyers to run them, with their own system of higher education as a complete alternative to Oxford and Cambridge: the Inns of Court in London. Common law thus created a second English learned profession alongside the clergy, boasting its own traditions, training and esprit de corps, a profession which did not exist in such a developed fashion anywhere else in Western Christendom. Cromwell, with his membership of Gray's Inn, was in a minor way one of these common lawyers, and many others sat in the Commons. Moreover, he and they were only too aware in 1532 that one of the most exalted among their number, Lord Chancellor More, had spent his three years of office aiding and abetting the Church courts in a heightened pursuit of heretics, both persistent Lollards and the new evangelicals.

As More felt himself increasingly boxed in and at odds with the King's plans, he turned to waging implacable war on enemies of the Church whom he could crush without inhibition. Gone were the days of Cardinal

Wolsey, when no one was burned at the stake for heresy: More had a positive relish for burning heretics. Since 1529, he had been saying so at savage length in print, in flat rejection of Wolsey's conciliatory line, and although claims by angry Protestants of the next generation that he personally tortured heretics have no evidence to back them up, his words now became Church policy.[16] It was bad enough that More was closely involved in justifying the death of the popular preacher and Cambridge don Thomas Bilney at the hands of old Bishop Nix of Norwich. Bilney had been burned at the stake the previous summer, after the last Parliamentary session. The burgesses of Parliament for Norwich (one of whom was of course Cromwell's friend Reynold Littleprow) were infuriated by Bilney's execution, which contrasted with his previous lenient treatment by Cardinal Wolsey, and they made it clear in September 1531 that they would raise the matter in the next Parliamentary session. One of the chief agitators testifying to the injustice of Bilney's death was John Curatt, whom we have met before, facing the wrath of Bishop Nix on behalf of Wolsey, Thomas Winter and Thomas Cromwell.[17]

In response, More first set up his own official but highly irregular inquiry as Lord Chancellor into Bilney's execution, and then he published a thoroughly skewed account of the affair in the course of a major attack on William Tyndale, *The Confutation of Tyndale's Answer*. Senior churchmen took their cue from More's encouragement to extend persecution. A few days before the 1532 session of Parliament opened, the evangelical Thomas Benet died in flames outside Exeter, and there were more harassments and burnings to come; even while this Parliament was sitting, Cromwell's friend the charismatic preacher Hugh Latimer ended up in a prison cell at Lambeth Palace on heresy charges levelled in the current meeting of Convocation. In response, therefore, the Supplication became as much an attack on Thomas More as on the traditional Church leadership. It was also the clearest sign yet that Thomas Cromwell was going to fight in the name of the new religion.

Common law is founded on precedent, and its lawyers are therefore disposed by their professional training to conservatism. By no means all of them would have thought it a bad thing for the Church to pursue heretics (in fact very few people in the sixteenth century, Catholic or Protestant, opposed the principle of burning, just the choice and quantity of those burned). What common lawyers generally did feel, however, was resentment against what they saw as excessive and unreasonable claims by high-flying practitioners of civil and canon law. More was an exception, for his professional instincts were overcome by his strong sense of being caught up in a cosmic battle for the soul of Europe between the

Papacy and the forces of Antichrist. English contemporaries of tradition-alist religious outlook did not generally follow him. Among Cromwell's developing clutch of propaganda writers was an elderly common lawyer called Christopher St German, who never showed the slightest warmth towards evangelical reformation, but who in retirement from legal prac-tice spent the 1530s vigorously defending the royal cause against Rome in a stream of anonymous pamphlets, which have only recently gradually been reassembled round his name. St German, who remained obstinately his own man despite initial patronage from Cromwell, did not approve of the manner in which the King eventually proclaimed a divinely granted royal supremacy, but he approved of papal power even less.[18]

A coalition of interests, therefore, evangelical, legal and royalist, fuelled the Commons' enthusiasm for attacking the Ordinaries in their Supplication. The perfect man to unite them was the King's manager in the Commons, Thomas Cromwell, but he had his own preoccupations in doing so, and we should not think that they were a perfect fit with the concerns of his royal employer. Much historians' ink and ingenuity have been expended on reconstructing the exact sequence of events which led to this measure taking on the importance that it did.[19] Suffice it to say that the most likely origin of this Supplication was in draft petitions pre-pared in the anti-clerical agitation of Parliament in the autumn of 1529, which had gone nowhere at that time apart from adding to the general political noise. Cromwell had probably not been greatly involved (if at all) in producing the drafts, given his likely position in that session (see above, Chapter 4), but he would have been well aware of them, and he gathered some of the material for his own archive – no doubt stored in his 'law parlour' at Austin Friars.

Chancellor More had made the issue of the Church courts personal with his championing of persecution, including of evangelicals whom Cromwell would have known well: the Supplication could now be used in remoulded form to bring the defiant Church authorities to heel. The King had gained very little from the modified declaration of the 1531 Convoca-tion that he was Supreme Head of the Church 'as far as the law of Christ allows'. Convocation's reopened proceedings in January and February 1532 reveal the churchmen showing an unwonted energy in producing measures of institutional reform, quite independent of anything the King and his chief councillors were planning. They must have been energized by their bruising confrontation with royal power the previous year, quite apart from the growing volume of heretical activity and popular icono-clasm throughout the kingdom.[20] No wonder Cromwell became involved in the royal effort to halt this self-assertiveness.

Now the early drafts of the Supplication in Cromwell's papers ceased to languish as sidelined gestures from radical back-benchers: fresh versions combined previous material with heavy new interventions from himself and no less a figure than the Speaker of the Commons, Thomas Audley, to produce a final text. In mid-March 1532, in a remarkable echo of the agitation for a *praemunire* pardon for the laity precisely a year before, a deputation led by Audley presented the King with the Supplication. The leading personnel in the room at this second meeting were the same as on that earlier occasion, as everyone would vividly have remembered; the presentation of the Supplication was something of a theatrical revival.

The King's reaction reflected several conflicting considerations, most of them negative, but some sympathetic. He would remember that, a year before, the previous Commons delegation had in the end forced him to do what they wanted. He was also furious that his new request for subsidy and the legislation on feudal rights had been lost, and he was no more fond of Lollards or evangelical heretics than was Chancellor More. On the other hand, the Supplication clearly attacked More, who had become one of the chief obstacles to royal plans when a Lord Chancellor should have been leading the charge for his Sovereign; it represented further pressure on the Church, whose senior Archbishop had just provoked Henry into rage by open defiance in the Lords' chamber in a speech on 15 March. The King's response was as confused as all this might suggest: he said he would not make any decision until he had heard 'the party that is accused' – that is, the clergy. Then in a non-sequitur he jumped to a diatribe about the defeat of the primer seisin legislation.[21]

Tempers did not subside over the Easter recess. There were more harsh words in Parliament about a financial grant, and one West Country burgess called Thomas Temys had the effrontery to seek a new Commons request to the King to take back Queen Katherine. The clergy returned an aggressive answer to the King's consultation on the Supplication against the Ordinaries, which angered first him then the Commons. There was thus now competition as to whether laity or clergy would infuriate the much tried monarch more. Amid the collapse of government legislative plans and some strikingly frank exchanges between a second Commons delegation and Henry about his marriage in the wake of Temys's outspokenness, the one constant was the King's animus against the independence of the Church.[22]

The sequence of three informal meetings between MPs and King in 1532 is remarkable. Each jolted the chaotic affairs of this Parliament a stage further in the direction of royal supremacy in the Church as a way of solving the King's Great Matter. The third came on 11 May, and in the meantime Easter had intervened, decisively swinging the balance among the King's conflicting priorities. He was infuriated at being hectored on two successive Sundays in his own chapel at Greenwich by members of the Palace's resident community of Observant Franciscan friars, for the most part fierce partisans of his ill-treated wife. Observants belonged to a variety of Franciscan enthusiasm which sought to recapture the early rigour of life among Franciscan friars. The austerity of the Observant Order appealed to many European monarchs, Henry VIII's predecessors included, hence the presence of Observant friaries alongside the principal royal palaces, a suitable foil for regal magnificence. Unfortunately Observant integrity included fearless commitment to moral stances which King Henry now found disconcerting and hugely inconvenient. Vigorous condemnations to his face of his annulment plans were not what he expected amid holy festivities, and with what was either sublime lack of self-awareness or an impulse to savage satire he wrote to the papal bureaucracy in Rome to demand a commission to try the obstreperous Observants. The Commons Supplication against the Ordinaries suddenly seemed a good deal more congenial.[23]

Accordingly when Henry met the Commons delegation on 11 May, flanked by eight senior peers, he declared himself outraged that the clergy 'be but half our subjects, yea and scarce our subjects; for all the prelates at their consecration make an oath to the Pope, clean contrary to the oath that they make to us'. He was conveniently armed with copies of the relevant oaths, which Speaker Audley took back to the Commons and read out, to general sensation.[24] What Audley may not have known, and naturally did not retail to MPs, was that these were precisely the oaths which John Foxe records Thomas Cromwell showing to the King at their fateful meeting in the garden at Westminster back in January 1530. Through all the confusion and noise of that Parliamentary spring, Cromwell had managed in the end to keep the focus on the subject of the Supplication and its assault on clerical power, aided by the vigour of senior churchmen's reaction to the King's attack.

Another recent archival discovery reveals Cromwell, right on the eve of Parliament in December 1531, trying to manipulate an uncontroversial land transaction in a way that not merely anticipated the struggle of these five strife-ridden months, but was prophetic of a much greater constitutional transformation in 1533–4. Cromwell was organizing a major royal land exchange with the ancient royal abbey of Waltham Holy Cross, part of a number of such exchanges whose confirmation was one of the more constructive aspects of the 1532 Parliament. We will return to this (see below, pp. 193–4), but what is relevant for the present is that in his draft of the agreement between the Abbot of Waltham and the King, Cromwell personally inserted as an afterthought, into an otherwise routine piece of royal verbiage, one word fraught with significance. To the phrase 'to the most serene and invincible Prince our Lord Henry the Eighth' (*serenissimo et invictissimo Principi Domini nostro Henrico Octavo*), he twice added the word 'Supereminenti' before 'Principi'. This unusual adjective (what exactly did it mean? 'the Supereminent'? 'the Overtopping'?) failed to make it into the formal enrolment of the deal on the Close Roll of Chancery; clearly someone had objected to it. That failure was a mark of what an empty concession the Church made on royal supremacy in the 1531 Parliament. Yet in those two carets written in the hand of Thomas Cromwell we see the first gleam of a new round of royal campaigning.[25]

Breaking the Church's resistance came to trump even the cause of getting money out of Henry's subjects. Abandoning the grudging grant of taxation that Parliament offered, on 14 May the King sent down an order proroguing the assembly. While MPs dispersed, no doubt with relief after a prolonged and bruising session, Henry turned his attention to Convocation. A day later, just after Archbishop Warham had read the formal instruments of dissolution, a party of senior royal councillors headed by the Duke of Norfolk abruptly arrived with a paper from the King, which took up an hour of agitated private discussion before the remaining clergy learned of its astonishing contents: a royal demand for an unreserved submission of the Church's powers to legislate or run its own affairs, and acceptance of a proposed royal commission to revise the whole range of canon law.

The next twenty-four hours were turbulent, but drawing on a rump representation of prelates and maybe no lower clergy at all, the government ended up on 16 May with a document which gave it all it wanted: a complete submission of the Church in the realm to the King, surprisingly couched in English within the usual Latin administrative framing. The royal commissioners receiving this questionable instrument were a curiously assorted bunch, three of whom look like whatever peers could be rounded up in Westminster for the purpose, Lords Abergavenny, Hussey and Mordaunt – but alongside that random trio of noblemen were two old collaborators at Court, Treasurer Fitzwilliam and Thomas Cromwell.[26] The submission was too much for Thomas More: he resigned as Lord Chancellor.

Here was a symbolic triumph for Cromwell, after three eventful years steadily advancing in the King's service. He celebrated that same day by clinching a deal with the London Austin Friars to extend his property-holding further into their premises on a ninety-nine-year lease, the basis for a lavish extension of his house there.[27] But it had been a very rough ride, and throughout the session some formidable opposition remained. In the Commons it was led by some politically weighty figures, who by their status as knights of the shire took their places on the benches in uncomfortably close physical proximity to the King's councillors: notably the senior knight for Warwickshire, Sir George Throckmorton.[28] We know of their activities from a detailed confession of Throckmorton, who in renewed political trouble in autumn 1537 was forced to give exact reminiscences as far back as 1532.[29]

Throckmorton had known Cromwell at least since his Wolsey years, and he came from a family inclined throughout the sixteenth century to express their often sharply contrasting political opinions with pugnacity. His literary style in letters to Cromwell is marked by its brisk straightforwardness, and he was not afraid to strike out on his own line against Crown interests on matters of local administration: all round, not a man to be trifled with.[30] He was one of the principals among a group of MPs, mostly knights of the shire, in the habit of dining together at the Queen's Head Tavern at the Westminster end of Fleet Street: a convenient venue at the city gates, particularly for lawyers getting back from Parliament to the Inns of Court and in urgent need of a drink.[31] Repeatedly discussions over supper turned to their unhappiness with royal moves in Parliament, 'such acts as the Appeals and other' – by which Throckmorton probably meant either the Supplication against the Ordinaries or the submission of the clergy; he went on in a later part of the confession to link 'the Act of Appeals' with the Restraint of Annates, which was indeed part of the royal programme of 1532.[32]

There was nothing particularly conspiratorial about these knights of the shire, stalwarts of royal government in the localities, meeting in a prominent inn in the middle of the lawyers' quarter; it was equally natural that Throckmorton's views brought him to speak to like-minded figures in the Lords led by Sir Thomas More, or in Convocation the prominent conservative London cleric Dr Nicholas Wilson. The convalescent John Fisher was still a member of the Parliament. In their own eyes, they were at this stage a loyal opposition in a grave matter of policy yet to come to a conclusion (Fisher is in a more dubious category, since as the situation worsened some of his communication with Ambassador Chapuys was downright treasonous, ranging as far as encouragement of foreign invasion).[33] They enjoyed in Parliament privileges of freedom of speech and from arrest recognized since the fourteenth century, even if the extent of those privileges was vague, like so much else in Tudor political practice.[34]

Throckmorton nevertheless had no doubts as to who was dominating events in the Commons in 1532: 'the common house was much advertised [admonished or warned] by [Cromwell] and . . . few men there would displease him.' When Throckmorton got a chance to speak to the King directly in private, Cromwell was in attendance at the meeting to provide any further required dose of 'advertising'. This meeting probably occurred during the session itself, since the conversation parallels surprisingly unbuttoned remarks Henry made about his 'grudge of conscience' to a Commons delegation after Thomas Temys's outspokenness on Queen Katherine. If a face-to-face meeting was meant to intimidate Throckmorton, Cromwell and the King had misjudged their man. Sir George recalled that he turned the King's talk of his conscientious scruples in an even bolder direction than Temys: 'I feared if ye did marry Queen Anne, your conscience would be more troubled at length, for that it is thought ye have meddled with the mother and the sister.' Caught badly off guard by this breathtaking directness, the King retorted defensively, 'Never with the mother,' while Cromwell lashed out in an effort to save the situation, 'Nor never with the sister neither, and therefore put that out of your mind.'[35]

So Henry had admitted adultery (or, in his eyes, fornication) with Mary Boleyn, though not with the Countess of Wiltshire. It was a tribute to a curious honesty in the King's conscience in sexual matters, as well as to his conscientious acceptance that those called to Parliament had to be recognized as his counsellors, however unwelcome or shocking their counsel. Outsiders beyond Parliament to whom they might then be indiscreet were in a different category, so Throckmorton took more risks in his conversations with other prominent dissidents such as his cousin William Peto, Minister-Provincial of the Franciscan Observants, keeping a gloomy eye on proceedings from a lodging provided by Archbishop Warham at Lambeth Palace just across the Thames from Westminster. Likewise, it was not Sir George but the friend beyond Parliament to whom he recounted the story of Henry's embarrassing admission, Sir Thomas Dingley, who eventually ended up on the executioner's block for sexual gossip about his sovereign. Worse still, Dingley had gossiped to foreigners.[36]

There could hardly be a more telling symptom of Cromwell's arrival at the centre of power than his presence at this tense interview, tugging at the King's sleeve. Henceforward, one significant silence is obvious in his correspondence: virtually no one bothered to put an address on letters to him, because his name would find him more easily than his exact location. Now, at last, came the beginnings of formal royal office. On 12 April 1532, the day when Archbishop Warham bleakly presented the Convocation of Canterbury with the Commons Supplication against the Ordinaries, the King signed a warrant for Cromwell's appointment as Master of the Jewels, vacant by the death of an old friend of his, Robert Amadas (who, curiously enough, had been named just before him in that list of New Year's gifts for the King).[37] In July came his appointment in a different ancient department of state, Chancery, to an office previously held by another old friend, the late Thomas Hall, one of his Ipswich circle of acquaintance.[38] This was the splendidly named Clerkship of the Hanaper – the custodianship of what was indeed once just a wicker travel-hamper, holding a great variety of documents produced by the various secretarial and legal activities of Chancery: charters, formal royal writs and much more.

Both these offices had reasonable fees and perquisites attached, but that was not really the point. What ought also to be considered was a vacant position which Cromwell did not gain, nor probably seek: the Lord Chancellorship of England, the highest legal office in the realm, formerly held by his master Wolsey and just vacated by Thomas More. No one for the moment was granted this, but the Keepership of the Great Seal of the realm, chief responsibility of the Lord Chancellor, was immediately granted on More's resignation to the Speaker of the Commons, Thomas Audley, who was then upgraded to Chancellor in January 1533.

What was in the minds of Cromwell and the King when these various appointments were made? Cromwell had watched the Cardinal being consumed by his enthusiasm for the Lord Chancellor's judicial business, spending an inordinate amount of his precious time on it. To land himself with the same burden would be foolish. Audley was more obviously a career lawyer; he was also a friend of Cromwell's going back at least to common service in the 1523 Parliament, and after that in Wolsey's household. Cromwell will already have noted his friend's combination of legal pernicketiness and political pliability: as Speaker of the Commons and knight of the shire for Essex, Audley was a convincing candidate for the post in professional terms, and while he clearly adored the excitement of affixing every fresh seal on every royal instrument, he showed no inclination to build up his own political following.

It might seem unnecessary to ponder the question of the Chancellorship, given that Cromwell was not especially distinguished or senior in legal practice, but in 1532 Henry made a choice of that kind generally

1. Putney was still rural in this view of the approach to Putney Church from 1820; the boy Thomas Cromwell would have known the church tower, and possibly the buildings in the foreground.

2–3. Holbein's portraits of the veteran bureaucrat Sir Henry Wyatt (*left*) and of his younger admirer and friend Thomas Cromwell (*below*) in 1532 adopt the same formula for a busy, preoccupied royal servant, grasping an administrative document.

4. Thomas Cromwell at the end of his career, with his coat of arms as augmented in 1537; there are several versions of this image, chubbier but in milder mood than in Holbein's earlier representation.

5–6. The heraldry of Thomas Cromwell (*left*) and Thomas Wolsey (*right*) shows how Cromwell took the chief of Wolsey's coat and made it the fess in his own achievement.

7. Cromwell may have commissioned this accomplished silver-gilt medallion to commemorate his first grandson's birth. The obverse describes him as royal secretary, with the date 1538; the reverse has his augmented arms of 1537 enclosed with the Garter. The coronet is that of an earl rather than a baron, and may have been added in 1540.

8–9. An heraldic 'Parliamentary Roll' of 1539/40 shows the arms of Cromwell as augmented in 1537 (*left*), delicately struck through at his attainder with the note *traditor* (traitor). Their similarity in format to the arms of Edward Seymour, augmented in 1536 (*right*), is striking; both augmentations recorded on the Roll result from marriages of Seymour sisters, to the King and to Gregory Cromwell.

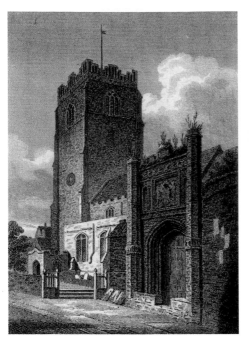

10. The one still-surviving fragment of Cardinal College Ipswich, possibly its watergate, beside the truncated St Peter's Church, in 1812.

11. Thomas Wolsey: a late sixteenth-century Italian version of a contemporary portrait.

12. An illustrated MS copy of George Cavendish's biography provides an Elizabethan take on Wolsey, captioned 'Mi Lorde rides to Westminster Hawle'.

13–15. Cromwell's enemies: (*clockwise from the top*) Anne Boleyn (*c.* 1501–36), Thomas Howard, third Howard Duke of Norfolk (1473–1554), and Stephen Gardiner, Bishop of Winchester (1483–1555).

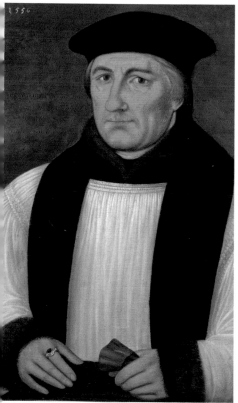

16. This well-known portrait by Gerlach Flicke (d. 1558), of Cromwell's great friend and ally Archbishop Thomas Cranmer, is not as straightforwardly naturalistic as it looks, but a statement of his evangelical and Augustinian theology of grace, commissioned at a moment of evangelical self-confidence in 1545 in Henry VIII's last troubled years. One of the books lying on the table is Augustine of Hippo's treatise *Of Faith and Works*, and recent restoration has revealed three broken panes in the window behind Cranmer. It is likely that they represent the true light of the Holy Trinity breaking through to our impaired vision of grace, which itself might be symbolized by the modish magnificence of the furnishings.

reckoned to be bizarre, for his new Archbishop of Canterbury: a Cambridge don with no experience of the wider Church until his very recent transformation into a royal diplomat. The difference was that in that case the promotion of Thomas Cranmer had the enthusiastic backing of Anne Boleyn. Moreover, as we will discover in the next chapter, Cromwell had made a different appropriation of very considerable power during 1532, without any public warrant at all. He had already begun to interfere in the English Church in ways broadly anticipating his formal grant of the titles Vicar-General and Vice-Gerent in Spirituals in 1534–5.

There is a pattern in these non-appointments and relatively minor appointments between 1530 and 1534; witness the furtive way Cromwell became a royal councillor in early 1531. The outward appearance clashed with the reality that he grew ever more important in government through these four years. Even by early 1533 no one under the King could match him, and so Ambassador Chapuys repeatedly affirmed that he was the man enjoying most credit with the King.[39] This is all more than an accident; it must represent deliberate choice. But whose? Most obviously, the King's. There were people at Court who would have been furious at Cromwell's public promotion to honourable office, and they were headed by Anne Boleyn and her uncle the Duke of Norfolk. Anne in particular was no slouch when it came to the staging of screaming rows.

It took time for Henry, a thorough coward when it came to personal confrontations, to manoeuvre his new minister into an unassailable public role. Most likely Anne could only be persuaded to accept something of the reality of Cromwell's position with good grace once he had triumphantly steered her through to marriage and coronation.[40] It is striking that his next preferment, and that merely the Chancellorship of the Exchequer (not then an exalted office), was finalized on the day the King first showed off Anne as his Queen – Easter Even 1533 – but it is equally remarkable that a month and a half later, when a large number of gentlemen and esquires were granted various ranks of knighthood at her coronation, Thomas Cromwell was not among them. This is all the more surprising because he was actually the man deputed to collect fines from those who refused knighthood at the coronation, and to adjudicate on the excuses people made to avoid accepting that honour. Unlike those shrinking violets, he had no reason to avoid the burdens of knighthood in service to the Crown, obligations he was already far exceeding.[41] It looks like a calculated snub. Knighthood and peerage followed for him only after Anne Boleyn's death.

As for the offices Cromwell did first take in 1532, both were convenient ways to have discreet but paramount control of the King's informal treasury, the royal Privy Coffers, without involving himself in routine work of the offices, undertaken instead by deputies.[42] The Clerk of the Hanaper dealt with a variety of fees due to the Crown for documents drawn up in Chancery, which ran yearly to two or three thousand pounds available for the King's purse, not to mention a decent if unspectacular income for Cromwell himself as Clerk. Cromwell kept that sizeable sum of royal profit under his own administration for the Privy Coffers. In doing so, in characteristic fashion he cut across what had become the normal route for dealing with profits from the Hanaper, by which they should have passed to Sir Brian Tuke, the Treasurer of the Chamber: a sore trial to that humourlessly acquisitive royal servant, who frequently complained (to Cromwell, among others) of being starved of cash. To add to Tuke's frustration, the Jewel House built by Henry VII gave the Master of the Jewels a base in the Tower of London, geographically at the polar opposite side of London to Tuke's headquarters in Westminster – from Cromwell's point of view, also conveniently near his home base at Austin Friars.[43]

The Mastership of the Jewels did not have the prestige of fourteenth-century antiquity which the Clerkship of the Hanaper enjoyed, but it presented a more obvious direct route to the King's presence. The department of the Jewels was not like Chancery, which had become a fossil from the everyday life of early medieval monarchs, turning in function to bureaucracy and litigation. It by contrast remained a very personal Court office in the daily life of King Henry, with a usefully general brief to fetch the King anything he wished to use or gloat over, out of his heap of royal baubles. The Master looked after whatever assets Henry chose to allot him, from the crown of the realm down to a silver-gilt chessboard. It may have been a consideration for Cromwell that a significant part of that store of valuables had very recently been in the possession of Cardinal Wolsey.[44] By its nature, much of this treasure could be readily and unobtrusively turned into coin, since all Tudor coinage was to a greater or lesser degree minted from precious metal. It was a logical consequence that Cromwell came to have a good deal to do with the operation of the royal mint (which, hardly coincidentally, had its London base in the Tower), and he made sure that his clients, particularly his trusted evangelical household servant John Whalley, were placed in charge there.[45]

These two posts, then, provided room for discreet initiative and informality in passing money on to tasks to which the King's enthusiasm or attention might be drawn, to the degree which Cromwell thought appropriate. Meanwhile he leaped acrobatically around the paper-and-parchment trail necessary for formal authorization. Geoffrey Elton, rather illogically for a proponent of a bureaucratic 'Tudor Revolution in Government' which formalized decision-making and removed it from Courtly informality, enjoyed excavating examples of retrospective expedients: 'Item, to cause warrants to be drawn for such money as is newly laid out by me for the King' – and better still the memorandum 'To know what things that I do lack warrant for, and to cause a warrant to be made thereof to sign'. Such warrants were far from trivial. In less than a year from September 1532, Cromwell sent north £20,000 from the Privy Coffers to his friend and former colleague in Wolsey's service George Lawson. This was the bulk of the money Lawson received during that period for various operations defending the border with Scotland, matters where it was sensible to react quickly and flexibly to sudden emergencies. As Elton noted, none of the warrants Cromwell signed were 'dormant'; in other words, they were not regularly occurring payments which needed no fresh decision to be triggered. Each represented a tiny fragment of policy.[46]

Meanwhile, Cromwell carried on supervising various important aspects of the King's building projects: his years with Wolsey gave him ample preparation for this, and the various royal moneys now under his control could swiftly be transferred to the task, once more without interference from Treasurer Tuke.[47] It was a shrewd move to keep buildings as part of his concerns, for building of all sorts, palaces to castles to coastal defences, was among the King's great enthusiasms, to rival jewels and books. Cromwell knew his man. Enjoyable discussions with Henry about progress on cherished projects were as useful a bonding experience for a rising minister as sifting royal treasure or perusing venerable volumes, though as early as autumn 1533 we find Cromwell contemplating how he might most tactfully suggest to the King a more structured and economical way of exercising the royal passion for building.[48] Neither would it harm his own growing domestic building projects in London to have a close working relationship with royal masons and carpenters.

These formal acquisitions of Court offices demanded a thorough overhaul of Cromwell's social status, which duly followed in no fewer than four different respects. First adjustment: it must be given substance by appropriate landholding. So far his landed property was insignificant: the episodically expanding footprint of his home in Austin Friars, plus a clutch of run-of-the-mill leases, mostly in the Home Counties. Now on 27 May 1532, between his two grants of office, he gained something very different: the ancient Marcher lordship of Rhymney or Romney in Glamorgan, which was King Henry's to grant out because after lately belonging to the attainted Duke of Buckingham it became available for redistribution on the death of Buckingham's widow in 1530.[49] By its nature Rhymney was in a more exalted league than rented farms or parsonages: besides rolling Welsh acres, there were substantial tenants with ancient obligations to bring condemned criminals to the county gallows, and provide furnishings for royal sessions of justice. There was also a good deal of tightening up to do after years of Crown mismanagement of the Dowager Duchess's assets.[50]

As Cromwell's landed estates expanded in a more predictable fashion in south-east England, his active interest in Rhymney seems to have receded, but his general interest in Wales did not. Among his papers is a long memorandum from a servant, Thomas Philips, written in the same month as the Rhymney grant, responding to a query of Cromwell's about the general state of Wales.* It was a litany of deficiencies, mainly caused by the administrative inadequacies of the Council in the Marches of Wales, then still maintained in the name of Princess Mary. Philips recommended a complete remodelling of the Council: a cause Cromwell duly took up, and turned into major legislation in 1536.[51]

Second adjustment: etiquette would demand that the holder of a feudal lordship, however minor, must obtain an official grant of a coat of arms from the College of Heralds if he did not have one. Cromwell's offices at Court in any case made heraldry a practical necessity, for everyday display – so much of Court life depended on purposeful display. The grant was duly made by Cromwell's friend Thomas Benolt, then Clarenceux King of Arms, and it fits Cromwell's new position at this moment, though confusingly dated in Benolt's records (he put it in the 23rd regnal year of Henry VIII, which would just work for the grant of the Mastership of the Jewels in mid-April 1532, but he then added the date 1533, spanning Henry's 24th and 25th years).[52] The crest of Cromwell's coat consists of a golden demi-lion rampant, holding a gold finger-ring with a ruby stone, which is surely a reference to the Mastership (maybe even specifically to that ruby ring given to the King the previous New Year). Heraldry is seldom without meaning; in the sixteenth century, people would be able to read it as we read road-signs, and from the same prudential motives. So let us follow their example. (See Plate 5.)

The fact that the allusion to jewels is merely in the crest, and not in the body of the coat itself, raises the suspicion that Cromwell had been using that coat of arms before, simply not bothering to get it authorized. That thought is strengthened by the nature of the coat, all of which suggests

---

* This Thomas Philips is almost certainly nothing to do with either Thomas Philips of London or Thomas Phelips of Dorset discussed at various points below.

his life in the later 1520s. Cromwell has chosen three lions rampant, probably from the heraldry of his brother-in-law Morgan Williams (see above, pp. 38–9), but then he has separated the trio of lions by a radical visual appropriation: he has lowered the *chief or* (the golden head-band) of Cardinal Thomas Wolsey's arms to form a *fess or* (a golden central band) across the middle of the shield. On Wolsey's *chief* and Cromwell's *fess* alike are a red rose between two Cornish choughs. The rose is of course a symbol of their common service to King Henry VIII. Choughs (heraldry's preferred species of crow) are the symbol of Thomas Becket of Canterbury, and therefore of all English Thomases, be they Wolsey or Cromwell – it would take a year or two for an extra layer of irony to appear in that symbol. So this coat was aggressively proclaiming a servant of Thomas Wolsey; maybe Cromwell had adopted it when the Cardinal appointed him to his council in 1527. To retain it in 1532, with the Cardinal's reputation at its nadir, was an extraordinary and admirably defiant statement, calculated in particular to infuriate that hypersensitive snob Thomas Duke of Norfolk.

Benolt's stumbling over the dating of the grant in his records does hint at a slightly untidy retrospective legitimization of Cromwell's arms, also suggested by the puzzling circumstance that at the same time Cromwell appears to have called on another friend, Thomas Audley, to use his newly acquired powers as Keeper of the Great Seal to issue a further royal confirmation of his grant of arms. It would be the first recorded occasion on which this happened, though the Crown was the fount of honour in the kingdom, and direct royal grants of arms did thereafter occur from time to time. A slow progress of a royal patent through the often tortoise-like procedures of Chancery after an initial grant by the heralds might account for Benolt's double dating of the grant. Proof of this does not survive elsewhere, but a great deal of documentation of Cromwell's honours (especially his heraldry) was hastily culled in 1540.

The evidence of this grant via Keeper Audley occurs in a letter to Cromwell from his deputy in the Hanaper, John Judd, that same summer of 1532. Judd had been up in Ipswich doing clear-up business for the widow of Cromwell's predecessor in the Clerkship of the Hanaper, Mistress Cecily Hall, and en route dropped off 'the patent of arms' at Audley's home at Berechurch near Colchester. The trip on to Ipswich prevented Judd from personally supervising Audley when he sealed the royal grant, and his professional pride was hugely wounded when he got back to Berechurch, because he found that Audley's staff (maybe unfamiliar with this little-used procedure for a grant of arms) had chosen the wrong colour of wax and silk laces for the patent. 'It is a perpetuity,' he lamented, and such grants without time-limit demanded the colour green, for which perpetuity Cromwell was after all paying a hefty fee.[53]

Third adjustment: a Crown official of some status (in fact rather more status than currently met the eye) needed his portrait painted, both to display in his own mansion and also as a model, if his influence and reputation so expanded that people would wish to have copies for their own walls. This portrait seems to have been preserved by the faithful Ralph Sadler, who must have acquired it in the break-up of his old master's house in 1540: the portrait was sighted in the long gallery of his grandson's house at Standon in 1623.[54] The go-to painter of 1532 was Hans Holbein the Younger, who duly produced the famous image of the Crown official in his black cap and gown, papers and a book as specimens of his administrative duties and library arranged with careful casualness on the table before him (see Plate 3). He is wearing his ring with a heart-shaped turquoise, already noted as 'upon my master's finger' when his inventory was made in 1527, and their may be the turquoise ring he had sent to the Duke of Norfolk during his quest for a Parliamentary seat in 1529: what could be more symbolic of his triumph in reaching his present fortunes?[55]

The letter lying on the table before the sitter handily dates the portrait to this time even if we had not presumed that new office occasioned it, for it is meticulously (if implausibly from a routine point of view) addressed as from his royal employer, 'To our trusty and right well beloved Councillor Thomas Cromwell, Master of our Jewel House'. The green cloth which covers the table also shouts his new formal access to the Court: the 'Board of Green Cloth' was coming at this time to be the name for the group of royal officers from Treasurer downwards who met to discuss the finances of the royal Household. The Master of the Jewels had no prescribed place among them, but that was hardly relevant to the way in which Cromwell's duties were now making him indispensable in finding cash for the insatiable demands of royal magnificence and commonplace consumption by thousands of individuals thronging the King's palaces through the year.

Holbein was a master of a realism which has left us riveting character-sketches of the Tudor Court, but he nevertheless found significantly few imitators in English portraiture over the next century. Cromwell's portrait may suggest why. No one has ever suggested that it is an endearing picture, and now the watchful, slightly hooded-eyed minister, within a minute of losing his temper, hangs in the Frick Collection in New York, paired with Holbein's image of bleakly fearless, clear-sighted Thomas More: not to the advantage of the Master of the Jewels. Hilary Mantel has engagingly imagined the reactions at Austin Friars when the painter delivers the result.[56]

Rather than the Frick's loaded juxtaposition, it is worth setting Cromwell's picture alongside that of an older friend and perhaps mentor from his circle of Kentish gentry: the veteran civil servant Sir Henry Wyatt, also in his time Master of the Jewels. Cromwell was one of the executors of Sir Henry's will in 1536, and benevolent patron of his problematic if very talented son Thomas. (See Plate 2.) We see the same black cap and befurred gown, the same little folded administrative paper in a tight grasp – above all, the same preoccupied, watchful expression. Both pictures share a visual formula signifying a busy, competent servant of the King, who owed his present fortunes to his prince: in Wyatt's case, his career had started among a whole set of forensically efficient administrators, some raised by their King from humble backgrounds, who shaped the achievements of Henry VII's government. Part of what they had achieved was deep unpopularity. Cromwell would be aware of this ambiguous history, but he had also seen Wyatt survive it, to become one of the grand old men of Henry VIII's government and enjoy a splendid retirement.

Clearly the sitter decided to accept his portrait as representing some truths about himself. It fed into many copies, as well as the negative image of him which prevailed in the Romantic era – yet no unfavourable comment emerges from the sixteenth or seventeenth centuries, and a remarkably faithful and accomplished copy of the Standon portrait was made eighty years after Holbein for the then Lord Cromwell, Gregory's descendant, which that peer must have considered worth the expense.[57] As we will see, Holbein did deliver other less rebarbative images of Cromwell and his family, and other portrait traditions represent different takes on the same physiognomic material. The fact that Cromwell did not consign Holbein's effort to the furnace, as Lady Churchill did with Graham Sutherland's hated portrait of Sir Winston, suggests once more his self-confidence and robust temperament, a parallel to the jaunty defiance in his coat of arms. He did not need his collateral descendant Oliver to invent a famous phrase about public representations, 'warts and all'. By contrast, Sir Thomas More's noble image in the Frick portrait took quite a lot of adjustment to get right.[58]

Fourth and last adjustment: no royal official with pretensions to gentle status could possibly tolerate not being named to that essential organ of local government, the county commission of the peace, which the Crown or its local delegates issued for every shire or county in England. Since the fourteenth century, the justices of the peace (JPs) had taken on more and more local powers: they were ideal agents from the monarchy's point of view, since apart from a fairly nominal daily payment for turning up at the 'quarter sessions' every three months, they cost nothing (most of them got ample reward from the prestige and power the office brought). Better still, they could be dismissed or appointed by the simple means of issuing another royal commission with a new list of names to sit on the county bench of JPs, cancelling out the previous commission. The first round-up of commissions in which Cromwell's name is known to appear is a book listing them kingdom-wide (a *liber pacis*) dateable by its content to 1532.[59] He was placed in commission only for counties where he had property: Essex, Kent, Middlesex and Surrey (Wales was not within the system at that stage). It was not until after the great traumas of 1536–7, now victorious and his son the King's brother-in-law, that his name appeared on every commission of the peace issued by the Crown.

This *liber pacis* from 1532 was Cromwell's own, for in the list for Surrey, the county of his birth, he has added in his own hand three new names: Thomas Heneage, Sir Anthony Browne and Sir Richard Page. All of them held office at Court, and in a significant faux pas Cromwell inserted these three names in the Surrey list out of their proper order. JPs were named in commission in a strict hierarchical arrangement jealously observed at meetings by all those involved, and royal servants should not have been tacked on the end of the list. Evidently he was still learning about such technicalities.[60] Yet he would have been well aware of the precise political significance of adding them to the Surrey bench. Not only were they all former servants of Wolsey, but in the badlands of Surrey's surprisingly contentious local politics they were ranged alongside Cromwell's friend Sir William Fitzwilliam against the faction maintained by the Duke of Norfolk. Heneage and Page were resuming careers as Surrey JPs after being dropped at Wolsey's fall.[61] So Cromwell's entry of them on his *liber pacis* is a tiny reflection of seismic shifts in national politics at the same time.

The circumstances of Cromwell's rise in spring 1532 involved two immediate political casualties, who would now be marked out as his enemies for life, however much public proprieties might be observed: Sir Thomas More and Bishop Stephen Gardiner. More had had enough of trying to reconcile his conscience with public office and, as we have seen, the submission of the clergy to the King provoked his resignation as Lord Chancellor, to be succeeded by Thomas Audley. Erasmus, far away in Freiburg im Breisgau, heard of Lutheran glee in Germany that one of Audley's first actions as Keeper was to release twenty evangelical heretics whom More had kept in prison; the great humanist did not think it impolitic to repeat this item of news about the changing political atmosphere in England promptly in print.[62] From the moment of his resignation, despite his considerable powers of public discretion, More became one of the chief symbols of opposition to the King's plans for marriage and religion. Consequently not only did Henry turn to hate him as only Henry could, but Thomas Cromwell became the chief agent in his destruction.

Bishop Gardiner did not return to London from his French embassy until 6 March, and he was appalled at how far the attack on the Church had gone in his absence. The presentation of the Supplication against the Ordinaries on 18 March provoked him into preparing a vigorous response, seized on by the beleaguered leadership of Convocation and the basis for their own aggressive reply delivered to King and Commons in late April. Gardiner did not expect the King to be so angry at his part in this, and his subsequent letter to Henry simply made matters worse: brave though it was of him to write at all, his characteristic gambit of wrongfooting his opponents by citing their own works was on this occasion rank idiocy.[63] John Foxe immortalized Gardiner as 'Wily Winchester', but his wiliness was compromised by an extremely quick temper.[64] Throughout his career, he was capable of surprising misjudgements, and this was the worst: his political position under Henry VIII never fully recovered from it.

Gardiner, on the verge of becoming the King's chief minister, now found even his role as Principal Secretary slipping away, displaced by Cromwell's increasing significance. He saw his fine new house at Hanworth surrendered to Anne Boleyn, and the Archbishopric of Canterbury which should have been his on the death of William Warham that summer of 1532 went to another. By the second half of 1533, it was clear that the Secretaryship was in fact if not in name in Cromwell's hands: one of those silent transfers of power to a man without a public face which characterized his first four years in royal service. Already during Gardiner's prolonged absence abroad on royal diplomatic business, Cromwell had the keeping of the crucial Signet seal which initiated large sections of royal business (it was the King's personal seal for correspondence, theoretically the signet ring on his finger); his assistant Ralph Sadler had power over the fees which suitors would have to pay for its use.[65]

Over the next few years, Gardiner lost the services of three talented servants who calculated that he was damaged goods, the same calculation that he had made with Thomas Wolsey; they all ended up in the service of his supplanter, Thomas Cromwell. Last was the talented and politically agile Thomas Wriothesley, so often misleadingly placed among

Cromwell's long-standing servants, the story of whose final move out of Gardiner's orbit into Cromwell's must wait for a later crisis at Court at the beginning of 1536.[66] Another was William Paget, a political escapologist even shrewder than Wriothesley: both men were high in Gardiner's affections after being favourite pupils of his at Trinity Hall Cambridge, which makes plain the limits of his wiliness.[67]

The third ungrateful young object of Gardiner's esteem is a real surprise: Thomas Cromwell's own nephew, Richard Cromwell alias Williams, who seems to have entered Gardiner's service after the death of his former master the Marquess of Dorset in 1530. Richard was with Gardiner on his French mission in winter 1532, acting among other things as a diplomatic courier; in winter 1533 his alert cousin Christopher Wellifed, seeking a way to get a wealthy parish benefice in Gardiner's gift, commented hungrily to his parents that 'I hear say my cousin Richard is in great favour with the bishop.' Within a month, however, that same Richard was described as Thomas Cromwell's servant by their relative George Lawson.[68] Now Richard Cromwell took his place alongside Ralph Sadler as one of Cromwell's talented young men.

Less immediately obvious casualties of events were the three great Court magnates in the King's counsels, the Dukes of Norfolk and Suffolk and Anne Boleyn's father the Earl of Wiltshire. Wiltshire was an able diplomat, but diplomats seldom have the qualities for leadership in government, and there was no question that he owed his sudden prominence to his daughter's increasingly certain marriage to the King. His fortunes rose and fell in relation to hers, and he was no match for the new arrival among royal ministers. One would have expected the two Dukes likewise to have benefited from Wolsey's final fall in 1529, just as they had done when his power briefly faltered over the Amicable Grant crisis in 1525, yet their ascendancy soon turned out to be fragile.

Charles Brandon Duke of Suffolk's remarkable staying power in the King's affections relied on his pliable charm and Henry's warm memories of their common youthful prowess in the tiltyard. Otherwise he lacked the administrative abilities required for celebrations in a brewery, let alone governing a kingdom. Brandon had married the King's sister Mary after the death of her husband King Louis of France back in 1515: a love match which had been an unpleasant surprise both to Henry and to her French in-laws. Despite royal forgiveness, their marriage remained as much a liability as an asset, particularly since the Dowager Queen Mary rapidly decided she loathed Anne Boleyn. While she was about the only person in the realm who could have got away with such open hostility, it meant that Suffolk's position at Court actually deteriorated after Wolsey's removal.[69]

Brandon and Howard did not protect their own interests by effectively combining against any newcomer at the top. They were never particularly warm allies; in fact at the moment of the Duke of Norfolk's fall from grace in 1546, in an understandably self-pitying though not inaccurate list of all the people who had hated him, Norfolk listed the Duke of Suffolk as leading a trio of noblemen who had encouraged Wolsey to destroy him back in 1515.[70] In their own region of East Anglia, the Dukes were competitors for influence, an unequal contest which the Duke of Norfolk generally won.[71] That very spring of 1532 a poisonous feud erupted between their followers, connected to the Dowager Queen's unkind comments on the prospect of a royal Boleyn marriage. This led to a sensational outrage in Westminster itself while Parliament was still sitting, when Suffolk's tenant and relative Sir William Pennington was murdered by the brothers Richard, Robert and Anthony Southwell, Norfolk gentlemen then in Howard's affinity. Both Dukes suffered from the public scandal.[72]

On 20 July 1532, the fallout from that affair provoked further trouble which summed up the now quadrangular relationship. Suffolk wrote plaintively to Cromwell, mildly reproaching him for letting the King know that servants of Norfolk had complained to him about death threats made by Suffolk's servants. Norfolk and Suffolk had both hoped to keep this from Henry's ears; they were not pleased at this short-circuiting of their affairs, but neither of them made much of a fuss about it.[73] In fact throughout the 1530s Suffolk was very happy to defer to Cromwell's ability to do him favours; he asked him to be godfather to his son and heir Henry in 1535 (presumably alongside the King), and acquiesced with only minor grumbles in the dramatic and wholesale removal of ducal estates and power from East Anglia up to Lincolnshire from 1537.[74] The only time that the Duke of Suffolk showed anything like open defiance of the wishes of the great minister was on a matter of policy towards Lincolnshire in 1536, after he had led the successful neutralization of the rising there, at a moment when Cromwell seemed at his weakest. It was still a very token squeak.[75]

The Duke of Norfolk was a man of much greater ability than his fellow-magnate: experienced as a diplomat and military commander, with a decent record in that most intractable of Tudor territories, Ireland, and ruthlessly determined to build on his own already exalted position in the realm. His niece Anne Boleyn's cause looked like an asset in pursuing that aim, but his own uneasy combination of religious traditionalism and brusque contempt for the Church's power at home and abroad did not produce results for the Great Matter after the fall of Wolsey any more impressive than the

Cardinal's strenuous efforts. During 1532, it became painfully apparent to those close to events that Cromwell's rise was edging Norfolk aside. It was in May that the late Marquess of Dorset's brother Lord Leonard Grey, wooing a rich widow, tried to enlist his 'loving friend and fellow Master Thomas Cromwell' in getting a supportive letter from the Duke (see above, p. 47), but in making his request Grey used that phrase now increasingly common in begging letters found in Cromwell's correspondence, even from members of the nobility: 'my whole trust *next God and the King* is in you.'[76] By July Dr Augustine, no amateur in reading political atmospheres, was sending Cromwell his letters to the Duke from Regensburg unsealed, so his friend could read them first.[77]

This shift must have been an unpleasant surprise to Norfolk, who had no previous reason to suppose that a quietly efficient servant of the fallen Cardinal could represent a threat to him. He had, of course, been the royal minister who secured the King's agreement for Cromwell to make his entry to Parliament in 1529. No one could have infuriated him more as political rival than a nonentity from Putney – apart from a butcher's son from Ipswich. Norfolk's aristocratic hauteur was all the more pronounced because of its fragility: for all the Howards' pretensions, someone as versed in history as Thomas Cromwell could have pointed out that the family's entry to the peerage had been no more than six decades before, and their ducal title had been granted around the time of Cromwell's own birth. Howard magnificence was borrowed plumage from their Mowbray predecessors in the Norfolk title, complete with an ancient Norfolk mausoleum in their Cluniac priory of Thetford, a funereal venue which meant a great deal to the Duke.

The next year was to make Norfolk's decline obvious. By December 1533, Chapuys was describing the Duke to his imperial master as a spent force, who spoke as poisonously of the Pope as he could 'for fear of losing the small credit he still enjoys, which scarcely goes beyond the limits allowed him by Cromwell, nowadays the man who has most influence with the King, at which, as I hear from all sides, the Duke is very much annoyed, and is seriously contemplating leaving the Court and retiring into private life'.[78] That was in fact what he did for the next few years, with the considerable exception of the emergency caused by the Pilgrimage of Grace in 1536–7. The Duke's full reappearance, replete with a rage seeking satisfaction for years of perceived slights, coincided with the final shaking down of Cromwell's power in 1540, and time did not mellow his hatred of the fallen minister in later years after the upstart's death. When he himself was thrown into the Tower of London as a result of his son's crazy dynastic indiscretions in 1546, he begged to be given at least the same hearing as that 'false man [Cromwell], and surely I am a true poor gentleman'.[79]

This was a relationship characterized by an unstable mixture of ducal anxiety and outward friendship. The Duke had all the ability of the professionally insincere to put up an effective act in the role of bluff honest comrade. It is a shame that we cannot certainly date or place in context the most extreme of his falsehoods, when the Duke avowed to Cromwell, in his own distinctive and rather pleasing handwriting,

> By my friends I have been advertised that since I saw you last, ye have most lovingly handled me, for the which . . . I assure you in few words you will always find me a faithful friend, grudge who will, *the King only reserved*, not doubting once to shew the same with effect, though ye shall have little need thereof, as I pray Almighty God ye never have . . .[80]

Cromwell on his side was always punctilious in maintaining the charade, until the pressure of events impaired his judgement in his last year of life. Nevertheless, he simultaneously kept up a remarkable friendship and correspondence with the Duke of Norfolk's estranged wife Elizabeth Stafford, daughter to the executed Duke of Buckingham: she and Cromwell stood godparents together to a son of one of Cromwell's nieces in 1537.[81] No one will claim that the Duchess was an easy character, but she had been deeply wronged by her husband: Norfolk was ensconced for the rest of his life with a Lincolnshire gentlewoman called Elizabeth Holland, and would never have dreamed of taking his wife back. For Cromwell to offer her his friendship was a strong statement, and not one of any direct political use. In fact with his usual candidly grim humour, Cromwell more than once in the 1530s said to the Duke, 'My lord, ye are an happy man that your wife knoweth no hurt by you, for if she did, she would undo you.'[82]

Norfolk reminisced that at the time of the trial and execution of his wife's father, the Duke of Buckingham, 'of all men living he hated me most.'[83] There was competition for that honour, and Cromwell was high among the contenders, given the Duke's enjoyment in destroying his old master the Cardinal. Shared antipathies as much as any political calculation drew Cromwell to Duchess Elizabeth – yet another person who made no secret of the fact that she detested Anne Boleyn.[84] The Duchess became, like her much loved brother Henry Lord Stafford, or the mad Lord Dudley's son Edward, or Wolsey's Thomas Winter and the mysterious Thomas Minterne, one of Cromwell's waifs and strays. They were among his old obligations, to be observed without reward, amid all the other business which crowded in upon him, until it was too late to do more.

8

Making a Difference: 1532

A fascination of Cromwell's years in power is deciding what difference he made, after subtracting what would have been the routine aims or achievements of any half-competent minister, and after assessing what is likely to have originated from his royal master – who had a quarter-century's experience of kingship by the time Cromwell became his chief minister, and was not a fool. Are there political initiatives attributable to his arrival at the centre of government? Straight away, the story of the later 1530s presents itself as the unfolding story of key Parliamentary decisions. We have already noted Cromwell's ability to seize the moment; nowhere is that more obvious than the use to which the King and his ministers put England's and Ireland's legislative assemblies. Henry summoned Parliament in autumn 1529 when Cromwell still had nothing to do with the King's government; if that had been the only session of what became the 'Reformation Parliament', its lack of significant achievement would hardly make it stand out from its predecessors. It did not even destroy Wolsey as some had clearly intended, and Cromwell may have had something to do with that failure – if only as one of the public voices to which the King hearkened as he brooded on the fate of his great minister.

Only after its recall in winter 1531 did this Parliament become remarkable and indeed unprecedented, not merely for the number of times it was summoned again, but for what it actually achieved in legislation. The 1531 session was the first in which Cromwell emerged as a government spokesman, but at that stage he was still one royal minister among several, and there was much disorder and failed business. We will have cause to see what Cromwell did in the later sessions of Parliament once his rivals had fallen away; and later it will become apparent that his use of the King's other Parliament in Dublin was equally novel and indeed without parallel during the century. The English Parliament could never be taken for granted at any stage while he was a royal minister: frustrating, but maybe also fascinating, for him.

Yet Cromwell's opportunism in using existing situations in and beyond Parliament and bending them to his purposes could have remained a matter of ambition and temperament, rather than shaping distinctive policy agendas which would have taken a different course without him. What remains to demonstrate is that in these years from 1531 up to 1540 one can isolate policy initiatives which seem peculiarly his. In order of importance, from the apparently ridiculous to the sublime, we begin with sewers, pass through public relations and end with the Church.

The word 'sewer' has suffered linguistic misfortune since the Tudor age. Then it had a much wider reference, and the 'commissions of sewers' given sweeping new statutory powers and structure by the 1532 session of Parliament were vital for proper functioning of transport, inland fisheries, marsh drainage and flood defences. In many ways, the work of these commissions over several centuries from 1532 created the modern geography of rural England: less spectacularly or rapidly than the Industrial Revolution, but cumulatively just as important in effect. The commissions' membership was not that different from the commissions of the peace, on the good grounds that one needed people with considerable social cachet in outfacing local vested interests in order to destroy weirs and other obstacles to free movement on rivers, or to galvanize local efforts to stand up to coastal erosion.[1]

This was an issue where one man's profitable weir or mill-race was an infuriating obstruction to many more people's community fishing, or the free flow of water to keep river silting at bay, or to boats at a time when water transport was the easiest way to move bulky goods, grain and agricultural produce included. Tudor people were more ready to judge problems in terms of morality than economics. Just like enclosure for sheep-farming, the matter of weirs took on moral dimensions: it demonstrated human greed and selfishness, which threatened to damage a frail social fabric by endangering food supplies. In Tudor society, famine still loomed, with all its capacity to poison human relations and cause very public suffering, let alone riot and rebellion; the moral outrage was not some academic debate. Weirs had been the subject of moral outrage long before Cromwell's years of power, when he was just a boy living in a Thames-side village (with a father who owned a mill); there was repeated agitation in the Parliaments of Henry VII about them, resulting in one or two pieces of legislation with a local focus and not much effect.[2]

Cromwell's own interest in weirs and waterworks dated back at least to his service with Wolsey on monastic suppressions. In administering wide areas of Thames-side marshland which formed the core estates of the dissolved abbey of Lesnes in Kent, he had been caught up in trying to remedy a catastrophic breach of flood defences in winter 1529, causing havoc in the low-lying countryside around; the breach may have resulted from lack of maintenance after that abbey's suppression in 1525, in which he had been an agent. Everyone right up to the King then tried to wriggle out of financing repairs, so it was several years before the huge costs were sorted. Meanwhile the drowning of land around Lesnes, Erith and Plumstead was so serious that it needed an Act of Parliament in the 1531 session, and Cromwell can probably take credit for steering this Act through to success before the general legislation on sewers the following year.[3]

Once the Act for commissions of sewers passed in 1532, Cromwell immediately put himself on the commission for the county of Surrey. At that stage he did not have much property in Surrey, but he did have plenty of clamorous relatives and friends there, and maybe a sense of local patriotism. Despite all the burgeoning business of a busy royal minister, this was not a nominal appointment. Sir Nicholas Carew of Beddington was clearly a little surprised in September to find that the writ empowering him to swear commissioners of sewers was also addressed to Cromwell. Carew wondered whether he would be coming in person to the oath-taking at Kingston upon Thames.[4] It is not certain that Cromwell made it to Kingston on that occasion, but he did indeed sit on the commission when it met in Southwark, a session which caused much local alarm by its decisions on river obstructions.[5] Other letters about the Surrey commission include one from his friend Sir William Fitzwilliam, hoping to see him come down to Kingston, and commenting optimistically in an autograph postscript, 'There is no man now in our quarter that reasons against it, but every man with it that has either learning or discretion.' That was a tactful way of saying how unpopular the new legislation on sewers was among landowners generally, and it continued to be well into the seventeenth century. Construed aggressively, as Cromwell intended it to be, its provisions undoubtedly threatened property rights.[6]

Cromwell's membership of the commission in Surrey was not just a piece of piety to his native county; it reflected his real ongoing preoccupation with the wider issue of land drainage. That was clear when he took a personal interest in a very different piece of marsh reclamation, in Calais, which many in the town believed threatened the defences of that perennially insecure outpost of the realm. The commissioners to examine the site included himself, and he had a chance to do something about it when he joined the King's spectacular meeting with the King of France in autumn 1532 (see below, pp. 206–9); it is piquant to think of him pondering banks and ditches amid the glamorous royal junketings. But then, this was an issue which fascinated King Henry too: another useful bonding opportunity between the two men, without the complications of their different theological outlooks which made questions of religion so tricky. Royal autograph musings as well as Cromwell's appear on one draft list of members of this Calais commission.[7]

Cromwell also began following Cardinal Wolsey in curbing sheep-farming enclosure. In 1534 he tried to interest the King as well, seeking his personal backing for legislation in Parliament that spring which would have limited any one person to running a flock of 2,000 sheep and no more. There must already have been signs of opposition in the Commons when he wrote, because it was after the Commons had made their contribution that he begged the King to intervene and urge the Lords to accept the bill. The draft of his letter to Henry survives in his own hand, full of second thoughts as to how best to express his extreme anxiety about the fate of his measure. In the end, in a revealing display of hyperbole, he affirmed that his Majesty would thus 'do the most profitable and beneficial thing that ever was done to the Common wealth of this your realm, and shall thereby increase such wealth in the same amongst the great number and multitude of your subjects as was never seen in this Realm since Brutus'.[8]

Landowners in both Houses in March 1534 will have remembered that this was the Cardinal's man pushing a programme which had already thoroughly infuriated them in previous years, and they combined to wreck Cromwell's bill. After a great deal of to-and-fro emendment, it emerged toothless and peppered with provisos, and it may have survived on the statute book as an occasionally activated measure only because it had little actual effect. Thereafter, Cromwell kept away from the enclosure issue for some years, and maybe his lack of success there is why he turned to weirs and water engineering. Fifteen-thirty-five saw Henry VIII and Cromwell embarking on further sewer-related adventures, in which both men invested a great deal of time and worry. The most spectacular single project was their effort to build an effective harbour for Dover, England's principal crossing-point to mainland Europe, a scheme which gobbled up money all through the 1530s and 1540s, only to face repeated disasters. It had to wait for a complete engineering rethink in the reign of Queen Elizabeth before it began working properly: one of the many ways in which the daughter outshone the achievements of the father.[9]

The Dover project reflected King Henry's fascination with his navy, but there was more to it than that. In the same year, King and minister launched an even more ambitious nationwide campaign: to use the commissions of sewers to destroy weirs and water-mills on rivers throughout lowland England, with its sluggish if charming water-courses. Their efforts were sparked early in the year with an approach to Master Secretary from the city authorities in Winchester, who succeeded in raising his concern about the city's economic plight, pinpointing the worst problem as obstructions to the city's river navigation down to Southampton.[10] Over the next months it became clear that this particular case was not unconnected to Bishop Gardiner's estate interest in water-mills on the River Itchen, as well as to an episcopal court jurisdiction which the city wished curbed. So in this instance Cromwell could add to his economic concerns and moral indignation the political satisfaction of harassing a rival.[11]

Nevertheless, the campaign greatly expanded beyond Winchester in late August 1535, with a nationwide launch by royal circular during the King's western progress (at the end of which King and minister had the chance to see how things were going in Winchester itself).[12] One can sense Bishop Roland Lee's lack of enthusiasm for prosecuting the campaign in his letters to Cromwell, coupled with resigned acceptance that he would have to do his duty on the matter in the west Midlands; for by then Lee was Lord President in the Welsh Marches.[13] Weirs form one of the constant worries in the correspondence of Lord and Lady Lisle over a couple of years after 1535, since a weir of Lady Lisle's at Umberleigh (Devon) was among those coming under threat, in this case from a commissioner who was a particular friend of Cromwell, Sir William Courtenay of Powderham. The Lisles' energetic and competent servant John Husee briefed them on the inevitability of demolition, given that the King and Cromwell alike were bafflingly pursuing the issue regardless of immediate economic rationales: 'his Grace is very earnest in it, for he hath lost himself more than 500 marks by the year in such weirs and mills as hath been pulled down. And Mr Secretary is very earnest in the same and will show no favour.'

Gloomily, Husee cited the words of the royal commission, which spelled out the social ills that it sought to combat: 'All weirs noisome to the passage of ships or boats, to the hurt of passages or ways and causeways shall be pulled down; and those that be occasion of drowning of any lands of pastures ... and also those that are the destruction of the increase of fish.' The consequence was that if any weirs could be defined as responsible for such grievances, 'then is there no redemption but pull them down, although the same weirs have stood since 500 years before the Conquest.'[14] The Lisles' other senior servant Leonard Smyth confirmed the apparent economic irrationality of what was happening: 'no man within the realm loseth so much therein as doth the King and the Queen, for *their* weirs (which are in all countries most commonly best) are destroyed.'[15]

Cromwell assiduously followed up the initial royal order of August 1535 to enforce compliance. It is astonishing to find among his remembrances preparing legislation for the Parliament of February 1536 (alongside the abolition of ecclesiastical sanctuary liberties and 'a reformation to diminish' monastic life) 'An Act that never weir nor water-mill shall hereafter be erected or made within this realm'. This particular Year Zero measure never made it to the statute book.[16] The Dissolution of the Weirs has not figured much in accounts of Henry VIII's reign, but in 1535–7 it must have caused as much alarm and anger among the gentry of lowland England as the simultaneous surveying and dissolution of lesser monasteries, without any compensating thought of possible profit for either themselves or the King. It therefore provides an interesting comparison with the monastic suppressions, because (as King Henry's puzzled subjects noticed) it did not march in step with his economic interests. Yet it also alerts us to the fact that, when Henry did dissolve monasteries, there was an analogous element of moral reformation in his thoughts, and in those of the Vice-Gerent as well. Cromwell was still alert for rogue water-mills in 1539, and might, had he lived longer, have gone down in history as the Hammer of the Weirs.[17]

There are signs that in the year before Cromwell's downfall the Cardinal's former assistants in his anti-enclosure campaigns were trying to interest him in renewing Wolsey's crusade against enclosures. Roger Wigston, a prominent Leicester and Coventry merchant, had been one of the most active movers in Wolsey's campaign against enclosures in the Midlands in the years after 1517, and given that he was *inter alia* a sheep-farmer himself, his interest in the moral issue clearly overruled his economic self-interest; we may take it that he felt that there was a socially justifiable code for enclosing land, alongside irresponsible and selfish enclosures. He was back on full throttle in summer 1539 in his efforts to enlist Cromwell:

> If God send me health, I intend to view the enclosures between this and Michaelmas that be grievously complained upon in the counties of Warwick, Leicester and Northampton, and to certify your Lordship of the actors and offenders with their qualities and quantities of their acts and offences, so that thereupon commissioners may be sent forth to make enquiry of the same according to the law.[18]

Yet it was not just the Cardinal's former agents who looked for remedy via Cromwell: Dr John London, who had not been among Wolsey's devotees and does not generally figure in history as a man with a social conscience, was urging Cromwell to action against Northamptonshire enclosures in January 1539. By that time, a series of accelerating political crises prevented the minister from moving on to this cause, but Wigston and London clearly judged that since the government's parallel campaign against weirs had finally run out of steam, it was time to revive a different crusade to protect the weak and vulnerable.[19]

Next in Cromwell's catalogue of innovation is the development of official printed propaganda in English directed to a domestic reading public, followed by a keen interest in other varieties of mass communication such as public drama. The efforts started in 1531–2. To use the vernacular printing press was to take a leaf out of Sir Thomas More's book in more senses than one. Apart from his own massive and bitter literary output, the Lord Chancellor had been doing his best to enrol others in his campaign to defend the old Church. The strategy produced an impressive group of publications or republications of devotional works at this time, designed to steady the traditional faith of those unnerved by the evangelical eloquence of the likes of Tyndale.[20]

Most threateningly for evangelicals, Lord Chancellor More intimidated William Barlow, a cosmopolitan young evangelical scholar and Augustinian canon, into recanting his heresy, and then got him to write a well-informed denunciation of evangelicalism Europe-wide, including vivid personal observations of Germany's troubles. The book was published in 1531 by More's nephew and principal publisher as a *Dialogue of these Lutheran Factions*.[21] Notable were dark words which Barlow put in the mouth of his alter ego, the disillusioned returned evangelical traveller: 'I let pass my Lord Cardinal's act in pulling down and suppressing of religious places, our Lord assoil his soul. I will wrestle with no souls: he knoweth by this time whether he did good or evil.'[22] It was time to meet such printed fire with fire.

One distinctive feature of the Parliamentary session in winter and spring 1531 was a new departure in the King's Great Matter: the decision to present his case to a wider public. For the international audience, there was the *Censurae*, published in Latin just after Parliament's dispersal that spring. We cannot know whether all the various English tracts circulated in Parliament remained in manuscript, or whether some were put into print for convenience of distribution; no printed copies apparently survive. Nevertheless, from this point on, a new feature of the King's proceedings was a commitment to presenting his case to a native public in the language most of them would find easiest to read. During 1531, Thomas Cranmer was put to the formidable task of making an English translation of the whole of the Latin *Censurae*, which when it appeared in November was entitled *The Determinations of the most famous and most excellent Universities of Italy and France*. Cranmer bravely tried to make the *Determinations* an endurable read, and made some interesting choices of English words, including what may actually have been his own neologisms – 'context' was one which we still find useful, though 'caroginous' has not found so many admirers for its useful purpose in describing something which seems to be carrion. Cranmer also tweaked the content itself, reflecting his own developing evangelical agenda. It was perhaps Tudor England's first work of abstract theology put into print in the vernacular, so to move beyond the Latin of scholarship he was forced into becoming a linguistic pioneer.[23]

The next step was to publish works which a public literate in English might find more enjoyable to read than the dry arguments of the *Censurae*. This policy was implemented in 1532, as the new session of Parliament pushed forward the aggression against the Church which had been such a feature of the session in early 1531. The results hardly matched the flood of evangelical propaganda which Martin Luther had unleashed in Wittenberg after 1517, but in the bucolic atmosphere of the English publishing market there was little precedent for Tudor government to seize the initiative in sponsoring such literature for political or religious purposes, particularly for such a radical purpose as this. The one new mind at work on the intractable problem of the Great Matter definitely identifiable at this time was Thomas Cromwell's.

It may seem a large claim to put Cromwell at the centre of this new departure. After all, Thomas Cranmer was the translator of the *Censurae*, that first public English expression of the case for the annulment in print. By his later achievement in presiding over the drafting of two successive versions of the Book of Common Prayer in 1549 and 1552, the Archbishop did indeed make an extraordinary and lasting contribution to the development of the English language. Yet throughout Cranmer's career his undoubtedly exceptional gifts in the vernacular went very specifically into creating formal liturgical prose or works of academic theological argument. His efforts at entering the arena of popular propaganda, such as his answer to the West Country rebels protesting against the new Prayer Book in 1549, are not distinguished, and his version of the *Censurae*, despite its linguistic interest, is not out of line with that.[24]

Cranmer was not the man to initiate the first hesitant English imitation of Lutheran *Flugschriften*. The likelihood is that Cromwell was doing what he did so often in the next few years, nudging the King into an enthusiasm which Henry then made his own. Cromwell was not himself inclined to authorship, but he was a vigorous impresario of many other voices, directing an increasingly formidable output of official propaganda not merely in print, but in the pulpit and popular drama. His hour for such enterprise had come: for, as we have seen, by the end of 1531 the King was allowing him the power to shape official policy: an opportunity through which he shaped a near-decade of English politics, and much more beyond.

Certainly the mood quickened in 1532, perhaps as Cromwell was better placed to defy disapproval from conservatives like the Duke of Norfolk, and while More's oppositional literary production continued its relentless forward march to provide an incentive. Probably during the Parliamentary session of winter and spring 1532, an elderly burgess of Parliament for Dorchester called Jasper Fyllol published a racy pamphlet attacking in unashamed evangelical terms clerical arrogance and greed: *Against the Possessions of the Clergy*. Fyllol went so far as to say it was against divine law for clerics to possess landed property, a proposition of John Wyclif's condemned by a General Council of the Church more than a century before.[25] The sentiment matches very well the Lollard petition and its contemporary update which we have already contemplated as circulating in the 1532 Parliament.

Fyllol followed this up in 1533 with an anonymous second effort in the same style, *Enormities used by the Clergy*, which has the distinction of including the first description of Bishop Fisher infuriating Parliament by his speech in autumn 1529 (see above, pp. 95–7). Fyllol would have been an eye-witness to that, and he may also quote his own Parliamentary speech commending the 1532 Supplication against the Ordinaries, which would be a rare survival of what was said in an early Tudor Parliament. He certainly takes the highly risky step of ventriloquizing a biting address to the clergy by King Henry himself. Fyllol's subsequent career does not suggest self-destructive lunacy, but it does involve important service to Thomas Cromwell (see below, pp. 282–3). The pamphlets were published by a printer who can be found a little later enjoying Cromwell's patronage, and who in this venture might have needed the minister's reassurance that he would not suffer bad consequences. Fyllol's own spirited if unsuccessful attempt at the end of 1532 to get a lucrative office in the London Customs service by alleging corruption among the existing officers lodged itself in Cromwell's archive. It thus seems likely that these fiery tracts had Cromwell's encouragement within the bounds of deniability. Notably, despite their radical content, they never appeared on the frequent official lists of banned literature.[26]

Much more openly associated with the King was the appearance in September 1532 of a rather well-written tract called *A Glass of the Truth*, a dialogue between a lawyer and a divine, which did better with the English public than the *Determinations*, and was widely supposed to have been written by the King himself.[27] It was a selection from what could have been very dry material in that research-mine of historical sources, the *Collectanea satis copiosa*, but its inclusion of some discussion of the late Prince Arthur's sexual exploits probably helped to boost sales: no worries in 1532 about sparing Queen Katherine's feelings. Two years further on, in 1534, the likely principal editor of the *Collectanea satis copiosa*, Edward Foxe, further cannibalized the manuscript compilation for his magisterial *De vera differentia*. That was a much more substantial Latin (and therefore international) defence of what was by then the established royal supremacy in the Church, but in 1532 the *Glass* was addressed to a popular English audience, and got it, running to three editions in Henry's reign.

There is indeed direct evidence that Henry took a keen interest in the writing of the *Glass*, but as with all Henry's literary compositions someone else did the donkey-work. Correspondence in September 1532 puts Cromwell himself in the editorial seat, fielding nervous attempts of colleagues to get round the King's possessive refusal to consider revisions of the text as it was about to be published.[28] There was a particular reason for publishing it then: the *Glass* was the first of a pair of publications calculated to make the best of October's meeting of the Kings of England and France at Calais to discuss Henry's imminent Boleyn marriage (see below, pp. 206–9). This summit was not guaranteed to please the English public, tutored to see the French as their hereditary enemies, nor those politicians who for perhaps more sophisticated reasons preferred an English alliance with the Holy Roman Emperor. The meeting needed presentation.

In late summer 1532, the *Glass* was translated into French by Cromwell's old friend and his son's former tutor John Palsgrave. That was published at much the same time as the English version, no doubt for distribution during the Calais festivities. The royal ambassador in Italy, Nicholas Hawkins (another Putney boy, nephew of Bishop West of Ely), attempted a Latin translation that same autumn on Henry VIII's instructions, but he was clearly worried that the work was too racy and personal to launch on an international audience, and nothing came of that idea.[29] What did immediately come out for an eager London public – with a speed that must have taken some forethought, before Henry's return to England – was a slim but action-packed description of the meeting of the Kings: *The Manner of the Triumph at Calais and Boulogne*. Complete with an exciting cover-illustration of the King of France on horseback, it did well enough for a second edition with added lists of French notables to drool over. It was published by one of London's most committed evangelical printers, a protégé of Cromwell, John Gough, in partnership with the veteran printer Wynkyn de Worde. The pamphlet was a departure from Gough's normal religious fare; maybe he was the only printer available to do a rush job.

Naturally the content did not reveal those connections, which would have been beside the point, and it diplomatically made much of the Duke of Norfolk's part in the Calais proceedings, while failing to mention Master Cromwell. Yet the text did contain an interesting little piece of political spin: the description of the chief dance drew attention to 'my Lady Mary' without further identification, in a fashion which would have led casual readers to think that Princess Mary was present, which emphatically she was not. The Mary who was dancing was Anne Boleyn's sister Mary, who did not inspire the public affection enjoyed by her namesake. Forming a pair with the *Glass*, this instant-news pamphlet is a remarkable piece of government public relations in print.[30] From then on, the outpouring of print in the interests of both Henry's plans and Cromwell's own religious agenda seemed unstoppable until the royal minister's fall. We will find him extending this engagement with the public to the stage, previously so much the property of traditional religion (see below, pp. 416–20).

Cromwell's third major preoccupation from late 1531 was one we have come to expect from Thomas Wolsey's sometime agent: monasteries, including a small and tentative but unmistakable trial of further dissolutions. This was part of a wider programme of interfering in the internal affairs of the English Church. The extensive intervention in monastic life which he now resumed is the most striking example of the way in which between 1530 and 1534 he was given a great many responsibilities without any formal royal title. What Cromwell did in Church affairs in 1532 has such important implications for the remainder of his career that it is worth examining in detail, sending us on journeys the length and breadth of Henry VIII's kingdom. Master Cromwell himself will not be coming with us, for he is too busy now with undertakings for his Majesty in London and Westminster, but his friends and servants will be our companions, as they ride out to do his and the King's bidding.

The variety of ecclesiastical business on which the royal minister now launched himself reproduces fairly completely what he would do with explicit formal powers after 1534 as Vicar-General and Vice-Gerent in Spirituals. The work seems to have started suddenly in December 1531 and thereafter remained constant and frequent. It morphed seamlessly out of all he had done in the previous year to expand the royal estate for new royal palaces, particularly transforming York Place into Whitehall and expanding north of Westminster, with land purchases and exchanges, the latter mostly with religious foundations. From then on, his activity showed all the signs of the later omnivorousness of the Vice-Gerency: thus on 30 December 1532 Sir Edward Guildford wrote from Kent protesting at Cromwell's order to the trustees of a local chantry to dismiss its priest and replace him with someone whom Sir Edward considered thoroughly unsatisfactory. They would have to talk about it when he came up for the next session of Parliament, he said crossly. Why, he might have asked, would Cromwell the Clerk of the Hanaper and Master of the Jewels have become involved in such a trivial ecclesiastical matter?[31]

Guildford and Cromwell were friends, and Guildford a familiar figure at Court, but it is remarkable that the wider general public were also already aware of the minister's interest in Church affairs. Moreover, the public knew him as the enemy of the traditional Church hierarchy, and that general impression gave a fine opportunity to three West Country wideboys to exploit the naivety of an aged priest in the Blackdown Hills entangled in a local dispute. In late September 1532, they rode up from the Somerset Levels to stage a mock-arrest of the priest, claiming a 'special commandment' from Cromwell to bring him before the royal Council. Their demands for money were accompanied by blood-curdling threats: 'if he knew how sore Master Cromwell was against priests, and how grievously he handled them, he would rather spend all the goods he had than come before him, for he [Cromwell] was a man without any conscience against priests.' It was the following January before the poor cleric got the chance to complain against the unscrupulous trio, and the minister thus slandered filed this sad tale in his papers.[32]

Cromwell's current interference in Church affairs was led by his relations with monasteries, just as in the open evolution of the Vice-Gerency a couple of years later. First, in December 1531 and the beginning of 1532 came his steering of major exchanges of property between the Crown and three royal monasteries around London, Waltham Holy Cross, Westminster Abbey and the Charterhouse of Sheen: part of a complex set of such transactions, the non-monastic elements of which do not seem to have concerned him nearly so much.[33] Draft agreements survive in all three cases, that for Waltham being entirely in Cromwell's hand, as we have already noted (see above, pp. 164–5); subsequent negotiations there involved his trusted servant Ralph Sadler. Cromwell seems to have taken over the Westminster agreement at a late stage, since that draft inserts into a long list of legal worthies his own name (as 'one of the King's Council') and that of Attorney-General Hales, a pair who in the other deal with Waltham were actually the original agents.[34]

Straight away, however, one finds Cromwell doing far more than supervising land transactions and business; there are more than 150 exchanges of letters between him and heads of religious houses between 1532 and 1534.[35] Monastic heads regarded him as the best person to write to in time of trouble. So in July 1532 the Abbot of Jervaulx (Yorkshire) wrote to him, despite being 'unacquainted', in order to stop the Bishop of London from sending back a runaway monk expelled from Jervaulx some years before.[36] Cromwell routinely took the lead in settling the choice of monastic heads all over the country, for all the world as if he were Cardinal Legate like his old master, but now on behalf of the King; actually he was intervening more frequently than Wolsey had ever done. Simply for the year 1532, evidence for his interventions survives from St Bartholomew's Smithfield in London, Bruton, Montacute and Muchelney (all Somerset), Holm Cultram (Cumberland), Tilty (Essex), Vaudey (Lincolnshire) and St James Northampton, and no doubt these identifiable instances are only a part of the story.[37]

In the case of Muchelney, the appointment of a new abbot for this ancient Benedictine foundation was of an indecorously young monk in his twenties, and it was effected with substantial money arriving informally in Cromwell's pocket.[38] This was not something that happened much in the later years of his ascendancy. Cromwell was offered many bribes in his career; following up the outcome usually reveals that they were not taken or, if they were, they proved a wasted investment. Acceptance of the Muchelney bribe was perhaps the result of over-excitement at his new power, or perhaps a reflection of the fact that at this early stage of his career in royal service his minor formal office and modest estates meant he was short of money. Already many monasteries, gentry and nobility were setting up a regular fee for him, as one would to a legal consultant, often with a formal grant of nominal office. Presents, of course, were always acceptable. They oiled the wheels of early modern government, particularly if offered with a little self-deprecating joke, such as that of Bishop West of Ely in March 1533, who in regretting that he could not do a requested favour sent Cromwell 'a poor token of St Audrey' (founder-saint of his cathedral, from whose proverbially downmarket fair our word 'tawdry' derives). The present, not tawdry at all, could have been anything from a gold coin to a pie. What is missing in general from the evidence of Cromwell's finances is the huge bribe. That was not his style.[39]

Cromwell acted in both monastic and general Church business in concert with his great friend Roland Lee. We have met Lee before: a Northumberland man with a Cambridge doctorate in canon law, Cromwell's former colleague in dissolutions under Wolsey. Like Cromwell, Lee had been loyal to their old master to the bitter end – one strong element in their enduring friendship – and in the early 1530s Lee's gruff fondness for the early-teenaged Gregory Cromwell gave him a special place in the proud father's esteem.[40] That avuncular interest, which Lee extended to a variety of his own nephews and nieces, suggests a man whose clerical vocation did not include much sympathy for the cloistered life. Indeed, he was not an especially clerical clergyman (which may have commended him to Cromwell): Archbishop Cranmer distinguished him from various other possible Lees as 'Dr Lee the lawyer' when letting Ambassador Hawkins know of new episcopal appointments in December 1533.[41] Nor was the civil lawyer an enthusiastic preacher; on one occasion soon after becoming a bishop, Lee approached the task of preaching the royal supremacy with the gingerliness of a man who claimed to have been 'never hithertofore in pulpit'.[42]

Lee's letters to Cromwell sparkle with sharp humour, of which that last claim might be an example. The pair's informal rapport is perceptible even when Cromwell in his years of greatness, constrained by other demands and pressures, behaved high-handedly towards his old friend (see below, pp. 423–4). Lee brought an extensive northern gentry cousinage of Lees and others to his partnership with Cromwell, many of whom proved their usefulness in various ways, not least in giving Cromwell lines of communication into a part of the kingdom which he did not know personally. Now in 1531–2 their old co-operation in matters ecclesiastical revived, extending royal control over the Church in England, at the same time as Cromwell pushed forward that programme in Parliament.

The powers which were to become the Vice-Gerency and once had been Wolsey's as papal legate *a latere* were not as yet wholly in Cromwell's hands. There were various English monastic jurisdictions which the Cardinal had been able to override by virtue of his legatine powers, and which on the eve of a major confrontation with the Papacy now needed fresh attention. The Cistercian Order, for example, was part of an international corporation with its mother house in France at Cîteaux, and its current visitor was a Frenchman, the Abbot of Chaalis. Wolsey had substituted a homegrown Cistercian visitor, the Abbot of Waverley, but in April 1532 the King replaced Chaalis with a wider commission of English Cistercian abbots instead. This had happened before, but the royal commission justified it now by saying that it was not convenient to admit a stranger into the realm – a full year before the break with Rome. Despite that provision, the new mood of 1532 was such that Cistercians or their patrons wishing to challenge the abbots in royal commission turned to Cromwell; this happened at Bruerne, Vaudey and Tilty alike in 1532–3.[43] At the same time Roland Lee intervened in a developing crisis at Rievaulx Abbey in Yorkshire: he was the agent whereby his relative the Earl of Rutland, hereditary patron of Rievaulx, turned to Cromwell to get a judgment of the abbatial commissioners overturned.[44]

By contrast, the Premonstratensian Order was an exempt jurisdiction which the Crown could not override with the excuse of excluding a stranger from the realm, because very early in Henry VIII's reign the English Premonstratensians had patriotically secured exemption from their mother house in France and were therefore headed in the realm by the Abbot of Welbeck in Nottinghamshire.[45] Nevertheless it was to Cromwell, once more via Roland Lee, that the Master of Christ's College Cambridge turned about a Premonstratensian abbatial election at Coverham in Yorkshire. He wanted to advance a monk who was probably Roger Horsman, brother of a Fellow of Christ's by the name of Leonard Horsman (a Yorkshireman and himself already a client of Cromwell). Lee first approached Cromwell about Coverham in late 1531 or 1532. On that occasion, Cromwell was distracted by 'manifold business', perhaps diplomatically in order to avoid a face-off with Welbeck, but a little later Roger Horsman duly got his promotion as Abbot of Coverham, for a while, at least.[46] Working towards that goal, Lee made a shrewd effort to get his friend's interest focused back on what he represented as a troubled house, in the course of a long letter to Cromwell on New Year's Day 1533:

> There be two things to be remembered: one, the reformation of such enormities; the second, the interest of the King his Highness being founder there, whereby in that religion and Order of the Premonstratenses might as well something grow to the King's advantage as in other [orders], and that discreet father [the Abbot of Welbeck], as ye know, partly to be let of [prevented from exercising] his lordly jurisdiction.[47]

Lee thus alerted his friend to possibilities of neatly combining monastic reform with the clipping of abbatial wings: that was to be the hallmark of Cromwell's ecclesiastical policy over the next few years.

Alongside all these transactions, and perhaps concentrating the minds of the various monks involved in them, was what looks remarkably like an opportunistic programme of specimen dissolutions during 1532. This clutch of suppressions followed the profile of Wolsey's programme: one major monastery, in this case the large and prominent London Augustinian house

MAKING A DIFFERENCE: 1532

of Holy Trinity or Christ Church Aldgate. Alongside this equivalent of St Frideswide's Oxford in Wolsey's dissolutions came satellite suppression of small houses. In each case, there was a good reason: the houses were in trouble. Christ Church, despite its stately church and honourable position in the city (its Prior was an alderman *ex officio*), was deep in long-term debt. Its suppression came first and very suddenly in late February 1532, with Drs Roland Lee and John Oliver in charge of proceedings.[48]

A mark of the novelty of the action at Christ Church was the government's uncertainty about how to redeploy its redundant assets. In various suppressions over the previous 150 years, monarchs or churchmen had redeployed the estates and buildings of dissolved monasteries for new uses within the Church system, especially for chantry colleges, mostly at Oxford and Cambridge – Wolsey's being the last.[49] New chantries were not going to be founded now, particularly if Cromwell had anything to do with the disposals. One scheme (clearly mooted just before Christ Church's surrender, because it involved the then current royal exchange of estates with Waltham Abbey) was to make the priory the basis for a new city hospital. The memorandum survives in Cromwell's papers, together with a draft bill for the 1532 Parliament, but nothing came of it.[50] There was even less substance to a rumour that the troublesome Greenwich Observant Franciscans would be moved to the empty buildings; after their truculent sermonizing to the King at Easter 1532, that was never going to happen.[51]

Instead, the outcome at Christ Church anticipated the main programme of monastic suppressions. The beneficiary was a layman, Thomas Audley, gaining some of the income and property appropriate to a Lord Chancellor (a deficiency which sadly did not then cease to occupy his thoughts). Audley was a little uncertain of the proprieties in receiving this bonanza without exact precedent. He suggested to Cromwell that he would keep some liturgical use for the stately church, but that came to nothing after the neighbouring parish of St Katherine Cree refused to move their worship there, worrying about how permanent their title might prove to be. John Stow reminisced with some satisfaction that Audley's subsequent partial demolition of the church had been badly botched.[52] Despite all these as yet unsolved questions, the surrender in late February passed without major incident or protest in London, other than muted expressions of unhappiness such as those of St Katherine's parishioners. That must have emboldened Cromwell and his team for further efforts.

Roland Lee had other problems on his mind. Besides an increasingly heavy involvement in the legal side of the King's Great Matter, he currently led a team with a major ecclesiastical task: supervising on behalf of the King the diocese of Coventry and Lichfield, which covered a vast area of the west Midlands and northern Welsh borders. The aged Bishop, Geoffrey Blythe, died some time in late 1531. This initiative is in itself odd, because administration of a vacant diocese was the prerogative of the Archbishop of Canterbury, and indeed in the subsequent correspondence within the team we hear a mention of Archbishop Warham's official stoically carrying on his conventional visitation of Coventry and Lichfield *sede vacante* alongside Lee's own activities.[53] Lee's group of royal administrators was appointed (as was admittedly the King's right) to deal with the Bishop's 'temporalities' – his landed possessions as a subject of the Crown. They interpreted that brief as generously as they could, busying themselves with collecting clerical taxes which the old Bishop had allegedly maladministered, plus investigating his laxity over the treatment of prisoners in the episcopal gaol and irregularities around his will.[54] Evidently, as was becoming Cromwell's custom, they were pushing their luck.

Even more unusual was the accompanying circumstance that a process for making Roland Lee himself the next Bishop of Coventry and Lichfield began on 24 January 1532, but was not then completed until 1534, after the break with Rome and under a different archbishop, who in the course of his administration of that bizarrely prolonged process explicitly noted that there had been opposition to it.[55] What was going on? Lee was actually a natural choice for the diocese: he knew it well, having previously been Chancellor and Vicar-General to the late Bishop Blythe from 1525 to 1528. The stop-start nature of this process suggests that Lee's appointment was seen as a first attempt to break the power of the old Church hierarchy, but by making its move in January 1532 the Crown had struck too soon. As the tightlipped struggle around his preferment progressed, Lee headed the constitutionally odd royal team in the diocese regardless, and was evidently told to report direct to Cromwell. Their actions blatantly marginalized Warham's jurisdiction before any formal submission of the clergy had taken place, particularly in one respect: a further monastic dissolution.

The local team administrator was the Archdeacon of Salop, Richard Strete (who at the outset of their work called Cromwell 'my good master'). On 6 April 1532 Strete reported to Lee that the Prior of Calwich, a small Augustinian priory in Staffordshire, had just died, leaving only one canon in occupation.[56] Strete's follow-up letter to Cromwell of 26 April reported the house now void and therefore escheated to the Crown (this was stretching a point, given the continuing presence of the surviving canon). The following day he had an indenture drafted, granting Calwich to Ralph Longford, a minor courtier and prominent local gentleman, who claimed to be founder. After reciting Longford's claim, the deed rather confusingly proclaimed the King's intention 'the possession and inheritance to dispose and convert' (altered from 'descend and revert', thus radically changing the direction of the sentence) 'to other godly and charitable uses and purposes, after his Grace's intent'. The document was in fact a legal mess, ending up as a lease of Calwich at an economic rent (yet to be decided) to Longford or anyone else whom the King chose. Inept or not, if operative it removed the rights of any monastic founder other than the King.[57]

This was a remarkable precedent, but even when the team bothered to set up a formal 'office' or inquisition to complete the settlement (a month after they had declared Calwich void and taken an inventory of its possessions), that did not end the problems the little monastery raised.[58] Longford, alas, was not the only local man with a keen interest in the Calwich estate, for whatever the priory lacked in spiritual athleticism, its barns were full and its cattle fecund. More than a year later Cromwell was still being dragged into irritable correspondence on competing claims – 'I well perceive who granteth such men an inch they will take an ell,' he snapped to Archdeacon Strete.[59] And what would happen to the remaining canon? He was still hanging around Calwich when Cromwell wrote that letter to Strete in June 1533, and he must be sent to 'some good house of that religion being near unto you'. There did not seem much remaining of the King's 'godly and charitable uses and purposes'.

We have generous documentation on the Calwich affair, but only one letter survives to illuminate the obscure end of a little Augustinian priory in north Wales at Beddgelert in the same year. The mechanism for its suppression is not clear, since the local Bishop was still in place in 1532 and so there was no question of diocesan temporalities needing royal supervision as there was in Coventry and Lichfield. Beddgelert may simply have ended up with no canons, and thus escheated to the Crown within earshot of the nearby commissioners – maybe via that local boy and common friend of Cromwell and Lee, Master Ellis ap Rhys. News of its fading away reached as far as the household of the teenaged Princess Mary in Kent by 30 November of that year. Her leading servants, Margaret Countess of Salisbury and John Lord Hussey, wrote to Cromwell asking for a lease of the priory for one of the Princess's footmen, 'for that ye have the letting thereof'. Both signatories were destined to die on the block for defending the world of monasteries and traditional religion, but the fact that they had no hesitation in approaching Cromwell is another little indication that Mary's household did not regard him as a hostile force at this stage.[60]

The clinching proof of the link between Calwich and Beddgelert is that Cromwell bundled their supervision into one administrative job, which he kept personally under his wing. Many people knew this: so the Anglesey magnate Sir Richard Bulkeley riskily presented him with a fait accompli, sending his brother to occupy the tenancy of Beddgelert, relying on a previous face-to-face promise from Cromwell. This chutzpah unsurprisingly did not produce a long-term lease for the Bulkeleys, because soon Dominican Friar-Provincial John Hilsey was after it, for a Welsh protégé from his order studying at Oxford. Hilsey added diplomatically that Friar Griffith 'would have made friends to the King's Grace for the gift of the same, unless I commanded him the contrary, for to avoid and escape your Mastership's displeasure'.[61] It was no doubt with relief that in 1535 Cromwell formally handed over this tedious little task to John Gostwick, a gourmet of financial trivia as well as another former senior servant of Wolsey.[62] The fate of Beddgelert remained complicated and bound up in monastic tangles: first the Crown granted it out in January 1536 in a property exchange with a royal monastery, Chertsey Abbey in Surrey, and hence it passed in 1537 to the very last monastery founded in Henry's England, a new Bisham Abbey just up the Thames, which was actually only Chertsey moved to different buildings. When the refounded Bisham closed after only a year, Beddgelert Priory really was gone, leaving nothing but a modest parish church in a quiet Welsh valley.[63]

There is a possibility that a fourth monastery escaped these experiments in dissolution, thanks to some second thoughts from Cromwell: another little Augustinian house, at Hardham in Sussex. Bishop Sherburne of Chichester said gratefully in either late 1532 or 1533 that by Cromwell's 'prudent counsel and charitable words, the priory of Hardham (the which was decreed to have been suppressed) standeth and prospereth'.[64] This is a piquant compliment, since in 1525 Cromwell had been the means of stopping Bishop Sherburne himself from suppressing the similarly minor Augustinian priory at Shulbrede (see above, pp. 60–61). Sherburne's letter is annoyingly difficult to date precisely, with a chance that he was referring to Cromwell securing a reprieve of Hardham under Wolsey. The relationship between Hardham's survival and Cromwell's previous defence of Shulbrede Priory is thus difficult to recover, but a later deed preserves intriguing straws in the wind: Hardham really did meet its end in autumn 1534 in a collusive sale to its gentry patron – shades of Calwich – a transaction involving both Cromwell himself with his servants and friends, and some of the erstwhile local friends of Shulbrede. Before that extinction, just as at Shulbrede in 1525, the temporarily reprieved Prior of Hardham had gratefully granted Cromwell an annuity.[65]

There are clear common threads in the dissolutions of 1532. All concerned Augustinian houses. A problem for the Austin canons was the very flexibility and brevity of their Rule. What was an asset in the twelfth-century glory-days of their foundations was now their weakness, as an excess of small institutions languished both economically and in spiritual morale. Otherwise, all four cases were notable for the extreme untidiness of what happened to the assets of the unfortunate monasteries, and for the general drift towards their ending up in the hands of laymen. This latter result was a complete innovation in late medieval English monasticism – it had last happened in the Anglo-Saxon period, but it was now to be the dominant motif in King Henry's dissolutions.

From the late fifteenth century, a new attitude is perceptible towards struggling monasteries, best exemplified in that unsentimental monarch Henry VII. Between 1494 and 1507, he had likewise dissolved four semi-derelict monasteries for his own benefit, and although some of that benefit was for the wealth of his soul, material wealth also entered into his redeployments, for he extracted a tidy sum in three suppressions from the institutions which received their estates.[66] Yet still, the end-result was a redistribution for spiritual and educative purposes, as with Wolsey's suppressions. Now, in 1532, the rules had not simply broken down: as the untidy outcome of these four suppressions shows, they were being rewritten. Moreover, if monasteries with flourishing farms were to be disposed of on a large scale, and their remaining monks dealt with, there needed to be a system in place, with officials dedicated to handling such minutiae. It would not do to take up Cromwell's valuable time. All this was a lesson learned. The consequence, in 1536, was the Court of Augmentations.

It is not a new idea that the dissolutions of 1532 were a test of public reaction. That shrewd commentator Thomas Fuller, looking back in the 1650s to the end of Christ Church Aldgate, noted wryly that 'Some conjecture this was King Henry's design . . . to make a discovery in people's affections, how they resented the same. He dispatched this convent first . . . and if he had found the people much startled thereat, he could quickly knock off, retrench his resolutions, and (dexterous to decline envy for himself) handsomely cast the same on his instruments employed therein.'[67] That nicely nails King Henry's devious sense of self-preservation. Moreover, it is possible to see in the manner of these dissolutions a debate which resumed three years later, when the royal Councillors began considering really ambitious plans for resuming Wolsey's cull of small monasteries. Among the family papers of Cromwell's Kentish Protestant friends the Wyatts there survives a fragmentary reminiscence in a late Tudor account of the Reformation which is in other respects independently well informed.

Its story is that when the question of a major programme of dissolutions came up (from the context, in early 1536), Cromwell counselled caution on the King and his Council, with good reason:

> For when the late Cardinal Wolsey had obtained your Majesty's favour and licence of the Bishop of Rome to dissolve certain monasteries for the building of his Colleges at Oxford and Ipswich, yet the same (were it never so gently done and circumspectly used and that by one and one) was not done without some disquiet, as everybody knoweth. Wherefore mine advice is that it should be done by little and little, not suddenly by Parliament. And I doubt not but seeing how horrible this kind of religion [that is, the monastic life] is and how odious to the wiser sort of people, they may be easily persuaded to leave their [monastic] cowls and to render their possessions to your Majesty, by whose progenitors they were first erected.[68]

The writer then claims that Lord Chancellor Audley and his colleague the ambitious lawyer and civil servant Richard Rich prevailed against this advice, successfully arguing for a Parliamentary Act to dissolve the lesser monasteries and the erection of a Court of Augmentations to administer their wealth. Considering the vigorous Protestant partisanship throughout this manuscript, its story here is so out of line with the general Elizabethan exaltation of Cromwell as scourge of the monasteries that it deserves to be taken seriously. It fits exactly Cromwell's cautious mode of procedure in 1532. The leading role of Richard Rich corresponds to a remark of the French ambassador at the moment of Cromwell's fall in 1540, that Rich 'was first deviser of the casting down of abbeys and all that was newly done in the Church, so that he devised and Cromwell lent his authority'.[69]

In this policy discussion Cromwell was, as the anonymous writer pointed out, speaking from experience, including his uncomfortable time as scapegoat for popular fury against monastic dissolutions in autumn 1529. In 1532, amid his discreet suppressions, there had been the prudent snub to Audley by the parish of St Katherine Cree, and a rumble of discontented talk. That summer of 1532, for instance, Cromwell and his old London friend Alderman John Allen investigated a claim that on 24 July the Prior of the London Crutched Friars said to his guests in expansive mood over dinner 'that a certain religious man should come unto him who privily should say that the King's highness was determined to put down certain religious houses; adding these words, "that if he so did, whereas tofore he was called *Defensor Fidei*, he should be called *Destructor Fidei*"'.[70] This reflected what was actually going on that year, and was the precursor of much bilious comment to come. Cromwell would remember the Crutched Friars when urging caution in the policy debates of 1535. The anonymous narrator tells us that 'the rest of the Council, making the King believe he should at all times be able to repress easily all insolency and fury of the people, agreed it should be done by Act of Parliament.' Yet 'that [which] he [Cromwell] feared after came to pass': namely the Pilgrimage of Grace.

There is a festive tailpiece to all this monastic adventuring in 1532. Our journey now leads us to Cambridge and then to Norfolk. Among the slew of exchanges of land confirmed by Act of Parliament in 1532 consolidating Henry's royal estates around London was one between the Crown and Christ's College Cambridge: the Act recited a grant by the King on 2 January 1532, in return for the College's manor of Roydon in Essex, of yet another small Augustinian priory, Bromehill up in Norfolk Breckland.[71] It was then some three years since Stephen Gardiner, Roland Lee, Thomas Rush and Thomas Cromwell had wound up the affairs of Bromehill Priory for Cardinal Wolsey; so the tale links those earlier dissolutions to the fresh crop in 1532.[72]

The deal is interesting in a number of ways: first, it was the only one of the whole batch of exchanges from this time to involve an Oxbridge college. Second, the newly arrived Master of the College, Henry Lockwood, was not very happy about it, and sounds at odds with his own Fellows on the subject, describing it plaintively to Cromwell in the middle of its passage through Parliament as '*their* busy exchange of lands'. The fact that one of Lockwood's most senior and distinguished Fellows, Robert Gunthorpe, had long been Rector of the two churches in Weeting, the parish in which Bromehill lies, probably tells us all we need to know about that.[73] More interesting still are the intimate links between Cromwell and Christ's College at that moment. In 1534, the ever-lugubrious Lockwood reminded Cromwell that 'I was one of the first suitors to you after you were put in authority under the King's Grace.' If he had thought further about it, this was perhaps not the most tactful thing to say to a patron, but for us it at least suggests a first contact in summer 1531, as the College's land exchange was taking shape.[74]

Maybe Christ's had intended Bromehill as a summer or plague retreat as Poughley Priory had been for Cardinal College Oxford (they are in fact respectively about the same distance away), but this was not how it turned out: no less a person than Roland Lee intervened in June 1532, drafting a letter in his own hand for Cromwell to send to the Master, arranging a sixty-year lease of the Priory from the College for Roger Fowler, who was Lee's brother-in-law.[75] This was only one element in a skein of sudden associations between Cromwell, Lee and Christ's, at the

heart of which was the education of little Gregory Cromwell, who transferred from tuition at Pembroke Hall to Christ's at this time. Prioress
Vernon of Little Marlow was still keeping a jealous eye on her old charge,
vigilant in her agreement with Cromwell to retain control of Gregory till
he was twelve, but by 1532 she was doing so in amicable co-operation
with the Master of Christ's, who wrote from a visit to Marlow to report
Gregory as 'merry'. It must be said that this is the first phase of Gregory's
schooling which did not involve some sort of contention or trouble.
Cromwell even offered Henry Lockwood the rich London benefice of St
Sepulchre's Holborn in summer 1532, though in the end it was agreed
that Dr Lee would have it instead.[76]

At the end of that Michaelmas Term, Roland Lee cheerfully set out for
Norfolk from his Essex parsonage of Ashdon with 'your little man'
Gregory – 'not only well and cleanly kept, but also profits in his learning';
they were off to spend the vacation over Christmas and New Year into
1533 at Bromehill Priory, with some of Gregory's young friends from
Cambridge, hosted by Master and Mistress Fowler.[77] The following
August, 1533, Lee and Gregory were back at Bromehill with the Fowlers
for another holiday, which Lee certainly needed after an exceedingly
stressful though successful six months of royal business. He amused himself on that trip by directing Gregory's fumbling thirteen-year-old archery
practice on the deer in one of the Duke of Norfolk's nearby parks (with
permission, doubtless): 'the skins were so hard that the flesh would not
be hurt,' he reported back to Austin Friars with affectionate sarcasm.[78]

But let us finally return Dr Lee to Bromehill on New Year's Day 1533,
'among a husfull of childern, God help', as he groaned in mock-weariness
and vigorous northern orthography to Gregory's father back in London.
Surrounding Lee would be a bustle of Gregory and the Wellifed and Sadler boys, plus any small Fowlers; it was a decade or two before most
clergy of the English Church grew accustomed to such an experience.[79]
So with the Rector of Ashdon and his sister and brother-in-law enjoying
family festivities where once Austin canons had meditated, and shouts of
over-excited early teenagers echoing round derelict monastic chambers in
a Breckland winter, an old order gave place to the new world which
Thomas Cromwell was now steering into existence.

9

A Royal Marriage: 1532–1533

By summer 1532, there was no doubt that Anne Boleyn was on her way to marrying the King. The only question was when and how. She was installed in the house at Hanworth lately and briefly Stephen Gardiner's, very near Hampton Court, and her wardrobe was expanding to suit the role of a queen. Cromwell's varied royal building portfolio now included a radical refit of the royal apartments in the Tower of London, musty and old-fashioned at this time because their main customary use in late medieval England was as backdrop to the first stage in a coronation ritual, and the last coronation had been in 1509. In December 1532, Cromwell was host to King and prospective consort, accompanied by loyalist courtiers and the French ambassador, at his fiefdom in the Jewel House of the Tower, to show them both the rich display of plate selected for the Queen and how his modifications of the royal lodgings were progressing.[1] As the group of advisers round the King accepted with varying degrees of enthusiasm the royal determination to marry Anne and puzzled their way forward, they were dealt one ace: the death of Archbishop Warham in August 1532, forestalling defiance to which he seemed to have been nerving himself that spring.

Normally the vacancy of such a great and wealthy Church office would provide a year or so's windfall income for the Crown, but there was now a more important consideration: securing a compliant Primate of All England, who in the right circumstances might move the Great Matter to its conclusion.[2] The choice came speedily, and was possibly mooted before Warham's death, though apparently not to the man concerned. He was one of the leading chaplains of the Boleyn family, Thomas Cranmer, currently Archdeacon of Taunton, and since January far away on a strenuous embassy to the Holy Roman Emperor in Germany and Italy. Given the difficulties of early modern communication, it was the end of October before Archdeacon Cranmer heard of his promotion, apparently no less astonishing to him than to the rest of the political and ecclesiastical world beyond Anne Boleyn's bedchamber. This was more than just unexpected good fortune for Cranmer, but also a deep embarrassment, because that formerly very conventional cleric had by now travelled away from his quiet Cambridge days in more than one sense. During a prolonged stay that summer in the newly Lutheran city of Nuremberg, he did something almost as surprising as the King choosing him for archbishop, by marrying a local lady who was niece to Nuremberg's chief evangelical pastor, Andreas Osiander. It was his second marriage; the first, abruptly ended by his wife's death in his early Cambridge days, had taken place when he was still a layman, but the groom was now an ordained priest.

In marrying Margarete in Nuremberg, Cranmer defied four or five centuries of legislation in the Western Church extending celibacy from monks to secular priests: it was clearly a principled decision, which showed he had embraced evangelical reformation, for Margarete was not to remain a concubine like so many female companions of late medieval clergy, but became a lawfully wedded wife in the face of the world, alongside godly spouses of such reformers as Martin Luther and Martin Bucer. Yet the Archbishop-elect was not temperamentally inclined to dramatic public gestures (at least not till the last two hours of his earthly life), and he omitted to tell the authorities back in England about his new circumstances. For the time being, maybe for two or three years, Mistress Margarete Cranmer stayed with her relatives in Germany (and, when she did come to England, contrived to remain totally out of the public eye all through the 1530s). Now her new husband made his way with significant lack of speed back to England, to prepare for the throne of St Augustine and much more.

Meanwhile Cromwell was busily readying something more momentous than refurbishments at the Tower of London: diplomacy and choreography for the extraordinary international summit between France and England across the Channel in autumn 1532, a jamboree without parallel since his old master Wolsey had been impresario of the meeting of King Henry and King François at the Field of the Cloth of Gold a dozen years before. The principal actors were the same as in 1520. The English aim was to secure explicit French acceptance of the coming marriage in the most direct way possible, by presenting the French King in decorously festive company with Madame Boleyn before the eyes of a whole continent. The choreography was delicate in the extreme, involving the exchange of royal jollities both on the English soil of Calais and in the adjacent French fortress town of Boulogne.

The French had every interest in binding Henry VIII into the alliance they were patiently constructing against the Habsburgs. He would be a major catch in comparison with the German princes, mostly Lutherans, who had so far been the object of King François' diplomacy.[3] Yet the French were also perfectly well aware how much less they had to gain than the English from any agreement at Calais. Too splendid a reception of Anne would jeopardize French plans for an alliance with the Pope which would itself outflank the Habsburgs. It is likely that King Henry actually proposed holding a wedding ceremony in Calais, but then received emphatic advice from the French that this was a step too far. Out of such considerations, magnificence of display was curtailed, but there was splendour enough, and the event was instantly trumpeted in print for an English audience.[4] Amid the elaborate preparations, it would be useful to confuse suspicious ears in southern Europe until all was safely done: this was achieved by that most effective of counter-intelligence devices, false news. Cromwell's own spy Dr Augustine reported to his patron from Bologna that he had heard the meeting had been put off or even cancelled – this on 14 October, three days after the King and Anne sailed to Calais.[5]

An essential preliminary step had been to raise Anne's formal status to a level fitting for one about to enjoy polite conversation with the Most Christian King. Accordingly, on 1 September 1532, she became a peeress in her own right: Marquess (not Marchioness) of Pembroke – an honour modelled on Henry's elevation of Edward IV's niece Margaret Pole as Countess of Salisbury in her own right, twenty years before. Irony runs as a constant stream through Henry VIII's reign: he would eventually dispatch both peeresses he had created to be beheaded in the Tower. But for the time being the Marquess, her title given substance by lands of princely value, had her moment in the October sun with the French King, including a carefully arranged invitation to step through a pair of dances. It was time for Anne finally to bestow her ultimate thanks on her suitor for her extraordinary advancement. At some stage in this adventure, after six years of technical continence, she and Henry at last fully consummated their love. Maybe they did even stage some discreet form of betrothal or marriage in November, having for the time being abandoned the possibility of a public event. Bearing in mind the difficulties that still lay ahead, one peculiarity of the Marquess's already peculiar title was that it would descend to a son of hers even if born outside wedlock; this putative boy would have similar status to Henry's existing illegitimate son the Duke of Richmond.[6]

All this was a triumph for Cromwell. Among nearly 3,000 English hangers-on accompanying the King across the Channel, from the Duke

of Norfolk downwards, he was officially still a low-profile figure, not even
possessing a knighthood: the meticulous local chronicler who adored
listing notables did not name him in an exhaustive and exhausting catalogue of the company who crowded the town.[7] Yet he was the man who
worked out the finance, dipping into the King's ready reserves in his
capacity of Master of the Jewels to send 2,000 pounds directly over to the
Vice-Treasurer of Calais; there must have been much expenditure besides
this to put in place.[8] By now his real role in the King's affairs meant that
he accompanied the royal party to Boulogne on the male-only venture to
the French Court, while the Marquess of Pembroke was left to amuse
herself in Calais. A dissident friar from the Greenwich Observant Franciscans took the opportunity to have a confidential conversation with
him in Boulogne.[9] Thomas Alvard, left behind at Whitehall and keeping
him up to date with London news, observed with friendly envy, 'I am
very glad to hear the good report how the King's Grace hath you in so
great favour, and the French king also . . . and also of your housekeeping,
it is showed me there is never an Englishman there, the King's grace
except, that doth keep and feast Englishmen and strangers as ye do.'[10]
Even allowing for a good friend's exaggeration, this is quite a compliment, since there was considerable competition for lavish hospitality.

Given that as yet Cromwell had little income from rolling acres to sustain this sort of expenditure, this was also a calculated financial risk, but,
for a Putney yeoman's son who in the course of those events won the
good opinion of a monarch far more powerful than the King of England,
it was well worth it. He took with him his own set of musicians, useful
to enhance his hospitality.[11] He made careful advance provision for himself in lodging and catering, because such an occasion was obviously
going to strain the limited resources of Calais to breaking-point. His old
friendships there gave him an advantage. John Benolt, genial secretary of
the town, was chief among them (John's brother Thomas was the Clarenceux herald who had granted Cromwell his coat of arms). The Benolt
brothers arranged well ahead for the Marshal of Calais, Sir Edward
Ringley, to find Cromwell a good lodging, with stabling and that all-
important amenity for this festive trip, 'a cellar for your drink . . . and all
in one house' (not surprisingly, Cromwell made sure that John Benolt
was soon handsomely rewarded with further lucrative preferment).[12]

Despite the thoroughly satisfactory outcome, the journey to Calais
and Boulogne represented a turning-point in Cromwell's life: for a man
who had travelled more than nearly all his countrymen, it was his last
venture beyond English shores. Henceforth he was tied to the King's
journeys, which despite occasional more expansive plans were themselves

confined during Cromwell's lifetime to lowland England and usually just the counties round the capital. More frustratingly still, he might be left behind in London when the King went holidaying into deep country. It was symptomatic that at what was to prove an anxious Christmas and New Year 1532/3 he had not been able to join Gregory with Dr Lee and the Fowlers at Bromehill, despite Lee's hopes. He would never go to Ireland, maybe never again visit northern England nor even Wales, that part of the kingdom with special resonance for him. In Wales, thanks to family and friends, he had ample and effective eyes and ears, but in Ireland and the North, he was much more at a disadvantage, constantly relying at a distance on the perceptions and agendas of others.

The spectacle of Calais was safely past, but further pieces of the jigsaw remained. Cranmer must be retrieved in safety from his year-long mission, escorted home, installed as Archbishop of Canterbury and set to work to give a public face to what may already have become a royal marriage. Late on Sunday 1 December, Cromwell hastily sent off his old servant Stephen Vaughan for this task, ordering him to ride through the night to Dover and take a boat to Calais on Monday as soon as it was light. The urgency and secrecy of the task are remarkable, and may reflect a sudden decision by Anne that she was pregnant. From Dover, Vaughan had a wretched Channel crossing and a worse journey to Paris, including a bad fall with his horse in frozen weather. To add to his troubles, he had no idea where 'the man' (as he cryptically referred to his quarry) might be. It was eight days after his departure, in an inn at Lyon, that the first news came of the elusive envoy, around 30 miles off. Vaughan could at last fulfil his mission to convey a highly confidential oral message to the Archbishop-to-be.[13]

Despite Vaughan's optimism that they might be back by Christmas, Cranmer managed to prolong the journey till the beginning of January 1533. On the 24th or 25th of that month there was a clandestine royal wedding in Westminster, possibly the second between Henry and Anne (after all, in his own eyes, he had been a bachelor, free to marry whom he liked). Roland Lee may have been the presiding priest. Cranmer, meanwhile, took up residence next to Whitehall in lodgings of the canons of St Stephen's Chapel, handy for consultations on the next legal and theological moves and convenient for his attendance at the imminent meetings of Convocation and Parliament.[14] It was worth investing in the considerable sums of money necessary to obtain the papal bulls for his coming consecration as Archbishop, so that all should seem to be done properly and without the possibility of challenge. Since Cranmer had nothing like enough cash, he was loaned a thousand pounds by the King from the

Privy Coffers via Cromwell in his capacity as Master of the Jewels. It was processed through one of Cromwell's Italian friends in London, the Genoese merchant Arrigo Salvago, who would be accustomed to arranging such large international transactions.[15]

From now on, Cromwell and Cranmer enjoyed an intimate cooperation which went beyond business. As we have seen, their relationship had evolved over four years or so from administrative transactions at Ipswich, and now a genuine trust and affection overcame the delicacy of their allegiances to two conflicting patrons. Alexander Alesius or Alane, an Anglophile Scotsman who knew the Court of Henry VIII well, later told Queen Elizabeth that when King Henry made Cranmer Archbishop of Canterbury he presented him with a ring that had once been Cardinal Wolsey's, a ring which Alesius now possessed; that would have been a resonant gift.[16]* Cranmer never became another Wolsey for Cromwell – it was rather the other way round – but the special nature of their relationship is illuminated by an archival paradox worth exploring.

When Richard St George, an early seventeenth-century herald and antiquary, decided to fill blank pages in an old notebook he owned with his own genealogical collections, he saved from destruction a century-old letter-book of Archbishop Cranmer's, running from the Primate's entrance into office in spring 1533 through to summer twelve months on, plus a few later items.[17] Evidently as Cranmer took up unfamiliar and daunting new responsibilities, he decided to get a grip on them as did many conscientious Tudor gentry: he ordered his secretary to copy outgoing letters into this book, together with a little relevant incoming correspondence to act as templates for future imitation (the most interesting of which is a rare official letter of the King's elder brother Prince Arthur, from just before his death in 1501 – maybe Cranmer thought it might be useful in the Great Matter).[18] The collection is extraordinarily varied, from matters of national importance to trivial business of his domestic establishment, though there is nothing strictly private: this was a document designed for use and consultation. It is probable that, as the Archbishop gained more confidence in his office, he decided he could do without such an aid; certainly in the later months the original intention of keeping the collection thematic began breaking down and clashed with chronological copying.

The volume's contents have one remarkable feature: an almost total absence of the Archbishop's letters to Cromwell. Of Cranmer's 111 outgoing

* Alane had changed his birthname with humanist affectation to the biographically resonant Alesius, a version of the Greek for 'wanderer', and I will use this name for him hereafter.

letters, only one in the main period of the collection is addressed to the royal minister, and this in a period during which we actually possess no fewer than seventeen original letters from the Archbishop to Cromwell in the State Papers, surviving from what was obviously an intense correspondence. Of those seventeen, on three separate occasions Cranmer wrote twice to Cromwell on the same day.[19] There is only one plausible explanation for this absence: a second letter-book contained Cranmer's letters to Cromwell, probably supplemented by the Archbishop's letters to the King. After three letters to King Henry, the existing book has fifteen blank pages (in which St George wrote his notes), as if an early decision was made not to carry on entering such material, but thereafter to put them elsewhere. Another strong indication is that at folio 47 the clerk has written out a complete address for a letter to Cromwell, and then nothing further, as if he then realized he had inadvertently picked up the wrong letter-book, and so moved to enter his copy in the other one. Alas, Cranmer's second volume joined so many of his papers in oblivion.[20]

A pair of ultimately incompatible ideals united Cranmer and Cromwell: loyalty to the King and the furthering of evangelical reformation. In view of Henry's capricious approach to theology and frequent religious traditionalism, this was never going to be an easy combination to manage. On the second matter, Cranmer could always write in an unbuttoned fashion to his colleague about promoting godliness and the Gospel, but there was a marked difference between them. Cranmer was totally unwavering in his enthusiasm for the cause. For him, the recent convert, the world divided into strivers after truth and deluded or depraved followers of Antichrist, although his gentle and thoughtful disposition meant he could always hope for the deluded to be persuaded to follow the path of righteousness (he was a predestinarian, and believed God would guide those whom he had decreed for salvation). The Archbishop's household and the clergy associated with it were consistently aggressive in their evangelicalism; each promotion of Cranmer's clients was a little pinprick against false teaching in the Tudor Church, and there was no comfort for those of traditional religious outlook from him.

Cromwell was both more flexible and more ruthless than Cranmer. It was all very well for a priest and a former Cambridge don to enjoy his ideological purity; the politician was managing a far more complex job, doing the dirty political work he was sparing Cranmer. The Archbishop only really learned the art of political survival when he had to, after Cromwell had been brought to the scaffold. In subsequent crises he did acquire a hard-headed toughness in public life which met its match only in the wholly unexpected national reversal of direction on Edward VI's death. In tussling with the growing pile of business on his desk, Cromwell had much to weigh up and balance beyond the concern of his high-minded colleague.

Cromwell's picaresque life and clubbability brought him plenty of traditionalist-minded friends. There were not only folk from Putney days, up the social scale as far as Bishop West of Ely, but a throng of convivial relationships acquired in his peripatetic service under Wolsey. It was in fact this latter group who provided the main supporters for his entrance into the King's service. Only a fool would have abandoned such good friends now, and it is arguable that only a knave betrays friendships solely to promote an idea. In any case, Cromwell's theological radicalism perhaps already not only outstripped that of the Archbishop of Canterbury, but also outran what would ever be possible to change in Henry's realm, even with the extraordinary powers over the Church that the royal Councillor was now steadily acquiring.[21]

One personal clash in Cromwell's circle is especially revelatory of his multiple loyalties in his years of power: an astonishing outburst of pique from his old servant and friend Stephen Vaughan over the nomination of Cromwell's other great friend, Roland Lee, to be Bishop of Coventry and Lichfield. Vaughan was not himself immune to the pull of family over conviction: he was very fond of his wife's brother, the talented priest-musician John Gwynedd, whose traditionalist outlook must have been apparent to him, but whom he consistently commended to Cromwell for promotion.[22] Despite this, his attack on Roland Lee, written from Antwerp on 1 November 1533, by which time Lee's prospective advancement was public knowledge, is an extreme example of Vaughan's lack of proportion, and of a propensity for self-righteous ranting which in the end curtailed his own career.[23]

Vaughan appended his philippic against Lee to a plea to be recalled from a long and unrewarding tour of diplomatic duty in the Low Countries; a lesser man would have realized this was not an ideal combination. 'That which follows is superfluous, though my mind is such as condescendeth not to silence,' he began ominously:

> You have lately holpen an earthly beast, a mole, and an enemy to all godly learning, into the office of his damnation: a Papist, an idolater, and a fleshly priest unto a Bishop of Chester.* Remember God in all your facts

___

* That is, Bishop of Coventry and Lichfield, then informally known as Bishop of Chester, the city where his cathedral had formerly been situated. The present diocese of Chester dates only from 1541, and its cathedral is the former abbey church of St Werburgh; the Norman former cathedral of St John is a thrilling fragment on the other side of the city.

[deeds], let no affections of persons lead you to condescend or work so evil a deed. You cannot undo that you have done . . . Who knoweth more of the Bishops' iniquity than you? Who knoweth more of their tyranny, false-hood and untruth against God, prince and man than you? And should you help ['in this time specially', Vaughan added as an afterthought] to increase the number of wicked men where there is a lack and so great a need of good and virtuous men? Be you sorry for it, and help him with your good counsel, for I am more sorry for this deed done by you than for all the things that ever I knew you do.

'I write not for any malice to the man whom you have so holpen, but rather to show you my judgement therein,' Vaughan continued – the cry of the passive-aggressive in every age – and after much moralizing on true friendship he rounded off with 'fare you well with long continuance and increase of all your godly enterprises.' The parting barb was in the 'godly', and his 'mole' insult is a striking image for Lee's traditionalist blindness in religion.

What jealous incomprehension of a rival friendship resounds through this diatribe! It would not be the last time he exploded in indignation against his patron, and one has to admire his courage, when more and more of the pile in Cromwell's in-tray resounded with sycophancy. Vaughan's next letter from the Low Countries three weeks later was not-ably and uncharacteristically brief, after receiving a letter from Cromwell as usual now lost, but which we may suppose told him in no uncertain terms to mind his own business.[24] It was hardly surprising that Cromwell ignored Vaughan's ill-natured eloquence, not least given the obvious rap-port between Roland Lee and Gregory Cromwell. Yet it is also a tribute to the minister's forbearance that after this he went on using Vaughan on the same sort of diplomatic and general tasks as before, and even put him in the way of minor promotions.

We glimpse here the awkward faultline separating Cromwell's gentry or clerical friends of Wolsey days from his older circle of godly mercantile Londoners like Vaughan. Archbishop Cranmer did not face similar div-ided loyalties as he joyfully exploited his new resources and promoted his own godly Cambridge friends to infuse the archiepiscopal machine of the Province of Canterbury with evangelical purpose. Nevertheless, the rap-port between minister and Archbishop did begin to draw together the various evangelical circles. Not completely: as we have seen, Cromwell's reconciliation with Anne Boleyn's evangelical clientage did not extend to Thomas Goodricke (even though Cranmer consecrated Goodricke and Lee as bishops on the same day, 19 April 1534), nor did it include Anne's almoner John Skip.[25] Other evangelicals benefiting from Anne's favour probably had pre-existing and separate acquaintance with Cromwell from Cambridge. The most important was Hugh Latimer, whose frequent letters to Cromwell throughout the 1530s were enlivened with the same sort of savage and informal wit as Roland Lee's, albeit with a swaggering godliness. Latimer and Lee had a rather similar hand, rapid and semi-italic, which seems to have been common among academics arriving in the universities around the turn of the century. Both clearly enjoyed dispensing with a secretary when writing to Cromwell.

Now Parliament must meet again, to make its contribution to the matrimonial jigsaw. As in 1531, foreign affairs caused its prorogation through autumn 1532 – in this latter case, the King's absence in Calais. Before leaving London for that diplomatic fiesta, Henry decided on a further date of 4 February 1533, which as Lord Keeper Audley observed to Cromwell in October 1532 was 'a very good time, for it is about the midst of Hilary Term, and the days then shall wax somewhat fair again' (a saving on morning candles, in other words).[26] Audley finally got his eagerly anticipated promotion to Lord Chancellor a week before Parliament reconvened. This had consequences: now he presided over the Lords rather than the Commons, in place of Sir Thomas More.

Audley's substitute as Speaker of the Commons was Humphrey Wingfield, an appointment reeking of Cromwell's contrivance, since Wingfield was a friend from Ipswich days and former senior legal consultant for Wolsey.[27] Cromwell, Audley and Wingfield were tasked with passing legislation to give Archbishop-elect Cranmer powers to declare the Aragon marriage null. The vehicle of this final solution of Henry's obsession was an Act 'in Restraint of Appeals' to any jurisdiction beyond the realm, taking the sting out of Queen Katherine's appeal to the Pope. But before that measure was launched on Parliament there were other matters to attend to.

Cromwell made meticulous preparations for what past experience suggested would be an extremely testing session. One apparent innovation had lasting significance: a regular system of what were later called by-elections, to replace MPs who could no longer sit (usually because they were dead). Accordingly, in summer 1532 Cromwell got the Clerk of the Crown to give him an annotated list of current membership. He then handed over the list not to a member of Lord Keeper Audley's staff, which would have been the correct procedure for such a piece of paper, but to a Crown official with whom he was developing a fruitful administrative relationship: Thomas Wriothesley, Clerk of the Signet. Wriothesley drew up a list of seats to be filled, and so they were, in time for the new session of Parliament in February 1533. One of these new MPs was Cromwell's friend Thomas Alvard, left high and dry when spurned by the electors of Orford back in 1529. Cromwell went on attending to such vacancies: one of his memoranda in October 1533 preparatory to yet another session of this Parliament was 'The new election of such burgesses, knights, and citizens as are lacking in Parliament'. The practice of choosing replacement MPs through by-elections became one grievance raised in the northerners' Pilgrimage of Grace in 1536, though one feels that as a cause of major national rebellion it was a bit of a makeweight.[28]

Such by-elections were a necessary innovation in a Parliament which eventually sat over an extraordinary and unprecedented seven years. Yet this apparently minor piece of administrative creativity was also the outward sign of the momentous decision of the 1530s. In these years there was so much business of national importance and controversial character being transacted that it would have been foolish to impose it on the kingdom by royal fiat. Rather, it demanded the appearance of consensus, even initiative, from the highest assembly of the realm. As a result of this need, it was during the 1530s that the assembly of 'commons' became a 'House' with a status equal at least in terms of function to the Lords, and most legislation was introduced in the Commons. Soon afterwards in 1548 it acquired its own permanent chamber in the Palace of Westminster.[29] Official propaganda and public pronouncements put out through these years fully exploited this rhetoric of consensus in a variety of ways, emphasizing the active role of Parliament in a manner with little precedent.

The customary form of opening for a Parliamentary statute was some variation on 'Be it enacted by the King our Sovereign Lord and the Lords Spiritual and Temporal and the Commons in this present Parliament assembled and by authority of the same, that . . .'. Several of the most important statutes of the early 1530s changed this formula, to suggest an approach by subjects to the sovereign; that was the form of 'English Bills' initiating a lawsuit in Chancery or in the prerogative courts such as Star Chamber and Requests, on which the form of privately introduced bills in Parliament was traditionally based. It may not be coincidental that these were the courts Cromwell had known best as a practising lawyer. So the first Act of Succession in 1534 (which we will scrutinize later) took the form of a petition to the King from 'your most humble and obedient subjects the Lords Spiritual and Temporal and the Commons in this present Parliament assembled'. They demanded action 'to foresee and provide for the perfect surety of both you and your most lawful succession and heirs . . .'. Similarly, some of the most important royal proclamations of this period studiously linked themselves to previous Parliamentary action. So the proclamation depriving Queen Katherine of her royal style on 5 July 1533 referred back to legislation by the 'common assent' of the recent Parliament and the two Convocations. The King, in this constructed pageant, was a wise and thoughtful ruler, listening to the worries and fears of his subjects and giving them judicious remedy.[30]

This intensive use of Parliament in the 1530s, a crucial moment in its consolidation and growth when many other such assemblies in Europe were atrophying, had implications not merely for the religious future of Tudor England, but for the shape of national history thereafter. When, over the next 400 years, other European commonwealths evolved into something like nations, it was usually through an exercise of will by monarchs who felt little need of their medieval representative assemblies. Cromwell the Parliamentary veteran is the most likely candidate for having promoted Parliament in the kingdom of England at this moment. It is much less likely that his plans encompassed later centuries, and there was another immediate negative consequence. If the official theory of the 1530s ran that the realm was united with one voice as expressed in Parliament, once this expression had been made anyone dissenting was not a true subject, or churchman, lord, knight or burgess. The fate of such individuals could be dire. If Cromwell crafted the rhetoric, he was also put in charge of enforcing the consequences.

Given the stormy atmosphere of the 1532 Parliament, there is no doubt that Cromwell would have done his best to influence in a useful direction the choices of replacement MPs for the new Parliamentary session, though the ability of the Crown to achieve perfect obedience was strictly limited. The Lords too were augmented with compliant votes. The Abbot of Burton-on-Trent was summoned for the first time in Burton Abbey's history, but then he was Thomas Cranmer's good friend William Benson alias Boston, already involved in the preparations for annulment legislation, and in any case about to be rewarded with promotion to Westminster Abbey. Benson did not actually actually sit in the Lords as Abbot of Westminster till the following session of Parliament a year later, so this summons was anticipating that promotion, with Cromwell's usual creative distortion of precedent. The King also used his latitude in summoning to the Lords to bring in three eldest sons of noblemen (Lord Rochford most senior among them) plus one young peer lately a concern of Cromwell's during his wardship, Lord Monteagle, who was retrieved from his home in the North despite a previous dispensation not to attend.[31]

Then there was the crucial bill itself. The future Act in Restraint of Appeals took a great deal of drafting and redrafting, which may have started even before the King left for Calais in autumn 1532: eight full drafts and four fragments survive in the State Papers, littered with corrections, mostly Cromwell's but including contributions from Henry himself.[32] Its predecessor was a rather less ambitious bill drafted by Thomas Audley which simply dealt with 'the King's matter', narrating the trouble that he had been put to, providing for the two English archbishops to decide the matter and enjoining the realm to ignore any sanctions imposed on it by Rome. This was scrapped, and the earliest version of the eventual legislation substituted, which sidestepped the immediate issue of Henry's case and turned negative defiance towards a positive general statement of why the Papacy was irrelevant to any such case. It achieved the remarkable feat of not mentioning either Katherine of Aragon or Anne Boleyn, or marriage to either of them.[33]

That first draft already contained the resonant opening preamble already quoted on England's status as an empire, proved by 'sundry old authentic histories and chronicles', but also had a great deal more abuse of the Pope than was thought politic in the final version. Not only might that have offended some members of Parliament to no good purpose, but it was unwise when simultaneously seeking the papal bureaucracy's co-operation with the legal formalities to get Cranmer his Archbishopric. In fact in the end the papal nuncio was invited to Parliament's opening ceremony on 4 February, which might have been intended to suggest to the gullible that the Papacy did not disapprove of the forthcoming Boleyn marriage.[34] Nevertheless, one of Cromwell's subsequent corrections which did last into the text of the Act was his alteration of 'the See Apostolic' to 'the See of Rome'; this was a hint much taken up in Protestant England when the Pope was commonly (and, it has to be said, accurately) called 'the Bishop of Rome'. Contrariwise, in the drafts Cromwell repeatedly and in the end successfully removed references which the King liked (and kept putting back) to the proposition that all jurisdiction in English law was 'derived and depended of the imperial Crown of this realm'. That might be a clear expression of the proposition behind this legislation, but it was a real hostage to fortune in the rough and tumble of Parliamentary debates, and best left out.[35]

Dogged opposition continued in and out of Parliament, and the finished version of the bill was only introduced into Parliament as late as 14 March, the beginning of some fraught weeks. Cranmer, now armed with those very expensive papal bulls, was meanwhile consecrated Archbishop in St Stephen's Chapel in the Palace of Westminster on 30 March. The ceremony did credit to no one present, being conducted under papal authority which at several stages in the proceedings Cranmer formally rejected if it

Parliamentary bills were customarily drafted in double space for emendation. On this page of a draft of the Act in Restraint of Appeals, King Henry himself inserts 'and off and fromme the sayd imperiall crowne and non otherwyse' into the text of the bill.

clashed with his duty to God and the King. On 1 April the new Primate of All England took his place in the chair across the road in Convocation, a week before a not overwhelming majority in the clerical assembly agreed to accept the King's dismissive view of a papal dispensation to marry one's deceased brother's wife.[36]

Then finally a hardly altered bill became the Act in Restraint of Appeals that first week in April. Rome had lost its role as ultimate court of spiritual appeal in the realm. Katherine was henceforth to be styled the Princess Dowager, and her daughter the Lady Mary, while her most prominent champion in the capital, Bishop Fisher, was put under house arrest in the care of Bishop Gardiner. No public announcement was made about when the King's latest wedding had taken place. On Holy Saturday, 12 April, the Queen of England processing in regal finery at Court to the Vigil Mass of Easter was Anne Boleyn.[37] On Easter Day Prior George Browne, Cromwell's landlord at Austin Friars, used his festal sermon or liturgical bidding of the bedes to pray for Anne as Queen, at which a large section of the congregation marched out in protest,

Cromwell's emendments on the penultimate draft of the Act show him underlining for removal various phrases, including 'deryved and dependeth frome and of the same Imperiall Crowne', and producing a more concise text. The King's emendments did not survive into the final Act.

provoking Henry to fury and prohibition of any further such demonstrations in the City. It was his second Easter in a row soured by public criticism of his marriage plans.[38]

In the flurry of events still necessary to get to the finishing line, Cranmer now had the starring public role, with Cromwell barely visible, though one can glimpse some frenetic scrambling in the background.[39] In the very delicate business of the Primate's letter summoning the newly minted Supreme Head of the Church to an ecclesiastical court hearing, to end the public scandal of his supposed Aragon marriage, there is no manuscript trace of Cromwell intervening.[40] Likewise, trusting to the competence of Cranmer and archiepiscopal staff, he did not attend the hearing of the royal case during May at Dunstable Priory, relying on reports via the ecclesiastical lawyer Thomas Bedell, whom the King had poached from senior office in the Archbishop of Canterbury's administration immediately after Warham's death. Bedell was now a loyal satellite of Cromwell, and later became his chaplain.[41] While Cranmer was busy at Dunstable, the assent of the Northern Convocation in York needed to be secured. Cromwell entrusted this task to Roland Lee, a sensible choice in view of Lee's northern links and the likely awkwardness of some of the northern senior clergy. Lee did his job with his usual brusque efficiency, against some initially formidable opposition.[42]

In the middle of all this delegation is a fascinating glimpse of what made Cromwell so adept at negotiating the opening years of his rise to power. At the height of his busyness, he took an evening off to throw a cheerful supper-party for the Duke of Norfolk's sister Anne Dowager Countess of Oxford. Dr Lee, a close neighbour of hers in north-west Essex, and a man who knew how to have a good time, warned him of that redoubtable lady's imminent descent on the capital for coronation duties: 'I am always bold of you for remembrance of your lovers and mine . . . my good Lady of Oxford . . . comes to the Court upon Sunday, and intends to be merry with you Monday or Tuesday [28 or 29 April 1533] at supper, only to be merry and give you thanks of your goodness; praying you for my sake, the rather so accept her. She is a woman of high wit, and loving to her friends.' Cromwell had a way with dowagers, as we have already seen. Lady Oxford was lavish in her thanks afterwards for 'your great cheer, and also for your kindness to me showed' – he would go on doing her favours.[43]

The last tessera was placed into the mosaic in a very discreet ceremony at Lambeth Palace, which symbolized the new partnership of Cranmer and Cromwell in achieving the long-sought aim. At Dunstable on 23 May, Cranmer had delivered his sentence on the invalidity of the King's marriage to Katherine of Aragon. On Wednesday 28 May, now back at Lambeth, the very day before the coronation festivities began, he complemented that decision by declaring valid the previous royal wedding to Anne.[44] This took place 'in a certain well-known high gallery in the manor of Lambeth', in the presence of only five witnesses and a notary public, Thomas Argall, whom his master Thomas Bedell had already assured Cromwell was ultra-reliable.[45] The witnesses besides Cromwell himself look like two paired teams: for Cromwell (and the King) there were the ever-faithful Thomas Alvard and Roland Lee's younger cousin and fellow-civil lawyer Dr Thomas Lee, while on Cranmer's side there were the Treasurer of his household John Goodricke and his Steward Henry Stockheath.

One can almost hear the exhalation of relief as the last seal went on that document, while over the river City aldermen and civil servants fretted over dress rehearsals, favoured schoolchildren repeated their lines, gunners checked that their weapons would not prove lethal and tavernkeepers drafted in extra staff for the morrow. Some clerk of Chancery then sat out the Friday drawing up a formal inspection of the paperwork, while Londoners slept off their celebrations of Thursday's deafening river pageant, and Henry and his new wife busied themselves in further ceremonial in the Tower. Further cogs in the medieval machine of Chancery creaked into motion on 4 and 6 June to cap the formality of record, while the capital sorted out its impressions of a weekend filled with spectacle, alcohol and vast outpourings of money.

The efforts leading to these culminating events of 29 May to 1 June 1533 had brought down Cardinal Wolsey and radically changed the direction of Cromwell's life, to say little of other lives already remade or ruined, with many more to come. The centrepiece was a coronation, not a wedding, for, as the discreet meeting at Lambeth legally confirmed, the wedding had already happened; maybe in reality twice. In fact, this was the only solo coronation to be held for any of the six ladies who married King Henry VIII (Katherine of Aragon had been crowned alongside him), and as such it was a symptom of the constant over-assertion which characterized the establishment of the Boleyn marriage. Cromwell was its behind-the-scenes impresario, however little official position he could claim in the public face of it: there was not even a knighthood for him in the various knightings held during the festival. Once more, this reflected his very partial visibility in government over the previous three years. His friend at Court Sir Anthony Browne nevertheless testified to his role when replying in June from embassy in Paris to a 'kind loving letter' from

Cromwell: the success of proceedings 'was not a little to your praise in my mind, for I am sure that there was none that had the pain and travail that you had, and I think no man has deserved more thanks than you have, which is not a little comfort to your friends'.[46]

Just as in the Calais festivities, a commemorative printed souvenir of the events spelled out the meaning of the pageantry, complete with pictorial cover. Once more John Gough took on the job in partnership with Wynkyn de Worde: *The noble triumphant Coronation of Queen Anne, Wife unto the most noble King Henry VIII*.[47] Cromwell, with his usual eye for creative talent, employed the historian John Leland and the rackety Oxford don Nicholas Udall to produce a script for the civic festivities, in Latin and English. There was also some French verse to reinforce the point made at Calais that the King of France supported the match, and a number of the French ambassador's staff were given a prominent place in the procession in Westminster Abbey.

The other dominant note in the imagery of the pageants and ceremonies intended to calm public worries or resentments was traditional piety: all the more reason to keep Cromwell's name out of proceedings. It was important not to present the Boleyn marriage as in any way disruptive of the faith which still commanded the allegiance of the overwhelming majority in the kingdom. A shame, therefore, that the new Queen was not called Mary, but much use was made of the name Anne, that saint being mother of Our Lady among others, and grandmother of Jesus: the pageant en route at Leadenhall was a tableau of St Anne presiding over the extended Holy Family. They appeared without Jesus and Joseph, whose presence might have been a devotional step too far, given that the spectacle included mechanical devices in which an angel crowned Anne Boleyn's heraldic falcon; by implication, her expected child would step into the vacant role of England's Messiah.

To the disappointment of those looking for God's judgement on wickedness, the weather was perfect. Cranmer did all that could be demanded of an archbishop, and Anne showed extraordinary stamina over the ceremonial marathon, no doubt energized by the fulfilment of all her plans. So much in these events was not quite what it claimed. The Queen's prolonged feast in Westminster Hall would have offered plenty of quiet amusement for Cromwell, the ultimate insider to events. In the middle of Henry III's long stone-trestled royal table on the dais, suitably cushioned on its medieval throne, sat a new queen in a not particularly concealed advanced state of pregnancy, while to focus the occasion on her alone her one seated companion at the great table (at slightly less than shouting distance) was an archbishop who (as she may or may not have known) was somebody else's lawfully wedded husband, despite his metropolitan-ate in the Western Church. The Dowager Countess of Oxford was standing beside the Queen's chair, one of a pair of senior noblewomen equipped with cloths ready to conceal and receive royal expectoration or the like during the meal; she was certainly earning Cromwell's private supper beforehand. By convention the King watched the whole event from an elevated royal box. (See Plate 17.)

Cromwell was surely hovering there in the background. He could look on in satisfaction, as one of the most lavish spectacles ever staged in Tudor England wooed the public mood over four days from sullen com-pliance or angry denunciation towards excited fascination. His jealous eye on proceedings did not prevent him being alert to satellite events. The canons of King Henry's College Oxford were unpleasantly surprised to find the minister's habitual attention to their affairs extended to a sharp reprimand for absence from their duties at Whitsuntide, when of course they should have been praying for the new Queen in their College chapel, in parallel to events in the capital. Instead, most of them had taken a jaunt up to London to enjoy the coronation jamboree. They excused their frivolity to their benefactor and protector with a masterpiece of academic unctuousness: 'our joy was so great to see the effect of the truth for the which we had so earnestly laboured, and of long time so heartily desired, that it was a marvel that any one of us all could and did refrain himself from the sight of the same.'[48] One can imagine Cromwell's enjoyment of this self-serving pomposity.

As we noted in Chapter 7, on the very night that Anne was first paraded around Court as Henry's Queen, 12 April or Easter Even, Cromwell had been conceded one more small promotion in his snail-pace progress to outward signs of his already formidable power under the King, by being appointed Chancellor of the Exchequer.[49] This office, unlike the Clerk-ship of the Hanaper or the Mastership of the Jewels, has in more recent constructions of the government of this realm got ideas above its Tudor station. In 1533, it was nothing like as important an office of state as nowadays: the Chancellor had rather ill-defined duties, but that lack of definition was among the post's advantages, which could bend it to Cromwell's purposes. He made this clear only a couple of months after gaining the office, when he observed expansively to Edward Lee Arch-bishop of York that he would be perfectly entitled without further ado to discharge Lee from payment of clerical taxation owing from Wolsey's time, 'having a room of authority in the said Exchequer'.[50] The neat-ness of his acquiring his new office in the second of the two ancient departments of government, a counterpart to his Clerkship of the Hanaper in Chancery, looks more than coincidence.

Unlike Hall of the Hanaper or Amadas of the Jewels, the previous Chancellor of the Exchequer was not some obscure working civil servant but a peer of the realm: the distinguished diplomat and literary translator John Bourchier Lord Berners, late Deputy of Calais. Just as with Cromwell's previous two acquisitions of office, he knew his predecessor well, for instance in amicable business correspondence when Berners had needed an approach to Wolsey back in 1529.[51] Given Berners's other occupations, it is unlikely that he paid much attention to the Chancellorship beyond collecting his fee, but Cromwell did. He took an interest in acquiring documents giving him some idea of the Exchequer's history and functioning: all part of his self-education in royal government. He also immediately acted on his position by sitting in the Exchequer Court, as demonstrated by his order to the barons (judges) of the Exchequer in June 1533 not to pursue Archbishop Lee over that clerical taxation. As usual, once appointed he never relinquished his grip on the office, and as late as 1540 he sat in the Exchequer from time to time in a judicial capacity. An Elizabethan reminiscence has preserved the equally typical circumstance that, when doing so, he displaced the accustomed formal order of seating, parking himself next to the Lord Treasurer (who happened to be the Duke of Norfolk): a usurpation of status gratefully continued by some later chancellors.[52]

In immediate practical terms the Chancellorship brought Cromwell one chore, but in the longer term one highly important opportunity for patronage. The chore was to collect the fines or hear excuses from a wide range of gentlemen and esquires who had to their dismay been confronted with a demand to come to Queen Anne's coronation and be knighted, or face a fine. In fact it may have been to undertake this imminent task that Cromwell was given the Chancellorship as the most immediately vacant office in the Exchequer. Knighthood was of course an honour, but came with the expectation of much ill-rewarded public service, and many were genuinely unable to contemplate such a lifetime's financial burden. In any case, this was in reality a windfall tax on the moderately well-off, with the actual knighting as the alternative. The protests of those claiming they should not have to pay the fine because their income fell below the forty-pound-a-year income threshold for knighting, plus wheedling letters from their friends, built up to a considerable correspondence, which in itself gave Cromwell the chance to dole out favours right across the realm.[53]

Among those letters of concerned friends was the first surviving direct letter to him from the King's daughter Mary, now seventeen years old. The very day before the coronation festivities began, 28 May 1533, Mary wrote from what was by now gilded custody in the Archbishop of Canterbury's vast palace at Otford, addressing her note to 'Mr Cromwell' (no more, no less). This was early in what turned into a long and intense correspondence, but it was not the start, for she did not address Cromwell 'as unacquainted' in what was an informal note. She begged him to excuse the aged father of one of her servants from appearing to receive knighthood, 'as I am advertised that all such men shall first resort unto you to know the King my father's further pleasure therein'. She could not bring herself to mention what the occasion of Mr Wilbraham's knighting might be, and she carefully and spiritedly superscribed her secretary's text 'Mary Princess'. Yet, as before in the matter of Beddgelert Priory, we get the sense she expected a fair deal.[54]

The longer-term attraction of the Chancellorship was that its occupant's place among the judges of the Exchequer Court gave him a say in nominations each November of the shortlist of three possible candidates for each county sheriff, to serve from spring the coming year. Cromwell had been alerted to this possibility in November 1532, when Lord Keeper Audley went out of his way to describe how the system worked, and sent him a full list of that year's names. Sheriffs did their ancient formal accounting in the Exchequer, so it was natural that choosing them should be associated with it. Come the following February or March, as Audley explained (Cromwell was learning a lot about government in 1532), the King would in a picturesque piece of ancient ceremonial take a silver bodkin and prick through the parchment beside one of the three names, guided no doubt in his choice by a good deal of informal discussion. Then the new Sheriff's year would begin.[55]

The November shortlisting in the Exchequer was therefore an important moment in government: a chance to wield influence and bestow favours throughout the realm. Some people were just as anxious to avoid being Sheriff as others were anxious not to be knights, for it was a year of burdensome office and much expense not reimbursed. Some by contrast wanted the Shrievalty very much, for it offered all sorts of opportunities to exercise power: harassing neighbours and favouring friends, influencing lawsuits and, in Parliamentary election years, swaying the choice of representatives in the Commons. Shrieval business came to Cromwell very quickly; during the bustle of the coronation itself, the current Sheriff of Cornwall buttonholed him in his capacity as Chancellor of the Exchequer to obtain licence not to appear in the Exchequer Court to account in the following Michaelmas Term.[56] From then on, begging letters about the Shrievalty were another common item in Cromwell's in-tray, a further useful opportunity to intervene in local government, complementing his scrutiny of commissions of the peace through the Hanaper.

Lord Berners's death also left vacant his more important office, the Deputyship of Calais. His successor, appointed on 23 March 1533, three weeks before Cromwell's own promotion, was Arthur Plantagenet Viscount Lisle, an illegitimate son of King Edward IV and therefore by way of being the King's uncle. It is a tribute to Lisle's likeable nature and evident lack of political ambition that the King never for one moment seems to have applied his normal dynastic fears to his relative; when Lisle did eventually suffer the catastrophe of arrest and imprisonment in the Tower, it was on other grounds. His appointment to this crucial post on England's frontiers was the first made in one of the Tudors' regional governorships during Cromwell's years of power, and although it looks more like a personal decision of the King's, it will not have displeased him. Until religious disputes drove them apart and ranged Lisle among Cromwell's opponents in his final struggles, the Lisles regarded the great minister as a reliable if often frustrating source of favour and support in their frequent legal troubles, not least because Cromwell's entanglement with the upper gentry of Kent gave him a hold over their troublesome relatives, Edward Seymour and John Dudley.

The coronation represented a real moment of achievement, but no one could suppose that the consequences had ceased to ripple outwards. The Emperor Charles was determined to see Queen Katherine and her daughter Mary properly treated, and Chapuys pressed Henry's Council hard on this. He was surprised at how warmly Cromwell spoke of Katherine, but that was in accord with the official line that she was Princess Dowager and should be given all possible respect as such.[57] Beyond those already formidable worries were incalculable consequences if the Pope excommunicated the King for all he had done in the previous few years: at worst, foreign invasion or internal rebellion, or both. Such nightmares must be countered with the most ambitious programme possible of intellectual and diplomatic warfare, though it is unlikely that the King's advisers as yet saw quite where that might take them.

The new phase of the campaign had various elements. One was to go even further in building up a case from history to show that Henry enjoyed an imperial jurisdiction by right, which inexplicably his predecessors had long neglected. The *Collectanea satis copiosa* had been a start, but who knew what else was sitting in monastic libraries in the

kingdom and beyond? So, soon after the city pageants had been dismantled, Cromwell's deviser of elegant verse for the coronation, John Leland,
already marked out as a precocious investigator of antiquity, was dispatched to travel the length and breadth of the kingdom looking for further
manuscripts, armed with a royal commission to secure entry to ancient
abbeys, priories and friaries. Thus began Leland's marvellous investigative
journeys across Tudor England which have left us so much, but which in
their antiquarian excitements, overwhelming possibilities and distressing
witnesses of destruction eventually robbed him of his sanity.[58]

All through the monastic visitations and subsequent dissolutions,
Cromwell's agents remained alert for relevant historical manuscripts.
Some of his men, like the scholarly Welshman John ap Rhys of Brecon
(who in 1534 married a niece of Cromwell's), had their own antiquarian
interests. The King's library, as well as Archbishop Cranmer's, was
regularly enlarged with monastic literary spoils.[59] At the same time that
Leland set out on his journeys, a very different historian of England, the
Italian Polydore Vergil, obtained royal permission to leave his Archdeaconry of Wells Cathedral to travel abroad in some style, overseeing the
first printed version of his long-awaited *Anglica historia* in Basel. He had
outraged patriotic historians such as Leland by his scepticism about
Geoffrey of Monmouth's stories of King Arthur, which lay behind the Act in
Restraint of Appeals, but he was still a highly respected historian of international standing. Evidently someone at Court felt his decades of historical
writings might be helpful, even if he did take a different line to most of
those researching for the King. That person was probably not Cromwell,
who would be well aware of how much Vergil had always hated Cardinal
Wolsey. This was one Italian with whom he did not have a rapport.[60]

A month after the coronation Cromwell was among those witnessing
yet another legal transaction, vital but for the moment top secret: a record
at Greenwich Palace on 29 June 1533 of the King's appeal to a future
General Council of the Church, in case he was excommunicated by 'our
most holy Lord the present Pope' (*sanctissimus Dominus noster Papa
modernus*) over his repudiation of Katherine of Aragon. This might seem
simply a wise precaution, and indeed far away in Rome a fortnight later
the Pope did provisionally excommunicate Henry. But it was far more
than that; such appeals to a General Council had been formally forbid-
den by Pope Pius II in 1460, and the courtesy of the address belied the
revolutionary nature of the action. In this respect at least, Henry was
imitating the man he detested, Martin Luther, whose own appeal to a
General Council in 1518 had been a sensational escalation of his quarrel
with Rome. It was a mark of the ambiguity in all the King's proceedings

in religion from now on: were they part of the continent-wide Reformation or not? Cromwell would use his developing power to provide one set
of possible answers to this never-resolved question.

Once more the small group witnessing the King's declaration were
headed by an archbishop: this time, however, not Cranmer but his northern colleague and Wolsey's successor as Archbishop of York, Edward
Lee.[61] Lee, a veteran diplomat, was no relation to the various northern
Lees captained by Roland Lee, and unlike Roland his religious traditionalism was not offset in Cromwell's eyes by close past links to Wolsey, or
by his protracted and rather silly academic feud with Desiderius Erasmus. In fact Lee was a long-standing protégé of Bishop Fisher, who had
done his best to mediate fairly between his two friends in Lee's squabble
with the great European humanist.[62] He had been made Archbishop of
York in late summer 1531, when Cromwell did not have enough influence
in government to point the King in another direction. Stephen Gardiner
became Bishop of Winchester at the same time, and these appointments
have the fingerprints of the Duke of Norfolk on them. Throughout the
1530s, Lee's continuing presence as Archbishop of York was an irritation
to both Cromwell and the Archbishop of Canterbury, Cranmer. His
obstructive fussiness was reminiscent of Thomas Audley's, but mitigated
by his desperate sense of his own vulnerability and his anxiety to please.*

Lee was not quick to help in passing royal legislation in the 1533 Parliament, in sharp contrast to Cranmer. It is likely he was called back
south now specifically to bind him into the King's ongoing campaign by
his presence at this declaration; Cranmer could easily have been called up
from his palace at Croydon, where he had been spending the previous
week, to play the same role.[63] Archbishop Lee travelled down to London
after he had finished presiding over the troublesome Convocation of York
in mid-May. A fortnight before witnessing the King's appeal at Greenwich, he certified his Convocation's acceptance of the King's annulment
from a relative's country house outside Southwark (the archbishops had
of course just lost their grand Westminster house of York Place to the
King, so he had no official London base of his own).[64] We have already
glimpsed Cromwell doing Lee a favour over his back-taxes in the
Exchequer during these weeks in London (see above, p. 223), and that
looks like a reward for good behaviour.

Bishop Tunstall of Durham was also pursued for his signature endors-
ing the two formal copies of this appeal at Greenwich. He had initially

* The fussiness was also reflected in his habitual dating of his letters by year, a highly
unusual gift to posterity among his contemporaries, for which one must be grateful.

been extremely reluctant to attend the Northern Convocation at all, and when he did comply with the royal order he caused enough obstruction at its meetings to win admiring comment from Chapuys, before Roland Lee managed to browbeat a majority of the clergy present into accepting the King's demands. Tunstall's signature on the appeal, like Lee's, was a sign that for the time being the leading traditionalists had struggled with their conscientious dilemma between loyalty to King Henry and resistance to a cruel marital injustice and the break with Rome, to the point of compliance with the royal demands. It looks like part of the same set of deals that in mid-June Bishop Fisher was set at liberty to return to his diocese; Chapuys specifically recorded that this gesture of goodwill to the grand old man of the episcopal bench was thanks to Cromwell's intercession with the King.[65] The mood the government were trying to set was that all reason for conflict was past; all was now agreed. That would lead up to a happy event both tailpiece and finale to the great celebrations of the coronation.

The way of nature postponed this resolution for a couple of months: the birth of an heir to the King and Queen, on 7 September 1533.* Henry would naturally have preferred a boy to have been born, since that quest lay at the heart of his proceedings over the previous six years. He had prepared elaborate celebrations for such an eventuality, but at least a healthy girl delivered without fuss was a good sign for Anne's presumed future pregnancies. A splendid christening for Princess Elizabeth a few days later took place in the church of the Observant Friars at Greenwich, a setting both logical as it was in effect Greenwich Palace's Chapel Royal and also a deliberate put-down to the recalcitrant majority in the community there. The emphasis among participants was to unite two contending groups in the nobility: partisans of Queen Katherine and Princess Mary – the Marquess and Marchioness of Exeter, Lord Hussey, the Duke of Suffolk – with the aristocrats who had supported Boleyn throughout her struggle to power – Wiltshire and Norfolk, and a generous showing of Howards. Once more Cromwell played no ceremonial part in proceedings, being just an observer alongside his courtier friends William Paulet and William Fitzwilliam. His low official profile

---

* What turned out later to have been an historic occasion is still commemorated in the Church of England's Book of Common Prayer. In its very minor revision in 1604 a feast-day was inserted on 7 September into the Book's Kalendar of holy days: the imaginary St Enurchus, at best a misprint for the risibly obscure St Evurtius of Orleans. With admirable liturgical conservatism, no one has subsequently subtracted St Enurchus's Day from the Anglican Kalendar. It was probably a private joke by a well-informed printer at the expense of the new monarch King James I.

continued, even while fading stars of the Howard interest paraded in the limelight around the Duke of Norfolk's niece Anne and her baby.[66]

The fragile show of goodwill at the christening, a public unanimity which the government pursued with increasing ruthlessness, belied the fact that a hard-core opposition had not been at all cowed by the success of the King's plans. Queen Katherine was not going to co-operate with the fiction of unity, and her old allies among the royal convents of Franciscan Observants were prominent in keeping her in touch with sympathizers abroad, led by their former Provincial William Peto, who left England around the end of 1532 to orchestrate opposition from the Low Countries. Another source of worry for the government was increasingly political stridency from a visionary nun of Kent, Elizabeth Barton, who turned her visions into denunciations of the Boleyn marriage and linked her sabotage of royal hopes with the efforts of the Observants. This combination promised a nightmare of internal sedition and external intervention.

During summer 1533 Cromwell was already directing efforts to confront these menaces, making full reports to the King. According to his Franciscan Observant informant John Laurence, two Observant friars had arrived from abroad, collecting texts on the Great Matter to fuel Peto's continuing propaganda campaign against it.[67] Two other Observants from the Greenwich community had been covertly visiting Queen Katherine in the household assigned to her as Princess Dowager at Wolsey's old Hertfordshire retreat of The More; Cromwell had them arrested near by at Ware.[68] Of the Greenwich friars, Cromwell commented, 'It is undoubted that they have intended and would confess some great matter, if they might be examined as they ought to be, that is to say, by pains.' In other words: torture. So far, the greatest human casualties in the King's Great Matter had been Katherine of Aragon's wrecked marriage and the associated misery of her daughter Mary. Now the tally of suffering rippling out from King Henry's determination rolled on through a decade and more into imprisonment, terror and death for scores of others. The agent over the next seven years, whatever his own private inclinations, was necessarily the minister whom Chapuys described as now really in charge of government, transacting all matters in the realm.[69]

PART THREE

Touching Pitch

Whoso toucheth pitch, shall be [de]filed withal, and he that is familiar with the proud, shall clothe himself with pride.

Ecclesiasticus 13.1, in the translation
of Miles Coverdale, 1535

More threateneth them which enterprise difficult and urgent matters than those which only seeketh easy and light matters.

Stephen Vaughan to
Thomas Cromwell, 3 February 1530

10

Treason in Prospect: 1533–1534

Fifteen-twenty-five was a tense year in Kent, disrupted by Cardinal Wolsey's monastic dissolutions and by the ultimately successful resistance to his attempts at innovative taxation. At Eastertide, a young woman of the county, Elizabeth Barton, began having a series of divine visions, enlivened by violent fits at least temporarily cured by visiting a local shrine of Our Lady at Court-at-Street. Such spiritual demonstrations were not uncommon in early Tudor England. Archbishop Warham, the chief local magnate disapproving of both of Wolsey's initiatives, and lord of the parish where Barton was a domestic servant, took a special interest in her, and in the course of time she was installed as a nun in a small convent at Canterbury. Enclosure did not curb her public pronouncements and prophecies. As with the very similar activities of the daughter of Sir Roger Wentworth at Ipswich a decade before (which may indeed have inspired Barton to imitation), her public renown was much boosted by retelling her wondrous doings in both manuscript and print.[1]

The difference between Wentworth's demonstrations at Ipswich and Barton's was that after the initial drama the Maid of Kent persisted in mediating divine messages. As soon as the King's marital troubles became public knowledge in 1528, she turned to fierce and apocalyptic criticisms of his relationship with Anne Boleyn. She could rely on the stream of visitors to Canterbury, many delighted to add a living saint to the experience of pilgrimage. In addition, for a nun, she got out and about rather a lot. Beyond her first patron Archbishop Warham, she visited the great Bishop Fisher in Rochester; as early as 1528 she interviewed Cardinal Wolsey on Warham's recommendation; and on at least two occasions she reached to the very pinnacle of power, the King himself. Her clerical supporters fanned out across the country, and included Observant Franciscans, dangerously integrating her campaign of opposition into their own. Her monastic backers at Canterbury Cathedral translated her words into Latin, so papal diplomats could bear them back to Rome. She mightily impressed the papal auditor Silvestro Dario, on annulment business in England in 1529, and may have been the cause of his turning against the King's case thereafter.[2]

This was an astonishing use of the cultural niche which Barton occupied as divinely inspired innocent: she is reported as making prophecies of destruction to the King's face which far exceeded the reported words for which the Duke of Buckingham had been executed a decade before. Meanwhile, her tally of interviews included at least two partisans of Katherine of Aragon who had been choreographed into the show of unity at Elizabeth's christening in September 1533: John Lord Hussey and the Marchioness of Exeter. Sir Thomas More carefully avoided an interview with her for some years, but after Anne's coronation he agreed to meet her at Syon Abbey, one of that complex of royal monastic foundations surrounding King's Henry's birthplace at Richmond Palace. That same summer Barton's supporters brought out a new pamphlet containing her latest angry denunciations in an edition of 700; the printer was arrested and cross-examined, and not one copy now survives. This comprehensive and effective censorship of the printing press was without English precedent, and a tribute to Cromwell's efficiency.[3]

Barton was probably doomed from the moment she claimed to have been supernaturally uprooted in autumn 1532 from Canterbury and flown over to Calais in the wake of the King and his Court (she would have heard the noise of his progress past her nunnery on the Dover road). After she had soared in spirit across the Channel, she landed in the midst of a royal mass in Calais, where an angel presented her with the consecrated wafer the priest was about to elevate before King Henry. This theft by teleportation, in the presence of Anne Boleyn herself, directly denied the King's divinely conferred authority to rule. The government must recover from its previous dithering in face of her charisma: Barton could not be allowed to persist in sabotaging reunion in the political nation. In the same week in late July 1533 that Cromwell was contemplating torture for dissident Observants, on the King's orders Archbishop Cranmer began decisive action against the Maid. Newly arrived in his palace at Otford (recently vacated by Princess Mary), he summoned Barton in company with her Prioress for the first interview of many she was to undergo that summer.[4]

Cromwell prepared the interrogatories Cranmer used with the Maid as he would with so many suspected traitors over the next seven years. The technique was sophisticated: as Chapuys noted for Charles V after the interrogations had achieved their desired result, Cromwell and his team consistently treated her *comme une grosse dame*, as if she were a great lady.[5] We might compare the process to a decompression chamber, steadily extracting her extraordinary charisma to create a new and unfamiliar atmosphere. At first the Archbishop played the role which came naturally to him, that of gently probing scholar; he even licensed the Maid to refuel herself spiritually with an Assumptiontide visit to the Marian shrine at Court-at-Street which had launched her public career. It was a sign that the King's party were confident they had her where they wanted.

After Cromwell's return from the King's progress into Surrey, interviews resumed in London. Cromwell and Cranmer were joined there by Hugh Latimer, a remarkable turnaround in Latimer's fortunes little more than a year since he was Archbishop Warham's prisoner at Lambeth Palace accused of heresy. The presence of the unashamedly evangelical Latimer on the team was a sign the regime was now going for the only option possible in the face of Barton's inspired utterances. If her revelations did not come from God, they must be the work of the Devil, who had bent her human weakness to increasingly diabolical purposes, with the aid of malicious papist clergy. The new strategy was also a testimony to the waning influence on the King of instinctive traditionalists captained by the Duke of Norfolk; one did not have to be an evangelical to sneer at the Maid's revelations, but it certainly helped. Faced with sudden cold scepticism, Barton's self-belief totally crumbled; she confessed that after her initial manifestations her campaign had indeed been orchestrated by treacherous clergy of Kent.

Through the autumn, the Maid's network of clerical supporters was rounded up, arrested and interrogated, and a welter of incriminating papers scrutinized. The regime presented the damning parts of all this information to an extraordinary Great Council of notables, which met in Westminster for three days in mid-November. Cromwell was later to describe it in the course of a bad-tempered correspondence with Bishop Fisher as being 'as great assembly and council of the Lords of this realm as hath been seen many years heretofore, out of a Parliament'.[6] Fisher could have retorted that this was not true, for it was merely the first such meeting since the Great Council which had humiliated Cardinal Wolsey in October 1529. Just as then, the subject was exhibited in person before the assembled company; evidently the government were now sure enough of Barton's self-annihilation to risk this public exposure.

Chancellor Audley's speech to this Great Council summarized the state of play on the King's quarrel with the Pope, before proceeding to evidence on the Maid. He named prominent people implicated in her seditious conversations, such as Archbishop Warham, but ostentatiously confined identifications only to those (like Warham) no longer alive, while making it clear that others could be named. With that encouragement, the assembled company of England's great and good roared for Barton's execution at the stake: another extraordinary turnaround from nationwide burnings of evangelical heretics only a year before. The rhetorical destruction of the Maid and her indicted associates was then carefully crafted for a wider public, in a sermon preached on 23 November from England's most prominent pulpit, the open-air 'Paul's Cross' beside St Paul's Cathedral. The first performer was one of a new crop of bishops, John Capon alias Salcott, elect of Bangor, brother of Cranmer's and Cromwell's old associate ex-Dean William Capon of Cardinal College Ipswich.* Sir Thomas More was among the audience, whether willingly or under coercion he does not record.[7] The same text was then repeated a fortnight later in Canterbury by one of Cranmer's staff, just after Cranmer's triumphant enthronement; on both occasions, Barton and her chief supporters were paraded as objects of shame.

Audley's speech menacingly left open the fate of the long list of notables who had hearkened to the Maid. It was worth trying to preserve the show of unity created at Princess Elizabeth's christening, and so a week after the Great Council King Henry began to place boundaries around those to suffer, by pardoning the Marchioness of Exeter for her contacts with Barton. Vastly relieved, she begged Cromwell to protect her and her husband from any further royal anger and enclosed for his information a draft of the abject response she had sent to the King's letter of pardon.[8] In the course of her reply to Henry, she had played up the useful rhetorical escape-route that she was 'a woman, whose fragility and brittleness is such as most facilely, easily and lightly is seduced and brought into abusion and light belief', and prudently emphasized how angry the Marquess was with her for what she described to Cromwell as misjudgements out 'of simplicity and for lack of knowledge'. These two fine performances of femininity, no doubt crafted by the Marquess's secretaries, for the moment saved the Exeters' position at Court and carefully insulated them from whatever judgement might fall on 'so many wise persons who have been equally abused, as I hear say'. Pardoning the Marchioness also gave the King one less reason to confront her father, William Lord Mountjoy, who was in the process of shedding the increasingly intolerable office of Chamberlain to ex-Queen Katherine.

The printed propaganda that accompanied the destruction of the

---

* John Capon, being also a Benedictine abbot, was normally known by his name in religion from the family home village, Salcott in Essex.

Maid's reputation during the autumn took the form of uninhibited public statements of England's independence from papal jurisdiction, published for domestic consumption. This was an audacious rejection of five centuries during which the Pope's ultimate place in English Christianity had never been officially denied, whatever his quarrels with previous monarchs like King John and Edward I. Cranmer led a campaign of sermons attacking the notion of papal authority in the universal Church. A pamphlet, whose wide distribution throughout the realm necessitated a second edition, proclaimed instead the final authority of a General Council, just as in the King's formal appeal lodged with the Pope, and it vigorously defended the Boleyn marriage through history and theology. Maybe its text incorporated parts of Audley's speech to the Great Council, which might be implied by the pamphlet's title *Articles devised by the Whole Consent of the King's Most Honourable Council*. It is notable as the first official English publication to deploy an evangelical sneer-word with a long future, 'papist'.[9] In an apparent innovation, a meeting of the regular royal Council ordered the separate printing of a single Parliamentary statute as if the text were a royal proclamation, and ordered it set on every parish church door in the land. That statute was, of course, the Act in Restraint of Appeals.[10]

These moves were designed to convince every subject of Henry VIII just how very wrong the Maid was. 'Surely I think that she did marvellously stop the going forward of the King's marriage by her visions,' Cranmer reflected to his friend Ambassador Hawkins on 20 December, relaxing after the drama and in the wake of his own emphatic assertion of authority in Kent by his enthronement and first visitations. The Archbishop had gone so far as to ensure that in that twice-repeated sermon Barton was labelled a heretic, laying her open to being burned at the stake as the Great Council had demanded. All this official blackening of her reputation did have an effect. Two ultra-conservative monastic chroniclers, one a monk of St Augustine's Canterbury in Barton's heartland and the other Wolsey's former critic the anonymous Austin canon of Butley in Suffolk, both used their very traditional vehicle of historical record to reflect on her career as a story of imposture; in fact both used the word 'hypocrite', meaning actor, prominent in the official propaganda.[11]

All this was the domestic counterpart of King Henry's momentous defiance of his papal excommunication in July. The breach was exacerbated by the diplomatic incompetence of the principal royal envoy in southern Europe, Bishop Gardiner. If anything was necessary to convince the King that Cromwell was a better option as chief minister than the Bishop of Winchester, it would have been events in the south of France in autumn

1533. The Pope had travelled to Marseille to confer with King François over their carefully prepared alliance, sealing it with his niece's marriage to the King's second son, so the English diplomatic delegation were outsiders to one of the decade's most important meetings. Gardiner and his colleagues were joined by the civil lawyer Edmund Bonner, chosen to deliver in person the royal appeal to a General Council initiated in Greenwich after Anne's coronation. Bonner's partnership with Gardiner was inherently uncomfortable; he had been a Wolsey loyalist to the last, and further bonded with Cromwell through their mutual enthusiasm for all things Italian, from literature to Parmesan cheese.[12] Bonner's own Italian was coming on, but in case conversation with the Pope or his entourage became too quickfire for him he took to the meeting William Penizon, a native Italian-speaker long in Tudor service, and friend to Cromwell.[13]

The 7th of November was an exhausting and humiliating day for them. Their much deferred personal interview with the Pope was interrupted by the King of France, arriving with elaborate casualness, paying little attention to the English delegation and pointedly engaging his newly acquired papal relative in cheerful conversation for three-quarters of an hour. After that, his Holiness enjoyed himself making Bonner feel uncomfortable for two more hours while Vatican officials reviewed the paperwork. Over the next few days, Bonner and Gardiner between them managed to infuriate both the papal delegation and the King of France, who had been doing his best for a year now to save King Henry from papal wrath and who nevertheless now found himself harangued by an English bishop for his unhelpfulness.

Gardiner's report back to the King was at least admirably full in depicting this disaster, perhaps under pressure from his fellow-envoys to cover their backs. What his appalled sovereign would have carried away from that report was the Most Christian King's crisp judgement to Winchester that 'ye have marred all'.[14] Henry would have been even less impressed had he learned that Gardiner was keeping his own future options open with Rome during his prolonged embassy. In summer 1533 he had clandestinely obtained a papal indulgence to hear mass even during any prospective interdict, via the genial permanent English ambassador to the Vatican, William Benet, an old friend. One could argue that he and other English envoys needed such permission if they were not to stand out uncomfortably during their embassies by not attending mass, but that does not apply to some others named in this and other grants of the same period, patently those unreliable in the King's break with Rome – Archbishop Lee of York, the Marquess and Marchioness of Exeter, William Lord Sandys.[15]

There was no going back now. Parliament once again must push matters forward, enacting a clutch of measures branching out of the King's
defiance of the Pope.[16] For the third year in a row, a planned session,
sixth of this freakishly prolonged Parliament, was postponed through the
autumn by pressure of events, finally reassembling on 15 January 1534.
Informed observers saw that the logic of previous moves suggested a
major trimming of the Church's landholdings – their 'temporalities'.
'Some presuppose the spiritualty shall depart with their temporalities,
whereof many be glad and only few bemoan them,' reported John Husee
to Lord Lisle in Calais. Chapuys heard from the Scots diplomatic delegation that Cromwell had said much the same thing to them. This was not
just talk, and might have led to major confiscations of Church institutions and estates earlier than actually happened over the next few years.[17]
In fact through 1534 some startlingly radical proposals had less spectacular outcomes for churchmen, but action enough began in the first
session affecting both Church and realm: clerical taxation and privilege,
explicit statements on succession of the Boleyn line, plus the major task
of tidying away the Maid of Kent and her associates, defined as widely as
politically necessary. The result was the first round of political executions
since the death of the Duke of Buckingham in 1521. It was characteristic
of Wolsey's years in power that fewer people had died for political reasons than over many previous decades; that was about to change.

With so much to process in bringing the Church to heel, it would be useful to manage the bench of bishops in the Lords (mitred abbots in the
Lords rarely caused difficulties to government plans). It was already
depleted by a handy crop of vacancies through death. Cromwell took
pains to license Archbishop Lee's absence, a move suiting them both.[18]
Bishop Tunstall was one of the other episcopal absentees in 1532, and so
he was again in 1534; that meant that the Northern Province was represented only by the never-troublesome John Kite of Carlisle.* John Fisher
made the excuse (more than an excuse) of illness, and there was no sign
of the venerable Richard Nix of Norwich either, cowed as he was by the
government's politically inspired charge of *praemunire*, with a crushing
fine to follow.

There can rarely have been so few bishops present in the House before
the 1640s when the English Civil Wars swept them all away for a while;

---

* The Province of York did actually include a fourth diocese, that of Sodor and Man, but
this diocese comprising only the Isle of Man has never been represented in the English or
British Parliaments.

but the one virtually constant attendee among the episcopal contingent was Archbishop Cranmer (forty-one days out of forty-six) during the passage of legislation which furthered the ruin of traditional religion. The attending bishops were forced to show their loyalty in public by joining a rota of preaching against the Pope at Paul's Cross. Meanwhile, most unusually, the Convocation of Canterbury was hardly allowed to meet at all during the Parliamentary session; its substantive business had to wait until the Lords and the Commons had gone home. The government probably did not trust its membership to refrain from distracting and negative noise, even after the submission of the clergy two years before.[19]

The show of unity which the government sought from Parliament was once again best achieved by exclusion or voluntary absence. There are signs that in the Commons some of the prominent knights of the shire who had met during previous sessions at the Queen's Head Tavern to share their unhappiness were unenthusiastic about being in a position where they would have to express further dissent. Cromwell had given Sir George Throckmorton pointed advice in 1533 'to live at home and serve God and meddle little', counsel which that spirited gentleman quoted back to its author on two occasions.[20] It looks as if Throckmorton sat out most if not all the Parliamentary session of winter 1534 back home at Coughton Court, for halfway through he asked Cromwell to do his best to get him leave of absence for the rest of the session. Throckmorton's fellow-diner at the Queen's Head Sir Marmaduke Constable used the same excuse of local administrative duties in Yorkshire to ask Cromwell for licence to arrive three weeks late into Parliament's sittings.[21]

Often in previous accounts of this Parliament and similar occasions, these absences have been interpreted as the result of government pressure, but that is too crude an interpretation of the transaction. Unity was a prized good in medieval and Tudor England: division was an aberration from the norm, hence the government's use of voting by division in Parliamentary proceedings as a way to shame people into conformity. Respected county leaders like Throckmorton or Constable, or long-term Crown servants, would not wish to show open defiance to royal policy: absence was a useful middle way between defiance and assent. We should compare these absences with the retirement of two major figures in Court life in the previous months: Cromwell's friend and patron Vice-Chamberlain Sir John Gage, and William Lord Mountjoy, Chamberlain to Queen Katherine. Gage said goodbye to the King in August 1533 'with the water standing in his eyes'; his final departure for the Charterhouse of Sheen came that December, around the same time Mountjoy also got his discharge. Mountjoy had begged Cromwell to get him released from his long-held office, sickened by constant confrontations with Katherine and her loyal servants as he tried to impose the fiction of her dowager status upon her.[22]

The two sessions of Parliament in 1534 transacted a great deal of routine business which was in effect catch-up; so much legislation had rained down from above in sessions from 1529 that many private suits were held up.[23] Now it was a sensible ploy to please members by beginning the session with a substantial succession of private bills for completion: such matters as protection for trades and their gilds, remedies for problems in particular cities and boroughs, and private matters for magnates and churchmen. Yet one of the earliest pieces of legislation, actually the first considered in the Lords after Parliament opened, was a curious initiative for which one would expect a history of previous public grievance or discussion, but there is little previous trace. It was a statute making buggery a felony, that is a criminal offence in common law, with the death penalty attached to it.

The annoyingly unnamed peer who advocated this Act for the Punishment of the Vice of Buggery linked it to misuse of ecclesiastical sanctuary jurisdictions, which suggests a context: this was the first symptom of the new attack on Church privilege. That well-informed anonymous commentator on the Reformation whose fragmentary account remains in the Wyatt papers directly linked its enactment not just to the unnaturalness of clerical celibacy generally but to monastic corruption in particular, and so the buggery statute looks like a new try-out in Cromwell's programme of intervention in the affairs of monasteries and friaries.[24] Over the previous four years, William Tyndale in his literary duel with More had launched the long English Protestant tradition of linking sodomy to clerical celibacy. Yet the Act had a wider significance, quite apart from forming the basis of all punitive action in England against male homosexuals up to the nineteenth century. After the Papacy had created a body of canon law and church courts to administer it in the eleventh and twelfth centuries, such matters of morality as this had been the concern of church lawyers in the Western Church, and not of the King's courts. The Act was the first major encroachment in England on that general principle, a phenomenon which occurred right across sixteenth-century Europe, Catholic and Protestant alike, and actually rather earlier in other European temporal jurisdictions. It is one of the features of Cromwell's innovations which England's official Protestant Reformation steadily expanded.[25]

Rather more directly tied to current struggles was much skirmishing on heresy, which continued beyond the first session. First it involved the

Commons raising the case of the last-remaining prisoner from Thomas More's evangelical victims, a citizen of London called Thomas Philips. Philips had been arrested by the Bishop of London, John Stokesley, for charges including reading the Bible in English. Cromwell clearly enjoyed disliking Stokesley, on several grounds. He was one of the main agents of Wolsey's humiliation in autumn 1529; additionally, despite his religious conservatism, he was a client of the Boleyns, as that had revealed.[26] His appointment as Bishop in 1530 had predated Cromwell's ability to deflect it, like the promotions of Archbishop Lee and Bishop Gardiner, but Cromwell took care to harass him throughout his episcopate. The Philips brouhaha was the first in their confrontations. It linked to Cromwell's concerns on another front: while still Lord Chancellor, Thomas More took up the Philips case and used his powers in a highly unusual move to get the accused diverted to the Tower of London from incarceration in Bishop Stokesley's prison.

Defending his action subsequently, More observed that he had wanted to avoid Philips suffering the fate of Richard Hunne, the London Lollard whose death in 1514 in the episcopal prison had caused nationwide outrage against the Church hierarchy. The similarities of the cases, More would have realized, were uncomfortable. He made this comment in print in 1533, when he was out of office but still struggling to champion traditional religion and, as far as he could, hold the regime to it against Cranmer and Cromwell. His discussion of the Philips case came in his *Apology*, during the last stages of his literary spat with William Tyndale. Philips was the only new heretic he named in his text, and he was careful to underline that the King had told 'certain of the greatest Lords of his Council' that Philips should have been obedient to Stokesley.[27] Parliament's pursuit of justice for Philips was therefore handily an assault on both the traditionalist Church authorities and on Thomas More. Moreover, the City's fury at Philips's continuing imprisonment produced a direct confrontation between Commons and Lords.[28]

On 7 and 9 February the Lords considered Philips's petition outlining his grievances against Stokesley and eventually sent it back to the Commons, saying it was beneath the dignity of the peers to consider. No doubt the cheerleaders against it were Stokesley himself and Gardiner, who were among the few bishops actually present in the House. Stokesley is named in the Lords' Journal leading a further rejection of Commons complaints on 2 March. The Commons were so enraged by this rebuff that they arranged another of their occasional conferences with the King at Whitehall Palace on 5 March to discuss 'reformation of the acts made by the Spirituality in the Convocation against His Grace and his subjects'.[29] This resulted in an Act setting up a royal commission for reform of canon law in England: potentially a revolutionary outcome of the developing royal supremacy.

But now an opposite cause was making its way through Parliamentary business, with the capacity to embarrass and divide conservatives: the bill of attainder against Elizabeth Barton and her associates. Attainder by Parliamentary Act was a convenient way of avoiding any formal trial in the law courts, but its finality made it a dangerously drastic procedure. Four days after the Lords' rejection of the Philips bill, they found themselves having to ask the King whether he really wanted Sir Thomas More and others called before them to answer charges which would result in their inclusion in the attainder. The King's rage against his former friend had got to the point where the first draft of the bill included More along with Bishop Fisher and one of Fisher's chaplains. In the end More's name was omitted, but not Fisher's; he was forced to pay a substantial (though not crushing) fine to avoid penalties.

At the end of March a new heresy bill emerged from the Commons. At this point, proceedings became unusual: the Lords did not deign to give any readings to the Commons bill, but instead passed it to Lord Chancellor Audley. On 28 March (a rare day on which Archbishop Cranmer was not present), they gave three rapid readings to a bill of their own devising, which looks as if it considerably defanged the Commons initiative; the final copy of this bill unusually contains several alterations which must reflect a rough ride right up to the end, and it only cleared the Commons for royal assent on the very last day of the session. It still abolished the main heresy statute which since 1401 had been the means of killing Lollards and, in the past few years, evangelicals as well. Significant is its only specific provision defining heresy, or rather not defining it, by making clear that speaking against the 'pretended power of the Bishop of Rome' was not heretical.

These paired conflicts illustrate the dynamic of the murderous confrontations through the 1530s. Two causes could incite the King to destructive fury. On the one hand was heresy, particularly anything looking like an attack on the doctrine of the real presence in the eucharist (the trigger-word was 'sacramentarianism'). On the other was treason, including anything which Henry might decide was a threat to the succession of his rightful heirs. The normal logic was that evangelicals were vulnerable to accusations of heresy, usually as 'sacramentaries'; it was generally traditionalists who laid themselves open to treason charges, and so the delicate art of persuading the King to homicidal sadism demanded opposite strategies for those seeking to destroy their enemies. The traditionalists still pressed forward with their attack as Parliament ended.

Some time in late 1533 or early 1534, Thomas More's usual publication outlet headed by his nephew William Rastell printed a long letter from Bishop Gardiner's nephew and confidential servant Germain Gardiner, ostentatiously dated from the Bishop's palace at Esher on 1 August 1533.[30] Any alert reader could identify Germain's unnamed correspondent as the diplomat, Boleyn client and champion of the King's Great Matter Edward Foxe, apparently away from London and therefore needing to be filled in on what had happened.[31]* The work is hardly a letter, more a carefully composed tract of forty-two folios incorporating verbatim documents and records of conversations, and it will have been worked up a good deal in the six months or so before publication. Principally it tried to justify a parallel act of persecution to Philips's: the burning on 4 July 1533 of an evangelical associate of William Tyndale's, John Frith, who had like Philips been imprisoned in the Tower. The tract makes much of Bishop Gardiner's part in Frith's trial, and his elaborate efforts to persuade the condemned man back to orthodoxy. The Philips case is mentioned as if in an afterthought at folio 14, since his examination by the same team on 26 June 1533 had taken place a week after Frith's; of his case, Germain observed, 'I shall not need to write unto you, for there be other enough which both can and I am sure would.'

More continued to influence persecution of heretics even after resigning as Lord Chancellor, via such kindred spirits as the Duke of Norfolk and Bishops Gardiner and Stokesley; this is witnessed in a narrative petition from yet another of his victims, an evangelical called John Field.[32] A Commons initiative which threw a bad light on another example of co-operation between Stokesley and More could not have displeased Cromwell or Cranmer. Putting all this evidence together, it is possible to suggest a place for Cromwell in Parliament's proceedings on Philips and heresy. A measure against the heresy laws based on the Philips case survived the Lords' contemptuous dismissal of the Commons petitions and the peers' subsequent sabotage of the more general Commons bill on heresy. That indicates dogged persistence in those backing it, and official encouragement. Philips himself subsequently found paid employment in the Tower of London which had once imprisoned him. In that capacity he made himself useful to Cromwell in managing the imprisonment of the aristocratic prisoners in the purge of 1538; he even converted one of them,

---

* Foxe had been away in France on embassy earlier in the year, but it is not clear where he was in August 1533, except that Germain writes to him from 'these parts', suggesting Foxe was again away from London, maybe simply performing his duties as Provost of King's College Cambridge.

Sir Nicholas Carew, to reading the English Bible, for which Stokesley had indicted Philips himself six years earlier.[33]

Germain Gardiner's elaborate account of Frith's destruction, published at the close of this Parliamentary session, drew attention to a spectacular case of heresy which the previous year had severely embarrassed both Cromwell and Archbishop Cranmer and threatened King Henry's trust in them. Their names are resoundingly absent from his very circumstantial narrative, even though Cranmer had conducted careful examinations of Frith before the final trial, in which Cromwell had also been involved. Frith's interrogation in June 1533 preceded by only a month Cranmer's and Cromwell's opening assault on the Maid of Kent's psychological defences. Their credibility in the Maid's case was threatened by associating them with Frith, and Cranmer did his very best to distance himself from Frith's radical views on the nature of the eucharist, always the theological topic most calculated to arouse King Henry to destructive anger.[34] Germain's coy passing reference to the Philips case was an unsubtle effort to tar Philips with the same brush as Frith. Coming from More's tame press, this tract was a last-ditch attempt to rally religious traditionalists divided by the Great Matter to a greater common cause; but other events in Parliament meant the effort was too late.*

The buggery statute and the confrontation over heresy were subplots of the larger drama played out in the first session of 1534. Anne might already be Queen and her daughter a princess, but the King now demanded that the whole realm should add a guarantee of this royal succession. On 7 March Parliament passed with only minor emendments a bill defining Katherine of Aragon's status as Princess Dowager, widow of Prince Arthur – a measure which gave extra weight to the royal proclamation saying the same thing eight months before. The major companion of the Act on Katherine, culmination of the Parliamentary session with only ten days to go before closure, was a bill 'for the establishment of the King's Succession' in the Boleyn marriage. It had major and lasting political implications, since it laid down penalties for opposing that marriage and succession, and began widening treason in significant ways beyond definitions standard since Parliamentary legislation enacted as long ago as 1352.

This move did not leap straight out of the minds of government drafters in 1534. Drafts and discussions about new treason legislation dated at

---

* It is relevant that in 1534 William Rastell ceased to operate as a printer. In effect, the More propaganda machine in England then closed down, until Rastell revived it in Queen Mary's reign with a great edition of the martyr's collected works.

least back to late 1530, a year or so before Cromwell became a significant player in the King's Council. Subjects proposed for fresh treasons at that time, such as holding one of the King's castles against him or illegally fleeing the realm, concerned neither succession nor royal supremacy; indeed those first drafts may have been aimed at dealing with Wolsey's treasonable activities and were therefore put aside when his death by natural causes pre-empted any punishment at the King's hands. Then, amid the bundle of matters which the King ordered Cromwell to push forward in late summer 1531 was 'the bill of Augmentation of Treasons', ready for one of those autumn sessions of Parliament which never happened.[35]

We can glimpse Cromwell through his handwriting on drafts, tinkering with and steadily expanding and refining this legislation all through 1532, as confrontation with Rome became ever more serious, and the Boleyn marriage project marched inexorably towards Anne's coronation. The Parliament of 1533 had to clear the ground for those events; in its two sessions the 1534 Parliament provided the means. Thus, at a late stage of drafting, the bill so long in formation turned into an Act concerning the Boleyn succession, and acquired the preamble turning it into an expression of concern from the King's loyal subjects – Ambassador Chapuys later entertained himself before the royal Council in ridiculing this rhetorical device.[36] The drafts reveal how many anxious hands other than Cromwell's contributed to getting the legislation and its criminal penalties for the realm's most serious temporal crime into a form likely to be acceptable to Parliament. Not only was the range of activities defined as treason much expanded, but crucially the 'overt deed' of treason at the heart of the 1352 legislation was now more closely defined to include opposition 'by writing or imprinting'.

Technological advance – the rise of printing – demanded this expansion from the fourteenth-century statute. It was a logical but radical consequence of the years after 1529, when William Tyndale and Thomas More began their literary duel, turning the nation's divisions into polemical printed text, and from 1531, when Cromwell started marshalling the printing press for government propaganda purposes. Any work challenging that official message now made its author liable to suffer the new penalties for treason. Treason by words had always been one of possible grounds for conviction, but the evidence was often too vague to satisfy lawyerly precision. Accordingly, and rather adroitly, the royal Council agreed before presenting the bill to Parliament that oral treason would now be covered in the Act of Succession by a lesser though very serious offence in existing law, misprision of treason. This covered oral attacks on the Boleyn marriage and refusal to swear an oath upholding the

succession. Those convicted of misprision were still liable to imprisonment at pleasure and loss of all possessions.

This legislation hardly concerned Elizabeth Barton. Any action against
her under its provisions would have been awkwardly retrospective, but in
any case she could have been charged only with misprision: she had committed no treason in writing, for others had written down and printed
her words. Was King Henry himself guilty of abetting misprision by listening to her treasonous words in their interviews prophesying his doom,
and then doing nothing about it? It was best to play safe and simply enact
her legal destruction by a separate Parliamentary attainder, together with
whichever of her supporters the King wished to see die immediately. She
was hanged and beheaded (at least not burned at the stake) at Tyburn on
20 April, along with five of her clerical promoters from Canterbury and
the Greenwich Observant Friary. She gained an unenviable distinction
as the only woman in English history to have her severed head placed
among those spiked on London Bridge. Her fate may have been a useful
spur to those administering and taking the oath to the succession nationwide, a hugely ambitious plan to secure explicit consent to the Boleyn
succession from the people of England as a whole.[37] The Act of Succession was a programme for combating not Barton's past crimes but current
or future acts of wickedness which the campaign of oath-taking might
soon reveal.

As that initiative was in preparation, further humiliation came for the
clergy. The day after the Lords and Commons had stood down on 30
March, the Convocation of Canterbury was recalled and forced to vote
on a motion that 'the Bishop of Rome has no greater jurisdiction given
him by God in holy scripture in this realm of England than has any other
foreign bishop.' The main reason for delay in calling Convocation is
manifest: now that Parliament had safely voted through the Act of Succession and its penalties for treason by words, any discussion of the papal
supremacy would be hobbled by the possibility of infringing the provisions of the new Act. Accordingly, a large majority assented. This was
followed by a round-up of signatures from senior clergy not present, then
fanning out to hundreds if not thousands of England's churchmen both
regular and secular over the next few months. If that were not enough,
also beginning in April was the separate campaign of oath-taking, in
which clergy and laity alike were made to sign up to the provisions of the
Act of Succession itself. These were operations as vast as collecting the
names of taxpayers or adult males fit to serve the King in war, and no
doubt they drew on the same methods of local compilation.[38]

Once more, the successful conclusion of a Parliamentary session

offered the King a chance to reward Cromwell with further outward confirmation of his real power. Probably this April he became royal Principal
Secretary in place of Stephen Gardiner. This was as definitive a confirmation of Cromwell's central place in the King's counsels as circumstances,
and maybe Anne Boleyn, would allow. It had clear implications for the
balance of forces between traditionalists and evangelicals around the
King. The outcome of the Barton affair had been catastrophic for conservatives. The balance of death would now shift from evangelical heretics
to conservative traitors.

Gardiner inadvertently made the transfer of office easier by his recent
conduct. Remarkably, there is no record of his contributions to business
in either Lords or Convocation, even though on his return from France in
late January he was almost as regular an attender in the Lords as Cranmer. His lack of diplomatic success in France that autumn would be
reason enough for his demotion, but maybe presence did not make Henry's heart grow fonder. In any case, Lord Lisle's alert agents in London
reported first on 6 April that 'my Lord of Winchester is gone to his diocese of Winchester, and not to return back again till the King's Grace
send for him,' and then on 15 April that 'My Lord of Winchester is out of
the Secretaryship and resteth in Master Cromwell.'[39] The second of these
informants, Sir Thomas Palmer, was brother to one of Cromwell's servants, and the precision of Palmer's observation is confirmed by the fact
that the first surviving signet warrant to be signed by Cromwell as Secretary is dated that very day, 15 April. In fact Cromwell had been usurping
Gardiner's signature on such warrants on a regular basis in the Bishop's
absence through the previous autumn.[40]

Cromwell is therefore irredeemably associated with the campaign of
official cruelty that followed. Nevertheless, one can see him doing his
best to rein it in while conscientiously doing the King's ruthless will,
being as candid a friend as he dared with the most prominent victims, Sir
Thomas More and Bishop Fisher, in their long-postponed showdown
with the King. He engaged in lengthy and testy correspondence with the
ailing Fisher throughout the winter during the Bishop's absence from the
Lords. The one surviving letter of Cromwell's, maybe from halfway
through the Parliamentary sitting and in draft seven pages in length, was
schoolmasterly in tone about the Bishop's contacts with the Maid, and
tartly remarked how seriously Fisher had taken 'the matter whereupon
she made her false prophecies, to which matter ye were so affected (as ye
be noted to be on all matters which ye enter once into) that nothing
could come amiss that made for that purpose'. That was nothing less
than the truth.[41]

Archbishop Cranmer, given personal responsibility for collecting signatures from More and Fisher to the Act of Succession, suggested to Cromwell and the King a number of ways in which they might accept some compromise, and thus give good example to Katherine and Mary. But the twelve months during which Henry sought to enfold the ex-Chancellor and Bishop into his show of unity were past. Cromwell's letter to the Archbishop conveying his consultation with the King on Cranmer's suggestion reveals him in his own hand toughening up the initial draft dictated to his clerk. He struck out an emollient final phrase asking Cranmer to use his 'approved wisdom and dexterity' to get a full oath, and bluntly spelled out that the King 'specially trusteth that ye will in no wise suppose, attempt or move him [Henry] to the contrary, for his Grace supposeth that that manner of swearing, if it shall be suffered might be an utter destruction to his whole cause, and also to the effect of the law made for the same'.[42]

At More's final examination at Lambeth Palace on 13 April leading up to the offer of compromise, Cromwell was equally vehement, as he saw the chance of agreement slipping away for ever. He was desperate to bring the former Lord Chancellor back from the brink. More recalled him swearing a great oath 'that he had liever [rather] that his own only son' ('which is of truth a goodly young gentleman, and shall I trust come to much worship', More added) 'had lost his head than that I should thus have refused the oath. For surely the King's Highness would now conceive a great suspicion against me, and think that the matter of the nun of Canterbury was all contrived by my drift [encouragement].'[43] Cromwell could only remind More of the obvious: old friendship counted for nothing against the minister's loyalty to the King, and his awareness of how difficult it could be to head off Henry's destructive whims – particularly if, as More's well-informed son-in-law and biographer William Roper later claimed, Queen Anne was nerving Henry against compromise 'by her importunate clamour'.[44]

So More and Fisher went to the Tower, and over their remaining year of life the King's harshness towards them only increased. Cromwell went on trying to talk them round, and mutual respect continued, at least from More: writing from the Tower, he went out of his way to praise Cromwell's prudent handling of the Elizabeth Barton affair (this was the prospective martyr's only letter written in prison which his hagiographer Roper did not choose to reproduce in 1556).[45] Cromwell's patient efforts extended to others, notably the most respected community of monks in the City of London, the Carthusians by Smithfield. They were not treated like the Franciscan Observants, whose whole order was dissolved because of their connection with the Maid, and to whom both Cromwell and Cranmer increasingly displayed blanket hostility. Some English Carthusian communities consistently remained loyal to Henry's schism, notably Hinton Charterhouse in Somerset under its much respected Prior Dr Edmund Horde, and Cromwell clearly hoped that this could be made more general.[46]

The regime treated the London Charterhouse much as it did the aristocratic ladies and retired Oxbridge dons of the Bridgettine house at Syon, that is with reasoned argument as well as occasional coercion. In both cases Cromwell was prepared to argue face to face, as with Thomas More and Bishop Fisher. At the beginning of 1534, about the time he began tense conversations with More and Fisher about their relationship to the Maid's campaigns, he resolved 'To go to the Charterhouse myself' to interview the community.[47] The first serious open clash of the London Carthusians with royal policy came in April, when like the rest of the King's subjects they were faced with the oath to the Act of Succession. The confrontation was untidy: Prior John Houghton and his Proctor (assistant) Humphrey Middlemore were the driving force behind the community's refusal and spent a short time in the Tower of London alongside Fisher and More. They agreed to give way; but not all their brethren followed suit, even after repeated efforts to persuade them.

At this stage the Carthusians were still trying to avoid extending the confrontation more widely to the royal supremacy. Yet that issue could not long be avoided. Cromwell visited the Charterhouse in person several times during 1534, trying to get them to take the oaths, and probing ways of exploiting the tensions which affect any intensely devout enclosed community. On one occasion in June 1534, he interviewed a dissident Carthusian of the house called Thomas Salter, who united his personal clashes with his superiors to the royal cause.[48] In August Cromwell's trusted old servant John Whalley was at the Charterhouse and passed on to his master a letter from Salter full of usefully negative reports about life under the current Carthusian leadership and the widespread failure of morale in Carthusian houses in mainland Europe. Whalley additionally sent over a batch of Charterhouse apples for Cromwell's pleasure; they had a special reputation in the City.[49]

The regime did score significant successes, permanently reeling in prominent conservatives from pursuing further opposition. Bishop Fisher, stricken with what looked to Roland Lee like terminal illness when the two of them spoke, was past caring what the King thought, but not his fellow-bishops Gardiner, Tunstall and Edward Lee.[50] On the day the Maid and her associates died, 20 April, it was common knowledge in London that these three bishops had been sent for from their dioceses. John Husee told Lord Lisle that 'some thinketh they shall to the Tower' (he was too discreet to point out they would be joining Fisher and More there).[51] Ever since Gardiner migrated to the King's service, he had been torn between ambition and principled anger at attacks on ecclesiastical power, but his loss of the Secretaryship to Cromwell and exile to his diocese in April 1534 were far too reminiscent of what had happened to his old master Wolsey. From now on up to his royal master's death, Gardiner devoted his considerable talents to making the royal supremacy work in the interests of traditional Catholicism.

Likewise Edward Lee was not going to cause any further open trouble. Cuthbert Tunstall had been much more straightforwardly part of the opposition to the annulment and break with Rome than either Gardiner or Lee, and he might well have become entangled with the Maid had he not been so far away in the north. We can gauge how closely he was associated with More and Fisher from a later report to Cromwell, who in late 1539 was building up evidence against Tunstall in a further round of political crisis. The deponent testified that Burton, one of the Bishop's servants, was in London 'when the bishop of Rochester [Fisher] and Thomas More were dangered' – this must have been in mid-April just before their examination and then imprisonment in the Tower, 'and the said More asked Burton, "Will not thy master come to us [and] be as we are?" And he said he could not tell. Then said More, "If he do, no force, for if he live he may do more good than to die with us." '[52]

In the light of the debacle around the Maid, the King was understandably paranoid about Bishop Tunstall's intentions, and just as the Bishop was travelling south in late April he ordered Cromwell to organize a raid on Tunstall's chief houses in his diocese, ransacking his private papers for incriminating evidence. It was the first occasion on which Cromwell used as his personal agent a servant later very busy in his monastic affairs, Dr John ap Rhys. Ap Rhys acted as secretary to the northern magnates authorized to undertake the search; he took care to append a postscript to their report, in their names, commending his own diligence.[53] The commissioners found little, attributing their failure to Tunstall's foresight in removing dangerous papers, but the intimidating effect of their ostentatiously disruptive action was more than enough for Cromwell's purposes. Just as with Gardiner and Lee, it permanently ended the Prince-Bishop's efforts at opposition. By 19 May Chapuys was reporting to the Emperor that he had listened with disgust to Bishop Tunstall commending the Act of Succession, which the ambassador linked directly to the raids in County Durham. It was also the memory in Tunstall's own household that this was a turning-point in his allegiance.[54]

Henry showed his confidence in Lee's and Tunstall's acquiescence by immediately ordering them to join a high-powered commission alongside the newly consecrated Bishop Roland Lee, Almoner Edward Foxe and the lawyer Thomas Bedell; their Mission Impossible up in Huntingdonshire was to persuade Katherine of Aragon to accept the reality of the new shape of politics. Tunstall went out of his way to tell her (and the King, who would be reading his report) that he had changed his mind about the validity of her case. The fact that Katherine was rather splendidly contemptuous of the whole delegation and its purpose was almost less important than the fact that the only two bishops of the Northern Province who mattered had irrevocably demonstrated their subservience to the King and his plans for the future of the realm.[55]

With all official pretence of allegiance to Rome now gone, it was the moment to fill some of those episcopal vacancies pending for some time, without any more scrabbling around for papal approval. Accordingly Cranmer took time off in the middle of the April campaign for oaths, the day before the execution of the Maid of Kent, to perform the first consecrations of bishops in his archiepiscopate. They were a trio recently helpful in the King's Great Matter: Thomas Goodricke for Ely; John Capon alias Salcott for Bangor; and at long last, after no less than three years of frustrating delay, Roland Lee for Coventry and Lichfield. Goodricke and Salcott were straightforward Boleyn protégés, but the real prize for Cromwell was landing his old friend Lee in the vast west Midlands diocese. When their mutual friend Lancelot Collins, Treasurer of York, first heard of the prospective appointment six months earlier, he had written cheerfully to Cromwell, 'If it be, as I hear say, that my own good friend Mr Dr Lee by your help shall be Bishop of Chester, I am thereof glad, for then I reckon you bishop there yourself.'[56]

Lee was indeed Cromwell's first protégé on the episcopal bench. The new Bishop gratefully doled out the usual crop of favours: a bailiwick of a chief episcopal manor for Ralph Sadler, and a prebend in Lichfield Cathedral for Christopher Wellifed, Master Secretary's omnivorous clerical nephew and schoolmate of Gregory Cromwell – this latter only two days after Lee's consecration.[57] But the Bishop of Chester's promotion was even more important because he was already chosen as next President of the Council in the Marches of Wales, which enjoyed sweeping powers either side of the Welsh border, and jurisdiction formal and informal in the rest of the Principality as well. From 1525 to 1533 its status was as governing Council for Princess Mary; up to the annulment crisis she was resident in the Marches, with her own stately little Court in the Council's capital Ludlow Castle, and another bishop was President of her Council, John Veysey of Exeter. Veysey was not the most energetic of administrators and, particularly as Katherine and her daughter had been eclipsed, good order in Wales rapidly deteriorated.

Cromwell, with his own particular Welsh preoccupations, was eager to solve this vexation: he noted in a remembrance of May 1533 the need for 'the establishing of a Council in the Marches of Wales', since Mary's demotion from being Princess of Wales meant that her Council had lost its authority. Again a couple of months later, he fretted 'in whose name the council in Wales shall direct their letters and process from hencefor-wards?'[58] Veysey must go: Lee was the ideal replacement. He knew what Border country was like from childhood, though it had been a different border, and it so happened he was personally linked to two of Veysey's predecessors as Lord President in the Marches: Bishop William Smyth of Lincoln who had ordained him, and Bishop Blythe who had made him Chancellor of Coventry and Lichfield.[59] Lee could be confident that he was leaving the work of his diocese in trustworthy hands, since the team of reliable administrative colleagues led by Archdeacon Richard Strete which Cromwell constituted in 1531 was still in place. That meant the Bishop could concentrate on the Presidency of the Council and the strenu-ous business of imposing the rule of law on Wales.

The Lord President threw himself with relish into his new post. While still engaged in persuading the London and Sheen Carthusians, Syon and the Observant convents to take the oath of succession, he briskly for-warded to Cromwell a list of local magnates whom he would like to have placed in commission with him.[60] When Lee set out for the west Mid-lands at the beginning of July, he travelled with a very important young guest: Gregory Cromwell. No more bucolic frolicking in East Anglian parsonages and converted priories for Gregory: this was a new stage in his education, appropriate to the son of the leading royal minister. Lud-low Castle effectively showcased a royal Court, without the dangers of the real thing.

Fourteen-year-old Gregory had the rest of the summer and autumn to watch and learn under the benevolent but unsparing eye of his honorary uncle Roland: 'Ye shall not need to care for him in his order,' the Bishop promised Cromwell. Gregory's long-suffering tutor Henry Dowes was probably trying to accentuate the positive when he listed the shower of hunting invitations from local magnates that the boy had received: it 'cannot be but greatly to his breaking, and profit in good manners, to see the fashions of such men of worship'.[61] The tutor's equine use of 'break-ing' suggests an excess of high spirits in his young charge; Dowes refrained from commenting that being lionized by the Staffordshire gentry was unlikely to curb them. When Bishop Lee sent Cromwell's 'treasure' back to London with evident regret just after the Christmas celebrations, his affectionate end-of-term report also suggests that Gregory was physically small for his age (as do Gregory's later portrait miniatures): 'although nature worketh not in bodily strength, yet it surmounteth in good, gentle and virtuous conditions, which I pray God to continue.'[62]

Around the time Gregory was having his bags packed for Ludlow, Crom-well received an alarming letter from Ireland. Quite when it was sent and when it arrived are both alas uncertain. That was one of the big problems with Ireland, for even letters containing news of emergencies might some-times take three weeks or a month to reach the English capital. This letter probably left its sender in early July. The writer was Robert Cowley, a senior Anglo-Irish lawyer, breaking the news that the Earl of Kildare's son Lord Thomas Fitzgerald (titular Lord Offaly, but known to posterity as 'Silken Thomas') along with members of the great Geraldine family affinity had 'committed infinite murders, burnings and robbings in the English Pale abouts the city of Dublin, specially the King's lands and pos-sessions'. Worse still, they were proclaiming that they were 'of the Pope's sect and band, and him they will serve against the King and all his par-takers, saying further that the King is accursed, and as many as take his part and shall be openly accursed'.[63]

Cowley, a veteran critic of the Geraldines, did not hold back his frus-tration and fury. 'It had been good that the said Earl's heir had been still kept in England. I am sure your wisdom gave no advice to send him home and whosoever counselled the King's Grace thereto was far overseen [utterly crazy].' What had happened in the Pale was treason: Cowley, not immune from pomposity, called Offaly's outrages 'seditious and prodit-orious'. The news became worse again: on 27 July Cromwell's friend and colleague John Allen Archbishop of Dublin fell into the hands of Silken Thomas while trying to flee the country, and Offaly had him murdered along with some of his companions. This atrocity took place amid con-fused scenes which the Fitzgeralds later tried to present (particularly to the Pope) as an unfortunate accident, but it was noticeable that the sur-vivors were a couple of the Archbishop's senior attendants who happened to have the cash for ransom.[64]

As Cowley made clear, all this was a disaster long in the making, which Cromwell might have averted had he not been so occupied on other matters. It is worth tracing how the explosion had built up. We have noticed Cromwell establishing friendly relations with Cowley's patron Piers Butler Earl of Ossory, sworn foe of the Geraldines, back in autumn 1531 (see above, pp. 153–5). At that stage, the Earl of Kildare could still exploit his rival contacts with the Duke of Norfolk and Anne Boleyn, and in July 1532 he got himself reappointed as Deputy of Ireland, after six years out of office. Cromwell's own steady cultivation of other informants in Irish administration reinforced his opinion that this was a bad idea, and in September 1533 the Earl was summoned to the English Court. Not surprisingly suspicious, and moreover seriously ill from a gunshot wound, he procrastinated, but eventually arrived in February 1534, with Offaly appointed as his lieutenant back home. As Cowley noted in fury, the government had missed the chance to keep Silken Thomas in England the previous year.

Kildare's status during his English stay remained uncomfortably ill-defined. While he fretted at Court through winter and spring 1534, Cromwell took time off from many other worries to produce careful and comprehensive plans for a complete overhaul of government in the historically Anglo-Norman parts of the island: *Ordinances for Ireland*. Their contents were not particularly novel among English efforts to govern the normally ungovernable island: not so much an Irish 'Revolution in Government' as a proposed restoration of an idealized version of the past. The main novelty was that, with his usual perception of the usefulness of the new medium, Cromwell had copies printed; that made them far less easy to consign to forgetfulness in the back of a chest in Dublin than previous efforts. Drawing on memoranda from trustworthy Anglo-Irishmen who knew the situation at first hand, Cromwell proposed a thoroughgoing assault on the usurpation of royal power by the Anglo-Norman nobility, the re-establishment of English-ruled territory to the maximum it had achieved in the fourteenth century and the setting up within it of an English style of local government (rather optimistically, this envisaged English-style compliant noblemen and conscientious gentry to do the necessary work). If these innovations really did take root, then the medieval central institutions of government in Dublin might be made to work much as they did in contemporary England.[65]

However unrealistically ambitious all this was, it was clear that within this scheme there was no place for the overweening power of the Earl of Kildare, whatever place a cowed Fitzgerald interest might thereafter play alongside other nobility. By May Kildare had lost the Deputyship to an ally of Cromwell's and of the Butlers, Sir William Skeffington, a military man from Leicestershire with long experience of Ireland including a spell as Deputy, plus a healthy detestation of the Geraldines. But Skeffington, increasingly handicapped by ill-health, fatally delayed his return from London.[66] Offaly was furious at the snub to Fitzgerald honour in Skeffington supplanting his father, and there were parallel sinister events at the English Court: the arrest of another magnate from the Tudor borders, William Lord Dacre of Gilsland, and the abrupt summoning to London and intimidation of Bishop Tunstall of Durham. To treat thus the great men of northern England suggested an equal menace for Geraldines.[67]

Offaly's growing displays of defiance in Dublin precipitated his father's arrest in London on 29 June, and the Earl's ill-health led to his death in the Tower a couple of months later, with no direct involvement in swelling Irish unrest.[68] Thanks to Offaly, unrest had become island-wide rebellion, with a particularly dangerous twist. Cowley's summer report to Cromwell made it clear that Offaly was already expressing strident defiance of royal religious policy; he had vigorous backing among senior clergy in the Anglophone parts of the island, from Meath to Armagh. They were not just angry locals from the Geraldine affinity, but included a brand-new arrival in Ireland as Chancellor of St Patrick's Cathedral Dublin, Dr John Travers, an Oxford academic prominent enough to have been University Preacher the year before he set out for his new office. In other words, Travers knew exactly what Thomas Cromwell was up to back in England. Several of his fellow-dissidents in the Irish Church had plenty of Oxford links from their days studying there. This group were as dangerously motivated as the admirers of the Maid of Kent, but additionally had an army at their backs.[69]*

In the wider world, the Holy Roman Emperor's advisers showed a lively interest in Irish developments. The old alliance between England and Empire had been severely strained first by King Henry's despicable treatment of Katherine of Aragon, and then by his flirtation with Protestant reformers. Habsburg diplomats had started taking notice of Ireland in 1528 when the King's plans for the Aragon annulment became apparent, but Chapuys became freshly alert to Irish trouble as the Boleyn marriage took shape in spring 1533. That summer Thomas Batcock, a merchant in Spain and an old informant of Cardinal Wolsey's, approached the new chief minister to warn him that Spanish Court gossip had the Emperor planning to 'set the Scots and Irishmen against us, with a great number of Spaniards. All shall be as pleaseth God.'[70] The Mayor of

---

* I am puzzled by the general emphasis in recent Irish historiography on downplaying the element of stridently papalist activism in the rebellion. The very circumstantial account in Cowley's letter to Cromwell shows that it was there from the outset.

Waterford wrote drawing Cromwell's attention to the ongoing reality of these plans just as Silken Thomas's rebellion broke out.[71]

In fact Charles V never committed substantial resources to helping the Irish rebels beyond some arms shipments to another Anglo-Norman magnate in alliance with Offaly, Thomas Fitzthomas Earl of Desmond. That hardly mattered: the Irish noblemen's offer to transfer their allegiance from the Tudor Crown to the Habsburgs, and their open proclamation of loyalty to the Pope, were important assets for the Emperor, won at remarkably little expense. The modest imperial investment was an exact equivalent of what the English were doing against Habsburg interests in Germany and the Baltic (see below, pp. 262–3), but much more cost-effective. Members of the Irish nobility withdrawing their allegiance from the English Crown had no precedent.

The possible consequences deeply alarmed King Henry and his ministers, though in public and in documents which might become public they played down their fears, for obvious reasons. Chapuys reported to the Emperor with frank *Schadenfreude* Cromwell's fury as ever more dire reports poured in from Ireland in August; Master Secretary had the cleric who brought the news of Archbishop Allen's murder detained, accusing him of treason for stirring alarm in England by leaving Ireland so hastily.[72] It was plain that Sir William Skeffington must make a reality of the Deputyship to which he had been appointed in the spring, and return to face the spreading insurrection. Skeffington set out at the end of July with the makings of a hastily assembled expeditionary force, but he delayed in Chester and Holyhead for weeks before crossing the Irish Sea, suffering from his recurrent illness, and reluctant to leave before even more reluctant English levies trickled in to give him the semblance of a convincing army.[73]

Attending Skeffington and doing his best to chivvy him on to Ireland was another Leicestershire man, Cromwell's servant William Brabazon, accompanied by a more junior Cromwell household colleague also from the Midlands, Thomas Agard. Brabazon was a key and long-standing member of Cromwell's personal administrative team, and sacrificing him was a major statement of intent: clearly he and Agard were to be the Secretary's eyes and ears in Ireland. Appointed Under-Treasurer of the Irish Exchequer on 26 August, Brabazon was one of the few Englishmen whom Cromwell sent to Ireland on a permanent basis, and he stayed long after his patron's fall. On his death on campaign in Ulster in 1552 after a long and successful career in Irish government, he was commemorated with a handsome tomb and monument in St Catherine's parish church in Dublin.[74] Appropriately, these were remarkably modish, among the first examples of Renaissance art in the island; they symbolized a new era for

Ireland, though not exactly a new dawn. Skeffington's reappointment as Deputy had marked the end of centuries in which Anglo-Norman noblemen had effectively kept Ireland in their own hands, and inaugurated an almost unbroken period of government by Englishmen which only drew to its messy conclusion in 1921.

Not surprisingly after the Irish catastrophe, the already vindictive atmosphere in English politics grew ever more poisoned, and over the next few years the fear of treason produced ever more murderous results. Right away, furious recriminations flew around, exposing strains normally discreetly veiled. Chapuys continued to derive much amusement from them, particularly the chasm which opened up between Cromwell and the Duke of Norfolk, resulting in the Duke retreating from Court once more. Furious rows at the Council board included an incident around the beginning of September 1534, concerning the King's illegitimate son the Duke of Richmond, that the ambassador rightly found very interesting:

> I am told that among other accusations which Cromwell brought on that occasion against the Duke [of Norfolk], one was that he was more the cause of the present disaster than anyone else, inasmuch as he had wanted to keep the Duke of Richmond near him and his daughter, [Richmond's] wife; and that, had he consented to allow him to go to Ireland eight months ago, as he had been advised, none of this would have happened.[75]

Henry Fitzroy, the King's illegitimate son by a Staffordshire gentlewoman called Elizabeth Blount, was a dynastic asset whose value waxed and waned in relation to the prospect of the King acquiring a more satisfactory male heir. The King was proud of him while he was his only son, and brought him up in appropriate splendour. At six he was created Duke of Richmond and Somerset; in June 1529, aged ten, he was made Lord Lieutenant of Ireland (thus all the Irish Deputies we have met were Deputies to him). His godfather Cardinal Wolsey also sent him to Yorkshire with his own regional council to match Princess Mary's position in Wales. Thereafter, Richmond's advancing years made him more credible as a governing figurehead, as well as a political asset to be fought over; at Wolsey's fall he was one of the prizes available for distribution. The Duke of Norfolk as part of his triumph over Wolsey did his best to annex the boy, no doubt in co-operation with Anne Boleyn, leading in stages to the fourteen-year-old Richmond marrying Norfolk's daughter Mary in November 1533.

That curiously delayed event showed bad timing, as it coincided with Norfolk's rout in national politics. His grip on the teenager began almost immediately to be contested, and his refusal to allow Richmond to be sent to Ireland that winter was clearly part of the struggle. Instead, at the end of May 1534 the little Duke was separated from his father-in-law to live on his estates at Canford on the Dorset coast, arriving to the sort of local excitement and acclaim which was to greet his slightly younger contemporary Gregory Cromwell in the Marches a month or two later. It is interesting that the Duke's 'Governor' George Cotton immediately wrote to Cromwell to let him know how successful the welcome in the West Country had been, going out of his way to thank the Secretary for his long-term 'manifold goodness'.[76]

Just as indicative was a letter from Richmond himself to Cromwell a week later, about the appointment of a West Country abbot. It was part of a correspondence that summer in which the boy carefully showed Master Secretary how conscientiously he was playing the role of a local magnate. He also displayed a teenage enthusiasm for accompanying the King on a proposed visit to France which others of more mature years were doing their best to avoid; this letter in his own hand is rather touching in its eager adolescent awkwardness.[77] Ireland would have given Richmond a larger-scale apprenticeship in government than Dorset offered, and his presence there would have allowed Cromwell to populate the Irish administration with more allies alongside Brabazon and Agard. Thanks to Norfolk's stubbornness in February 1534, that plan was now impossible.

There were, nevertheless, compensations. Norfolk's effective disgrace left a much less contested space in government, the last convulsion of a sequence of events in which Cromwell's rivals had conveniently suffered falls from power or complete eclipses, not least thanks to treason in prospect. Five years before, Cromwell had set off from Wolsey at Esher 'to make or mar' in the 1529 Parliament. Now Bishop Gardiner was licking his wounds in that same episcopal palace, Thomas More had exchanged the Lord Chancellor's seat for a cell in the Tower and the conservative bishops who had sneered at Cromwell's master that autumn were humbled. Out of his ill-wishers, there remained Anne Boleyn to deal with, and she would have done well to understand what one of Cromwell's West Country friends and former colleagues under the Cardinal said to him appreciatively that summer of 1534: 'I do well perceive, as ye have often times said to me, that although ye were slow, ye be sure at length.'[78] Above them all was one neither slow nor sure: the never-predictable King Henry. Where would the royal whim next take Master Secretary?

11

Spirituals: 1534–1535

In 1534 the first substantial signs appeared of Cromwell grafting his own evangelical religious enthusiasm on to Henry VIII's break with Rome. Over the previous three years, his undoubted relish for curbing the independent power of the Church had matched the King's own fury at leading churchmen's opposition to the Aragon annulment. Yet nothing Cromwell had accomplished for his master so far in government policy moved beyond that particular agenda, towards the Reformations across the water. To go further was a delicate task, given that Henry VIII detested most of what developing Protestantism stood for. Nevertheless, with the destruction of the Maid and her allies, closely followed by the shock of an Irish rebellion driven by an increasingly open papalist rhetoric, he was emboldened in efforts to move the King's various inconsistent religious agendas towards his own, and in Archbishop Cranmer he had a sympathetic collaborator. The often rash ways in which Cromwell pursued his plans over the next few years are some of the best proofs that he was more than a politician shaped by cynical ambition.

The first signs of his efforts to promote evangelical reformation in England were initiatives in foreign policy, the area in which he was least experienced or competent. In reaching out to evangelicals overseas, he had been forced to embrace King Henry's emphatic snub to the exiled William Tyndale in 1531, and none of the government's other tentative approaches abroad that year had come to anything. The year 1533 saw the King sending embassies to both Catholic and Protestant rulers in the Empire; although they were led by Cromwell's evangelical agent Stephen Vaughan and the resident diplomat Christopher Mont, it was clear that religion mattered far less to Henry than the task of outflanking or harassing Charles V and finding backing for his marriage to Anne Boleyn. The missions proved even more humiliatingly fruitless than two years before; yet Cromwell did not give up. He put intensive drafting work into fresh memoranda for the King in December 1533, concentrating on embassies to German princes who explicitly rejected papal authority.[1]

When at the end of January 1534 a trio of English ambassadors set off to various parts of Germany and to the King of Poland, they were once more associates of Cromwell and Cranmer: Dr Thomas Lee, William Paget (freshly acquired as Cromwell's client from the fading Bishop Gardiner) and Cranmer's friend Archdeacon Nicholas Heath. They were all equipped with generous cash on a royal warrant channelled to them via the Master of the Jewels.[2] Given their official status, there was a curious slant to the message when in May Heath and his companions presented themselves to the Diet (assembly) of the Schmalkaldic League of Protestant states in Nuremberg, soliciting a return official embassy from the League to England. The records of the Diet noted that the ambassadors' arrival was 'counselled and set up through a few of the most distinguished people of the realm, *though not endorsed by the King*'.[3]

The memorandum comments further on this group (its members unnamed), their purpose and the likely benefit of a Protestant embassy to England. 'The English councillors and distinguished people who favour the Gospel and have requested such an embassy will have greater cause to prompt the King, so that through this means, which the Almighty in His grace has now miraculously set forth, the Gospel may be brought to England, and from a persecutor [Henry] will become a lover of the Word of God.' More followed in the same vein, from which it is evident that while the English missions to mainland Europe had many purposes in King Henry's mind, this was not one of them. The feelers to Nuremberg were an embassy within an embassy, and no one other than Cromwell would have had the chutzpah to try something like this. Maybe the King knew about the wooing of the League, and allowed it to go forward, subject to deniability. Maybe he did not.

The leaders of the Schmalkaldic Diet were clearly interested in the English approach, given the care with which they considered and minuted it, but they were also hard-headed politicians who recognized a dubious prospect when they saw one. Why waste money and energy on an embassy which might face a direct snub from the King of England? The timing of the English embassies that winter and spring could not have been worse: Germany was far more interested in the evangelical states' military action to claw back from the Habsburgs the territory of the exiled Duke of Württemberg, and by a political meltdown in the kingdom of Denmark, likewise potentially involving Habsburg power. Henry did in fact back the winners in the short, sharp Württemberg campaign, though his contribution was at one remove: he agreed to divert to the cause the current instalments of a substantial pension France had been paying England for decades, in view of the common interest of England, France and the Schmalkaldic League in harassing the Emperor. At least that promised a little English goodwill stored up for the future with the League.[4]

The first apparently productive Protestant contacts with England this year came not from the League but from the Hanseatic cities of Lübeck and Hamburg to the north, where Thomas Lee followed up a royal mission he had undertaken the previous year. The two great trading ports were strongly opposed to the Emperor and the Pope, saw England as a valuable ally, were prepared to declare their firm conviction that the Aragon annulment was good and godly, and sensationally declared that if Henry backed their plan to invade Denmark and oust its present monarch they would offer him the vacant Danish throne. Henry always showed a touching confidence in other people's admiration of his abilities as a ruler, and the prospect of anyone in mainland Europe expressing unalloyed support for his marital troubles was additionally thrilling. As far as Cromwell and Cranmer were concerned, Lübeck and Hamburg were as attractive a prospect as the Schmalkaldic League, being good Protestants as well as major trading partners with England on the North Sea and Baltic coasts.[5]

Accordingly, in mid-June 1534, two stylish Hanseatic diplomatic delegations arrived in England to a warm welcome at Court. They were followed a few weeks later by their leader, delayed through illness: Johannes Aepinus (Johann Huck before Latinizing himself), Superintendent – effectively evangelical Bishop – of the Church of Hamburg. His appearance was a new and exotic experience for the English: Aepinus was a theological heavyweight among German Protestant clergy, and so an inspiration to still tentative and thinly spread evangelical imitators in the infant Church of England. Chapuys, bewildered by this diplomatic initiative, but correctly assuming it was not good news for the Emperor, reported a lavish banquet for the Hanseatics thrown by Cranmer at Lambeth Palace, with a significant guest-list: the newly consecrated Bishops Salcott and Goodricke, Edward Foxe and inevitably Cromwell. It was not surprising that apparently 'the conversation turned principally on several articles of the Lutheran sect, such as the authority of the Pope and other matters, on which these people wished to have the opinion and advice of the Lubeckian doctors, and find the best means of persuading the English to such a radical change in religious matters.'[6]

The home team at Cranmer's dinner-table sounds remarkably like 'the

English councillors and distinguished people who favour the Gospel' in the Schmalkaldic minute at Nuremberg. Yet the relationship never crystallized: futility and cross-purposes stumbled on in dismal succession, doing the godly cause no favours. The English had no real grasp of the intricacies of Baltic politics, and the internal affairs of both Hamburg and Lübeck were chaotic. The regime in Lübeck might be godly, but it had come to power through insurrection, boasting a populist agenda which would have appalled King Henry if he had experienced it at first hand, and which infuriated the rest of the Hanseatic League. Blatant piracy by Lübecker shipping against Habsburg vessels right down as far as the Channel seriously embarrassed the English authorities in their dealings with the Habsburg Low Countries, a far more important commercial partner for England than Lübeck.[7] By autumn 1534, having reversed alliances in the Danish dynastic struggles, Lübeck was brazenly backtracking on the thought of promoting Henry to the Danish crown, though the King blindly persisted in thinking he could benefit from intervening in Denmark.[8] This irresponsible English diplomatic adventuring left the Schmalkaldic League deeply unimpressed, and offset goodwill gained through Henry's financial contribution to the Württemberg campaign. It was a miracle that any further negotiations with Germany took place the following year: really a tribute to the narrowness of King Henry's international options, thanks to his own domestic and external follies.

In England itself, the evangelical cause was marked by equal confusion. Over the next year the regime discovered that even if the existing structures of the Provinces of Canterbury and York might now be described in official documents with a new phrase, 'the Church of England', that left a great many questions unanswered about the new Church. This was embarrassingly revealed by Archbishop Cranmer's launch in May 1534 of a metropolitical visitation for his own Province, patently aimed at laying his clergy open for whatever measures of reformation the King would allow him.[9] Cranmer had already dealt with his own diocese of Canterbury in 1533; that was the easy part. Now he launched the wider programme on the most obvious starting-point, the diocese of London, and extended it outwards month by month, evidently intending to cover the whole of the Southern Province during the next twelve months or so.

Straight away Bishop Stokesley of London spotted a fatal flaw in the plan: Cranmer's own official title, under whose powers he acted, still contained the phrase 'Legate of the Apostolic See'. Astonishingly, no one had thought to get rid of it. With infuriating punctiliousness, Stokesley and his Cathedral Chapter of St Paul's (no friends to reformation there) courteously pointed out that to accept the Archbishop's visitation was to accept this obnoxious papal title and lay themselves open to all the disgrace and horror of *praemunire*. Over the next months Bishops Longland of Lincoln, Nix of Norwich and lastly Gardiner of Winchester all took their cue from Stokesley, ingeniously ringing the changes on legal obstructions to their metropolitan's jurisdiction. Looking back over events of the previous five years, they had genuine reason to fear further encounters with the arbitrariness of *praemunire* charges.

Cranmer therefore only had a clear run for visitations in the vacant diocese of Worcester and the effectively vacated Rochester (Fisher being in the Tower). He took some care to avoid personal encounters with his episcopal colleagues whenever he launched himself in person on the wider countryside, preaching and doling out injunctions, including orders for far more sermons of biblical exposition, and warnings to the clergy to avoid ostentatious living. He did not reach the further dioceses in the west or any of the four dioceses which covered Wales, perhaps hoping that Bishop Roland Lee would supply the deficit there in due course, and naturally he had no formal powers at all in the Province of York. In the Northern Province his colleague as Archbishop, Edward Lee, was never going to pay sympathetic attention to what Canterbury wanted, and would need constant bullying from Cromwell to forward any measure smacking of evangelical reformation.

In parallel to this effort came a lesser royal visitation of the various orders of friars in the realm, which would among its other tasks take the friars' oaths to the supremacy. That was a matter of some importance, since friars were by vocation the chief preachers within the Church and could do much to influence public opinion. How was such a general visitation of the fraternal orders to be achieved, without any good precedent, now the break with Rome had taken effect? It was in practice done by a royal warrant delivered to Archbishop Cranmer in spring 1534, appointing as visitors two leading friars from the Dominicans and Austin Friars, both evangelical in their outlook. Since the pair were personally closer to Cromwell than to Cranmer, there can be little doubt these were appointments which Cromwell arranged. He soon saw to it that their efforts were rewarded with promotion to bishoprics.[10] For the Dominicans, there was John Hilsey, who had abandoned his traditionalism during raucous pulpit wars in Bristol in 1533, and now emerged as a strong preacher for evangelical reformation.[11] For the Austins, there was none other than Cromwell's landlord at the London Austin Friars, Prior George Browne. He can previously be glimpsed writing to Cromwell in a note of the early 1530s about a piece of Cambridge preferment, in terms not only evangelical but as hostile to 'schoolmen' as the most fashionable humanist could be.[12]

Hilsey and Browne ran into difficulties over jurisdiction just as Cranmer did. We have a record of direct defiance from the Warden of the Southampton Observant Franciscans, who with spirited unwisdom appealed straight to Master Secretary against the visitors reciting their commission in his convent. The unwelcome intruder was probably the visitors' assistant Richard Ingworth, Dominican Prior of King's Langley and another reliable satrap of Cromwell's.[13] Browne was evidently nervous when he ventured into the Northern Province, and reported with relief to Cromwell when the assembled inmates of the two friaries in Beverley 'all did agree according to my commission'.[14] Alas, the two commissioners themselves eventually fell out; Hilsey was furious when in autumn 1534 the Austin Friar Browne tried to assume jurisdiction over the Dominicans as Master-General, 'the which your Mastership appointed to *me* . . . and where that we by the counsel of our whole General Chapter hath made certain assignations, he hath changed and broken them . . . saying that he is our Master-General and that we shall do nothing but under him'.[15] It was all becoming extremely messy, and needed a firm referee with clear, unchallengeable authority.

Unlike the dilemmas posed by England's international weakness, Cromwell could tackle these domestic headaches with comparative ease in his favourite arena, Parliament. In the first autumn Parliamentary session actually to take place without prorogation since 1529, the main business was to tidy up the weaknesses in legislation about Church and succession exposed by Cranmer's visitation and the great campaigns of oath-taking.[16] An essential first step was an Act of Supremacy, which briskly passed Parliament over the first fortnight; really it said nothing that had not been practice since the spring, but it implicitly saluted the serried ranks of clergy and religious who had taken the oath against papal authority, and it made routine the name that was still an unfamiliar novelty: 'the Church of England'. It recognized the King as Supreme Head of that Church, enjoying 'all honours, dignities, pre-eminences, jurisdictions, privileges, authorities, immunities, profits and commodities, to the said dignity . . . appertaining': a round-up to which no single individual had ever previously been entitled, given that the dignity had not existed.[17]

This magniloquently comprehensive list was ripe with possibilities, particularly as far as 'profits and commodities' were concerned. A further Act 'for First Fruits and Tenths' relieved churchmen of wealth many lay-people regarded as surplus, by granting the King a sum equivalent to the first year of a cleric's income in any newly acquired office, and a tenth of all subsequent income in these offices. 'First Fruits' was an innovatively weasel phrase: simply a new description of the tax which in papal times had been called 'annates', and which over the previous few years had been regularly denounced in royal propaganda for its burdensomeness. 'First Fruits', however, had a good evangelical ring, derived from the Old Testament's institution of a thank-offering to God of the harvest's first produce. Cromwell did a lot of the work drafting this bill alongside Chancellor Audley, and was responsible in particular for furnishing it with one of his most elaborate and silkily worded statutory preambles, praising the King, his achievements in bringing his subjects 'tranquillity, peace, unity, quietness and wealth' and his 'excessive and inestimable charges' in attaining this happy result. Given the current level of awareness of treasonable words, it would have been risky to make any hurtful remarks in Parliament about that encomium. The preamble was thus worth the verbal elaboration, particularly since a more modest measure of royal appropriation of papal revenues, including annates, had actually failed to pass the Lords in the first session of 1534.[18]

The present bill's progress past the bishops and abbots in the Lords was speeded by a number of concessions to current clergy, remitting some of the burdens the King had opportunistically heaped on them during his various campaigns of intimidation, and exempting the poorest from payment. Its provisions were decidedly less radical than proposals to be found in government papers for general confiscation of church lands in return for clergy both monastic and non-monastic receiving fixed stipends: these schemes may have been intended primarily to scare leading clergy into accepting the more moderate package.[19] Nevertheless, the legislation permanently increased fiscal exactions on the clergy of the Church of England way above the comparatively minor demands previously made by popes.

All this was alongside the long-standing 'occasional' tax demands from the Church which medieval kings of England had always made. In the 1520s Cardinal Wolsey had much increased these exactions, to general fury from his fellow-clergy – once more, Wolsey can be seen as anticipating measures that Thomas Cromwell then took further. The Convocations of Canterbury and York no longer had any real part in agreeing those rounds of taxation when the demand was made; they were simply to vote them through parallel to any Parliamentary vote of a grant. They must have gasped to find that the new system would begin straight away: New Year's Day 1535.[20]

Further Acts laid down discipline and punishment for opposition to reformation. One dealt with a serious technical fault in administering the oath of succession nationwide since the earlier session of Parliament.

The wording of the oath went beyond that contained in the Act of Succession, as Thomas More damagingly pointed out from his prison cell, particularly in its explicit provision that those sworn should repudiate the power of any 'foreign authority or potentate' and any oath previously made to them. Either More or his biographer – the text does not make it plain – saw these additions as an arbitrary decision of Cromwell and Chancellor Audley, which had thus to be remedied in legislation, 'espying their own oversight in that behalf'.[21] The Act retrospectively legalized the wording used throughout the oath-taking campaign; that simple move made the continued imprisonment and eventual conviction of Fisher and More legally easier. More difficult to secure, though a comparatively short and tightly constructed bill, was a much more general Act refining the provisions for treason passed in the spring.[22]

The government were painfully aware that the Act of Succession had not provided effective sanctions on indignant comment about either the King's marriage plans or his confrontation with the Papacy and Church hierarchy. Accordingly they decided radically to narrow the category of misprision of treason, and gave an unenviable promotion to most of the offences which misprision had covered. It now became high treason 'to wish, will or desire by [spoken] words or in writing' challenges to the royal succession or supremacy; or to use language about the King such as heretic, tyrant or usurper. The change went down very badly. John Fisher's brother Robert, one of Rochester's MPs, told the Bishop that 'there was much sticking at the same' in the Commons, and made it clear that the chief worry was still the vagueness of this offence by words.[23] Members were fearful of being trapped in frivolous but fatal accusations. Their similar worries in the 1531 Parliament about laypeople not being explicitly exempted from *praemunire* prosecution had created a real hold-up, on which the Crown had given way rather than imperil its legislative timetable.

The only way that this opposition could be outfaced was to stress that the treason legislation solely covered 'maliciously' speaking on such topics. Surprisingly, this carried the day. Official insistence on the importance of this adverb was so emphatic that common memory (represented not just by Robert Fisher but by another MP who was a client of Cromwell, John Rastell) held that the Commons themselves had insisted on its inclusion, even though 'maliciously' already appeared both in the text of the Act of Succession passed in the spring and in official drafts of this Treason Bill prepared before the Parliamentary session. It is difficult to see how there could be any speaking against these high matters not construable as malicious, but somehow the supposed concession quelled further trouble for the time being, and the Treason Bill passed without material change. Even so, it left a bitter taste, and its partial repeal proved an easy way for Edward Seymour Duke of Somerset to gain popularity early in his Protectorate after King Henry's death.

For those anxious about arbitrary use of the new legislation, the Act in fact contained a more important statement of precision about proof than the flannel about 'maliciously': all those convicted must be 'lawfully convicted according to the customs and laws of this realm', which meant the common law of England. However imperfectly that principle might be applied, it was still a principle, and it had not appeared in the legislation of 1352 or thereafter in its application, which had often been by the arbitrary will of the monarch. As ecclesiastical law and privilege retreated in the 1530s, so did the common law expand, and by implication its restraining power on the Crown. This was one of many ways in which Thomas Cromwell's work on the immediate needs and policies of Henry VIII pushed the future of England's government and polity in a direction which would not have been apparent to him at the time.

One other tiny pair of words in the Treason Act shows how alert Cromwell and his drafters were to dangers unfolding around the King from dissident churchmen. It occurs in a saving clause protecting the rights of those who might, though innocent, be deprived of property by a felony committed by a traitor. That might seem generous, but it made an exception for 'such persons as shall be so convict, and their heirs *and successors*'. Those last two words are a significant novelty, unprecedented in exceptions for punishment in common law. 'Heirs' meant what it said: heirs in families. 'Successors' were those in corporations, in particular clergy who held possessions or estates by virtue of their office. They could be clergy like the Maid's backers who had been parish priests, like Archbishop Warham's chaplain Henry Gold, Vicar of Hayes, or even the successor of a bishop like John Fisher; but more likely they would be the head of a monastery or friary with predecessors convicted of treason. The phrase had clearly been in Cromwell's mind for some time, since it reflected a proposal in his remembrances of October 1533, while the Maid of Kent's destruction was unfolding, for legislation in a future Parliament.[24]

Now, therefore, an unfortunate monastery or friary could be permanently forfeit to the Crown, as if it was a piece of property belonging to the family of a traitor. At that juncture, Cromwell would probably be thinking of the head of a Franciscan Observant house. By autumn 1534, the Observant Order in England had disappeared (dissolved that summer, although their friaries had been handed over to other 'Conventual'

Franciscans rather than suppressed), but the Observants still flourished in vigorous traditionalism in chaotically rebellious Ireland, and as late as autumn 1539 they hung on in one house in the Channel Islands outside Parliament's jurisdiction.[25] In the next few years, the word 'successors' would come to have multiple applications for dissolving a much wider range of monasteries.

The Act of Supremacy was background to the greatest expansion of Cromwell's power so far: his appointment to perhaps the most important and far-reaching office he ever held, despite his later promotions. In early 1535 the King granted him a peculiar title, which in English usage had no precedent and saw no successors, 'Vice-Gerent in Spirituals'. Vice-Gerent was simply a translation of the Latin for 'exercising in place of' – the exercise in this case being of King Henry's powers as Supreme Head of the Church.* In terms of jurisdiction, Cromwell's creation as Vice-Gerent was reliant on that grandiloquent list in the Act of Supremacy, reciting the Supreme Head's 'honours, dignities, pre-eminences' etc. etc. 'to the said dignity . . . appertaining'. With such a cornucopia of power, Henry could easily farm out some to a subordinate.

Despite the novelty of the confected name, it did have an exact and recent precedent of which Cromwell was of course aware: the special papal legateship *a latere* exercised by his old master Cardinal Wolsey. Wolsey had been deputy of the Pope in the Tudor realms; Vice-Gerent Cromwell enjoyed the same powers, overriding the two Archbishops in England (and possibly the Archbishops in Ireland too, though like everything in Ireland that was more complicated). When he fully unveiled a bureaucracy for his new office, it was strikingly like Wolsey's legatine administration, and included some of the same people as its officials. The glaring difference, of course, was that in exercising such powers over the Church Wolsey, like the Pope, was an ordained priest and consecrated bishop, while Cromwell, like the King, was a layman.

It is one of the amusing symptoms of this that once the Vice-Gerency had been constituted as possibly the most important executive office in the whole Church of England, no one was quite sure about the appropriate form of respectful address for such a beast as a Vice-Gerent. He could hardly be called 'your Grace', certainly not 'your Holiness'. During 1535, someone on his visitatorial team (maybe the expertly oleaginous Dr Richard Leighton) must have intimated to those worried by the problem that an equally novel 'your Goodness' might be the solution. The sycophantic

---

* It is in no way related to an imaginary compound 'Vice-Regent', which remains a favourite mistake among undergraduates and others.

among his staff and the Church hierarchy rather self-consciously adopted it, once in a while, before the conferring of a peerage on Cromwell happily enabled them to say 'your Lordship'.[26] One hopes that the Vice-Gerent was saved by his sense of humour from encouraging its adoption. In fact, usages of the vice-gerential title itself are not that common in addresses on Cromwell's letters, and generally heralded some administrative or patronage query relating to the Church. Still fewer bothered with the title annexed to it, 'Vicar-General'.[27]

The run-up to creating the Vice-Gerency was complex and crabwise, as was characteristic of Cromwell's promotions. All those involved were feeling their way through the momentous experiment created by the supremacy legislation. There is also the usual suspicion that its gradual unfolding was designed to neutralize the unfavourable exclamations of Queen Anne.[28] The journey began in the early 1534 Parliament, which legislated to replace an important aspect of papal power by setting up a new 'Faculty Office' under Archbishop Cranmer. Its job was to issue various dispensations formerly the Vatican's prerogative: licensing monks and friars to become secular clergy, for instance (that would soon become major business), providing for clergy to be non-resident in one or more of their benefices, or enabling men and women to marry despite infringing the Church's complicated regulations on prohibited degrees of relationship. Cardinal Wolsey, by virtue of his legatine powers, had very handily provided just such an office, saving those seeking dispensations having to apply to Rome; after his fall, multiple inconveniences piled up, even before the formal break with the Papacy. The passage of the legislation setting up the Faculty Office in spring 1534 marked the moment that the sort of influential laypeople who had always sought dispensations realized the reality of the royal supremacy. Papal authority was definitively at an end, and they must look elsewhere to sort out their problems. 'After this day, the Bishop of Rome shall have no manner of authority within the realm of England,' John Grenville wrote to his master Lord Lisle on 20 March 1534.[29]

One problem with the newly established Faculty Office, up and running only a fortnight after the end of the first 1534 Parliamentary session, was its dependence on a highly clumsy dual system of authorizing more expensive dispensations: there was to be a clerk in Chancery looking after them in tandem with the Lambeth Palace administration. The clumsiness no doubt reflected the government's uncomfortable awareness that, even if Cranmer's ancient title was 'Primate of All England', his actual powers over the Province of York were non-existent, and just as diaphanous for Ireland. In a similar fashion, an Act for the Submission of the Clergy, passed in the same Parliamentary session, had replaced appeals to the Pope with a structure of appeals in Chancery – thus currently to the incumbent Lord Chancellor, Thomas Audley.

If the system thus created was clunky, it had the additional drawback that it allowed no formal place for Thomas Cromwell, despite the fact that he had been playing an all-pervasive part in ecclesiastical administration since the beginning of 1532, without any office to justify it. Even a teen-age apprentice in government like the Duke of Richmond knew that. When he wrote to Cromwell on 11 June 1534, Richmond asked him to allow a free election of a new abbot to the Dorset Cistercian house of Bindon, 'as the King's Highness hath (as I think) constituted and author-ised you that ye by your wisdom and discretion shall take an order and direction in all such causes'.[30] Audley's continuance as one half of the new duo of Archbishop of Canterbury and Lord Chancellor was unavoid-able, in view of his clear competence at his job and constant usefulness in drafting vital government legislation. In any case, if he had been shoul-dered aside to provide Cromwell with the leading legal office in the realm, even a worm as pliable as Audley might have turned.

Accordingly, and probably with this matter of ecclesiastical jurisdic-tion mainly in mind, on 8 October 1534 Cromwell gained another promotion in Chancery: the office of Master of the Rolls.[31] He elbowed aside a colleague in his anxiety to acquire it: on 31 May 1534 his old colleague in Wolsey's service and in the annulment proceedings, the ecclesiastical lawyer Dr John Tregonwell, wrote to him anxiously check-ing that Cromwell's long-standing promise of the Mastership of the Rolls on the likely vacation by its present holder Dr John Taylor would be ful-filled.[32] Tregonwell's qualifications made him an obvious choice for the office, but Taylor survived till October without apparently resigning. By then, Cromwell had changed his mind and took it himself, thus as it turned out permanently transferring the Mastership of the Rolls from the domain of Chancery-trained clerics to lay common lawyers. On a lesser scale, this was as symbolic a moment as the re-creation for a layman of Wolsey's legatine powers.

Theoretically Cromwell thus became Audley's deputy in Chancery, but this meant that he did not need to be dragged into the everyday liti-gation business afflicting his superior, even though it gave him a major place in England's legal hierarchy. From then on until an even greater promotion in 1536, it was as Master of the Rolls that contemporaries generally addressed letters to him. The Mastership was a rich source of fees and perquisites, in an average year a very handsome 300 pounds-plus, and brought a further exceptional benefit: The Rolls, the Master's

stately and venerable house in Chancery Lane, worth having for its geographical position alone. This new base put Cromwell at a much more
convenient distance from the Court and Parliament in Westminster –
right on the western edge of the City, unlike Austin Friars up in the far
north-east. He moved in straight away.[33]

What The Rolls would save Cromwell in time and decorum is apparent from a cheerful passing comment by his friend Attorney-General
Christopher Hales in a business note of 1533: Hales needed to consult
him, but could not leave his own legal chambers, so 'if it may please you
to put your mule out of her direct way of Westminster towards Gray's
Inn, I will be at your commandment.'[34] This gives us a vivid glimpse of
Master Secretary trotting through the City crowds on his endless journeys from Austin Friars, down Cheapside and Ludgate Hill to the Strand
and onwards west. His steadily increasing dignity must be spared such
commuting. In a serious health crisis in March and April 1535, decorum
worked the other way, for Cromwell fell very ill with a fever at The Rolls,
confined to the house for around a month. Towards the end of it the King
took the most unusual step of visiting him in person, dining and transacting a little formal business. It was an unusual sign of Henry's personal
concern, because unlike Wolsey Cromwell was normally only with the
King for business discussions; their relationship did not normally have
the trappings of easy friendship. Queen Anne did not accompany the
monarch on this errand of mercy.[35]

The Rolls was thus a house fit for a King. Austin Friars remained
Cromwell's more domestic retreat, and he went on adding to its splendour, but The Rolls housed much of his archive – alongside the repository
of official Chancery records, another convenience. He even had his own
handsome private chapel next door (not that such amenities seemed particularly to concern him).* In fact Cromwell liked the house so much that
he did not release it to the Master of the Rolls who succeeded him in July
1536: coincidentally Attorney-General Hales. Hales does not seem to
have kicked up a fuss about this while Cromwell lived, despite the house
specifically forming part of his grant of office. He was remembered rather
sadly as dining habitually at an inn in Chancery Lane, and 'during his
time at the Rolls to have kept very small house or none at all'.[36] This
was as much an example of Cromwell's high-handedness as taking the
Mastership in the first place.

---

* The splendid Renaissance tomb of Master of the Rolls John Young, d. 1516, remains in
the Victorian reconstruction of the chapel now contained in the Maughan Library, King's
College London: formerly the Public Record Office, successor to that Chancery archive.

Through the year, conversations continued about staging an alternative to the unfolding fiasco of Cranmer's archiepiscopal visitation: a royal visitation of Church institutions across the realm.[37] The plans got steadily more ambitious, as we can see from fortunately dateable drafts of measures setting it up. The first draft, from summer or early autumn 1534, envisaged a team of three visitors-general, unnamed, merely to make tours of inspection of exempt religious houses – in other words, monasteries and colleges previously answering only to the Pope and so outside the powers of visitation of the Archbishops of Canterbury and York. Their work would parallel the commission on the friaries already falteringly under way.[38] Next came a much broader draft commission for the visitation of any ecclesiastical institution, which internal evidence dates between 17 November and 19 December 1534.

This expanded plan arose directly from the recent passage of the Act of Supremacy. For the first time it used the unfamiliar Latin word 'vicegerentes' – in the plural, since three commissioners were to exercise those powers. This time they were named: Cromwell, John Tregonwell and their old collaborator on the annulment campaign Thomas Bedell. But that document was busily corrected, and in the alterations Cromwell emerged as sole Vice-Gerent (poor Tregonwell, disappointed once more). He was also styled Vicar-General – the difference between the two titles was never clear, but a Vicar-General at least sounded like a familiar official in a diocesan hierarchy.[39] This revision formed the basis of the royal warrant waved benevolently on through the system by a variety of Cromwell's own administrative personae, finally arriving in Chancery on 21 January 1535.[40] The grant was closely followed by a procession of declarations from the bishops, starting with Cranmer on 10 February, proclaiming their loyalty to the Crown and to no external authority.[41]

That was not the end of the story. The warrant setting up the Vice-Gerency was limited in focus to the staging of a nationwide royal visitation, which sounds like a one-off, time-limited event. Cromwell did not even begin making any moves till the following summer – rather later in the Province of York, after facing down legal quibbles from Archbishop Lee. Meanwhile, he set up an administration on the basis of his new title, but his officers waited till 18 September 1535 to suspend the administrative powers of all bishops (including the archbishops), soon after Cranmer's metropolitical visitation had been finally put out of its misery by formal termination on 1 August. Over the next few months it became clear that the mass suspension was made so that Cromwell could selectively restore powers to the episcopate as he thought fit.[42]

A fresh stage of his grab for power in the Church began in January

1536, with the setting up of a vice-gerential court to process the most high-value wills (and thus take especially lucrative business from archbishops and bishops alike). All this open-ended exercise of the royal supremacy was on the basis of a visitation which was never actually brought to a formal end during Cromwell's lifetime; he used his powers, for instance, to visit the vacant diocese of Hereford as late as 1539.[43] In fact, if Cromwell had formally ended his visitation, it is a moot point whether the Vice-Gerency would legally have continued to exist. It is all a perfect example of his genius for improvisatory administration with amoeba-like properties of expansion.

Amid these manoeuvres, it comes as no surprise that when the Act for First Fruits and Tenths was passed by the autumn 1534 session of Parliament the administration of these new taxes was placed firmly in the hands of the Lord Chancellor and Master of the Rolls. In practice, Audley played no significant part, and Cromwell appointed as Treasurer and General Receiver for the money another of his former close colleagues under Wolsey, John Gostwick, already in charge of a portmanteau of royal revenues at his master's disposal (Calwich and Beddgelert priories had come under Gostwick's wing at this time). It was a conveniently personal arrangement; while Cromwell lived, Gostwick was not allowed a formal department or 'court' to support his administration of First Fruits and Tenths, even though he also undertook a vast swathe of other financial business which the royal minister had previously found time to consider in person. Instead Gostwick got an extremely generous salary – paid initially without any formal warrant.[44]

Financial supervision of churchmen meshed very nicely with the jurisdictional powers which Cromwell increasingly enjoyed through the Vice-Gerency. Characteristically, as in earlier years with his first arrival on the commissions of sewers and of the peace, he had himself placed on regional commissions for assessing the new clerical taxes in those areas most directly his concern: Kent, Middlesex and Surrey, together with the city of Bristol, which had shrewdly chosen him as Recorder the previous year. He went so far as to send in his own auditors to deal with three wealthy religious institutions in Surrey, perhaps in order to see how the new system was working at first hand.[45] Inevitably, his personal involvement quickly ceased, and the commissioners busily worked in the localities with no more central consultation than necessary.

The commissioners were authorized to begin work in January 1535. The scale of their labours, whose results largely survive, was deeply impressive. They recorded for the first time since Domesday Book (and in far more detail) what financial assets belonged to the Church: the *Valor ecclesiasticus*, which in its early nineteenth-century edition runs to six volumes. The work was done by a mixture of local gentry and diocesan financial officials, reinforced with some civil servants from Westminster, and although assessments erred somewhat towards generosity, particularly for secular clergy, the records have been shown to be broadly realistic. The initial requirement of completing the work by 30 May was ridiculously optimistic, but virtually all was done in nine months from issuing the commissions, plus inevitable corrections to come: a staggering achievement given the administrative conditions of the time. The King now knew how much the Church might have to offer him in terms of assets and estates, and where it all was.[46]

One final component of Cromwell's intimidating clutch of powers was his supervision of England's two universities, where an increasing proportion of its clergy did their final training, alongside a growing section of the English gentry. By now he had a decade's worth of close personal relations with both Oxford and Cambridge, and had chosen Cambridge for the education of little Gregory and cousins. His saving of Cardinal College Oxford under a different name (albeit for the moment with lessened ambitions) ensured him a golden reputation and continued direct involvement there. Somehow by 1534 he had also wrested the Visitorship of New College from its customary holder as Bishop of Winchester, Stephen Gardiner, and arbitrated in a major College row between the Warden and evangelically inclined Fellows. Surprisingly, he did not show especial favour to the evangelicals, partly because Warden John London was good at trimming his own traditionalist instincts and had been very helpful in annulment business. London, close friend for decades with another protagonist of the annulment on Cromwell's staff Thomas Bedell (lately Fellow of New College), went on to become one of Cromwell's chief roving assistants.[47]

Cromwell's wider interference at Oxford remained to some extent hobbled by the obstinate persistence of John Longland Bishop of Lincoln as Chancellor of the University. Longland was a religious conservative who, like Warden London, had banked a generous deposit of goodwill with the King through long-standing support for the Aragon annulment. He was thereafter equally adroit in rarely stepping too far out of line, so Cromwell never displaced him at Oxford, despite occasional clashes between their respective religious clients. Nevertheless it was principally Cromwell to whom University and town authorities looked when locked in a prolonged struggle about their respective jurisdictions; he might be seen as more of an honest broker between the two sides than Longland.[48] Subsequent correspondence shows that he was never a blind partisan of the University in disputes which frequently descended into violence.

In 1533 the alert University authorities in Cambridge also began recognizing their need to honour Cromwell's new power by granting him a modest annual fee. In 1534 they could do better, thanks to the death of their High Steward, Lord Mountjoy; Cromwell duly took that office deferentially proffered to him.[49] Mountjoy, until recently veteran Chamberlain to Queen Katherine, was by the time of his death the symbol of a previous age. So too was the then University Chancellor, no less a figure than Bishop John Fisher: a colossus in Cambridge affairs since the early years of the century, and particularly associated with St John's College, founded at his urging by Henry VIII's grandmother Lady Margaret Beaufort.

It was sadly symptomatic of Fisher's changed circumstances that on 3 October 1534 he announced (or was ventriloquized from his cell in the Tower as announcing) that he was nominating deputies to adjudicate in Cambridge's own row between town and gown, over jurisdiction at the mammoth annual Stourbridge Fair. Fisher's nominees were mainly Cambridge academic notables, but also included Queen Anne's almoner Nicholas Shaxton, her cousin Dr William Butts and Cromwell's man Dr Thomas Lee.[50] The last stage in this transfer across generations and allegiances awaited Fisher's judicial murder in June 1535. A little over two months afterwards, the University was still locked in battle with the town, sometimes literally, and that was no time to be sentimental (it rarely is with academic administrators). So, just before the next round of town/ gown hostilities at the Fair in September, Cromwell was gratified to hear that he had been elected Chancellor of Cambridge. It was the culmination of a year in which power in the Church under the Supreme Head decisively shifted from a variety of clergy to a single layman.[51]

Deaths for Religion: 1535

English relations with Rome had entered a curious twilight zone. There was still a resident royal ambassador there: the now veteran diplomat Gregorio Casali, doing his charming best to hold on to some sort of normality against overwhelming odds. In the wake of his English colleagues' diplomatic debacle at Marseille before the Pope and French King, Casali travelled to England and stayed for no less than six months in the first half of 1534, both in order to defend his own efforts in a thankless embassy and to embed himself and his family anew in England's alternative diplomacy. He had to do some quick footwork, since his relations with men of influence in England were some years out of date: Gardiner and the Duke of Norfolk had previously figured most highly among his correspondents, and he needed to adjust to new realities.

Casali did his best to interest Cromwell in expanding the range of his European missions to Venice and to János Szapolyai, pretender to the Hungarian throne. This might produce a grand if ramshackle alliance with the French against the Habsburgs, but far-off central European powers and potentates were hardly major players for the English, and it was a mark of English diplomatic desperation that Casali was taken at all seriously in these schemes.[1] Cromwell's investment in them was modest, and no more came of them than from the simultaneous English missions to the Schmalkaldic and Hanseatic Leagues. The final disaster came in spring 1535, when Henry's designated envoy to the Hungarian pretender, Gregorio's brother Giambattista Casali, was recognized and imprisoned by Habsburg officials in Dalmatia. As Chapuys observed to the Emperor with grim realism, 'Had the King of the Romans ordered [Giambattista] to be hanged, [Cromwell] would not have cared a fig for it.'[2]

On returning to Rome in July 1534, Gregorio Casali briefly became important once more, as a new pope was soon to be chosen. The death of the much harassed Clement VII in September caused rejoicing at the English Court (and alas also among the faithful in the Eternal City). Chapuys disgustedly reproduced more callous remarks: Cromwell could not 'refrain from saying in public, to anyone he meets, that "at last that great devil was dead", and it seems as if he was sorry not to be able to give that Pope a worse title'.[3] With the conclave for a successor opening on 11 October, events of the last few years did not inhibit the King of England from sending his envoy the customary blank letters of credence for lobbying the cardinals during the election: a diplomatic place-holder which will have cut little ice with anyone. The English were lucky that the candidacy of Cromwell's nominal former employer Cardinal Campeggio, a serious early contender, soon languished, for he was furious at being deprived of the See of Salisbury, as well as personally loathing Casali. The successful candidate, Alessandro Farnese, now Pope Paul III, did not have any such baggage. This at least meant that Casali could play for time to postpone further announcement of the King's excommunication.[4]

In reality, Rome had become a sideshow in Henry's plans, as Cromwell's tardy responses to Casali's conscientious stream of letters demonstrated. The royal supremacy flattered the King's ego and had at long last delivered Cromwell the open consolidation of his existing powers in the Church into the Vice-Gerency. Neither of them would seriously have contemplated surrendering these gains to the Holy Father. In May 1535, the new Pope took a symbolic step prompting Henry VIII to his most reprehensible act of judicial cruelty yet, which in turn made the breach well-nigh irreparable. Pope Paul decided to appoint as cardinals six internationally respected churchmen who compensated for his first two appointments (members of his own family worse than undistinguished). Two among the new half-dozen were likely to infuriate the King of England: one was Girolamo Ghinucci, admittedly an Anglophile with a long record of faithful service to the English Crown, but recently ejected *in absentia* from his English diocese of Worcester alongside Campeggio's removal from Salisbury. The other was John Fisher, a year into his imprisonment in the Tower of London.

The Pope probably intended this honour to give Cardinal Fisher some protection from harm, but he soon realized how badly he had miscalculated. The announcement cut across continuing efforts by the King's servants to secure a full declaration of conformity from Fisher and Thomas More: on 7 May Cromwell had led a deputation of royal councillors to them, at which he read Fisher the Act of Supremacy and spelled out that a denial of the supremacy now meant treason. After news of the Cardinal's hat, there was no more effort at dialogue, merely detailed examination of Fisher's servants to push forward a final verdict.[5] On 22 June the aged Bishop, already desperately ill, was beheaded. Thomas

More followed him on 6 July. Incredulity and horror in mainland Europe for once united the Emperor and the King of France, and made Casali's position in Rome untenable; after feeble attempts to justify Fisher's death, he stayed away from the city for the rest of the year.[6] His eclipse had not been reversed when he died at the end of 1536.

No one serving prominently in royal government can be dissociated from the King's actions. Stephen Gardiner, former voice of dissidence, devoted his energies in late summer and early autumn to writing a reply to the papal denunciation of Fisher's death, stressing the newly made Cardinal's treason. Bishop Tunstall, who had sailed even closer to the wind, wrote a telling letter to Cromwell six months after Fisher's execution in which he had occasion to refer to Wolsey and Fisher in the same sentence: as a good traditionalist, he added the customary 'whose soul God pardon' to his reference to Wolsey, but not to his mention of Fisher.[7] Over the next few years, while traditionalists did their best to defend the Catholic faith expounded in Fisher's magisterial writings, very few dared to cite his name until his complete rehabilitation in the reign of Queen Mary. Even then, it remained an embarrassment that Gardiner, the Queen's first Lord Chancellor, had written the most effective of all the denunciations of Fisher as a traitor to his King.

Amid the collective guilt, it is still inescapable that Cromwell had been in charge of the two prisoners' fates since the beginning of 1534, and once the King had shown the depth of his malevolence in Fisher's death, the minister choreographed the judicial procedures which briskly led to More's execution.[8] The court's decision was based on evidence from Richard Rich, Solicitor-General and already firmly within Cromwell's circle of patronage, in front of jurors carefully picked by Master Secretary. Few historical accounts have managed to make the tale of Rich's career anything better than despicable in its opportunism and chameleon-like profession of religious belief; he is likely to have distorted what he had heard in interviews with More on 12 June.[9]

At the trial itself, More left inhibition behind, liberated by the prospect of death from years of watching every phrase he uttered. His attack on the King was devastating. He accused him of nothing less than perjury in breaking his coronation oath by which he had sworn to defend the Church. His final words on the scaffold were equally searing; there was no propaganda advantage for the King in any of this. At least Henry remembered their old friendship enough to allow More to die cleanly by beheading alone, a small mercy the King had already afforded his grandmother's favourite priest. His head and Fisher's nevertheless stood spiked among the traitors on London Bridge. Does anything mitigate the record?

It can only have been with Cromwell's permission that Antonio Buonvisi, so long his friend as well as More's, had continued to supply wine and decent food which sustained the morale of the two prisoners in the Tower until early spring.

It is also noticeable that Cromwell's feelings towards More remained much more ambiguous than towards Fisher, who had contributed to Wolsey's humiliation in autumn 1529 (and who, though Cromwell did not know it, had recently advocated invasion of the realm by Habsburg armies). It is significant that in Cromwell's jottings of remembrances for action in late June he could not bring himself to name More in relation to the business of execution, amid a series of references to them both: the note read 'When Master Fisher shall go to execution, and also the other.'[10] The squeamishness continued in his circle: three years after the event, his servant Thomas Knight, a former Oxford don turned diplomat, reported to Cromwell from the Low Countries about devotional pamphlets on sale on local bookstalls commemorating More and Fisher as holy martyrs and calling them saints, but Knight could only describe them likewise as 'the Bishop of Rochester *and the other*'.[11]

There is an equal ambiguity in Cromwell's attitude towards further Catholic martyrs in England whose deaths just predated Fisher and More, and had stirred fury across mainland Europe before the news of those paired atrocities spread.[12] The victims were various members of the Carthusian Order, who after their uncomfortable confrontation with oath-taking the previous summer continued despite the Treason Act ostentatiously to refuse the oath of supremacy and would not co-operate with commissioners for the *Valor ecclesiasticus* who appeared at their houses. Their tragic story and its aftermath reveal much about the subtleties of Cromwell's relationship with this most austere and impressive of late medieval English monastic orders, and also how personal and intense that relationship was.

The victims of the King's savagery on 4 May 1535 were heads of the Carthusian convents in the Midlands at Beauvale and Axholme, with Prior John Houghton of London, accompanied by one non-Carthusian, a prominent priest of Syon, Richard Reynolds. In April, after the Carthusians had travelled to London on business, Cromwell personally examined them during his convalescence at The Rolls in what turned into preliminaries to a hearing for treason.[13] He also licensed the verbose intellectual Thomas Starkey to make an effort to win over Father Reynolds, as Starkey reported meaningfully to his former patron in Italy, Reginald Pole, rehearsing the arguments in a further effort at persuasion. These

conversations may have been a response to a plea from Archbishop Cranmer, who knew Reynolds and the Prior of Axholme well, and after
previous discussions with them hoped they could be brought round.[14]

Before Father Houghton had been tried and condemned, Cromwell
took a startling gamble. The maverick Carthusian polymath Andrew
Borde had been imprisoned in the London Charterhouse under the discipline of the order; it is not often remembered in the Carthusian story
that until this moment the monks had their own powers of coercion and
intimidation. There was something of a tussle for Borde's soul between
Cromwell and the Carthusians. While he was still their prisoner, his
fellow-monks had forced him to write to Prior Houghton in the Tower to
encourage him in his defiance. Yet Borde was a spirit too wild for Carthusian or probably any discipline, and like his former fellow-prisoner
Thomas Salter (whom we encountered in the previous round of Carthusian confrontation) he saw Cromwell as a lifeline out of his tangled
relationship with the order.[15] Cromwell equally recognized his talent, and
constituted Borde as the most extraordinary of roving ambassadors overseas. Among his other purposes, Borde must visit the Grande Chartreuse
itself, mother house of all Carthusian houses.[16]

In that remote valley amid Provençal mountains, Borde used his
undoubted charm on the Prior-General, along with a no doubt edited
version of events in England, to secure a remarkable open letter to all the
Carthusians of England. The addressees were headed by the Prior and
Convent of the London Charterhouse; it is clear that at this stage Borde
was blissfully ignorant that Prior Houghton had been executed soon
after his own departure. The Prior-General exhorted his English brethren to obedience to King Henry, and more astonishing still, as Borde
reported to his now-deceased Prior, 'the aforesaid reverend father hath
made the right honourable Esquire Master Cromwell and my Lord of
Chester brethren of all the whole religion, praying you that you do nothing without their counsel.'[17] 'My Lord of Chester' was of course Roland
Lee, one of Cromwell's commissioners in the first unsuccessful round of
trying to secure oaths from the Charterhouse monks, as well as from
Bishop Fisher.[18] For good measure, Borde secured a positive verdict from
the Prior-General on Henry VIII's annulment of his marriage to Katherine of Aragon, among a string of other favourable verdicts on the same
theme from French provincial universities. Subsequent news of the executions of Houghton, Fisher and More would have changed all their minds,
and Borde's audacious adventure led nowhere.[19]

While Borde was in France that summer, the government put special
efforts into keeping the remaining Carthusian communities in obedience,

both in the provinces through Cromwell's nationwide monastic visitors and in the London house through representatives whom he chose specially for the task.[20] Just after Prior Houghton's death on 5 May, Thomas Bedell, a near neighbour of the Charterhouse in Aldersgate, visited the house to argue with them about papal supremacy. Sebastian Newdigate, a former gentleman of the King's Privy Chamber turned monk, who had a sister among the nuns of Syon, was one of the spokesmen who faced him down. Bedell disillusioned Cromwell of any expectations that the execution might have intimidated the monks, 'regarding no more the death of their father, in word or countenance, than he were living and conversant among them'.[21] That summer Newdigate, the acting head Humphrey Middlemore and the Proctor of the house William Exmew followed Prior Houghton to the scaffold, three days before Bishop Fisher.

Bedell's letter to Cromwell in May gives a glimpse of the high-temperature atmosphere of inspired utterance he faced in the house: he warned his defiant audience that their truculent attitude came from the false spirit in the mouths of the deceitful prophets of King Ahab of Israel. Perhaps this led Cromwell to determine on an extraordinarily elaborate and painstaking strategy, mapped out in special vice-gerential instructions for lay 'governors' who took over the running of the house from the executed Prior. The aim was not to dissolve the house but to turn it into a reformed evangelical monastic community with a changed ethos, based on intensive Bible study (Bibles to be provided). All this was backed up by a royal pardon for any of the surviving community 'for all heresies and treasons by any of them committed before that day'.[22]

Cromwell envisaged a two-pronged programme to persuade to conformity those members of the Charterhouse who had not been executed. One in a conservative direction included more visits from Bedell, a staid traditionalist lawyer, plus a sequence of sermons from well-known preachers of the same character who were toeing the royal line on supremacy. Yet Cromwell also confronted the Carthusians with a different variety of religion, as high-temperature and extrovert as their own. His agents as 'governors' were not clergy but laymen, two of his intensely evangelical associates from the London mercantile community, Jasper Fyllol and John Rastell. Fyllol, at his own request, was installed in a cell in the Charterhouse itself to work more systematically on the monks.[23] By the end of September 1535, he had produced a critical report and financial analysis of the community for Cromwell to decide on the house's future.[24]

Fyllol and Rastell make a close and resonant pair. Both were MPs in the Reformation Parliament still in session in 1535. Both were elderly, which had not stopped them embracing evangelical religion. Fyllol, a servant of Cromwell, was probably nearly seventy and it may be remembered that at the height of the break with Rome, perhaps at Cromwell's instigation and certainly with his approval, he published two pamphlets so radically anti-clerical that he might be suspected of Lollard connections.[25] Rastell, at the end of a long printing career as a Catholic, likewise made an abrupt about-turn when he published an anti-clerical tract around 1532. He was such an identifiable evangelical that after his Charterhouse service traditionalists secured his arrest, probably during a temporary political advantage in autumn 1536. He died in prison, most likely in 1537.[26]

Maybe Cromwell hoped that their venerable years in combination with their evangelical opinions and their enthusiasm for clerical poverty would strike a chord with the Carthusian fathers. Just as importantly, Rastell was Thomas More's brother-in-law, showing the Charterhouse traditionalists that despite that relationship he had seen the error of his ways and enthusiastically embraced evangelical truth: Carthusians could do so too. In fact this bold and labour-intensive initiative did not produce very impressive results. Fyllol could report that three of the convent had been encouraged to leave and enter the wider ministry of the Church, but otherwise both he and Rastell met with consistent hostility from senior monks in distributing literature in favour of the royal cause, and the seniors forced the rest of the community into line in opposition.[27]

Fyllol's efforts at importing more evangelicals for face-to-face discussions with individual dissidents met with no more success. Neither Rastell's fellow-printer William Marshall nor an outspoken Scotsman called John McDowell or Maydewell (a friar about to leave the Dominican Order) made any more impression on them.[28] Not long afterwards, the imperial ambassador noted that Cromwell was having to forbid printed pamphlets with new Carthusian visions of the martyrs' crowns bestowed on Henry VIII's spring and summer crop of victims.[29] Still Cromwell did not give up on his efforts with the house. In December 1535, while John Husee was trying to satisfy his master Lord Lisle's worries about the demolition of weirs, he said he would try to find the minister in a good mood, 'but he is now much busied with the monks of the Charterhouse.' At the same time Cromwell made similar strenuous efforts with the priests and nuns of Syon, as did a number of other senior figures including Queen Anne herself.[30]

In his report to Cromwell Fyllol had left open the possibility of suppressing the London Charterhouse, no doubt thinking of the Observants' fate in summer 1534, but the instructions to the 'governors' had not envisaged that, and it did not happen. John Gostwick clearly thought the Charterhouse's future was secure when in October 1535 he wrote to Cromwell for the appointment of a protégé to the vacant chaplaincy for Sir Robert Rede's chantry in the monks' church. Gostwick, now administrator of First Fruits and Tenths for Cromwell, was in a position to know his thinking, and was always alert for personal advantage. Any hint of imminent suppression would no doubt have brought an eager request for some pickings from the house's dissolution.[31] The London Charterhouse remained without a prior until April 1536, when Cromwell appointed William Trafford, previously Proctor at Beauvale Charterhouse to the martyred Prior Laurence. This was one of Cromwell's successes in wooing the Carthusians, because it was a clear message that Trafford had abandoned defending papal power 'usque ad mortem', his defiant proclamation when his Prior was arrested.[32]

Trafford's appointment can be read alongside an exceptionally revealing later letter to Cromwell from his old servant Ralph Sadler, who had become Cromwell's eyes and ears in the King's private apartments. The letter was written on 27 September 1536 last thing at night because of its urgency. It reminds us that Cromwell (now Lord Privy Seal) was not a free agent in dealings with the Charterhouse, and that much of the murderous violence there was the responsibility of his master.[33] Sadler told Cromwell that that evening he had happened to remind the King that the Bridgettines at Syon needed a new superior; this jerked Henry's memory to an allied subject, and not in a good way. The King snapped at Sadler:

> 'the Charterhouse in London is not ordered as I would have had it. I commanded', quoth he, 'my Lord Privy Seal a great while ago to put the monks out of the house; and now he wrote to you . . . that they be reconciled, but seeing that they have been so long obstinate, I will not now . . . admit their obedience, and so write to my Lord Privy Seal.' This His Grace commanded me to write to your Lordship (as I do), which as you shall have opportunity ye may temper with His Grace, as by your wisdom shall be thought convenient.

In other words, Sadler knew that Cromwell was trying to preserve the Charterhouse against the King's evident determination that it should be destroyed. After appropriate 'tempering' with his royal master, Cromwell succeeded for two more years.

Ultimately one cannot expect the chief minister of an angry and ruthless king to do much more than obey his will or face the consequences. Yet there are other reasons to view the executions of the Carthusians, Fisher and More as Cromwell will have seen them in order to understand his sense of retribution, emergency and opportunity; they died alongside a varied array of other deaths for religion across the seas. First and most immediately relevant was the betrayal and arrest in the Habsburg Low Countries of William Tyndale; his execution in 1536 was as emblematic and as much a perversion of justice as those of the English Catholic martyrs.[34] By 1535 Tyndale had been living in Antwerp for around six or seven years, fearsomely productive in propaganda and Bible translation, and benefiting from the indulgence of the city's leading printers, who were happy to publish his works with a false imprint; the considerable demand for this sacred contraband back in England was too good to neglect, whatever the risks. For much of this time he counted on protection and shelter from evangelical English merchants living in Antwerp, latterly the well-connected London merchant Thomas Poyntz, who was of the same family as the West Country knight to whom Tyndale had acted as domestic tutor in the early 1520s. Poyntz was to sacrifice his prosperity and inheritance in the cause of Tyndale and godly religion.[35]

The Bible translator was nevertheless a marked man, already having more than once earned King Henry's displeasure through his obstinately principled refusal to conform to royal wishes. In time of trouble he could expect little sympathy from the King. His downfall came through the plotting of a shady young English gentleman of Dorset called Henry Phelips, who was no doubt able to gain Tyndale's confidence because of his links to Thomas Cromwell. Cromwell had done various favours for Phelips's father Richard at least since his days with Wolsey, particularly in strenuous efforts to get Henry's brother Thomas out of serious legal trouble in the West Country during 1534.[36] Henry repaid this goodwill by treachery. He obtained a 'commission' to arrest Tyndale and also the passing English envoy Robert Barnes, who he would have known was a protégé of Cromwell's, together with Cromwell's old acquaintance George Joye, another Antwerp resident; in the event he managed to entrap only Tyndale, probably on 24 April 1535.[37] While it is not clear to whom Phelips owed his authorization, strong suspicion fell on Bishop Stokesley of London, who loathed 'the arch-heretic' and had clashed with Tyndale's brother Edward over diocesan estates in Gloucestershire.[38]

Cromwell would have heard the news of Tyndale's arrest in the week that the Carthusian monks were executed. He could do nothing to influence Tyndale's fate, given King Henry's continuing coldness towards the translator and England's current lack of diplomatic clout with the Emperor; it is easy to imagine his frustration and fury, all the worse for the dangers of expressing his feelings openly. It would have made it easier to see Fisher and More die that summer. In September 1535 he sent two

letters 'devised [that is, carefully drafted] for Tyndale' to his most influential contacts in the Low Countries, the Lord of Bergen op Zoom and
the Archbishop of Palermo, via Stephen Vaughan and associated evangelical English merchants. Their answers were courteous but non-committal,
hardly surprisingly when the memories of the executions in the Tower
were still raw, and when everyone knew that the English were launching
their biggest mission yet to the Emperor's turbulent princes of the
Empire.[39] Tyndale lingered for more than a year in prison, like Fisher
before him. In September 1536, imploring God to open the King of England's eyes, he was strangled by the Brussels executioner and his corpse
burned. Cromwell did not forget Phelips's part in his death, nor Stokesley's likely role in the background.

The most exotic of slaughters, and most nightmarish in the various European religious atrocities of 1535, occurred in the city of Münster in
north-west Germany. In February 1534, growing crowds of 'Anabaptists'
from all over northern Europe hijacked the city's initially Lutheran rejection of its Prince-Bishop and set up their own apocalyptic kingdom as a
beacon for the whole continent. 'Anabaptist' is a catch-all and abusive
term for a great variety of sixteenth-century Europe's radical adventures
in Christian belief beyond the rebellions of Martin Luther or Huldrych
Zwingli. Such radicals made many individual theological choices in
pushing the logic of Luther's remoulding of tradition. Their widespread
affirmation of baptizing only adults into Christian community was just
one of these decisions, but it earned them that general label as 'rebaptiz-
ers', Anabaptists. They would themselves have regarded this Greek sneer
as a canard, since in their eyes baptism done to infants was not true
baptism at all. In the early 1530s, some radicals turned to contemplating
violence against all powers in contemporary society, not merely the old
Church authorities. It would hasten the return of Christ to perfect all
things in the Last Days of the world. This was an idea to appal any evangelical who felt it perfectly possible to live out godly reformation in
obedience to the existing powers ordained to rule by God.

This truly revolutionary mood crystallized in the northern Low Countries. Cromwell was kept well informed about the build-up of trouble by
his old mercantile friends there, principally John Hacket in Brussels. At
first, in March 1534, Hacket exploited reports of increasing disorder
caused by 'these new sects of rebaptisement' to slap down snide comments from Habsburg courtiers about English popular unrest, but as
the situation deteriorated, and as the English realized how it was linked
to growing turmoil in Münster, *Schadenfreude* dropped away and real

alarm took over.[40] The long siege of Münster by a joint expeditionary force of Protestants and Catholics had not yet reached its appalling conclusion in starvation, betrayal and execution when in spring 1535 the English authorities realized that they also had Anabaptists in their midst.

These were no mere strays in the immigrant diaspora of south-east England, but part of a targeted international mission spreading out from Münster to bring on the Last Days of the world. If Cromwell had but known it, one of those coming to England was Gerrit Geyle, one of nine people in a room in Amsterdam in December 1533 who witnessed Jan Matthys launch his prophetic mission from God before gathering followers to march on Münster, the first leader of its revolution.[41] Yet maybe Master Secretary did indeed learn of this catalytic moment in Amsterdam, because Geyle was one of those burned in a short, sharp English campaign against Anabaptists in spring 1535. A royal proclamation in March ordered them all to leave the realm; both Cromwell and Cranmer were involved in the examinations of those who did not.[42] After a dark note in Cromwell's 'remembrances' to ask 'what the King will do with the Anabaptists', up to twenty-five were burned at the stake in London and neighbouring towns in May – one of the most spectacular co-ordinated burnings of heretics in England in the whole century, outclassing any single set-piece of Queen Mary's reign twenty years later. Both the King and Cromwell took especial care to let Chapuys know about this, and they sent those professedly penitent back to the Habsburg authorities in the Low Countries. Even Bishop Fisher in his cell pricked up his ears at the news.[43]

The Anabaptists were a nightmare for Master Secretary and Archbishop Cranmer in more than one way. First was the fear familiar from present-day neuroses about terrorism that this was only the start: when Münster was finally taken in June and its Anabaptist defenders butchered, another of Cromwell's informants in Antwerp told him that many survivors were fleeing to England.[44] An English-language pamphlet about the reign of 'Jan of Leyden' in Münster, printed probably in Antwerp soon after the city's fall, was colourful and exciting, but did not especially condemn the insurrectionists; it might give the English ideas.[45] Henry's autos-da-fé of 1535 did not end Anabaptist activities in England, nor break their links with regrouped radicals in the Low Countries in the wake of Münster. Even when Protestantism triumphed in England under Edward VI, Elizabeth and James I, the Protestant authorities went on burning radicals at the stake. It has often and plausibly been suggested that one of the most lasting achievements of the Vice-Gerency, certainly one which has left Cromwell's memory golden with historians, is a direct result of official fears of Anabaptism: his order in his vice-gerential

injunctions of autumn 1538 that every parish in the kingdom must keep
a register of marriages, christenings and burials. Keeping a full record of
babies christened could make each parish aware of those who were not,
and the authorities could act accordingly.

An equal anxiety for Cromwell and his evangelical allies was how to
separate their own religious agenda from Jan of Leyden in the mind of
King Henry. It was embarrassing when Anabaptists died at the stake in
May 1535 displaying similar heroic fervour to 'mainstream' martyrs with
evangelical views like Cromwell's and Cranmer's own. Seventy years
later that perceptive Jesuit polemicist Robert Parsons gleefully highlighted this worry: he recalled a troubled comment to one of King Henry's
courtiers by an evangelically inclined gentlewoman, who in 1535 had
watched Anabaptists burn at Smithfield, 'singing, and chanting scriptures, as I began to think with myself, whether their device was not of
some value or no'.[46] Cromwell's own occasional printer the evangelical
John Gough was among Londoners picked up for examination, for printing 'the Confession of the City of Geneva'.[47] The Protestant Reformation
in a city about to welcome John Calvin might seem remote from Münster, but who was to say in 1535? What, indeed, of populist ferment in the
city of Lübeck, Henry VIII's difficult ally?

The austere reformer John Calvin shared Cromwell's concern not to
be linked with Münster's other John, of Leyden. The Preface in the first
version of his master-work of systematic theology, the Institutes, has a
dedication to his sovereign King François of France, dated less than two
months after the fall of Münster in 1535. Calvin kept this dedicatory text
in all later versions of this eventual best-seller, long after the King was
dead. Why retain this passionate appeal to a monarch who was one of the
greatest disappointments among many for sixteenth-century reformers?
Because Calvin needed to emphasize that he and his fellow-evangelicals
in France were peaceful and law-abiding, really the King's best and most
truly Catholic subjects, rather than the self-styled Catholics who per-
secuted them. One might say that the whole of Calvin's later theological
development was shaped by his obsessive need to show he was not John
of Leyden. In 1553 he too burned an 'Anabaptist', the maverick theologian Michael Servetus.[48]

Calvin's Preface was an embarrassed comment not simply on Münster
but on evangelical excesses in France. In October 1534, just as François
was pulling together plans for a reunion of Europe's divided Christianity
through talks with the German Protestants, the French King was appalled
to find printed attacks on the mass posted in prominent public settings,
and on the door to his own private apartments too. In his fury, he

endorsed the most severe round of persecution of evangelicals that France had known, and ostentatiously reaffirmed his traditional Catholic loyalty.[49] Those heretics burning in France were part of the wider context for the deaths of More and Fisher; like Tyndale's arrest, they showed that evangelicals were menaced from both ends of the ideological spectrum, radical and papal.

In fact Cranmer and Cromwell could rhetorically link Anabaptist radicals with the monks of the London Charterhouse; they were both 'sects'. This might also have a useful appeal to King Henry. By now he had become fond of seeing himself as holding the middle way in religion; it was his sacred duty to punish extremes, up to and including executions.[50] As 'sects', both papist religious orders and radicals cut themselves off from the Church's mainstream life. Tyndale had pioneered the application of such terms to orders of monks and friars, 'as one holdeth of Francis, another of Dominic'.[51] It was easy to extend the same rebuke to radicals. By their actions both extremes had 'divided, rent and torn in pieces the quiet unity and friendly concord of the holy religion', Archbishop Cranmer's chaplain Thomas Becon proclaimed in a remarkable recasting of early Reformation history; he was writing in 1550, by which time English monks had been dispersed and Protestant magistrates were themselves burning Anabaptists.[52] In a sermon of the same period Hugh Latimer condemned monks and Anabaptists alike because neither could 'abide the company of men'; they shunned ordinary society, forgetting the 'commandment of love and charity'.[53] By this logic, religious persecution of Carthusians and radicals redressed the balance of Christian love: a conclusion which that strident evangelical preacher fully endorsed.

In 1535, in an indirect piece of luck for Cromwell, King François reined in his revenge on French religious dissidence enough to resume negotiations with the Schmalkaldic League, in pursuit of his long feud with the Emperor. That spring he even began serious attempts to persuade Philip Melanchthon, Luther's colleague in Wittenberg, to come to Paris. King Henry was stirred to jealousy, fearing agreement between the German Protestants and France which would exclude him. He had other worries too. Having made such a fuss appealing to a General Council in the business of his marriage in 1533–4, he was now terrified that the Pope would call his bluff and summon just such a Council backed by the Catholic powers of Europe. It would be worth the King's while to reach out to resist a papally convened Council. Cromwell therefore had an excellent opportunity to put past disappointments behind him and revive his overtures to the Schmalkaldic League.[54]

This was a dramatic turnaround from the very recent English failures to engage successfully with German Protestantism. Preparations reached their height in summer 1535, just as Henry was making himself a pariah in Catholic Europe by executing Fisher and More. As we have seen, Cromwell's allies and sympathizers had led previous embassies to Protestant Germany, but this year he scored a notable coup by persuading the King to appoint two new envoys even more unequivocally evangelical: his friend the ex-friar Robert Barnes and the Cambridge don Dr Simon Haynes, who had just become Vicar of Stepney, the parish where Cromwell's country home was situated. Barnes was a particularly significant choice, since he knew Wittenberg well and was the most obvious card-carrying Lutheran among English evangelicals; in March 1535 Cromwell had persuaded the King to send him on an urgent mission to Wittenberg to talk about the Boleyn marriage.[55] No one was better placed to argue Philip Melanchthon out of going to Paris. Yet the choice of Dr Haynes is remarkable too, because (as he admitted) he had no experience of diplomatic missions. Cromwell must have convinced the King that this evangelical enthusiast would have credit with Melanchthon. If Barnes failed to work his magic in Germany and the great German reformer did reach Paris, Haynes's brief was to warn him against the wiles of the French, and pass on official English propaganda in print and manuscript.[56]

Melanchthon was Cromwell's trump card throughout these negotiations. Despite being Luther's right-hand man, he seemed immune from Henry's hatred of Luther himself: the King respected his formidable reputation as a humanist scholar which outweighed that unfortunate connection, and the renewed English embassy to Germany was the first of Henry's attempts at a charm offensive on Wittenberg's Professor of Greek for a personal meeting in England. The planning was very careful on both sides. In August 1535, before the main English mission set off, the King received the first dedication of a major Protestant book not penned by one of his own subjects. It was no less a work than a new edition of Melanchthon's theological textbook which was already shaping theological thought in the infant Lutheran Churches, his *Loci communes*.

The author was well briefed, doubtless by Robert Barnes during his lightning visit to Wittenberg in March. In the dedicatory Preface, appropriately and flatteringly larded with Greek, alongside pointed condemnations of both Anabaptists and 'the dreams of monks', Melanchthon declared that he had been told 'you are admirably learned as well in theology as in the rest of philosophy, and especially in that most exquisite of studies, the contemplation of movements and workings of the heavens.'[57] This last thought was especially deft, in view of the King's fascination with astronomical instruments, and perhaps Nikolaus Kratzer, the ingenious German in royal service who made them, had prompted Barnes. A monarch who in past years had consumed Erasmus's flattery would be delighted with this endorsement of his abilities.

The main text was calculated to draw Henry into a more positive assessment of German theology. Melanchthon's revision of his book in 1535 proved to be the decisive version in future Lutheranism. He had done more than write a flowery new preface; he had shifted his theological analysis in the fashion best calculated to please the King, who had always found the starkness of Luther's formulation of justification by faith unacceptable. Melanchthon meticulously constructed a niche for good works in assisting the process of salvation, to the frank alarm of some Lutheran colleagues.[58] Lutherans in fact took decades to decide among themselves what they thought of this move, but in the short term it further eased Henry's fears of conversations with German Protestants. In September Archbishop Cranmer introduced the Scots theologian Alexander Alesius to the King, as envoy from Melanchthon; Alesius proffered the dedication copy of the *Loci communes*. Henry sent off a handsome reward of 300 crowns to Wittenberg with his thanks, referring Melanchthon further to a letter from 'our most faithful and confidential Principal Secretary, Thomas Cromwell'. No Protestant theologian had previously been honoured thus.[59]

This royal letter of 1 October left England in Alesius's baggage a week or two before the most high-powered English embassy yet to the Schmalkaldics, led by Edward Foxe, now Bishop of Hereford, with Nicholas Heath in his wake. Barnes, back in Germany since July, now served as the essential link with the Germans, whom he knew better than any other Englishman. Foxe's promotion to the episcopate signalled how far Henry VIII was prepared to identify his Church with the Protestant Churches of Germany. The royal instructions to the ambassadors even gave space to the line to take if Henry was invited to join the Schmalkaldic League: cautious but not negative. This was a great advance on the previous year's plausibly deniable overture to the Diet of Nuremberg.[60] Cromwell's skills in international diplomacy were maturing: so far, everything fitted perfectly into his diplomatic jigsaw in 1535, and we will watch the consequences of these manoeuvres unfolding the following year. They did so amid a startling reversal of English politics: an equal culmination of Cromwell's aims and hopes, to which we must now turn.

13

Progresses and Scrutinies: 1535–1536

In June 1535, Ambassador Chapuys told the Emperor of an encounter that had left him puzzled:

> Cromwell said lately to me that were the Lady [Anne Boleyn] to know on what familiar terms he and I are, she would surely try to cause us both some trouble, and that only three days ago they spoke angrily together, the Lady telling him, among other things, that she would like to see his head off his shoulders. 'But', added Cromwell, 'I have so much confidence in my master, that I fancy she cannot do me any harm.' I cannot tell whether this is an invention of Cromwell, in order to raise the value of what he has to offer. All I can say is that everyone here considers him Anne's right hand, as I myself told him some time ago.[1]

It is hardly surprising Chapuys did not know what to make of what would in principle be pleasing intelligence. In the echo-chamber of angry conservative noblemen who apart from Master Secretary were his chief informants around the Tudor Court, it was self-evident that the heretical Queen and the heretical minister were hand in glove in efforts to destroy true religion. Previously, the ambassador had been puzzled by Cromwell's apparently positive attitude to Katherine of Aragon's daughter Mary. In October 1534 Cromwell went so far as to say that King Henry loved Mary 'a hundred times more than his last-born' and that personally he 'had no doubt that in time everything would be set to rights'. Chapuys suspected this was intended 'to bamboozle the world in general [*amuser le monde*]' and lessen the Emperor's fears about Mary's treatment, but if Cromwell indeed meant to confuse, it seems a high-risk strategy.[2]

Cromwell's remark was made at a time in autumn 1534 when the King's affections had apparently moved away from Anne to first one then another young lady of the Court. Anne's stock fell further with another biological setback, a miscarriage of her second child.[3] It is always difficult to judge the seriousness of such emotional breaches in a relationship which had always been about high emotion between two strong-willed people, but then the King's relationship with his elder daughter Mary was equally stormy and changeable, beyond the usual teenage reasons. Henry's fury with Mary at her refusal to play his shadow-game with royal titles was balanced by his genuine affection for her, and Cromwell was perfectly aware of the contradiction. Coming to Court affairs after Mary's eclipse in status, he had so far not seen much of her – in that dispatch of 24 October 1534 Chapuys said that as far he knew they had only ever met once – but, as we have seen, the record of their contacts so far consists of her asking him for favours. He would make his own calculations about placing himself in the triangle of husband, wife and stepdaughter.

That vigilance makes it all the more intriguing that Cromwell was prepared in June 1535 to speak to Chapuys of his deep rift with Queen Anne, because it came at a moment when the royal marriage seemed very much back on track. The centrepiece of events that summer was a royal progress around western England and on to the south coast. King and Queen triumphantly paraded before their subjects with every appearance of harmony, in one of the most politically significant and successful progresses of the Tudor age, prolonged into late October by the King's characteristic fears of plague back in the capital.[4] It ran alongside the belated inauguration of Thomas Cromwell's vice-gerential visitation, taking advantage of the royal presence to lend authority to what could have been a shaky start, given Cranmer's recent experience. Joining the royal couple at Winchcombe in the Cotswolds on 23 July, three weeks after their departure from Windsor, Cromwell personally involved himself in its work when he could.

It was certainly time to begin turning vice-gerential powers into visitation, because spring 1535 exposed an extraordinary eight months of scandalous impersonation in the provinces worthy of Gogol's Khlestakov. This Government Inspector *avant la lettre* was a parish priest gone to the bad called James Billingford. He was from a respectable Norfolk gentry family with links to the Duke of Norfolk, but also bizarrely an Edmund Billingford (probably his elder brother) became one of Cromwell's extended gentry entourage.[5] In the 1520s James was Rector of South Elmham St George in Suffolk, presented to the living by a local gentleman likely to have been his brother-in-law.[6] One can imagine the deep boredom of a high-spirited young graduate in his Waveney valley rectory, under the eye of his relations, and with a couple of curates to do any real work. South Elmham was a principal lordship of Bishop Nix of Norwich, and the episcopal manor-house was actually in Billingford's parish. Maybe it was after witnessing the collapse of the aged Bishop's resistance to Archbishop Cranmer's visitation in September 1534 that the Rector of St George had the idea of embarking on a wild adventure of deception and extortion from monasteries. If his brother was already by then linked to Cromwell, family talk could also have provided inspiration for this parody of visitation.

James Billingford was evidently adept at namedropping and acting like a gentleman. Banking on the state of nerves about monastic dissolution up and down the country, he went on tour claiming to be the official representative of various prominent people, Cromwell included. He kept himself and his Osip-like attendant in high style on their Tudor road-trip; there were some riotous evenings dicing and carding in assorted hostelries between the serious business of intimidating abbots. From early in Billingford's campaign that September in his native East Anglia, two letters forged in Cromwell's name survive in the minister's papers. They demanded money with menaces from a couple of Norfolk monasteries, since 'the King of his regal power' was undertaking selective dissolutions and reform of abuses. The letters have deceived some modern historians into thinking they represent Cromwell's authentic methods of procedure; whether their amateurish production equally duped the monastic heads of house is not clear.[7]

Despite some near-misses that winter, it was May Day 1535 before Billingford's extended spree of deception in the Midlands fatally collided in Oxfordshire with cold scepticism from one of Cromwell's friends, the local JP Anthony Cope.[8] Billingford at first tried to present it as all a big joke to that gentleman (who happened to be a classical historian of some distinction, used to dissecting tall tales), before resorting to dark talk of all the monastic conspiracies he could reveal to Master Secretary. Cope recommended a merciful discharge for the 'poor lad' his servant. James's own fate is alas unknown, though when the commissioners for the *Valor ecclesiasticus* did their work that same spring, one of his former curates was listed as Rector of South Elmham St George in his place.[9] It must be said that Cromwell had a distinctly soft spot for wild young men whom the rest of the world deplored – maybe he remembered his own adventurous early days, and hazarded that some of them combined wildness with talent.[10]

Once Cromwell had emerged from the dire distraction of Carthusian and other executions that spring and summer, Billingford's remarkably long-lasting scam needed remedying by something more official and systematic – not least to quell the widespread confusion and demoralization which the trickster's pseudo-visitatorial adventures had caused among regular clergy. The royal progress in summer 1535 provided the perfect launchpad. The visitation was far more comprehensive than has been understood until recently: over seven months, the visitation commissioners visited over 85 per cent of the kingdom's religious houses and secular cathedrals, hospitals and major chantry colleges, including colleges in Oxford and Cambridge Universities.[11] Cromwell allowed two existing arrangements of visitation to stand. One, set up under his own powers the previous year, was for the orders of friars. The other was for the Gilbertine Order, whose Master was Robert Holgate, an evangelically inclined protégé of his. Though some of Cromwell's visitors did on occasion infringe Gilbertine privilege, the order was quietly exempted from suppression which ought substantially to have affected it under the legislation of 1536. Was this because, uniquely among the religious, the Gilbertines were a purely English order uncontaminated by foreign interference?[12] By contrast, the Abbot of Welbeck's long-standing royal grant of visitation for his Premonstratensian Order in the realm, which Roland Lee had already suggested back in 1532 needed curbing, was effectively ignored and superseded by the vice-gerential visitors. This makes all the more telling Cromwell's decision to preserve Holgate's independent jurisdiction.[13]

One of the visitation's main tasks, like Cranmer's metropolitical visitation over the previous year, was to gather more formal acceptances of the royal supremacy and Boleyn succession. That was paired with a vigorous nationwide campaign in summer 1535, featuring sermons and detailed alterations of the liturgy removing references to the Papacy, supervised (under careful government scrutiny) by the diocesan bishops.[14] Nevertheless, the inquiries of Cromwell's visitors had diverse purposes, not all negative. Often their findings have been seen to further a complete suppression of monasteries, and to concentrate on ferreting out sexual scandal, but their investigations covered many other topics on which arguably reform was needed, at least from an evangelical humanist point of view: for instance, detailed provisions for preaching and biblical study to enrich the devotional life of monastic communities.

As so often in Cromwell's innovations, purposes changed to suit new circumstances. During the royal progress the Vice-Gerent personally visited Winchester College, feeder school for New College Oxford, in company with Dr John London the Warden of New College, and prescribed it a revised curriculum. That irresistibly recalls Wolsey putting his name to a textbook for Cardinal College Ipswich.[15] The visitors also made detailed provisions for changes at Oxford and Cambridge, and there were no inquiries into moral lapses there, so the visitation's purpose was never universal dissolution. One glaring and consistent absence from the visitors' inquiries anywhere was much concern with proper attendance at or conduct of community worship, a staple matter of inquiry for centuries in bishops' visitations. The vice-gerential team, not least the Vice-Gerent himself, apparently had no great investment in the traditional liturgy of the Western Church.[16]

Consistent with that contrast with past practice on visitation, the personnel of Cromwell's visitation were a new mix for a new purpose. They were civil and canon lawyers of Oxford and Cambridge, and straddled the boundary between clerical and lay status, for such lawyers might choose whether or not to take holy orders. Church benefices or headships of collegiate institutions generously bolstered their incomes regardless, but their experience in diocesan or metropolitical administration gave them little rapport with the monastic life which was now their prime concern. Closeness to Cromwell was the main criterion for selection. Dr John ap Rhys, vice-gerential Registrar, was married to Cromwell's niece, and we have previously met Dr Ellis ap Rhys (no relation) as Sub-Dean of Cardinal College Ipswich. Dr Francis Cave was from a family long friendly with Cromwell, while Dr John Tregonwell was Roland Lee's colleague in visiting Thetford Priory for Wolsey in 1528–9. There were only three ordained clerics in the team, but they were similarly tied to Cromwell's circle: Dr John London's connections to him have already become apparent, Dr Richard Leighton was his Rector at Stepney and Dr Adam Beconsaw was one of the Essex parsons who hosted young Gregory Cromwell's peripatetic education in autumn 1533.[17]

Marshalled thus, the list reveals how close were Cromwell's ties to canon and civil lawyers, but then many of them had been involved alongside him in sorting out technicalities of the King's Great Matter. Additionally, hovering behind virtually all of them was another canon lawyer, Bishop Roland Lee, via friendship or relationship: not least his boisterous cousin Dr Thomas Lee, or equally boisterous former colleague in Wolsey's service Ellis ap Rhys, whom Bishop Lee stoutly defended to Cromwell against justified complaints from his fellow-visitors about personal indiscretion and ostentation.[18] This boisterousness is repeatedly evident in the visitors' letters or comments from others both favourable and abusive; one feels they were having an extremely good time, sometimes with uncomfortable shades of James Billingford. Their reunions after travels would generally have been convivial, though the high spirits also resulted in vicious rows. Noticeable too is how Cromwell tended to match the visitors with the regions they knew best: the Welshmen went to Wales, Cornish Dr Tregonwell to the West Country, Northamptonshire Dr Cave to the Midlands, Drs Leighton and Lee eventually to their native North. Generally this worked, quelling future local trouble, but the opposite was true of that last-named pair in the Province of York; the northern rebels of 1536 hated both Leighton and Lee and would have loved to exact vengeance for their visitations. As so often, Cromwell's touch faltered in the North.

Cromwell remained close to the King and Queen for much of August, September and October as they travelled around south-western counties, mixing his government duties with close personal supervision of his visitation. He prolonged his absence from London so much that by late September his household were growing anxious about provisioning and re-engaging staff laid off for the summer.[19] This may have been the longest period away from London that he enjoyed in the 1530s, and it was certainly one of the longest times he spent on a royal progress, which normally left him behind on government drudgery back in the capital. The western progress and visitation in 1535 had still wider significance. When the North rose in rebellion a year later, nearly bringing down the regime, the equally traditionalist West Country and border country with Wales beyond it remained quiet. They had been gratified by the royal presence but will also have noted how closely King and minister were aligned, and that the principal secular hosts in Gloucestershire and Wiltshire were gentry openly identified with evangelical reformation. In these regions, the traditional fiction which sustained English rebellions – that the King was ignorant of his evil ministers' conduct – was difficult to sustain.

The evangelical tone of the summer progress launching the visitation is very noticeable; Henry did not discourage it, fresh from having destroyed those twin symbols of traditional religion, Thomas More and John Fisher. Never predictable in matters religious, the King achieved a first at this time by commissioning the first Bible printed in the British Isles, published in July 1535 – yet not an English but a wholly Latin text, consisting of selections from the Vulgate Old Testament and all of the New Testament.[20] He took a keen interest in this project, furnishing it with a very personal preface which discreetly plagiarized Erasmus rhapsodizing on the central spiritual role of a prince in his kingdom. Among other wise pieces of counsel, the King commended the typeface, which he had personally chosen for ease of reading. He was beginning to have trouble with his eyesight and was using spectacles for reading, though his preface did not confide this to his subjects. In fact, the royal Latin Bible project remained incomplete; a promised second volume with the rest of the biblical text never emerged from the press, and even this first book is exceedingly rare. Cromwell had more ambitious ideas on biblical instruction, as we will see in Chapter 15.

Ambassador Chapuys heard how effective the evangelical preaching of

Court chaplains had been with West Country people, though he consoled himself that those hearkening to the message were mere 'simpletons [*idiotes*]' who would soon return to truth in the right circumstances.[21] The furthering of religious change was a purpose which Cromwell and Anne Boleyn shared whatever their other differences. Staying at Winchcombe in late July, the Queen took the trouble to send her chaplains down the road to Hailes Abbey, Cistercian home of one of late medieval England's more controversial relics, the Holy Blood, to bring sceptical reports back to the King. The relic may even have been removed for a while, before it was destroyed in Cromwell's more general round-up three years later.[22] From this time on, the cataloguing of relics in a sarcastic spirit, together with occasional confiscations, became a major part of the vice-gerential visitors' work.

By contrast with the Queen's forcefully negative intervention, Abbot Sagar alias Whalley remembered gratefully Cromwell's own 'comfortable words' when he visited Hailes Abbey. It sounds distinctly as if Master Secretary was pouring oil on waters troubled by the Queen, and certainly he told the Abbot to get in touch in the event of problems; he also contrived that the Abbot became a royal chaplain.[23] Cromwell's interventions were not confined to Hailes. He took a particular interventionist interest in this whole area, which he knew of old through his friendships at neighbouring Winchcombe Abbey going back to the days of the great Abbot Kidderminster. The royal progress was the ideal moment to revive that old relationship, and Cromwell arranged a second stay at Winchcombe Abbey a couple of weeks after the royal couple had left.[24] His effect on the monastic community was galvanizing (or divisive, if one prefers), reminiscent of his personal concern for the London Charterhouse.

It is possible that one monk of Winchcombe, John (surnamed in religion Placet or Placidus), had long-standing family links to Cromwell's household, as his surname in the world was Horwood, like the John Horwood who received a generous legacy in Cromwell's will of 1529. He was anyway an old servant of Abbot Kidderminster, and they would have got to know each other then.[25] Now Placet played a major role in the evangelical faction within the abbey, inspired by personal conversations with Cromwell from which he recalled that the minister 'full discreetly and catholicly declared the efficacy of our three vows in which we trust too much' – that is, the monastic vows of poverty, chastity and obedience. Placet followed the royal progress for a further conversation with Master Secretary in Hampshire in early October.[26] He and his sympathizers in the abbey allied with an evangelical Oxford don of Merton called Anthony Saunders, whom Cromwell personally appointed to preach at Winchcombe – probably prompted by the evangelical local gentleman and Oxford graduate Richard Tracey, whose father William's posthumous exhumation for heresy in his will had recently been a national *cause célèbre*. Tracey was now himself on familiar terms with Cromwell, who had taken a close interest in his father's case.[27]

As local factions jostled for Cromwell's favour, a great many eyes, not least in Oxford, were watching the developing situation in the great reforming abbeys of the Cotswolds.[28] The Abbots of Winchcombe and Hailes proved unhelpful to Anthony Saunders. Abbot Sagar of Hailes actually sponsored a rival preacher, a more conservative don from Magdalen College Oxford, George Cotes. Cotes aroused strong opinions and created puzzling alliances of disapproval across the religious divide; Cromwell seemed to think well of him despite it all.[29] Sagar may already have realized this curious regard for Cotes, and he covered his back by sending the preacher off to follow the Court down to Wiltshire to take the oath of succession, which so far Cotes had contrived to avoid. There was a remarkably intimidating trio of oath-takers in this ceremony – Cromwell himself, plus Dr Richard Leighton and Captain of the Guard Sir William Kingston – but Cotes was by then safely ensconced at Hailes. Hugh Latimer found him an unwelcome presence in the diocese on taking up office as Bishop of Worcester that autumn.[30]*

Despite such eddies of relationship as his tolerance of Cotes's unmistakable religious conservatism, it is striking how Cromwell's promotion of the royal supremacy in these Gloucestershire monastic encounters was so openly linked to his evangelical programme. His conversations with John Placet criticizing the monastic vocation inspired the monk to write a treatise commending the supremacy, which he sent on to the Vice-Gerent after the progress. The same thing happened following Cromwell's visit to the Cistercian Kingswood Abbey, 40 miles south of Winchcombe. Prior Thomas Redinge wrote to him afterwards in markedly evangelical terms, looking back to Cromwell's 'charitable and divine words' to him at Kingswood, which likewise prompted Redinge to write a tract on the supremacy. When the abbey was dissolved in 1538, one of its monks, possibly the same person under a different surname, was acting as a roving evangelical preacher.[31]

The visitation was still taking shape as the summer went on. The disadvantage for Cromwell of the King being close at hand was that his Majesty might be seized by one of his periodic fits of interest in what was going on. At the beginning of August, the King became irritably aware

---

* Cotes ended his career as Queen Mary's choice for Bishop of Chester.

that proposed general injunctions for the visitors to enforce had not yet been issued, contrary to traditional good practice in episcopal visitations. He scolded Cromwell for the negligence, who in turn scolded his visitors; a defensive letter from Richard Leighton ill-conceals irritation and anxiety. Leighton realized the serious implications for his master of the King's displeasure; 'rather I may be buried quick [alive] than to be the occasion why the King's Highness should diminish any part of the affiance, confidence or the expectation of your assured and proved mind towards His Grace.' Leighton rushed back to the Court at Berkeley Castle from Cirencester Abbey, to help in a major drafting of injunctions 'which should stand for ever', for use in all houses to be visited.[32]

A draft of these injunctions survives maybe from that very day at Berkeley: a fair copy with some practical tinkerings in Cromwell's own hand, none of which was in the end used. One of his emendations modifies the ban on boys in the company of monks (a measure which would bear considerable fruit as the visitors decided to look for sexual scandal) by proposing an exception for boys serving at mass. Equally sensible, and yet not taken up, was a provision for a licensing system for women visiting monasteries. Finally Cromwell tried to remove an order for monks to say a daily mass for the souls of the monastic founder, converting it instead into a simple provision for prayers for the King and his wife. The King must have decided that this undermining of intercessory masses was too radical a move, and the visitors did not enforce it.[33]

Altogether the King's sudden enthusiasm for radical monastic austerity was not helpful, suggesting a delight in ordering reforms without thinking through the consequences, characteristic of the man. The blanket order excluding women from male religious communities was all very well, but alongside its laudable aim of excluding ladies of lurid reputation, it omitted any consideration of the eminently respectable elderly folk who had made formal arrangements for a devout retirement alongside communities of their choice. It was particularly embarrassing when the ban affected a towering authority-figure among Cromwell's gentry friends in Kent, Jane (or Joan) the widow of Sir Richard Guildford. She had been tutor to a succession of royal children down to Princess Mary – an elderly matriarch of such intimidating piety and social connection that she was reverently known at Court as 'Mother Guildford'. What would happen to her dignified residence at Bristol's Hospital of the Gaunts? Lady Guildford's coldly correct letter to Cromwell must have made him squirm; it was addressed pointedly not from the Gaunts but from a Gloucestershire manor of her stepson Sir Nicholas Poyntz, who had recently hosted the King in exceptional style at Acton Court. This

In regulations for monasteries drafted by the vice-gerential scribe Robert Warmington, Cromwell tries to create a sensible regulation for the presence of women in monasteries: to the provision that they be 'utterly excludid', he adds in his own hand 'onles they ffyrst optayne lycens of the Kynges Highnes or his Vysytor'. His alteration disappears in the published version.

dowager would need an exceptional application of charm.[34] By January 1536, the visitors were quietly making exceptions to that particular rule, and thereafter for all practical purposes it lapsed.

But that was not all. One brief and novel order, 'that no monk or brother of this monastery by any means go forth of the precinct of the same', caused immediate problems and then months of appalled reaction from monastic heads. What would the prohibition mean when communities needed to collect their rents that Michaelmas, let alone any more general business? The immediate result was a vicious row between Dr Leighton and Dr Thomas Lee. Leighton the priest applied the orders flexibly; Lee the lawyer applied them strictly; John ap Rhys the nephew-by-marriage implicitly criticized Lee to their master. Even when Cromwell made it clear that flexibility was permitted, Lee remained obstinate, strengthened by his jealousy of Leighton's seniority.[35] Matters descended into farce at Bruton Abbey in Somerset when, on 23 August, Lee directly contradicted Leighton's recent permission to the Abbot to leave the precinct, and then wrote in fury to the Vice-Gerent denouncing his colleague. He claimed that his own interpretation of the injunctions did 'nothing but upon the King's pleasure and yours'.[36] It was a personality clash reminiscent of the spat the previous autumn between the commissioners Friars Browne and Hilsey. Both rows were a result of entering uncharted waters in jurisdiction, with insufficient guidelines or precedents.

This explosive situation sent Cromwell haring down 40 miles from Court in south Gloucestershire to stay with Lord Chief Justice Fitzjames at Redlynch, a mile or so from Bruton.[37] Headmasterly rebukes could be delivered there in the presence of the kingdom's most senior common lawyer, though a later reminiscence shows that Lee got off lightly, and Cromwell did not pay much attention to the Abbot of Bruton's complaint about his officer's high-handedness.[38] An unsuccessful day's hunting in Lord Daubeney's park at Wincanton (a few miles south) cannot greatly have enhanced the expedition.[39] Cromwell's temper was not improved when he rejoined the Court in its next location in Wiltshire to discover that in his absence the King had rifled through his postbag and opened a whining letter from Stephen Vaughan complaining about money: a revealing glimpse of how monarch and minister related.[40] Gradually, messily, the situation on monastic enclosure resolved itself. A stream of begging letters from heads of house to the Vice-Gerent offered useful multiple opportunities to be gracious to them, and from 1536, the order was quietly put aside unless it was politic not to, until the time when there were no more enclosures to observe.

*

Cromwell's return to Court took him to Bromham Hall, home of the Queen's Chamberlain Sir Edward Baynton, but within a day or two everyone had moved on to another great Wiltshire house, Wolf Hall: home to Sir John Seymour and to his unmarried eldest daughter Jane, a junior lady-in-waiting of the Queen. Master Secretary wrote from there on 4 September; the Court, including Queen Anne, stayed there for a week.[41] Wolf Hall is now a name shrieking hindsight; Anne Boleyn's biographer Eric Ives was wise in his caution against such assumptions. Jane had in fact been an Inconspicuous presence at Court under the eyes of Henry VIII since the days of Katherine of Aragon. Rather more significant was the public affirmation that this visit gave to her brother Edward, who was in any case at that stage more prominent at Court than Jane, an Esquire of the Body who had accompanied the royal couple to Calais on their crucial visit of 1532.[42] Edward Seymour soon emerged as a key player in Cromwell's story. They had known one another for a long while: Seymour had been in Wolsey's household in his youth alongside John Dudley, that other rising courtier in Cromwell's circle who in King Edward's reign would become fatefully tangled in Seymour's career.[43]

Cromwell would not habitually have moved in the smart circles of Seymour and Dudley while in service to the Cardinal, but in 1530, as part of the clear-up of Wolsey's financial affairs, he had supervised a Yorkshire estate transaction involving Edward and Sir Anthony Ughtred, who was by then husband to Gregory Cromwell's future wife Elizabeth Seymour, Edward's sister.[44] Once he was in power under the King, he met Seymour and Dudley on much more equal terms. By the end of 1533 Arthur Lord Lisle, newly appointed Deputy of Calais, was soliciting Cromwell for help in what became an immensely complicated lawsuit about inheritance in Somerset, with Seymour and Dudley on the one side and Lord and Lady Lisle on the other. Lisle was confident that Dudley would co-operate 'the rather . . . if it would please you to move it to him'.[45] Cromwell proved an honest broker between the Lisles and their opponents; if anything he favoured Lord Lisle in what was not a strong legal position against some considerable aggression from Seymour. When Seymour and Cromwell met again at Wolf Hall in September 1535, the long-drawn-out negotiations and Seymour's reluctant acceptance of Cromwell's judgement were quite a recent memory.[46]

For the time being, there was no pressing circumstance to alter that relationship dramatically. The royal marriage seemed as secure as it had ever been, with numerous reports of how 'merry' Henry and Anne had been during the latter stages of their travels.[47] Anne's discovery at some stage in October that she was once more pregnant testified that all was well in the royal bed, and offered a sign of hope for her future. Yet all this was dependent on their relationship remaining strong, in the face of continuing sullen resentment of the Queen and sympathy for her step-daughter among the London public. Sometimes that old loyalty was openly expressed: a public demonstration in favour of the Lady Mary in late summer involved no lesser figures than Anne's own aunt Lady William Howard and her sister-in-law, Jane Lady Rochford. They spent some time in the Tower as a rebuke for this extraordinary indiscretion; but that would not be the last of Lady Rochford in the affairs of Queen Anne.[48]

The summer progress reached Winchester in mid-September, for its most prolonged and magnificent phase; the Court paused in its wanderings for more than a fortnight before further travels west and south. Cranmer took over the diocesan Bishop's cathedral to consecrate three bishops of unambiguously evangelical reputation: Hugh Latimer, Edward Foxe and Fisher's successor Friar John Hilsey. That signalled a shift in power on the episcopal bench, but it was also just one of several snubs at Winchester to its Bishop, Stephen Gardiner. Gardiner had made a reasonably successful bid for rehabilitation after previous indiscretions through loyalist publications: a vindication of Fisher's execution and a major work of propaganda for the royal supremacy, *De vera obedientia*. Nevertheless, during the Winchester visit Thomas Starkey presented the King with the manuscript of another major vernacular publication of conservative-flavoured loyalism, which would remind Henry that others could deliver a similar product.[49]

It is as if the King decided to test Gardiner's loyalty to the hilt during his visit. Chapuys, ever alert to significant details, noted that Henry ordered an inventory of Winchester Cathedral's treasures to be made, appropriating some of the most remarkable items, and also seized from the Bishop 'certain [water-]mills to give them away to the community, and thereby gain the people's favour'.[50] This was an acute pairing of observations. We have seen how both King and minister personally cherished this cause of river navigation in general and the Winchester case in particular. Just as some of Cromwell's actions in Cotswold abbeys were a dramatic demonstration of his visitatorial powers over monasteries, this was a set-piece in the launch of the national campaign against weirs, besides being a personal blow to Gardiner's prestige.

One of Lord Lisle's servants anxiously reported the minister's vehemence in the case: 'there is commandment that the sea shall have his course to Winchester, and that the mills shall be stopped along upon the river; for I heard Master Secretary speak in the premises to Thomas Fisher of Woodnyll, commanding him not to speak against the said water course.'[51] The same vehemence jumps out of Cromwell's sharp comment to Bishop Gardiner himself in a private postscript in response to Gardiner's protest about the demolition of one of the episcopal mills: 'I doubt not but your Lordship, knowing what good is like to ensure to the commonwealth by the pulling up of the said mill, will be as glad thereof as I have been, for that only respect, to further the doing of it.' A personal moral crusade meshed conveniently with harassing his political rival.[52]

At the same time an important series of conversations took place both at Winchester and at Gardiner's country home of Bishop's Waltham, involving the King, the Vice-Gerent, Leighton, Lee and ap Rhys, about the visitation's further direction. The most formal business was to suspend the powers of all bishops while the visitation continued, an explicit acknowledgement that there was more than visitation of monasteries going on. That was accompanied by preparations for a proper vice-gerential court for Cromwell to take over major business from the episcopate. Soon afterwards, late in October, Dr Tregonwell took on a new title while moving round his circuit in the West Country: 'general visitor ... throughout the dioceses of Salisbury, Bath and Wells and Exeter' – in other words, visitor to any ecclesiastical establishment he or Cromwell pleased, not just monasteries and nunneries.[53]

Yet monasteries were still the visitation's central concern. We know of two dissident monks visiting Cromwell at Bishop's Waltham, from the two monastic communities which personally concerned him most: Winchcombe Abbey and the London Charterhouse. From Winchcombe came John Placet; from the Charterhouse, Andrew Borde, who appropriately after his recent travels brought as a present his manuscript gazetteer of all Europe (Cromwell amid his busyness alas irretrievably mislaid it). Their appearances came alongside important supplements to the agenda for the visitors, not to the advantage of monasteries. First, the commissioners were told to gather up papistical writings: soon after John Placet had spoken with the Vice-Gerent at Waltham, we can find him helpfully sending down just such a batch to save the visitors going back to his monastery.[54] More significantly for future events, the visitors were now first enjoined to inquire more broadly about cases of 'sodomy' and 'incontinence', to include *voluntariae pollutiones*: masturbation.

There was no precedent in canon law or visitatorial practice for such a systematic inquiry on this embarrassing subject. That stately royal foundation of Chertsey Abbey, so often host to the King on his holidays, has the dubious distinction of being the first foundation to make an affirmative response to the question, around 26 or 27 September 1535. This was occasioned by a visit from Dr Lee, who gratuitously pointed out to his

master that he was superseding an earlier verdict by Bishop Gardiner and
Sir William Paulet that all was well in the house.[55] Thereafter, Dr Leighton's
Act Book (now lost, but preserved in summary form in a later publication
of that prurient Protestant Bishop John Bale) was suddenly full of sexual
misdemeanour, previously no more than a gentle trickle of cases.

From now on the visitation began collecting scandal with the aim of
discrediting the monastic life in the eyes of the English public. We cannot
know for certain whose idea this was, but it does suggest the fussy prud-
ishness of Henry VIII, wedded to a new determination to close as many
monasteries as he could get away with.[56] A clutch of evidence points to
new directions in royal policy on monasteries coming out of the consultations at Winchester and Bishop's Waltham. Chapuys, whom someone
was clearly briefing about the English Court's travels, noted that in
Cromwell's close personal visitation of the monasteries alongside the progress 'it is certain that both brothers and nuns are given to understand
that it is in their interest to leave their houses, inasmuch as a reformation
of all religious congregations is shortly intended, so very rigorous and
exceptional that probably all will have to go – which is what this King is
trying to bring about in every possible way, so he may have better occasion to seize the whole of Church property without provoking discontent
and murmurs among his subjects.'[57]

Almost at a tangent from the main work of monasteries was the inclusion in visitation of those other great religious corporations, the
Universities of Oxford and Cambridge.[58] Here the relationship of visitor
and visited was very different: the visitors themselves included a good
number of Oxbridge dons, and all were veterans of university study.
Cromwell's own intimate relationship to both universities, and his intense
interest in their studies, is clear. At Cambridge, as newly elected Chancellor of the University, he was in the curious position of both insider and
outsider as visitor. It was a role which emphasized the revolutionary
character of what he had initiated: this was the first time secular government had intruded on the internal affairs of Oxford and Cambridge, an
interference that has never thereafter ceased.

The orders imposed by the visitors did much to revolutionize teaching
in both universities. They banned lecture courses based on the great
medieval textbooks of theology and biblical commentary, emphasized
direct engagement with the biblical text, strengthened the teaching of
Greek (hardly studied at all in medieval Oxbridge) and even specified
Luther's colleague and Henry VIII's new friend Philip Melanchthon as
one of the authorities for instruction. Most radical of all was the complete abolition of the teaching of canon law, the basis of organization in

the Western Church for four centuries. That could be regarded either as King Henry's act of spite against the Papacy or as the logical outcome of the assertion in the Act in Restraint of Appeals that this realm was an 'Empire'.

Since the Church's law remained in place as a living system, operated in the network of English Church courts, the ending of canon law teaching resulted in an absurd situation: senior canon lawyers could learn their principles only by studying the parallel system of Roman law called civil law still taught in the universities. If they wanted to go further into the study of their own practice, they had to go abroad to papist Europe to study: principally to the University of Padua, which in good Venetian spirit tolerated a certain amount of religious deviance in the interest of good international relations and solid financial gain.[59] Other parts of Oxbridge's curriculum revolution were finessed, as is the way of universities. Curriculum reform proved less radical than the external reformers wished: Peter Lombard's great medieval textbook the *Sentences* remained much studied in both universities for decades. It would be pleasing to believe that intellectual curiosity proved a healthy brake on official diktat.

During the autumn Cromwell continued to make up visitation policy on the hoof, and his visitors were sometimes slow to catch up with the latest alteration. By mid-October, perhaps prompted by the discovery of Wolsey's twenty-three-year-old daughter among the nuns of Shaftesbury Abbey, he had thought better of the visitation requirement for monks and nuns younger than twenty-four to leave their communities. John ap Rhys wrote a harassed letter to him on 22 October about the changed requirement. Cromwell, never tolerant of recalcitrance, had been constrained to repeat ('eftsoons') an order to the visitors not to expel anyone over twenty, and 'it shall be followed as far as it may lie in me; but many there be already dismissed in places where we have been above the age, and whether ye would have any restraint again made of them, let your Mastership see.'[60]

One could describe this change as responsiveness to reality; Cromwell was becoming aware that the cohort of twenty- to twenty-four-year-olds was more reluctant to quit monastic life than he had expected, quite apart from one distressed young nun at Shaftesbury. A further development was an order to the visitors to inquire into the history of monastic founders, to see which houses were royal foundations and might therefore be more easily commandeered. This was encouraged by a memorandum from some government lawyer suggesting that merely by examining royal foundations and seizing the property of those in breach of the founder's regulations (no doubt that would turn out to be all of them) the King would regain £40,000 of revenue every year.[61] The proposal was nevertheless at this stage absurdly impractical. As so often in schemes around attacks on church wealth, it represented a possible direction of travel, to be taken in the right political circumstances.

Yet the inquiry had another dimension. Among all noblemen who could count themselves heirs to pious Anglo-Norman monastic founders, the greatest tally of ancient titles was clutched by the Duke of Norfolk, who was smarting from his political marginalization, and never neglectful of his own profit. Cromwell soon became aware that Norfolk had launched a private enterprise of dissolution in his own heartland that autumn, closing down a sequence of small East Anglian family monasteries associated with his predecessors. The complaisant monks of his dynastic mausoleum Thetford Priory leased him their cell at Wangford; Cistercian Sibton sold itself outright to him; at the end of November, so did the nuns of Bungay beside his ancient castle – 'before it was suppressed, I showed the King and Mr Secretary that the nuns would not abide in the house,' the Duke blandly reminisced soon afterwards, while pointing out that he had also told the King of a similar disinclination to remain among the debt-ridden canons of Woodbridge, prior to a private suppression.[62]

Where the Duke led the way, other East Anglian gentry enthusiastically followed: William Woodhouse at Ingham, John Derick at Marham nunnery. It was enough to make many other little houses convert as much of their assets into ready cash as they could.[63] This flow of private asset-stripping must be stopped, and surrenders at least regularized; yet in autumn 1535 there was no legal way of actually preventing them. It was not surprising that in this deteriorating situation Cromwell resumed the policy of individual monastic dissolutions in the Crown's interest which he had tried out in 1532. The new closures had the same justification, failure in finance, which at that earlier juncture had been the pretext for the closure of Christ Church Aldgate. In a series of seven royal dissolutions from November 1535 to February 1536, almost identical wording was used in the deeds of surrender, despite the fact that in some cases there really was lurid sexual scandal which might have provided good reason for suppression.[64]

The last two in the sequence, Bilsington Priory in Kent and Tilty Abbey in Essex, both eventually surrendered on the same day, 28 February 1536, despite being around 90 miles apart across the Thames. Both these monasteries were linked to Cromwell via his web of Kentish gentry friendships, centred on Margaret Wotton, widow of his former employer

Thomas Marquess of Dorset. We have met both houses before (see above, pp. 48–9, 60–61). Bilsington was spared dissolution by Wolsey in 1525, no doubt through its connections to Dorset's brother-in-law Sir Henry Guildford and Cromwell's friend Anthony St Leger; St Leger leased it after its present dissolution. Tilty Abbey contained the retirement home of the widowed Marchioness. Its closure was arranged in person by her old servant, Thomas Cromwell's nephew Richard; his friend and contemporary Ralph Sadler had boyhood memories from his father's stewardship for the Greys at Tilty. The rather unusual paperwork around the surrender manages to omit any mention of the Marchioness's stately mansion in the abbey precinct, which continued to be occupied by her family well into the Elizabethan age. Still odder was the agreement that for the time being the Abbot of Tilty and his seven monks should remain in their communal life along with their staff, until the King told them to go. Perhaps the Marchioness saw them as agreeable adjuncts to her retirement.[65]*

While nothing at this stage suggests a general plan to end monasticism, the visitation's work up to the beginning of Parliament consistently reveals the intention of thinning out the ranks in the regular life, using criteria of misdemeanour, youth or repudiation of a false vocation. The terms of the visitors' injunctions resulted in far more dismissals from the monastic life than historians have previously realized: perhaps 1,700 monks out of a total of around 9,000, mainly relying on the provisions for dismissing those younger than twenty-four.[66] During winter 1536, the commissioners made elaborate plans to transfer monks and nuns wishing to remain in religion, but they were taken aback by the administrative load created by the unexpectedly large numbers, particularly in the North.[67] Nevertheless the sequence of ad hoc but sequenced dissolutions in autumn and winter 1535/6 strongly suggests that, on the very eve of the first Parliament of 1536 which enacted the first general measure of dissolution, no definite decision had been taken on how to proceed.

That likelihood is further reinforced by the behaviour of Drs Leighton and Lee in their visitation of monasteries in the Northern Province in winter 1536. They were arbitrary and bullying enough to provoke much of the anger which exploded later in the year, but some of their bullying, such as Leighton's considerable and unsuccessful efforts to secure the suppression of Marrick Priory in February 1536, would clearly have been unnecessary if there had been a plan prepared for the general legislation

---

* The Marchioness's eldest son by her first marriage, George Medley, went on living at Tilty till his death in 1562, and is commemorated by a monumental brass in the parish church, the former *capella extra portas* of the monastery.

put through Parliament a month or so later. Altogether, the conduct of the visitation as late as that winter gives backing to the story we have already encountered: that in discussions in the royal Council at this time Cromwell championed a continuing programme of piecemeal closures, such as those he had supervised since his days with Wolsey, and once more between November 1535 and February 1536, and that he was then defeated by a combination of Lord Chancellor Audley and Richard Rich. Instead, Audley's and Rich's proposal for systematic legislation to close lesser monasteries on the basis of annual income followed in the coming Parliament.[68]

Before that resolution, the configuration of power at Court was convulsed by successive deaths, though these were accidents of nature rather than the murderous design of the previous spring and summer's run of executions. The first might seem to lessen the King and Queen's difficulties; this is certainly how Henry viewed the news of the passing of Katherine of Aragon on 7 January 1536. His unconcealed rejoicing and that of Queen Anne, accompanied by her family's hopes that the Lady Mary would be next, are not endearing.[69] Cromwell's feelings may have been more ambiguous. The huge relief of the situation was that Katherine's death diminished the obstacles to his preferred alliance overseas with the Emperor rather than the King of France; it also left Mary as a political and diplomatic wild-card. Given that virtually no one in mainland Europe had ever been persuaded by King Henry's case for his annulment, the departure of Katherine was one small step to removing that embarrassment from current diplomatic considerations. As Bishop Gardiner piously put it in a memorandum to Cromwell soon afterwards, 'God hath given sentence . . . by the death of the Dowager.'[70]

Cromwell, as he emphasized to the grief-stricken Chapuys, did his best to make the ceremonies around the ex-Queen's funeral in Peterborough Abbey as dignified as befitted the widow of the King's elder brother, and the preparations included a hearse with appropriate tapers in St Paul's Cathedral as an accompanying tribute in the capital. Workmen began to put it up, but, as Chapuys observed, the plans were then abruptly halted. This was thanks to a fit of royal spite. Ralph Sadler, as usual acting as Cromwell's go-between with the King when Cromwell could not do business in person, wrote from Greenwich Palace reporting his fruitless interview with the King about this. Henry's wayward mood that day was only partly assuaged by Sadler's presentation of Cromwell's diversionary novelty gift of an ingenious lock. Henry dismissed the hearse plans regardless: 'surely it should be to his Grace more charge than is either requisite or needful.'

Sadler did his best to change the royal mind, in the interests of decency. He pointed out that this honour had recently been given at St Paul's to the King's sister Mary, widow of Louis XII of France, but that was a bad misstep, producing the snarl 'that *she* was a Queen'; enough was already being spent on Katherine's funeral, Henry commented sourly.[71] In fact the ceremonies leading Katherine's coffin from Kimbolton to Peterborough were miserable, despite dutiful magnificence and the presence of noble ladies who had been Katherine's partisans. Chapuys refused to travel up to the Fens, given that he could not recognize Katherine's style as Dowager Princess in the ritual. The preacher was the wildly inappropriate John Hilsey of Rochester, chosen expressly to repeat a message of the royal supremacy over the royal corpse, before an audience all well aware that his predecessor at Rochester had been John Fisher. There was no chance of Katherine's aged Spanish confessor George de Athequa, still nominally Bishop of Llandaff, occupying the pulpit that day.[72]

In this moment of Anne's heartless rejoicing, a second death cheated her of further triumph; in fact, there were no more triumphs for her. Energized by the lifting of Katherine's shadow, the King had plunged gleefully into the sporting pastimes of his vigorous young manhood, and resumed jousting. As is the way for middle-aged men in denial about the passage of time, disaster followed: a very serious fall in full armour in the tiltyard. He lay unconscious for two hours. Five days later on 29 January, badly affected by shock at the accident, the Queen miscarried another child, after something like three or four months of pregnancy. Malicious later Catholic commentary produced a story of a malformed foetus; there is no good contemporary warrant for this, despite the gullibility of some modern historians, and actually not much more certainty that the child was male.[73]

It was disaster enough for Anne that her pregnancy had once more resulted in miscarriage, just as her late predecessor had been so regularly afflicted. The King's chance of acquiring a legitimate male heir receded still further. At the very moment when Katherine was no longer around to infuriate him into supporting his true wife Anne, here was a source of dark thoughts as to why all his efforts to regularize his marital life had not after all met with the Deity's approval. Chapuys was happy to record the King's unfeeling expressions of self-pity: 'he had been seduced and forced into this marriage through spells and charms ... God had well shown his displeasure at it by denying him male children.' Worse still for Anne, Chapuys heard of the increasing royal interest in Jane Seymour.[74] Another lady was also bound to benefit in status: the Lady Mary. Behind the infant Princess Elizabeth, she and the slightly younger Duke of

Richmond came suddenly into clearer focus as possible heirs to the throne on the brink of adulthood. Both now enjoyed fitful displays of affection and attention from the King.

All this was significant material for Cromwell to weigh up, particularly as Anne's many conservative enemies began considering their options. Later depositions (taken in an entirely different political crisis) reveal that in February 1536 he made quiet feelers to the Lady Mary about securing a deal in which she could become heir apparent in return for acceptance of her present status. This was the deal Cromwell went on to secure from her the following summer. Mary's historical legacy is fatally prone to hindsight. We have to remember that in winter 1536 she was a very young woman, just twenty, and was not yet the symbol of religious intransigence, triumph and tragedy, that she undoubtedly later became. Granted, she was Katherine of Aragon's daughter, but she was also simply not Anne Boleyn. That would override any other consideration as various leading courtiers and politicians, Cromwell included, decided what their approach to her would be.

Cromwell's February negotiations with Mary took place in co-operation with Sir Nicholas Carew, a courtier who had always loathed Anne but had been protected from the consequences of that by his friendship with the King. Carew was another Surrey man, in fact knight of the shire in Parliament alongside Cromwell's old friend Sir William Fitzwilliam. What happened is described in a deposition from an anonymous former servant of Katherine of Aragon, who also seems to have been in Cromwell's service, or at least suborned by him. Events are dateable to February by the mention of Mary being moved to Hunsdon:

> about the time that the King's council had sent to her to Hunsdon, [Carew]
> sent for me to his chamber at Westminster, bidding me welcome, saying
> that the cause he sent for me was for that he did know I did give my heart
> and service to her for her mother's sake; and he showed me a letter of his
> own hand to her, wherein he besought her for the love of God (and so in
> likewise did all her friends here) desire her to follow the King's desire, and
> they were sure that his Majesty was minded at that Parliament to make her
> heir apparent till God should send his Majesty other issue. At which time
> I made answer, I durst not, except I did know my Lord's [Thomas Crom-
> well's] pleasure, then being Secretary; who [that is, Carew] bade me not
> fear, for he would show him his-self, saying that he was sure Master
> Secretary would give a hundred pounds that she would consent. And so
> thereupon I went with his letter to her Grace, who showed me that her
> Grace had received the same day a letter from his [Carew's] wife by her

servant; and the same day Tomyou, servant to the said Master Secretary, being there with her Grace, unto whom I showed the cause of my coming. And that night [Tomyou] and I came to London about midnight.[75]

The fact that these talks involved Cromwell's senior servant, Richard Tomyou, shows the seriousness of the overture. Tomyou was a highly appropriate choice to speak to Mary. The surname Tomyou is so odd that his father may have been Italian, but in any case he was one of the smart Italianate young men who (like his friend Richard Morison) had enjoyed Wolsey's patronage, probably with the thought that they could be useful in educating Thomas Winter. Cromwell's financial colleague in the Cardinal's desperate last months, Tomyou was subsequently placed as Clerk Controller first to Katherine of Aragon and then in late 1533 to Lady Mary – surely on the recommendation of Master Secretary.[76] Apart from now being Cromwell's own Clerk Controller, Tomyou went on (once a revolution had occurred) to marry a lady-in-waiting to Sir Nicholas Carew's erstwhile protégé Queen Jane Seymour; later, in 1538, the Lady Mary was giving Tomyou presents which indicated he still had at least an honorary position among her servants.[77] Given the collaboration of Carew and his friends with Cromwell to secure Mary's future in the succession, a formidable tangle of roots was now burrowing under Queen Anne's endangered position.

As if that were not enough, Cromwell heard a story with the potential to overturn all the political changes of the previous seven or eight years. It is preserved in a remarkably circumstantial reminiscence addressed in 1559 to Anne Boleyn's daughter, the newly enthroned Queen Elizabeth, by that self-renamed wanderer Alexander Alesius, writing from abroad to tell Elizabeth what he knew of her mother's downfall back in 1536.[78] For some of those events Alesius had been a privileged insider/outsider: a pioneer among the procession of sententious Scotsmen explaining the English to themselves over the centuries. The reader may recall that he had arrived in England in September 1535, bearing the presentation copy of Philip Melanchthon's *Loci communes* for the King (see above, pp. 289–91). Alesius actually claimed responsibility for the book's dedication to Henry, but that probably usurps credit from Robert Barnes in his mission to Melanchthon that spring.

In all Alesius's narratives in print and manuscript spread over three decades, after discounting his assumption that the history of early Tudor England revolved round himself, he proves a reliable witness to events in which he was involved, wherever they can be cross-referenced. There is a scrupulosity in his writing despite his self-importance; for instance, in his letter to Queen Elizabeth, he makes it clear that he and her mother never met personally despite his visits to the English Court, so his esteem for Anne was based solely on her reputation and the major role she had played in furthering evangelical religion, for instance in the promotion of bishops like Cranmer and Latimer. His witness to the tangled events of that spring has not been taken seriously enough.[79] From autumn 1535 he was first the guest of Cranmer and Cromwell in London, a useful cog in their plans for an international Protestant alliance, and then a lecturer in Cambridge at royal expense (in fact the precursor of the later Regius professors), still visiting the capital on occasion, as he did at the time of Anne's arrest.[80] He was therefore well placed to observe events at Court, and even to understand them. His message is that, from the beginning, Cromwell took the initiative in Queen Anne's downfall.

Alesius's tale begins in winter 1536, and although he presents it as a conspiracy against the good name of innocent Queen Anne, sparked by the papist malice of Bishop Gardiner, the story develops so that Cromwell becomes the Queen's principal nemesis. Stephen Gardiner (by then on embassy to the King of France) wrote from Paris to friends at Court that the French Court was full of rumours after letters had been discovered accusing Anne of adultery. Chief among his correspondents in England was his old servant Thomas Wriothesley, whom Alesius observes Bishop Gardiner had placed at Court to look after his interests ('ad sua negocia curanda'). Crucially, Wriothesley passed the news to Cromwell. Given that over his career Alesius expressed much gratitude to Cromwell for favour in the later 1530s, it is remarkable that he was prepared to make the Protestant hero an ally of Wily Winchester in these events, particularly when recounting them to the Protestant Queen. Not only does this unexpected narrative texture give his account plausibility, but it corroborates what Cromwell himself later said to Chapuys about how he had engineered Anne Boleyn's fall.

The detail of Wriothesley's communicating his news to Cromwell lends the story a further air of authenticity. To appreciate why, it is necessary to clear up a long-standing myth that Wriothesley was very early in Cromwell's employment, a mistaken notion that has obscured the plausibility of Alesius's tale.[81] Wriothesley was in reality associated with Gardiner and then through him was in royal service, before moving to Cromwell's clientage now in February 1536.[82] Wriothesley's move thus only followed Gardiner's departure from England for his French embassy in autumn 1535, an absence prolonged in the end for around three years. This is the real moment at which Wriothesley transferred his allegiance from his old Cambridge tutor to Master Secretary.

By summer 1536 Wriothesley was fully in the employment of the triumphant minister as secretary and gate-keeper to his power. The following year John Husee observed of his present position with Cromwell that 'The man standeth in place where he can please or displease.'[83] It is noticeable that by that time people were in the habit when they wrote to Cromwell of writing a more unbuttoned letter in parallel to Wriothesley, glossing their formal requests and asking for a little boost to what they sought: exactly the same relationship which obtained for those writing to the King when they added a supplementary letter to Cromwell. Wriothesley spent the second half of the 1530s in bitter confrontation with Stephen Gardiner, who naturally felt deeply betrayed after his earlier trust.

Yet for the moment, Cromwell and Gardiner did not necessarily have divergent interests if a rumour came from Paris which might undermine Anne. In fact, beyond personal antipathies to her and to each other, both men were instinctively in favour of alliance with the Empire. This ranged them in this crucial matter of policy against the consistent tendency of Queen Anne and her uncle the Duke of Norfolk to stay close to the French: Anne through her happy memories of more than six teenage years in the household of Queen Claude of France, Norfolk because of a handsome pension paid annually to him by the French King. Cromwell's correspondence with Gardiner from this period goes out of the way to mend fences with gestures of friendship and confidential gossip, and he even sang Gardiner's praises to Chapuys, commending his scepticism about French diplomatic overtures to King Henry. The ambassador noted his extraordinary vehemence on the French manoeuvres – 'in a passion – so much so that he could hardly get his words out'.[84]

Alesius tells us that between them Cromwell and Wriothesley told the King about the rumours circulating in France; Gardiner from now on ceases to figure in his narrative. The King reacted with an extreme of fury, but throughout his life he was perfectly capable of dissimulating his feelings when necessary. He needed agents to turn the rumours into a case. This was exactly the same procedure he later adopted against Archbishop Cranmer in the conservative vendetta of 1543 which came to be known as the 'Prebendaries' Plot' (in that case, an unsuccessful effort at the victim's destruction).[85] So Henry put Cromwell and Wriothesley secretly to work, alongside certain others (unnamed by Alesius) with a reputation for detesting the Queen. She had, he says, sharply reproved them and threatened to denounce them to the King for serving their own interests under a pretence of evangelical religion, making everything available for sale and being bribed into making unworthy ecclesiastical appointments for enemies of the Gospel.[86] This very specific set of charges sounds unmistakably like an unfriendly description of the vice-gerential bureaucracy, particularly the visitation commissioners, and it agrees with evidence of clashes between Cromwell and Anne later in the spring.

Investigations quietly continued. They involved contacts with a number of ladies of the Queen's bedchamber. It would not be surprising if one of these was Mistress Margery Horsman, who had written to Master Secretary warmly and confident of favours in the preceding autumn, and whose family were precocious evangelicals with links to Cromwell via Christ's College Cambridge; she seamlessly sailed through the coming revolution into the service of Jane Seymour.[87] The message conveyed to the ladies, said Alesius, was that the King now hated the Queen, since she had not provided an heir, and indeed there was no hope that she would.[88] That observation dates these proceedings to mid-winter or very early spring 1536, after Anne's miscarriage of 29 January.

Alesius's account parallels the evidence already described of Cromwell's and Carew's contacts with the Lady Mary in February; and on the day of Queen Anne's trial in May, Cromwell reminded Chapuys of a significant hint he had made back on St Matthias Eve (that is, 23 February 1536), both about Anne and about a change in Mary's position: 'he had implicitly made clear enough and predicted what would follow from it.'[89] That reminiscence illuminates what Chapuys noted from that same conversation just after it had taken place: Cromwell had invited him 'to consider what marvellous things he had achieved ever since he had been in charge of administering the King's affairs; whereby he seemed to imply that it was in his power to undo part of what he had already done'.[90] A fortnight afterwards, at the beginning of March, Edward Seymour was appointed a gentleman of the Privy Chamber: a reminder that there was now a third person in the King's marriage.[91]

In mid-March, Cromwell sent his son away from the darkening political atmosphere in the capital, back to scenes of old pleasures in East Anglia. Gregory was hosted at Woodrising in Norfolk, home of Richard Southwell, now a senior servant of Cromwell's, with the murder of William Pennington in 1532 apparently no black mark against him as mentor of the young. Over the next few months the teenager was fêted by local notables, right up to the Duke of Norfolk himself. Given all that happened that year, it was a prudent decision to leave Gregory in his rural idyll right up to Christmas 1536.[92] This was also the last chance to complete his education, as he neared seventeen. His indefatigable tutor Henry Dowes wrote with prim satisfaction from Woodrising, 'Whereas the last summer was spent in the service of the wild goddess Diana, this shall

(I trust) be consecrated to Apollo and the Muses.'[93] In other words, during summer 1535, Gregory had enjoyed a thoroughly good time at Rycote House with his relative John Williams, getting to know Oxfordshire society out on the hunting field, just as in the west Midlands with Bishop Lee in 1534. (See Plate 22.) To judge by a lovelorn letter addressed to Master Secretary from Rycote by a slightly older friend of Gregory, desperate for support in wooing a local gentlewoman, the long stay in Oxfordshire had been marked by adolescent emotional drama.[94] This year, it was important to cocoon the boy from the not much more sophisticated emotional tangles developing at Court.

Alesius's story and all that flanks it provide a coherent account of how the terminal crisis in Anne Boleyn's life began to unfold in winter 1535/6. The story is perfectly consistent with the shape of politics we have uncovered since Cromwell entered the King's service. Two powerful advocates of evangelical reformation, Cromwell and Anne, had very good reasons for detesting each other dating back to Thomas Wolsey's humiliation. In this unstable situation their mutual hatred came to override their joint enthusiasm for promoting a religious revolution, which had held through 1535. During the 'reign' of Queen Anne, Thomas Cromwell had quietly accumulated power, yet his place in the King's counsels remained anomalous: clearly now the leading royal minister, yet without great offices and honours to express that reality – not even a knighthood. He was at last in a position to begin remedying this deficiency.

14

Surrenders and the Scaffold: 1536

While discreet probings continued at Court around Queen Anne, public affairs were taken up with what proved the last meeting of the Parliament begun so long ago. Opening on 4 February 1536, it lasted little more than nine weeks, but was in legislative terms one of the busiest and most productive sessions.[1] It passed an exceptional number of private bills, thirty-five in this session (surpassed in the Tudor age only by one Parliament, in Henry VII's time), plus much government business. This was clearly because Parliament's work was no longer distorted by the King's Great Matter and the consequent break with Rome; a logjam was released. Major legislation now passed not just on monasteries but on the nationwide problem of poverty, on land law and inheritance and on a new governing structure for Wales: projects on which Cromwell had expended a good deal of effort and drafting over the last year or two. These were not his only preparations. In a typical example of his acquiring apparently trivial office for a purpose, he obtained a grant from Westminster Abbey of the position of abbey Gate-Keeper, a separate duty beside the far more honourable Stewardship they had already given him. We need not think of Master Secretary brooding like his Holbein portrait from the gatehouse lodge: the point was that the office gave him or nominated underlings free access to the abbey precincts while the House of Commons sat in the refectory, together with the right to exclude on the spur of the moment anyone who might be a political nuisance.[2]

The first major measure introduced and debated in Parliament concerned yet more steps to curtail the jurisdiction of bishops, including their rights to administer justice in the territory of certain privileged 'liberties' which would normally be the prerogative of royal officials; the greatest of these liberties was the Palatine Bishopric of Durham. The Act also revived plans, repeatedly pursued and never completed till the twentieth century, to produce a comprehensive revision of canon law for England. This attack on the Church hierarchy followed closely on a menacing pair of circulars to the bishops in January, both characterizing them in remarkably schoolmasterly terms as negligent and untrustworthy. One letter from the King brusquely ordered them to call in all preaching licences, with a covering letter from Cromwell as Vice-Gerent even more scolding: 'I write frankly,' he growled, 'compelled and enforced thereunto both in respect of my private duty and otherwise for my discharge, forasmuch as it pleaseth his Majesty to use me in the lieu of a councillor; whose office is an eye to the prince.' There was an illuminating definition of the Vice-Gerency.[3]

All this was part of general criticism of the institutional Church that winter; yet it concealed much uncertainty among King and Council about turning this into action, particularly on the matter of monasteries. Suspicion of clergy, greed for monastic wealth and genuine desire for a satisfactory measure of reformation contended untidily in this debate. One symptom is a surviving fair-copy draft of a bill on the monasteries; it bears no relation to the end-result in Parliament, and has therefore been neglected and misunderstood. It concentrates on denouncing the promotion of pilgrimages, miraculous images and relics by monks and provides for the ejection of those who did so. Thinning out the ranks of religious was an alternative to systematic suppression of monasteries, a possibility that was not mentioned at all. Instead, the draft spent much time denouncing religious who exploited their 'pretensed holiness and piety' and 'simulate[d] poverty' to give respectability to popish errors. The implication was that other monks, nuns and friars managed to avoid such pitfalls; it is a programme for a reformed but drastically slimmed-down monastic polity.

It was also a rambling and moralizing document, ineptly trying to straddle the boundaries of common and canon law. That has been taken to suggest it had nothing to do with government plans, but in fact it is in the hand of Robert Warmington, one of the most senior clerks to Cromwell's visitation commissioners. Not only does it reflect what they had done in selectively dismissing monks and nuns and gathering discreditable data, but it closely echoes wording in some of their injunctions. It highlights the reforming work of the visitation past and future, and places a broad power of dispensation in Cromwell's hands as Vicar-General. This, therefore, was no mere kite-flying speculation, but an official path not trodden.[4] It also dovetails with Cromwell's preferred plan presented in the Wyatt narrative fragment, in which he not only advocated piecemeal closures but also envisaged conversations in monasteries about 'how horrible this kind of religion is and how odious to the wiser sort of people', to persuade them 'to leave their cowls'. That was exactly the strategy his visitors had been attempting under his instructions at the London Charterhouse.[5]

Ambassador Chapuys, in a dispatch to the Emperor while Parliament was still sitting, also confirms the Wyatt narrative's picture of Cromwell thwarted:

> I am told, besides, that although Cromwell was at one time the adviser and promoter of the demolition of the English convents and monasteries, yet perceiving the great inconveniences likely to arise from that measure, he has since made attempts to thwart it, but that the King had resolutely declined to make any modification of it whatever, and has even been rather indignant against his Secretary for proposing such a thing.[6]

The impression of indecision or continuing argument over monasteries is supported by yet another witness who could not have been better informed: William Popley, one of Cromwell's oldest friends, recently transferred to his service from that of Lord Lisle. He remained a consistent bridge between these two royal servants. Popley wrote to Lisle from The Rolls on 22 February, more than a fortnight after Parliament had opened, to discourage that predatory peer questing after Beaulieu Abbey: 'I cannot perceive that the same or any like shall be suppressed, nor any of like lands, forasmuch as at the session of this Parliament they ordain statutes and provisions for the maintenance and good order of the clergy, as well religious as secular.'[7] Those 'provisions' do not suggest any general measure of suppression. Rather, they sound very like the bill against hypocritical monks promoting popish superstition, and if so, that proposal must then still have been in play in Parliament. Members would have registered how much initiative and power it would confer on the Vice-Gerent, and many of them would have felt every incentive to stop it in its tracks.

This may have been the moment when Thomas Audley and Richard Rich outbid their colleague with their preferred strategy, as now events moved quickly in a different direction. By 3 March, the Calais worthy Sir Richard Whethill, over in London monitoring the passage of important legislation for the enclave, had heard 'that abbeys and priories under three hundred marks by year and having not twelve in convent shall down'. On 9 March, Popley told Lisle the same tale, though he was still uncertain whether legislation would happen. He also referred to the individual surrenders culminating little more than a week earlier at Tilty and Bilsington: 'divers have forsaken their houses, so that by dissolution thereof and certain sales made by the heads of such houses, the King's Grace hath obtained divers houses.' His letter briskly dismissed Lisle's typically unrealistic further hopes of rich pickings from Glastonbury Abbey: 'there is no such purpose, not yet any worshipful house.'[8]

By the end of the month a suppression measure indeed passed

Parliament, affecting only smaller monasteries with an annual income of less than £200, as Whethill and Popley had previously heard.[9] Its preamble took pains to praise 'divers great and solemn monasteries, where, thanks be to God, religion is right well kept and observed', language which was reflected in remarks about 'worshipful houses' by the insider commentator Popley. We need not think that in 1536 suppression of the smaller monasteries was a blind to hide a covert scheme for eventual universal dissolution. The lower limit of twelve in community of which Whethill had learned, with its echo of Christ's twelve apostles, was that chosen by Wolsey and his staff for their proposed systematic suppressions in 1528, aimed at streamlining English monasticism.

What was genuinely new was that the legislation also addressed the evidence of monastic vice provided by Cromwell's visitors, specifically employing the term 'comperts' which they had used for their summary findings. The evidence of these *comperta* (records of 'things discovered'), however much it might be considered muck-raking, did indeed reveal the largest concentration of misdemeanours as being in the smaller monastic houses: 'the bigger the monastery, the lower the rate of crime'.[10] It is also clear that the documentation represented in the *comperta*, or at least as much as was available that March, did its job in outraging Lords and Commons when presented to them. For those who might feel outrage in general terms, excepting any small monastery that they actually knew at first hand, the legislation artfully made provision for grants of exemption from suppression, which must have satisfied a good many fears. In the largest single exemption thus made, the entire fleet of Gilbertine houses large and small came through unscathed.

Despite the exceptions, the suppression of rather more than 200 monasteries represented a huge administrative task, the scale and detailed slog of which were already made apparent in Cromwell's specimen dissolutions of 1532. The answer was a further Act of Parliament creating a 'Court of Augmentations', a government department whose name perhaps too frankly defined its purpose in dealing with this very considerable new 'augmentation' of the King's income. The obvious implication was that the Crown fully intended to hang on to its new gains. The Court's first Chancellor was Richard Rich, lending additional plausibility to the assertion by the anonymous historian in the Wyatt papers that Rich and Audley rather than Cromwell bore responsibility for creating it. Audley was Rich's first patron in government, and Audley's servant Thomas Pope became Receiver of the new Court as deputy to Rich. The account observes that 'they placed only their friends and servants to be ministers' in it.[11]

The Court modelled itself on the most coherently organized department of land revenue in government, the Duchy of Lancaster, taking detailed advice from Duchy officials on how to set things up. Rich was very familiar with Duchy practice, having been one of its senior officers since 1532. He was perfectly capable of combining liberal doses of sycophancy in letters to Cromwell with a relish for an independent (indeed high-handed) exercise of his new Chancellorship, which earned him a good deal of public ill-will. On occasion, as dissolutions of monasteries expanded beyond those affected by the 1536 legislation, Rich even dared to express annoyance at Cromwell's suppression commissioners, whom he regarded as obstructing the Augmentations officials under his own control.[12]

In practice, Cromwell was rarely anything less than helpful to the work of Augmentations. If he had indeed been overruled in Council on the way forward, it was not in his nature to allow pique to stand in the way of acquiring power and influence. Augmentations officials soon included many civil servants close to him or from his household, including his servant Robert Southwell, whom he esteemed enough as early as 1533 to recommend to his Devon friend Sir William Courtenay for a good marriage.[13] Others among local Augmentations receivers were Robert's brother Richard (Gregory's host in Norfolk) and from the Cromwell payroll William Blythman, John Scudamore, John Freeman and George Gifford.[14]

Parliament had much else to consider besides monasteries. One of the most remarkable new measures from the government was a pioneering attempt to deal with Tudor England's growing problem of poverty and unemployment through comprehensive legislation. It was the first stage in creating a coherent national system of poor relief in subsequent centuries. The statute actually passed was based on a far more ambitious sixty-six-page draft, whose importance was first realized by Geoffrey Elton; it is avowedly intended for this Parliamentary session, dateable to the previous months.[15] The form of the draft is unusual, which might make it seem just one of the many utopian schemes of reform from enthusiastic would-be policy-makers that Cromwell gathered in his archives, but there is a strong indication that the minister was closely involved in its creation. Its proposal for a 'Council to avoid vagabonds', to supervise the category of able-bodied unemployed in undertaking public works, concentrates on his favourite and then topical preoccupation, river and sea engineering, beginning with the great new harbour works at Dover.

Under the draft scheme (avowedly time-limited in the first instance to 1540, an unusual measure of cautious experiment), administration of poor relief would be paid for by a graded national tax, but there would also be parish collections and encouragement of further parish charity through a poor-box, 'before [in front of] the sacrament there as nigh as can be reasonably devised'; set-piece homilies would be prepared by the diocesan bishops for their clergy to preach. Such a national poor-box scheme actually became permanent under Edward VI, although the reserved sacrament in its pyx at the high altar was no longer there in churches. Overseers would be appointed in parishes, responsible for both vagabonds and the poor for good reasons unfit to work. There are even suggestions that physicians be appointed and paid to attend to those who would be able to work if given medical attention.

There are two remarkable features of this bill's history. First is that Cromwell persuaded King Henry himself to come to the Commons to present it and speak in its favour, 'they to see it for a common wealth to his subjects': that is, a great public benefit. Second, the Commons were unimpressed by this show of majesty. The government were forced to withdraw the measure and present a more modest proposal. The Act that passed was much less comprehensive, and the proposed Council on vagabondage disappeared; perhaps the Court of Augmentations was enough setting up of new central institutions for Parliament to stomach in one session. Nevertheless the provisions for parish almsgiving and poor-box remained, as did the requirement for local officials to find work for the able-bodied unemployed. The subsequent fate even of this watered-down measure was confused; whatever continuing life it had was merely on the sufferance of a royal proclamation of 1538.

At the end of Elizabeth's reign a much greater economic crisis than Henrician England ever experienced forced action on Parliament, and thereafter the poor law system glimpsed in 1536 endured till the nineteenth century.[16] Like Parliament's equally firm refusal to be bossed about in curbing agricultural enclosures in March 1534, the stuttering start to poor law legislation underlines the fact that in the 1530s it was perfectly possible for Parliament to show determined and successful opposition to measures proposed by the King's chief minister, provided they did not focus on the two issues which aroused Henry's murderous rage: religion and the future of the dynasty. Tudor England was never a simple monarchical tyranny.

The King and his ministers may have been fairly relaxed about the fate of a measure of social engineering because alongside it they appeared to have gained a victory in an important matter of royal revenue that had been vexing the Crown long before Cromwell's arrival in power.[17] The theory of landholding in England was still that of the feudal system, set up to guarantee effective armies at the Crown's disposal. All land ultimately belonged to the King, and landholders were royal tenants, some directly ('tenants-in-chief'), and others as tenants of tenants. It was all intended for a military system which had long vanished, but the law had not changed, and the Crown could exploit it. Thanks to the vagaries of landownership since the twelfth century, the category of tenant-in-chief effectively netted in anyone above the level of the humblest village landowners, and some of them too; monarchs therefore had a great deal of room to interfere in their subjects' estates by primer seisin, the right to step in and meddle in various profitable ways on the death of a landholder.

Late medieval lawyers, happy like lawyers in every age to provide tax-avoidance schemes for those prepared to pay for them, evolved a system of trusts by which legal estate in a property was conveyed to trustees ('feoffees'). These feoffees held estates for the benefit or 'use' of the real owner of the land (who was known in common law French as the *cestuy que use*); their existence defeated the Crown's feudal rights. The group of feoffees to uses was renewable and hence as a body the feoffees never died; the beneficiary or *cestuy que use* avoided all the Crown's rights of primer seisin. The device of the use was invaluable to stop the Crown getting its hands on a landowner who was a child (and so in ancient feudal theory too young to serve in the King's army). The monarch could not take advantage of his profitable powers to administer the child's lands in wardship. Equally important, uses allowed landowners to leave land in their wills to whomever they pleased; feudal law simply forbade bequests of land by will.

The existence of feoffment to uses was infuriating to those acquisitive monarchs Henry VII and Henry VIII, but it took time for the Crown to work out how to defeat the stratagems of the legal profession. We have noticed in passing the sturdy rebuff which Parliament gave to royal efforts to regain its rights on primer seisin in 1529 and 1532 (see above, pp. 158, 163), and after that another way was taken: a specimen court case, attacking family trusts which Lord Dacre of the South had set up before he died in September 1533. In devising this route, someone must have realized that lawyers might be set against lawyers on the issue. Case-law on uses had been developed in the relatively flexible legal culture of the Court of Chancery, whose original speciality as a forum for natural justice against legal rigidity made it the appropriate setting for judgments on disputes about trust. Lawyers practising in the much more formulaic world of common law courts – King's Bench or Common Pleas – did not share in this lucrative business and might be inclined to cut their Chancery colleagues down to size.

The Crown duly first brought its case against the late Lord Dacre's trust before Chancery, as was to be expected, but the judges there (who naturally included Lord Chancellor Audley and Master of the Rolls Cromwell) adjourned the matter to be argued before the entire body of common law judges, who assembled in the Court of Exchequer Chamber in Easter Term 1535. The Crown won, albeit narrowly: the Dacre trust was declared fraudulent, by a bare majority of the judges, and that applied to all the thousands of similar family trusts then in operation. The landowners of England (and their lawyers) were aghast. Not surprisingly in the Parliament of spring 1536 they meekly voted through Crown legislation which regularized their trusts but also restored many feudal rights to the King. This Statute of Uses became one of the fundamental pieces of legislation in English land law up till 1925, not least because lawyers now applied their customary evasive genius to further variants on the use, for purposes both admirable and dubious.

The legislation also left massive questions unresolved about how land might be left by will. That issue was prominent among the grievances of the Pilgrimage of Grace, and the continuing discontent of England's nobility and gentry after the Pilgrimage's defeat led effectively to a capitulation by the Crown on property bequests, by the passage of a further Statute of Wills in the 1540 Parliament (see below, p. 518). Cromwell should not be given the entire credit, if that is the word, for masterminding this bold but flawed outcome of the uses problem in 1536. In the 1520s, his future colleague Thomas Audley had taken advantage of an autumn reading (lecture) at the Inner Temple to launch a blistering attack on the fraudulent nature of uses in Chancery, a formal diatribe which at that stage doubled as an attack on the then Lord Chancellor, Cardinal Wolsey. That particular political clash was long in the past, the passage of events having conferred the Lord Chancellorship on Audley himself, but his guiding hand in this legislation must be a strong possibility.

Nevertheless Audley was working very closely with Cromwell and probably even in cahoots with Lord Dacre's principal feoffee, the lawyer Thomas Polstead. Once the judgment had been secured, Polstead was subject to an inquisition, apparently initiated by Cromwell himself, indicting him for fraud in drawing up his employer's conveyances. The sting may have been taken out of this accusation by the fact that Thomas was brother to Cromwell's principal servant Henry Polstead – they came from a Surrey gentry family – and only a few months after the judgment in Exchequer Chamber Thomas Polstead acted as a feoffee for Cromwell himself in a matter of wardship.[18] This reeks of collusion to get the Crown its result, overseen by Cromwell. The Polstead connection may explain why it was Lord Dacre who was singled out; not all legal teams for the nobility would have a weak link like that. It is noticeable that, after all this, Cromwell was extremely protective of the teenage grandson and heir of Lord Dacre, now exposed to the wardship rights of the Crown. The ninth Lord Dacre of the South turned into an extreme example of the minister's rackety young men, to the point of being executed in 1541 – but he seems to have been fond enough of his near-contemporary Gregory Cromwell to have named his son and heir Gregory in 1539.[19]*

Finally among other varied Acts passed in this Parliament came a clutch of measures which taken together moved further towards a uniform royal jurisdiction in law and government throughout the mosaic of territories making up the Tudor realms. We have already noted the legislation at the beginning of this session which undermined ecclesiastical liberty jurisdictions; to that was added a comprehensive restructuring of government in the anomalous enclave of Calais. This was the fruit of a great deal of worry and preparation dating back to Wolsey's time and continued during Cromwell's visit to Calais with the King in 1532. It culminated in 1535 with a high-powered royal commission of inquiry under Sir William Fitzwilliam; the commissioners were appalled by evidence of local mismanagement. One of the measures of reconstruction brought Calais further into the community of the realm by granting it two MPs in the Westminster Parliament.[20]

A much larger-scale integration began with a trio of measures for Wales. Its provisions eventually created a single framework of government there, closely resembling that of England, with a new network of shires named after their county towns, justices of the peace meeting in sessions, and MPs in the House of Commons. This much improved on previous legislation on Wales passed in the autumn 1534 session of Parliament, which had been a ragbag of tidying-up measures to enforce justice. No doubt useful, and prepared with the full approval of Bishop Lee after six months of experience in his Presidency of the Marches, they had not seriously altered the existing tangle of Welsh jurisdictions.[21] Now that would drastically change, but, like the proposed poor law of this session, the legislation was avowedly experimental, allowing the King to suspend any part of it he saw fit, which in fact he did by proclamation in the national state of disarray in February 1537. Evidently there were some nerves in royal circles about what was being proposed, and no certainty that conditions in Wales would make the scheme practical.

---

* Dacre's son Gregory was baptized at Hurstmonceaux on 25 June 1539, when Gregory Cromwell was living at Leeds Castle, 35 miles away (I am indebted to Teri Fitzgerald for pointing this out to me).

The tentative nature of the statute shiring Wales in 1536 reflects not only the fact that the administrative preparation was sketchy (certainly compared with the mammoth effort put into preparing the Calais legislation) but also the embarrassment that it had not involved any consultation with the chief local actor, Lord President Bishop Lee. Cromwell licensed the unsuspecting Bishop to be absent from this Parliamentary session because of his workload in the borders, so there was nothing that Lee could say until it was too late. Indeed, while Parliament was sitting, the Bishop sent up his own detailed and quite different suggestions for reform to Cromwell, responding to a previous royal request, and he seemed confident that the minister's 'politic wisdom' would see his ideas enacted forthwith.[22] The sharp divergence of Parliamentary action on Wales from what the leading actor in Welsh government expected is notably parallel to the indecision and sudden change of direction surrounding Parliamentary proposals on the dissolution of the smaller monasteries.

There may in fact be a direct connection between these two U-turns. It is possible that Lee's proposals were swept aside, and the bill on Wales drafted in a totally new form, as a result of the decision on a general measure to dissolve the lesser houses. The point is that, thanks to the general poverty of Welsh monasteries, the suppression legislation of 1536 resulted in the vast majority being closed – no fewer than forty-four out of forty-seven. A promise to shire Wales could make the work of closing monasteries easier to enforce there, because it offered a considerable compensating prospect to Welsh gentry, of universal access to English rights and representation. In any case, by the time that Bishop Lee learned what was actually happening in Parliament, it was 12 March, and too late for him to do anything about it. All he could do was express deep disapproval of the whole new scheme. He had no confidence in the Welsh gentry's ability to act like English justices of the peace, and pointedly reminded Cromwell that his post at Ludlow Castle battling with disorder was only through 'your means and pleasure'. Lee appended some comments on a Welsh gentleman arsonist, just to underline his sentiments.[23]

Having once vented his spleen, and perhaps placated by assurances of the avowedly provisional nature of the legislation, the Bishop grudgingly got on with his job. On 29 April (innocent of current turmoil at Court) he wrote again in reply to a warm letter from Cromwell, reminding him that 'Your continual favour is to me life and health, next under God and the King my sovereign lord,' and inviting him to use one of his various houses if the King's progress went north that summer.[24] In the end, Lee survived his friend to die in 1543 still in harness as Lord President; he rested to the last in the Marches, for his stately tomb graced not his cathedral at Lichfield but Shrewsbury's largest parish church. He clearly enjoyed the strenuous work of the Presidency and his vice-regal status more than the tedious business of being Bishop of Coventry and Lichfield, and making further fuss about the shiring of Wales might have brought all that to an end. Ultimately the work of creating the new local institutions necessary for Welsh reorganization was completed only in 1541. The final result was confirmed by a further great statute in 1543, in what was also the first Parliament containing Welsh MPs able to join in the business of voting it through. By then, the likely chief author of the original legislation was unable to savour the outcome.[25]

The greatest task of all, dwarfing the problems of Wales, was beyond the competence of the Westminster Parliament: what to do about Ireland. There was no question of immediately trying to reduce the island to the sort of uniformity envisaged in the shiring of Wales: its division between 'Old English' and Gaelic territories was too profound and the boundaries between them too uncertain to do more than expand Old English jurisdictions back to where they had been when English rule was at its most effective. Before even that could happen came the hard slog of crushing the Kildare rebellion. After a shaky start, the Tudor Crown did not regain the military initiative until spring 1535, and it was early autumn before 'Silken Thomas' Fitzgerald finally surrendered.

Cromwell immediately began to plan for a workable reconstruction of Ireland, embodied in a crisp two-page memorandum.[26] Much of it amounted to detailed military provision and a thorough tidying-up of administration, which could be entrusted to the reliable English and Anglo-Irish civil servants he had already identified in Ireland. But two provisions were far-reaching: first, a question about long-term Crown policy in the latest expedition to Ireland. 'Whether it shall be expedient to begin a conquest or a reformation?' A conquest would entail ending the historic division of cultural regions, fulfilling ancient English hopes of possessing the whole island and opening the possibility of a shiring as in Wales. Second: '[the Dublin] Parliament to be summoned against the octaves of Hilary [20–26 January 1536], and so to be prorogued . . . at the King's pleasure'.

The second question in effect answered the first: it was best not to think big for the time being. The Irish Parliament, thus cautiously convened for whenever the military and political situation made a proper meeting feasible, represented only that part of the island historically under Crown control. Yet even to call a new Parliament and to use it as Cromwell now did was an innovation in terms of English government in Ireland. When Parliament eventually met in Dublin on 1 May 1536, its two years of subsequent sessions produced forty-two statutes, virtually all on

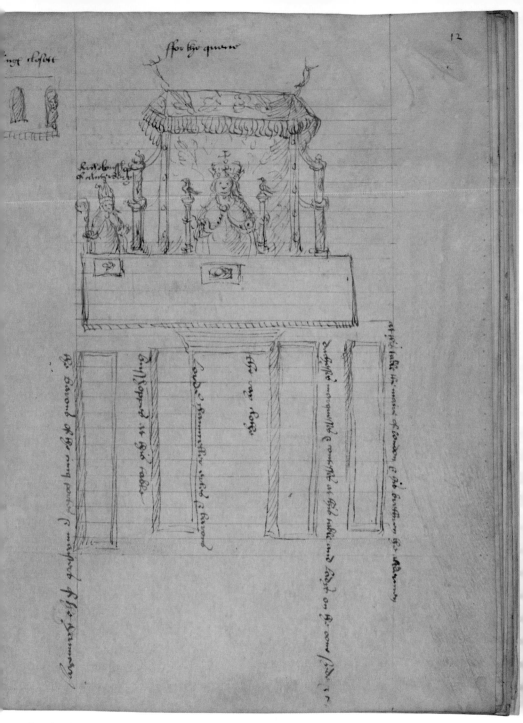

12

17. Sketch-plan for Anne Boleyn's coronation feast in Westminster Hall, 1 June 1533: Cranmer alone shares her table, while King Henry watches from a 'closet' above. From right to left, the lower tables seat the Lord Mayor of London and his brethren; peeresses; Lord Chancellor Audley heading earls and barons; the bishops; 'barons' (officials) of the Cinque Ports and Masters in Chancery.

18. Queen Katherine of Aragon (1485–1536): watercolour miniature on vellum, c. 1525, possibly by Lukas Horenbout.

19. Queen Jane Seymour (1508/9–37) soon after her marriage, 1536, by Holbein.

20. Queen Anne of Cleves (1515–57) by Bartolomaeus Bruyn the Elder: this may be the portrait that in 1539 did not satisfy the English ambassadors and led to a royal commission for a replacement by Holbein.

21. Queen Katherine Howard (1523–42): few likenesses survived her fall, save this Holbein miniature in two versions.

22. Of the vast Rycote House, Sir John Williams's Oxfordshire home, where Gregory Cromwell spent a happy summer in 1535, only parts survived demolition late in the eighteenth century.

23. Cromwell spent great sums on Brooke House, Hackney, former London home of the earls of Northumberland, before returning it to Henry VIII in 1536; this is its nineteenth-century state. Its demolition in 1954–5 after Second World War bomb damage was inexplicable official vandalism.

24–5. This recently identified Holbein miniature of Gregory Cromwell (*left*), now in The Hague, probably commemorated his marriage in 1537. It may have been intended as a pair with that of his proud father (*right*, shown wearing his Garter collar, granted just after Gregory's marriage).

26. A second Holbein miniature of Gregory Cromwell, aged twenty-four in 1543, has strayed even further than The Hague, and via Danzig and the Second World War is currently held in Moscow; this photo was taken just before the First World War. Both are evidently informal domestic treasures.

·ETATIS· ·SVÆ·21

27. There can be little doubt that this Holbein masterpiece, the original in Toledo, depicts Elizabeth Seymour (*c.* 1518–68; successively Lady Ughtred, Lady Cromwell and Lady Paulet), though it has been much claimed for other sitters. Aged twenty-one, she was then Gregory's wife, and already a mother three or four times. Her brooch depicts God the Father enthroned, a reasonably safe choice for an evangelical household.

28. Monument to Gregory Lord Cromwell, *d.* 1551, in the private chapel, formerly the monastic choir, at Launde Abbey, Leicestershire. Erected by his widow Elizabeth Seymour, it is a specimen of the early flowering of Protestant Renaissance architecture associated with the Seymours, and amply deserves Nikolaus Pevsner's description as 'one of the purest monuments of the early Renaissance' in England.

29–30. Two houses successively chosen by Thomas Cromwell as homes for his son and family. *Above*: Lewes Priory (Sussex), only partly converted from its monastic glory before Gregory's hasty move to Leeds. This eighteenth-century view, with town and castle as backdrop, shows desolation even before further ruthless intervention by Victorian railway engineers. *Below*: Leeds Castle (Kent), previously home to the Guildfords, much cherished and enhanced in its splendour by later lovers of the Romantic.

31–4. Henry's courtiers in the 1530s: Holbein studies. (*Clockwise from top left*) Thomas Wyatt the Elder (1503–42), Thomas Wriothesley (1505–50), Nicholas Carew (*c.* 1496–1539) and Ralph Sadler (1507–87).

Cromwell's initiative, whereas the six previous Irish Parliaments back into the 1490s had managed only twenty-five, discounting routine renewals.[27]

One provision in the bundle of proposed legislation Cromwell sent over to Master of the Rolls Allen just after preparing his memorandum was to suspend 'Poynings' Law', the famous provision of a Parliament held in 1494–5 by Lord Deputy Sir Edward Poynings 'that no Parliament be holden in this land until the Acts be certified into England'. It might seem paradoxical that Cromwell should nullify this measure intended by English administrators to control Irish Parliamentary initiatives, but actually what he was removing was an official power of veto in Westminster which had made it virtually impossible to take any positive action in the assembly. Poynings' Law would have severely hampered him in producing and then the Dublin Parliament in scrutinizing and making adjustments to the bundle of statutes designed to pull Ireland into conformity with current English government policy: vital matters like the royal supremacy, along with other local recommendations from reliable administrators of the Pale. For decades, Irish government had been in the hands of the Fitzgeralds, with occasional temporary and in the long term ineffectual interventions from Westminster. Now, after vast expenditure of money, effort and human life, the Geraldines had been broken. Westminster could lead in making changes, rather than struggle against autonomous Geraldine power thinly disguised as lieutenancy for the Crown.[28]

Who would replace the great Anglo-Norman noblemen? We have seen how from 1532 or so Cromwell was steadily identifying local Old English gentlemen marked by loyalty and competence, and reinforcing them with one or two imported Englishmen he knew well, principally his servants William Brabazon and Thomas Agard. Had he been able to send the Duke of Richmond with a suitable staff in 1534, the process could have continued more smoothly; instead, Sir William Skeffington arrived perforce as military fire-fighter. Skeffington's death while war was still sputtering on left his office of Deputy vacant, and what seemed like the dream choice to replace him was Cromwell's friend Lord Leonard Grey, brother of his former employer the late Marquess of Dorset. Already senior military commander in Ireland, Grey knew Ireland well and might be able to build bridges with the discontented, since his sister had married the late Earl of Kildare. In summer 1535 he escorted over to England his nephew by marriage, Silken Thomas, for whatever treatment the King saw fit.

After Lord Leonard had returned to Ireland, he was kitted out with a brand-new Irish peerage in January 1536; this was unusual for an English governor, but perhaps Cromwell felt that Grey might find it useful to have his own vote in the proposed meeting of the Dublin Parliament. His new title – Viscount Graney – came from a grant of a nunnery and its estates in Kildare territory. In a portent of things to come in Ireland, the nuns of Graney evaded suppression and Grey's predations for a couple more years; maybe one reason why Lord Leonard virtually never used the title.[29] The attempted dissolution of Graney paralleled Cromwell's piece-meal English dissolutions of that autumn and winter, particularly those for Grey's own relatives at Bilsington and Tilty. Its suppression would have been a precocious action in England, and was still more so in war-torn County Kildare: the fact that it was bungled was a sign of that perennial English lack of realism about conditions over the Irish Sea.[30]

The disadvantages of a lord deputy who was a military man with a short fuse and an affection for his surviving Fitzgerald relatives emerged over the next few years, but for the moment in spring 1536 Lord Leonard presided efficiently over the opening session of the Irish Parliament. Ably assisted by William Brabazon, he processed the government's first batch of legislation, including the royal supremacy (they were in fact too efficient, since the Dublin legislators dutifully passed an Act for the Boleyn succession, as Brabazon reported to Cromwell on 17 May, in blissful unawareness of recent English events).[31] The Deputy's troubles started with the rejection in September of a watered-down version of the Westminster Parliament's monastic dissolution bill from the spring; the frustration of his designs on Graney Abbey should have been a warning.

This government defeat represented not so much devout Catholic resistance to the Reformation (after all, the Dublin Parliament had just passed the royal supremacy) as annoyance among Anglo-Irish gentry that a favoured few benefiting from Cromwell's alliance with the Earl of Ossory and the Butlers looked set to monopolize sources of power and profit, which was to be expected after the collapse of both Fitzgerald and Boleyn influence. Once members were reassured of open season on monastic property, the suppression legislation passed scarcely amended the following year.[32] Yet neither Cromwell nor Henry VIII succeeded in total monastic dissolution in Ireland, despite grievously wounding Irish regular religious life. We will glimpse further examples of Irish ecclesiastical confusion as the next few years unfold.

Haplessly sucked into the Irish morass was Cromwell's other choice of senior agent in Ireland: a new archbishop of Dublin to replace his friend John Allen (lately murdered by Geraldines), with a brief to move forward religious reform wherever possible. The lucky winner was his landlord at Austin Friars, Prior-Provincial George Browne. One advantage of sending a friar was that in theory at least he ought to have modest financial expectations, which was just as well, since Cromwell envisaged devoting most of the archiepiscopal revenues to administrative expenses in Ireland. Browne had proved himself as a royal visitor of friaries over the previous two years; this huge leap in promotion might be considered a reward for effort, just as his once uncomfortably yoked colleague John Hilsey was now gracing the diocese of Rochester.

Hilsey, in what may have been intended as a gesture of reconciliation after their quarrels, was one of the two bishops assisting Archbishop Cranmer at Lambeth in Browne's consecration for Dublin on 10 March 1536. In a slightly uncomfortable additional ceremony, redolent of loose ends in the royal supremacy (to say nothing of the untidy fit of jurisdictions between England and Ireland), Cranmer invested the new Archbishop with the pallium: this was a garment of both authority and subordination, just as Canterbury himself had received it from the Pope back in 1533.[33] Browne took some time to travel to his new charge, perhaps further delayed by the momentous events of the spring and early summer. It was 19 July before he and William Body, another of Cromwell's trusted servants, arrived in Dublin, 'in a readiness to execute and follow all your pleasure and commandment according unto the effect of your good counsel', as he affirmed in a note dashed off straight away to his patron. Browne had absorbed a barrage of advice on Irish politics and reformation from Master Secretary before leaving, which he now did his best to put into action, against daunting odds.[34]

On 14 April 1536, as this third component of government reorganization took its shaky course in Ireland, the Westminster Parliament drew to an end. By then alert members would be aware that some very odd things were going on at Court. One of the oddest, which would instantly have told the world of a serious rift between the Queen and Thomas Cromwell, was a technicolor sermon in the Chapel Royal on Passion Sunday, 2 April, preached by Queen Anne's almoner, John Skip.[35] We know in detail what Skip said, because the preacher found himself facing unsympathetic interrogation as events unfolded over the following months. The text alone, John 8.46, 'Which of you can convict me of sin?', was a trumpet-call against accusations that most of the world had no idea had been made. To begin with, in a rambling and complex discourse, Skip defined 'you' and 'me' in relatively innocuous terms: his audience and the clergy of the Church respectively. Yet even that would be enough to make a congregation stir uneasily, given the barrage of attacks on the Church hierarchy Cromwell had been orchestrating both inside and outside Parliament, and the current passage of legislation about the lesser monasteries. What was a known evangelical like Skip up to, taking this rhetorical line?

Worse followed when the preacher turned to criticizing royal councillors (not specified) 'for the malice that they bear toward many men or
toward one man', and especially for their attempts at 'the renovation or
alteration of any old or ancient customs or ceremonies' in religion, and
'renovations or alterations in civil matters' as well. What possible instance
might he be thinking of? The answer quickly followed: the story of 'gentle
King Ahasuerus' of Persia, his virtuous wife Esther and the wicked royal
councillor Haman, who had planned a massacre of the Jews until Esther
interceded for them with the King. Skip subtly altered the story: in the
original, Haman offered King Ahasuerus a great sum to finance the massacre, whereas in Skip's recension he assured the King that this great sum
would be raised as a result, intending in reality to end up with the money
himself. The massacre clearly equated to the monastic suppressions: in
Haman we see personified those false venal evangelicals whom Alesius
described as having been denounced by Queen Anne, but more specifically the single persona of Master Secretary Cromwell. In the end, Haman
was hanged. It is uncertain whether Skip pioneered the description of
Cromwell as Haman the wicked royal councillor, but it quickly became a
regular trope about the royal minister, used by the rebels in the Pilgrimage
of Grace and by a host of ill-wishers or moralists thereafter.[36]

Skip's identification of Anne as champion of monasteries against
'Haman' reflected her vigorous efforts in these weeks to oppose the
programme of suppression which Parliament had just passed. No doubt
aware of Cromwell's discomfiture over that legislation, she was making a
bold bid to become herself the champion of a positive and evangelical
reform of monastic life. Her erstwhile chaplain William Latimer later
reminisced (Alesius-like) to Queen Elizabeth about a preaching campaign which Anne launched in her last month of life. She ordered Bishop
Hugh Latimer (no relation) to use his first available sermon before the
King to implore him not to persist in 'the utter subversion of the said
houses and to . . . convert them to some better use'. Latimer says the
Queen then bullied heads of monastic houses who came to her encouraged by this message into providing money for university scholarships,
and it is true that in the later 1530s there was a surge in monks taking
university degrees.[37] Archbishop Cranmer, out of the loop of Court politics down at his Kentish palace of Knole, was alarmed at the confusing
messages he was getting, and wrote to Cromwell to seek a face-to-face
clarifying word, as 'the cause of religion [monasticism] . . . goeth all contrary to mine expectation, if it be as the fame goeth'.[38] Anne was bidding
to wrest leadership of reformation from its other chief champions, especially Cromwell.

It was too late. The day before Skip preached, Chapuys wrote excitedly to his master on a variety of developments, one of which (as we noted) was Cromwell's royal rebuff on monastic legislation; he also relayed his perception that there was a deep rift between Queen and minister. This followed an engrossing conversation with the Secretary. 'I told him that I had purposedly avoided visiting him many a time for fear of arousing his royal mistress's suspicions, for the reasons he himself explained to me.' Chapuys immediately recalled that conversation of June 1535, when Cromwell had said that Anne 'would like to see his head off his shoulders'. He then proceeded to pass on hugely satisfying information from Anne's ill-wisher the Marchioness of Exeter, that the King's dalliance with Jane Seymour had moved to a far more serious level. Taking a leaf out of Anne Boleyn's book back in the 1520s, that young lady was modesty itself when Henry offered her a rich gift; she vowed that she could not accept it 'until God might send her some good determination of marriage [*quelque bon party de mariage*]'.[39]

Chapuys commented that Jane had been well briefed. The King, his passion fired by this rectitude, 'had taken away from Master Cromwell's apartments in the Palace [of Whitehall] a room, to which he can when he likes have access through certain galleries without being seen, of which room the young lady's elder brother [Edward] and his wife have already taken possession for the express purpose of her repairing thither'. There is no need to suppose that Cromwell would have felt any inclination to resist this appropriation. Those few days he spent at Wolf Hall in the progress six months before were now bearing fruit. The central issue fatally escalating the long-standing tensions at Court seems to have been foreign policy, in manoeuvres we can follow largely in a monumentally long dispatch of Chapuys on 21 April.[40] The prize for both King Henry and the Holy Roman Emperor could not have been higher: a proper alliance after the missteps and bitterness of the last few years, leading if possible to English reconciliation with Rome on some new basis. Part of the prize would also be a decisive rejection of the pragmatic French relationship (with its encouragement of France to pursue reformation) which Henry had forwarded throughout most of his marriage to Anne Boleyn. Even Anne and her party, including her brother George Lord Rochford, saw the way the wind was blowing and made the right diplomatic noises about being friendly with the Empire.

All seemed to be going well until on 18 April, Easter Tuesday, the vital player, the King himself, suddenly behaved with extreme petulance in Chapuys's presence, rehearsing years of real and imagined slights to his dignity and English interests from the Emperor, all the way back to

Charles V's accession; he blustered that Charles would never have gained his throne without Henry's help. Cromwell and Audley were appalled and did little to conceal their feelings, on which Cromwell enlarged on the following day when he and Chapuys met to lick their wounds. After they had both sunk into gloom, 'Cromwell suddenly recovered his spirits, and said that the game was not entirely lost, and that he had still hopes of success.'[41] Later, in another very frank conversation with Chapuys when Anne was no more, he represented this as the moment when he 'set himself to think up and plot out the whole business [il se mist a fantasier et conspirer le dict affaire]'.[42] He was going to destroy the Queen.

The stakes were now very high. The King's tantrums are amply accounted for by the strain of his multiple deceptions and conflicts of loyalties, while at one stage in this crucial month, as Chapuys confided to his friend Granvelle, Cromwell took to his bed out of sheer anxiety.[43] Much that happened is hidden from us, not least because of the unmistakable way in which Cromwell's in-tray archive thins during the crisis, then resumes its normal amplitude after the Queen's arrest on 2 May. Someone has evidently weeded out some of the more explosive material, probably at his fall in 1540. What did happen, happened very fast; between the King's outburst on 18 April and the first arrest on 30 April of a suspect in the scandal around Anne (the musician Mark Smeaton), a mere twelve days went by. Events rushing towards tragedy tangled with an increasingly hollow Court normality.[44] The King made plans to visit his cherished harbour works at Dover for the beginning of May; Lord Rochford, in his capacity as Warden of the Cinque Ports, wrote hastily on 17 April to Lord Lisle asking for help with the arrangements – the last surviving fragment of everyday correspondence from the Queen's brother.[45]*

St George's Day, 23 April, brought to Greenwich the usual gathering of the Knights of the Garter, arranging their annual feast for the following month. The King did not intend to be at the feast, given his plans to visit Dover, and he nominated in his stead Henry Percy Earl of Northumberland – on the face of it a puzzling choice, given the Earl's unstable health, both mental and physical. A new knight was to be elected, and there were two possible candidates. One of them was Lord Rochford, but the King chose the other: the undoubtedly dashing and martial Sir Nicholas Carew. Chapuys noted for his master both Rochford's disappointment and the fact that Carew was Anne's enemy.[46] It will be recalled that back in February

---

* The Cinque Ports are a medieval association of ports in Kent and Sussex (many more in fact than the principal five), organized for coastal defence, with appropriate privileges.

Carew had been quietly involved in negotiations with the Lady Mary alongside Cromwell.

If the crisis was beginning to reveal itself even among public magnificence, much more stirred behind the scenes. A quiet frenzy of bureaucratic activity filled the day after the Garter Ceremony, the most neutral parts being formal appointments which in less crowded hours might have concentrated Anne Boleyn's fury, in her new capacity as champion of the monasteries: all the senior officers in the new Court of Augmentations. Yet far more devastating was an enrolment that day of unspecified life grants for Jane Seymour to the value of 100 marks derived from lands and annuities.[47] That might seem modest enough, but it was coupled with the appointment of two special commissions of oyer and terminer ('to hear and determine') for the counties of Middlesex and Kent, consisting of national notables and senior judges. The agenda of these ad hoc commissions, whose purpose was customarily to try the most serious criminal offences, was not stated, and it is unlikely that many of those named to them were immediately told they had been thus singled out for service – least of all Anne Boleyn's father, the Earl of Wiltshire, listed on the Middlesex commission. Among those listed, one wonders how much the Dukes of Norfolk and Suffolk knew, but there can be few doubts about the part of Lord Chancellor Audley and Secretary Cromwell.[48]

An eggshell-thin façade continued to mask reality. Bustle around the King's supposed preparations for Dover was a fine distraction, justifying the Council's unusually long and frequent meetings. So on 28 April Thomas Warley wrote to his master Lord Lisle from London, telling him that Queen Anne expected to meet Lady Lisle at Dover, 'as Mistress Margery Horsman informed me' (what did Mistress Horsman really know?); the King and Queen were planning to pause on their journey at Rochester on 3 May. Lisle and his household were being made the useful idiots in all this; that same 28 April, Cromwell dropped broad hints to an excited John Husee that he himself would pay a visit to Calais during the Dover expedition, so the Lisles should prepare accordingly.[49] Nevertheless by the fateful 24 April or the following day at the latest, Anne already suspected that she was facing some major disaster. Yet another cleric looking back from the beginning of Queen Elizabeth's reign, no less a figure than her Archbishop of Canterbury, Matthew Parker, Anne's trusted chaplain in 1536, recalled to another survivor of those years, Sir Nicholas Bacon, that 'not six days before her apprehension' he made a special promise to Anne to look after her little daughter Elizabeth.[50]

Chapuys glimpsed the truth as well, but only in part. He was distracted by genuine ongoing diplomatic pirouettes around the French, but nonetheless gathered snippets from his conservative aristocratic friends. Lord Montague's brother Sir Geoffrey Pole told him that on 27 April Bishop Stokesley of London had been consulted in his capacity as canon lawyer and old hand at dispensing with royal wives, as to whether the King might rid himself of Anne. Stokesley, understandably cautious, shut down the legal question by a pragmatic response that 'he would, before he answered, try to ascertain what the King's intentions were'. On 29 April, when the juggernaut had actually begun rolling, Chapuys had still not made this all add up to the news for which he would have so ardently wished: to his confidant Granvelle in the same post he said that he had nothing of importance for the Emperor's information, but he had written anyway 'for suspicion of negligence'.[51]

If only Chapuys had known that two days earlier writs had been prepared for a completely new Parliament, less than a month after the dissolution of the previous one. These writs would have needed the King's consent, which suggests that he was already inclining towards arrangements for his wife's downfall; but the most likely use for such an assembly would have been another annulment of marriage, such as was discussed with Bishop Stokesley that same day.[52] Simple annulment was only one possible option to be considered. Anyone keeping a watch on the erratic movements of Sir Nicholas Carew's brother-in-law and the King's old hunting companion Sir Francis Bryan would tabulate much of interest. Bryan, who had been absent from Court after quarrels with the Boleyns, reappeared briefly early in the month, but then left for home in Buckinghamshire.[53] There his friend the Abbot of Woburn saw the arrival of Cromwell's letter recalling Bryan to Court, 'wheresoever he was in this Realm upon the sight of the letter . . . a marvellous and peremptory commandment . . . [which] would [have] astonished the wisest man in the realm'. Bryan was called to Cromwell's presence for a briefing before he saw the King.[54]

Matters were going so fast now that we cannot put an exact day to Bryan's recall. It fits somehow into the action beginning on Saturday 29 April, when there came a charged encounter between the Queen and her young and infatuated musician Mark Smeaton – according to her afterwards, the first time the two of them had been alone together since an evening of music-making back on the autumn progress at Winchester. She insisted later that she had sharply rebuked Mark for his tantrum and over-familiarity in this encounter, but fatally their exchanges were overheard, and within hours Smeaton was under interrogation in Cromwell's house at Stepney. That was the ideal place for such a crucial component of his plans: secluded, and more or less equidistant by river from Greenwich Palace and the Tower of London. By Monday evening Smeaton's nerve broke under questioning, and he confessed to adultery with the Queen, which may have been no more than a combination of wishful thinking and current terror. He completed an enforced journey from Greenwich via Stepney to the Tower, from which, like several others in this affair, he would not re-emerge.

The Queen in her bewilderment and fear exploded in fury at her close friend at Court Henry Norris, and then fatally tried to remedy the resulting susurration of gossip by sending Norris to the King to testify to her good name. Throughout this awful weekend, one is reminded of how difficult it was to get any privacy at the Tudor Court, even among those for whose benefit it was all supposed to be functioning. Alexander Alesius, who happened to have travelled from Cambridge to Greenwich Palace on business at the most dramatic of many dramatic moments of his life, witnessed the extraordinary sight of the Queen with the infant Elizabeth in her arms, pleading with the King. They were at a window out of his earshot, but the body-language told him of King Henry's rage.[55]

Alesius's account does not make it clear whether that tableau occurred on Sunday 30 April or Monday 1 May. What certainly happened on Sunday was the sudden announcement of a week's postponement of the Dover plans, duly noted for Lord Lisle by his servant Warley, though placed amid so much other news that it did not read as the symptom of crisis.[56] It was hardly surprising that Warley did not understand the whole picture, for on that same Sunday Cromwell shows us how much he was controlling information. In the aftermath of Smeaton's interrogation, he wrote from Stepney to Ambassador Gardiner in Paris, blandly passing on standard business about the ongoing French negotiations and routine compliments to the English diplomatic staff. The compliments included a gift of cramp-rings, traditionally blessed by the monarch on Good Friday and distributed to the faithful for their sacred curative powers. The gesture to traditional piety, in these circumstances, may have amused him.[57]

The noisy rows of the weekend and the emotions they revealed seem to have been the catalyst to transform what might have been a relatively decorous set of annulment proceedings into steadily more insane charges of treason, adultery and incest, and the judicial murders that were their consequence. Henry's paranoia was best provoked by making the most extreme of accusations. Monday 1 May was the moment for Cromwell to feed in whatever information he had gained from the unfortunate Smeaton, packaged as suggesting the Queen's infidelity. The King abruptly left the May Day tournament at Greenwich and sailed up-river to Whitehall with a mere six attendants.[58] At this point Jane Seymour discreetly retired from the scene to Beddington in Surrey, home of the recently Gartered Sir Nicholas Carew. Anne was arrested at Greenwich the next day, Tuesday 2 May, arriving at the Tower about six o'clock in the evening, and Norris was soon under arrest as well, likewise bound for the Tower.[59] Lord Rochford followed the King to Whitehall, perhaps trying to defend his sister, but later that day he too was arrested.

Over the next week, arrest after arrest sent a variety of courtiers to join those already in the Tower. Cranmer, Anne's protégé, showed his mettle when on Wednesday 3 May he wrote to the King, replying to a letter Cromwell had sent him on the King's behalf summoning him up from Kent to Lambeth Palace. It is Cranmer at his finest: trying to comfort the King, frankly pointing out his own debt to the Queen's patronage, reminding his master of her part in promoting reformation and imploring him 'to bear no less entire favour unto the truth of the Gospel than you did before'. Finally, in a sad postscript after being briefed in Star Chamber across the river from Lambeth, he acknowledged the serious and specific nature of what the Lord Chancellor and others had told him. No one else had the courage to write any of these things to the King at his most dangerous.[60] What Cranmer's letter also reveals is that Cromwell had kept him as much in the dark as he had Bishop Gardiner.

By 8 May, Master Secretary had secured all those he wanted neutralized, plus one or two whom he may have felt were best off in protective custody. His protégé Thomas Wyatt was the most obvious among them, for before the King's marriage Wyatt had undoubtedly been Anne's lover – some said dangerously close in time to the King's own first passion for her. Sir Richard Page, Cromwell's friend in Wolsey's service, was another arrest; both Wyatt and Page survived the experience, though Page was told firmly never to come back to Court, and did not.[61] The problem was to provide enough damning evidence about Anne: the really imperilled prisoners were remarkable in the consistency of their denials of charges levelled against them of adultery with the Queen – or, in the case of her brother George, of incest. Only Mark Smeaton, no gentleman born, so treated more harshly than the courtiers, was forthcoming, after unspecified pressures physical and psychological at Stepney. Various ladies of the Court provided further bits and pieces, and Anne in her understandable hysteria and collapse of morale furnished still more. None of it, in the fragmentary state of the evidence we have, amounted to the sexual betrayal in which the King wanted to believe to sustain the hatred he had discovered for her. At worst it was witty flirtation, but

perhaps the worst thing was indeed that it was witty, and Henry felt himself the target of other people's sniggers.

Anne was now victim of the most extreme example of Henry's ability
to turn deep affection into deep hatred, and then to believe any old nonsense to reinforce his new point of view. Cromwell was his minister and
must do his bidding, but (if the reader has been in any measure convinced
by this retelling of Court politics in the 1530s) the minister had his own
reasons for enthusiastically pursuing the Queen to destruction. That is
what he did, eliminating both her and the courtiers whom he and the
King had singled out. Now the oyer and terminer proceedings provided
for so long ago on 24 April, and involving much manic legal and administrative activity, reached conclusions. On 12 May Westminster Hall
witnessed the trials of Mark Smeaton, Sir Francis Weston, William Brereton and Henry Norris. The accused might look with a sinking heart on
the jurymen who sat in deliberation on them; what attention to detail
Cromwell had shown in assembling this team of ill-wishers![62] Anne and
Rochford followed on 15 May.

The various charges of sexual crimes and treasonous talk were full of
fictions that can easily be dismissed for putting the accused in locations
where they certainly had not been at the time of their supposed offences.
As Lord Steward, it was the Duke of Norfolk's duty to preside at these
trials, including those of his niece and nephew. In the case of Anne, Norfolk wept as he pronounced the guilty sentence, though one cynical
modern historian may be justified in speculating whether these were tears
of relief at his own survival.[63] The trial was by Anne's peers, that is, the
nobility of England. That meant that Cromwell was not among those
pronouncing the Queen guilty; he was not a nobleman – and, though a
royal councillor, not even a knight of the realm. It was not necessary: he
had done enough. After his formal naming in the oyer and terminer back
in April, his task now was simply to make sure that everything went
according to plan. It would be a congenial duty.

Anne died on 19 May, beheaded in the Tower of London before a
thousand spectators. Chapuys, not permitted to watch since he was a foreigner, heard that Cromwell was prominent among those royal councillors
close to the scaffold. Like her brother a couple of days before, she died
with dignity, saying nothing that could be considered a specific confession of guilt, and her body was given quiet burial in the chapel of St Peter
within the Tower. Meanwhile, Cromwell would not have been pleased to
know that one of his servants was sitting in a London inn where Alexander Alesius was staying, cheerfully telling the assembled company that,
while the Queen was beheaded, the King 'consoled himself with another

woman [*se oblectavit cum alia*]' in a secluded country house, the gates shut on royal orders to all except councillors and secretaries. The landlord, another of Cromwell's servants, joined with Alesius and others terrified at the indiscretion in telling him to hold his tongue, but the landlord did not say that he was wrong.[64] After all, in the King's own eyes, this diversion was not committing adultery.

On the day the Queen's brother Rochford was executed, Henry VIII was officially informed by his Archbishop of Canterbury that he had for a second time inadvertently entered a marriage which had never existed. This judgment is in dismal contrast to Cranmer's letter of defence to the King, and it is not clear on what grounds the Archbishop once more pronounced an annulment: the relevant papers have disappeared, not surprisingly in view of later Tudor history.[65] John Stokesley was only one among several senior canonists discreetly approached before the arrests: Chapuys noticed that from 25 April Cromwell had spent the best part of four days with Richard Sampson. Sampson was Dean of both the Chapel Royal and St Paul's, and also happened conveniently to be Rector of the parish of Stepney, Cromwell's centre of operations for much of the crisis.[66]

One direction not in the end taken in pronouncing an annulment was to explore a possibility that back in the 1520s Anne Boleyn had been contracted to marry Henry Percy Earl of Northumberland. If true, this would have invalidated her marriage to the King. That needs to be considered alongside an odd circumstance at the height of the turmoil, when everything still hung in the balance. The day following Smeaton's arrest, 1 May, and the day before Anne herself was arrested, Cromwell surrendered back to the King a splendid house at Hackney which he had been granted only the previous September, during the last stages of the West Country progress; he had spent very great sums of money on improving it even before the formal grant.[67] It seems strange to have taken time off in the middle of mayhem at Court to arrange a land transaction.

This gift (or rather regift) to Henry might just seem like a sweetener, a larger version of the ingenious lock for which Ralph Sadler had been courier to the King in January, but why would the King want a house back which he had given away only seven months before? Until now, Cromwell had intended it to become his main country seat, and had actually entertained Chapuys there on Easter Day, the ambassador remarking on its magnificence (see Plate 23).[68] The answer must lie in the fact that before Henry's grant to Cromwell the owner had been the Earl of Northumberland. He had only just surrendered it to the King in 1535, as part of a forced land deal by which the Crown evidently hoped to save the bulk of the Percy inheritance from the Earl's own vindictiveness towards his heirs.[69] Now this same hapless representative of a great and ancient dynasty might be the mechanism to unlock the royal marriage which had taken so much blood and sweat to create. It would be worth offering him the house he clearly loved in return for evidence of a pre-contract.

Cromwell's surrender of Hackney therefore looks like the addition of one more card to the Crown's pack of possibilities for declaring the marriage annulled. In the end it could not be played. On Saturday 13 May, with courtiers already condemned and Anne's trial opening on the Monday, Northumberland wrote to Cromwell from his current lodging at Newington Green indignantly refusing to contradict the denial of any pre-contract which he had solemnly sworn in 1532; the pre-contract option was not going to work.[70] It is remarkable that the Earl could be so firm, for the strain on his fragile health at this time was enormous. He had to be helped out of the chamber after casting his vote for Anne's condemnation on 15 May. Six days later he had a pitifully public panic attack while trying to fulfil the presidency at the Garter Feast so bafflingly imposed on him in April (perhaps that honour had also been a clumsy attempt to flatter him into compliance). He persevered in the excruciating festivity with some difficulty.[71] It is pleasing to record that a year later, after much further national drama had passed, Cromwell yielded to the Earl's pleas for royal permission to return to Hackney during his last illness. That is where Henry Percy died, attended by Drs Thomas Lee and Richard Leighton, two northerners who rather unexpectedly seemed genuinely fond of him and able to bring him comfort at the last. He was only around thirty-five years old.[72]

Confusion about the shape of the coup against Anne has been aided by the embarrassment of Protestant commentators from John Foxe onwards that one Protestant champion should eliminate another, and a consequent lack of comment on the subject. As we have seen, Alexander Alesius, writing in private to Anne's daughter, had no such inhibitions. Foxe's informants would have known the truth about Anne Boleyn's fall, but it was an unnecessary complication to his heroic picture of Cromwell: pointing out in addition that Cromwell was destroying the chief agent of Cardinal Wolsey's destruction would make matters even more confusing. Modern historians too have made heavy weather of Anne Boleyn's fall, because they have taken up these early-established and persistent beliefs that the Queen and Cromwell were allies, and that she had advanced his career because of their mutual enthusiasm for promoting evangelical reformation. The evidence for either proposition hardly exists, and the weight of circumstances in fact shows the reverse, allowing events to take on a much greater clarity and straightforwardness – though they do not make Cromwell's part in Anne's destruction any more engaging.

The evidence for an original Catholic conspiracy which Cromwell then belatedly took over is equally flimsy. Of course conservatives at Court enthusiastically joined in the destruction of Anne and had great hopes for it, as did every Catholic in the land and beyond. We should start from that glimpse of Nicholas Carew and Thomas Cromwell working together to rehabilitate Mary on the King's terms in February 1536, and the way in which Carew has appeared in the story after that. Some straws in the wind also involve that other southern magnate Sir Anthony Browne, who had been such a long-standing ally of Cromwell from Wolsey days, despite their different religious outlooks.[73] During winter and early spring, there was no definite way forward, as Anne's various enemies discreetly cast around for nuggets to aid their intentions, always watchful of the King's changing moods. Then came the sudden resolve on 18 April of which Cromwell spoke to Chapuys on 24 May, when after their mutual shock at Henry's public tantrum Master Secretary had 'set himself to think up and plot out the whole business'.

As that famous observation indicates, the responsibility for Anne's destruction remains squarely with Cromwell, as he cheerfully admitted. At least he thought of her as a worthy adversary, as he observed in that remarkably frank debriefing with Chapuys on 24 May: 'he emphatically praised the sense, wit and courage of the late Concubine, and of her brother.'[74] Cromwell did not abandon or betray a partner in reformation. With Anne dead, the Reformation which he sought suddenly became much less complicated, though he would always have to work in a roller-coaster collaboration with the King's tempestuous emotional appetites. If the royal passions had not veered so decisively towards Jane Seymour that Henry once again broke all decencies, destroying Anne and then immediately marrying a successor, no one could have achieved the result of May 1536. Yet the person who did was Wolsey's best servant. From the sidelines, other wounded admirers of the Cardinal, including those who had helped to bring Cromwell into the King's service in 1530, rejoiced at what the architect of Wolsey's legacy project had achieved. It was a monument for the Cardinal far beyond the skill of Italian craftsmen.

PART FOUR

Power and its Reward

*He taketh a burden upon him, that accompanieth a more honour-
able man than himself. Therefore keep no familiarity with one that
is richer than thyself. How agree the kettle and the pot together?
For if the one be smitten against the other, it shall be broken.*

Ecclesiasticus 13.2, in the translation
of Miles Coverdale, 1535

*Good it is, the obedience and right of the King's most honourable
laws regarded, to have the favour of the commonalty, and not
to lose the favour and honour with justice under the King's
highness . . .*

William Maunsell to Cromwell, 27 July 1533

15
Summer Opportunities: 1536

On 30 May 1536, eleven days after Anne Boleyn's execution, King Henry married Jane Seymour: in his own eyes this was his first proper marriage. The new Queen had an easy task in creating a new atmosphere of unity, after the public confrontations and partisanship which had been the product of Anne Boleyn's temperament. Chapuys adroitly conferred on Jane at their first interview the title of 'peacemaker', which had a fairly obvious diplomatic purpose, but which was seized on with pleasure by the King, a little nervous about how his demure bride might perform in front of the most important foreign envoy in the realm.[1] Whatever courtiers thought about the rights and wrongs of destroying the Boleyns, the sense of relief among them after months of storms or brooding atmospheres is palpable. Readers will recall the satisfied comment of Cromwell's early patron Sir John Russell, now restored to a prominence at Court he felt to be his due after years of political eclipse, that 'the King hath come out of hell into heaven for the gentleness in this, and the cursedness and unhappiness in the other.'[2] For Cromwell and various much tried diplomats sent to lie abroad for their King, there was no further need to pursue the thankless task of getting anyone to agree that repudiating Queen Katherine of Aragon had been a good and godly thing to do: the issue could just be quietly forgotten.

The new Queen did little to disturb the narrative of peace, after making one or two early efforts to exercise some initiative. As the story reached Chapuys, even before Anne was securely gone, Jane expressed her warm sympathy to King Henry for his eldest daughter Mary, and suggested that she should be replaced 'in her former position'. The King, incredulous that anyone close to him should express an altruistic opinion, slapped her down, snapping that 'she ought to be mindful of the welfare and advancement of her own children, if she had any by him.' Chapuys credited her with a generous-minded and spirited reply.[3] In the following month, she was the last port of call in a vigorous campaign to stop the dissolution of the much respected Northamptonshire nunnery of Catesby (Cromwell's visitors had just given the nuns a star report), but once more Henry was furious at being the subject of a pincer movement by various people lobbying him on Catesby's behalf, even with the promise of 2,000 marks for him from the Prioress. Soon the convent closed its doors.[4] It may have been a reminiscence of this case which fuelled the French rumour-mill later in the year representing Queen Jane as suppliant for monasteries to be spared, with the King brutally 'reminding her that the last Queen had died in consequence of meddling too much with State affairs'.[5]

Thereafter Jane devoted herself more successfully to making sure Henry had a good time, playing havoc with the sleeping patterns of their entourage. At the end of September, Ralph Sadler ruefully penned a weighty report for his old master after a long day coping with the King's wilfulness, 'at twelve o'clock of the night, which is our accustomed hour in the Court to go to bed'.[6] When early in the New Year the Queen found that she was pregnant, it is likely that matters settled down; a delighted Henry was not going to risk the health of his wife and child. Maybe Jane's early attempts to assert herself were her own doing, evidence of a generous-hearted but naive spirit. Yet we should remember that observers felt that her much more important initiative, insisting on marriage before sexual congress, was the result of careful tutoring. Both her unsuccessful efforts at intercession with the King would fit well with Thomas Cromwell's own agendas that summer. He was doing his best to divert the King from picking off virtuous monastic houses, twice making his own pleas to him for Catesby (as Prioress Bickley noted gratefully), and likewise trying to save the London Charterhouse, now that it was firmly under his control.[7] As we will see, he was also following up his moves of the previous winter to benefit the Lady Mary.

In keeping with the current emphasis on reconciliation and unity, the summer saw a doling out of good news in religion to both traditionalists and evangelicals, neither of whom could really have been said to have won when Anne was destroyed. In the middle of the new Parliamentary session, the King and Queen led a solemn procession from Whitehall Palace to Westminster Abbey to the most elaborate possible celebration of Corpus Christi Day (15 June 1536), accompanied by the two archbishops, peers and courtiers.[8] Conservatives received the appointments to vacant dioceses, but on the other hand Bishop Latimer was only the most prominent figure among various evangelicals allowed to preach attacks on such aspects of traditional religion as purgatory, pilgrimages and devotion to images – the sorts of issues Cromwell had envisaged making the subject of a campaign in monasteries the previous winter.

The most striking expression of this mood of concession to old and new alike was the first effort to define what the infant Church of England believed: ten Articles of religion approved by Convocation that summer. Reflecting what was obviously quite a tussle between evangelicals and conservatives in Convocation, they uncomfortably amalgamated material from several months of Bishop Foxe's gritty theological discussion with Lutherans in Germany, with stout rearguard action from bishops like Cuthbert Tunstall in defence of traditional doctrine. Confession to a priest, for instance, was defended in traditional style, but that sat side by side with a very Lutheran-sounding exposition of justification by faith. Theologically alert commentators spotted the pantomime-horse dual character of the Articles and were displeased from opposing points of view. Alesius, particularly upset, complained bitterly to Johannes Aepinus the Superintendent of Hamburg, and unsuccessfully petitioned Cromwell to let him leave the country.[9]

There were of course spoils to be distributed from the wreck of the Boleyn fortunes. A day after the King's new wedding, George Lord Rochford's father-in-law, Cromwell's congenial fellow-bibliophile Lord Morley, was granted the honorific and profitable Stewardship of the large royal lordship of Hatfield Park, just forfeited by Rochford. It was a reward, which clearly did not strike the royal grantee as in poor taste, for a useful contribution made by Morley's daughter Jane Lady Rochford to the evidence condemning her husband and sister-in-law.[10] In fact, after a heart-rending letter to Cromwell from the less-than-grieving widow about her poverty in the wake of her husband's execution, she succeeded in getting both minister and King to bully the far more genuinely bereaved Earl of Wiltshire into an arbitrary increase of the dowry agreed on her marriage to his late son.[11]

Other rewards were marginally less disreputable. As he was now the Queen's brother, Edward Seymour needed a boost in status, so within a week of her marriage he became Viscount Beauchamp, a suitably grand title which the heralds managed to resurrect for the King's consideration from an extinct barony enjoyed by one of his family name nearly two centuries before. Viscounts were at the time decidedly rare sights in the English honours system, though there was a significantly recent precedent in that granted to Lord Leonard Grey in the Irish peerage a few months before.[12] For rather more professional services rendered as canon lawyer to facilitate the new marriage, Dean Richard Sampson got a Bishopric, moreover one that was not actually vacant: he supplanted the aged Robert Sherburne at Chichester. Sherburne, in earlier days a model of episcopal energy who had successfully kept Wolsey at bay from his diocese, had long been in Cromwell's sights for removal. Five days after Anne Boleyn's arrest, the old Bishop learned of Cromwell's pleasure that he was acquiescing in these arrangements for his retirement. He was dead within three months, prudently bequeathing Cromwell a gilt cup and ten pounds to leave his executors alone in seeing to his other bequests.[13]

Less fortunate than Richard Sampson was his fellow-traditionalist Bishop Gardiner, who benefited less from the Boleyns' tragedy than he might have expected, particularly given his catalytic role the previous winter. In Cromwell's letter spelling out for the ambassadors in Paris an official account of Anne's crimes to pass on to the French Court, he let Gardiner know he was being remitted £200 from two annual pensions from his episcopal estates amounting to £300 which in sunnier times the King had ordered him to pay the late Henry Norris and Lord Rochford. The Bishop would continue to be liable for Norris's £100, but it was now to be paid to 'the Vicar of Hell' – the Court nickname for Sir Francis Bryan. This was evidently Bryan's reward for whatever transpired in that urgent summons back from Buckinghamshire and for subsequent services. Cromwell relayed the royal message to the Bishop that 'though it be some charge unto you, his Highness trusteth ye will think it well bestowed.' If Gardiner had had more sense, he would have taken this broadest of hints in thankfulness for what was after all more than a small mercy. Instead he made a fuss, and went on making his fuss for months: once more, Winchester at his least wily.[14]

No obvious bounty at first appeared for the chief architect of the new order. Cromwell's gratification was a little deferred. The easy part was to make sure he would have reliable subordinates at the heart of the King's private apartments, so central to the revolution just effected. So his friend and colleague back to Wolsey days Thomas Heneage was promoted within the Privy Chamber in June, replacing the executed Henry Norris as Groom of the Stool, and the faithful Ralph Sadler became a groom of the Privy Chamber in July, formalizing a role he had played for some time as go-between and facilitator of business, whenever monarch and minister were apart.[15] Obviously the huge rewards Cromwell was now pursuing needed much preliminary negotiation and planning, but more importantly, before anything was decided, there was a further price: King Henry paid by results.

One of these results was a successful outcome for Parliament and Convocation, which met on 8 June with remarkable speed, after particular care that nationwide elections effectively renewed membership in the House of Commons. The assembly was an achievement in itself, given that Parliament virtually never met in the agriculturally intensive seasons of summer or early autumn. All the legislative adjustments about succession and treason that one would expect after recent excitements sailed through; apart from the evangelicals grouped around Anne's clients among the bishops and their correspondents abroad, the Boleyns had had no natural constituency, dependent as they had been on Anne basking in the King's affections. Parliament also successfully hustled though a large backlog of private business remaining from the spring. The only official measure triggering that now characteristic sign of serious disagreement, a division of the Commons, was further tinkering with ecclesiastical dispensations after the break with Rome. The bill probably caused widespread concern about the status of past papal dispensations affecting marriages, but evidently it was resolved.[16]

Yet behind this business so familiar from Cromwell's Parliamentary management lurked something even more important, and much more dangerous and unpredictable: a binding in of the Lady Mary to the new royal settlement, the task Cromwell had begun while Queen Anne's position crumbled the previous winter. Throughout the unedifying struggle that followed, Mary saw Cromwell not as her enemy but as a firm source of support in her quest to regain her father's favour.[17] There were four key players: the King, his minister, the Princess without a current title and the imperial ambassador, determined to undo nigh on a decade of accumulating slights and petty cruelties to his protégée. Chapuys did try lobbying the new Viscount Beauchamp, emphasizing that it would be in the Seymour family's interests to have Mary restored to her proper title, but Beauchamp, while expressing sympathy, was a lightweight compared with Master Secretary.[18] Cromwell was his master's servant, still as firm as he was in February in insisting that any deal with Mary would be on the King's terms, but he was also as punctilious in informing Chapuys as was consistent with his allegiance. They never worked more closely together than in this anxious spring and summer.

Cromwell's early exchanges with Mary, and his sensitive guidance of her responses to her father, contrasted sharply with the bullying from the Duke of Norfolk and Bishop Sampson when on 15 June they went to Hunsdon to present the King's demands: acceptance of her father's Supreme Headship in the Church of England, and her own illegitimate status. After that wretched confrontation, in which in agony of mind Mary gave no ground, the King angrily prepared legal proceedings which might have led to her death for treason. Maybe there was a good-cop/bad-cop strategy here, but Cromwell made a point of telling Chapuys that he recognized that 'the almost excessive love and affection' of Henry's subjects for Mary had become much more obvious after Anne's fall.

He realized what a catastrophe the execution of the King's daughter would be for the monarchy, far outclassing the destruction of More and Fisher.[19] His own continued position was now entirely dependent on Mary giving way, and his desperation generated his own fury in answering her steadily more emotional pleas.

Acute tension was undermining Mary's already fragile health. She surrendered in the end on 22 June, explicitly accepting the demands conveyed by Norfolk and Sampson: a bitter moment, which amply explains some of the bitterness in her later years of power. Many eyes across the nation were trying to penetrate official darkness around these proceedings, and there was general relief when news gradually filtered out that further savagery had been averted. A week later Richard Sparkford, an influential and well-informed clergyman from Hereford diocese who was up in London for Convocation, wrote back home to his good friend John Scudamore that 'My Lady Mary, as far as I can know, hath submitted herself like a wise and virtuous lady to the King's pleasure, of the which we may be glad.' No one now symbolized the world as it had been before 1533 better than Mary, and for conservatives like Sparkford (earlier in his career he had been personal chaplain to Cuthbert Tunstall) her surrender would be a considerable comfort for their consciences, troubled by submissions to the King's religious adventures over the previous half-decade.[20]

On Chapuys's testimony, Mary herself felt real gratitude to Cromwell for his goodwill towards her, and she expressed it extravagantly: 'how much I am bound unto you, which hath . . . travailed, when I was almost drowned in folly, to recover me before I sunk and was utterly past recovery.'[21] Cromwell himself told the ambassador he was convinced that his own imprisonment loomed. In his fury at his daughter's intransigence, the King had arrested Cromwell's friends and probable fellow-conspirators against Anne, Sir Anthony Browne and Sir William Fitzwilliam, who in turn yielded up the name of a definite fellow-conspirator, Sir Nicholas Carew. Add to that the arrest of Lady Anne Hussey, wife of Mary's longstanding Chamberlain, and things looked desperate indeed. Knowledge of their plight must have swayed Mary in her decision: she sacrificed her own integrity to save others.

Mary's capitulation swiftly brought her reward: the first meeting with her father for five years. On 6 July 1536 she was brought to spend twenty-four hours with him and her new stepmother. The meeting took place in strict secrecy, though Cromwell let Chapuys into his confidence about it the day before. Its setting was that spare royal house at Hackney, so lately Cromwell's, but then surrendered and left purposeless by the way that the Boleyn annulment had worked out. Hackney was a subtle choice, for after Cromwell's extensive rebuilding programme, and with its previous history in the Percy family, the house held no distressing memories for any of the royal trio; it proclaimed a new start. So Henry's family was apparently bound together once more, amid scenes of tearful reconciliation and regret, which must have convinced Mary at least for the moment that she had done the right thing. Her three-year-old half-sister Elizabeth was left behind at the country house at Hunsdon which the two royal daughters currently shared; a Boleyn child was too much of a complication for this event.[22]

Mary's gratitude to Cromwell for her decision was profound, but so was his to her, and he expressed it in a remarkable way: commissioning a commemorative gold medal, edition of one, specifically for presentation to her. Such personalized medals were still exotic in Tudor England, a culture on the fringes of European sophistication, but they had been regular objects of display in Renaissance Italy since the late fifteenth century. This was another tribute to Cromwell's Italian taste, which he repeated for himself or his son a couple of years later (see Plate 7). If this specimen was as handsome and modish as that portrait medallion, it is unsurprising that King Henry seized on it and insisted on presenting it to his daughter as if it were his idea; Cromwell was forced to substitute another gift. Equally predictably, the medal no longer exists, but Chapuys had the chance to take a detailed description of it: relief portraits of Henry and Jane on one side and of Mary on the other, with a poem on the subject of humility surrounding her image. The verses went so far as to include the resonant words 'respexit humilitatem' from the Magnificat, the song in which another Mary, God's own mother, praised divine regard for her lowliness – but this second Mary's obedience was also an example of how to obey parents and country alike.[23]

Historians have concentrated on the undoubted humiliation of Mary's submission, so soon after losing the mother who had been denied her presence even at the deathbed. Understandably that has obscured Cromwell's major role in sustaining her in this crisis against real danger stemming from her father's anger; he remained a resource of support for her. Cromwell had 'never refused to further my continual suits to you', she testified to him in December 1536; 'you were always a mean' to arrange her allowance that year of forty pounds a quarter from the King, which significantly was first paid the previous winter, during those early stirrings against Anne Boleyn.[24] The following summer Elizabeth Duchess of Norfolk, never one to hold her tongue and a good friend to Mary, praised Cromwell because 'I hear say how good you were to the lady Mary, the King's daughter, in her great trouble.'[25] Mary now became an honoured presence at the Seymour Court; her excellent relations with Cromwell continued.

Such was the intensity in the relationship between Mary and Cromwell set up in this traumatic struggle of May and June that a rumour was born that they might marry. It worried some of her household, who deputed her mother's former doctor to warn Chapuys that Henry might 'farm her out' to Cromwell. The ambassador, having observed the past weeks of intense drama so closely, dismissed this as fantasy, 'which I cannot in any wise believe; if the King were indeed to have wished for it, Cromwell would not hear of it'.[26] Cromwell was indeed assigned a role of public gallantry for her at Court, so on 22 February 1537 his account-books reveal him dispatching Wriothesley to Mary with the handsome present of fifteen pounds 'because my Lord was her Valentine'. Given that Cromwell was now around fifty-two and she was twenty-one, this was a symbolic courtship, more the attention of a second father-figure. The message was reinforced that same day at the christening of Lord and Lady Beauchamp's first-born child. The baby's aunt Queen Jane stood as godparent alongside the Lady Mary and Master Secretary himself – yet another touching scene of family reconciliation, this time in company with the man who had arranged it all.[27] Soon thereafter came another happy christening to bind them together (see below, pp. 440–44).

Stories of Cromwell's marital intentions did not go away, resurfacing in particular around the months of his fall in 1540. It is not entirely implausible that this was in his portfolio of possible outcomes, given the astonishing further ascent which we will trace, but if so it was one of the most dangerous thoughts he ever entertained. There were more immediate rewards for securing Mary's submission. After years of anomaly between his real power and its lack of outward expression, he now gained a peerage and one of the highest secular offices in the land, that of Lord Privy Seal, then the third-ranking office of state after the Lord Chancellor and Lord Treasurer, with control over a crucial stage in the procession of documents for sealing after the initial royal signature on any grant or decision. Possession of the privy seal forged yet another link in Cromwell's increasingly comprehensive chain of control of access to the King for anyone seeking action or favours. This promotion came immediately after he had placed Ralph Sadler in the King's Privy Chamber, where Sadler could look after the informal first stages of these processes – tactfully finding the right moment when the King was disposed to scrawl his signatures ('signs manual') on papers before they moved on through the system.[28]

In obvious symbolism, Cromwell replaced in office Anne Boleyn's father the Earl of Wiltshire, who was now 'clear dispatched from the Court', as Richard Sparkford told John Scudamore in his round-up of news on 30 June 1536. Cromwell's appointment as Lord Privy Seal was first announced that day, and came as a considerable surprise, as the gossip had been that Lord Beauchamp had won this crucial post. Sparkford actually said in the body of his letter, 'as it is thought, my Lord Beauchamp the Queen's brother should be Lord Privy Seal', and recorded Cromwell's capture of the office only in a postscript. Evidently there was a last-minute tussle about it lasting some days, with victory to Cromwell, which Chapuys considered was his reward for clinching the Lady Mary's submission eight days before.[29]

The drama of Cromwell's promotion can be savoured in Richard Sparkford's letter of 30 June, because just as he was addressing his missive for dispatch, he had to scribble his hasty postscript updating it on three vital matters. News had just reached him that his master the Bishop of Hereford had finally docked in London after the nine-month mission in Germany; then 'this day, the Privy Seal was given to Master Secretary, and he continue Secretary also', with all the consequent shuffling of offices below that to prominent lawyers, whose names Sparkford excitedly listed.[30] Cromwell's peerage was agreed before the end of Parliament, but he postponed his actual entry into the Lords to the ceremonies of the last day, 18 July, because the Commons still needed his management while he could hold his seat as an MP. The new Speaker Richard Rich could not be trusted to dominate the chamber; he was a surprising choice, given an evident unpopularity which meant that unusually it took two days to get his appointment through at the outset of the session. Rich's arrogant use of his Chancellorship of the Court of Augmentations was no doubt a major factor in infuriating landed gentry seeking their share of the monastic lands bonanza.[31]

The grant of Cromwell's barony was actually finalized on 9 July. He was accompanied in elevation by John Bourchier Lord Fitzwarren, who advanced to the Earldom of Bath. This honour for one described by a well-informed commentator a couple of years later as 'old and foolish'* might seem an odd coupling with a peerage for the new Lord Privy Seal, until one notes that Fitzwarren was uncle to Beauchamp's formidable second wife Anne.[32] Fitzwarren's earldom was a statement about Beauchamp's and Cromwell's political harmony, nine days after Master Secretary had edged past him to become Lord Privy Seal. Then as just the

---

* Bath was sixty-eight in 1538.

final curlicue on Cromwell's triumph: 'at the breaking up of the Parliament', in other words at the same time as his peerage grant took effect, he gained a knighthood, the normal prelude to a peerage and the normal accompaniment of a newly conferred barony, but an honour that had strangely eluded him in the Boleyn years.[33]

When we first met young Thomas Cromwell in Putney, we noted the significance of the peerage title he gained in July 1536: Baron Cromwell of Wimbledon.[34] It was a deliberate blow against the snobbery sparked by the rise of any low-born minister in the Tudor age, and was backed up with a princely grant of the appropriate estate: the ancient lordship of Wimbledon formerly belonging to the Archbishop of Canterbury which included in its rolling acres the hamlet of Putney. Cromwell gained this by a Parliamentary statute in this session, ratifying an unmistakably unequal three-way property transaction between himself, the King and Archbishop Cranmer. It is worth considering the processes described in this Act in some detail, because they tell us a great deal about the realignments of summer 1536.[35]

The business began in the previous Parliament in winter and spring 1536, when an Act recognized an exchange of lands between the King and Cranmer centring on the Archbishop surrendering Wimbledon, in return for Henry granting him the Abbey of St Radegund's Bradsole just outside Dover. This was a royal foundation earmarked for dissolution (in fact the Act wrongly said that it had already been dissolved, on 1 February). At that stage this arrangement bore no obvious relation to Cromwell; it was among a number of exchanges then enacted, resembling the group of such transactions between the monarchy and corporate bodies in 1531–2, likewise ratified in Parliament (see above, Chapter 8). There was nothing especially rapacious about these, apart from the common factor of convenience for the Crown's consolidation of landholdings, especially near royal palaces. The lordship of Wimbledon, lying along the Thames, was a perfect example.

By contrast, the new Act in the summer session completely remodelled the deal between Cranmer and the King. Although Henry kept his title to Wimbledon, he was at pains to say that his previous choice of St Radegund's was not a fair exchange for it, 'his Highness not willing that the same Archbishop or his successors should have or sustain any loss, detriment or hindrance in that behalf'. So instead the King offered as a replacement for St Radegund's Abbey the small priory of St Gregory in Canterbury (even though neither house was yet dissolved). This royal pretext was flimsy, and grew flimsier still when the Act incorporated Cranmer's sale of a desirable part of the St Gregory's property to the new

Master of the Rolls, Christopher Hales.* That looks like a sweetener to Hales for the fact that (as we have seen) he was not destined to enjoy the Master's fine house in Chancery Lane, despite having just succeeded to the Mastership after Cromwell, and having been specifically promised it in his grant of office.[36]

Meanwhile the Act went on to divest Cranmer of a further property in Sussex, and then conferred the whole ensemble on Cromwell. Completely changing tack, it then threw into his grant some of the most desirable Norfolk properties lately owned by the Bishop of Norwich, principally the ancient episcopal manor of North Elmham. This royal gift to Cromwell, made on 12 June actually during the Parliamentary session, has significant political resonances in itself.[37] Six months previously the King had taken the opportunity offered by the death of old Bishop Nix to acquire the entire Norwich episcopal estates for himself, in a land exchange of startling boldness. The new Bishop was William Rugge alias Repps, Abbot of St Benet's Hulme in Norfolk Broadland, and for some years a client of Cromwell's. In return for surrendering diocesan lands he had never occupied, on promise of promotion, Repps was allowed to keep his abbatial title and the reasonably ample estates of his Benedictine monastery for himself and his episcopal successors. In future, these lands would be the sole support for the bishops of Norwich, who lost for ever a body of lands whose nucleus had belonged to bishops in East Anglia well before there had been any kingdom of England.[38]

Cromwell probably steamrollered the diocesan deal through in order to stop the Duke of Norfolk getting his hands on large quantities of East Anglian episcopal land to add to the Duke's recent digestion of local monasteries. A bundle of evidence around Bishop Nix's death cumulatively reveals a local move in concert with Cromwell to stop the Duke taking advantage of Nix's chaotic last weeks at his palace at Hoxne and their even more chaotic aftermath. Cromwell's friend of Wolsey days Sir Thomas Rush headed the move to enlist him in this noble cause, when Norfolk sent his agents over to Hoxne in a bid to take over Nix's affairs and put a stop to the dying Bishop's last campaign of charitable giving: 'If my lord of Norwich were at liberty to use his goods at his pleasure you would have much honour by it – either by the King's Highness or by you,' Rush pleaded. There was great drama when the Bishop died, as Nix's senior chaplain Richard Redman galloped from Suffolk to London to secure Cromwell's support. Nix's principal servants did indeed win his

---

* Cranmer did at least get a reversion on St Radegund's in 1538, probably indicating a sense that he had been badly done by.

sympathy, with long-term benefits for their futures in the diocese. The exchange with Abbot Repps followed from this.[39]

Repps was the most astute of choices as bishop. The Duke of Norfolk could hardly object to the new Bishop's considerable distinction as a conservative theologian (he had a Cambridge DD), and Repps showed himself eager to please the Howard interest alongside careful expressions of obligation to Master Secretary. None of this would have stopped the Duke feeling a sense of defeat when seeing his chief political rival luxuriating in the gift of North Elmham. It may be significant that Cromwell chose to send his son to Norfolk this year, after Gregory had spent summer 1535 with his Williams relatives in Oxfordshire.[40] During his travels round Norfolk, the young man cannot have failed to inspect Elmham, which lies just 13 miles north of Woodrising, home of his principal host Richard Southwell. The stylish little episcopal castle there would make an ideal capital mansion for Gregory, but it lay in the heart of the Duke of Norfolk's country.

Before the spectacular grants of summer 1536, Cromwell's build-up of landed estates outside London and its suburbs was not impressive. Apart from bits and pieces across the south-east, his single most resonant territory remained his Welsh lordship of Rhymney, acquired as long ago as 1532. Now he really did possess estates worthy of a nobleman. At the heart of his new lordship by the Thames was the splendid former archiepiscopal house of Mortlake, which straight away that July he proceeded to develop with relish and bagfuls of cash, as the memory of his recent comparable efforts at Hackney faded.[41] Mortlake had the huge advantage over Hackney of being a stone's throw from the Thames, and within an easy ride or barge-trip of Hampton Court, 7 miles upstream. Richmond Palace, if Henry ever chose to reactivate it as his residence (and he did at a crucial juncture this year), was even closer; in the other direction, Westminster was about the same distance as Hampton. Mortlake and the lordship of Wimbledon provided a whole new dimension to Cromwell's power.

It is of course an irony that Cranmer, the champion of evangelical reformation, should be the first victim among incumbent bishops of what over the next two decades became an accelerating royal policy of stripping the episcopate of much of its prime estates. Asset-stripping was probably not the intention when the exchange was first arranged between Cranmer and the King in the winter of 1536. Whatever the smooth talk in the later Parliamentary enactment, St Gregory's Canterbury was not such a good deal as St Radegund's Dover, described that spring by Cromwell's servant John Whalley (who knew about such things) as 'one of the properest houses and the most commodious pieces of ground in Kent'.[42]

It is likely that Cranmer's treatment in the summer statute was a form of punishment for speaking up for Anne Boleyn, or more generally for his symbolic role as 'her' bishop, in which case he and his advisers would have regarded his compliance as acres well spent in return for survival. He lost much more than Wimbledon in subsequent years of exchange, though he did devise some evasive action (including protection for that hard-won compensation, St Gregory's Priory) through obstructive long leases, such as one of sixty years to Cromwell's servant Henry Polstead, another outlying Sussex property. At least things got better for the Archbishop under Edward VI, when many of his colleagues went on experiencing serious losses of estates.[43]

After all the political adjustment wrapped up in Cromwell's peerage, promotion in office and grant of lands, two additional blows of fate dealt him another political bonus and brought further misery to the Duke of Norfolk, with hardly any effort on his own part. First came a massive indiscretion by the Duke's younger half-brother Lord Thomas Howard, who pursued the possibility of marrying the King's Scottish-born niece Lady Margaret Douglas – a twenty-one-year-old loose cannon in the realm and, as daughter of Henry's sister Margaret, then senior ranking royal female of the Tudor dynasty, given that her cousins Mary and Elizabeth both now counted as illegitimate. Howard and Douglas were arrested, and on the morning of Parliament's dissolution on 18 July one of the very last pieces of legislation (introduced with extreme haste and several additions on the text of the final version) provided for Lord Thomas's execution. Its preamble outdid in bitterness any public condemnation since Elizabeth Barton, denouncing the wickedness of Howard's marriage proposal cynically made 'lately within the King's own mansion place at Westminster . . . his Majesty there being for the affairs of his Parliament'. It declared as high treason any attempt to marry one of the royal family without royal assent under the Great Seal. Lord Thomas never left the Tower of London before a fatal illness; Lady Margaret, after piteous appeals to Cromwell, graduated from the Tower to Syon nunnery, and thence to an adventurous career which culminated rather better than one might expect, as grandmother to King James VI and I.[44]

One reason for the King's extreme of fury at the Douglas/Howard affair was his consciousness that he was about to lose his only acknowledged son: Henry Fitzroy Duke of Richmond died on 22 July after contracting a lung infection. The death of a teenager, particularly one by all accounts possessed of charm and perhaps even talent, would be a tragedy in any circumstances. His father was fond of him, and his contemporary Henry Howard Earl of Surrey, the Duke of Norfolk's son and heir, was utterly devastated: according to Norfolk, not the most empathetic of men, Surrey was an emotional and physical wreck for months afterwards 'for thought of [grief for] my Lord of Richmond'.[45] Yet there was no escaping the calculations to follow Richmond's passing. As we have observed, the young Duke was always an asset requiring custodianship, with something of a tussle between Cromwell and the Duke of Norfolk after Wolsey's fall (see above, Chapter 10). Even though Norfolk had gained the prizes of Richmond's marriage to his daughter and the boy's intense friendship with his son, Cromwell had lately been making ground, particularly when Richmond was removed out of Norfolk's orbit to Dorset and the Court.

Now the young Duke's usefulness was ended. That summer Norfolk thus lost two potential routes to royal influence, his niece Queen Anne and his son-in-law, and he also gained a massive liability in the shape of a brother under attainder for treason. By contrast, the stock of Cromwell's protégée the Lady Mary (who had good reason to detest Norfolk) was considerably improved in the absence of a male child for the King. The Lord Privy Seal wrote Mary what Chapuys felt amounted to a letter of congratulation. The Duchess of Norfolk more than once thereafter praised Cromwell for his goodness to Richmond's former servants as the ducal household broke up, taking many of them into his own service.[46] Cromwell's kindness was of course another stick with which the Duchess could beat her detested husband, who made his situation still worse by badly mishandling the oversight of Richmond's corpse from London for burial at Thetford Priory, a last permanent custodianship of the royal child for the Howards. Chapuys reported with unfeeling glee on the ghastly procession of a decaying cadaver enclosed only in straw, trundling in a waggon across the counties to Norfolk for all the world to see, a mere couple of attendants trailing behind it.[47]*

The King was furious with Norfolk for this hideously public incompetence, which looked remarkably like callousness, never an implausible attitude in connection with Thomas Howard. One does not have to speculate wildly on Cromwell's feelings as he read the Duke's mortified letter of excuses and apologies: 'It is further written to me that a great bruit doth run that I should be in the Tower of London. When I shall deserve to be there, Tottenham shall turn French,' he wrote, 'with the hand of him that is full, full, full of choler and agony.' When this lament

---

* Richmond's post-mortem wanderings were not over, for he now lies beneath a comparatively modest tomb in Framlingham parish church, having been moved from Thetford Priory after the dissolution.

was penned on 5 August, none other than Gregory Cromwell was staying with the Duke at Kenninghall, revelling in the delights of its deerpark as part of his nine-month immersion in Norfolk high society.[48] In August 1536, Cromwell had Norfolk just where he wanted him; and he had the stately Norfolk manor of North Elmham as well, sitting squarely in the centre of the Duke's home territory.

After this run of luck, Cromwell may have felt that the atmosphere of studied religious neutrality in which the King's marriage to Jane Seymour had opened was ripe for manipulation in the evangelical cause. Two routes for dialogue in the opposite direction, towards Rome, closed down during the summer. The more promising was from Cardinal Lorenzo Campeggio, previously seen in England in 1529 at the legatine court at Blackfriars. He had been observing recent English turbulence with great interest, and he calculated that his previous role in obstructing the Boleyn marriage might now have a rather different valence. In the intervening years Campeggio had quietly kept open lines of communication to Cromwell. One of his letters survives, thanking the minister for continued benevolence in England and speaking in extravagant terms of the Cardinal's devotion to King Henry – just about believable when the letter was written in January 1535, after Campeggio's earlier anger at losing the Bishopric of Salisbury had cooled and before the King got round to executing Fisher and More.[49]

Accordingly on 6 June 1536, now assured of Anne Boleyn's fall, Campeggio commissioned his brother Marc'Antonio to plan an expedition to England, armed with letters of introduction to Bishop Tunstall, the Duke of Suffolk and probably a raft of others whom the Cardinal regarded as his English friends; punctiliously he omitted from his signatures any claim to be Bishop of Salisbury. The recovery of his Bishopric was nevertheless one of the items on his brother's diplomatic shopping-list, plus a courteous suggestion to King Henry that if he needed a cardinal-protector at the proposed forthcoming General Council at Mantua, Campeggio was just the man.[50] Matters did not proceed quickly. Campeggio knew the right people to involve, especially that veteran Anglo-Italian Antonio Buonvisi, but by August and September the political situation in England had swayed too much against any conservative encouragement in England to open talks via the Cardinal. Marc'Antonio's servant Lodovico got as far as a personal interview with Cromwell, but he reported back that Cromwell's message was more polite than promising. He noted in particular the Duke of Norfolk's dire situation. Marc'Antonio himself was in England during the autumn, but Cromwell and the King were unlikely to feel any better disposed to reconciliation with Rome during the desperate months facing the Pilgrimage of Grace. It all came to nothing.[51]

Campeggio's approach was in any case sabotaged almost before it began by his own colleague in Italy, Reginald Pole. In spring 1536, Pole finally resolved to confront and admonish his royal cousin. He had come a long way from that time in 1529–30 when he was among the English representatives abroad seeking sympathy for Henry's marital adventures. After leaving England in 1531, he watched developments at home with increasing horror, and during 1535, still in discreet conversation with Cromwell via various agents, principally their mutual client Thomas Starkey, turned his thoughts into a long treatise. It was resonantly entitled *Pro ecclesiasticae unitatis defensione* ('To defend the unity of the Church'), known more snappily as *De unitate*. He sent a copy to Bishop Tunstall, who read it in July 1536 and was appalled at its misjudgement; Starkey shared Tunstall's dismay.

Pole's hectoring effusion, including unflattering accounts of the King's behaviour back to his accession, based on first-hand observation, and clarion-calls for him to return to papal obedience, was the opposite of Campeggio's emollient overtures. Its contents were, as Pole's biographer perceptively comments, the sort of unvarnished truths that a conscientious spiritual adviser might present to a penitent in the privacy of confession. The vital difference was that they had already been said in draft to a wider audience than the recipient, and that audience was widening all the time.[52] Pole seemed oblivious to this discrepancy. He envisaged his text as addressed to the entire English people; it is understandable that, in his rage after Henry's atrocities against his relatives in 1538, he allowed his Latin text to appear in print for the whole world to read.

In replying to Pole with what was in itself a considerable treatise, Tunstall did not take any chances. Being down in London for Parliament and Convocation, he made sure that Cromwell had a copy before it was dispatched to Rome, and no doubt Starkey did the same with his own more concise letter of reproach.[53] Tunstall emphasized to Pole what a strategic error it was to send such a long document. Henry would inevitably give it to others to read for him, thus spreading the wildly overpersonal comments, which extended in the original in Rome to the King's former dalliance with Mary Boleyn (it looks as if wiser counsels omitted that particular section from the version sent to England). Possibly Henry only ever saw the summary of the diatribe prepared by Richard Morison, loyally labelled 'Abbreviations of a certain evil-willed man', but that would be bad enough.[54] The King felt deeply betrayed by Pole's volte-face. How could he be expected to understand that Pole saw offering the frankest pastoral advice as an act of gratitude for all the previous royal bounty? As for Cromwell, unlikely to share any residual regrets felt by Starkey and Tunstall about the priggish humanist, Hugh Latimer later reminisced, 'I heard you say once after you had seen that furious invective of Cardinal Pole that you would make him to eat his own heart.'[55]

Cromwell had very different plans for the future of English religion. He extended the scope of his Vice-Gerency beyond its first focus on visiting monasteries and corporate bodies into the whole Church. That was starkly emphasized during June by his presence in meetings of the Convocation of Canterbury a couple of miles away in St Paul's Cathedral.[56] His official Dr William Petre claimed a presiding place for him as representative of the Supreme Head of the Church, and Archbishop Cranmer readily granted him an equal seat. Cromwell openly 'sat divers times in the Convocation house among the bishops, as head over them'.[57] He therefore had first-hand observation of how difficult Convocation could be, including on 23 June when clergy of its Lower House (always the likely origin of trouble rather than the bishops) presented a long list of heretical opinions to be condemned, some of which he undoubtedly held himself, on matters such as the eucharist, devotion to images and justification by faith. He would also note the perennial problem of getting the King's will approved in the Church of England: whatever one did in the Convocation of Canterbury needed to be echoed in the Convocation of York, smaller to manage but a lot further off, and inclined to belligerent traditionalism. There must be another way.

    The beginning of that alternative became apparent after Convocation dispersed in Parliament's wake. In late July or August, the Vice-Gerent issued on his own authority a set of injunctions for the religious life of the entire kingdom.[58] If, as is likely, he notionally issued them on 1 August, he was doing so after conference with Archbishop Cranmer, for that day he addressed a letter from Cranmer's great Kentish palace at Otford, on his way home from accompanying the King on the postponed visit to the Dover harbour works.[59] Cranmer would rejoice in the evangelical tone of the injunctions, and may have made suggestions for content; but the fact remained that this was the first time that a layman had done anything of the sort since Anglo-Saxon kings in very different times. Naturally where it suited the Vice-Gerent they referred back to various ecclesiastical decisions made earlier that summer: so they cited and reinforced Convocation's abolition of various holy days, and drew on and commended critical discussion of devotion to images and pilgrimages which had formed part of the Ten Articles. Yet they contained much else that was really new.

In autumn 1535, Cromwell's visitors to the universities brought radical intentions to the reform of higher education: now his injunctions dealt with the other educational extreme, children's earliest steps in schooling. They enlisted parish clergy in a campaign of sermons and addresses to get families to teach their children the first building-blocks of the Christian faith – Lord's Prayer, Apostles' Creed and Ten Commandments. Clergy must preach over a long period on each clause or article in these texts, having made them available (obviously in English); or 'shew where printed books containing the same to be sold, to them that can read or will desire the same'. It is true that clergy of the Western Church had been trying to get children to learn the Lord's Prayer, Creed and Commandments as far back as the reforming Lateran Council in 1215, but the difference here was that secular authority led the campaign, and advocated every possible contemporary method for doing so, including Cromwell's favourite medium of print. The order was a striking if perhaps premature vision of a kingdom united in basic educational instruction, and the purpose was laid out at some picturesque length: such teaching would combat juvenile idleness which led over time to a depressing list of vices right up to murder, followed by the bitter reproaches of the perpetrators to their thoughtless families who had been slow to bring them up 'in some good literature, occupation, or mystery'.

This was reminiscent of moves to public instruction which Martin Luther had been encouraging since the mid-1520s, using those same basic Christian texts. The seventh clause of the injunctions was an even more direct affirmation that Cromwell's Church was embracing evangelical reformation of religion: 'every parson, or proprietary of any parish church within this realm shall on this the feast of St Peter ad Vincula next coming [1 August 1537] provide a book of the whole Bible, both in Latin, and also in English, and lay the same in the choir for every man that will, to look and read thereon.'[60] This was for the moment another expression of future intent. It must have bewildered and worried those parishes which took it seriously, while exciting others – for no such single book existed at the time. It would certainly have been possible to buy a large Latin Vulgate for display, and loyalists might conceivably have searched out King Henry's brand-new edited-down Vulgate if it had been easily available (see above, p. 297); but what was this English Bible?

There was indeed no legally permitted English Bible text on the market in August 1536. Cromwell had given clandestine encouragement to the publication the previous October of the first complete English Bible in print, by his old friend the ex-Austin Friar Miles Coverdale. Coverdale's Bible looked remarkably official with its large format, handsome title-page designed by Hans Holbein the Younger and dedication to the King, and caused quite a stir when copies arrived in London (see Plate 37). With an irony characteristic of Cromwell's plans, Coverdale's work was based on the pioneering efforts of William Tyndale, who despite all the Lord Privy Seal's diplomatic efforts was still lying in prison in the Low Countries, soon to suffer execution, with King Henry's connivance. The Coverdale edition could not come from the same Antwerp press as Tyndale's precisely because of the crackdown sparked by his arrest. It had to be printed elsewhere, maybe Cologne, with some batches being given a little finishing under Cromwell's patronage by an evangelical printer in Southwark, James Nicholson.[61] National provision of Bibles unsurprisingly got off to a slow start, though over the next year some sympathetic bishops did repeat this vice-gerential order in their own visitations. Twelve months of patient persuasion by Cromwell and Cranmer elapsed before the King authorized yet another modification of the existing biblical texts for national use.

The King probably never realized that Cromwell was manipulating his power as Supreme Head to promulgate a translation inspired by the man he had grown to hate and whose destruction he had helped to engineer. It is to be hoped that he never saw a meaty little edition of Tyndale's *Parable of the Wicked Mammon*, which James Nicholson also daringly issued from his Southwark press in 1536 without any attempt at disguise. Not only did it prioritize on the title-page the theme of justification by faith, a doctrine Henry detested, but it openly proclaimed Tyndale's name in the author's preamble to the reader. The title-page block, with a prominent use of the Tudor royal arms, was actually an import, once more a creation of Hans Holbein, previously used by Tyndale's former publisher in Antwerp for an edition of Melanchthon's *Loci communes*.[62] Surely none of this was done without Cromwell's approval; it suggests how much he was testing the boundaries this promising summer.

It is possible Henry did eventually fathom an even more audacious stratagem of Cromwell's, though he could not possibly have understood its profound effect over time. This moved the course of English religion not merely towards the Protestant Reformation but towards a particular strand within it that the King would unquestionably consider obnoxiously heretical: the newly established Protestant Church in the Swiss city of Zürich. Cromwell did not originate this initiative, which to begin with heavily implicated Archbishop Cranmer, but in his characteristically improvisatory fashion he sustained the enterprise when theological considerations checked Cranmer's enthusiasm, and did so in ways that have left a permanent mark on the Church of England and its various world offshoots till the present day. Put simply, the move to embrace Zürich turned English Protestantism's path away from Lutheranism and towards what became the Reformed Protestant family of Churches. This move we can trace back to the year 1536.[63]

The first stirrings in the story came from Strassburg and its far-seeing chief pastor, Martin Bucer, keenly interested in the progress of the English mission led by Bishop Foxe to the Schmalkaldic League in 1535–6. Strassburg was not a member of the League, and its Protestantism did not look to Martin Luther and Saxony but south and west, to cities of the Empire and Switzerland taking their cue from a different and indeed rival reformer, Huldrych Zwingli, chief pastor of Protestant Zürich until his death in 1531. There was no escaping the fact that the two Protestant blocs had disagreed very quickly on fundamental issues. Most importantly, Luther, like the Pope and Henry VIII, believed that in the mass bread and wine became the body and blood of Christ (though he disagreed with Pope and King as to how this miracle took place). By contrast, the Swiss and south Germans saw this liturgical drama as 'the Lord's Supper': a memorial of Christ's great sacrifice on the Cross, mystically symbolized in bread and wine, which nevertheless remained bread and wine still.

The southerners also abhorred idolatry, by which they principally meant sacred images in churches. Luther, after some thought, decided that the issue was unimportant and let most images stand in his church buildings. Even the music of the two groupings differed. To a toleration of traditional Latin church music (and pipe-organs), Luther added his own freshly composed hymns, usually to new tunes. The southerners considered all that on the edge of idolatry – indeed, Zürich abolished all music in churches as potentially idolatrous in distracting worshippers for God, and kept the ban right into the 1590s. Other communities which in general followed Zürich did not take that extreme position, but still allowed congregations only biblical music, by which they principally meant the 150 psalms. Even Luther's Protestant hymns were beyond the pale.

This formidable chasm among Protestants crystallized by mid-century into two hostile camps with names to identify them: Lutherans and the Reformed – both Protestants, but irredeemably at odds (as, formally, they still are). That was in the future, but the gulf was already wide and Martin Bucer was anxious to bridge it, encouraging a series of discussions which ultimately foundered both on Luther's unwillingness to see other people's points of view and Bucer's inability to think of simply expressed ways of smoothing over theological complexities. Negotiations reached a peak in spring 1536, as was duly noted for Cromwell by William Clifton, a sharp-eyed merchant of some note, and as Customer of London in overall charge of levies on goods in and out of England's principal port. Clifton was at that stage in Germany, accompanying Ambassador Foxe to the diplomatic meeting which led to Bucer's best shot at reunion, the document later known as the 'Wittenberg Concord'.

Clifton enumerated the various principalities and cities involved in the rival theological camps: with a clutch of Cambridge dons in his family and acquaintance, right up to Archbishop Cranmer, he was well qualified to do so. If Cromwell had not appreciated the difference between the two sides before, he certainly did now, as Clifton told him how the cities led by Strassburg and Zürich

> which be of the Evangeli [use the Bible translation] and use the ceremonies and laws of Zwingli, which be contrary to Dr Martin Luther and his law and constitutions, and those that be of his part, as the land of Saxony and Hessen, with divers other great cities and towns, went to assemble and meet together in Eisenach . . . in the land of Thuringia: to make and take a way for both parties how to execute and use their ceremonies in the Church and other constitutions that they have ordained and made, that the common people shall not murmur and grudge their conscience as it [sic] do now, to see one of one part and another of another part, and the one learned man writing against another. Wherefore if their agreement may take effect amongst themselves, I think it will be a godly way and do much good among the common people.[64]

Alas, it did not.

At the same time as Bucer reached out to the Lutherans, he wanted to do as much as possible to bind the enigmatic religious proceedings in England into what was happening in mainland Europe. He wanted the point of view of Strassburg and the Swiss to register in London; it would counteract the Lutherans, who up to now had been the chief focus of interest for English diplomacy, given that their Schmalkaldic League had military clout which might intimidate the Holy Roman Emperor. It was difficult to know what Strassburg had to offer in competition. The city's general policy throughout the century, an extremely sensible one, was to keep out of other people's fights.

Bucer therefore wooed the English in the way he knew best, through books. In the first place in late 1535 he used the unlikely medium of

Stephen Gardiner's exposition of the royal supremacy, *De vera obedientia*, which he now had newly printed in Strassburg with lavish extra praise not only for that unappreciative prelate but also for Foxe and his colleague in embassy Nicholas Heath – plus Archbishop Cranmer. Bucer and Cranmer had actually been writing in very friendly terms to each other for four years, after contact facilitated by the Basel scholar Simon Grynaeus during his sociable tour of English worthies in 1531. Second gambit in Bucer's charm offensive was to dedicate a couple of his own books to Cranmer and Foxe in 1536. The books concerned were major works of biblical commentary and eucharistic discussion: this was serious literary diplomacy. If Cromwell needed any prompting to notice Bucer's compliment, it was provided by the distinguished French evangelical poet Clément Marot, now in exile from France along with John Calvin for his religious radicalism; Marot said that he could arrange similar dedications to Cromwell himself by 'the learned men there'.[65] The Lord Privy Seal had his own, more effective plans.

Closely following Bucer's literary diplomacy was the current chief pastor (*Antistes*) of Zürich, Zwingli's successor Heinrich Bullinger, a man with as keen a nose for international contacts as Bucer himself. On the face of it, Zürich was even less promising as a continental partner for England than Bucer's Strassburg. Strassburg was at least an international commercial centre enjoying frequent contacts with London, but there really were no natural links between the valleys of the Thames and the Limmat. The only possible asset was a personal relationship based on religious sympathy. Bullinger persuaded Grynaeus, who had been so helpful to Bucer, to effect an introduction by letter. Out of this a friendship by correspondence blossomed between Bullinger and Cranmer, using evangelical publisher/printers of London and Zürich as unobtrusive envoys in the course of their business in the book trade. Over the next year, the Archbishop of Canterbury wrote to Bullinger in remarkably relaxed (even calculatedly indiscreet) style. After this success, Bullinger encouraged the leader of another Swiss Protestant city, Joachim von Watt ('Vadianus') in St Gallen, to get in touch with Cranmer and follow Bucer's example by sending him his own theological writings.

Most remarkable fruit of all these manoeuvres early in 1536 was a journey by three enthusiastically evangelical young Englishmen, John Butler, Nicholas Partridge and William Woodroffe, to pay a long educational visit to the far-away Swiss city. Some in England would consider the destination suspect, so the public story was that they were off to explore Italy. They arrived in Zürich in August 1536, so probably set out from England in July. A fourth, William Peterson, arrived in September.

The visit was a great success; Bullinger took a keen personal interest, helping the young men settle into advanced biblical study in the city.[66] It became reciprocal when Bullinger's eighteen-year-old adopted son Rudolph Gwalther arrived in England in spring 1537, conducted by Partridge and Woodroffe. His two-month stay left Gwalther with golden memories for the rest of his life's work as one of the leading pastors of Zürich. English Protestantism benefited hugely, particularly when Zürich warmly welcomed Protestant exiles in Mary Tudor's reign. Gwalther returned to Switzerland in company with Partridge and three more Englishmen, and yet another appeared a few months later. That added to the circus Nicholas Eliot, John Finch, another now nameless and lastly in September 1537 Bartholomew Traheron – in all, eight evangelical English travellers. Some ranged further, reaching St Gallen and Konstanz, and even that turbulent city beyond the Swiss Confederation, Geneva.

It would be easy to read all this as Archbishop Cranmer's initiative, and certainly until the summer of 1536 he was chief apparent actor in creating England's evangelical axis to Strassburg and Zürich. Yet the pioneering student exchange came after that. Ferreting into the origins and connections of the young Englishmen, it is striking how little they linked to Cranmer, and how much to Cromwell. Those with a university connection came from Oxford, not Cambridge; Cranmer's connections were all the other way. Magdalen College, of which Nicholas Partridge was a Fellow, was prominent in their stories. That has added interest because over previous months Cromwell and his vice-gerential visitors were pulled into internal rows at Magdalen over the search for a new president and allied matters. On 9 September 1535 a group of mostly junior Fellows of Magdalen, Partridge included, clubbed together to write to Cromwell in warm support of the visitors' orders for a Greek lecture and dismantling of traditional scholastic teaching, expressing themselves in unbuttoned evangelical terms. Two Thomas Marshalls, brother and son of Cromwell's favoured evangelical printer, William Marshall, were also Magdalen men. The Magdalen squabbles may have been a catalyst to assemble travellers to Switzerland.[67]

One Fellow of Merton College Oxford, John Parkhurst, did not make it to Zürich at this time, but he was a linchpin in all this and emphasizes the Cromwell connection. He was one of Zürich's greatest friends in later years, spending a happy exile there under Mary before becoming first Elizabethan Bishop of Norwich. In the 1530s he was a protégé of Cromwell's Gloucestershire protégé Richard Tracey, foster-father to the eighth traveller Bartholomew Traheron. Parkhurst was from Guildford, which brings us another link among the Swiss travellers: to Nicholas Eliot, a

Student (Fellow) of King Henry's College Oxford, and the most obviously charismatic among the whole group (alas he died young). Eliot, probably son of the Master at Guildford's Free School, was in turn a close relative of Cromwell's employees Thomas and Henry Polstead, the latter of whom was also the subject of an elegant complimentary Latin verse from Parkhurst. Finally in these various Cromwell links, Peterson cannot be traced at Oxford, but unexpectedly he was brother to Robert Peterson, the Prior of Lewes, who was indeed an Oxford man, and whose great monastery as we will see soon became home to Gregory Cromwell.

Other features stand out among the eight visitors to Zürich. If Cranmer was really their patron, one would expect them to show some interest in clerical careers. One, William Woodroffe, was apparently already a priest, but with a curiously obscure clerical career before the Elizabethan period, including his flight from Oxford University at a time of witch-hunts against evangelicals in 1529, leaving behind a cache of books revealing his fascination with Erasmus.[68] In contrast to the clerical vocations of their friends in Zürich, as well as in contrast to Cranmer's clientage, none of the others sought a primarily clerical path into the Church of Henry VIII. This is not surprising, given their pronounced partisanship for Zürich religion (one or two considered even Bucer an unsound compromiser with Lutheranism); the Henrician Church was just too tainted, even when led by Cranmer. Instead, the Lord Privy Seal and his friends directed them into secular paths: a royal bursary to study law for Eliot, direct employment by Cromwell for Traheron, and for Partridge not a clerical title but a lectureship in divinity paid by Cromwell's client Bishop William Barlow. Eliot acted for a while as tutor in the household of Cromwell's servant Anthony Aucher, down at Dover. Peterson and Butler simply became merchants, which took them to Strassburg's newly forming evangelical English community.

All this fits together, but the most persuasive evidence comes from Rudolph Gwalther's visit to England in 1537. Being both conscientious and Swiss, he kept a detailed diary of this exciting and exotic trip, complete with accomplished sketch-maps.[69] Naturally, he started out via Basel and an interview with Simon Grynaeus. Coming from the Zürich humanist elite, Gwalther also reverenced the brand-new monument of the late Erasmus in the former cathedral, and being of Swiss theological persuasion he showed equal reverence for Luther's bugbear Andreas Karlstadt, then lecturing in Basel. Further humanist tourism en route involved a friendly meeting in Bruges with Princess Mary's old tutor Juan Luis Vives, perhaps for a briefing on how a foreigner should behave in England. That was a couple of days before facing the delays and miseries of the Channel, its marine terrors an unfamiliar experience for the Swiss. After a grim Calais–Dover crossing, Gwalther's idyll began among Partridge's relatives in Kent, then a sequence of distinguished hosts up to Cranmer at Lambeth: Sir Edward Wotton at Boughton Malherbe (3 miles from the Partridges at Lenham) and in London Wotton's brother-in-law Lord John Grey. This was the same Lord John Grey who back in 1526 had so singularly saluted Cromwell as his brother, and the common factor here was Margaret Wotton Dowager Marchioness of Dorset, Thomas Cromwell's former employer.[70]

By now it was early March 1537. The sight of the Lady Mary with her father and stepmother at Greenwich Palace provoked Gwalther to edifying reflections on the dangers of courtly life and riches, but he was still young enough to be delighted with Greenwich's whale skeleton, chaperoned by the genial Clerk of the Royal Kitchen Michael Wentworth, a relative of his companion William Woodroffe (the lions in the Tower of London also entertained him).[71] Then at last, on 11 March, it was Oxford, and Magdalen College, where the voyagers were greeted by an enthusiastic party of Oxford dons, six of whom were among the twenty Fellows of Magdalen signing the petition to Cromwell back in September 1535 – seven, counting in Gwalther's fellow-traveller Partridge. John Parkhurst also came across from Merton to join the fun.[72]

Gwalther had many more delights during his tour: Syon Abbey impressed him mightily, and Nicholas Udall the erudite headmaster of Eton seems to have kept his hands to himself. Further warm hospitality from Lord John Grey and Cranmer enlivened the journey back to a much easier Channel crossing from Margate. While in Kent, Gwalther enjoyed an antiquarian tour of Leeds Castle, lately home in succession to Cromwell's friends Sir Henry and Edward Guildford. Throughout, one senses a friendly absence of the unifying personality behind all this, the Lord Privy Seal. It was natural and politic that Bullinger as chief clergyman of the city of Zürich should make his approaches and sustain open friendship with the chief clergyman of the kingdom of England. Cromwell would have been ill advised to show open involvement. The importance of his keeping out of the limelight in regard to the Swiss exchange was underlined by what happened next.

Gwalther was guileless courier back to Switzerland of a packet of letters from Cranmer, one appropriately to Bullinger and another to be forwarded to Vadianus in St Gallen. Vadianus would have been disconcerted by the contents: a thank-you note for his present of his theological *Aphorisms* from 1536, but actually a hatchet-job on their eucharistic theology. Cranmer found Vadianus's 'remembrance' view of the eucharist unacceptable, and said so at length.[73] Thus Cranmer, like his royal master (and like Luther), still at this stage vigorously affirmed the real presence in the eucharist against the Swiss and Strassburgers. Not long afterwards, he sent an equally astringent reply to another literary overture, from Bucer's colleague as Strassburg pastor Wolfgang Capito. This was even more serious, because Capito had dedicated his book to King Henry, and after having it read and analysed for him, the King seized just as sharply as Cranmer on its statements about the eucharist.[74] Although Cranmer did not thereafter end contacts with Zürich, he was much more circumspect and deliberately dilatory in letter-writing. It was not until King Henry's death in 1547 that he felt able to abandon his scholarly caution about the eucharist; the removal of the terrifying charisma of King Henry then allowed him to make the great leap across the theological divide, jettisoning a real-presence theology resembling Luther's and embracing the symbolist view of the eucharist that Zwingli had pioneered.

Yet still Zürich was never high among Cranmer's priorities across the sea, certainly compared with Strassburg.[75] In the meantime, the overseas contacts continued without him, and the young men from 1536–8 continued in wanderings and warm correspondence with their friends across the water. The Polsteads sustained their Surrey relatives, and so rather unexpectedly did yet another connection of the Marchioness of Dorset, her son-in-law Henry Fitzalan, then Lord Maltravers before succeeding to his father's Earldom of Arundel. Fitzalan was thus also part of the Grey circle. He has often been seen as more conservative in religion than was really the case in his early career.[76] Finally, in early 1540 Lord Chancellor Audley sounded out Bullinger on a return visit to England by Rudolph Gwalther, perhaps again ventriloquized by Cromwell. From 1538 Audley had been brother-in-law to both Maltravers and Henry Grey, Marquess of Dorset.[77]

Although Gwalther's second trip did not materialize (hardly surprisingly in view of events in 1540), in Edward VI's reign a procession of talented scholars and theologians followed his footsteps from Zürich to Oxford, playing a significant part in counteracting the still powerful conservatism of the University. Their consistent patrons were the Marchioness of Dorset's son Henry Grey, now Duke of Suffolk, plus his scholarly daughter Lady Jane Grey: both receiving praise from Heinrich Bullinger. We must remember too how the same Kentish gentry cousinage spread outwards to embrace both leaders of Edward VI's government, Edward Seymour and John Dudley. Once Jane Grey's coerced venture in queenship was crushed by the Lady Mary's coup d'état in 1553, Zürich became the most welcoming of hosts for shell-shocked Protestant English refugee scholars, and on return to the England of Elizabeth I they provided most of the first bishops in her restored Protestant Church of England. They fostered decades of close relationships with the Alpine city so far away, and made Queen Elizabeth's Church resemble Zürich's Church much more than Geneva's.

This has been a complex tale to tease out, founded on sideways glances and glimpses of relationships, yet it is perhaps the most important story in Cromwell's career. It is dependent on seeing how his early service to the second Marquess and Marchioness of Dorset in the 1520s created links into the Kentish upper gentry and a common disposition not just towards Protestant religion, but to the crystallizing identity of that form of Protestantism later called Reformed. Quietly, with extraordinary discretion, Cromwell put friends and household to support an enterprise of international theological matchmaking with no immediate strategic relevance, and which would have aroused the suspicion and rage of King Henry if he had fully known about it. No cynical, 'secular-minded' politician would have taken such risks. Cromwell was deliberately laying foundations for a Protestant future. Many in England in 1536 could already perceive at least that broader intention. Their moment was at hand to strike against the heretical minister.

Grace for the Commonwealth: 1536

In autumn 1536 rebellions in Lincolnshire and the North nearly brought down the Tudor regime; the rising of northern England is remembered as the 'Pilgrimage of Grace'. Widespread rage at the policies of Thomas Cromwell, indeed his very existence in government, lay at its heart. As we excavate its course, two events need placing in the prehistory. First is the rising that did not happen in summer 1535. Early that June, widespread riots broke out in the Craven region of the Pennines; the rioters cast down fences and field-walls from enclosures to lay them open for common use. The business touched on quarrels among the gentry. One of the most significant local landowners, Sir Marmaduke Tunstall (nephew of Bishop Tunstall), was accused of raising around 200 armed men to intimidate followers of Thomas Stanley Lord Monteagle, in what was no doubt a long-standing feud.

Though a serious disturbance, this was all still routine stuff. Cromwell had some reliable friends in the right area to tip him off about it, including Dr Thomas Lee's cousin and godfather Sir James Layburn, a local servant of the Duke of Richmond who owed Master Secretary many favours, so the news reached him by 18 June. He sent a strong circular letter to local JPs (plus one he wrongly thought was a JP, who was nevertheless very willing to help), and they swung into action, holding a prolonged emergency sessions at Craven in which eighty-two people were indicted for riot in three different locations. Some of those convicted were then distributed around various prisons.[1]

The justices reported reassuringly if a little ungrammatically as soon as 5 July: 'as far as we can perceive at this time, all the country is quiet at this present day as ever they were, and the malefactors is sorry for their offences, and as soon as they were sent for in the King's name and yours, came unto us without denier, and submit themselves unto the King's Highness to be punished at his pleasure.'[2] So everyone in the Pennines behaved according to script: rioters showed their anger and made their point, gentry stepped in armed with menaces including Cromwell's authority and, once outward peace had been restored, any gentry participation was quietly forgotten, no doubt accompanied by severe words in private. Sir Marmaduke Tunstall had quickly enlisted in the ranks of his fellow-gentry in exercising retribution, as Sir James Layburn reported back to Cromwell, without comment. The prisoners were left to endure what was no doubt a stuffy and unpleasant time in gaol until late August and September 1535, when local magnates all advised Cromwell that they would have learned their lesson and could be released.[3] No deaths and, above all, at no stage did anyone mention religion.

The second northern incident, in early 1536, was a complete contrast. It centred on the murder of a prominent merchant and indeed former Mayor of Newcastle, Ralph Carr, at Malton in Yorkshire. This was the fallout of a prolonged family dispute whose epicentre was 60 miles north of Malton, in the village of Wycliffe on the Yorkshire/County Durham border. The supposed murderer was William Wycliffe of Wycliffe, arrested and brought to trial before the assize judges at York, where a jury acquitted him, to the horror of Mistress Carr (née Wycliffe) and to the judges' strong disapproval. While the case was rescheduled for a second hearing, Cromwell summoned the entire jury to London to face the Council in Star Chamber, and in May the jurors were punished with a crushing fine, to be paid in instalments over years.[4]

This uncorked a toxic mix of furies. The victim was an outsider to Yorkshire, the accused a local gentleman of ancient lineage; the jury as was normal in such serious cases included a wide spectrum of local worthies from knights to yeomen, now all humiliated by southerners.* Sir Thomas Tempest, a Yorkshire knight who became deeply involved in the Pilgrimage of Grace, bitterly referred back to the jurors' treatment in a memorandum that he offered the rebels' assembly at Pontefract in October 1536, specifically laying the blame on 'the Lollard and traitor Thomas Cromwell', but also on 'his servants and eke [also] his servants' servants'.[5] The Wycliffe case meant that Cromwell's local agents in the North were perceived as interfering in the processes of justice as they had not been during the Craven disorders.

One of those agents, James Rokeby, happened to be a perfect symbol of these betrayers of northern values, all the worse because he hailed from a prominent north Yorkshire gentry family of antique genealogy,

---

* Not surprisingly after this history, the Wycliffes remained staunch Catholic recusants in later years. John Wyclif[fe], inspiration of the Lollards much earlier, was a Yorkshireman, but not a close relative.

immediate neighbours of the Wycliffes.[6] Rokeby's public activities could not have been more obnoxious to partisans of William Wycliffe. He was one of the financial officials promoting the recent series of government moves in the North, such as the *Valor ecclesiasticus* and the monastic dissolutions, and he was soon on the payroll of the new body administering the results, the Court of Augmentations. Another northern gentleman gone to the bad, Dr Thomas Lee, reckoned James's brother Dr John Rokeby among his closest childhood friends, and strongly recommended him to Cromwell in autumn 1535 for the work of monastic dissolution. To cap it all, Dr Rokeby, a civil lawyer, was already a senior member of Archbishop Cranmer's staff in the archiepiscopal Court of Arches, as well as a contemporary of Dr Ellis ap Rhys at the same university hostel in Cambridge. An uncle of his, William Rokeby, was one of the surveyors of the monasteries being dissolved that summer.[7]

James Rokeby was drawn into the feud because William Wycliffe had granted him the right of presentation to the vacant parish of Wycliffe, 2 miles down-river from the Rokebys' childhood home at Mortham Tower; it may be that James already intended to appoint his almost clerical brother John to this familiar church.[8] William Wycliffe's peril presented James with a problem: worried about his legal position if the patron of the living was convicted, he made what would then have seemed a sensible move by going direct to Cromwell, and getting letters of appointment to the parish directly from the Lord Privy Seal, before heading back to plunge himself into the work of dissolving monasteries. It was a bad mistake: his arrival in August 1536 with these obnoxiously southern credentials not only exacerbated local anger but catapulted him into disputes about the parish appointment which detained him in the North until he was trapped by the violence of the autumn. In those dire circumstances, he became a ready-made figure of hatred, an unfortunate reminder of the summer's *cause célèbre*. As he later testified, at a particular moment of peril in the autumn an angry crowd yelled at him that he was 'a Lollard, and a puller-down of abbeys'. The latter was certainly true.[9]

In the background of this immediate unpleasantness was Westminster's decades-long neglect of northern interests, symbolized by the lack of a resident Archbishop of York between Thomas Savage's death in 1507 and Wolsey's belated arrival in 1529, but above all by Henry VIII's laziness in never having visited his northern shires. That was in sharp contrast to his father, who went to York three times. In the fickle memory of northerners, who had once given Richard III his only taste of popularity, Henry VII was now the focus for nostalgia.[10] James Rokeby, terrified at the sound of a roar from the Pilgrims' assembly at Pontefract that

October, was told they were shouting 'that they would have all the governance of the realm in like estate as it was *in the latter end* of King Henry the Seventh's days'. That sentiment, on which Sir Thomas Tempest's contemporary memorandum enlarged at length (maybe Tempest sparked the thought), was remarkably precise in its chronology and referred directly to the good old days before the death of the popular and flamboyant Archbishop Savage.[11] What an archbishop could achieve simply by being resident was shown in the impact that the equally flamboyant Wolsey made in a short time when he at last came north – too effective for his King's liking, in fact.

Then had followed the rapid changes of the Cromwell era, particularly and overwhelmingly the dissolution of monasteries, but also the vague threat of much more, the possibility of new taxation adding injury to insult. Such challenges to old certainties needed explanation or at the least forceful personal statement. For western England, the King's presence, unusually extended on the 1535 progress as far as Bristol and the Severn valley, provided just such messages. The Welsh borders had the powerful personality of Bishop Roland Lee, brutally willing to enforce anything the government wanted and not brook contradiction. West Cornwall, which was extremely troublesome to Henry VII and would be so again to Henry VIII's son, was currently under the sway of a good friend of Cromwell's, Sir William Godolphin, greatest entrepreneur of the Cornish tin industry, who notably lobbied Cromwell in 1537 to restore individual patronal festivals to Cornish churches; Cromwell listened and agreed. The amalgamation of patronal days into a national feast on a single day in the year was one of the grievances that provoked Lincolnshire and the northern Pilgrims in 1536, and the concession delighted Cornwall, with its especial profusion of local sanctities.[12]

Contrast northern England in the 1530s, where three bishops led the Church in the Province of York. Archbishop Edward Lee and Bishop Tunstall of Durham were both patently unhappy with the direction of change, even though they went through the motions of implementing and promoting it. Bishop Kite of Carlisle was cut from the same cloth, but in any case was hardly visible. There were virtually no well-motivated and well-informed evangelical preachers in the North to counterbalance this underwhelming endorsement of government changes or maybe even enthuse people. Two exceptions were imported by an evangelical Yorkshire gentleman in Cromwell's circle, Sir Francis Bigod, friends from Bigod's Oxford days as a protégé of Cardinal Wolsey. One was a former senior monk of Canterbury Cathedral and Canterbury College Oxford, William Jerome, who decided around 1534 to leave the monastic life; the other was that firebrand whom we met long before at Boston and Oxford, Thomas Garrett. Now in high favour with Hugh Latimer and armed with a general preaching licence from Archbishop Cranmer plus the title of chaplain to Bigod, during 1534 and 1535 Garrett preached a message of religious revolution so exotic in the North that it sparked widespread offence and open contradiction.[13]

Bigod was not the best person to introduce Jerome and Garrett to suspicious Yorkshire folk, being extravagant, debt-ridden and unstable. His conflicted personality, first a sycophantic client of Cromwell and then belated rebel leader, highlights a neglected aspect of the Pilgrimage of Grace. Much recent research has emphasized its wide reach across social divides: it was a movement of anger from the commons which the gentry and nobility actively failed to resist, since they were equally unconvinced of the government's good intentions. Commons and rulers united to defend the traditional religious culture and social relationships of northern England. Yet the Pilgrimage also needs to be recognized as a northern civil war: a confrontation first perceptible in the Wycliffe affair, between northerners who were benefiting from and helping to implement southern policies, and those who failed to see either profit or reason in the changes. The latter group blamed Cromwell for perverting their fellows in the North, and in the disturbances to come sought forcibly to reintegrate the strays back into northern society.

Anger thus festered among northerners. It was bad enough when there was no obvious religious component. So in a malign coincidence, the same week that Rokeby set out on his ill-starred journey north, far away in Limerick on 10 August Lord Leonard Grey wrote in a mood of deep despondency to Cromwell of chaos and plummeting morale among his English levies, sparked when 'the northern men about their wages began a sore mutiny and insurrection'; they encouraged others in what was turning into a general mutiny over pay in the Irish expeditionary force, crippling the war effort in the south and west.[14] Probably the troubles in England had already broken out by the time his letter limped its way through Ireland's uncertain communications towards Westminster. Meanwhile, Cromwell's attention was turned away from the imminent catastrophe towards other challenges to the King's policies. In fact the expression of dissent most worrying the Lord Privy Seal in August and September was a set of wild words from a parish priest in Worcestershire.

On 20 August, the parson of the village of Crowle outside Worcester, James Pratt, relaxed at the end of his round of Sunday services 'amongst many wives and men in the hall' of the village alehouse. Thus inspired, he ranted furiously about the arrival that week of Augmentations commissioners to survey the Augustinian priory at Studley, 13 miles away over the Warwickshire border. The ale did not improve the clarity of his remarks, but they were forceful enough: 'the Church went down and would be worse until there be a shrap [cock-fighting pit] made, and said that he reckoned there were 20,000 nigh of flote [armed company], and wished there were 20,000 mo[re], so that he were one, and the rather tomorrow than the next day, for there shall never be good world until there be a shrap.' His audience got the point; the landlord's sister-in-law tartly observed that Pratt 'spake there many words of war that might be spared'.[15] There are no prizes for guessing whom those thousands in Pratt's imagination might take on in the cockpit.

A fortnight later, two local JPs rounded up depositions on Pratt's fighting talk for Cromwell's perusal. By return of post on 7 September, after consulting the King, he authorized them to interrogate Pratt under torture in Worcester Castle ('pinch him with pains,' he wrote). Torture was a most unusual procedure in the English provinces, but one of the two justices was a member of the Council in the Marches of Wales, so this extreme measure was in line with the King's Council in London signing off similar procedures there. In fact Pratt fairly effectively withstood the 'pinching' they administered, admitting very little, and in the meantime he was visited in his prison by an alarming number of well-wishers topping up his intake of wine and ale. By the time Cromwell received the justices' further findings on Pratt at the end of September, troubles were stirring elsewhere. It was a sign of the rapid shift in priorities that an immediate dissolution of Studley Priory did not follow the Augmentations commissioners' survey on 18 August; it waited till the following February.[16]

Worcestershire was not the direction in which Cromwell should have been looking, but the only report he received during September suggesting unrest in Lincolnshire or Yorkshire sounded relatively innocuous and already satisfactorily sorted. A trio of south Lincolnshire villagers sat miserably in the stocks on 7 September while four local gentlemen cross-questioned them on a rumour they had spread the previous day: that the King was dead 'and that it must be in secret kept till such time as my Lord Privy Seal had levied the tax' – that is, an imminent collection of the latest instalment of the Parliamentary subsidy granted back in 1534. The main examiner, John Freeman, was close to Cromwell and one of the receivers of the Court of Augmentations. This was a break from his current campaign of closing the smaller Lincolnshire monasteries, heading a substantial force of labourers to strip them immediately of bells, lead and valuable building materials. The men sitting in the stocks at Donington would be perfectly aware of these outrages; and so, 40 miles to the north in the Lincolnshire Wolds, were the people of Louth.[17] Elsewhere in Lincolnshire, the Abbot of Barlings heard the widespread rumour that, after Michaelmas, Freeman and his fellows would be back from London to make a start on greater monasteries. One of the first houses to go was to be Barlings.[18]

Michaelmas, 29 September, was a resonant feast in the Tudor calendar. Its only rival in the rhythm of everyday life was Lady Day (25 March), but Michaelmas had much more heft, for the harvest was in and folk could afford to relax a little and find time for matters both solemn and festive. It was the main season at which leases were renewed and rents paid, so money (or its absence) was much on people's minds. All sorts of administrative decisions were taken at Michaelmas: most cycles of local elections took place then, together with all sorts of regular courts, borough, manorial and diocesan, and one of the quarterly meetings of justices of the peace. Folk gathered to exchange gossip, opinions, grievances, drink too much. This year there were many surprising and distressing novelties to announce in the regular Michaelmas meetings of bishops, archdeacons and their officials with diocesan clergy: all the measures from the summer Convocation and Cromwell's pioneering vice-gerential injunctions.

The most immediately offensive new injunction was a drastic simplification of saints' days, so that all parochial dedication festivals from now on must be celebrated on 1 October, regardless of the local saint. Following immediately after Michaelmas itself, this was a bolt from the blue to offend the most compliant church official, not least for its insensitive indifference to the preparation time needed for such an important local festival. Among other new provisions, the threat that clergy would be examined to assess their learning hugely offended parsons and curates satisfied with their own estimate of their pastoral abilities: a common clerical reaction in every age to such demands.[19] Small wonder that all over the country Michaelmas 1536 invited trouble. As tax officials gathered their files and as monasteries shut their doors in Lincolnshire, Lancashire, Yorkshire and all points north, not only Lincolnshire was poised on the edge of explosion.

The first outbreak was in Dentdale, an area of the western Pennines in the vast parish of Sedbergh, rather similar territory to Craven 30 miles to its south where trouble had erupted the previous summer. At the end of September, an outsider stumbled innocently into a ferment of furious posturing at Dent, including the swearing of oaths to defend local churches and abbeys from royal confiscations. William Breyar was a restless individual who at one stage in wandering round the kingdom picked up work transporting baggage for the Queen's household. From that, he acquired royal livery clothing, which proved less than an asset when he rode into Dent. His distinctive outfit attracted unwelcome attention from a trio of street idlers, who began a vigorous argument when they realized this was the royal livery. Who was responsible for closing monastery churches in their area? Not the King, they eventually decided, 'but the deed of Crumwell, and if we had him here we would Crum him and Crum him that he was never so Crumwed, and' (an afterthought of distinctly ambivalent deference to the King) 'if thy [royal] Master were here, we would new crown him.'

Thus the very first public expression of the great stirs in this chaotic autumn named the hated Lord Privy Seal. The crowd around William Breyar grew, and turned violent. He managed to scramble to his horse and did not feel safe till he had ridden the 10 miles to Kirkby Lonsdale. The Kirkby folk reproached him for having blundered into the hornets' nest at Dent; they told him the oath-taking had started the previous Monday, 25 September, and that it had already spread over three other neighbouring parishes. These were not the small neat compact units of lowland England: parishes in the thinly populated Pennine uplands could rival the size of an Italian diocese, and the comfortably endowed rectory of Sedbergh was no exception.[20]

Dentdale was the first outbreak of real English resistance to the Reformation of Cromwell and Henry VIII to resemble the Irish rebellion of summer 1534.[21] For almost a month, the Dentdale men kept to their own territory, but others began imitating their example. Dentdale pioneered an aspect of the northern troubles which became characteristic, the taking of oaths, and it eventually provided a full-scale contingent joining the Pilgrimage by 21 October, a fortnight after the big outbreak in south-east Yorkshire around 8 October. There had been no hint of oath-taking in Craven's popular disturbances the year before, and it is interesting that Breyar learned in his flight to Kirkby that 'one of Dent who would not be sworn had fled to Sir Marmaduke Tunstall.' That gentleman-dabbler in trouble in 1535 was apparently now a symbol of loyalty to the Crown.

Why was Dentdale the trigger for the great explosion? The likely key is a monastic dissolution, just as Studley Priory's closure provoked James Pratt's drunken outburst in Worcestershire. In this case, the victim was the Premonstratensian house of Coverham, 30 miles east, corporate rector of the parish of Sedbergh and therefore of Dentdale. Coverham was dissolved on 14 August, by none other than that ill-starred seeker after the benefice of Wycliffe, James Rokeby, along with Cromwell's servant and Augmentations official William Blythman. They left in charge a local man, Robert Asporner; as the insurgency flared, he was chased out, eventually taking refuge with the King's army.[22] Yet a further circumstance related to Coverham Abbey and its closure in August directly concerned Dent: the death of the Vicar of Sedbergh, Roger Horsman.

We have met Horsman before, when some three or four years previously Dr Roland Lee had lobbied Cromwell to get him appointed Abbot of Coverham; the connection was through Horsman's brother Leonard, Fellow of Christ's College Cambridge.[23] Horsman was quickly replaced as Abbot of Coverham by Christopher Rokeby, whom it is tempting to link to his namesake James. On Horsman's resignation the abbey evidently appointed him to its living at Sedbergh, but his recent death left Sedbergh vacant. When Coverham Abbey surrendered to James Rokeby and William Blythman, the Crown gained the right to present a successor parson for Sedbergh, which the King duly exercised far away in Windsor on 1 October, blissfully oblivious to all that was happening in Dent.

Horsman's old link to Lee and Cromwell – and beyond them, to Christ's College Cambridge and to Mistress Margery Horsman at Court – seems too much of a coincidence amid all this trouble. We should not think of Dentdale and its vicinity as some benighted region, cut off from events in the south: Sedbergh boasted a school then only ten years old, with strong links to St John's College Cambridge, a college currently very angry about the fate of its late benefactor and virtual founder, Cardinal John Fisher.* Maybe, ironically, the rebels' idea of oath-taking came from the royal campaigns for oaths to the royal succession and supremacy which were such prominent features of recent years, thanks to Thomas Cromwell.[24] As that shout of Crumming menace to poor frightened Breyar in Dent showed, there was a hesitation in the insurgents' attitude to the Crown which in the end proved fatal: they knew they hated Cromwell, but could they effectively distinguish his wickedness from the actions of his royal master? Was it possible to 'new crown' Henry VIII with a new set of policies?

Seventy miles across the north Pennines, at Hexham, came an exactly contemporary outburst of resistance to the government's plans, and once more the main target was James Rokeby. He was one of four dissolution commissioners who found themselves repelled from Hexham Priory on 28 September. This was no token resistance, for according to the alarming report brought to the commissioners while still on the road to Hexham,

---

* Conversely, one talented local boy who defected via Cambridge to the evangelical world the Dentdale men so hated was Miles Coverdale, Cromwell's favoured Bible translator.

it included guns and artillery as well as an angry crowd. The Austin canons
there were well equipped for such eventualities, being the last significant
English monastic presence before the Scottish border, and they faced up to
the commissioners just as they had done over centuries to a Scots raid –
with the additional intimidation, they claimed, of a royal letter under the
Great Seal for their exemption from suppression, despite their coming
within the terms of the Act: probably the fruit of Archbishop Lee's intervention with Cromwell immediately after the spring Parliament.[25]

Nonplussed, the commissioners slunk away to Corbridge, 5 miles closer
to the safety of Newcastle, leaving the canons in triumphant battle array
on Hexham Green. The rapid unfolding of events elsewhere meant that no
further official action took place against the priory until the following
February (shades of Studley Priory). The canons were no doubt well
aware, despite waving their exemption at the commissioners from their
battlements, that Cromwell had already designated their house for a grant
to Henry Percy Earl of Northumberland's favourite servant, Sir Reynold
Carnaby. Sir Reynold had only recently completed a very satisfactory deal
with Cromwell, selling him family lands in Kent. The Carnaby family
straight away sent down an indignant report about the Hexham outrages
to the Earl and Sir Reynold in London, alongside the commissioners' own
memorandum to Cromwell. Rokeby, Carnaby, even Percy himself: here
were yet more examples of northerners doing southerners' bidding, and
now getting their just deserts.[26]

Effectively the government had now lost control of two widely separated regions of northern uplands, but so far these unprecedented
expressions of defiance had not resulted in the insurgents moving beyond
their home bases – yet, crucially, neither had anyone in authority tried to
restore order, as they had done so quickly in Craven the previous year.
Everyone was waiting to see what would happen next. On Sunday 1
October came the events which began unravelling royal power across
half England, not just north of the Humber but right into the English
lowlands. The spark was in the Wolds of Lincolnshire, within the octave
of Michaelmas – the time expected for the return of the detested John
Freeman and his agents of monastic destruction and maybe more destruction still. That Sunday Thomas Kendall, Vicar of Louth, mounted the
pulpit in the town's magnificent church to preach an excitable sermon in
tune with the general mood, amid seething local rumours of confiscation
of church goods: the universal Church, as well as his own church, was in
danger. As the town's prized silver crosses were solemnly processed in the
liturgy, a prosperous yeoman of Louth prophesied that he and his fellows
should never have the chance to follow the crosses again.[27]

Affronted faith combined with fierce local pride amid the splendour of Michaelmas devotion and festival excitement. A crowd gathered in front of the rood screen after evensong, and relieved the churchwardens of their keys to the church treasury, entrusting them to a Louth shoemaker named Nicholas Melton. Shoemakers both in sixteenth-century Europe and later had a recurrent tendency to adventurous thoughts and radical talk, and Melton was the perfect exemplar; his name resounded through subsequent events as 'Captain Cobbler'.[28] What would the crowd do with their righteous indignation? They turned on the local incarnations of Thomas Cromwell. First was John Heneage, brother to Cromwell's friend and colleague, the newly promoted courtier Thomas Heneage; he was in town to take oaths of a very different sort to those of Dent in the annual Michaelmas election of new town officers.[29]

In doing so, Heneage was acting in his capacity as Steward of the Bishop of Lincoln, John Longland, Lord of the Manor of Louth. As a cleric of unmistakably traditionalist outlook, Longland might seem an unlikely pairing with Cromwell as the symbol of obnoxious religious change, but the very nature of the Bishop's jurisdiction in Louth invited local resentment. Borough manors dominated by great churchmen rarely had an easy relationship with their clerical overlords. If they had become prosperous boroughs on their own account, they sought rights and freedoms unimagined in the remote ages when episcopal lordship was first imposed; but clerical lordship never died. That structural problem fatally entwined Longland's evident unpopularity in Louth with Thomas Cromwell's. It did not help that, in the Lincolnshire section of Longland's vast diocese stretching from the Humber to the Thames, the Bishop was largely an absentee magnate: born at Henley-on-Thames and an Oxford man (currently University Chancellor), he divided his time between London and his fine house at Wooburn in Buckinghamshire. More immediately pertinent in 1536, Longland was widely perceived to be the chief fomenter of Henry VIII's moral scruples about his marriage with Katherine of Aragon.[30]

Heneage was thus the unwitting focus of a great many resentments both traditional and contemporary. Far from administering oaths himself, on Monday 2 October he was manhandled into the parish church and sworn to be true 'to God, the King and the commonalty' – the first of a series of notables forcibly sworn over the next few months. Heneage insisted he would find out the truth of proposals for church confiscation from the King himself, a plausible promise given his brother's position in the Privy Chamber, and he was allowed to ride south to the Court. Simultaneously, the mob rounded up in the marketplace a servant of the

Bishop's Chancellor, in town for Michaelmas episcopal business, and ceremonially burned his administrative papers. For centuries such action had symbolized defiance of clerical power, though the most famous recent example, Martin Luther burning the Pope's bull in 1520, would not have commended itself to Louth folk. Around them, crowds swelled with excited and vengeful recruits from the surrounding country.[31]

The next move was unequivocally aimed at Cromwell and his employees. Alone among Lincolnshire monasteries recently suppressed and despoiled, the little Cistercian nunnery of Legbourne, 4 miles out of Louth, was actually Cromwell's own rented property. Why he decided to invest in this small convent is a mystery: it was far from his other estates, and he had shown no previous interest in acquiring monastic lands. Nevertheless his Augmentations lease of 7 August sits in the Court's books flanked by leases to his nephew Richard of two priories in Huntingdonshire, and former monastic rectories in Lincolnshire to none other than Mr John Hencage.[32] There must have been an historic connection of Legbourne to one of Cromwell's properties elsewhere to explain this otherwise apparently random acquisition. That is suggested by a letter of the previous spring from the Prioress, Jane Missenden, one of a local gentry family: she begged him (in vain) to get her house exempted from the suppression legislation, 'as God has endowed you with the just title of founder of the priory of Legbourne'.[33]

The new landlord's servants were enjoying lunch in the former nunnery on 2 October when a crowd from Louth arrived. John Milsent (Cromwell's household receiver) and John Bellow were carried off to Louth and another servant, George Parker, was rounded up en route. Many wanted to hang them or stab them to death, but more moderate counsels led to Bellow and Milsent sitting in the stocks in Louth marketplace before being thrown in gaol.[34] In their place, the insurgents installed a nun back at Legbourne, and at the recently surrendered Louth Park Abbey, a nearby male Cistercian counterpart to Legbourne, the monks were put in possession once more. These were the first restorations of recently suppressed monastic houses, in a pattern which characterized the northern stirs everywhere.[35] Later in this insurgency, associates of Cromwell or the equally obnoxious Archbishop Cranmer continued to be victimized: the Lincolnshire homes of John Freeman and Cranmer's friend John Tamworth were among the few the rebels chose systematically to wreck.[36]

When first reports of the Louth stirs reached Windsor, the most vivid and horrifying early information came via a report from Christopher Ayscough, royal Gentleman Usher and Lincolnshire man (brother of the

future Protestant martyr Anne Ayscough) who had been sent up to rec-
onnoitre. Amid generally accurate intelligence, he reported that Milsent
had been hanged and Bellow baited to death with dogs.[37] This was all the
more plausible because a day or two later exactly parallel outrages really
did occur at Horncastle, a small episcopal market town very like Louth
(though here its absentee landlord was the Bishop of Carlisle). A Horncastle mob beat to death Bishop Longland's Chancellor John Rayne, and
hanged an unfortunate memorably called George Wolsey, surely not
coincidentally an old servant of the Cardinal.[38]

The fake news of Milsent's and Bellow's atrocious deaths quickly
spread in London, and was in fact relayed to Brussels in an otherwise
strikingly well-informed report by Chapuys's nephew, who added the significant detail that the hanged man was cook to Dr Thomas Lee.[39] In fact
both Milsent and Bellow survived their ordeal, despite a fortnight's
imprisonment, as did George Parker, who was at large and doing the bidding of royal commanders against the insurgents within a week of the
Louth insurrection.[40] That drawing back from the most extreme mili-
tance was a mark of how the very large armed gatherings mustered in
Lincolnshire were fairly quickly contained. Yet it remained alarming that
in the first week of their action the insurgents had a very precise shopping-
list of leading figures whom they wished rounded up and delivered to
them or banished the realm, nearly all identifiable evangelicals: Bishops
Cranmer, Hilsey and Latimer; other bishops including Lincoln and Ely;
Cromwell, Rich and Master of the Rolls Christopher Hales. No more
than the men of Dentdale were the leaders in the Lincolnshire stirs political innocents abroad; one did not have to be a gentleman or nobleman
to show political sophistication in Tudor England.[41]

The King reacted to the first reports from Lincolnshire with incandescent rage and a thirst for revenge. Yet he recovered fast from initial panic,
and made an adroit choice of commander in the Duke of Suffolk for a
substantial military force, hastily gathered from those regions the regime
calculated would remain loyal, in southern and eastern England. Brandon may not have been especially bright, but he was as physically
imposing as the King himself, genuinely experienced in real warfare in
France as well as tournaments, and possessing a unique asset in the situation. While Bishop Longland was reckoned in popular memory as a key
player in the betrayal of Queen Katherine of Aragon, it would also be
remembered that the Duke's first wife (King Henry's sister Mary) was
among Katherine's greatest defenders, and his remarkably young current
wife was daughter to a former Spanish attendant of Katherine's, María
de Salinas. Truth be told, María, Dowager Lady Willoughby, was not a

popular landlord in Lincolnshire and faced trouble on her estates during the rising. Nevertheless, unlike his present mother-in-law, the Duke had the advantage of landed prospects in the county without (as yet) the actual possession of estates to compromise his popular reputation.[42]

There was no question of Thomas Cromwell getting anywhere near confrontations with the rebels. It would have been the height of folly to inflame their passions still further, quite apart from his indispensable role in shuttling between Windsor Castle and London, busily drafting statements and letters for the King to send out to insurgents and loyalists alike, and frantically scrabbling to finance this totally unexpected and deeply expensive eventuality.[43] Cranmer was sent off into virtual invisibility in deepest Kent to keep an eye on any local trouble, not an especially demanding task in that region, while Bishops Foxe and Sampson remained at Court and active on the Council: they were probably considered more politically capable figures than him, and certainly less provocative, considering the obvious hatred most northerners felt for the Archbishop.[44]

The silence of another bishop throughout the autumn crisis is notable, and rather puzzling. Not a single definitely dateable letter from Roland Lee survives from the Welsh Marches amid the heap of strategic correspondence between Cromwell and provincial commanders confronting the Pilgrims. Maybe they were weeded out later for some political reason around Cromwell's fall, or perhaps he simply got on with his job at Ludlow with his usual brusque efficiency; in one of his later letters he referred back to a particular set of arrangements he made to recruit 500 men while raising forces against the insurgents back in 1536.[45] His next unquestionably dateable letter is from 15 January 1537, when he wrote from Wigmore Castle to reassure Cromwell about the lack of Welsh reaction to renewed stirrings in the North: 'to my knowledge, little amongst them [is] conceived of the matters in England, forasmuch as their language doth not agree to the advancement thereof.'[46]

Cromwell himself made no effort to hide his considerable contribution to military efforts confronting first the Lincolnshire insurgents and then the northern Pilgrims. Gregory Cromwell was still far too young to become involved, and remained out of harm's way in East Anglia, but Gregory's honorary elder brother Richard Cromwell alias Williams was plunged into the affair straight away, according to the circumstantial account of Chapuys's nephew. As soon as the King heard of the Louth outrages, on 4 October, 'he summoned the gentlemen then at London to go thither under the command of Richard Cromwell, and ordered the mayor of London to supply them with horses,' on the pretext of welcoming the Habsburg military commander the Count of Nassau on a visit to the City.[47] Chapuys himself reported further developments to Charles V: Richard moved on 7 October to take from the Tower of London 'a quantity of ammunition, as well as arrows and other weapons of war', while Uncle Thomas's new building works at Mortlake and in London supplied sixty or seventy craftsmen.[48]

Soon Richard was riding north with his uncle's allocation of 100 cavalry, and energetically recruiting further forces from the Fens just south of Lincolnshire, which had become his home country over the previous few years. Among his tasks was to liaise with the Lord Privy Seal's victimized servants, including John Freeman, spoiling for vengeance after the sacking of his house, and a dazed John Milsent. By 2 November Richard was confident enough of Lincolnshire's security to send back John Bellow to sort out the situation at Legbourne Priory.[49] From his stream of urgent and informative letters back to Cromwell, one gets the feeling that the young man was having the time of his life, despite appropriate remarks asking his uncle to calm his wife's anxieties. He won avuncular praise from the senior commanders in Lincolnshire for his energy and efficiency, particularly from Cromwell's friends Sir William Fitzwilliam and Sir John Russell.[50]

Richard's troop was only half the Lord Privy Seal's contribution to the war effort. Cromwell sent off a second detachment of 200 under a former senior servant of the late Duke of Richmond, Sir Richard Cotton (Richard's brother Sir George, also previously in Richmond's service, joined Richard Cromwell's troop). Cotton was deputed to round up Cromwell's dispersed servants in eastern England, as well as commanding domestic staff from the Cromwell household; he weeded them down to the best 160 (including, he apologetically admitted, one of Cromwell's cooks), and detailed the arrangements he made to keep them smart, well paid and in high morale. He tactfully made it clear that this would be effort and money well spent, since this second Cromwell troop was to serve with Thomas Duke of Norfolk. The symbolism of the Cotton brothers leading the Cromwell contingent into possible battle would not be lost on Richmond's late father-in-law, after the painful events that summer.[51]

There was a political minefield to negotiate here. The Duke of Norfolk showed unfeeling glee on first hearing of the crisis in Lincolnshire. The news came at the nadir of his fortunes after the hammer-blows of the summer. As the Bishop of Carlisle commented to Chapuys in the first week of the crisis, Norfolk was convinced that 'it will work the ruin and destruction of his competitor and enemy, Cromwell, on whom he puts all the blame for these events, and whose head it's said the insurgents demand.'[52] It was a shattering blow, therefore, though one the Duke ought to have predicted, when his long-standing rival Suffolk gained command of the army for Lincolnshire, while Norfolk was fobbed off with the undemanding duty of guarding East Anglia. He was, after all, hereditary Earl Marshal, who might expect the senior command by ancient right. 'God give me grace honestly to die shortly and not to live with this shame. My Lords of Oxford and Sussex might have stayed [kept peace in] this country as well as I,' he stormed to Cromwell and Council colleagues on his eastward journey on 8 October, alongside an even more emotional lament to the King from 'your foolish old servant' – both written in his own hand.[53]

Norfolk continued to seethe while given confusing and inconsistent instructions about mustering troops, in what look suspiciously like moves to keep him occupied but which may just reflect indecisiveness in King and Council about what to do with the angry nobleman. Then, in the middle of October, just as it appeared that the Duke of Suffolk had succeeded in containing the situation in Lincolnshire, and Norfolk was ordered not to advance any further out of East Anglia, news started filtering south that official concentration on neutralizing the Lincolnshire insurgents was drawing attention away from something far more serious across the Humber.[54] The Yorkshire stirs had found a charismatic leader, Robert Aske. He was from a well-connected local gentry family but was also a lawyer in London – Thomas Cromwell would know him well, for they were both members of Gray's Inn. Aske was turning the swelling mobs of commons into a single force of rebellion, converging in triumphant assemblies in York and Pontefract, and intimidating more and more nobles and gentlemen into making peace with the people's assemblies. But more than intimidation was at work. Aske was able to present events as a sacred mission, not some run-of-the-mill tax protest or enclosure riot or howl of hatred against Cromwell. Soon the whole vast movement called itself a 'Pilgrimage', and its full name is too often shortened in modern writing to 'Pilgrimage of Grace'. It was a 'Pilgrimage of Grace for the Commonwealth' – representing the whole of northern society.[55]

By 20 October, Thomas Howard was back in the game as a major player. He successfully advocated a two-pronged expedition for the North, with the Earl of Shrewsbury leading troops recruited from the Midlands and the West, and his own army from the South and East. Suffolk was left in a now subordinate role, clearing up the situation in Lincolnshire. Three days later, Norfolk was in Newark-on-Trent with a small advance force, on the verge of negotiating with the Pilgrims in their assembly in Doncaster; the King's future seemed to lie in his hands. Even more satisfyingly, he seemed to have the prospect of deciding Cromwell's future. Might he throw in his lot with insurgents, whose religious views he found a good deal more congenial than those of the Lord Privy Seal, and who now included most of the nobility and gentry he had so long known from northern service?[56]

While the Duke of Norfolk considers his options, it is worth surveying the fate of Cromwell's associates stranded amid the triumph of the Pilgrims, now controlling so much of northern England. Monastic heads of house regarded as collaborators with Cromwell were expelled. The Master of Cromwell's favoured order the Gilbertines, Robert Holgate, whom he had made Prior of its wealthiest and most influential house at Watton in Yorkshire, fled in late October to join the Lord Privy Seal in London. He did not return till spring 1537, by which time Cromwell had consoled him with a bishopric.[57] James Cockerell, veteran Prior of Augustinian Guisborough, who had resigned under pressure from Drs Lee and Leighton in February 1536, was restored by Sir Francis Bigod around 12 November (the earliest sign that Bigod was deserting Cromwell's cause). Cockerell replaced Cromwell's nominee Robert Pursglove, who like Holgate gained a bishopric, albeit only the suffragan title of Hull, in 1538.[58] As a second rebellion in the North gathered momentum in January 1537, the commons took into custody the monk of St Mary's York whom Cromwell and the Duke of Norfolk had nominated to head its Cumberland cell of St Bees, as he travelled across the Pennines to take up his duties.[59]

Some of Cromwell's lay collaborators also faced punitive action, particularly those directly associated with monastic despoliation, showing the minimum awaiting the likes of Drs Lee and Leighton if they had been trapped in the North. The Augmentations official Leonard Beckwith (now a refugee in the south like John Freeman) had his house ransacked; so did William Blythman.[60] We have already seen Robert Asporner homeless after his expulsion from Coverham Abbey – he was one of those 'servants' servants' of Cromwell denounced at the Pontefract assembly by Sir Thomas Tempest. Sir George Lawson, Cromwell's friend and relative, one of the Crown's chief financial and military agents in the North, was targeted in renewed northern violence that winter. He was afraid to leave York to join Cromwell in London, he said, because he had been warned by several friends that 'the commons will not only spoil all my farms and goods but also put me in jeopardy of life'.[61] A servant of Sir Reynold Carnaby had his house burned down. Carnaby's designs on Hexham Priory were only one cause of his low reputation among both the commons and some of his fellow-magnates.[62]

The most violent of these acts took place in what became a second phase of the Pilgrimage in winter 1537, when far fewer of the northern governing class were involved in disturbances and therefore less able to moderate them. One feature of the main outbreaks in the autumn was that many northern people directly associated with Cromwell were not treated in this extreme fashion. Once identified, they were ritually humiliated, but then given a chance to be reintegrated into the newly fashioned society of the North by oath-taking. It is fortunate for our understanding of events that most of them complied, because this forced them to explain themselves at length to the government after the rising's defeat; their depositions and other excuses are very informative.

The most striking case is Dr John Dakyn. He could not have been a more obvious victim for Pilgrim rage: former principal of St Nicholas Hostel Cambridge (also alma mater to John Rokeby and Ellis ap Rys), he began his Yorkshire legal career as Vicar-General to the heroically pluralistic William Knight, Archdeacon of Richmond. There he was the everyday face of an Archdeaconry that in size and powers was more like a diocese, covering the Pennine region from which the 1536 stirs emerged. Dakyn had been helpful to Roland Lee in managing the Northern Convocation over the King's Boleyn marriage. His hospitality to William Blythman and Drs Lee and Leighton in their northern work was well known, as was the fact that a close kinsman of his surname was a servant of Richard Cromwell. All that earned bitter reproach from the Pilgrims that he was a traitor, not true to the commons. At Pontefract, Dakyn was forced to become Chief Clerk to the assembly's proceedings.[63]

Naturally Dakyn tried to account for this afterwards. He explained that even before the triumphal entry to York and the Pontefract assembly, in his own town of Richmond, 'I being a stranger not born in that country, having example of death before me . . . seeing also the gentlemen of the country, as James Rokeby, Anthony Brackenbury and other . . . for the time [being] said as they [the rebels] said and did as they did for jeopardy of my life.' There in his account is the name of James Rokeby once more. Rokeby provided his own squirmings to Cromwell about becoming a delegate to the Pontefract assembly, who had thus accepted the 'Lollard, and a puller-down of abbeys' back into the commonwealth of Yorkshire. Elsewhere, some of Cumberland's leading gentlemen known to be close to Cromwell were made to take the Pilgrims' oath of loyalty: one was Sir John Lamplugh, on his payroll both before and after the rising. Another forced oath-taker, cousin to Drs Roland and Thomas Lee, was John Lee of Isel in Cumberland, an old friend of Cromwell with a penchant for sending him breezy letters accompanied by slightly bizarre presents, such as a roll of leeches.[64]

Also conspicuous was the treatment of the two men most readily identified with Cromwell in the city of York, Sir George Lawson and the veteran Minster Treasurer, Lancelot Collins. When Robert Aske arrived with thousands of supporters for liturgical celebrations of his Pilgrimage with Archbishop Lee in the week of 16 October, this pair were singled out to play a prominent role in the triumph. Collins, as we noted when observing his first contacts with Cromwell way back in 1514, had put up the heraldry of his two greatest patrons, Cromwell and Cardinal Bainbridge, over his front door: threatened with having his house burned down, he hastily dismantled the display, unfortunately along with the King's arms. Sir George was forced to be Aske's host during his stay in the city, while Collins was made to treat Aske to a lavish dinner and furnish him with payments of ready cash.[65]

All this amounted to a form of the sacrament of penance: repentance and promise of amendment of life, followed by reconciliation with the community. The most likely source of this remarkable idea is Robert Aske himself. He was precisely the type of the potential collaborator with Cromwell's regime represented by John Dakyn or James Rokeby: rooted in northern gentry society, but equally at home at Gray's Inn, where as a lawyer who understood the North he regularly did business for northern magnates like the Earls of Northumberland and Cumberland. Moreover, the government understood the psychology, and after defeating the Pilgrimage sought with some success to reverse it. When on 8 and 9 May 1537 the Duke of Norfolk set forth in York the indictments of participants and empanelled the juries to try them, he not only expected the largest gathering of county gentry seen in the city for many years, but made a particular point of appointing as jurors people close to those indicted, including near relatives of Thomas Lord Darcy and Sir Robert Constable – and, most strikingly of all, Robert Aske's own brother John.[66]

Not everyone played to the Pilgrims' script. Cranmer later commended the Controller of his household, John Wakefield, to Cromwell. Wakefield was one of a Yorkshire gentry family to whom the Archbishop gave much patronage; since the late 1520s he had been plugging away like Francis Bigod at the thankless task of promoting evangelical reformation in the North. For that and his notorious connection to the hated Cranmer, Wakefield was brought to the Pontefract assembly by Thomas Lord Darcy of Templehurst, being particularly vulnerable as a near-resident to the town, but he pointedly withdrew from the gathering. He was punished with the 'loss of all his goods, which at that time were specially spoiled, because he was so unobedient unto their minds'. Cranmer would have liked him to receive the Cluniac Priory at Pontefract in reward for his sufferings, beyond compensation the Duke of Norfolk had already allotted to him, but it was not to be.[67]

Another less than penitent sinner fared rather better. William Maunsell was one of Yorkshire's leading financial officials: long-standing county Under-Sheriff and Escheator, with consequently many local enemies and a good friend in Thomas Cromwell, not least because an escheator had much to do with administering the consequences of the new Statute of Uses. William's brother Thomas, a priest, was unmistakably an active and enthusiastic participant in the Pilgrimage, but still felt protective towards his wayward sibling. Hearing that William 'was in great danger of his life because he would not take the oath' at York, on 16 October Thomas persuaded an angry Robert Aske to allow him to administer it to William in person and in private. Granted this favour, Thomas turned up at his brother's door, where William proceeded to hit him, hard. Taking this as a no, Thomas decided nevertheless with fraternal loyalty to report to Aske that the oath had been duly administered; and that was that.[68] Maunsell was rewarded for his recalcitrance after the rebellion by being made Gentleman Usher of the King's Privy Chamber.[69]

By now it will be apparent that the Lincolnshire Rising and Pilgrimage of Grace were aimed at Cromwell and his associates more precisely and carefully than has generally been appreciated. The unpardonables were (as the Sawley Abbey ballad written for the Pilgrims ran) 'Crim, Cram and Rich / With three Ls and their like', the 'three Ls' or hells probably being Lee, Leighton and Hugh Latimer, or maybe just the whole clan of Lees, Bishop and all.[70] Early on in events, on 15 October 1536, John Freeman advised Cromwell 'if there shall be any one matter of the requests of the false rebels of Yorkshire redressed, that it may appear to them and all others that ye shall be a suitor for it, that the ignorant wretches may the better goodwill bear you'. In 1525, this policy had stood Cardinal Wolsey in good stead and helped bring a face-saving end to the Amicable Grant, but no similar charade would ever have worked for Cromwell.[71]

Indeed, any direct involvement of the Lord Privy Seal or his surname in Yorkshire proved deeply counter-productive. When negotiations for a truce reached a delicate stage on 27 October, with the Duke of Norfolk's small royal advance guard eyeing the much greater rebel force at Doncaster, proceedings were nearly derailed by a violent quarrel between one of the Pilgrims and one of the Cromwell contingent. There was also great indignation at reports of Richard Cromwell's 'extreme' words against the Lincolnshire insurgents (all too plausible; he spoke very violently of them in his letters to his uncle).[72] Another near-catastrophe came in November when the Pilgrims intercepted one of the Lord Privy Seal's letters to the royal garrison at Scarborough; it promised that the commander 'shall see them so subdued as their example shall be fearful to all subjects whilst the world doth endure'.[73] This was a very different message from the government's conciliatory public line presented in negotiations by the Duke of Norfolk, and the fact that we have two copies suggests that the rebels circulated it for propaganda purposes.

At the beginning of November, after the Duke of Norfolk had concluded a truce with the Pilgrims, the King contemplated sweeping concessions to the rebels. These were to be conveyed by the Duke. To be complete, they should have included the sacrifice of Cromwell. That possible way forward is strongly implied by the first draft of an answer which Henry composed in the first week of November to demands brought to Windsor on 2 November by Norfolk and gentry delegates from the Pilgrims (Sir Ralph Ellerker and Robert Bowes). The royal reply was a long document, frequently peevish in tone, more like a rather testy and defensive contribution to a conversation than a proclamation. This is because it was intended as a printed tract for wide distribution. A similar printed tract answering the Lincolnshire rebels was issued from Thomas Berthelet's press at much the same time, late in 1536, but the surviving manuscript is an early and shorter draft of the Yorkshire printed text. Ralph Sadler took down the copy, which the King then corrected in his own hand. It is no scrawl, but a considered, almost final text. It is worth examining and comparing with the printed outcome for what it does and does not say on one vital matter.[74]

Both draft and printed text included a lengthy treatment of the Pilgrims' criticism of royal councillors, designed to refute the claim that the Council now contained fewer noblemen than in the past. Henry recalled his first Council back in 1509, in which 'I note none but two, worthy calling noble.' Now his Council was overflowing with noblemen 'both of birth and condition'. He listed them in detail, along with two knights who did not have peerages at all, but whom he clearly considered appropriate to include: Treasurer Sir William Fitzwilliam and Comptroller Sir William Paulet. 'Now how far be ye abused, to reckon that then there were mo[re] noblemen in our Privy Council, than now?' he concluded triumphantly. A silence shouted out from this practical syllogism. The peer whose name was conspicuously absent was Lord Cromwell of Wimbledon, and there was no mention of the office of Lord Privy Seal either, even though Henry troubled to name those of Cromwell's two friends Fitzwilliam and Paulet. Instead the reference to Cromwell was oblique, linked directly to that other unnamed Councillor Archbishop Cranmer, and breathtakingly equivocal in contemplating their joint fates:

Where ye, the Commons, do name certain of our Council to be subverters
both of God's law and the laws of this realm; we do take them and repute
them as just and true executors, both of God's laws, and ours, as far as their
commissions under us do extend. And if any of our subjects can duly prove
the contrary, we shall proceed against them, and all other offenders therein,
according to justice, as to our estate and dignity royal doth appertain . . .
And one thing amongst others maketh me think that this slander should be
untrue: because it proceedeth from that place which is both so far distant
from where they inhabit, and also from those people, which never heard
them preach nor yet knoweth any part of their conversation.

This was open-ended musing rather than ringing defence. It positively
invited denunciation of those unnamed, and could not have been written
with Cromwell anywhere near the King's chamber. In fact he was not in
permanent residence at Windsor at this time, but commuting from Mortlake or The Rolls; so Thomas Heneage and Fitzwilliam had to write to
him urgently from Windsor on 5 November, telling him to intercept
Ellerker and Bowes after they had left the castle, to stop them going
north from London.[75] Cromwell was sometimes away for days at a time
at this crucial juncture, causing another Pilgrim emissary at Court, Percival Cresswell, looking round the Council board at Windsor, to conclude
that he had been dismissed from their number.[76] For a day or two, there
was a real possibility that this might happen. At least Cromwell had
Ralph Sadler to keep him informed of danger – and, in the end, this first
version containing the King's betrayal of all the Lord Privy Seal's service
never reached the North. Was it the very text taken from Ellerker and
Bowes when they were intercepted?

Berthelet's printed version, among several expansions, reveals a major
addition amid the King's discussion of his Council. Cranmer's name was
inserted to head the names of the bishops, and there then followed a
strong character reference for two other figures hated by the rebels:

And for because it is more than necessary, to have some of our Privy Council learned in the laws, and acquainted with the policies and practices of the
world, we, by the advice of our whole Council before named, did elect and
choose into our Privy Council, and also into their rooms, Sir Thomas Audley knight, our Chancellor, and the Lord Cromwell, Keeper of our Privy
Seal, thinking them men in all our opinions most meet for the same rooms.[77]

Given that explicit support, the sting was removed from the later passage
about the naming and proving of 'certain of our Council'. That was
nevertheless retained unaltered.

The newly endorsed councillors are therefore given carefully bounded treatment, but at least Cromwell, Cranmer and Audley now had the King's explicit backing. This represents a crucial shift of atmosphere in Court politics during that first week of November. By 11 November Gervase Clifton, a young Nottinghamshire gentleman serving in the royal army at Nottingham, had reported back to the Earl of Derby's servant Richard Banks news of how the royal negotiations with Ellerker and Bowes had concluded – both Clifton and Banks had known Cromwell since the days when he was much involved in the affairs of Wolsey's wards, of whom Clifton had been one. The King insisted just as in his draft reply that he would 'be at his liberty and to choose his Council at his pleasure', but now there was a difference: 'he will not forego my Lord of the Privy Seal for no man living.'[78] Late in November, relying on his London informants, Aske had told Lord Darcy gloomily, 'The King lieth at Richmond, and Cromwell only the ruler about him.' Richmond was a significantly unusual choice of retreat from Windsor for the King: not a palace where he had spent much time since boyhood, and needing significant repair in 1536. It was, however, very near Mortlake – and invariably the secret of winning King Henry's favour was to contrive to remain as close to him as possible.[79]

After a terrifying moment of peril, Cromwell was safe. The royal armies were still dangerously weak in relation to the thousands of insurgents across a swathe of the North, and the appearance of concession and conciliation must continue, particularly in religion; hence the retention of that passage in the printed text suggesting that the King would listen to complaints against his ministers. Yet that did not stop the reviser of the King's original draft adding a page and a half in print vigorously defending the suppression of monasteries, with detailed and accurate historical examples right back to Edward III, taking in on the way 'the Cardinal of York' and his suppressions 'for a College in Oxford'. Such a positive mention of Wolsey, possibly the first in a government publication since his fall, reeks of Cromwell's editorial hand.[80]

At this moment of balance, it was especially important to rein in aggressive evangelicals in southern England. Some of them were taking their lead from a high-profile and confrontational sermon at Paul's Cross preached by Bishop Hugh Latimer on 5 November. Latimer exploited the epistle text of the day from Ephesians (about putting on 'the whole armour of God') to create an extended military metaphor of evangelical faith as weaponry. He scathingly attacked the northerners, added ominous remarks about some of his episcopal colleagues unnamed, and vigorously rejected the common characterization of evangelical religion as 'the New Learning'. As was not unusual, Latimer was pleased with his own performance, but it is not difficult to see how it would enrage traditionalists.[81] A week later, a prominent evangelical London merchant, Robert Packington, was sensationally murdered with a handgun on a city street. There followed the arrest and imprisonment of a series of leading 'heretical' preachers, including Robert Barnes, who had preached with fury at Packington's funeral.

The round-up might seem at first sight illogical, but it is likely that it was a decision by Cromwell, both as a gesture to please conservatives and as protective custody for his protégés. It was he who had commissioned Latimer to preach in his absence, and the Bishop's rather defensive account of his peroration suggests that the Lord Privy Seal was not pleased with the result. That move was followed on 19 November by a royal circular to the bishops ordering them to implement the Ten Articles agreed by Convocation in the summer, and to crack down on radical preaching and the like.[82] All this action represented a concerted orchestration of soothing conservatism, which continued as negotiations moved to what seemed to most of the Pilgrims to be a satisfactory conclusion in the first week of December, including a general pardon, the prospect of a Parliament summoned to York, all suppressed monasteries restored and a freeze on further monastic dissolutions. With a settlement agreed, the King finally moved to spend Christmas at Greenwich Palace on 22 December. He took advantage of the blockage of the Thames by ice to travel from Whitehall not by barge but on horseback in procession through Westminster and the City, all the way down to a river crossing in the East End.[83]

This last-minute royal public outing was turned into a massive display of traditionalist festivity and loyalty: 'the streets richly behanged with rich gold and arras; the four Orders of friars standing in Fleet Street in copes of gold with crosses and candlesticks and censers', and so on through City streets: Bishop of London and abbots and cathedral choir and two priests from every City church, gildsmen, noise, triumphal cheers. Unrecorded by Charles Wriothesley who chronicled all this was my Lord Privy Seal sitting in his house at The Rolls, within earshot just off Fleet Street, checking amid much correspondence that all was going to plan. The perfect culmination to restoring harmony in the realm, friars and abbots and all, it was virtually the last time such a scene could have taken place in Henry's capital, though no one could know that at the time. One reassuring letter Cromwell wrote from The Rolls that same festive 22 December went to the Abbot of Kirkstead in Lincolnshire, which the Abbot received with joy, grateful that he was 'having pity and charity upon me'; his monks had turned up with their staff at the Louth demonstrations in October, so he had need to worry. He was hanged in March 1537.[84]

The government had made an apparently almost complete surrender to the Pilgrims' demands. Yet the Pilgrims' delight in their victory was utterly misplaced. The fatal fact remained: Cromwell was still in place. Both King and minister were furious at what they had been made to agree, and were just waiting for a chance to overturn it. Both were good at keeping their counsel; and what better time could there be to show spurious goodwill than at Christmas? An extraordinary royal house-party ensued. Aske was invited to lead a delegation of northern gentry to spend Christmas with the Court at Greenwich, under safe conduct until Twelfth Night. Such an extravagant gesture must have helped to quell his doubts. He spent part of the festivities writing his own account of the Pilgrimage, at the King's request.[85] The Duke of Norfolk was also there, but it is doubtful whether Cromwell spent much time in the presence of either adversary. His son Gregory arrived back to spend Christmas with him after an East Anglian stay of nearly nine months, their longest sep-aration ever. Richard Southwell seemed to regret the youth's departure from Woodrising.[86]

Aske duly left Greenwich in secrecy on Twelfth Night and hastened back to Yorkshire, and Norfolk rode away for some well-earned rest at Kenninghall Lodge, preparatory to resuming what turned out to be a prolonged lieutenancy in the North. Cromwell was not at Greenwich to see them off. He was in his own house at The Rolls, sorting out the government's financial woes, and firing off menacing letters to begin examinations of suspects. It must have been a particular satisfaction to open a letter of 4 January from the Coventry Carthusians, nervously let-ting him know they had unwittingly been harbouring none other than the fugitive Vicar of Louth, Thomas Kendall, who in his militant sermon after Michaelmas had triggered the whole conflagration.[87] Kendall was hanged on 29 March 1537, by which time many others were sharing his fate, enemies of the regime and of the Lord Privy Seal.

The Pilgrimage was a watershed in Tudor England and in Cromwell's career. It so nearly succeeded, and so nearly destroyed him, revealing a stark and much simpler new configuration of politics. No longer did Anne Boleyn's existence complicate England's ideological divide, yoking together those of otherwise disparate views who supported or detested her. The injustices done to Queen Katherine and Princess Mary became far more obviously a cause allied to traditional religion, and the golden memory of Cardinal Wolsey ebbed in its capacity to bind Cromwell to those of very different religious outlook. Former friends and allies, even courtiers who had helped him enter the King's service like William Fitzwilliam and William Paulet, now became much more ambiguous in their relationship to him – even, perhaps, opponents. He would not have forgotten their inclusion in that poisonous royal draft of early November. That was a future problem. In the meantime, many more than Thomas Kendall faced retribution.

17

The Reckoning: 1537

The formal position at the beginning of 1537 was that the Pilgrims had secured everything they wanted – short of the removal of Thomas Cromwell. One permanent change in Henry's government was the definition of a small set of councillors around the King as his 'Privy Council'. This was not a new term: it had often been used over the previous decade, either to distinguish those councillors meeting at Westminster from those named to the Council in the Marches of Wales, the Council in the North or other subsidiary conciliar bodies, or as a shorthand description for councillors attendant on the King for a particular purpose. So Cromwell was addressed on letters in summer 1532 as 'of the King's Privy Council' while he was one of the group intensively working on the all-important agreement with France. The usage from 1537 was new, implying a set number of people specifically named to that position, no more than twenty or so. The phrase continued into the early Stuart age to describe the main body for executive government, and still remains fossilized in the British governmental system.[1]

Geoffrey Elton saw this change as part of Thomas Cromwell's 'Revolution in Government', formalizing executive power and taking it 'out of Court'. That puts the matter the wrong way round. Until the fall of Anne Boleyn in 1536, Cromwell thrived on indeterminacy in government, which allowed full rein to his improvisatory skill. After that, his own position crystallized much more clearly into office and formal honour, and the Pilgrimage was at least in part an expression of fury at that development. The crisis in royal government which followed nearly destroyed him in early November. The King, in the printed *Answer* to the Pilgrims, publicly used that phrase 'Privy Council', implying that the whole Council had recommended Cromwell to the monarch as suitable for office.[2] That made him one Councillor among several. He thus paid a price for survival: this newly formalized body sat not as a vehicle for his power, but to check it. The Privy Council's further formalization, with its own clerk and minute-book, occurred immediately on his fall in 1540: a move designed to prevent any fresh Thomas Cromwell from emerging to usurp the power now distributed among Henry VIII's closest advisers.[3]

From now on, Cromwell became far more single-minded in pursuing evangelical reformation. He would still have to step very carefully, for he was conscious of many enemies. His new caution may explain why his protégé printer William Marshall, arrested in the little conservative purge of November 1536, never rejoined Cromwell's stable of radical publishers.[4] Monks, friars and traditional-minded nobility had all revealed themselves as seeking Cromwell's destruction. At the beginning of 1537 he did not yet have the sheaves of depositions which he and his assistants extracted from the frightened men rounded up during the spring, but he knew enough already, from all that had happened.

Henry Clifford Earl of Cumberland, not the greatest of intellects but impeccably loyal to the Crown throughout the crisis, put it clearly (though tactlessly) on 12 January 1537 in making excuses to Cromwell for not sending any letters to him during the Pilgrimage: 'the commons in every quarter throughout this country are so wilfully minded against you, in case any man should have chanced to have been taken therewith, he had [would have] died without help; and as yet they continue in the same fury against you, so that in case any man speak of you, he is despised of all the country.'[5] Cromwell would therefore have no compunction in encouraging an already vengeful King to deceit and savagery. The policy was laid out in a memorandum of mid-December (maybe from Cromwell himself): divide the gentry from the commons, and bombard the North with preaching on national unity and the sinfulness of rebellion, while quietly preparing institutions of government in the hands of proven loyalists, led by the Duke of Norfolk.[6] The rebels were given a comprehensive pardon as part of the settlement, but that only applied to their actions up to the moment of the pardon, and if anything else should happen, punishment could begin.

Something else did happen: a rising in the East Riding of Yorkshire as early as the second week of January 1537. Among several bills of complaint by then circulating, one document best expresses the swiftly rising tide of suspicion and disillusionment among the common people, and it may have served as their main manifesto. Twenty days had passed since the agreement, the deadline for summoning a Parliament at York, and still no sign of an assembly, it noted. 'Cromwell and other evil counsellors should have been banished the Court, and they are now in higher favour than ever they were before.' Worse still, the paper now ranged 'Captain' Aske among the traitors: in the south, he 'had great rewards given to betray the commoners; and since that he came home, they [the government] have made Hull against the commons ready to receive ships by the sea to destroy all the North parts. Wherefore now is the time to arise.'[7]

With Aske discredited among many former Pilgrims, and gentry and nobility reasserting their normal loyalty to the Court, the gentry leader to whom the renewed rebels now turned was a rather strange figure: Sir Francis Bigod. With a surname redolent of twelfth-century Norman nobility and ancient estates in Yorkshire, he was a convincing local man, but in every other respect a bizarre choice, long an active evangelical client of Cromwell. Strangest of all, Bigod had published a substantial tract (probably in 1535), explaining why the widespread impropriation of parish revenues by monasteries was a thoroughly bad thing. Yet after he had been captured by the Pilgrims in October while trying to flee to London, he proved their most successful brand plucked from the fire of Thomas Cromwell, and had thrown himself into the work of dismantling all that Cromwell meant in the North. Struggling inside a troubled personality were two conflicting identities, and loyalty to his local roots won out.

Bigod was partner in rebellion with a yeoman from the Beverley area, John Hallom, who had been unhappy about the December agreement from the beginning. Hallom seems to have been entirely traditional in his religious outlook, petitioning the Pilgrim leadership in late November to ensure punishment for Cromwell, Cranmer, Audley, Latimer and the usual evangelical suspects.[8] Two causes seem to have united their contrasting outlooks. The first was Bigod's personal exploration of his evangelical faith, which made him decide that the royal supremacy was wicked. The second was their common resentment of Cromwell's nominees for head of Watton and Guisborough Priories, respectively Holgate and Pursglove; Aske, conscientiously offended by the illegality of deposing this pair during the Pilgrimage, restored them both to office. It is difficult to decide whether Hallom or Bigod was the leading spirit in rebellion, but the most recent historians of these events are inclined to credit Hallom, which would make more sense than looking to a confused and idealistic gentleman, whatever his charisma. Bigod's decisive contribution was to turn his literary talents to rousing new circulars, oaths and proclamations, and to persuade the commons of the East Riding that great multitudes waited once again in the North and West for a call to rebellion.

It was all in vain. An attempt to take Hull on 16 January showed the weakness of the commons, now enjoying minimal co-operation from any gentry or nobility. Hallom was captured and executed by the end of the month. Bigod had reached Cumberland by the time he was seized by government forces on 10 February. His flight to the north-west reflected the fact that disturbances rumbled on there, a pale reflection of his fantasies of renewed rebellion, with barns being raided, enclosures cast down and traditional liturgical observances turned into studied acts of rebellion. Dentdale, where the very first stirs had begun in September 1536, was one of the main centres supplying men and leadership for the last major clash with loyalist forces outside Carlisle, a week after Bigod's capture. Before his execution, his curiously tangled relationship with Cromwell was illustrated in a long letter to the Lord Privy Seal. This confessed his part in the risings, but ended with a plea for favour for his evangelical preacher-protégé William Jerome, the ex-monk of Canterbury. Cromwell listened: at the end of May he instructed his servant and Rector at Stepney, Richard Leighton (so hated by the Pilgrims), to present Jerome as Vicar of Stepney, after the renegade monk had been equipped with a dispensation from monastic life in order to take up the post. Only five days later Bigod was executed. One hopes he knew about this gesture of grace.[9]

February and March were mostly occupied with mopping-up operations, but fresh small-scale resistance still flared, each incident an excuse for more government retribution. The most serious was actually a gentry conspiracy by Sir John Bulmer and his common law wife Margaret Cheyney intended to raise Ryedale and areas beyond, but by now arrests, trials and the beginning of executions were sapping any enthusiasm among the commons who had sustained the stirs over six months. This last effort produced the most horrible of all the deaths in the long programme of punishment after the Pilgrimage: on 25 May Margaret was burned at the stake in Smithfield, the fate reserved not just for heretics but for female traitors. Only a year before Anne Boleyn had likewise been threatened with burning for her supposed treason, to the alarm of some judges. This time, no dissent was expressed.[10]

Among those examined, tried and executed were some very senior political figures, now firmly defined as traitors and treated accordingly. One was John Lord Hussey, whose main crime was to dither and, as a nobleman of Lincolnshire, not to show himself strong enough to lead the county's trouble-makers away from full-scale revolt. Nevertheless, there was more: Hussey had drifted into the group of traditional-minded noblemen (still represented as far into King Henry's personal circle as Lord Montague and the Marquess of Exeter) who habitually offloaded their anger at Cromwell's religious policy on to Ambassador Chapuys. In 1534 Hussey even went so far as to seek Charles V's intervention in England on behalf of the true faith. Cromwell must have known enough about such mutterings to decide that Hussey must have an exemplary if mercifully swift death. There is rich irony here, because Lord Hussey was not some scion of ancient nobility resentful of parvenus, a Percy or a Dacre, but one of the last survivors of the clique of ambitious and efficient 'new men' in government, a collective Thomas Cromwell *avant la lettre* who had been the focus of so much public anger in Henry VII's regime.[11]

Then came Thomas Lord Darcy of Templehurst, degraded from the Order of the Garter on conviction by his peers and eventually executed on 30 June 1537. It was said later that Cromwell had promised the Lords at Darcy's trial 'that he would do that was in him that the said Lord Darcy should neither lose life nor goods', but matters turned out differently, despite the rather nebulous character of the evidence against the accused.[12] In the judgement of the most authoritative recent student of Darcy's behaviour, he 'neither planned nor encouraged the rebellion of October 1536. But he was guilty of flirting with rebellion.'[13] He had not exploited his capacity to raise a defensive army against the Pilgrims and, knowing his military weakness, had surrendered Pontefract Castle to the rebels, providing them with their most imposing stronghold and place of assembly. Even more than Hussey, Darcy had made a heavy investment both financially and emotionally in traditional religion. He hated the 'New Learning' and, like Hussey, talked treasonably to Chapuys about Scottish or imperial invasion. A short deposition from a Yorkshire chantry priest during the trial recorded in Cromwell's own hand provided some of the most damning evidence: it included Darcy's wistful remark on first hearing of the Lincolnshire rising, 'If they had done this three years ago, it had been a much better world than it now is.'[14]

Yet others with similar black marks came through the scrutinies of spring 1537 and survived. There was certainly no witch-hunt against Darcy's family, as we will see from the cordial relations of his second son Sir Arthur Darcy with Thomas Cromwell (see below, pp. 423–5). Something more about Darcy may have decided his fate; something that would have given the Lord Privy Seal particular satisfaction. The evidence was supplied (ironically in the circumstances) by the Duke of Norfolk, who in late April reported to Cromwell his discovery of a cache of papers from 1528–9 in Darcy's extensive archive. They related to his plans with other noblemen (Norfolk himself included) to destroy Cardinal Wolsey; the documents included a mass of detailed charges in Darcy's own hand against Wolsey, for extravagance, vainglory and government mismanagement.[15] Not many people, least of all Thomas Howard, would have taken much interest in this material, for it was hardly relevant to the current charges, and indeed after Wolsey's fall it could hardly be regarded as treasonous. Yet one person that spring took a very great interest. As charges against Darcy were framed, clerks catalogued his actions and his archive. In the margins, Cromwell carefully annotated items which could be used against him because they postdated the December pardon.

One version of these listings opened with a memorandum by Cromwell's servant Richard Pollard which had no immediate relevance, since it consisted of two notes relating to Wolsey: 'First, the destruction of the Cardinal in the Chancery. Item, the book that the lord Darcy made against the Cardinal.'[16] As if that were not enough raking over of old coals, there survives a further memorandum of 'Articles against Lord

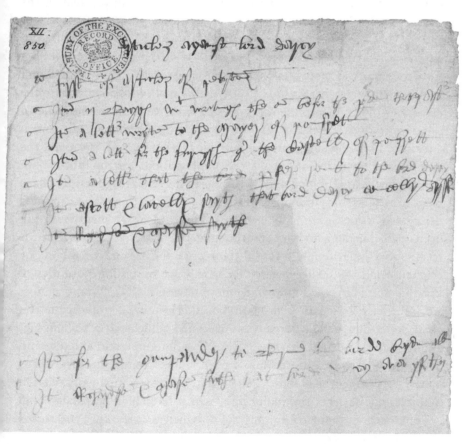

In a memorandum in Cromwell's hand of 'Articles agenst Lord Darcy', he adds two items kept separate at the foot, since they do not relate to the Pilgrimage of Grace: 'It'm For the gunpowder to burne my Lorde Cardinall' and 'It'm Richardson and Mason saithe that Lorde Darcy d'd off theym'.

Darcy', on a scrap of paper in Cromwell's own most scrawling hand. It is a brief classification of the evidence, noting the most damning items, such as supplying Pontefract Castle and counselling Aske. In an after-thought below, Cromwell made two extraordinary notes: 'Item For the gunpowder to burn my Lord Cardinal. Item Richardson and Mason saith that Lord Darcy delivered of them.'[17] This could not be more startling. It suggests a northern nobleman of the Pilgrimage of Grace anticipating Guy Fawkes, another unsuccessful Roman Catholic conspirator. Did Cromwell really believe that Darcy's plotting back in 1529 included this precocious plan for terrorist action? Yes or no, in the course of a year, he had achieved a double act of revenge against the Cardinal's two most implacable though contrasting enemies. First was Anne Boleyn; now came Thomas Darcy.

After the Pilgrimage, religion could make old friendships grow cold: at Court, no one was more identified with the evangelical cause than Crom-well. An embarrassing episode exposed this reality from an unexpected direction. In summer 1537, while Lord Darcy was still in the Tower of London awaiting execution, Cromwell made final arrangements to send a team of four English commissioners into Ireland to assess the military and political situation and make recommendations for the future. Over the last few years, Ireland and its problems had cost the English govern-ment terrifying sums of money, perhaps £46,000 in three years; the King demanded action on the ruinous price of his Lordship.[18] That would have been reason enough for the commission, but correspondence from the Irish Council alarmingly revealed the factional divisions in Dublin gov-ernment, and the depressing reality that since becoming Lord Deputy Lord Leonard Grey had only made matters worse.

Grey was drawn into Irish factionalism. He was partisan against the great Butler clan, and favoured what remained of the lately rebellious Ger-aldine affinity; beyond that, he governed in an autocratic and arbitrary fashion. Yet there might be faults on all sides. Cromwell tended not to believe everything the Dublin Council told him. He consistently drew on multiple reports from the island and, where he judged necessary, made appointments without consulting them. Much to their fury, he treated them as a subsidiary English provincial council, like the Council in the Marches of Wales or the Council of Calais. That in itself was a new bal-ance between Westminster and Dublin; consistent with that shift in power, while the English commissioners were in Ireland, from September 1537 to April 1538, they effectively superseded Lord Leonard's authority.[19]

The commission has its own significance. It was Cromwell's greatest intervention in Irish government reform: it established a more regular system of English garrisons, reflecting his belief that the English Lordship in Ireland could be treated like a giant version of Calais. It produced many more direct links between Irish notables and the Lord Privy Seal, and thoroughly equipped one of its members, Sir Anthony St Leger, for his later service as Lord Deputy. The commission's work additionally has a precious archival value, for its secretary compiled a little letter-book of Cromwell's early letters to the commissioners, useful not only for what they say but also for pinning down his whereabouts in summer and early autumn 1537. The book may owe its existence to an embarrassment: more than a month after setting out from Court, the commissioners had to confess that while Cromwell was firing off multiple letters to them they were still at Holyhead on Anglesey, kicking their heels waiting for the right wind to take them to Dublin. After that, a letter-book would be a help in making sure all his demands were met.[20]

Even more unfortunately, one of the commissioners went severely off the rails, in the process furnishing some revealing and unkind glimpses of the atmosphere around the King in the first half of 1537, and of Thomas Cromwell's position in particular. Ireland had this disorienting effect on some Englishmen: it must have been exhilaration at arriving in an exotic society where nevertheless a great many people spoke English, no doubt linked to being hospitably plied with unfamiliar forms of alcohol. Cromwell's financial servant William Body suffered the same experience in 1536, on an earlier fact-finding tour which had also brought out the worst in him.[21] In this case, the victim of Ireland Syndrome was George Paulet, brother to Sir William, now Treasurer of the Household. Very soon after arriving, George began showing off to his new Irish friends with astonishing indiscretions.

News of Paulet's words got back to Cromwell before the commissioners returned, maybe around Christmas 1537; the two Kentish men among the four commissioners, Sir Anthony St Leger and Sir Thomas Moyle, discreetly took a lead in gathering up accusations for him. St Leger and Moyle liaised with Cromwell's Anglo-Irish confidant Robert Cowley, who in a letter written before the commissioners had even set out for home namechecked as witnesses other people Cromwell considered reliable in Ireland: William Brabazon and John Allen the Irish Master of the Rolls.[22] Cowley, 'fearing that by secret malicious practice, the King's Majesty (as God forbid) should be misinformed upon your Lordship, if others would be timorous to advertise your Lordship of the truth', provided specimens of malice from the man he discreetly described as 'the person': 'there was no lord or gentleman in England that loved or favoured your

Lordship because your Lordship was so great a taker of money, for your Lordship would do or speak for no man, but all for money.' That was standard abuse which Cromwell would have heard before, and he could smile at the assertion that he had sent a Welshman to St Patrick's Purgatory in Ulster to inquire about dangerous prophecies. Cowley had no need to repeat the worst; that was waiting in the depositions St Leger had gathered.

The depositions show that Paulet quickly decided to break ranks with his fellow-commissioners in their capacity as neutral external observers. He threw in his lot with the Fitzgerald faction, furious at what they saw as Cromwell's partisanship for the Butlers. As had already become apparent, such Geraldine supporters had the sympathy of Lord Leonard Grey. Paulet spoke dismissively of the commission itself as a device of Cromwell's: he 'and his fellows were sent hither in commission but for a flim-flam to stop the imagination of the King and his Council', in other words, to put them off from making their own decision.[23] All Paulet's negative remarks about Cromwell, with his Geraldine audience in mind, emphasized Cromwell's shaky position at Court in the wake of the Pilgrimage of Grace. He said to Chief Justice Aylmer, 'The lord Privy Seal drew every day towards his death, and that he escaped very hardly at the last insurrection.'[24] Master of the Rolls Allen enlarged on this in his report of Paulet's words:

> I would not be in his case for all that ever he hath, for the King beknaveth him twice a week, and sometime knocketh him well about the pate; and yet when he hath been well pummelled about the head and shaken up, as it were a dog, he will come out into the great chamber, shaking of the bush [head] with as merry a countenance as though he might rule all the roost. I (saith he [Paulet]) standing at the lower end of the chamber perceive these matters well enough, and laugh at his fashion and ruff [pride], and then my brother [William Paulet] and my lord Admiral [Sir William Fitzwilliam] must drive a mean to reconcile him to the King again.[25]

Perhaps of all the things Paulet said, this naming of names was the most damaging, both for Cromwell's prestige in Ireland and for his vulnerability at Court in early 1537. Chief Justice Aylmer heard him tell a similar tale to Lord Leonard, with one more significant character added: on Paulet's return to England, 'he would laugh at this gear [talk] with my lord of Norfolk, Master Treasurer [William Paulet], and my lord Admiral when they were secretly together,' and 'would hit [deal a blow to] my Lord [Butler] and me [Aylmer], and that none of us would know from whence it came, by secret information to the King'.[26] So here, at least in

Paulet's account, was a line-up of conservative-minded courtiers ready to mock Cromwell's turbulent relationship with King Henry and damage his Irish allies. Two were his early friends and supporters, though another, the Duke, had never been one.

What were the implications of this in Court politics? In normal circumstances, leading courtiers like William Paulet or Admiral Fitzwilliam would heal breaches between monarch and minister, who everyone knew were both men quick to lose their temper. The convention in such contests was for the King always to win, as Cromwell well understood: hence the rueful smirk as he came into the great chamber 'shaking of the bush'. A royal slap accepted was a strategic withdrawal, before further efforts to get his way: his accustomed 'tempering' of the King to which Ralph Sadler referred in autumn 1536 over the fate of the London Charterhouse. There were occasions in the next few years, however, when mediators held back from smoothing over conflict. Cromwell must now anticipate that possibility, reinforcing the stark message of his near-fall in November 1536. Not surprisingly, George Paulet paid for his astonishing indiscretions after his return home with a spell in the Tower of London, and he needed every ounce of credibility his brother possessed to resume any sort of career thereafter. His evident closeness to Lord Leonard Grey while in Ireland also permanently damaged Cromwell's trust in the Lord Deputy, for all his family ties.[27]

While the Duke of Norfolk and his assistants cleared up remnants of the renewed risings in the North in February 1537, Cromwell made it clear that the autumn's brief cosmetic show of reconciliation with traditional religion was over. In the privacy of diplomacy, he brutally rejected fresh overtures from Reginald Pole in December 1536. Pole used as intermediary his servant Michael Throckmorton, younger brother to that abrasive friend of Cromwell's Sir George Throckmorton. Michael might seem a good choice, since he was one of the cultured young Englishmen who had spent years in Italy, on warm terms with such Anglo-Italian clients of Cromwell as Thomas Starkey and Richard Morison, as well as a familiar figure to Cromwell himself. Nevertheless Pole's initiative could not have been worse timed, as King Henry prepared to betray his promises to the northern Pilgrims.

The chances of Michael Throckmorton's success were not improved when he fell seriously ill near Calais just before New Year 1537; that delayed his meeting with Cromwell at the point when Henry VIII took the measure of Robert Aske at Greenwich, and the English Court regained its self-confidence.[28] Yet, in any case, Pole's utter lack of political sense made a constructive outcome impossible. One can imagine Cromwell's satirical reaction to Pole's follow-up proposal that 'if he [Cromwell] can obtain [royal consent] (my Lord himself being so pleased), I think he [Pole] would be most best content to speak with him of any other' in person – but in Flanders. This was less than six months after the death of William Tyndale at the hands of the imperial authorities in Flanders, trapped by men not a million miles from Pole's own circle of acquaintance. The offer came alongside Throckmorton's own awkward admission that he had returned to Rome in mid-February to find his master 'in a foul array and very strange apparel': his way of conveying the news that Pole was now a cardinal and the Pope's legate to England.[29]

Small hope, then, of a courteous exchange of views in Brussels. Quite the reverse: Cromwell and Henry regarded the offer of a meeting as nothing less than a trap (probably rightly), and promptly set up their own. As Pole arrived in Flanders in his official capacity as legate to England, they sought to arrange for him to be kidnapped and brought to England. The agents were Cromwell's closest friends over there: in Calais the Knight Porter Sir Thomas Palmer, and in Brussels the permanent English representative John Hutton. As Hutton probed Pole's movements and contacts, he realized that among his servants was the man who had betrayed William Tyndale to the authorities, Cromwell's former protégé Henry Phelips, who was now hand in glove with Michael Throckmorton.[30] Far from being an honest broker or even double agent, Throckmorton was Pole's man through and through. When Michael wrote again from Rome on 20 August 1537, acknowledging the hopelessness of the prospect that Cromwell might come to Flanders, Cromwell's reply was five sides of concentrated fury at the betrayal of personal friendship. It is not often that we have the chance of hearing my Lord Privy Seal at full throttle, a privilege best enjoyed at a safe chronological distance.[31]

Addressing Throckmorton throughout as 'Michael', Cromwell stormed, 'if you were either natural towards your country, or your family, you would not thus shame all your kin. I pray God they bide but the shame of it': those difficult but fundamentally loyal Throckmortons of Coughton Court. 'This am I sure of, though they by and by suffer no loss of goods, yet the least suspicion shall be enough to undo the greatest of them' – the greatest of them, of course, being Sir George. 'Wherefore if ye will yet turn to your country, and shew yourself sorry for that ye foolishly have done, I dare assure you ye shall find the King's Highness much more ready to seek commendation of clemency than of justice, at your faults.' As for the Cardinal, 'Pity it is that the folly of one brain-sick Poole, or, to say better, of one witless fool, should be the ruin of so great a family.'

Cromwell was in a good position to make those words prophetic. He made no bones about spelling out the King's inclination towards his former remittance-man: 'There may be found ways enough in Italy to rid a traitorous subject. Surely let him not think but where justice can take no place by process of law at home, some times she may be enforced to seek new means abroad.' These were two Anglo-Italians in correspondence: the implications could hardly be clearer.

Cromwell also renewed his pressure on the London Charterhouse; brutal threats once more became action, but he also made a genuine effort to reconcile to Henry's Church and Reformation a monastery in whose fate he was strikingly invested. Few matters have damaged his reputation as much as the Charterhouse. In April 1536 he had reinstated a monk to head the community in place of his lay commissioners; William Trafford remained in place unhappily heading the house while further dire fates befell his more consistently defiant brethren. Exiled members of the Charterhouse, Dom John Rochester and Dom James Walworth, were executed in the North on 11 May 1537. They had been removed from London to Hull soon after Trafford's arrival, and in the wake of the Pilgrimage they were caught up in the Duke of Norfolk's ruthless crackdown on those he defined as traitors: 'Two more wilful religious men in manner unlearned I think never suffered,' Howard observed to the King.[32] Their examination seems to have prompted a fresh and final attempt to get their mother house to conform. On 18 May 1537 Cromwell's vice-gerential commissioners Thomas Bedell (by now a veteran in visits to the Charterhouse) and Richard Gwent confronted the community with a demand for acceptance of the King as Supreme Head of the Church in England. Twenty agreed, ten refused.[33]

The fate of the ten refuseniks was to be sent to Newgate, confined in the worst conditions which that never hospitable prison offered. Within a month, five of the ten were dead and two others appeared on the point of death.[34] Their deaths have provoked some of the darkest accusations against Henry VIII and Cromwell amid many that cannot be denied; but the notion that they were deliberately starved to death is a myth, founded on the heroic actions of Thomas More's adopted daughter Margaret Giggs, who brought them comfort in their imprisonment. Such a calculated atrocity is impossible, given that a great many eyes (many sympathetic) were upon them in London, including that vigilant observer John Husee, reporting back to his master Lord Lisle in Calais.[35] What seems to have happened, certainly suggested by Thomas Bedell's report to Cromwell that the Carthusians had died 'by the hand of God', was that they were carried off by an outbreak of infectious disease, the scourge of always crowded and ill-run Tudor prisons: perhaps typhus, or the plague which was particularly virulent in London that summer.

We know that more than one of the remaining five Carthusians survived, since a year later Bishop Hugh Latimer (a man less admirable the more one gets to know him, not least for his grim single-mindedness towards his enemies) complained to Cromwell about the mild conditions for the monks of the Charterhouse in Newgate, 'in a fair chamber more like to indurate [harden] than to mollify'.[36] In a curious triangulation of opposite partisan agendas, evidence against deliberate starvation is provided by the Carthusian hagiographer Maurice Chauncy, who wrote that when Cromwell heard that most of the monks had died he was furious, and said with an oath that he had had something far more unpleasant in mind for them.[37] No doubt Cromwell meant a public traitor's death; that would not have been out of character for him. One of the imprisoned monks, William Horne, listed as sick in Bedell's report of June 1537, survived another three years, when his execution was part of a fresh round of belated savagery from Henry VIII.

For all the wretchedness of the Carthusian deaths, the fact remains that in May 1537 Cromwell secured assent to the royal supremacy from the majority of the Charterhouse community, in fact two-thirds of them. Maurice Chauncy records with deep remorse and commendable honesty in the later version of his reminiscences that he was one; they were trying to preserve the community for the future. For the moment the monks must have felt justified, for the Charterhouse was still there. They were living on borrowed time: on the urging of Cromwell and Bedell, they formally surrendered their house to the King within a month of the fatal vote.[38] Perhaps this surrender was Cromwell's latest effort to 'temper' the King's fury with them. Meanwhile, as revealed in final suppression accounts at the end of 1538, they meticulously maintained their celebrated orchard and gardens.[39] This contrasts with the growing demoralization, asset-stripping and decay among the kingdom's friaries that year. No doubt gardening was a welcome distraction from Cromwell's widening Reformation.

The power of the Vice-Gerent in Spirituals found new uses in 1537. Building on his issue of ecclesiastical injunctions in summer 1536, Cromwell called together leading clergy under his own auspices – not a Convocation of Canterbury or York or a joint session of the two, but a body for which contemporaries found it difficult to provide a name, vaguely calling it an 'assembly'. It did in fact have a model in both past and future: the legatine synods for all England called by Cardinal Wolsey in 1519 and later by Cardinal Pole in Mary's reign for the restored Roman Catholic provinces of Canterbury and York. Once more Wolsey had set a pattern which Cromwell creatively adopted. We can be justified, therefore, in calling it a vice-gerential synod; it began meeting on 17 or 18 February 1537.[40]

The great advantage of such a new body, apart from the fact that it straddled the York/Canterbury border, was that since it had no exact precedent, its membership was up to Cromwell. If he needed any model for such a free-form assembly apart from Wolsey's, it was the secular Great Council, which was simply a gathering of whichever notables the King decided to choose. A Great Council had in fact just met for a number of days beginning on 26 January. It achieved little beyond showing that King Henry had decided to repudiate his agreement with the Pilgrims to summon a Parliament at York; subsequently in the Tudor age only Queen Mary briefly revived any such meeting. Cromwell's synod went on to be a good deal more drawn out and constructive than the January Great Council. It sat in the end for around six months, though increasingly as a private committee which the Vice-Gerent left to get on with doctrinal business: the goal was a comprehensive book-length statement of what the new Church of England believed. For its membership, he chose all the bishops of the kingdom able to attend (including Archbishop Lee of York) plus a hand-picked set of senior clergy, archdeacons and academics – notably, not a single monk or friar, suggesting that by now he did not see the regulars as having anything especially useful to contribute to the future of English theology.[41]

We are lucky to have another intervention of the garrulous Alexander Alesius to illuminate the early stage of the synod, while Cromwell still presided over it in person. Alesius had been forced out of his Cambridge lectureship during 1536 and was now in London badgering Cranmer and Cromwell for further support. His narrative formed part of an English polemical work printed in Germany (intended for subsequent Latin translation, since it was addressed to Johann Friedrich Elector of Saxony); it was too personal and indiscreet for any English printer to handle.[42] The Scots theologian's entrance to the synod came after a chance encounter with the Lord Privy Seal on the road to Westminster. Cromwell ordered him to accompany him to the meeting.[43] On Cromwell's entrance,

> all the bishops and prelates did rise up and did obeisance unto him as to their Vicar General; and after he had saluted them, he sat him down in the highest place, and right against him sat the Archbishop of Canterbury, after him the Archbishop of York, and then London, Lincoln, Salisbury,

Bath, Ely, Hereford, Chichester, Norwich, Rochester and Worcester and certain other whose names I have forgotten. All these did sit at a table covered with a carpet, with certain priests standing about them.[44]

The business that day concerned the sacraments – three or the traditional seven in number? – one of the issues left untidy in the Ten Articles the previous summer. Cromwell opened proceedings with a plea in the King's name for calm debate on the business solely on the basis of scripture, without reference to 'any papistical laws or by any authority of doctors or Councils', still less to Church tradition – tradition or 'unwritten verities' were a constant refuge for conservative theologians, who maintained the authority of 'unwritten verities' independent of scripture.

The bishops immediately divided on predictable party lines, set out accurately by Alesius, with Cranmer taking advantage of not being in the chair to put forward a frankly evangelical view of the sacraments, reducing them to the two central sacraments of eucharist and baptism, undeniably witnessed in scripture. Cromwell then showed how cavalier he could be, given the lack of fixed rules in his new assembly; he asked Alesius himself to speak, to the fury of the conservative Bishop of London, Stokesley. After some charged exchanges, the following day one of Cranmer's staff indicated that it might be better if the Scotsman held his peace, as some of the bishops resented his irregular presence there. Cromwell saw the point, but he made sure that Alesius left his notes for his intended speech for the benefit of Stokesley and others in the meeting.

Cromwell did not attend the gathering in person for more than a few days; he had plenty else to do, while the clergy's professional business was theological construction (and horsetrading). They continued this in a variety of less formal settings, where they might be less inclined to strike aggressive party attitudes, far into the summer. On the way, the synod was diverted from preparing doctrinal instruction by the need for some robust statements denouncing current papal plans for a General Council of the Church at Mantua. The King was still terrified of such a council formally denouncing him, backed by combined support from the King of France and the Holy Roman Emperor. Manuscript treatises clearly related to the synod survive on this subject, and an allied tract printed in 1538 by the royal press of Thomas Berthelet has often been attributed to Alesius; Cromwell would have found this a useful alternative means of occupying his talents.[45]

The synod's work on General Councils served the useful purpose of uniting the opposed camps in the episcopate, smoothing the way to steady evangelical encroachment on the uncomfortable doctrinal balance set out in the Ten Articles of 1536. The extent of evangelical success was evident when in autumn 1537 Berthelet published the synod's work, after much final tinkering by Bishop Foxe, as *The Institution of a Christian Man*. Reflecting the combined authorship of prelates and ecclesiastical dignitaries announced in its preface (interestingly not including the Vice-Gerent), it quickly acquired the informal name 'the Bishops' Book'. It was a long and comprehensive theological statement in terms which any thoughtful person could understand. In a manner pioneered for teaching documents by Martin Luther, it was structured on the principal Christian texts everyone would encounter from an early age: Apostles' Creed and Ten Commandments, Lord's Prayer and Ave Maria. Discussion of sacraments followed, now seven not three, though the four lesser sacraments (confirmation, ordination, unction, marriage) were carefully differentiated from the greater.[46]

This document was the high-water mark of evangelical doctrinal change in Henry VIII's Church. He wrote a rather lukewarm endorsement not in the end printed in the book; it would not have enhanced its credibility. He had in fact not completed his read-through by the publication date, and took some time after that, for understandable and tragic reasons after the death of his third Queen, but it was his custom in emotional crises to bury himself in theology, and he soon decided on a revision. He scribbled detailed comments on his copy, which after much theological sparring with Cranmer and others formed the basis of a rather different and more conservative text.[47] Events nevertheless postponed its publication until 1543, and in the meantime the Bishops' Book stood as the statement of English Church belief. Henry's lack of enthusiasm was more justified than he realized, because via a primer (lay devotional book) published by Cromwell's favoured printer William Marshall in 1535 certain passages entered the text which started life in the German of Martin Luther. It is another example of Cromwell quietly slipping unacceptably evangelical material past the King's notice.

One distinctive feature of the Bishops' Book had a major effect on the future of the Church of England: its numbering of one basic building-block of the text, the Ten Commandments. The importance of this requires some explanation. Although all Christians agree on the sacred number ten, they have never agreed on how to divide up the biblical passages which make up the Commandments into that number. The issue is whether to classify a rather long-winded commandment to destroy 'graven images' as a separate free-standing commandment, or amalgamate it with the snappy first commandment to 'have no other Gods but me'. In the latter case, the rationale is to assume that this anomalously wordy piece of text is just a comment on the basic thought (having done that, the total of ten commandments is made up by dividing commands about covetousness towards the end of the commandment material). If on the other hand the graven image commandment stands separately, as Commandment Number Two, rather than Commandment Number 1B, then it forms one of God's basic priorities. The issue extended in the Reformation beyond graven images as such, since devotion to images shaded into devotion to physical objects and locations generally, in shrines and sacred places. That in turn was the basis of the vast medieval enterprise of pilgrimage.

Protestants all agreed that shrines and pilgrimages were bad ideas, but they flatly disagreed on numbering the Commandments, and therefore on the status of sacred art in church. Because Luther considered sacred images not a matter of importance either way, he was as ready as Roman Catholics to downgrade the image prohibition into an appendix to the First Commandment, and indeed he often even omitted it when discussing the Commandments. It was the Swiss who made the change back to a separate image prohibition and an independent Second Commandment, recalling that this was the ancient custom of the Jews and indeed of the Eastern Christian Churches (Easterners scrupulously observe it by not allowing 'graven' or carved images in churches, but making a great many painted images on flat painted surfaces: icons). The Swiss were followed by all Protestants in the Reformed tradition. The Reformed made idolatry into a major theological issue, one of the greatest human sins and a constant danger to the worship of God, especially in church buildings.[48]

Which way would the Bishops' Book jump on this vital matter of numbering the Commandments? It parted company with Luther as well as with the Pope and joined the Swiss in making the prohibition of graven images the Second Commandment. Its discussion under that heading was admittedly not long and was also cautiously phrased, concentrating on inappropriate devotion to images, but this was the first sign that Protestant sympathies within Henry's Church might move away from Luther towards the Reformed. It came in the very year that the young Züricher Rudolph Gwalther paid his visit to England.[49] In Cromwell's absence, Archbishop Cranmer or Bishop Foxe chaired the discussions which resolved the question; in the end the bishops rejected a draft text from conservative bishops which would have included an explicit defence of shrines and pilgrimage in the Bishops' Book. Cromwell would fully have backed the evangelical bishops in approving this change of direction. It was in line with the attacks which from summer 1535 his visitors made on relics in monasteries, and with his wider campaign against shrines and venerated images, which actually began at the same time as his synod, in winter 1537.

The pioneering example was a dissolution under the 1536 Act of a small Cluniac priory on the Norfolk coast. Bromholm happened to be home to a fragment of the True Cross, filched from Constantinople during its Western occupation in the thirteenth century. This 'Good Rood of Bromholm' had become a major national goal of pilgrimage. Revenue from pilgrims made up for the priory's modest endowment in land which nevertheless brought it within the scope of the dissolution Act. No comparably charismatic sacred site in the kingdom had so far faced closure, but Cromwell followed the logic of the Act, using as his agent Richard Southwell, Gregory Cromwell's Norfolk host from the previous year. Bromholm was dissolved in February 1537 and Southwell's brother got the lease, specifically including the income from offerings to the Rood.[50]

That provision might suggest some uncertainty in government circles about tackling such a popular focus of devotion: might the relic and pilgrimage survive the closure of the host monastery? Southwell seems to have had an equal sliver of doubt when he wrote to Cromwell on 2 February: he had taken possession of the Rood, he said, 'which in case it may so stand with your pleasure, I will personally (after the suppression finished) bring unto you, or more soon as it shall like you [to] devise for the convenient conveyance of the same'. By the end of the month Southwell had his instructions; Cromwell wanted custody of the relic in London. It duly travelled down in the reliable care of one of Southwell's friends, the ex-Prior of Pentney, another little Norfolk house dissolved that month.[51] Six months later, the discussion of the Second Commandment finally agreed in the Bishops' Book went out of its way to praise representations of the Rood in churches 'as an open book' of Christ's Passion; evidently this did not apply to relics which purported to be the real thing.[52]

The Good Rood of Bromholm began a collection of such items quarantined in Cromwell's houses for eventual destruction. The fact that this was the future direction of policy was confirmed in May, when the Duke of Norfolk included in his thorough and otherwise unsentimental survey of the late priory at Bridlington in Yorkshire a proposal to save the shrine of St John of Bridlington in the priory church, now designated for the use of the parish there. Cromwell and the King briskly vetoed that idea and told him to send the metal fabric of the shrine down to London. Interestingly, the message Cromwell relayed to Norfolk was that the King would have the shrine taken down 'to the intent that his people should not be seduced in the offering of their money'. This was a very Erasmian sentiment, one of the points at which King Henry's jackdaw's nest of theology happened to coincide with the developing Protestant Reformation.[53]

A parallel story of reformation this summer was Cromwell's final securing of an officially authorized vernacular Bible. A Bible available for all to read or hear was essential if Henry's idiosyncratic Church could make any claim to evangelical godliness. The Vice-Gerent pursued this goal in close partnership with Archbishop Cranmer and an ideologically committed printer, Richard Grafton, who supervised the production in Antwerp of yet another development of William Tyndale's texts into a complete Bible. This time the general editor was John Rogers, chaplain to the English merchants in Antwerp when Tyndale was in the city, and the man responsible for rescuing unpublished parts of the pioneer translator's work on his arrest.[54]

Obviously the name of King Henry's *bête noire* could not be mentioned in the new complete work, so it appeared under the name of the non-existent 'Thomas Matthew', and so is known to posterity as the 'Matthew Bible'.[55] (See Plate 38.) Cromwell had undoubtedly been preparing the ground for the King to accept this and give it a royal licence, because when on 4 August Cranmer wrote to him asking him to show Henry a copy for approval, only a few days passed before assent came through to authorize it for general sale. Henry was in cheerful mood, with his Queen's pregnancy reaching its end. The authorization of the Matthew Bible remains one of Thomas Cromwell's greatest achievements in sneaking evangelical reformation past the King. A translation largely created by the man in whose destruction Henry had connived was now to be placed in every significant church in the realm. It has remained the basis of every English biblical translation until modern times. Around nine-tenths of the New Testament text in the King James Bible of 1611 was in fact produced by Tyndale just under a century earlier.[56] That same year, 1537, saw the publication by James Nicholson in Southwark of a second edition of Coverdale's previous translation: the first Bible in English wholly to be printed in England.

An English Bible was essential to instruct the kingdom in reformation, but in this year we also begin to find definite evidence of Cromwell extending the effort beyond printing press and pulpit to the medium of drama. Now he had a peerage, it was seemly for him to spend money on a group of players; that was one sign of a great household. Apart from the King himself, such ancient noble families as the Percys, Howards, de Veres and Staffords all sustained players at some stage in the late fifteenth or early sixteenth century.[57] Cromwell's patronage was distinctive in concentrating on plays which were evangelical propaganda, with one principal writer and impresario, carefully selected for obvious talent. He could have chosen others. At some point early in 1537, an east Suffolk parson by the name of Thomas Wylley wrote to him, seeking protection from the malice of local traditionalist clergy and listing the titles of plays he had written since the early 1530s: they were suitably anti-papal in theme, but also touched on sensitive subjects such as the eucharist and purgatory.[58]

Since Wylley does not appear again in his correspondence, this seems to have been an offer Lord Cromwell felt able to refuse, but at just the same time a much more promising playwright appeared from exactly the same area: John Bale, a former senior Carmelite who had quit the order for the secular priesthood, after transitioning from an extrovert Carmelite piety to an even more extrovert evangelicalism. He got into trouble in Suffolk for similar reasons to Wylley, but had useful support after arrest and detention at Greenwich Palace around Christmastide 1536 on charges of preaching heresy: on the one hand from the evangelical circle in east Suffolk around Thomas Lord Wentworth – reputedly a great influence in Bale's conversion – and, more unexpectedly, from John Leland, through their common interest in history. It was Leland who, despite his conservative religious opinions, appealed directly to Cromwell to get Bale released 'in the name of good letters and charity'.[59]

Bale was not a new name to the Lord Privy Seal in 1537. While still a professed Carmelite and Prior of the Doncaster Whitefriars in 1534, he had run into trouble with Archbishop Lee and Bishop Stokesley for his evangelical sermons, but Cromwell repeatedly made sure that he suffered no ill consequences, for the sake of the plays he was writing.[60] Now this second round of favour rapidly unfolded into a specialized ministry of drama under Cromwell's patronage. Bale wrote about two dozen polemical evangelical plays in the 1530s, though only five have survived, all associated with his burst of creative activity inspired by Cromwell's aggressive promotion of reformation in 1537–8. Bale toured them across the country with a company of actors, Lord Cromwell's Players; the first reference to them performing occurs at King's College Cambridge on 8 September 1537, where the Provost was that establishment evangelical Bishop Foxe of Hereford. Over the next year, the company can be found presenting its material in widely dispersed and not automatically sympathetic centres: Shrewsbury, Leicester, the Guildhall of Cambridge, New College Oxford and Thetford Priory.[61] It is a pity that we do not know whether Lord Chancellor Audley's players, recorded in Cromwell's accounts as performing before him in London during Christmas 1537 and in January 1538, delivered the same sort of message.[62]

Cromwell's players may link to efforts to neutralize the effect of the Pilgrimage of Grace by strenuous preaching of obedience to the Crown. The Leicester visit, for instance, may have coincided either with a preaching visit from Bishop John Hilsey in Rogation Week (early May) 1537 or with Dr Thomas Lee's vice-gerential visit that August; both men were obvious symbols of Cromwell's new dispensation. One can imagine Dr John London, Warden of New College, eagerly agreeing to any enterprise of his patron Cromwell, but the Howard family monastery at Thetford is a more surprising venue, and the players seem to have gone there a second time before its suppression. If the plays performed there were the trilogy opening with *The Chief Promises of God*, then the structure of this first play around the great 'O' Antiphons in the liturgy of Advent suggests a date at the end of autumn. Autumn 1537, as we will see, was the moment when the Duke of Norfolk and Cromwell were at their most co-operative – and co-operation centred on closing Thetford's Cluniac sister houses at Lewes and Castle Acre (see below, Chapter 18).

For Thetford Priory, the message might be especially pointed. In Act 5, Bale riskily deploys a parallel common at the time between Henry VIII and King David, turning in this instance to explicit reference to David's notorious adulterous sin. 'Of late days, thou hast misused Bathsheba,' God consequently admonishes the now repentant King:

> Thou shalt not die, David, for this iniquity,
> For thy repentance; but thy son by Bathsheba
> Shall die, forasmuch as my name is blasphemed
> Among my enemies, and thou the worse esteemed.

Lying entombed in Thetford Priory church for a twelvemonth was the prime example of a royal 'son by Bathsheba', Henry Fitzroy Duke of Richmond. Could Bale's actors really have said these explosive lines at Thetford? Or might he have explained that it all really referred to the King's unfortunate entanglement 'of late days' with the wrong woman, Anne Boleyn, and her miscarriage of January 1536?

Equally pointed, unambiguous and topical in any setting in 1537 are references to the recent events of the Pilgrimage of Grace in the next play of this trilogy: *John Baptist's Preaching in the Wilderness*. Bale contrasts Christ humbly accepting his baptism at John's hands with rebel arrogance: 'Where the froward sects continually rebel / Ye shall see Christ here submit himself to baptism.' When Christ appears on stage, he has majesty enough, styling himself 'the great grand captain', with the sacrament of baptism as the 'livery token' of his followers. No audience could fail to think of Captain Aske, or the badge of the Five Wounds of Christ which had been adopted Pilgrims as their 'token'. There was no place for monasticism in this new army of the Saviour, as the final monologue of the play in Bale's own persona made clear:

> Give ear unto Christ, let men's vain fantasies go,
> As the Father bade by his most high commandment;
> Hear neither Francis, Benedict nor Bruno [the Carthusian founder],
> Albert [the Carmelite] nor Dominic, for they new rulers [rules?] invent.

Cromwell's players continued with their evangelical adventures in his service up to his fall, in some very carefully targeted performances, which lends plausibility to the notion that they would indeed have dared to present this trilogy when visiting Thetford. One of their most significant later shows was staged in Canterbury on 8 September 1538, amid a triumphal display of the Reformation at its most destructive, when King Henry himself visited the city. Their play 'before my Lord' (Cromwell himself) took advantage of the royal trumpets and 'loud pipes' being on hand, and was staged during an entertainment at Sir Christopher Hales's grand house in the Canterbury suburb of Hackington. This was a fitting setting, as Hales acquired it in 1532–3 from Archdeacon William Warham, an absentee cleric rather reminiscent of Thomas Winter, in one of the earliest outright lay spoliations of church property in England, just after William's uncle Archbishop Warham had died.[63]

This first week of September brought massive change to Canterbury around the destruction of St Thomas Becket's shrine in the Cathedral. Who can doubt that the play on this occasion was Bale's *On the Treasons of Becket*? Moreover, another play of Bale's which includes a celebration of destroying shrines can be dated exactly to this period. This is his *Three Laws of Nature, Moses and Christ, corrupted by the Sodomites* – the latter theme a major preoccupation for Bale.[64] The text of *Three Laws* includes a remarkable East Anglian in-joke about the Trinitarian Norfolk priory of Ingham, irregularly dissolved in 1536, which could not have had currency more than a year or two later, but in a speech from Infidelitas, one of the villains, the play also has direct references to East Anglian shrines closed in autumn 1538:

> It was a good world, when we had such wholesome stories
> Preached in our church, on Sundays and other feryes
>   [feria or ordinary weekdays].
> With us was it merry,
> When we went to Bury,
> And to Our Lady of Grace,

To the Blood of Hailes,
Where no good cheer fails,
And other holy place.[65]

Given its East Anglian allusions – Bury, Ipswich, Ingham – this play
was probably designed for Ipswich in the throes of the evangelical take-
over of the town that autumn, in the wake of Cromwell's burning of
Ipswich's wonder-working image of Our Lady of Grace in his bonfire of
images at Chelsea at the beginning of September – St Edmund's shrine at
Bury had come down earlier in the year.[66] And so the campaign of agit-
prop drama continued. Cranmer had Bale's players back at his Kentish
palace of Ford over the Christmas season of 1538/9, performing at least
one other play, *King John*: a radical re-presentation of that previously
reviled foe of Pope Innocent III, now turned into an evangelical hero.
The performance provoked much local interest and alcohol-fuelled seasonal ill-will.[67] Bale operated at the outer limit of what was possible in
Henry VIII's Church of England. When Cromwell fell, he fled the country, until more promising times dawned under Edward VI.

Cromwell's Vice-Gerency always operated on a tricky line between lay
and clerical status, given the exalted claims of the Supreme Headship
which it reflected. A most surprising overstepping of the line occurred on
1 October 1537, when Cromwell became Dean of Wells Cathedral, by
royal appointment. There was little or no English precedent for a layman
taking such an office. Admittedly the lately deceased Richard Wolman,
his immediate predecessor (an old colleague in Wolsey's service ultra-
loyal to the King throughout all his twists and turns), was one of the
greatest pluralists of his age among the English clergy, but he was still a
cleric. Cromwell's appointment was a remarkable departure, based no
doubt on some antiquarian on his staff pointing out that there was no
need for a cathedral dean to be a priest. The Latin word for 'dean' was
decanus, which simply meant head of a church. Surely the Vice-Gerent's
already sweeping powers could embrace that idea? In any case, handsome revenues and perquisites were attached, and the Deanery gave
useful control over an important West Country institution.

The complaisant Bishop Clerk of Bath and Wells could see the advantages in having such a protector, particularly since the protector was
never likely to be uncomfortably near to hand. The cathedral Chapter
also fulsomely expressed its pleasure.[68] Cromwell coupled his new office
with requiring Bishop Clerk to grant him the presentation to a cathedral
prebend once occupied by Thomas Winter, culled from the young man in
the drastic slimming down of Wolsey's prodigal provision for his future.

It had passed to Cromwell's own senior ecclesiastical agent Thomas Bedell, now deceased, a clutch of ecclesiastical delights available from his own formidable pluralism. The Dean-elect of Wells proceeded to grant the right of presentation to the prebend jointly to his servants Thomas Wriothesley and Dr William Petre; one William Wriothesley duly appeared in the prebendal stall in succession to that evocative pair of previous occupants.[69]

Cromwell's tenure as Dean of Wells set a precedent for several such appointments of laymen as cathedral deans in the Tudor age: they were generally civil lawyers, such as the celebrated Crown servant and intellectual Sir Thomas Smith, who graced the Deanery of Carlisle Cathedral with his absence for much of Queen Elizabeth's reign. Through this opportunistic acquisitiveness at Wells, the Vice-Gerent may unwittingly have saved cathedrals from their logical extinction in a Reformed Protestant Church, by providing them with a number of powerful lay protectors in their most vulnerable decades. That had remarkable consequences for the future course and theological complexion of the Church of England, since cathedrals brought to a Reformed Church an entirely alien flavour of ceremony and the beauty of holiness.[70] Such a long-drawn-out example of the law of unintended consequences would no doubt have surprised Cromwell. As he rejoiced in his Deanery in autumn 1537, he had far greater and far more immediate causes for celebration. He had survived some extraordinarily dangerous times over eighteen months, and had pulled off a coup which few could equal.

18

The King's Uncle? 1537–1538

In the fraught period after Anne Boleyn's death, religious divisions increasingly mapped themselves on to family alliances. That accelerated in summer 1537 around a dynastic marriage that has been seriously underplayed in previous accounts of events: Thomas Cromwell's son Gregory, now around seventeen and ready for adulthood after his long and careful education, married Elizabeth Seymour, the King's sister-in-law. This signalled the construction of a Seymour/Cromwell bloc which, but for the premature death of Queen Jane Seymour, might have carried all before it and radically reshaped the last years of King Henry's reign. As it was, the results were dramatic enough, both immediately and in the long term.

As Cromwell moved close to the Seymours, with political results satisfactory for everyone concerned, Elizabeth Seymour, younger sister of Jane, emerged as significant. Probably in 1530 she became second wife to a rather older Yorkshire gentleman, Sir Anthony Ughtred, while in her early teens.[1] Such unions were not uncommon in the higher reaches of English society, though convention would dictate a decorous interval before the pair cohabited. In 1533 or even early 1534 they had a son, Henry, and then came a girl, Margery, not yet born when Ughtred died in 1534.[2] Cromwell was involved on Wolsey's behalf in the Ughtreds' chaotic family affairs and became particularly friendly with Sir Anthony, who by 1530 or so was paying him a handsome yearly fee.[3] From 1532 Sir Anthony was Captain of the island of Jersey. When he wrote to Cromwell excusing the fee's late payment the following year, they also had a professional relationship: Cromwell in his characteristically amorphous duties of those years was responsible for repairs to Mont Orgueil, the Captain's residence on Jersey. Sir Anthony promised his friend a fine consignment of French wine.[4]

It was therefore no surprise when the now-widowed though still teenaged Lady Ughtred approached the Lord Privy Seal in March 1537, asking for the lease of some abbey in Yorkshire, from a list of possibles (some not yet suppressed, but worth trying anyway) which she thoughtfully enclosed. By now, she had returned from Jersey to the North; her daughter Margery was being schooled in a little Yorkshire nunnery, Wilberfoss.[5] Elizabeth's letter was a frank appeal for substantial help, on the basis of close acquaintance:

> My Lord, insomuch as my husband (whose soul God pardon) did bear ever unto your Lordship both his heart and service next under the King's Grace, I am therefore the more bolder to write and sue . . . besides that I do put mine only trust in your Lordship . . . and intend not to sue to none other . . . Further at my last being at the Court I desired your Lordship that I might be so bold as to be a suitor to you, at which time your Lordship gave unto me a very good answer . . . I was in Master Ughtred's days in a poor house of mine own, and ever since have been driven to be a sojourner, because my living is not able to welcome my friends, which for my husband's sake and mine own would sometime come and see me. Wherefore if it please your Lordship now to help me, so that I might be able to keep some poor port after my degree in mine own house, now being a poor woman alone, I were the most bound to you that any living woman might be, and more with a little help now, than if ye advised me to be bound to thing of a thousand marks a year.

Lady Ughtred ended by referring Cromwell to her friend Sir Arthur Darcy, a close colleague of her husband while they were respectively Captains of Guernsey and Jersey. She evidently regarded Arthur as an acceptable emissary to the Lord Privy Seal, despite the fact that he was younger son to the now imprisoned Thomas Lord Darcy of Templehurst. Equally, the doomed Sir Francis Bigod was a close relative of her late husband's family, and mentioned them casually in a letter to Cromwell not long before Elizabeth wrote.[6]

Lady Ughtred (as she continued to be known until her second husband Gregory was made a peer – before that, formally she outranked him) comes across in this and her other correspondence as already capable, businesslike and ready to seize the moment when needed. Her neat and confident signature in a masculine 'secretary-hand', not the usual female sprawling italic, is symptomatic. Now was the time for Elizabeth to put out feelers for a replacement husband, with a decent period of mourning for Sir Anthony out of the way, and the inconveniences of the Pilgrimage of Grace dealt with. Evidently Cromwell saw ideal consort material in her, quite apart from the fact that she was the Queen's sister. Less than a fortnight after Lady Ughtred's letter, Bishop Roland Lee fell foul of the Lord Privy Seal's alliance with the Seymours. Lee was appalled to learn from Cromwell that the King wanted the fine London residence of the

Bishops of Chester in exchange for Edward Lord Beauchamp's house on the Thames at Kew, so that Beauchamp could have the London house on the Strand as his base near Whitehall.[7] Kew was actually not such a bad compensation, placing the Bishop in the middle of the upper-river royal palaces, but it robbed Lee and his successors of a very convenient head-quarters for Parliamentary sessions, a sine qua non for the English episcopate, and he felt deeply betrayed by his friend.

Next day Lee's senior adviser John Packington (brother of the lately assassinated evangelical merchant Robert) wrote discreetly behind his master's back to Cromwell, alarmed by the Bishop's evident depression during Easter festivities at Wigmore Castle and pointing out how much his performance in Wales had outshone any predecessor in the post. Surely, suggested Packington, he deserved a proper equivalence of exchange beyond the Kew house. Cromwell did make himself a 'remembrance' about extra dissolved monastic property, which Lee rather belatedly received, 'and to thank him for granting his house for Lord Beauchamp', but a month after the initial bombshell Lee continued reproachful just the respectable side of resentment: 'although I am not so able to do your Lordship pleasure as the Lord Beauchamp, yet I bear your Lordship as good a heart to my little power, and more than that, ye cannot have.' It took some time before the old friendship settled down again; and today we may hear the Bishop's ghostly sigh as we pass the grand entrance to Somerset House on the Strand where his lost mansion stood.[8]

Meanwhile, Lady Ughtred, launched on a trip south to join the Seymours, was having a good time playing the marriage market and enjoying a newfound influence in Court circles. Sir Arthur Darcy flirtatiously wrote to her from Yorkshire on 15 June, in what some might consider over-sprightly vein, seeing that his father was in the Tower of London awaiting degrading from the Garter and execution. He offered his friend a handsome present of money and a 'fair bed' (a topical present) if she could secure a Yorkshire monastic lease for him from Augmentations: 'if ye speak but a word to the King, ye may have it.' He also teased her about her marital quest – 'sure it is, as I said: that some Southern lord shall make you forget the North' – and suggested that John de Vere, fifteenth Earl of Oxford (elderly, no doubt massively dull and a widower for the last decade), might be the lucky man: 'I heard say that ye should have your train borne at [Castle] Hedingham; my Lord of Oxford can tell you whose castle it is.'[9]

It is difficult to sift the layers of Sir Arthur's levity, yet he and his correspondent would be perfectly well aware that the de Veres' Norman blood of the deepest azure was polar opposite in hue to that of England's most recent addition to the baronage. A sequence of payments for Lord

Cromwell's summer excursion on 24 and 25 June, little more than a week after Darcy wrote from Yorkshire, tells its own story: a barge-trip between London and Mortlake, a reward to Lord Beauchamp's servant for a present of artichokes, rewards to other members of the Beauchamp household at Twickenham – and 'to Lady Ughtred's servants there', forty shillings. Soon the secret was out: on 17 July 1537, John Husee told his master in Calais, 'The saying is that my lord Privy Seal's son and heir shall shortly marry my Lady Ughtred, my lord Beauchamp's sister.'[10]

Husee was showing his usual discretion in thus describing the eligible young widow. Even a man as slow on the uptake as Lord Lisle would have realized that Elizabeth Seymour had a far more important pair of relationships, as Jane Seymour's sister and the King's sister-in-law. That would make Gregory Cromwell the King's brother-in-law by marriage, and Gregory's father would be in some sense the King's uncle. Genealogists may baulk at such a description, and in a strict sense they would be right, but in the murderous genealogy of the previous century, and in King Henry's brooding in the watches of the night, it will not have escaped royal notice that the most convincing of the generally unconvincing hereditary claims of the Tudors to the throne of England was the marriage of a king's widow to her Steward, the Welshman Owain ap Maredudd ap Tewdwr: Henry VIII's great-grandfather. It was an explosive thought, and one which would occur not just to the King, but to every meticulous scrutineer of family trees among the English nobility.

From having been a child bride previously, Elizabeth Seymour was at the time of her second marriage a year or two older than her new husband: around twenty, perhaps. She was by now possessed of considerable personal presence (see Plate 27). A remarkable letter of hers to her father-in-law survives in her own characterful hand; it may date from this summer or possibly from another, slightly later juncture in her marriage, which we will consider in due course.[11] Amid many respectful compliments, 'because I would make unto you some direct answer', Lady Ughtred is indeed direct in saying that for the time being, despite Cromwell's kindness in giving her the 'co-use of your own houses as others', his 'liberal token' and her pleasure that he is 'contented' with her, she is 'very loth to change the place where I now am'. She wishes for the time being to go on lodging with her brother Edward, though she is considering a lodging a quarter-mile away from one of Cromwell's houses. There is some stately skirmishing going on in this letter, but one gets the impression that Cromwell would consider the young lady who signed herself 'your humble daughter-in-law, Elizabeth Ughtred' a duellist worthy of his steel.

Elizabeth and Gregory went on to have a large family who carried on the Cromwell family name into the baronage for another century and a half. Their first child (a son and heir, loyally named Henry, her second son of that name) was christened just seven months after their marriage, which suggests some enthusiastic anticipation by the young couple.[12] Later letters to her from her formerly wild young spouse suggest real affection. It may have been for the wedding that Thomas Cromwell commissioned a portrait miniature of his son as a present for his wife, though its natural pairing is another Holbein miniature, of the Lord Privy Seal himself. Put side by side, the pride of the father in his son is palpable (see Plates 24–5). The boy has the same looks, the same long turned-up nose and a slightly odd, hooded cast to the eyes, though it all looks rather more appealing in a teenager. One would not expect this vigorously individual depiction to be an accident; the same cast to the eyes is there in a second miniature of Gregory which Holbein created in 1543: now approaching his mid-twenties, but again a rather informal, intimate image. This was perhaps again created for his wife, in a marriage which had survived more than one severe trial.

The wedding required careful public handling, and it may be no coincidence that one of the periodic sparse patches in the Cromwell archive is precisely from these summer months of 1537, suggesting archival weeding in the Seymour interest during the crisis of 1540. The marriage took place with the minimum of public fuss – though, again, the ever-alert Husee reported it to both his master and his mistress on the day, 3 August. This time Husee dared to point out that the bride was the Queen's sister.[13] The venue was 9 miles from London, at Cromwell's country house at Mortlake, a hasty journey for the Lord Privy Seal from accompanying the King on his summer progress further west in Surrey, at Sunninghill and Guildford. Richard Cromwell handed over fifty pounds to Gregory as a present from his father, then the Lord Privy Seal himself distributed generous gifts of cash round the household.[14]

Apart from any political discretion about the wedding, the plague was currently raging in London, and every public ceremony was low key. A rural location like Mortlake would not only alleviate the wedding party's anxieties, but soothe the King's perennial obsession with outsiders bringing infection to the Court, an anxiety heightened at the time by the Queen's advanced pregnancy. It was frustrating for a prominent conservative clergyman, Nicholas Wilson. He desperately wanted to buttonhole Cromwell at Mortlake on business, but was stuck in London and therefore under suspicion of taint; on the very day of the wedding he pleaded by letter with Thomas Wriothesley (acting as gate-keeper) to allow him in. Wilson was probably disappointed, given that after only forty-eight hours Cromwell hastened to return to Court at Windsor, leaving the newly-weds to adjust to married life.[15]

Cromwell's rapid return to Windsor after the wedding had a particular and pressing purpose. The choreography of these events demanded some enhancement of his own status, if his son's marriage to Elizabeth Seymour was not to seem even more incongruous than it actually was. Accordingly, his appointment at Windsor Castle on 5 August was with the Chapter of the Order of the Garter, who in a rather summary assembly of a mere five knights before the King in the royal closet were tasked with finding a replacement for the recently executed Thomas Lord Darcy. They presented Henry with a substantial long-list of candidates with votes in various combinations, from which the King without much show of deliberation chose Cromwell, leaving a further place vacant for the Prince he was sure was soon to appear. The Lord Privy Seal 'being immediately summoned, fell down before the Sovereign, giving with all the eloquence he was master of (and certainly he was master of the best)' a suitably modest speech of acceptance.[16]

After that there were opportunities for some family time with his son and daughter-in-law, and with Richard Cromwell too, still acting in his discreet elder-brother role for the young couple. The addresses of Cromwell's letters and his accounts reveal him back at Mortlake at the beginning of September, then for a substantial stay in early October, by which juncture he would have known he was to become a grandfather for the first time.[17] His close current links to the Seymours come across vividly in a warm letter from Lord Beauchamp on 2 September, writing from Wolf Hall; amid commendations to his sister and her husband, Seymour hoped God would soon send him a nephew.[18] The letter is no mere piece of formal diplomacy, because various names in the Wolf Hall hunting-party (the incompetence of whose hounds and hawks Beauchamp jokingly deplored) were the sort of friends of Cromwell who stayed under the political radar, people with whom he could relax – including a Wiltshire gentleman called Thomas Edgar. 'Monsieur' Edgar, who benefited from a string of small favours from Cromwell, appears in his correspondence only sporadically, but usually with some joke or frivolity attached to him, and in the public mind Edgar was sufficiently distinguished for foul language that in 1540 Robert Barnes devoted some finger-wagging admonition to him in his final remarks before being burned at the stake.[19]

Cromwell's new status was publicly emphasized by a further development of his heraldry; he had already shown himself alert to the messages which heraldry presented, and if he needed any prompting, then his new chief of staff Thomas Wriothesley was son and grandson of two Garter Kings of Arms. His old coat in 1532 defiantly proclaimed his loyalty to Cardinal Wolsey: the new coat, which he was discussing with the present Garter King Christopher Barker during July, additionally trumpeted his closeness to the Seymours.[20] The whole achievement now became a quarterly coat, so its new component in second and third quarters appeared as if they were the coat of a spouse, which in a sense they were. But primarily this was what is known as an augmentation of honour, even while also reflecting Gregory's marriage to a Seymour.

The new quartering may look fairly straightforward, but is actually unusual in heraldic terms, being based on a sixfold division. Within the six compartments, fleurs de lys alternate with pelicans, doing what pelicans do in heraldry, which is to peck their breasts to bring forth blood for their young, in the manner of Christ shedding his blood for humanity.[21] 'Pelicans in their piety' were by then a symbol of evangelical commitment among members of the Tudor elite inclined that way: in the same years, Archbishop Cranmer changed the three cranes on his family coat of arms to three pelicans.[22] So on two successive occasions Cromwell had nailed his colours to the mast in a very literal sense: first for Wolsey and second for Reformation, both now displayed side by side.

But why the sixfold arrangement, and why the fleur de lys? All becomes clear in the arcane technicalities of heraldry, when these new arms are viewed beside another augmentation of honour granted the year before, for the arms of Edward Seymour when he was made a viscount after his sister's marriage to the King: a quartering of *or on a pile gules between six fleurs de lys azure, three leopards of the field*. That is remarkably similar to the new second and third quarters in the Cromwell arms: it exhibits the same unusual threefold structure, same metal and colours, fleurs de lys and a feral creature. In Cromwell's case, the creature was not a leopard (too royal and therefore risky, given Henry VIII's paranoia), but a bird: the pelican carried an evangelical message, yet it could also echo the main motif of the original Seymour family coat, birds' wings conjoined.[23]

The full ceremony of entering Cromwell into his stall at St George's Chapel Windsor under a banner of this new design took place at the end of August. By then Henry was off elsewhere enjoying himself. The King rather pointedly deputed his presiding role to the (no doubt not entirely delighted) Marquess of Exeter. Another Knight who might have felt something of a pang was the Earl of Wiltshire, absent down in Kent at Hever Castle, from whom Cromwell hastily borrowed his best collar of St George for the ceremony: a former royal father-in-law obliging a new royal uncle by marriage.[24] Maybe Viscount Beauchamp would not have

been pleased at the false rumour reaching John Husee that he was like-
wise to be installed as Knight that day; but evidently, as became apparent,
he had traded that possibility for a future earldom. One Knight of the
Garter did not deign to travel to Windsor for the occasion from his East
Anglian home, but instead grimly set out back to his lieutenancy in the
North: Thomas Duke of Norfolk.[25]

On 20 July Dr Richard Corwen, Archdeacon of Oxford, up at Sheriff
Hutton Castle, the Duke's Yorkshire headquarters, sent Cromwell some
extended memoranda about the last days of Robert Aske before his execution at York. Corwen, a veteran Oxford don and canon of the royal
chapel at Westminster, had been chosen as a safe pair of hands to minister to the condemned rebel's last spiritual needs; he included a great deal
of useful information from Aske, which he punctiliously noted was part
of their general conversation and not gleaned in the confessional. One
was Aske's opinion that Cromwell 'did not bear so great favour to my
lord of Norfolk as he [the Duke] thought he did', 'which thing', commented Corwen tactfully, 'I have kept secret from my said lord of
Norfolk'.[26] In this, as in much else, Aske was a shrewd judge of atmospheres. In all the very extensive correspondence between Cromwell and
the Duke in spring and summer 1537 about affairs in the North, on the
Duke's side full of extravagant affirmations of friendship and general
indebtedness to the minister, there is not the slightest hint that Cromwell
told him anything of his son's marriage plans. They would have been of
some interest to the Duke even if Gregory had not been happily hunting
his deer the previous summer.

Thus when Norfolk arrived for a much sought and long-postponed
visit to Court at Grafton Regis on 15 August, it may have been the first
time he heard the news of the wedding celebration by the Thames twelve
days before, or that the Lord Privy Seal had joined him in the Order of
the Garter. If he needed telling on either count, Cromwell was on hand
on his arrival.[27] Norfolk had certainly not included any congratulations
to the happy young couple in his series of testy letters early in the month,
complaining in increasingly emotional terms about being kept away from
the King on progress, and culminating in a postscript in his own hand to
Cromwell on 8 August: 'I pray you think that the loss of one of my fingers
should not be so much to my sorrow, as to be in fear not to see my master
at this time.'[28] Given all he had done for the government in the North
over the previous months, he had a legitimate grievance.

It is not unlikely that the Duke used his precious few days of access to
the King at Grafton and Ampthill to make it clear that there needed to be
some political rebalancing. Now tectonic plates did indeed move in the

political configuration of the kingdom, the chief of which was a bold but
sensible scheme which ended up more or less satisfying everybody. It
involved shifting the power base of Charles Brandon Duke of Suffolk
almost totally away from the county which gave him his title and into
Lincolnshire, where he had in the end distinguished himself pacifying the
rising of autumn 1536, and where his fourth wife's ancestral Willoughby
estates lay. This would remove the long-standing friction between Brandon and Howard in East Anglia which in the recent past had even led to
murder (by Richard Southwell, no less). This left the Duke of Norfolk
unrivalled regional magnate in Norfolk and Suffolk, while providing a
second impressive ducal presence in an area which, the events of 1536
showed, sorely needed it. Of the two dukes, it was always going to be
Brandon who would be the more amenable to such treatment.[29]

The transfer actually began in spring 1537: in April the King told
Suffolk to move his household to a still unstable Lincolnshire, rather as
Norfolk was acting as lieutenant in the North. As an incentive, he gave
him the splendid castle at Tattershall for a headquarters. Suffolk was
perfectly willing to go, though he pointed out that such a complex move
needed time, and illness in the family further complicated matters. Yet at
this stage there seems no sense of a long-term strategic aim. At the end of
May, Cromwell asked him his own opinion as to whether staying in Suffolk 'should do more good than [his] being in Lincolnshire'. Moreover, the
Duke went on accumulating gains of estates from dissolved Suffolk monasteries into 1537, in fact doing rather better out of them than the Duke of
Norfolk.[30]

The agenda changed and widened that summer. Suffolk's estate officials launched all sorts of legal moves to safeguard his long-term interests,
totting up his historic assets and enhancing the income of his East
Anglian estates, with a forthcoming great exchange in mind. This was a
huge operation. Intricate haggling between King and Duke began producing concrete proposals only in spring 1538, and the 'Last Agreement'
was completed on 30 September that year, though the mechanics ground
on into 1540. In the place of his accumulation of East Anglian properties,
many of them ancient possessions of the Suffolk title from older families
before his own recent elevation, Charles Brandon gained an impressive
array of Lincolnshire estates and great houses, sprinkled through his new
home county from the Humber down to Rutland and the borders of the
Wash. A duke had been moved like a chess-piece across the expanses of
lowland England.[31]

There was an important corollary of this new understanding. Given
that the Duke of Suffolk was no longer to complicate the East Anglian

political scene with his presence, that must also apply to Cromwell's own son and heir, the newly married Gregory. If Cromwell had gained the major episcopal estate of North Elmham in 1536 with the intention of placing Gregory's capital mansion there, that must not now happen. It was very much in the Duke of Norfolk's interest to suggest a good alternative. Accordingly, instead of North Elmham, by an intricate agreement worked out during autumn 1537, Gregory would be installed nearly 200 miles to the south, in deepest Sussex. This change of direction was all the more striking because the developing Cromwell dynasty had neither existing estates nor historic connections with the area. The place chosen was the stately Cluniac priory of Lewes, which if Cluniac monasteries were not all constituted priories of their mother house in France, would amply have justified the name of abbey alongside the greatest Benedictine houses. It was the senior Cluniac house in England, delectably situated in a river valley and spreading comfortably out below the town which clambered up the hillside above, crowned with an ancient castle.[32]

The idea of Lewes may have appealed to Cromwell all the more because living 5 miles from the town was his sometime benefactor Sir John Gage of Firle, still a good friend despite their considerable religious differences. Sir John might be a useful grandfatherly influence on his excitable offspring, a good successor to Roland Lee. Yet that was not the prime reason for the new focus on Lewes Priory. Its founder by succession from eleventh-century Warenne Earls of Surrey was none other than Thomas Duke of Norfolk. Lewes offered a very suitable case for dissolution, since it was pleasantly remote from his main territorial concern (his interest in the dramatic but now fairly useless castle above the town was blunted by a complicated part-inheritance). The Duke had already brought the priory to Cromwell's attention in 1534, though with precisely the opposite intent: at his request, Cromwell had met with Prior Peterson during a visit to London and ordered him to avoid any grants of Lewes demesne lands to predators. In the meantime matters had moved on considerably, including an extremely negative result at Richard Leighton's vice-gerential inspection.[33]

Lewes Priory was handily linked to a subsidiary Cluniac house which, by contrast, interested the Duke very much, and which he proceeded to obtain for himself as a virtual gift from the King: Castle Acre in Norfolk. The fact of that royal gift would in itself be a sure sign that Castle Acre was part of a wider deal. The Duke of Norfolk's own letter to Cromwell of 4 November 1537 from Hampton Court described with considerable satisfaction how the King was 'content to give us Lewes, if we might bring the bargain to pass, saying and rehearsing further concerning your

service done to him, no less than I said to you in your garden'. Cromwell
was to get two parts and the Duke the third – that is, Castle Acre.[34] In
summer 1538 Cromwell acquired a licence from the Crown to sell North
Elmham to the Duke to round off the whole transaction. Yet by that time
Norfolk had thought better of it; he had viewed the estate in the spring
and thought the woods and park 'nothing of such goodness and value as
I weened they had be'. The Elmham property stayed with the Cromwells,
and in Queen Elizabeth's reign it did become their family home.[35]

This intricate deal had other elements. Another royal gift brought Cromwell his first outright possession of a monastery, also in Sussex: Augustinian
Michelham, a lesser house than Lewes.[36] Sixty miles west along the south
coast, at the same time as matters moved forward at Lewes, Cromwell's
principal secretary Thomas Wriothesley was set up with a third royal gift:
a substantial monastery for his capital mansion, Premonstratensian Titchfield Abbey, just outside Southampton.[37] Wriothesley's servant John White
spelled out the significance of Titchfield's part in the great plan, with unctuous gratitude to both God and his master, when congratulating the latter on
the happy final result of the rather protracted process:

> All we your ministers and servants and a great multitude of loving hearts
> were on St. Stephen's day last past [26 December 1537] merry, thanks be first
> therefore given to Our Lord, and secondly to you, whom I trust He hath
> chosen specially to rule in this my native country, which is in these parts
> both barren of good rulers, and the rulers barren of the faithful and loving
> hearts of the people.

What White meant was that the newly created mansion was usefully
located to skew power structures in Hampshire away from the control of
Wriothesley's former master Bishop Gardiner; Wriothesley had the opportunity to demonstrate the potential of his new position in contests for
county elections to Parliament in 1539. Together with Lewes, Titchfield
gave Cromwell the prospect of two reliable centres of power in southern
counties.[38]

The tangle of arrangements uniting East Anglia and Sussex was personified in the last Abbot of Titchfield, John Simpson alias Salisbury: a
very recent import from Norfolk. He was a former monk of Bury St
Edmunds and although involved in the scandalous outbreak of evangelicalism in Oxford in 1528, became Prior of the Norfolk Benedictine house
of Horsham St Faith (an appointment courtesy of Cromwell).[39] Despite
being a Benedictine, he managed at the same time to be Prior of the small
Premonstratensian Sussex house of Durtford, and with both Horsham
and Durtford dissolved in 1536 he continued this versatility to move to

the Premonstratensian house at Titchfield. Salisbury was flexible in geographical terms as well, remaining suffragan Bishop of Thetford in Norwich diocese during his brief tenure of Titchfield, before surrendering the house on 28 December 1537. Soon the Bishop nimbly leaped in a different ecclesiastical direction, first as prebendary and then as long-serving Dean of the newly secularized foundation of Norwich Cathedral (to name but his principal preferments – in Elizabeth's reign, he ended up as Bishop of Sodor and Man, which diocese he is unlikely to have visited).

Simpson's counterpart at Lewes, Prior Robert Peterson, was confronted with the prospect of dissolution in early November 1537. His contacts with Cromwell had been numerous. Not only was his brother, the evangelical London merchant William Peterson, one of the favoured travellers to Zürich at this time (see above, Chapter 15), but in April 1537 Sir John Gage drew Prior Peterson to Cromwell's attention, as an expert on the Lord Privy Seal's own pet enthusiasms, land reclamation and coastal defence, a matter of direct relevance in that part of Sussex. The Prior, who was on the commission of sewers for Sussex, even travelled to Flanders to see how things were done there.[40] Rather remarkably and probably not coincidentally, Peterson became a prebendary of Lincoln Cathedral in the same month Sir John wrote to Cromwell, despite still being a Cluniac monk; a fortnight before surrendering the priory, he added a prebend of St Paul's Cathedral. Certainly the second promotion looks like a sweetener. His horizons already stretched well beyond the precincts of Lewes.[41]

Also striking in the Lewes business is the extreme haste with which Cromwell completed the deal. It was a slightly unorthodox transaction, involving simultaneous surrender of a substantial and far-distant cell at Castle Acre which would in other circumstances have been itself a major monastic dissolution. He and the Duke of Norfolk were nervous about getting it right. The negotiators rather rashly tried to make their deal absolutely foolproof by adding to its other elements a legal fiction used in the Court of Common Pleas to secure land transfers, known as levying a fine: a common law conveyance from monastic head to the Crown. Lord Chancellor Audley, punctilious to a fault in matters of common law, pointed out to Cromwell the problems of legal logic in such a process as it related to Titchfield, but thereafter the levying of a fine was repeatedly used in monastic surrenders. Consequently, one of the elements in the Parliamentary legislation of 1539, tidying up what by then had become an avalanche of dissolutions, was to give full statutory backing to this shaky procedure.[42]

Still it needed the personal touch. The Duke of Norfolk rode down

himself from Court to Reigate in Surrey to meet Cromwell's senior officials and make sure all passed smoothly. It was the day after Jane
Seymour's funeral, so the Duke had to get permission from the King for
his journey; moving things along was important enough to risk proprieties. Richard Cromwell, whom Cromwell had put in charge of the whole
Lewes venture, went with him.[43] The Prior of Lewes did indeed make
things awkward, playing off the two sides against each other, and then
there was the business of getting the whole community to co-operate. To
still some objections it was decided that the deed of surrender should not
include a grovelling preamble confessing the sins of Lewes Priory, even
though such preamble admissions were common in earlier surrenders
and would be used a great deal the following year in the surrender of
friaries. At Lewes, there might have been material enough for confession,
to judge from earlier reports.[44]

Apart from sparing the community's blushes, the surrender was
clinched by throwing money at the problem. Cromwell made an unprecedented offer of permanent pensions for all the monks unless they were
granted or obtained preferment in the Church of equivalent value, plus a
gratuity, plus a year's wages for the staff. Wriothesley immediately copied the pattern at Titchfield in December and January, as did that other
beneficiary of the great rebalancing of 1537–8, Charles Duke of Suffolk,
at Revesby.[45] This provided the model followed by all surrenders of co-
operative monasteries thereafter, though henceforth pension liability fell
on the Crown, not on the beneficiaries. This was a move of much general
significance; no member of a threatened monastic community need fear
a future of poverty out in the world: a great incentive to accept dissolution, especially when the alternative might be death by attainder.[46]

Gregory Cromwell's wedding in August 1537 thus had momentous
consequences. Immediately, it produced new areas of demarcation in
local politics across lowland England, pivoting on deals between Cromwell and the Duke of Norfolk, but additionally it created patterns for the
remaining monastic dissolutions up to 1540. The aftermath of the Pilgrimage saw the Crown close not only all smaller monasteries reopened
by the Lincolnshire rebels and Pilgrims but, additionally, larger houses
with heads implicated in the stirs. Whalley, Hexham, Bridlington,
Jervaulx, Kirkstead, Barlings were all declared forfeit to the Crown by
the attainder of their heads for treason; that followed the provision
thoughtfully inserted to this effect in the Treason Act of 1534 (see above,
pp. 268–9). Further suppressions were swelling beyond a trickle, to the
extent that Cromwell found himself financially disadvantaged. In the
course of his long involvement in monastic affairs, he had accumulated

so many grants of fees from monasteries that he now felt their loss. A partial solution emerged only in spring 1538, when he was awarded the Stewardship of all suppressed monasteries north of the Trent, plus a set of named dissolved houses around the kingdom: an office with a handsome fee of £100 per annum.[47]

As surrenders accumulated, it became clear that a mode of proceeding was necessary for monastic houses outside the scope of the first dissolution Act, and for which there was neither a pretext of treason nor that rationale of debt or misrule first employed at Christ Church Aldgate back in 1532. That is precisely what the closure of Lewes and Titchfield provided: surrender with full compensation for livelihood. Still, even at this late date, there seems no general plan for monastic dissolution, certainly not in the mind of the Duke of Norfolk. He took care to translate with all due reverence the principal relic of Castle Acre Priory, the arm of St Philip, to the Cluniac house of Thetford, which he was encouraging to act as a local hub for conservative forces in East Anglian religion. Various accompanying items of splendour also made the journey south to Thetford from Castle Acre. This was a radical contrast to Cromwell's and Wriothesley's treatment of the churches of Lewes and Titchfield, but it was all of a piece with Norfolk's unsuccessful effort earlier in the year to save the shrine and cult of St John of Bridlington in the former priory church.[48]

While Norfolk and Cromwell moved forward on their deal, a royal tragedy intervened, stemming from what had seemed to be triumph. The King's longed-for legitimate male heir, the central object of so much grief and toil over the previous decade, was born to Queen Jane at Hampton Court, on 12 October 1537. She sent the happy news via one of her gentleman ushers directly to Cromwell, in his capacity as her High Steward (the note was in fact written by Ralph Sadler); he was lodging in St James's Palace transacting London business as near the City as was safe with the plague still virulent, so he distributed a celebratory twopence each to the poor in the surrounding hamlet.[49] Amid nationwide relief at the successful outcome of all the King's anxieties, this was a great personal moment for him: really the apogee of his career, if he had but known. His son was unchallengeably uncle to a future king, when the greatest magnate in the land, the Duke of Norfolk, could only chalk up being great-uncle to a royal girl now declared illegitimate.

Such realities were glossed over on 15 October at the baby's christening as Edward, a name whose unfortunate associations with the previous boy-king of that name mislaid in the Tower of London were counter-balanced by martial royal predecessors and by the Queen's brother. Like Queen Jane's marriage, this was a time for coming together. There were enough godparents to satisfy every faction: the Duke of Norfolk and Archbishop Cranmer shared the honours at the font, the Lady Mary and the Duke of Suffolk at the confirmation which followed, and in a gesture to another layer of the recent past (possibly at Cranmer's gentle prompting) the Earl of Wiltshire bore the Archbishop's confirmation present to the little Prince. The four-year-old Lady Elizabeth had the honour of carrying in her half-brother's chrisom robe in front of the baby, though to avoid mishaps she was herself carried by Lord Beauchamp and her great-uncle Lord Morley.

Although the Lord Privy Seal was present, he had no ceremonial duties: perhaps it might have seemed provocative. There were reports of earldoms to come in the next few days: John Husee thought that Cromwell would be Kent or Southampton and Sir William Fitzwilliam Warwick. His colleague Thomas Palmer heard Southampton for Fitzwilliam and Salisbury for Lord Beauchamp.[50] It would have been remarkable if Edward Seymour had indeed become Earl of Salisbury, because there was currently a countess of that title in her own right: Margaret Pole, mother of the disgraced Cardinal. Maybe Henry did contemplate this massive snub, since the only dark notes of the christening-day concerned the group of notables associated with Pole. Reginald Pole's elder brother Lord Montague was given a part in the ceremony, but a second brother Sir Geoffrey Pole was not admitted to Court when he appeared, and on the very day of the christening Michael Throckmorton's brother Sir George was committed to the Tower of London – a fulfilment of that threat in Cromwell's furious letter to Michael a few weeks before (see above, pp. 408–9).

In this dire moment, Sir George produced the abject and very informative depositions on his behaviour which have illuminated earlier events. He was saved from the fate increasingly nearing the Pole circle by making some uncharacteristically evangelical noises of enthusiasm in his depositions, affirming how much he had learned from the two books produced under Cromwell's auspices that summer, the Matthew Bible and the Bishops' Book. This capitulation was a start. In addition, one of those tipped for honours from the King, Throckmorton's relative Sir William Parr, may have used his own deposit account of favour with Cromwell (Parr had been a senior servant of the late Duke of Richmond) to steer Sir George back over the next year to a remarkably complete rehabilitation.[51]

In the wake of the christening, the honours the King actually granted fell short of the suggestions being bandied about in the first euphoria after the Prince's birth. A pointed little geographical dance with titles was involved. Sir William Fitzwilliam did become Earl of Southampton, which maritime title matched his long-term naval interests as Lord Admiral. Nevertheless, his power-base lay in Surrey, and the new figure actually emerging in the Southampton region at Titchfield Abbey was Cromwell's lieutenant Thomas Wriothesley (who did gain the title of Southampton a decade later). Lord Beauchamp, who unlike Fitzwilliam actually lived in Hampshire, was advanced at the same time to an earldom of Hertford even longer in abeyance than his previous viscountcy. The antiquarian revival of this thirteenth-century title for a man who had no connection with Hertfordshire is even odder than his previous Beauchamp viscountcy, and the name may actually have been suggested by the then well-known Hartford Bridge in the Hampshire parish of his home at Elvetham. Both Fitzwilliam and Seymour got some small annual financial support from revenues of the port of Southampton.[52]

Cromwell in the end received no formal advancement. The new Earl of Hertford was uncle to a future King by blood, not just by marriage like Gregory Cromwell, and Seymour's promotion balanced Cromwell's edging ahead of him into the Order of the Garter three months before. Cromwell naturally showed no hint of disappointment; he played a leading role in the creation, ceremonially reading aloud the two patents of earldom in his continuing role as Principal Secretary, with his new best friend the Duke of Norfolk looking on. Nevertheless, in a matter fully under his control as Lord Privy Seal, he was able to advance himself in a significant respect just as if he had obtained some new peerage promotion: his name began appearing on every county commission of the peace in the kingdom. Although he was more than unlikely to appear at quarter sessions in Cumberland, for example, he now had the right to do so if he pleased.

Previously, even while gaining a barony, the Vice-Gerency and the third most senior office in the realm as Lord Privy Seal, Cromwell continued to be named only to the counties where he had substantial estates: Essex, Kent, Middlesex and Surrey. When a new commission was issued for Oxfordshire on 28 June 1537 he gained a place on the bench there, once more reflecting a substantial land purchase he was contemplating in that county. Then on 26 October came his first known commission outside lowland England, in Derbyshire.[53] The only exceptions to his being named to every commission from that November until his fall were a number of episcopal and monastic liberties with their own commissions of the peace, which is a remarkable example of his legal scrupulosity, considering his consistent drive to get rid of ecclesiastical exempt jurisdictions.[54]

It was on 24 October that a terrible tragedy overcame the delight of Prince Edward's birth. The Queen had never properly recovered from childbirth; her sickness increased and suddenly became desperate with the onset of septicaemia; she sank into delirium. At eight that evening the Duke of Norfolk scribbled an urgent note to Cromwell: 'My good lord, I pray you to be here tomorrow early to comfort our good master, for as for our mistress, there is no likelihood of her life, the more pity, and I fear she shall not be on live [alive] at the time ye shall read this.'[55] Queen Jane died at around midnight; she was only twenty-eight. King Henry was devastated; this was one marriage where his love had no time to cool.

Even in death Jane performed her unifying role: at her funeral on 12 November, Lady Mary was the chief mourner. Nevertheless it is notable how well represented in the ceremonies were what one can now call the Cromwell affinity; their principals were, after all, close relatives of the deceased Queen. Among the half-dozen notables bearing banners along-side the heralds in procession were Gregory Cromwell (his first ever public duty), his cousin Richard and Richard's father-in-law Sir Thomas Denys, together with one of Cromwell's great supporters in Cornwall, Sir William Godolphin. Lady Ughtred and Richard Cromwell's wife were among the principal mourners, as was the lady-in-waiting who had married Cromwell's senior servant Richard Tomyou.[56] Formally nothing much had changed. Edward was still heir apparent, the Seymours in the King's high favour. Their joint interest with the Lord Privy Seal was per-haps greater than ever, for the one great difference in Court politics was that the King was in marital terms a free agent once more.

Once Henry got over his genuine grief at Jane's death, he would be seeking another wife, to provide him with the spare son he would feel necessary for his fragile and complicated dynastic line. That would inter-est other members of the English nobility; it certainly interested the Duke of Norfolk, who, in the letter of November telling Cromwell of Henry's agreement to their bargain over Lewes and Castle Acre, also recounted his talk of succession with the King,

> (though peradventure not wisely, yet after mine accustomed manner plainly) exhorting him to take in good part the pleasure of Almighty God in taking out of this transitory life the Queen our late mistress, and recom-fort himself with the high treasure sent to him and his realm, that is to say, the Prince, with many other persuasions to advise him to tract no longer time than force should drive him unto, to provide for a new wife, by whom of likelihood more children might be brought forth to our most rejoice and consolation.[57]

The King would be more suspicious than ever of any nobleman who appeared to threaten the life of his son, even by passively possessing an unhealthily large dose of potential royal blood. In the eternal calculation of factors influencing Henry's attitude to his nobility, three days before that conversation the Duke of Norfolk was relieved of one past embarrassment of that sort, in the shape of his half-brother Lord Thomas Howard, attainted for his unauthorized marriage to Lady Margaret Douglas. Lord Thomas died still a prisoner in the Tower of London. It was a consortium of Cromwell, Wriothesley and Lord Hertford who diplomatically cited maternal grief to negotiate the King's consent for Howard's quiet burial by his mother the Dowager Duchess. She took him up to Thetford Priory, to lie near that other victim of fate, the Duke of Richmond.[58]

These various dynastic preoccupations shaped Henry's actions over the next two years. In the aftermath of Jane's death, Cromwell stuck as close to Court as he could. Having secured his foothold in St James's Palace, thanks to the plague's unusually prolonged virulence, he made little effort to return to The Rolls from this useful entrée to the royal precinct of Whitehall. Many of his surviving letters this autumn are dated from St James's or the subsidiary royal house in Westminster called The Neat (in what is now Pimlico).* At this time of mourning, we should guard against the temptation to read everything in terms of faction and self-interest. That thoughtful and scholarly prelate Cuthbert Tunstall, writing from York to Cromwell, added to a long business letter a postscript in his own hand, urging comfort for the King: 'Of his mirth, all our mirth depends, and of his heaviness all our heaviness; wherefore my singular good Lord, show yourself a solicite and diligent servant, as I am sure ye do.'[59]

Cromwell was exhausted from the strain of autumn events. In mid-December, 'somewhat acrazed [ill]', he announced to suitors he was retiring to Mortlake, and for the next week or more would undertake only the King's business. The unspoken message was that he wanted time with his son and daughter-in law.[60] This may explain why they failed to arrive promptly in their new home in Sussex. There was excitement in Lewes at the prospective arrival of the Lord Privy Seal's son (and probably more so at the prospect of his wife, the King's sister-in-law). John Milsent, uncomfortably camping out in the vast empty buildings on 12 December, confided his worry about any further delay to Henry

---

* This had been a rural retreat of the Abbot of Westminster, granted to the Crown a few years earlier.

Polstead: 'The people hereabouts are very sorry because that Master Gregory and my Lady do not come down before Christmas; they think that they shall not come at all, and so the house to be broken up here.' It was encouraging locals to break into the precinct and steal anything they could lay their hands on while Milsent and his three companions were occupied in other parts of the site.[61]

After New Year, arrangements at Lewes and Titchfield resumed their pace. Wriothesley was quick off the mark beginning the conversion of his abbey, which involved a particularly ruthless conversion of the church into splendid domestic apartments: the ruins of the results can still be viewed. His plans were already advanced around New Year 1538, with neighbours agreeing to buy up materials in the building right down to the gravestones in the floors (John Husee urgently consulted Lord Lisle to see whether he would like the coffin of his first wife removed to the local parish church).[62] One senior local conservative cleric, contemplating the resulting havoc in company with a fellow-visitor, Cromwell's servant Richard Tomyou, expressed his dismay rather ambiguously: 'it was [would be] a good deed to save the walls of the church there standing to a use, and a piteous sight to see them thrown down where they might stand to a use.' A thrifty Wriothesley would have agreed.[63]

Cromwell's plans at Lewes were even more ruthless: total destruction of the majestic priory church by one of the kingdom's foremost Italian engineers, Giovanni Portinari, eventually carried out in March. Portinari even proposed speeding up the work with gunpowder, and had on hand some of the most skilled construction workers in London (in other words, the King's employees).[64]* That left the residential parts of the monastic complex intact for Gregory and his wife. That month they moved into a property probably already much improved from the half-sacked premises of Christmastide. They left for Sussex soon after the christening of their son Henry on 1 March, probably at Hampton Court. What looks like an associated entertainment, mounted by Lord Cromwell's players and musicians, was staged for the benefit of King Henry himself: Portinari, a Renaissance Man as well as a demolition man, was in charge of this masque.[65] The Lady Mary almost certainly stood godmother at the christening of this loyally named boy; she gave an expensive cup at the christening and the substantial sum of forty shillings to the nurse and midwife, with messages before to the Lord Privy Seal and afterwards to

---

* The work moved so quickly that it left the founders' coffins still buried and intact, to be rediscovered during the Victorian construction of Lewes railway station.

the young couple at Lewes. This fits well with the other evidence of Mary's warm relations with Cromwell in the mid-1530s.[66]

On Gregory's arrival in Sussex, he was straight away put to apprenticeship as a county gentleman. He proudly signed a joint letter with old Sir John Gage on 19 March about examining a rogue ex-monk of Lewes Priory, committing him to Bishop Sampson's commissary for imprisonment.[67] The young man had never been the most prompt of correspondents, but in his first proper private letter home, on 11 April, he explained with a silkiness perhaps borrowed from his tutor Henry Dowes that 'I have long deferred to write unto you of my state and condition, and how both my wife and I like this country,' wanting 'more experience in the same than I could have in a day or twain's proof'. He professed himself delighted with Lewes, fêted by local nobility and gentry as in his previous rural tours, and 'as concerning the house and the situation of the same, it doth undoubtedly right much please and content both me and my wife, and is to her so commodious as she thinketh herself to be here right well settled.'[68] The letter was in his own neat secretary-hand, a touchingly close if slightly clumsy imitation of Dowes's. Gregory, very grown up now, even tried an elegant little play on words about the welcome from Sussex society 'with their presences and also presents'.

Cromwell was preoccupied with the future of his dynasty at least as much as the King was with his. Gregory had reached a milestone in a future so carefully constructed for him: now the young Sussex magnate, fulfilling one main goal in all his father's striving and scheming over the last decade. Cromwell even arranged a secondary house for him 10 miles to the north of Lewes, Sheffield in the parish of Fletching, apparently part of the estates of that lesser Sussex monastery King Henry had given him at Michelham. This pairing of capital mansion and satellite-house was a classic arrangement for upper county gentry, in imitation of the King's own more spectacular arrangements west of London. The Lord Privy Seal spent some time at Sheffield himself that summer while the Court was on progress in the area.[69]

When Gregory wrote his letter from Lewes on 16 April 1538, he was sitting as JP at quarter sessions in the town. He conducted an examination of some malefactors, all on his own. These vandals were being indicted for digging up and casting down a wayside cross, part of a popular craze in the 1530s for seeking hidden treasure in such places.[70] Back in London, Gregory's father was contributing rather more officially to the tally of ecclesiastical demolition in a variety of ways. The keynote of the year 1538 was destruction.

19

Cutting Down Trees: 1538

In 1564 a clergyman-doctor and author called William Bulleine published what turned out to be his most popular work, *A Dialogue Against the Fever Pestilence*, a medley of moralizing, medical advice and travel fantasy carefully positioned for the Protestant mass market. In one section of the fantasy, the hero conducts his wife round the parlour of an inn ornamented with instructive pictures, sententiously answering her eager questions about their subjects and meaning. After falling for some misogynistic teasing, she admires a particular portrait. 'Oh wife,' says her husband, 'it was the picture or *effigium* of a nobleman, which in his days served a great King, and was like the cutter down of trees by the ground. But if God had not (upon some secret purpose) prevented his labour in the wood of Antichrist, he would have utterly eradicated all papistry.' This is the only picture in their exhaustive scrutiny to be identified by name: the margin notes that it is 'the Lord Cromwell', who died when Bulleine was in his mid-twenties.[1]

Religious and political forestry was Cromwell's business in 1538 more than in any other year of his royal service: all the kingdom's friaries, many of its monasteries and its principal shrines and their relics tumbled, and in the end one of the greatest noble affinities, including some of the King's oldest friends, crashed down as well. In this year the Vice-Gerent's promotion of evangelical reformation in the kingdom reached its height, but he also found frustration in his boldest plan yet to link England to the Protestant Reformations in mainland Europe. It was part of the wider question of foreign policy, and – dangerously as always – it concerned the King's marriage. Foreign affairs was always a problem for Cromwell, as the King considered this area of government peculiarly his own, with no hint of the formal delegation that the Vice-Gerency represented in religion; Henry had a continuous experience of international diplomacy now stretching back nearly thirty years. At a moment of particular irritation with Cromwell for obstinately persisting with his own line of foreign policy that spring, the King was prepared to say to the French ambassador that the Lord Privy Seal 'was a good manager, but not fit to meddle in the concerns of kings'.[2]

Cromwell's current problem was to turn a vital question away from domestic into foreign policy. Should the King's new wife be from within the realm or from abroad? Rather remarkably, King Henry allowed this question to be a subject for discussion, at least formally and in his presence: the great civil servant Sir Thomas Smith reminisces that, as a young Fellow of Queens' College Cambridge, he first came to the attention of Henry VIII when he debated with Sir John Cheke at Court after the death of Queen Jane as to 'whether his Majesty should wed someone from overseas or one of his own people'.[3] One can see the King, with his pretensions as a patron of learning, seeing this as an ideal demonstration of the practical uses of humanist rhetorical skills.

Cromwell himself had no doubts about the answer, as was starkly revealed in a private argument with Cranmer, who took the opposite view.[4] The two men's disagreement nicely demonstrates their different priorities. Cranmer was solicitous for Henry's personal happiness, as a royal chaplain should be. He said he did not wish to see the King 'marry without [outside] the realm'. The Archbishop 'thought it most expedient the King to marry where that he had his fantasy and love, for that would be most comfort for his Grace'. Cromwell snapped back furiously, 'There was none meet for him within this realm.' One can see exactly why the Lord Privy Seal should say that: a marital alliance with any noble family of the kingdom, but with the Howards in particular, would suck further value out of his alliance with the Seymours. Cranmer retorted with spirit 'that it would be very strange to be married with her that he could not talk withal'. Given that he probably had to teach English to his own German wife Margarete back in 1532, he spoke from experience. In the event the supposedly politically naive Cranmer got the King's psychology right; if only Cromwell had listened to him.

King Henry himself agreed with Cromwell, at least on the general principle. During the next two years of long-distance courting, his clear priority was the overseas option; the question was where to place his marriage in the European diplomatic balance.[5] His requirements were unrealistically high; not only did he seek beauty and the prospect of more children, he wanted to kill as many diplomatic birds with one stone as possible, in a situation where the two European dynasties greater and more secure than the Tudors, the Habsburgs and Valois, seemed dangerously close to finding real agreement after years of warfare. Grave dangers for England and its excommunicated monarch loomed from these Catholic rulers making common cause; inevitably that would exclude Henry, and maybe lead to something much worse. This was perfectly realistic. In August 1538, Chapuys once more delicately raised with the Lady Mary the prospect of flight abroad; although she discounted the idea for the moment, looking instead for better treatment from her father, she did not definitively reject it, and significantly told the imperial ambassador that she might herself write to the Emperor.[6] At the end of the year, the current French ambassador in England, the Sieur de Castillon, wrote to his friend Constable de Montmorency at a moment of especial exasperation with the English government, outlining at some length a proposal for a joint invasion of England by King François and Charles V.[7]

What dynastic marriage would best minimize such a risk? Apart from himself (whom some observers might have considered a dubious asset), King Henry now had three children to offer, at various levels of diplomatic attractiveness. Obviously Edward was the prime exhibit, but Mary and Elizabeth gained much from being part of the portfolio. Accordingly, King Henry was promiscuous in his approaches to the most senior eligible ladies in western Europe, in ways entertaining to members of Europe's political elite with a greater sense of the absurd than himself. Perhaps his most ambitious effort, a parody of Cardinal Wolsey's efforts at universal peace, was a suggestion retailed to a carefully straight-faced Castillon in February 1538 that the King himself should marry the twenty-three-year-old French Duchess Marie de Guise (from one of France's greatest ducal houses), while Edward should marry the Emperor's daughter, Mary wed the heir to the throne of Portugal and Elizabeth the heir of Charles V's brother King Ferdinand. Three days before, Cromwell sent his protégé Thomas Wyatt (at present ambassador to the Emperor) a version of this scheme minus any reference to its principal French component, to offer Charles V. It is unlikely that that well-informed monarch would have failed to ask about the missing element in the package.[8]

Cromwell was not an honest broker in all this. His emphatic preference was as ever for a Habsburg alliance, all the more so because the Duke of Norfolk, both from general inclination and because of his long-standing pension from the French, was equally consistent in supporting a French marriage. Their fragile alliance of convenience of autumn 1537 disappeared, particularly when their differences led to Cromwell's humiliation at Court at the beginning of May. The French ambassador was perfectly aware of these alignments and found them highly amusing; he relished describing to Montmorency Cromwell's discomfiture when King Henry's affections veered decisively towards a French alliance cemented by a Guise marriage. This was the same letter in which Castillon reported

Henry's dismissive remarks about Cromwell's fitness for foreign policy. 'On that, he sent for Norfolk, whom the Lord Privy Seal was preventing as much as he could from coming to Court. And my said Lord is utterly thwarted [*bien camus*], and so suspect in matters concerning France that at the moment his advice is not much sought; and now most of the leading men at Court visit me, which is a very good sign . . . in a nutshell, M. de Norfolk is more welcome than for a long time, and my Lord under suspicion for too much Spanish passion.'[9]

This was Cromwell's lowest point in the King's esteem so far in seven years of service, apart from that moment of near-shipwreck during the Pilgrimage of Grace. He was actually being kept away from Council meetings held on the King's progress in Essex. Richard Cromwell had to report to his uncle that there was no answer to a packet of letters he had taken to Court, as 'his Highness was all this day very busy in Council with the Lords, and talked long with the French ambassador.' Henry curtly told Richard to wait for his response the following day.[10] Particularly unfortunate was the recent death on 8 May of Edward Foxe, Bishop of Hereford: a major blow not just to Cromwell (who was supervisor of his will), but to the general reconciliation of quarrels at Court. Foxe was the smoothest of evangelical statesmen – too smooth for some: Melanchthon experienced him as 'prelatical', and the fiery reformer George Joye later put him in a corner of Hell alongside Wolsey and More.[11] But Foxe was also the sort of man whom the piously conservative Lord Lisle could see as a reliable ally at Court, while still impressing most of the German Protestants he encountered on his long embassy in 1535–6. He would be sorely missed in the diplomatic tangles to follow.[12] This was also the time that George Paulet returned from Ireland after relentlessly badmouthing Cromwell to Irish notables. It is not surprising that the Lord Privy Seal concentrated his fury on Paulet for his indiscretions over there, sending him to the Tower.

In his usual style Cromwell also fought back against his ill fortune, inserting himself into the Essex royal progress through a lavish entertainment. The day after Richard's embarrassed letter to his uncle, John Husee reported to Lord Lisle (alongside news of Paulet's imprisonment) that 'on Tuesday next, or Monday [21 or 22 May], the King shall have a great banquet at Havering, of my lord Privy Seal's gift'.[13] More than fifty pounds' worth of expenditure appears in Cromwell's accounts, probably additional to stores in his own cellars. To divert the easily bored monarch, there appeared six Cornish wrestlers (a speciality act Cromwell had considered before, courtesy of his Cornish friend Sir William Godolphin), and a porpoise was centrepiece for the table.[14] Cromwell went out of his way to be pleasant to the French ambassador, following what Castillon heard was a severe talking-to from the King.[15]

The danger passed. The wrestlers and the porpoise may have helped, but it turned out that this same month Marie de Guise had already married King Henry's nephew the King of Scots, to his uncle's considerable chagrin. Cromwell's exhibition of Francoscepticism did not seem so heinous after all. It would be tedious to follow the twists and turns of Henry's unrequited courtships during 1538. By the end of the year, the King remained unmarried, while circumstances changed in many other ways. Meanwhile Cromwell had pressed home his other grand passion in foreign affairs: a closer alliance with the Schmalkaldic League and other evangelical cities of the Empire and Switzerland. His enthusiasm for a Habsburg alliance was an uneasy bedfellow with this, for the Protestantism of the Schmalkaldic princes and cities was anathema to their overlord Charles V. Yet the League had its own military resources which might give the Emperor pause if he threatened England, so long as its members were sufficiently motivated to take an interest in the island kingdom – they possessed the only Protestant military force of any significance in mainland Europe. This was a useful thought when presenting the King with any proposal for negotiations.

During 1537, dealings with the Schmalkaldic League had stalled.[16] While discreet exchanges between Zürich and England gathered momentum (see above, Chapter 15), the Schmalkaldeners badly mishandled a renewed overture to King Henry in the spring, entrusting a formal statement on the common threat of a papal General Council to a totally unqualified and unaccredited sailor of Hamburg. He made the worst possible impression on the English Court and the King. Horrified at this misstep, Cromwell, Cranmer and Foxe sent a quiet private rebuke to the League via a godson of the Earl of Wiltshire, Thomas Theobald, who had spent time in Germany as a student and had been providing the Archbishop with information on central Europe. They also extended their feelers beyond the League to the city of Strassburg; this was in parallel with the Zürich initiatives, but Cranmer's old correspondent Martin Bucer, on friendly terms with many leading figures in the League, would also be a useful voice in getting a renewed Schmalkaldic embassy to England.

By autumn 1537 the German Protestants were enthusiastic about this proposal, though they also had a healthy understanding that King Henry must not be allowed to realize the extent of the discreet groundwork the English evangelicals had already undertaken: 'in these matters, the King is not to be trifled with,' as Philip Melanchthon anxiously reminded the Elector of Saxony.[17] With discretion maintained, it was promising that

Henry was still worried about a General Council, and was happy to consider his own embassy to the only significant power in western Europe immune from papal overtures. By February 1538, the ever-faithful Christopher Mont was travelling to the League's Diet with letters and confidential oral instructions. Cromwell's name was very carefully kept out of all Mont had to say, for it was important to represent the whole initiative as the King's, but the evangelical expression of the message was entirely the Lord Privy Seal's, and Mont's visit had been preceded by Cromwell's own private letter to the leading Schmalkaldic prince Philipp of Hessen.[18]

The German embassy, a joint mission in the names of Landgraf Philipp and Johann Friedrich Elector of Saxony, assembled with four principal members. One of them did not stay in England long, leaving leadership in the hands of the Hessian diplomat Georg von Boineburg and the Saxon ducal Vice-Chancellor, Franz Burchard. They were both distinguished and highly competent, but the German conception of the mission was still merely to explore something more ambitious. A mark of this preliminary character was that the third active member and the mission's theological consultant, Friedrich Myconius, Superintendent of Gotha, was something of a second-ranker among Lutheran reformers. He was certainly not the equivalent of Philipp Melanchthon, the only Lutheran for whom King Henry felt real respect on account of Melanchthon's formidable scholarly reputation. Melanchthon was as always deeply unenthusiastic about meeting the King of England, and had made his excuses. This was an initial mistake if anything was to come of the discussions. So was the fact that the Germans were sure they had more to offer to the English than vice versa: they had already achieved properly godly Reformations which should set England an example.

The mission came armed with a list of four points to be resolved on German terms: allowing communion 'in both kinds' (bread and wine) to all communicants; abolishing 'private masses' (directed towards particular prayer intentions, especially prayers for the dead); denying the value of monastic vows and, finally, abolishing universal clerical celibacy. Even monastic vows remained an open question in England, despite everything that was happening to the regular life, and all the other points were likely to arouse King Henry's disapproval. On the German side, the issue of 'both kinds' was particularly important: for centuries the Western Latin Church had restricted the laity to taking only bread at mass, on the infrequent occasions that they received communion at all, and the restoration of the cup had become one of the chief symbols of the Reformation. The hopelessness of resolution on these matters would not be obvious to begin with, since the ambassadors' first contacts were with Cromwell and Cranmer, in the Whitehall complex and at Lambeth Palace. Cromwell, full of optimism, told them that the only real problem for the King would be the issue of clerical celibacy.[19]

The following day, 2 June, Henry himself met the ambassadors with his leading councillors, including both Norfolk and Cromwell. Straight away the King raised the question of the missing Melanchthon, who was best placed to discuss with him some problematic points in the Augsburg Confession of 1530 (Melanchthon had drafted it in the first place). At least in public Henry accepted the substitution of Myconius with good grace, and a week later Myconius did his best with the King. The atmosphere remained cordial, the Germans optimistic about progress. Cromwell's actions as Vice-Gerent at this time offered plenty to please them, as will become apparent, and Myconius would be gratified to be invited as regular guest preacher to the largely foreign congregation in the church of the Austin Friars, no doubt after judicious pressure from Cromwell on his landlord and neighbour Prior Hammond. Myconius was probably the first foreign Protestant to be allowed such public exposure in England.[20]

Yet Cromwell would see a wider picture than that available to the German Protestants. There were just too many diplomatic negotiations in progress for comfort. Thomas Wyatt rushed back from his embassy in France (arriving on 3 June, the day after the Germans' interview with the King), but in a matter of days he had to hare south again over the Channel, because of a critical moment in high diplomacy. The long-dreaded agreement had arrived: the King of France and the Emperor were concluding a deal, the Treaty of Aigues-Mortes. Mortifyingly it was concluded without reference to Wyatt and his English mission. Meanwhile Henry was now pursuing at full tilt a Habsburg princess, the Duchess of Milan.[21] Consequently there were now two imperial ambassadors in England for red-carpet treatment: Don Diego de Mendoza, entrusted with a particular brief for the Milan marriage, and the veteran Chapuys. Both would be deeply suspicious of the Schmalkaldic delegation. It was vital to keep those two sets of envoys apart, and in fact when the imperialists saw King Henry on 6 June, the appointment was neatly quarantined between the two royal interviews first with the whole Schmalkaldener mission and then with Myconius.

Whatever his private enthusiasms, the Lord Privy Seal realized that the Emperor and his representatives far outclassed his Protestant vassals in importance. It was symptomatic that Cromwell secured the Schmalkaldeners lodgings in the City which Cranmer for one thought cramped and thoroughly unsuitable, but lodged the two imperial envoys in his own properties in solicitous rural comfort, away from the danger of City plague, though on opposite sides of London: one in Stepney and one in Mortlake.[22] Since the King's marital fantasies still involved eligible French ladies if no progress emerged with the Duchess of Milan, there could be no question of ignoring the French ambassador Castillon. He was currently installed in Sir Thomas More's old house in Chelsea; Cromwell was a temporary near neighbour in a small royal house there after yielding his two rural residences to the imperialists. The Lord Privy Seal made sure that he saw plenty of Castillon in Chelsea.[23] The essential criterion for this diplomatic version of a Feydeau farce was for everyone to be within hailing distance of a Thames barge.

Cromwell thus straddled desperately conflicting agendas, and his recent contretemps over the French marriage proposals was a reminder that the King was listening to multiple voices. That became apparent when the English team to negotiate with the Schmalkaldeners took shape. Its membership accurately reflected the breadth of opinion among English higher clergy. Alongside Cranmer, assisted by his old friend Archdeacon Nicholas Heath, were two bishops who were articulate and uncompromising traditionalists: Sampson of Chichester, a regular antagonist of the Archbishop, and, most remarkably, Bishop Stokesley of London, who had just come through some torrid times, centring on a charge of *praemunire* which looks like Cromwell's doing. Sampson and Stokesley deployed as adviser a favourite Court conservative, Dr Nicholas Wilson, in order to balance Heath.[24] The veteran Anglo-German Robert Barnes was a participant in the discussions, but, at the Germans' request, on their side!

The combination of viewpoints spoke to the self-image the King had chosen for himself amid the debates of the 1530s: proponent of the 'middle way', weighing opinions from both extremes and sternly holding the balance between them. At the time it was a favourite pose to claim oneself as the centre-point of extremes, and the King's centre-point did not coincide with any of those espoused by his theological team – not least because it was liable to shift without warning.[25] That was one good reason why Cromwell left the theologians at Lambeth Palace to get on with their business, just as he had in his vice-gerential synod the previous year. It was far more important for him to stick as closely as he could to the King, who was then on a long summer progress through Sussex and Kent. Other matters intertwined with the work of the Lambeth negotiators needed the sort of personal attention only he could provide. One difficulty was a build-up of tensions in summer 1538 with Lord and Lady Lisle, to whom Cromwell had previously been friendly and helpful. From now on, his increasingly less sympathetic interventions in their enclave of Calais contributed to the growing atmosphere of religious faction there.

Archbishop Cranmer was involved in rows with the Lisles almost as soon as he and Lisle arrived in their respective offices in 1533. He strongly disapproved of their traditionalist religious outlook, particularly Lady Lisle's, and provoked them by choosing John Butler, an aggressive proponent of evangelical reformation and a local man, as his Commissary for the enclave.[26]* Cromwell generally kept his distance from these spats, but in September 1537, in a foretaste of what was to come, he spectacularly lost his temper with his friend Sir Thomas Palmer, loosely in service to both Cromwell and the Lisles. Religion was at stake, in particular the arrest that summer of two conservative priests in Calais, who had been denounced by John Butler. Cromwell was convinced that the Lisles showed undue lenience to the pair, and as Palmer reported it to Lord Lisle, he 'swore by God's blood we were all papists, and looked through out our fingers' to sedition – or, as we would say, turned a blind eye to it. A shouting-match developed between Palmer and Cromwell in which 'he that was a stone's-cast off might hear us'. Their conversation settled down more constructively, and Cromwell's own letter to Lord Lisle written the same day as Palmer's made no mention of the incident.[27]

Now this following summer matters became much more fraught, over another Calais priest under suspicion for opposite reasons. Adam Damplip held views on eucharistic presence that were so advanced that they caused Cranmer some awkwardness in defining an acceptable version of them to let Damplip escape the worst. Despite this, Cromwell threw himself into this case.[28] Thomas Master's seventeenth-century notes from then extant State Papers preserve a precious glimpse of the Lord Privy Seal's incandescent letter to Lord Lisle on 14 August, otherwise now lost, defending Damplip. He stormed at the Deputy 'for persecuting those who favour and set forth God's word and favouring those who impugn it'; worse still, 'for suffering bruits to be scattered that the Bishop of London is Vicar-General of England, and all English books shall be called in, etc.'. There were secular complaints about Calais government too, and Cromwell invoked the ultimate sanction, 'to inform the King of him'.[29]

Cromwell was then on progress in Sussex with Henry, but he made a point of posting this letter via Cranmer at Lambeth Palace for forwarding to Calais, with a copy for the Archbishop's files. Cranmer was delighted by 'how frankly and freely you do admonish [Lisle]'.[30] Cromwell, Wriothesley and Richard Morison personally drew up the

---

* This John Butler should not be confused with the visitor to Zürich introduced in Chapter 15.

interrogatories for Damplip's chief opponent, Prior Dove of the Calais Carmelites, who was now under arrest as well. Among the questions was the very dangerous 'whether he was privy to the Bishop of London's letters to the Lord Deputy of Calais?' Questions followed about Dove's dealings with the Bishops of Chichester and Durham.[31] It is clear that both Cromwell and Cranmer saw Dove's interrogation as a means not merely to save Damplip, but also to save the German negotiations from disaster, by attacking the conservative bishops best placed to wreck them. Cranmer actually wrote Cromwell two letters on 18 August: the second detailed his efforts to stop the German envoys leaving for home in frustration at the lack of progress.[32]

Bishops Stokesley and Sampson remained delegates in the team at Lambeth, but extending Dove's interrogation to include Bishop Tunstall witnessed the fact that he was now a major player in the Schmalkaldic negotiations: not in person at Lambeth Palace but at the King's side on progress. After some very anxious years before the Pilgrimage of Grace, a sudden turnaround in Tunstall's fortunes came when in late June 1538 King Henry rewarded him for his steady service heading the Council in the North by summoning him to Court. It was soon clear that this was no punitive invitation to cause dread, when a royal letter told the Council that since Tunstall's arrival Henry had become 'minded to continue his demore [attendance] here about our person'. Cromwell made the best of an unwelcome situation by securing as Tunstall's replacement to lead the Council at York his reliable protégé the Yorkshire Gilbertine Robert Holgate Bishop of Llandaff, who had the potential to be a second Roland Lee for him in the North.[33]

That did not lessen the damage that Tunstall could do to evangelical hopes in his new close access to the King. In a list of abusively alliterative nicknames for conservative clerics he loathed, John Bale could think of nothing worse for Tunstall than 'Dreaming Durham', which suggests that what was so dangerous about the Bishop was a quality of quiet reflection he shared with Cranmer. Tunstall had none of the clerical arrogance which so infuriated Henry in other great prelates, and his nuanced analytical approach to theology produced broadly traditionalist conclusions. He was one of the best travelled and least provincial of English bishops, uniquely able among them to reflect from first-hand experience on Eastern Orthodox Christian custom.[34] Tunstall's household later recalled that through the subsequent summer progress months of 1538, 'the King's Majesty did call upon my Lord many times and talk with him on the way.'[35]

By September, Tunstall was formally installed on the Privy Council, to replace the deceased Bishop Foxe, with opposite partisan effect. It revealed how this new slimmed-down and bounded version of the King's Council created in 1536 put checks on Cromwell's freedom of manoeuvre. The promotion reflected the King's appreciation of Tunstall's help in dealing with the German delegation. Henry's disenchantment with them was much encouraged when they committed another faux pas: unwisely prompted by Cromwell, von Boineburg and Burchard wrote directly to the King at the beginning of August, asking him to clarify his position on various specified theological points under dispute. The King relished this sort of theological nitpicking and, as he responded, it was for the most part with Tunstall on hand as theological adviser. The disruptive business at Calais also reached its climax in August. The very fact that the Calais disturbances involved the arrest of opposing clergy highlighted the presence of conflict, which the King abhorred, and which in combination with his irritation at the direct manner of the German delegation easily turned towards sympathy with a conservative set of answers to their theological demands. By the time Henry had returned to London in September, it was clear that there would be no further progress. The Germans, not prepared to prolong the farce, were gone by the early days of October, with nothing achieved.[36]

This was a considerable setback for Cromwell's plans and for the evangelical cause in general. Yet it was only one half of the story of attempted reformation which needs completing before turning to the dynastic drama of autumn 1538. From the beginning of the year, Cromwell moved ever more decisively to knock down two pillars of traditional religious life in England and Wales: one, the friaries, and the other, pilgrimages to shrines and relics. These twin campaigns can be followed through together to the watershed of October 1538. Both treated the supremacy as a weapon of violent reform, purging old superstition. However much Cromwell loved his vice-gerential power, and King Henry relished the wealth gained from these acts of spoliation, there was a moral and theological dimension of which we must not lose sight. It was no coincidence that these campaigns were launched with an affirmation of vernacular Bible-reading. This came in February with a set-piece meeting of as many JPs who could be gathered from across the kingdom to meet the Lord Chancellor and Privy Council in Star Chamber: not a common event. They were told to spell it out to priests and people in their shires that it was now perfectly legal to own an English Bible, and that any clerical accusations of heresy should be filtered through secular legal process in quarter sessions.[37]

As we have seen, the downfall of shrines began in earnest in 1537, with Cromwell's confiscation of the Good Rood of Bromholm; yet even after the new round of monastic dissolutions represented by his deal with the Duke of Norfolk over Lewes and Castle Acre, Castle Acre's arm of St Philip still sat secure in new splendour, cared for by the Cluniac monks of Thetford. Now came much more public noise about a general destruction. It began in earnest on 24 February 1538, when Bishop Hilsey preached before a huge audience at Paul's Cross denouncing two relics, the Rood of Boxley Abbey (just dissolved) and the Holy Blood of Hailes Abbey. Hilsey ridiculed the Hailes relic even though it was still enshrined in its Gloucestershire monastery, but the Boxley Rood was on hand beside him, for exhibition and then gleeful destruction by his audience.[38] The Rood was a twelfth-century wooden crucifix from a period when (for devotional and not fraudulent purposes) some images were provided with moving parts. Hilsey and Cromwell seized on this antiquarian curiosity to highlight the frauds of the old faith, even though the 300-year-old contrivance had no current cult of significance.

It was the perfect launch of a campaign that would occupy the rest of the year. Swiss observers were gleeful at the reports; John Husee warned the Lisles in March about the scale of the campaign in mainland England, and suggested that the chief devotional image of Calais would be next. In deepest Suffolk, a prudent lady making her will in May left money to her parish church to make a picture of the Assumption of Our Lady 'if images still continue' – if not, for a font cover.[39] This was the moment when Gregory Cromwell reported to his father how the official campaign had sparked private-enterprise iconoclasm in Sussex. After a Sunday evening's fun in the alehouse, one likely lad said to another, 'There be many crosses digged up hereabouts, and men say there is much money under Willingdon Cross, which, if thou wilt be ruled by me, we will have.' The cross duly fell the following Saturday, but, alas for them, no treasure emerged and instead they faced an uncomfortable time before the Sussex bench. Nevertheless, the incident showed that Cromwell's campaign was achieving what it had set out to do: to rob sacred images of their power to intimidate or inspire.[40]

The campaign against the friars was launched slightly later, in April 1538, but thereafter was astonishingly complete and rapid. At the beginning of the year the whole tally of friaries created in the kingdom since the early thirteenth century stood intact. Even when the Observant Franciscans were dissolved as an order in 1534 for defying the King, their houses and communities were allowed to stand, transferred to compliant Conventual Franciscans. By the first months of 1539, all friaries had been closed. The speed of their demise (and in the English-speaking Pale of Dublin too) revealed that what had once been their greatest strength was now a fatal weakness: they were reliant on the lay public, in a much more profound way than monasteries or nunneries. Cromwell played on that weakness.[41]

To understand this paradox of rapid collapse, one should appreciate the difference between monks and friars. Monks predate friars; their name comes for the Greek for 'single' or 'solitary', not because monks were generally single hermits, but because their communities withdrew from the everyday world to concentrate on prayer. To achieve this, they would expect to be self-supporting, relying on their own landed estates, to minimize contact with disruptive secularity. The movement producing the friars in late twelfth-century Europe represented a criticism of the separateness of the monastic way of life, which many devout folk felt led to laziness and self-indulgence. The orders of friars made sure they would never be led into a life of inappropriately comfortable prosperity by the simple structural device of forbidding their communities to hold property.

This rule was never absolute, and law on property trusts evolved partly to get round it, but in general the principle held: friaries were never great landowners, and generally held no more than their own site and some minor rented property. Despite this, no attempt was made to include them in the Act of 1536 dissolving the lesser monasteries and nunneries, which left them unaffected. Indeed in 1536 the Norfolk monastery of Ingham tried to escape suppression (or at least unwelcome attention to its private deal with a local gentleman) by pretending that its quite rare affiliation to the Trinitarian Order made it a house of friars.[42] The consequence of the principle of true poverty was that friars could survive only by begging from the laity; they were 'mendicants', from the Latin *mendicare*, to beg. Since, unlike monks, they needed everyday contact with laypeople or they would perish, they were necessarily out in the world. Laypeople continued funding friars only for benefits in return, principally preaching and hearing confessions, but since such spiritual services brought friars much esteem, friary churches also became greatly in demand for intercessory masses in the purgatory industry.

Friars rapidly became the Western Church's specialists in preaching, so they needed to be intellectually alert and well informed. Soon they established friaries in university towns to get the best intellectual training they could, and Martin Luther the Austin Friar was only the latest among their academic stars. As a result, many of them followed Luther into that great rebellion of the intellect, the Reformation. Far more friars than monks turned into campaigning Protestant leaders: one might consider the Reformation as a revolution of friars faced with a pastoral crisis. Anguished at how they had collaborated in deceiving the laity, gabbling masses for the dead and doling out cheap forgiveness in the confessional, they now determined to make amends by preaching Luther's message of salvation by God's grace alone. We have met some English friars who took that route from early in Cromwell's public career, Miles Coverdale, Robert Barnes and later John Bale, and seen two prominent friars, John Hilsey and George Browne, transmogrify into reforming leaders of the Church under Cromwell's patronage.

To that list can be added another leading friar, Richard Ingworth, friend to Cromwell at least since becoming Prior of the royal Dominican foundation at King's Langley in the mid-1520s. Ingworth was associated with Hilsey and Browne in their visitations of friars under Cromwell's powers (see above, p. 265), and in December 1537 he followed them into the episcopate, though only as suffragan Bishop of Dover to Archbishop Cranmer. It is likely that all three ceased to believe in their vocation as friars during 1535, when Cromwell was prepared to let them loose on the wider Church as leaders in the name of evangelical reform. That is suggested in Ingworth's frank and spirited riposte to Cromwell in 1538, referring to his promotion as Bishop the year before: 'It hath pleased your Lordship to write to me as ye judge that though I have changed my habit, I have not changed my friar's heart. Good my Lord, judge me not so, for God shall be my judge, my friar's heart was gone two years before my habit, saving only my living.'[43]

What was now the point of being a friar? The structure of their orders linked them far more than most monastic orders to the centralizing power of Rome, which had formalized their existence at the height of the Papacy's medieval self-assertion in the thirteenth century. Their chief offering to the everyday life of the Church, confession and masses for the dead, formed part of the old superstition. Many friars used their talents in preaching and teaching to defend traditional religion, which in Cromwell's eyes made them worse than useless; they were enemies of the Gospel. The more friars who could be made to see this, the better. We find Cromwell early in 1538 personally doing just that in the prominent London house of the Franciscans: the Warden wrote to him in the course of other important business, in similar terms to Ingworth: 'Your Lordship spoke to me of changing my coat; of truth, my Lord, I put no confidence in my coat, neither in the colour nor fashion, neither toward life of body nor toward life of my soul, and that shall appear whensoever your Lordship shall command us to change, as ye may when ye will, and we will obey gladly, for we know that it is not against God's law.'[44]

On 6 February 1538 the King issued a commission to the newly consecrated Bishop Ingworth to visit all orders of friars under Cromwell's
vice-gerential authority.[45] Throughout his subsequent work Ingworth
was referred to as the 'Lord Visitor': a title partly dependent on his style
of address as Bishop, but also with a slightly novel and even secular feel
to it, a reminder that this was an enterprise under the Vice-Gerent.
Ingworth, perhaps preoccupied with duties for Cranmer, took until the
beginning of April to put his commission into effect; his first visit in what
turned out to be a destructive mission was a dash into East Anglia. This
was prompted by a close ally of Cromwell's, Thomas Lord Wentworth,
a peer with pronounced and articulate evangelical views, who had no
doubt heard of the imminence of national visitation. His intervention
showed the way to what became a general pattern.

On 1 April Wentworth wrote to Cromwell from his Suffolk home of
Nettlestead Hall, outlining the plight of the Franciscans of Ipswich, a
friary of exceptional splendour founded by his ancestors. They were 'in
great necessity and poverty, for that the inhabitants within the said town
and of the county be not so beneficial in showing their charity towards
them as they have been in times past'. The Ipswich Greyfriars in their
consequent destitution had sold their possessions just to survive, as their
wretched Prior confessed on being summoned to account for himself to
his founder at Nettlestead. Wentworth thoroughly approved of this shift
in public opinion. As he said at some didactic length, Suffolk's charity
was now directed to more worthy aims: a move which Wentworth himself, now the county's leading resident magnate after the Duke of Suffolk's
departure, had no doubt encouraged.[46] Wentworth 'called to remembrance' to the receptive ears of his correspondent that the orders of friars
were 'neither stock nor graft which the Heavenly Father hath planted,
but only a spiritual weed planted of that sturdy Nimrod the Bishop of
Rome, to rob Christ of his merits'. One sees how this opinionated nobleman might indeed have been the agent of John Bale's conversion. His
mini-sermon had a practical corollary: the friars had sold their house
to their founder, and he sought Cromwell's blessing on this convenient
acquisition of what he frankly pointed out could become his own residence in Ipswich. Both men would think of their mutual friend Sir
Humphrey Wingfield, with just such a pair of town and country residences in Tacket Street Ipswich and the nearby village of Brantham.

The result was immediate. Bishop Ingworth, who had set out from the
London Blackfriars probably towards the Midlands to start on his visit-
ation, was abruptly summoned back to St James's for a briefing with
Cromwell, and then made straight for Ipswich.[47] He inventoried the

house on Sunday 7 April, in the presence of the two town bailiffs and Cromwell's local agent William Laurence, together with members of Lord Wentworth's staff. This was a business of some delicacy, requiring maximum official presence, since another noble personage besides Wentworth was casting a frosty neighbourly eye on proceedings: the widowed Margaret Lady Curzon, whose husband's very recent tomb stood in Greyfriars church amid a remarkable heritage of aristocratic monuments, and who lived only a street away. Yet it all went off satisfactorily, as Laurence reported with relief to Cromwell: Ingworth showed 'much discretion, having so busy matters as ever I see man [anyone]' in the face of havoc and asset-stripping by the friars.[48]

No one really knew how to achieve the desired result at the Ipswich Greyfriars; there was no precedent to follow. There was no policy of general dissolution at this stage; that was not Cromwell's message in his briefing to Ingworth at St James's. Laurence summarized Ingworth's speech to the friars in their chapter house. The Bishop assured them that 'he was sent by your Lordship under the King not to dissolve any house or to destroy any house, but to reform; wherefore if that the house hereafter was dissolved, it was through their own negligence and by their own act.' He would leave them with enough goods to survive 'till their own fact [deed] put them out', at which point they should resort to Laurence, 'and he there delivered letters for each of them to go to another place' – that is, another Franciscan friary. One of the inventories noted that Laurence had custody of these letters 'whensoever the friars depart'.[49]

No deed of surrender survives for Greyfriars, and maybe the friars' previous sale to Lord Wentworth was silently accepted. Later on in the year, Augmentations officials noted that they had not interfered with the dissolved Greyfriars 'because of certain commandments given by my Lord Privy Seal, as it is said'.[50] Ingworth did not dissolve Ipswich's other two friaries until the autumn, though in the meantime he seized money the Carmelites had made from a sale of borough tenements and left them only part of the proceeds, in the hands of an Ipswich worthy, to loan to them as needed.[51] There were deep personal resonances for Cromwell in this untidy launch of the campaign on friaries at Ipswich: it must have pulled him back to those rain-soaked celebrations in September 1528 when he so lovingly orchestrated the opening of Cardinal College (see above, Chapter 4). Lord Wentworth was guest at the festivities that day, along with Sir Humphrey Wingfield. Guest of honour, however, had been Our Lady of Ipswich, whose shrine still stood in her chapel as Greyfriars tottered into oblivion.

In the same letter detailing Ingworth's proceedings, Laurence asked his master what to do with the shrine chapel and its priests, and whether he wanted Our Lady's offertory box emptied (Cromwell's senior servant John Milsent had the key). The priests had been funded for two decades by the father of the Maid of Ipswich, whose visions of Our Lady had anticipated those of the Maid of Kent; the late Lord Curzon had published a vivid eye-witness account of the wonders. Laurence also reminded Cromwell that the parishioners of St Peter's were still agitating to get back their church and its devotional furnishings from its dereliction after Cardinal College's closure – the same building hosting the College dedication in 1528.[52] After negotiations had sorted out the fate of Greyfriars, Lady Curzon transferred the remains of her late husband to the restored St Peter's Church, to lie with her under a new tomb made safe from the friary's dissolution; Lord Curzon, a parishioner, had been one of those concerned to see the church up and running again.[53]

To remedy the procedural difficulties exposed at Ipswich, the King issued Ingworth with a second mandate at the beginning of May, including explicit mention of his experiences of embezzlement in friaries, and spelling out his powers to seize and inventory their goods.[54] That did not end the Bishop's uncertainties. Writing in late May from a circuit of visitation in the Midlands and West Country, he detailed how he was using his supplementary powers. The picture was of general poverty and desperation: 'before the year be out, there shall be very few houses able to live, but shall be glad to give up their houses and provide for themselves otherwise.' In urban and lowland England, the public overwhelmingly hearkened to one message of Henry's Reformation: they were wasting their money on friars.[55]

The government encouraged this process not merely through Ingworth's prodding at demoralized communities, but also with specific moves to cripple the friars' traditional sources of income and curtail their pastoral activities. Roland Lee commissioned a set of injunctions for his clergy in his diocesan visitation of Coventry and Lichfield in June 1538. One order was that in future the laity were not to go to friaries for their Easter confessions. Lee presented this formerly routine practice as a slight to secular clergy, and moreover a sign that such layfolk must have particularly sleazy sins they wanted hidden from their parish priest. The Bishop would not have thought up this provision for himself; he would have copied it from some general pro-forma for visitation from the vicegerential office, and he asked Cromwell for his approval of the text of his injunctions before Berthelet printed it.[56] Yet there was still no vision of general suppression in Ingworth's letter of 23 May; 'very few' might survive amid what was becoming a general rout, but still some would. It was rather reminiscent of Cromwell's early advocacy of gradual and selective suppression of monasteries.

The Vice-Gerent's joint campaigns against friars and images were thus well launched by May. They came together even more pointedly than at Ipswich in London on 22 May, in one of the most horrific incidents of the Henrician Reformation: the burning of Friar John Forest for heresy.[57] Forest was a former member of the Greenwich Observants, who in early 1538 was living with the London Conventual Franciscans. Up to this time he had publicly accepted the royal supremacy, but his true opinions lay elsewhere. He was arrested (probably on Cromwell's authority as Vice-Gerent) for encouraging sedition when hearing confessions; one major issue was that he had used the confessional to encourage acceptance of the supremacy while rejecting it in conscience. The heresy charge centred on his affirmation that the Catholic Church was the Roman Church, and that priests in confession might turn the eternal pains of Hell into the time-limited pains of purgatory. In the background was the King's continuing terror of what might happen at the apparently imminent meeting of the General Council at Mantua; everything Forest had to say on the subject of Church Councils and papal authority over them contributed to his condemnation.

At first Forest recanted, but he was imprisoned in a cell of Newgate gaol with a conservative Carmelite and survivors of the imprisoned London Carthusians. That stiffened his resolve. He thus became a lapsed heretic, condemned for returning to 'heresies' that were actually commonplaces of late medieval Western Christianity. Instead of providing government theatre with a recantation at Paul's Cross, he burned at Smithfield. His cruel fate reflected what King Henry would have liked to have done to Reginald Pole; it was deliberately pitched beyond the normal ghastly drama of heretic-burning. Forest hung in chains roasting over a fire partly fuelled by the chopped-up remains of a particularly aggressive wooden cultic image from north Wales, a warrior-saint called Dderfel Gardarn ('mighty Dderfel'). At the beginning of April Dr Ellis ap Rhys (for whom Cromwell had engineered appointment as diocesan Commissary in St Asaph), alerted his master to Dderfel's seditious potential, having witnessed the crowds at a festival for the saint. Cromwell immediately ordered the image to be carted up to London, and it arrived by the end of the month.[58]

The massive, beast-like wooden setting-block for Dderfel's image still survives in Llandderfel church, a bleak and direct link to a Tudor atrocity (see Plate 43). The effigy's public destruction at Smithfield despite outraged Welsh demands for its restoration, even offers of substantial cash, spread an intransigent message of religious change beyond lowland England. Everything about this event could be a lesson for the audience of thousands, led by Cromwell, Cranmer, the Dukes of Norfolk and Suffolk, the Earls of Sussex and Hertford, and Bishop, Mayor and Sheriffs of London. Pinned to the scaffold were simple racy verses mocking both image and human victim, composed by William Grey (or Gray), one of Cromwell's literary clients who appears to have been a recently secularized Dominican friar: they were excerpted from a gleeful ballad Grey published that year celebrating official iconoclasm, in the same knockabout style as Bale's plays.[59]

The drama of this occasion included a sermon from England's star evangelical preacher Hugh Latimer, addressed to Forest before he burned. The main topic was idolatry. This was a preaching opportunity to which Latimer looked forward with more relish than some may consider decent, but he had an excellent record of success in converting friars to the evangelical cause, and this was too good a moment to miss.[60] The fiery display following Latimer's oratory jointly punished idolatry, papistry and Catholic views of penance. Ap Rhys had told Cromwell of the Welsh belief that Dderfel could fetch anyone out of Hell who made him an offering; this paralleled Forest's exalted view of the efficacy of confession. It also underlined the fate of those exercising casuistry in stating their faith, particularly in taking oaths: Grey's doggerel included the line 'Forest the Friar, that obstinate liar'. Confession was a powerful weapon of traditional religion, and confessors must take note of Forest's fate.

This was calculated educational terrorism, but, compared with Hilsey's barnstorming performance at Paul's Cross in February as the Boxley Rood was destroyed, it was not an unqualified success. Some already committed to the evangelical cause did celebrate Forest's execution: that night a crowd took up the message of iconoclasm by breaking into the parish church of St Margaret Pattens and destroying its rood, a major object of devotion in the City. When outraged City officials rounded up those they could catch, the iconoclasts claimed the Lord Privy Seal's authorization; their leader was the radical printer John Gough, whom we have seen benefiting from Cromwell's custom.[61] Yet Forest's death must also have offended many in the vast audience by marginally exceeding the acceptable level of gruesomeness in burning heretics.

Tellingly, Latimer's sermon that day has not survived, and it was not included in any of the early editions of his pulpit oratory. Even more significantly, the Henrician regime quietly gave up on presenting papalist or traditionalist convictions as a crime of heresy. There was a doctrinal standard under which it could have done so, the Bishops' Book of the year before, but in the middle of Henry's omnivorous marital overtures abroad in the shadow of a Franco-Imperial alliance against England, pursuing this line would be very unwise. Any potential bride from European royal houses might theoretically be liable to heresy charges the moment she landed in England, an idea both embarrassing and absurd. Small wonder that Henry himself, and his more straightforwardly Protestant successors, henceforth killed Catholics (when required) not as heretics but as traitors or fomenters of sedition, with a different set of sadistic punishments.

This set of prudential thoughts probably took some time to crystallize, but Cromwell's evangelical propaganda machine forged ahead. His tame printers John Gough and James Nicholson published a fierce attack on the friars, attributed mendaciously but with imaginative commercial acumen to Geoffrey Chaucer and almost certainly a Lollard tract from his time. The printers used the same Holbein-designed title-page previously used for works by Melanchthon and Tyndale.[62] Fifteen-thirty-eight saw Nicholson's enterprising press produce a surprising novelty: the earliest known English translation of a text by a Zürich theologian, not something for which the King would have shown any enthusiasm. It was a commentary by Heinrich Bullinger on the Second Epistle to the Thessalonians, perhaps part of a projected set of companions to Bible-reading of which the publisher then thought better. As yet, there was not enough of an English market for this sort of expository text. Its most prominent theme was appropriate for this year of confrontation and turmoil: how to endure Antichrist's persecution, Antichrist being the Pope, as Bullinger helpfully pointed out. The tract was spiced up with local colour, in the form of sneers at named English shrines closed by Cromwell that same year.[63]

Together these two publications emphasized the links between the campaigns against shrines and friars exemplified in Forest's execution. That June a royal order went out in London that former monks and friars must cease to wear their habits in public. John Foxe preserves a story about the Scottish-born poet-friar Alexander Barclay from a source which could not be more reliable, Cranmer's publisher the immigrant evangelical Reyner Wolfe, probably an eye-witness. A parallel reference in Charles Wriothesley's London Chronicle pins the incident precisely to the time of the order against friars. Barclay had been an Observant Franciscan, like Forest. After that he sailed very close to the wind in an itinerant ministry of preaching and counselling on theology, with a conservative agenda. He now had a bruising encounter with the Lord Privy Seal, who happened to be walking through Paul's Churchyard and spotted Barclay in Reyner Wolfe's bookshop, still defiantly wearing his habit. ' "Yea, said [Cromwell], will not that cowl of yours be left off yet? An if

I hear by one o'clock that this apparel be not changed, thou shalt be hanged immediately, for example to all other." And so putting his cowl away, he never durst wear it after.' Eventually Barclay did became a convinced Protestant, through the rather more gentle persuasion of Archbishop Cranmer.[64]

While the scales were thus increasingly weighted against the survival of friaries, public uncertainty still remained. Cromwell bypassed Ingworth in dealing with the Oxford and Cambridge friaries, which were in a different category of usefulness, and possibly worth saving. Dr London reported with annoyance that one of his fellow-commissioners at Oxford had returned from the capital in early July saying that 'the four Orders in Oxford and Cambridge should stand', and this stiffened the Dominicans against surrender.[65] Cromwell's intentions were more decisively expressed in the case of Queens' College Cambridge, home to senior evangelicals who knew him well, like Simon Haynes, Thomas Smith and William May. Here the Fellows ignored all the niceties: they simply demanded the Carmelite friary next door, sending an admittedly flowery Latin letter to the Lord Privy Seal on the same day in August that they accepted a private surrender from the Carmelites (the College did not trouble Cromwell with that detail). Remarkably, they got their wish straight away. Smith and a colleague chased Cromwell right down to Petworth in Sussex on the King's progress, and came away with his personally countersigned royal order to them for a more formal surrender, which they duly executed, for all the world as if they were Bishop Ingworth himself.[66]

Ingworth was still treating his own commission as a genuine visitation in late July. Amid the general meltdown, he repeatedly left open those friaries in good order, but was at a loss to know how to distribute among them the considerable number of friars from others still wanting to continue in their vocations.[67] It was 28 July before he received Cromwell's evidently testy answer to his report, at last spelling out a revised purpose: a general suppression. Even then, Ingworth punctiliously insisted on doing everything by the book: he must have the right paperwork to give friars a new career as secular priests.[68] He continued to deploy the same rhetoric as before. A memorandum of the formula he used survives from his visit to Stafford, with houses of Franciscans (his most troublesome order) and Austin Friars. The Bishop assured the friars that he had no commission for suppression, 'nor I use no such fashion in any place. I am sent to reform every man to a good order and to give injunctions for preservation of the same.' On hearing these injunctions, neither community felt motivated to continue. A local gentleman in a consortium who had given a meadow in return for the saying of masses for the dead wanted his land back, since they would no longer take place.[69]

And so the picking apart of English friaries continued. Ingworth and Dr London led the charge, with occasional help from Bishop Hilsey. On the way, many urban corporations, Ipswich among them, picked up useful buildings for civic purposes, not least through some steady pressure on Cromwell from Dr London. After some characteristically courtly begging letters, the Universities of Oxford and Cambridge also benefited. Ingworth's pleas to Cromwell for capacities for friars to become secular clergy were answered by Cranmer's Faculty Office in a big round-up on 10 September, a significant incentive to other friars to secure their future by co-operating.[70] A notably poignant moment occurred in November 1538, when Bishop Ingworth evicted his Dominican brethren from his own priory of King's Langley. Thereafter his letters to Cromwell rarely lacked a postscript reminder that he wanted Langley for an episcopal residence, given that he had no other, which heroic persistence eventually produced a formal grant in February 1540.[71] By late spring 1539, the friars were dispersed from their houses throughout the kingdom, even in the furthest North. With customary male cowardice, the government took a little longer to evict the aristocratic ladies of the four female convents which followed Franciscan or Dominican Rules.

Those days of September when so many friars were processed by Cranmer's bureaucracy into the wider Church were also a symbolic moment in a gradual dissolution of the uniquely English Order of the Gilbertines, so carefully spared in the first Dissolution Act of 1536. On 24 September the Master, Robert Holgate, another religious fortified in his evangelical conversion by a mitre, surrendered the nominal head house of Sempringham in Lincolnshire, where St Gilbert had begun the whole enterprise four centuries before. The task might be relatively straightforward, because the whole order was a single corporation headed by Holgate, and it did not require the sort of strenuous tour of visitation made by Ingworth and London for the friars. Nevertheless, in significant contrast to the friars, the Gilbertines were not extinguished in a single operation. It was not until early December 1539, while the very last monasteries went down, that Holgate surrendered his own house of Watton Priory in Yorkshire, long the real chief house of the order. Holgate needed a home base as President of the Council in the North, and he got a life grant of the house (including, very usefully, the Master's London residence), together with another major Yorkshire Gilbertine priory at Malton, the last to surrender, two days after Watton.[72]

*

September 1538 was a watershed in Cromwell's dual campaign, for it also saw the climax of his steady assault on cultic images. In the premier league was Our Lady of Walsingham, collected by royal commissioners from Walsingham Priory in mid-July along with her jewellery and taken to Lambeth Palace to impress the German delegates with English commitment to the theological dialogue. Cromwell and Lord Chancellor Audley were among those on hand to receive her on 18 July.[73] It was not then clear what would happen to her, but images of the second rank were gathered at the Lord Privy Seal's home at Austin Friars, stowed among his spare beds, stripped bare of their clothes, candles and prayers. Our Lady of Ipswich was among the first, shipped down along the coast by William Laurence, with Lord Wentworth grimly making sure there was no trouble in the borough. Laurence saw to it that her shrine church was swiftly demolished, and the stone used in repairing his own parish church near by.[74] By the beginning of September she had been joined at Austin Friars by St Anne of Buxton, St Modwen from Burton Abbey and, from Basingstoke, an image of the Holy Spirit (whatever that can have been).[75]

The culmination of all this in September was another ideological public bonfire, this time only of wooden images with no human victim. Our Lady of Walsingham was chief fuel, but alongside her burned the other figures in Cromwell's collection at Austin Friars and probably some not otherwise recorded. They were taken out to Cromwell's temporary rural home at Chelsea; the location obliquely spoke of the difficulty of the occasion and perhaps of the ambiguous reception of Friar Forest's death back in May. Chelsea was near enough London for the interested to congregate, but not so near that casual passers-by could coalesce into hostile demonstrations.[76] One hesitates to suggest that a subsidiary consideration may have been to annoy Ambassador Castillon, lodged so close by. At the same time, a further cultic image was solemnly cremated in another place with memories for Cromwell: a rood at Boston, where a Dominican preached to the onlookers justifying its destruction. That event was orchestrated by a former colleague from Cardinal College Ipswich days, the composer John Taverner.[77] Cromwell himself was elsewhere, having rejoined the King on his progress in Kent, for the greatest set-piece of all in his campaign: the destruction of St Thomas Becket's shrine at Canterbury, rival to Walsingham in international renown (both were recent victims of Erasmus's literary satire).

Even before the break with Rome, William Tyndale had warned King Henry that Becket was his enemy. Reading Tyndale's evangelical refashioning of English history in *The Practice of Prelates*, the King saw the point.[78] Becket's cult was from the outset an assertion of the Church's moral and political superiority over the English monarchy. His centuries-old popularity (attested by Thomas Cromwell's own forename, along with that of a host of other Tudor Englishmen) was firmly rooted in popular belief that he had been killed by Henry II's henchmen for opposing tyrannical royal taxation: that was a favourite theme of pardoners as they sold their indulgences.[79] How many reasons did the latest King Henry and his chief financial genius need for hating the saint's memory? And what better occasion could there be for humiliating Becket and the pretensions of the traditional Church than the progress of its new Head through Canterbury?

On his visit the King lodged in his most recent royal palace, the lately dissolved abbey of St Augustine, Canterbury's second grand and ancient monastery. The city was thronged with notables, ranging from Lord Lisle (for once allowed to leave Calais, after many pleas) to Ralph Sadler, plus a generous selection of Cromwell's servants from Wriothesley downwards. This latter group were busy pulling down Becket's shrine, before they moved on to Winchester Cathedral to perform a similar service for St Swithin, before Bishop Gardiner returned from his long embassy in France.[80] The jewels of Becket's shrine were naturally cannibalized for the King's Privy Coffers. Cromwell had at least part of Becket's bones burned – with the same theological justification as Friar Forest's fate: defending the heresy of faith in the Papacy. He said as much in a draft pamphlet prepared probably for international use the following year. Though it claimed that the majority of the remains had been 'put away secretly' to avoid superstition, the burning was what stuck in the public imagination, as far away as Rome.[81] The jollification at Canterbury included John Bale's latest drama of evangelical triumph, on the subject of Becket's treasons (see above, Chapter 17).

In one of those coincidences of which 1538 was full, Bale's play was staged on the Nativity of Our Lady, 8 September, the day Cardinal College Ipswich had been officially launched ten years before. Three days earlier, the Vice-Gerent 'exhibited' his latest official injunctions to the Church of England, that word almost certainly meaning that this was the occasion on which he formally presented them to the King. Once more these injunctions included an order for every parish to furnish itself with a Bible (now much more feasible than in 1536, thanks to the Vice-Gerent's encouragement of Bible printing); there was also the famous requirement for parish registers for baptisms, marriages and funerals. Versions of these injunctions had been circulating since May, as at that time one set was used for visitation by Cranmer's officials in the vacant diocese of Hereford. September represented a formal relaunch, and added some new items specifically condemning Becket and his cult.[82] Back in London, the Mercers' Chapel dedicated to St Thomas on the site of his childhood home was thoroughly purged of anything to do with its saint, who had unsurprisingly been richly celebrated in the building. The injunctions were clearly hostile to the provision of and attention to images generally; it has been observed that, thereafter, virtually no new images were provided in churches until Queen Mary ordered them again two decades later.[83] Altogether in enactment, theatre and action this represented the most forward moment of the Vice-Gerency's reforming zeal: for once – and for a moment only – it was done with the unambiguous and enthusiastic consent of King Henry himself.

Looking back over these eventful nine months, it is apparent how much they represented a farewell to earlier episodes in Cromwell's career. One silent farewell was to Thomas Wolsey, when in the last days of August 1538 the abbey of St Mary at Leicester surrendered to Cromwell's commissioners, his servants John Freeman and Dr Francis Cave. The abbey held the grave of the fallen Cardinal, stricken on his last journey south back in 1530. After that, Cromwell had taken a special interest in the house, usually via his nephew Richard. Its last Abbot, John Bourchier, was his appointment, over which he had taken some trouble in 1534, and in 1540 Bourchier was lined up to be Bishop for a new diocese of Shrewsbury, had it been established.[84] When Leicester Abbey closed, it is likely that quiet arrangements ensured a decent reburial for the Cardinal's corpse, but since everyone involved in the smoothly executed surrender knew each other well, nothing needed to be committed to paper. Dr Cave meaningfully asked the Lord Privy Seal what should be done with the abbey buildings, as yet intact, with the implication that the institution or its church might continue in some way; he remarked that 'a hundred marks yearly will not sustain the charges in repairing this house if all buildings be let stand.'[85]

By contrast to the discretion at Leicester, we have viewed rich surviving evidence which recalled Cromwell to his service to the Cardinal at Ipswich. The town of Ipswich was transformed in 1538. Wolsey had intended his native borough to be a showcase of a reformed humanist Catholicism, its wonder-working Marian shrine nestling amid a dozen and more parish churches. Around this ensemble in stately guardianship would stand the three friaries and surviving Augustinian priory, alongside the greatest institution of all, Cardinal College. Instead, thanks to close co-operation between the Lord Privy Seal and Thomas Lord Wentworth, Ipswich became a model borough of the continent-wide Protestant Reformation. Parish church towers still jostled the skyline, but all others were gone, and in the former Dominican friary the town now cherished its restored school alongside a public workhouse and accommodation for the destitute. Wentworth installed Thomas Becon, a future star of Protestant reformation, as priest of Ipswich's largest parish chantry (founded by Cardinal Wolsey's rich uncle Edmund Dandy), in anticipation of the Puritan lecturers cherished by the town in later years. Ipswich's transformation and its notoriously Puritan future paradoxically came courtesy of the man who cherished the Cardinal's memory most.[86]

In the middle of this destruction of shrines and friaries in September, in a curious and poignant chance, Cromwell's turning of the page was symbolized by the death of an elderly *grande dame* who meant much to him. Jane Vaux, widow of a famous pilgrim to Jerusalem, Sir Richard Guildford, stepmother of Sir Edward and mother of Sir Henry, was 'Mother Guildford' to the royal Court, and dowager of all dowagers. We met Lady Guildford in 1535 in some dudgeon about her residence at Bristol's Gaunts Hospital, and her annoyance with Cromwell may well have been soothed in early 1537 by the lease of a small dissolved Bristol nunnery, over which Cromwell took some considerable trouble for her sake. 'Clearly I perceive your especial mind towards her,' said Richard Rich of Augmentations, restraining his irritation, after a second badgering from the Lord Privy Seal on the subject.[87] Such profit from the dissolution did not unsettle Lady Guildford's conservative piety. When not in Bristol, she lodged palatially in the precinct of the London Blackfriars, where long ago the Guildfords' dear family friend Sir Thomas Brandon had been buried. It was at Blackfriars that she died on 4 September, just as Cromwell's commissioners set out to do their work at Canterbury.[88]

Lady Guildford's executors were Cromwell's friend (and sometime patron) Sir John Gage and her Anglo-Italian cousin Sir William Penizon. She made the Lord Privy Seal supervisor of her will, to be good lord to them and her household 'in like manner as he hath been to me in life'. He got a gold and jewelled crucifix for his trouble. In this will, last revised only a week before her death, she left a generous legacy to the London Dominicans to pray for her, and her funeral there was of a traditional splendour which made Penizon a little nervous for the messages it might convey to the general public.[89] For Cromwell, that would be a minor concern. All due respect had been paid to a matriarch of Tudor high society who would have expected nothing less. Two months later Blackfriars closed along with all other London friaries, part of a general round of dissolutions that month that at a stroke removed all save one of the capital's religious houses, including at long last the London Charterhouse. Only St Bartholomew's Priory in Smithfield, a satellite of the King's favoured abbey of Waltham, survived, for another year.

Lady Guildford was gone, and with her an era. Others that autumn and winter did not receive such an honourable dispatch. Fifteen-thirty-eight was a turning-point, as more and more of the country's political elite perfectly prepared to accept King Henry's new dispensation were nevertheless pushed to the conclusion that Thomas Cromwell was too dangerous to lead it. Those whom they would have considered their inferiors watched the drama with cynical interest. At the beginning of the year, in the course of his ever-vigilant scrutiny of seditious words noted and sent in by conscientious local magistrates, Cromwell read of some smallholders on the edge of the Cambridgeshire fens. Wherever truth lay in recollections of relaxed conversations during the harvest of 1536, these words formed a well-observed commentary on the two years since Cromwell had gained his greatest office as Lord Privy Seal. John Raven and William Marshall accused each other of saying 'Was not my Lord Cardinal a great man, and ruled all the realm as he would? What became of him? Is he not gone? Also Sir Thomas More, High Chancellor of England – did not he in like wise rule all the whole realm? What became of him? Is he not gone?' Raven then admitted to spelling out the logic of these truths: 'And now my Lord Privy Seal in like manner ruleth all, and we shall see once the day that he shall have as great a fall as any of them had . . .'[90] As Cromwell turned the page, he may have brooded on how many others agreed, particularly among those close to the King.

PART FIVE

Nemesis

Woe be unto them that have lost patience, forsaken the right ways, and are turned back into froward ways. What will they do, when the Lord shall begin to visit them?

Ecclesiasticus 2.14, in the translation of Miles Coverdale, 1535

God preserve you in long life in the finishing of many things well begun, and to the performance of many things yet unperfect.

Hugh Latimer Bishop of Worcester to Cromwell, summer 1538

20

Shifting Dynasties: 1538–1539

In July 1538 a monastery was dissolved at Bisham in Berkshire. That might not seem worthy of remark when houses of religion were disappearing all over the realm, but there was one bizarre feature here: the monastery was founded less than a year before, by royal charter, as 'the King's monastery of Bisham', dedicated to the Holy Trinity and conceived as no mean foundation: a Benedictine abbey with a mitred abbot. Only a few months before Abbot Cordrey received his charter in December 1537, he and his monks had possessed a different identity, as the ancient royal foundation of St Peter's Chertsey, surrendered to the Crown. Now moved up-river to Bisham, Cordrey had not previously enjoyed the privilege of a mitre (which potentially carried with it a seat in the House of Lords). Appropriately for that honour, he was named as a county JP on two successive commissions of the peace in Berkshire, in March and May 1538.[1]

The puzzle becomes all the more acute on visiting Bisham and viewing the bumpy field beside the Thames where once stood this new abbey and its predecessor on the site, an Augustinian priory dissolved in July 1537. Not a stone remains visible, but what the new occupants from Chertsey would have found on their arrival was a church stuffed full of the tombs of nobility. No more than a few brisk paces away loomed a great mansion, part of which does survive. It was then principal home to Margaret Pole Countess of Salisbury, mother to Henry Pole Lord Montague and his younger brothers Reginald and Geoffrey; the tombs housed their ancestors. What are we to make of all this? Pursuing the story backwards, it is worth noting that Thomas Cromwell knew this stretch of the Thames well: 3 miles away across the river was Little Marlow Priory, where Prioress Vernon had tutored Gregory Cromwell in his childhood.

In April 1535, Cromwell took a decisive interest in a new prior of Bisham in the middle of a disputed election. Against opposition from the Countess of Salisbury, who tried to get the incumbent Prior to stay on, Cromwell's militantly evangelical protégé William Barlow gained the post; Master Secretary clearly judged that this institution needed his variety of firm leadership.[2] Barlow was in fact absentee as diplomat and soon Bishop in Wales, and as Bisham's commendatory head he surrendered the priory to the Crown.[3] Given how obnoxious Barlow would be to the Countess, she may not have mourned his removal, but her thoughts would then turn to how to preserve the family mausoleum. What better device than an elaborate scheme for a new monastery, carefully honouring her royal cousin and the memory of his lately deceased Queen Jane, staffed by a set of monks of impeccable Catholic respectability from Chertsey?

Those were the terms on which the new Bisham Abbey opened, handsomely endowed, in December 1537. Ironically, one of its new possessions was the dissolved priory of Beddgelert in Wales, for which the Countess herself had solicited Cromwell back in 1532, looking for a grant to a servant of the Lady Mary. When the abbey closed six months later, it is clear that Cromwell and his staff had no regrets. Richard Leighton, in charge of the operation, went out of his way to be sarcastic about a community he portrayed as already in dissolution: 'the monks of small learning and much less discretion' scrambling over themselves to auction off even their habits, and the Abbot a drunk and 'a very simple man'. All this despite the fact that someone the previous year had considered Abbot Cordrey worthy of a seat in the House of Lords. Yet Leighton also noted scrupulously for his master that 'the church we stir not, nor no part thereof.'[4] This was in June 1538, but in fact it was soon gone. That autumn, amid a welter of depositions about treason, a suspect canon of Chichester Dr George Crofts deposed that 'he had heard Sir Geoffrey Pole lament the pulling-down of Bisham, because his kin and ancestors lay there.' The Countess had deplored it too, although in one of her depositions in the autumn she also admitted that this venture had brought its own doom: she 'much lamented the living' of the Chertsey monks 'which was the cause' of the new dissolution.[5]

Altogether the untidy end of Bisham Abbey in July 1538, abruptly terminated after hardly having begun, its mausoleum church demolished in front of the Countess of Salisbury's windows, looks like a calculated insult to a great noble affinity: the first shot in a conflict breaking into the open during autumn, in which Cromwell encouraged the King to harry and cull the group of Court nobility who had never been reconciled to religious change. Prominent among them were Lord Montague and his cousin the Marquess of Exeter. With Montague's mother the Countess of Salisbury as their general matriarch, they had long flirted with sedition, back to their interest in the Maid of Kent and through constant private conversations with Ambassador Chapuys about foreign intervention.

Worse still, the Countess's evident closeness to her former charge the Lady Mary fuelled the King's suspicions that she had stiffened Mary's obstinacy at various key junctures. After the business had reached its bloody conclusion, Cromwell spelled out that possibility to Chapuys, tartly observing that he and his imperial colleagues must have known of these intrigues, and worse: attempts to marry Mary to the Marquess and sideline Prince Edward.[6]

Lurking behind all this was the uncomfortable fact that King Henry and his family had a lesser share of historic royal blood than the Courtenays and Poles between them possessed through their Yorkist ancestry. This mattered all the more to King Henry now that his legitimate heir was a robust one-year-old. History has come to call the autumn debacle the Exeter or Montague Conspiracy. How much actual conspiracy was involved is not clear, but the events were not short of the conspiratorial on all sides. On the Exeter group's most exposed flank were victims already: the Maid herself, More, Fisher, Hussey, Darcy, plus one whom the King would dearly love to become his victim, Reginald Pole. At their other extreme was the ultra-loyalist and amiably harmless Lord Lisle, Deputy of Calais, whose own Plantagenet blood quotient was 50 per cent, but illegitimate. As noted in the previous chapter, Calais provided the first open battleground in summer 1538, but while trouble there rumbled through that summer, Cromwell took advantage of his journeys in southern counties around the royal progress to gather intelligence on the Countess and her circle.

As early as June a group of friends, whose common link was Chichester Cathedral and who included a servant of Cromwell's, fell out over whether to reveal 'a great confederacy' between the Marquess of Exeter, Lord Montague, Lord Sandys and Lord De La Warr, all conservative peers of the region.[7] In fact, the vital information came from a different informant, Gervase Tyndale alias Clifton, a client of Cromwell who had been on the staff of Cardinal College Oxford.[8] Tyndale was no relation to the Bible translator, but was closely related to the Midlands family of Clifton, sires to more than one Cambridge don and kin to Archbishop Cranmer. He returned from Oxford to the Midlands as schoolmaster of Grantham, one of a select group of activists promoting evangelical reformation in the region and keeping Cromwell informed on dissent.[9] By autumn 1537 the Provost of Eton was thanking the Lord Privy Seal for providing Tyndale, 'your own true scholar and bedeman', to replace the raffish Nicholas Udall as schoolmaster at the College.[10]

In some mischance of health the following summer, Tyndale became a patient resident with a doctor called Richard Eyer, on the Hampshire

coast at Warblington. This happened to be the second residence of the
Countess of Salisbury. It will have been via Bisham and Eton that she and
her household knew Tyndale, and she detested his religious opinions,
ordering him to leave Warblington in July or August 1538. That ulti-
matum provoked Tyndale and his host to talk of the general atmosphere
of conservative religious dissent in the Salisbury circle, but more specifically about her contacts abroad, up to and including sending letters to
Cardinal Pole. These new accusations concerned John Helyar, the Countess's senior chaplain and parson of Warblington, whom Cromwell had
already examined about his travel abroad; Helyar was spending more
and more time overseas. On the previous occasion, Reginald's brother Sir
Geoffrey Pole and Sir William Paulet between them 'made such shift that
the matter was cloaked [concealed]'. Tyndale now hurried to use his various contacts with Cromwell to convey further alarms, including news of
renewed correspondence with Helyar from the Countess and Sir Geoffrey. He buttonholed the Lord Privy Seal, then staying with his son at
Lewes, but yet again Sir Geoffrey persuaded Cromwell that there was
nothing in it. Matters had now arrived into the last days of August.[11]

This sequence of events sounds all very haphazard and circumstantial,
and twice the Poles had exercised their credit with the King to slide the
family circle away from trouble. Yet it was part of a gathering storm of
little incidents and conflicts all tending in the same direction. The troubles at Calais involving the Lisles were part of that pattern. The result
was only accidental in the sense that the fall of Anne Boleyn was accidental; both convulsions were triggered by happenstance, no single incident
of which would have proved fatal without the vigilance and helping hand
of a man looking out for such matters, waiting for the right moment to
persuade the King of their significance.[12] There was an odd recruit to the
Surrey commission of the peace in summer 1538: Jasper Horsey, a Devon
man and servant to the Marquess of Exeter. Horsey became a key witness against the Courtenay/Pole circle, and was later also useful against
the collateral victim of these stirs, Sir Nicholas Carew. He was granted
some of Carew's property and what can only be a reward for services
rendered: a position as Gentleman Usher of the Chamber, just before 22
February 1539. Horsey looks suspiciously like Cromwell's agent of investigation within the Courtenay household.[13]

So matters continued into September 1538. There was talk in Sussex
that 'if my Lady of Salisbury had been a young woman, the King and his
Council would have burnt her at their late being in the country' on the
royal progress: that is, she would have suffered the prescribed penalty for
female traitors. For a moment in early September Sir Geoffrey seemed

safe, but one of his henchmen, Hugh Holland, was taken up to London a bound prisoner for examination.[14] Just at this juncture, Richard Cromwell's father-in-law Sir Thomas Denys arrested a Breton priest down in Devon, after mysterious journeys which had begun in Sussex. The man told wild tales about the Poles and in particular a clandestine visit to England by Cardinal Pole which mostly seem fantasy, but he clearly did know the family.[15]

This was the tipping-point. By the end of the month, Sir Geoffrey was in the Tower, so crushed by the turn of events that he attempted suicide. As he and others added their fragments to a picture of discontented posturing and occasionally treasonous words, enough was pieced together from early November to justify the arrest of Exeter, Montague and eventually the Countess of Salisbury herself.[16] Ambassador Castillon, still lodged in Chelsea, straight away saw this crisis for what it was: 'Long ago this King said to me that he would like to wipe out this House of Montague, which still represents the White Rose [of York] – and the House of Pole from which the Cardinal comes.'[17] Now those sharing the King's inclination in that direction, principally Cromwell, had the task of keeping their master fixed to that destructive aim.

This agenda had its problems, because the autumn of 1538 proved a switchback of religious extremes, always dangerous for what by now we can call a new evangelical establishment. Among the peerage they numbered Cromwell, the Grey network, the Seymour family interest and their circle of friendship, and on the ecclesiastical side Cranmer and the group of like-minded bishops from Hilsey to Latimer to Shaxton, backed up by their clientage in the universities.[18] The evangelical clergy were much more clear-cut in their views, more committed by vocation and hence more exposed, than the noblemen. Nevertheless, all were painfully aware of their vulnerability, particularly now that one of their most determined opponents, Stephen Gardiner, had returned from near three years of embassy in France, vigilant for any opportunity to arouse the King's suspicions of evangelical proceedings.

The evangelicals' strategy to cover their backs was to show themselves as severe as possible to those on their more radical flank. In any case they saw the persecution of Anabaptists as a necessary and congenial task to protect godly religion, as was apparent when the threat first appeared in 1535 (see above, Chapter 12). It was helpful that a renewed warning of Anabaptist activity in England came in a letter to King Henry from their own allies in mainland Europe, Philipp of Hessen and Johann Friedrich of Saxony. Radical activity, it turned out, had extended to a printed English tract challenging orthodox views on the nature of Jesus Christ.

Cromwell acted straight away, appointing vice-gerential commissioners from the areas around London where the threat was most acute; the commissioners were balanced between evangelicals and conservatives. Burnings of Anabaptists followed in the capital and in Colchester.

Alongside that campaign was an affair potentially far more dangerous to the evangelical cause, because it involved one of their own, a former don of Queens' Cambridge called John Lambert alias Nicholson. In 1531, when the old Church leadership was still fighting its corner, Convocation singled Lambert out for prosecution alongside such figures of the future establishment as Hugh Latimer. By winter 1536 it was Cranmer and Latimer who found themselves constrained to get Lambert imprisoned by Chancellor Audley for sounding off about prayer to saints. Now, in autumn 1538, Lambert confronted a prominent London evangelical and royal chaplain, John Taylor, with outspoken scepticism about the bodily presence of Christ in eucharistic bread and wine. Taylor called on Robert Barnes to help him defend a real-presence theology which avoided papal error (Barnes was, after all, the most obvious and authentic Lutheran in all England), and he then brought in Cranmer. The Archbishop prudently put Lambert in confinement again – but all in vain: fatally convinced of his own rightness, Lambert appealed to the King to hear his case.

This was a disastrous misjudgement. Henry's customary inclination to occupy himself with theology when lacking a wife made him take a particular interest in the case, and his mood was currently veering towards the conservative end of his volatile spectrum. That was apparent from a new royal proclamation on religion: a personal public intervention, side-lining his Vice-Gerent, who one might have thought had already produced enough regulation for the Church less than two months before. The proclamation followed up various of Cromwell's orders, and repeated condemnations of Anabaptism and Becket, but it also imposed censorship on the printing press, including unauthorized versions of the Bible, and it expressly forbade clergy to marry – a reaction to the fact that in southern England a number of clergy were doing just that (not to mention the Archbishop of Canterbury's wife Margarete, lurking obscurely in one of his palaces in Kent).

Even if we did not possess a draft of this proclamation emended in the King's own hand, the general shapelessness and theological incoherence of the final version is redolent of brusque royal papering-over of disagreements among his bishops. Worse still for John Lambert, this document was issued on 16 November as part of the theatrics in the most high-profile heresy trial that early Tudor England had seen, with Lambert himself and King Henry as joint and opposed stars of the proceedings.

The Supreme Head of the Church of England chose to preside himself over the event in Westminster Hall, symbolically clad in white, with his bishops merely as assistants to undertake the theological detail of prosecution. Cromwell's only substantial part was to house the condemned prisoner, presumably at The Rolls, before Lambert was taken to the stake at Smithfield on 22 November: the same fate as Forest had suffered there six months before, but for polar-opposite beliefs.

The whole Lambert business hugely embarrassed John Foxe when he wrote it up in *Acts and Monuments*, given that it implicated some of his chief Protestant heroes in burning a man who looked in retrospect like a good Protestant. Cranmer in particular has come in for plenty of abuse for inconsistency among later writers.[19] Yet the Archbishop's own theology of the eucharist at the time was opposed to the views of Lambert, who may also have affirmed some real radicalism on infant baptism and the nature of Christ, and the Lutheran princes of Germany expressed no disapproval of the condemnation. Cromwell kept his counsel. Two days later, effectively in a continuation of the same theatre, Bishop Hilsey returned to Paul's Cross to deliver a definitive exposure and mockery of the Holy Blood of Hailes, this time with the relic on hand as his visual aid – in careful pairing with this symbol of old error, new error was represented by four immigrant Anabaptist prisoners standing beside the pulpit bearing their heretics' faggots, preparatory to burning at the stake. The occasion was a necessary act of damage limitation for the evangelical establishment in relation to King Henry.[20]

Lurking in the background for evangelical advantage was the chief factor balancing the King's affirmation of traditional theology and keeping him savagely inclined against the Poles and Courtenays: the threat from Rome. From the early autumn, letters reached Cranmer and Cromwell, principally from their man in Italy Thomas Theobald, reporting proceedings against the King in Rome. Imminent was a final publication of the papal excommunication long hanging over Henry, and there was a prospect of equally damaging practical action to follow: the Pope was urging the King of France and the Holy Roman Emperor to impose a trade embargo on England. That had been a standard move against the Infidel in the great days of the Crusades, and though obstinately religion-blind merchants had tended to ignore such orders in the interests of commerce, there was no knowing whether it might not work this time, backed by two great monarchs with modern resources. Accompanying this alarming prospect were Theobald's caustic reports on Reginald Pole's household, which included their dealings with William Tyndale's betrayer Henry Phelips and the Welsh would-be rebel leader James ap Hywel.[21]

Royal action against the Montague circle therefore anticipated the formal promulgation of the papal excommunication in Rome on 17 December.[22] By then a fortnight had elapsed since the trials, heavily managed by Cromwell, and although the Countess of Salisbury was for the time being spared in the Tower of London, most of the other principals were dead. The one long-term survivor was Sir Geoffrey Pole, who in his state of psychological collapse had babbled out extra evidence of his family's contacts with the Cardinal. He gained his life at the expense of any remaining self-esteem; his second unsuccessful suicide attempt followed during the Christmas season. Many years later, in changed times, the surviving heir of the Courtenays, a pardonably unstable young man, came across Sir Geoffrey travelling in Liège, and only hasty government security work prevented a revenge killing.[23]

The evangelicals thus survived some testing times, and disposed of old friends of the King who, had they succeeded in regaining Henry's old affection, could have destroyed the Lord Privy Seal and all he stood for.[24] Cromwell had been doing his best gradually to place his friends in the King's Privy Chamber; the arrival of Thomas Heneage as Chief Gentleman and Groom of the Stool after the fall of Anne Boleyn had been a satisfying milestone in that process. Now in January 1539, matters decisively speeded up: Sir Francis Bryan, flamboyant (and conservative-minded) veteran of the Privy Chamber, was sidelined in favour of the straitlaced evangelical Anthony Denny, and the senior courtier Sir Anthony Browne was also discountenanced. Most dramatically of all, Cromwell himself was at the same time named Chief Nobleman of the Privy Chamber: a satisfaction for the Putney boy, and another pointed snub to ancient nobility. More and more Privy Chamber staff were evangelicals: joining Denny and Ralph Sadler were Philip Hoby, Richard Morison and John Lascelles, all of whom were Cromwell's servants before they were the King's, and did not radically change their allegiance now.[25] In regional politics, the counterpart of this was to set up an institution to deal with residual Courtenay or Pole influence in the West Country: a Council like that in the Marches of Wales, to have oversight of Cornwall, Devon, Somerset and Dorset, under Cromwell's old ally John Russell, who was granted a barony and a Garter knighthood. In fact this 'Council of the West' proved an unnecessary precaution, and was closed down without fuss after only a few years.[26]

Ripples of evangelical advantage spread outwards from the political upheavals. Notable was a peerage for Cromwell's colleague and (in most circumstances) collaborator, Lord Chancellor Audley, who gained his barony of Walden on 29 November 1538. His title came from his recent acquisition of the rich Benedictine house of Saffron Walden Abbey in Essex; its Abbot moonlighted for some time before the dissolution not only as suffragan Bishop of Colchester but as Steward of Audley's estates.[27] Today we know the Jacobean successor of the resulting stately home as Audley End. Cromwell hoped for more. The Duke of Norfolk's later angry reminiscence in 1546 reveals that the Lord Privy Seal had probed whether it might be possible to draw Norfolk into the net of accusation in the course of his interrogations: 'Cromwell, at such time as the Marquess of Exeter suffered, examined his wife more straitly of me than of all other men in the realm, as she sent me word by her brother the Lord Mountjoy.'[28]

This was one of the first signs that the always fraught relationship of Norfolk and Cromwell was badly breaking down. Master Secretary's questions to the Marchioness about the Duke remained private, but the fate of the White Rose group increasingly convinced the remaining conservative grandees that Cromwell, his policies and ambitions, threatened them too. Amid the general settling of accounts, the Lord Privy Seal grimly pushed change forward. In December, he secured a circular on religious reform in the King's name to county JPs, vigorously reasserting and further explaining his September injunctions. It went out so abruptly that its last instruction, presumably addressed to a hastily chosen set of local magnates, was to get the letter copied for distribution to all their neighbouring JPs.[29] Amid all this fast-moving high politics, one is inclined to forgive Cromwell for badly losing his temper with Lady Lisle when she turned up in London. She badgered him on a range of private business concerns and royal favours sought by the myopic couple, oblivious to how wrong the moment was: 'how he handled me and shook me up, I will not now write, nor it is not to be written,' she reported to her husband in great and ungrammatical indignation.[30]

On New Year's Eve came an unexpected addition to the cull among King Henry's oldest friends: Sir Nicholas Carew, Cromwell's fellow-conspirator against Queen Anne back in 1536. Carew's destruction is puzzling and the charges against him so miscellaneous as to suggest an even greater degree of improvisation than in the trials earlier that month. The only previous sign of anything untoward was that he had been passed over in the King's choice of Sheriff for Surrey in November, which may reflect a suspicion he was too close to the White Rose group to be a reliable agent in their imminent trials.[31] Carew was nevertheless on the jury condemning the prisoners. That may have triggered his arrest, since one of the charges in his own indictment was that he commented sceptically about the proceedings, 'I marvel greatly that the indictment against the

Lord Marquess was so secretly handled and for what purpose, for the like was never seen.'[32] Diplomatic spin-doctoring about the White Rose conspiracy to foreign powers made much of Carew's letters found among the papers of the condemned, but it is hardly surprising such letters existed in this small Court circle.[33]

Ultimately, given King Henry's volatility this autumn, there may be some truth in a Carew family tradition preserved by Thomas Fuller that a quarrel during a game of bowls turned sour: Henry 'gave this knight opprobrious language, betwixt jest and earnest; to which the other returned an answer rather true than discreet'.[34] When Carew was eventually executed on 3 March 1539, he was not treated in death with the same fury as the White Rose group. Like Anne Boleyn before him, he did not have his head spiked up in public as a traitor, but it was reunited with his body in a grave near hers in the Tower chapel. That consideration, and Carew's public announcement from the scaffold that he had converted to evangelical belief in prison, suggests quiet intervention by Cromwell on his old collaborator's behalf.[35] The widowed Lady Carew acknowledged Cromwell's kindness in getting a royal grant of some of the considerable Carew property, and she sought a supplement to emergency financial support already doled out to her via Richard Cromwell and others of his team. It may be significant that Elizabeth Lady Ughtred's great friend Arthur Darcy had married Sir Nicholas's daughter.[36] Still the best that could be done was to mitigate, not overturn, the effects of King Henry's rage.

The successful resolution of this blood-soaked autumn created another chance to extend Cromwell's activity in Ireland: in effect, a delayed version of the forward policy in religion he adopted in England during 1538.[37] The commission of inquiry he had sent over in 1537 proved a golden opportunity for various groups in Irish government opposed to Lord Deputy Grey, including Cromwell's trusted old servant William Brabazon and the increasingly embattled Archbishop Browne, plus a good many in the Anglo-Irish governing clique. Their advantage was even greater now the White Rose affinity in England was smashed: they could draw attention to Lord Leonard's undoubted favour to his Fitzgerald relatives, who might be painted as the Irish equivalent of Poles and Courtenays. That was not an unreasonable line: there was every sign that autumn that the Geraldines were intensifying their links to Rome and to Cardinal Pole's growing attempts at orchestrating what amounted to a crusade against the Tudor dominions.

A corollary of complaints against Grey was vigorously to impose English-style reforms in religion within the Lordship. Lord Leonard's

increasing stonewalling in defence of traditional religion in his jurisdiction gave additional advantage to his enemies. During autumn 1538, it
looked as if Grey might be replaced as Lord Deputy by the former member of the commission team Anthony St Leger, to the delight of Grey's
opponents.[38] Lord Leonard nevertheless enjoyed his own lines of communication to London, and although news of dissension in Ireland was the
last thing Cromwell wanted to hear, that worked both ways: Grey might
represent his opponents as the source of conflict in his blustering letters
to the King and Lord Privy Seal. It may be that Cromwell's own long-
standing links with the Greys stayed his hand for the time being.

   Although Cromwell left the Deputy in place, he gave Grey's opponents
independent control over Ireland's religious life, in what was also a
remarkable power-grab for himself. He prompted the King arbitrarily to
extend the jurisdiction of the Vice-Gerency to Ireland. This meant that,
under the King, Cromwell was the only man with jurisdiction throughout all the Tudor dominions. The vice-gerential commission authorized
on 3 February 1539 was charged with suppressing images and dissolving
monasteries. It was a triumvirate of Archbishop Browne, Brabazon and
his close ally, John Allen the Irish Master of the Rolls. Soon they were
joined by the like-minded Robert Cowley and Thomas Cusack, veteran
informants for Cromwell in Ireland. The one person definitely not in
commission with them was Lord Deputy Grey – a straightforward insult,
since the commissioners were also named as deputies not to Grey but to
the Vice-Gerent.[39]

   This team in true Cromwellian style began work before receiving their
February commission, setting out with a selection of allies in January on
an energetic tour of much of southern Ireland. They proclaimed Cromwell's injunctions, accompanied by copies of the official English
translations of the Lord's Prayer, Creed, Commandments and Ave Maria
for general use in the dioceses, and among much else they made a point
of hanging in his habit a friar convicted on a theft charge.[40] While Cromwell's power endured, the commissioners spared no effort to bring the
English Reformation of 1538 to the Irish Lordship. Their major achievement was to dissolve Ireland's only monastic cathedral, Christ Church
Dublin, refounding it in January 1539 as a secular college with dean and
chapter, just as King Henry had done in England the previous year at
Norwich.[41] This really did show the Vice-Gerency in action, and in fact
the inauguration became a rare moment of public harmony between the
commissioners, Lord Deputy and the corporation of Dublin. This cathedral church at the heart of the capital, down the street from the Deputy's
castle, thus continued in all its ceremonial magnificence, despite the

bizarre circumstance of a second Dublin cathedral, St Patrick, already
governed by a dean and chapter, outside the city walls.[42]

Nevertheless, the vice-gerential commissioners became part of Ireland's current political problem. In May they announced they were
looking for total suppression of monastic houses in the parts of Ireland
under English rule; this caused a storm of indignation and counter-
proposals from Lord Leonard and other members of the Irish Council.[43]
This rift was paired with the patent reality that once more the whole Irish
situation was spiralling out of control, descending towards a further
outbreak of open war with the Gaelic regions of the island. Fitzgeralds
provided a figurehead identity in what was now an unequivocally papalist revolt against all that Cromwell had been sponsoring over the previous
half-decade – an even more serious situation than Silken Thomas's rising
in 1534.

We must leave this developing crisis to unravel a more domestic but still
dire contretemps for Thomas Cromwell. While the White Rose trials and
executions took their course in autumn 1538, something different and
rather strange was happening in Sussex. Events there are shrouded in discretion and dependent on reconstruction from fragments of evidence,
crucial parts of which have been in the past misdated. The most important item bears no date at all. It is a letter from Richard Sampson Bishop
of Chichester written in his own hand to his 'loving friend' Richard
Cromwell, the text of which deserves reproducing in full:

> Master Cromwell, I commend me heartily unto you. And whereas yesterday,
> at yours and other my friends' desires, I was content at your own assignment
> that the young man should come into the church of Chichester upon a Sun-
> day at the time of high mass, and before the high altar with a low voice to
> the priest that shall sing mass, say these words: 'I knowledge myself to have
> offended Almighty God and the world; I desire mercy of God'; and to have
> two bushels of wheat ready baken in loaves of half pennies the piece, and
> cause them to be distributed to poor folks either by his own hand or by some
> other: the young man hath been with me this morning and scornfully
> refused this penance. Wherefore I advertise you of it, praying you to weigh
> it as a matter that toucheth much the honesty of your friend. For surely
> if there be any business [disturbance] for it, I will advertise the King's Maj-
> esty of the whole. And I doubt not but when my Lord Privy Seal shall hear
> the truth, he will assist me in it. Thus fare you most heartily well.[44]

This is a most remarkable missive, far from the normal emollient tone
adopted by Bishop Sampson addressing the Cromwell administrative

machine. At the end of summer 1538, in his capacity as Dean of St Paul's, he had complied with orders to dismantle major devotional objects; there followed an abject letter to the Lord Privy Seal affirming his commitment to whatever religious policy the King wanted next, and just before Christmas 1538 he acquiesced without public fuss in the removal of Chichester Cathedral's splendid shrine to his predecessor St Richard.[45] One of his Chichester canons and conservative soulmates, George Crofts, had just been arrested and would be executed for his part in the White Rose affair. Despite all that, this letter to Richard Cromwell is not just self-confident, but bristling with controlled anger. Notable is the curious reversal of the natural order of threat: if necessary, Sampson will tell the King, then (ultimate sanction) he is sure that the Lord Privy Seal will back him up, given all the facts.

The reader will probably have guessed that the recalcitrant young man in the case can only be Gregory Cromwell. That would account for Richard Cromwell's involvement; he had no natural connection with the diocese of Chichester other than his elder-brother watching brief on his cousin. Given that the eighteen-year-old's misdemeanour brought him within discipline of the Church courts, it is likely to have been sexual in nature; the only real alternative possibility as a serious offence demanding punishment by the Bishop would be a heresy charge, and nothing in Gregory's career before or afterwards suggests high-temperature or enthusiastic religion. Whatever it was, was serious enough to shock not merely the Bishop but the county elite and Richard Cromwell, and raise the possibility of further 'business' – it was more than what Tudor society regarded as routine sin, such as seducing a servant girl. This affected Gregory's 'honesty', that is, his reputation, and therefore the reputation of the King's sister-in-law Lady Ughtred. It is tempting to read her very direct undated holograph letter to her father-in-law, refusing to live under his roof and announcing that she would stay with friends near by, in relation to this family crisis (see above, p. 425).

Sampson offered the most face-saving of deals to Gregory, a murmured penance at a considerable distance from Lewes, amid the comparative privacy and liturgical chanting of the cathedral's community mass in choir; and still Gregory refused. Though we will probably never know what he did, given the present fragmentary state of Chichester's diocesan archives, more important is the effect.[46] Cromwell decided abruptly to remove his son and family from Sussex altogether, and give them a fresh start. All that urgency in autumn a year before; that lavish expenditure on securing Lewes Priory's surrender; that massive outpouring of resources on demolition and rebuilding; that setting up of Gregory as local JP: all had been for nothing. The first sign of this humiliating about-turn comes in a letter to Cromwell from Sir John Gage at Firle, down the road from Lewes. Gage wrote on 18 December, which places Bishop Sampson's letter earlier that month or in November. He observed without further comment that since the writing of his previous letter (so this was quite sudden news) 'I was informed that your pleasure is to let to farm all your lands now being in your hands at Lewes'; he therefore asked to lease a substantial part of them.[47]

Over the next few months, tidings spread, though no one thought it a good idea to comment on the cause in writing. It is likely that John Husee would have enlarged on a report to Lord Lisle if speaking face to face when on 5 March 1539 he wrote that 'Mr Polstead goeth into Sussex to dissolve my Lord's house at Lewes, and tarrieth out fourteen days.'[48] We probably have Polstead's own report of this expedition in his careful memorandum for Cromwell from Lewes, dated only 'Friday' but obviously written in March 1539. It is evident from arrangements Polstead was by then making at Lewes for transferring livestock to a new home that Cromwell began devising a workable second plan for Gregory's future straight away in December 1538.[49] That meant a good deal of frantic improvisation, and keeping options open: it would be unwise to embark on a new permanent arrangement for his wayward son as precipitate as the great scheme of autumn 1537.

We can watch the anxious father considering options. In view of whatever happened at Lewes in November or December, it is interesting to find him on 26 November 1538 reconveying his Norfolk property at North Elmham to Gregory and Elizabeth and their heirs, together with the major lordship of Oakham in Rutland.[50] Yet any fresh move to use Elmham would mean renewed confrontation with the Duke of Norfolk, and while Oakham was promisingly remote from London, it was perhaps too much so. Cromwell was also negotiating for a major estate at Painswick in the Cotswolds with the Lisles and the Earls of Hertford and Bridgewater, but that was still enmired in ill-tempered three-way haggling.[51] A sensible course would be a holding operation: finding some temporary but dignified home for the young couple at a decent distance from Lewes. An ideal candidate emerged: Leeds Castle in Kent. We have visited Leeds on more than one occasion, most recently in the cheerful company of Rudolph Gwalther during his English tour. It was a Crown property once in the Constableship of Cromwell's close acquaintances the Guildfords; Gwalther's visit in 1537 shows that the castle gates still hospitably opened there for a young Swiss evangelical. The then Constable of Leeds in succession to the late Sir Edward Guildford was another local magnate, the courtier Sir

Edward Neville, who became unhappily tangled in the White Rose conspiracy and was executed on 9 December 1538.

Now, on cue, on 4 January 1539, none other than Thomas Lord Cromwell himself succeeded the Guildfords and Neville as Constable of Leeds Castle.[52] The castle thus lay available for his use, more importantly for occupation by Gregory and Lady Ughtred, who promptly arrived in March. They would be getting used to the sound of workmen doing hasty refits as background to their married life.[53] No doubt Reginald Pole, with his view of Cromwell as the English Machiavelli, would have seen this sequence of events as proof of conspiracy to destroy Neville alongside his own relatives, purely for the sake of Leeds Castle. It looks more like another example of Cromwell's genius for seizing the main chance. Perhaps as he looked through schedules of the executed man's estates and offices (which were much solicited by others immediately on Neville's death), the germ of his idea for Gregory's new home blossomed.

The Lord Privy Seal had more to add to the scheme, from the same circle of old Kentish acquaintance. Two days before the grant of Leeds Castle, he came to an agreement with Sir John Dudley, heir by marriage of Sir Edward Guildford, to buy the chief family mansion at Halden, 14 miles south of Leeds. This included an impressive array of Guildford estates spilling over from Kent into the Sussex marshes, which the family had turned into richly productive farmland, and to which Dudley had recently gained title after some bruising legal battles. The purchase price was staggering, at least £3,500, which would both transform Dudley's uncertain fortunes and make Cromwell and his dynasty into the greatest magnates of the area, successor to the Guildfords at their most magnificent.[54] All these plans were reflected in Henry Polstead's report to his master in March on refiguring the Sussex and Kent estates. Cromwell wanted the Lewes livestock driven straightaway to Leeds and Halden, but the season demanded a gradual transfer via an intermediate estate. Gregory's new symbolic position in Kent was eased by the death precisely at this time, 13 March, of the man who had briefly been the county's most prominent nobleman, Thomas Boleyn Earl of Wiltshire. Wiltshire would never have tried to rival the Cromwells, even though there were signs he was now regaining a limited amount of royal favour after the catastrophe of his daughter's execution, but his disappearance from the scene did remove a complication.

The prompt arrival of Gregory and his wife in the splendour of Leeds in March was politically necessary to provide minimum propriety for one of Cromwell's most audacious moves yet. His nineteen-year-old son, within about a month of taking up residence in Kent, was to sit as one of its pair of knights of the shire in a new session of Parliament. Writs of summons went out on 1 March and Parliament assembled on 28 April – a very narrow window of opportunity. In all Cromwell's seizing of chances, this was one most at risk of offending convention, though it had a certain dynastic logic. In 1529 the knights for Kent were the half-brothers Edward and Henry Guildford; they both died during the Reformation Parliament, and we know for certain that Sir Edward's replacement in 1534 was, logically, his son-in-law Sir John Dudley. Given that, it is tempting to suppose that likewise on Henry's death in 1532 Cromwell took advantage of his rapidly rising career to quit his carpet-bagging Parliamentary borough seat at Taunton for a far more appropriate place as knight of the shire for Kent. As general Parliamentary manager, he would then naturally have sat for Kent in the second Parliament of 1536 as well. One indication that this was the case comes in the rumour recorded by John Husee at the time of Prince Edward's baptism in 1537, that Cromwell was about to be advanced to the Earldom of Kent: that would be natural promotion for a knight of the shire for that county.[55]

For the moment all that can only be supposition, but, if it is correct, Gregory's move to follow his father in Parliament could just about seem respectable, particularly thanks to Leeds Castle and his rolling acres of former Guildford lands. Even so, the stretch was considerable, and the haste in which it was done is revealed by the fact that at no stage in 1539– 40 can Gregory be found named to the commission of the peace in Kent. Whatever had happened in Sussex probably made that seem for the moment unwise.[56] That indicates hesitation, and the sight of Gregory sitting in the Commons in spring 1539 was the first sign of what became increasingly apparent over the next twelve months. Cromwell was losing his grip on his previous acute sense of what was not just politically possible but also politically wise. It is significant that the most obvious trigger for this corruption of Cromwell's judgement was dynastic: his fatherly love for the erratic, energetic boy who was his only legitimate heir. Yet the sheer scale of the problems facing any would-be reformer in the Tudor realms and the increasing turmoil of politics would have tested anyone's powers of management, even someone with Cromwell's exceptional talent and energy. From now on, events reveal his deteriorating sense of discretion and control.

Stumbling Blocks: 1539

Some time around February 1539, amid preparations for a new Parliament, Cromwell commissioned his senior clerk Thomas Derby to draw up a sixteen-page 'Summary Declaration of the Faith, Uses and Observations in England'. He took great interest in getting its contents right, personally annotating and emending the document, though it was never finished.[1] The text, which is written in English, would be appropriate for MPs and peers to read, but matters overtook it, and this is its only surviving version. Probably a final version was intended for translation and distribution in Germany, perhaps particularly in the territories of Cleves, where a new marital possibility was emerging. It is a remarkable insight into Cromwell's thinking at the end of tumultuous changes in 1538: a forthright and vigorous celebration of England's religious revolution written by one of the participants, taking the story right back to the destruction of Elizabeth Barton.

The tract celebrated a Church of England orthodox in doctrine, detesting the heresies of Anabaptists (Cromwell prudently added 'Sacramentaries, and all others'), and rejoicing in dignified liturgy with daily masses (here Cromwell balanced his previous thought by striking out 'private and public' from masses – that phrase would not have pleased German Protestants). Cromwellian achievements were trumpeted, with little hint of the trials along the way: an English Bible, the Parliamentary poor law (an interesting inclusion), clipping of clerical wings, a still-projected reform of canon law, superstitious holidays curtailed, indulgences banned, shrines dismantled. The pamphlet celebrated the King's prudence in executing a variety of traitors, from 'Thomas More the jester' and 'Fisher of Rochester, the [vain]glorious hypocrite', through to the White Rose group. The Maid of Kent and Becket came in for particularly extended dishonourable mention. All had been done by due legal process, the pamphlet insisted. 'Who can find in his heart knowing this, to think the same prince that so hath judgments ministered by the law and by ordinary jurisdiction, to be a tyrant? It is plain malice and iniquity so to defame and misreport his noble Grace.'[2]

A long passage on monastic dissolutions is still notably open-ended. It celebrates all the steps taken in suppressions up to early 1539. Just as in the published version of the King's answer to the Pilgrims in 1536 (see above, Chapter 16), it compares the similar dissolutions made 'by the Bishop of Rome's authority in the Cardinal of York's time'. Nevertheless the section discussing what would happen next has some curious hesitations. A sentence about 'religious persons' which in its original form said that they '*did almost* throughout the realm surrender their houses' is altered to they '*have been disposed* throughout the realm *to* surrender their houses'. That change might suggest greater finality, yet the passage continues overleaf after further second thoughts: 'some other house[s], for respect of the places they stand in, his Grace will not dissolve.'[3]

This document offers a glimpse of royal policy on the monasteries as it stood in winter 1539. Crucially, even now it did not include total dissolution. The houses still standing untouched were the bedrock of the English monastic system, mostly the greatest Benedictine monasteries of Anglo-Saxon antiquity. Even an evangelical might regard them as ornaments to 'the places they stand in'. There is good evidence that such houses would have responded quite positively to Cromwell's injunctions for their good conduct back in 1535. Once the impractical regulations on monastic enclosure were quietly laid aside, it was possible for a conscientious abbot to warm to the Vice-Gerent's instructions for scholarship, study, Bible-reading, proper communal life and dignified abbatial hospitality. The model the injunctions reinforced reflected a conscious shift in style in a group of leading Benedictine and Cistercian monasteries which was in progress well before Cromwell came to power.[4]

These flagships of an ancient monastic tradition were moving of their own accord towards a life more resembling the great chantry colleges of England. Such a policy was precisely what Cardinal Wolsey, ably assisted by Thomas Cromwell, had forwarded in the 1520s with St Frideswide's Priory Oxford and St Peter's Priory Ipswich: he had turned them into colleges. One should not be misled by the automatic modern association of the word 'college' with higher education: all *collegia* then were first and foremost corporations of secular (non-monastic) priests, and their primary function was not education but prayer, particularly prayer for the dead – even the colleges of Oxford and Cambridge. To turn monasteries into colleges might be regarded as a measure of Catholic reform, but an evangelical reformer could equally well sympathize; secular clergy could pray as well as any monk, and also contribute more to the Church as a whole.

Colleges so far remained untouched by government policy, and for the most part flourished: such institutions as Fotheringhay, St Mary's Warwick and St George's Chapel Windsor. They were closer in their life and even architectural layout to the new clutch of Oxbridge colleges of Tudor foundation than they might seem today. Stoke-by-Clare College in Suffolk provided a textbook example of how colleges beyond the universities might continue in a moderate evangelical splendour, combining solemn liturgical observance with preaching and provision for children's education. A favourite retreat for Cambridge dons, its Master Matthew Parker (an appointee and chaplain of Anne Boleyn) doubled as head of a Cambridge college, Corpus Christi. Parker took the trouble to write new statutes for Stoke when he became Dean in 1535, getting John Cheke to turn them into mellifluous humanist Latin.[5]

This, then, is how a group of Benedictine abbots had been thinking for some decades – such heads of house as Islip and Benson of Westminster, Cromwell's friend Kidderminster of Winchcombe or his protégés Sagar of Hailes and Hawford of Evesham. They were encouraged by the proliferation of specifically monastic colleges at Oxford providing accommodation for Benedictines and Augustinians studying in the universities. These institutions were rather paradoxical, a contradiction of monastic enclosure, but an affirmation of monastic scholarship. They began emerging in the late thirteenth century, but a remarkable development among them is specific to the 1530s. In the last five years before the final monastic dissolutions, more Benedictine monks took Oxford degrees than in any period in the previous forty years. The highest numbers were in the last two years – some members continued studying in the universities after the dissolutions. Indeed it is not at all certain how final the dissolution of the Oxbridge monastic colleges was; unlike the former friaries, most eventually saw refoundation under new names, beginning with Lord Chancellor Audley's remodelling of Buckingham College Cambridge as Magdalene College.*

This phenomenon is a tribute to intellectual liveliness in English Benedictines, and had it continued on the same trajectory it would have resulted in the greatest English monasteries behaving more and more like Oxbridge colleges. That looks like deliberate policy on the part of the elite abbots.[6] The last survivor of Queen Mary's restored Westminster Abbey in the 1550s reminisced that the new community lived more in the manner of Oxford

---

* At Oxford, Canterbury College is now part of Christ Church and St Mary's College belongs to Brasenose, but the others all survive independently under different guises: Durham as Trinity, Gloucester as Worcester and St Bernard's as St John's.

and Cambridge or the Inns of Court than a strict Benedictine community.[7] That also reflected government thinking during 1538. There was much anticipation that major Benedictine and Augustinian monasteries would be remodelled as colleges. As central a government figure as Chancellor Audley proposed Colchester and St Osyth's, the fiery evangelical Bishop Latimer mooted Great Malvern, further suggesting two or three such refoundations in each county; Abbot Sagar of Hailes put forward his own house.[8]

The unanimity across the religious spectrum is striking. Cromwell himself invested some effort in proposing Little Walsingham (purged of its shrine, like Hailes), his northern evangelical client Prior Robert Ferrar was advocate like Sagar for his own Nostell Priory as preaching centre and school, and the Duke of Norfolk similarly for the Howard mausoleum church of Thetford, envisaging a lavishly funded replacement in precise detail. The Duke, remarkably, proposed to use Matthew Parker's evangelically inspired new statutes for Stoke College as his model, having already obtained the King's consent for the transformation, and Ferrar's plan also sounds like an imitation of Stoke.[9] Nearly all these ideas cluster in August and September 1538, just as the destruction of the friaries and shrines climaxed. They culminated in the Vice-Gerent summoning the monastic community of Canterbury Cathedral during the King's visit to the city in early September; he personally ordered them to change their monastic habits for the garments of secular priests, as the Benedictine monks of Norwich Cathedral had already done in May.

For reasons unclear to the monks at the time, this transformation of Canterbury was postponed for another couple of years, which reflects the fact that the plans for new colleges were in general drastically slimmed down.[10] Nevertheless, they were not totally abandoned, and the initiatives in late summer 1538 ought to be seen alongside Cromwell's other plans for reformation in this year, not simply as a diffused scramble for survival by the monasteries. The atmosphere did change in the next few months, while the White Rose arrests spooled out. Alternative voices emerged in Cromwell's correspondence, from servants of his actually involved in the business of dissolution. John Freeman, at work in Lincolnshire since 1536, suggested in October after detecting asset-stripping by Gilbertine houses there that 'they are in a readiness to surrender without any coming.' Only a day later, Cromwell's old friend John Uvedale said of the thirty-nine remaining abbeys and priories in Yorkshire that he would like to see them all dissolved – not without self-interest: he was after a little nunnery called Marrick, and eventually got it.[11]

Neither of these comments really addressed the Benedictine or Augustinian heart of England's remaining monasticism. The decisive blow to an expansive plan of remodelling many greater houses came from a voice not to be ignored: King Henry. Now that the Holy Roman Emperor and the King of France had come to an understanding, Henry felt desperately vulnerable, and from January 1539 onwards this sent him scurrying to his military engineers for a great southern coastal defence programme. It has left state-of-the-art Tudor strongpoints from St Michael's Mount to Lowestoft, brand-new fortifications costing huge amounts. No other single country-wide scheme was built on the same scale before the nineteenth and twentieth centuries.[12] Such expenditure made a confiscation of estates from the remaining monasteries all the more tempting.

At every stage in 1539, Henry and not Cromwell can be seen taking the decisions. The King was on the move, in the thick of defence preparations, while Cromwell was back in London. Thus it was Ralph Sadler who in mid-March let Cromwell know from Dover that Henry 'will omit none opportunity in the devising here of such things as bulwarks, blockhouses and fortilaces as shall be meet for surety and defence'. The King ordered Cromwell to get on with implementing his vision.[13] As early as 26 January, Ambassador Castillon had heard that the King had decided to grasp the nettle of the many surviving nunneries, whose closure would anger not only the nuns but also their families (generally nobility and gentry), who took advantage of their schooling for girls and young boys – Lady Ughtred with her little daughter at Wilberfoss would be an instance, not to mention Gregory Cromwell. Henry was nevertheless ready to confiscate them all. Sensitivities were such that many nunnery closures were delayed until the end of the year, along with the last of the male communities.[14]

Nevertheless, despite the financial windfall from great monastic closures during 1539, fragments of the previous plans remained. Two great abbeys, Thornton in north Lincolnshire and Burton in Staffordshire, did indeed become colleges on a generous scale, pure specimens of the scheme, and remained on their new course into the 1540s. Adding to the sense of open-endedness in these events, they must have continued in their communal life before their official refoundation in the years after Cromwell's death, rather like supposedly dissolved monastic colleges in Oxford and Cambridge. In the case of Burton Abbey, the continuing encouragement may have come from the former Abbot, now Abbot of Westminster, William Benson, who also secured an extraordinarily lavish future settlement for Westminster. Besides these two survivors, the remaining monastic cathedrals were remodelled and some abbeys promoted to cathedrals (Westminster among them), in numbers which remained a major debate of policy right up to Cromwell's fall in 1540. As preparations for Parliament took shape in early 1539, the future of the monasteries remained untidy and uncertain. The dissolution of the monasteries was not a certainty until it was complete. What it was not was a long-term scheme authored by Thomas Cromwell.

Cromwell had good reasons to feel well pleased as Parliament approached in April 1539, quite apart from turning a difficult family situation in Sussex into the planting of a new Cromwell dynasty in Kent. He could rejoice in fulfilling one of his greatest long-term plans, a lasting memorial to his Vice-Gerency: the publication at last of a fully official English Bible.[15] This had been a long time in the making. It was a thorough revision of the Matthew Bible whose authorization he had obtained in 1537, and was prepared in Paris, through an ambitious co-operation between the French printer François Regnault and Cromwell's regular London printers Richard Grafton and Edward Whitchurch, with the hugely experienced Miles Coverdale in charge of textual revision. From a technical point of view, working in Paris made sense, for the French printing industry was far better able to cope with such a complex print-run. Yet the enterprise ran constant risk of sabotage from a suspicious Catholic monarch and an even more suspicious Inquisitor-General and University Faculty of Theology (the Sorbonne).

All through 1538 the operation painfully staggered ahead. Cromwell kept a watchful eye on progress amid all his other concerns that eventful year. There was near-shipwreck over Christmas, just as the work was completed: the Inquisitor-General seized the finished copies. Cromwell now brought all his diplomatic resources to bear on the problem, including some tense meetings with Ambassador Castillon. His advantage as the King's minister was that he could survey the whole range of Anglo-French concerns to find a useful bargaining counter. The perfect lever emerged, wholly unrelated to the Bible or even religion: a commercial dispute over an English seizure of a French ship for piracy. It was owned by the Sieur de La Rochepot, brother to the very influential Constable of France, Castillon's great friend Anne de Montmorency.

The pressure worked. Over the winter, 2,500 copies of the Bible were rescued and brought to England, along with vital type and craftsmen prepared to carry on the project, to supply enough copies for the 9,000 or so churches of England and Wales. It was a prodigious operation, without any precedent in the English printing industry, and culmination of Cromwell's encouragement of the vernacular press. He set up his team in the buildings of the London Greyfriars, so recently dissolved. Curiously, once the French-produced Bibles were safe and the press was busy in London churning out more, negotiations stalled on returning Rochepot's ship. The French were still angrily pursuing the grievance when

Cromwell lay prisoner in the Tower more than a year later; his last date-able letter, four days before his execution, is actually his rejoinder to the King of France's renewed complaint.[16] Cromwell's recovery of the Bibles was an extraordinary success for *Realpolitik* applied to a godly cause. The resulting volume in the warehouses in April 1539 was magnificent, and has justly been called the 'Great Bible'; it was the basis for all official Bibles in England right up to 1611. Thanks to a preface by Cranmer which appeared in the 1540 editions onwards, it has sometimes been called 'Cranmer's Bible', but that is a totally misleading branding: rather, it is Cromwell's Bible.

The book's famous title-page, traditionally and wrongly credited to Hans Holbein (the actual artist remains controversial), does indeed give equal credit to both Archbishop and Vice-Gerent, though of course visual pride of place goes to King Henry VIII.[17] The King liked the title-page format so much that in subsequent editions, it appears three times at appropriate places in the volume.[18] The design exploits the binary format of a title-page to tell two simultaneous descending stories around the title-panel, connected appropriately at the head by the Supreme Head himself. He hands out Bibles in two directions: one side to Cranmer and the bishops, the other to Cromwell and the Privy Council. Cranmer and Cromwell then pass them out to the kingdom's respective clerical and temporal notables. Cartouches beside them bear their respective coats of arms, to identify the pair for anyone with heraldic knowledge (that is, a great many). At the foot, crowds of the King's subjects benefit from godly preaching as a result. In the printed editions, a prison at the bottom right-hand corner shows the fate of those who do not listen; one lavish hand-painted version of the title-page in Cromwell's own surviving copy in Cambridge omitted this warning. (See Plate 39.)

This was not the only hopeful sign for future progress in religion as elections to Parliament proceeded in April. Diplomacy offered new possibilities, though really they were a by-product of England's narrow-ing diplomatic options in relation to the Emperor and the King of France. First was the continuing search for a royal bride. None of the King's overtures to ladies eligible and available in Europe in 1538 came to any-thing. The one major marital corridor left relatively unexplored so far beyond France, the Empire and southern Europe was some suitable bride in the evangelical camp in the north; unhappily possibilities were not numerous, either in the Empire or in Scandinavia. The King of England could not be expected to drop further than a duchess in the Tudor equiva-lent of the *Almanach de Gotha*, which narrowed the field considerably.

Very early in the whole saga of royal remarriage, in December 1537, Cromwell asked his friend John Hutton, permanent English representative in Brussels, to draw up an overall shortlist. It did not look at all promising. Hutton, never very confident in his own qualifications as a diplomat, said nervously, 'I have not much experience amongst ladies' (Mistress Hutton presumably excepted). His tally, apart from the Duchess of Milan, included the widow of the Count of Egmont, who with irresistibly Gilbertian echoes he said 'passeth forty years of age, the which doth not appear in my judgement by her face'. Last, and least, 'the Duke of Cleves hath a daughter, but I hear no great praise neither of her personage nor beauty': a young lady called Anna.[19] Thereafter the Cleves idea festered somewhere towards the bottom of the heap, surfacing briefly according to the imperial ambassadors in a proposal from the Germans early in their mission of summer 1538.[20]

Once the Protestants had left unsatisfied in October 1538, it was the end of the year before the manifest reluctance of the Duchess of Milan (or, perhaps more importantly, her Habsburg relatives) for an English royal marriage left the Cleves option as the best on the table.[21] The United Duchies of Jülich-Cleves-Berg, scattered territories on the western flank of the Empire bordering the Low Countries, were not part of the Schmalkaldic League. In fact they had not broken with the Pope, but under Duchess Anna's father Duke Johann, a great admirer of Erasmus, they went their own way in Church reorganization as much as Lutheran principalities and cities, and Anna's sister Sybille married Luther's protector Johann Friedrich Elector of Saxony. Duke Johann of Cleves might be said to have created his own 'middle way' in religion between old and new, just like Henry VIII. Moreover, the ducal family was at odds with the Emperor over further territories whose title was in dispute between them. This mixture might be made to look very attractive to King Henry.

Accordingly, in January 1539, Christopher Mont found himself once more entrusted with a vital mission in Germany, alongside an English diplomat associated with Robert Barnes, Thomas Paynell. Cromwell added his own briefing-notes to those provided in the King's name, and his instructions (unlike the King's) explicitly ordered the ambassadors to pursue with the Court of Cleves the idea of Henry marrying Anna. Everything must be as casual as possible, merely indicating that the Lord Privy Seal was well disposed to the idea, and that it might be a good plan to 'send her picture hither, to the intent his Lordship might persuade his Majesty thereby'. Much was to follow from that.[22] This is the most likely moment for Cromwell's tetchy exchange with Archbishop Cranmer, in which Cranmer insisted that the King needed a common language with his wife for conversation.[23] In view of the King's excellent French, this would not have been a problem with the Valois or Habsburg candidates on display during 1538, but it was sadly true of Duchess Anna. At the same time, the Lord Privy Seal scotched any move to promote into the King's affections a young lady of the Court, Katherine Howard by name, who lived with her grandmother, the Dowager Duchess of Norfolk, just across the river from Westminster at Lambeth. The fact that she was yet another niece of the Duke of Norfolk would have been enough to arouse his alarm.

The other task for Mont and Paynell was to get the Schmalkaldeners back to England for further talks on theology and diplomatic alliance. That would not be easy after the previous summer's fiasco. The Germans were well informed on the twists and turns of English religious policy, they had come to an understanding with the Habsburgs which relieved previous possible military anxieties, and they were particularly annoyed by the stridently traditionalist tone of Henry's proclamation of 16 November 1538 which had accompanied John Lambert's heresy trial. In the end, they agreed to send over yet another preliminary embassy, once more featuring Franz Burchard. It left Frankfurt in the first week of April and arrived on the 23rd, just before Parliament was due to open. The delegates' instructions and message to the King from the Elector and Landgraf Philipp were coldly correct. It was up to Cromwell to use all his powers of persuasion to produce the right atmosphere between the prickly delegates and a King once more thwarted in hopes of showing off his learning to Melanchthon.[24]

While these pieces of his political jigsaw fell into place, the Lord Privy Seal made his usual careful preparations for the first Parliament since the multiple crises of 1536. A great deal of official legislation needed pushing through, as is apparent in one of his 'remembrances' from early March.[25] Chief among immediate concerns was the official oblivion of the Courtenay/Pole circle. Most were dead already, but attainders in Parliament would add the additional solemnity of consent by the whole realm, useful both domestically and in diplomacy, and Reginald Pole needed to be treated as if he were dead. The resulting Act of Attainder was frighteningly extensive in numbers, comprising a third of all those attainted in sixteenth-century England. Besides that, the King's ambitious programme of coastal defence loomed large, and would have to be paid for. Among other expedients, this might involve Parliamentary taxation or a forced loan, requiring 'the names of all the wealthy men of the realm, as well priests, merchants, and others'. There were also necessary tidying-up measures on still half-complete plans for poor relief and government in Wales.

Cromwell also added a note into the list which took on a significance he definitely did not expect: 'A device in the Parliament for the unity in religion'. This proposal was the twin of a surviving draft proclamation emended in the King's own hand that was notably savage in tone. It complained indeed about lack of unity in religion, and anticipated Parliamentary legislation to remedy this: what began in the text as the promise of 'terrible laws' in Parliament, Henry, in momentarily more emollient mood, changed to 'good and just laws', before deciding to shelve the declaration for the moment.[26] We will discover what the King meant by 'terrible laws'.

Cromwell's own letters survive in unusual quantities for this period, reflecting partly a cache of correspondence with his protégé Thomas Wyatt, who was on various diplomatic missions abroad, and partly his letters to the King, who was away from the capital inspecting coastal defence works. The royal archive would have preserved these latter, which would then have been cherrypicked by the team trawling for evidence to destroy the fallen minister in summer 1540. Among the most important letters to Henry is one of 17 March, running the gamut of current concerns from Ireland, defence and overseas trade restrictions amid international tension to preparations for Parliament.[27] In it, Cromwell expansively promised the King that 'I and other your dedicate councillors be abouts to bring all things so to pass that your Majesty had never more tractable parliament.' As an example, he told Henry that he had ensured the election to Parliament of the man who was now the most effective international propagandist for the regime, Richard Morison, newly appointed to the Privy Chamber in reward for his efforts so far.[28] In Cromwell's necessary absence in the Lords, Morison would be the best government spokesman 'to answer and take up such as would crack or face [brag or show off] with literature of learning or by indirected ways, if any such shall be, as I think there shall be few or none'.

It is worth noting that Cromwell presented the government electioneering as the united work of ministers eager to smooth over possible electoral confrontations: 'I and other your dedicate councillors' – regardless (he did not need to add) of any religious differences they might have. To put it another way, from the outset of what turned out to be a highly polarized assembly, Cromwell was not as much in charge as he wished.[29] There was a significant amount of careful government pairing of different interests in electing the two knights of the shire for each county, as the election in Kent showed. Gregory Cromwell was elected as knight with another newcomer to Parliament, Sir Thomas Cheyney. As a pillar of local and national government, Cheyney was a much more obvious choice than Gregory: Warden of the Cinque Ports and this same month appointed Treasurer of the royal Household, as well as leading actor in the King's current obsession, building coastal defences. Cheyney's appointment as Warden in succession to Lord Rochford immediately after Anne Boleyn's fall was at the time ascribed to Cromwell's decision, but much had happened since, and one important fact about Cheyney does not suggest he was at the top of the Lord Privy Seal's personal list of candidates in 1539: he was a notorious religious conservative who fiercely clashed with that other Kentish power, Archbishop Cranmer.[30]

Other results also suggest conscious pairing. In Norfolk, Gregory's former long-term host Richard Southwell was elected knight alongside the classic Norfolk magnate (naturally therefore a relative and something of a client of Thomas Howard) Sir Edmund Wyndham. Both were presented to the electorate as choices of the King and Cromwell, but a complication arose, annoying and embarrassing both Cromwell and the Duke of Norfolk: an unscheduled and typically egotistical candidacy by the Duke's nephew, Edmund Knyvet, which they combined to see off, having him summoned to Star Chamber to explain himself.[31] Sussex saw the election of the ever-reliable but traditionalist Sir John Gage as knight of the shire along with a local evangelical, William Goring of Burton, an old friend of Cromwell, and one of those who had played a useful part in destroying the Courtenay/Pole group.[32]

Inevitably untidinesses abounded in a never predictable process. In Hampshire and Surrey, a long letter to Cromwell from William Fitzwilliam Earl of Southampton and the newly created Lord St John (William Paulet) dutifully described a broadly based process of sorting out borough and county seats, amid much other business on the coastal defence scheme; a further letter from Fitzwilliam the week before dealt with Sussex in similar terms.[33] The reality was not so simple. Southampton and St John had been Cromwell's friends, but their religious conservatism (plus the enormous faux pas by Paulet's brother George in Ireland in 1537) was creating increasing distance in that relationship. They emphasized that they had given Cromwell the lead role in picking suitable candidates, but in Hampshire in particular there was the problem of Bishop Gardiner's standoff with Thomas Wriothesley. Both Gardiner and Wriothesley were returning from embassies abroad. The Bishop was now in a position to assert himself after his long absence in France; he was still furious with his former servant for his desertion to Cromwell in winter 1536, and the detestation was mutual.

A much less discreet view of Hampshire proceedings appears in two entertainingly malicious reports about the election from the county Sheriff John Kingsmill, addressed to Wriothesley himself.[34] Despite being the returning officer by virtue of his office, Kingsmill was not a neutral party in religious faction: brother-in-law to William Goring and in later decades the foundation of the county's Protestant ascendancy in Elizabeth's reign. He sneered at the opposition to Wriothesley's candidature in Hampshire, fuelled by fury from Gardiner and local clergy at Wriothesley's destruction of Winchester Cathedral's shrine of St Swithin while the Bishop had been in France. More generally 'you are the man that is like to purge the cankered and rusty hearts from their old superstitions.' Kingsmill described how much Gardiner's return and the prospect of his influence at Court had heartened local traditionalists; these included not only the elderly Lord Sandys but also William Paulet Lord St John, who back in 1529 had been Cromwell's benefactor in entering Parliament. Delighted that Wriothesley planned to turn up at quarter sessions, Kingsmill begged him to stay in Hampshire to 'cause men to be bold in the good opinion wherein they know you bear of the best' – that is, the cause of evangelical religion.[35] Perhaps with the Sheriff's help, the Hampshire election emerged as a triumph for Cromwell. The King's intention early in March had been merely to place Wriothesley as burgess for Southampton, but he became knight of the shire along with another of Cromwell's local servants, Richard Worsley.[36] That seemed to bode well for containing any threat from Gardiner and his conservative sympathizers in Parliament.

In the middle of electioneering, Cromwell's senior clerk Thomas Soulemont passed on to Secretary Wriothesley the Lord Privy Seal's confidence that 'the Parliament will not last long,' but events derailed his careful planning.[37] Cromwell fell ill: he described his affliction in rueful letters of excuse to the King as ague and tertian fever, which in Tudor England probably implies malaria. As early as 4 April, John Husee told his ever-importunate employer in Calais that the Lord Privy Seal had not left his house for two days, and towards the end of the month he was confined to his house in London, unable to talk to the King at Richmond or steer Parliament, which formally opened on 28 April. It was 10 May before he finally risked even the short journey to Westminster.[38] In the meantime he did his best, moving closer to Parliament in his old lodgings at St James's Palace, and carrying on conversations with the German ambassadors when he could. Later he reminisced to the Germans that his illness had given the conservative bishops their chance to mould Parliament's proceedings.[39] Significantly the man chosen as Speaker of the Commons was for the first time since 1529 not a close ally of his: the lawyer Sir Nicholas Hare, a senior servant of the Duke of Norfolk and, unusually for the Speakership, only a burgess and not a knight of the shire.

Whatever Cromwell meant in his remembrance of March about 'A device in the Parliament for the unity in religion', the erratic progress of discussion on six articles of religion in the House of Lords took a very different direction from any intended by him. The Duke of Norfolk introduced it, and Cromwell and Cranmer were increasingly marginalized in its formulation. Its commendations were all traditional: real presence in the eucharist, the acceptability of communicants receiving only bread without wine, compulsory clerical celibacy and perpetuity of monastic vows of celibacy, 'private' masses (such as Cromwell's draft tract had omitted to discuss) and the importance of sacramental confession to a priest. Alongside the Parliamentary debates were meetings of the clergy in St Paul's Cathedral which extended beyond the Convocation of Canterbury's normal membership to include representatives of the Province of York. If this body had any name at all, it would have been a vice-gerential synod, just as back in 1537, but with events rapidly spiralling out of control Cromwell was not the dominant figure in the assembly's proceedings. Even the abbots of the remaining great monasteries, not in evidence at all in the previous synod meeting, were active participants, and the synod's conclusions broadly supported Parliament's traditionalist line, with very few voices against.

The Germans watched all this in horror and disbelief. Their last meeting with the King on 26 May involved a 'hefftige disputation' (violent row) about clerical marriage, whose prohibition formed part of the Parliamentary bill of the Six Articles. Cromwell's pleas did not stop them leaving the country on 31 May, bearing letters of complaint from King Henry and of deep regret from the Lord Privy Seal, who assured the Elector of Saxony he would do his best to advance the Gospel.[40] All informed analyses of this crisis for Cromwell's and Cranmer's programme of evangelical reform have put the spotlight back on King Henry, away from the long Protestant tradition which made Bishop Gardiner the chief villain; that view is reinforced by Henry's personal confrontation with the Germans.

As always, Henry decided which voices rang most loudly in his ears at any one time, and at the moment they were those of Gardiner and the Duke of Norfolk. What needs explaining is his decision. The main answer lies in the festering crisis in Calais, where religious disagreements and wild public statements from both extremes represented exactly the mix the King hated.[41] They centred on arguments about the eucharist. Henry was particularly adamant about real presence – that was why John Lambert had died – and this was actually where the Six Articles had originated, with a draft by Chancellor Audley on the single matter of the eucharist. The articles then expanded, possibly as a result of the King's anger with the aggressive attitude of the German ambassadors; certainly the other five topics closely echoed the points under contest between the English and the Germans in 1538 and 1539.[42]

Cromwell was now deeply involved in a partisan way in these Calais disputes, backing the evangelicals under investigation there with increasing recklessness. A combination of conservative prelates and lay magnates, some former friends of his like Sir Anthony Browne, was now ranged against him. Many of the names also hovered round the partisan correspondence of John Kingsmill about Hampshire and neighbouring counties. Prominent among them was William Lord Sandys, Hampshire man and Lord Chamberlain, but also Captain of Guines Castle in Calais. He would not have forgotten Cromwell's demand that he surrender the cult-image of the Holy Spirit from his dynastic chapel at Basingstoke the previous September, to add to the destruction of such objects, any more than Gardiner forgot the dismantling of St Swithin's shrine. The matter of Calais spread across southern England because evangelical networks were both interconnected and increasingly militant. The Calais radical Adam Damplip, for instance, was revealed as a client of Nicholas Shaxton, the notoriously evangelical Bishop of Salisbury, once Anne Boleyn's protégé, but now dependent on Cromwell. John Goodall, one of Shaxton's senior servants in Salisbury, a former MP, was arrested earlier that spring for unwise iconoclasm with a sacramentarian character in the Cathedral.[43]

Events through June rolled out relentlessly against the evangelical cause. Fresh prisoners arrived in London not merely from Calais but from Bristol and Archbishop Cranmer's diocese. These even included Thomas Brooke, one of the two MPs elected from Calais, who was brave enough to speak up at length in Parliament against the Six Articles and foolish enough to concentrate on eucharistic presence when he did so, despite Cromwell's warnings. Bishop Shaxton himself was kept away from Parliament and Convocation in London by order of the Privy Council until the last few days when everything about religion was already decided, although the excuse had been plague.[44] Cranmer's German wife probably left England at this juncture, with one little clause added to Parliament's prohibition of clerical marriage delaying its deadline, probably designed to let her depart with some dignity. Cranmer's pioneering clerical marriage is famous, but the most prominent Archbishop in the Irish Church, George Browne of Dublin, was now also secretly a married man, eventually with three children. As the effects of the Six Articles legislation rippled out to Ireland, this handicap dramatically curtailed Browne's capacity and willingness to push forward a Cromwellian-style Reformation in the island.[45]

In this situation, not only Cranmer was in despair. Latimer and

Shaxton resigned their dioceses, and suffered house arrest under the care
of clerical colleagues. Alexander Alesius, urgently prompted by Cranmer,
fled abroad with his wife, his experiences of Henry's England seared into
his memory. 'Our Lord save you from all the power of your adversaries,
Amen,' Shaxton wrote miserably to the Lord Privy Seal in the first week
of July.[46] Cromwell did his best to counter-harass conservatives, for
instance summoning up the aged and flamboyantly traditional parson of
Cold Ashton in Gloucestershire for interrogation by the Privy Council,
but the balance of advantage in such matters was now emphatically with
his opponents.[47]*

The Act of Six Articles continued to trouble evangelicals up to the
early months of Edward VI's reign, but mitigating factors may have
consoled Cromwell and perhaps Cranmer too. First, close scrutiny of its
terms would reveal that it did not actually reverse any of the measures of
reform they had put in place in the previous few years. On the sixth article, the status of sacramental confession in the life of the Church, Henry
exercised the Supreme Head's prerogative of contrariness to side with the
evangelicals, dropping a reference to confession being 'necessary according to the law of God'. This probably reflected his deep distrust of the
power of clergy, which declaring confession to be of divine institution
could only enhance. He was also furious with Bishop Tunstall for openly
opposing this change in the Lords, and wrote him a long and incandescent letter on the subject: a mark of how much he cared about the issue,
for Henry normally loathed putting pen to paper.[48]

Cromwell could also be consoled by the number of plans put in place
before his illness, which went forward satisfactorily alongside the religious debacle. One was a second Act concerning monastic dissolutions. It
did not itself dissolve any monasteries, but was an overdue recognition of
doubts which the lawyers had expressed over the hasty surrenders made
in the great deal between Cromwell, the Duke of Norfolk and Thomas
Wriothesley in autumn 1537. All surrenders falling outside the terms of
the 1536 Act were affected by similar doubts and, given how many had
now happened, it made perfect sense to declare the King's unblemished
title to the estates he had gained. There was unlikely to be much opposition in Parliament to this: alongside the King and the favoured few who
benefited from royal near-gifts, many others who bought or leased estates
at commercial prices, plus a host of monks and heads of house who needed
their pensions assured, would all hasten to cheer on the legislation.

---

* Thomas Key's splendid rebuilding of Cold Ashton church, liberally strewn with his device
of a key, is a monument to both piety and self-advertisement.

Above all, this bill offered no point of principle to which to object. Its deliberately undramatic preamble concentrated on the fact of dissolution without any comment on its rights and wrongs.[49] Monasteries continued to stand for nearly a year, and no legislation in the English Reformation ever stated that monasticism in itself was a bad thing. That was helpful in later twists and turns of that strange evolution in Christianity called Anglicanism. Moreover, the Act was paired with a further piece of legislation offering hope for a new future to an elite group of monastic heads of house: a bill passed through both Houses on a single day, 23 May, giving the King authority to establish new bishoprics and therefore cathedrals (which could hardly be other than great monastic churches), plus any collegiate bodies Henry cared to create. Cromwell introduced this measure into the Lords. It reflected plans Cardinal Wolsey had made but never implemented, yet it was also close to the King's heart. The expansive and visionary preamble promising all sorts of good results from the new foundations (education and biblical lecturing, poor relief and almsgiving) most unusually exists in the distinctive royal handwriting. Henry took a great personal interest in subsequent discussions on who would be the lucky winners. No numbers or names were specified in the Act, one of the ways in which the future of the monasteries remained open that summer.[50]

A further measure passed without trouble was a brief and innocently titled 'Act for the Placing of the Lords in the Parliament'. For all that this might sound rather technical, it was a major shake-up in the order of precedence for the most powerful men of the realm, a matter of huge importance when political realities were expressed through public ceremony and formal rankings in seating and processions. The remarkable feature of the Act, a true Tudor Revolution in Government, was that offices of state would now automatically modify any other system of noble precedence: even the classic ladder of noble title from baron up to duke, where antiquity of creation decided precedence within every rung. Now, if a royal Chief Secretary were a baron, he was at the head of the barons. Likewise the Lord Chancellor, Lord Treasurer, Lord President of the Council and Lord Privy Seal, if peers, would sit above any duke apart from dukes in the King's own family. This meant that service to the monarch outfaced any other form of dignity in the realm. Overmighty subjects, particularly those who preened themselves on Plantagenet blood, should take due note, assuming that they had survived recent events to be able to do so.

These provisions of course sent Thomas Cromwell shooting up the scale of precedence from the lowliest baron in the peerage, in more than one respect. The very first clause after the preamble's opening verbiage spelled out that, because the King had made Thomas Lord Cromwell his Vice-Gerent, that officer and his successors should be placed 'on the right side of the Parliament-Chamber and upon the same form that the Archbishop of Canterbury sitteth on, and above the same Archbishop and his successors; and shall have voice in every Parliament to assent or dissent as other the Lords of the Parliament'. The other bishops would trail along on the bench in accustomed measure of antiquity, but Cromwell would always outrank them. This was something to savour amid the tactical defeat over the Six Articles. The bill quickly cleared the Lords and Commons. If the Duke of Norfolk had been inclined to any harrumphing, he would quickly realize that the Lord Treasurer in the new system was himself; and at least Cromwell was now sitting on a bench healthily remote from his own.[51]

The precedence bill gave formal expression to a spectacular event which took place in the middle of its passage on 8 May, but which of course also reflected plans made before Cromwell's illness. This was the most prominent display in the kingdom-wide bustle around defence, a muster of all military forces of London before the King himself. During a Parliamentary session, it attracted maximum attention and excitement, and was in fact the largest such muster in the entire century. It was orchestrated to show Lord Cromwell's close collaboration with the City authorities: some might see it rather as expressing his dominance in London. John Husee's excited report to Lord Lisle emphasized the place of Cromwell and his family: the Lord Privy Seal personally spent nearly £400 on wages, tips and new uniforms in City colours for the day for 1,500 men amid a total of somewhere around 15,000 to 20,000.[52]

The armed bands all mustered near Richard Cromwell's home at Stepney, which made for the maximum processional value across the main streets of London to Whitehall, where the King viewed the vast gathering. Richard was prominent among the captains, with Gregory at his side making a ceremonial military reality of his new public role as a knight of the shire. Ralph Sadler headed the troops as they set off, commanding the artillery and guns repeatedly firing off rounds, most spectacularly in front of the King at Westminster. Cromwell dragged himself from his sickbed at St James's to a ceremonial viewing in the park before the soldiers returned to the City – he was not yet well enough to attend Parliament or even to get as far as Whitehall, but he could hardly miss this triumph. The all-day event defined his place as one of the greatest armed men in the realm.

The equivocal consequences of this Parliament, which did deliver more or less what Cromwell had assured the King it would, were summed up by Henry's peculiar attempt to put everything right among his principal advisers by abruptly summoning them all to someone else's dinner party.

Just after Parliament had ended on 28 June, he told Archbishop Cranmer to hold a feast at Lambeth Palace for all members of the House of Lords who were available, headed by Cromwell and the Dukes of Norfolk and Suffolk. It is to be hoped that the Vice-Gerent and Lord Treasurer Norfolk between them ensured that the Archbishop got a royal subvention for this major occasion. It was charged with tension, amid the ongoing investigations into heresy, and as a means of reconciling the principal parties was the reverse of successful. The atmosphere that evening remained vividly with Cranmer's secretary Ralph Morice, whose reminiscences of it fuelled the narrative of John Foxe in no fewer than three different places in his great book, though omitting a further conversation he thought better than to reproduce.[53]

First worth noting is this anecdote Foxe chose to ignore, evidently because it would complicate his straightforward narrative of his two Reformation heroes. The secretary overheard an exchange between the Lord Privy Seal and the Archbishop at the table which showed Cromwell at his most unbuttoned. His words combine brutal frankness and rueful envy:

> You were born in a happy hour, I suppose . . . for, do or say what you will, the King will always well take it at your hand. And I must needs confess that in some things I have complained of you unto his Majesty, but all in vain, for he will never give credit against you, whatsoever is laid to your charge; but let me or any other of the Council be complained of, his Grace will most seriously chide and fall out with us. And therefore you are most happy, if you can keep you in this estate.

Here, in a moment of startling clarity, we are transported to the heart of early Tudor politics, as the leading men at Court eyed one another and judged the moment to plant a negative thought in the mind of their terrifyingly unpredictable royal master. The remark also parallels that glimpse of Cranmer and Cromwell when they quarrelled over what sort of bride was suitable for the King. They could fight because they were friends, and appreciated each other's very different temperaments. They had just experienced a grave test that was not yet complete, and might still result in their destruction. Together, they might succeed in their joint project of reformation.

One wonders at what stage in the evening this conversation took place in relation to another, more public confrontation: a venomous row between the Lord Privy Seal and another principal guest. Foxe did not name him, but the content of the exchange shows that it was the Duke of Norfolk. Morice would have known the identity, and so, clearly, did Foxe. He chose to conceal it, a charitable instinct when he published the story in 1570: his former pupil the fourth Duke, Thomas Howard's grandson, was currently languishing in the Tower of London on treason charges. It would have been tactless to depict the previous Duke in such a direct clash with one of the heroes of Foxe's Reformation story, particularly because the tale included a reminder of Norfolk's potential role in a papal election. The Duke seized on the general brief of the evening, which was to comfort the Archbishop and reassure him of the King's favour, in order to make a malicious comparison with Cardinal Wolsey. Cranmer 'was much to be preferred for his mild and gentle nature, whereas the Cardinal was a stubborn and a churlish prelate, and one that could never abide any noble man, and that . . . know you well enough, my Lord Cromwell, for he was your master, etc.' 'Etc.' is always the sign in a Tudor text of further offensive material omitted, and there was offence enough already.

The Lord Privy Seal at first controlled his temper, riposting coldly 'that he could not deny but he was servant sometime to Cardinal Wolsey; neither did repent the same, for he received of him both fee, meat and drink, and other commodities', but he then made a wounding thrust at the Duke: '[Cromwell] was never so far in love with him [Wolsey], as to have waited upon him to Rome, if he had been chosen Pope, as he understood that *he* [Norfolk] would have done, if the case had so fallen out.' This was a deadly blow: to Norfolk's outraged denial, Cromwell furiously shot back in his most combative style, specifying 'what number of florins he should have received, to be his Admiral [of the Fleet]' to conduct the Cardinal to Rome. That was a characteristic grasp of detail long squirrelled away in his memory until it proved useful. The Duke, as Earl of Surrey, was indeed Admiral of England at the time of Wolsey's second unsuccessful bid to be Pope in 1523. Horrified at what was turning into a full-scale shouting-match with dangerous political overtones, Cranmer and other peers intervened to calm things down; 'yet it might be', as Foxe or Morice observed, 'that some bitter root of grudge remained behind, which afterward grew unto him [Cromwell] to some displeasure.'[54]

Now there was an understatement. The incident stripped bare the reality of a decade of mutual hatred and resentment. We must trace how the grudge festered in the claustrophobia of Court and City, and follow Cromwell to a meeting at the Council board twelve months later.

Downfall: 1539–1540

In an absorbing piece of detective work, two bibliographers recently reassessed a unique woodcut in the collections made by Samuel Pepys, now at Magdalene College Cambridge (see Plate 46). They have restored to the record one of the most striking examples of Thomas Cromwell as patron of evangelical publishing, but, more than that, have illuminated England's political situation in late 1539. The woodcut would be a remarkable specimen in any circumstances, because its vivid picture includes one of the earliest portraits of Martin Luther, still a friar, in mortal combat with the then Pope, Leo X, therefore dateable to 1521. The image is securely attributable to the great Hans Holbein, whom we have so often met in this story, but still more pleasing is the unexpected union of this woodcut from Basel in 1521 with English descriptive verses below, in a single printed composition. Meticulous argument narrows down the production to the second half of 1539 and to the evangelical London publisher John Mayler, the verses probably translated from a German original by the most obvious author of such things at the time, Miles Coverdale. Only Cromwell could have made this publication possible.[1]

This picture and poetry, binding Luther at his most combative into the developing literature of the English Reformation, is a perfect symbol of the evangelical possibilities that survived the debacle of the Six Articles that summer, and of the continuing future developments in Cromwell's Reformation. It is surprising how quickly the conservative triumph began to stall.[2] Several bishops who would have championed the Six Articles, including the extremely safe choices as successors to Latimer and Shaxton, went off to do their duty in their dioceses, while Cromwell followed the King on a long summer progress into Surrey, back up to Woodstock in Oxfordshire and Henry's favourite retreats in that area. In August and September he enjoyed more strokes of luck than might have been predicted. First was an instantly failed coup, based on the same pattern of antagonisms we witnessed in the spring's Parliamentary elections.

A conservative coalition of leading politicians was already in place. They included former friends of Cromwell now deeply alienated by his religious programme and his increasing dominance even in the King's Privy Chamber. In August, 'there was great murmuring in the progress time, and saying that the lord Privy Seal should be out of favour.' Encouraged by this rumour, the Earl of Southampton, Sir William Kingston and Sir Anthony Browne secretly tried to persuade Bishop Tunstall over an intimate supper to make a bid 'to have had rule and chief saying under the King's Highness'. Tunstall simply refused to play along; 'he draweth all towards [wholly joins the party of] my Lord Privy Seal, and will not follow them,' complained one of his chaplains to a fellow-servant in disappointment at hearing the news.[3]

Cromwell may not have known of this failed initiative at the time, but simultaneously he scored a notable victory that probably explains Tunstall's reluctance to lead a coup (quite apart from the Bishop's rueful memories of King Henry's stinging letter about the status of sacramental confession during the Six Articles debates). The Lord Privy Seal directly faced off Bishop Gardiner, who levelled accusations of heresy at that storm petrel of Anglo-German relations Robert Barnes. Barnes had been a royal ambassador that spring, and once more Gardiner completely misjudged the effect of outspokenness on the King. After the eclipse of Bishops Latimer and Shaxton, such heresy charges might have seemed a promising line to take; instead, they earned Gardiner expulsion from the Privy Council, at Cromwell's request. Bishop Sampson of Chichester was ejected at the same time, for reasons unclear to the observer at Court who recorded it, but surely connected to Sampson's current enthusiasm for backing Lord Lisle in proceeding against heretics in Calais.[4]

All this was good news for Cromwell. Then came a bonus: the death on 8 September of Bishop Stokesley, leading champion of traditional religion. The diocese of London now lay effectively at the Lord Privy Seal's disposal, just at his moment of maximum favour. His choice to fill the see was Edmund Bonner, recently Edward Foxe's successor as Bishop of Hereford, through now on mission in France. Bonner's qualifications could not be more satisfying: a friend of Cromwell from Wolsey days, he had been a huge help during the efforts to save the Great Bible materials from confiscation by the Parisian Inquisitor-General. He was on excellent terms with everyone in Cromwell's household from Wriothesley and Richard Cromwell downwards, and, best of all, was a bitter enemy of Stephen Gardiner. The good news reached Bonner on embassy at Compiègne by 1 October; loud were his thanks to the King conveyed via the Lord Privy Seal. Hindsight is a depressing gift; we know that Bonner

turned very quickly to alliance with Gardiner and a pronounced and
henceforward lifelong religious traditionalism, but that hardly makes
sense in relation to what went before in his career. Cromwell cannot have
known he was making a serious mistake.[5]

The developing royal match with Anne of Cleves also seemed very
much the right move in autumn 1539. If anything promoted the Lord
Privy Seal's swing back to good fortune, it was the King's decision to
reward his months of advocacy of a Cleves marriage, bringing with it
new approaches to the Schmalkaldic League. Henry made those drastic
changes to his Privy Council in August just as he received the reply of
his ambassador to Cleves, Nicholas Wotton, telling him that Anne of
Cleves's brother the Duke had appointed ambassadors for England to
discuss terms. Wotton was as positive about the prospective bride as he
could be, also letting his master know that 'Your Grace's servant Hans
Holbein hath taken the *effigies* of my Lady Anne and the Lady Amalia,
and hath expressed their images very lively.'[6] (See Plate 20.) Amalia, then
aged twenty-two and youngest of the Cleves sisters, was perhaps considered less eligible than Anne, two years older, so Anne would remain first
choice, despite Holbein's additional effort. As the Cleves delegation
moved towards England, so once more did Franz Burchard and colleague
from the Elector of Saxony. Both groups arrived in England on 18 September to warm welcomes from suitably distinguished people.

Cromwell met the Saxons on 20 September in frank and expansive
mood, and told them the dire consequences for true religion of his illness
in the spring. Enemies of the Gospel had their opportunity to try to
remove him, together with Chancellor Audley and Cranmer: 'yet nevertheless, up to now, no implementation [of the Six Articles Act] has taken
place, and he is also taking the greatest possible care that the moment
will not arrive for this now to happen.' Cromwell assured them that he
was back in charge: the King was not favouring those who had backed
the legislation, and 'some of these have since that time been excluded and
discharged from the Privy Council.'[7] Even Henry showed himself agreeable when meeting the Germans again, and so matters proceeded for the
rest of the month. The marriage treaty was signed on 6 October, and
both German delegations set out home, with further large-scale negotiations with the Schmalkaldic League once more a realistic prospect.
Cromwell emphasized to the Saxons how important it was for the Cleves
marriage to go ahead if the Six Articles were to be repealed. All that
remained was for Henry's fourth attempt at a bride to begin her journey
to meet her betrothed.

*

The alignment of forces in Cromwell's favour continued to crystallize in a last tragedy of England's medieval monasticism: the execution in late autumn of three abbots of great and venerable Benedictine monasteries, Glastonbury, Reading and Colchester.[8] Their turnaround in fortunes was remarkable: the Abbots of Reading and Colchester actually attended Parliament in spring and summer. The sudden catastrophe may be explained by their bleak realization that summer that there was no likely future for their houses: that despair led them into varied and unconnected indiscretions, all of which provoked sudden retaliatory action from Cromwell's agents at a time when he knew that conservative forces were marshalling against him. Was the final flurry of dissolutions from late autumn 1539 a reaction to the discoveries and the consequent executions? It is by no means clear that even Cromwell had any plan to make a clean sweep of all monasteries until that moment. Indeed in one sense, the clean sweep never happened.

The charges against Abbot Cook of Reading in September are particularly mysterious, though he had never been a particular favourite of Cromwell's evangelical associates. His arrest may be a delayed spasm of the White Rose affair. Abbot Marshall of Colchester had a history of deploring the religious changes of the 1530s, and was charged with concealing abbey valuables. Abbot Whiting of Glastonbury was the most spectacular and surprising casualty: aged, much respected and a courteous if not intimate correspondent of Cromwell. In a gesture that would have appealed to Master Secretary's sense of humour, he chose him to succeed Sir Thomas More as abbey Steward after More's execution.[9] The sudden turnaround in atmosphere at Glastonbury was striking. On 30 June, William Popley, a man in the counsels of both Lord Privy Seal and Lord Lisle, wrote from Court to Calais to soothe a West Country quarrel in which Lisle had taken great offence against Whiting: 'the man is sage, circumspect, and of good estimation,' Popley said reassuringly. Lord Stourton wrote much the same to Lady Lisle from the West Country the previous day.[10]

Mid-September saw a complete change. Richard Leighton, currently engaged in winding up Reading Abbey, had to write to Cromwell with a grovelling apology for praising Whiting to the King back in 1535, when he was vice-gerential visitor to Glastonbury: 'which now appeareth neither then nor now, to have known God, neither his prince, neither any part of a Christian man his religion'. The new information was revealed by Cromwell's 'discreet inquisition', presumably only in the last few weeks.[11] Objects of suspicion piled up to incriminate the Abbot as the visitors searched the vast abbey and its estates: various traditionalist pamphlets and (unsurprisingly) an array of papal documents, but, more materially in every sense, a great deal of concealed plate and money. Dean William Capon had done the same on a smaller scale at the closure of two-year-old Cardinal College Ipswich (see above, p. 112); one can imagine the feelings of such an eminent figure nearing not only the end of his own life but nigh on a millennium in the life of his house. Capon, Cromwell's friend and just about on the right side of Henrician politics, survived. Abbot Whiting had the most deliberately humiliating and cruel death on 15 November: hanged, drawn and quartered as a traitor on Glastonbury Tor, from where he would have looked down on the beauty of the abbey and its lands stretching to the far horizon.

Matters around the greater monasteries nationwide were nevertheless still open. That would discourage other senior figures from following this trio into desperate actions as much as the executions themselves. This is particularly noticeable among the reform-minded monasteries of the Cotswolds, with their long-intimate relationship to Cromwell. On 17 August 1539, the Abbot of Winchcombe wrote Cromwell a dignified reply to his 'most favourable and loving letter'. He was not minded 'for any preferment or any worldly affection or pleasure' to surrender the house 'of my own motion', yet he would follow whatever was the King's will and Cromwell's advice, 'of whom and by whom I count myself under God and the King to enjoy all that I have'. Their actual will and advice was still to be known, and one possible version of Winchcombe's future that summer was implicit in the Abbot's lease of all its demesne lands to Cromwell's protégé Richard Tracey. Tracey was not sure whether the house would actually decide to surrender.[12] In November, with the fate of the three imprisoned abbots under discussion, Cromwell made a note of remembrance for Winchcombe which still gave no indication of suppression, next to a very specific memorandum of the suppression of other great monasteries.

Winchcombe in fact surrendered just before Christmas. Abbot Munslow retreated as prebendary to a neighbouring great Benedictine monastery that made it through to a new cathedral status, St Peter's Gloucester, with the prospect of a life not too dissimilar from the past.[13] That same summer the Abbot and Convent of Evesham, another of the Cotswold elite, likewise still thought it worth writing to Cromwell to propose that their house be added to the list of colleges: Evesham Abbey could be a centre of preaching, of poor relief and of hospitality for Court and nobility.[14] Abbot Hawford actually became Dean of Worcester, a 'New Foundation' cathedral previously a Benedictine monastic cathedral. All these new cathedrals were styled 'colleges', for that was what in constitution they were. Hawford's other neighbour among the Cotswold abbeys, Stephen Sagar of Hailes, was noted at the dissolution in January 1540 as having kept the abbey in such good order 'as though he had looked for no alteration of his house'. That was perhaps nothing less than the truth: the same letter of the royal commissioners dealt with the still unresolved question of who would be 'master' of the new collegiate cathedral of St Peter's Gloucester.[15]

There were thus some stories resolving into continuation, but no one knew what to expect. One confident tale in Bishop Tunstall's household as late as December 1539 was that Peterborough Abbey was not going to be refounded as a college after all, but would simply be dissolved; the reverse happened. Only a fortnight later, the head of that house made his New Year's gift to the King, and was already described in the royal inventory as 'the Warden of the King's College of Peterborough'; there the cathedral stands to this day.[16] Such uncertainties were the inevitable consequence of the lack of specifics in the Parliamentary Act authorizing new bishoprics the previous summer. The last monastic closures took place between January and March 1540. Surreally that same New Year's gift-list still included gifts from three monastic heads of house – Waltham, Westminster and Christ Church Canterbury – and since two of those institutions survived, it is likely that the Abbot of Waltham expected continuance too; he was, after all, head of one of the most senior royal foundations in the kingdom, and his house was on the more expansive draft lists of new dioceses and cathedrals.[17] In the event Waltham was the very last abbey to be suppressed without a successor institution, on 23 March 1540. Still no decision to close all monasteries had ever been made public.

Among the final houses to be closed for good, on 16 February 1540, was Thetford Priory. We have repeatedly visited this Cluniac house, mausoleum of earls and dukes of Norfolk for centuries, for which the Duke had made elaborate proposals in 1538 to survive as a college. Prior Burden was in a panic about dissolution in summer 1539, but was comforted by reassurances from Agnes Dowager Duchess of Norfolk (the Duke's stepmother), 'notwithstanding now that greater houses than this is, are suppressed in sundry places'. Then in an urgent letter, 'now that the common bruit and voice is that none house of religion shall stand', he appealed to her and the Duke, still hoping the priory could be a college, even if he was not its 'minister'.[18] The pleas were in vain. With surely deliberate delay, the suppression of Thetford was postponed to a few days after the Duke had left England on a brief and hastily organized embassy to France.

After Thetford's surrender, the Duke maintained the priory church,

whose fate was still not clear; he was granted the priory and all its extensive possessions in July 1540, as Cromwell lay in the Tower.[19] During the
1540s, he and his stepmother took exceptional measures to preserve the
family tombs at Thetford. Most were eventually transported 40 miles
away to Framlingham in Suffolk, complete with their occupants, or
replaced with brand-new tombs; in Queen Mary's time in the swansong
of his long career, the Duke rebuilt the choir of Framlingham parish
church to receive them. That was trouble and effort enough but, even
more extraordinarily, a different resting-place awaited not only the Dowager Duchess (as she specified in her will) but also her husband the second
Duke, buried magnificently at Thetford in 1524: his coffin travelled from
Thetford all the way to an alternative Howard family mausoleum she had
provided for herself in the parish church across the road from her home
at Lambeth, at the gates of Cranmer's palace. There they lay amid many
children and relatives already commemorated, and graves of relatives
continued to accumulate in the Duchess's Lambeth chapel. This double
set of moves was the most extreme example of family relocation of tombs
in the whole English monastic dissolution.[20]

Thetford's closure in February 1540 and the failure to re-create it as a
college, when Burton and Thornton Colleges continued to flourish and
Henry's 'New Foundation' cathedrals settled down into a refreshed existence, was a direct blow to the always brittle family pride of Thomas
Duke of Norfolk. Whatever nuances there may be in Cromwell's orchestration of the dissolution of the monasteries, his old enemy would see this
as yet another deliberate insult to Howard honour from the Lord Privy
Seal. Such injuries were dangerously accumulating, and more arrived in
the spring of 1540. This was no time for Cromwell to confront his old
enemy so recklessly, for in the same months a royal dynastic catastrophe
became painfully apparent, emerging inescapably from Thomas Cromwell's plans for the future of the realm. Those plans were dependent on
successfully directing the King's affections to Cleves.[21]

Everyone saw the Cleves marriage as another triumph for Cromwell's
campaign of reformation. Bishop Tunstall's servants said gloomily that
the Lord Privy Seal had contrived to get Henry married to 'one of his
own sort', adding the unlikely detail that Duchess Anna 'will not come
into England as long as there is one abbey standing'.[22] At the same time
a message of evangelical triumph was literally being hammered home in
a royal palace in the Westminster complex, as craftsmen hastily created
a splendid ceiling for the chapel in the subsidiary palace of St James's,
where Cromwell had so frequently lodged in recent years (see Plate 45).
With rare and modishly Italian magnificence it still celebrates the

forthcoming marriage, amid a riot of Tudor emblems and, for the first time in such a display, even the harp of Ireland, a foretaste of plans for integrating the Lordship further into the King's control. Three times the fatal conjunction of initials 'HA' leaps out of the panels; six times 'BERG', five times 'GULICK [Jülich]', four times 'CLEVE', but also four times there occurs the only specifically religious reference in the whole ceiling design: to the Word of God, 'VERBUM DEI'. This was the programme for the reign of King Henry and Queen Anne: dynastic splendour and strictly evangelical iconography.[23]

The flagship dynastic enterprise had an attendant flotilla of purposes. One which Cromwell discreetly launched in December was yet another examination of the affairs and opinions of Bishop Tunstall, who only that summer had seemed so much part of the conservative triumph in Parliament – this while the Bishop was deeply engaged in drafting final marriage agreements with the representatives of Cleves.[24] Matters went so far as the arrest and interrogation of his brother John Tunstall, parson of the comfortable Yorkshire living of Tanfield, together with several members of the Bishop's household; events immediately following stopped any further move against Cuthbert Tunstall in its tracks, but the depositions taken have left us much useful information stretching back over a decade.[25]

At the same time there was discussion of a second German marriage, of the Lady Mary to Philipp, Duke of Bavaria.[26] This would be an ideally similar match to the Cleves marriage: the Duke had not formally broken with the Papacy, but he was at odds with his Habsburg overlords. Remarkably, the Duke had journeyed in person with little fanfare to England and was currently in London. Mary seemed happy enough with this prospect, even consenting to meet him on Boxing Day in the garden of the (soon-to-be-former) Abbot of Westminster. On this occasion she went still further by allowing him against all protocol to kiss her – well, he was German, and a prince. 'Since the death of the late Marquess [of Exeter] no lord of this kingdom has dared to go so far,' commented Ambassador Marillac, an observation which illuminates both the exalted status of the Courtenays at Court before their fall and the reason why that fall was necessary.[27]

All remained well while the new royal bride embarked on her long and difficult overland journey from Cleves during autumn 1539. Her reception at Calais at the beginning of December was suitably splendid, and showcased Gregory Cromwell in his first international role, attendant on the principal notable, Lord Admiral Southampton. Ably assisted by his old tutor Henry Dowes, Gregory was assiduous in writing informative and even witty letters about developments, both to his father and to his wife (all sign of trouble there was past, with two sons already in their cradles at Leeds Castle). The welcoming deputation from Dover did suffer an ominous false start: they had to return to port for lack of wind, though at least this first experience of the sea reassured the young man that he was less prone to sea-sickness than his companions, as he reported proudly to his father.[28]

They had a fortnight to recover before Anna reached Calais. Here, amid the awkwardness of adjusting the social customs of two countries unfamiliar to one another, the Lady insisted on an informal supper, Cleves-style, with the leading men of the Court deputation. Lord Admiral Southampton and Ambassador Wotton reported this with slight discomfort to the King, listing all those at table to cover their backs against criticism: a roll-call of peers and veteran courtier knights, with Master Gregory last of all, 'and Master [Richard] Morison should have sitten there, but there lacked room.' Cromwell's representatives at the festivities were being carefully kept in their place.[29]

So Anna and her escort finally arrived in Canterbury for Christmas, the Lady gamely bearing up against really vile weather with the aid of huge festivity, gunfire and a shower of presents including fifty gold sovereigns from Cromwell himself, Cranmer acting as postman.[30] It was at Rochester on New Year's Day that King Henry had his first and famously disastrous glimpse of his new bride. Amid many mysteries around that monarch, his taste in beauty is one of the least easy to fathom. The great passion of his life, Anne Boleyn, was not conventionally beautiful. Conversely, nothing in the remaining images of Anne of Cleves hints at anything to inspire such instant repugnance in 1540. Meekness had clearly appealed to Henry in his third effort at matrimony, Gregory Cromwell's sister-in-law, but this time perhaps there was a lack of vivacity even outwardly perceptible, accentuated by a careful educational programme in dullness at the Court of Cleves.

It was to Sir Anthony Browne that the King first confided his utter dismay. Browne did nothing to contradict his master's feelings, only worrying that his half-brother Lord Admiral Southampton would be in trouble for singing Anne's praises from Calais.[31] Cromwell was aghast at a grim royal response to his own cheerful enquiry on 2 January, and when he had a chance to take Southampton aside he duly berated him in what the victim indignantly saw as an attempt 'to turn all the King's miscontentment upon the shoulders of the said Earl'. It was not wise to have antagonized the Earl of Southampton thus. The leading men at Court subsided into discreet panic, to the accompaniment of outward triumphal celebration. Cromwell organized a 3-mile-long guard of honour of citizens of London on the approach to Greenwich Palace for the prospective bride and groom for 3 January. He controlled his feelings by manic supervision: an unsympathetic Spanish observer thought he 'looked more like a post-runner than anything else, running up and down with his staff in his hand', while the King looked openly glum.[32]

Frantic examination of the marital paperwork revealed no loopholes. Postponements of the wedding ceremony by a day were in vain, though they puzzled and worried the bride-to-be, stranded amid incomprehensible whispers and rather too comprehensible confusion. After some farcical missteps of choreography in which Cromwell nearly had to substitute for the aged Earl of Essex leading the Lady to meet her groom, all was accomplished in the chapel of Greenwich Palace, twenty-four hours late: the gloomiest royal wedding of the Tudor age, followed by the gloomiest wedding night.[33] Matters did not improve. What could Cromwell do in these circumstances? This was about the most serious blow to his position that could be imagined, because his own protracted diplomacy had resulted in the King's sexual humiliation. Over the next few months Cromwell's delicate enquiries on that subject always yielded similar answers. It became increasingly apparent that the only way out of the situation was a full-scale annulment on grounds of non-consummation. That would inevitably put royal humiliation into the public domain, however discreetly handled.

The Lord Privy Seal would have to exercise immense self-control in the face of a growing wave of quiet *Schadenfreude* from his enemies among the small group of courtiers who had some idea of what was going on. He was most vulnerable to attack on the matter of religion. He made that clear to the most sympathetic audience he had, the various Schmalkaldic ambassadors, reinforced just then by Ludwig von Baumbach, a Hessian diplomat who joined them to bring worrying information about hostile moves against England by Charles V. Baumbach reported home that Cromwell had observed to them that 'he sets great store by our opinions concerning matters of the faith, but the world standing as it does now, whatever his lord the King holds, so too will he hold, and die on that account.'[34]

Emphatically that remark does not mean that Cromwell in his royal service would blindly follow any religious policy the King dictated. He was saying precisely and with bitter realism that at this catastrophic juncture it would be madness to take any further religious initiatives of his own.[35] The problem was that, under the pressure of desperate worry, necessary discretion was deserting him. Also part of his thoughts at this tumultuous time was a moment of fury preserved in the Act of Attainder destroying him the following summer, among a number of observations which sound all too like the Lord Privy Seal in a towering rage: 'If the Lords would handle him so, that he would give them such a breakfast as never was made in England, and that the proudest of them should know'. There need not be a prize for guessing that the person uppermost in his mind was the Duke of Norfolk. This was said, according to the Act, on 31 January 1540.[36]

This combustible situation simply needed one trigger to set conflict in motion. That was provided by those old enemies Bishop Stephen Gardiner and Dr Robert Barnes. Over the previous year, Barnes was riding high: royal ambassador in Germany, catalyst for Gardiner's humiliating ejection from the Council in August, with rewards (admittedly small and overdue) in the shape of cathedral prebends from the evangelical bishops.[37] Now, from 12 February until Easter, the Bishop turned his wrath on Barnes, who was unwise to react badly to a traditionalist sermon of Gardiner's. More evangelical preachers were then provoked into pulpit aggression alongside Barnes: William Jerome and Thomas Garrett in particular. They were a resonant pairing, for as Gardiner may have remembered (and may have reminded King Henry) they had preached in the North under the auspices of that enigmatic Pilgrim of Grace, Sir Francis Bigod. Thanks to Cromwell's forgiving attitude, they had continued in evangelical prominence thereafter, Jerome as Cromwell's own Vicar at Stepney, and Garrett as chaplain to the now disgraced Bishop Latimer.

Cromwell realized how vulnerable this made him. He sent his son's trusted servant Henry Dowes to Stepney to provide a detailed report on Jerome's recantation sermon ordered by the King (the recantation did not save Jerome from the Tower).[38] Simultaneously the King was showing himself aggressively uncompromising to the Schmalkaldic delegation: Henry 'had been sufficiently advised by his learned men that ours [the German Lutherans] have gone too far with regard to priestly marriage, communion in both kinds and the private mass'.[39] There could be no more learned man among the conservative episcopate than Stephen Gardiner, and in March Cromwell even went so far as to stage an extended dinner party in an attempt at fire prevention.[40]

Yet the minister's fierce temper could always let him down when trying to relax among his intimates. The Gardiner dinner party and Jerome's humiliating performance at Stepney just predated a furious outburst on 31 March, when according to the Act of Attainder Cromwell was at Austin Friars and heard that the evangelicals had been committed to the

Tower. His shout reversed his words to the Schmalkaldic ambassadors about true religion: 'If the King would turn from it, yet I would not turn; and if the King did turn, and all his people, I would fight in the field in mine own person, with my sword in my hand, against him and all others.' There was more in the same vein, and waving of fists 'as though he had a sword in his hand'; it sounds a perfectly plausible outburst of passion in the privacy of home.[41] It was just at the moment Ambassador Marillac heard that in a major shift among the King's ministers the two bases of Cromwell's power, the Vice-Gerency and the office of Lord Privy Seal, were to be reassigned to bishops Tunstall and Clerk. The Vice-Gerency looked especially vulnerable.[42]

In an atmosphere of intense political activity, everything was ripe for capture by factional forces as the King, with his own dark personal pre-occupations, leaned first one way, then another. The effect of the Barnes/Gardiner conflict shaped royal choices in a new pair of committees to consider doctrine and liturgy in the Church: the majorities on them were conservative, and they quickly occupied themselves with harassing another evangelical cleric whose chaplaincy to the Duke of Suffolk did not protect him from hostile investigation.[43] Worse still were the first signs of activity for commissions under the Act of Six Articles, which the previous autumn Cromwell had boasted he had rendered inoperable. Then a new session of the Parliament elected in 1539 opened on 12 April. Although the Commons would be much the same in membership, the Lords had changed in the meantime, and not in Cromwell's favour. While it had lost without replacement the still substantial number of abbots who attended the previous year, the balance on the bishops' bench had shifted towards conservatism. Just how much was not yet apparent in the public actions of Bishop Bonner of London and Heath of Rochester (a replacement for the reliable and high-profile evangelical John Hilsey), but the loss of Latimer and Shaxton was obvious.

The agenda for Parliament was full enough without considering the future of religion. The King still had an urgent need for ready money for his coastal defences, having curiously shied away from fiscal demands on his subjects in the 1539 session, after initial exploratory noises about taxation.[44] The arrival of major monastic estates in government hands could do little immediately to solve cashflow, so one of the first pieces of business was to get agreement to new rounds of taxes which required justification as usual in an explanatory preamble. This must conceal one uncomfortable reality whose disclosure would unnecessarily alarm the public: growing rebellion in Ireland across the Gaelic parts of the island was becoming extremely serious, and would need a major military response. Instead, after a couple of major redrafts, the preamble was a ragbag of all the usual suspects in such justificatory flimflam; as in 1534, Cromwell threw in the general idea of gratitude to the King from his taxpayers for all his energy in religion and defence, as well as a list of particular demands, Ireland figuring in a relatively minor capacity.[45]

The preamble was repeated more stylishly in a major speech prepared by Richard Morison and corrected in precise and rather pedantic detail by Cromwell himself: precisely the sort of task for which Morison was elected the year before, as the minister's and the government's mouthpiece in the Commons. It is in fact one of only two full texts of Parliamentary speeches from early Tudor Parliaments, the other being Cromwell's sceptical speech about a French war back in 1523. In 1540, unlike that earlier effort, the government got everything it wanted in taxation, but at the price of widespread hatred for the man who clinched the grant.[46] Writing in the seventeenth century of the first royal closure of monasteries in 1532, Thomas Fuller judged that Henry had tried that out with the intention of hiding behind his minister's actions should the effort prove unpopular. His contemporary Lord Herbert of Chirbury considered that that same royal instinct was on display in 1540, and that the unpopularity of the taxation was yet another consideration to throw on the scales when Henry allowed Cromwell to be destroyed.[47]

Besides the tax grant was a huge volume of legislation both public and private: so much that Geoffrey Elton commented it was almost as though Cromwell knew this would be his last Parliament.[48] It certainly demonstrated the minister's frantic energy in trying to cope with the continuing pile of legislative needs built up over three years: the volume of demands itself witnessing how both King and people now saw Parliament as the forum for securing change. Among government bills, the most important concerned land tenure, principally a new right for the King's subjects to use their wills to make decisions on leaving land to whom they pleased. This was a necessary royal retreat from the great kingdom-wide groundswell of fury against the Statute of Uses of 1536, which, as we observed, swept aside a century and more of legal evasions of feudal inheritance law. The Statute of Wills was a lasting and sensible modification of the King's reasserted feudal rights, drawing the sting from the previous legislation; the mark of its success was how little it needed supplementing in later centuries.[49]

All this had to be accomplished alongside Cromwell's two main challenges: to counter the King's profound sense of disappointment in his chief minister over the Cleves marriage, and to defeat the build-up of pressure from his enemies. With his eyes placed around Court, he will have been chilled to see signs of the King's renewed interest in that petite and lively lady-in-waiting to Queen Anne, the Duke of Norfolk's niece Katherine Howard. The first administrative evidence of this came near the end of April in the most bizarre of personal gifts to Katherine: a grant of goods and chattels confiscated by a Sussex coroner from the homes of two fugitive rural murderers. It suggests the King impulsively seizing on the first bureaucratic instrument on his desk which was convertible to cash; one hopes that he added a bouquet of flowers.[50]

Such straws in the wind demanded counteraction. One move might seem a rare example of Cromwell ceding power to others. By a warrant personally signed by the King, arrangements were made for him to surrender the office of Principal Secretary, which he had held in title from 1534 and in practice from about two years before that. The office was regranted jointly to a pair of courtiers, but their names reveal that this was a consolidation of his power or an attempt to disguise it, not a concession, because they were his own principal secretary Thomas Wriothesley and his oldest principal servant Ralph Sadler. A mark of their subordinate relationship was a provision for Sadler's formal seating: when the Lord Privy Seal was dining at Court, Sadler 'shall accompany him at his table'. The Secretaries' position in a formal meeting of the Council when it sat judicially in Star Chamber was down below every other office-holder present, although to provide the minimum political clout expected in their position they were granted knighthoods.[51]

Both new Secretaries were currently MPs, and the warrant appointing them arbitrarily modified the Statute on Precedence of the previous year, which had been designed to accommodate Cromwell's exalted place as Secretary in the Lords. Now, remarkably, one of the pair would alternate week by week in Lords and Commons during a Parliamentary session. Given that Wriothesley and Sadler were Cromwell's close associates, this move was designed to strengthen his position in Parliament, and of course it could also be presented as streamlining the King's business. Later Tudor and Stuart monarchs returned to the arrangement of two Secretaries, with the obvious motive of avoiding dominance by any one single politician.

Nevertheless, Cromwell needed something much more thoroughgoing. In typical style, it came in the form of some wild improvisation, leapfrogging on the back of events that might have stayed unrelated, to 'make or mar'. Within a fortnight of each other there were the bizarrely coincidental deaths of two elderly Essex noblemen: on 13 March, the Earl of Essex, Henry Bourchier (he broke his neck falling from his horse), then on 21 March, the Earl of Oxford, John de Vere. On consecutive days in April, the Crown united dignities enjoyed by these scions of ancient nobility in the person of Thomas Cromwell. It was a sign of the extraordinary instability of these months, and the way in which the King might reward whom he pleased amid the battle of factions. Cromwell could still win his master's favour. On the 17th he became sixteenth Earl of Essex (the first Earl was granted the title back in the early twelfth century), with substantial county estates to match. On the 18th, he was granted the fifteenth Earl of Oxford's title of Lord Great Chamberlain: titular (and, in the right hands, actual) head of the royal Household. The Garter ceremony on 23 April and his creation ceremony two days later emphasized the magnificence of the newly created Earl amid his peers.[52]

There was a price, and a heavy one. In a move strikingly reminiscent of the surrender of Hackney House in the middle of the Anne Boleyn crisis, Cromwell made a major sale of estates to the Crown, and they were no mean estates: his whole lordship of Wimbledon, with his great house at Mortlake.[53] This might be presented as a logical consequence of his elevation to the Earldom of Essex. His barony was as Lord Cromwell of Wimbledon; now that that lesser title was a mere adjunct for his dramatic promotion to one of the oldest earldoms in the realm, Wimbledon became less emblematic. Yet it was still an astonishing sacrifice: sprawling acres that had brought him in triumph home to Putney in 1536 and the mansion on which he had spent so much. In 1539 Cromwell had bought substantial adjacent estates in Dunsford, Wandsworth and Wimbledon from the Duke of Suffolk, evidently intending permanently to extend his property block in this Thames-side corner of Surrey; those new acquisitions went to the King as well.[54] The problem was that all these lands neighboured the King's expanding empire of parks and palaces from Hampton Court through Richmond to his new fantasy palace at Nonsuch, all now forming 'The Honour of Hampton Court'. After Henry's death, safe from reprisals the Privy Council frankly noted that this great scheme had been an answer to the King's increasing ill-health and obesity, to give him easy retreats not involving much travel.[55]

The other price to pay would be obvious to anyone not so desperate and besieged by the pace of events: his enemies were spurred into risking drastic action. So many of Cromwell's bravura improvisations over the last twelve months had the corollary of enraging traditionalist nobility, moving them towards the conclusion that he must be stopped. Now his promotions were a wild lunge forward. This dynamic continued into the month of May, as Cromwell showed a new self-confidence in what amounted to a slow-rolling attempted coup against his opponents. It is significant that, just as in spring 1536 at a moment of intense political crisis, the State Papers archive thins out. Various interested parties subsequently saw to the removal of embarrassing evidence, and much of what we know has to come from reports back home of the French ambassador Marillac, absorbed and darkly entertained by the unfolding drama.

And what drama it was. The opening was a great tournament on May Day, long planned to celebrate the Cleves marriage and of course an unavoidable celebration, given that the King had still not fully disclosed his private agonies to anyone. Fifty noblemen and gentry took part, and Cromwell contrived that three of the six ceremonial challengers were his close associates: Sir John Dudley, Sir Thomas Seymour and, a notable public affirmation of the King's confidence in the Cromwell brand, his own nephew Richard, who was only knighted during the course of proceedings.[56]* Among other conjunctions produced by this great ceremony and the meeting of Parliament in May, the Dukes of Norfolk and Suffolk were together at Court for the first time in a long while. Quite exceptionally, two lieutenants of the King's extended dominions were also making their way to London: Lord Leonard Grey from Ireland and Lord Lisle from Calais. Both of them suffered from getting what they wished for, for they had long been agitating to return to Court, confident that they could charm the King in explaining why all was not as it should be in their territories.

The case of Ireland would demand a great deal of charm. The evidence of Grey's quarrels with the Irish Council stretched back years. Over the previous few months a string of alarming letters from the Lord Privy Seal's informants in Ireland showed not just how much the military situation was deteriorating, but how Grey was obstructing the efforts of the Earl of Ormond and Archbishop Browne to further Cromwellian-style reformation.[57] Cromwell's promotion of Grey's candidacy for Lord Deputy back in 1535 had been a bad misjudgement. On 1 April Grey was summoned back from Dublin. He arrived at Westminster surprisingly speedily, only about six weeks later. His position was then unclear; but then so was much else. Parallel royal summonses had gone out to the Earl of Ormond, Chancellor Allen and Vice-Treasurer Brabazon, but they said firmly that the developing crisis prevented them from coming, and interestingly the English government did not press the point. In Lord Leonard's absence the situation in Ireland was becoming dire, nothing less than a Gaelic insurrection inspired by papalist religious fury.[58]

---

* Richard commemorated this occasion with a wall-painting at his new Huntingdonshire mansion converted from Hinchingbrooke Priory, which is still extant though alas very damaged.

Steadily more damning news of Grey's failure percolated to London. In one especially poisoned bullet of information after he had left, Archbishop Browne reminisced pointedly to Cromwell, 'I cannot say that his Lordship favoureth that false traitor Reginald Pole, whom in communication between his Lordship and me I called papish cardinal; and he in a great fume called me poll-shorn knave friar; and shortly after that, his Lordship took his journey towards Galway and Limerick, where as it was commonly bruited, the said Cardinal should arrive, leaving there the King's chief ordnance [artillery].'[59] Perhaps this thrust provided the coup de grâce for Grey, though probably thanks to delays in the Irish post his arrest came two days after Cromwell's own. The official announcement of it would be some comfort to Cromwell's friends on the Dublin Council, reaching them two days after a previous letter from Westminster bearing news of their ally's fall.[60]

Calais, such a running sore in recent English politics, now provided a decisive nudge for Cromwell's plans: as in Ireland, the toxic name of Pole was the key. The unstable balance of advantage between conservatives and evangelicals tipped over against Lord Deputy Lisle and his household when one of his chaplains, Gregory Botolf, fled to Rome.[61] When the news broke in mid-April, it became quickly apparent that several members of the Lisle household had known this was about to happen. This was even more straightforward than Archbishop Browne's insinuations against Lord Leonard: Rome meant Reginald Pole, and Lisle's family contacts already leaned so much in that direction. When Lisle obeyed his summons to London, he was full of expectations that his visit would prove much to his advantage, and in fact at first all seemed well; he was present on 23 April at the Garter ceremonies to witness Cromwell's new triumph, and even sat in sessions of the Lords.

Then on 19 May, while Lord Leonard still tarried uncertainly at Court, Lord Lisle was arrested and interrogated, and Lady Lisle and their children detained in Calais. The rumours of a Pole conspiracy in Calais spread rapidly through London and nearly entangled Cromwell's old foe Sir John Wallop, then on embassy in France: the Lord Privy Seal sent one of the royal Secretaries to Marillac to seek any news of him from Paris, and Marillac knew perfectly well what that was about. Cromwell's sudden advantage struck down prominent conservatives previously untouched: Bishop Sampson of Chichester and Dr Nicholas Wilson, both closely linked to the Lisles, were arrested and sent to the Tower. The speed of this is underlined by the fact that the pair had just been marked for episcopal promotions – in fact Sampson was publicly recognized as Bishop-elect of the new diocese of Westminster on the very day of his arrest.[62] Ralph Sadler promptly opened discussions with his old master about what to do with Sampson's goods; the Duke of Suffolk wanted the use of Sampson's mule.[63] Calamity for traditionalists was spreading: a leading city merchant, Richard Farmer, was savagely punished by the Court of King's Bench for maintaining a papalist chaplain, and two other citizens fled abroad, fearing a similar fate.[64]

Behind these casualties, a further target was Bishop Tunstall. Cromwell was scrutinizing the body of evidence gathered six months before, which he had been forced to lay aside amid the disaster of Anne of Cleves's arrival. To emphasize to the public what all these moves meant, Archbishop Cranmer stepped into the pulpit at Paul's Cross to fill a slot assigned to Sampson before his imprisonment, and the French ambassador heard a message very different from that preached by Stephen Gardiner in Lent. Marillac saw that a final resolution loomed, but he was still baffled as to what it might be. He was now certain that the chief contenders still at large were Cromwell and Gardiner.

The answer came on 10 June: a total reversal of direction. The first week in June, Cromwell was still interrogating Wilson and Sampson, taking his place in Council and Parliament and dealing with routine administration. His last surviving ordinary letter, on 4 June, is addressed appropriately enough to one of his oldest friends, Sir George Lawson, passing on signed royal instructions for financing defensive works at Berwick-upon-Tweed.[65] On 6 June he had a difficult and tense meeting with Henry, the King's misery now all too obvious to those close to him at Court. The King at last made the excruciating admission that he was still impotent with the Queen, and allowed Cromwell to confide in one other royal intimate, Lord Admiral Southampton. Maybe the Earl of Essex actually refused to support an end to the Cleves marriage; one of Archbishop Cranmer's senior staff had that impression.[66] Either that day or the next, Cromwell returned from Court to Austin Friars: the burden was too much for him. In what should have been domestic privacy, he let his chief of staff Thomas Wriothesley into the secret. A couple of conversations followed about what might be done, but Cromwell could say little more than 'it was a great matter,' 'and then brake off from him'.[67]

Here was a man staring into the abyss, as Wriothesley could see. Maybe it was at this stage that the Secretary made the decision to abandon a loser, just as he had abandoned Gardiner in winter 1536 – in effect, to reverse the decision which he had made then. Maybe his resolution had come earlier, and some at least of the antagonism we have seen between Wriothesley and the Bishop was not all it seemed. Another Bishop, Edmund Bonner, so recently appointed to London, might also have been

instrumental in swapping alliances. His friendship with Cromwell went
back to the 1520s, but in the past few years he and Wriothesley had
become very close in diplomatic service.[68] William Palmer, a minor courtier who hated Stephen Gardiner, wrote a venomous poem ventriloquizing
the Bishop's voice in events of the 1530s and 1540s. His verses sketched
Cromwell's downfall as a gradual betrayal; for once it was Cromwell and
not Gardiner who misjudged an intimate friend. Here is 'Gardiner'
speaking with relish of the betrayer:

> The next way I thought was to find one out
> That Cromwell trusted and of his counsel were;
> As God would have it, such a one I found,
> My secret friend and of old acquaintance;
> There was no evil that against me could sound
> But thereof I had true intelligence.
> And Cromwell thought him my mortal enemy –
> The more loved him above all other;
> And on my part, I shewed not contrary –
> Yet we were friends as brother and brother.[69]

It is difficult to decide whether Wriothesley or Bonner is the better candidate for this traitor. The treachery would include revealing the two stories
of Cromwell's rash private pronouncements which were rehearsed in his
attainder. Wriothesley is the more likely to have been present, and was
certainly of Gardiner's 'old acquaintance', but Bonner would not have
been far behind.

These revelations were only part of the poison. Evidently the King was
convinced that Cromwell had been indiscreet about his sexual performance, beyond the royal permission to confide in the Earl of Southampton.
Here was the fatal opportunity to alter course once more. In the next two
or three days those determined to foil the spreading evangelical coup said
the right things to the King to achieve the desired result. The psychology
with Henry was to find an oblique reason why he should feel savage fury
with a victim, to fuel his self-righteousness and draw attention away
from his own sense of humiliation. With Anne, it had been the notion
that she had committed the crimes of adultery with all and sundry, and
incest with her own brother. With Cromwell, the obvious (and in fact
accurate) direction was religion: his constant private initiatives, often
amounting to deception of his prince, which could be construed as
heresy. Maybe, in Henry's final rage against his great minister, casting
around for pretexts to hate Cromwell, he was fed enough clues about the
various exchange visits of young evangelicals to Zürich to realize that the

Lord Privy Seal had stealthily aided English 'sacramentaries' to roam highly suspect regions of Europe. If so, the King had good reason to execute Cromwell as a heretic: much more than with the accompanying charges of treason.

Just as with Bishop Sampson, the arrest on Thursday 10 June represented a total reverse of fortune. Cromwell and Cranmer are among those recorded as present in the Lords that morning. In the afternoon, the Lord Privy Seal arrived still dressed formally as for Parliament to find the majority of his colleagues already assembled, with the choreography of the event worked out between them. Our best description comes from Ambassador Marillac's account to Constable Montmorency, polished after a fortnight of careful enquiry.[70] The Captain of the Guard told Cromwell that he was a prisoner:

> Cromwell in a rage ripped his cap from his head and threw it to the ground
> in contempt, saying to the Duke of Norfolk and others of the Privy Coun-
> cil assembled there that this was the reward of the good service he had
> done to the King, and that he appealed to their consciences to know
> whether he was a traitor as in their accusations; he added that since he was
> thus treated, he renounced all pardon and grace that he might be offered,
> as one who had never thought to have offended, and only asked the King
> his master if he had such an opinion of him, not to make him linger long.

It was a moment for furious recriminations: among those who called him traitor, some sarcastically reminded him of his own legislation on treason, and inevitably the Duke of Norfolk led the way in humiliating him, ripping the collar of St George from his neck, while Admiral Southampton, 'to show himself as great an enemy in adversity as he had been considered a friend in prosperity', untied his Garter decoration. From there an unobtrusive barge took him from a palace watergate downstream to the Tower of London. The first that the capital knew of his fate was the sight of Sir Thomas Cheyney and the royal guard arriving at Austin Friars to inventory his goods.

Back in the Council chamber, the Privy Council busily sent off letters to ambassadors and to the various regional Councils and Ireland, explaining what had happened. Wriothesley did the drafting; it was after all his job, but also his insurance policy. The letters showed how carefully the conspirators had drawn up their plans, because they anticipated material in the eventual Act of Attainder, including the anecdote about Cromwell's furious words at the time of Robert Barnes's imprisonment (that was not good news for Barnes either). They concentrated on Cromwell's 'oultrage', that is, his mad behaviour, and his subversion of the King's constant quest for 'the mean indifferent, true and virtuous way'.[71] Speed was of the essence to make this counter-coup work: Ambassador Pate in Brussels received his copy of the letter (the contents of which utterly delighted him) as soon as Sunday the 13th.

The signs are that current English embassies abroad had been carefully weighted by Cromwell's opponents at Court towards those who would welcome the news. Foreign affairs, as we have seen, were always Cromwell's Achilles heel. Sir John Wallop, English ambassador in France, had been Cromwell's enemy since the 1520s. In April Ambassador Pate, who defected to Rome the following year before becoming a papalist bishop, replaced Cromwell's evangelical protégé Thomas Wyatt at the imperial Court – so that decision was made during the conservative offensive in March. It is revealing that on 16 June Pate addressed what was formally a reply to the whole Privy Council to the Duke of Norfolk alone.[72] King François of France wrote to Marillac expressing his satisfaction, revealingly observing that his 'cousin' Norfolk would be able to tell him about their conversation during his recent embassy on the prospect of getting rid of Cromwell.[73]

Wallop was punctilious in promptly feeding back to the King the various damaging reports of Cromwell circulating in foreign Courts: the fallen minister had wished to make himself king, and marry the Lady Mary. Anything discreditable, particularly mood-music about threats to the dynasty, could help to buoy up Henry's level of hatred. Abstracts survive of the ambassadors' letters and French commentary on events, summarized for the King's benefit and Cromwell's further damnation (alas in the hand of Ralph Sadler, doing his job as Secretary like Wriothesley).[74] Marillac noted that those searching Cromwell's papers promptly cherrypicked his correspondence with Schmalkaldic princes, and that the King was particularly infuriated by their content: with some justification, since Cromwell had indeed consistently negotiated beyond his brief without his master's knowledge.[75]

A fascinating study could be made of the marks on Cromwell's surviving papers showing how they were scrutinized and annotated when seized in 1540. I have suggested that the household committed an act of loyal destructive vandalism on the out-tray files before royal commissioners could remove them, but plenty remained. Besides that, a formidable armoury was stored at Austin Friars, of which the inventory at confiscation survives: 400 pikes, 759 bows, 459 bills, 272 handguns and armour for more than 600 men, which explains how Cromwell could put up such an impressive show at the great City muster of 1539, and reminds us of his formidable contribution to the forces marching against the Pilgrimage of

Grace three years before.[76] There was no secret: in 1539 Cromwell boasted to the King of intimidating Ambassador Marillac with a tour of his armoury, during which he had made the point that twenty other lords or gentlemen could have done the same. His military resources were not a problem while Henry favoured his minister; they were fuel for paranoia when paranoia had already been stirred.[77]

In such circumstances, who would stand up for the fallen minister? Countless people on receiving favours over the last decade had expansively promised to recompense his goodness if it were in their little power; none came forward now.[78] There were honourable reasons not to. With the triple arrests of Lisle, Cromwell and finally Lord Leonard Grey, large swathes of the King's dominions under lieutenancy were formally leaderless; this was no time to add to destabilization. The remaining provincial governors were Cromwell's two bishops, Roland Lee and Robert Holgate in the Welsh Marches and the North respectively, together with his friend Lord Russell as absentee head of the very recently created Council in the West; they all needed to get on with their job. One man alone had the courage to be a voice of reason, just as when Anne Boleyn lay helpless in the Tower: Archbishop Cranmer.

Either the day after Cromwell's arrest or at that very meeting, Cranmer heard at the Privy Council table that Cromwell was a traitor, and next day he wrote to the King in the prisoner's defence. We have only part of the text, printed by Lord Herbert probably from State Papers lost a century later in a fire among manuscripts at Westminster, but it is so like Cranmer's tormented defence of Anne Boleyn four years before that he may well have got out his 1536 files to find a model of how to write on behalf of a fallen patron and friend to whom he was devoted. The same three elements are there: warm praise of the victim, horror if the charges proved true and pastoral concern for the King in the loss of a brilliant adviser:

> who cannot be sorrowful and amazed that he should be a traitor against your Majesty, he that was so advanced by your Majesty, he whose surety was only by your Majesty, he who loved your Majesty (as I ever thought) no less than God; he who studied always to set forwards whatsoever was your Majesty's will and pleasure; he that cared for no man's displeasure to serve your Majesty; he that was such a servant, in my judgement, in wisdom, diligence, faithfulness, and experience, as no prince in this realm ever had . . .

Cranmer turned adroitly to the theme of treason, starting with that recently rehabilitated evangelical hero of the English monarchy's struggle with the Papacy:

If the noble princes of memory, King John, Henry II and Richard II had had such a Councillor about them, I suppose they should never have been so traitorously abandoned, and overthrown as those good princes were . . . I loved him as my friend, for so I took him to be; but I chiefly loved him for the love which I thought I saw him bear ever towards your Grace, singularly above all other. But now, if he be a traitor, I am sorry that ever I loved him or trusted him, and I am very glad that his treason is discovered in time; but yet again I am very sorrowful; for who shall your Grace trust hereafter, if you might not trust him? . . . But I pray God continually night and day, to send such a counsellor in his place whom your grace may trust, and who for all his qualities can and will serve your Grace like to him.[79]

This was an astonishingly brave letter to write, given Cranmer's own danger. He was on his own, for the first time since becoming Archbishop, without the protection of the hard-nosed operator always able to deal with political crises. In 1563 John Foxe printed a plausible story in *Acts and Monuments* about the Archbishop's peril at this time, which he may later have considered indecorous, and dropped from later editions. Cranmer was due for arrest, but he avoided a group waiting to buttonhole him at 'the common stairs of Court Gate' in Whitehall when he 'suddenly shot into the privy stair' (the private stair to the royal apartments) to see the King in person. The King gave Cranmer his signet-ring, with a rather typical Henrician anti-clerical growl, 'Go thy ways; if thou deceive me, I will never trust bald-pate again while I live.' The signet was Henry's favourite device for lending his authority to protect his intimates: a talisman to preserve Cranmer, just as in a renewed attempt to destroy him in 1543.[80]

Cranmer could do nothing else for Cromwell, any more than for Anne Boleyn. He took his place in the Lords, absenting himself from the deliberations only one day that month, and dutifully voted through the first reading of Cromwell's attainder on 19 June with everyone else.[81] The attainder charges, only finally decided on 29 June after some tinkerings, focused on treason and heresy: in the sardonic words of Lord Herbert a century later, 'that the Head of the Church's Vicegerent in Spiritual Affairs should be an heretic and favourer of them, to some seemed strange, to others gave occasion of merriment.'[82] By that Act, Cromwell was legally dead: useful to the King only for what evidence he could provide to bolster Henry's arguments about the nullity of the Anne of Cleves marriage, hastening yet another royal wedding. The delicate task of annulment was launched on 5 July, and was thereafter a brisk minuet round Parliament and the two Convocations of the kingdom.[83] Queen Anne, utterly shocked at first on being told what was afoot, soon proved heroically resilient at the prospect of not being married to Henry VIII. She took a handsome settlement of English estates from her relieved non-husband, and concentrated very happily on not being married to anyone for another seventeen years of life, generally esteemed by those who remembered her, from Queen Mary downwards.[84]

Once one marriage was safely ended and another in sight, Cromwell could be taken from his cell in the Tower and disposed of. The vital task for Norfolk, Gardiner and others was to stop him having the face-to-face contact with Henry that twice saved Cranmer, and might have broken the spell of the King's malice. All he was allowed to do was to write a series of detailed letters contributing what he could to the pile of evidence. They do everything possible to remind the King of his good service in government: 'I am a right simple man to be a witness in this matter, but yet I think next your Grace, I know as much as any one man living in this realm doth.'[85] It was perhaps more true than tactful to point out the perils of being an indispensable minister: 'hard it is for me or any other, meddling as I have done, to live under your Grace and your laws, but we must daily offend.'[86]

Interspersed among the testimony were pleas for the Cromwell family: 'I most humbly beseech your gracious Majesty [to be] good and gracious lord to my poor son, the good and virtuous [Lady] his wife and their poor children.'[87] One letter was used formally as evidence in the ecclesiastical judgment of annulment, and hence a copy survives in a logical but still surprising place: transcribed with extreme accuracy by a notary into the archive of the Archbishop of York, whose Convocation needed to add assent to the annulment proceedings.* The York notary was extremely thorough. Heart-stoppingly, he included Cromwell's postscript to the King: 'Most gracious prince: I cry for mercy, mercy, mercy!' One wonders whether Henry was given the chance to hear these letters read out to him verbatim.[88]

On the day of Cromwell's execution, 28 July 1540, the King took his mind off it by getting married to Katherine Howard. One doubts whether he reflected on his previous diversion with a young lady while disposing of Anne Boleyn. Just as in Anne's case, Cromwell could with full legal propriety have been burned at the stake, and maybe his enemies sought that. In July Parliament enacted a general pardon; in itself that was a customary piece of routine to sort out various legal liabilities for officials

---

* With an acute sense of hierarchy in the current situation, the officials placed Cromwell's testimony in a sequence after all the current politicians, but before the ladies. Yet the writer is still referred to in the heading as 'the Lord Thomas Crumwell Earl of Essex'.

and private individuals, but this contained some extraordinary provisions. Not only was Cromwell of course among those excluded by name
from pardon, but the exclusions were widened from merely 'sacramentar-
ians' (a heresy of which Cromwell was attainted): a proviso added by the
Lords on 9 July tacked on a carefully specified set of eight radical beliefs,
all of which characterized supposed Anabaptists. That suggests smear
tactics aimed at increasing the noise-levels about heresy around the fallen
minister.[89] Yet, as in 1536, Henry drew back from a degree of frightful-
ness: the Earl of Essex would die by simple beheading, which might
indicate that the King was once more beginning to think of him as a peer
of the realm, rather than as Thomas Cromwell, shearman. That was the
mercy which emerged from Cromwell's pleading postscript.

He was brought from his cell to the scaffold on Tower Hill. Beside him
in death was Walter Lord Hungerford. This relatively minor nobleman's
fate was connected to Cromwell's because he undertook administrative
tasks for the Lord Privy Seal in his West Country homeland, and because
he provided discredit by association. His arrest seems to have arisen out
of traditionalist remarks about the King by his chaplain, but investigation triggered a wave of lurid accusations against Hungerford himself
which at the very least showed what a dysfunctional life he led, not for
the first time in the Hungerford family: a spectrum of wife-beating, incest
and buggery, sickening if even half true. It was the last charge that
ensured Hungerford's execution, under a statute Cromwell himself had
steered through Parliament in earlier years. All this distracted usefully
from the initial charges against Hungerford's chaplain, which suggests
that the wretched peer may actually have been arrested in the course of
the Lord Privy Seal's normal round of scenting out conservative religious
dissidence. Hungerford did not die gracefully or with tranquillity: 'at the
hour of his death [he] seemed unquiet, as many judged him rather in a
frenzy than otherwise,' one chronicler observed.[90]

By contrast, Cromwell was the model of control. His duty, customary
for prominent condemned people, was to make an appropriate speech
expressing repentance and saying something about the offence for which
he was dying.[91] Unless one had nothing to lose, the limits on what could
be said were considerable. Cromwell was conscious of performing a last
service for his much loved son and grandchildren, to distance them from
his own attainder and give the King reason to look well on them in the
future. So he chose his words carefully, though actually giving no ground
to his enemies. Yes, he had lived a sinner – but have not we all under
Christian teaching? – 'and it is not unknown to many of you that I have
been a great traveller in this world, and being but of a base degree, was

called to high estate, and sithence the time I came thereunto, I have offended my prince.' All statements of fact.

Given the heresy charges against him, the most important task was to protect his family by being precise in refuting the charge. 'And now I pray you that be here, to bear me record, I die in the Catholic faith, not doubting in any article of my faith, no, nor doubting in any sacrament of the Church.' He repeated that he died in the Catholic faith of the holy Church. The Tower official Anthony Anthony's slight expansion of the chronicler Edward Hall's version of his speech made him say ambiguously, 'I intend this day to die God's servant,' and recorded a remark more precise than Hall: 'I believe in the laws ordained by the Catholic Church.' Yet no one was to say what he actually believed by all that, or indeed how many sacraments of the Church he was affirming; any mainstream Protestant could make exactly the same affirmations. The overriding concern was to distance himself very precisely from the Anabaptism with which his foes wished to associate him. Of course he prayed for the King and his son Prince Edward, 'that godly imp', and ended with a substantial prayer committing his soul to God.

Anthony Anthony said that Cromwell pointedly finished on a prayer 'for the King's noble Council; and put off his gown, and the hangman asked forgiveness'. Another version adds a very personal touch directed to Sir Thomas Wyatt, a protégé who may have owed him his life back in 1536: Wyatt was admirably prepared literally to stand by his patron and friend at this last moment. Allowing this courtier and ambassador to be there beside the scaffold may be another sign that the King was treating the death less gracelessly than he had done in early June. 'He turned him about, and said "Farewell Wyatt", and "Gentle Wyatt, pray for me".'[92] It was in that respect a suitably stylish end. According to Hall, the executioner needed forgiveness indeed, for he did an unskilful job. The occasionally reliable anonymous Spanish chronicler disagreed in his own eye-witness account, and said the head was off in a stroke.[93] Either way, even botched beheadings are soon over.

23

Futures

His body did not have far to travel: buried in the Tower's chapel of St Peter-in-Chains (ad Vincula). Thanks to his busyness for the King in dissolving religious houses, the doors of Austin Friars church beside his great house were locked, its many monuments gathering dust. There were no friars to give him a kindly grave amid the bones of City merchants and pious gentlefolk, unlike so many earlier traitors. He lay near Anne Boleyn, the woman whose cause had brought him so high, and whose destruction he had choreographed.

His own death did not end the killing. Two days later a notorious event embodied the King's idiosyncratic notion of the 'middle way'. Six priests were executed: three evangelicals for heresy, and three papalist Catholics for treason. They suffered the respective customary punishments: in the former case burning, in the latter hanging, drawing and quartering. Robert Barnes, Thomas Garrett and William Jerome were clearly identified with Cromwell, and their clashes with Gardiner had sparked the six months of violent political turmoil. Barnes, who unlike Cromwell had no family to worry about, gave the sermon of his life, vigorously affirming a clear Lutheran faith to ward off charges of radicalism with which his trio were being smeared. In a rhetorical masterstroke, he capped the assertion of his theological respectability by a plea for marriage to 'be had in more reverence than it is; and that men, for every light cause invented, cast not off their wives'.

That was deliciously *ad hominem*, as was Barnes's plea that the monastery lands be put to good use. John Foxe recorded a surprising amount of not unsympathetic audience participation in Barnes's performance. His burning remained a subject of contest between Catholics and Protestants for years, and added lustre to a reputation as a scholarly champion of Reformation which long resonated across Europe, even across the division between Lutheran and Reformed Protestants.[1] Barnes's death nevertheless signalled a significant change in direction for English

Protestantism. He had known Martin Luther more intimately than any other Englishman, and represented Luther's theology more completely than any other English theologian. His death removed a powerful English advocate for the Wittenberg version of the European Reformation, against other Reformations to the south, to which Thomas Cromwell had covertly reached out: Zürich and Geneva. It was the beginning of what has been called 'the strange death of Lutheran England'.[2]

Still the slaughter continued, as Ambassador Marillac noted. On 4 August came ten more executions for treason, one of which was a bastard son of Sir Nicholas Carew, another a Carthusian, and a former monk of Westminster seems to have been among their fellows: a sprinkling of names suggesting traditionalist victims, left over from previous political mayhem, rather than any relentless pursuit of Cromwell's supporters.[3] True, the destroyers of Cromwell now felt free to make prosecutions under the Act of Six Articles. In the diocese of London, Bishop Bonner and a traditionalist Lord Mayor elected in 1539 against the City's normal reformist preferences instituted extensive action even before Cromwell's death. In September, ex-Prior Robert Ferrar had to take evasive action in the diocese of York against charges of heresy levelled by a newly emancipated Archbishop Lee.[4] Yet the striking feature about the London persecution is how swiftly it was curtailed – the day after Barnes and his fellows had died, and by the King's command. In the political rather than religious sphere, not a single prominent evangelical politician lost his place at Court.[5] After a vicious pamphlet war in bad verse about Cromwell's religion broke out between Cromwell's former pamphleteer William Grey and Thomas Smith, a minor gentleman in Court service, the Privy Council intervened to shut them both up.[6]

This must reflect a conscious royal decision not to allow the conservative counter-coup to become more than a surgical excision of the Lord Privy Seal. The Privy Council was left balanced between evangelicals and traditionalists; a fortnight after his execution, on 10 August 1540, its proceedings were bureaucratized as they never had been under Cromwell himself, by instituting a minute-book of proceedings with its own clerk. That would give the King a chance to scrutinize their proceedings, if he ever felt they were trying to act beyond his control.[7] Rumours that Cuthbert Tunstall would succeed Cromwell as Vice-Gerent in Spirituals proved untrue. No one individual apart from the monarch ever again held the fate of the Church of England in his hands, for no one else ever enjoyed this innovation in English office-holding. Its archive disappeared from sight, remnants resurfacing only in the twentieth century.[8] The Vice-Gerency was a Tudor Revolution in Government that never happened.

By contrast to Cromwell's own fate, during his last lonely weeks in his cell in the Tower, favour for his friends went on trickling placidly through royal bureaucracy. One as close to him as his nephew Richard was granted a licence to alienate (sell or convey) a Huntingdonshire manor on 23 June, and Richard had a further licence on 28 June, although on this latter occasion he took the sensible precaution of being named Sir Richard Williams, rather than Sir Richard Cromwell alias Williams, as he had been only five days before. The 28th of June was, after all, the day before his uncle's attainder passed all its stages in Parliament.[9]

It was not simply that Norfolk and Gardiner failed to secure a witch-hunt against Cromwellians: Cromwell's friends and allies moved forward into new positions as crucial as the two vacant lieutenancies in Ireland and Calais. That was settled within a fortnight of Cromwell's arrest, when Sir Anthony St Leger was given the funds to take him to Dublin as Lord Deputy, an appointment first canvassed in 1538 (to Lord Leonard Grey's fury); Henry Fitzalan Lord Maltravers set off with appropriate finance for Calais.[10] St Leger was simultaneously made Keeper of Leeds Castle, no doubt easing the fears of Gregory Cromwell and his wife about their immediate future. A month later Sir Ralph Sadler was granted the Clerkship of the Hanaper, one of Cromwell's first formal offices back in 1532, and which he had been clutching jealously ever since.[11] Naturally, courtiers once friends but prominent in the betrayal were also involved in this redistribution, the chiefest beneficiary being the Earl of Southampton, who succeeded as Lord Privy Seal. It would be easy to justify the grant of Austin Friars in July to Thomas Wriothesley; he knew the house very well.

Yet those perquisites of the coup run alongside some rather unlikely pieces of continuity: the King reappointed Cromwell's leading domestic administrators to their previous jobs. His late controller John Ryther was to be Keeper of Austin Friars and, jointly with his late Steward Henry Polstead, Ryther had oversight of all the attainted Earl's lands. We know from the minute-books of the Privy Council that one responsibility for Ryther and Polstead was to look after the fallen minister's archive at Austin Friars while it was further sifted for useful material.[12] This is strikingly like a grant nine years before, giving oversight of Cardinal Wolsey's late lands to the person who knew them best, Thomas Cromwell. Other smooth promotions that same August were of Henry Polstead's brother Thomas as King's Attorney of the Court of Wards, and Cromwell's patronage secretary Anthony Bellasis, stepping over the ashes of Thomas Garrett to become Rector of the plum Worcestershire living of Hartlebury.[13]

This delicate tidying of debris from the Earl of Essex's fall was an indication that the evangelical revolution had some sort of future, as long as it avoided showing too much open regret for the late minister. In a significant negotiation of the new situation, a further edition of his beloved Great Bible appeared soon after his destruction – with one noticeable alteration. The monumental title-page, as we have seen, originally displayed two cartouches of the arms of Cranmer and Cromwell, identifying their figures distributing Bibles to the kingdom. Now, anticipating modern airbrushing of photos, Cromwell's arms were simply removed from their cartouche, leaving a blank oval amid the busyness of the design. It was so obvious as to be almost a statement. A further eloquent evangelical adjustment of it can be found in a spectacular Bible designed specifically for the royal library. In 1541 the evangelical printer Anthony Marler secured a publishing coup in persuading King Henry to reissue Cromwell's order for a Bible in every church, with a very effective additional refinement that parishes would be fined forty shillings for not buying one. To many observers, this was the moment when the order really became effective after half a decade of nationwide procrastinating.[14]

Such a success deserved a thank-you present for the King, and in a spectacular and intricate job of printing Marler printed off a special presentation copy of his Bible: three volumes on vellum, no less. He realized that his artist's embellishment of the pictorial title-page needed some tactful manipulation. Not only did he replace both heraldic cartouches with some innocuous foliage, but he altered the very recognizable clean-shaven figure of Thomas Cromwell receiving the Bible from the King to someone else entirely, sporting a beard. Tatiana String suggests that it may be the bearded John Lord Russell, who from late 1542 held the office of Lord Privy Seal once enjoyed by Thomas Cromwell. In fact, amid the swings of policy that characterized the last years of Henry's reign, Marler gained no further advantage from the King, but it was a spirited try.[15]

Once Cranmer, the Church and Parliament had so speedily delivered the King his marriage annulment, and after Queen Anne had made her happy co-operation clear, Henry's venom began to evaporate, as he turned from enjoying his latest wedding on 28 July to reports of his late minister's dignified last performance that day. Behind all the attainder's bluster about treason and heresy, it was the Cleves marriage that had brought Cromwell down. Appropriately enough, during August 1540, the splendid furniture of his house at Austin Friars was raked through to set up the Lady Anne in comfort in her new country house (Bletchingley, Surrey, available thanks to the recent execution of Sir Nicholas Carew).[16]

One is tempted to date Henry's regrets slightly earlier, to a letter from

Comparison with the title-page of the 1541 edition of the Great Bible, where the removal of Cromwell's arms has left an embarrassing oval blank cartouche in the design, shows how the title-page of Anthony Marler's presentation copy for Henry VIII has not only filled the blank with foliage but replaced Cromwell with a bearded figure.

a man who on other occasions profoundly irritated him, Sir John Gostwick. Gostwick had enjoyed friendly relations with Cromwell since Wolsey days, but he was a religious conservative who began harassing evangelicals as early as 1536 and thereafter among those steadily more alienated from the Vice-Gerent's forward religious policy. On 9 July 1540 Gostwick wrote to the King in his capacity as Treasurer of First Fruits and Tenths, letting him know with smug venom that he had been concealing some funds from these taxes 'which, if I had declared unto him [Cromwell], he would have caused me to disburse by commandment without warrant, as heretofore I have done'. That would certainly be consistent with Cromwell's easy-going attitude to authorization in government, but Gostwick no doubt calculated on it reinforcing current accusations in the attainder Act about the fallen minister's arrogation of royal authority.[17]

Now this money needed disbursing, and over four pages Gostwick

· ANNO · ETATIS ·   · SVÆ · XLIX ·

35. This version of Holbein's numerous intimidating images of Henry VIII, now in Rome and the most sumptuous example surviving, is dated by Henry's age to 1540. It depicts him in the clothes he wore at his wedding to Anne of Cleves, an embarrassment that may account for its early departure from England.

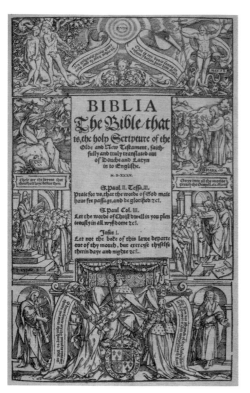

36. Holbein's title-page for Coverdale's Bible (1535) features Henry VIII as Supreme Head of the Church, offering the Bible to his bishops; in the dominant position is God, significantly presented not as an image but as his Hebrew name (the Tetragrammaton).

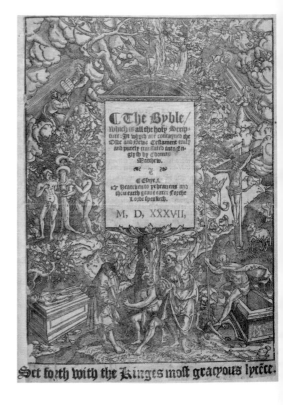

37. The title-page of the 'Matthew' Bible (1537), by an artist now unknown, concentrates on the theological theme of the Fall of Adam and Eve, in apposition with the Crucifixion and Resurrection.

38. The hand-coloured title-page to the Apocrypha in Cromwell's de-luxe parchment copy of the Great Bible, probably the presentation copy for him from Miles Coverdale and Richard Grafton. Now in the Old Library at St John's College, Cambridge, it may have descended to the donor Bishop John Williams from Cromwell's Welsh relatives. At the foot of the title-page, loyal crowds shout in Latin in response to preachers and JPs 'VIVAT REX'; children at the pulpit and under instruction from their parents do their best with 'GOD SAVE THE KYNGE/KINGE'. No sound comes from the prison on the right.

39. Catholic martyrdom: the executions in the Tower of London of John Fisher and Thomas More in 1535 and of Margaret Pole Countess of Salisbury in 1541 are here conflated in Richard Verstegan's Catholic polemic *Theatrum crudelitatum haereticorum* (1587).

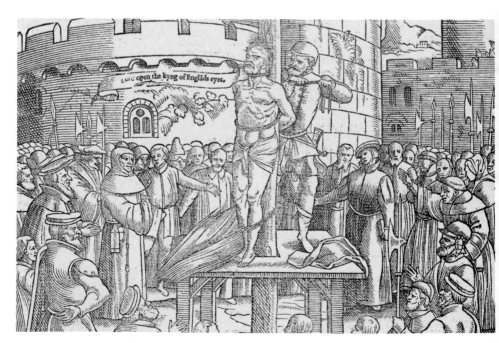

40. Protestant martyrdom: the execution of William Tyndale in 1536 in Brussels is here also imaginatively portrayed in the 1563 edition of John Foxe's 'Book of Martyrs' (*Acts and Monuments*).

11. Carthusians throughout Europe have not forgotten their brethren's sufferings in England in the 1530s. In 1617 the Charterhouse in Granada commissioned the talented painter turned Carthusian Juan Sánchez Cotán to reimagine the executions of May 1535 (along with Richard Reynolds of Syon), in rather Spanish terms. The spectators lounging in an upper balcony no doubt include Cromwell.

42. This now rather shapeless beastie seems to be the wooden base-block for the statue of Dderfel Gardarn, astonishingly still surviving in the porch of Llandderfel parish church (Gwynedd), even though Cromwell had the image which stood on it carted off to London in 1538.

43. In this early nineteenth-century image of the martyrdom of John Forest from an angry Catholic polemic against Foxe's *Book of Martyrs*, the recumbent image of Dderfel Gardarn in the flames looks as human as the friar above.

4. The superb ceiling of the chapel of St James's Palace is a little-known relic of Henry VIII's
opes for his Cleves marriage: installed around the beginning of 1540, it is scattered with the
oyal couple's monogram HA and the names of the Duke of Cleves's territories.

¶ The husbandman.

¶ Doctor Martin Luther.

¶ The Pope.

¶ The Cardinall

45. Magdalene College, Cambridge, possesses an apparently unique copy of a broadside printed in late 1539 by Cromwell's client John Mayler, first issued possibly in Basel in 1521; the portrait of Martin Luther is one of the earliest known, while Miles Coverdale may have provided the translation of the original German verses below. There is irony in this evangelical depiction of Luther as a friar in 1539, since by then all English friaries had been closed.

laid out a frighteningly wide spectrum of payments already made and costs to be met, from naval defences to the royal tomb to repairing fences in Kent. Throughout resounded the deferential but relentless 'Item, to know your Majesty's pleasure ... whereof I must humbly require your Majesty's warrant ...'. The King's fury at Cromwell's procedural high-handedness may have been somewhat mitigated by the depressing realization that his minister was no longer around to make decisions like that. The next few years proved full of administrative drift in the regime. That reflected a general incoherence of political and religious decision-making in Henry's government as it lurched between factional conflicts in Privy Council and Privy Chamber.

As late as May 1546, the King noticed a lamentable laxity in stock-taking of his possessions since Cromwell's days. Among preparations for other comprehensive measures of inventorying, Master of the Jewels Sir John Williams found himself facing a high-powered commission of Privy Councillors headed by Lord St John, whose warrant coldly noted that no proper survey had been made since the time of the previous holder of Williams's office: 'Sir Thomas Lord Cromwell, attainted'.[18] More seriously, the 1540s saw a new revenue-raising measure that Cromwell had always kept at bay, with the exception of one desperate expedient in the Lordship of Ireland: a debasement of England's silver coinage. This accelerated in King Henry's last years, and continued into the next three reigns, disastrously disrupting the economy. Debasement was a cynical confidence trick against the monarchy's subjects whenever money returned to the mint for recoinage, and was ultimately deeply damaging to government itself. Although Northumberland's regime tried to grapple with the problem under King Edward VI, it took some determined work on Queen Elizabeth's part to make an end of it – one of the achievements of which she was most proud.[19]

In the months after Cromwell's execution, the King's change of attitude to the treacherous and heretical 'shearman' became palpable. It was revealed in November 1540 when he picked Sir Richard Cromwell to be Sheriff of Cambridgeshire and Huntingdonshire for a second time.[20] Henry's continuing dissatisfaction with the ministers now haplessly coping with his histrionics reached the ears of Marillac, ever alert for English political comedy. He reported in winter 1541 that the King had reproached his Council for Cromwell's death, 'saying that, upon the pretexts of trivial faults that he had committed, they had laid several false accusations on him, by which he been made to put to death the most faithful servant he ever had'.[21] Self-pity has a talent for rewriting events. Such a mood, acutely observed for the appropriate opportunity, was a perfect matrix into which Lady Ughtred could insert a plea for royal favour for her husband and family, left stranded by the Lord Privy Seal's fall.

Elizabeth Seymour always inspires admiration; in 1537 she had likewise shown herself past mistress of timing in her overtures to Cromwell. Her letter in autumn 1540 was carefully judged, tailored in its brevity to Henry's notoriously short attention-span, as well as handsomely penned by her secretary above her own confident signature.[22] After deploring Thomas Cromwell's 'heinous trespasses and most grievous offences', she warmly thanked her royal brother-in-law for extending 'your benign pity towards my poor husband and me, as the extreme indigence and poverty wherewith my said father-in-law's most detestable offences hath oppressed us, is thereby right much holpen and relieved'. Once the King was less burdened by his 'most high and weighty affairs', she hoped for his 'accustomed pity and gracious goodness towards my said poor husband and me, who never hath nor (God willing) never shall offend your Majesty'. And Lady Ughtred took the plunge into signing herself 'Elizabeth Cromwell'.

It worked. On 5 December the King (during a brief Surrey holiday with his young bride) put his signature to the grant of a new peerage. Gregory Cromwell, not even knighted at the time, was to become Baron Cromwell. Henry was also generous this month to Sir Ralph Sadler and Stephen Vaughan. A fortnight after Gregory's grant, the Privy Council gathered at Whitehall (instructed that month to do so whenever 'they had advertisement of the same from his Highness') to witness its finalization. The meeting was not recorded in their new minute-book, but would have afforded immense entertainment to the shade of the late Lord Privy Seal. Present as signatories were not merely such old friends as Cranmer, Audley, Suffolk and Sir John Gage, but a number of deserters such as Southampton and St John – and, most deliciously of all, the Duke of Norfolk.[23]

Unlike his father's barony in 1536, Gregory's peerage was not given a location, which probably reflects ongoing discussions about which fragment of his father's huge accumulation of lands he should have. He already possessed two or three estates in joint tenure with his father. One was the Welsh lordship of Rhymney, the first significant property Thomas had obtained, back in 1532: it took some time to regain a firm hold on Rhymney, but by 1544 it was assured to Gregory at least for life.[24] More significant, though perhaps of less sentimental value, were the Norfolk lordship of North Elmham and Rutland lands at Oakham. The Crown also held back from challenging title there, and a couple of months later Baron Cromwell was also granted his father's recently acquired property of Launde Priory in Leicestershire. This was a monastery that Thomas

The end of Elizabeth Seymour's letter of autumn 1540, successfully pleading for Henry VIII's 'accustomed petie and gracious goodnes towardes my saide pore husbonde and me, who never hath nor Godde willynge never shall offende your Maiestie'. She signs herself 'Your most bonde woman Elysabeth Cromwell'.

had known well since at least Wolsey days; its aged Prior had only surrendered after around forty years in post during the final scramble of dissolutions in December 1539. Just before that, Cromwell made a special note among a set of beneficiaries of suppressions, 'myself for Launde'.[25]

Launde was a sensible choice, a fresh start in a new shire. To move to the former episcopal mansion at North Elmham would have unnecessarily annoyed the Duke of Norfolk, so Gregory and Elizabeth made their home in Leicestershire. Gregory died there in 1551, in the same summer epidemic of sweating sickness which tragically carried off the two Brandon boys of the ducal Suffolk line; he was little more than thirty years old. His grieving widow commissioned a monument in the private chapel they had created from the choir of Launde Priory church, and there it still stands. One of the finest products of England's Protestant Renaissance, devoid of popish imagery, it centres on a sumptuous display of Gregory's heraldry. Elizabeth, who herself survived a bout of the illness, placed her initials ES in central position on the tomb, which is probably an eloquent comment on the realities of this eventful marriage. The epitaph could not be simpler, simply reciting Gregory's name, titles and date of death; strikingly it does not record the name of his father.[26] (See Plate 28.)

After all that had happened, Gregory cannot be regarded as a fool for keeping a reasonably low profile in mid-Tudor politics, but he had not been invisible. He took an appropriate part in county government; his uneventful rural life can be glimpsed in surviving letters of his tenants in one Northamptonshire manor. They were the Johnson family, who like himself were more exotic than they seemed: sprung from Dutch roots, with a background in Calais and London commerce, and closely linked to such old Cromwell associates as the Cave family and Sir John Gage.[27] Gregory conscientiously attended Parliamentary sessions between 1542 and 1547, though he gave a proxy to his brother-in-law the Earl of Hertford in 1544, when he may have been in poor health – that same year he also asked for an exemption from serving in the King's French war.[28] The fact that Gregory sat for a charmingly informal miniature portrait from Hans Holbein the Younger in 1543 suggests that he was then also no stranger at Court (see Plate 26). It was the high noon of King Henry's sixth and last attempt at matrimony, with the eirenic if evangelically inclined Katherine Parr. The Parr family had long enjoyed excellent relations with Gregory's father, while Queen Katherine's connection to Lord Thomas Seymour is the stuff of romantic fiction.

Suddenly, at Henry VIII's death, Gregory was especially visible. As the King's coffin solemnly processed from its lying-in-state at Westminster on 14 February 1547, six noblemen bore the staves of the canopy above it; one was Lord Cromwell. The ceremonies at both the funeral and young King Edward's coronation were deliberately traditional, to emphasize the unity of the realm in a moment of transition; placing this young peer at the centre was therefore a notable intrusion of a past memory unwelcome to many peers both temporal and spiritual. At his nephew's coronation a week later, Gregory was one of the leading men of the realm dubbed a knight of the Bath.[29] Later, in May 1548, he and his wife were granted a fine new estate in Rutland, much expanding their Midland holdings; nor was this a regrant of any of his father's confiscated lands – rather it was a former possession of the Bishop of Lincoln.[30] True, Gregory was the new King's uncle and brother-in-law to the new Lord Protector, Edward Seymour, but here is a wider symbolism. Baron Cromwell was unlikely by temperament or inclination to be a high flyer in the Edwardian regime, unlike his exact contemporary Henry Grey Marquess of Dorset and Duke of Suffolk, but he was still a Cromwell.

What happened in the opening weeks of 1547 was a coup of Cromwellians against Thomas Cromwell's enemies: a brisk reversal of the debacle of summer 1540. Just as then, they built on the pre-existing whims of Henry VIII, but to opposite effect. Old King Henry retained his wits almost to the last, but terrible health and constant pain in his last months of life magnified the habitually errratic quality of his decision-making and the arbitrary violence of those decisions. Through 1546 they swayed from his final bout of burning evangelicals for sacramentarian heresy, with the possibility that even Queen Katherine might be brought down, to the Earl of Surrey's sudden arrest in December. Surrey had with increasing recklessness staked his claim to royal blood, and by implication a claim to be Lord Protector for the prospective young King Edward VI. When he was arrested, so was his father the Duke of Norfolk, utterly bewildered by this turn of events. Meanwhile, Bishop Gardiner, with hopeless timing once more refusing a royal demand to exchange some of his episcopal estates, brought his own disgrace; he was removed from the list of councillors to govern the realm in the event of a royal minority.[31] Surrey was executed just before the old King's death; the government then spared Norfolk and Gardiner, though they both spent the whole of Edward's reign in the Tower.

When Henry died in January 1547, the eclipse of the Howards and Gardiner should still have left a Council carefully balanced according to the King's wishes, but that did not happen. Already in December the imperial ambassador could see that the coming regime was going to be dominated by Edward Seymour and John Dudley. As the King lay dying, careful adjustments were made to his will, signed with the dry-stamp version of his signature, much used when he was disinclined to sign or incapable of doing so. A new clause allowed one councillor to act alone, so long as he gained permission from the majority of his colleagues. With events having swept aside Gardiner, new recruits to the Council made that possible: Sir William Herbert, Sir Anthony Denny and the Kentish brothers Nicholas and Edward Wotton. Denny was a veteran evangelical in the Privy Chamber; the name of Wotton will by now be familiar from Cromwell days.[32] Soon Edward Seymour was recognized as Lord Protector, with a new title: Duke of Somerset. Little more than a fortnight after King Edward's coronation, the arch-betrayer of 1540, Thomas Wriothesley, lost his current position as Lord Chancellor, on trumped-up charges of misusing his office. He had clearly gained a taste for betrayal, because just a few months before he had been behind Surrey's arrest too; much good had it done him.[33]

The realm was in the hands of evangelicals, who with careful pacing over the six years of Edward VI's reign laid down a religious 'Revolution in Government' of unmistakably Reformed Protestant character.[34] The young King vigorously backed their aims, with increasing personal intervention. Their chief partner overseas was not now any Lutheran polity: the Schmalkaldic League had in any case been consigned to history by its defeat at the hands of Charles V in 1547. Instead, England looked to that city of Zürich which had first made an unexpected connection to the faraway island thanks to Cranmer and Cromwell. Now the Grey family enthusiastically sustained those old personal links with Heinrich Bullinger and the Reformed Church in the city. Only Edward's death and the ineptitude of John Dudley and Henry Grey in establishing the royal succession brought this revolution juddering to a halt, with the unexpected success of the Lady Mary in seizing the throne from Queen Jane Grey.

Mary's death in 1558 brought to the throne the last of Henry's children, Princess Elizabeth, to re-establish a carefully static version of her half-brother's dynamic Protestant revolution; in the words of her favourite royal minister Sir Christopher Hatton to a not over-sympathetic House of Commons, the Queen 'placed her Reformation as upon a square stone, to remain constant'.[35] Elizabeth had good reason to detest the nexus of politicians with Cromwell at their centre who had first destroyed her mother and then tried to divert the succession from herself and her half-sister; yet she was irreversibly tied to them in her role as Europe's leading Protestant monarch; and, like Cromwell, she was a Nicodemite who had kept quiet about her Protestantism in her sister's return to Roman Catholicism. At least some of the old resentments fell away when she was drawn into an intimate and indeed passionate relationship with John Dudley's son Robert, but quite apart from his place as favourite and leading Councillor, much else bound her to the Protestant elite of her father's Court.

Cromwell's evangelical religion had included a strange sort of Nicodemism, which ran alongside and contributed to the Reformation that he promoted openly and aggressively in the name of Henry VIII during the

1530s: it was hidden in plain sight. Its permanent results became apparent only after his death, in the Reformations under Edward VI and Elizabeth.[36] These later developments of the English Reformations fulfilled many venerable Lollard hopes, including the destruction of sacred imagery and the promotion of a Reformed sacramental theology which the old King had murderously loathed. Because of this posthumous result, Cromwell's religious programme must count as the most successful Nicodemite enterprise of the whole Reformation. While the Italian Reform of the Spirituali and their Nicodemite fellow-travellers was in the 1540s and 1550s exposed, crushed and scattered abroad by the Counter-Reformation, to diffuse into central European Reformed Protestantism and into varied Unitarianisms in eastern Europe, Thomas Cromwell's Nicodemite version of Reformed Protestantism endured. Under the tutelage of his most accomplished imitator, Queen Elizabeth I, it became the Church of England.[37]

Elizabeth was herself the product par excellence of King Henry's break with Rome, which break she repeated on her accession, though she and her advisers shrank from the title of 'Supreme Head' that Henry and Cromwell had created for the monarch and opted merely for 'Supreme Governor' of the Church of England. Many of her leading politicians, particularly the brothers-in-law Sir William Cecil and Sir Nicholas Bacon, saw their careers in government administration begin in the evangelical circles around Cromwell: Nicodemites all. In her first two decades she was also served by that erstwhile friend of Cromwell's, William Paulet, now formidably old as Marquess of Winchester, but also formidably in charge of her treasure. If the Queen met the wife of Paulet's son John, then she was face to face with Elizabeth Seymour, who embarked on a third marriage after Gregory Cromwell's death, and finally lies in the Paulet family vault at Basing in Hampshire. On her coffin, Elizabeth's Cromwell baronial title trumps both her third marriage and her old customary address as Lady Ughtred.[38]*

What else endured into Elizabeth's reign and beyond? By now the reader will have seen Geoffrey Elton's particular vision of a bureaucratic 'Tudor Revolution in Government' dispersed, for all the fruitful consequences of that thesis in historical argument over the last half-century.[39] There was revolution enough, in Cromwell's steady, careful plans to make all the Tudor realms work in the same way, on the model of England, which was a polity with a unique degree of centralization in Europe

---

* In the vault, she is 'Domina Cromwell, quondam coniux Johannis, Marchionis Winton.'; she died before her third husband succeeded to the title.

and, by the standards of the time, exceptionally well run even before Cromwell took over its supervision. Symbolic of his work was the first reliable service of relays of horses for royal messengers 'riding post' on certain vital routes, for example to Berwick or Dover from London, inaugurated in 1533.[40] The drawing together of the realm was easiest for the little enclave of Calais, and it was hardly Cromwell's fault if later government incompetence left Queen Elizabeth permanently resentful at her sister's loss of this last English continental possession. Wales was a larger-scale task, but with due caution its shiring, with local sessions of JPs on something like the English model, was successfully rolled out in the 1540s after the principal author's death. That system endured into the twentieth century.

There were plenty of incentives for Welsh gentry and higher clergy to feel enthusiastic about the proposed changes. They reinforced existing paths of Welshmen to social advancement, particularly in the Church and the law, affording plenty of access for the talented to the English universities – especially Oxford, where certain colleges had long been hospitable to the Welsh, and one founded in Elizabeth's reign, Jesus College, became peculiarly their own. We have seen numerous connections between Cromwell's administrative team and the Welsh: not merely the ambiguous asset to Wales of *y Doctor Coch*, Ellis ap Rhys, but also his southern namesake John ap Rhys. Sir John went on from the Vice-Gerent's service to become not only Secretary to the Council in the Marches, but an enthusiastic historian and evangelical author of the first printed book in Welsh, which vigorously defended worship in the Welsh language.[41] In an overwhelmingly traditionalist society apparently remote from the sources of early Reformation fervour, there were already enough influential and motivated evangelicals to mould the future of Welsh religious identity into Protestant and not Catholic forms. Cromwell played his part in that.

Ireland was a totally different story. The degree of separation was much greater than between Wales and England: because of the far greater distance not merely between Westminster and Dublin (to say nothing of the distance between Westminster and Galway) but between the two cultures within the island. One was a decayed version of high medieval England; the other was a Gaelic society of much greater antiquity. Their relationship to the English Crown was radically different, both in formal terms and in practice. Cromwell, like his old master Wolsey, chose to see this situation as a problem to be solved: his answer, partly forced on him by events, was an effort to restore old Anglo-Irish institutions to force much more direct English intervention, reviving the Dublin Parliament as instrument for royal policy and imposing an outsider to represent royal power. This policy failed, only partly thanks to the inadequacies of Lord Leonard Grey. By then, Ireland was costing the King a minimum average of around 4,000 pounds a year, when before the interventions of the 1530s it had cost nothing. Now a long-standing stability based on all sorts of informal understandings and local realities had been sacrificed by confrontation with various Irish magnates, principally the Fitzgeralds. There was a fatal conjunction at work, because Cromwell's intervention-ist policy also revealed sources of Irish revenue which were incentives to further intervention, only exacerbating the instability.[42]

Cromwell was not a fool in Ireland any more than elsewhere. He began exploring alternative ways forward by sending the commission of 1537, and its most talented member, his client Sir Anthony St Leger, then pioneered a promising strategy. St Leger came to agreements with three Gaelic lords whose lands bordered territories of the Lordship; they offered to submit wholly to the sovereignty of the Tudor Crown in return for titles of nobility in the English manner, with royal letters patent to estab-lish their hereditary possession of their lands. Alongside that was another constructive suggestion from Bishop Staples of Meath in the course of the commission's work; Staples was a consistent rival to Archbishop Browne, but, as a Wolsey appointee to the Irish episcopate, someone with his own commitment to change in the island. Staples pointed out that within the Gaelic lordships the Pope was historically considered the ultimate sover-eign in the island, with the English Crown deriving its power from papal grant in feudal fashion. Why not simply replace the feudal overtones of the Lordship of Ireland and erect Ireland into a sovereign kingdom whose monarch was Henry VIII? The idea had all the logic (and lack of authen-tic historical justification) of the English Act in Restraint of Appeals.[43]

Military crisis in Ireland and growing political crisis in England meant that Cromwell had too much else on his mind to carry this out, but on St Leger's return as Lord Deputy in 1540 the proposal's time had come. The kingdom of Ireland was erected, and a policy of 'surrender and regrant' rolled out across the Gaelic lordships. During St Leger's long years as Deputy, this remained the foundation of policy: a characteristic example of a Cromwellian flexibility in policy to meet a particular situation.* In 1542 the Irish Parliament transformed the medieval shire of Meath, for a century and more a mere geographical expression, into two new

---

* It is baffling that Brendan Bradshaw throughout his *Irish Constitutional Revolution* chose to see St Leger's policies as a rejection of Cromwellian policy, and anachronistically labelled them 'liberal'. He did not sufficiently appreciate St Leger's lifelong close ties to Cromwell.

shires with as close an approximation to the English model as local conditions allowed; this was parallel to what Cromwell had done in Wales
from 1536, implemented with a similar caution and attention to local
realities.[44] St Leger was as averse to conflict as Grey his predecessor
had gleefully embraced it: that shaped the religious policies for a new
dispensation.

Archbishop Browne, mightily relieved at Grey's disappearance, was
happy to survive in post as a much less confrontational agent of religious
change, pushing forward the royal supremacy in what was now the Kingdom of Ireland. This did involve him in one huge personal concession; he
did not simply send his wife away, as did Archbishop Cranmer in 1539,
but divorced her, with suitable arrangements to support her and his
children (among other details, she remarried one of his own servants). St
Leger carefully held off the King's attempts to criminalize clerical marriage in Ireland until this was satisfactorily sorted. Thereafter a version
of Cromwellian reformation in Ireland proceeded at a far more conservative pace agreed between St Leger and Browne, consonant with what
royal government was allowing in England. It also reflected the way that
English government learned lessons from the Pilgrimage of Grace, con-
ciliating those in northern England whose goodwill made government in
the region easier.[45] St Leger's time as Lord Deputy right up to 1556 represents the most hopeful period in the steadily more dismal story of relations
between Tudor government and Ireland, and it should be seen as a working out of the late Lord Privy Seal's principles of government. Subsequent
failures right up to the present day are no more Cromwell's fault than was
the loss of Calais.

If Cromwell lurked behind St Leger, how much greater a shadow over
Cromwell was cast by his old master Cardinal Wolsey, whose heraldry he
bore. There is much in his career in government which continued Wolsey's legacy project, even though completion of the Cardinal's tomb and
chantry colleges was no longer possible or perhaps desirable. In the
government of England, template for the changes in all the territories we
have surveyed, Wolsey set a pace which Cromwell then continued. Wolsey increased the number of JPs in every county; as Lord Chancellor, he
turned meetings of the royal Council sitting in Star Chamber at Westminster into a tribunal to control misbehaviour among the justices, and
ordered as many as possible to appear annually to renew their oath of
loyalty to the Crown. Cromwell kept all this up, and also improved on it
in his far greater programme of change. He sent out constant circular
letters to the provinces. In an adroit piece of psychology, they bypassed

his interest in the printing press and were handwritten to suggest personal attention from the King – both flattering and intimidating.

Notably for a supposed agent of bureaucratic revolution, Cromwell did not foster a great network of royal officials, like the 40,000 or 50,000 who came to run the kingdom of France by the early seventeenth century. English government was largely provided for free by local volunteers, which made for a fruitful and complex relationship between provincial and central governors. It was hardly surprising that local magistrates in the 1530s, conscious that Wolsey's keen gaze was still falling on them in intensified form, hastened to make sure that they knew their duty. A standard guide to the office first published in 1506, the *Boke of Justices of the Peas*, went through six editions in a decade, and in 1538 came a brand-new competitor in the market, imaginatively entitled the *Newe Boke of Justices of the Peas*, from the leading lawyer Sir Anthony Fitzherbert.[46]

Because of Cromwell's sensitivity to the grand bargain in Tudor government between monarch and magistrate, he elaborated on Wolsey's agenda by hugely developing Parliament's role in both England and Ireland, confirming it as the instrument of government when elsewhere its role was dwindling; woe betide any later English monarch who tried to dispense with it. In fact he extended Parliamentary participation to the vast majority of the Tudors' possessions, in the course of building a Church independent of Rome and creating new institutions in the realm. The process was never complete, for outlying islands are still excluded. It took till 1673 to bring the episcopal palatinate of County Durham into the House of Commons, but Cromwellian momentum rolled on after his death to bring in the lesser palatinate of Cheshire in 1543 alongside Wales, and the Channel Islands scored a near-miss at the same time.[47] It was a back-handed compliment to the dramatic and effective way that Cromwell had enlisted Parliament in the King's extraordinary (indeed outrageous) enterprises in the early 1530s that among the demands of the Pilgrimage of Grace was the insistence that Parliament be called to the North, with increased representation for the region.

As Geoffrey Elton observed, Parliament was chief among the King's 'points of contact' with his subjects. The frequent awkwardness and lack of co-operation in Parliamentary proceedings produced ultimate if grudging and ungracious consent. The relative stability of Tudor England was the product of 'moderate contentment'. The King's leading men were far more frequently Parliament men from the 1530s – more precisely, they became Commons men, if a peerage did not bar them and provide a seat in the other place. That produced a very different dynamic in the royal Council in the 1530s from the time of Henry VII or indeed the earlier years of Henry VIII, and matters did not change thereafter. From Thomas Cromwell's time onwards, royal advisers mostly knew what it was to sit through the squabbles, the excitement and the tedium of a Tudor Parliamentary session. Other European rulers would have done well to foster such a political culture.[48]

The corollary of this was that not all planned government policy had an easy ride. One of the most fiercely debated aspects of Cromwell's policy occurred in the 1539 Parliament. After both Houses had accepted the Six Articles, a bill trying to define punishments for the defiance of royal proclamations ran into considerable trouble. The problem was to know how proclamations' status in law related to Parliamentary enactments: that was one of Cromwell's first preoccupations when he became a councillor in 1531. What did he intend by introducing this measure? Was it an attempt to introduce Tudor despotism by the back door? If so, the modifications to the eventual statute made by Parliament stymied that possibility. It is far more likely that this was another example of Cromwell's tidy-mindedness, kicked around in Parliament by critical legal minds including Elizabeth's future Lord Keeper of the Great Seal Nicholas Bacon, then a young evangelical and in other respects a beneficiary of Cromwell's interest. Anything stronger would be inconsistent with Cromwell's awareness that Tudor government was a process of negotiation with an alarmingly large number of interested parties.[49]

Some readers may consider that this book underplays the theme of rapacity in Cromwell's public career, which did witness the single greatest land transfers in this country's history since the Norman Conquest. I have tried to show that while there was selfish greed enough among the King and his leading councillors, eagerly imitated by the wider group of his subjects who had funds to invest in suddenly available church lands, there was a degree of idealism and reforming enthusiasm in Cromwell's vision of what it all meant. The balance between idealism and rapacity was easily tipped. Fifteen-forty-eight saw outbursts of popular rage against the governing classes which fully erupted nationwide a year later. They were sparked by the greed of two former servants of Thomas Cromwell, and yet the risings also appealed to the idealism embodied in his own reforms.

The stirs of 1549 displayed two contrasting rhetorics: traditionalist in the West Country and the Midlands, evangelical in eastern and southern England. Yet both were directed against acquisitive gentry, and had been anticipated the previous year by attacks on two distinctly unlikeable individuals. In the West it was William Body, a former financial official of Cromwell who, despite being a layman, in 1537 acquired the office of Archdeacon of Cornwall from the egregious son of Cardinal Wolsey, Thomas Winter, against strong opposition from the diocesan authorities. In 1548 a mob at Helston lynched Body while he was visiting parish churches to carry out Edwardian government orders on destroying 'superstitious' images. Trouble simmered through the next year and, when Devon folk rose in fury against the new English Prayer Book at Whitsun 1549, Cornishmen were ready to join them.[50]

Anti-enclosure riots in Hertfordshire in 1548 targeted the lord of the manor of Northaw, Sir William Cavendish, current Auditor of the Court of Augmentations, and incidentally ancestor of the present Duke of Devonshire.[51] Cavendish was like Body an old servant of Cromwell's, and has the distinction of writing one of the most nauseatingly sycophantic among hundreds of sycophantic letters Cromwell received in his public career – 'patron of my poor living, and the rather because all that I have or intend to have, report, doth and always shall sound that it cometh of you' – this was in fact written at Northaw.[52] Cavendish made himself unpopular in the area; in 1548 he obtained a royal commission to enclose very extensive common land there. Large crowds protested against his scheme and devastated his rabbit warrens, allegedly killing nearly 2,000 rabbits and even blowing up the burrows with gunpowder. The protesters claimed that such a far-reaching commission as Cavendish's had no validity while King Edward was still a minor (the Helston mob's spokesman said exactly the same about Body's authority for iconoclasm). According to one prosecution witness, they also anticipated events a year later in setting up a camp on the disputed commons; such actions bequeathed the traumatic events in summer 1549 the name of 'the camping time'.

Tudor politicians and administrators certainly remembered Northaw. In 1579 another enclosure riot broke out there, attracting extraordinary worry from the Privy Council and local JPs; two participants were hanged, which had not happened in 1548. Fifteen-forty-eight indeed saw remarkably little retribution, reflecting the uncomfortable fact that both Wolsey and Cromwell had regarded enclosures as all too prone to abuse. Another former protégé of Cromwell's, an idealistic evangelical government official called John Hales (who held Cromwell's old office of Clerk of the Hanaper), enlisted Protector Somerset's enthusiasm in a fresh official campaign to curb the evil, which was an encouragement to ordinary folk to pull down enclosures themselves. This was part of the complex mix of events in 1548–9: a reminiscence of the man who enthusiastically backed King Henry in his hatred of weirs, and who was remembered by many for his goodness to the poor.

No one will expect a simple legacy from a politician whose brief years of power extended in so many directions and whose energy transformed so much. His own family is complex enough. His grandson Henry Lord Cromwell married Mary Paulet, stepdaughter to Thomas's daughter-in-law. Henry left little impression on Elizabethan politics apart from sponsoring a government-backed scheme to improve coastal defences in Norfolk; it was in principle sensible, but he turned it into a project to improve his own shaky finances, thereby infuriating some of the most conscientious county governors in a notoriously contentious shire.[53] Henry's son Edward was one of the rakish young noblemen who drifted into the orbit of Robert Devereux Earl of Essex and shared in Essex's self-inflicted catastrophe of rebellion against Queen Elizabeth in 1601. In disgrace, with the Launde and Rutland estates gone, Edward relocated to Ireland, following the example of his uncle Henry Ughtred, another disappointment to their complicated family; maybe, if Thomas Cromwell's father indeed came from Ireland, this was actually a return of the native. The line of the Barons Cromwell lasted a couple of generations, with an extra couple of Irish peerage titles to its credit, but became extinct on the death of Vere Essex Cromwell, Lord Cromwell, fourth Earl of Ardglass, in 1687.[54]

Looming inevitably over that unsatisfactory if surprisingly prolonged tale is the name of another Cromwell, who until the last few years was the one whose name most people would first remember: Richard Cromwell alias Williams's descendant Oliver, Lord Protector of England. It is one of the accidental ironies of history that Richard's great-grandson removed the head of Lady Margaret Douglas's great-grandson, whose collateral ancestor performed a similar service for Richard's uncle. The execution of Charles I in 1649 was as great a national trauma as England's break with Rome in 1533, though in the end it may have had the unintended effect of curbing this country's enthusiasm for destroying monarchy. More than a century after Richard Cromwell alias Williams/Williams alias Cromwell made his will as a knight of the realm in 1544, one of his descendants reversed their ambiguity of surname once more.

Henry Cromwell of Ramsey in Huntingdonshire was Oliver Cromwell's cousin, and at the Restoration of Charles II he found the name deeply embarrassing, particularly as he continued to sit as knight of the shire for his native county, Oliver's county, in a dozen years of the Cavalier Parliament. He became Henry Williams. Whatever the sincerity of Henry's conversion to staunch royalism, that of his poetically inclined wife Mrs Anna Williams can hardly be doubted, for she painstakingly

copied prayers for the royal family and verse extolling Thomas Cranmer's Book of Common Prayer into her devotional commonplace book.
For this couple, it was a relief to become once more Williams, without
qualification: posterity for Morgan Williams the Welsh gentleman so
long before.[55] The rest of the nation did not find it so easy to slough off
the memory of two Cromwells: one who came to the executioner's block
at the order of a king of England; the other who repaid the compliment.

Thomas Cromwell did so much in a decade. He served his king with
careful attention to what Henry wanted, and an even more careful attention to insinuating his own plans and hopes into the King's proceedings.
Partly he wanted to forward a religious revolution; partly his aim was
more predictably to forward his own family's dignity in the realm, and
his success in that respect was astonishing: the grandson of a Putney
brewer married the sister-in-law of a king. It was hardly surprising that
some believed him capable of planning a marriage to the King's daughter
Mary; what an alteration that would have made to history! The actual
alteration was profound enough: not just the break with Rome which had
sprung from King Henry's ego, but a committed Protestantism for
Edwardian and then Elizabethan England – steered by men who had
benefited from his patronage and guidance, from noblemen like John
Dudley, Edward Seymour and Henry Grey, to civil servants and lawyers
as diligent and talented as himself, Elizabeth's trusted servants Nicholas
Bacon and William Cecil. Still part of that political elite until his death
full of years and honour in 1587 was Sir Ralph Sadler, now far from boyhood service to a rising London man of affairs, reputedly dying England's
richest commoner, having lately acted as gaoler to a Catholic queen,
Mary Queen of Scots.

Protestant England endured, gradually outstripping the great powers
which in the Tudor age had made it seem marginal in Europe. It took a
new and steadily more dominant place on the world stage. Even in Anna
Williams's time in the 1650s, it was beginning to assume that role, as
Thomas Cromwell's namesake Oliver won victories in ocean-wide warfare against the popish power of Spain. Lord Protector Oliver had at his
disposal the national navy once the pride of old King Henry; Henry had
spent so much of his wealth on it, mostly gained lately at the expense of
the Church. The kingdom of England restored in 1660 built on Oliver
Cromwell's achievements, in partnership with a now Protestant Scotland. The new alliance, naming itself Great Britain in 1707, implausibly
for a small archipelago created a seaborne world empire that rose and fell
from the seventeenth century to the twentieth. That imperial story lies
behind the formation of another world power whose time may similarly

pass, the United States of America. This, and much more, for better or worse, remains the legacy of Thomas Cromwell.

> *All transitory things shall fail at the last, and the worker thereof*
> *shall go withal. Every chosen work shall be justified, and he that*
> *meddleth withal, shall have honour therein.*
>
> Ecclesiasticus 14.19, in the
translation of Miles Coverdale, 1535

Abbreviations and Conventions Used in Bibliography and Notes

In citations of State Papers in the National Archives, I have adopted the numbering stamped in print on the manuscripts by archivists at the old Public Record Office, as opposed to various other systems in pencil or ink which their successors added in attempts to do better. I am aware of the deficiencies of these printed numbers, which do not always cover all the pages in volumes (particularly in the Lisle Letters, TNA, SP 3), but they have been adopted by *State Papers Online* as the means of citation, and that is how most scholars worldwide will now locate them. I apologize to my colleagues who have used the other notations on the manuscripts, as I have myself in the past. In papers in the British Library, I have adopted the most recent sequence of numbering out of what is sometimes a range of possibilities, as that is generally how *SPO* cites the documents.

In the Notes, all citations are to page numbers, unless foliation (f.), signature (sig.) or membrane (m.) numbers are specified. Foliation is normally customary though not universal in manuscripts and is noted below, but otherwise pagination should be assumed. To lessen the confusion and ire of others amid all this complication, I have provided the entry numbers in *Letters and Papers* (also employed by *SPO*) as a reference guide to material from the State Papers and other primary sources calendared in *LP*. Where *State Papers Online* has nodded in its great enterprise, and keyed in the wrong folio reference or omitted it, I have supplied it; where *SPO* has not provided images, I have cited where possible an edition of the text in print, particularly that prodigious pre-Victorian work of scholarship, *State Papers published under the Authority of His Majesty's Commission*. Where applicable, I have generally substituted the reference number of manuscript material edited in the *Lisle Letters* in place of a *Letters and Papers* reference, since Miss St Clare Byrne's editorial comment to that collection is so valuable, as well as richly enjoyable, and her transcriptions almost always accurate.

Baker	J. H. Baker, *The Men of Court 1440 to 1550: a prosopography of the Inns of Court and Chancery and the courts of law* (2 vols., Selden Society supplementary series 18, 2012). Where information on lawyers is given without further citation in endnotes, it has been taken from Baker
BL	Manuscripts in the British Library

Bodl.	Oxford, Bodleian Library (some material MS, some printed)
Bradford (ed.), *Correspondence of Charles V*	W. Bradford (ed.), *Correspondence of the emperor Charles V and his ambassadors at the courts of England and France . . .* (London, 1850)
Burke, *General Armory*	B. Burke, *The General Armory of England, Scotland, Ireland and Wales . . .* (London, 1884)
Chambers (ed.), *Faculty Office Registers*	D. S. Chambers (ed.), *Faculty Office Registers 1534–1549* (Oxford, 1966)
Complete Peerage	G. E. C[okayne], rev. V. Gibbs *et al.* (eds.), *The Complete Peerage of England, Scotland, Ireland . . . Extant, Extinct, or Dormant* (13 vols., London, 1910–59)
Cross, Loades and Scarisbrick (eds.), *Law and Government under the Tudors*	C. Cross, D. Loades and J. J. Scarisbrick (eds.), *Law and Government under the Tudors* (Cambridge, 1988)
CS	Camden Society publications
EETS	Early English Text Society
EHR	*English Historical Review*
Elton, *Studies*	G. R. Elton, *Studies in Tudor and Stuart Politics and Government* (4 vols., Cambridge, 1974–92)
Emden, *Oxford 1501 to 1540*	A. B. Emden, *A Biographical Register of the University of Oxford A.D. 1501 to 1540* (Oxford, 1974)
ERP	A. M. Querini (ed.), *Epistolarum Reginaldi Poli . . . Collectio* (5 vols., Brescia, 1744–57)
Foxe	Foxe, *Acts and Monuments*, various editions, specified by date of publication; see also Primary Sources in Print below, and easily available via *The Acts and Monuments Online*: http://www.johnfoxe.org
Hall	E. Hall, *The Triumphant Reigne of Kyng Henry the VIII*, ed. C. Whibley (2 vols., London, 1904)
HC 1509–1558	S. T. Bindoff (ed.), *The History of Parliament: the House of Commons 1509–1558* (3 vols., London, 1982)
HC 1558–1603	P. W. Hasler (ed.), *The History of Parliament: the House of Commons 1558–1603* (3 vols., London, 1981)
HJ	*Historical Journal*
JEH	*Journal of Ecclesiastical History*
Kaulek (ed.), *Correspondance*	J. Kaulek (ed.), *Correspondance Politique de Mm. de Castillon et de Marillac . . .* (Paris, 1885)
Lambeth	London, Lambeth Palace Library MS collections
Le Neve, *Fasti*	J. Le Neve, *Fasti Ecclesiae Anglicanae*, revised by various editors (London, 1962–, in progress). Two sequences, arranged by diocese or group of dioceses: *1300–1541* and *1541–1857*

Lisle Letters	M. St C. Byrne (ed.), *The Lisle Letters* (6 vols., London and Chicago, 1981)
Lords Journals	*Journals of the House of Lords*, 1509 *et seq.* (10 vols., London, s.a.)
LP	J. S. Brewer *et al.* (eds.), *Letters and Papers, Foreign and Domestic, of the reign of Henry VIII, 1509–47* (21 vols. and 2 appendix vols., London, 1862–1932)
MacCulloch (ed.), *Reign of Henry VIII*	D. MacCulloch (ed.), *The Reign of Henry VIII: politics, policy and piety* (Houndmills and London, 1995)
Merriman	R. B. Merriman, *Life and Letters of Thomas Cromwell* (2 vols., 1902, repr. Oxford, 2006)
Muller (ed.), *Letters of Gardiner*	J. A. Muller (ed.), *The Letters of Stephen Gardiner* (Cambridge, 1933)
ODNB	*Oxford Dictionary of National Biography* (60 vols., Oxford, 2004) [updated online resource, subscription only]
Pocock	N. Pocock (ed.), *Records of the Reformation: the Divorce, 1527–33* (2 vols., Oxford, 1870)
PP	*Past & Present*
RSTC	A. W. Pollard and G. R. Redgrave, rev. W. A. Jackson and F. S. Ferguson and completed by K. F. Pantzer, *A Short-Title Catalogue of Books Printed in England, Scotland, and Ireland and of English Books Printed Abroad, 1475–1640* (revised edn, 3 vols., London, 1976–91)
Rymer (ed.), *Foedera*	T. Rymer (ed.), *Foedera, conventiones, literae, et cujus-cunque generis acta publica* ... (20 vols., London, 1704–35)
SCJ	*Sixteenth Century Journal*
Smith	D. M. Smith (ed.), *The Heads of Religious Houses: England and Wales III: 1377–1540* (Cambridge, 2008). Where information on monastic heads is given without further citation in endnotes, it has been taken from Smith
SP 1	TNA, SP 1 plus volume and folio number: State Papers Domestic, Henry VIII
SP 3	TNA, SP 3 plus volume and folio number: Lisle correspondence
SP 60	TNA, SP 60 plus volume and folio number: State Papers, Ireland
Spanish Calendar	P. de Gayangos, G. Mattingly, M. A. S. Hume and R. Tyler (eds.), *Calendar of State Papers, Spanish* (15 vols. in 20, London, 1862–1954). I have made my own adaptation of the translations offered where appropriate

SPO | *State Papers Online, 1509–1714*: https://www.gale.com/uk/primary-sources/state-papers-online15091714.aspx [subscription only]

State Papers | *State Papers published under the Authority of His Majesty's Commission, King Henry VIII* (11 vols., London, 1830–52)

Statutes of the Realm | *The Statutes of the Realm printed by Command of his Majesty King George the Third* . . . (11 vols., London, 1810–28)

Survey of London | *Survey of London*, individual volumes by area; a variety of editors

TNA | The National Archives, Public Record Office, Kew, with call number

TRHS | *Transactions of the Royal Historical Society*

TRP | P. L. Hughes and J. F. Larkin (eds.), *Tudor Royal Proclamations* (3 vols., New Haven and London, 1964, 1969)

VCH | *Victoria County Histories*, individual volumes by county; a variety of editors

VE | J. Caley and J. Hunter (eds.), *Valor ecclesiasticus temp. Henrici VIII: Auctoritate regia institutus* (6 vols., London, 1810–33)

Venetian Calendar | R. Brown, G. Cavendish Bentinck, H. F. Brown and A. B. Hinds (eds.), *Calendar of State Papers, Venetian* (38 vols. in 40, London, 1864–1947)

Wilkins (ed.), *Concilia* | D. Wilkins (ed.), *Concilia Magnae Britanniae et Hiberniae* (4 vols., London, 1737)

Wing | D. G. Wing, *Short-Title Catalogue of Books Printed in England, Scotland, Ireland, Wales, and British America and of English Books Printed in Other Countries, 1641–1700*, 2nd edn, rev. and ed. J. J. Morrison and C. W. Nelson with M. Seccombe (4 vols, New York, 1972, 1982, 1988, 1998)

Wriothesley's Chronicle | W. D. Hamilton (ed.), *A Chronicle of England . . . by Charles Wriothesley, Windsor Herald* (2 vols, CS 2nd series 11, 20, 1875, 1877)

Bibliography

PRIMARY SOURCES UNPUBLISHED

Cambridge, Corpus Christi College, Parker Library

Parker MSS: collections of Archbishop Matthew Parker and contemporaries

Cambridge, Queens' College

Magnum Journale: College accounts

Cambridge University Archives

Register of Wills 1

Hatfield House, Hertfordshire

Cecil Papers

London: British Library

Additional MSS, Charters and Rolls
Arundel MSS
Cotton MSS
Harley MSS and Charters
Lansdowne MSS and Rolls
Royal MSS
Stowe MSS

London: College of Arms

MS 2 G.4: Grants of arms by Thomas Benolt, Clarenceux King of Arms
MS M 7: Armorial, Knights
MS Num Sch 6/40: 'Parliamentary Roll', 1539/40

London: Lambeth Palace

Cranmer's Register (no classification)
MSS 616–17: Carew Manuscripts
MS 751: Eighteenth-century transcript of the records of the Convocation of Canterbury

London: Metropolitan Archives

MS CLC/270/MS01231; formerly Guildhall Library, MS 1231: MS collections relating to Henry VIII

London: The National Archives, Kew

C 1: Early Proceedings in Chancery
C 244: Returned commissions in Chancery
CP 40: Proceedings in the Court of Common Pleas
C 54: Close Rolls
C 82: Warrants for the Great Seal, Henry VII to Anne
E 30: Exchequer: Treasury of Receipt, diplomatic documents
E 36: Exchequer: Treasury of Receipt, miscellaneous documents
E 101: Exchequer: King's Remembrancer, various accounts
E 135: Exchequer: miscellaneous ecclesiastical documents
E 315: Augmentations: miscellaneous books
E 321: Exchequer: legal proceedings in the Court of Augmentations
E 322: Exchequer: deeds of monastic surrenders
PROB 11: Prerogative Court of Canterbury wills
REQ 2: Proceedings in the Court of Requests
SC 6: Ministers' and Receivers' accounts
SP 1; SP 2; SP 6; SP 10; SP 11; SP 12; SP 15; SP 46: State Papers, Domestic, Henry VIII–Elizabeth I
SP 3: Lisle correspondence
SP 5: Exchequer: King's Remembrancer papers
SP 7: Wriothesley correspondence
SP 60: State Papers, Ireland
SP 70: State Papers, Foreign, Elizabeth I, 1559–77
STAC 1–4: Star Chamber Proceedings, Henry VII–Philip and Mary

Oxford: Bodleian Library

MS Ashmole 861: Elias Ashmole's transcripts from the (mainly lost) Chronicle of Anthony Anthony

MS Jesus College 74: collections by Thomas Master for Lord Herbert's *Life of Henry VIII* [q.v.], arranged by topic. Contains extracts from much material of State Paper character otherwise unknown, probably from that part of the Cottonian collection totally destroyed in the Ashburnham House fire of 1731, an exceptional catastrophe for manuscripts: that part of the collection on the shelves with the classifications 'Otho' and 'Vitellius' seems to have been particularly badly hit, and the likelihood is that the unknown material is from there

Folio Δ 624: Edward Lord Herbert of Chirbury, *The Life and Raigne of King Henry the Eighth* (London, 1649, Wing H1504: see also Secondary Sources: Books and Articles below), interleaved with extracts from the Chronicle of Anthony Anthony

Oxford: Christ Church

MS D&C vi.c.2: Wolsey's statutes for Cardinal College Ipswich

Suffolk Record Office, Ipswich

Archdeaconry of Ipswich Wills, IC/AA2

Washington, DC: Folger Shakespeare Library

Items of Cromwell's correspondence

West Sussex Record Office, Chichester

Lavington MS/646: deed relating to Hardham Priory

Woking: Surrey History Centre

Loseley MSS, LM 59/150: inventory of Cromwell's armoury

York Minster

Borthwick Institute, York: Abp. Reg. 28 [Register of Archbishop Edward Lee], ff. 141Av–150r: notarial transcript of proceedings in annulment of Anne of Cleves marriage. Freely available via https://archbishopsregisters.york.ac.uk

PRIMARY SOURCES IN PRINT

All items printed before 1640 are given their RSTC number, and those from 1641 to 1700 their Wing number.

A. Alane [Alesius], *Of the auctorite of the word of God agaynst the bisshop of London* . . . (?Leipzig, ?1538, *RSTC* 292)

?A. Alesius, *A treatise concernynge Generall Councilles, the Byshoppes of Rome and the Clergy* . . . (London, 1538, *RSTC* 24237)

A. Alesius, *De Authoritate Verbi Dei* . . . *contra Episcopum Lundensem* (Strassburg, 1542)

P. S. Allen, H. M. Allen and H. W. Garrod (eds.), *Opus Epistolarum Des. Erasmi Roterodami* . . . (12 vols., Oxford, 1906–58)

[Anon.], *The maner of the tryumphe at Caleys [and] Bulleyn* (London, 1532, *RSTC* 4350, 4351)

[Anon.], *The noble tryumphaunt coronacyon of quene Anne, wyfe vnto the moost noble kynge Henry the .viij* (London, 1533, *RSTC* 656)

[Anon.], *Articles deuisid by the holle consent of the kynges moste honourable counsayle, his gracis licence opteined therto, not only to exhorte, but also to enfourme his louynge subiectis of the trouthe* (London, 1533, 1534, *RSTC* 9177, 9178)

[Anon.], *A treuue nyeuu tydynges of the wo[n]derfull worckes of the rebaptisers of M[u]nster in Westuaell* (Antwerp, 1535, *RSTC* 564)

[Anon.], *Jack vp Lande compyled by the famous Geoffrey Chaucer* (Southwark, ?1538, *RSTC* 5098)

J. Anstis (ed.), *The register of the most noble Order of the Garter* . . . *usually called the Black Book* . . . (2 vols., London, 1724)

I. W. Archer, S. Adams, G. W. Bernard, M. Greengrass, P. E. J. Hammer and F. Kisby (eds.), *Religion, Politics, and Society in Sixteenth-Century England* (Camden 5th series 22, 2003)

J. Ayre (ed.), *Prayers and other pieces of Thomas Becon* (Parker Society, 1844)

J. Bale, *The Epistle Exhortatorye of an Englyshe Christyane* . . . (Antwerp, ?1544, *RSTC* 1291a)

J. Bale, *A comedy concernynge thre lawes, of Nature[,] Moses, & Christ, corrupted by the sodomytes. Pharysees and Papystes* (Wesel, ?1547, *RSTC* 1287)

M. Bandello, *Novelle*, ed. G. Mazzuchelli (9 vols., Milan, 1813–14)

M. Bandello, *The novels of Matteo Bandello Bishop of Agen now first done into English prose and verse*, ed. and trans. J. Payne (6 vols., London, 1890)

W. Barlow, *A dyaloge describing the originall ground of these Lutheran faccyons* . . . (London, 1531, *RSTC* 1461)

Marquess of Bath, *Report on the Manuscripts of the Most Honourable the Marquess of Bath preserved at Longleat IV: Seymour Papers 1532–1686* (Historical Manuscripts Commission, 1968)

P. Boesch (ed.), 'Rudolph Gwalthers Reise nach England im Jahr 1537', *Zwingliana* 8/8 (1947), 433–71

A. Borde, *The fyrst boke of the introduction of knowledge* . . . (London, 1555, *RSTC* 3383)

W. Bradford (ed.), *Correspondence of the emperor Charles V and his ambassadors at the courts of England and France* . . . (London, 1850)

J. S. Brewer *et al.* (eds.), *Letters and Papers, Foreign and Domestic, of the reign of Henry VIII, 1509–47* (21 vols. and 2 appendix vols., London, 1862–1932)

S. Brigden (ed.), 'The Letters of Richard Scudamore to Sir Philip Hoby, September 1549–March 1555', *Camden Miscellany* 30 (Camden 4th series 39, 1990), 67–148

R. Brown, G. Cavendish Bentinck, H. F. Brown and A. B. Hinds (eds.), *Calendar of State Papers, Venetian* (38 vols. in 40, London, 1864–1947)

J. Bruce and T. T. Perowne (eds.), *Correspondence of Matthew Parker, D.D . . .* (PS, 1853)

W. Bulleine, *A dialogue both pleasant and piety-full, against the fever pestilence* (London, 1564, *RSTC* 4036)

M. W. and A. H. Bullen (eds.), *A Dialogue Against the Feuer Pestilence, by William Bullein, from the Edition of 1578, Collated with the Earlier Editions of 1564 and 1573* (EETS extra series 52, 1888)

H. Bullinger, *Heinrich Bullinger: Briefwechseledition*, various editors (Zürich, 1973–, in progress)

M. St. C. Byrne (ed.), *The Lisle Letters* (6 vols., London and Chicago, 1981)

Calendar of Patent Rolls . . . Edward VI . . . (6 vols., London, 1924–9)

Calendar of State Papers Foreign . . . Elizabeth [I] . . . (23 vols., London, 1863–1950)

J. Caley and J. Hunter (eds.), *Valor ecclesiasticus temp. Henrici VIII: Auctoritate regia institutus* (6 vols., London, 1810–34)

G. Cavendish, *The Life of Cardinal Wolsey*, ed. S. W. Singer (2nd edn, London, 1827)

D. S. Chambers (ed.), *Faculty Office Registers 1534–1549* (Oxford, 1966)

M. Chauncy, *Historia aliquot martyrum Anglorum maxime octodecim Cartusianorum: sub Rege Henrico Octavo ob fidei confessionem et summi pontificis jura vindicanda interemptorum* (London, 1888)

J. Clark (ed.), *The Various Versions of the Historia aliquot martyrum anglorum maxime octodecim Cartusianorum . . .* (Analecta Carthusiana 86, 3 vols., Salzburg, 2006)

P. D. Clarke in Clarke and M. Questier (eds.), *Camden Miscellany XXXVI: papal authority and the limits of the law in Tudor England* (Camden 5th series 48, 2015), 1–100

H. Cole (ed.), *King Henry the Eighth's scheme of bishopricks: with illustrations of his assumption of church property, its amount and appropriation, and some notices of the state of popular education at the period of the Reformation; now first published from the originals in the Augmentation Office, Treasury of the Exchequer, British Museum, etc.* (London, 1838) [main contents, 1–74, are *LP* 14 ii no. 429]

Corpus Reformatorum, ed. C. G. Bretschneider *et al.* (101 vols. to date, 1834–)

G. E. Corrie (ed.), *Sermons by Hugh Latimer . . .* (Parker Society, 1844)

G. E. Corrie (ed.), *Sermons and Remains of Hugh Latimer . . .* (Parker Society, 1845)

M. Dowling (ed.), 'William Latymer's Chronickille of Anne Bulleyne', *Camden Miscellany* 30 (Camden 4th series 39, 1990), 23–65

D. Dymond (ed.), *The Register of Thetford Priory II: 1518–1540* (Norfolk Record Society, 60, 1996)

Early English Books Online http://eebo.chadwyck.com/home [subscription only]

H. Ellis (ed.), *Original Letters illustrative of English History . . . from autographs in the British Museum and . . . other collections* (11 vols. in 3 series: London, 1824, 1827, 1846)

G. R. Elton, 'Two unpublished letters of Thomas Cromwell', *Bulletin of the Institute of Historical Research* 22 (1949), 35–8

G. R. Elton (ed.), *The Tudor Constitution: documents and commentary* (2nd edn, Cambridge, 1982)

Epistolae Tigurinae de rebus potissimum ad ecclesiae Anglicanae Reformationem pertinentibus . . . (Parker Society, 1848)

D. Erasmus, *Liber . . . de praeparatione ad mortem . . . accedunt aliquot epistolae seriis de rebus, in quibus item nihil est non novum ac recens* (Basel, 1534)

J. Foxe, *Rerum in ecclesia gestarum . . . commentarii* (Basel, 1559)

J. Foxe, *Actes and Monuments of these latter and perillous dayes* . . . (London, 1563, *RSTC* 11222)

J. Foxe, *The first volume of the ecclesiasticall history contaynyng the actes and monumentes of thynges passed in euery kynges tyme in this realme . . . The second volume of the ecclesiastical history, conteynyng the actes and monumentes of martyrs* (London, 1570, *RSTC* 11223)

J. Foxe, *Actes and monuments of matters most speciall and memorable, happenyng in the Church* (London, 1583, *RSTC* 11225)

[J. Foxe], *The Unabridged Acts and Monuments Online* or *TAMO* (HRI Online Publications, Sheffield, 2011). Available from: http//www.johnfoxe.org

W. H. Frere with W. M. Kennedy (eds.), *Visitation Articles and Injunctions of the Period of the Reformation II: 1536–1558* (Alcuin Club 15, 1910)

J. Gairdner (ed.), ' "The Spousells" of the Princess Mary . . .', *Camden Miscellany* 9 (CS new series 53, 1895), 1–38

G. Gardiner, *A letter of a yonge gentylman named mayster Germen Gardynare, wryten to a frend of his, wherin men may se the demeanour [and] heresy of Ioh[a]n Fryth late burned, [and] also the dyspycyo[n]s [and] reasonynge vpon the same, had betwene the same mayster Germen and hym* (London, 1534, *RSTC* 11594)

S. Gardiner, *Obedience in Church and State: three political tracts by Stephen Gardiner*, ed. P. Janelle (Cambridge, 1930)

P. de Gayangos, G. Mattingly, M. A. S. Hume and R. Tyler (eds.), *Calendar of State Papers, Spanish* (15 vols. in 20, London, 1862–1954)

R. Glover, *The visitation of Cheshire in the year 1580* . . ., ed. J. P. Rylands (Harleian Society 18, 1882)

E. Hall, *The Triumphant Reigne of Kyng Henry the VIII*, ed. C. Whibley (2 vols., London, 1904)

W. D. Hamilton (ed.), *A Chronicle of England . . . by Charles Wriothesley, Windsor Herald* (2 vols., CS 2nd series 11, 20, 1875, 1877)

[Hatfield House], *Calendar of the manuscripts . . . preserved at Hatfield House, Hertfordshire* (24 vols., Historical Manuscripts Commission, series 9, 1883–1976)

A. Heal, 'A great country house in 1623', *Burlington Magazine* 82 (1943), 108–16

T. Hearne (ed.), *Titi Livii Foro-Juliensis, Vita Henrici Quinti, Regis Angliae: accedit, Sylloge Epistolarum, a variis Angliae Principibus scriptarum* (Oxford, 1716)

T. Hearne (ed.), *Benedictus, abbas Petroburgensis, De vita & gestis Henrici II. et Ricardi I. E Codice MS. In Bibliotheca Harleiana descripsit* . . . (2 vols., Oxford, 1735)

[Henry VIII], *Ansvvere made by the Kynges Hyghnes to the Petitions of the Rebelles in Yorkeshire* (London, 1536, RSTC 13077)

E. V. Hitchcock (ed.), *The Lyfe of Sir Thomas Moore, knighte, written by William Roper* . . . (Early English Text Society original series 197, 1935)

L. Howard (ed.), *A collection of letters, from the original manuscripts of many princes, great personages and statesmen* (London, 1753)

R. W. Hoyle, 'Thomas Master's narrative of the Pilgrimage of Grace', *Northern History* 21 (1985), 53–79 [material from Bodl. MS Jesus College 74 ff. 322r–327v]

R. W. Hoyle (ed.), 'Letters of the Cliffords, Lords Clifford and Earls of Cumberland, *c.* 1500–*c.* 1565', *Camden Miscellany* 31 (Camden 4th series 44, 1992), 1–189

P. L. Hughes and J. F. Larkin (eds.), *Tudor Royal Proclamations* (3 vols., New Haven and London, 1964, 1969)

M. A. Sharp Hume (trans. and ed.), *Chronicle of King Henry VIII. of England* . . . (London, 1889)

The Institution of a Christen man, conteynynge the Exposytion . . . *of the commune Crede, of the seuen Sacramentes, of the .x. Commandementes* . . . (London, 1537, RSTC 5164)

P. Janelle, 'An unpublished poem on Bishop Stephen Gardiner', *Bulletin of the Institute of Historical Research* 6 (1928–9), 12–25, 89–96, 167–74

Journals of the House of Lords, 1509 *et seq.* (10 vols., London, s.a.)

G. Joye, *The Refutation of the Byshop of Winchesters derke Declaratio[n] of his false Articles* . . . (London, 1546, RSTC 14828.5)

J. Kaulek (ed.), *Correspondance Politique de Mm. de Castillon et de Marillac* . . . (Paris, 1885)

C. L. Kingsford (ed.), 'Two London Chronicles from the collections of John Stow . . .', *Camden Miscellany* 12 (Camden 3rd series 18, 1910), iii–59

V. Klinkenborg and H. Cahoon (eds.), *British Literary Manuscripts, series I: From 800 to 1800* (New York [Pierpont Morgan Library], 1981)

P. H. Lawrence (ed.), *Extracts from the Court Rolls of the Manor of Wimbledon, extending from 1 Edward IV. to AD 1864* (London, 1866)

S. M. Leathes (ed.), *Grace Book A* (Cambridge Antiquarian Society, Luard Memorial Series 1, 1897)

J. Leland, *The itinerary of John Leland in or about the years 1535–1543*, ed. L. Toulmin Smith (5 vols., repr. London, 1964)

J. Leland, *De Uiris Illustribus: On Famous Men*, ed. J. P. Carley (Toronto, 2010)

D. M. Loades (ed.), *The Papers of George Wyatt Esquire* . . . (Camden 4th series 5, 1968)

T. Lott, 'Account of the Muster of the Citizens of London in the 31st Year of the Reign of Henry VIII', *Archaeologia* 32 (1847), 30–37

D. MacCulloch (ed.), 'The *Vita Mariae Angliae Reginae* of Robert Wingfield of Brantham', *Camden Miscellany* 28 (Camden 4th series 29, 1984), 181–300

F. Madden (ed.), *Privy purse expenses of the Princess Mary* . . . (London, 1831)

G. W. Marshall (ed.), *The Visitations of the County of Nottingham in the Years 1569 and 1614* . . . (Harleian Society 4, 1871)

T. F. Mayer (ed.), *The Correspondence of Reginald Pole: a calendar* (3 vols., Aldershot, 2000–2004)

R. B. Merriman, *Life and Letters of Thomas Cromwell* (2 vols., 1902, repr. Oxford, 2006)

G. C. Moore-Smith (ed.), *Gabriel Harvey's Marginalia* (Stratford-upon-Avon, 1913)

T. More, *The apologye of syr Thomas More knyght* (London, 1533, RSTC 18078)

T. More, *The vvorkes of Sir Thomas More Knyght, sometyme Lorde Chauncellour of England, wrytten by him in the Englysh tonge* (London, 1557, RSTC 18076)

J. A. Muller (ed.), *The Letters of Stephen Gardiner* (Cambridge, 1933)

A. R. Myers (ed.), *English Historical Documents 1327–1485* (London, 1996)

R. Newcourt, *Repertorium Ecclesiasticum Parochiale Londinense* ... (2 vols., London, 1708–10)

J. G. Nichols (ed.), *The Chronicle of Calais, in the reigns of Henry VII and Henry VIII, to the year 1540* (CS 1st series 35, 1846)

J. G. Nichols (ed.), *Narratives of the days of the Reformation* ... (CS 1st series 77, 1859)

H. Nicolas (ed.), *Proceedings and Ordinances of the Privy Council of England VII* (London, 1837)

C. B. Norcliffe (ed.), *The Visitation of Yorkshire in the years 1563 and 1564, made by William Flower* ... (Harleian Society 16, 1881)

R. Parsons, *A treatise of three conuersions of England from paganisme to Christian religion* (3 vols., Saint-Omer, 1603–4, RSTC 19416)

N. Pocock (ed.), *Records of the Reformation: the Divorce, 1527–33* (2 vols., Oxford, 1870)

N. Pocock (ed.), *A treatise on the pretended divorce between Henry VIII. and Catharine of Aragon, by Nicholas Harpsfield* ... (CS 2nd series 21, 1878)

G. Puttenham, *The Art of English Poesy*, ed. F. Whigham and W. A. Rebhorn (Ithaca, NY, 2007)

Messrs. Puttick and Simpson, *Catalogue of an extraordinary collection of autograph letters, of the highest interest, rarity, and importance, and in the finest condition, with portraits and other illustrations ... which will be sold by auction, by Messrs. Puttick and Simpson ... at their new and very spacious premises, No. 47, Leicester Square, on Monday, March 10th, 1862, & three following days* ... (London, 1862)

A. M. Querini (ed.), *Epistolarum Reginaldi Poli* ... *Collectio* (5 vols., Brescia, 1744–57)

J. Raine (ed.), *Wills and Inventories from the Registry of the Archdeaconry of Richmond* ... (Surtees Society 26, 1853)

R. Rex (ed.), *A Reformation Rhetoric: Thomas Swynnerton's The Tropes and Figures of Scripture* (Cambridge, 1999)

G. Ribier (ed.), *Lettres et mémoires d'estat ... sous les règnes de François premier, Henry II. et François II.* (2 vols., Paris, 1666)

H. Robinson (ed.), *Original Letters relative to the English Reformation* ... (2 vols., Parker Society, 1846–7)

E. F. Rogers (ed.), *St Thomas More: selected letters* (New Haven, 1961)

E. F. Rogers (ed.), *The Letters of Sir John Hackett 1526–1534* (Morgantown, VA, 1971)

F. X. Roth (ed.), *The English Austin Friars 1248–1538 2: The Sources* (*Augustiniana* supplement, 1961)

T. Rymer (ed.), *Foedera, conventiones, literae, et cujuscunque generis acta publica* . . . (20 vols., London, 1704–35)

G. W. Sanders (ed.), *Orders of the High Court of Chancery* . . . (2 vols., London, 1845)

W. G. Searle (ed.), *Grace Book Γ* (Cambridge University Press, 1908)

D. G. Selwyn, *The Library of Thomas Cranmer* (Oxford Bibliographical Society 3rd series 1, 1996)

T. Starkey, *Exhortation to the people, instructynge theym to vnitie and obedience* . . . (London, 1536, RSTC 23236)

State Papers published under the Authority of His Majesty's Commission, King Henry VIII (11 vols., London, 1830–52)

The Statutes of the Realm printed by Command of his Majesty King George the Third . . . (11 vols., London, 1810–28)

John Stow, *A Survey of London. Reprinted From the Text of 1603*, ed. C. L. Kingsford (2 vols., Oxford, 1908)

E. Surtz and V. Murphy (eds.), *The Divorce Tracts of Henry VIII* (Angers, 1988)

R. S. Sylvester (ed.), *The Life and Death of Cardinal Wolsey by George Cavendish* (Early English Text Society original series 243, 1959)

W. Tyndale, *A Treatyse of the Justificacyon by faith only, otherwise called the parable of the wyked mammon* (Southwark, 1536, RSTC 24455).

H. Walter (ed.), *Doctrinal Treatises and introductions to different portions of the Holy Scriptures. By William Tyndale* . . . (Parker Society, 1848)

H. Walter (ed.), *Expositions and Notes on sundry portions of the Holy Scriptures, together with The Practice of Prelates. By William Tyndale* . . . (Parker Society, 1849)

H. Walter (ed.), *An Answer to Sir Thomas More's Dialogue, The Supper of the Lord* . . . *and W[illia]m Tracy's Testament expounded. By William Tyndale* . . . (Parker Society, 1850)

S. J. Weinreich (ed. and trans.), *Pedro de Ribadeneyra's Ecclesiastical History of the Schism of the Kingdom of England* (Jesuit Studies 8, 2017)

D. Wilkins (ed.), *Concilia Magnae Britanniae et Hiberniae* (4 vols., London, 1737)

C. H. Williams (ed.), *English Historical Documents 1485–1558* (London, 1967)

[T. Wolsey], *Rudimenta grammatices et docendi methodus, non tam scholae Gypsuichianae per reuerendissimum D. Thoma[m] cardinale[m] Ebor. feliciter institutae q[uam] o[mn]ibus aliis totius Anglie scholis prescripta* (Southwark, 1529 etc.; RSTC 5542.3)

SECONDARY SOURCES: REFERENCE

J. H. Baker, *The Men of Court 1440 to 1550: a prosopography of the Inns of Court and Chancery and the courts of law* (2 vols., Selden Society supplementary series 18, 2012)

S. T. Bindoff (ed.), *The History of Parliament: the House of Commons 1509–1558* (3 vols., London, 1982)

W. M. Brady (ed.), *The episcopal succession in England, Scotland and Ireland, A.D. 1400 to 1875* (3 vols., Rome, 1876–7)

B. Burke, *The General Armory of England, Scotland, Ireland and Wales* ... (London, 1884)

J. P. Carley, *The Libraries of Henry VIII* (London, 2000)

J. P. Carley, 'The Libraries of King Henry VIII: an update of the Westminster inventory of 1542', *Library* 7th series 16 (2015), 282–303

Clergy of the Church of England Database: http://theclergydatabase.org.uk

G. E. C[okayne], rev. V. Gibbs *et al.* (eds.), *The Complete Peerage of England, Scotland, Ireland* ... *Extant, Extinct, or Dormant* (13 vols., London, 1910–59)

Dizionario Biografico degli Italiani (1960–, in progress)

W. Dugdale, *Monasticon Anglicanum* ... , ed. J. Caley, H. Ellis and B. Bandinel (6 vols., London, 1817–30)

A. B. Emden, *A Biographical Register of the University of Oxford* A.D. *1501 to 1540* (Oxford, 1974)

J. Foster, *The Register of Admissions to Gray's Inn, 1521–1889* ... (London, 1889)

J. Greatrex, *Biographical Register of the English Cathedral Priories of the Province of Canterbury c. 1066–1540* (Oxford, 1997)

P. W. Hasler (ed.), *The History of Parliament: the House of Commons 1558–1603* (3 vols., London, 1981)

G. Hennessy, *Novum Repertorium Ecclesiasticum Parochiale Londinense* ... (London, 1898)

J. Le Neve, *Fasti Ecclesiae Anglicanae*, revised by various editors (London, 1962–, in progress). Two sequences, arranged by diocese or group of dioceses: *1300–1541* and *1541–1857*

Oxford Dictionary of National Biography (60 vols., Oxford, 2004) [updated e-resource subscription only: http://www.oxforddnb.com]

A. W. Pollard and G. R. Redgrave, rev. W. A. Jackson and F. S. Ferguson and completed by K. F. Pantzer, *A Short-Title Catalogue of Books Printed in England, Scotland, and Ireland and of English Books Printed Abroad, 1475–1640* (revised edn, 3 vols., London, 1976–91)

W. A. Shaw, *The Knights of England* (2 vols., London, 1906)

D. M. Smith (ed.), *The Heads of Religious Houses: England and Wales III: 1377–1540* (Cambridge, 2008) [statements about monastic heads in the text are taken from here unless otherwise referenced]

R. Spalding, *Contemporaries of Bulstrode Whitelocke 1605–1675* (Records of Social and Economic History new series 14, 1990)

State Papers Online, 1509–1714: https://www.gale.com/uk/primary-sources/state-papers-online [subscription only]

Survey of London, individual volumes by area; a variety of editors

J. and J. A. Venn (eds.), *Alumni Cantabrigienses* (4 vols., Cambridge, 1922–7) [http://venn.lib.cam.ac.uk is the extended version of Venn, and statements about Cambridge University residence in the text are taken from there unless otherwise referenced]

Victoria County Histories, individual volumes by county; a variety of editors

A. Wagner, *Historic Heraldry of Britain* (Oxford, 1948)

D. G. Wing, *Short-Title Catalogue of Books Printed in England, Scotland, Ireland, Wales, and British America and of English Books Printed in Other Countries, 1641–1700*, 2nd edn, rev. and ed. J. J. Morrison and C. W. Nelson with M. Seccombe (4 vols., New York, 1972, 1982, 1988, 1998)

SECONDARY SOURCES: BOOKS AND ARTICLES

S. Alford, *London's Triumph: Merchant Adventurers and the Tudor city* (London, 2017)

J. D. Alsop, 'Cromwell and the Church in 1531: the case of Waltham Abbey', *JEH* 31 (1980), 327–30

P. Arblaster, G. Juhasz and G. Latré, *Tyndale's Testament* (Turnhout, 2002)

M. Aston, *England's Iconoclasts I: Laws against Images* (Oxford, 1988)

M. Aston, *Broken Idols of the English Reformation* (Cambridge, 2016)

J. Aubrey, *The natural history and antiquities of the county of Surrey . . .* (5 vols, London, 1718–19)

G. J. Aungier, *The History and Antiquities of Syon Monastery, the parish of Isleworth, and the chapelry of Hounslow . . .* (London, 1840)

M. Axton and J. P. Carley (eds.), *'Triumphs of English': Henry Parker, Lord Morley, translator to the Tudor Court. New essays in interpretation* (London, 2000)

P. Ayris, 'The public career of Thomas Cranmer', *Reformation and Renaissance Review* 4 (Dec. 2000), 75–125

J. H. Baker, *The Oxford History of the Laws of England 6: 1483–1558* (Oxford, 2003)

D. Baker-Smith, 'Antonio Buonvisi and Florens Wilson: a European friendship', *Moreana* 43 (2006), 82–108

R. Barrington, 'Two Houses both alike in dignity: Reginald Pole and Edmund Harvell', *HJ* 39 (1996), 895–913

K. R. Bartlett, 'Morley, Machiavelli, and the Pilgrimage of Grace', in Axton and Carley (eds.), *'Triumphs of English': Henry Parker, Lord Morley*, 77–86

G. W. Bernard, *War, Taxation and Rebellion in Early Tudor England* (Brighton and New York, 1986)

G. W. Bernard, 'Anne Boleyn's religion', *HJ* 36 (1993), 1–20

G. W. Bernard, *The King's Reformation: Henry VIII and the remaking of the English Church* (New Haven and London, 2005)

E. L. Blackburn, *An architectural and historical account of Crosby Place, London* (London, 1834)

J. Blatchly and D. MacCulloch, *Miracles in Lady Lane: the Ipswich shrine at the Westgate* (Dorchester, 2013)

P. W. M. Blayney, *The Stationers' Company and the Printers of London 1501–1557* (2 vols., Cambridge, 2013)

F. Blomefield and C. Parkin, *An Essay towards a Topographical History of the County of Norfolk . . .* (11 vols., London, 1805–10)

M. Bowker, *The Henrician Reformation: the diocese of Lincoln under John Longland 1521–1547* (Cambridge, 1981)

A. Boyle, 'Hans Eworth's portrait of the Earl of Arundel and the politics of 1549–50', *EHR* 117 (2002), 25–47

B. Bradshaw, *The Dissolution of the Religious Orders in Ireland under Henry VIII* (Cambridge, 1974)

B. Bradshaw, *The Irish Constitutional Revolution of the Sixteenth Century* (Cambridge, 1979)

B. Bradshaw and E. Duffy (eds.), *Humanism, Reform and the Reformation: the career of Bishop John Fisher* (Cambridge, 1989)

S. Brigden, 'Tithe controversy in Reformation London', *JEH* 32 (1981), 285–301

S. Brigden, 'Thomas Cromwell and the "brethren"', in Cross, Loades and Scarisbrick (eds.), *Law and Government under the Tudors*, 31–50

S. Brigden, *London and the Reformation* (Oxford, 1989)

S. Brigden, 'Henry Howard, Earl of Surrey, and the "conjured league"', *HJ* 37 (1994), 507–37

S. Brigden, *Thomas Wyatt: the heart's forest* (London, 2012)

A. D. Brown, *Popular Piety in Late Medieval England: the diocese of Salisbury, 1250–1550* (Oxford, 1995)

A. J. Brown, *Robert Ferrar: Yorkshire monk, Reformation bishop and martyr in Wales (c. 1500–1555)* (London, 1997)

K. Brown, 'Wolsey and ecclesiastical order: the case of the Franciscan Observants', in Gunn and Lindley (eds.), *Cardinal Wolsey*, 219–38

G. Burnet, *The History of the Reformation . . .* (2 vols., London, 1679, Wing B5797)

L. Busfield, 'Men, women and Christ crucified: Protestant Passion piety in sixteenth-century England', *Reformation & Renaissance Review* 15 (2013), 217–36

M. L. Bush, *The Pilgrimage of Grace: a study of the rebel armies of October 1536* (Manchester, 1996)

M. L. Bush, 'A progress report on the Pilgrimage of Grace', *History* 90 (2005), 566–78

M. L. Bush and D. Bownes, *The Defeat of the Pilgrimage of Grace: a study of the postpardon revolts of December 1536 to March 1537 and their effect* (Hull, 1999)

C. C. Butterworth and A. G. Chester, *George Joye 1495?–1553: a chapter in the history of the English Bible and the English Reformation* (Philadelphia, 1962)

B. Buxton, *At the House of Thomas Poyntz: the betrayal of William Tyndale with the consequences for an English merchant and his family* (Lavenham, 2013)

G. Byng, 'The contract for the north aisle at the church of St James, Biddenham', *Antiquaries Journal* 95 (2015), 251–65

J. P. Carley, '"Her moost lovyng and fryndely brother sendeth gretyng": Anne Boleyn's manuscripts and their sources', in M. P. Brown and S. McKendrick (eds.), *Illuminating the Book: makers and interpreters* (London, 1998), 261–80

J. P. Carley, 'Religious controversy and marginalia: Pierfrancesco di Piero Bardi, Thomas Wakefield, and their books', *Transactions of the Cambridge Bibliographical Society* 12 (2002), 206–45

J. P. Carley, 'Hannibal Gamon and two strays from the library of King Henry VIII', *The Book Collector* 64 (2015), 213–19

J. P. Carley, 'Thomas Wolsey's Epistle and Gospel lectionaries: unanswered questions and new hypotheses', *Bodleian Library Record* 28 (2015), 135–51

J. P. Carley and A. M. Hutchison, 'William Peto, O.F.M.Obs., and the 1556 edition of *The folowinge of Chryste*: background and context', *Journal of the Early Book Society* 17 (2014), 94–118

J. P. Carley and P. Petitmengin, 'Pre-Conquest manuscripts from Malmesbury Abbey and John Leland's letter to Beatus Rhenanus concerning a lost copy of Tertullian's works', *Anglo-Saxon England* 33 (2004), 195–223

P. R. N. Carter, 'The fiscal Reformation: clerical taxation and opposition in Henrician England', in B. Kümin (ed.), *Reformations Old and New: essays on the socio-economic impact of religious change, c. 1470–1630* (Aldershot, 1996), 92–105

P. Cavill, *The English Parliaments of Henry VII 1485–1504* (Oxford, 2009)

C. E. Challis, *The Tudor Coinage* (Manchester and New York, 1978)

D. S. Chambers, *Cardinal Bainbridge in the Court of Rome 1509 to 1514* (Oxford, 1965)

A. Chibi, 'Henry VIII and his marriage to his brother's wife: the sermon of Bishop John Stokesley of 11 July 1535', *Historical Research* 67 (1994), 40–56

J. G. Clark, 'Humanism and reform in pre-Reformation English monasteries', *TRHS* 6th series 19 (2009), 57–93

N. Clark, 'The gendering of dynastic memory: burial choices of the Howards, 1485–1559', *JEH* 68 (2017), 747–65

P. Clark, *English Provincial Society from the Reformation to the Revolution: religion, politics and society in Kent 1500–1640* (Hassocks, 1977)

P. D. Clarke, 'Canterbury as the New Rome: dispensations and Henry VIII's Reformation', *JEH* 64 (2013), 20–44

A. Coates, *English Medieval Books: the Reading Abbey collections from foundation to dispersal* (Oxford, 1999)

C. Coleman and D. Starkey (eds.), *Revolution Reassessed: revisions in the history of Tudor government and administration* (Oxford, 1986)

[J. P. Collier, forger], 'Transcript of an original manuscript, containing a memorial from George Constantyne to Thomas Lord Cromwell', 'ed.' T. Amyot, *Archaeologia* 23 (1831), 50–78

P. Collinson, 'Puritans, men of business and Elizabethan Parliaments', *Parliamentary History* 7 (1988), 187–211

P. Collinson, 'Geoffrey Elton', *Proceedings of the British Academy* 94 (1997), 429–55

H. M. Colvin (ed.), *The History of the King's Works 3–4: 1485–1660* (London, 1982)

I. Cooper, 'The speed and efficiency of the Tudor south-west's royal post-stage service', *History* 99 (2014), 754–74

J. Corder (ed.), *The Visitation of Suffolk 1561 made by William Hervy* . . . (2 vols., Harleian Society, new series 2 and 3, 1981, 1984)

J Craig and C. Litzenberger, 'Wills as religious propaganda: the testament of Richard Tracy', *JEH* 44 (1993), 415–31

C. Cross, D. Loades and J. J. Scarisbrick (eds.), *Law and Government under the Tudors* (Cambridge, 1988)

P. Cunich, 'Benedictine monks at the University of Oxford and the dissolution of the monasteries', in H. Wansbrough and A. Marett-Crosby (eds.), *Benedictines in Oxford* (London, 1997), 155–82

C. W. D'Alton, 'Charity or fire? The argument of Thomas More's 1529 *Dyaloge*', *SCJ* 33 (2002), 51–70

D. Daniell, *William Tyndale: a biography* (New Haven and London, 1994)

E. Jeffries Davis, 'The beginning of the Dissolution: Christchurch, Aldgate, 1532', *TRHS* 4th series 8 (1925), 127–50

J. F. Davis, *Heresy and Reformation in the South East of England 1520–1559* (London, 1983)

C. S. L. Davies, 'The Cromwellian decade: authority and consent', *TRHS* 6th series 7 (1997), 177–95

C. S. L. Davies, 'Tournai and the English Crown, 1513–1519', *HJ* 41 (1998), 1–26

E. J. Devereux, 'Elizabeth Barton and Tudor censorship', *Bulletin of the John Rylands Library* 49 (1966), 91–106

A. G. Dickens, *Thomas Cromwell and the English Reformation* (London, 1959)

A. G. Dickens, *Lollards and Protestants in the Diocese of York 1509–1558* (2nd edn, London, 1982)

A. G. Dickens, *Late Monasticism and the Reformation* (London and Rio Grande, 1994)

A. Dillon, 'John Forest and Derfel Gadarn: a double execution', *Recusant History* 28 (2006), 1–21

E. Duffy, *Reformation Divided: Catholics, Protestants and the conversion of England* (London, 2017)

T. F. Dunn, 'The development of the text of Pole's "De Unitate Ecclesiae" ', *Papers of the Bibliographical Society of America* 70 (1976), 455–68

A. J. Eagleston, *The Channel Islands under Tudor Government, 1485–1642: a study in administrative history* (Cambridge, 1949)

J. Edwards, *Mary I: England's Catholic queen* (New Haven and London, 2011)

J. Edwards, *Archbishop Pole* (Farnham and Burlington, VT, 2014)

S. G. Ellis, 'Thomas Cromwell and Ireland, 1532–1540', *HJ* 23 (1980), 497–519

S. G. Ellis, *Reform and Revival: English government in Ireland 1470–1534* (Royal Historical Society Studies in History 47, 1986)

S. G. Ellis, *Tudor Frontiers and Noble Power: the making of the British state* (Oxford, 1995)

S. G. Ellis, *Defending English Ground: war and peace in Meath and Northumberland 1460–1542* (Oxford, 2015)

G. R. Elton, *The Tudor Revolution in Government: administrative changes in the reign of Henry VIII* (Cambridge, 1953)

G. R. Elton, *Star Chamber Stories* (London, 1958)

G. R. Elton, 'The law of treason in the early Reformation', *HJ* 11 (1968), 211–36

G. R. Elton, *Policy and Police: the enforcement of the Reformation in the age of Thomas Cromwell* (Cambridge, 1972)

G. R. Elton, *Reform and Renewal: Thomas Cromwell and the Common Weal* (Cambridge, 1973)

G. R. Elton, *Studies in Tudor and Stuart Politics and Government* (4 vols., Cambridge, 1974–92) [I have cited Elton's articles from this collection if they are included in it, rather than in their original setting, since frequently he added to the collected versions new footnotes with useful second thoughts]

G. R. Elton, 'Thomas Cromwell's decline and fall', in Elton, *Studies* 1, 189–230

G. R. Elton, 'Why the history of the early-Tudor Council remains unwritten', in Elton, *Studies* 1, 308–38

G. R. Elton, 'Henry VIII's Act of Proclamations', in Elton, *Studies* 1, 339–54

G. R. Elton, 'Parliamentary drafts, 1529–1540', in Elton, *Studies* 2, 62–81

G. R. Elton, 'The evolution of a Reformation statute', in Elton, *Studies* 2, 82–106

G. R. Elton, 'An early Tudor poor law', in Elton, *Studies* 2, 137–54

G. R. Elton, 'The political creed of Thomas Cromwell', in Elton, *Studies* 2, 224

G. R. Elton, 'Tudor government: the points of contact', in Elton, *Studies* 3, 3–57

G. R. Elton, 'The materials of Parliamentary history', in Elton, *Studies* 3, 58–155

G. R. Elton, 'Taxation for war and peace in early-Tudor England', in Elton, *Studies* 3, 216–33

G. R. Elton, 'Thomas Cromwell Redivivus', in Elton, *Studies* 3, 373–90

G. R. Elton, 'Thomas More and Thomas Cromwell', in Elton, *Studies* 4, 144–60

G. R. Elton, 'How corrupt was Thomas Cromwell?', *HJ* 36 (1993), 905–8

M. C. Erler, *Reading and Writing during the Dissolution: monks, friars and nuns 1530–1558* (Cambridge, 2013)

M. Everett, *The Rise of Thomas Cromwell: power and politics in the reign of Henry VIII* (New Haven and London, 2015)

D. Fenlon, *Heresy and Obedience in Tridentine Italy: Cardinal Pole and the Counter Reformation* (Cambridge, 1972)

[M. Finch] for Lincolnshire Archives Committee, 'A Boston guild account', *Archivists' Report* 16 (1 April 1964/31 March 1965), 40–43

J. Finot, 'Le commerce de l'alun dans les pays-bas et la bulle encyclique du Pape Jules II en 1506', *Bulletin Historique et Philologique* (1902), 418–31

T. Fitzgerald and D. MacCulloch, 'Gregory Cromwell: two portrait miniatures by Hans Holbein the Younger', *JEH* 67 (2016), 587–601

A. Fletcher and D. MacCulloch, *Tudor Rebellions* (6th edn, London, 2016)

C. Fletcher, *Our Man in Rome: Henry VIII and his Italian ambassador* (London, 2012)

A. Fox, 'Sir Thomas Elyot and the humanist dilemma', in Fox and Guy, *Reassessing the Henrician Age*, 52–75

A. Fox and J. Guy, *Reassessing the Henrician Age: humanism, politics and reform 1500–1550* (Oxford, 1986)

A. Freeman, 'To guard his words', *Times Literary Supplement*, 14 December 2007, 13–14

A. Freeman and J. Ing Freeman, *John Payne Collier: scholarship and forgery in the nineteenth century* (2 vols., New Haven and London, 2004)

T. S. Freeman, 'Research, rumour and propaganda: Anne Boleyn in Foxe's "Book of Martyrs"', *HJ* 38 (1995), 797–819

R. Fritze, '"A rare example of godlyness amongst gentlemen": the role of the Kingsmill and Gifford families in promoting the Reformation in Hampshire', in Lake and Dowling (eds.), *Protestantism and the National Church in Sixteenth Century England*, 144–61

T. Fuller, *The Church-History of Britain from the birth of Jesus Christ until the year M.DC.XLVIII* (London, 1655, Wing F2416)

T. Fuller, *The Worthies of England*, ed. J. Freeman (London, 1952)

S. R. Gammon, *Statesman and Schemer: William, first Lord Paget, Tudor minister* (Newton Abbot, 1973)

L. R. Gardiner, 'Further news of Cardinal Wolsey's end, November–December 1530', *Bulletin of the Institute of Historical Research* 57 (1984), 99–107

L. R. Gardiner, 'George Cavendish: an early Tudor political commentator?', *Parergon* new series 6 (1988), 77–87

E. Gerhardt, 'John Bale's adaptation of parish- and civic-drama's playing practices', *Reformation* 19 (2014), 6–20

D. Gerhold, *Thomas Cromwell and his Family in Putney and Wandsworth* (Wandsworth Historical Society Papers 31, 2017)

J. B. Gleason, *John Colet* (Berkeley, CA, and London, 1989)

J. M. Gray, *Oaths and the English Reformation* (Cambridge, 2013)

G. B. Graybill, *Evangelical Free Will: Philipp Melanchthon's doctrinal journey on the origins of faith* (Oxford, 2010)

S. Gunn, *Charles Brandon, Duke of Suffolk, 1484–1545* (Oxford, 1988)

S. Gunn, 'Peers, commons and gentry in the Lincolnshire Revolt of 1536', *PP* 123 (1989), 52–79

S. Gunn, 'The structures of politics in early Tudor England', *TRHS* 6th series 5 (1995), 59–90

S. Gunn, *Henry VII's New Men and the Making of Tudor England* (Oxford, 2016)

S. Gunn and P. G. Lindley (eds.), *Cardinal Wolsey: Church, state and art* (Cambridge, 1991)

J. Guy, *The Cardinal's Court: the impact of Thomas Wolsey in Star Chamber* (Hassocks, 1977)

J. Guy, *The Public Career of Sir Thomas More* (Brighton, 1980)

J. Guy, *Christopher St German on Chancery and Statute* (Selden Society supplementary series 6, 1985)

J. Guy, 'The Privy Council: revolution or evolution?', in Coleman and Starkey (eds.), *Revolution Reassessed*, 59–86

J. Guy, 'Thomas Cromwell and the intellectual origins of the Henrician revolution', in Fox and Guy, *Reassessing the Henrician Age*, 151–78

J. Guy, 'Wolsey and the Parliament of 1523', in Cross, Loades and Scarisbrick (eds.), *Law and Government under the Tudors*, 1–18

J. Guy, *Henry VIII: the quest for fame* (London, 2014)

J. Guy, *Thomas More: a very brief history* (London, 2017)

P. Gwyn, *The King's Cardinal: the rise and fall of Thomas Wolsey* (London, 1990)

S. W. Haas, 'The *Disputatio inter clericum et militem*: was Berthelet's 1531 edition the first Henrician polemic of Thomas Cromwell?', *Moreana* 14 (Dec. 1977), 65–72

S. W. Haas, 'Henry VIII's *Glasse of Truthe*', *History* 64 (1979), 353–62

S. W. Haas, 'Martin Luther's "Divine Right" kingship and the royal supremacy: two tracts from the 1531 Parliament and Convocation of the Clergy', *JEH* 31 (1980), 317–25

C. Haigh, *The Last Days of the Lancashire Monasteries and the Pilgrimage of Grace* (Manchester, 1969)

C. Haigh, *Reformation and Resistance in Tudor Lancashire* (Cambridge, 1975)

E. M. Hallam, 'Henry VIII's monastic refoundations of 1536–7 and the course of the Dissolution', *Bulletin of the Institute of Historical Research* 51 (1978), 124–31

E. A. Hammond, 'Doctor Augustine, physician to Cardinal Wolsey and Henry VIII', *Medical History* 19 (1975), 215–49

A. Harmer [H. Wharton], *A Specimen of some errors and defects in the History of the Reformation of the Church of England wrote by Gilbert Burnet, D.D., now Lord Bishop of Sarum* (1693, Wing W1569)

A. L. Harris, 'Tombs of the New English in late sixteenth and early seventeenth-century Dublin', *Church Monuments* 11 (1996), 25–41

I. Harris, 'Some origins of a Tudor revolution', *EHR* 126 (2011), 1355–85

E. Hasted, *The history and topographical survey of the County of Kent . . .* (2nd edn, 12 vols., Canterbury, 1797–1801)

A. Hawkyard, *The House of Commons 1509–1558: personnel, procedure, precedent and change* (Parliamentary History: Texts and Studies 12, 2016)

D. Hay, *Polydore Vergil: Renaissance historian and man of letters* (Oxford, 1952)

P. Hayward, 'Gregory the Great as "Apostle of the English" in post-Conquest Canterbury', *JEH* 55 (2004), 19–57

F. Heal, 'What can King Lucius do for you? The Reformation and the early British Church', *EHR* 120 (2005), 593–614

M. Heale, 'Dependent priories and the closure of monasteries in late medieval England, 1400–1535', *EHR* 119 (2004), 1–26

M. Heale, *The Abbots and Priors of Late Medieval and Reformation England* (Oxford, 2016)

E. Lord Herbert of Chirbury, *The Life and Raigne of King Henry the Eighth* (London, 1649, Wing H1504)

A. Higgins, 'On the work of Florentine sculptors in England in the early part of the sixteenth century: with special reference to the tombs of Cardinal Wolsey and King Henry VIII', *Archaeological Journal* 51 (1894), 129–220, 367–70

E. Hildebrandt, 'Christopher Mont, Anglo-German diplomat', *SCJ* 15 (1984), 281–92

E. J. Hobsbawm and J. Wallach Scott, 'Political Shoemakers', *PP* 89 (1980), 86–114

N. Holder, *The Friaries of Medieval London: from foundation to dissolution* (Woodbridge, 2017)

C. Holmes, 'G. R. Elton as a legal historian', *TRHS* 6th series 7 (1997), 267–79

P. J. Holmes, 'The last Tudor Great Councils', *HJ* 33 (1990), 1–22

W. F. Hook, *Lives of the Archbishops of Canterbury* (12 vols., London, 1860–76)

A. Hope, 'Lollardy: the stone the builders rejected?', in Lake and Dowling (eds.), *Protestantism and the National Church in Sixteenth Century England*, 1–35

I. B. Horst, *The Radical Brethren: Anabaptism and the English Reformation to 1558* (Nieuwkoop, 1972)

S. B. House, 'Cromwell's message to the regulars: the biblical trilogy of John Bale, 1537', *Renaissance and Reformation/Renaissance et Réforme* new series 15 (1991), 123–38

R. W. Hoyle, 'Henry Percy, sixth Earl of Northumberland, and the fall of the House of Percy, 1527–1537', in G. W. Bernard (ed.), *The Tudor Nobility* (Manchester, 1992), 180–211

R. W. Hoyle, 'The origins of the dissolution of the monasteries', *HJ* 38 (1995), 275–305

R. W. Hoyle, 'War and public finance', in MacCulloch (ed.), *Reign of Henry VIII*, 75–99

R. W. Hoyle, 'Place and public finance', *TRHS* 6th series 7 (1997), 197–215

R. W. Hoyle, *The Pilgrimage of Grace and the Politics of the 1530s* (Oxford, 2001)

R. Hutton, 'The local impact of the Tudor Reformations', in C. Haigh (ed.), *The English Reformation Revised* (Cambridge, 1987), 114–38

E. W. Ives, 'The genesis of the Statute of Uses', *EHR* 82 (1967), 673–97

E. W. Ives, 'The fall of Wolsey', in Gunn and Lindley (eds.), *Cardinal Wolsey*, 286–315

E. W. Ives, *The Life and Death of Anne Boleyn 'The Most Happy'* (Oxford, 2004)

E. W. Ives, 'Anne Boleyn on trial again', *JEH* 62 (2011), 763–77

E. W. Ives, R. J. Knecht and J. J. Scarisbrick (eds.), *Wealth and Power in Tudor England: essays presented to S. T. Bindoff* (London, 1978)

M. E. James, 'Obedience and dissent in Henrician England: the Lincolnshire Rebellion 1536', in James, *Society, Politics and Culture: studies in early modern England* (Cambridge, 1986), 188–269 (repr. from *PP* 48 (1970), 3–78)

L. Jardine and A. Grafton, ' "Studied for action": how Gabriel Harvey read his Livy', *PP* 129 (1990), 30–78

H. A. Jefferies, 'Tudor Reformations compared: the Irish Pale and Lancashire', in C. Maginn and G. Power (eds.), *Frontiers, States and Identity in Early Modern Ireland and Beyond: essays in honour of Steven G. Ellis* (Dublin, 2016), 71–92

C. Johnson, 'The travels and trials of a sixteenth-century Wirral recusant', *Cheshire History* 47 (2007–8), 22–33

M. Jurkowski, 'The history of clerical taxation in England and Wales, 1173–1663: the findings of the E 179 project', *JEH* 67 (2016), 53–81

H. A. Kelly, *The Matrimonial Trials of Henry VIII* (Stanford, CA, 1976)

M. Kelly, 'The submission of the clergy', *TRHS* 5th series 15 (1965), 97–119

R. J. Knecht, 'Francis I, "Defender of the Faith"?', in Ives, Knecht and Scarisbrick (eds.), *Wealth and Power in Tudor England*, 106–27

D. Knowles, 'The last abbot of Wigmore', in V. Ruffer and A. J. Taylor (eds.), *Medieval Studies Presented to Rose Graham* (Oxford, 1950), 138–45, repr. in Knowles, *The Historian and Character* (Cambridge, 1963), 171–8

D. Knowles, *The Religious Orders in England III: the Tudor age* (Cambridge, 1959)

P. Lake and M. Dowling (eds.), *Protestantism and the National Church in Sixteenth Century England* (Beckenham, 1987)

S. Lander, 'Church courts and the Reformation in the diocese of Chichester, 1500–58', in R. O'Day and F. Heal (eds.), *Continuity and Change: personnel and administration of the Church in England 1500–1642* (Leicester, 1976), 215–37

K. Lanz, *Correspondenz des Kaisers Karl V . . .* (3 vols., Leipzig, 1844–6)

G. Latré, 'The 1535 Coverdale Bible and its Antwerp origins', in O. O'Sullivan (ed.), *The Bible as Book: the Reformation* (New Castle, DE, and London, 2000), 89–102

S. E. Lehmberg, *The Reformation Parliament 1529–1536* (Cambridge, 1970)

S. E. Lehmberg, *The Later Parliaments of Henry VIII 1536–1547* (Cambridge, 1977)

G. Leveson-Gower, 'The Howards of Effingham', *Surrey Archaeological Collections* 9 (1888), 395–436

P. Lindley, 'Playing check-mate with royal majesty? Wolsey's patronage of Italian Renaissance sculpture', in Gunn and Lindley (eds.), *Cardinal Wolsey*, 261–85

P. Lindley, 'Materiality, movement and the historical moment', in Lindley (ed.), *The Howards and the Tudors: studies in science and heritage* (Stamford, 2015), 43–75

C. Litzenberger, *The English Reformation and the Laity: Gloucestershire, 1540–1580* (Cambridge, 1997)

A. H. Lloyd, *The Early History of Christ's College, Cambridge, Derived from Contemporary Documents* (Cambridge, 1934)

F. D. Logan, 'Thomas Cromwell and the Vicegerency in Spirituals: a revisitation', *EHR* 103 (1988), 658–67

F. D. Logan, 'The first royal visitation of the English universities, 1535', *EHR* 106 (1991), 861–88

R. Lutton, 'Richard Guldeford's pilgrimage: piety and cultural change in late fifteenth- and early sixteenth-century England', *History* 98 (2013), 41–78

K. D. Maas, *The Reformation and Robert Barnes* (Woodbridge, 2010)

D. MacCulloch, *Suffolk and the Tudors: politics and religion in an English county 1500–1600* (Oxford, 1986)

D. MacCulloch, 'Two dons in politics: Thomas Cranmer and Stephen Gardiner, 1503–1533', *HJ* 37 (1994), 1–22

D. MacCulloch (ed.), *The Reign of Henry VIII: politics, policy and piety* (Houndmills and London, 1995), including D. MacCulloch, 'Henry VIII and the reform of the Church', 159–80

D. MacCulloch, 'The consolidation of England, 1485–1603', in J. Morrill (ed.), *The Oxford Illustrated History of Tudor and Stuart England* (Oxford and New York, 1996), 35–52

D. MacCulloch, 'A Reformation in the balance: power struggles in the diocese of Norwich, 1533–1553', in C. Rawcliffe, R. Virgoe and R. Wilson (eds.), *Counties and Communities: essays on East Anglian history presented to Hassell Smith* (Norwich, 1996), 97–115

D. MacCulloch, *Tudor Church Militant: Edward VI and the Protestant Reformation* (London, 1999)

D. MacCulloch, *The Later Reformation in England 1547–1603* (2nd edn, Houndmills, 2001)

D. MacCulloch, *Reformation: Europe's house divided 1490–1700* (London, 2003)

D. MacCulloch, 'The latitude of the Church of England', in K. Fincham and
P. Lake (eds.), *Religious Politics in Post-Reformation England: essays in honour of Nicholas Tyacke* (Woodbridge, 2006), 41–59

D. MacCulloch, 'Heinrich Bullinger and the English-speaking world', in E. Campi
and P. Opitz (eds.), *Heinrich Bullinger (1504–1575): Leben, Denken, Wirkung*
(Zürcher Beiträge zur Reformationsgeschichte 24, 2007), 891–934

D. MacCulloch, 'Calvin: fifth Latin Doctor of the Church?', in I. Backus and
P. Benedict (eds.), *Calvin and his Influence, 1509–2009* (Oxford, 2011), 33–45

D. MacCulloch, *Silence: a Christian history* (London, 2013)

D. MacCulloch, *Thomas Cranmer: a life* (revised edn, New Haven and London,
2016)

D. MacCulloch, 'The Church of England and international Protestantism, 1530–
1570', in A. Milton (ed.), *The Oxford History of Anglicanism I: Reformation
and Identity, c. 1520–1662* (Oxford, 2017), 316–32

D. MacCulloch, 'Thomas Cromwell and the London Charterhouse', in J. P. Carley
and J. Luxford (eds.), *The Carthusians in the City: history, culture and martyrdom at the London Charterhouse c. 1370–1475* (forthcoming, 2020)

D. MacCulloch and J. Blatchly, 'A house fit for a queen: Wingfield House, Tacket
Street, Ipswich and its heraldic room', *Proceedings of the Suffolk Institute of
Archaeology and History* 38 pt 1 (1993), 13–34

R. McEntegart, *Henry VIII, the League of Schmalkalden and the English Reformation* (London, 2002)

A. M. McLean, ' "A noughtye and a false lyeng boke": William Barlow and the
Lutheran factions', *Renaissance Quarterly* 31 (1978), 173–85

H. Mantel, *Wolf Hall* (London, 2009)

P. Marshall, 'The Rood of Boxley, the Blood of Hailes and the defence of the Henrician Church', *JEH* 46 (1995), 689–96

P. Marshall, 'Papist as heretic: the burning of John Forest, 1538', *HJ* 41 (1998), 351–74

P. Marshall, 'The other Black Legend: the Henrician Reformation and the Spanish
people', *EHR* 116 (2001), 31–49

P. Marshall, 'The shooting of Robert Packington', in Marshall, *Religious Identities in Henry VIII's England* (Aldershot, 2006), 61–79

P. Marshall, ' "The greatest man in Wales": James ap Gruffydd ap Hywel and the
international opposition to Henry VIII', *SCJ* 39 (2008), 681–704

P. Marshall, 'The making of the Tudor Judas: trust and betrayal in the English
Reformation', *Reformation* 13 (2008), 77–101

P. Marshall, 'Crisis of allegiance: George Throckmorton and Henry Tudor', in Marshall and G. Scott (eds.), *Catholic Gentry in English Society: the Throckmortons
of Coughton from Reformation to emancipation* (Farnham, 2009), 31–67

P. Marshall, *Faith and Identity in a Warwickshire Family: the Throckmortons
and the Reformation* (Dugdale Society Occasional Papers 49, 2010)

P. Marshall, *Heretics and Believers: a history of the English Reformation* (New
Haven and London, 2017)

P. Marshall and A. Ryrie (eds.), *The Beginnings of English Protestantism* (Cambridge, 2002)

T. F. Mayer, *Reginald Pole: prince and prophet* (Cambridge, 2000)

S. Menache, 'Papal attempts at a commercial boycott of the Muslims in the Crusader period', *JEH* 63 (2012), 236–59

A. de Mézerac-Zanetti, 'Reforming the liturgy under Henry VIII: the instructions of John Clerk, Bishop of Bath and Wells (PRO, SP6/3, fos 42r–44v)', *JEH* 64 (2013), 96–111

J. F. Mozley, *William Tyndale* (London, 1937)

M. Murphy, 'Thame, Tübingen, Kraków and Reading: the itinerary of Leonard Cox, humanist and schoolmaster (*c.* 1495–1550)', *Humanistica Lovaniensia* 64 (2015), 75–95

V. Murphy, 'The literature and propaganda of Henry VIII's first divorce', in MacCulloch (ed.), *Reign of Henry VIII*, 135–58

J. Murray, 'Archbishop Alen, Tudor reform and the Kildare Rebellion', *Proceedings of the Royal Irish Academy* 89C (1989), 1–16

J. Murray, *Enforcing the English Reformation in Ireland: clerical resistance and political conflict in the diocese of Dublin, 1534–1590* (Cambridge, 2009)

J. G. Nichols, 'Some additions to the biographies of Sir John Cheke and Sir Thomas Smith . . .', *Archaeologia* 38 (1860), 98–127

G. Nicholson, 'The Act of Appeals and the English Reformation', in Cross, Loades and Scarisbrick (eds.), *Law and Government under the Tudors*, 19–30

M. Ó Siochrú, 'Foreign involvement in the revolt of Silken Thomas, 1534–5', *Proceedings of the Royal Irish Academy* 96C (1996), 49–66

N. Orme, *The History of England's Cathedrals* (Exeter, 2017)

G. Ormerod, *The history of the county palatine and city of Chester* (2 vols., London, 1819)

M. D. Orth, 'The English Great Bible of 1539 and the French connection', in S. L'Engle and G. B. Guest (eds.), *Tributes to Jonathan J. G. Alexander* (London, 2006), 171–84

D. Paisey and G. Bartrum, 'Hans Holbein and Miles Coverdale: a new woodcut', *Print Quarterly* 26 (2009), 227–53

G. Parks, *The English Traveller to Italy* (2 vols., Rome, 1954)

T. Penn, *Winter King: the dawn of Tudor England* (London, 2011)

J. Phillips, 'The Cromwell family', *Antiquary* 2 (1880), 164–8; 'The Cromwells of Putney', *Antiquarian Magazine & Bibliographer* 2 (1882), 56–62, 178–86; *Wandsworth Notes and Queries* (1898), part 3, 42–3

J. Pierce, *The Life and Work of William Salesbury: a rare scholar* (Talybont, 2016)

C. Platt, *Medieval Southampton: the port and trading community, A.D. 1000–1600* (London and Boston, 1973)

A. F. Pollard, 'Thomas Cromwell's Parliamentary lists', *Bulletin of the Institute of Historical Research* 9 (1931), 31–43

D. Potter, 'Foreign policy', in MacCulloch (ed.), *Reign of Henry VIII*, 101–33

J. Prise, *Historiae Britannicae Defensio / A Defence of the British History*, ed. and trans. C. Davies (Oxford, 2015)

J. S. Purvis, 'The registers of Archbishops Lee and Holgate', *JEH* 13 (1962), 186–94

G. D. Ramsay, 'The undoing of the Italian mercantile colony in sixteenth century London', in N. B. Harte and K. G. Ponting (eds.), *Textile History and Economic History: essays in honour of Miss Julia de Lacy Mann* (Manchester, 1973), 22–49

V. B. Redstone, 'South Elmham Deanery', *Proceedings of the Suffolk Institute of Archaeology and History* 14 pt 3 (1912), 323–31

G. Redworth, *In Defence of the Church Catholic: the life of Stephen Gardiner* (Oxford, 1990)

R. Rex, 'The English campaign against Luther in the 1520s', *TRHS* 5th series 39 (1989), 85–106

R. Rex, *The Theology of John Fisher* (Cambridge, 1991)

R. Rex, 'The early impact of Reformation theology at Cambridge University, 1521–1547', *Reformation & Renaissance Review* 2 (Dec. 1999), 38–71

R. Rex, 'Jasper Fyloll [*sic*] and the enormities of the clergy: two tracts written during the Reformation Parliament', *SCJ* 31 (2000), 1043–62

R. Rex, 'The friars in the English Reformation', in Marshall and Ryrie (eds.), *Beginnings of English Protestantism*, 38–59

R. Rex, 'Redating Henry VIII's *A Glasse of the Truthe*', *Library* 7th series 4 (2003), 16–27

R. Rex, 'New additions on Christopher St German: law, politics and propaganda in the 1530s', *JEH* 59 (2008), 281–300

M. Riordan and A. Ryrie, 'Stephen Gardiner and the making of a Protestant villain', *SCJ* 34 (2003), 1039–63

J. Roberts, *Holbein and the Court of Henry VIII: drawings and miniatures from the Royal Library Windsor Castle* (Edinburgh, 1994)

P. Roberts, 'Wales and England after the Tudor "union": Crown, Principality and Parliament, 1543–1624', in Cross, Loades and Scarisbrick (eds.), *Law and Government under the Tudors*, 111–38

M. L. Robertson, ' "The art of the possible": Thomas Cromwell's management of West Country government', *HJ* 32 (1989), 793–816

M. L. Robertson, 'Profit and purpose in the development of Thomas Cromwell's landed estates', *Journal of British Studies* 29 (1990), 317–46

J. Robinson, 'The slippery truth of George Buchanan's autobiography', *SCJ* 39 (2008), 71–87

J. Röhrkasten, *The Mendicant Houses of Medieval London 1221–1539* (Münster, 2004)

E. G. Rupp, *Studies in the Making of the English Protestant Tradition* (Cambridge, 1947)

A. Ryrie, 'The strange death of Lutheran England', *JEH* 53 (2002), 64–92

A. Ryrie, *The Gospel and Henry VIII: evangelicals in the early English Reformation* (Cambridge, 2003)

J. J. Scarisbrick, *Henry VIII* (London, 1968)

J. J. Scarisbrick, 'Cardinal Wolsey and the Common Weal', in Ives, Knecht and Scarisbrick (eds.), *Wealth and Power in Tudor England*, 45–67

J. J. Scarisbrick, 'Henry VIII and the dissolution of the secular colleges', in Cross, Loades and Scarisbrick (eds.), *Law and Government under the Tudors*, 51–66

J. J. Scarisbrick, 'Fisher, Henry VIII and the Reformation crisis', in Bradshaw and Duffy (eds.), *Humanism, Reform and the Reformation*, 155–68

J. Schofield, *Philip Melanchthon and the English Reformation* (Aldershot, 2006)

J. Schofield, *The Rise and Fall of Thomas Cromwell, Henry VIII's Most Faithful Servant* (Stroud, 2008)

W. G. Searle, *The History of the Queens' College of St Margaret and St Bernard in the University of Cambridge . . .* (2 vols., Cambridge, 1867–71)

E. H. Shagan, 'Print, orality and communications in the Maid of Kent affair', *JEH* 52 (2001), 21–33

E. H. Shagan, 'Clement Armstrong and the godly commonwealth: radical religion in early Tudor England', in Marshall and Ryrie (eds.), *The Beginnings of English Protestantism*, 60–83

E. H. Shagan, *Popular Politics and the English Reformation* (Cambridge, 2003)

D. J. Shaw, 'Books belonging to William Warham, Archdeacon of Canterbury, c. 1504–1532', in D. E. Rhodes (ed.), *Bookbindings & Other Bibliophily: essays in honour of Anthony Hobson* (Verona, 1994), 277–86

C. M. Sicca, 'Consumption and trade of art between Italy and England in the first half of the sixteenth century: the London house of the Bardi and Cavalcanti company', *Renaissance Studies* 16 (2002), 163–201

C. M. Sicca, 'Fashioning the Tudor Court', in M. Hayward and E. Kramer (eds.), *Textiles and Text: re-establishing the links between archival and object-based research* (London, 2007), 93–104

C. M. Sicca and L. A. Waldman (eds.), *The Anglo-Florentine Renaissance: art for the early Tudors* (New Haven and London, 2012)

C. A. J. Skeel, *The Council in the Marches of Wales: a study in local government during the sixteenth and seventeenth centuries* (London, 1904)

M. C. Skeeters, *Community and Clergy: Bristol and the Reformation, c. 1530–c. 1570* (Oxford, 1993)

A. J. Slavin, 'Cromwell, Cranmer and Lord Lisle: a study in the politics of reform', *Albion* 9 (1977), 316–36

A. J. Slavin, 'The Rochepot Affair', *SCJ* 10/1 (Spring 1979), 3–19

A. J. Slavin, 'The Gutenberg galaxy and the Tudor revolution', in G. P. Tyson and S. S. Wagonheim (eds.), *Print and Culture in the Renaissance: essays on the advent of printing in Europe* (Newark, NJ, 1986), 90–109

A. H. Smith, *County and Court: government and politics in Norfolk, 1558–1603* (Oxford, 1974)

T. A. Sowerby, ' "All our books do be sent into other countreys and translated": Henrician polemic in its international context', *EHR* 121 (2006), 1271–99

T. A. Sowerby, *Renaissance and Reform in Tudor England: the careers of Sir Richard Morison c. 1513–1556* (Oxford, 2010)

T. A. Sowerby, 'The coronation of Anne Boleyn', in T. Betteridge and G. Walker (eds.), *The Oxford Handbook of Tudor Drama* (Oxford, 2012), 386–401

H. M. Speight, ' "The politics of good governance": Thomas Cromwell and the government of the southwest of England', *HJ* 37 (1994), with reply by M. Robertson, 623–41

D. Starkey, *The Reign of Henry VIII: personalities and politics* (London, 1985)

D. Starkey, 'Court and government', in Coleman and Starkey (eds.), *Revolution Reassessed*, 29–58

D. Starkey, 'Intimacy and innovation: the rise of the Privy Chamber, 1485–1547', in Starkey (ed.), *The English Court from the Wars of the Roses to the Civil War* (London, 1987), 71–118

D. Starkey (ed.), *Henry VIII: a European Court in England* (London, 1991)

M. Stephenson, *The Gilbertine Priory of Watton* (Borthwick Paper 116, 2009)

T. C. String, 'Henry VIII's illuminated "Great Bible"', *Journal of the Warburg and Courtauld Institutes* 59 (1996), 315–24

T. C. String, 'A neglected Henrician decorative ceiling', *Antiquaries Journal* 76 (1996), 139–51

T. C. String, *Art and Communication in the Reign of Henry VIII* (Abingdon, 2008)

J. Strype, *Ecclesiastical Memorials, relating chiefly to Religion . . .* (3 vols., London, 1721)

J. Strype, *Memorials . . . of . . . Thomas Cranmer . . .*, ed. P. E. Barnes (2 vols., London, 1853)

D. Stuart, *Manorial Records: an introduction to their transcription and translation* (Chichester, 1992)

A. Suckling, *The History and Antiquities of the County of Suffolk* (2 vols., Ipswich, 1846–8)

R. N. Swanson, *Indulgences in Late Medieval England: passports to paradise?* (Cambridge, 2007)

J. G. Taylor, *Our Lady of Batersey: the story of Battersea church and parish . . .* (London, 1925)

B. Thompson, 'The laity, the alien priories, and the redistribution of ecclesiastical property', in N. Rogers (ed.), *England in the Fifteenth Century* (Stamford, 1994), 19–41

T. Thornton, 'Henry VIII's progress through Yorkshire in 1541 and its implications for northern identities', *Northern History* 46 (2009), 231–44

S. Thurley, 'The domestic building works of Cardinal Wolsey', in Gunn and Lindley (eds.), *Cardinal Wolsey*, 76–102

S. Thurley, *Whitehall Palace: an architectural history of the royal apartments, 1240–1698* (London and New Haven, 1999)

S. Thurley, *Houses of Power: the places that shaped the Tudor world* (London, 2017)

N. S. Tjernagel, *Henry VIII and the Lutherans: a study in Anglo-Lutheran relations from 1521 to 1547* (St Louis, MO, 1965)

N. Tyacke (ed.), *England's Long Reformation, 1500–1800* (London, 1998)

W. Underwood, 'Thomas Cromwell and William Marshall's Protestant books', *HJ* 47 (2004), 517–39

M. Vale, *Henry V: the conscience of a king* (London and New Haven, 2016)

S. Wabuda, 'Cardinal Wolsey and Cambridge', *British Catholic History* 32 (2015), 280–92

K. R. Wark, *Elizabethan Recusancy in Cheshire* (Chetham Society 3rd series 19, 1971)

J. C. Warner, 'A *dyaloge betwene Clemente and Bernarde, c.* 1532: a neglected tract belonging to the last period of John Rastell's career', *SCJ* 29 (1998), 55–65

J. C. Warner, *Henry VIII's Divorce: literature and the politics of the printing press* (Woodbridge, 1998)

S. R. Westfall, *Patrons and Performance: early Tudor household revels* (Oxford, 1990)

W. E. Wilkie, *The Cardinal Protectors of England: Rome and the Tudors before the Reformation* (Cambridge, 1974)

D. Willen, *John Russell, first Earl of Bedford: one of the King's men* (London, 1981)

M. Williamson, 'Evangelicalism at Boston, Oxford and Windsor under Henry VIII: Foxe's narratives recontextualized', in D. Loades (ed.), *John Foxe at Home and Abroad* (Aldershot, 2004), 31–45

B. Winchester, *Tudor Family Portrait* (London, 1955)

J. Woolfson, *Padua and the Tudors: English students in Italy 1485–1603* (Cambridge, 1999)

C. J. Wright, 'The man who wrote on the manuscripts in the British Museum', *British Library Journal* 12 (1986), 76–85

M. Wyatt, *The Italian Encounter with England: a cultural politics of translation* (Cambridge, 2005)

J. Youings, 'The Council of the West', *TRHS* 5th series 10 (1960), 41–59

J. Youings, *The Dissolution of the Monasteries* (London, 1971)

W. G. Zeeveld, *Foundations of Tudor Policy* (Cambridge, MA, 1948)

UNPUBLISHED DISSERTATIONS

W. Bakker, 'Civic reformer in Anabaptist Münster: Bernard Rothmann, 1495?–1535?' (University of Chicago PhD, 1987)

C. Boswell, 'The culture and rhetoric of the answer-poem, 1485–1625' (Leeds University PhD, 2003)

A. Boyle, 'Henry Fitzalan, twelfth Earl of Arundel: politics and culture in the Tudor nobility' (University of Oxford DPhil, 2003)

L. Busfield, 'Protestant epistolary counselling in early modern England, c. 1559–1660' (University of Oxford DPhil, 2016)

C. Euler, 'Religious and cultural exchange during the Reformation: Zürich and England, 1531–1558' (Johns Hopkins University PhD, 2004)

N. Holder, 'The medieval friaries of London: a topographic and archaeological history, before and after the Dissolution' (University of London PhD, 2011)

J. Hyde, 'Mid-Tudor ballads: music, words and context' (University of Manchester PhD, 2015)

A. Laferrière, 'The Austin Friars in pre-Reformation English society' (University of Oxford DPhil, 2017)

N. Lewycky, 'Serving God and King: Cardinal Thomas Wolsey's patronage networks and early Tudor government, 1514–29, with special reference to the archdiocese of York' (University of York PhD, 2008)

P. S. Needham, 'Sir John Cheke at Cambridge and Court' (Harvard University PhD, 1971)

W. B. Robison III, 'The justices of the peace of Surrey in national and county politics, 1483–1570' (Lousiana State University PhD, 1983)

A. N. Shaw, 'The *Compendium Compertorum* and the making of the Suppression Act of 1536' (University of Warwick PhD, 2003)

P. J. Ward, 'The origins of Thomas Cromwell's public career: service under Cardinal Wolsey and Henry VIII, 1524–30' (London School of Economics PhD, 1999)

Notes

Introduction

1. George Gifford to Cromwell, 10 December 1536, SP 1/112 f. 164, *LP* 11 no. 1278. The catalogue of 1533 is analysed in *LP* 6 no. 299: see at 139.   2. Curiously, Sir Geoffrey Elton, despite his acute archival sense and the nature of his great thesis about Cromwell's bureaucratic revolution, did not make this deduction: see G. R. Elton, *The Tudor Revolution in Government: administrative changes in the reign of Henry VIII* (Cambridge, 1953), 76.   3. The obituary by Collinson, 'Geoffrey Elton', *Proceedings of the British Academy* 94 (1997), 429–55, manages to be both balanced and affectionate; on Elton and biography, see ibid., 440.   4. G. R. Elton, 'Thomas More and Thomas Cromwell', in Elton, *Studies* 4, 144–60, at 146–7 (my italics), and see Elton, 'Thomas Cromwell's decline and fall', in Elton, *Studies* 1, 189–230.   5. A refreshing reassessment is L. R. Gardiner, 'George Cavendish: an early Tudor political commentator?', *Parergon* new series 6 (1988), 77–87.   6. Cromwell to Michael Throckmorton, late September 1537, SP 1/125 f. 71, *LP* 12 ii no. 795.   7. Pilgrims' song, SP 1/108 f. 186r, *LP* 11 no. 786[3]; deposition of William Breyar, 22 October 1536, SP 1/109 f. 37v, *LP* 11 no. 841.   8. BL MS Cotton Otho C/X f. 246, *LP* 15 no. 822[3] is the King's original holograph draft of questions to be put to Cromwell about the Anne of Cleves marriage, *c.* 29/30 June 1540, and he heads it 'Questions to be axid of Thomas Cromell'. This holograph disproves Geoffrey Elton's assertion ('Thomas Cromwell's decline and fall', 228–9) that Henry did not make any move to strip Cromwell of his honours and titles; matters were more complicated than that.

1. Ruffian

1. J. Schofield, *The Rise and Fall of Thomas Cromwell, Henry VIII's Most Faithful Servant* (Stroud, 2008), 14–15, carefully sets out the not entirely conclusive evidence.   2. T. Fuller, *The Worthies of England*, ed. J. Freeman (London, 1952), 547.   3. Foxe 1570, 1386.   4. D. Gerhold, *Thomas Cromwell and his Family in Putney and Wandsworth* (Wandsworth Historical Society Papers 31, 2017).   5. The traditional evidence is summarized in Merriman 1, 2–5, drawing on the wildly untrustworthy research of John Phillips. It is carefully analysed and much

discarded in Gerhold, *Thomas Cromwell and his Family*. The articles to be treated with scepticism are J. Phillips, 'The Cromwell family', *Antiquary* 2 (1880), 164–8; 'The Cromwells of Putney', *Antiquarian Magazine & Bibliographer* 2 (1882), 56–62, 178–86; *Wandsworth Notes and Queries* (1898), part 3, 42–3. Gerhold's excellent research substitutes facts for fiction, such as the exact location of land held by Walter Cromwell in Putney, Wandsworth and Roehampton.   6. See e.g. D. Stuart, *Manorial Records* (Chichester, 1992), 4. I am very grateful to the Rev. Thomas Steel for putting me back on the right course of interpretation of these entries. 7. Anthony St Leger to Thomas Cromwell, 17 October [1536], SP 1/108 f. 114, *LP* 11 no. 746. The year date derives from the address to Cromwell as Lord Privy Seal, while subsequent years are very unlikely: in October 1537, St Leger was in Ireland, on royal business which permanently transformed his fortunes for the better. 8. See below, p. 37, for what was certainly a link of the Wellifed family to Archbishop Warham's kitchen in the 1520s.   9. In the earlier letter, SP 1/76 f. 162, *LP* 6 no. 604, St Leger to Thomas Cromwell, 8 June, possibly 1533, St Leger attributes him 'half the living that I have'. He is writing from Slindon, an archiepiscopal demesne leased to him by the Archbishop; he had given his son and heir the Christian name Warham. The later letter is St Leger to Cromwell, 20 June, probably 1534, SP 1/84 f. 193, *LP* 7 no. 862.   10. C. L. Kingsford (ed.), 'Two London Chronicles from the collections of John Stow . . .', *Camden Miscellany 12* (Camden 3rd series 18, 1910), iii–59, at 15; report by William Berners on Paulet's conversation, SP 60/6 f. 52, *LP* 13 i no. 471[4].   11. [Unknown] to Thomas Broke, 3 January [1535]), SP 1/89 f. 6, *LP* 8 no. 11.   12. On Cromwell and Francis Meverell: Thomas Abbot of Croxden to Cromwell, 13 January ?1533, SP 1/74 f. 25, *LP* 6 no. 35. Francis Meverell's mother was from the prominent Derbyshire family of Babington of Dethick (*HC 1509–1558* 2, 597), and her nephew John Babington of Dethick (on whom see *HC 1509–1558* 1, 356) was a servant of Cromwell's by 1536: Sir Anthony Babington to Cromwell, 2 May 1536, SP 1/103 f. 216, *LP* 10 no. 787. For John Babington's lobbying of his master on behalf of the evangelical musician William Senhouse, see papers on Senhouse at SP 1/123 ff. 201–4, *LP* 12 ii no. 436; Babington to Cromwell, 16 October 1537 (SP 1/125 f. 182, *LP* 12 ii no. 925) and 21 August 1538 (SP 1/135 f. 133, *LP* 13 ii no. 149). Oddly enough, a century later, the last of the direct line of the Meverells married Thomas, fourth Lord Cromwell of the third creation and first Earl of Ardglass (1594–1653), great-great-grandson of Thomas Cromwell: *Complete Peerage* 1, 192–3.   13. Cranmer to Cromwell, 8 April 1539: SP 1/150 f. 98, *LP* 14 i no. 720. For Francis Bassett's part in bringing defaced pilgrimage images to Cromwell in London, see a letter from his elder brother Sir William Bassett to Cromwell, late August 1538, BL MS Cotton Cleopatra E/IV f. 285, *LP* 13 ii no. 244.   14. See a tangle of references to troubles in Derbyshire involving the relatives of the Earl of Shrewsbury's leading servant Ralph Leche, the Basfords, Lekes and Sacheverells, all of whom claimed kinship to Cromwell: 25 July ?1534, SP 1/85 f. 69, *LP* 7 no. 1006; 26 August ?1534, SP 1/85 f. 121, *LP* 7 no. 1089; ?October 1534, SP 1/86 f. 56, *LP* 7 no. 1268; 1 August 1537, SP 1/123 f. 177, *LP* 12 ii no. 417.   15. Nicholas Glossop to

Cromwell, 24 June ?1533, SP 1/77 f. 77, *LP* 6 no. 696. **16.** D. MacCulloch, *Thomas Cranmer: a life* (revised edn, New Haven and London, 2016), 2. **17.** West to Cromwell, 18 February 1533, SP 1/74 f. 167, *LP* 6 no. 167. **18.** For West's anti-Lutheran addition to the oath sworn by those being admitted as incumbents in the Ely diocese, see Thomas Goodricke Bishop of Ely, Somersham, to Cromwell, 29 July 1535, and accompanying enclosure, SP 1/94 ff. 186–8, *LP* 8 no. 1131[1, 2]. **19.** MacCulloch, *Thomas Cranmer*, 15. **20.** West to Cromwell, 18 February 1533, SP 1/74 f. 167, *LP* 6 no. 167. **21.** Thomas Megges to Cromwell, 10 April 1535, SP 1/91 f. 194, *LP* 8 no. 578. On the royal appointment, see Megges to Cromwell, 22 July ?1535, SP 1/94 f. 118, *LP* 8 no. 1088, and 8 April [1536], SP 1/103 f. 100, *LP* 10 no. 634, where Megges is not more specific than saying that Cromwell has preferred him into the King's service. **22.** Thomas Goodricke Bishop of Ely to Cromwell, 29 December [1534], SP 1/87 f. 130, *LP* 7 no. 1583; a series of letters from Megges to Cromwell, including 10 March [1535], SP 1/91 f. 71, *LP* 8 no. 367; 22 July ?1535, SP 1/94 f. 118, *LP* 8 no. 1088; 3 November ?1535, SP 1/98 f. 159, *LP* 9 no. 754. **23.** Richard Cromwell to Cromwell, 11 July 1537, SP 1/122 f. 228, *LP* 12 ii no. 241. See Goodricke's detailed and deeply hurt letter to Cromwell, 18 August 1537, SP 1/124 ff. 52–3, *LP* 12 ii no. 533. **24.** Henry Polstead to Cromwell, 30 July 1538, SP 1/134 f. 284, *LP* 13 i no. 1499. **25.** References to Cromwell's servant Thomas Avery (not to be confused with a close friend of Cromwell's from Suffolk, Thomas Alvard) litter *Letters and Papers*, but he also appears in the manorial records of Wimbledon, amerced for breaking rules on appropriating wood for fuel: P. H. Lawrence (ed.), *Extracts from the Court Rolls of the Manor of Wimbledon, extending from 1 Edward IV. to AD 1864* (London, 1866), 85. He was son-in-law of another of Cromwell's most trusted servants, Thomas Thacker: Thacker to Avery, 26 September 1537, SP 1/125 f. 30, *LP* 12 ii no. 751. **26.** For Cromwell's sponsorship of Wandsworth's promotion to Bodmin, see John Veysey Bishop of Exeter to Cromwell, 18 February *recte* 1534, SP 1/74 f. 168, *LP* 6 no. 169; for Wandsworth's lavish acknowledgement of what he owed Cromwell, Wandsworth to Cromwell, 23 February *recte* 1535, SP 1/82 f. 176, *LP* 7 no. 222. Prior Wandsworth was thoroughly enmeshed in the London mercantile community of evangelicals: see Wandsworth to William Lock, 28 May *recte* 1535, BL MS Cotton Cleopatra E/IV f. 139, *LP* 10 no. 981. Gerhold, *Thomas Cromwell and his Family*, 15–19, 28–9, provides the evidence of Walter Cromwell's move from Putney to Wandsworth soon after 1500, and he has made the important discovery that the fragment of will appended to Thomas Cromwell's own will, *LP* 4 iii no. 5772, can be identified as that of William Sharparow, 1526, TNA, PROB 11/22/130, who owned a mill at Wandsworth. **27.** For malicious Cornish reference to his links to Cromwell, Wandsworth to Cromwell, 21 July ?1536, SP 1/105 f. 95, *LP* 11 no. 133. **28.** E. Lord Herbert of Chirbury, *The Life and Raigne of King Henry the Eighth* (London, 1649, Wing H1504), 462.

Chapter 2: The Return of the Native

1. Eustace Chapuys to Nicolas de Granvelle, 21 November 1535, *Spanish Calendar* 5 i no. 228, at 568. 2. The first English translations of Bandello material were made by William Painter in 1566; the standard edition is M. Bandello, *The novels of Matteo Bandello Bishop of Agen now first done into English prose and verse*, ed. and trans. J. Payne (6 vols., London, 1890). The Italian original of this story can be found in M. Bandello, *Novelle*, ed. G. Mazzuchelli (9 vols., Milan, 1813–14), 5, at 227–46. On Bandello's opinion of Henry VIII, see M. Wyatt, *The Italian Encounter with England: a cultural politics of translation* (Cambridge, 2005), 66–7. 3. Bandello, *Novels of Matteo Bandello*, ed. and trans. Payne, 4, 103–16, abridged in Foxe 1570, 1396–7. On the alteration, cf. Bandello, *Novels of Matteo Bandello*, ed. and trans. Payne, 4, 107 with Foxe 1570, 1396. 4. Foxe adds (Foxe 1570, 1386) from recollections of Archbishop Cranmer conveyed to his secretary Ralph Morice that Cromwell had been 'in the wars of Duke Bourbon at the siege of Rome' [1527], which is chronologically impossible, and may result from misremembering the Duke of Bourbon's earlier Italian campaigns for France in the years following Garigliano – for instance, at the French siege of Genoa in 1507. That would make perfect sense alongside Bandello's story. 5. Bandello, *Novels of Matteo Bandello*, ed. and trans. Payne, 4, 107; Foxe 1570, 1396. 6. For Frescobaldi's plea to Cromwell, 4 October 1533, SP 1/79 f. 122, *LP* 6 no. 1215. I am grateful to Dr Simone Maghenzani for helping me with the Italian of this letter. 7. *Dizionario Biografico degli Italiani* (1960–, in progress), s.v. Frescobaldi, Francesco. In his letter to Cromwell of 4 October 1533, he called himself a young man. 8. Francesco Frescobaldi to [Wolsey], ?1529, SP 1/55 f. 142, *LP* 4 iii no. 5974, and cf. memoranda of 1519 on the debts owed by the Frescobaldi brothers to the Crown, SP 1/232 ff. 153–9, *LP Addenda* 1 i no. 238, or other copies of the same material at SP 1/18 ff. 18–21, *LP* 3 i no. 54, *LP* 3 i no. 54; SP 1/29 f. 166, *LP* 3 ii no. 3694, 1530. 9. On Dr Augustine's chequered career, see E. A. Hammond, 'Doctor Augustine, physician to Cardinal Wolsey and Henry VIII', *Medical History* 19 (1975), 215–49; for samples of his monotonous pleas to Cromwell for the payment of subventions as agreed via Frescobaldi, see SP 1/70 f. 170, *LP* 5 no. 1188 (22 July 1532); SP 1/70 f. 174, *LP* 5 no. 1197 (28 July 1532); BL MS Cotton Vitellius B/XIII f. 217, *LP* 5 no. 1413 (12 October 1532); BL MS Cotton Vitellius B/XIII f. 218, *LP* 5 no. 1422 (14 October 1532), BL MS Cotton Vitellius B./XIII f. 142, *LP* 6 no. 22 (5 January 1533). 10. T. Penn, *Winter King: the dawn of Tudor England* (London, 2011), 201–4, and see J. Finot, 'Le commerce de l'alun dans les pays-bas et la bulle encyclique du Pape Jules II en 1506', *Bulletin Historique et Philologique* (1902), 418–31. 11. C. Platt, *Medieval Southampton: the port and trading community*, A.D. 1000–1600 (London and Boston, 1973), 204, and ibid., 258 and *passim*, for references to the port's Italian trade. 12. A useful summary account of Huttoft is ibid., 244–5. On his son John's service to Cromwell, John Huttoft to Thomas Wriothesley, 20 August ?1537, SP 1/124 f. 64, *LP* 12 ii no. 546. 13. Henry Huttoft to Cromwell, 16 June 1535, SP 1/93 f. 77, *LP* 8 no. 878. 14. George Elyot, mercer, to

Cromwell, 28 June [1535], SP 1/104 f. 211, *LP* 10 no. 1218, misdated to 1536 by *LP*, but Dover Priory had been dissolved by then. Elyot dated his letter from Calais, but depositions relating to events in summer 1535 name him as a mercer of London: SP 1/99 f. 173v, *LP* 9 no. 1059.   **15.** For Hacket's thirty years in the Low Countries, see Stephen Vaughan to Cromwell, 7 December 1534, SP 1/87 f. 81, *LP* 7 no. 1515. Hacket was according to his wishes buried in Calais, and it may be that his surname should rightly be Hacquet. His letters are collected in E. F. Rogers (ed.), *The Letters of Sir John Hackett 1526–1534* (Morgantown, VA, 1971).   **16.** For Hacket's connection with the Frescobaldi, and Bernardo de' Pigli's claim on his estate, see Vaughan to Cromwell, 7 December 1534, SP 1/87 f. 81, *LP* 7 no. 1515. An English copy of Hacket's will, made on 26 October 1534, is SP 1/86 ff. 93–6, *LP* 7 no. 1309; Cromwell's fellow-executor was no less a figure than the Archbishop of Palermo, the leading figure in Habsburg administration in the Low Countries.   **17.** For one example of many, illustrating how Hacket's letters passed on a routine basis via Calais, see Hacket to Cromwell, 22 April 1533, SP 1/75 f. 156, *LP* 6 no. 372. For Stephen Vaughan's praise of Hacket, see Vaughan to Henry VIII and Cromwell, 26 January 1531, BL MS Cotton Galba B/X ff. 46–7, *LP* 5 no. 65[1, 2].   **18.** Foxe 1570, 1385.   **19.** TNA, C 1/482/33: complaint of Cromwell against Anthony Wells and William Thomas about a dispute in the regnal year 5 Henry VIII [1513–14].   **20.** Vaughan to Cromwell, 13 April 1536, SP 1/103 f. 122, *LP* 10 no. 663.   **21.** TNA, CP 40/1038 (Hilary Term 1523), mm. 263d, 595d: the gentleman defendant was Edward Fetyplace, whom we will meet again as an uneasy colleague of Cromwell's at Poughley Priory later the same decade.   **22.** On abuse of Cranmer, MacCulloch, *Thomas Cranmer*, 22, 169–70. For the 'shearman' trope from an Essex parson who had been in the North just before the Pilgrimage of Grace, see SP 1/116 f. 9, *LP* 12 i no. 407[2]; and for the same in a long poem against Cromwell by the friar Dr John Pickering from east Yorkshire in late 1536, SP 1/118 f. 292v, *LP* 12 i no. 1021[5].   **23.** Kaulek (ed.), *Correspondance*, 194: 'seulement Thomas Cramvell, tondeur de draps'. In practice, the King quickly drew back from this extreme, and even Cromwell's enemies such as Bishop Gardiner often could not help themselves referring to him as the Earl of Essex after his fall: cf. SP 1/161 f. 1, *LP* 15 no. 821[1].   **24.** S. Alford, *London's Triumph: Merchant Adventurers and the Tudor city* (London, 2017), 46–51.   **25.** Lisle to Cromwell, 17 June [1536], SP 3/9 f. 18, *Lisle Letters* 3 no. 727. For another Calais acquaintance, see Henry Lacy to Cromwell, 18 August 1522, SP 1/25 f. 117, *LP* 3 ii no. 2445; 30 April 1527, SP 1/41 ff. 179–80, *LP* 4 ii no. 3079. Laurence Giles of Calais was also important to him, and a man to introduce to friends: see *inter alia* John Croke at Calais to Cromwell, 16 July 1527, SP 1/235 f. 216, *LP Addenda* 1 i no. 539.   **26.** Katherine of Aragon wrote to Cromwell, 1 September 1534, SP 1/85 f. 135, *LP* 7 no. 1126, an extremely personal letter. Rather unusually in Cromwell's correspondence, he had the letter carefully and accurately translated into English, the fair copy of this being BL MS Cotton Otho C/X. f. 176, *LP* 7 no. 1126[2], but that may have been for the benefit of his fellow-councillors, or even for Katherine's royal husband. Cf. Chapuys's letter of farewell to Cromwell, 21 March 1539, SP 1/144 f. 153, *LP* 14 i no. 579: this is a notably friendly and informal note from a man who could now afford to relax at the end of many duels over the previous decade.   27. See the letter in Italian of Joachim Hochstetter of Augsburg to Cromwell, 24 August 1528, SP 1/50 ff. 23-49, *LP* 4 ii no. 4662[1]. Augustine to Cromwell, 16 May 1532, SP 1/70 f. 38, *LP* 5 no. 1027. For Ambassador Nicholas Hawkins's forwarding of a German pamphlet via Thomas Cranmer for Cromwell to find a translator, see Hawkins to Henry VIII, 21 November 1532, SP 1/72 f. 46, *LP* 5 no. 1564. A letter from Wolf Reittwiser to Cromwell, 26 November 1539, SP 1/155 f. 47, *LP* 14 ii no. 589, is nevertheless written in German and seems to be couched in personal terms as if its writer expected Cromwell to be able to read it.   28. Creke to Cromwell, 17 July 1522, SP 1/25 f. 55, *LP* 3 ii no. 2394. For the ongoing importance of Spain in Creke's life, see below, pp. 131-2.   29. Confidential final sentence: Morison to Cromwell, ?May 1537, BL MS Cotton Cleopatra E/VI ff. 323-4, *LP* 12 i no. 1311; see also Morison to Cromwell, ?1537, SP 1/127 f. 158, *LP* 12 ii no. 1330.   30. Edmund Bonner to Cromwell, ?April 1530, SP 1/57 f. 75, *LP* 4 iii no. 6346.   31. On Morley, see M. Axton and J. P. Carley (eds.), *'Triumphs of English': Henry Parker, Lord Morley, translator to the Tudor Court. New essays in interpretation* (London, 2000), 77-86.   32. Morley to Cromwell, 13 February s.a., SP 1/143 f. 74, *LP* 14 i no. 285, and useful contextual commentary in K. R. Bartlett, 'Morley, Machiavelli, and the Pilgrimage of Grace', in Axton and Carley (eds.), *'Triumphs of English': Henry Parker, Lord Morley*, 77-86. The dating of this letter is controversial: see discussion in Bartlett, 83 n. 2. I suggest that related correspondence of Morley to Cromwell, 18 January s.a., SP 1/114 f. 151, *LP* 12 i no. 128 and 25 March s.a., SP 1/117 f. 120, *LP* 12 i no. 728, has been wrongly dated to 1537, and that all these three letters are of 1538; the last item refers to the likelihood of the imminent suppression of Beeston Priory in Norfolk, which in fact took place in May or June 1538 (see Smith, 374). Nothing in any of the three letters precludes a date in early 1538.   33. A. J. Slavin, 'The Gutenberg galaxy and the Tudor revolution', in G. P. Tyson and S. S. Wagonheim (eds.), *Print and Culture in the Renaissance: essays on the advent of printing in Europe* (Newark, NJ, 1986), 90-109, at 95, and G. Parks, *The English Traveller to Italy* (2 vols., Rome, 1954).   34. On Collins as Bainbridge's nephew, and his and Cromwell's testimony in the Stratford Langthorne tithe case, see D. S. Chambers, *Cardinal Bainbridge in the Court of Rome 1509 to 1514* (Oxford, 1965), 77, 115-16.   35. Le Neve, *Fasti 1300-1541: Northern Province*, 15: he was admitted to the Treasurership by proxy on 5 May 1514 and in person on 14 November 1514, suggesting he had just returned from Rome then.   36. Lee to Cromwell, 14 April 1538, SP 1/131 f. 91, *LP* 13 i no. 762.   37. See Collins's testimony after the Pilgrimage, SP 1/118 f. 268r, *LP* 12 i no. 1018. Note also his reference to 'my late Lord' when writing to Cardinal Wolsey, Bainbridge's successor at York, 27 March 1529: SP 1/53 f. 130, *LP* 4 iii no. 5400.   38. TNA, C 244/163/92. A memorandum on the Empson family dated by *LP* to 1512 with a possible endorsement by Cromwell, SP 1/3 f. 73, *LP* 1 no. 1473, offers no proof of date at all, and probably relates to material in later legal cases involving the Empsons, e.g. TNA, C 1/512/71.   39. SP 1/53 f. 37v, *LP* 4 iii no. 5330, a summary record from 1529 or 'Dettes due unto me, Thomas

Crumwell, by statutes, billes, and obligations', and see below on the Ughtred transaction about Kexby, p. 596 n. 39. The same folio has a record of a slightly earlier bond in Cromwell's possession, between Robert Croxton and Thomas Barley, but that does not involve Cromwell himself. For Allen, the Archbishop and Alderman John Allen, see Thomas Allen to Cromwell, August 1534, SP 60/2 f. 57, *LP* 7 no. 1109.   40. A decline ably analysed in G. D. Ramsay, 'The undoing of the Italian mercantile colony in sixteenth century London', in N. B. Harte and K. G. Ponting (eds.), *Textile History and Economic History: essays in honour of Miss Julia de Lacy Mann* (Manchester, 1973), 22–49.   41. John Stow, *A Survey of London Reprinted from the Text of 1603*, ed. C. L. Kingsford (2 vols., Oxford, 1908), 1, 132. For Cromwell's Fenchurch residence in 1522–3, see Wm Popley to Cromwell (dwelling by Fenchurch), 15 January ?1522, SP 1/23 f. 271, *LP* 3 ii no. 1963; Thomas Twesell to Cromwell at Fenchurch London, 20 October 1522, SP 1/26 f.108, *LP* 3 ii no. 2624 .   42. SP 1/233 ff. 334–8, *LP Addenda* 1 i no. 400. For Antonio Duodo and Venice, see Duodo to Cromwell, 10 September 1535, BL MS Cotton Nero B/VII f. 110, *LP* 9 no. 327, and for an account of a colourful night out in which Duodo behaved very badly among his fellow-Italians, [unknown] to Cromwell, ?1533, SP 1/81 f. 148, *LP* 6 no. 1701.   43. This is part of the treatise which its eighteenth-century editor called *Apologia Reg. Poli ad Carolum V. Cæsarem* drastically summarized in *LP* 14 i no. 200 from *ERP* 1, 66–171, and to which we will return. Charles V was probably spared the pleasure of ever reading it. See *ERP* 1, 126–7 (sect. xxviii); repr. in Merriman 1, 18.   44. See correspondence concerning the travels of Wolsey's illegitimate son Thomas Winter, both 2 August 1532, Winter to Cromwell, SP 1/70 f. 182, *LP* 5 no. 1210, and Rullo himself to Cromwell, BL MS Harley 6989 f. 36, *LP* 5 no. 1211. On Rullo's career in heterodoxy, see below, pp. 72–3.   45. SP 1/21 f. 120rv, *LP* 3 i no. 1026 is a summons to the contending parties, the Prioress and Vicar of Cheshunt, to Rome in early December 1520. It is evident from later stages of papers, heavily corrected by Cromwell (SP 1/31 ff. 31–2, *LP* 4 i no. 368; SP 1/234 ff. 94–8, *LP Addenda* 1 i no. 427), that this document was exhibited in Chancery proceedings in 1524, and there is no suggestion in this case that Cromwell's involvement was in Rome itself; he was attorney in England for the Prioress.   46. R. N. Swanson, *Indulgences in Late Medieval England: passports to paradise?* (Cambridge, 2007), especially 172–4, 375–9. A good account of the workings of the Gild is [M. Finch] for Lincolnshire Archives Committee, 'A Boston guild account', *Archivists' Report* 16 (1 April 1964/31 March 1965), 40–43. BL MS Egerton 2886 is the Compotus book of the Gild of St Mary Boston 1514–1525; for later books, see [Finch], 'A Boston guild account', describing a further account book for 1525–6, and there are subsequent accounts for 1526–35 and 1536–8, now deposited at Lincolnshire Archives as 6-CHAR/2/1. I am indebted to Dr Rod Ambler for pointing me to these later volumes.   47. BL MS Egerton 2886 f. 101r itemizes the expenses of the clerk, William Hasill, including riding to Wolsey for the suspension of the pardon made by the Austin Friars.   48. BL MS Egerton 2886 f. 112r: part of the account of Thos Parowe, Gild Alderman Whitsun 9 Henry VIII [1517] to Whitsun 10 Henry VIII [1518].   49. Foxe 1570, 1385. Foxe also made a gratuitous link in his account to

Chamber meeting Cromwell in Antwerp; Foxe probably added this with the aim
of connecting his narrative, whereas the Boston accounts make clear that Cromwell travelled to Rome via Calais.   50. There has been much confusion in dating
this trip, beginning with John Foxe repeatedly putting it in 1510. The reality can
be reconstructed from entries in BL MS Egerton 2886, first at f. 125r, which specifies the size of Cromwell's fee. Being in the account for 1518–19, it can only refer
to a journey in that accounting year, since the full account by Geoffrey Chamber
(ibid. f. 181rv) covers the whole Rome enterprise over three years between Whitsun 1517 and Whitsun 1520, and it specifies two journeys to Rome, the first of
which was undertaken by Chamber and his servants alone and not in company
with Cromwell, and that must have been in 1517 (less likely early 1518).   51. SP
1/232 f. 199, *LP Addenda* 1 i no. 267. Sixteen years later Stephen Vaughan referred
to the widowed Mistress Addington as Cromwell's 'great friend': Vaughan to
Cromwell, 10 September 1535, BL MS Cotton Titus B/I f. 345, *LP* 9 no. 330.   52.
Swanson, *Indulgences in Late Medieval England*, 375.   53. Foxe 1570, 1385–6.
54. The Austin Friars' indulgence is *RSTC* 14077c.1.   55. John Robinson to
Cromwell, s.a., SP 1/27 f. 286, *LP* 3 ii no. 3015. John Robinson was Alderman of
the Gild between Whitsun 1519 and Whitsun 1523, and was responsible as Alderman for printing costs in the accounts between those years; he was answering a
letter from Cromwell of 5 May s.a., yet was unlikely to be replying to it as late as
12 June 1519, which was Whitsun in that year.   56. BL MS Egerton 2886 ff.
264v–265v, in the account of Geoffrey Chamber as Secretary for the year ending
Thursday in Whitsun Week 16 Henry VIII [1524]. Cromwell is also found drafting
a letter from Wolsey to an unidentified bishop in the Gild's favour, which is likely
to date from after he entered the Cardinal's service in 1524: SP 1/235 ff. 32–5, *LP
Addenda* 1 i no. 471.   57. On regular gifts of ling, see Richard Tomyou to Cromwell, 18 August 1536, SP 1/106 f. 17, *LP* 11 no. 321. On wildfowl gifts, see e.g.
John Williamson to Cromwell, 4 November [1532], SP 1/72 f. 13, *LP* 5 no. 1512;
Robert Tomlynson, Alderman of Our Lady's Gild in Boston to Cromwell, 29 May
1533, SP 1/76 f. 119, *LP* 6 no. 554; John Wendon to Cromwell, 8 January 1534/6,
SP 1/89 f. 16, *LP* 8 no. 29; Nicholas Robertson to Cromwell, 4 May 1538, SP 1/132
f. 26, *LP* 13 i no. 925. Cromwell does not seem to have been involved in the Gild's
next major negotiation with Wolsey and Archbishop Warham for a papal bull of
confirmation in 1525: [Finch], 'A Boston guild account', 43.   58. G. Byng, 'The
contract for the north aisle at the church of St James, Biddenham', *Antiquaries
Journal* 95 (2015), 251–65; Byng discusses TNA, E41/318, which is a draft contract dated 16 December 1522, in the same hand (a clerk of Cromwell's) as a
petition drafted for Somer in the early 1520s: SP 1/2342 f. 25, *LP Addenda* 1 i no.
429[2].   59. Foxe 1583, 1231. For Somer's friendship with Cromwell, see an
unknown correspondent from the Middle Temple to Cromwell, early 1530s, SP
1/88 ff. 42–3, *LP* 7 no. 1618, writing after Somer's death.   60. F. Blomefield and
C. Parkin, *An Essay towards a Topographical History of the County of Norfolk . . .* (11 vols., London, 1805–10), 9, 488, provides an alternative pedigree for
Cromwell's wife then in the possession of Blomefield, which could be compatible
with this possibility: 'he is said to have married *Elizabeth*, a daughter and coheir

of *John Prior*, (widow of *Thomas Williams*,) by *Isabel* his wife, daughter of *Richard* Lord *Talbot*, which *John* was son of Sir *John Prior*, by *Joan* his wife, daughter of *Edward Grey*, 2d son of *Reginald* Lord *Grey* of *Rutheyn*, and bore for his arms, *azure*, a bend, per pale, *gules*, and *or*, in a bordure ingrailed, counterchanged.' That might also explain Cromwell's undoubted relationship to the Williams family of Oxfordshire. This pedigree does name the mother as Isabel, and it goes on to make a mistake about Cromwell's later peerage title, so doubts remain.   61. Henry Wykes to 'my faithful cousin' Cromwell, 2 November [?1523], SP 1/29 f. 26, *LP* 3 ii no. 3502. The only other trace of him in Cromwell's papers is a letter asking a favour for a friend, calling on Cromwell's affection for Surrey and signing himself 'your servant and bedeman': Wykes to Cromwell, 29 January 1539 (not 1538 as in *LP*), SP 1/128 f. 136, *LP* 13 i no. 172. On the Wykes family at Thorpe, see *VCH: Surrey* 3, 437–40. Lawrence (ed.), *Extracts from the Court Rolls of the Manor of Wimbledon*, 87, records John Wykes among the court homage in Henry VIII's time.   62. She can be seen to have her own chamber at f. 102v in the inventory of Cromwell's house at Austin Friars taken in 1527, SP 1/42 ff. 101–16, *LP* 4 ii no. 3197. *LP* suggests that at f. 113r there is also a reference to the chamber of 'Mr' Prior, but this is a misreading of a rather faded and indistinct word; the page is in a secondary hand to the main writer of the inventory and patently replaces the much altered inventory of Mistress Prior's chamber at f. 102v. The contents of both lists are what one would expect a lady of the house to concern herself with: almost entirely household linen (plus in the latter case a couple of altar frontals).   63. Morison to Cromwell, probably summer 1536, SP 1/113 f. 181, *LP* 11 no. 1481, and earlier note e.g. the Cambridgeshire farmer William Cowper to Cromwell, 5 June ?1525, SP 1/34 f. 232, *LP* 4 i no. 1385, who asks 'my mistress your mother for another plaster for my knee'. Stephen Vaughan to Cromwell, 15 December 1528, SP 1/51 f. 105, *LP* 4 ii no. 5034.   64. Cromwell's accounts, 29 December 1539, *LP* 14 ii no. 782, at 344: 'Mistress Pryour, by Mr. Gregory, 40s.'.   65. The names of Anne and Grace are erased from the original text of Cromwell's will of summer 1529, SP 1/54 ff. 234–44, Merriman 1, 56–63. Nothing absolutely specific proves that the daughters were younger than Gregory, but there were no moves to get them married off in the 1520s, which if the marriage had taken place early in the 1510s might well have started in 1528–9. The original text of the will speaks of 'my little daughter Grace' (SP 1/54 f. 240v), but just 'my son Gregory', suggesting that she is younger than Gregory, but both girls get the same legacies: not just 100 marks for marriage when they come of lawful age to be married, but also £40 for providing for them till then, suggesting that they are not far apart in age, with Anne slightly older.   66. Elizabeth's death is likely to have been in February or early March 1529, as Stephen Vaughan refers to money in Mistress Prior's custody, suggesting that her daughter was dead by then: Vaughan to Cromwell, 23 March [1529], SP 1/53 f. 128, *LP* 4 iii no. 5398. Then two correspondents in April 1529 send Cromwell good wishes for finding a new wife: Eleanor Scrope to Cromwell, 6 April [1529], SP 1/236 f. 76, *LP Addenda* 1 i no. 639; Edward Lewkenor to Cromwell, 13 April 1529, SP 1/236 f. 77, *LP Addenda* 1 i no. 640. His daughters were evidently still alive when he first drafted his will in summer 1529.   67. The first culprit in print, basing himself on 'the research of J. S. Brewer', seems to be W. F. Hook, *Lives of the Archbishops of Canterbury* (12 vols., London, 1860–76), 6, 122.   68. See Merriman 1, 11–12, and his particularly crass remarks on Gregory at 53–4. For detailed reappraisals, see M. C. Erler, *Reading and Writing during the Dissolution: monks, friars and nuns 1530–1558* (Cambridge, 2013), 88–106, and T. Fitzgerald and D. MacCulloch, 'Gregory Cromwell: two portrait miniatures by Hans Holbein the Younger', *JEH* 67 (2016), 587–601.   69. In 1536 Gregory Williams, named as Cromwell's nephew, was put into possession of two benefices on Anglesey by local ecclesiastical officials: Sir Richard Bulkeley to Cromwell, 17 December 1536, SP 1/112 f. 218, *LP* 11 no. 1329. The fact that Sir Richard's brother Prebendary Arthur Bulkeley was resisting this move may suggest that Gregory Williams was still young enough to raise questions as to whether he was suitable to hold the benefices.   70. P. Hayward, 'Gregory the Great as "Apostle of the English" in post-Conquest Canterbury', *JEH* 55 (2004), 19–57.   71. Cf. John Williamson to Cromwell, 15 October 1532, SP 1/71 ff. 110–11, *LP* 5 no. 1435, with Williamson to Cromwell, 16 August 1535, SP 1/95 f. 89, *LP* 9 no. 105.   72. Thomas Cromwell's will of 12 July 1529, SP 1/54 ff. 234–47, *LP* 4 iii no. 5772, refers to his late wife's sister Joan, wife to John Williamson. John's children were numbered among Cromwell's 'poor kinsfolk' in his will. For outline details of family relationships, see Merriman 1, 5.   73. *LP* 4 ii no. 3403: an indenture with Wellifed's deputy Thomas Maneryng, 6 September; Wellifed had custody of Lambeth Palace alongside his office as chief cook. On the cook, Merriman 1, 17, translates Eustace Chapuys to Nicolas de Granvelle, 21 November 1535, *Spanish Calendar* 5 i no. 228, at 568, though Chapuys muddies the waters with an apparent reference to Richard Williams alias Cromwell as son of this cook; Morgan Williams, Richard's father, was Cromwell's brother-in-law.   74. Christopher Wellifed's preferments or hoped-for preferments are too numerous to list here. For his arrival at the King's Hall, see Christopher Wellifed to Cromwell, 26 January ?1535, SP 1/89 f. 64, *LP* 8 no. 107.   75. Burke, *General Armory*, 246, s.v. Cromwell of Hinchingbrooke. For 'Mr Morgan', see William Brabazon to Cromwell, 14 August ?1528, SP 1/55 f. 45, *LP* 4 iii no. 5849.   76. J. Leland, *The itinerary of John Leland in or about the years 1535–1543*, ed. L. Toulmin Smith (5 vols., repr. London, 1964), 3, 17.   77. The evidence for Walter's change of name comes only from the later 1530s: *LP* 13 ii no. 119/2, 17 August 1538, and Thomas Legh to Thomas Cromwell, 3 September 1538, SP 1/136 f. 70, *LP* 13 ii no. 275.   78. Henry Sadler to Ralph Sadler, 16 December 1529, BL MS Cotton Titus B/I f. 163, *LP* 5 no. 584. *LP* misdates this letter to 1531, but it has to be 1529; the Marquess of Dorset mentioned in it, together with his wife, died on 10 October 1530, at which time his young son was unmarried. Richard was still called Williams in Thomas Cromwell's will in summer 1529.   79. See the jovial remarks about Richard's household in Thomas Brooke (Thomas Cromwell's gentleman servant) to Cromwell, 24 August 1535, SP 1/95 f. 159, *LP* 9 no. 172, and same to same, 11 September 1535, SP 1/96 f. 134, *LP* 9 no. 345.   80. On this, see below, pp. 172–3.   81. Thomas Cromwell's coat was *azure on a fess between three lions rampant or, a rose gules between two Cornish choughs proper,* the fess and charges thereon being the tribute to Wolsey; for further discussion of the heraldry, see below, pp. 427–8. Interestingly, his coat makes no reference to the heraldry of the Meverells of Throwley: *or, a griffin segreant sable*. For these blazons, see Burke, *General Armory*, 246. 82. *Gules, 3 chevronels argent between as many lions rampant or* (in some cases, the colours/metals are reversed; see Burke, *General Armory*, 246, s.v. Cromwell, alias Williams, and Cromwell of Hinchingbrooke). 83. *LP* 5 no. 1065(33): 17–27 May 1532. For an introductory letter explaining the customs of the lordship and its overlordship, Sir William Morgan (a relative of Morgan Williams?) to Cromwell, 21 November 1532, SP 1/72 f. 44, *LP* 5 no. 1562. 84. On 21 December 1523, Cromwell was a signatory to and one of the scribes for an inquest of wardmote in Broad Street ward, which includes Austin Friars: SP 1/29 ff. 117–22, *LP* 3 ii no. 3657. A list of Cromwell's papers in 1524 includes the bill of Thomas Smith, 'for the house in Fanchurche' and four acquittances 'for this my howse': SP 1/32 f. 234r, *LP* 4 i no. 955. For the accusations in the Attainder Act, see Chapter 22. 85. Cromwell's building programme at Austin Friars and the medieval background are admirably analysed in N. Holder, 'The medieval friaries of London: a topographic and archaeological history, before and after the Dissolution' (University of London PhD, 2011), ch. 5. 86. Ibid., 142. 87. On Cavalcanti and the financial scandal and collapse in morale at Austin Friars in Bellond's time, see F. X. Roth (ed.), *The English Austin Friars 1248–1538 2: The Sources* (*Augustiniana* supplement, 1961), no. D1032. I am very grateful to Dr Anik Laferrière for leading me to this latter material. On Cromwell, see below, p. 62. 88. The commission was made in 1526, while Cromwell was resident at Austin Friars. For an excellent account of the Austin Friars, Italian connection, see C. M. Sicca, 'Consumption and trade of art between Italy and England in the first half of the sixteenth century: the London house of the Bardi and Cavalcanti company', *Renaissance Studies* 16 (2002), 163–201, especially on this point at 187. She points out, 170, that Nunziata had come to London in 1519 in connection with the projected tomb for Henry VIII. 89. E. L. Blackburn, *An architectural and historical account of Crosby Place, London* (London, 1834), 51–4. 90. D. Baker-Smith, 'Antonio Buonvisi and Florens Wilson: a European friendship', *Moreana* 43 (2006), 82–108, usefully modifies the account in C. T. Martin, rev. B. Morgan, in *ODNB*, s.v. Bonvisi, Antonio. 91. Sicca, 'Consumption and trade of art between Italy and England', 172. 92. On Cromwell and Casali, see below, pp. 277–8. 93. On Gigli and Ghinucci and their relationship with Wolsey, see Wyatt, *Italian Encounter with England*, 58–9. For one example among many of Ghinucci's pleas to Cromwell, which also stresses Ghinucci's contacts through his nephew Dr Augustine, Ghinucci to Cromwell, 27 December 1532, BL MS Harley 6989 f. 17, *LP* 5 no. 1666. For his relationship with Buonvisi, Ghinucci to Cromwell, 28 June 1535, SP 1/93 f. 150, *LP* 8 no. 940, and for his admirably generous reaction to his deprivation by Henry VIII as Bishop, John Boroughbridge to Cromwell, 26 May 1535, SP 1/92 f. 171, *LP* 8 no. 763. 94. M. Everett, *The Rise of Thomas Cromwell: power and politics in the reign of Henry VIII* (New Haven and London, 2015), 27, lists the relevant letters. 95. On Popley as courier, see *Lisle Letters* 2, no. 277, and on Salisbury, SP 1/32 f. 36, *LP* 4 i no. 611, wrongly dated by *LP* to 1524, but redateable to 1517–18 via

Le Neve, *Fasti 1300–1541: Salisbury*, 62. On Knight, see *ODNB*, s.v. Knight, William.   96. C. M. Sicca, 'Fashioning the Tudor Court', in M. Hayward and E. Kramer (eds.), *Textiles and Text: re-establishing the links between archival and object-based research* (London, 2007), 93–104, at 98.   97. Wyatt, *Italian Encounter with England*, 50.   98. I am indebted to Dr Susan Brigden for letting me know of her so far unpublished research on the Bardi/Cavalcanti papers in the Archivio di Stato in Florence, revealing the social contacts of the Bardi/Cavalcanti at Austin Friars. On Wyatt's relationship with Sir Henry Guildford see S. Brigden, *Thomas Wyatt: the heart's forest* (London, 2012), 173–6.   99. For a detailed discussion of this function of the London Austin Friars, see A. Laferrière, 'The Austin Friars in pre-Reformation English society' (University of Oxford DPhil, 2017), ch. 4.   100. On this, see S. Brigden, *London and the Reformation* (Oxford, 1989), 153–5.   101. John Gough to Cromwell, 24 March probably 1532, SP 1/69 f. 189, *LP* 5 no. 896. Richard Williams alias Cromwell, writing to Lord Lisle on 11 May 1535, calls Gough his 'cousin and kinsman', which would suggest that he was a Welshman like ap Reynold: SP 3/2 f. 156, *Lisle Letters* 2 no. 388.   102. On the debt, see two letters of ap Reynold to Cromwell, SP 1/73 ff. 131–2, *LP* 5 no. 1756[1, 2]. For later good turns by Cromwell to ap Reynold in 1534–5, see ap Reynold to Cromwell, SP 1/92 f. 121, *LP* 8 no. 668, and SP 1/84 f. 168, *LP* 7 no. 830, and Sir Thomas Palmer's letter of thanks to Cromwell on ap Reynold's behalf, 16 October probably 1535, SP 1/98 f. 18, *LP* 9 no. 623.   103. SP 1/22 ff. 106–60, *LP* 3 ii no. 1289. Knyvett's protection as a member of the Calais retinue is SP 1/22 f. 160r, *LP* 3 ii no. 1289[7]. He was a debtor to Cromwell in a bond payable on 1 August 1527: SP 1/53 ff. 43r and 45v, *LP* 4 iii no. 5330.   104. Aubrey, *Natural history and antiquities of Surrey*, 5, 236.   105. SP 1/162 ff. 83–92 at f. 88v, *LP* 15 no. 1029/6, 512. The Marquess's arms do not appear in two copies of a second inventory of the same hall made soon afterwards in the late 1520s, the original of them dated to 1527 (SP 1/42 ff. 101–16, *LP* 4 ii no. 3197; SP 1/243 ff. 70–88, *LP* Addenda 1 ii no. 1467, the latter there wrongly thought to be another part of that in SP 1/162). The former inventory in SP 1/162 is damaged and incomplete, so the absence of Wolsey's arms in it is not significant; in any case it also certainly postdates Cromwell's entry into Wolsey's service in 1525, since at f. 86r it refers to 'a cloth stained with a table of the taking of the French King [at the battle of Pavia, February 1525]'.   106. The items are first Cromwell, holograph, to Margaret Marchioness of Dorset, April 1523, SP 1/41 f. 160v, *LP* 4 ii no. 3053[ii]. Cromwell has confused historians in this letter by mentioning an incorrect date, Wednesday 17 April, which has pointed readers to 1527, the only such date in the 1520s. However, the letter refers to the Marquess's Scottish expedition, which took place in April 1523 (the Marquess was elsewhere in April 1527). What seems to have happened is that Cromwell wrote on Thursday 16 April 1523, and in correcting his initial reference to 'yesterday' to a specific day, Wednesday, inadvertently projected *tomorrow's* Friday 17 April on to *yesterday*, Wednesday 15 April. The second item is Cecily Dowager Marchioness of Dorset to Cromwell, Thursday before the Assumption [13 August 1523], BL MS Cotton Vespasian F XIII, f. 173, *LP* 3 ii no. 2437. This letter can be no later than 1523, as Cromwell had entered Wolsey's service by August 1524, but it can be no earlier than 1523, since

Cecily Bonvile's second husband the Earl of Wiltshire died on 6 April 1523, and only after his death would she have reverted (as she did) to styling herself Cecily Dorset, ignoring Wiltshire's title. See *Complete Peerage* 4, 419 and n.   107. For 'Mr Morgan ... with the Marquess of Dorset', William Brabazon to Cromwell, 14 August ?1528, SP 1/55 f. 45, *LP* 4 iii no. 5849. For Richard and Dorset, SP 1/54 f. 238v, *LP* 4 iii no. 5772; when Cromwell's will was revised in 1530–32, an alteration shows that Richard had left the service of the Greys.   108. Lord George Grey to Cromwell, Friday before Whitsunday 1527 or 1528, SP 1/53 f. 258, *LP* 4 iii no. 5542. The letter refers to Sir John Allen as Alderman, whereas he was knighted in his year as Lord Mayor 1525–6, and Friday before Whitsunday 1526 would have been in his mayoralty. The threeway involvement of Lord George with Cromwell and Alderman Allen mentioned in the letter must relate to two bonds also involving the three of them catalogued among debts owing to Cromwell's in SP 1/53 f. 49v, *LP* 4 iii no. 5330, none of which is later than February 1529.   109. John Grey to 'my good frende' Cromwell, 12 January [1526], SP 1/37 f. 6, *LP* 4 i no. 1881, dateable to 1526 by its reference to the dissolution of Tickford and Ravenstone priories. On his later part in Cromwell's story, see below, p. 369.   110. Lord Leonard Grey to Cromwell, 24 May [1532], SP 1/70 f. 56, *LP* 5 no. 1049; see below, especially p. 329.   111. Lady Cecily Dudley to Cromwell, 24 February 1538, SP 1/141 ff. 211–12, *LP* 13 ii Appendix no. 6.   112. Edward Dudley to Cromwell: 3 June 1536, SP 1/104 ff. 106–7, *LP* 10 no. 1045 (3 June [1536]); 20 December 1537, SP 1/241 ff. 250–51, *LP Addenda* 1 i no. 1276. This last should be read alongside Edward Dudley to Thomas Wriothesley, 20 December 1537, SP 1/141 ff. 213–14, *LP* 13 ii Appendix no. 6[2].   113. Lord Leonard Grey to Cromwell, 31 October [1536]: SP 60/3 f. 169, *LP* 11 no. 933.   114. Lord Leonard Grey to Cromwell, 1 April 1538, SP 60/6 f. 82, *LP* 13 i no. 653, and several other references put Budgegood in Cromwell's and Richard Cromwell's service by 1536: cf. e.g. Budgegood to Cromwell, 26 March 1536, SP 1/103 f. 33, *LP* 10 no. 567. He was being called the Dowager Marchioness's servant in 1533: Charles Duke of Suffolk to Margaret Marchioness of Dorset, 28 July [1533], SP 1/82 f. 138, *LP* 7 no. 153[2]. On his previous service to the Marquess, see the Marquess's will of 1530, TNA, PROB 11/24 ff. 72v–76r, and Budgegood's own reminiscence of his service in France with the Marquess in 1512, *LP* 14 i no. 186[iii].   115. On his flight to Italy: e.g. Budgegood to Cromwell, 26 September [1538], SP 1/137 f. 30, *LP* 13 ii no. 433; Alban Hyll to Cromwell, 25 October 1538, SP 1/138 f. 9, *LP* 13 ii no. 694; the reports of the many eyes following his adventures are circumstantially confirmed in his own report to papal officials from prison, 29 December 1538, *LP* 14 i no. 1.   116. There is a summary of Cromwell's involvement, not always correctly dated, in 'Houses of Cistercian monks: abbey of Tilty', in *VCH: Essex* 2, 134–6.   117. Cf. e.g. Henry Sadler (from Tilty) to Ralph Sadler 'dwellynge with Master Crumwell', 16 December [1529], BL MS Cotton Titus B/I f. 163, *LP* 5 no. 584; on dating, see p. 592, n. 78 above. The year 1529 represented a low ebb in the Marquess of Dorset's fortunes, before his final acquisition of great wealth sadly only just before his death in 1530.   118. Margaret Marchioness of Dorset to Cromwell, 4 February [1534], SP 1/82 ff. 136–7, *LP* 7 no. 153[1]. Later, in 1537 or 1538, the Dowager Marchioness also entrusted her younger son Lord Thomas to the now ennobled Cromwell's service and protection: Marchioness of Dorset to Cromwell, 24 January [1538], SP 1/128 f. 117, *LP* 13 i no. 136, and 8 February 1538, SP 1/129 ff. 12–13, *LP* 13 i no. 231 (see in that letter her special appeal to Cromwell 'who hath always borne so good heart towards my Lord my late husband'). **119.** John Guy, 'Wolsey and the Parliament of 1523', in Cross, Loades and Scarisbrick (eds.), *Law and Government under the Tudors*, 1–18, at 15–16, argues that Cromwell's speech might be seen as a plant for Wolsey's covert strategy of avoiding a French campaign and invading Scotland. It is a fine balance, but I suspect that this is over-subtle. **120.** On the Marquess's financial, political and legal troubles, see *ODNB*, s.v. Grey, Thomas, second Marquess of Dorset. **121.** SP 1/41 f. 157r, *LP* 4 ii no. 3053[iv]. SP 1/235 ff. 203–5, *LP Addenda* 1 i no. 532, are adroit redraftings by Cromwell of the Parliamentary bill turning it into a petition to the King's Council. **122.** SP 1/233 ff. 315–16, *LP Addenda* 1 i no. 396: draft lease of lands in the Barony of Egremont, 22 December 1523, in the hand of Cromwell's clerk, with some corrections by him. **123.** Other aristocratic patrons would have been involved there, respectively the great rivals the Barons Dacre and Clifford Earls of Westmorland. Another straw in the wind is that Sir Christopher Dacre, one of the knights of the shire for Cumberland in 1523, was a cousin of and friendly with the Lees or Leghs, a northern clan who included Cromwell's longstanding friends and colleagues Dr Roland Lee and Dr Thomas Lee: see Sir Christopher Dacre to Cromwell, 28 September 1533, SP 1/79 f. 78, *LP* 6 no. 1167. **124.** All currently known information on the membership of the 1523 Parliament is summed up in *HC 1509–1558* 1, 29–164. Bristol was the first urban community spontaneously to appoint Cromwell to office, as Recorder in succession to his friend Lord Chief Justice Sir John Fitzjames: William Appowell to Cromwell, 8 August ?1533, SP 1/78 f. 97, *LP* 6 no. 956. Cromwell and his clerk were responsible for formulating two bills concerning London livery companies, the Glaziers and the Skinners (the latter against the Skinners' leadership), neither of which succeeded in the form proposed: see Guy, 'Wolsey and the Parliament of 1523', 11–12. The draft bills are SP 1/233 ff. 291–5, *LP Addenda* 1 i nos 384–5. **125.** Cromwell to Creke, 17 August 1523, SP 1/28 f. 154, *LP* 3 ii no. 3249. **126.** G. R. Elton, 'The political creed of Thomas Cromwell', in Elton, *Studies* 2, 224. **127.** The letter, properly dated only in the last thirty years, is Sir Richard Cornwall to Cromwell, 28 September [1523], SP 1/55 f. 129, *LP* 4 iii no. 5962. For the redating and an explanation of the 'business', see *HC 1509–1558* 1, 705–6. **128.** For excellent comment on the background, see A. Hawkyard, *The House of Commons 1509–1558: personnel, procedure, precedent and change* (Parliamentary History: Texts and Studies 12, 2016), especially 3–5, and on More's rueful exchange with Cardinal Wolsey, ibid., 209.

Chapter 3: In the Cardinal's Service: 1524–1528

1. P. J. Ward, 'The origins of Thomas Cromwell's public career: service under

Cardinal Wolsey and Henry VIII, 1524–30' (London School of Economics PhD, 1999), efficiently disposes of attempts to land Cromwell in Wolsey's service in earlier years (in chs. 1 and 2). Within the bounds it sets itself, Ward's excellent thesis is a reliable guide to these years, particularly valuable in its meticulous listing and analysis of documents relating to Wolsey involving Cromwell, 1524–30, ibid., 246–316. 2. S. Thurley, 'The domestic building works of Cardinal Wolsey', in S. Gunn and P. G. Lindley (eds.), *Cardinal Wolsey: Church, state and art* (Cambridge, 1991), 76–102, at 80. The Robert Cromwell in Wolsey's household (alongside a John Cromwell) after the Rector of Battersea's death in 1517 has to be a younger and less significant member of the family: see J. G. Taylor, *Our Lady of Batersey: the story of Battersea church and parish . . .* (London, 1925), 401, and *LP* 4 ii no. 2972 and *LP* 4 iii no. 6185. 3. G. Cavendish, *The Life of Cardinal Wolsey*, ed. S. W. Singer (2nd edn, London, 1827), 67. On the benefice, see *ODNB*, s.v. Wolsey, Thomas. 4. On Allen, see *ODNB*, s.v. Alen, John. One of the most remarkable clusters of connections is that between Dorset, Thomas Cromwell, Richard Cromwell, Dr John Allen and Roger Beverley, a former abbot of Tilty. In 1529/30 Beverley was induced by the second Marquess of Dorset to resign his abbacy, and as a secular priest may have become schoolmaster to the third Marquess, before he accompanied Allen to Dublin as Archbishop's chaplain, and found himself destitute after Allen's murder. All this can be reconstructed from John Palmer Abbot of Tilty to Cromwell, late 1533 or early 1534, SP 1/88 f. 91, *LP* 7 no. 1658; Margaret Marchioness of Dorset to Cromwell, 10 April [1534], SP 1/69 f. 216, *LP* 5 no. 926; Roger Beverley to Thomas Cromwell, 17 May 1535, SP 60/2 f. 113, *LP* 8 no. 728; Roger Beverley to Richard Cromwell, 18 May 1535, SP 60/2 f. 115, *LP* 8 no. 729. 5. SP 1/31 f. 72, *LP* 4 i no. 388 7/2–4, which are records of these conveyances on 1–3 March, following on from SP 1/31 f. 72, *LP* 4 i no. 388 7/1, Allen's purchase of the manor of Kexby (Yorks.) from Sir Robert Ughtred, 19 February 1524. Cromwell seems to have been arranging all this, judging from the costs of the recovery in Common Pleas recorded at SP 1/31 ff. 58–9, *LP* 4 i no. 388[1]. For further discussion of this material, see Ward, 'Origins of Thomas Cromwell's public career', 25–9. It is interesting to note that thirteen years later Cromwell's son Gregory married the widow of Sir Anthony Ughtred, Sir Robert's son. 6. [T. Wolsey], *Rudimenta grammatices et docendi methodus, non tam scholae Gypsuichianae per reuerendissimum D. Thoma[m] cardinale[m] Ebor. feliciter institutae q[uam] o[mn]ibus aliis totius Anglie scholis prescripta* (Southwark, 1529 etc., *RSTC* 5542.3). 7. Wolsey to Cromwell, February 1530, Bodl. MS Jesus College 74 f. 193v, completing the loss of this part of the text in BL MS Cotton Appendix XLVIII f. 18, *LP* 4 iii no. 6204, printed as far as it goes in *State Papers* 1, 354. Wolsey repeated the phrase in instructions to Ralph Sadler for Cromwell: Bodl. MS Jesus College 74 f. 192r. 8. Cromwell witnessed Wallingford Priory's surrender (for the time being abortive) on 19 April 1524, so in itself that indicates that he must have been taken on no later than March: *LP* 4 i no. 1137. On Wallingford's faltering end, see Smith, 154; Ward, 'Origins of Thomas Cromwell's public career', 64n, puts its surrender in 1525, and while some evidence might seem to suggest that, the dates of the various promotions of heads of house with evidence provided by Smith, 499, 502, puts it fairly securely in 1524.   9. Everett, *Rise of Thomas Cromwell*, 36 and nn.   10. S. Gunn, *Henry VII's New Men and the Making of Tudor England* (Oxford, 2016), 221–3, provides a good summary of the Monteagle affair; for Cromwell's pension from Hussey (an irony in view of his later role in Hussey's downfall in 1537), see ibid., 303. See the roll call of combatants in the articles of agreement, Cromwell among them, 2 June apparently 1528, SP 1/59 ff. 106–7v, *LP* 4 iii Appendix no. 109.   11. There is a securely dated letter of congratulation on 'your good promotion that I hear of through the favour of My Lord's Grace' from Henry Lacy of Calais to Cromwell, going out of its way to address him as 'my Lord Cardinal's servant and of his Council', 30 April 1527, SP 1/41 f. 179, *LP* 4 ii no. 3079.   12. The tomb is admirably discussed in P. Lindley, 'Playing check-mate with royal majesty? Wolsey's patronage of Italian Renaissance sculpture', in Gunn and Lindley (eds.), *Cardinal Wolsey*, 261–85.   13. Bodl. MS Jesus College 74 ff. 189r–191r, *LP* 4 iii no. 5743[I and II]; discussed with transcript as Appendices III and IV in A. Higgins, 'On the work of Florentine sculptors in England in the early part of the sixteenth century: with special reference to the tombs of Cardinal Wolsey and King Henry VIII', *Archaeological Journal* 51 (1894), 129–220, 367–70. Since then, this correspondence has been curiously neglected by historians, surely not because the key letter is in Latin and left without translation in *LP*. Lindley, 'playing check-mate with royal majesty?', 264, follows *LP*'s mistake in the date of Rovezzano's letter; it is 31 January 1530.   14. See the letter from Cavallari's widow Helen to Cromwell, probably early 1530, SP 1/52 f. 64, *LP* 4 ii no. 5120.   15. 'virum magni ingenii maximæque dexteritatis': Bodl. MS Jesus College 74 f. 189r.   16. Helen Cavallari to Cromwell, probably early 1530, SP 1/52 f. 64, *LP* 4 ii no. 5120; same (now Helen Wryne) to Cromwell, ?late 1536, SP 1/113 f. 203, *LP* 11 no. 1497.   17. Cavendish, *Life of Wolsey*, ed. Singer, 258.   18. John Bigges, 'To the right worshipful Master Cromwell, with my lord Cardinal's grace abiding' (so Bigges had no idea where Cromwell actually lived), 13 April [1525], SP 1/235 f. 53, *LP Addenda* 1 i no. 485. Bigges wrote to Cromwell 'as yet unacquainted'. *LP* puts this letter in 1526, but there is no evidence of the monastic dissolution programme being active in April 1526, whereas it was at its height around April 1525, and Bigges was actively interested in the process of suppression.   19. Thomas Bennet to Wolsey, 4 March 1525, SP 1/34 f. 34, *LP* 4 i no. 1150.   20. Bigges to Cromwell, 13 April [1525], SP 1/235 f. 53, *LP Addenda* 1 i no. 485. For the relationship of Bishop and corporation, see also Nicholas Shaxton Bishop of Salisbury to Cromwell, 3 July 1537, SP 1/241 f. 106, *LP Addenda* 1 i no. 1235.   21. For an example of Cromwell's negotiations with Campeggio's officials in Salisbury diocese, one of them being his brother Marc'Antonio Campeggio, see Thomas Byrd to Cromwell, 1 September 1528, SP 1/50 f. 64, *LP* 4 ii no. 4690. Another obvious Wolsey appointee via Campeggio was Sir Thomas Heneage as episcopal Steward, an office held during the Bishop's pleasure: see Bishop Shaxton to [Sir Robert] Tyrwhitt, 29 May 1536, SP 1/104 f. 67, *LP* 10 no. 986.   22. See an exasperated letter from the Corporation of Salisbury to Cromwell, 6 April ?1534, SP 1/65 f. 189, *LP* 5 no. 182. On Bennet's continuing role and Cromwell's lack of involvement in appointing his own deputy, see Bennet to Cromwell, 2 January

1530, SP 1/236 f. 292, *LP Addenda* 1 i no. 683, and Thomas Chaffyn to Cromwell, 2 January 1530, SP 1/56 f. 190, *LP* 4 iii no. 6136. On Winter's appointment, see Le Neve, *Fasti 1300–1541: Salisbury*, 18. **23.** On Littleprow, see *HC 1509–1558* 2, 557–8, s.v. Lytilprowe, Reginald. **24.** For all this, D. MacCulloch, *Suffolk and the Tudors: politics and religion in an English county 1500–1600* (Oxford, 1986), 227–30. **25.** On Sherburne, see *ODNB*, s.v. Sherborne, Robert, and S. Lander, 'Church courts and the Reformation in the diocese of Chichester, 1500–58', in R. O'Day and F. Heal (eds.), *Continuity and Change: personnel and administration of the Church in England 1500–1641* (Leicester, 1976), 215–37, particularly 223–8. Events at Shulbrede can be reconstructed from three sources: first, two letters of 1525, Prior and Brethren of Shulbrede to Richard Bedon, s.a., SP 1/65 f. 137, *LP* 5 no. 107, and Richard Bedon to Cromwell, 'Thursday after St Valentine' (16 February if 1525), SP 1/65 f. 136, *LP* 5 no. 106. *LP* dates these to 1531, but the reference to 'Lord Percy' dates them to before the death of Henry, fifth Earl of Northumberland, who died on 19 May 1527, and Cromwell was active in dissolutions in Kent and Sussex in early 1525. The story is completed by a damaged letter from Richard Leighton to Cromwell, 4 October 1535, SP 1/97 f. 92, *LP* 9 no. 533, though *LP* misunderstood the fragmentary text, asserting that the demolitions had been carried out by the current Abbot. Leighton clearly had no idea of Cromwell's earlier involvement. **26.** TNA, SP 2/O f. 133, *LP* 6 no. 1625[7], is a draft grant of annuity by William Burrey, Prior of Shulbrede, of 26s 8d, a half-mark more than promised in Bedon's letter; this has to date before Burrey ceased to be Prior, so before 1529. A catalogue of Cromwell's financial papers in 1532, *LP* 5 no. 1285, makes a reference to this under vi, 'My master's patents'. For Cromwell saving a second small Augustinian house in Sussex, Hardham, almost certainly during his later round of dissolutions in 1532, see below, p. 200. **27.** Sir Henry Guildford to Cromwell, 30 March [1525], SP 1/47 f. 141, *LP* 4 ii no. 4117, misdated in *LP*; it can only be 1525, because of its reference to the dissolution of Tonbridge. **28.** On Bilsington, see Smith, 379, and on Leeds, *VCH: Kent* 2, 162–5. Anthony St Leger to Thomas Cromwell, 17 October [1536], SP 1/108 f. 114, *LP* 11 no. 746, and see above, p. 16. **29.** Stephen Vaughan to Cromwell, probably spring 1525, SP 1/52 f. 38, *LP* 4 ii no. 5115; misdated by *LP* to 1529. **30.** On Bayham, Sir Edward Guildford to Sir Henry Guildford, 8 June [1525], and associated papers, SP 1/34 ff. 240–48, *LP* 4 i no. 1397. On Tonbridge, Warham to Wolsey, 2 July [1525], SP 1/35 f. 48, *LP* 4 i no. 1470, and Warham to Wolsey, 3 July 1525, SP 1/35 f. 50, *LP* 4 i no. 1471. For comment, see P. Clark, *English Provincial Society from the Reformation to the Revolution: religion, politics and society in Kent 1500–1640* (Hassocks, 1977), 22. On background in the Amicable Grant, see G. W. Bernard, *War, Taxation and Rebellion in Early Tudor England* (Brighton and New York, 1986). **31.** *LP* 4 i no. 2024[vi]; this was a recognizance before local JPs, 4 March 17 Henry VIII [1526]. **32.** John ap Rhys was referring to his colleague in visitation Thomas Lee, when writing to Cromwell on 16 October [1535], SP 1/98 f. 16, *LP* 9 no. 622. William Knight to Wolsey, 19 August [1527], SP 1/44 f. 3, *LP* 4 ii no. 3360. **33.** A letter of congratulation on 'your good promotion that I hear of through the favour of My Lord's Grace' from Henry Lacy

of Calais to Cromwell, 30 April 1527, SP 1/41 f. 179, *LP* 4 ii no. 3079.
34. Smith, 499, 502. Cromwell's presence in the area is attested by his witnessing
the surrender of Wallingford Priory, as noticed above, on 19 April 1524: *LP* 4 i no.
1137.   **35.** See e.g. John Abbot of Osney to Cromwell, 16 January 1534, SP 1/82 f.
85, *LP* 7 no. 79, in which he thanks Cromwell not merely for his goodness but also
for his 'great cheer at my last being with you'. On the High Stewardship, see Prior
and Convent of Osney to Cromwell, 23 November 1537, SP 1/126 f. 151v, *LP* 12
ii no. 1120.   **36.** SP 1/88 ff. 105–6, *LP* 7 no. 1670, in a notably old-fashioned
hand for the 1520s. *LP* misdated this to 1534, but since it refers to the Prior as
'aged' it must be from the time of Bellond rather than his successors Gilbert Roos
and George Browne, and should be seen in the context of Bellond's mismanagement which led to his forced retirement in 1525. See e.g. Roth (ed.), *English Austin
Friars 2: The Sources*, nos. D1041, D1049–50.   **37.** Ingworth to Cromwell, early
December 1538, SP 1/140 f. 73, *LP* 13 ii no. 1021.   **38.** Abbot of Pershore to
Cromwell, n.d. but 1538, SP 1/141 f. 174, *LP* 13 ii no. 1259.   **39.** D. Starkey,
'Intimacy and innovation: the rise of the Privy Chamber, 1485–1547', in Starkey
(ed.), *The English Court from the Wars of the Roses to the Civil War* (London,
1987), 71–118, at 78–9, 82, 86–7, 91, 94, 103, 105.   **40.** See the copy of Sir William Compton's will annotated by Wolsey himself, SP 1/49 f. 3, *LP* 4 iii no. 4442.
Wolsey provided for the education of the young heir, Peter Compton: John Gost-
wick to Cromwell, 14 March ?1529, SP 1/59 f. 127, *LP* 4 iii Appendix no. 233. For
Compton's close involvement in the rebuilding of Winchcombe parish church and
his local links, see C. Litzenberger, *The English Reformation and the Laity:
Gloucestershire, 1540–1580* (Cambridge, 1997), 26.   **41.** For Cromwell and Tottenham, see SP 1/236 f. 171, *LP Addenda* 1 i no. 614. For the Escheator and drafts,
LP 4 ii no. 5117[3] and *LP* 4 iii no. 4442.   **42.** Kidderminster to Cromwell, 3
November probably 1532 or 1533 (*LP*'s suggestion of 1531 seems too early), SP
1/68 f. 38, *LP* 5 no. 510. See also same to same, 21 October ?1529, SP 1/55 f. 171,
LP 4 iii no. 6014. See also *ODNB* s.v. Kidderminster, Richard, though Dr Cunich
has elided two Richard Abbots of Winchcombe in his account of the correspondence with Cromwell.   **43.** Richard Munslow Abbot of Winchcombe to Cromwell,
30 June probably 1529, SP 1/235 f. 346, *LP Addenda* 1 i no. 593, and 13 January
?1532, SP 1/69 f. 14, *LP* 5 no. 716. By 1535, Cromwell's relationship with Winchcombe was still close, but had become much more complex: see below, pp.
298–9.   **44.** On this theme, see J. G. Clark, 'Humanism and reform in pre-
Reformation English monasteries', *TRHS* 6th series 19 (2009), 57–93, at
80–92.   **45.** See entries at SP 1/53 ff. 41r–42r, 48r, *LP* 4 iii no. 5330; they include
the houses of Welbeck, St James Northampton, Christ Church Canterbury, Lewes,
Wenlock, Merevale, St Mary York, Butley and Hinton Charterhouse.
46. Edmund Whalley Abbot of St Mary's York to Cromwell, 6 January [?1529], SP
1/52 f. 97, *LP* 4 iii no. 5143. There is a strong presumption that Abbot Whalley
was of the same Nottinghamshire family who supplied Thomas Cromwell with
his servants Hugh, John and Thomas. For the reversionary lease, which in fact
was overtaken by complications, see William Thornton Abbot of St Mary's
York to Cromwell, 24 July ?1532, *LP* 5 no. 1192.   **47.** Frisby to Cromwell,

14 January s.a., BL MS Cotton Titus B/I f. 358, *LP* 4 iii no. 6146, but also *LP* 5 no. 718. *LP*'s redating from 1530 to 1532 seems less likely, given that Frisby does not refer to Cromwell as a councillor. A letter of Cromwell to Wolsey, 24 July s.a., is written from 'Londe', which *LP* thinks is London, but is more likely Launde: SP 1/57 f. 252, *LP* 4 iii no. 6530. From its content, it can only be assigned to 1530, hence is 24 July 1530, and for obvious reasons it cannot have been written on the same snowy visit. A letter written by the Prior to Cromwell, 2 March 1528 or 1529, SP 1/235 f. 275, *LP Addenda* 1 i no. 574, shows Cromwell performing multiple favours for Launde in return for the right to present to one of its benefices. **48.** We await Dr Hope's own presentation of his fascinating findings, especially on the Hidden family of Hungerford discussed below; meanwhile, see A. Hope, 'Lollardy: the stone the builders rejected?', in P. Lake and M. Dowling (eds.), *Protestantism and the National Church in Sixteenth Century England* (Beckenham, 1987), 1–35. **49.** John London to John Longland Bishop of Lincoln, 25 February 1528, SP 1/47 f. 16, *LP* 4 ii no. 3968. The narrative of events by Anthony Dalaber, fleshing out London's letters, is in Foxe 1563, 660–66. **50.** Thomas Elyot to Cromwell, 25 March [1528], SP 1/235 f. 280, *LP Addenda* 1 i no. 577. **51.** Canner to Cromwell, 27 December ?1528, SP 1/51 f. 122, *LP* 4 ii no. 5069. **52.** John Sone to Cromwell, ?January 1527, SP 1/236 f. 12, *LP Addenda* 1 i no. 611. **53.** Petition of William Cockes, SP 1/106 f. 4r, *LP* 11 no. 301[2]. Cockes also indicated that Cromwell's interest in his case was not casual, for he was responsible for getting Cockes released from Bishop Fox of Winchester's prison at Wolvesey fifteen weeks after this arrest, when Wolsey took over Winchester diocese on Fox's death. See also Emden, *Oxford 1501 to 1540*, 147. **54.** For money paid out to Dr Robert Shorton (Dean of Wolsey's chapel) for the conveying of 'sondrie' scholars from Cambridge to Oxford, rounding up the payments on 13 February 1526, see Cromwell's accounts for the suppression of monasteries and the founding of the Colleges, SP 1/44 ff. 207–314, *LP* 4 ii no. 3536, at f. 217v. Far from being an evangelical sympathizer, Shorton rapidly alienated himself from Wolsey by his fierce partisanship for Katherine of Aragon: H. A. Kelly, *The Matrimonial Trials of Henry VIII* (Stanford, CA, 1976), 61, 202. T. A. Sowerby, *Renaissance and Reform in Tudor England: the careers of Sir Richard Morison c. 1513–1556* (Oxford, 2010), follows the suggestion of W. G. Zeeveld, *Foundations of Tudor Policy* (Cambridge, MA, 1948), 29–30, that Edward Foxe was the prime mover in choosing the Cambridge contingent. There is no reason why Foxe should not have been involved, and later he showed himself an evangelical ally of Cromwell in the 1530s, but his initiative does not account for all the evidence presented here. **55.** MacCulloch, *Thomas Cranmer*, 28–9. **56.** For a good summary of early Tudor Boston's peculiar religious atmosphere, see M. Williamson, 'Evangelicalism at Boston, Oxford and Windsor under Henry VIII: Foxe's narratives recontextualized', in D. Loades (ed.), *John Foxe at Home and Abroad* (Aldershot, 2004), 31–45. **57.** BL MS Egerton 2886 f. 202r (Tyndale); ff. 295r–296v. **58.** Williamson, 'Evangelicalism at Boston, Oxford and Windsor under Henry VIII', 39–40, shows how the shadow of Garrett's evangelicalism linked his London parish and Boston clergy even after his death. **59.** Edward Fetyplace to Cromwell, 12

February [1525, misdated by *LP* to 1529], SP 1/52 f. 219, *LP* 4 iii no. 5285. On Fetyplace, see S. Gunn, *Charles Brandon, Duke of Suffolk, 1484–1545* (Oxford, 1988), 88.   **60.** Edward Fetyplace to Cromwell, 13 January 1527: SP 1/59 ff. 104–5, *LP* 4 iii Appendix no. 103. This letter is dateable by Fetyplace's statement in it that 'it is not yet ii yeres complete sithe the tyme of the suppression of the seid monastery'. Poughley was suppressed on 14 February 1525: *LP* 4 ii no. 1137.   **61.** Wolsey's irritable remarks about the desertion of the College for Poughley come in a memorandum to three of his senior officials (not including Cromwell) dateable to summer 1526, *LP* 4 i no. 1499/26, at 673. In 1526 Cambridge recorded the disruption of its Trinity term because of the plague: W. G. Searle (ed.), *Grace Book Γ* (Cambridge University Press, 1908), 220.   **62.** John Clerk, canon of Cardinal College, from Poughley, to Cromwell, 4 August 1526 or 1527, SP 1/49 f. 196, *LP* 4 ii no. 4607. *LP* misdates this 1529, by which time Clerk was dead, and misses the reference to 'Sir Frith'. According to Emden, *Oxford 1501 to 1540*, 218, Frith vacated his Fellowship at Cardinal College in 1526, though he was among those imprisoned there in the 1528 round-up.   **63.** In Cromwell's accounts for the suppression of monasteries, SP 1/44 ff. 207–314, *LP* 4 ii no. 3536, at ff. 212v and 292v, are payments of 26s 8d to John Eden for gathering the rents of the late monastery of Poughley.   **64.** Foxe 1583, 855, 856, 858, 861. It is likely that the family were originally Scots, from Clydesdale, and that their alternative name was derived from the manor of Hidden in Hungerford, with which they continued to be associated: see *VCH: Berkshire* 4, 192, 199. John Clydesdale alias Hidden made his will on 10 August 1549, TNA, PROB 11/33/192, which has some unusual features: he proclaimed his belief in soul-sleep, and made arrangements for security for a large list of named tenants, looking suspiciously like a gathered community. One of his supervisors was John Wilmot, yeoman, perhaps the son of his sister Alice's first husband John Wilmot. The family has been meticulously researched by Nicholas and Norman Hidden in two privately printed volumes, 1988 and 1996.   **65.** TNA, C 1/516/42, bill of John Glydesdall, provides genealogical details.   **66.** 'Articles of agreement made between Thomas Doyley and Alice his wife, ordained, ended, and determined by the Right Worshipful Master Doctor Taylor, Master of the Rolls', 11 October 1527, SP 1/44 ff. 144–5, *LP* 4 ii no. 3486; the documents are in the hand of Ralph Sadler and Thomas Cromwell. On Anne Cottismore alias Doyle, née Eden alias Clydesdale, Foxe 1570, 1000, and for elucidating comment, Hope, 'Lollardy: the stone the builders rejected?', 8–9.   **67.** John Croke to Cromwell, 16 July [1527], SP 1/235 f. 216, *LP Addenda* 1 i no. 539, which usefully specifies that this is the case before the Master of the Rolls. Croke knew what he was talking about; he was an official in Chancery. He also figures prominently in Cromwell's will of 1529: see below, p. 88.   **68.** K. D. Maas, *The Reformation and Robert Barnes* (Woodbridge, 2010), 16–21.   **69.** Miles Coverdale to Cromwell, 1 May ?1526, SP 1/65 f. 238, *LP* 5 no. 221; the fact that Coverdale signs off calling himself 'friar' means that this letter cannot be any later than 1527, since by Lent 1528 he had unilaterally left his order and was wearing the garb of a secular priest: Foxe 1570, 1229. It may be as early as 1525, since Cromwell had been much involved in monastic business in

East Anglia that year.   70. Coverdale to Cromwell, 27 August [1527]: SP 1/44 f. 34, *LP* 4 ii no. 3388. It is worth cautioning the reader that the 'Master More' and his family referred in this correspondence is unlikely to have been Sir Thomas More, though commentators have usually assumed that. Cromwell had various friends in Surrey and London called More (e.g. Christopher More of Loseley in Surrey, on whom see More to Cromwell, possibly October 1534, SP 1/86 f. 129, *LP* 7 no. 1344), but most probably this is the London-based Roger More, servant of the King's bakehouse, who was named supervisor of Cromwell's will in 1529 (SP 1/54 ff. 234–47 at f. 243v, *LP* 4 iii no. 5772); see also below, p. 607, n. 40.   71. A mass of evidence from Foxe involving Barnes and Coverdale is summarized in J. F. Davis, *Heresy and Reformation in the South East of England 1520–1599* (London, 1983), 59–65.   72. Erler, *Reading and Writing during the Dissolution*, 88–106, provides a good overview of the relationship between Cromwell and Vernon.   73. For disparaging (if self-serving) references to the poor results of Palsgrave's teaching, see John Cheking to Cromwell, 27 July probably 1529, SP 1/49 f. 152, *LP* 4 ii no. 4560; Margaret Vernon's letter to Cromwell, SP 1/65 f. 37, *LP* 5 no. 17, is dateable to 1529 (for the arguments on this, see Fitzgerald and MacCulloch, 'Gregory Cromwell', 589–90), and must have been written shortly before that.   74. The run of Cheking's letters to Cromwell is dated by *LP* to 1528, which is probably a year or two too early given that they must postdate Margaret Vernon's letter cited in the previous note: SP 1/49 f. 152, *LP* 4 ii no. 4560; SP 1/50 f. 179, *LP* 4 ii no. 4837; SP 1/51 f. 2, *LP* 4 ii no. 4916.   75. R. Rex (ed.), *A Reformation Rhetoric: Thomas Swynnerton's The Tropes and Figures of Scripture* (Cambridge, 1999), 15–16; Rex there gently corrects an earlier error of mine in confusing John Cheking with John Cheke. Elsewhere he points out what will be obvious to anyone with experience of Oxbridge colleges, that in Reformation disputes they did not behave like a well-drilled football team in their theological outlook: R. Rex, 'The English campaign against Luther in the 1520s', *TRHS* 5th series 39 (1989), 85–106, at 92–3. For a reminiscence of Cheking dateable to 1527, see G. Joye, *The Refutation of the Byshop of Winchesters derke Declaratio[n] of his false Articles . . .* (London, 1546, *RSTC* 14828.5), f. 81v, and cf. f. 82v for the dating, nineteen years before 1546.   76. MacCulloch, *Thomas Cranmer*, 166, 196–7, and see below, pp. 362–3, 493.   77. For a discussion of the theme of Nicodemism, both in the Reformation and beyond, see D. MacCulloch, *Silence: a Christian history* (London, 2013), ch. 7.   78. For further discussion, see Hope, 'Lollardy: the stone the builders rejected?'   79. For summary discussion of the *Spirituali* see D. MacCulloch, *Reformation: Europe's house divided 1490–1700* (London, 2003), 213–37, 261–3.   80. On Rullo's career in heterodoxy, D. Fenlon, *Heresy and Obedience in Tridentine Italy: Cardinal Pole and the Counter Reformation* (Cambridge, 1972), 72, 76, 78, 280n.   81. J. J. Scarisbrick, 'Cardinal Wolsey and the Common Weal', in E. W. Ives, R. J. Knecht and J. J. Scarisbrick (eds.), *Wealth and Power in Tudor England: essays presented to S. T. Bindoff* (London, 1978), 45–67; see also below, pp. 187–8.   82. P. Gwyn, *The King's Cardinal: the rise and fall of Thomas Wolsey* (London, 1990), 293–9, provides a useful overview on Wolsey and the English episcopate, though he is probably too sanguine about the good relations between Wolsey and Warham.   83. M. Heale, 'Dependent priories and the closure of monasteries in late medieval England, 1400–1535', *EHR* 119 (2004), 1–26, at 24.   84. The MS reminiscence is BL MS Harley 422 ff. 84–8, conveniently printed in G. E. Corrie (ed.), *Sermons and Remains of Hugh Latimer . . .* (Parker Society, 1845), xxvii–xxxi.   85. Gunn and Lindley (eds.), *Cardinal Wolsey*, 9–13, and K. Brown, 'Wolsey and ecclesiastical order: the case of the Franciscan Observants', in ibid., 219–38. On Ireland and Allen, see J. Murray, 'Archbishop Alen, Tudor reform and the Kildare Rebellion', *Proceedings of the Royal Irish Academy* 89C (1989), 1–16, especially 8.   86. For the limitations of Wolsey's achievement in Star Chamber and more generally, see J. Guy, *The Cardinal's Court: the impact of Thomas Wolsey in Star Chamber* (Hassocks, 1977), 119–31.   87. Augustine to Cromwell, 16 May 1532, SP 1/70 f. 38, *LP* 5 no. 1027, full text at Pocock 2, 259: 'quod vellem ut semper in animo haberes, quod mihi et aliis dictitare solebas, Reverendissimum nostrum herum non ob aliam causam ita omnibus hominibus exosum fuisse quam propter illam longam suam procrastiationem, et plurima verba factis vacua.' Augustine added unctuously, though with due note of Wolsey's other merits, 'I hope you will not imitate him in this (although I would wish that in other things), but rather imitate yourself: that is, an excellent man' – 'In hoc nollem te eum imitari, in ceteris vellem. Immo potius te ipsum imiteris velim, hoc est virum optimum.'

Chapter 4: Managing Failure: 1528–1529

1. For fuller discussion of Wolsey and the shrine, see J. Blatchly and D. MacCulloch, *Miracles in Lady Lane: the Ipswich shrine at the Westgate* (Dorchester, 2013), 17–45. A full description of the event, from which the following details are taken, was sent to Wolsey by the College's Dean: William Capon to Wolsey, 26 September 1528, BL MS Cotton Titus B/I ff. 281–2, *LP* 4 ii no. 4778.   2. The statutes of Cardinal College Ipswich survive in an imperfect vellum copy in the archives of Christ Church Oxford, the first twenty folios of which are missing (a final list of contents tells us the headings of the missing material at f. 57r): MS D&C vi.c.2. Provision is made for the annual procession to Our Lady's shrine on 8 September, as Dean Capon apologetically acknowledged in his letter to Wolsey.   3. For Cromwell's legal headaches in completing the transfer of the College site, see Cromwell to Thomas Arundell, 30 June [1528], SP 1/49 f. 1, *LP* 4 ii no. 4441, and William Capon to Cromwell, probably 1 July 1528, SP 1/55 f. 18, *LP* 4 iii no. 5810. The legal hitch most likely explains the abandoned foundation stone of the College bearing the date 20 June 1528 and discovered in fragments in an Ipswich well in the eighteenth century: BL Stowe 881 f. 51r.   4. Capon to Cromwell, 24 October 1529, SP 1/50 f. 203, *LP* 4 ii no. 4872. *LP* dates this to 1528, but it can be reassigned to 1529 by the securely dated receipt from Cromwell to Capon for a reward payment from Jesus College on 18 February 1530 consequent on the work mentioned in this letter: SP 1/57 f. 24, *LP* 4 iii no. 6230.   5. Testwood arrived at Boston in 1524: BL MS Egerton 2886 f. 295r. For his excellent service

at Ipswich, William Capon to Wolsey, 12 April 1529, SP 1/52 f. 174v, *LP* 4 iii no. 5458, and for the letter which may have resulted in Cromwell furthering his next appointment at St George's Chapel Windsor, Testwood to Cromwell, 1531 or 1532, SP 1/73 f. 141, *LP* 5 no. 1766. 6. Memorandum to Cromwell, dated plausibly to January 1530 in *LP*: SP 1/56 ff. 216–18, *LP* 4 iii no. 6186. 7. For his continuing loyalty to Wolsey, see Cavendish, *Life of Wolsey*, ed. Singer, 385, and Wolsey to the Chief Baron of the Exchequer, ?August 1530, SP 1/57 ff. 263–4, *LP* 4 iii no. 6555: that letter is interestingly a draft in Cromwell's hand which must then have been transferred to Yorkshire to be emended by Wolsey. 8. See below, pp. 296, 459. An overview of ap Rhys's extraordinary career can be gained by combining the accounts in *HC 1509–1558* 3, 151–2 and *ODNB*, s.v. Price [Prys], Ellis. A. N. Shaw, 'The *Compendium Compertorum* and the making of the Suppression Act of 1536' (University of Warwick PhD, 2003), 169, also provides a useful addition. 9. Hall 2, 57. 10. See the meticulous reconstruction in E. W. Ives, *The Life and Death of Anne Boleyn 'The Most Happy'* (Oxford, 2004), ch. 6, with useful summary at 90. 11. Bernard, *War, Taxation and Rebellion in Early Tudor England* is too indulgent to the Dukes of Norfolk and Suffolk in arguing for their disinterested support of government aims in this affair: cf. his comments at ibid., 92. 12. Hall 2, 144. 13. Ives, *Life and Death of Anne Boleyn*, ch. 8. 14. For two letters about foreign shipping, see Cromwell to Thomas Arundell, 30 June [1528], SP 1/49 f. 1, *LP* 4 ii no. 4441, and Capon to Cromwell, probably 1 July 1528, SP 1/55 f. 18, *LP* 4 iii no. 5810. *LP* asserts that SP 1/50 ff. 9–16, *LP* 4 ii no. 4656[2], an important draft on foreign affairs which it dates to late August 1528, is in Cromwell's hand. Although it does resemble his hand, many key characteristics show that it is not. 15. Thomas Rush to Cromwell, 9 January [1529], SP 1/236 f. 69, *LP Addenda* 1 i no. 632. 16. John Chaffcombe Abbot of Bruerne to Cromwell, 11 March [1529], SP 1/53 f. 101, *LP* 4 iii no. 5373, securely dateable by its reference to Sir Simon Harcourt as Sheriff of Berkshire and Oxfordshire; John Smart Abbot of Wigmore to Cromwell, summer 1529, SP 1/52 f. 65, *LP* 4 ii no. 5121. For dating, as well as an excellent sketch of context, see D. Knowles, 'The last abbot of Wigmore', in V. Ruffer and A. J. Taylor (eds.), *Medieval Studies Presented to Rose Graham* (Oxford, 1950), 138–45, repr. in Knowles, *The Historian and Character* (Cambridge, 1963), 171–8, at 174. 17. On these two, see respectively pp. 63 and 56. On the document of June 1528, SP 1/59 ff. 106–107v, *LP* 4 iii Appendix no. 109. Gunn, *Henry VII's New Men*, 223, convincingly redates this much damaged document. 18. For Cromwell's memorandum to prepare Winter's lease of the mineral rights, 1528, see SP 1/47 f. 279r, *LP* 4 ii no. 4229[7 iii] (1528), and for Winter's surrender of the lease, which shows that he had finally received it on 10 February 1529, just as the Cardinal resigned the see, *LP* 4 iii no. 6094. See also a clutch of papers relating to Durham as Wolsey's affairs were wound up there, and referring to lead and the coal supply for Cardinal College Ipswich, SP 1/52 f. 19, *LP* 4 ii no. 5111[4], and John Metcalfe, Wolsey's auditor at Durham, to Cromwell, 18 March probably 1529, SP 1/236 f. 75, *LP Addenda* 1 i no. 637. For an overview of Cromwell in relation to Durham business, Ward, 'Origins of Thomas Cromwell's public career', 172–81. 19. John Clasey to Cromwell,

?August 1535, SP 1/96 f. 34, *LP* 9 no. 228.   **20.** Minterne's career is summarized with only a few slips in Emden, *Oxford 1501 to 1540*, 411. His letters to Cromwell, misdated by *LP* but probably both of 1538, are 5 June [?1538], SP 1/104 ff. 118–19, *LP* 10 no. 1065, and 7 December [1538], SP 1/72 f. 117, *LP* 5 no. 1613; Minterne to the King, writing from Orleans, 12 February 1542, is SP 1/169 f. 26, *LP* 17 no. 99. The first reference to his royal pension paid at Lady Day 1538 is in the book of royal payments, Arundel MS 97 f. 11v, *LP* 13 ii no. 1280, at 525; his payment at Lady Day 1540, *LP* 16 no. 380, at 186, is sandwiched between wages of a stable-hand and the Court rat-catcher.   **21.** For Morison as petty canon of Cardinal College Oxford, see BL MS Cotton Appendix L f. 82, *LP* 13 ii no. 817. Wolsey also arranged a pension out of Worksop Priory for Morison: *VE* 5, 175. On Winter and Morison, Sowerby, *Renaissance and Reform*, 20, 24, 27–8.   **22.** Winter to Cromwell, 9 July probably 1534, SP 1/85 f. 43, *LP* 7 no. 964.   **23.** John Curatt to Cromwell, 24 April 1529, SP 1/53 f. 215, *LP* 4 iii no. 5491; same to same, 25 April 1529, SP 1/53 f. 216, *LP* 4 iii no. 5492; Nix to Wolsey, 23 May 1529, SP 1/54 f. 29, *LP* 4 iii no. 5589. For a more extended account of Nix's relations with Wolsey, see MacCulloch, *Suffolk and the Tudors*, 151–3, and for Curatt's later clashes with Nix over the treatment of Thomas Bilney, see J. Guy, *The Public Career of Sir Thomas More* (Brighton, 1980), 167–8.   **24.** Ives, *Life and Death of Anne Boleyn*, 114–15.   **25.** William Capon to Wolsey, 12 April 1529, SP 1/52 f. 174r, *LP* 4 iii no. 5458. It is worth pointing out that a house inventory often attributed to Felixstowe from this period has nothing to do with it, concerning instead private business of Cromwell's with Robert Studley at Filston (Kent) in 1528: SP 1/52 f. 101, *LP* 4 iii no. 5145; SP 1/48 f. 37, *LP* 4 ii no. 4295.   **26.** For an example of Wolsey's continuing lavish expenditure on beautiful liturgical books in 1529, and excellent discussion of the plunder of his possessions which followed, see J. P. Carley, 'Thomas Wolsey's Epistle and Gospel lectionaries: unanswered questions and new hypotheses', *Bodleian Library Record* 28 (2015), 135–51, especially 145 and 151.   **27.** Ives, *Life and Death of Anne Boleyn*, 114–20.   **28.** The documents in Darcy's own hand against Wolsey are SP 1/54 ff. 202–10, *LP* 4 iii no. 5749[1, 2]. For their discovery, see Duke of Norfolk to Cromwell, 29 April [1537], SP 1/119 f. 53, *LP* 12 i no. 1064. Cf. Guy, *Public Career of Sir Thomas More*, 106–7; as will become apparent below (pp. 95, and 609 n. 61), I have one significant disagreement with Guy and others as to whether Darcy and his fellows were contemplating large-scale dissolutions in those papers.   **29.** The letters are undated, Cromwell's being SP 1/55 f. 19v, *LP* 4 iii no. 5812, with Claybrook's now f. 19r (*LP* 4 iii no. 5813), but dateable here by the mention of Blackfriars. For the context in Wolsey's administration, see P. D. Clarke in Clarke and M. Questier (eds.), *Camden Miscellany* XXXVI: *papal authority and the limits of the law in Tudor England* (Camden 5th series 48, 2015), 1–100, at 25–7.   **30.** Edward Brysby to Cromwell, 28 August [1529], SP 1/55 f. 71, *LP* 4 iii no. 5876 (Cromwell was then at Barnwell Priory, just outside Cambridge, probably dealing with a protracted struggle over whether Wolsey could effect its Prior's move to become next Prior of the Suffolk house of Butley); John Williamson from London to Cromwell in Ipswich, 5 September [1529], SP 1/59 f. 133, *LP* 4 iii Appendix no. 237. In administrative documents of the College internally dateable to 1529, there is mention of 'Books that came last with Master Cromwell the 7 day of September': SP 1/236 f. 106, *LP Addenda* 1 i no. 651.   31. BL MS Cotton Vitellius B/XII f. 168, *LP* 4 iii no. 5953. The text, damaged in the Cottonian fire, is efficiently augmented in H. Ellis (ed.), *Original Letters illustrative of English History . . . from autographs in the British Museum and . . . other collections* (11 vols. in 3 series: London, 1824, 1827, 1846), 1st series 1, 307, though one has to correct one important error in the reconstruction, followed by *LP*, by correcting Ellis's reading of 'Greenwich' to 'Grafton'. 32. T. F. Mayer (ed.), *The Correspondence of Reginald Pole: a calendar* (3 vols., Aldershot, 2000–2004), no. 245 (a draft of Pole's *Apologia ad Carolum Quintum*), 1, 212. The dating is clear from Pole's movements in 1529, and the fact that he says (ibid.) of Cromwell that 'Tunc in familia Car. Eb. fuit'. Mayer's arguments for believing that this interview never took place are unimpressive: T. F. Mayer, *Reginald Pole: prince and prophet* (Cambridge, 2000), 99–100.   33. Mayer (ed.), *Correspondence of Pole*, 1, 212: 'cum a me qureret quo pacto se consiliarius principis cum principe se gerere deberet, si quando principis animus ab eo quod vulgo honestum videbatur inclinaret, cum vero hoc re quereret illo quidem nulla tum authoritate preditus erat.' The translation is mine, as Mayer's manages to obscure the point of the passage.   34. Ives, *Life and Death of Anne Boleyn*, 117–20; E. W. Ives, 'The fall of Wolsey', in Gunn and Lindley (eds.), *Cardinal Wolsey*, 286–315, at 294–300.   35. Ives, *Life and Death of Anne Boleyn*, 120–26; Guy, *Public Career of Sir Thomas More*, 31. The date of 17 October seems confirmed by Hall 2, 156, though he makes a slip by naming the month November.   36. Cavendish, *Life of Wolsey*, ed. Singer, 248, 251–2.   37. *ERP* 1, 127 (sect. xxviii): 'Hic vero notus esse coepit . . . in hac vero statim celebris esse coepit, et pluribus notus . . . ut cum Cardinalis . . . ab administratione Reipublicae remotus esset . . . ipse omnium voce, qui aliquid de eo intellexerant, ad supplicium posceretur . . . Hoc enim affirmare possum, qui Londini tum adfui, et voces audivi, adeo etiam ut per civitatem universam rumor circumferretur, eum in carcerem fuisse detrusum, et propediem productum iri ad supplicium.'   38. SP 1/53 ff. 36–51, *LP* 4 iii no. 5330: the transactions listed stretch all the way back to 8 December 1518. *LP* asserts that the majority of the document is in the hand of Thomas Wriothesley, as it also does of Cromwell's will, discussed next. This is not so; they are in a commonplace formal clerk's hand. The identification by *LP* of Wriothesley's hand in Cromwell's papers of the 1520s is the basis for the oft-repeated supposition that Wriothesley was in Cromwell's employment then. The positive evidence suggests that this is wrong: see below, pp. 314–15.   39. SP 1/54 ff. 234–44, *LP* 4 iii no. 5772. As just noted, the assertion in *LP* that this document is in the hand of Wriothesley is wrong. An extra folio of provisions added by Cromwell himself includes mention of the lordship of Rhymney, which was formally granted to him on 17 May 1532 (*LP* 5 no. 1065[33]); his other alterations to the text are probably earlier.   40. More achieved his moment in the limelight in May 1536, when he was one of a round-up of minor court officials who formed the Westminster jury presenting a remarkably fictional list of charges against Queen Anne Boleyn: *LP* 10 no. 876[7]; John Avery was also among them. There are various references to 'Mistress More' as a close friend and neighbour of Cromwell, and she may have been Roger More's wife: cf. e.g. Launcelot Colyns to Cromwell, 27 September 1533, SP 1/79 f. 73, *LP* 6 no. 1159.   **41.** Cf. e.g. Cromwell to Wolsey, 2 April 1528, SP 1/47 f. 153, *LP* 4 ii no. 4135.   **42.** On Gregory as delicate, see the remarks of Roland Lee to Cromwell, 27 December 1534, SP 1/87 f. 129, *LP* 7 no. 1576.   **43.** Cavendish, *Life of Wolsey*, ed. Singer, 258–9; modified as noted, my italics. This reading is admittedly not present in the text of the version in BL MS Egerton 2402, which is the supposedly autograph version used in R. S. Sylvester (ed.), *The Life and Death of Cardinal Wolsey by George Cavendish* (Early English Text Society original series 243, 1959); cf. 104. Sylvester did not prove that this MS was autograph, as is observed by Gardiner, 'George Cavendish: an early Tudor political commentator?', 81. Maybe Cavendish himself changed his mind on the wording.   **44.** Cavendish, *Life of Wolsey*, ed. Singer, 260–70.   **45.** Sadler's letter to Cromwell, 1 November 1529, is BL MS Cotton Cleopatra E/IV f. 211, *LP* 4 iii Appendix 238. Elton, *Tudor Revolution in Government*, 77–80, provides excellent comment on the letter without seeing that it was possible to reconcile Sadler's letter with Cavendish's account. Indeed, the one remaining apparent discrepancy actually provides further confirmation that Cavendish's account reproduces the course of events: Cavendish asserts that Thomas Rush provided Cromwell with a Parliamentary seat (Cavendish, *Life of Wolsey*, ed. Singer, 273–4). That is what Cromwell would have assumed when speaking with Cavendish at Esher on 1 November, and Cavendish would not necessarily have been told of the change of plan which occurred in the next few days in London.   **46.** Satisfyingly, this very ring is likely to be that in Cromwell's household inventory of 1527, alongside a great many others: 'A gold ring, with a turquoise like a heart, upon my master's finger', worth six pounds, SP 1/42 ff. 101–16 at f. 112r, *LP* 4 ii no. 3197. As noted by S. E. Lehmberg, *The Reformation Parliament 1529–1536* (Cambridge, 1970), 27n, there is no evidence of bribery in any of these transactions.   **47.** Once more, commentators, including Lehmberg, *Reformation Parliament*, 27, have not seen how to reconcile Sadler's letter with Cavendish's statement that Cromwell 'had chanced to meet with one Sir Thomas Rush . . . whose son was appointed to be one of the burgesses of that Parliament, of whom [i.e. Sir Thomas] he [Cromwell] obtained his room'. The interpretation I provide removes the problem; Cavendish recorded what he knew of Rush and Alvard's situation that All Hallows' Day, and he does *not* say that Cromwell substituted for Alvard.   **48.** *HC 1509–1558* 1, 191–3 on Ipswich and Orford, and corresponding biographies, and on the Orford disputes, MacCulloch, *Suffolk and the Tudors*, 63, 70, 306–7, 322–3. Hunt's role in the fight is related in TNA, STAC 2/20/400.   **49.** BL MS Cotton Otho C/X f. 218v, *LP* 10 no. 40[ii], is a slip in Cromwell's hand listing certain names headed by the three Winchester episcopal boroughs 'Taunton, Downton, Hindon', which suggests that for the new 1536 Parliament he designated his fellow of 1529, a locally based lawyer called William Portman, alongside his own servant Richard Pollard, to be burgesses for Taunton. He himself may have moved on to be knight of the shire for Kent, which would be far more appropriate for his status by that time: see *HC 1509–1558* 1, 112–14, and below, pp. 485–6.   **50.** For Cromwell's recent purchase of long leases at Sutton-at-Hone and Dartford (Kent), also mentioned in the first draft of his will, see TNA, SP 2/J ff. 159–69, *LP* 4 iii no. 6336. On the possible role of Gage in Cromwell's choice of Lewes Priory for his son's first marital home, see below, p. 431.   **51.** Ives, 'Fall of Wolsey', 287–8, 307, drawing on Cavendish, *Life of Wolsey*, ed. Singer, 270–71, and Wolsey to Henry VIII, *c.* 3 November 1529, SP 1/55 f. 191, *LP* 4 iii no. 6024.   **52.** Vaughan to Cromwell, 30 October 1529, SP 1/55 f. 198, *LP* 4 iii no. 6036.   **53.** For slightly exiguous information on Morris, see *HC 1509–1558* 2, 636–7 and Baker 2, 1126–7, s.v. Morris, John V.   **54.** Lehmberg, *Reformation Parliament*, 22–6, and see the relevant biographies in *HC 1509–1558*. Hall hosted Wolsey on his journey north in April 1530 (Cavendish, *Life of Wolsey*, ed. Singer, 313), and his family had a host of connections with Cromwell, many via Calais. Confusingly, there was a second Sir William Fitzwilliam, not an MP, who was Treasurer of Wolsey's household (the other Sir William the MP was royal Treasurer), and lived near Peterborough: on him, see Cavendish, *Life of Wolsey*, ed. Singer, 310–17. Hawkyard, *House of Commons 1509–1558*, 119n, adds on the basis of Wolsey connections George Acworth (Bedfordshire), Thomas Audley the later Lord Chancellor (Essex), William Gascoigne (Bedfordshire), Nicholas Hare (Downton) and William Nanfan (Dorchester). Thomas Alvard needs to be subtracted from Hawkyard's list, since (as we have seen) he did not become an MP till a by-election of 1533; Hawkyard, *House of Commons 1509–1558*, 88, also points out that Richard Page was replaced at York within two weeks of Parliament opening.   **55.** Chaffyn to Cromwell, 2 January [1530], SP 1/56 f. 190, *LP* 4 iii no. 6136 (see on the same matter Thomas Bennet to Cromwell, 2 January [1530], SP 1/236 f. 292, *LP Addenda* 1 i no. 683). *HC 1509–1558* 1, 608, wrongly reassigns Chaffyn's letter to 1536; the decorum of the address of both letters makes that impossible.   **56.** Hall 2, 155–6; P. J. Holmes, 'The last Tudor Great Councils', *HJ* 33 (1990), 1–22, at 1, 6–8.   **57.** Lehmberg, *Reformation Parliament*, 76–85, provides a sound narrative of opening events in Parliament.   **58.** SP 1/236 ff. 168–9, *LP Addenda* 1 i no. 663; cf. Lehmberg, *Reformation Parliament*, 96.   **59.** SP 1/56 ff. 39–42, *LP* 4 iii no. 6043[7]; the main body of text, *pace* G. R. Elton, 'Parliamentary drafts, 1529–1540', in Elton, *Studies* 2, 62–81, at 65, does not resemble the hand of any of his clerks at the time. Elton associated another anti-clerical petition with this Parliament, but the evidence points fairly clearly to a date in 1530–31, and it is amusing to observe Lehmberg struggling between respect for Elton and logic in his commentary on it: Lehmberg, *Reformation Parliament*, 85 and n. 4.   **60.** On those plans, see R. W. Hoyle, 'The origins of the dissolution of the monasteries', *HJ* 38 (1995), 275–305, at 282.   **61.** SP 1/54 f. 208v, *LP* 4 iii no. 5749[1]. Guy, *Public Career of Sir Thomas More*, 106, has misunderstood the import of this clause in the document (which he prints in transcript, at 206–7) to imply that Darcy was exploring the possibility of complete monastic dissolution in 1529; this idea has gained considerable circulation in historiography on the Tudors. Yet Darcy clearly intended his clause as part of a denunciation of Wolsey's jurisdictional excesses. Hoyle, 'Origins of the dissolution of the monasteries', 288, concurs with my conclusion here.   **62.** 'ad nostrae religionis [i.e. the Augustinian Order] obprobium, scandalum, dessipacionem et ruinam non solum nostrae Religionis sed etiam

Monachorum, Monacharum ac Monialium quasi per totam Angliam': A. G. Dickens, *Late Monasticism and the Reformation* (London and Rio Grande, 1994), 46–7. **63.** Lehmberg, *Reformation Parliament*, 86–94. **64.** J. J. Scarisbrick, *Henry VIII* (London, 1968), 250–51; J. J. Scarisbrick, 'Fisher, Henry VIII and the Reformation crisis', in B. Bradshaw and E. Duffy (eds.), *Humanism, Reform and the Reformation: the career of Bishop John Fisher* (Cambridge, 1989), 155–68, at 158. For relevant comment on Fisher's extraordinary vehemence, Hoyle, 'Origins of the dissolution of the monasteries', 286, and he also favours taking the dissolution proposal seriously, at 289. **65.** *LP* 4 iii no. 5411. **66.** For Pole's comments on his position in October, see above, p. 87; for Foxe reporting similar opinions of him at Court at the beginning of 1530, see below, p. 106, and see also the comments of Thomas Rush, below, pp. 101–2. **67.** Guy, *Public Career of Sir Thomas More*, 121–6. **68.** The full document is preserved only in seventeenth-century recensions respectively published by Sir Edward Coke and Lord Herbert of Chirbury: see Herbert, *Life and Raigne of King Henry the Eighth*, 266–74. Ives, 'Fall of Wolsey', 295–8, 307–10, deals with the document; his interpretation of it as the coming together of a 'grand faction' (at 312) seems to me over-elaborate, and it is much more straightforward to see its introduction as thanks to a decision of the King, as I argue here. **69.** For the Cardinal's signature on the petition, see Hall 2, 171, which gives a much abbreviated account of what is nevertheless clearly the same text. **70.** Cavendish, *Life of Wolsey*, ed. Singer, 274–5; cf. comment in Elton, *Tudor Revolution in Government*, 81. **71.** Shele to Cromwell, 27 November [1529], SP 1/68 f. 58, *LP* 5 no. 551. *LP* was uncertain how to date this, but it clearly refers to Parliament and none other sat in November before 1534, which is far too late for the address and content. Shele also sent greetings to Mistress Prior and gifts and promises of waterfowl. For Cromwell's esteem of his 'clerk' Shele, who had a small benefice in Essex (R. Newcourt, *Repertorium Ecclesiasticum Parochiale Londinense* ... (2 vols., London, 1708–10), 2, 638, makes him vicar of the marshy parish of Walton to 1546), see John Longland Bishop of Lincoln to Cromwell, SP 1/68 f. 108, *LP* 5 no. 623, dateable to January 1534 by reference to Longland to Cromwell, dateable as 3 January 1534, SP 1/82 f. 249, *LP* 7 no. 322, discussing the chantry of Chalgrave of which Shele was thereafter Master. **72.** Herbert, *Life and Raigne of King Henry the Eighth*, 274. **73.** Wolsey to Cromwell, [17 December 1529], BL MS Cotton Vespasian F/ XIII f. 147, *LP* 4 iii no. 6080. The Duke's visit to Esher in December will have been that described in detail by Cavendish, and dated as after the publication of the petition: Cavendish, *Life of Wolsey*, ed. Singer, 277–85. **74.** *LP* 4 iii no. 6094. For Winter's recall, see Chapuys's report to Charles V, 25 October 1529, Bradford (ed.), *Correspondence of Charles V*, 291, *Spanish Calendar* 4 i no. 194. **75.** SP 1/56 ff. 139–41, *LP* 4 iii no. 6115, probably of December 1529. **76.** Sadler to Cromwell, dated only 'Thursday', but December 1529, BL MS Cotton Titus B/I f. 375, *LP* 4 iii no. 6112. **77.** Bodl. MS Jesus College 74 f. 193r, *LP* 4 iii no. 6076, at 2714. **78.** Ibid.: extracts of a letter probably of December 1529. **79.** Bodl. MS Jesus College 74 ff. 189r–190r, *LP* 4 iii no. 5743. **80.** For a representative sample, see William Capon to Cromwell, 29 October [1529], SP

1/55 f. 197, *LP* 4 iii no. 6034; Capon to Cromwell, 22 November [1529], SP 1/56 ff. 88–9, *LP* 4 iii no. 6061; parson of Horsmonden to Cromwell, 17 November [1529], SP 1/56 f. 87, *LP* 4 iii no. 6058.   81. Rush to Cromwell, 29 December [1529], SP 1/56 f. 124, *LP* 4 iii no. 6110. Thomas Bonham was Receiver-General of the Duchy of Lancaster, and Audley was the Duchy's Steward in his native Essex.   82. Orford is 3 miles from Butley Priory, home of the chronicler whose furious opinion of Wolsey's dissolution we have already heard.   83. Cromwell's accounts, payment for 23 May 1539: *LP* 14 ii no. 782, at 341.   84. C. Johnson, 'The travels and trials of a sixteenth-century Wirral recusant', *Cheshire History* 47 (2007–8), 22–33, at 22: a meticulous study which is unnecessarily sceptical about the Cromwell connection.   85. G. Ormerod, *The history of the county palatine and city of Chester* ... (3 vols., London, 1819), 2, 304.   86. Johnson, 'The travels and trials of a sixteenth-century Wirral recusant', which once more is over-cautious, at 26, on identifying Sander. K. R. Wark, *Elizabethan Recusancy in Cheshire* (Chetham Society 3rd series 19, 1971), 153, 168, unfortunately gets in a muddle over Christian names, but, apart from that, provides further illumination on the Houghs and their recusant relatives.

Chapter 5: Serving Two Masters: 1530

1. Vaughan to Cromwell, 3 February 1530, SP 1/56 f. 227, *LP* 4 iii no. 6196.   2. Littleprow to Cromwell, 6 February [1530], SP 1/65 f. 122, *LP* 5 no. 86. *LP* misdates this letter to 1531, but Littleprow's reference to a rumour that Wolsey is dead, 'which I think is not true', shows that it must predate the Cardinal's actual death in November 1530; even Norfolk's modern reputation would preclude a merchant of Norwich not having heard of that event after three months. Wolsey had indeed been very ill in January 1530. Elton, *Tudor Revolution in Government*, 83, concurs.   3. This and what follows are from Foxe 1570, 1386–7. Foxe attributes to Hales the office of Master of the Rolls, which he did not in fact hold till later in the 1530s – parallel with his premature styling of Sir John Russell as Earl of Bedford: one has to remember that these titles are how many of Foxe's readers would remember and identify these individuals in 1570. Elton, *Tudor Revolution in Government*, 71–6, is much more sceptical about the idea of a single interview between Cromwell and the King (though he veers in his opinion of Foxe's reliability).   4. Hales to Cromwell, 19 July 1536/9, SP 1/152 f. 140, *LP* 14 i no. 1287.   5. Hales to Cromwell, 2 December [1526], SP 1/235 f. 181, *LP Addenda* 1 i no. 494, dateable by reference in London's Common Council Book to what was clearly a major row about this appointment, copied in SP 1/40 f. 12, *LP* 4 ii 2639.   6. Hales to Cromwell, 26 December ?1526, SP 1/235 f. 75, *LP Addenda* 1 i no. 495.   7. Hales to Cromwell, 28 December [1533], SP 1/81 f. 29rv, *LP* 6 no. 1574. Mr Bedell was Thomas Bedell, not yet in Cromwell's service; many other documents group Hales with Cromwell, Lee and Bedell, who evidently had a lot in common. This and the case of Nicholas Caunton both represent instances of Hales disapproving of Cromwell's young protégés; he evidently did not suffer fools

gladly, as is also apparent from his treatment of his young cousin John Hales: John Hales to Cromwell, late September 1534, SP 1/85 f. 197, *LP* 7 no. 1210. **8.** Brigden, *Thomas Wyatt*, deals well with both these relationships: see the appropriate index entries.   **9.** Chapuys to Charles V, 6 February 1530, Bradford (ed.), *Correspondence of Charles V*, 308–9, *Spanish Calendar* 4 i no. 257.   **10.** Russell to Cromwell, 1 June [1530], SP 1/57 f. 139, *LP* 4 iii no. 6420; my italics. For Sandys's impatience to see this grant completed, see Sandys to Cromwell, 16 June [1530], SP 1/57 f. 160, *LP* 4 iii no. 6460, and for drafts of it corrected by Cromwell, SP 1/57 ff. 162–4, *LP* 4 iii no. 6460[2–3].   **11.** Respectively the examination of Sir Francis Bryan, mid-June 1536, BL MS Cotton Otho C/X f. 174r, *LP* 10 no. 1134[4], the deficiencies supplied from Bodl. MS Jesus College 74 f. 249r (my italics); Russell to Lisle, 3 June [1536], SP 3/7 f. 36, *Lisle Letters* 3 no. 713.   **12.** For Gage's resignation, reported to Cromwell by their mutual friend Sir William Fitzwilliam, 10 August 1533, SP 1/78 f. 104, *LP* 6 no. 965. For a letter written from the Sheen Charterhouse seeking Cromwell's help in employing a former servant, John Gage to James Gage, 19 December 1533/5, SP 1/68 f. 90, *LP* 5 no. 588.   **13.** Starkey, 'Intimacy and innovation', 108–9, has some brief remarks on these lines.   **14.** Foxe 1570, 1387; he adds that this 'was about the year of our Lord 1530'. For the significance of these oaths in 1532, see below, p. 164.   **15.** See the patent roll entries for January, *LP* 4 iii no. 6187.   **16.** The section on Cromwell's interview with the King from *Apologia Reg. Poli ad Carolum V* is *ERP* 1, 118–21 (sect. xxvii).   **17.** J. Edwards, *Archbishop Pole* (Farnham and Burlington, VT, 2014), 25–31.   **18.** *ERP* 1, 123–4 (sect. xxvii): 'non possum affirmare me expressisse, qui non interfui, tamen hoc possum affirmare, nihil in illa oratione positum alicujus momenti, quod non vel ab eodem nuncio eo narrante intellexi, vel ab illis, qui ejus consilii fuerunt participes, sparsim quidem ab illis, et diversis temporibus dicta, quorum ego summam in unum collegi, quae minime ex meo ingenio excogitavi, ut verisimilia, sed ex illorum ore excepi, quae profero ut vera.'   **19.** Geoffrey Elton's repeated assertion against this passage that Pole and Cromwell only ever met once (e.g. Elton, *Studies* 2, 124, 217) is curious, and seems to rest on his misunderstanding of Pole's phrase elsewhere that they met 'semel et iterum' (*ERP* 1, 132). Pole actually says that he heard one thing from Cromwell in public (respectable sentiments) and another (discreditable) in private, 'semel et iterum, nunquam amplius' – once or twice, never more: a comment on the infrequency of the deplorable sentiment, not of their meetings. On Pole's time in England through most of 1531 see e.g. Edwards, *Archbishop Pole*, 40–42.   **20.** *ERP* 1, 121 (sect. xxvii).   **21.** Ives, *Life and Death of Anne Boleyn*, 132–4.   **22.** Scarisbrick, *Henry VIII*, ch. 9, 'The Campaign against the Church', remains the most concise and convincing account of the development of Henry's ideas about the royal supremacy. On Cranmer's promotions in 1530, MacCulloch, *Thomas Cranmer*, 48–51.   **23.** Cavendish, *Life of Wolsey*, ed. Singer, 295.   **24.** Bodl. MS Jesus College 74 f. 192r, and see commentary in Lindley, 'Playing check-mate with royal majesty?', 265–7, which includes a fascinating reconstruction of the tomb components (see p. 59 above).   **25.** BL MS Additional 20030 f. 48, *LP* 5 no. 1799: payment in December 1530.   **26.** For the happy resolution of the angels' fate,

NOTES TO PP. 112–14

see http://collections.vam.ac.uk/item/O1278468/sculpture-da-rovezzano-benedetto. See also H. M. Colvin (ed.), *The History of the King's Works 3–4: 1485–1660* (London, 1982), 3, 320–22, and on Portinari working for Cromwell on a masque at Court and in demolition at Lewes Priory, see below, p. 440. For important studies on the tombs of Henry and Wolsey and their Italian connections, see C. M. Sicca and L. A. Waldman (eds.), *The Anglo-Florentine Renaissance: art for the early Tudors* (New Haven and London, 2012).   **27.** William Laurence to Cromwell, 31 May [1531], SP 1/66 f. 21, *LP* 5 no. 273. One notes also in a list of Cromwell's archive of summer 1534 a 'paper of the schoolhouse in Ipswich': *LP* 7 no. 923[xii], 343. On the destruction of the shrine, see below, p. 464. **28.** William Sabine and William Nottingham to Cromwell, 20 March [1540], SP 1/117 f. 65, *LP* 12 i no. 688 (misdated in *LP*).   **29.** D. MacCulloch (ed.), 'The *Vita Mariae Angliae Reginae* of Robert Wingfield of Brantham', *Camden Miscellany* 28 (Camden 4th series 29, 1984), 181–300, at 184–8; D. MacCulloch and J. Blatchly, 'A house fit for a queen: Wingfield House, Tacket Street, Ipswich and its heraldic room', *Proceedings of the Suffolk Institute of Archaeology and History* 38 pt 1 (1993), 13–34.   **30.** Petition of Thomas Gyllott, Merchant of the Staple of Calais, to Cromwell, ?1534, SP 1/88 f. 68, *LP* 7 no. 1639.   **31.** The inventories of church goods, misdated in *LP*, are SP 1/47 f. 256r, f. 258r, *LP* 4 ii no. 4229[2, 3], and the petition is SP 1/240 f. 261, *LP Addenda* 1 i no. 1171, misdated by *LP* but dateable by a note of the parishioners' concern to retrieve the goods in William Laurence to Cromwell, ?8 April 1538, SP 1/242 f. 3, *LP Addenda* 1 ii no. 1312. Cromwell had by 1538 returned the church 'stuff' to Roger Austen, the Duke of Norfolk's park keeper at Earl Soham: for Austen at Soham, see TNA, SC 6 H VIII 6305. For its arrival in Cromwell's custody from Rush, see the identical list in Thomas Thacker to Cromwell, 11 September [1535], SP 1/96 f. 129, *LP* 9 no. 340. For Robert Lord Curzon's previous worries about the reconstruction of St Peter's parish and church, see Curzon to Cromwell, 20 December [1532], SP 1/72 f. 145, *LP* 5 no. 1650, and for the very informative later churchwardens' accounts, 1563–1664, BL MS Additional 25344.   **32.** Starkey, 'Intimacy and innovation', 96–7.   **33.** SP 1/65 ff. 262–7, *LP* 5 no. 260; SP 1/65 f. 268, *LP* 5 no. 261: all documents corrected by Cromwell or in his hand, one of which at least is probably from May 1531. For details of the King's ambitious plans to expand Whitehall and other palaces at this time, see S. Thurley, *Houses of Power: the places that shaped the Tudor world* (London, 2017), especially 120–48.   **34.** SP 1/58 f. 19, *LP* 4 iii no. 6598. Ward, 'Origins of Thomas Cromwell's public career', 229–31, provides excellent commentary on this.   **35.** Cavendish, *Life of Wolsey*, ed. Singer, 297. **36.** Ives, *Life and Death of Anne Boleyn*, 207–9 and 396 n. 19.   **37.** On Cranmer and the Boleyns, MacCulloch, *Thomas Cranmer*, 47–8, 54, 82–3, 93, 157–9. On Goodricke and the Boleyns, ibid., 47; Richard List to Anne Boleyn, 4 February 1533, BL MS Cotton Cleopatra E/IV f. 31, *LP* 6 no. 115 (using Goodricke as a go-between); S. Gunn, 'The structures of politics in early Tudor England', *TRHS* 6th series 5 (1995), 59–90, at 74; and cf. above, pp. 19–20.   **38.** The exact sum that Cromwell paid is unknown, but one payment was part of a sum of £99 15s which he made in 1535 also for a lease at Waltham from another lessor and for

wine and robes: account of his receiver Henry Polstead, *LP* 9 no. 478, 157.
39. £400 in fact at her death: SP 1/103 f. 318r, *LP* 10 no. 912.   40. Ives, *Life and Death of Anne Boleyn*, 210.   41. On the marriage proposal, William Courtenay to Cromwell, 15 July 1533, SP 1/77 f. 211, *LP* 6 no. 837. So far, I have not been able to track down a marital alliance involving Courtenay and Cromwell.
42. Anne Boleyn to Cromwell, May 1534/5, BL MS Cotton Cleopatra E/V f. 350, *LP* 7 no. 664. Anne was right about Harman and Wolsey: Brown, 'Wolsey and ecclesiastical order', 236–7. One letter to Cromwell has been seen as relating to service he did for Anne Boleyn as Steward on her Welsh estates: William Brabazon and Hugh Whalley to Cromwell, 26 March [1532], SP 1/74 f. 196, *LP* 6 no. 200. In fact 'My Lady' mentioned in it is Lady Katherine Howard, widow of Rhys ap Gruffydd, who was executed in December 1531, as is apparent from two letters misdated by *LP*: Brabazon to Cromwell, 1 March [1532], SP 1/53 f. 129, *LP* 4 iii no. 5399, and Cromwell to Brabazon and Whalley, 3 April [1532], SP 1/103 f. 85, *LP* 10 no. 617[i] (the last misdating has affected Merriman 2 no. 141).   43. These points are well made in Schofield, *Rise and Fall of Thomas Cromwell*, ch. 7.
44. That can be painfully demonstrated by reading the various sixteenth-century editions of that great work, but is also apparent from silence if one reads T. S. Freeman, 'Research, rumour and propaganda: Anne Boleyn in Foxe's "Book of Martyrs"', *HJ* 38 (1995), 797–819. The only subtraction to make from his authoritative account is his acceptance as evidence of the spurious material in [J. P. Collier, forger], 'Transcript of an original manuscript, containing a memorial from George Constantyne to Thomas Lord Cromwell', 'ed.' T. Amyot, *Archaeologia* 23 (1831), 50–78.   45. The election is well described in M. Heale, *The Abbots and Priors of Late Medieval and Reformation England* (Oxford, 2016), 287–8.   46. See below, Chapter 14, and Ives, *Life and Death of Anne Boleyn*, 202–4, 294–5.   47. One of those who do doubt is Prof. George Bernard; but I judge his various attempts to prove his case, notably G. W. Bernard, 'Anne Boleyn's religion', *HJ* 36 (1993), 1–20, to have been effectively answered by the various writings of E. W. Ives, lastly and concisely in Ives, 'Anne Boleyn on trial again', *JEH* 62 (2011), 763–77. The knockout blow is in any case the evidence of Anne's evangelical library presented in J. P. Carley, ' "Her moost lovyng and fryndely brother sendeth gretyng": Anne Boleyn's manuscripts and their sources', in M. P. Brown and S. McKendrick (eds.), *Illuminating the Book: makers and interpreters* (London, 1998), 261–80.   48. R. McEntegart, *Henry VIII, the League of Schmalkalden and the English Reformation* (London, 2002), 93, comes to the same conclusion.   49. On the move, Cavendish, *Life of Wolsey*, ed. Singer, 288–99 (see his specific assertion that the move to Richmond was without the Council's knowledge and 'through the special motion of Master Cromwell': 293); Ives, 'Fall of Wolsey', 313. Simon Thurley elucidates the complex relationship between Henry's and Wolsey's occupation of Hampton Court and Richmond in the late 1520s in 'The domestic building works of Cardinal Wolsey', 90–91.   50. Wolsey to Cromwell, first week of February, BL MS Cotton Appendix XLVIII f. 22, *LP* 4 iii no. 6249. Full text in *State Papers* 1, 361.   51. Cavendish, *Life of Wolsey*, ed. Singer, 299, 303–4.   52. *LP* 4 iii, nos. 6213, 6220. For the negotiations, see especially Wolsey to Cromwell, late January/

beginning of February 1530, BL MS Cotton Appendix XLVIII f. 20, *LP* 4 iii no. 6226. Full text in *State Papers* 1, 361: Wolsey urged Cromwell to speak directly with the King, but we cannot know that he did.   **53.** Cavendish, *Life of Wolsey*, ed. Singer, 294–5.   **54.** Cavendish is a meticulous and reliable witness on Wolsey's movements from now on, and will not further be referenced: Cavendish, *Life of Wolsey*, ed. Singer, 307–404.   **55.** SP 1/57 ff. 38–42, *LP* 4 iii no. 6294[1–5], drafts where the crossings-out of 'Councillor' are consistent. See also a finished specimen dated 28 March 1530, BL MS Cotton Caligula B/VII f. 162, *LP* 4 iii no. 6295; this would have come back into the archive when Dacre's papers were seized in 1534. For Wolsey's request to Cromwell for these letters of recommendation, Bodl. MS Jesus College 74 f. 193r, *LP* 4 iii no. 6076, at 2714. Wolsey had also lost the title of 'Councillor' in a royal privy seal of 29 March addressed to him, concerning his relinquishing of control in the diocese of Winchester: BL MS Cotton Titus B/I f. 61, *LP* 4 iii no. 6298. In a final irony, the King was then lodging at Wolsey's favourite Hertfordshire retreat of The More.   **56.** Gage to Cromwell, 13 April 1530, SP 1/57 f. 67, *LP* 4 iii no. 6335. Gage ended by hoping to see Cromwell at Court at Windsor 'these Easter holidays'.   **57.** D. M. Loades (ed.), *The Papers of George Wyatt Esquire . . .* (Camden 4th series 5, 1968), 152–3. This intriguing account of the English Reformation from *c.* 1600, not apparently authored by Wyatt himself, is notable for its original perspectives and circumstantial detail, though alas is incomplete and damaged.   **58.** Donington to Cromwell, 10 August 1530, SP 1/57 f. 265, *LP* 4 iii no. 6556. For uncomplimentary opinions of Donington, see e.g. Lancelot Collins to Wolsey, 27 March [1529], SP 1/53 f. 130, *LP* 4 iii no. 5400; Robert Smith to Wolsey, 10 June [1530], SP 1/57 f. 155, *LP* 4 iii no. 6447. **59.** Vaughan to Cromwell, 1 December 1530, SP 1/58 f. 173, *LP* 4 iii no. 6754. **60.** Vaughan to Cromwell, 30 November 1530, SP 1/58 f. 147, *LP* 4 iii no. 6744; the end of this correspondence about the whale-oil is Vaughan to Cromwell, 26 February 1532, BL MS Cotton Galba B/X f. 5, *LP* 5 no. 808.   **61.** For the wine licence, of 20 December 1532, see *LP* 5 no. 1693[10].   **62.** Cromwell to Wolsey, n.d., Bodl. MS Jesus College 74 f. 192r, and same to same, [17 May 1530], f. 194r, the latter *LP* 4 iii no. 6076, at 2715 (the Luther fragment of the latter is also cited in chronological position by *LP* from an intermediate source as *LP* 4 iii no. 6391). For the background to the King's summons, which culminated on 24 or 25 May 1530, reinforcing the date of this letter fragment as 17 May, see Guy, *Public Career of Sir Thomas More*, 103–4.   **63.** C. Euler, 'Religious and cultural exchange during the Reformation: Zürich and England, 1531–1558' (Johns Hopkins University PhD, 2004), 223.   **64.** E.g. Vaughan to Cromwell, 9 December 1531, BL MS Cotton Galba B/X ff. 23–5, *LP* 5 no. 574; Vaughan to Cromwell, 27 August 1533, SP 1/78 f. 167, *LP* 6 no. 1040. See Cromwell to Wolsey, 18 August 1530, SP 1/57 f. 272v, *LP* 4 iii no. 6571, Merriman 1 no. 18, 333.   **65.** MacCulloch, *Thomas Cranmer*, 60–66, 71, 153–4.   **66.** Ives, 'Fall of Wolsey', 313–15, concisely rounds up the evidence; see also Hammond, 'Doctor Augustine', 217–20.   **67.** Chapuys made the claim to Charles V about his regular contact with Wolsey in a letter of 20 August 1530, *Spanish Calendar* 4 i no. 411, at 692. The claim of the French ambassador about Wolsey's intrigues, at third hand via Chapuys, is in Bradford (ed.), *Correspondence of Charles V*, 325–6, *Spanish Calendar* 4 i no. 509; Ives, 'Fall of Wolsey', 314–15, provides good commentary on this.   68. See William Brabazon to Cromwell, early May 1530, SP 1/53 f. 227, *LP* 4 iii no. 5507; William Capon to Cromwell, 7 May [1530], SP 1/53 f. 250, *LP* 4 iii no. 5526; Capon to Cromwell, 15 May [1530], SP 1/54 f. 4, *LP* 4 iii no. 5550; Robert Smyth to Wolsey, 10 June [1530], SP 1/57 ff. 155–6, *LP* 4 iii no. 6447 (in which the reference to Alvard occurs, apparently ready to take liturgical books to York from Ipswich). This whole sequence apart from the last letter is misdated in *LP* to 1529, but that is clearly wrong, not merely because of Capon's thanks but because the principal actor is Brabazon. For much of the spring of 1529 he was lying severely ill at Walton in Suffolk: cf. the reference to his five-week illness in Cromwell's accounts, SP 1/44 f. 310r, *LP* 4 ii no. 3536, with John Smith to Cromwell, 31 March [1529], SP 1/53 f. 135, *LP* 4 iii no. 5405, a letter which has to be of 1529 in view of the content.   69. Wolsey to Cromwell, BL MS Cotton Appendix XLVIII f. 25, *LP* 4 iii no. 6524, printed in full in *State Papers* 1, 362. As usual with Wolsey's holograph notes, it is undated, but what seems like a reply to it by Cromwell appears to have been dated 12 July 1530: Bodl. MS Jesus College 74 f. 193v, *LP* 4 iii no. 6076, at 2715.   70. All these strands can be conveniently sampled in the extracts gathered by Thomas Master, Bodl. MS Jesus College 74 f. 194v, *LP* 4 iii no. 6076, but they are present in many of the original letters which survive. From them must be subtracted a peremptory letter from Cromwell to an Archbishop of York which can conclusively be reassigned to 1538 thanks to Ward, 'Origins of Thomas Cromwell's public career', 219–20: Cromwell to [Edward Lee Archbishop of York], 5 May [1538], SP 1/57 f. 87, *LP* 4 iii no. 6368.   71. Cromwell to Wolsey, 18 August [1530], SP 1/57 ff. 270r–273r, *LP* 4 iii no. 6571; Merriman 1 no. 18, efficiently displays the emendments, though not the change in hands, and I have made some modifications to his readings. The draft is not in Wriothesley's hand, as *LP* claims. Thomas Master made extracts from the vanished fair copy of this letter, but conflated it with an earlier letter of Cromwell's in August containing less reassurance, which had probably generated Wolsey's anxious letter of 10 August mentioned in this present text of 18 August: Bodl. MS Jesus College 74 f. 194rv, *LP* 4 iii no. 6076, at 2715–16.   72. The geldings are also mentioned in a letter of Thomas Donington to Cromwell, sent down with Wolsey's letter of the same day, 10 August 1530, SP 1/57 f. 265, *LP* 4 iii no. 6557; Donington also thanked Cromwell for his 'gracious goodness' to their common master.   73. Chapuys to Charles V, November 1530, *Spanish Calendar* 4 i nos. 804–5. Ives, 'Fall of Wolsey', 314–15, efficiently introduces the complex evidence; see also Ives, *Life and Death of Anne Boleyn*, 131.   74. Bodl. MS Jesus College 74 f. 194v, *LP* 4 iii no. 6076, at 2716.   75. Cromwell to Wolsey, 21 October 1530, BL MS Cotton Appendix XLVIII f. 110, *LP* 4 iii no. 6699, the much damaged text partially reconstructed in Merriman 1 no. 19, 334–5; part is excerpted in Bodl. MS Jesus College 74 f. 194v, *LP* 4 iii no. 6076, at 2716, which suggests that the text from Cromwell's lost letter about Wolsey's distrust, excerpted before this, was the opening of the now fragmentary text of 21 October in the Cottonian Appendix. On Wellifed and Sadler, see above, pp. 70–71.   76. Cavendish, *Life of Wolsey*, ed. Singer, 348, 351.   77. See especially L. R. Gardiner, 'Further news of Cardinal Wolsey's end, November–December, 1530', *Bulletin of the Institute of Historical Research* 57 (1984), 99–107, and useful supplementary comment in Ives, 'Fall of Wolsey', 314–15nn.   78. An abbreviated version is in *Spanish Calendar* 5 i no. 228, Chapuys to Nicolas de Granvelle, 21 November 1535, missing some important nuances, especially the crucial subjunctive 'auquel il deust promettre', 'at which he *must have* promised'. It is surprising that Geoffrey Elton did not appreciate this: Elton, *Tudor Revolution in Government*, 72. The French original from Vienna which I have translated is conveniently presented via a TNA transcript in Merriman 1, 17.   79. Hawkyard, *House of Commons 1509–1558*, 137, 204–5.   80. See the good account of him by Alan Bryson in *ODNB*, s.v. Wallop, Sir John.   81. Wolsey used that phrase to Cromwell's annoyingly persistent relative Henry Carbot, while postponing the fulfilment of promises of promotion which Cromwell had secured for Carbot the previous March at Sheen Charterhouse: Carbot to Cromwell, 11 August 1530, SP 1/57 f. 266, *LP* 4 ii no. 6558.   82. Cavendish, *Life of Wolsey*, ed. Singer, 297.   83. Russell to Cromwell, 1 June [1530], SP 1/57 f. 139, *LP* 4 iii no. 6420.

Chapter 6: Council and Parliament: 1531

1. G. R. Elton, 'Why the history of the early-Tudor Council remains unwritten', in Elton, *Studies* 1, 308–38.   2. TNA, E 101/421/1, *LP* 5 no. 341, for the July reference. For two from December 1531, see Henry VIII to Surveyors and Auditor, 11 December 1531, SP 1/68 f. 82, *LP* 5 no. 577 (interestingly, concerning finances for the refounded King Henry's College Oxford); Abbot of Waltham to Cromwell, 'of the Council', 31 December 1531, SP 1/73 f. 7, *LP* 5 no. 1684 (convincingly redated by J. D. Alsop, 'Cromwell and the Church in 1531: the case of Waltham Abbey', *JEH* 31 (1980), 327–30). A variety of letters addressing him with such honorifics as 'Councillor to the King's Majesty' are misdated in *Letters and Papers* to 1531, when many of them can definitely be reassigned to a later year, and few definitely placed in this period.   3. Creke to Cromwell [winter 1531], SP 1/69 f. 138, *LP* 5 no. 840. Cromwell's papers include a number of instances of his involvement in Creke's business in Spain and Crete over the previous decade.   4. [Creke] to Cromwell, [early April 1531], SP 1/68 f. 137, *LP* 5 no. 652: 'I stand at point of preferment, by the labour of the Spaniards and other my friends to enter service with the Queen in 7d halfpenny a day.'   5. Creke to Cromwell, [April 1531], SP 1/81 f. 95, *LP* 6 no. 1642, where it is misdated to 1533, correctly reassigned to 1531 in Corrigenda to that volume; the italics are mine, indicating the final clue to the firm dating of this correspondence. It is interesting that Creke did not use the title 'Councillor' in his slightly earlier letters to Cromwell already cited. There is a further emotional appeal from Creke to Cromwell, SP 1/81 f. 94, *LP* 6 no. 164, which probably does come from 1533. Cromwell evidently then got him a secretarial post with Archbishop Cranmer, in whose correspondence he appears, before a good deal of complicated business after his death into which Cromwell was drawn once more. For the most usefully clarifying letter about that tangle, badly timed in the

middle of the Pilgrimage of Grace crisis, see William Heydon to Cromwell, 25 October 1536, SP 1/109 f. 103, *LP* 11 no. 867.   6. For a report of the Hanworth grant to Gardiner, see Robert Smith to Wolsey, 10 June 1530, SP 1/57 ff. 155–6, *LP* 4 iii no. 6447. In the same month the Marquess of Dorset in his will left £20 to 'Dr Stephens now secretary to the King's Grace' (TNA, PROB 11/24 ff. 72v–76r); surprisingly, Cromwell does not figure in the bequests.   7. On the trade dispute, Customers of Bristol to Cromwell, 1 March 1535, SP 1/91 f. 5, looking back on events in 1531. On the proclamation, Cromwell to Norfolk, 15 July [1531], BL MS Cotton Titus B/I f. 318, *LP* 8 no. 1042; this was convincingly redated from 1535 by G. R. Elton, *Reform and Renewal: Thomas Cromwell and the Common Weal* (Cambridge, 1973), 117–18.   8. Augustine to Norfolk, 3 June 1531, BL MS Cotton Galba B/X f. 10, *LP* 5 no. 283; Piero de' Bardi to Cromwell, 14 October 1531, SP 1/68 f. 18, *LP* 5 no. 474.   9. *Venetian Calendar* 4 no. 694, at 297. Falier had arrived back in Venice at the beginning of November after thirty-seven months' absence: ibid., nos. 689, 690. For Falier's period of service, from December 1528 to September 1531, see 'Venetian Diplomatic Agents in England', in *Venetian Calendar* 1, cxxii–cxxix. Elton, *Tudor Revolution in Government*, 91, failed to notice that Falier was describing the situation in England at his departure from it in September, and hence dated Cromwell's rise into the 'inner ring' of councillors to November; in this, he has been followed by many commentators since.   10. In the list of names, the *Venetian Calendar*'s identification of 'il maggior Contarvolo Ary cavaliere dell' ordine' as Thomas Lord Darcy KG is clearly wrong, and it has to be Sir *Henry* ['Ary'] Guildford KG, then Comptroller of the Household.   11. BL MS Cotton Titus B/I f. 486, *LP* 5 no. 394, with useful commentary in *State Papers* 1, 380–83. The document is endorsed by the King himself.   12. C. Fletcher, *Our Man in Rome: Henry VIII and his Italian ambassador* (London, 2012), 161.   13. We are indebted to the excellent analysis of McEntegart, *Henry VIII, the League of Schmalkalden and the English Reformation*. For my own attempts to cut the Gordian Knot of Henry's theology, see D. MacCulloch, 'Henry VIII and the reform of the Church', in MacCulloch (ed.), *Reign of Henry VIII*, 159–80.   14. See the account in Fletcher, *Our Man in Rome*, 156–68, and see above, p. 134.   15. McEntegart, *Henry VIII, the League of Schmalkalden and the English Reformation*, 13.   16. McEntegart, ibid., 13 and n., argues that the English overtures of 1531 to Germany were biconfessional in direction. This is true, but misses the point that, besides those missions concerned with the electoral challenge to the Habsburgs, there was a series of specifically evangelical missions which I now discuss, which had a wider reference geographically and in intention, and which included the Swiss. He does actually pick up this point later, with useful discussion: ibid., 39–41.   17. Maas, *Reformation and Robert Barnes*, 25–6.   18. MacCulloch, *Thomas Cranmer*, 60–66.   19. MacCulloch, *Thomas Cranmer*, 59, 68, 77, and D. MacCulloch, 'Two dons in politics: Thomas Cranmer and Stephen Gardiner, 1503–1533', *HJ* 37 (1994), 1–22.   20. E. Surtz and V. Murphy (eds.), *The Divorce Tracts of Henry VIII* (Angers, 1988), and see commentary in MacCulloch, *Thomas Cranmer*, 51–5, and V. Murphy, 'The literature and propaganda of Henry VIII's first divorce', in MacCulloch (ed.), *Reign of Henry VIII*,

135–58. **21.** Chapuys to Charles V, 24 June 1531, *Spanish Calendar* 4 ii no. 753, at 201. There really is no other candidate for this reference, given Richard Rex's convincing redating of the *Glasse of the Truthe* to 1532: R. Rex, 'Redating Henry VIII's *A Glasse of the Truthe*', *Library* 7th series 4 (2003), 16–27. The *Disputatio* is also likely to be the 'book in writing' renouncing papal power which Simon Grynaeus saw in the King's chamber in early summer 1531: MacCulloch, *Thomas Cranmer*, 62–3. **22.** The work is *RSTC* 12510 and 12510.5, and the English translation of 1533 is 12511 and 12511a; S. W. Haas, 'The *Disputatio inter cleri cum et militem*: was Berthelet's 1531 edition the first Henrician polemic of Thomas Cromwell?', *Moreana* 14 (Dec. 1977), 65–72. Of Haas's attempts to date various works to 1531, this is the most secure: the printing of the Latin version of the *Disputatio* directly relates to the English version of the *Censurae* published as the *Determinations* in November 1531 (*RSTC* 14287), for that work reused its type-face ornaments, especially the title-page. **23.** Vaughan to Henry VIII and Cromwell, 26 January 1531, BL MS Cotton Galba B/X f. 46r, *LP* 5 no. 65. **24.** Vaughan to Cromwell, 16 December [1530], SP 1/68 f. 85, *LP* 5 no. 585 (misdated in *LP* but assignable to 1530 because of its reference to the recent publication of Cornelius Agrippa's *De vanitate scientiarum*, first published at Antwerp in September 1530, and by Vaughan's reference to this letter of 16 December by date ('the eighth day before Christmas') in a further letter to Cromwell on 3 January 1531, SP 1/65 f. 46, *LP* 5 no. 26. **25.** Haas, '*Disputatio inter clericum et militem*', 66, is too confident in identifying this work with the book bought by Vaughan, tempting though the identification is. On the genuine dialogues by Ockham which we know to have been in Henry VIII's library, see J. P. Carley, *The Libraries of Henry VIII* (London, 2000), 56–7, no. 170 (this is corrected in J. P. Carley, '*The Libraries of King Henry VIII*: an update of the Westminster inventory of 1542', *Library* 7th series 16 (2015), 282–303, at 298); 188, no. 1060; 189–90, no. 1077; see also J. P. Carley, 'Hannibal Gamon and two strays from the library of King Henry VIII', *The Book Collector* 64 (2015), 213–19. I am grateful to James Carley for discussions on this. **26.** See above, pp. 66, 68–9, 69–70. On Coverdale's uncertain movements at this time, probably in Antwerp, see *ODNB*, s.v. Coverdale, Miles. **27.** C. C. Butterworth and A. G. Chester, *George Joye 1495?–1553: a chapter in the history of the English Bible and the English Reformation* (Philadelphia, 1962), 30, 40–43; on Frith, John Clerk to Cromwell, 4 August 1526 (dateable to that year by its reference to Frith before he fled abroad), SP 1/49 f. 196, *LP* 4 ii no. 4607. **28.** Vaughan to Cromwell, 1 December 1530, SP 1/58 f. 173, *LP* 4 iii no. 6754; my italics. **29.** Cromwell to Stephen Vaughan, early May 1531, BL MS Cotton Galba B/X ff. 354–7, *LP* 5 no. 248; Merriman 1 no. 21 effectively presents the complicated alterations. Despite *LP* numbering this as 248, it is clearly this letter to which *LP* 5 no. 246 is a response. **30.** Vaughan to Henry VIII, 20 May 1531, SP 1/65 f. 252, *LP* 5 no. 246. **31.** Maas, *Reformation and Robert Barnes*, 22–6. **32.** MacCulloch, *Thomas Cranmer*, 65–6; Maas, *Reformation and Robert Barnes*, 25–6. Elton, *Tudor Revolution in Government*, 91–3, is a judicious assessment of the Cromwell/Vaughan transactions in this year. **33.** Carley, *Libraries of Henry VIII*, Introduction. **34.** Ibid., lvii–lviii. **35.** J. P. Carley, 'Religious controversy and marginalia: Pierfrancesco di Piero Bardi, Thomas Wakefield, and their books', *Transactions of the Cambridge Bibliographical Society* 12 (2002), 206–45; Carley's fascinating reconstruction suggests that Bardi offered these books to the King as a New Year's gift for the beginning of 1532.   **36.** *LP* 5 no. 506[1].   **37.** McEntegart, *Henry VIII, the League of Schmalkalden and the English Reformation*, 15–16, 90. See also E. Hildebrandt, 'Christopher Mont, Anglo-German diplomat', *SCJ* 15 (1984), 281–92, and *ODNB*, s.v. Mont, Christopher.   **38.** Cromwell to Christopher Mont, probably late summer 1533, SP 1/80 f. 54, *LP* 6 no. 1374.   **39.** Vaughan to Cromwell, 21 November 1533, SP 1/80 f. 106, *LP* 6 no. 1448.   **40.** Vaughan to Cromwell, 1 November 1533, SP 1/80 f. 75, *LP* 6 no. 1385.   **41.** G. Nicholson, 'The Act of Appeals and the English Reformation', in Cross, Loades and Scarisbrick (eds.), *Law and Government under the Tudors*, 19–30. The main *Collectanea* MS is BL MS Cotton Cleopatra E/VI ff. 16–135. For a crisp analysis of the theory of 'empire', usefully limiting Cromwell's role in formulating it, see J. Guy, 'Thomas Cromwell and the intellectual origins of the Henrician revolution', in A. Fox and J. Guy, *Reassessing the Henrician Age: humanism, politics and reform 1500–1550* (Oxford, 1986), pp. 151–78. See also F. Heal, 'What can King Lucius do for you? The Reformation and the early British Church', *EHR* 120 (2005), 593–614, particularly 599–600.   **42.** The narrative in the next two paragraphs reflects the excellent account in Guy, *Public Career of Sir Thomas More*, 133–40, although he probably dates Cromwell's active agency in this manoeuvres too early, if my account of Cromwell's interview with the King in December 1530 is accepted.   **43.** As Guy points out, ibid., 137, Hussey was already a proctor in the Court of Arches, but he also may have been acting as Registrar of the Province of Canterbury by this time; he was certainly scribe of the diocesan Official of Middlesex in the diocese of London by 1526 (Emden, *Oxford 1501 to 1540*, 684).   **44.** Cromwell to Wolsey, 21 October 1530, BL MS Cotton Appendix XLVIII f. 110, *LP* 4 iii no. 6699, efficiently reconstructed in Merriman 1 no. 19, 334–5.   **45.** R. W. Hoyle, 'War and public finance', in MacCulloch (ed.), *Reign of Henry VIII*, 75–99, at 77.   **46.** Lehmberg, *Reformation Parliament*, 109–11; the proceedings of this 1531 session of Convocation are fairly fully recorded in an eighteenth-century transcript, Lambeth MS 751, 55–75, with some small lacunae provided in Wilkins (ed.), *Concilia* 3, 724–6. On the Commons meeting in the refectory, see Hawkyard, *House of Commons 1509–1558*, 189–91.   **47.** Two addresses by Convocation to Henry VIII, TNA, E 135/8/36 (4 March 1531) and E 135/8/37 (22 March 1531, reciting the previous instrument and specifying that the grant was made on 24 January).   **48.** Lambeth MS 751, 59, 61–2. Lehmberg, *Reformation Parliament*, 114, says that Warham and his delegation were referred to some councillors, but this is incorrect; it was not surprising that the King should send them to the judges who had overseen the earlier *praemunire* indictments.   **49.** Lambeth MS 751, 61: 'Dominus Cromewell intravit et habuit secretam communicationem cum Reverendissimo'; Rochford appears at Lambeth MS 751, 62.   **50.** Lambeth MS 751, 63–4: 'Ecclesiae et cleri Anglicani, cuius singularem protectorem, unicum et supremum dominum, et quantum per Christi legem licet etiam supremum caput ipsius . . .'.   **51.** S. W. Haas, 'Martin Luther's "Divine

NOTES TO PP. 147–50

Right" kingship and the royal supremacy: two tracts from the 1531 Parliament and Convocation of the Clergy', *JEH* 31 (1980), 317–25.   52. Quoted. in ibid., 322.   53. 'The cause of the vexation of Roger Dycker, prisoner in the Marshalsea': SP 1/68 f. 109, *LP* 5 no. 628; since *LP*'s misreading of 'Kyrkhollam', the place has consistently been mistakenly styled Kirk Holland, which does not exist. For Cromwell's relationship with the Babingtons and Meverells, see above, p. 17.   54. Steven Haas, in making a decent enough case for those two examples of manuscript tracts coming from this 1531 Parliament, pointed to other docu ments surviving in the State Papers that might also belong to the campaign: Haas, 'Martin Luther's "Divine Right" Kingship and the royal supremacy', 320n.   55. Hoyle, 'Origins of the dissolution of the monasteries', 284–5, and especially 303: he cites Berkeley Castle, Select Roll 153, and prints the text of the second petition, ibid., 302–5. The bulk of the Lollard text from one of the more or less contemporary copies is provided in A. R. Myers (ed.), *English Historical Documents 1327–1485* (London, 1996), 668–70. Hoyle attributed this to the earlier Parliamentary session of 1529, but it actually sits rather better either amid the King's menacing demands for an unprecedented sum of money from an unnerved Church hierarchy in winter 1531 or in the following Parliament of 1532.   56. SP 1/56 f. 13r, *LP* 4 iii no. 6043[3]; for comment on this list (before the discovery of the Berkeley Castle documents) likewise suggesting a redating to 1531, see Elton, *Reform and Renewal*, 92.   57. *Pace* Hoyle, there is nothing specifically to tie down this list of bills to the 1529 session of the Reformation Parliament, where the Church hierarchy put up a fairly effective resistance to any moves to curb its power and privilege; there is a much more natural home for the list, including the paired petitions, amid the fierce assault to which Convocation succumbed in 1531. There is some overlap between the bills listed in the memorandum of lost bills and Cromwell's list from September 1531 of bills being proposed for an autumn session of Parliament: for instance on primer seisin, pluralities and export of unwrought cloth (cf. SP 1/56 f. 13, *LP* 4 iii no. 6043[3] and BL MS Cotton Titus B/I f. 486, *LP* 5 no. 394), and the list of lost bills included the thorny question of uses and recoveries, which remained unresolved in the spring 1531 Parliament after some bitter arguments.   58. Hall 2, 184–5; Chapuys to Charles V, 2 April 1531, *LP* 5 no. 171, at 83; this was not published in the *Spanish Calendar*.   59. Lehmberg, *Reformation Parliament*, 128–30.   60. Wilkins (ed.), *Concilia* 3, 745–6. Tunstall's protestation was subsequently cut out of his own register but by oversight remained in that of York, as in Wilkins's transcript: see the account of these events, slightly misdated, in the deposition of Christopher Chaitor, 16 December 1539, SP 1/155 f. 155v, *LP* 14 ii no. 750. For Henry's reply, BL MS Cotton Cleopatra E/VI f. 220, *LP* 5 Appendix 9, and on its dating to 1531, see A. G. Dickens, *Lollards and Protestants in the Diocese of York 1509–1558* (2nd edn, London, 1982), 158, though he is there too sanguine about the pliability of the Northern Convocation. Guy, *Public Career of Sir Thomas More*, 161, and Lehmberg, *Reformation Parliament*, 157n, have been misled by misdating in *LP* into thinking that there is direct evidence of Cromwell participating in management of this session of the York Convocation: unfortunately the two letters of

Dean Brian Higdon they cite are from 1533. **61.** Chapuys to Charles V, 2 April 1531, *LP* 5 no. 171, at 85; Lehmberg, *Reformation Parliament*, 129–30. **62.** Chapuys to Charles V, 17 July 1531, *Spanish Calendar* 4 ii no. 765. **63.** Ives, *Life and Death of Anne Boleyn*, 146–7, and on the private letters, the anonymous reminiscence of one of Katherine's old servants, possible Anthony Roke (see below, p. 656, n. 75), SP 1/142 ff. 201v–202r, *LP* 14 i no. 190. **64.** SP 1/141 f. 125rv, *LP* 13 ii no. 1223, in a fair formal hand, likely to be the secretary of the unnamed author. Elton, *Reform and Renewal*, 26–8, does a good deal of the work on elucidating this text; his suggested identification of its author is fully justified, but he gets some of the dating wrong. The text is misdated in *LP*; it is likely to date to autumn 1536 as it talks of Cranmer's servant Robert Wakefield as alive (he died no later than October 1537), but was written after Cromwell had gained his peerage; it calls on Robert Barnes to confirm 'what he hath heard of my doctrine and communication in Wales this last summer', and whereas Barnes was in London through the summer of 1537, in 1536 he was in hiding in an unspecified place (Martin Luther to Nicholas Hausmann, *LP* 11 no. 475). Among Oliver's many preferments, he was parson of Ross-on-Wye and at least by the end of the decade a canon and bursal prebendary of St David's (Emden, *Oxford 1501 to 1540*, 425); the latter may suggest common patronage to Oliver and Barnes from William Barlow, Bishop there from June 1536. **65.** *LP* 5 no. 306[2, 5]. *LP* 13 ii no. 1223 misreads 'law parlour' as 'low parlour', but the text is quite clear. The reference to 'your old house at the Austin Friars' distinguishes it from the new house created by Cromwell's massive building programme there in 1535. For Oliver as royal chaplain on 24 February 1532, when he took the surrender of Christ Church Aldgate with Roland Lee, see Rymer (ed.), *Foedera* 14, 411–12, and for an interesting glimpse of Oliver's rapport and colleagueship with Lee soon after that, Oliver to John Scudamore, 7 March [1532], BL Add. 11042 f. 66. **66.** I have argued that consideration of the royal supremacy was what first brought Thomas Cranmer to the Reformation, at about the same time: MacCulloch, *Thomas Cranmer*, 59–60. **67.** On Walter Cromwell's possible Irish ancestry, see above, pp. 16–17. For a fine overview of Irish government in this period and Cromwell's relationship to it, see S. G. Ellis, 'Thomas Cromwell and Ireland, 1532–1540', *HJ* 23 (1980), 497–519. **68.** Piers Earl of Ossory to Cromwell, 2 January 1532, Lambeth MS 616 f. 46, printed in *State Papers* 2, 153–5. For the accompanying memorandum referred to below, Lambeth MS 616 f. 47, printed in *State Papers* 2, 156–8, and the copy of Ossory's letter to Wiltshire is Lambeth MS 616 f. 48. All these are calendared at *LP* 5 no. 688[i–iii]. **69.** Murray, 'Archbishop Alen, Tudor Reform and the Kildare Rebellion', especially 14, and B. Bradshaw, *The Irish Constitutional Revolution of the Sixteenth Century* (Cambridge, 1979), 91. **70.** S. G. Ellis, *Reform and Revival: English government in Ireland 1470–1534* (Royal Historical Society Studies in History 47, 1986), 31–48. **71.** Bradshaw, *Irish Constitutional Revolution*, 92 (citing TNA, E 36/139, 17, briefly mentioned at *LP* 7 no. 923[iv], 340); Bradshaw's comment on Ossory's letter, ibid., 92–4, is very perceptive. On Cusack, see also *ODNB*, s.v. Cusack, Thomas, and Ellis, *Reform and Revival*, 223.

Chapter 7: New Year's Gifts: 1532

1. *LP* 5 no. 686, 329. Cromwell had plenty of ruby rings to choose from – rubies seem to have been a favourite of his: SP 1/42 f. 112r, *LP* 4 ii no. 3197. 2. 9 January 1532: SP 1/69 f. 9, *LP* 5 no. 701. Cromwell's job informally extended to anything which might be considered part of Wolsey's former possessions, and was no sinecure: for the King's outburst of bad-tempered suspicion about revenues from The More which only a personal interview with Cromwell could be expected to allay, see Thomas Heritage to Sir John Russell, 30 April [1532], SP 1/69 f. 266, *LP* 5 no. 976. 3. Lambeth MS 751, 75. The heretic was the lately dead William Tracey, friend of William Tyndale, whose will became a *cause célèbre* – J. Craig and C. Litzenberger, 'Wills as religious propaganda: the testament of William Tracy', *JEH* 44 (1993), 415–31 – and whose equally evangelical son Richard became a client of Cromwell's. 4. MacCulloch, *Thomas Cranmer*, 79–82; Lehmberg, *Reformation Parliament*, 131; A. Fox, 'Sir Thomas Elyot and the humanist dilemma', in Fox and Guy, *Reassessing the Henrician Age*, 52–75. 5. Christopher Hales to Cromwell, 31 December 1531, SP 1/68 f. 105, *LP* 5 no. 620. Hales wrote 'if he hear' when he clearly meant 'if ye hear' about the meeting of Parliament. 6. Lehmberg, *Reformation Parliament*, 132, rounds up some of those asking for absence, and one can add to that list the Abbot of Abingdon, who was first off the mark in early December (William Button to Cromwell, 9 December 1531, SP 1/68 f. 79, *LP* 5 no. 571). 7. Edgecombe to Cromwell, 23 March [1534], SP 1/83 f. 8, *LP* 7 no. 365; Hawkyard, *House of Commons 1509–1558*, 253, though Hawkyard there confuses Piers with his son Richard. 8. Edwards, *Archbishop Pole*, 42–3. 9. Above, p. 150. 10. Lehmberg, *Reformation Parliament*, 153–6. 11. Ibid., 133–5. On the rocky ride for primer seisin legislation, see E. W. Ives, 'The genesis of the Statute of Uses', *EHR* 82 (1967), 673–97, and see below, pp. 158, 163 12. Wilkins (ed.), *Concilia* 3, 746 (now BL MS Additional 48012 ff. 57v–58): 24 February 1532. The minutes of Convocation noted that the Archbishop did not attend that day, and the Abbot of Westminster presided in his place: Lambeth MS 751, 79. 13. Cromwell to Gardiner, late February 1532, SP 1/69 f. 40, *LP* 5 no. 723. 14. Hawkyard, *House of Commons 1509–1558*, 331–5. 15. *Spanish Calendar* 4 ii no. 926, and for discussion of this phase of the 1532 Parliament, see Lehmberg, *Reformation Parliament*, 135–8. 16. For a brilliant summary of this question, J. Guy, *Thomas More: a very brief history* (London, 2017), 32–8, 53–5, and for perceptive if perhaps indulgent analysis of More's dark mood in this period, E. Duffy, *Reformation Divided: Catholics, Protestants and the conversion of England* (London, 2017), chs. 1–3, and C. D'Alton, 'Charity or fire? The argument of Thomas More's 1529 *Dyaloge*', *SCJ* 33 (2002), 51–70. 17. On all this, see Guy, *Public Career of Sir Thomas More*, 164–71. On Curatt, above, p. 83. 18. J. Guy, *Christopher St German on Chancery and Statute* (Selden Society supplementary series 6, 1985); R. Rex, 'New additions on Christopher St German: law, politics and propaganda in the 1530s', *JEH* 59 (2008), 281–300. 19. The most recent survey of the bewilderingly technical debate, G. W. Bernard, *The King's Reformation: Henry VIII and the remaking of the English*

Church (New Haven and London, 2005), 58–61, has much to commend it, apart from its culminating intention of reducing Cromwell's part in contemporary events, based on an unreasonably selective reading of evidence.   20. H. A. Kelly, 'The submission of the clergy', *TRHS* 5th series 15 (1965), 97–119, at 98–102.   21. Hall 2, 202–5; Lehmberg, *Reformation Parliament*, 138–46.   22. Lehmberg, *Reformation Parliament*, 147–8.   23. Guy, *Public Career of Sir Thomas More*, 192–3.   24. Hall 2, 209–11.   25. Alsop, 'Cromwell and the Church in 1531: the case of Waltham Abbey'; the Close Roll enrolment is TNA, C 54/400, m. 24.   26. The proceedings are recorded in Lambeth MS 751, 91–3. Various copies and drafts of the submission are rounded up in *LP* 5 no. 1023, and the English text without the witnesses is printed in Pocock 2, 257–8, where doubts are expressed about the source of the extended text in Wilkins (ed.), *Concilia* 3, 754–5, relating it to what is now BL MS Additional 48012 ff. 63v–64r. Kelly, 'Submission of the clergy', remains the best overview of this crucial session of Convocation and its culmination.   27. TNA, SP 2/L ff. 183–8, *LP* 5 no. 1028.   28. Hawkyard, *House of Commons 1509–1558*, 205, is a useful counterweight to dismissive assessments of these magnates.   29. SP 1/125 ff. 200–206, *LP* 12 ii no. 952: the source of what follows. A fair copy made from Throckmorton's own challenging handwriting is SP 1/125 ff. 207–10, *LP* 12 ii no. 952[2]. The confession's date is slightly later than that given by *LP* or elsewhere, since Sir George wishes a long life to the King and Prince Edward but does not mention Queen Jane Seymour, who died on 24 October 1537. The text is conveniently presented in Guy, *Public Career of Sir Thomas More*, 207–12. The events described in it map well on to the 1532 Parliament, though Throckmorton puts them at 'six or seven years past' and in his reminiscence of his meeting with Friar Peto he speaks of 'a little before the beginning' of Parliament, when he means a little before the end: cf. Guy, *Public Career of Sir Thomas More*, 210; SP 1/125 f. 204v.   30. P. Marshall, 'Crisis of allegiance: George Throckmorton and Henry Tudor', in Marshall and G. Scott (eds.), *Catholic Gentry in English Society: the Throckmortons of Coughton from Reformation to emancipation* (Farnham, 2009), 31–67, is an excellent overview of Throckmorton and the material dealt with here; for a wider view of the family in the period, see P. Marshall, *Faith and Identity in a Warwickshire Family: the Throckmortons and the Reformation* (Dugdale Society Occasional Papers 49, 2010).   31. The connection to Fleet Street is made in two other confessions from 1537 of Throckmorton and Sir William Essex (SP 1/113 f. 60v, *LP* 11 no. 1406, and cf. *LP* 11 no. 1405) which reveal them as still in the habit of taking supper at the Queen's Head in 1536. It was 'betwixt the Temple Gates', and Throckmorton and Essex were members of the Middle and Inner Temple respectively. Similarly to 1532, on that occasion their private conversation on delicate matters was after supper, 'every man departed'.   32. The text at that point appears anachronistically to continue to the Act of Supremacy of 1534, but it should probably better be repunctuated and so read 'and had much communication as well of the Act of Appeals as of that of Annates, and of the supremacy and authority that Our Lord gave to Peter above the other disciples'; thus there is no anachronism. Cf. Guy, *Public Career of Sir Thomas More*, 211; SP 1/125 f. 205r.   33. See Chapuys's report of a conversation with Fisher about invasion backing rebellion: Chapuys to Charles V, 10 October 1533, *Spanish*

Calendar 4 ii no. 1133, at 821. **34.** Hawkyard, *House of Commons 1509–1558*, 233–46. **35.** It is necessary to understand that this text was composed in 1537, which is why Throckmorton then referred properly to 'Queen Anne'. He would not have done so at the time of the original version of his retort to the King, when she was still merely Mistress Boleyn. **36.** Dingley's execution was postponed until 1539, but should be associated with this episode. Bernard, *King's Reformation*, 211–12, tries to argue that Throckmorton was merely boasting to Dingley that he said these words to the King, and that he was 'pretending' to have done so. There is nothing in the text of the confession to justify this. Throckmorton expresses remorse for having rehearsed the conversation to Dingley, a bad faux pas since Dingley was not an MP, then goes on to say that he repeated it to Sir Thomas Englefield (Justice of the Common Pleas) and Sir William Barrington, who were indeed in the Lords and Commons respectively. Marshall, 'Crisis of allegiance', 41–2, concurs in my judgement on other grounds. **37.** *LP* 5 no. 978[13]; the process was completed on 14 April. **38.** *LP* 5 no. 1207[36]. There were several Thomas Halls in government circles at the time. **39.** Chapuys to Charles V, 10 and 18 May 1533, *Spanish Calendar* 4 ii nos. 1072, 1073, at 669, 677. **40.** J. Guy, *Henry VIII: the quest for fame* (London, 2014), 28, 44, and see G. Puttenham, *The Art of English Poesy*, ed. F. Whigham and W. A. Rebhorn (Ithaca, NY, 2007), 374. **41.** For further discussion of this duty, which was probably attached to his new post of Chancellor of the Exchequer, see below, pp. 224–5. **42.** On all this see Elton, *Tudor Revolution in Government*, 98–112, 139–57, and Starkey, 'Intimacy and innovation', 94–9. The Mastership of the Wards, another office which he was strongly rumoured in autumn 1532 to be obtaining, and which has often been ascribed to him, in fact stayed with his friend and benefactor Sir William Paulet and another trusted associate, Sir Thomas Englefield: Elton, *Tudor Revolution in Government*, 428–30. **43.** Elton, *Tudor Revolution in Government*, 112 n. 2; for a representative whinge from Tuke to Cromwell, 22 May 1537, SP 60/4 f. 77, *LP* 12 i no. 1297. For the Master's base in the Tower, see Thurley, *Houses of Power*, 128–9. **44.** *LP* 5 no. 1799 is the summary of a 92-page vellum book recording the royal jewels and plate handed over to Cromwell on coming into office, 2 June 1532, including much obviously from Wolsey. **45.** C. E. Challis, *The Tudor Coinage* (Manchester and New York, 1978), 84–5. **46.** Elton, *Tudor Revolution in Government*, 148–9, 155. For Sir John Gostwick's attempt of July 1540 to intensify Henry VIII's anger about Cromwell's casualness in warranty, see below, pp. 535–7. **47.** Cf. e.g. SP 1/70 ff. 100–103, *LP* 5 no. 1086: an agreement of 11 June 1532 between Cromwell as Master of the Jewels and the royal Master Carpenter for works at the Tower of London. **48.** Cromwell's remembrance, BL MS Cotton Titus B/I f. 455, *LP* 7 no. 143; *LP* dated this to early 1534, but the content looks more directly related to November 1533. **49.** *LP* 5 no. 1065[33]: a grant in survivorship to Thomas Cromwell and Gregory, his only son. A general round-up of Cromwell's land acquisitions, with occasional misunderstandings, is provided by Everett, *Rise of Thomas Cromwell*: see ibid., 184–95 and index, 353, s.v. Land, Property and Wealth. **50.** William Walwyn to Cromwell, 24 September [1532], SP 1/71 f. 52, *LP* 5 no. 1342; Sir William Morgan to Cromwell, 21 November [1532], SP 1/72 f. 44,

LP 5 no. 1562.   **51.** Below, pp. 326–8. Thomas Philips wrote from Ludlow, head-quarters town of the Council in the Marches, on 3 May [1532], SP 1/70 f. 11, *LP* 5 no. 991. The reference to 'Princess' Mary makes this document no later than 1532, and Cromwell as point of reference for Philips makes it very unlikely to be earlier.   **52.** London, College of Arms MS 2 G.4 f. 35v. I am very grateful to Robert Yorke, Archivist Emeritus of the College, for our discussions of Cromwell's heraldry. The full formal blazon of this first version of his achievement is *azure on a fess between three lions rampant or, a rose gules between two Cornish choughs proper.* Crest: *a demi-lion rampant double-queued or, holding a gem-ring or, stoned gules.*   **53.** John Judd to Cromwell, 4 August [1532], SP 1/70 f. 186, *LP* 5 no. 1214. Judd's embarrassment makes his letter somewhat incoherent, but his meaning is clear. The business for Mistress Hall at Ipswich concerned professional debts left by Thomas Hall, the nature of which is specified in a draft grant to her, TNA, SP 2/M ff. 183–5, *LP* 5 no. 1730.   **54.** The inventory of Standon for the then Ralph Sadler records among much material from the first Ralph's time 'Cromewells picture' in the long gallery: A. Heal, 'A great country house in 1623', *Burlington Magazine* 82 (1943), 108–16, at 113.   **55.** SP 1/42 ff. 101–16 at f. 112r, *LP* 4 ii no. 3197, and see above, p. 91.   **56.** H. Mantel, *Wolf Hall* (London, 2009), Part 5, ch. 3. Frick collection accession no. 1915.1.76.   **57.** Now National Portrait Gallery, London, NPG 1727.   **58.** J. Roberts, *Holbein and the Court of Henry VIII: drawings and miniatures from the Royal Library Windsor Castle* (Edinburgh, 1994), 28–9.   **59.** TNA, SP 2/M ff. 126–47, *LP* 5 no. 1694. Cromwell appears in the Essex list at f. 132v, Kent at f. 136r, Middlesex at f. 138v and Surrey at f. 140v.   **60.** On Cromwell's inexperience in local government up till then, see sensible remarks in H. M. Speight, '"The politics of good governance": Thomas Cromwell and the government of the southwest of England', *HJ* 37 (1994), with reply by M. Robertson, 623–41, at 627–8.   **61.** W. B. Robison III, 'The justices of the peace of Surrey in national and county politics, 1483–1570' (Lousiana State University PhD, 1983), 167–8, 171–5.   **62.** P. S. Allen, H. M. Allen and H. W. Garrod (eds.), *Opus Epistolarum Des. Erasmi Roterodami . . .* (12 vols., Oxford, 1906–58), 10, 116 (5 October 1532), 135 (late 1532), 180 (21 March 1533). The second of these letters, to Johannes Faber, Bishop of Vienna, appears in D. Erasmus, *Liber . . . de praeparatione ad mortem . . . accedunt aliquot epistolae seriis de rebus, in quibus item nihil est non novum ac recens* (Basel, 1534), 93.   **63.** Kelly, 'Submission of the clergy', 105, 110; Muller (ed.), *Letters of Gardiner*, 48–9.   **64.** For a masterly assessment of the myth around Gardiner, his character flaws and real talents, see M. Riordan and A. Ryrie, 'Stephen Gardiner and the making of a Protestant villain', *SCJ* 34 (2003), 1039–63.   **65.** Leonard Smyth to Lord Lisle, 15 December [1533], SP 3/7 f. 160, *LP* 1 i no. 886, *Lisle Letters* 1 no. 97. See also Elton, *Tudor Revolution in Government*, 124–5, 261–86.   **66.** Below, pp. 314–15.   **67.** For Paget jumping ship, see S. R. Gammon, *Statesman and Schemer: William, first Lord Paget, Tudor minister* (Newton Abbot, 1973), 25–7.   **68.** Richard is named in Thomas Cromwell's will of 1529, with the phrase 'servant with my Lord Marquess Dorset' erased. See two references to Gardiner's servant 'Mr Cromwell' on mission with him in letters of Henry VIII to Gardiner, 9 and 16 February 1532, Pocock 2, 184, 190, *LP* 5 nos. 791, 807;

Christopher Wellifed to his parents, 23 January [1533], SP 1/74 f. 66, *LP* 6 no. 70 (he failed in his quest for Cottenham; the Bishop of Ely had obtained it for his Chancellor Robert Cliffe); George Lawson to Cromwell, 1 February [1533], SP 1/74 f. 121, *LP* 6 no. 107.   **69.** Gunn, *Charles Brandon, Duke of Suffolk*, 115–27; Ives, *Life and Death of Anne Boleyn*, 165.   **70.** Norfolk's testimony to the Privy Council, mid-December 1546, BL MS Cotton Titus B/I f. 101r, *LP* 21 ii no. 554. He was describing a conversation with Wolsey at Esher, which must have been the memorable encounter described by Cavendish in December 1529: Cavendish, *Life of Wolsey*, ed. Singer, 277–85. He said that Suffolk's initiative had been fourteen years before that, so 1515, just at the time that Brandon had first gained the ducal title.   **71.** MacCulloch, *Suffolk and the Tudors*, 57–71, 228–30.   **72.** Gunn, *Charles Brandon, Duke of Suffolk*, 125. Richard and Robert Southwell's escape from punishment in this affair and total rehabilitation (at the expense of a property surrender to the Crown) is remarkable, and needs further explanation. They were clearly already on excellent terms with Cromwell and seem to have at this stage left Norfolk's service for his.   **73.** Duke of Suffolk to Cromwell, 20 July [1532], SP 1/70 f. 165, *LP* 5 no. 1183.   **74.** On the removal, see below, Chapter 18. On Cromwell as godfather, see Duke of Suffolk to Cromwell, [18 September 1535], SP 1/96 f. 172, *LP* 9 no. 386; dateable as *LP* observes by the birthday of Henry Brandon.   **75.** Duke of Suffolk to Cromwell, 27 November [1536], SP 1/112 f. 21, *LP* 11 no. 1180: a letter in which he bluntly recommends the payment of royal debts in the county. It is his boldest surviving letter to Cromwell.   **76.** Lord Leonard Grey to Cromwell, 24 May [1532], SP 1/70 f. 56, *LP* 5 no. 1049; my italics. See above, p. 47.   **77.** Augustine to Cromwell, 22 and 28 July 1532: SP 1/70 f. 170, *LP* 5 no. 1188; SP 1/70 f. 174, *LP* 5 no. 1197.   **78.** *Spanish Calendar* 4 ii no. 1158, at 876.   **79.** Norfolk's testimony to the Privy Council, mid-December 1546, BL MS Cotton Titus B/I f. 100r, *LP* 21 ii no. 554.   **80.** Duke of Norfolk to Cromwell, 'Ascension Day' [?1535], SP 1/92 f. 124, *LP* 8 no. 673; my italics. 'Grudge who will', a favourite phrase of the Duke's, was borrowed as a motto by his niece Anne Boleyn, although she may also have purloined it from Margaret of Austria: Ives, *Life and Death of Anne Boleyn*, 141. Elton, 'Thomas Cromwell's decline and fall', 193–7, usefully rounds up the course of the Cromwell/Norfolk relationship.   **81.** Elizabeth Duchess of Norfolk to Cromwell, 10 November [1537], BL MS Cotton Titus B/I f. 389, *LP* 12 ii no. 1049. It is unfortunate that we cannot pin down the exact relationship of the child's mother 'Mistress Abram' to Cromwell, though she was presumably the wife of the younger of two Thomas Abrams who were London merchants and friends of his.   **82.** Norfolk's testimony to the Privy Council, mid-December 1546, BL MS Cotton Titus B/I f. 101r, *LP* 21 ii no. 554.   **83.** Ibid.   **84.** Ives, *Life and Death of Anne Boleyn*, 141–3.

Chapter 8: Making a Difference: 1532

1. For the medieval background on commissions of sewers, see J. H. Baker, *The Oxford History of the Laws of England 6: 1483–1558* (Oxford, 2003), 265.   **2.** P. Cavill, *The English Parliaments of Henry VII 1485–1504* (Oxford,

2009), 162-3.   3. Elton, *Reform and Renewal*, 121-2. The disaster can be seen first unfolding in William Harris to Cromwell [Sunday 17 January 1529], SP 1/40 f. 101, *LP* 4 ii no. 2759 (misdated by *LP* to 1526), and an appalled Thomas Cromwell to Stephen Gardiner, 18 January [1529], SP 1/52 f. 146, *LP* 4 iii no. 5186.
4. Sir Nicholas Carew to Cromwell, 23 September [1532], SP 1/67 f. 83, *LP* 5 no. 429 (misdated in *LP* to 1531, but it has to be after the passage of the 1532 Act).
5. Erasmus Forth to [Thomas] Stidolf, ?autumn 1532, SP 1/73 f. 103, *LP* 5 no. 1728.   6. Fitzwilliam to Cromwell, probably autumn 1532, SP 1/84 f. 102, *LP* 7 no. 760 (misdated by *LP* to 1534, but the address to Cromwell as Master of the Jewels renders that unlikely *a priori*). John Browning Abbot of Waverley to [Thomas] Stidolf, probably 1532, SP 1/73 f. 142, *LP* 5 no. 1765, no doubt relates to that or another meeting of the commissioners at Southwark. For long-term argument about the Act, see C. Holmes, 'G. R. Elton as a legal historian', *TRHS* 6th series 7 (1997), 267-79, at 273-4.   7. Cromwell's first draft of the commission is SP 1/73 f. 61r and a later draft with the King's and Cromwell's emendations, SP 1/73 f. 59r, *LP* 5 no. 1705.   8. For a thorough account of this ill-fated legislation, see Elton, *Reform and Renewal*, 90-92, 100-106; Cromwell's draft letter to the King, of late March 1534, is SP 1/82 f. 82, *LP* 7 no. 73.   9. On the Dover saga, see Colvin (ed.), *History of the King's Works* 4, 729-68.   10. Robert Bager, Mayor of Winchester, to Cromwell, 19 January [1535], SP 1/89 f. 35, *LP* 8 no. 63.   11. See Chapuys's shrewd comments on the political dimensions of the case, *Spanish Calendar* 5 i no. 203, at 542; for stages of the dispute running into 1536 and 1537, Mayor, Recorder and citizens of Winchester to Cromwell, 10 January [1536], SP 1/101 f. 44, *LP* 10 no. 67, and Mayor and citizens of Winchester to Cromwell, 9 August 1537, SP 1/105 f. 266, *LP* 11 no. 252 (misdated in *LP*).   12. For an early stage in the campaign, see William Burton Abbot of St Augustine's Bristol to Cromwell, 24 August [1535], SP 1/95 f. 156, *LP* 9 no. 169; for Cromwell following up early circulars, Cromwell to Roland Lee, early September 1535, SP 1/96 f. 50, *LP* 9 no. 241[II]. For more on the visit to Winchester, see below, pp. 304-6.   13. For specimens, Roland Lee to Cromwell, 19 and 24 August 1535, SP 1/95 f. 111, *LP* 9 no. 126; SP 1/95 f. 154, *LP* 9 no. 166.   14. John Husee to Lord Lisle, 19 November [1535], SP 3/5 f. 110, *Lisle Letters* 2 no. 483.   15. Leonard Smyth to Lord Lisle, 10 December 1535, SP 1/99 f. 114, *Lisle Letters* 2 no. 495; my italics.
16. SP 1/102 f. 5rv, *LP* 10 no. 254. There was a reaffirmation in that Parliament of previous related legislation against streaming for tin in Devon and Cornwall: Lehmberg, *Reformation Parliament*, 234.   17. For Cromwell pursuing action in 1539, John ap Rhys to Cromwell, 21 August 1539, SP 1/153 f. 37, *LP* 14 ii no. 72.   18. Wigston to Cromwell, ?July 1539, SP 1/152 f. 210, *LP* 14 i no. 1350; Scarisbrick, 'Cardinal Wolsey and the Common Weal', 58, draws attention to the prominence of Roger Wigston in Wolsey's campaign.   19. John London to Cromwell, 10 January [1539], SP 1/142 f. 31, *LP* 14 i no. 42.   20. J. P. Carley and A. M. Hutchison, 'William Peto, O.F.M.Obs., and the 1556 edition of *The folowinge of Chryste*: background and context', *Journal of the Early Book Society* 17 (2014), 94-118, at 94-6.   21. W. Barlow, *A dyaloge describing the originall ground of*

these Lutheran faccyons . . . (London, 1531, *RSTC* 1461). There have been nearly two centuries of debate on the confusing number of William Barlows and their relationship to this work: all is sorted out effectively by A. J. Brown, *Robert Ferrar: Yorkshire monk, Reformation bishop and martyr in Wales (c. 1500–1555)* (London, 1997), 266. See also E. G. Rupp, *Studies in the Making of the English Protestant Tradition* (Cambridge, 1947), 62–72, and for a link between Barlow and More as early as 1525, A. M. McLean, ' "A noughtye and a false lyeng boke": William Barlow and the *Lutheran factions*', *Renaissance Quarterly* 31 (1978), 173–85, at 176–7. **22.** Barlow, *Dyaloge describing the originall ground of these Lutheran faccyons*, sig. P4v. **23.** MacCulloch, *Thomas Cranmer*, 55–8. **24.** Ibid., 438–40. **25.** For what follows in this and the next paragraph, see the excellent detective work of R. Rex, 'Jasper Fyloll and the enormities of the clergy: two tracts written during the Reformation Parliament', *SCJ* 31 (2000), 1043–62. Rex (pp. 1061–2) is curiously reluctant to credit the sincerity of Fyllol's evangelicalism, despite providing much evidence for his radicalism, and in view of his action for Cromwell a year or two later at the London Charterhouse. His arguments from the nature and contents of Fyllol's prayer book do not seem to me to be enough to contradict that evidence. **26.** Fyllol's petition is TNA, SP 2/M f. 125, *LP* 5 no. 1690. **27.** The first edition is *RSTC* 11919. Rex, 'Redating Henry VIII's *A Glasse of the Truthe*', is a convincing refutation of S. W. Haas, 'Henry VIII's *Glasse of Truthe*', *History* 64 (1979), 353–62, which argued for a dating of this tract to 1531, and also made the serious mistake of confusing the *Collectanea* and the *Censurae/Determinations*. **28.** Richard Croke to Cromwell, 17 September 1532, SP 1/71 f. 36, *LP* 5 no. 1320; Croke to Cromwell, 23 September 1532, SP 1/71 f. 48, *LP* 5 no. 1338. These two letters cannot be any earlier than 1532, as Croke with characteristic pretentiousness signs himself 'Sub-Dean' in Greek characters, and he did not become Sub-Dean of King Henry's College Oxford until that year. **29.** Hawkins to Henry VIII, 21 November 1532, SP 1/72 f. 48r, *LP* 5 no. 1564. On the French translation, John Williamson to Cromwell, 20 October [1532], SP 1/71 f. 128, *LP* 5 no. 1454. **30.** [Anon.], *The maner of the tryumphe at Caleys [and] Bulleyn* (London, 1532, *RSTC* 4350, 4351), and see comment, Ives, *Life and Death of Anne Boleyn*, 160–61. This John Gough should be distinguished from the John Gough of Calais mentioned previously (above, p. 45). The best previous precedent for such government instant news was for the proposed marriage of the King's sister Mary in 1508: J. Gairdner (ed.), ' "The Spousells" of the Prinsess Mary', *Camden Miscellany* 9 (CS new series 53, 1895), 1–38. **31.** Sir Edward Guildford to Cromwell, 30 December [1532], SP 1/72 f. 171, *LP* 5 no. 1678. **32.** *LP* 6 no. 87. It is a circumstantial story; the conmen were well informed enough to know that Cromwell was about to leave for Calais with the King. **33.** Everett, *Rise of Thomas Cromwell*, 77–8, rounds them all up. Below we will meet the one exception to that: the exchange with Christ's College Cambridge, still therefore involving an ecclesiastical corporation of royal foundation. **34.** Alsop, 'Cromwell and the Church in 1531: the case of Waltham Abbey', discussing TNA, E 407/8/180/4. The Westminster draft is TNA, SP 2/L ff. 66r, 70r, 71r, *LP* 5 no. 673, with some small further emendments in Cromwell's hand; cf. the enrolment of an earlier version of the grant on 23 December 1531, which mentions neither Cromwell nor Hales, *LP* 5 no. 627[23]. No. 627[24] is a royal grant to Wolsey's former abbey of St albans, also signed on 23 December, of one of the nunneries dissolved by Wolsey, which likewise does not explicitly involve Cromwell, though it is precisely the sort of business in which he would have had a major interest. I have noted (above, p. 110) Cromwell's simultaneous appointment at the beginning of January 1532 as royal Receiver-General of estates belonging to Wolsey's former Colleges, all of them former monastic lands.   35. Heale, *Abbots and Priors of Late Medieval and Reformation England*, 284.   36. Robert Thornton Abbot of Jervaux to Cromwell, 30 July [1532], SP 1/70 f. 178, *LP* 5 no. 1203.   37. The following citations are simply representative of much other documentation, and should be compared with the appropriate new appointments noted by Smith. St Bartholomew's Smithfield: Robert Fuller Abbot of Waltham to Cromwell, 22 May 1532, SP 1/70 f. 53, *LP* 5 no. 1044; Bruton and Montacute: Sir John Fitzjames to Cromwell, 9 September [1532], SP 1/71 f. 23, *LP* 5 no. 1304; Muchelney: see next note; Holm Cultram: John Lord Hussey to Cromwell, 19 November [1532], SP 1/72 f. 41, *LP* 5 no. 1556; Tilty: Margaret Marchioness of Dorset to Cromwell, 17 October [1532], SP 1/79 f. 186, *LP* 6 no. 1304 (misdated in *LP*); St James Northampton: George Gifford to Cromwell, 19 May [1536], SP 1/104 f. 30, *LP* 10 no. 916, commenting on an election of May 1532. On Vaudey, see below, n. 43.   38. Cf. e.g. Thomas Ine Abbot of Muchelney to Cromwell, 15 June 1533, SP 1/77 f. 44, *LP* 6 no. 651 (also wrongly calendared as *LP* 5 no. 295) referring to the events of 1532, about which there is much other correspondence.   39. Nicholas West Bishop of Ely to Cromwell, 9 March [1533], SP 1/74 f. 213, *LP* 6 no. 218. G. R. Elton's characteristically crisp and informed answers to the question 'How corrupt was Thomas Cromwell?', *HJ* 36 (1993), 905–8, are an effective valedictory defence of his hero.   40. See Lee writing to Cromwell on the business of Wolsey's pardon, winter or spring 1530, SP 1/57 f. 1, *LP* 4 iii no. 6212.   41. Cranmer to Nicholas Hawkins, 24 December 1533, BL MS Harley 6148 f. 41r, *LP* 6 no. 1546. Cranmer's phrase does not suggest any warm acquaintance with Lee.   42. Roland Lee to Cromwell, 7 June [1535], SP 1/93 f. 29, *LP* 8 no. 839.   43. See Henry Saxton, Abbot of Vaudey to Cromwell, 28 October [1532], SP 1/71 f. 152, *LP* 5 no. 1477; Cromwell to the Abbot of Woburn, probably November 1532, SP 1/77 f. 175, *LP* 6 no. 778; John Lord Hussey to Cromwell, 20 April [1533], SP 1/83 f. 101, *LP* 7 no. 516; Robert Hobbes Abbot of Woburn to Cromwell, 7 July [1533], SP 1/77 f. 176, *LP* 6 no. 779.   44. *LP* 5 no. 978[6]; see G. R. Elton, *Star Chamber Stories* (London, 1958), 147–73, and for background on the Cistercians, D. Knowles, *The Religious Orders in England III: the Tudor age* (Cambridge, 1959), 28–38.   45. For an account of the Premonstratensians' exemption, see Richard Bowyer alias Strelley to Cromwell, n.d. but 1537–40, SP 1/123 f. 162, *LP* 12 ii no. 400.   46. Smith, 568–9, noticed a Horsman as Abbot at Coverham without fixing him to a date in the early 1530s or to this letter, but he must be the Roger Horsman who died in 1536 as Vicar of Sedbergh, a Coverham living (*LP* 11 no. 943[16]), and who must have previously resigned the Abbacy to the Abbot at the dissolution, Christopher Rokeby. For the possible significance of this in the early stages of the Pilgrimage of Grace, see below, pp. 379–80. On Leonard Horsman, see Lee to Cromwell, summer 1532, SP 1/81 f. 26, *LP* 6 no. 1566; Horsman to Cromwell, 2 August [1532], SP 1/70 f. 184, *LP* 5 no. 1212.   **47.** Roland Lee to Cromwell, 1 January [1533], SP 1/237 f. 5, *LP Addenda* 1 i no. 724. *LP* misdated this letter, which fits into a sequence of letters in 1532–3. Lee's observation that the King was founder was true only to the extent that Henry II had confirmed the founder's gift – see 'Premonstratensian houses: abbey of Coverham', in *VCH: Yorkshire* 3, 243–5 – but it was clearly a well-established idea by now; see *LP* 10 no. 364, 142. Contrast Archbishop Cranmer's punctiliousness in approaching the Abbot of Welbeck for a preferment to the Abbacy of Newsham, Cranmer to [Abbot of Welbeck], May 1534, BL MS Harley 6148 f. 20r, *LP* 7 no. 685.   **48.** E. Jeffries Davis, 'The beginning of the Dissolution: Christchurch, Aldgate, 1532', *TRHS* 4th series 8 (1925), 127–50, remains a model of research, and Geoffrey Elton was unwise to sneer at the idea embodied in the title: Elton, *Star Chamber Stories*, 147. For the surrender, see Rymer (ed.), *Foedera* 14, 411–12.   **49.** For fine surveys of such redeployments, see B. Thompson, 'The laity, the alien priories, and the redistribution of ecclesiastical property', in N. Rogers (ed.), *England in the Fifteenth Century* (Stamford, 1994), 19–41; Heale, 'Dependent priories and the closure of monasteries in late medieval England'. It will be apparent that my account here slightly modifies or amplifies Heale's lists of suppressions given ibid., 26.   **50.** The bill is SP 1/238 f. 96, *LP* 1 i no. 864, which also notes the memorandum on hospital foundation, including its mention of the Waltham exchange, TNA, E 135/8/48; that memorandum was clearly the same as 'Paper reciting an order for a hospital devised of Christchurch lands made by the King' mentioned in a catalogue of Cromwell's papers for the early 1530s, *LP* 7 no. 923 [xxxvii].   **51.** Richard Lyst to Cromwell, 4 February 1533, BL MS Cotton Cleopatra E/IV f. 34, *LP* 6 no. 116.   **52.** Audley to Cromwell, SP 1/78 f. 60, *LP* 6 no. 927: dateable to late July 1533 by grants which Audley signed at his house of Brettons in Barking, a prospective stay mentioned in his letter, *LP* 6 nos. 929[51–2], 1060[1–4]. For Stow's narrative, Stow, *Survey of London*, ed. Kingsford, 1, 142.   **53.** Richard Strete to Cromwell, 26 April [1532], SP 1/75 f. 174, *LP* 6 no. 389 (misdated by *LP*).   **54.** Richard Strete to Roland Lee, 25 February 1532, SP 1/237 f. 158, *LP Addenda* 1 i no. 771; Strete to Cromwell or Roland Lee, 12 May [1532], BL MS Cotton Cleopatra E/IV f. 283, *LP* 10 no. 857 (misdated by *LP*).   **55.** Le Neve, *Fasti 1300–1541: Coventry and Lichfield* 3, sets out the evidence: licence for election was sought on 24 January 1532 (Lichfield *Acta Capitularia* 4 f. 93v). Lee was granted custody of the temporalities, which had presumably been the responsibility of his team since early 1532, only on 18 December 1533 (*LP* 6 no. 1595[20]); licence to elect was granted on 23 December 1533 (*Acta Capitularia* 4 f. 108v). Election came on 9/10 January 1534 (Lambeth Palace, Cranmer's Register ff. 150, 153), but was then prorogued until 20 January (Cranmer's Register f. 155). Royal assent was delayed until 19 and 22 March 1534 (Cranmer's Register ff. 154–155v). Opposition to election was cited by Cranmer on 26 March (Cranmer's Register f. 149v). Cranmer's confirmation was granted on 16 April (Cranmer's Register f. 149) and he finally consecrated Lee on 19 April (Cranmer's Register f. 156v).   **56.** Richard

Strete to Roland Lee, 25 February 1532, SP 1/237 f. 158, *LP Addenda* 1 i no. 771; Strete to Roland Lee, 6 April [1532], SP 1/57 ff. 55–6, *LP* 4 iii no. 6313 (misdated by *LP* to 1530).   57. Richard Strete to Cromwell, 26 April [1532], SP 1/75 f. 174, *LP* 6 no. 389 (misdated by *LP* to 1533); draft indenture of 27 April 1532, SP 1/69 f. 260, *LP* 5 no. 969.   58. Strete to Cromwell, 22 May [1532], SP 1/70 f. 54, *LP* 5 no. 1045; commission for the inquisition, undated, SP 1/238 f. 17, *LP Addenda* 1 i no. 813.   59. From a sequence of correspondence, the most important item is Cromwell to Strete, 14 June 1533, SP 1/77 f. 41, *LP* 6 no. 645, including this irritated remark (securely dated by the previous letter of Sir Anthony Fitzherbert to Cromwell, SP 1/238 f. 77, *LP Addenda* 1 i no. 851, which refers to 'Sir' Ralph Longford – he was knighted at Anne Boleyn's coronation, 1 June 1533). For the later accounts detailing Longford's rental payments, see SP 1/113 ff. 80–811, *LP* 11 no. 1411[i and ii], *LP* 8 no. 802[20].   60. Countess of Salisbury and John Lord Hussey to Cromwell, 30 November 1532, SP 1/99 f. 97, *LP* 9 no. 900 (misdated by *LP* to 1535; they did not recognize the Countess's signature).   61. Sir Richard Bulkeley to Cromwell, 23 June probably 1533, SP 1/77 f. 69, *LP* 6 no. 690; John Hilsey to Cromwell, undated but after April 1534, SP 1/91 f. 152, *LP* 8 no. 472. Friar Morris Griffith named in his petition became his diocesan Chancellor when Hilsey became Bishop of Rochester in August 1535.   62. *LP* 8 no. 802[20].   63. *LP* 10 no. 226[17]; Smith, 374.   64. Sherburne to Cromwell, 8 December 1532/3, SP 1/72 f. 119, *LP* 5 no. 1618.   65. West Sussex Record Office, Lavington MS 646, a deed of 1590 which includes a recital of a deed of 1535, describing arrangements made after the collusive sale of Hardham to its patron Sir William Goring (a friend of Cromwell's) in autumn 1534; among the feoffees for Goring were Sir Giles Covert, who had lobbied for Shulbrede's survival, Cromwell himself with two of his own household officers and Richard Bedon, another gentleman involved in the Shulbrede affair; curious, since Shulbrede and Hardham are not at all close to each other in the county. For the sale itself, see 'Priory of Hardham', *VCH: Sussex* 2, 74–5. For Cromwell's annuity from Hardham, see *LP* 5 no. 1285, 557, where the priory appears under its alternative name of Heringham: annuities in that list are no later than autumn 1532.   66. Heale, 'Dependent priories and the closure of monasteries in late medieval England', 22–3.   67. T. Fuller, *The Church-History of Britain from the birth of Jesus Christ until the year M.DC. XLVIII* (London, 1655, Wing F2416), Bk VI, 307.   68. Loades (ed.), *Papers of George Wyatt*, 159. The previous folio of this narration is, infuriatingly, lost.   69. Marillac to Montmorency, 23 June 1540, Kaulek (ed.), *Correspondance*, 195, *LP* 15 no. 804: 'qui a esté premier inventeur d'abattre les abbayes et de tout ce qui a esté innové en l'Église, de sorte que cestuy inventoit et Cramvell prestoit l'auctorité . . .'. For the evident complication of dissolution legislation in the 1536 Parliament, see below, pp. 319–22.   70. *LP* 5 no. 1209.   71. 23 Henry VIII cap. 22: *Statutes of the Realm* 3, 392–4.   72. Papers on the suppression, 18 and 20 September 1528: SP 1/50 f. 102rv, *LP* 4 ii no. 4755; SP 1/44 f. 308v, *LP* 4 ii no. 3536.   73. Henry Lockwood to Cromwell, 4 March [1532], SP 1/69 f. 140, *LP* 5 no. 847; my italics. Before becoming Master in 1531, Lockwood had himself been a Fellow of the College from 1523. While all the indications are that Lockwood was a traditionalist in religion, getting a Lincolnshire benefice on a presentation from Syon Abbey and resigning as Master in 1548, Gunthorpe was at least by the late 1530s noted as an evangelical in a warm testimony from his old Cambridge friend Thomas Cranmer: Cranmer to Cromwell, 26 May [1537], SP 1/120 f. 194, *LP* 12 i no. 1281. On Weeting, see Blomefield and Parkin, *Topographical History of the County of Norfolk*, 2 159–73.   74. Lockwood to Cromwell, 4 January [1534], SP 1/82 f. 13, *LP* 7 no. 16.   75. Cromwell to Lockwood (draft in the hand of Roland Lee), 7 June [1532], SP 1/238 f. 74, *LP Addenda* 1 i no. 845. Note also in Cromwell's list of deeds in his archive in 1535 among material going back years, an 'Indenture of goods of the late monastery of Bromehill, sold to Roger Fowler': SP 1/96 f. 41r, *LP* 9 no. 234.   76. For all this, see Lockwood to Cromwell, 12 September [1532], SP 1/71 f. 26, *LP* 5 no. 1309, and the undated letter of Lockwood to Cromwell, [1532], SP 1/73 f. 120, *LP* 5 no. 1745, addressed from Vernon's priory of Marlow and reporting Gregory as 'merry' there. Lee became Rector of St Sepulchre's in August 1532. In the College audit book for 1532/3 are payments to Cromwell, his servant and 'Mr Lee the Archdeacon' [of Cornwall] 'for the quicker expedition in our College business': A. H. Lloyd, *The Early History of Christ's College, Cambridge, Derived from Contemporary Documents* (Cambridge, 1934), 234–5.   77. Lee to Cromwell, 9 December [1532], SP 1/237 f. 79, *LP Addenda* 1 i no. 744 (misdated in *LP*). Lee actually had a benefice in Norfolk 23 miles from Bromehill, at Banham, and it is interesting that he did not choose to take Gregory there; no doubt the Rectory, designed for a celibate parson, was too small for the visiting party.   78. Lee to Cromwell, 15 August [1533], SP 1/78 f. 111, *LP* 6 no. 981; 21 August [1533], SP 1/78 f. 143, *LP* 6 no. 1011. Gregory went on to spend the autumn in Essex with Lee and various of his prosperous clerical neighbours: Gregory Cromwell to Cromwell, 17 and 25 October [1533; both letters previously misdated]: SP 1/68 f. 22, *LP* 5 no. 479; SP 1/68 f. 32, *LP* 5 no. 496.   79. Lee to Cromwell, 1 January [1533], SP 1/237 f. 5, *LP Addenda* 1 i no. 724 (*LP* misdates to 1531).

Chapter 9: A Royal Marriage: 1532–1533

1. Ives, *Life and Death of Anne Boleyn*, 156–7; Thurley, *Houses of Power*, 129–30, 241.   2. For this and what follows, see MacCulloch, *Thomas Cranmer*, 69–77.   3. R. J. Knecht, 'Francis I, "Defender of the Faith"?', in Ives, Knecht and Scarisbrick (eds.), *Wealth and Power in Tudor England*, 106–27, at 123.   4. See above, pp. 191–2. For all the usual suspects involved in sorting out the final stages of the Anglo-French treaty at home – Gardiner, Cromwell, Oliver, Roland Lee – see Gardiner to Cromwell, c. 21 August 1532, SP 1/70 f. 205, *LP* 5 no. 1245. On the prospects of a Calais wedding, Ives, *Life and Death of Anne Boleyn*, 166.   5. Augustine to Cromwell, 14 October 1532, BL MS Cotton Vitellius B/XIII f. 218, *LP* 5 no. 1422. In the same letter Augustine reported that ambassador Gregorio Casali had left for England, which was at best a half-truth fed to him, since Casali was actually meeting the King at Calais: Fletcher, *Our Man in Rome*, 178–9.   6. Ives, *Life and Death of Anne Boleyn*, 157–61, summarizes events at

Calais, and makes the point about descent at ibid., 167. Anne's estates, with a rental value of *c.* £5,000, outdid the £4,000 rental value of Richmond's estates at his creation in 1525: see Hoyle, 'War and public finance', 77. On marriage possibilities, see MacCulloch, *Thomas Cranmer*, Appendix II.   7. J. G. Nichols (ed.), *The Chronicle of Calais, in the reigns of Henry VII and Henry VIII, to the year 1540* (CS 1st series 35, 1846), 41–4.   8. Marquess of Bath, *Report on the Manuscripts of the Most Honourable the Marquess of Bath preserved at Longleat IV: Seymour Papers 1532–1686* (Historical Manuscripts Commission, 1968), 1–3, is a list of those going to Calais, 2,773 in all, with twelve staff of the Jewel House.   9. John Laurence to Cromwell, 30 November 1532, BL MS Cotton Cleopatra E/IV f. 132, *LP* 5 no. 1591. For Laurence's previous curious and not yet fully explained links to a dissident group among the Greenwich Observants given patronage by Wolsey, see Brown, 'Wolsey and ecclesiastical order', 231–8.   10. Thomas Alvard to Cromwell, 2 November [1532], SP 1/72 f. 10, *LP* 5 no. 1509.   11. John Williamson to Cromwell, 23 October [1532], SP 1/71 f. 139, *LP* 5 no. 1464: Thomas Farmer was sent over 'with your viols'.   12. John Benolt to Cromwell, 2 September 1532, SP 1/71 f. 12, *LP* 5 no. 1284. Benolt's reward in Crown preferment and ecclesiastical office ran into complications, detailed in extensive correspondence in the State Papers; the jumping-off points are Thomas Goldwell Prior of Christ Church Canterbury to Cromwell, 23 October [1532], SP 1/71 f. 140, *LP* 5 no. 1465, and 10 November 1532, SP 1/72 f. 19, *LP* 5 no. 1528. Thomas Baschurch to Cromwell, n.d. but around 12 February 1533, SP 1/74 f. 152, *LP* 6 no. 154, makes it clear that Cromwell was responsible for arranging the exchange which was the means of Benolt's preferment.   13. Vaughan [unsigned to remain confidential; significantly misidentified in *LP* as Wriothesley] to Cromwell, SP 1/72 f. 96, *LP* 5 no. 1602; Vaughan to Cromwell, 5 December 1532, SP 1/72 f. 99, *LP* 5 no. 1609; Vaughan to Cromwell, 9 December 1532, SP 1/72 f. 121, *LP* 5 no. 1620.   14. MacCulloch, *Thomas Cranmer*, 83–5, 637–8.   15. For the loan from the Privy Coffers, 6 February 1533: TNA, E 101/421/9, *LP* 6 no. 131. Salvago's involvement is uniquely attested in a wayward but occasionally invaluable Spanish source: M. A. Sharp Hume (trans. and ed.), *Chronicle of King Henry VIII. of England . . .* (London, 1889), 19. For Salvago's links with Cromwell, see two letters to Cromwell from their mutual friend (and another Genoese) Antonio di' Vivaldi: 24 August 1535, BL MS Cotton Galba B/X f. 65, *LP* 9 no. 175; 2 March 1536, BL MS Cotton Vitellius B/XIV f. 221, *LP* 10 no. 403.   16. Alexander Alesius to Elizabeth I, 1 September 1559, TNA, SP 70/7 f. 11v, *Calendar of State Papers Foreign . . . Elizabeth [I], 1: 1558–59*, no. 1303, 533.   17. BL MS Harley 6148: the spirit of recycling seems to have haunted this manuscript, since it was the object of a bizarre attempt at historical forgery in the late Victorian period. On this, see C. J. Wright, 'The man who wrote on the manuscripts in the British Museum', *British Library Journal* 12 (1986), 76–85.   18. Prince Arthur's letter of 8 June 1501, concerning reforms at the Cistercian house at Abbey Dore, is BL MS Harley 6148 f. 151r.   19. See *LP* 6 nos. 1473, 1474 (26 November 1533); *LP* 7 nos. 17 and 20 (5 January 1534); *LP* 7 nos. 806, 807 (7 June 1534). Archbishop Lee of York was also in the habit of writing double letters to Cromwell on the same day, perhaps in the hope that their different subjects might get individual attention from him. The one letter from Cranmer to Cromwell in the collection's main sequence is 19 July 1533, BL MS Harley 6148 f. 30v, *LP* 6 no. 868, and there is one further letter to Cromwell beyond the main dateline, 1 March 1535, right at the end of the collection, BL MS Harley 6148 f. 50v, slightly abbreviated from the original, SP 1/91 f. 2, *LP* 8 no. 306. Its presence here and in this position may well suggest that the letter-book scheme did not survive the first pair of volumes. **20.** I explained this archival paradox in MacCulloch, *Thomas Cranmer*, 135. Since Everett, *Rise of Thomas Cromwell*, 137–8, was apparently unable to understand it, I have provided this further explanation. **21.** See below, pp. 363–71. **22.** Vaughan to Cromwell, August 1535, SP 1/90 f. 193, *LP* 8 no. 301; same to same, 4 September [1535], SP 1/96 f. 74, *LP* 9 no. 275. On Gwynedd, see ODNB, s.v. Gwynneth, John. **23.** Vaughan to Cromwell, 1 November [1533], SP 1/80 f. 75, *LP* 6 no. 1385. **24.** Vaughan to Cromwell, 21 November [1533], SP 1/80 f. 106, *LP* 6 no. 1448. **25.** On Skip's attack on Cromwell from the pulpit in Anne Boleyn's final crisis, see below, pp. 331–3. **26.** Audley to Cromwell, beginning of October 1532, SP 1/72 f. 15, *LP* 5 no. 1514; slightly misdated by *LP*, since it predates Audley's next letter about the mechanics of the prorogation on 4 November and has in any case to have been written before the King left for Calais around 8 October: cf. Audley to Cromwell, 20 October 1532, SP 1/71 f. 121, *LP* 5 no. 1450. **27.** An additional mystery detailed in *HC 1509–1558* 3, 640, remains to be unravelled. Wingfield may have been the first Speaker promoted from a borough constituency (which would be another innovation attributable to Cromwell), or (far more likely) he may already have been knight of the shire for Suffolk in replacement for Thomas Wentworth, promoted to the Lords in December 1529. **28.** A good discussion of all this is Hawkyard, *House of Commons 1509–1558*, 96–101, with specimen illustrations of the two crucial documents, SP 1/56 f. 7, *LP* 4 iii no. 6043[i], and SP 1/82 f. 52, *LP* 7 no. 56. Cromwell's memorandum of October 1533 is BL MS Cotton Titus B/I f. 464, *LP* 6 no. 1382. **29.** On this and what follows, see G. R. Elton (ed.), *The Tudor Constitution: documents and commentary* (2nd edn, Cambridge, 1982), 233–40, 248–9. **30.** J. C. Warner, *Henry VIII's Divorce: literature and the politics of the printing press* (Woodbridge, 1998), 44–6. For the Act of Succession, see Elton (ed.), *Tudor Constitution*, 6–12, and for the proclamation of 5 July 1533, *TRP* no. 140. **31.** Lehmberg, *Reformation Parliament*, 170–71. On Monteagle, see above, pp. 56, 80. Benson's successor at Burton, William Edys, did actually sit for four days in the 1534 session: Lehmberg, *Reformation Parliament*, 257. **32.** It was one of Geoffrey Elton's early achievements to sort out these drafts: see G. R. Elton, 'The evolution of a Reformation statute', in Elton, *Studies* 2, 82–106. The diagram of how they relate to each other at 83 makes one grateful for not having to do the work again, though Lehmberg, *Reformation Parliament*, 164n, testifies that he did exactly that. What follows draws generously on Elton's analysis. **33.** Slightly abridged text in Elton (ed.), *Tudor Constitution*, 350–53. **34.** On the papal nuncio's presence, Lehmberg, *Reformation Parliament*, 171, and Ives, *Life and Death of Anne Boleyn*, 169. **35.** Nicholson, 'Act of Appeals and the English Reformation', 29. **36.** On all this, MacCulloch,

Thomas Cranmer, 88–9. 37. Ives, *Life and Death of Anne Boleyn*, 164; Mac-
Culloch, *Thomas Cranmer*, 89–93. 38. *Spanish Calendar* 4 i no. 1062, at
646. 39. Thomas Audley to Cromwell, *c.* 22 April 1533, SP 1/75 f. 151, *LP* 6 no.
366: the scrabbles to locate a vital misplaced set of 'opinions of doctors and
learned men in the King's great case' involve Audley, Cromwell, Cranmer, the
Duke of Norfolk, the Earl of Wiltshire, Roland Lee, Bishop Gardiner and a
not very pleased Henry VIII. 40. MacCulloch, *Thomas Cranmer*, 90–92.
41. Thomas Bedell to Cromwell, 12 and 14 May 1533: BL MS Cotton Otho C/X
f. 164, *LP* 6 no. 461; SP 1/76 f. 34, *LP* 6 no. 469. For an account of Dunstable,
MacCulloch, *Thomas Cranmer*, 90–94. 42. The successful result of the York
Convocation, after much fraught correspondence from Lee and others to Cromwell, is reported by Lee's colleague there Thomas Magnus (Archdeacon of the East
Riding and Canon of Windsor) to Cromwell, 15 May 1533, BL MS Cotton Caligula B/III f. 169, *LP* 6 no. 486. Previously Lee had been the messenger considered
robust enough for the unenviable task of summoning Queen Katherine to Cran-
mer's court at Dunstable, meeting a predictable rebuff: Archbishop Cranmer to
Nicholas Hawkins, 17 June 1533, BL MS Harley 6148 f. 25r, *LP* 6 no. 661.
43. Roland Lee to Cromwell, 24 April [1533], SP 1/75 f. 167, *LP* 6 no. 381; Anne
Countess of Oxford to Cromwell, 11 May [1533], SP 1/76 f. 33, *LP* 6 no. 468. For
Cromwell's rapport with the Dowager Marchioness of Dorset and other ladies of a
certain age, see above, pp. 47–9, 300–302, 467–8. 44. *LP* 6 no. 737[7]. 45. Thomas
Bedell to Cromwell, 12 May 1533, BL MS Cotton Otho C/X f. 164, *LP* 6 no. 461.
46. Anthony Browne to Cromwell, 12 June [1533], SP 1/76 f. 198, *LP* 6 no. 631.
The best accounts of what follows are Ives, *Life and Death of Anne Boleyn*, 172–
83, and T. A. Sowerby, 'The coronation of Anne Boleyn', in T. Betteridge and
G. Walker (eds.), *The Oxford Handbook of Tudor Drama* (Oxford, 2012), 386–401.
47. [Anon.], *The noble tryumphaunt coronacyon of quene Anne, wyfe vnto the
moost noble kynge Henry the .viij* (London, 1533, *RSTC* 656). 48. Canons of the
King's College Oxford to Cromwell, 19 June [1533], SP 1/77 f. 54, *LP* 6 no.
673. 49. *LP* 6 no. 417[22]. 50. Edward Lee Archbishop of York to Cromwell, 27
September 1533, SP 1/79 f. 71, *LP* 6 no. 1158, recalling a conversation which
would have been in the previous June. 51. John Lord Berners to Cromwell, 11
April 1529, SP 1/53 f. 173, *LP* 4 iii no. 5456. 52. Elton, *Tudor Revolution in
Government*, 113–14; I am drawing on his further account of the office up to
120. 53. For a royal letter to a county sheriff outlining the process of fines for
recalcitrants with the summoning of defaulters before Cromwell, see Henry VIII
to the Sheriff of Oxford, 31 May [1534], SP 1/239 f. 191, *LP Addenda* 1 i no. 988
(misdated in *LP*). What appears to be a final round-up of actions against those
owing the Crown money for distraint of knighthood occurs in the Chief Justice of
Common Pleas' Plea Roll for Hilary 26 Henry VIII [winter 1535], TNA, CP
40/1084, in which a commission of Cromwell, William Paulet and Brian Tuke
prosecuted more than a hundred actions against esquires. It is puzzling to find
these cases here. In a previous round of distraints in 1501 they had been recorded
in a special Exchequer roll, TNA, E 159/279: Baker, *Oxford History of the Laws
of England* 6, 162n. 54. Princess Mary to Cromwell, 28 May [1533], BL MS

Cotton Vespasian F/XIII f. 282, *LP* 6 no. 550.   **55.** Thomas Audley to Cromwell, 4 November [1532], BL MS Cotton Titus B/I f. 281, *LP* 5 no. 1518.   **56.** Sir Hugh Trevanion to Cromwell, 18 October [1533], SP 1/79 f. 191, *LP* 6 no. 1309, reminding Cromwell of their conversation during the coronation.   **57.** Chapuys to Charles V, 11 July 1533, *Spanish Calendar* 4 ii no. 1100, at 739. See the commands for appropriate respect, particularly and pointedly directed at her household, in the proclamation of 5 July 1533, *TRP* no. 140.   **58.** J. Leland, *De Uiris Illustribus: On Famous Men*, ed. J. P. Carley (Toronto, 2010), lii–liii; and what follows in Carley's introduction is a wonderful reconstruction of Leland's itineraries. **59.** See Carley, *Libraries of Henry VIII*, 318–21; D. G. Selwyn, *The Library of Thomas Cranmer* (Oxford Bibliographical Society 3rd series 1, 1996), 203– 14.   **60.** *LP* 7 no. 737[5]: a licence to travel abroad with six servants, first signed at Greenwich on 1 May 1533 and completed at Westminster on 6 June. In general, see D. Hay, *Polydore Vergil: Renaissance historian and man of letters* (Oxford, 1952), which has not yet been superseded.   **61.** Two copies of the King's declaration are TNA, E 30/1026–7, *LP* 6 no. 721, which notes that both are endorsed by Cuthbert Tunstall; otherwise the full text is given in Rymer (ed.), *Foedera* 14, 476–9. On the excommunication, see Scarisbrick, *Henry VIII*, 317–19.   **62.** R. Rex, *The Theology of John Fisher* (Cambridge, 1991), 52–4.   **63.** For Cranmer at Croydon both before and after this date, see BL MS Harley MS 6148 ff. 23v, 24v, 28r, *LP* 6 nos. 770, 702–4, 771. For Lee in Parliament, Chapuys to Charles V, 23 February 1533, *Spanish Calendar* 4 ii no. 1053.   **64.** Lee's certification of Convocation's resolution on 14 June 1533 is TNA, E 30/1022, *LP* 6 no. 640; full text in Rymer (ed.), *Foedera* 14, 472. On the Lee manor-house at Stockwell, see *Survey of London: 26, Lambeth: Southern Area*, 81–2.   **65.** Chapuys to Charles V, 16 June 1533, Spanish Calendar 4 ii no. 1081, at 706, where his comments on Lee and Fisher are linked. Lee's letter to Cromwell about his tense negotiations with Tunstall, 4 May [1533], SP 1/76 f. 13, *LP* 6 no. 437.   **66.** See the account of the christening in Ives, *Life and Death of Anne Boleyn*, 184–5. Cromwell's presence is attested only by the attendance list in a notarial instrument concerning the christening, which necessarily had to be a complete record: Corpus Christi College Cambridge MS 105, 274, *LP* 6 no. 1111[4]. Richard Watkins the notary worked closely with Cromwell: see his letter about the election of a new abbot of Burton-on-Trent, Watkins to Cromwell, 27 June [1533], SP 1/77 f. 90, *LP* 6 no. 716.   **67.** Cromwell to Henry VIII, SP 1/80 f. 50, *LP* 6 no. 1369. *LP* dates this letter to October 1533, but it probably predates the letter cited next.   **68.** Cromwell to Henry VIII, 23 July [1533], SP 1/78 f. 25, *LP* 6 no. 887.   **69.** Chapuys to Charles V, 20 November 1533, *Spanish Calendar* 4 i no. 1153, at 859.

Chapter 10: Treason in Prospect: 1533–1534

1. The best recent accounts of Barton are E. H. Shagan, *Popular Politics and the English Reformation* (Cambridge, 2003), 61–88, and E. H. Shagan, 'Print, orality and communications in the Maid of Kent affair', *JEH* 52 (2001), 21–33. For print and the Wentworth miracles, see Blatchly and MacCulloch, *Miracles in Lady Lane*, 21–3, 69–74; it is not certain whether the Wentworth girl's name was Anne or Jane, as discussed at 27–9.   2. See the denunciation of Dario's reverence for her in a Cromwellian pamphlet of 1539, SP 1/143 f. 205r, *LP* 14 i no. 402. Previously Dario had been helpful to King Henry in 1529: Kelly, *Matrimonial Trials*, 158–9.   3. Cromwell's remembrances dateable just before 24 September 1533, partly in his own hand, give details of the printing: Cotton Titus B/I f. 493rv, *LP* 6 no. 1194. See E. J. Devereux, 'Elizabeth Barton and Tudor censorship', *Bulletin of the John Rylands Library* 49 (1966), 91–106. This lost work has to be distinguished from the earlier and apolitical printed account of Barton's wonders partly preserved by William Lambarde.   4. Where not otherwise referenced in this and subsequent paragraphs, see my account of these events in MacCulloch, *Thomas Cranmer*, 103–5.   5. Chapuys to Charles V, 20 November 1533, *Spanish Calendar* 4 i no. 1153, at 863.   6. Cromwell to John Fisher, probably late February 1534, BL MS Cotton Cleopatra E/IV f. 102v, *LP* 7 no. 238. See also the vivid description of events in the Council supplied by Chapuys to Charles V, 20 November 1533, *Spanish Calendar* 4 i no. 1153.   7. He alluded to his presence in his letter to Cromwell of early March 1534, saying that he had not seen Father Risby from Christmas 1532 until Risby's exposure at the Paul's Cross sermon: BL MS Arundel 152 f. 296, *LP* 7 no. 287, and see text in E. F. Rogers (ed.), *St Thomas More: selected letters* (New Haven, 1961), 195.   8. Gertrude Marchioness of Exeter to Henry VIII, [26 November 1533], BL MS Cotton Cleopatra E/IV ff. 94–5, *LP* 6 no. 1464; Marchioness of Exeter to Cromwell, Wednesday [26 November 1533], SP 1/80 f. 116, *LP* 6 no. 1465. The correspondence is dateable from the Marchioness's mention in her letter to the King of having just received his letter of pardon dated (Tuesday) 25 November from Greenwich, and from the Wednesday date of her letter to Cromwell. *LP* states that the draft of her letter to the King is corrected by Cromwell, but the corrections do not appear to be in his hand, and it is unlikely that he would have gone down to West Horsley in Surrey, from where she writes.   9. [Anon.], *Articles deuisid by the holle consent of the kynges moste honourable counsayle, his gracis licence opteined therto, not only to exhorte, but also to enfourme his louynge subiectis of the trouthe* (London, 1533, 1534, *RSTC* 9177, 9178); the text is reproduced in Pocock 2, 523–31. P. Marshall, *Heretics and Believers: a history of the English Reformation* (New Haven and London, 2017), 208.   10. The three copies of the memorandum for the Council including the order for printing, one of them a draft extensively corrected by Cromwell, are described in *LP* 6 no. 1481[1–3]; for comment, see G. R. Elton, 'The materials of Parliamentary history', in Elton, *Studies* 3, 58–155, at 101. No copy of this printing is known to survive. On the Act, see also above, pp. 216–19.   11. J. G. Nichols (ed.), *Narratives of the days of the Reformation* ... (CS 1st series 77, 1859), 280, from BL MS Harley 419 ff. 112f, which is an incomplete English translation of the Latin original at Corpus Christi College Cambridge MS 298 pt iv, here at f. 29r. On Butley, Dickens, *Late Monasticism and the Reformation*, 65–6.   12. See Edmund Bonner to Cromwell, ?April 1530, SP 1/57 f. 75, *LP* 4 iii no. 6346; 24 December [1532], SP 1/72 f. 150, *LP* 5 no. 1654; early February 1533, SP 1/74 f. 118, *LP* 6 no.

103.   **13.** On Penizon, see A. Coates, *English Medieval Books: the Reading Abbey collections from foundation to dispersal* (Oxford, 1999), 126–7; also for his links to the Guildford family, below, p. 467, and R. Lutton, 'Richard Guldeford's pilgrimage: piety and cultural change in late fifteenth- and early sixteenth-century England', *History* 98 (2013), 41–78.   **14.** On all this, see Bonner's report, *LP* 6 no. 1425 (a reconstruction via Bishop Burnet of the now badly fire-damaged BL MS Cotton Vitellius B/XIV f. 71), and Gardiner and others to Henry VIII, mid-November 1533, *LP* 6 no. 1427.   **15.** *LP* 6 Appendix no. 6, which lists various similar grants to ambassadors including Bonner, and others not on embassy, during 1533 and 1534. I am unconvinced by efforts to exonerate Gardiner from knowledge of this grant in G. Redworth, *In Defence of the Church Catholic: the life of Stephen Gardiner* (Oxford, 1990), 56–7. For Gardiner's friendship with Benet, see their part in the will of John Purgold, Fellow of Trinity Hall Cambridge, 30 January 1527: Cambridge University Archives, Register of Wills I ff. 42v–43v; they had both been colleagues under Wolsey.   **16.** Where not otherwise referenced below, my account of this Parliament follows citations in Lehmberg, *Reformation Parliament*, 182–99. He makes the point that this is the only session of the Reformation Parliament for which the journal of the House of Lords has survived, making it much easier to trace the timing and progress of particular pieces of legislation.   **17.** Husee to Lisle, 7 January 1534, SP 3/5 f. 22, *Lisle Letters* 2 no. 108; Chapuys to Charles V, 28 January 1534, *Spanish Calendar* 5 i no. 7, at 24. Hoyle, 'Origins of the dissolution of the monasteries', 290–91.   **18.** Edward Lee Archbishop of York to Cromwell, 28 December 1533, SP 1/72 f. 164, *LP* 5 no. 1669. *LP* pardonably misdated this letter to 1532, as the final arabic 3 of the date is not well formed. It is however firmly dateable to 1533 by the fact of Lee's presence in the 1533 Parliament and his absence from the session of 1534. Lee also thanks Cromwell for a favour in an 'injunction', probably concerning his back-taxes in the Exchequer, about which he had previously agitated to Cromwell on 21 November 1533: Lee to Cromwell, SP 1/80 f. 108, *LP* 6 no. 1451.   **19.** On Cranmer's attendance, Convocation and the Paul's Cross preaching, see MacCulloch, *Thomas Cranmer*, 115.   **20.** Sir George Throckmorton to Cromwell, 29 October [1533], SP 1/80 f. 47, *LP* 6 no. 1365; same to same, 14 June [1534], SP 1/84 f. 176, *LP* 7 no. 838.   **21.** Sir George Throckmorton to Cromwell, 29 October [1533], SP 1/80 f. 47, *LP* 6 no. 1365; Sir Marmaduke Constable to Cromwell, 9 January [1534], SP 1/82 f. 41, *LP* 7 no. 31.   **22.** On Gage, see especially Sir William Fitzwilliam to Cromwell, 10 August [1533], SP 1/78 f. 104, *LP* 6 no. 965, and Chapuys to Charles V, 3 January 1534, *Spanish Calendar* 5 i no. 1, at 4; William Lord Mountjoy to Cromwell, 10 October [1533], SP 1/79 f. 158, *LP* 6 no. 1252.   **23.** Lehmberg, *Reformation Parliament*, 182.   **24.** Loades (ed.), *Papers of George Wyatt*, 156.   **25.** For general discussion, see MacCulloch, *Reformation: Europe's house divided*, 620–30, and for the English legal background, Baker, *Oxford History of the Laws of England* 6, 563. For Tyndale and clerical sodomy, see H. Walter (ed.), *Doctrinal Treatises and introductions to different portions of the Holy Scriptures. By William Tyndale . . .* (Parker Society, 1848), 438–9; H. Walter (ed.), *An Answer to Sir Thomas More's Dialogue, The Supper of the Lord . . . and*

W[illia]m Tracy's Testament expounded. By William Tyndale . . . (Parker Society, 1850), 52, 171.   **26.** On Stokesley and Wolsey's downfall, E. V. Hitchcock (ed.), *The Lyfe of Sir Thomas Moore, knighte, written by William Roper* . . . (Early English Text Society original series 197, 1935), 38–9.   **27.** T. More, *The apologye of syr Thomas More knyght* (London, 1533, RSTC 18078), ff. 211v–213v.   **28.** What follows can be traced through the *Lords Journals* 1, 65–81.   **29.** BL MS Harley 2252 ff. 34–5, *LP* 7 no. 399; see the text quoted in Lehmberg, *Reformation Parliament*, 193.   **30.** G. Gardiner, *A letter of a yonge gentylman named mayster Germen Gardynare, wryten to a frend of his, wherin men may se the demeanour [and] heresy of Ioh[a]n Fryth late burned, [and] also the dyspycyo[n]s [and] reasonynge vpon the same, had betwene the same mayster Germen and hym* (London, 1534, RSTC 11594). The date 1534 might seem decisive as putting publication after 25 March 1534, but More testified to Cromwell that Rastell had published another work with a 1534 date although he had in fact issued it before Christmas 1533: T. More, *The vvorkes of Sir Thomas More Knyght, sometyme Lorde Chauncellour of England, wrytten by him in the Englysh tonge* (London, 1557, RSTC 18076), 1422.   **31.** For accurate discussion of the identification of Edward Foxe as recipient, see Butterworth and Chester, *George Joye*, 104–6.   **32.** Field's petition of late 1533 refers to events in the second half of 1532: SP 1/78 ff. 219–20, *LP* 6 no. 1059. Confusingly, there is extensive correspondence in Cromwell's papers about a Thomas Phelips and his troubles at the hands of a Sir Thomas More just at this time. Both these were different men with the same names, and both came from Dorset; that case had nothing to do with religion, but see also below, p. 285.   **33.** On Carew and Philips, Hall 2, 284, with pointed reference to Philips's own earlier troubles; for Philips's reports a year later on the welfare of the Marchioness of Exeter and the Countess of Salisbury, SP 1/140 ff. 218–19, *LP* 13 ii no. 1176. *LP* dates these too early, as Philips refers (f. 219r) to the care of one of the prisoners having lasted a year; the report is therefore of autumn 1539.   **34.** MacCulloch, *Thomas Cranmer*, 101–2. John Day added his note on Cromwell's involvement in the Frith case very late in his expansion of Foxe's text, in fact in an appendix: Foxe 1583, 2149–50. As usual, one must subtract his updating of the titles of those involved, as he anachronistically describes Cromwell as already Vice-Gerent and a peer.   **35.** BL MS Cotton Titus B/I f. 486, *LP* 5 no. 394; see above, p. 134. My discussion is shaped by G. R. Elton, 'The law of treason in the early Reformation', *HJ* 11 (1968), 211–36. Elton repeated this material in *Policy and Police: the enforcement of the Reformation in the age of Thomas Cromwell* (Cambridge, 1972), 263–92. Some commentators place the previous Treason Act of Edward III in 1351, but sorting out the complications of his regnal years, sessions of Parliament and Old Style dating places it firmly in early 1352.   **36.** For the text of the final Act, see Elton (ed.), *Tudor Constitution*, 6–12. See Chapuys's account of his meeting with the Council on 16 May: *Spanish Calendar* 5 i no. 58, at 157.   **37.** Effectively studied in J. M. Gray, *Oaths and the English Reformation* (Cambridge, 2013), especially ch. 2.   **38.** MacCulloch, *Thomas Cranmer*, 121–5.   **39.** John Rookwood to Lord Lisle, 6 April [1534], SP 3/7 f. 14, *LP* 7 no. 441; Sir Thomas Palmer to Lord Lisle, 15 April [1534], SP 3/6 f. 102, *Lisle*

Letters 2 nos. 156, 162. See discussion in Redworth, *In Defence of the Church Catholic*, 57–62.   40. Elton, *Tudor Revolution in Government*, 124–5: Gardiner's last surviving signed signet warrant had been as long before as 3 February 1534. He had actually initiated this custom of the Secretary signing the warrants. 41. Cromwell to Fisher, *c.* late February 1534, BL MS Cotton Cleopatra E/IV f. 102r, *LP* 7 no. 238.   42. Cromwell to Cranmer, probably 18 April 1534, SP 1/83 f. 88, *LP* 7 no. 500. Significantly, this very important letter is not in Cranmer's surviving letter-book. See also MacCulloch, *Thomas Cranmer*, 124–5.   43. Thomas More to Margaret Roper, *c.* 18 April 1534, More, *The vvorkes of Sir Thomas More Knyght*, 1430, *LP* 7 no. 575. More interestingly repeated his reminiscence and the remark about Gregory in another letter to Margaret Roper in 1534: ibid., 1448, *LP* 7 no. 1118.   44. Hitchcock (ed.), *Lyfe of Sir Thomas Moore*, 74.   45. BL MS Arundel 152 ff. 296f, *LP* 7 no. 287, and see text in Rogers (ed.), *St Thomas More: selected letters*, 193–201.   46. On Horde, see Edward Lee Archbishop of York to Cromwell, 9 July 1535, BL MS Cotton Cleopatra E/VI f. 245, *LP* 8 no. 1011, and Edmund Horde Prior of Hinton Charterhouse to Cromwell, 1 September [1535], SP 1/85 f. 136, *LP* 7 no. 1127 (misdated by *LP* to 1534).   47. A remembrance of Cromwell's dateable by other content to late December 1533 or January 1534, BL MS Cotton Titus B/I f. 430, *LP* 7 no. 52.   48. Thomas Salter to Cromwell, 7 August [1534], SP 1/85 f. 98v, *LP* 7 no. 1046, speaking of a visit on 5 June 1534. M. Chauncy, *Historia aliquot martyrum Anglorum maxime octodecim Cartusianorum: sub Rege Henrico Octavo ob fidei confessionem et summi pontificis jura vindicanda interemptorum* (London, 1888), 106, talks about Cromwell's multiple visits to put the oath to the community 'quoties ad nos venit'.   49. John Whalley to Cromwell, 7 August [1534], SP 1/92 f. 63, *LP* 8 no. 601. *LP* places this in late April 1535, but there is no good reason to accept this, and the reference to apples suggests the first of the crop in late summer. It is dated merely 'Friday', which is also the day of Salter's letter of 7 August 1534.   50. Roland Lee to Cromwell, dateable to just before 17 April 1534, BL MS Cotton Cleopatra E/VI f. 160, *LP* 7 no. 498.   51. Husee to Lisle, 20 April [1534], SP 3/5 f. 130, *Lisle Letters* 2 no. 171.   52. Deposition of Christopher Chaitor, from internal evidence *c.* 16 December 1539, SP 1/155 f. 155v, and cf. the deposition of . . . Cray, f. 163r, both *LP* 14 ii no. 750.   53. Earls of Westmorland and Cumberland and Sir Thomas Clifford to Cromwell, 2 May [1534], SP 1/70 ff. 4–5, *LP* 5 no. 986; the letter and postscript are in the hand of ap Rhys, who made his own report to Cromwell the same day, SP 1/70 ff. 6–7, *LP* 5 no. 987. *LP* misdated these letters to 1532.   54. *Spanish Calendar* 5 i no. 58, at 157–8; deposition of Christopher Chaitor, SP 1/155 f. 155v, and of . . . Cray, f. 163r, both *LP* 14 ii no. 750. 55. Edward Lee and Cuthbert Tunstall to Henry VIII, 21 May [1534], SP 1/84 ff. 59–61, *LP* 7 no. 695. Tunstall went on to prove the truth of More's shrewd observation that in surviving 'he may do more good than to die with us': on his part in sabotaging negotiations with the Lutheran ambassadors in 1538, see below, pp. 451–2.   56. Lancelot Collins to Cromwell, 6 October 1533, SP 1/79 f. 145, *LP* 6 no. 1226.   57. The draft undated grant of the Stewardship and Keepership of Brewood, Staffordshire, remains in Cromwell's papers: TNA, SP 2/P f. 148, *LP* 7

no. 416[2]; the Prebend for Wellifed was Curborough.   58. Cromwell's remembrances, beginning of May 1533, SP 1/75 f. 171v, *LP* 6 no. 386[ii], and early July
1533, SP 1/77 f. 95, *LP* 6 no. 727.   59. C. A. J. Skeel, *The Council in the Marches
of Wales: a study in local government during the sixteenth and seventeenth centuries* (London, 1904), 59.   60. Roland Lee to Cromwell, early May 1534, SP
1/84 f. 100, *LP* 7 no. 758; Lee and Thomas Bedell to Cromwell, 7 May 1534, SP
1/83 f. 228, *LP* 7 no. 622.   61. Roland Lee to Cromwell, 3 July [1534], SP 1/85 f.
22, *LP* 7 no. 940; Lee wrote to Cromwell the very day he arrived at Beaudesert
Castle. Henry Dowes to Cromwell, SP 1/85 f. 44, *LP* 7 no. 967.   62. Roland Lee
to Cromwell, 27 December [1534], SP 1/87 f. 129, *LP* 7 no. 1576.   63. Robert
Cowley to Cromwell, ?July 1534, SP 60/2 f. 48, *LP* 7 no. 915, *State Papers* 2, 197–
8; this must predate his knowledge of Archbishop Allen's murder on 27 July, and
although it has a contemporary filing endorsement for June, that seems a little too
early. For Cowley's hostility to the Geraldines, see Bradshaw, *Irish Constitutional
Revolution*, 77.   64. Hugh Halgrave, Registrar to Archbishop Allen, to Thomas
Allen, 8 November [1534], SP 60/2 f. 62, *LP* 7 no. 1404. Halgrave confirms the
ransom story previously reported by Chapuys to the Emperor on 11 August 1534:
Spanish Calendar 5 i no. 84, at 244. A remarkably efficient summary of Cromwell's six months of anxieties and preoccupations from the beginning of Parliament
to this moment of crisis was provided for Lady Lisle by the family servant Thomas
Warley on 13 August 1534, by way of excuse for not getting results that the Lisles
wanted: SP 3/14 f. 52, *Lisle Letters* 2 no. 245.   65. This account draws on Bradshaw, *Irish Constitutional Revolution*, 98–104, 120–21; see also sensible remarks
in Ellis, 'Thomas Cromwell and Ireland, 1532–1540', 503.   66. The date of Skeffington's appointment is uncertain, but can be placed in late May by his letter to
Cromwell about offices in his gift, 24 May 1534, SP 60/2 f. 40, *LP* 7 no. 705. The
letter also shows that the Earl of Ossory, bane of the Fitzgeralds, was hand in
glove with Skeffington, and in London at the time of his appointment; they wished
to confer with Cromwell at Court. See also Ellis, 'Thomas Cromwell and Ireland,
1532–1540', 501–2.   67. On Tunstall, see above, p. 251. A convincing reconstruction of these links between the situations in northern England and in Ireland
is S. G. Ellis, *Tudor Frontiers and Noble Power: the making of the British state*
(Oxford, 1995), 174–8; Ellis points out the very different outcomes of the northern
arrests of 1534.   68. Where not otherwise referenced, this and following paragraphs are based on the excellent summary account in M. Ó Siochrú, 'Foreign
involvement in the revolt of Silken Thomas, 1534–5', *Proceedings of the Royal
Irish Academy* 96C (1996), 49–66.   69. Emden, *Oxford 1501 to 1540*, 575; on
clergy involvement in Silken Thomas's rebellion, see J. Murray, *Enforcing the English Reformation in Ireland: clerical resistance and political conflict in the diocese
of Dublin, 1534–1590* (Cambridge, 2009), 84–8, though he may underestimate the
amount of subsequent cover-up of clerical activism.   70. Thomas Batcock to William Pratt, a London merchant, 13 July 1533, BL MS Cotton Vespasian C/VII f. 42,
LP 6 no. 821.   71. William Wise Mayor of Waterford to Cromwell, 12 July [1534],
BL MS Cotton Titus B/XI/2 f. 359, *LP* 6 no. 815. Ó Siochrú, 'Foreign involvement
in the revolt of Silken Thomas', 54, draws attention to the misdating of this letter

in *LP*.   72. Chapuys to Charles V, 11 August 1534: *Spanish Calendar* 5 i no. 84, at 243–4. Chapuys was probably wrong in calling this cleric a bishop, as he appears to be Richard Rawson, Archdeacon of Essex, to judge by a letter of his brother John Rawson, Commendator of Kilmainham, to Henry VIII, 7 August 1534, *LP* 7 no. 1045, *State Papers* 2, 201. They had left via Waterford, knowing of the Mayor's previous report to Cromwell.   73. From a variety of depressing correspondence about Skeffington's faltering efforts to reach Ireland, see John Allen to Cromwell, 24 September [1534], SP 60/2 f. 59, *LP* 7 no. 1186.   74. On Brabazon, see *ODNB*. For Brabazon and Skeffington, see letter cited in previous note; for his first appointment as Under-Treasurer, Ellis, *Reform and Revival*, 222, and for Cromwell's ease with using Anglo-Irishmen in government rather than Englishmen, Bradshaw, *Irish Constitutional Revolution*, 98–9, 144–5. For Brabazon's monument (both it and the church have disappeared), A. L. Harris, 'Tombs of the New English in late sixteenth and early seventeenth-century Dublin', *Church Monuments* 11 (1996), 25–41, at 29.   75. Chapuys to Charles V, 10 September 1534, *Spanish Calender* 5 i no. 87, at 254: 'Quil estoit plus de la dite royne que autre pour austant quil avoit voulu tenir le duc de Richemont aupres de luy et de sa fille, sa femme, et que sil eust voulu laisse[r] aller au dit Yrlande sont passez huit mois, comme auoit este advise, ces choses ne fussent survenues.'   76. George Cotton to Cromwell, 2 June [1534], SP 1/84 f. 108, *LP* 7 no. 772. For George's closeness to Cromwell during the Pilgrimage of Grace, together with his brother Richard Cotton, see below, p. 386.   77. Richmond to Cromwell, 11 June [1534], SP 1/84 f. 162, *LP* 7 no. 821; 13 June [1534], SP 1/84 f. 169, *LP* 7 no. 831; his holograph letter about the Calais visit is 30 June [1534], SP 1/85 f. 5, *LP* 7 no. 904. For contrasting reluctance to go to France, see John Lord Mordaunt to Cromwell, 26 June [1534], SP 1/84 f. 212, *LP* 7 no. 884.   78. Sir Thomas Arundell of Dorset to Cromwell, 12 June [1534], SP 1/76 f. 196, *LP* 6 no. 629. *LP* acknowledged the incorrect date of this to 1533 in Corrigenda, and by giving it a place-holder at *LP* 7 no. 825.

Chapter 11: Spirituals: 1534–1535

1. McEntegart, *Henry VIII, the League of Schmalkalden and the English Reformation*, 14–20.   2. Warrant under the signet, 31 January 1534, SP 1/82 f. 128, *LP* 7 no. 137[1]; see also the remembrance in his hand to secure these payments and their passports, BL MS Cotton Titus B/I f. 430, *LP* 7 no. 52.   3. McEntegart, *Henry VIII, the League of Schmalkalden and the English Reformation*, 20: 'durch etliche furtreffliche des reichs Engellandt rethen und ingesessen, doch unvermerckt des kunigs'; my italics. I have modified Dr McEntegart's translation at this point, and in what follows, ibid., 21–5. Heath can be identified as being at Nuremberg by his earlier letter to Cromwell, 31 March [1534], BL MS Cotton Vitellius B/XXI f. 103, *LP* 7 no. 395.   4. On the pension and its current diversion, D. Potter, 'Foreign policy', in MacCulloch (ed.), *Reign of Henry VIII*, 101–33, at 125–6, and McEntegart, *Henry VIII, the League of Schmalkalden and the*

English Reformation, 24–5. Cromwell strongly denied that Henry had contributed any money for the Duke of Württemberg's restoration, while actually virtually admitting the transaction: Chapuys to Charles V, 5 May 1535, *Spanish Calendar* 5 i no. 157, at 458.   5. On this, see additionally to McEntegart, N. S. Tjernagel, *Henry VIII and the Lutherans: a study in Anglo-Lutheran relations from 1521 to 1547* (St Louis, MO, 1965), 128–34.   6. Chapuys to Charles V, 16 July 1534, *Spanish Calendar* 5 i no. 71, at 206. Chapuys speaks of only two of the bishops 'created by this new Pope' (Cranmer), and of course Roland Lee was by now in the west Midlands.   7. Amid copious papers relating to Lübeck's piracy, see in particular Vice-Admiral Sir Edward Guildford to Cromwell, 22 August 1533, SP 1/78 f. 144, *LP* 6 no. 1013; Chapuys to Charles V, 9 December 1533, *Spanish Calendar* 4 ii no. 1158, at 877–8; petition of Thomas Browne to Cromwell about stolen goods, summer 1534, SP 1/85 f. 16, *LP* 7 no. 918.   8. Jürgen Wullenweber Burgomeister of Lübeck to Cromwell, 17 October 1534, SP 1/86 ff. 59–60, *LP* 7 no. 1272; for background, see Tjernagel, *Henry VIII and the Lutherans*, 131–4.   9. On what follows, where not otherwise referenced, see MacCulloch, *Thomas Cranmer*, 123–35.   10. For their commissioning via Cranmer, see Chapuys to Charles V, 22 April 1534, *Spanish Calendar* 5 i no. 46, at 31. Shaw, 'Compendium Compertorum', 281, notes the rediscovery of the visitation articles they used: London Metropolitan Archives, MS CLC/270/MS01231 ff. 1–2.   11. On these events, see M. C. Skeeters, *Community and Clergy: Bristol and the Reformation, c. 1530–c. 1570* (Oxford, 1993), 34–46, and see also the commendation of him by Michael Drum, referring to Oxford preaching probably in Lent 1533, Michael Drum to William Marshall, 9 March ?1534, SP 1/82 f. 239, *LP* 7 no. 308.   12. George Browne to Cromwell, ?1533, SP 1/246 ff. 105–6, *LP Addenda* 1 ii, Appendix no. 5. This has the distinction of being the very last item in *LP*.   13. Gabriel Peacock, Warden of Southampton Observants, to Cromwell, 16 July [1534], SP 1/85 f. 50, *LP* 7 no. 982: for Ingworth's assistant role, Thomas Bedell to Cromwell, 15 September [1545], SP 1/96 f. 161, *LP* 9 no. 373.   14. Browne to Cromwell, 6 July [1534], SP 1/85 f. 35, *LP* 7 no. 953.   15. Hilsey to Cromwell, 16 October [1534], SP 1/86 f. 53v, *LP* 7 no. 1265; my italics.   16. On what follows, where not otherwise referenced, see Lehmberg, *Reformation Parliament*, 201–15.   17. Elton (ed.), *Tudor Constitution*, 364–5. The bill was accompanied by Cranmer's declaration to Convocation on 11 November that he was to be called Metropolitan, not *Legatus natus* – the official end to that embarrassment: Lambeth MS 751, 106.   18. Lehmberg, *Reformation Parliament*, 190–91.   19. Hoyle, 'Origins of the dissolution of the monasteries', 291–4, is a useful discussion of these proposals.   20. Elton (ed.), *Tudor Constitution*, 53–6. M. Jurkowski, 'The history of clerical taxation in England and Wales, 1173–1663: the findings of the E 179 project', *JEH* 67 (2016), 53–81, provides an essential overview on the sources, and the immediate impact is excellently analysed by P. R. N. Carter, 'The fiscal Reformation: clerical taxation and opposition in Henrician England', in B. Kümin (ed.), *Reformations Old and New: essays on the socio-economic impact of religious change, c. 1470–1630* (Aldershot, 1996), 92–105.   21. Hitchcock (ed.), *Lyfe of Sir Thomas Moore*, 78.   22. On this, see Elton, 'Law of treason in the early Reformation', 227–36.   23. Deposition of Bishop John Fisher, 12 June 1535, BL MS Cotton Cleopatra E/VI f. 165, *LP* 8 no. 858. Misprision of treason did not disappear entirely as an indictable offence: see Baker, *Oxford History of the Laws of England* 6, 589–90.   24. Hoyle, 'Origins of the dissolution of the monasteries', 290–91, commenting on a 'remembrance' of mid- to late October 1533, BL MS Cotton Titus B/I f. 150, *LP* 6 no. 1381[3]: 'Item an Act that any bishop, dean, abbot, abbess or any other head or ruler of any body politic within this realm or the King's dominions commit or do any of high treason, and be thereof convict, that then they shall forfeit all the lands and tenements temporal to the King's Highness, which they had in the right of their churches, dignities or houses, and the King's Highness to have those to dispose for defence of his realm.'   25. For that Observant house on Guernsey, see Chambers (ed.), *Faculty Office Registers*, 197.   26. An early example is John Burton Abbot of Osney to Cromwell, 15 September [1535], SP 1/96 f. 163, *LP* 9 no. 375. For examples from two sequential days interestingly far apart in location, which suggests some general order, see Thomas Chard Abbot of Forde to Cromwell, 11 December [1535], SP 1/99 f. 115, *LP* 9 no. 948, and Richard Leighton from Syon Abbey to Cromwell, 12 December [1535], BL MS Cotton Cleopatra E/IV f. 152, *LP* 9 no. 954. 27. Even more vanishingly elusive was the effort of one clerk who, in the course of a grant with an exceptionally long-winded preamble of titles for both King and Cromwell, added the third flourish 'Officiarius Principalis': SP 1/102 ff. 51–7, *LP* 10 no. 328, possibly of October 1535. Officials principal were, like vicars-general, familiar figures in diocesan administration, and it may have simply been a clerk of St Paul's Cathedral running on autopilot who created this office for the Vice-Gerent, rather than one of Cromwell's own staff in his new court. The document gave Cromwell's colleague at Court Richard Sampson custodianship of the mentally disturbed Dean, Richard Pace, and his cathedral responsibilities and estates.   28. On the setting up of the Vice-Gerency where not otherwise referenced below, see MacCulloch, *Thomas Cranmer*, 122–3, 129–35, and now the important discussions in P. D. Clarke, 'Canterbury as the New Rome: dispensations and Henry VIII's Reformation', *JEH* 64 (2013), 20–44, and Clarke in Clarke and Questier (eds.), *Camden Miscellany XXXVI: papal authority and the limits of the law in Tudor England*.   29. John Grenville to Lord Lisle, 20 March [1534], SP 3/3 f. 136, *Lisle Letters* 2 no. 147.   30. Richmond to Cromwell, 11 June [1534], SP 1/84 f. 162, *LP* 7 no. 821. We have already noted above (p. 265) that Cromwell had taken it upon himself to appoint a master-general for the Dominicans in 1533 or 1534.   31. For a good discussion of the Mastership, Elton, *Tudor Revolution in Government*, 127–33.   32. John Tregonwell to Cromwell, 31 May [1534], SP 1/84 f. 91, *LP* 7 no. 743.   33. See his letter addressed from The Rolls on 17 October [1534], *LP* 7 no. 1271, Merriman 1 no. 83, 389.   34. Christopher Hales to Cromwell, 20 May [1533], SP 1/76 f. 70, *LP* 6 no. 514.   35. Cromwell's illness at The Rolls from around 21 March to 24 April 1535 is best summarized in John Husee to Lord Lisle, SP 3/5 f. 48, *Lisle Letters* 2 no. 373. Henry visited him on 7 April: Husee to Lord Lisle, SP 3/5 f. 44, *Lisle Letters* 2 no. 365, and for specimens of their business discussions on that day, Sir Thomas Audley to Henry VIII, BL

MS Cotton Titus B/XI/2 f. 367, *LP* 8 no. 519, and Chapuys to Charles V, 17 April 1535, *Spanish Calendar* 5 i no. 150, at 438.   36. G. W. Sanders (ed.), *Orders of the High Court of Chancery* . . . (2 vols., London, 1845), 1, 17–18: a memorandum by 'old Mr Valence' from the 1590s, BL MS Lansdowne 163 f. 95. It continues to a peculiar anecdote about Hales which must originally have been thought a humorous parallel to these circumstances: 'He resting at the side bar at Westminster after the Lord Audley Lord Chancellor had gone up to sit, and being sent to that that was not his place *sedente Curia*, answered that he wist well enough where his place was.' As late as 10 August 1539 Cromwell's servant Henry Polstead was writing to his master from his office in The Rolls, SP 1/153 f. 13, *LP* 14 ii no. 29. There is no record of Cromwell leaving the property after that. For Hales's grant of office on 10 July 1536, 'with custody of the house or hospital of Converts', see *LP* 11 no. 202[17].   37. For what follows, unless separately referenced, see F. D. Logan, 'Thomas Cromwell and the Vicegerency in Spirituals: a revisitation', *EHR* 103 (1988), 658–67.   38. Dr David Skinner has kindly let me know of the evidence in the accounts of Fotheringhay College, Northamptonshire Record Office MS 4.xviii.6, that Cranmer visited in person and had to admit defeat over Fotheringhay's exempt jurisdiction in September 1534. This might have been one material incentive for the first draft commission.   39. The documents are respectively TNA, E 36/116 ff. 12–117, and TNA, SP 2/R ff. 2A–4, *LP* 8 no. 73.   40. TNA, C 82/692, *LP* 8 no. 75[1].   41. There is a round-up of these in *LP* 8 no. 190.   42. On the end of Cranmer's visitation, Richard Leighton to Cromwell, late June 1535, BL MS Cotton Cleopatra E/IV f. 56, *LP* 8 no. 955. On the inhibition and the workings of the vice-gerential office, see some notes from its lost archive in A. Harmer [H. Wharton], *A Specimen of some errors and defects in the History of the Reformation of the Church of England wrote by Gilbert Burnet, D.D., now Lord Bishop of Sarum* (1693, Wing W1569), 52–3, and BL MS Additional 48022 ff. 84r, 90r, 92r, 98v; cf. also M. Bowker, *The Henrician Reformation: the diocese of Lincoln under John Longland 1521-1547* (Cambridge, 1981), 77–8.   43. See the letter to Cromwell from Thomas Evans, who seems to have acted as a local representative of the Vice-Gerency in the West Country, 15 April [1539], SP 1/150 f. 129, *LP* 14 i no. 774. Hereford was effectively vacant from May 1538 to October 1539. This crucial evidence of Cromwell's continual activation of the vice-gerential visitation does not seem to have been generally noticed before.   44. Elton, *Tudor Revolution in Government*, 133, 190–201. If anything demonstrates that the Eltonian 'Revolution in Government' was based on a false premise, it is the administration of First Fruits and Tenths.   45. See the various commissions listed in *LP* 8 no. 149[35–82], 30 January 1535, and on his auditors at the Surrey houses of Merton, St Saviour's Southwark and St Thomas's Hospital, Sir William Fitzwilliam to Cromwell, 1 August [1535], SP 1/95 f. 5, *LP* 9 no. 4.   46. The best summary discussion of the *Valor* is still Knowles, *Religious Orders in England III*, 241–54.   47. Cromwell was receiving a fee from New College perhaps from the late 1520s, augmented in 1532: John London to Cromwell, 3 October [1532], SP 1/71 f. 79, *LP* 5 no. 1384. On Cromwell as visitor, London to Cromwell, 24 October [1534], SP 1/86 ff. 80–81, *LP* 7 no. 1299, and the letter of evangelical scholars of New College to Cromwell, 24 October [1534], SP 1/86 f. 82, *LP* 7 no. 1300. On the friendship of London and Bedell, e.g. London to Cromwell, probably 18 May 1532, SP 1/70 f. 41, *LP* 5 no. 1034.   **48.** Oxford University and town authorities to Sir William Fitzwilliam and Cromwell, 4 January [1533], BL MS Cotton Faustina C/VII ff. 208–9, *LP* 6 no. 20; Mayor of Oxford and other townsmen to Cromwell, 4 January [1533], SP 1/76 f. 30, *LP* 6 no. 21.   **49.** For the fee, S. M. Leathes (ed.), *Grace Book A* (Cambridge Antiquarian Society, Luard Memorial Series 1, 1897), 227, and Searle (ed.), *Grace Book Γ*, 286. For the Stewardship, Searle (ed.), *Grace Book Γ*, 301.   **50.** Corpus Christi College Cambridge MS 106, 195.   **51.** Cromwell to University of Cambridge, 5 September [1535], Merriman 1 no. 116, *LP* 9 no. 278.

Chapter 12: Deaths for Religion: 1535

1. For excellent analysis of this phase of Casali fortunes, see Fletcher, *Our Man in Rome*, 194–202, 205–9.   **2.** Chapuys to Charles V, 11 July 1535, *Spanish Calendar* 5 i no. 181, at 510.   **3.** Chapuys to Charles V, 13 October 1534, *Spanish Calendar* 5 i no. 97, at 281.   **4.** Fletcher, *Our Man in Rome*, 202–5.   **5.** Note of the meeting on 7 May occurs in deposition of Richard Wilson before the Lieutenant of the Tower and three of Cromwell's servants, Thomas Lee, Henry Polstead and John ap Rhys, 7 June 1535, *LP* 8 no. 856.   **6.** Fletcher, *Our Man in Rome*, 209–11.   **7.** On Gardiner, see S. Gardiner, *Obedience in Church and State: three political tracts by Stephen Gardiner*, ed. P. Janelle (Cambridge 1930), xvii; Cuthbert Tunstall to Cromwell, BL MS Cotton Cleopatra E/VI f. 249, *LP* 10 no. 202.   **8.** For an effective overview of these last days of Fisher and More, see Guy, *Thomas More: a very brief history*, 43–6.   **9.** On the eve of these events, see Richard Rich to Cromwell, 3 April [1535], SP 1/91 f. 162, *LP* 8 no. 490, in which he solicits a lucrative office with the promise of a handsome cash gift 'and over that pray for you'. The record of the trial of 26 June to 1 July 1535, *LP* 8 no. 974, contains the crucial testimony of Rich in regard to 12 June.   **10.** Remembrance, BL MS Cotton Titus B/I f. 474, *LP* 8 no. 892.   **11.** Thomas Knight to Cromwell, 5/6 October 1538, SP 1/137 f. 110, *LP* 13 ii no. 542. My italics: *LP* misreads as 'the others'.   **12.** Cf. the reaction in Venice: Edmund Harvel to Thomas Starkey, 15 June 1535, BL MS Cotton Nero B/VII f. 107, *LP* 8 no. 874.   **13.** Interrogatories for Robert Laurence Prior of Beauvale and Augustine Webster Prior of Axholme, 20 April 1535, SP 1/92 ff. 26–7, *LP* 8 no. 565. For Chauncy's account of their visit to London and confrontation with Cromwell, Chauncy, *Historia aliquot martyrum Anglorum*, 98–9.   **14.** Thomas Starkey to Reginald Pole, May 1535, BL MS Cleopatra E/VI f. 373rv, *LP* 8 no. 801; Cranmer to Cromwell, 30 April 1535, SP 1/92 f. 102, *LP* 8 no. 616.   **15.** Borde reminded Cromwell of this during his further adventures in Scotland, 1 April 1536, SP 1/103 f. 61, *LP* 10 no. 605. On Salter, see above, p. 250.   **16.** See Borde's report back to Cromwell from Bordeaux on his way to the Grande Chartreuse, 20 June 1535, SP 1/93 f. 119, *LP* 8 no. 901; he asks that Cromwell would be a 'good friend *as you ever have been* to

Master Prior of the Charter House [my italics]'.   17. Andrew Borde to Prior and Convent of the London Charterhouse and all priors and convents of the said Order in England, 2 August 1535, BL MS Cotton Cleopatra E/IV f. 70, *LP* 9 no. 11; John Gaillard Prior of the Grande Chartreuse to Roland Lee, 1 August 1535, BL MS Cotton Vitellius B/XIV f. 125, *LP* 9 no. 8, now much damaged. The fact that the Prior calls Bishop Lee John rather than Roland is probably scribal error rather than deliberate sabotage.   18. On the Charterhouse, Roland Lee to Cromwell, probably very early May 1534, SP 1/84 f. 100, *LP* 7 no. 758. On Fisher, Lee to Cromwell, just before 17 April 1534, BL MS Cotton Cleopatra E/VI f. 160, *LP* 7 no. 498.   19. Andrew Borde to Cromwell, writing from London probably in early September 1535, SP 1/96 f. 45, *LP* 9 no. 238. For Borde's summary of his mission and delivery of his letters from the Grande Chartreuse to Cromwell at Bishop's Waltham, between 18 and 24 September 1535, SP 1/96 f. 46, *LP* 9 no. 239.   20. On efforts in Somerset at Witham and Hinton, see Shaw, '*Compendium Compertorum*', 41 and 43, and Prior of Hinton Charterhouse to Cromwell, 1 September [1535], SP 1/85 f. 136, *LP* 7 no. 1127 (misdated in *LP* to 1534), and cf. Cromwell's remembrance 'Of the Charterhouse of Henton', dateable to the end of August 1535, TNA, E 36/143 f. 33, *LP* 9 no. 498.   21. Thomas Bedell to Cromwell, 6 May [1535], BL MS Cotton Cleopatra E/VI f. 259, *LP* 8 no. 675.   22. BL MS Harley 604 f. 2. This seventeenth-century copy of the instructions has been given a misleading heading, 'Instructyones to be performed by governores appointed to enter the possessyone of the Charterhowse of Londone upon the suppressyon thereof', but it clearly relates to the events of summer 1535.   23. John Whalley to Cromwell, 29 May [1535], SP 1/92 f. 188, *LP* 8 no. 778. Chauncy and then Nicholas Sander, echoed by the Jesuit historian Ribadeneira, say that two of Cromwell's servants were installed in the Charterhouse, and overall confirm the reports of Fyllol, Rastell and Whalley themselves, though with the most negative possible interpretation: Chauncy, *Historia aliquot martyrum Anglorum*, 109–10, and S. J. Weinreich (ed. and trans.), *Pedro de Ribadeneyra's Ecclesiastical History of the Schism of the Kingdom of England* (Jesuit Studies 8, 2017), 225.   24. Jasper Fyllol to Cromwell, 5 September [1535], BL MS Cotton Cleopatra E/IV f. 42, *LP* 9 no. 283, and Fyllol to Cromwell, September 1535, SP 1/96 f. 82, *LP* 9 no. 284.   25. Above, p. 190: Rex, 'Jasper Fyloll and the enormities of the clergy', 1043–62.   26. The date of 25 June 1536 suggested in *ODNB*, s.v. Rastell, John, for Rastell's death is far too early; his last extant letter (SP 1/113 f. 188, *LP* 11 no. 1487) addresses Cromwell as Lord Privy Seal, which Cromwell only became on 30 June 1536, and details of Rastell's final arrest seem to be associated with the crackdown on evangelicals in November 1536 (below, p. 395). That is also the judgement of J. C. Warner, 'A *dyaloge betwene Clemente and Bernarde*, c. 1532: a neglected tract belonging to the last period of John Rastell's career', *SCJ* 29 (1998), 55–65, at 65.   27. On the monks' reaction to Rastell, John Whalley to Cromwell, ?late spring 1535, SP 1/92 f. 61, *LP* 8 no. 600.   28. Fyllol to Cromwell, 5 September [1535], BL MS Cotton Cleopatra E/IV f. 42, *LP* 9 no. 283.   29. A report via Dr Ortiz to the Empress Isabella, 24 October 1535, BL MS Additional 28588 f. 31, *LP* 9 no. 681.   30. John Husee to Lord Lisle, 11 December [1535], SP 3/5 f. 84, *Lisle*

Letters 2 no. 496; Ives, *Life and Death of Anne Boleyn*, 265.   **31.** John Gostwick to Cromwell, 5 September 1535, SP 1/96 f. 76, *LP* 9 no. 279.   **32.** On Trafford's defiance, Sir John Markham and others to Cromwell, 18 April 1535, SP 1/92 f. 22, *LP* 8 no. 560, and Markham to Cromwell, 9 May [1535], SP 1/92 f. 135, *LP* 8 no. 692. On his appointment to the London Charterhouse, Henry Man Prior of Sheen to Cromwell, 23 April [1536], SP 1/92 f. 51, *LP* 8 no. 585 (misdated to 1535 by *LP*).   **33.** Ralph Sadler to Cromwell, 27 September [1536], SP 1/106 f. 217, *LP* 11 no. 501.   **34.** J. F. Mozley, *William Tyndale* (London, 1937) is still the most scholarly overall account of his life, and where not otherwise referenced I have followed its narrative and analysis, particularly in the account of his fall, 294–342. It must nevertheless now be supplemented by P. Arblaster, G. Juhasz and G. Latré, *Tyndale's Testament* (Turnhout 2002).   **35.** B. Buxton, *At the House of Thomas Poyntz: the betrayal of William Tyndale with the consequences for an English merchant and his family* (Lavenham, 2013) makes clear that the traditional notion that Tyndale lived in the English House in Antwerp has no foundation.   **36.** The complex but very suggestive history of Richard Phelips and his sons is well presented in *HC 1509–1558* 3, 103–5, which produces intriguing possible links between the Phelips family and Cromwell via the Marquess of Dorset and even a possible Cromwell relative, Richard Wykes. Using the conventional spelling for this gentry family usefully distinguishes them from the London victim of religious persecution Thomas Philips, discussed above: pp. 242–5.   **37.** The most vivid account here is of Thomas Theobald to Archbishop Cranmer, 31 July [1535], BL MS Cotton Galba B/X f. 119, *LP* 8 no. 1151. For elucidation and correction on the dates of Tyndale's arrest and death, see Arblaster, Juhasz and Latré, *Tyndale's Testament*, 176–7.   **38.** For Stokesley's letters to Cromwell on 26 and 29 January [probably 1533] about Edward Tyndale, denouncing William Tyndale as well, see SP 1/74 f. 83, *LP* 6 no. 81, and SP 1/74 f. 89, *LP* 6 no. 95. Despite Stokesley's honeyed words, these letters suggest that Cromwell was not sympathetic to the Bishop in that land dispute.   **39.** Stephen Vaughan to Cromwell, 4 September [1535], SP 1/96 f. 74, *LP* 9 no. 275; Vaughan to Cromwell, [11 September 1535], SP 1/90 f. 195 with a dummy placement as SP 1/96 f. 135, *LP* 8 no. 303 and now *LP* 9 no. 346; Robert Flegge to Cromwell, 22 September 1535, BL MS Cotton Galba B/X f. 68, *LP* 9 no. 409.   **40.** John Hacket to Cromwell, 12 March 1534, SP 1/82 ff. 246v–247r, *LP* 7 no. 317. See also vivid accounts of the Netherlands mayhem in Hacket to Cromwell and John Cooke to Cromwell, both 31 March 1534, SP 1/83 f. 23, *LP* 7 no. 397, and SP 1/83 f. 20, *LP* 7 no. 394; and Cooke to Cromwell, 5 April 1534, SP 1/83 f. 64, *LP* 7 no. 440.   **41.** W. J. de Bakker, 'Civic reformer in Anabaptist Münster: Bernard Rothmann, 1495?–1535?' (University of Chicago PhD, 1987), 241. For a compendium of much evidence of the Anabaptist witness in England in 1535, I. B. Horst, *The Radical Brethren: Anabaptism and the English Reformation to 1558* (Nieuwkoop, 1972), 37–9, 49–77.   **42.** It is difficult to disentangle Cromwell's and Cranmer's contributions from the evidence: MacCulloch, *Thomas Cranmer*, 146.   **43.** Cromwell's remembrance, early May 1535, BL MS Cotton Titus B/I f. 424, *LP* 8 no. 475; Chapuys to Charles V, 5 June 1535, *Spanish Calendar* 5 i no. 170, at 484; deposition of Bishop Fisher's servant

Richard Wilson, *LP* 8 no. 856.   **44.** Walter Mersche to Cromwell, 4 July [1535], SP 1/93 f. 190, *LP* 8 no. 982.   **45.** [Anon.], *A treuue nyeuu tydynges of the wo[n]derfull worckes of the rebaptisers of M[u]nster in Westuaell* (Antwerp, 1535, *RSTC* 564).   **46.** R. Parsons, *A treatise of three conuersions of England from paganisme to Christian religion* (3 vols., Saint-Omer, 1603–4, *RSTC* 19416), 1, 565.   **47.** SP 1/237 f. 284r, *LP Addenda* 1 i no. 809. There is no reason to date this set of memoranda any earlier than 1535, *pace* Horst, *Radical Brethren*, 49–50, 53–4. Even if one accepts that the work mentioned can be identified with one published in 1532, the memorandum is not necessarily asserting that this *Confession* has only just been published. Really nothing suggests Anabaptist activity in England earlier than 1534–5.   **48.** For my development of these themes, see D. MacCulloch, 'Calvin: fifth Latin Doctor of the Church?', in I. Backus and P. Benedict (eds.), *Calvin and his Influence, 1509–2009* (Oxford, 2011), 33–45.   **49.** Knecht, 'Francis I, "Defender of the Faith"?', 119–24.   **50.** On Henry and the 'middle way', see MacCulloch, *Thomas Cranmer*, 114, 137, 164, 183, 193, 212, 216, 238, 241–2, 265, 267, 275, 335, 348, 351, 617.   **51.** Tyndale, *The Parable of the Wicked Mammon*, in Walter (ed.), *Doctrinal Treatises by Tyndale*, 124.   **52.** J. Ayre (ed.), *Prayers and other pieces of Thomas Becon* (Parker Society, 1844), 40–41.   **53.** Corrie (ed.), *Sermons and Remains of Hugh Latimer*, 197.   **54.** For the following paragraphs where not otherwise referenced, see McEntegart, *Henry VIII, the League of Schmalkalden and the English Reformation*, 26–34.   **55.** Maas, *Reformation and Robert Barnes*, 27–8.   **56.** Royal diplomatic instructions to Cromwell via the Duke of Norfolk and Lord Rochford, [19 July 1535], BL MS Cotton Cleopatra E/VI f. 337, *LP* 8 no. 1062. In fact Melanchthon had a healthy fear of the French invitation and had made his own arrangements to avoid it: Melanchthon to Joachim Camerarius, 31 August 1535, *Corpus Reformatorum*, ed. C. G. Bretschneider *et al.* (101 vols. to date, 1834–), 2, cols. 918–19. For Haynes's nerves about his inexperience, see Simon Haynes to Cromwell, 22 July [1535], SP 1/94 f. 115, *LP* 8 no. 1086.   **57.** *Corpus Reformatorum* 2, cols. 920–30, at 927: 'Accipimus te cum in sacris literis praeclare doctum esse, tum in reliqua philosophia, ac praecipue in illa pulcherrima parte, videlicet in consideratione motuum et effectuum coelestium . . .'.   **58.** For decent summary discussion, J. Schofield, *Philip Melanchthon and the English Reformation* (Aldershot, 2006), 61–7, and for monograph-length treatment of this highly nuanced question, G. B. Graybill, *Evangelical Free Will: Philipp Melanchthon's doctrinal journey on the origins of faith* (Oxford, 2010).   **59.** Henry VIII to Melanchthon, 1 October 1535, *Corpus Reformatorum* 2, cols. 947–8; the letter from Cromwell does not appear to have survived. For Cromwell's memorandum probably from August 1535 to arrange for the 300 crowns, BL MS Cotton Titus B/I f. 433, *LP* 9 no. 219.   **60.** Cromwell arranged credit with an Italian firm in Germany to sustain Foxe and his colleagues in their mission through his old neighbour in Austin Friars, Antonio de Vivaldi: SP 1/97 f. 129, *LP* 9 no. 589, credit note dated 11 October 1535. Chapuys, ever vigilant, immediately reported this to his master: Chapuys to Charles V, 13 October 1535, *Spanish Calendar* 5 i no. 213, at 555.

Chapter 13: Progresses and Scrutinies: 1535–1536

1. Chapuys to Charles V, 5 June 1535, *Spanish Calendar* 5 i no. 170, at 484.   2. Chapuys to Charles V, 24 October 1534, *Spanish Calendar* 5 i no. 102, at 295.   3. Ives, *Life and Death of Anne Boleyn*, 191–7.   4. For what follows on the progress and visit-ation, see respectively the excellent summary account in D. Starkey (ed.), *Henry VIII: a European Court in England* (London, 1991), 120–26 (including a useful map of the itinerary), and Shaw, '*Compendium Compertorum*', *passim*: an exem-plary piece of archival research and analysis, which effectively replaces the study of the visitation in Knowles, *Religious Orders in England III*, ch. 22.   5. Edmund Billingford appears in Thomas Cromwell's service in 1538 as one of the 'Gentle-men not to be allowed in my Lord's household aforesaid but when they have commandment or cause necessary to repair thither': SP 1/140 f. 229r, *LP* 13 ii no. 1184[iii]. Edmund Billingford esquire is recorded as supervisor of the will of Thomas Bateman of Flixton (adjacent to South Elmham) in the 1550s (TNA, C 1/1406/26). On the Billingfords of Stoke Holy Cross (Norfolk) and their relation-ship to the Batemans, see Blomefield and Parkin, *Topographical History of the County of Norfolk*, 5, 523–4, 526, and J. Corder (ed.), *The Visitation of Suffolk 1561 made by William Hervy . . .* (2 vols., Harleian Society, new series 2 and 3, 1981, 1984), 2, 379; these show that Edmund was son and heir of Thomas Billing-ford. Thomas Billingford, probably the same as Thomas Bateman's father-in-law as well as Edmund Billingford's father (and putatively James's father too), received deer from the Howard estate at Framlingham in the 1510s: BL Additional Rolls 17746.   6. The clinching identification of Billingford, described as beneficed in Suffolk and taking various prominent people's names in vain, including that of the Duke of Norfolk, is in Anthony Cope to Cromwell, 2 May [1535], SP 1/83 f. 185, *LP* 7 no. 600 (misdated by *LP*). On South Elmham St George, also known as Sancroft, and Billingford as Rector there on the presentation of Thomas Bateman, who farmed the benefice from the Bishop, see A. Suckling, *The History and Antiq-uities of the County of Suffolk* (2 vols., Ipswich, 1846–8), 1, 207–12; V. B. Redstone, 'South Elmham Deanery', *Proceedings of the Suffolk Institute of Archaeology and History* 14 pt3 (1912), 323–31, at 329, 331. Billingford was there described as 'Magister', implying a university degree.   7. SP 1/106 f. 189, *LP* 11 no. 484, to Horsham St Faith Priory, dated 23 September [1534]; SP 1/106 f. 190, *LP* 11 no. 485, to Coxford Priory, undated. Merriman 2 nos. 163, 180, misdated them as well as being fooled into considering them authentic.   8. Besides Cope's letter referenced above, see Anthony Cope to Cromwell, 10 May [1535], SP 1/84 f. 6, *LP* 7 no. 641. For previous depositions on Billingford's activities in Der-byshire, Leicestershire and Nottinghamshire, apparently all taken in Nottingham on 24 January 1535, see *LP* 7 Appendix no. 22, *LP* 8 no. 94, and SP 1/89 f. 50, *LP* 8 no. 81[i and ii].   9. On Billingford's successor as Rector, Robert Thompson, see *VE* 3, 447. Interestingly, he was deprived under Queen Mary, presumably as a married man, and restored under Elizabeth: Suckling, *The History and Antiqui-ties of the County of Suffolk*, 1, 212.   10. On Cromwell's clash with Christopher

Hales over John Brigenden, see above, p. 105. Other examples are Nicholas Caunton (Christopher Hales to Cromwell, 19 July 1536/9, SP 1/152 f. 140, *LP* 14 i no. 1287), Nicholas Gifford (Cromwell to Wolsey, 21 October 1530, BL MS Cotton Appendix XLVIII f. 110, *LP* 4 iii no. 6699) and indeed some of his vice-gerential visitors like Thomas Lee and Ellis ap Rhys. For his patronage of Richard Lee against snobs, see Miss St Clare Byrne's perceptive discussion in *Lisle Letters* 4, 361-2, and the arch-example apart from his own son is Sir Thomas Wyatt, whose relationship with Cromwell is perceptively described by Brigden, *Thomas Wyatt, passim.*   11. Shaw, 'Compendium Compertorum', 416; Shaw's work on the visitation has been extraordinarily illuminating.   12. On Holgate and the Gilbertine immunity from visitation, see John Tregonwell to Cromwell, 27 September [1535], SP 1/97 f. 28, *LP* 9 no. 457, but see also an infringement by Thomas Lee at the very small Gilbertine house of Fordham (Cambridgeshire), Shaw, 'Compendium Compertorum', 116, and an equally small house at Mattersey (Nottinghamshire), at 222. For the exception from suppression, see Shaw, 'Compendium Compertorum', 400-401.   13. On Lee, see above, p. 196; on the visitation of even Welbeck itself, see Shaw, 'Compendium Compertorum', 202. A stand-off between Welbeck and the visitors about the election of a new abbot for the Premonstratensian house of West Dereham (Norfolk) in autumn 1535 inevitably ended in Cromwell making the nomination: the final pieces of correspondence in this long-running story are Thomas Lee and John ap Rhys to Cromwell, 11 November 1535, SP 1/99 f. 34, *LP* 9 no. 808, and Margery Horsman to Cromwell, 18 November [1535], SP 1/87 f. 35, *LP* 7 no. 1446, misdated in *LP*.   14. On this campaign, see Marshall, *Heretics and Believers*, 217-20, and A. de Mézerac-Zanetti, 'Reforming the liturgy under Henry VIII: the instructions of John Clerk, Bishop of Bath and Wells (PRO, SP6/3, fos 42r-44v)', *JEH* 64 (2013), 96-111.   15. John London to Thomas Bedell, 3 August 1537, SP 1/123 f. 188, *LP* 12 ii no. 427, looking back on Cromwell's visit, which took place on 18 September 1535: see Shaw, 'Compendium Compertorum', 89. On Wolsey's textbook, see above, p. 55.   16. Shaw, 'Compendium Compertorum', 140.   17. Gregory Cromwell to Thomas Cromwell, 17 and 25 October [1533], SP 1/68 f. 22, *LP* 5 no. 479, and SP 1/68 f. 32, *LP* 5 no. 496, both misdated by *LP*, written from Toppesfield, Beconsaw's benefice.   18. Roland Lee to Cromwell, 18 November [1535], SP 1/87 f. 32, *LP* 7 no. 1443, misdated in *LP* but subsequently corrected.   19. Richard Tomyou to Cromwell, 23 September 1535, SP 1/96 f. 201, *LP* 9 no. 415.   20. A. Freeman, 'To guard his words', *Times Literary Supplement*, 14 December 2007, 13-14. Henry's own copy survives: Carley, *Libraries of Henry VIII*, 95 (Westminster H2 no. 446).   21. Chapuys to Charles V, 10 August 1535, *Spanish Calendar* 5 i no. 193, at 529.   22. M. Dowling (ed.), 'William Latymer's Chronickille of Anne Bulleyne', *Camden Miscellany* 30 (Camden 4th series 39, 1990), 23-65, at 60-61. Latymer was nevertheless mistaken in saying that the relic was destroyed at this time; see discussion in Ives, *Life and Death of Anne Boleyn*, 264-5.   23. Stephen Sagar alias Whalley Abbot of Hailes to Cromwell, 28 January [1536], SP 1/101 f. 161, *LP* 10 no. 192. On the chaplaincy, see Cromwell's remembrance of *c.* May 1537, SP 1/120 f. 257, *LP* 12 i no. 1323, and NB Bishop Latimer's disapproval of the promotion, Latimer to

Cromwell, [21 July 1537], SP 1/123 f. 33, *LP* 12 ii no. 295.   24. See a reference to a letter of his dated from Winchcombe on 9 August, Sir George Throckmorton to Cromwell, 30 September [1535], SP 1/97 f. 55, *LP* 9 no. 488.   25. SP 1/54 f. 240v, *LP* 4 iii no. 5772. The bequest is in a mixed list of senior servants and friends, and probably does not relate directly to this John Horwood but to the Putney lawyer of the same name, since the monk had been serving Winchcombe's neighbouring church of Gretton since Abbot Kidderminster's time: cf. his petition probably of 1535, SP 1/100 f. 86, *LP* 9 no. 1145, and John Placet to Cromwell, probably September 1535, SP 1/96 f. 116, *LP* 9 no. 322. Note Placet's reminiscence of a papalist text on absolution which had brought Kidderminster 'in great scrupulosity, almost in desperation' – a reminiscence worthy of Luther – Placet to Cromwell, ?October 1535, SP 1/98 f. 131, *LP* 9 no. 723. A William Horwood was third Prior at the suppression in 1539: *LP* 14 ii no. 728.   26. John Placet to Cromwell, September 1535, SP 1/96 f. 116, *LP* 9 no. 322, and 9 September [1535], SP 1/96 f. 115, *LP* 9 no. 321; Placet to Cromwell, ?October 1535, SP 1/98 f. 131, *LP* 9 no. 723.   27. For Cromwell's promoting (in the end successfully) a property lease for Richard Tracey from Tewkesbury Abbey, see Henry Beeley Abbot of Tewkesbury to Cromwell, 16 February [1533], SP 1/74 f. 160, *LP* 6 no. 161. For the presence in Cromwell's papers of a copy of William Tracey's 'heretical' will and Archbishop Warham's warrant for the exhumation of his body for burning, listed in 'A declaration of "escriptes and writings" in my master's [Cromwell's] custody, which came into his possession from Mich. 21 [1529], to Mich. 23 Hen. VIII. [1531]', *LP* 7 no. 923, 341, 352.   28. Anthony Saunders to Cromwell, 2 November 1535, BL MS Cotton Cleopatra E/IV f. 60, *LP* 9 no. 747, and 3 February probably 1536, SP 1/89 f. 123, *LP* 8 no. 171; on Saunders and Cotes, see also Emden, *Oxford 1501 to 1540*, 506, 140.   29. For Cromwell's favouring of Cotes to be Master of Balliol over the strong objections of Bishop Longland, see Longland to Anthony Bellasis, early November 1539, SP 1/154 f. 111, *LP* 14 ii no. 477; Owen Oglethorpe to Cromwell, 11 November 1539, SP 1/154 f. 121, *LP* 14 ii no. 498; Cromwell to Fellows of Balliol, 22 November 1539, Merriman 2 no. 325, 240, in which Cromwell calls Cotes his 'friend'.   30. Memorandum of Cotes taking the oath, 2 September 1535, SP 1/96 f. 59, *LP* 9 no. 251 (Magdalen paid his travel expenses: F. D. Logan, 'The first royal visitation of the English universities, 1535', *EHR* 106 (1991), 861–88, at 875n), and cf. Stephen Sagar alias Whalley Abbot of Hailes to Cromwell, 31 August [1535], SP 1/88 f. 155, *LP* 7 Appendix no. 35, misdated in *LP*. Latimer to Cromwell, ?autumn 1535, BL MS Cotton Cleopatra E/V f. 393, *LP* 9 no. 1118.   31. Thomas Redinge Prior of Kingswood to Cromwell, 21 January 1536, SP 1/89 f. 48, *LP* 8 no. 79 (misdated to 1535 in *LP*); Cromwell to Richard Rich, 23 May [1538], *LP* 13 i no. 1051, Merriman 2 no. 264, 143. The preacher 'Thomas Lacock' mentioned in the second letter does not figure in the monks of the house listed at suppression in the same month, Chambers (ed.), *Faculty Office Registers*, 131, so may be the same as Redinge listed (though misspelled) there.   32. Richard Leighton to Cromwell, [11 August 1535], SP 1/94 f. 182, *LP* 8 no. 1127; Shaw, '*Compendium Compertorum*', 37, was the first to correct the misdating of this important letter.   33. SP 6/6 ff. 6–11 at ff. 7v, 9r, 10v, *LP* 8 no. 76[3]; Shaw,

'*Compendium Compertorum*', 288, identifies the main hand of this document as that of the vice-gerential scribe Robert Warmington. For excellent analysis of the evolution and implementation of the visitation injunctions, see Shaw at 279–327.   34. Jane Lady Guildford to Cromwell, 6 September [1535], SP 1/96 f. 83, *LP* 9 no. 289, written from the Poyntz manor of Hill in Gloucestershire; for the Master of the Gaunts' letter to Cromwell the following day, having received the injunctions, SP 1/96 f. 86, *LP* 9 no. 296.   35. Shaw, '*Compendium Compertorum*', 319.   36. SP 1/95 f. 147, *LP* 9 no. 159: a note of proceedings in the chapter house of Bruton, 23 August 1535 (misdated as September in the text); Thomas Lee to Cromwell, 24 August [1535], SP 1/95 f. 155, *LP* 9 no. 167.   37. Shaw, '*Compendium Compertorum*', 82 n. 39 acutely recognized that the draft letter to Exeter Cathedral Chapter of 27 August and dated from Redlynch, SP 1/95 f. 179, *LP* 9 no. 191, was not from Fitzjames but from Cromwell. To that can be added a reminiscence of Cromwell's Somerset friend Sir Nicholas Wadham of the 'merry word' Cromwell spoke to him over dinner with Fitzjames at Redlynch: Wadham to Cromwell, 21 October [1535], SP 1/98 f. 45, *LP* 9 no. 655. See also Shaw's useful comment, '*Compendium Compertorum*', 83–4, on Cromwell's likely personal involvement with dispensation at Sherborne at this time, and its wider implications.   38. See the letter of John ap Rhys to Cromwell, 16 October 1535, SP 1/98 f. 16, *LP* 9 no. 622.   39. Henry Lord Daubeney, 9 September [1535], SP 1/96 f. 109, *LP* 9 no. 316: an apology for the lack of game at Marsh Park on Cromwell's visit. Nor was Cromwell able to get the Parkership of Marsh which he asked for from Daubeney, whom one can see casting round desperately for some consolation prize.   40. Cromwell to Stephen Vaughan, [31 August 1535], *LP* 10 no. 376, Merriman 2 no. 177; a bad-tempered and frank scolding from minister and King misdated by *LP* and Merriman, but placeable here by context and by the reference to it by date and content in John Williamson to Cromwell, 3 September 1535, SP 1/96 f. 65, *LP* 9 no. 259. A more polite letter on the same subject from Cromwell to Vaughan, *c*. 2–4 September 1535, SP 1/102 f. 115, *LP* 10 no. 377, is clearly intended for others to read besides its putatively chastened immediate recipient.   41. Cromwell to the Abbess of Wilton, 4 September [1535], SP 1/96 f. 70, *LP* 9 no. 271.   42. Ives, *Life and Death of Anne Boleyn*, 291–2.   43. I. W. Archer, S. Adams, G. W. Bernard, M. Greengrass, P. E. J. Hammond and F. Kisby (eds.), *Religion, Politics and Society in Sixteenth-Century England* (CS 5th series 22, 2003), 123.   44. SP 1/47 f. 259v, *LP* 4 iii no. 4229; SP 1/50 f. 120v, *LP* 4 iii no. 4794[3]. These transactions, although here listed in the same documents as Wolsey's monastic dissolutions, did not result from dissolutions, as Barrett L. Beer assumed in his *ODNB* entry on Edward Seymour, but represent an earlier and problematic land purchase of Wolsey's from the Ughtreds, in which Cromwell had been involved from the outset in March 1524. There is a very large cache of papers relating to the Ughtred transactions in Cromwell's papers, SP 1/31 ff. 58–92, *LP* 4 i no. 388, together with SP 1/31 ff. 3–4, *LP* 4 i no. 294, which is a draft in his hand; see above, p. 54 and n. 5.   45. Lord Lisle to Cromwell, 21 December [1533], SP 1/81 f. 13, *LP* 6 no. 1550. *Lisle Letters* 1, 665–8, introduces this tangled affair.   46. From a long correspondence which can conveniently be followed in

Lisle Letters, the agreement is finally celebrated in Leonard Smyth (now Cromwell's servant and formerly Lord Lisle's) to Lord Lisle, 31 March [1535], SP 3/7 f. 168, *Lisle Letters* 2 no. 359.   **47.** Ives, *Life and Death of Anne Boleyn*, 293.   **48.** Ibid., 291–4.   **49.** T. Starkey, *Exhortation to the people, instructynge theym to vnitie and obedience* ... (London, 1536, *RSTC* 23236); for the Winchester presentation, see ibid., preface to the King, sig. A3v.   **50.** Chapuys to Charles V, 25 September 1535, *Spanish Calendar* 5 i no. 205, at 542. The inventory, specifically delivered to Cromwell, is Corpus Christi College Cambridge MS 149 f. 355, *LP* 9 no. 1171[1], printed in J. Strype, *Memorials* ... *of* ... *Thomas Cranmer* ... , ed. P. E. Barnes (2 vols., London, 1853), 2, 271–5. It duly includes two staffs of 'unicorn's horn' also mentioned by Chapuys, which took the King's fancy and which he appropriated.   **51.** Richard Towrys to Lord Lisle, 28 September [1535], SP 3/2 f. 149, *Lisle Letters* 2 no. 454. For further general action on Hampshire weirs, see Sir Anthony Windsor to Lord Lisle, 9 October [1535], SP 3/8 f. 115, *Lisle Letters* 2 no. 459, and for a reminiscence of Cromwell personally viewing a major weir near Southampton during the 1535 progress, Henry Huttoft to Cromwell, 30 January [1537], SP 1/128 f. 143, *LP* 13 i no. 177, misdated in *LP*.   **52.** Cromwell to Gardiner, 4 February [1536], Merriman 2 no. 137, *LP* 10 no. 255.   **53.** Shaw, '*Compendium Compertorum*', 141: the earliest example of such a title he has found is at Wells Cathedral on 25 October 1535.   **54.** Placet to Cromwell, ?October 1535, SP 1/98 f. 131, *LP* 9 no. 723. For Borde at Bishop's Waltham, see Andrew Borde to Cromwell, 1 April [1536], SP 1/103 f. 61, *LP* 10 no. 605; A. Borde, *The fyrst boke of the introduction of knowledge* ... (London, 1555, *RSTC* 3383), sig. E1v: rather coyly (writing in 1542 and dedicating his present work to Princess Mary) Borde says of his gazetteer 'one Thomas Cromwell had it of me, and because he had many matters off to dispatch for all England, my book was lost.'   **55.** Thomas Lee to Cromwell, 29 September 1535, SP 1/97 f. 47, *LP* 9 no. 472, together with a copy of his report on Chertsey, SP 1/97 f. 48, *LP* 9 no. 472[2].   **56.** Shaw, '*Compendium Compertorum*', 329–41.   **57.** Chapuys to Charles V, 25 September 1535, *Spanish Calendar* 5 i no. 205, at 541–2.   **58.** For what follows, see the excellent account in Logan, 'First royal visitation of the English universities'.   **59.** J. Woolfson, *Padua and the Tudors: English students in Italy, 1485–1603* (Cambridge, 1998), 39–72.   **60.** John ap Rhys to Cromwell, 22 October [1535], SP 1/98 f. 48, *LP* 9 no. 661. On Wolsey's daughter, see above, p. 81.   **61.** Shaw, '*Compendium Compertorum*', 370–79; this document, undated, but almost certainly of this period rather than the dating of February 1536 in *LP*, is SP 1/101 f. 197, *LP* 10 no. 242. The November 1535 dating is reinforced by Thomas Lee's recommendation of his friend Dr John Rokeby to Cromwell for employment, 'whether it be in examination of the foundations of religious houses or otherwise': Thomas Lee to Cromwell, 4 November [1535], SP 1/98 f. 173, *LP* 9 no. 762.   **62.** Memorandum from the Duke of Norfolk on Bungay and Woodbridge, early 1536, SP 1/104 f. 226, *LP* 10 no. 1236. On Sibton and Wangford, MacCulloch, *Suffolk and the Tudors*, 66.   **63.** On Ingham, cf. e.g. Richard Wharton to Cromwell, 7 November [1535], BL MS Cotton Cleopatra E/IV f. 147, *LP* 9 no. 785. On the others, Richard Southwell and Robert Hogan to Cromwell, 27 March 1536, SP 1/103 ff. 28–9, *LP*

10 no. 563.   64. Shaw, 'Compendium Compertorum', 124, 202, 238, 376; the houses were Dover, Langdon, Folkestone, Bilsington, Hornby, Tilty and Marton. A list of these houses with valuations contains two other names, Thurgarton and Horsham St Faith, which were spared for the time being: SP 1/239 f. 281, LP Addenda 1 i no. 1038. Hornby's surrender likewise did not take effect at this time, as it turned out to be a cell of Croxton Kerrial Abbey. In all these three cases of survival, the heads of house had personal links to Cromwell which they must have exploited.   65. The chief papers concerning this interestingly individual transaction can be found in TNA, E 322/243 (which gives the date 28 February 1535); SP 1/102 ff. 135–8, LP 10 no. 408 (Richard Cromwell's indenture with the Abbot, 3 March 1535). The expenses to the commissioners dissolving the two houses were substantial, 22s 7d to Thomas Parry at Bilsington and £4 8s 4d to Richard Cromwell at Tilty: SP 1/106 f. 67r, LP 11 no. 381.   66. Shaw, 'Compendium Compertorum', 316.   67. Ibid., 402–4.   68. Loades (ed.), Papers of George Wyatt, 159; see above, pp. 201–2. For Dr Shaw's convincing conclusions on these matters, see Shaw, 'Compendium Compertorum', 408–22.   69. Ives, Life and Death of Anne Boleyn, 295–6.   70. Muller (ed.), Letters of Gardiner, 75, LP 10 no. 256.   71. Ralph Sadler to Cromwell, 11 January 1536, SP 1/101 f. 50, LP 10 no. 76; my italics. Chapuys to Charles V, 21 January 1536, Spanish Calendar 5 ii no. 9; he picked up the fact that work on the hearse had been stopped.   72. On de Athequa's position, see Elton, Policy and Police, 244n.   73. Ives, Life and Death of Anne Boleyn, 296–8.   74. Chapuys to Charles V, 29 January 1536, Spanish Calendar 5 ii no. 13, at 28; same to same, 17 February 1536, Spanish Calendar 5 ii no. 21, at 39–40; MacCulloch, Thomas Cranmer, 149.   75. A deposition 'touching Sir Nicholas Carew' of early 1539, SP 1/142 f. 202rv, LP 14 i no. 190; lacunae in the damaged MS efficiently supplied by LP, which also suggests from the hand that the deponent is Anthony Roke, later a servant of Thomas Wriothesley. Tempting though it is to make that connection, the secretary hand is too commonplace to be certain.   76. On Tomyou with Cromwell in Wolsey's crisis in 1530, see 'The answer of Mr [Thomas] Cade and Richard Tomyou to Master Cromwell upon a bill of Richard Basden', SP 1/56 f. 217r, LP 4 iii no. 6186[2]; Wolsey also granted Tomyou a prebend in Southwell Minster in 1530, rather as Morison received a pension from Worksop Priory. On Tomyou's appointment first to Katherine of Aragon and then to Mary, see Duke of Suffolk and others to Norfolk and to Cromwell, 19 December [1533], SP 1/81 ff. 1, 3, LP 6 nos. 1542, 1543; on a compliment and greetings to him from Morison in Venice, Richard Morison to Thomas Starkey, probably late 1535, BL MS Cotton Nero B/VI f. 160, LP 10 no. 320.   77. For a very personal and anguished letter from the future Mistress Tomyou at Court to Cromwell, asking him to intervene with her unsympathetic father over the marriage, May ?1537, see SP 1/127 f. 186, LP 12 ii Appendix no. 26 (written in fact by her husband-to-be). For Mary's gifts to Tomyou and his wife, cf. e.g. F. Madden (ed.), Privy purse expenses of the Princess Mary . . . (London, 1831), 52.   78. Alexander Alesius to Elizabeth I, 1 September 1559, TNA, SP 70/7 ff. 3–13, Calendar of State Papers Foreign . . . Elizabeth [I], 1: 1558–59, no. 1303. Where not otherwise indicated, what follows here about this particular story is at

ff. 6r–7r. **79.** TNA, SP 70/7 ff. 7r, 11r, *Calendar of State Papers Foreign ...
Elizabeth [I], 1: 1558–59*, no. 1303, 527, 532. Even Eric Ives is dismissive: Ives, *Life
and Death of Anne Boleyn*, 329. **80.** On Alesius in Cambridge, see R. Rex, 'The
early impact of Reformation theology at Cambridge University, 1521–1547', *Reformation & Renaissance Review* 2 (Dec. 1999), 38–71, at 64–7. **81.** The myth
has been charmingly embellished by Hilary Mantel in the figure of 'Call-me-
Risley'. *Letters and Papers* started the error by attributing a great many of
Cromwell's early papers to Wriothesley's hand, but it is not especially distinctive
and in any case easily confused with that of Stephen Vaughan, who certainly was
Cromwell's servant in the 1520s. The one letter from Cromwell definitely in Wriothesley's hand, apparently from 1530, has been conclusively redirected to 1538 in
Ward, 'Origins of Thomas Cromwell's public career', 219–20: Cromwell to
[Edward Lee Archbishop of York], 5 May [1538], SP 1/57 f. 87, *LP* 4 iii no.
6368. **82.** The proof that Wriothesley was not in Cromwell's service early on
comes in a letter to Wriothesley from Cromwell's old servant William Brabazon,
writing from Ireland on 29 April [1537]: SP 60/4 f. 70, *LP* 12 i no. 1067. Brabazon
thanks Wriothesley for his kindness 'always shewed unto me *as unacquainted,*
desiring you of your continuance [my italics]'. As far as the early 1530s are concerned, Wriothesley was away in diplomatic service in 1533; Brabazon left for
Ireland in 1534. Thus they had had virtually no chance to know each other face to
face. Ellis ap Rhys also addressed Wriothesley 'as unacquainted' on 28 April 1538,
so Wriothesley had clearly not had an entrée into the Wolsey circle in earlier years:
TNA, SP 7/1 f. 1, *LP* 13 i no. 864. **83.** John Husee to [Lord Lisle], 21 August
[1537], SP 3/5 f. 61, *Lisle Letters* 4 no. 1001, 378. **84.** See e.g. Cromwell to Stephen Gardiner, 25/26 February 1536, Merriman 2 no. 139, from BL MS Additional
25114 f. 249 (not included in *LP*). Chapuys to Charles V, 24 February 1536, *Spanish Calendar* 5 ii no. 29, at 56. **85.** MacCulloch, *Thomas Cranmer*, ch. 8. **86.**
TNA, SP 70/7 f. 6v: 'dissimulata ira vocat ad se Crumwellum, Vrotesleum, et
quosdam alios, quos fama est odisse Reginam; quia graviter eos reprehenderat,
iisque comminata fuerat, se indicaturam Regi, quod praetextu Evangelii atque
Relligionis sua commoda quaererent, haberent omnia venalia, et acceptis muneri-
bus conferrent beneficia Ecclesiastica indignis, hostibus verae Doctrinae.' **87.**
Margery Horsman to Cromwell, 18 November [1535], SP 1/87 f. 35, *LP* 7 no.
1446, misdated by *LP* but securely in 1535 by its mention of the new Prior of Premonstratensian West Dereham. On the Horsmans, Christ's College and another
Premonstratensian house, Coverham Abbey, see above, pp. 196, 203, and below,
pp. 335, 338. Ives came to the same conclusion about her importance: Ives, *Life
and Death of Anne Boleyn*, 332. **88.** TNA, SP 70/7 f. 6v: 'Affirmant etiam
Regem odire Reginam, propterea, quae haeredem regni ex ea non sustulisset, nec
speraret quidem.' **89.** Chapuys to Charles V, 19 May 1536, *Spanish Calendar* 5
ii no. 55, at 123: 'si bien me souvenoye de ce que mavoit dit la veille sainct Mathias,
il mavoit tacitement assez declaire et pronosticque ce quen adviendroit.' **90.**
Chapuys to Charles V, 24 February 1536, *Spanish Calendar* 5 ii no. 29, at 58. A
mangled phrase in a note of Chapuys to Granvelle of 2 May also relates to this
incident in which ' "nen pour riens" told him ... and Cromwell since, that he hath

done and would do marvels': *LP* 10 no. 783.   91. Ives, *Life and Death of Anne Boleyn*, 302.   92. For the beginning and end of Gregory's longest childhood or teenage venture from home, see Richard Southwell to Cromwell, 20 March and 23 December 1536: BL MS Cotton Cleopatra E/IV f. 274, *LP* 10 no. 507, and SP 1/113 f. 22, *LP* 11 no. 1356.   93. Henry Dowes to Cromwell, 30 April 1536, SP 1/92 f. 104, *LP* 8 no. 618 (there misdated to 1535).   94. For Gregory's stay with John Williams at Rycote House in summer and autumn 1535, see his letters of 24 September [1535] and 25 November [1535]: SP 1/96 f. 209, *LP* 9 no. 422, and BL MS Cotton Titus B/I f. 357, *LP* 7 no. 1473 (misdated in *LP*); for the lovelorn letter from Rycote of one of his friends Thomas Farmer to Cromwell, 31 August [1535], SP 1/85 f. 133, *LP* 7 no. 1106 (misdated in *LP*). Farmer seems to have been a musician: see John Williamson to Cromwell, 23 October [1532], SP 1/71 f. 139, *LP* 5 no. 1464. He was still being lovelorn for a different lady to Cromwell in 1539: Farmer to [Cromwell], ?mid-September 1539, SP 1/153 f. 108, *LP* 14 ii no. 197. Gregory returned to Rycote with his tutor Henry Dowes for an extended working holiday from January to March 1537: Cromwell's accounts, *LP* 14 ii no. 782, at 328–9.

Chapter 14: Surrenders and the Scaffold: 1536

1. Where not otherwise referenced below on this Parliament, see Lehmberg, *Reformation Parliament*, 224–48.   2. Hawkyard, *House of Commons 1509–1558*, 337–8; Cromwell actually obtained this grant in September 1535 in anticipation of the autumn session which was then postponed to February 1536.   3. Henry VIII to the bishops, 7 January [1536], SP 1/101 f. 28, *LP* 10 no. 45, with an earlier variant draft in SP 6/2 f. 101, *LP* 7 no. 750 (misdated in *LP*); Cromwell to the bishops, 7 January [1536], BL MS Cotton Cleopatra E/IV f. 8, *LP* 10 no. 46. Elton, *Policy and Police*, 244–6, decisively resolves long doubts about the dating of the documents concerned; contrast Merriman 2 no. 236.   4. SP 6/1 ff. 115–20, *LP* 10 no. 246[16]; excellent discussion of the document in Shaw, 'Compendium Compertorum', 362–9.   5. Loades (ed.), *Papers of George Wyatt*, 159, and on the Charterhouse instructions, see above, pp. 282–3.   6. Chapuys to Charles V, 1 April 1536, *Spanish Calendar* 5 ii no. 43, at 83–4.   7. William Popley to Lord Lisle, 22 February [1536], SP 3/6 f. 144, *LP* 10 no. 339 (curiously not transcribed in full in *Lisle Letters*).   8. Sir Richard Whethill to Lord Lisle, 3 March [1536], SP 3/8 f. 77, *Lisle Letters* 3 no. 446; William Popley to Lord Lisle, 9 March [1536], SP 1/102 f. 177, *Lisle Letters* 3 no. 650.   9. £200 is the same as 300 marks, the sum that Whethill and Popley had mentioned. For discussion of the Act, Shaw, 'Compendium Compertorum', 386–406.   10. Ibid., 394.   11. Loades (ed.), *Papers of George Wyatt*, 159–60. The appointments of Rich and Pope were already known in political circles in London by 28 March: Thomas Warley to Lady Lisle, SP 3/14 f. 47, *Lisle Letters* 4 no. 668. For discussion of the Court, see Elton, *Tudor Revolution in Government*, 203–19, although Elton was characteristically insistent on the primacy of Cromwell's role in its creation. In particular (at 214) he wrongly cast

doubt on the idea that Pope had primarily been Audley's servant. Several letters between 1533 and 1536 place Pope in the household of Audley ('my Lord') at Christ Church Aldgate: cf. e.g. Pope to Cromwell, end of January 1533, SP 1/82 f. 150, *LP* 7 no. 180; ?1536, SP 1/100 ff. 92–3, *LP* 9 no. 1148.   **12.** Rich to Cromwell, 26 July [1538], SP 1/134 f. 248, *LP* 13 i no. 1465. For representative specimens of fury at Rich's high-handedness, John Husee to Lord Lisle, 6 September [1536], SP 3/4 f. 149, *Lisle Letters* 3 no. 765; 1 September [1537], SP 1/124 f. 157, *Lisle Letters* 4 no. 1004.   **13.** Sir William Courtenay to Cromwell, 14 October ?1533, SP 1/79 f. 177, *LP* 6 no. 1286.   **14.** See the appointments in *LP* 13 i no. 1520[II], 572–3, i.e. TNA, E 315/232, ff. 1v–7v.   **15.** BL MS Royal 18 C VI, not calendared in *LP*, but well discussed in G. R. Elton, 'An early Tudor poor law', in Elton, *Studies* 2, 137–54.   **16.** Elton, *Reform and Renewal*, 123–7, with as the centrepiece of its discussion the report of Thomas Dorset to burgesses of Plymouth on 13 March 1536, a letter which probably ended up in Cromwell's papers via its recipient, his client James Horswell, BL MS Cotton Cleopatra E/IV f. 131, *LP* 10 no. 462.   **17.** For an excellent and comprehensive discussion of the background, see Baker, *Oxford History of the Laws of England 6*, 653–86, from which the account below is taken unless otherwise referenced, but for the Crown's campaign against uses in the 1530s, see also Ives, 'Genesis of the Statute of Uses', and discussion in Lehmberg, *Reformation Parliament*, 235–8. For the controversial future of the Act, see Holmes, 'G. R. Elton as a legal historian', 274–8.   **18.** *LP* 8 no. 962[22]: a conveyance of 25 June 1536 which actually concerned a ward of Cromwell's, Thomas Rotherham junior, whose father had agreed that he should marry Cromwell's niece – see their draft agreement in 1533, TNA, SP 2/O ff. 119–31, *LP* 6 no. 1625[5].   **19.** Thomas Fiennes ninth Lord Dacre had a bad track record on violent game-poaching, which led to his execution in 1541, but which meanwhile resulted in an apologetic letter about an earlier incident to Cromwell, 4 December 1537, SP 1/127 f. 1, *LP* 12 ii no. 1169. Cromwell thereafter took the precaution of becoming Master of Dacre's game – Dacre to Cromwell, 25 January 1538, SP 1/128 f. 120, *LP* 13 i no. 143.   **20.** The relevant background documentation on the Calais commission is efficiently marshalled in Nichols (ed.), *Chronicle of Calais*, 98–135. C. S. L. Davies, 'Tournai and the English Crown, 1513–1519', *HJ* 41 (1998), 1–26, gives good reasons for rebutting the idea that Tournai had previously had Parliamentary representation when in English hands to provide a precedent. **21.** Lehmberg, *Reformation Parliament*, 209–11.   **22.** Roland Lee to Cromwell, 20 February [1536], SP 1/102 ff. 58–9, *LP* 10 no. 330.   **23.** Roland Lee to Cromwell, 12 March [1536], SP 1/102 f. 178, *LP* 10 no. 453.   **24.** Roland Lee to Cromwell, 29 April [1536], SP 1/103 f. 191, *LP* 10 no. 754.   **25.** P. Roberts, 'Wales and England after the Tudor "union": Crown, Principality and Parliament, 1543–1624', in Cross, Loades and Scarisbrick (eds.), *Law and Government under the Tudors*, 111–38, at 112–13.   **26.** SP 60/2 f. 83rv, *LP* 7 no. 1211: memorandum in a clerk's hand with many corrections by Cromwell, redated to autumn 1535 by Bradshaw, *Irish Constitutional Revolution*, 106–7.   **27.** Bradshaw, *Irish Constitutional Revolution*, 146–7.   **28.** Ibid., 147–9.   **29.** *Complete Peerage* 6, 79. A good overview of Lord Leonard's career is by M. A. Lyons in *ODNB*, s.v. Grey,

Leonard.   30. For a querulous memorandum (of late 1539 or early 1540) to Cromwell from Lord Leonard about this and other matters needing correction, SP 60/7
f. 168, *LP* 14 ii no. 795; for the whole sad story, B. Bradshaw, *The Dissolution
of the Religious Orders in Ireland under Henry VIII* (Cambridge, 1974), 66–
7.   31. William Brabazon to Cromwell, 17 May [1536], Lambeth MS 616 f. 44,
State Papers 2, 315. Cromwell's slightly embarrassed reply to Brabazon about the
Succession Act, saying that if not fully completed in its various stages, 'it must be
stayed till further knowledge of the King's pleasure', is SP 60/3 ff. 73–4, *LP* 10 no.
1051.   32. Bradshaw, *Dissolution of the Religious Orders in Ireland under Henry
VIII*, 47–65.   33. *LP* 10 no. 597[47 i and ii].   34. George Browne to Cromwell,
19 July [1536], SP 60/3 f. 112, *LP* 11 no. 120.   35. For an excellent account of
what follows, and crisp rebuttals of alternative interpretations, including those of
George Bernard, see Ives, *Life and Death of Anne Boleyn*, 282–3, 306–12. It will
be evident that Ives and I differ on Cromwell's intentions for monastic dissolution
at this stage, given my use above of the evidence about the dissolution legislation
provided by Dr Shaw, but in other respects our analyses of Skip's role in the crisis
concur: see MacCulloch, *Thomas Cranmer*, 155–6.   36. See verses composed by
Dr John Pickering, 1536/7, SP 1/118 ff. 292v–293r, *LP* 12 i no. 1021[5]; for Cranmer's chaplain Thomas Wakefield in the late 1530s, Carley, 'Religious controversy
and marginalia', 244, Appendix no. 38, and, for a later sixteenth-century use,
Chauncy, *Historia aliquot martyrum Anglorum*, 60. Bishop Aylmer in 1559 interestingly reapplied it to Wolsey 'and his company', in the course of an historical
reflection on Anne which contrived not to mention Cromwell by name: Dowling
(ed.), 'William Latymer's Chronickille of Anne Bulleyne', 42.   37. Dowling (ed.),
'William Latymer's Chronickille of Anne Bulleyne', 57–9; on the degrees, see
below, pp. 489–90.   38. Cranmer to Cromwell, 22 April [1536], SP 1/103 f. 151,
LP 10 no. 705.   39. Chapuys to Charles V, 1 April 1536, *Spanish Calendar* 5 ii no.
43, at 80–81, 84–5, and cf. Chapuys to Charles V, 5 June 1535, *Spanish Calendar*
5 i no. 170, at 484.   40. Chapuys to Charles V, 21 April 1536, *Spanish Calendar*
5 ii no. 43a. Good background comment in Ives, *Life and Death of Anne Boleyn*,
312–15.   41. Chapuys to Charles V, 21 April 1536, *Spanish Calendar* 5 ii no. 43a,
at 97–8.   42. Chapuys to Charles V, 6 June 1536, *Spanish Calendar* 5 ii no.
61.   43. Chapuys to Granvelle, 21 April 1536, *LP* 10 no. 700.   44. In what follows on Anne's fall and death, Ives, *Life and Death of Anne Boleyn*, 319–37, is a
generally reliable guide, though it will be apparent that we disagree in that I see
Cromwell as in charge of proceedings from February onwards. Where I take a
different line on other matters, I justify it in citations. I am convinced that at all
points one must subtract the evidence supposedly provided by George Constan-
tine, since his so-called 'memorial' of 1539 is one of the cleverest forgeries of that
Victorian master-forger John Payne Collier, despite not being detected in A. Freeman and J. Ing Freeman, *John Payne Collier: scholarship and forgery in the
nineteenth century* (2 vols., New Haven and London, 2004). So one must disregard in this and in all else [Collier, forger], 'Transcript of an original manuscript,
containing a memorial from George Constantyne to Thomas Lord Cromwell',
'ed.' Amyot.   45. George Lord Rochford to Lord Lisle, 17 April [1536], SP 3/7

f. 6, *Lisle Letters* 3 no. 677.   **46.** J. Anstis (ed.), *The register of the most noble Order of the Garter . . . usually called the Black Book . . .* (2 vols., London, 1724), 2, 398. Chapuys to Charles V, 29 April 1536, *Spanish Calendar* 5 ii no. 47, at 106. For details on Carew against Anne, see S. Lehmberg in *ODNB*, s.v. Carew, Nicholas.   **47.** *LP* 13 i no. 1520[II], 572–3, i.e. TNA, E 315/232, ff. 1v–8r.   **48.** *LP* 10 no. 848[i and vi].   **49.** Thomas Warley to Lord Lisle, 28 April [1536], SP 3/8 f. 65, *Lisle Letters* 3 no. 686; John Husee to Lord Lisle, 28 April [1536], SP 3/4 f. 47, *Lisle Letters* 3 no. 685.   **50.** J. Bruce and T. T. Perowne (eds.), *Correspondence of Matthew Parker, D.D. . . .* (Parker Society, 1853), 59.   **51.** Chapuys to Charles V, 29 April 1536, *Spanish Calendar* 5 ii no. 47, at 106; Chapuys to Granvelle, 29 April 1536, *LP* 10 no. 753, not included in the *Spanish Calendar*.   **52.** *LP* 10 no. 736. The writs included those to Lord Lisle and the mayor and burgesses of Calais to elect two representatives there.   **53.** Thomas Warley to Lord Lisle, 28 April [1536], SP 3/8 f. 65, *Lisle Letters* 3 no. 686.   **54.** Deposition of Robert Hobbes Abbot of Woburn, May 1538, BL MS Cotton Cleopatra E/IV f. 109v, *LP* 13 i no. 981[2].   **55.** TNA, SP 70/7 f. 7r, *Calendar of State Papers Foreign . . . Elizabeth [I], 1: 1558–59*, no. 1303, 527.   **56.** Thomas Warley to Lord Lisle, 2 May [1536], SP 3/14 f. 54, *Lisle Letters* 3 no. 690.   **57.** Cromwell to Gardiner, 30 April 1536, *LP* 10 no. 761, Merriman 2 no. 146.   **58.** Hall 2, 268.   **59.** The time of Anne's arrival is provided by Anthony Anthony, an eye-witness at the Tower, in a transcript in the Bodleian copy of Herbert, *Life and Raigne of King Henry the Eighth*, Bodl. Folio Δ 624, facing 385.   **60.** MacCulloch, *Thomas Cranmer*, 157–8.   **61.** Brigden, *Thomas Wyatt*, 145–6, 163–4, 280–81.   **62.** Ives, *Life and Death of Anne Boleyn*, 338–40.   **63.** Ibid., 340–42.   **64.** TNA, SP 70/7 ff. 9v–10r, *Calendar of State Papers Foreign . . . Elizabeth [I], 1: 1558–59*, no. 1303, at 530–31.   **65.** Kelly, *Matrimonial Trials of Henry VIII*, 250–59; MacCulloch, *Thomas Cranmer*, 158–9.   **66.** Chapuys to Granvelle, 29 April 1536, *LP* 10 no. 753.   **67.** See above, pp. 304–5. The grant is *LP* 9 no. 504[12], 24 September 1535, made from Audley's Essex home at Old Ford, so the decision would have been taken in the weeks before at Court in Winchester. Appended to it is a note of the personal surrender of the grant on 1 May 28 Henry VIII. On the house, see Colvin (ed.), *History of the King's Works* 4, 124–5; for a representative sample of Cromwell's spending on it and intentions for it, John Williamson to Cromwell, 3 September [1535] and 11 September [1535], SP 1/96 f. 65, *LP* 9 no. 259, and SP 1/96 f. 128, *LP* 9 no. 339; Richard Tomyou to [Cromwell], 23 September [1535], SP 1/96 f. 201, *LP* 9 no. 415.   **68.** Chapuys to Charles V, 21 April 1536, *Spanish Calendar* 5 ii no. 43a, at 86.   **69.** For a convincing rehearsal of the background, R. W. Hoyle, 'Henry Percy, sixth Earl of Northumberland, and the fall of the House of Percy, 1527–1537', in G. W. Bernard (ed.), *The Tudor Nobility* (Manchester, 1992), 180–211.   **70.** Earl of Northumberland to Cromwell, 13 May [1536], BL MS Cotton Otho C/X f. 221, *LP* 10 no. 864.   **71.** Anstis (ed.), *Register of the most noble Order of the Garter*, 2, 398–402.   **72.** Earl of Northumberland to Cromwell, 16 May [1537], SP 1/120 f. 99, *LP* 12 i no. 1211; Northumberland to Cromwell, 3 June [1537], SP 1/121 ff. 27–8, *LP* 12 ii no. 19; Richard Leighton to Cromwell, 29 June [1537], SP 1/121 ff. 187–8, *LP* 12 ii no. 165.   **73.** Miss St Clare Byrne meticulously if inconclusively marshalled the evidence: *Lisle Letters* 3, 378–84.   **74.** Chapuys to

Charles V, 6 June 1536, *Spanish Calendar* 5 ii no. 61, at 138: 'sur ce me loua grande-ment le sens, esperit, et cueur de la dicte concubine et de son frere.'

Chapter 15: Summer Opportunities: 1536

1. Chapuys to Charles V, 6 June 1536, *Spanish Calendar* 5 ii no. 61, at 158.   2. Sir John Russell to Lord Lisle, 3 June [1536], SP 3/7 f. 36, *Lisle Letters* 3 no. 713; see above, p. 107.   3. Chapuys to Charles V, 19 May 1536, *Spanish Calendar* 5 ii no. 55, at 124.   4. Joyce Bickley, late Prioress of Catesby, to Cromwell, end of June 1536, SP 1/102 f. 120, *LP* 10 no. 383. This is misdated by *LP* to February 1536 and therefore credited to Anne Boleyn, but there had been no moves against Catesby in her time, and the letter follows neatly on from Cromwell's commissioners to Cromwell, 12 May [1536], BL MS Cotton Cleopatra E/IV f. 241, *LP* 10 no. 858, and the commissioner (and Cromwell's servant) George Gifford to Cromwell, 19 June [1536] and 27 June [1536], BL MS Cotton Cleopatra E/IV f. 249, *LP* 10 no. 1166; SP 1/104 f. 210, *LP* 10 no. 1215.   5. Unknown correspondent to Cardinal du Bellay, 1536, *LP* 11 no. 860; Ridolfo Pio Bishop of Faenza (papal nuncio in France) to Ambrogio de' Recalcatia (papal secretary), 4 December 1536, *LP* 11 no. 1250.   6. Ralph Sadler to Cromwell, 27 September [1536], SP 1/106 f. 217, *LP* 11 no. 501.   7. Joyce Bickley, late Prioress of Catesby, to Cromwell, end of June 1536, SP 1/102 f. 120, *LP* 10 no. 383, and on the Charterhouse, see above, pp. 283-4.   8. *Wriothesley's Chronicle* 1, 47-8; Wriothesley did not mention Cromwell in his detailed list of those present.   9. On all this see MacCulloch, *Thomas Cranmer*, 159-66, and McEntegart, *Henry VIII, the League of Schmalkalden and the English Reformation*, 26-76; for Alesius's failed attempt to leave England at this time, TNA, SP 70/7 f. 11r, *Calendar of State Papers Foreign . . . Elizabeth [I]*, 1: 1558-59, no. 1303, at 533.   10. *LP* 10 no. 1256[2].   11. Jane Lady Rochford to Cromwell, late May 1536, BL MS Cotton Vespasian F/XIII f. 199, *LP* 10 no. 1010; Earl of Wiltshire to Cromwell, 1 July [1536], SP 1/105 f. 5, *LP* 11 no. 17.   12. *Complete Peerage* 2, 40 and 6, 478. Seymour's patent of creation, 5 June 1536: *LP* 10 no. 1256[4], and for Garter King of Arms's letter about the King's choice to Cromwell, beginning of June 1536, SP 1/104 f. 85, *LP* 10 no. 1017.   13. Robert Sherburne Bishop of Chichester to Cromwell, 7 May [1536], SP 1/103 f. 250, *LP* 10 no. 818, and see Richard Leighton's dismissive reference to him when writing to Cromwell on 1 October 1535, 'Tu ipse optime nosti hominem', SP 1/97 f. 74, *LP* 9 no. 509. For his will, *Lisle Letters* 3, 425, and for background, Lander, 'Church courts and the Reformation in the diocese of Chichester, 1500-58'.   14. Cromwell to Stephen Gardiner, 14 May [1536], Merriman 2 no. 147, *LP* 10 no. 873. For Husee's startlingly prompt and well-informed comment on this, see his letter to Lord Lisle, 24 May [1536], SP 1/104 f. 48, *LP* 10 no. 952. For Gardiner's protests, e.g. Cromwell to Gardiner, 8 June and 21 July 1536, Merriman 2 nos. 149 and 156, *LP* 10 no. 1084 and *LP* 11 no. 152.   15. D. Starkey, 'Court and government', in C. Coleman and D. Starkey (eds.), *Revolution Reassessed: revisions in the history of Tudor government and administration* (Oxford, 1986), 29-58, at 53-5.   16. S. E.

Lehmberg, *The Later Parliaments of Henry VIII 1536–1547* (Cambridge, 1977), 1–39, and on the division recorded in a later reminiscence of William Thomas, Hawkyard, *House of Commons 1509–1558*, 334.   17. The account below where not otherwise referenced follows the excellent summary in J. Edwards, *Mary I: England's Catholic queen* (New Haven and London, 2011), 43–51.   18. Chapuys to Charles V, 6 June 1536, *Spanish Calendar* 5 ii no. 61, at 160–61.   19. Chapuys to Charles V, 1 July 1536, *Spanish Calendar* 5 ii no. 70, at 185.   20. Richard Sparkford to John Scudamore, 30 June [1536], BL MS Additional 11042 f. 68r (not in *LP*). On Sparkford's career, see Emden, *Oxford 1501 to 1540*, 530, and for his chaplaincy to Tunstall (and also his long acquaintance with Cromwell), see William Popley to Cromwell, 27 September [1522], SP 1/26 f. 57, *LP* 3 ii no. 2577.   21. Princess Mary to Cromwell, 23 June 1536, *LP* 10 no. 1186: a text totally lost in the Cottonian fire and now preserved only in T. Hearne (ed.), *Titi Livii Foro-Juliensis, Vita Henrici Quinti, Regis Angliae: accedit, Sylloge Epistolarum, a variis Angliae Principibus scriptarum* (Oxford, 1716), 144.   22. Chapuys to Charles V, 8 July 1536, *Spanish Calendar* 5 ii no. 71, at 195–6. *Wriothesley's Chronicle* 1, 51 corroborates Chapuys's account. On Hackney in the Boleyn crisis, see above, pp. 340–41.   23. Chapuys to Granvelle, 23 July 1536, *LP* 11 no. 148 (not in *Spanish Calendar*), from an MS in Vienna. It is baffling that the *LP* translation made this object a ring rather than the medal which is patently what is described.   24. Mary to Cromwell, 8 December [1536], BL MS Cotton Otho C/X f. 277, *LP* 11 no. 1269, deficiencies in the damaged text supplied by Thomas Hearne.   25. Elizabeth Duchess of Norfolk to Cromwell, 26 June [1537], BL MS Cotton Titus B/I f. 388v, *LP* 12 ii no. 143.   26. Chapuys to Granvelle, 8 July 1536, *Spanish Calendar* 5 ii no. 72, at 198: 'et doubtent mesmement quil [Henry] ne la veuillie bailler a maistre cremuel, ce que ne crois en sorte du monde, et pense quicelluy cremuel, ores que le dict roy voulsist, ny entendroit . . .'.   27. John Husee to Lady Lisle, 22 February [1537], SP 3/12 f. 24, *Lisle Letters* 4 no. 868; it is not clear who this child was, nor how long s/he lived. See the payments in Mary's accounts around this christening, Madden (ed.), *Privy purse expenses of the Princess Mary . . .*, 16, 19, which also has a note partly in her own hand of Cromwell's New Year's gifts to her, at 6, 51. For the Valentine payment, see *LP* 14 ii no. 782, at 329.   28. For acute commentary on this, see Starkey, 'Court and government', 52–4.   29. Chapuys to Granvelle, 8 July 1536, *Spanish Calendar* 5 ii no. 72, at 198.   30. Richard Sparkford to John Scudamore, 30 June [1536], BL MS Additional 11042 f. 68r; it is extraordinary that historians have overlooked this remarkable letter. It confirms what has been doubted, e.g. by *Lisle Letters* 3, 439–40, that Lord Beauchamp was in the running for Lord Privy Seal: that is what John Husee had told Lord Lisle on 26 June [1536], SP 1/104 f. 208, *Lisle Letters* 3 no. 734.   31. That seems a more likely argument than that put forward by Lehmberg, *Later Parliaments of Henry VIII*, 16–17, and repeated since, that Catholic supporters of Mary and enemies of Cromwell objected; that is to mistake the atmosphere of this summer.   32. Bath is included in Anthony Budgegood's account of leading English nobility, end of 1538, *LP* 13 ii no. 732, printed from a document in the Vatican via W. M. Brady, *The episcopal succession in England,*

Scotland and Ireland, A.D. *1400 to 1875* (3 vols., Rome, 1876–7), 3, 493.   **33.** W. A. Shaw, *The Knights of England* (2 vols., London, 1906), 2, 50. For the peer- age grants for Cromwell and Fitzwarren, both completed on 9 July 1536, see *LP* 11 no. 202[14, 15] On 4 July one commission of the peace, for Essex, anticipated his peerage by naming him as Lord 'Crumwell' in the appropriate place on the bench after the earls: *LP* 11 no. 202[9].   **34.** See above, pp. 14–15. There has been confusion about Cromwell's title, first perpetrated by the great antiquarian Wil- liam Dugdale. For the quashing of his idea that the barony was of Oakham, see *Complete Peerage* 3, 556n, and for (actually rather rare) uses of the Wimbledon title: John Husee to Lord Lisle, 8 July [1536], SP 1/105 f. 17, *LP* 11 no. 46; Earl of Northumberland to 'my Lord Crumwell Lord of Wimbuldon', 30 March [1537], BL MS Cotton Vespasian F/XIII f. 159, *LP* 12 i no. 774; Henry Broke to 'Lord Cromwell of Wymlenton', 11 August [1538], SP 1/135 ff. 63–4, *LP* 13 ii no. 75.   **35.** The complex process can be followed in *Statutes of the Realm* 3, 585–6, 712–15: 27 Henry VIII, cap. 34; 28 Henry VIII, cap. 50.   **36.** See above, p. 272; Hales's grant of the Mastership, completed the day after Cromwell's patent of nobility, specifically referred to his custody of The Rolls: *LP* 11 no. 202[17]. On St Rade- gund's Bradsole, see *VCH: Kent* 2, 172–5. For the suppression of St Gregory's as late as 23 February 1538 after much litigation and trouble, Nichols (ed.), *Narra- tives of the days of the Reformation,* 264, 284, and TNA, E 321/34/6, 321/2/29.   **37.** *LP* 10 no. 1256[26].   **38.** For further discussion of this and what follows, see D. MacCulloch, 'A Reformation in the balance: power struggles in the diocese of Norwich, 1533–1553', in C. Rawcliffe, R. Virgoe and R. Wilson (eds.), *Counties and Communities: essays on East Anglian history presented to Hassell Smith* (Norwich, 1996), 97–115, especially 102–3. Repps had called himself 'Your extremely poor chaplain and assuredly perpetual bedeman' in asking to be excused attendance in Parliament in late 1535: Repps to Cromwell, 22 October [1535], SP 1/239 f. 86, *LP Addenda* 1 i no. 948 (misdated by *LP*).   **39.** Sir Thomas Rush to Cromwell, 15 December [1535], SP 1/99 f. 120, *LP* 9 no. 978; for the ride to Lon- don, TNA, E 315/128/85, deposition of Richard Redman.   **40.** See above, pp. 316–17.   **41.** Thomas Thacker to Cromwell, 24 July [1536], SP 1/105 f. 144, *LP* 11 no. 159, deals with the first building work at Mortlake and the partial removal of The Rolls household there, on the first day that parts of the house were in a condition to receive them.   **42.** John Whalley to Cromwell, 5 April [1536], SP 1/103 f. 95, *LP* 10 no. 624.   **43.** MacCulloch, *Thomas Cranmer,* 166–9.   **44.** Lehmberg, *Later Parliaments of Henry VIII,* 34–6; Margaret Douglas to Crom- well, ?August 1537, BL MS Cotton Vespasian F/XIII f. 241, *LP* 11 no. 294.   **45.** Duke of Norfolk to Cromwell, 12 July [1537], SP 1/122 f. 237, *LP* 12 ii no. 248.   **46.** Elizabeth Duchess of Norfolk to Cromwell, 28 September [1536] and 24 October [1537]: SP 1/106 f. 219, *LP* 11 no. 502 and BL MS Cotton Titus B/I f. 390, *LP* 12 ii no. 976.   **47.** On Cromwell's letter to Mary and the treatment of Richmond, see Chapuys to Antoine de Perrenot, *LP* 11 no. 221 (not in *Spanish Calendar*).   **48.** Duke of Norfolk to Cromwell, 5 August 1536, SP 1/105 f. 248, *LP* 11 no. 233.   **49.** Lorenzo Campeggio to Cromwell, 14 January 1535, SP 1/89 f. 26, *LP* 8 no. 51.   **50.** Campeggio to Tunstall, 5 June 1536, SP 1/104 f. 121, *LP* 10 no. 1067; Campeggio to Duke of Suffolk, SP 1/104 f. 122, *LP* 10 no. 1068. The Italian original of Marc'Antonio's instructions not only survives in the State Papers but was turned into a Latin version, presumably for the King's benefit, by the royal Italian secretary Peter Vannes. The Italian original is BL MS Cotton Vitellius B/XIV ff. 205–6, and the Latin translation SP 1/104 f. 126, *LP* 10 no. 1077[1–2].   **51.** W. E. Wilkie, *The Cardinal Protectors of England: Rome and the Tudors before the Reformation* (Cambridge, 1974), 229–32.   **52.** Edwards, *Archbishop Pole*, 51, 57. On the publishing history and prehistory of *De unitate*, see T. F. Dunn, 'The development of the text of Pole's "De Unitate Ecclesiae"', *Papers of the Bibliographical Society of America* 70 (1976), 455–68.   **53.** Tunstall's letter of 13 July 1536 to Pole is preserved in his own draft and also in a transcript by Wriothesley probably made for Cromwell: respectively BL MS Cleopatra E/VI. ff. 390–95, *LP* 11 no. 72[2], and SP 1/105 ff. 32–44, *LP* 11 no. 72[1].   **54.** Dunn, 'Development of the text of Pole's "De Unitate Ecclesiae"', 457, 462–3.   **55.** BL MS Cotton Cleopatra E/IV f. 323r, *LP* 13 ii no. 1036.   **56.** On what follows where not otherwise referenced, MacCulloch, *Thomas Cranmer*, 160–66, and Lehmberg, *Later Parliaments of Henry VIII*, 37–9.   **57.** *Wriothesley's Chronicle* 1, 52.   **58.** The best available text of the injunctions is to be found in C. H. Williams (ed.), *English Historical Documents 1485–1558* (London, 1967), 805–8. The fact that they specify 1 August 1537 as the date for acquiring a Bible for churches suggests that they were first launched exactly a year before that.   **59.** Cromwell to Lord Lisle, 1 August [1536], SP 3/2 f. 166, *Lisle Letters* 2 no. 152a, 96n.   **60.** For discussion about this clause, which is frequently and wrongly asserted not to have formed part of the original text of summer 1536, see MacCulloch, *Thomas Cranmer*, 166.   **61.** The account in G. Latré, 'The 1535 Coverdale Bible and its Antwerp origins', in O. O'Sullivan (ed.), *The Bible as Book: the Reformation* (New Castle, DE, and London, 2000), 89–102, needs modifying by D. Paisey and G. Bartrum, 'Hans Holbein and Miles Coverdale: a new woodcut', *Print Quarterly* 26 (2009), 227–53, particularly 244–6. See also James Nicholson to Cromwell, ?autumn 1535, SP 1/96 f. 33, *LP* 9 no. 226.   **62.** W. Tyndale, *A Treatyse of the Justificacyon by faith only, otherwise called the Parable of the wyked mammon* (Southwark, 1536, *RSTC* 24455), title-page and ff. 1–6r, 106r; see Paisey and Bartrum, 'Hans Holbein and Miles Coverdale', 248–9.   **63.** For what follows, unless otherwise cited, see MacCulloch, *Thomas Cranmer*, 174–84, and D. MacCulloch, 'Heinrich Bullinger and the English-speaking world', in E. Campi and P. Opitz (eds.), *Heinrich Bullinger (1504–1575): Leben, Denken, Wirkung* (Zürcher Beiträge zur Reformationsgeschichte 24, 2007), 891–934, at 891–910. In the latter piece, I go into remorseless detail on the prosopography of the visitors to Zürich discussed below, and will not repeat those citations here unless for clarification.   **64.** William Clifton to Cromwell, 11 May [1536], BL MS Cotton Vitellius B/XXI f. 178, *LP* 10 no. 847. There is a glitch in the Clifton family pedigree recorded in G. W. Marshall (ed.), *The Visitations of the County of Nottingham in the Years 1569 and 1614 ...* (Harleian Society 4, 1871), 18, as Customer Clifton (who died in 1564) cannot possibly be of the same generation as Dr Gamaliel Clifton, who was nevertheless Dean of Hereford, and who probably therefore accounts for William's presence in the diplomatic party of Bishop Foxe of Hereford. Probably this

William was the son of Gamaliel's brother William. On the remarkable Clifton family, see also MacCulloch, *Thomas Cranmer*, 17–18.   **65.** A tantalizingly brief summary of Marot's letter to Cromwell, clearly of the second half of 1536, is in Bodl. MS Jesus College 74 f. 134r.   **66.** Euler, 'Religious and cultural exchange during the Reformation', 101, 103.   **67.** Logan, 'First royal visitation of the English universities', 873–5, sums up the story broadly correctly, though he confuses Thomas son of William Marshall, junior Fellow of Magdalen, with William's brother Thomas (so uncle of the younger Thomas), former Demy of Magdalen and in 1535–6 Vicar of South Molton. To separate them, cf. Michael Drum to William Marshall, 9 March ?1534, SP 1/82 f. 239, *LP* 7 no. 308, with William Marshall to Cromwell, late December 1536, SP 1/113 f. 20, *LP* 11 no. 1355. The uncle's markedly conservative career probably indicates that it was not Cromwell but John Longland Bishop of Lincoln who wrote a recommendation of him in May ?1535, SP 1/92 f. 194, *LP* 8 no. 790, an unsigned contemporary copy of the original letter made for Cromwell's archive.   **68.** Emden, *Oxford 1501 to 1540*, 643, 742. If he is the same as the priest ordained in Exeter diocese on 29 March 1533, he probably links with the William Woodroffe revealed as having a Devon and Somerset clerical career taking off at the beginning of Elizabeth's reign: *Clergy of the Church of England Database*, s.v. Woodroff, William.   **69.** P. Boesch (ed.), 'Rudolph Gwalthers Reise nach England im Jahr 1537', *Zwingliana* 8/8 (1947), 433–71.   **70.** On Lord John, see above, p. 47. The one major error I made in MacCulloch, 'Heinrich Bullinger and the English-speaking world', was to identify this Lord John Grey as Henry Grey's brother; he would have been too young to undertake any hosting duties in 1537, and so it is Henry's uncle John who was responsible.   **71.** Wentworth's mother was a Woodroffe: *HC 1509–1558* 3, 582.   **72.** Boesch (ed.), 'Rudolph Gwalthers Reise nach England im Jahr 1537', 452: Michael Drum, John Somer, Nicholas Partridge, Richard Arderne, Thomas Slithurst, John Hoker, Simon Parrett. These are mostly the earlier and therefore probably the more senior names in the list of signatories in 1535. Several of them went on corresponding with Gwalther when he returned home: Euler, 'Religious and cultural exchange during the Reformation', 106.   **73.** MacCulloch, *Thomas Cranmer*, 179–81. Gwalther arrived back on 8 June 1537: Boesch (ed.), 'Rudolph Gwalthers Reise nach England im Jahr 1537', 459.   **74.** MacCulloch, *Thomas Cranmer*, 183–4.   **75.** Ibid., 354–5, 378–83, and cf. the concurrence of Euler, 'Religious and cultural exchange during the Reformation', 129.   **76.** An excellent account of him is provided by A. Boyle, 'Henry Fitzalan, twelfth Earl of Arundel: politics and culture in the Tudor nobility' (University of Oxford DPhil, 2003), and in Boyle, 'Hans Eworth's portrait of the Earl of Arundel and the politics of 1549–50', *EHR* 117 (2002), 25–47, especially 27–9.   **77.** Bartholomew Traheron to Heinrich Bullinger, 20 [*sic* – in fact about a week later] February 1540, H. Bullinger, *Heinrich Bullinger: Briefwechseledition*, various editors (Zürich, 1973–, in progress), 10, 51; H. Robinson (ed.), *Original Letters relative to the English Reformation* ... (2 vols., Parker Society, 1846–7), 316–17. MacCulloch, 'Heinrich Bullinger and the English-speaking world', 905, provides the possibility of more tangles along these lines than those with which I weary the reader here.

Chapter 16: Grace for the Commonwealth: 1536

1. Circular of Cromwell e.g. to the Earl of Cumberland, 18 June [1535], Merriman 1 no. 105, *LP* 8 no. 893; James Layburn to Cromwell, 8 July [1535], SP 1/94 f. 10, *LP* 8 no. 1008; Thomas Stanley Lord Monteagle to Cromwell, 4 July [1535], SP 1/93 f. 192, *LP* 8 no. 984. On Lee, Layburn and the Duke of Richmond, see Thomas Lee to Cromwell, 14 September [1533], SP 1/79 f. 53, *LP* 6 no. 1124 and Thomas Lee to Cromwell, 2 December 1537, SP 1/126 f. 177, *LP* 12 ii no. 1161. For the knight wrongly identified as a JP, who nevertheless offered his services, see Sir Stephen Hamerton to Cromwell, 5 July [1535], SP 1/93 f. 202, *LP* 8 no. 995, and for further background, see C. Haigh, *The Last Days of the Lancashire Monasteries and the Pilgrimage of Grace* (Manchester, 1969), 50.   2. Sir Richard Tempest, Sir Marmaduke Constable, Robert Chaloner and John Lambert the elder to Cromwell, 5 July [1535], SP 1/93 f. 198, *LP* 8 no. 992.   3. Henry Earl of Cumberland to Cromwell, 22 August [1535], SP 1/95 f. 127, *LP* 9 no. 150; Sir Richard Tempest to Cromwell, 27 August [1535], SP 1/95 f. 183, *LP* 9 no. 196; on Tunstall, Sir James Layburn to Cromwell, 24 September [1535], SP 1/96 f. 213, *LP* 9 no. 427.   4. Christopher Jenny to Cromwell, 27 March [1536], SP 1/91 f. 144, *LP* 8 no. 457 (misdated to 1535 in *LP*); see also M. L. Bush, *The Pilgrimage of Grace: a study of the rebel armies of October 1536* (Manchester, 1996), 132, 143, 166–7, 413. On the background, which reveals that in 1541 Mistress Carr came to an agreement with William Wycliffe, perhaps therefore not her husband's murderer, see 'Parishes: Wycliffe', in *VCH: Yorkshire North Riding* 1, 138–42, and R. W. Hoyle, *The Pilgrimage of Grace and the Politics of the 1530s* (Oxford, 2001), 40–41. William Wycliffe was still alive and honoured in 1562, when his relative Joan Wycliffe of Richmond made him supervisor of her will: J. Raine (ed.), *Wills and Inventories from the Registry of the Archdeaconry of Richmond . . .* (Surtees Society 26, 1853), 160.   5. Memorandum by Sir Thomas Tempest, October 1536, SP 1/112 f. 114v, *LP* 11 no. 1244. For the identification of Tempest as the author, see Bush, *Pilgrimage of Grace*, 167 n. 158.   6. For what follows where not otherwise referenced, see the deposition of James Rokeby, April 1537, SP 1/118 ff. 254–7, *LP* 12 i no. 1011: now much damaged and not attributed to him in *LP*, but Dr Bush and I independently arrived at Rokeby's identity (see Bush, *Pilgrimage of Grace*, 142n, 158–9).   7. For Dr Rokeby's old friendship with Thomas Lee, see Lee to Cromwell, 4 November [1535], SP 1/98 f. 173, *LP* 9 no. 762: 'we have been brought up together and the one have known the other ever since we were children.' Chambers (ed.), *Faculty Office Registers*, xxvi, mentions the appointment of James to an office in Cranmer's Faculty Office in 1544, though he also elides him with his brother John. John Rokeby and Ellis ap Rhys were both members of St Nicholas Hostel Cambridge.   8. For John Rokeby's clerical appointments, see *Clergy of the Church of England Database*: he was rather belatedly ordained deacon in 1547, and resigned Wycliffe in 1551 in the course of a hands-off clerical career up to his death in 1574. James Rokeby is glaringly absent from his mother's will made in 1540, while she made her 'son Doctor' one of the executors: Raine (ed.), *Wills and Inventories from the*

Registry of the Archdeaconry of Richmond, 17–19. **9.** Deposition of James Rokeby, April 1537, SP 1/118 f. 256r, *LP* 12 i no. 1011. **10.** T. Thornton, 'Henry VIII's progress through Yorkshire in 1541 and its implications for northern identities', *Northern History* 46 (2009), 231–44, at 232. **11.** Deposition of James Rokeby, April 1537, SP 1/118 f. 256v, *LP* 12 i no. 1011; my italics. On Savage, see *ODNB*, s.v. Savage, Thomas. Cf. Sir Thomas Tempest's memorandum, October 1536, SP 1/112 ff. 114v–115r, *LP* 11 no. 1244. **12.** For Godolphin's lobbying, see Sir William Godolphin to Cromwell, 3 May 1537, SP 1/119 f. 143, *LP* 12 i no. 1126, and for the result, John Tregonwell to Cromwell, 5 September [1537], SP 1/106 f. 134, *LP* 11 no. 405 (misdated in *LP*). For Godolphin possessing the greatest tin works in Cornwall, see Leland, *Itinerary of John Leland*, ed. Toulmin Smith, 1, 191. **13.** On Garrett, see above, pp. 65–6; for his preaching licence from Cranmer on 6 June 1534, Chambers (ed.), *Faculty Office Registers*, 39, and for patronage from Latimer, Thomas Bell to John Stokesley Bishop of London, 9 June [1536], SP 1/104 f. 147, *LP* 10 no. 1099. For adverse reactions to his preaching, John Lord Hussey to Cromwell, *c.* mid-April 1537, SP 1/118 ff. 123–4, *LP* 12 i no. 899, referring to 1534, and Sir Francis Bigod to Cromwell, 12 July [1535], SP 1/94 f. 24, *LP* 8 no. 1025. For Bigod's patronage to Jerome, see Bigod to Cromwell, 28 September [1536], SP 1/106 f. 220, *LP* 11 no. 503, and Dickens, *Lollards and Protestants*, 103–4, in the best (albeit perhaps over-sympathetic) account of Bigod, at 53–113. **14.** Lord Leonard Grey to Cromwell, 10 August [1536], SP 60/3 f. 127, *LP* 11 no. 266. **15.** Depositions accusing Pratt before Sir Gilbert Talbot and John Russell, 2 September 1536, SP 1/106 f. 139rv, *LP* 11 no. 407[2]. **16.** Sir Gilbert Talbot and John Russell to Cromwell, 5 September 1536, SP 1/106 f. 137, *LP* 11 no. 407, and report on Pratt's examination, SP 1/106 f. 138, *LP* 11 no. 407[2 ii]; Cromwell to Talbot and Russell, 7 September [1536], Merriman 2 no. 161 (not in *LP*); Cromwell to Russell, 8 October [1536], Merriman 2 no. 164 (not in *LP*). **17.** Report by John Freeman, Blaise Holland, Richard Wolmar and Roger Hilton, 7 September [1536], SP 1/106 f. 142, *LP* 11 no. 417, and see Freeman to Cromwell, 7 August [1536], SP 1/105 f. 257, *LP* 11 no. 242. For their friendship, see Freeman to Cromwell, ?September 1538, SP 1/136 f. 28, *LP* 13 ii no. 254. **18.** Deposition of Matthew Mackerell, Abbot of Barlings, BL MS Cotton Cleopatra E/IV f. 245, *LP* 12 i no. 702. **19.** For examples of the importance of this Michaelmas date directly referring to the Lincolnshire Rising, see Bowker, *The Henrician Reformation*, 148–52. **20.** Deposition of William Breyar, 22 October 1536, SP 1/109 ff. 36–49, *LP* 11 no. 841; the portion concerning Dent is effectively though belatedly analysed in Bush, *Pilgrimage of Grace*, 249. The Rectory of Sedbergh was worth £41 10s in the *VE*, 5, 243. **21.** The Dentdale initiative has been curiously downplayed by the most recent historians of the Pilgrimage of Grace. Hoyle, *Pilgrimage of Grace*, 213, talks of the 'qualitative difference' between it and the Pilgrimage outbursts from 11 October, with no real justification. Bush, *Pilgrimage of Grace*, deals with it in rather an afterthought at 249. **22.** Petition of Robert Asporner to Cromwell, ?spring 1537, SP 1/120 f. 265, *LP* 12 i no. 1326. **23.** For the succession of Richard Corney to Roger Horsman as Vicar of Sedbergh, see *LP* 11 no. 943[16], and for Cromwell's previous entanglement with the Horsmans and Coverham, see above, pp. 196, 316, 335. **24.** Useful discussion of this is Gray, *Oaths and the English Reformation*, 145–69. **25.** Report of Lionel Grey, Robert Collingwood, William Grene and James Rokeby 28 September 1536, SP 1/106 ff. 222–3, *LP* 11 no. 504. On Hexham's place in northern defence, see Edward Lee Archbishop of York to Cromwell, 23 April 1536, BL MS Cotton Cleopatra E/IV f. 286, *LP* 10 no. 716. **26.** See the Earl's plaintive letter about Hexham to Cromwell, 4 October [1536], SP 1/106 f. 251, *LP* 11 no. 535, only a day after he had written to Cromwell thanking him for sorting out Carnaby's grant of Hexham: Northumberland to Cromwell, 3 October [1536], SP 1/106 f. 246, *LP* 11 no. 529. For the culmination of some months of negotiation between Carnaby and Cromwell over estates in Kent in April 1536, see *LP* 10 no. 775[24] (Reynold is there misnamed Richard). For Carnaby's prompt journey north to resume the Hexham suppression, thwarted by events, see R. W. Hoyle (ed.), 'Letters of the Cliffords, Lords Clifford and Earls of Cumberland, *c.* 1500–*c.* 1565', *Camden Miscellany* 31 (Camden 4th series 44, 1992), 1–189, at 137–8. **27.** On this and what follows where not otherwise referenced, see depositions of Nicholas Melton and others, 21 October 1536, SP 1/109 f. 1, *LP* 11 no. 828[i]. See also for context and comment, Bowker, *The Henrician Reformation*, 148–56. **28.** See E. J. Hobsbawm and J. Wallach Scott, 'Political Shoemakers', *PP* 89 (1980), 86–114. **29.** M. E. James, 'Obedience and dissent in Henrician England: the Lincolnshire Rebellion 1536', in James, *Society, Politics and Culture: studies in early modern England* (Cambridge, 1986), 188–269 (reprinted from *PP* 48 (1970), 3–78), at 207. **30.** This was the observation of Eustace Chapuys's nephew to the Queen of Hungary in connection with the rising, mid-October 1536, *LP* 11 no. 714, but it was a belief widely shared at the time, and stated in one version of the rebels' demands to the King: cf. the articles, SP 1/108 f. 45, *LP* 11 no. 705; see also H. Walter (ed.), *Expositions and Notes on sundry portions of the Holy Scriptures, together with The Practice of Prelates. By William Tyndale . . .* (Parker Society, 1849), 309, 319–20; Loades (ed.), *Papers of George Wyatt*, 137–8; N. Pocock (ed.), *A treatise on the pretended divorce between Henry VIII. and Catharine of Aragon, by Nicholas Harpsfield . . .* (CS 2nd series 21, 1878), 175–6; Nichols (ed.), *Narratives of the days of the Reformation*, 219. **31.** Examination of Nicholas Melton, late 1536, SP 1/110 f. 133rv, *LP* 11 no. 968. **32.** TNA, E 315/209, ff. 7r–8r, *LP* 13 i no. 1520[iv]. **33.** Convent of Legbourne to Cromwell, *c.* April 1536, BL MS Cotton Cleopatra E/IV f. 329, *LP* 10 no. 384. **34.** Deposition of Nicholas Melton, 21 October 1536, SP 1/109 f. 1r, *LP* 11 no. 828[i (1)]; examination of George Brantwhet alias Browne, 30 October 1536, SP 1/110 f. 23, *LP* 11 no. 920[2]; examination of Nicholas Melton, late 1536, SP 1/110 f. 133rv, *LP* 11 no. 968; examinations before Sir John St John and Richard Cromwell, 3 November 1536, SP 1/110 ff. 161r, 162v, *LP* 11 no. 972. **35.** Christopher Ayscough to Cromwell, ?6 October 1536, SP 1/106 f. 291, *LP* 11 no. 567. **36.** S. Gunn, 'Peers, commons and gentry in the Lincolnshire Revolt of 1536', *PP* 123 (1989), 52–79, at 60; on the Tamworths and Cranmer, see MacCulloch, *Thomas Cranmer*, 17, 19. Gunn's article is a sensible corrective to the overstatements and general thesis about aristocratic faction in James, 'Obedience and dissent in Henrician England', which nevertheless remains useful in its careful narrative. **37.** Christopher Ayscough to

Cromwell, ?6 October 1536, SP 1/106 f. 291, *LP* 11 no. 567.   **38.** ?Thomas Bolles
to Sir Thomas Audley, 7 October [1536], E 36/121 ff. 116–17, *LP* 11 no. 585; for
the identification of Bolles, addressing himself from Gosberton, cf. Gunn, *Charles
Brandon, Duke of Suffolk*, 179. Some sources call George Wolsey Thomas, an
understandable slip.   **39.** Chapuys's nephew to the Queen of Hungary, mid-
October 1536, *LP* 11 no. 714.   **40.** On Milsent and Bellows, who frequently
appear in Cromwell's later business, Hoyle, *Pilgrimage of Grace*, 109; on Parker,
examination of George Brantwhet alias Browne, 30 October 1536, SP 1/110 f.
23v, *LP* 11 no. 920[2].   **41.** ?Thomas Bolles to Sir Thomas Audley, 7 October
[1536], E 36/121 ff. 116–17, *LP* 11 no. 585. I have written extensively on this theme
of yeoman leadership: see A. Fletcher and D. MacCulloch, *Tudor Rebellions* (6th
edn, London 2016), ch. 10.   **42.** Gunn, 'Peers, commons and gentry in the Lincolnshire Revolt of 1536', 60–63.   **43.** For a draft in his hand of a long angry
letter from the King to the Lincolnshire subsidy commissioners, berating them for
passivity and for interceding for the rebels, *c.* 6/7 October 1536, SP 1/106 f. 301,
LP 11 no. 569. For his efforts on the financial front, see Richard Eton to Thomas
Heneage, probably late October 1536, SP 1/240 f. 215, *LP Addenda* 1 i no. 1130,
and his memoranda about loans from November and December 1536, SP 1/113 ff.
83–6, *LP* 11 no. 1419.   **44.** MacCulloch, *Thomas Cranmer*, 170–71.   **45.** Roland
Lee to Cromwell, 3 September [1538], SP 1/136 f. 71, *LP* 13 ii no. 276. *LP* misreads
the number of soldiers as 100.   **46.** Roland Lee to Cromwell, 15 January [1537],
BL MS Cotton Cleopatra E/V f. 414, *LP* 12 i no. 93.   **47.** Chapuys's nephew to
the Queen of Hungary, mid-October 1536, *LP* 11 no. 714.   **48.** Chapuys to
Charles V, 7 October 1536, *Spanish Calendar* 5 ii no. 104, at 269.   **49.** Richard
Cromwell, [8 October 1536], SP 1/107 ff. 88–9, *LP* 11 no. 607 (for Cromwell's
allocation of 100 horse, see also *LP* 11 no. 580[5], 236); John Freeman to Thomas
Wriothesley, [17 October 1536], SP 1/108 f. 138, *LP* 11 no. 756; Richard Cromwell
to Cromwell, 2 November [1536], SP 1/110 f. 116, *LP* 11 no. 959.   **50.** Sir William
Fitzwilliam to Cromwell, 25 October [1536], SP 1/109 f. 99, *LP* 11 no. 865; Sir
John Russell to Cromwell, 25 October 1536, SP 1/109 f. 101, *LP* 11 no. 866.   **51.**
Sir Richard Cotton to Cromwell, 21 October [1536], SP 1/109 ff. 17–18, *LP* 11 no.
831; on Cotton, see *HC 1509–1558* 1, 711–13. For his brother Sir George in Richard Cromwell's troop, see Richard Cromwell to Cromwell, [8 October 1536], SP
1/107 ff. 88–9, *LP* 11 no. 607.   **52.** 'ce seroit la destruction et ruyne de son com-
petiteur et enemy Cremuel, auquel se imputoit la coulpe de tous ces affaires, et
duquel les mutins, comme lon dit, demandent la teste': Chapuys to Charles V, 7
October 1536, *Spanish Calendar* 5 ii no. 104, at 268.   **53.** Duke of Norfolk to
Cromwell, Edward Foxe Bishop of Hereford and Sir William Paulet, 8 October
1536, SP 1/107 f. 82, *LP* 11 no. 602; Duke of Norfolk to Henry VIII, 8 October
1536, SP 1/107 f. 80, *LP* 11 no. 601.   **54.** See the evident mood of relief at Windsor on 14 October, reflected in Cromwell's letter to the Earl of Cumberland, Hoyle
(ed.), 'Letters of the Cliffords, Lords Clifford', 148–9, and the orders received by
the Earl of Surrey for his father, dated from Windsor on the same day: Surrey to
Norfolk, 15 October [1536], SP 1/108 f. 95, *LP* 11 no. 727.   **55.** Bush, *Pilgrimage
of Grace*, 11. Superb and indispensable timelines of events are provided in ibid.,

424–36 (October to December 1536) and in M. L. Bush and D. Bownes, *The Defeat of the Pilgrimage of Grace: a study of the postpardon revolts of December 1536 to March 1537 and their effect* (Hull, 1999), 418–41 (through to 1537). **56.** Hoyle, *Pilgrimage of Grace*, 282–91. **57.** *LP* 12 i no. 6, at 6. Holgate was made Bishop of Llandaff in March 1537, but Cromwell had already decided on his appointment in January 1537: John Hilsey Bishop of Rochester to Cromwell, January 1537, SP 1/105 f. 199, *LP* 11 no. 188 (misdated in *LP* to 1536, because of misdating same to same, St Laurence day [3 February 1537], SP 1/105 f. 199, *LP* 11 no. 188, by the wrong St Laurence Day). On Watton's position in the order, see M. Stephenson, *The Gilbertine Priory of Watton* (Borthwick Papers 116, 2009), 33. **58.** For the sequence of events, see Thomas Lee to Cromwell, 10 February [1536], SP 1/102 f. 22, *LP* 10 no. 288; deposition of James Cockerell, quondam of Guisborough, April 1537, SP 1/119 f. 83r, *LP* 12 i no. 1087; Thomas Lee to Robert Pursglove alias Silvester, Prior of Guisborough, 8 March [1537], SP 1/102 f. 173, *LP* 10 no. 439. **59.** William Thornton alias Dent Abbot of York to Cromwell, 18 January [1537], SP 1/114 f. 159, *LP* 12 i no. 133. **60.** On Blythman, see the deposition of Lancelot Collins, SP 1/118 f. 268v, *LP* 12 i no. 1018; on Beckwith, examination of William Aclom, SP 1/116 ff. 169–70, *LP* 12 i no. 536, and his fairly honourable mention in Wilfrid Holme's poem on the Pilgrimage, Dickens, *Lollards and Protestants*, 118. **61.** Sir George Lawson to Cromwell, 24 January [1537], SP 1/115 f. 41, *LP* 12 i no. 219. For Lawson's calling Richard Cromwell 'brother', see Lawson to Cromwell, 9 January [1533], SP 1/74 f. 20, *LP* 6 no. 29. **62.** On Carnaby's servant, a remembrance of Cromwell in spring 1537, *LP* 12 i no. 973, and a memorandum detailing *inter alia* Sir Thomas Percy's campaign against Carnaby, SP 1/119 ff. 95–97r, *LP* 12 i no. 1090; for the Earl of Westmorland's reluctance to be seen publicly defending Carnaby, Duke of Norfolk to Cromwell, 12 April [1537], SP 1/118 f. 155r, *LP* 12 i no. 919. **63.** Petition of John Dakyn, *c.* March 1537, SP 1/117 ff. 201v, 204r–205v, *LP* 12 i no. 788; on his helpfulness in Convocation, Roland Lee to Cromwell, 29 July [1533], SP 1/78 f. 46, *LP* 6 no. 912. **64.** On Lamplugh, see Edward Lee Archbishop of York to Cromwell, 14 October [1535], SP 1/98 f. 3, *LP* 9 no. 606, and his employment by Cromwell at the dissolved Furness Abbey, 15 December 1537, SP 1/127 ff. 58–61, *LP* 12 ii no. 1216. On Lee's relationship to the other Lees and friendship with Cromwell, see John Lee to Cromwell, 18 October [1532], SP 1/71 f. 120, *LP* 5 no. 1446; on the leeches, Lee to Cromwell, 25 October [1533], SP 1/80 f. 23, *LP* 6 no. 1346. For their swearing to the Cumberland pilgrims, Bush, *Pilgrimage of Grace*, 350–51. **65.** Examination of Collins, 24 April 1537, SP 1/118 ff. 267v–268v, *LP* 12 i no. 1018. On his early acquaintance with Cromwell, see above, pp. 28–9. **66.** Duke of Norfolk to Cromwell, 8 May [1537], BL MS Cotton Caligula B/I f. 341, *LP* 12 i no. 1156. **67.** Cranmer to Cromwell, 28 February [1538], SP 1/129 f. 121, *LP* 13 i no. 369. **68.** Deposition of Thomas Maunsell, SP 1/113 f. 55r, *LP* 11 no. 1402. **69.** For William Maunsell, see Hoyle, *Pilgrimage of Grace*, 274, and for his troubles before the Pilgrimage, e.g. William Abbot of York to Cromwell, 2 March [1535], SP 1/91 f. 16, *LP* 8 no. 313, and Maunsell to Cromwell, 3 March [1535], SP 1/91 f. 24, *LP* 8 no. 320; note in the latter his friendly colleagueship and friendship with George Lawson and John Gostwick. Wilfrid Holmes's doggerel poem on the Pilgrimage singles out William Maunsell for praise for his loyalty: Dickens, *Lollards and Protestants*, 118.   70. Pilgrims' song, SP 1/108 f. 186r, *LP* 11 no. 786[3]. The interpretation of the Ls in Bush, *Pilgrimage of Grace*, 235, seems more plausible than including Bishop Longland, who had little relevance to the Yorkshire stirs.   71. John Freeman to Cromwell, 15 October 1536, SP1/108 f. 92, *LP* 11 no. 724; Mac-Culloch, *Suffolk and the Tudors*, 293.   72. Aske's answers to interrogatories, 11 May 1537, SP 1/120 f. 35rv, *LP* 12 i no. 1175[ii]; for Richard's sentiments on the Lincolnshire insurgents, Richard Cromwell to Cromwell, [11 October 1536], SP 1/107 f. 146, *LP* 11 no. 658.   73. Cromwell to Sir Ralph Eure junior, 10 November [1536], SP 1/111 ff. 41-2, *LP* 11 no. 1032, two copies, one mutilated. For further comment and context, see Hoyle, *Pilgrimage of Grace*, 329-30.   74. The draft is *LP* 11 no. 957, *State Papers* 1, 506-10 (my italics), discussed in Hoyle, *Pilgrimage of Grace*, 313-14, and Bush, *Pilgrimage of Grace*, 399, neither of whom discuss its most prominent silence; nor do they relate it to the longer printed version, [Henry VIII], *Ansvvere made by the Kynges Hyghnes to the Petitions of the Rebelles in Yorkeshire* (London, 1536, *RSTC* 13077). Its Lincolnshire fellow is *RSTC* 13077.5.   75. Thomas Heneage and Sir William Fitzwilliam to Cromwell, both 5 November 1536, respectively SP 1/110 f. 180, *LP* 11 no. 985, and SP 1/110 f. 181, *LP* 11 no. 986.   76. Examination of Percival Cresswell, E 36/119 f. 79rv, *LP* 12 i no. 1013; for background on Cresswell at Court, Hoyle, *Pilgrimage of Grace*, 318-19.   77. [Henry VIII], *Ansvvere made by the Kynges Hyghnes to the Petitions of the Rebelles in Yorkeshire*, sig. A4v. Another addition to the list of non-noble councillors here was Sir William Kingston; it is difficult to read the significance of this.   78. Gervase Clifton to Mr Banks, 11 November [1536], SP 1/111 f. 56, *LP* 11 no. 1042. On Clifton, see *HC 1509-1558* 1, 660-61, and for Cromwell's old involvement with Banks and Stanley wardship business, Laurence Starkey to Cromwell, 27 July ?1526, SP 1/39 f. 3, *LP* 4 i no. 2347.   79. Aske to Darcy, *c.* 21 November 1536, *LP* 11 no. 1128. Cromwell was among those councillors writing to the Duke of Norfolk from Richmond on 2 December: BL MS Harley 6989 f. 60, *LP* 11 no. 1228, and divided his time between there and London for the rest of the month. On Richmond at this time, Colvin (ed.), *History of the King's Works* 4, 228.   80. [Henry VIII], *Ansvvere made by the Kynges Hyghnes to the Petitions of the Rebelles in Yorkeshire*, sigs. A2v-A3r.   81. G. E. Corrie (ed.), *Sermons by Hugh Latimer* ... (Parker Society, 1844), 25-32; for Latimer's own defensive report of how well the sermon had gone down, Latimer to Cromwell, 27 December [1536], SP 1/113 f. 32, *LP* 11 no. 1374.   82. SP 1/111 f. 144 (and other copies elsewhere), *LP* 11 no. 1110. For context, see P. Marshall, 'The shooting of Robert Packington', in Marshall, *Religious Identities in Henry VIII's England* (Aldershot, 2006), 61-79, and MacCulloch, *Thomas Cranmer*, 171-2.   83. *Wriothesley's Chronicle* 1, 59-60.   84. Richard Harrison Abbot of Kirkstead to Cromwell, 29 January [1537], SP 1/115 f. 125, *LP* 12 i no. 278.   85. Hoyle, *Pilgrimage of Grace*, 368-9. For the King's movements at this time, see Sir William Paulet to Cromwell, [13 December 1536], SP 1/112 f. 177, *LP* 11 no. 1291: Henry was due to move to Whitehall on 19 December and to Greenwich on 21 December.

Wriothesley's Chronicle 1, 59, shows that he kept more or less to this timetable.   86. Richard Southwell to Cromwell, 23 December 1536, SP 1/113 f. 22, *LP* 11 no. 1356.   87. John Husee to Lord Lisle, 5 January 1537, SP 1/114 f. 22, *Lisle Letters* 4 no. 910, and for a distinctly nervous reply from the Earl of Oxford on 6 January 1537 to a request from Cromwell in regard to a volubly seditious northerner, SP 1/114 f. 24, *LP* 12 i no. 27. The Charterhouse next Coventry to Cromwell ('in haste'!), 4 January [1537], SP 1/114 f. 17, *LP* 12 i no. 19.

Chapter 17: The Reckoning: 1537

1. Stephen Gardiner Bishop of Winchester to Cromwell, *c.* 21 August 1532, SP 1/70 f. 205, *LP* 5 no. 1245; John Godsalve to Cromwell, a covering note just after previous, SP 1/70 f. 127, *LP* 5 no. 1118.   2. [Henry VIII], *Ansvvere made by the Kynges Hyghnes to the Petitions of the Rebelles in Yorkeshire*, sig. A4v, and see above, Chapter 16.   3. For sensible comment on these long-controverted matters, see J. Guy, 'The Privy Council: revolution or evolution?', in Coleman and Starkey (eds.), *Revolution Reassessed*, 59–86.   4. W. Underwood, 'Thomas Cromwell and William Marshall's Protestant books', *HJ* 47 (2004), 517–39, at 534–5.   5. Henry Earl of Cumberland to Cromwell, 12 January [1537], SP 1/114 f. 77, *LP* 12 i no. 72. Anthony Budgegood in his account of leading English nobility, end of 1538, *LP* 13 ii no. 732, described Cumberland as 'of good power, without discretion or conduct', and for another lukewarm opinion of his abilities, Duke of Norfolk to Cromwell, 12 April [1537], SP 1/118 f. 155, *LP* 12 i no. 919.   6. Hoyle, *Pilgrimage of Grace*, 365–7.   7. SP 1/114 f. 167, *LP* 12 i no. 138: well discussed in Bush and Bownes, *Defeat of the Pilgrimage of Grace*, 47, 151–4, who cogently argue for a date of 8–12 January 1537.   8. R. W. Hoyle, 'Thomas Master's narrative of the Pilgrimage of Grace', *Northern History* 21 (1985), 53–79, at 73. For what follows, see Bush and Bownes, *Defeat of the Pilgrimage of Grace*, 31–56.   9. Sir Francis Bigod to [Cromwell], ?late February 1537, SP 1/116 f. 164v, *LP* 12 i no. 533; for Jerome's dispensation to hold a benefice with change of habit on 20 May 1537, Chambers (ed.), *Faculty Office Registers*, 98, and his presentation to Stepney by Leighton on 29 May, G. Hennessy, *Novum Repertorium Ecclesiasticum Parochiale Londinense* ... (London, 1898), 411. Cranmer went on to present Jerome to an additional benefice in Kent on 16 December 1538 after the deprivation of the conservative Thomas Goldwell: Lambeth Palace, Cranmer's Register f. 366r.   10. Baker, *Oxford History of the Laws of England* 6, 588.   11. Gunn, 'Peers, commons and gentry in the Lincolnshire Revolt of 1536', 71–7, and Gunn, *Henry VII's New Men, passim.*   12. Deposition of George Croft, 12 November 1538, quoting a reminiscence of Lord De La Warr, who had been one of the peers at the trial: SP 1/138 f. 175, *LP* 13 ii no. 803.   13. Hoyle, *Pilgrimage of Grace*, 415, and see also 44, 68–70.   14. Deposition of John Richardson, chantry priest of Haddlesey (near Templehurst), 14 May 1537, SP 1/120 f. 83rv, *LP* 12 i no. 1200.   15. For the discovery, made by Dr Thomas Magnus, see Duke of Norfolk to Cromwell, 29 April [1537], SP 1/119 f. 53, *LP* 12 i no. 1064. The documents

themselves from 1529 are SP 1/54 ff. 202–10, *LP* 4 iii no. 5749[1, 2]. See above, pp. 83–4.   **16.** *LP* 12 i no. 848. For overlapping material but concentrating on events after the pardon and without any reference to Wolsey, see SP 1/118 f. 14, *LP* 12 i no. 847.   **17.** SP 1/118 f. 43, *LP* 12 i no. 850. I offer my best attempt at reconstructing the exceptionally scribbled final sentence, which partly repeats an erased line above ('Item Richardson and Mason saith'): my reading of 'delivered' is the most tentative, reading two squiggles which could be double a or double d, as the common abbreviation for that word. Everything else in that sentence is certain. Richardson and Mason must be local informants, but they do not seem to feature elsewhere in evidence about the Pilgrimage.   **18.** Ellis, 'Thomas Cromwell and Ireland, 1532–1540', 510.   **19.** Bradshaw, *Irish Constitutional Revolution*, 119–20, 141–5.   **20.** The admission comes in the commissioners' letter to Cromwell, 2 September [1537], SP 60/5 ff. 13–14, *LP* 12 ii no. 631; the letter-book is SP 60/5 ff. 1–5, *LP* 12 ii no. 389.   **21.** For the depressing details on Body, damning even if only 50 per cent true, Lord Leonard Grey to Cromwell, 24 November [1536], SP 60/3 f. 187, *LP* 11 no. 1157, and for the Irish background to his mission, Bradshaw, *Irish Constitutional Revolution*, 113.   **22.** Robert Cowley to Cromwell, 9 March [1538], SP 60/6 ff. 46–7, *LP* 13 i no. 470.   **23.** Deposition of John Allen, February/March 1538, SP 60/6 f. 49v, *LP* 13 i no. 471[2]. This whole bundle of depositions is interestingly annotated 'he is gone', suggesting that Cowley and his colleagues waited for the departure of the commissioners before sending it.   **24.** Deposition of Sir Gerald Aylmer, February/March 1538, SP 60/6 f. 51r, *LP* 13 i no. 471[3].   **25.** Deposition of Allen, February/March 1538, SP 60/6 f. 49r, *LP* 13 i no. 471[2].   **26.** Deposition of Aylmer, February/March 1538, SP 60/6 f. 51r, *LP* 13 i no. 471[3].   **27.** This is apparent in the fugitive Anthony Budgegood's attempt to provide a testimonial for them both to Cromwell, 26 September 1538, SP 1/137 f. 30, *LP* 13 ii no. 433. For William Paulet's holograph plea to Cromwell to show his brother mercy 'as you do to all others offending you', see Paulet to Cromwell, [14 May 1538], SP 1/132 f. 90, *LP* 13 i no. 999.   **28.** The central pieces of correspondence on Throckmorton's mission are Cromwell to the English ambassadors in France, 24 December [1536], BL MS Additional 25114 f. 237, *LP* 11 no. 1363, and Michael Throckmorton to Cromwell, 29 December [1536], SP 1/240 f. 242, *LP Addenda* 1 i no. 1156.   **29.** Michael Throckmorton to Richard Morison, ?15 February 1537, SP 1/116 f. 38v, *LP* 12 i no. 430 (this letter was presented in 1859 to the then Public Record Office by the notorious forger John Payne Collier, but comparison with other letters of Throckmorton confirms its authenticity). For Throckmorton's follow-up letter to Cromwell on 20 August 1537, acknowledging the hopelessness of the idea of Cromwell coming to Flanders, see BL MS Cotton Cleopatra E/VI ff. 386–8, *LP* 12 ii no. 552.   **30.** John Hutton to Cromwell, 26 May [1537], SP 1/120 ff. 205–7, *LP* 12 i no. 1293. The background to all this is meticulously set out in *Lisle Letters* 4, 220–25.   **31.** Michael Throckmorton to Cromwell, 20 August 1537, BL MS Cotton Cleopatra E/VI ff. 386–8, *LP* 12 ii no. 552; Cromwell to Throckmorton, late September 1537, SP 1/125 f. 71, *LP* 12 ii no. 795: an office copy in Stephen Vaughan's hand, perhaps for Hutton's benefit.   **32.** Privy Council to Duke of Norfolk, 7 April [1537], BL MS Harley 6989 f.

69v, *LP* 12 i no. 846; Duke of Norfolk to Henry VIII, 10 May [1537], SP 1/120 f. 26, *LP* 12 i no. 1172.   **33.** Rymer (ed.), *Foedera* 14, 588–9, *LP* 12 i no. 1232; SP 1/120 f. 140, *LP* 12 i no. 1233. The vice-gerential commission of 6 May 1537 to Thomas Bedell and Richard Gwent is BL MS Additional 48022 f. 95r.   **34.** Thomas Bedell to [Cromwell], 14 June [1537], BL MS Cotton Cleopatra E/IV f. 256, *LP* 12 ii no. 91.   **35.** John Husee to Lord Lisle, 29 June [1537], SP 3/5 f. 26, *Lisle Letters* 4 no. 973.   **36.** Hugh Latimer to Cromwell, 18 May [1538], SP 1/132 f. 106, *LP* 13 i no. 1024.   **37.** Chauncy, *Historia aliquot martyrum Anglorum*, 117: 'admodum aegre tulit, duriusque vexaturum se eos, si vixissent, cum magno juramento affirmabat.' Chauncy says nothing about death by starvation, but 'propter squalorem et foetorem carceris moriebantur': in other words, disease.   **38.** J. Clark (ed.), *The Various Versions of the Historia aliquot martyrum anglorum maxime octodecim Cartusianorum* ... (Analecta Cartusiana 86, 3 vols., Salzburg, 2006), 1, 11. For the surrender on 10 June 1537, see *LP* 12 ii no. 64.   **39.** For notes on these, with Cromwell and Richard Cromwell taking particular advantage of the trees and herbs, see the accounts from 24 November 1538 onwards, SP 1/139 ff. 148–9, *LP* 13 ii no. 903.   **40.** See Holmes, 'The last Tudor Great Councils', 10–16, and on Wolsey's legatine synod, Gwyn, *King's Cardinal*, 267–75.   **41.** For what follows on the vice-gerential synod where not otherwise referenced, see MacCulloch, *Thomas Cranmer*, 185–96.   **42.** A. Alane [Alesius], *Of the auctorite of the word of God agaynst the bisshop of London* ... (?Leipzig, ?1538, RSTC 292), especially sigs. A5–B8; there were later English printings at Strassburg. The work did indeed appear in an expanded version in Latin in 1542, with a formal preface to the Duke dated 1540: A. Alesius, *De Authoritate Verbi Dei* ... *contra Episcopum Lundensem* (Strassburg, 1542). There are anomalies in his account. Although he definitely states that the meeting took place in 1537 (by German and not English reckoning, therefore including February 1537 New Style), he speaks at *Of the auctorite* sig. B3r of Bishop Foxe as 'then new come out of Germany' (*De Authoritate* 26 is not quite so specific: 'nuperrime ex obita in Germaniam legatione redierat'), which might relate this whole incident to summer 1536, and therefore to some informal meeting while Parliament and Convocation were sitting. He also makes Cromwell refer in his speech more than once to an agreement 'by the consent of you and his whole Parliament' (sigs. A5v–A6r). Yet Alesius's reference to the summer 1536 Ten Articles as having previously forced him to leave Cambridge in protest means that the whole incident must have taken place in 1537.   **43.** This was said to be 'in the Parliament House' – in the longer Latin version Alesius is more explicit in calling this a 'sacrum senatum, qui Westmonasterii convenerat' ('holy assembly which [Cromwell] had convened at Westminster'): Alesius, *De Authoritate Verbi Dei*, 18.   **44.** Alane [Alesius], *Of the auctorite of the word of God*, sig. A5rv.   **45.** ?A. Alesius, *A treatise concernynge Generall Councilles, the Byshoppes of Rome and the Clergy* ... (London, 1538, RSTC 24237); MacCulloch, *Thomas Cranmer*, 193–4.   **46.** *The Institution of a Christen man, conteynynge the Exposytion* ... *of the commune Crede, of the seuen Sacramentes, of the .x. Commandementes* ... (London, 1537, RSTC 5164). For extended discussion, see MacCulloch, *Thomas Cranmer*, 191–3, 204–7.   **47.** MacCulloch, *Thomas*

Cranmer, 206–12.   **48.** Of the many works of Margaret Aston which have illumi-nated this question, the latest and most definitive is Aston, *Broken Idols of the English Reformation* (Cambridge, 2016), especially 552–9, but see also Aston, *England's Iconoclasts I: Laws against Images* (Oxford, 1988), ch. 7.   **49.** *Institution of a Christen man*, ff. 56v–58v. On Gwalther, see above, pp. 367–70.   **50.** Lease on 20 February, TNA, E 315/232 f. 45, *LP* 13 i no. 1520[ii], 574.   **51.** Rich-ard Southwell to Cromwell, 2 and 26 February 1537, SP 1/115 f. 171, *LP* 12 i no. 317, and SP 1/116 f. 126, *LP* 12 i no. 512.   **52.** *Institution of a Christen man*, f. 57v.   **53.** See Norfolk to Henry VIII, 10 May [1537], SP 1/120 f. 26, *LP* 12 i no. 1172, and his memorandum on Bridlington, 18 May 1537, SP 1/120 f. 235, *LP* 12 i no. 1307[2]; Cromwell's reply to him on 22 May [1537] outlining the King's response is SP 1/120 f. 165, *LP* 12 i no. 1257.   **54.** On this and what follows, see MacCulloch, *Thomas Cranmer*, 196–7.   **55.** For the slightly complex but con-vincing elucidation of this name, see N. Tyacke, 'Introduction', in Tyacke (ed.), *England's Long Reformation, 1500–1800* (London, 1998), 1–32, at 7–8, 28.   **56.** D. Daniell, *William Tyndale: a biography* (New Haven and London, 1994), 1.   **57.** A careful study is S. R. Westfall, *Patrons and Performance: early Tudor household revels* (Oxford, 1990), with a useful though not exhaustive list of patrons, Appendix D. She is however misled by the then current state of scholar-ship on John Bale to suppose that he received patronage from the fifteenth Earl of Oxford (d. 1540): see ibid., 118–19. This is intrinsically unlikely because there is no interval in Bale's career in the 1530s when the Earl could have provided such patronage. Bale himself speaks of patronage only from a John de Vere, Earl of Oxford; it is far more likely to be the sixteenth Earl, who succeeded just when Bale needed a new patron in 1540, who aroused Bishop Gardiner's ire through his play-ers disrupting the mourning for Henry VIII in 1547 and who initially supported Queen Jane Grey against Queen Mary. The length of Bale's exile abroad in the 1540s is not at all certain, but Oxford may have eased his return to England and provided employment before he took up a clerical post in Hampshire thanks to Bishop Ponet in 1551.   **58.** Thos. Wylley Vicar of Yoxford to Cromwell, ?Febru-ary 1537, SP 1/116 f. 157, *LP* 12 i no. 529. On 23 October 1544, still Vicar of Yoxford, he was dispensed to hold a second benefice (Chambers (ed.), *Faculty Office Registers*, 246), and is surely the Thomas Wyllye MA who became Vicar of Henlow that year on 25 November, though bizarrely he was then described as chaplain to Bishop Bonner and was presented on a grant from the late Llanthony Abbey.   **59.** John Leland to Cromwell, 25 January [1537], SP 1/115 f. 61, *LP* 12 i no. 230; for Bale's friendly letter of 1536 from Ipswich to Leland about antiquities, see Bodl. MS Jesus 74 f. 198v, printed in Leland, *Itinerary of John Leland*, ed. Toulmin Smith, 1, xi. On Bale in his Suffolk context, see MacCulloch, *Suffolk and the Tudors*, 143, 159–60.   **60.** Dickens, *Lollards and Protestants*, 140–43.   **61.** On this and what follows, S. B. House, 'Cromwell's message to the regulars: the biblical trilogy of John Bale, 1537', *Renaissance and Reformation/ Renaissance et Réforme* new series 15 (1991), 123–38. I find this a more convinc-ing analysis of the trilogy than E. Gerhardt, 'John Bale's adaptation of parish- and civic-drama's playing practices', *Reformation* 19 (2014), 6–20, though Gerhardt is correct in pointing out that a later performance of it was staged by Bale in Kilk-enny in 1553. The original context is clearly in 1537. **62.** *LP* 14 ii no. 782, at 333–4. **63.** For payments for the play, 8 September 1538, *LP* 14 ii no. 782, at 337, and further discussion of the context, MacCulloch, *Thomas Cranmer*, 226–8. On Hales's precocious acquisition, see Hales to Cromwell, late summer 1532, SP 1/82 f. 7, *LP* 7 no. 8; same to same, 29 September [1532], SP 1/71 f. 56, *LP* 5 no. 1354; same to same, 'Wednesday in Pentecost week' [4 June 1533], SP 1/92 f. 156, *LP* 8 no. 732 (wildly misdated by *LP* but redateable by its reference to the Duke of Norfolk's embassy to France). D. J. Shaw, 'Books belonging to William Warham, Archdeacon of Canterbury, C. 1504–1532', in D. E. Rhodes (ed.), *Bookbindings & Other Bibliophily: essays in honour of Anthony Hobson* (Verona, 1994), 277–86, at 277, cites a pedigree making the Archdeacon a son of the Archbishop's brother Nicholas. We have discussed this amicably, and I am still struck by the peculiarity of the Archdeacon's career, which might suggest that he was the Arch-bishop's illegitimate son. **64.** J. Bale, *A comedy concernynge thre lawes, of Nature[,] Moses, & Christ, corrupted by the sodomytes. Pharysees and Papystes* (Wesel, ?1547, *RSTC* 1287). The colophon at sig. G4r says explicitly that the play was 'compyled by Johan Bale. Anno M.D.XXXVIII, and lately inprented per Nicolaum Bamburgensem', implying a caesura between composition and publica-tion. The date of publication at Wesel is not at all certain, but it is likely to have been 1547, like Bale's other surviving plays. In the patently topically adjusted material at the end, the reader is exhorted at sig. G1r to 'praye for quene Kat-eryne [Parr], and the noble lorde protectour', which puts it in the time frame 1547–8. **65.** Bale, *Thre lawes*, sig. C4r. The reference to Hailes is the non-East Anglian exception proving the rule, since Hailes Abbey possessed the parish church of Haughley in Suffolk, with a subsidiary relic of the Holy Cross housed there and an object of pilgrimage. This particular scene assumes *inter alia* that the London Minoresses is as yet undissolved, which would have been the case in 1538, there is a sneering reference at sig. C3v to the consecration commemoration of the friary at Southampton, presumably the Austin Friars house dissolved on 6 October 1538 (*LP* 13 ii no. 545), and the whole ambience of the play is of a half-reformed Church appropriate to that era. The reference to 'Yngham Trynyte' is at sig. D2r. **66.** On Ipswich, see below, pp. 466–7, and for further context, Blatchly and MacCulloch, *Miracles in Lady Lane*, 53–6. **67.** For depositions on this of early January 1539, SP 1/142 f. 33, *LP* 14 i no. 47. **68.** John Clerk Bishop of Bath and Wells to Cromwell, BL MS Harley 283 f. 158, *LP* 12 ii no. 753; Canons Residen-tiary of Wells to Cromwell, 28 September [1537], SP 1/125 f. 50, *LP* 12 ii no. 768. **69.** On the prebend of Litton, see John Clerk Bishop of Bath and Wells to Cromwell, 13 September [1537], SP 1/124 f. 215, *LP* 12 ii no. 683, and Le Neve, *Fasti 1300–1541: Bath and Wells*, 55–6; *Fasti 1541–1857: Bath and Wells*, 72. William Wriothesley was deprived under Mary, presumably as married, by 22 May 1554. **70.** For summary discussion of lay deans and their significance in preserving cathedrals, anticipating a major theme in many of my writings, see D. MacCulloch, *The Later Reformation in England 1547–1603* (2nd edn, Hound-mills, 2001), 79–80.

Chapter 18: The King's Uncle? 1537–1538

1. The marriage had taken place by 16 January 1531, when they were jointly granted lands involved in the family transactions with Wolsey: *LP* 5 no. 80[14].   2. For Henry's career, see *HC 1558–1603* 3, 539–40.   3. See the note of it among many other patents in Cromwell's papers of 1532, *LP* 5 no. 1285, p. 557, and above, pp. 54, 303.   4. Sir Anthony Ughtred to Cromwell, 16 June [1533], SP 1/77 f. 46, *LP* 6 no. 659.   5. Lady Elizabeth Ughtred to Cromwell, 18 March [1537], SP 1/117 f. 36, *LP* 12 i no. 678. For Robert Southwell's noting 'a child of my Lady your daughter's' at Wilberfoss nunnery, see Southwell to Cromwell, 20 August 1537, SP 1/124 f. 73, *LP* 12 ii no. 549.   6. Sir Arthur Darcy and Sir Anthony Ughtred had been joint Stewards of the Forest of Galtres near York, and in October 1537 the office was regranted to Darcy along with that militant opponent of the Pilgrims William Maunsell: *LP* 12 ii no. 1008[27]. For Bigod mentioning 'my cousin Ughtred' (whom he expected Cromwell to be able to identify), see Bigod to Cromwell, late February 1537, SP 1/116 f. 163r, *LP* 12 i no. 533.   7. Roland Lee to Cromwell, 2 April [1537], SP 1/117 f. 232, *LP* 12 i no. 807; notably a holograph letter, unlike the accompanying letter to the King on the same subject: Lee to Henry VIII, same date, SP 1/117 f. 229, *LP* 12 i no. 806.   8. John Packington to Cromwell, 3 April [1537], SP 1/117 ff. 243–4, *LP* 12 i no. 821; Cromwell's 'remembrance' in late April 1537, *LP* 12 i no. 973; Roland Lee to Cromwell (with a notably more formal address than usual!), 5 May [1537], SP 1/119 ff. 175–6, *LP* 12 i no. 1139.   9. Arthur Darcy to Lady Ughtred, 15 June [1537], SP 1/121 f. 128, *LP* 12 ii no. 97. Oxford, whose ancient family seat was Hedingham Castle, was described in Anthony Budgegood's account of the peerage a year and a half later as sixty-six years old and 'a man of great power and little experience': *LP* 13 ii no. 732. His son and heir Lord Bulbeck was already married by this date.   10. Cromwell's accounts, 24 and 25 June 1537, *LP* 14 ii no. 782, at 330; John Husee to Lord Lisle, 17 July [1537], SP 3/5 f. 117, *Lisle Letters* 4 no. 981.   11. Lady Ughtred to Cromwell, n.d., SP 1/125 ff. 145–6, *LP* 12 ii no. 881. For the juncture, see below, pp. 482–6.   12. On Elizabeth's letter to the King in 1540, see below, pp. 538–9. Cromwell's accounts have payments on 1 March 1538 'for Master Richard's nurse and midwife, by Master Gregory, at the christening', then on 11 and 12 April things Lady Ughtred 'needed at her lying down', and for stuff being taken from Stepney to Lewes for her at the same time: *LP* 14 ii no. 782, at 334–5.   13. John Husee to Lord Lisle, 3 August [1537], SP 3/5 f. 109, *Lisle Letters* 4 no. 992; Husee to Lady Lisle, same day, SP 3/11 f. 132, *Lisle Letters* 4 no. 891.   14. For Cromwell at Sunninghill on 1 August, see Cromwell's letter of that day to the Irish commissioners, SP 60/5 f. 1, *LP* 12 ii no. 414, and for his plan to lodge at Guildford after that, Sir William Fitzwilliam to Cromwell, 1 August [1537], SP 1/123 f. 175, *LP* 12 ii no. 415; for his staying at Sir Richard Weston's house near Guildford on 2 August, referenced in Sir Roger Cholmley's letter to him, 26 August [1537], SP 1/124 f. 107, *LP* 12 ii no. 583, to be compared with a reference in Cromwell's accounts to a payment to a servant of Lady Weston's on 2

August, *LP* 14 ii no. 782, at 330 (where the payments at Mortlake on Gregory's wedding day may also be seen).   **15.** Nicholas Wilson to Thomas Wriothesley, 3 August [1537], TNA, SP 7/1 f. 87, *LP* 12 ii no. 425. Cromwell's staff were making payments at Windsor on 5 August: *LP* 14 ii no. 782, at 330.   **16.** Anstis (ed.), *Register of the most noble Order of the Garter*, 2, 407–9.   **17.** For various family payments around Mortlake in early September, see *LP* 14 ii no. 782, at 331.   **18.** Edward Lord Beauchamp to Cromwell, 2 September [1537], SP 1/124 f. 159, *LP* 12 ii no. 629.   **19.** Foxe 1563, 667, and for an overview of him, *HC 1509–1558* 2, 80–81. For examples of his relaxation with Cromwell apart from Beauchamp's letter, see Thomas Edgar to Cromwell, 18 August [1536], SP 1/106 ff. 20–21, *LP* 11 no. 324, and Thomas Thacker to Cromwell, 18 August [1538], SP 1/135 f. 113, *LP* 13 ii no. 125; Edgar is associated with Edward Seymour's uncle Robert in New Year's gifts to the King in 1540: *LP* 16 no. 380, at 179.   **20.** Christopher Barker, Garter, to Cromwell, 19 July [1537], SP 1/123 f. 21, *LP* 12 ii no. 286.   **21.** Its full heraldic description is *Per fesse azure and or, a pale counterchanged, charged alternately with fleurs de lys of the second, and pelicans with wings elevated vulning themselves gules.*   **22.** MacCulloch, *Thomas Cranmer*, 13–15.   **23.** I am very grateful to Jeremy Goldsmith for sending me in the right direction to make these deductions.   **24.** Thomas Earl of Wiltshire to Cromwell, 25 August 1537, BL MS Cotton Vespasian F/XIII f. 182, *LP* 12 ii no. 580; Anstis (ed.), *Register of the most noble Order of the Garter*, 2, 407–9. For Cromwell's expenses at Windsor around the ceremony on 26 August, see *LP* 14 ii no. 782, at 331.   **25.** John Husee to [Lord Lisle], 21 August 1537, SP 3/5 f. 62v, *Lisle Letters* 4 no. 1001, 382. Norfolk wrote to Cromwell on 27 August from Sheriff Hutton, having returned there the day before the Garter installation: SP 1/124 f. 113, *LP* 12 ii no. 588.   **26.** 'The saying of Robert Aske to me, Richard Corwen, out of confession to-for his death', 20 July [1537], *State Papers* 1, 558, *LP* 12 ii no. 292 [iii].   **27.** For Norfolk's presence at Grafton on 15 August (the feast of the Assumption), Duke of Norfolk to James V of Scotland, 27 August [1537], SP 1/124 f. 117, *LP* 12 ii no. 589; for Cromwell at Grafton that day, see his accounts, *LP* 14 ii no. 782, at 331.   **28.** Duke of Norfolk to Cromwell, 3 August [1537], SP 1/123 ff. 190–91, *LP* 12 ii no. 430; same to same, 8 August [1537], SP 1/124 f. 1v, *LP* 12 ii no. 479.   **29.** On the previous friction, see above, p. 179. For an overview of Brandon's part in dealing with the Lincolnshire Rising, see Gunn, *Charles Brandon, Duke of Suffolk*, 142–52.   **30.** Duke of Suffolk to Cromwell, 26 May [1537], SP 1/120 f. 198, *LP* 12 i no. 1284. On these early moves in the transfer, see also Gunn, *Charles Brandon, Duke of Suffolk*, 152–6, 167, and MacCulloch, *Suffolk and the Tudors*, 66–7.   **31.** Gunn, *Charles Brandon, Duke of Suffolk*, 168–74, and MacCulloch, *Suffolk and the Tudors*, 67–71.   **32.** Parts of the story which I tell here and in the following chapters on Gregory Cromwell, Sussex and Kent were spotted by Mary Robertson: 'Profit and purpose in the development of Thomas Cromwell's landed estates', *Journal of British Studies* 29 (1990), 317–46.   **33.** On the demesne prohibition, Robert Peterson Prior of Lewes to Cromwell, 2 August [1536], SP 1/105 f. 235, *LP* 11 no. 214, and same to same, 7 October [1536], SP 1/107 f. 59, *LP* 11 no. 583; for Leighton's transactions with Lewes,

Richard Leighton to Cromwell, [16 August and early October 1535], SP 1/95 f. 38, *LP* 9 no. 42, and SP 1/98 f. 22, *LP* 9 no. 632. For general discussion of Lewes Priory and Castle and Castle Acre Priory, see *VCH: Sussex* 2, 64–71 and 7, 19–31; *VCH: Norfolk* 2, 356–8.   **34.** Duke of Norfolk to Cromwell, 4 November [1537], SP 1/126 f. 58, *LP* 12 ii no. 1030.   **35.** Duke of Norfolk to Cromwell, 25 March [1538], SP 1/130 f. 126, *LP* 13 i no. 593; confirmation of estate to Cromwell and alienation licence, 4 July 1538, *LP* 13 i no. 1519[5], and Blomefield and Parkin, *Topographical History of the County of Norfolk*, 9, 489. For the previous and future transactions around this property, see above, pp. 355–6, and below, p. 484.   **36.** The grant went through on 1 October 1537: *LP* 12 ii no. 1008[3]. J. Youings, *The Dissolution of the Monasteries* (London, 1971), 65, began to glimpse the significance of all these relationships.   **37.** The earliest paperwork for this transaction just predates what remains for Lewes and Michelham, beginning with bonds from Wriothesley on 20 September 1537: see a note of various bonds, SP 1/127 f. 121, *LP* 12 ii no. 1275.   **38.** On the 1539 election, see below, pp. 497–8. John White to Wriothesley, 26 December [1537] ('at night'), TNA, SP 7/1 no. 85, *LP* 12 ii no. 1270. *LP* wrongly reads 'my Lord' for 'Our Lord' in this passage. For obvious reasons this John White needs to be distinguished from the Surrey man who was Bishop Gardiner's client, headmaster of Winchester College and himself future Bishop of Winchester.   **39.** On Salisbury at Oxford, see Foxe 1563, 666. For his appointment by Cromwell to Horsham in 1534, see Thomas Lee to Cromwell, 19 November [1535], SP 1/99 f. 60, *LP* 9 no. 849, and John Salisbury Prior of St Faith to Cromwell, 21 November [1535], SP 1/99 f. 69, *LP* 9 no. 865.   **40.** Sir John Gage to Cromwell, 20 April [1537], SP 1/241 f. 59, *LP Addenda* 1 i no. 1217.   **41.** Emden, *Oxford 1501 to 1540*, 672.   **42.** For excellent comment on the conveyancing problem and its consequences, see Youings, *Dissolution of the Monasteries*, 82–3; for Audley's doubts, see Audley to Cromwell, 1 and ?2 January 1538, BL MS Cotton Cleopatra E/IV f. 228, *LP* 12 ii no. 1153, and BL MS Cotton Cleopatra E/IV ff. 225–6, *LP* 12 ii no. 1159.   **43.** Norfolk to Cromwell, probably 11 November 1537, SP 1/127 f. 203, *LP* 12 ii Appendix no. 45.   **44.** For negotiations and meetings with the Duke, Henry Polstead to Cromwell, 12 November [1537], BL MS Cotton Cleopatra E/IV f. 279, *LP* 12 ii no. 1062; for the surrender of Lewes with Castle Acre on 16 November 1537, *LP* 12 ii no. 1101; for the pensions to monks and staff, SP 1/126 ff. 135–8, *LP* 12 ii no. 1101[2].   **45.** I am most grateful to Steven Gunn for pointing this latter case out: see Gunn, *Charles Brandon, Duke of Suffolk*, 156, 160.   **46.** For the process of pensioning or providing alternatives in preferment at work at Titchfield, see John Crayford and others to Wriothesley, 2 January [1538], TNA, SP 7/1 f. 13, *LP* 13 i no. 20. For discussion of the mechanics of the surrenders at Lewes and Titchfield, see Youings, *Dissolution of the Monasteries*, 62, 65–6, 73, 81–3, though she did not appreciate the wider political significance of these transactions.   **47.** *LP* 14 i no. 1355[I], 593, from TNA, E 315/252 II f. 32 (25 May 1538).   **48.** On Bridlington, see above, pp. 415–16. On Thetford and Castle Acre, D. Dymond (ed.), *The Register of Thetford Priory II: 1518–1540* (Norfolk Record Society, 60, 1996), 745–6, and MacCulloch, 'A Reformation in the balance', 105–6.   **49.** Queen Jane's letter to Cromwell as her High Steward, 12 October [1537], is BL MS Cotton Nero

C/X f. 1, *LP* 12 ii no. 889, which lists similar letters to other recipients. Receipt of the letter and consequent payments are recorded in Cromwell's accounts, *LP* 14 ii no. 782, at 332. Sadler had also let him know about the King's permission to him to use St James and the Neat interchangeably for lodging because of plague round The Rolls: Ralph Sadler to Cromwell, early October 1537, SP 1/127 f. 202, *LP* 12 ii Appendix no. 44. **50.** John Husee to Lord Lisle, 16 October [1537], SP 3/5 f. 91, *Lisle Letters* 4 no. 1024; Sir Thomas Palmer to Lord Lisle, same date, SP 3/6 f. 112, *Lisle Letters* 4 no. 1025. See also a detailed account of the christening, *LP* 12 ii no. 911, from BL Additional MS 6113 f. 81. **51.** The depositions are SP 1/125 ff. 200–206, *LP* 12 ii no. 952, and SP 1/113 f. 60v, *LP* 11 no. 1406. For illuminating discussion, see Marshall, 'George Throckmorton and Henry Tudor', 49–52. **52.** An account of the creation on 18 October is *LP* 12 ii no. 939, from BL MS Additional 6113 f. 87. **53.** Oxfordshire commission, *LP* 12 ii no. 157; Derbyshire: *LP* 12 ii no. 1008[43]; royal alienation licence for his Oxfordshire purchases of Standlake and Broughton Castle from the Earl of Huntingdon, 20 October 1537, *LP* 12 ii no. 1008[26]. **54.** For the first commissions placing him in every county, in November 1537, see *LP* 12 ii no. 1150, and for examples of exempt ecclesiastical jurisdictions, see *LP* 13 i no. 384[22] (4 February 1538: Archbishop of York's Liberty of Ripon, Yorkshire), *LP* 14 i no. 1354[1] (1 July 1539: Bishop of Durham's Liberty of Durham and Sedbergh), *LP* 14 i no. 1354[21] (4 July 1539: Liberty of the Abbot of St Albans). **55.** Duke of Norfolk to Cromwell, [24 October 1537], SP 1/126 f. 4, *LP* 12 ii no. 971. **56.** See the account at *LP* 12 ii no. 1060, from London, College of Heralds MS I 11 f. 37. **57.** Duke of Norfolk to Cromwell, 4 November [1537], SP 1/126 f. 58, *LP* 12 ii no. 1030. **58.** Earl of Hertford to Cromwell, [1 November 1537], SP 1/126 f. 48, *LP* 12 ii no. 1013. **59.** Cuthbert Tunstall Bishop of Durham to [Cromwell], 13 November [1537], SP 1/126 f. 118v, *LP* 12 ii no. 1077. **60.** John Husee to Lord Lisle, 14 December [1537], SP 1/127 f. 49, *Lisle Letters* 4 no. 1038. **61.** John Milsent to Henry Polstead, 12 December [1537], SP 1/241 f. 245, *LP Addenda* 1 i no. 1274. **62.** John Crayford and Roland Lathum to Thomas Wriothesley, 2 January [1538], SP 1/128 ff. 18–21, *LP* 13 i no. 19 (partly printed in Youings, *Dissolution of the Monasteries*, 246–8, with a plan of what Wriothesley did to the buildings), and John Husee to Lord Lisle, 3 January [1538], SP 1/128 f. 23, *Lisle Letters* 5 no. 1086. **63.** Examination of Geo. Croftes, *c.* 14 November 1538, SP 1/139 f. 17r, *LP* 13 ii no. 828. Their visit would probably have been while Cromwell was with the King on progress in summer 1538: see *LP* 14 ii no. 782, at 337. **64.** Giovanni Portinari to Cromwell, 20 and 24 March 1538, SP 1/130 f. 93, *LP* 13 i no. 554, and SP 1/130 f. 124, *LP* 13 i no. 590. **65.** Cromwell wrote from Hampton Court to Thomas Wyatt on 1 March [1538], BL MS Harley 282 f. 175, *LP* 13 i no. 387. On the same day there are payments in Cromwell's accounts to 'Master Richard's nurse and midwife, by Master Gregory, at the christening'; on 4 March to Robin Drum and his fellows 'for their waiting two nights the same time my Lord made the King a masque', and 'John Portynare, for the charges of the mask': *LP* 14 ii no. 782, at 334. **66.** Madden (ed.), *Privy purse expenses of the Princess Mary*, 66–7, 69; it is also interesting that the baby was referred to as 'Lady Ughtred's child', reinforcing the mother's formal social superiority over her husband.

I am very grateful to Teri Fitzgerald for drawing my attention to this material.   67. Gregory Cromwell and Sir John Gage to Cromwell, 19 March [1538], SP 1/130 f. 89, *LP* 13 i no. 549. This letter can only be of 1538, since Gregory had quit Sussex by March 1539.   68. Gregory Cromwell to Cromwell, 11 April [1538], SP 1/131 f. 62, *LP* 13 i no. 734.   69. Henry Polstead proposed to 'wait' on Cromwell while he was at Sheffield, 16 August 1538, SP 1/135 f. 95, *LP* 13 ii no. 106, and John Williamson's expenditure on works at Sheffield during Cromwell's stay in late August, *LP* 14 ii no. 782, at 337.   70. Gregory Cromwell to Cromwell, 16 April 1538, SP 1/131 ff. 110–11, *LP* 13 i no. 786[1, 2]. Compare Bishop Longland's complaint in May 1536 about an outbreak of such attempts 'to dig for money': John Longland Bishop of Lincoln to Cromwell, SP 1/103 f. 331, *LP* 10 no. 804.

Chapter 19: Cutting Down Trees: 1538

1. W. Bulleine, *A dialogue both pleasant and piety-full, against the fever pestilence* (London, 1564, *RSTC* 4036), f. 61r (I am indebted to Spencer Weinreich for drawing this to my attention).   2. 'il a chanté une chanson à mon milord Privé Séel, disant qu'il estoit bon pour le mesnaige, mais non pour entremettre des affaires des roys': Castillon to Constable de Montmorency, 14 May [1538], Kaulek (ed.), *Correspondance*, 50, *LP* 13 i no. 995.   3. 'super deliberatione, hospitem an popularem duceret': J. G. Nichols, 'Some additions to the biographies of Sir John Cheke and Sir Thomas Smith . . .', *Archaeologia* 38 (1860), 98–127, at 117, from BL MS Additional 325 f. 2.   4. Bodl. MS Jesus College 74 f. 299rv. This story forms part of a reminiscence involving Katherine Howard in friendly conversation with the Archbishop at the time of the annulment of Henry's marriage to Anne of Cleves in 1540, but actually the conversation between Cromwell and Cranmer which it recalls does not necessarily relate directly to Katherine. It is certainly of 1539 rather than 1538, as will be demonstrated below (pp. 494–5).   5. For what follows where not otherwise referenced, Scarisbrick, *Henry VIII*, 355–62, is an entertainingly sardonic guide.   6. Chapuys and Diego de Mendoza to Charles V, 31 August 1538, *Spanish Calendar* 6 i no. 7, at 26–7.   7. Castillon to de Montmorency, 30 December 1538, G. Ribier (ed.), *Lettres et mémoires d'estat . . . sous les règnes de François premier, Henry II. et François II.* (2 vols., Paris, 1666), 1, 341–4, *LP* 13 ii no. 1162.   8. Castillon to François I, 14 February 1538, Kaulek (ed.), *Correspondance*, 24, *LP* 13 i no. 273; Cromwell to Thomas Wyatt (English ambassador to the Emperor), 11 February [1538], Merriman 2 no. 238, *LP* 13 i no. 255.   9. Castillon to Constable de Montmorency, 14 May [1538], Kaulek (ed.), *Correspondance*, 50 (my translation), *LP* 13 i no. 995.   10. Richard Cromwell to Cromwell, [17 May 1538], SP 1/132 f. 100, *LP* 13 i no. 1015.   11. Butterworth and Chester, *George Joye*, 233; Rupp, *Studies in the Making of the English Protestant Tradition*, 103.   12. John Husee to Lord Lisle, 8 May [1538], SP 1/132 f. 50, *Lisle Letters* 5 no. 1158 and commentary; on the supervisorship, John Frere to [Cromwell], ?November 1538, SP 1/141 f. 142, *LP* 13 ii no. 1239.   13. John Husee to Lord Lisle, 18 May [1538], SP 3/4 f. 35, *Lisle Letters* 5 no. 1164. Havering-atte-Bower

was a royal manor in south Essex. **14.** William Earl of Southampton to Lord Lisle, 20 May [1538], SP 3/7 f. 176, *Lisle Letters* 5 no. 1167. See Cromwell's accounts for May and June, *LP* 14 ii no. 782, at 335. On Cromwell seeking wrestlers from Godolphin as early as a proposed royal visit to Calais in 1534, see Sir William Godolphin to Cromwell, 14 June and 12 July [1534], SP 1/70 f. 113, *LP* 5 no. 1093, and SP 1/70 f. 157, *LP* 5 no. 1168, both misdated to 1532 by *LP*. **15.** Castillon to François I, 31 May 1538, Kaulek (ed.), *Correspondance*, 52, *LP* 13 i no. 1101: 'j'entendz aussi que son maistre luy avoit chanté quelque chanson.' **16.** For what follows unless otherwise referenced, McEntegart, *Henry VIII, the League of Schmalkalden and the English Reformation*, 77–130. **17.** Ibid., 85: 'mit demselben konig in disen sachen nit zuschertzen ist' (I have slightly modified the translation). **18.** Ibid., 89–94. **19.** Ibid., 98–9. **20.** Ibid., 101–3; Cornelius Scepperus to Charles V, August 1538, and Chapuys and Diego de Mendoza to Charles V, 31 August 1538, *Spanish Calendar* 6 i nos. 4 and 7, at 13 and 31. **21.** Brigden, *Thomas Wyatt*, 385–96. **22.** Cromwell to Simon Haynes and Edmund Bonner, 8 June 1538, SP 1/133 f. 4, *LP* 13 i no. 1146. On Cranmer's opinion of the lodgings, Cranmer to Cromwell, 23 August [1538], BL MS Cotton Cleopatra E/V f. 225, *LP* 13 ii no. 164. The envoys themselves, at least in communication back home, expressed themselves perfectly happy: McEntegart, *Henry VIII, the League of Schmalkalden and the English Reformation*, 96–7. **23.** Castillon, to François I, 18 July [1538], Kaulek (ed.), *Correspondance*, 70, *LP* 13 i no. 1405; on Cromwell's house see Colvin (ed.), *History of the King's Works* 4, 64. **24.** McEntegart, *Henry VIII, the League of Schmalkalden and the English Reformation*, 102–4; see also MacCulloch, *Thomas Cranmer*, 216–21. **25.** For further discussion of Henry and the middle way, see MacCulloch, *Thomas Cranmer*, 183, 265, 275, 335, 348. **26.** On the beginnings of Calais conflict between Cranmer and Lisle, see MacCulloch, *Thomas Cranmer*, 111–13; for subsequent clashes, ibid., 140–42, 198, 204–5, 218–19, 247–8, 255–6, 262 **27.** Sir Thos. Palmer to Lord Lisle, 7 September 1537, SP 3/14 ff. 89–90, *Lisle Letters* 4 no. 1011; *Lisle Letters* following *LP* has a rare mistranscription of 'lokyd thorow out our fyngers' as 'lacked throughout our fiances', which of course makes no sense. Palmer's hand is unusually idiosyncratic. Cromwell to Lord Lisle, 7 September [1537], SP 3/2 f. 171, *Lisle Letters* 4 no. 1010. For background, see *Lisle Letters* 4, 347–51. **28.** On Damplip and Cranmer, see MacCulloch, *Thomas Cranmer*, 182, 218–19, and for a careful narrative of the Damplip affair itself, A. J. Slavin, 'Cromwell, Cranmer and Lord Lisle: a study in the politics of reform', *Albion* 9 (1977), 316–36, from 325 onwards. **29.** Cromwell to Lord Lisle, 14 August [1538], Bodl. MS Jesus College 74 f. 198v; Master misjudged the year. **30.** Cranmer to Cromwell, 18 August [1538], SP 1/135 f. 117, *LP* 13 ii no. 217. For Cromwell at Cowdray on 8 August and Arundel on 17 and 18 August, see John Tregonwell to Cromwell, 11 August [1538], SP 1/135 f. 61, *LP* 13 ii no. 74, Sir Robt. Wingfield to Cromwell, 21 August 1538, SP 1/135 f. 137, *LP* 13 ii no. 151, and Robert Rugge and Robert Palmer to Cromwell, 22 August [1538], SP 1/135 f. 138, *LP* 13 ii no. 154. **31.** SP 1/136 ff. 21–5, *LP* 13 ii no. 248. **32.** Cranmer to Cromwell, 18 August [1538], SP 1/135 f. 115, *LP* 13 ii no. 126. **33.** The royal letter appointing Holgate in

Tunstall's place survives in an undated draft by Wriothesley: SP 1/133 ff. 206–9, *LP* 13 i no. 1268. Tunstall's letter to Cromwell acknowledging the summons south was written from Newcastle upon Tyne on 27 June 1538: SP 1/133 f. 204, *LP* 13 i no. 1267.   34. J. Bale, *The Epistle Exhortatorye of an Englyshe Christyane* . . . (Antwerp, ?1544, *RSTC* 1291a), f. 14r; MacCulloch, *Thomas Cranmer*, 219–20.   35. Confession of Lancelot Thornton [end of 1539], SP 1/155 f. 164r, *LP* 14 ii no. 750[3].   36. McEntegart, *Henry VIII, the League of Schmalkalden and the English Reformation*, 115–33.   37. *Wriothesley's Chronicle* 1, 74, speaks of this meeting as at the end of Hilary Term, which would be 22 February 1538. The instruction to the clergy which they would have taken away must be BL MS Cotton Cleopatra E/V f. 344, printed in Strype, *Memorials . . . of . . . Thomas Cranmer*, ed. Barnes, 289–90.   38. P. Marshall, 'The Rood of Boxley, the Blood of Hailes and the defence of the Henrician Church', *JEH* 46 (1995), 689–96.   39. John Husee to Lady Lisle, 22 March [1538], SP 3/12 f. 90, *Lisle Letters* 5 no. 1131; will of Joan Jesope of Flixton by Bungay, made 31 May 1538, proved 27 April 1541, Suffolk Record Office (Ipswich), Archdeaconry of Ipswich Wills, IC/AA2/14/18 (I owe this reference to the late Peter Northeast).   40. Examination of malefactors by Gregory Cromwell, 16 April 1538, SP 1/131 f. 111r, *LP* 13 i no. 786[2]. The significantly named Golden Cross is still a place-name in the parish of Laughton named in the deposition. Willingdon may alternatively be the nearby village of Wilmington.   41. A generally accurate though angry overview is provided by Knowles, *Religious Orders in England III*, 360–66; on decay of popular support in the Irish Pale and Englishry, George Browne Archbishop of Dublin to Cromwell, 6 November [1538], SP 60/7 f. 155, *LP* 13 ii no. 769, and Bradshaw, *Dissolution of the Religious Orders in Ireland under Henry VIII*, 140–45.   42. Sir Roger Townshend, Sir William Paston, Richard Southwell and Thomas Mildmay to Cromwell, 10 August [1536], SP 1/105 f. 274, *LP* 11 no. 261.   43. Ingworth to Cromwell, BL MS Cotton Cleopatra E/IV f. 302, *LP* 13 i no. 1484[1].   44. Thomas Chapman Warden of the London Greyfriars to Cromwell, early April 1538, SP 1/131 f. 195, *LP* 13 i no. 880.   45. Lambeth Palace, Cranmer's Register f. 16r, *LP* 13 i no. 225.   46. Thomas Lord Wentworth to Cromwell, 1 April [1538], SP 1/130 f. 239, *LP* 13 i no. 651.   47. Ingworth to Cromwell, undated but first week of April 1538, SP 1/131 f. 190, *LP* 13 i no. 874.   48. William Laurence to Cromwell, ?8 April 1538, SP 1/242 f. 3, *LP Addenda* 1 ii no. 1312.   49. SP 1/141 ff. 225–6, *LP* 13 ii Appendix no. 16: one of two inventories made by Ingworth alongside *LP* 13 i no. 699. Laurence does not seem to be referring to capacities to hold secular benefices, which would later become the norm at surrenders of friaries.   50. TNA, SP 5/4 f. 126v.   51. Petition by Carmelites of Ipswich to Cromwell, ?April 1538, SP 1/141 f. 227, *LP* 13 ii Appendix no. 17.   52. See above, pp. 111–12, and William Laurence to Cromwell, ?8 April 1538, SP 1/242 f. 3, *LP Addenda* 1 ii no. 1312: there is a material misreading in the *LP* summary, which has read 'priests' for 'parishioners' in regard to St Peter's.   53. Robert Lord Curzon to Cromwell, 20 December [1532], SP 1/72 f. 145, *LP* 5 no. 1650. For background and context especially on the Curzons, see Blatchly and MacCulloch, *Miracles in Lady Lane*, 63–5.   54. Lambeth Palace, Cranmer's Register f. 16v, *LP* 13 i no. 926.   55. Ingworth to Cromwell,

23 May [1538], BL MS Cotton Cleopatra E/IV f. 301, *LP* 13 i no. 1052.   **56.** Lee to Cromwell, 16 June [1538], SP 1/133 f. 48, *LP* 13 i no. 1197; same to same, 21 June [1538], SP 1/133 f. 157, *LP* 13 i no. 1231. For the injunctions, see W. H. Frere with W. M. Kennedy (eds.), *Visitation Articles and Injunctions of the Period of the Reformation II: 1536–1558* (Alcuin Club 15, 1910), 19–24.   **57.** For what follows where not otherwise referenced, see P. Marshall, 'Papist as heretic: the burning of John Forest, 1538', *HJ* 41 (1998), 351–74. See also A. Dillon, 'John Forest and Derfel Gadarn: a double execution', *Recusant History* 28 (2006), 1–21.   **58.** Ellis ap Rhys to Cromwell, 6 April [1538], BL MS Cotton Cleopatra E/IV f. 72, *LP* 13 i no. 694; same to same, SP 1/131 f. 182, *LP* 13 i no. 863, and to Thomas Wriothesley, SP 7/1 f. 1, *LP* 13 i no. 864, both 28 April [1538].   **59.** Hall 2, 280–82. On Grey's ballad, Aston, *England's Iconoclasts I*, 429–30; the ballad does not survive in an original printing, but was reprinted in Foxe 1563, 655–6, then omitted from subsequent editions. On Grey, see R. Rex, 'The friars in the English Reformation', in Marshall and Ryrie (eds.), *Beginnings of English Protestantism*, 38–59, at 51–2.   **60.** On Latimer's conversion of friars, see Rex, 'Friars in the English Reformation', 46–7. Anthony Anthony supplies the theme of Latimer's sermon 'that we should not worship idols': Bodl. MS Ashmole 861 335.   **61.** Brigden, *London and the Reformation*, 290–91.   **62.** [Anon.], *Jack vp Lande compyled by the famous Geoffrey Chaucer* (Southwark, ?1538, *RSTC* 5098): it is important to realize against Paisey and Bartrum, 'Hans Holbein and Miles Coverdale', 249, that this is very specifically an attack on the friars and not on monasticism in general, which places it in 1538.   **63.** Euler, 'Religious and cultural exchange during the Reformation', 237–9.   **64.** Foxe 1583, 1212 (where Reyner Wolfe's name is garbled as 'Rheine'), an extended version of a reference to this story in Foxe 1570, 1398. For reference to Barclay's intransigence about his habit at the time of the order in 1538, see *Wriothesley's Chronicle* 1, 82. For good background on Barclay's career till then, see N. Orme in *ODNB*, s.v. Barclay, Alexander, and for the sequel, MacCulloch, *Thomas Cranmer*, 495–6.   **65.** John London to Cromwell, 7 July [1538], SP 1/134 ff. 114–15, *LP* 13 i no. 1335.   **66.** Master and Fellows of Queens' College Cambridge to Cromwell, 8 August [1538], BL MS Cotton Faustina C/VII f. 104, *LP* 11 no. 246 (where it is misdated to 1536); all the subsequent documentation is printed in W. G. Searle, *The History of the Queens' College of St Margaret and St Bernard in the University of Cambridge . . .* (2 vols., Cambridge, 1867–71), 1, 222–6 (I am grateful to Mark Earngey for alerting me to this material).   **67.** Ingworth to Cromwell, [both 25 July 1538], SP 1/134 f. 241, *LP* 13 i no. 1456, and SP 1/134 f. 243, *LP* 13 i no. 1457.   **68.** Ingworth to Cromwell, [28 July 1538], BL MS Cotton Cleopatra E/IV f. 302, *LP* 13 i no. 1484.   **69.** *LP* 13 ii no. 56.   **70.** Chambers (ed.), *Faculty Office Registers*, 162–5.   **71.** Ingworth to Cromwell, ?10 December 1538, SP 1/140 f. 73, *LP* 13 ii no. 1021; Chambers (ed.), *Faculty Office Registers*, 166 (20 November 1538); note of grant 7 February 1540, to be void if Ingworth advanced to benefices worth £100, *LP* 15 no. 1032, 542.   **72.** See Holgate's surrender of Sempringham, *LP* 13 ii no. 411, of Watton, 9 December 1539, *LP* 14 ii no. 663, and of Malton, 11 December 1539, *LP* 14 ii no. 671. For his grant of Malton, 26 June 1540, *LP* 15 no. 831[73], and of Watton and the London house, *LP* 16 no. 1550,

715.   73. Richard Vowell Prior of Walsingham to Cromwell, 14 July [1538], SP 1/134 f. 161, *LP* 13 i no. 1376; John Husee to Lord Lisle, 18 July [1538], SP 3/4 f. 44, *Lisle Letters* 5 no. 1193.   74. William Laurence to Cromwell, ?28–29 July 1538, SP 1/242 f. 5, *LP Addenda* 1 ii no. 1313; Thomas Thacker to Cromwell, 30 July [1538], SP 1/134 f. 290, *LP* 13 i no. 1501; on the reuse of materials at St Nicholas Ipswich, see Blatchly and MacCulloch, *Miracles in Lady Lane*, 58–63.   75. Thomas Thacker to Cromwell, 1 September [1538], SP 1/136 f. 29, *LP* 13 ii no. 256; William Lord Sandys to Thomas Thacker, 1 September [1538], SP 1/136 f. 33, *LP* 13 ii no. 259.   76. *Wriothesley's Chronicle* 1, 83, is the source for the Chelsea burning, but the ambiguity of its phrasing might be (and has been) taken to mean that the burning took place in July 1538. It is evident from Cromwell's correspondence that the images survived till September.   77. John Taverner to Cromwell, 11 September [1538], SP 1/136 f. 105, *LP* 13 ii no. 328; the actual burning was on 7 September.   78. Walter (ed.), *Expositions ... together with The Practice of Prelates*, 292.   79. On the anti-taxation theme, Fletcher and MacCulloch, *Tudor Rebellions*, 18, also, on pardoners and the theme, the petition of William Umpton, *c.* September 1532, SP 1/71 f. 2, *LP* 5 no. 1271, and Robert Ward to Cromwell, early summer 1535, SP 1/92 f. 108, *LP* 8 no. 626. For what follows where not otherwise referenced, see MacCulloch, *Thomas Cranmer*, 226–30.   80. For comments, see John Husee to Lady Lisle, 8 September [1538], SP 3/12 f. 81, *Lisle Letters* 5 no. 1217; same to same, 10 September [1538], SP 3/12 f. 13, *Lisle Letters* 5 no. 1218; John Husee to Lord Lisle, 5 October 1538, SP 1/137 f. 105, *Lisle Letters* 5 no. 1244.   81. For the admission of the burning of a supposed skull of Becket at Canterbury in suppressing the shrine, see SP 1/143 f. 204rv, *LP* 14 i no. 402; I discuss this pamphlet further below, pp. 487–8.   82. This is apparent from the record of them in Lambeth Palace, Cranmer's Register f. 101r, where they are related to that *sede vacante* visitation; note the visitation business at ff. 89v–92r. Less certain is the reference in Bishop Veysey's injunctions at Exeter in spring 1538 to vice-gerential injunctions lately given by Dr John Tregonwell: *LP* 13 i no. 1106.   83. R. Hutton, 'The local impact of the Tudor Reformations', in C. Haigh (ed.), *The English Reformation Revised* (Cambridge, 1987), 114–38, at 117–18.   84. See the schemes of bishoprics of April/May 1540, SP 1/243 f. 42r, *LP Addenda* 1 ii no. 1457.   85. Francis Cave to Cromwell, 29 August [1538], BL MS Cotton Cleopatra E/IV f. 252, *LP* 13 ii no. 211. Rather remarkably, in the following month, when Cromwell was at Burton in Sussex in the middle of important developing revelations in the White Rose conspiracy, he took the trouble to intervene personally in a trivial lease dispute long festering on a Leicester Abbey estate: cf. TNA, REQ 2/4/203, transcribed in G. R. Elton, 'Two unpublished letters of Thomas Cromwell', *Bulletin of the Institute of Historical Research* 22 (1949), 35–8, at 38. Elton misdated it to 1539: Cromwell's itinerary for 1539 makes it impossible for him to have been at anywhere called Burton in September that year, whereas it fits well into his 1538 itinerary, and immediately followed on the suppression at Leicester.   86. Principal document about Becon in the Dandy chantry of St Lawrence Church Ipswich is Thomas Lord Wentworth to Cromwell, soon after 15 December 1538, BL MS Cotton Vespasian F/XIII f. 211, *LP* 13 ii no.

1063. 87. Richard Rich to Cromwell, 15 August [1536], SP 1/106 f. 7, *LP* 11 no. 307; the lease, probably of March 1537, is noted in the Augmentations books, *LP* 13 i no. 1520[IV, f. 40v]. See above, pp. 300–301. 88. Sir John Gage and Sir William Penizon to Cromwell, 6 September [1538], SP 1/136 f. 82, *LP* 13 ii no. 289. For Sir Richard Guildford's interest and residence in Blackfriars, see Gunn, *Henry VII's New Men*, 257, 307, and for Lady Guildford's relationship with Sir Thomas Brandon, see her will, below, and *ODNB*, s.v. Brandon, Thomas. Lutton, 'Richard Guldeford's pilgrimage', makes a tantalizing association between the Guildfords, Penizon, Sir John Gage and Thomas Larke, chaplain to both Guildford and Cardinal Wolsey, plus Lollardy and Guildford's pilgrimage to Jerusalem via Italy just at the time when young Thomas Cromwell was also likely to be there. Alas, the one figure missing is Cromwell himself: that cries out for further investigation. 89. Her will made on 30 August 1538 is SP 1/135 ff. 252–5, *LP* 13 ii no. 219; see Penizon to Cromwell, 10 September [1538], SP 1/136 f. 98, *LP* 13 ii no. 316. 90. Depositions of John Cowper, John Raven, Richard Coke, William Marshall alias Glover, of Over, Cambridgeshire, SP 1/128 f. 80rv, *LP* 13 i no. 95; the words had only emerged on 17 and 18 January 1538, when a local JP promptly reported them to the Sheriff.

Chapter 20: Shifting Dynasties, 1538–1539

1. Surrender of Chertsey, 6 July 1537, *LP* 12 ii no. 220; new foundation at Bisham, 18 December 1537, *LP* 12 ii no. 1311[22]. Commissions of the peace: *LP* 13 i nos. 646[36] and 1115[69]. E. M. Hallam, 'Henry VIII's monastic refoundations of 1536–7 and the course of the Dissolution', *Bulletin of the Institute of Historical Research* 51 (1978), 124–31, begins discussion of this and the other refoundation of 1537, Stixwold in Lincolnshire, without noting the Pole dimension to the story. Stixwold would bear further probing. 2. Thomas Bennett to Cromwell, 16 April [1535], SP 1/92 f. 13, *LP* 8 no. 553; on the Countess of Salisbury's opposition, and Cromwell's writing for his preferred candidate, Sir Nicholas Carew to Cromwell, 27 April [1535], SP 1/92 f. 58, *LP* 8 no. 596. For Cromwell's remembrance on 'The vacation of Bisham and the demeanour of certain canons there' in June 1535, see BL MS Cotton Titus B/I f. 474, *LP* 8 no. 892. 3. For the complications of Barlow's career at this time, see Smith, 380; his surrender of Bisham is pinned to 1537 by TNA, E 322/54, *LP* 12 ii no. 220. 4. Richard Leighton to Cromwell, 22 June [1538], SP 1/133 f. 170, *LP* 13 i no. 1239. 5. Deposition (alas damaged) of Countess of Salisbury, 12/13 November 1538, SP 1/138 f. 200r, *LP* 13 ii no. 818. 6. Chapuys to Charles V, 9 January 1539, K. Lanz, *Correspondenz des Kaisers Karl V* . . . (3 vols., Leipzig, 1844–6), 2, 298–9, *LP* 14 i no. 37. 7. Examination of George Crofts, SP 1/139 f. 22r, *LP* 13 ii no. 829[II] (reporting events at Whitsuntide 1538), and for the same group of friends in more relaxed mood, see William Ernley, Steward of Chichester Cathedral, to John Hubberdine, a servant of Cromwell's, 15 December 1538, SP 1/140 f. 104, *LP* 13 ii no. 1062. 8. For the key clues about Tyndale's Oxford and Clifton connections, see his deposition of

October 1538, BL MS Cotton Appendix L ff. 82-4, *LP* 13 ii no. 817, which also provides the story below where not otherwise referenced.   **9.** Thomas Earl of Rutland to Cromwell, 25 August [1535], SP 1/95 f. 161, *LP* 9 no. 179; Richard Quiene to Cromwell, 14 October [1535], BL MS Cotton Cleopatra E/V f. 104, *LP* 9 no. 611; Gervase Tyndale to Cromwell, ?November 1535, SP 1/98 f. 146, *LP* 9 no. 740.   **10.** Robert Aldrich Provost of Eton to Cromwell, 7 October [1537], SP 1/125 f. 117, *LP* 12 ii no. 848.   **11.** This account has to be reconstructed from Cromwell's known presence at Lewes through letter addresses from 26–27 August, Tyndale's deposition October 1538, BL MS Cotton Appendix L. ff. 82–4, *LP* 13 ii no. 817; Oliver Franklin's deposition, 20 November 1538, SP 1/139 f. 122, *LP* 13 ii no. 875, plus entries in Cromwell's accounts in September, Arundel MS 97, *LP* 13 ii no. 1280, at 525, which relate to the episode: payments to 'two servants of the Bishop of Thetford for bringing Gervase Tyndale . . . and to the said Geffrey [*sic*] for his costs coming and returning, and tarrying at Lewes two or three days'. There may be garbling here, and hence a reference to Sir Geoffrey Pole as well as Tyndale. Bishop John Salisbury's late Titchfield connection with Wriothesley may explain his involvement in this Hampshire business.   **12.** It is on those grounds that I find unconvincing the presentation of the royal crackdown on the Poles as sheer accident without long-term antecedents in Bernard, *King's Reformation*, 410–18. Frankly, that seems a naive reading of events.   **13.** Robison, 'Justices of the peace of Surrey', 210–11.   **14.** Confession of John Wisdom, Joan Truslowe and Alice Patchett, SP 1/136 f. 157rv, *LP* 13 ii no. 392[2].   **15.** Depositions and covering letter from Sir Thomas Denys to Cromwell, 2 September [1538], SP 1/136 ff. 41–2, *LP* 13 ii no. 267; payments relating to this arrest in Cromwell's accounts for September 1538, Arundel MS 97, *LP* 13 ii no. 1280, at 525.   **16.** See John Husee's guarded reference to Lord Lisle about 'divers of the West Country . . . committed to the Tower', 26 September 1538, SP 1/137 f. 29, *Lisle Letters* 5 no. 1230; for his suicide attempt, same to same, 28 October [1538], SP 1/138 f. 35, *Lisle Letters* 5 no. 1259.   **17.** 'Il y a bien longtemps que ce Roy m'avoit dict qu'il vouloit exterminer ceste maison de Montagu, qui est encore de la Rose Blanche, et de la maison de Polle dont est le Cardinal': Castillon to Montmorency, 5 November 1538, Ribier (ed.), *Lettres et mémoires d'estat*, 1, 247–8, *LP* 13 ii no. 753.   **18.** On what follows where not otherwise referenced, see MacCulloch, *Thomas Cranmer*, 152–3, 231–6. Gunn, 'The structures of politics in early Tudor England', 74–5, is a model of how to derive a sense of such relationships without exaggeration or distortion, in this case by probing the Earl of Hertford's kitchen accounts.   **19.** For criticisms of the Archbishop on these grounds, see MacCulloch, *Thomas Cranmer*, 474–6.   **20.** Bodl. MS Ashmole 861 336; *Wriothesley's Chronicle* 1, 90.   **21.** The two major letters are Theobald to Cromwell, 1 October [1538], BL MS Cotton Nero B/VI f. 137, *LP* 13 ii no. 507, and same to same, 12 November 1538, BL MS Cotton Nero B/VI f. 55, *LP* 13 ii no. 812; see also P. Marshall, '"The greatest man in Wales": James ap Gruffydd ap Hywel and the international opposition to Henry VIII', *SCJ* 39 (2008), 681–704, and S. Menache, 'Papal attempts at a commercial boycott of the Muslims in the Crusader period', *JEH* 63 (2012), 236–59.   **22.** *LP* 13 ii nos. 1087–8.   **23.** On the suicide attempt, Chapuys to Charles V, 9 January 1539, Lanz, *Correspondenz des Kaisers Karl V*, 2, 306, *LP* 14 i no. 37. On Courtenay and Pole, imperial ambassadors in England, to Charles V, 19 September 1553, *Spanish Calendar* 11, at 239. **24.** For what follows, see Starkey, 'Intimacy and innovation', 114–15, and D. Starkey, *The Reign of Henry VIII: personalities and politics* (London, 1985), 120–21. **25.** See the list of members of the Privy Chamber, SP 1/142 f. 1, *LP* 14 i no. 2. **26.** All one needs to know about it is to be found in J. Youings, 'The Council of the West', *TRHS* 5th series 10 (1960), 41–59. **27.** For Abbot More of Walden as Audley's Steward even before becoming Bishop of Colchester, see Audley to Cromwell, 29 August [1536], SP 1/106 f. 51, *LP* 11 no. 369, and same to same, 18 September [1536], SP 1/106 f. 179, *LP* 11 no. 465. More's grant of episcopal office on 26 September 1536 was sealed at Audley's then country home of Berechurch. **28.** Norfolk's testimony to the Privy Council, mid-December 1546, BL MS Cotton Titus B/I f. 101r, *LP* 21 ii no. 554. Gertrude Blount/Courtenay, Marchioness of Exeter, was sister to Charles Blount Lord Mountjoy, who was actually on the panel for the trial of his brother-in-law in December 1538. **29.** Elton, *Policy and Police*, 259–60, discussing SP 6/4 ff. 266–82, *LP* 13 ii no. 1183. **30.** Lady Lisle to Lord Lisle, 3 December [1538], SP 3/1 f. 52a, *Lisle Letters* 5 no. 1298. **31.** Robison, 'Justices of the peace of Surrey', 211–15. **32.** *LP* 14 i no. 290[3], 113. **33.** Thomas Wriothesley to Cromwell, 2 February [1539], SP 1/142 f. 224, *LP* 14 i no. 208. **34.** Fuller, *Worthies of England*, ed. Freeman, 548. **35.** John Butler and others to Conrad Pellican and others in Zürich, *Epistolae Tigurinae de rebus potissimum ad ecclesiae Anglicanae Reformationem pertinentibus* … (Parker Society, 1848), 404–6, *LP* 14 i no. 466. **36.** Elizabeth Lady Carew to Cromwell, *c.* March 1539, SP 1/242 f. 222, *LP Addenda* 1 ii no. 1404; Maud Carew (widow of Sir Nicholas's father) to Cromwell, 20 November [1539], SP 1/155 f. 9, *LP* 14 ii no. 556. **37.** For what follows where not otherwise referenced, see the excellent account in Murray, *Enforcing the English Reformation in Ireland*, 113–24. **38.** Thomas Allen (brother of the Irish Master of the Rolls) to Cromwell, 20 October [1538], SP 60/7 f. 150, *LP* 13 ii no. 658. **39.** Murray, *Enforcing the English Reformation in Ireland*, 121. The commission of 3 February is *LP* 14 ii Appendix[5]. **40.** John Allen, William Brabazon and Gerald Aylmer to Cromwell, 18 January [1539], SP 60/8 f. 1, *LP* 14 i no. 88. **41.** Murray, *Enforcing the English Reformation in Ireland*, 122–3. **42.** For the correspondence about this new settlement, misdated in *LP* to 1538, see Lord Leonard Grey to Cromwell, 19 January [1539], SP 60/6 f. 11, *LP* 13 i no. 109, and Mayor and aldermen of Dublin to Cromwell, 23 January [1539], SP 60/6 f. 13, *LP* 13 i no. 130. **43.** Deputy and Council of Ireland to Cromwell, 21 May [1539], SP 60/8 f. 35, *LP* 14 i no. 1005. **44.** SP 1/133 f. 53, *LP* 13 i no. 1200. *LP*'s positioning of this letter was entirely arbitrary and was occasioned by a letter which has no relevance to it. **45.** On Sampson's demolitions at St Paul's on 23 August 1538, see *Wriothesley's Chronicle* 1, 84; for his letter of self-defence to Cromwell, 4 September [1538], BL MS Cotton Cleopatra E/V f. 306, *LP* 13 i no. 278. For the demolition of St Richard's shrine, *LP* 13 ii no. 1103 (20 December 1538). **46.** I am very grateful to Dr Andrew Foster for arranging for me to see the main possible source, the surviving fragment of the register for Bishops Sampson, Day and Scory, West Sussex Record Office, Chichester, Ep I/1/6, which alas concerns itself only with national business relating to the diocese. 47. Sir John Gage to Cromwell, 18 December [1538], SP 1/140 f. 125, *LP* 13 ii no. 1091. 48. John Husee to Lord Lisle, 5 March [1539], SP 3/4 f. 133, *Lisle Letters* 5 no. 1114. This letter and its fellow to Lady Lisle written from Gravesend represent a rare piece of misdating in the *Lisle Letters*, following *LP* 13 i no. 421 and *LP Addenda* 1 ii no. 1309, where they are attributed to 1538. They will be seen to fit in between *Lisle Letters* 5 nos. 1361a and 1362, 4 and 7 March 1539. 49. Henry Polstead to Cromwell, Friday ?14 March 1539, SP 1/129 f. 46, *LP* 13 i no. 293, misdated in *LP*. The farming arrangements described in it are certainly of late winter or early spring. 50. Alienation licence is *LP* 13 ii no. 967[54], passing on 30 November. The conveyance to Gregory after that appears to have been a month later, 26 December 1538: Blomefield and Parkin, *Topographical History of the County of Norfolk*, 9, 489. 51. The exhausting twists and turns of the Painswick affair can be traced throughout the *Lisle Letters*, best approached by index entries for Painswick. 52. *LP* 14 i no. 191[2]. 53. See various payments for the move and dissolution of the Lewes household between March and May 1539 in an account of John Williamson, *LP* 14 i no. 1049, and payments for repairs and provisions in April and May, *LP* 14 ii no. 782, at 341. The Lewes Priory precinct was leased on 21 June 1539 to Nicholas Jenny or Jennings, a Sussex yeoman who was a longstanding servant of Cromwell's, and who organized the winding up of the household there; he was given a new Crown lease on Cromwell's fall: *LP* 16 no. 305[70] (27 November 1540). For Jennings's role in organizing the move from Lewes to Leeds, John Williamson to Cromwell, 2 August [1539], SP 1/153 f. 6, *LP* 14 ii no. 12. 54. The indenture on the Close Roll is *LP* 14 i no. 9, the alienation licence (1 January 1539) *LP* 14 i no. 191[1], and for the payments to Dudley in Cromwell's accounts on 13 and 25 February 1539, *LP* 14 ii no. 782, at 340. 55. John Husee to Lord Lisle, 16 October [1537], SP 3/5 f. 91, *Lisle Letters* 4 no. 1024. For what other evidence there is in this reconstruction, see *HC 1509–1558* 1, 112–14. 56. Gregory's absence from the bench was first noticed by Mary Robertson: 'Profit and purpose in the development of Thomas Cromwell's landed estates', 332.

Chapter 21: Stumbling Blocks: 1539

1. SP 1/143 ff. 198–205, *LP* 14 i no. 402; see discussion in Elton, *Policy and Police*, 195–8. 2. SP 1/143 f. 205v, *LP* 14 i no. 402. 'Tyrant' has been altered from 'traitor', which one can dismiss as a slip of the pen. 3. SP 1/143 f. 202rv, *LP* 14 i no. 402. 4. A fine reassessment is Clark, 'Humanism and reform in pre-Reformation English monasteries', especially 87–92. 5. MacCulloch, *Suffolk and the Tudors*, 138–9, 162–3. 6. On the background, see the essays in H. Wansbrough and A. Marett-Crosby (eds.), *Benedictines in Oxford* (London, 1997), and on this development of the 1530s, Cunich, 'Benedictine monks at the University of Oxford and the dissolution of the monasteries', in ibid., 155–82, at 171–2. The largest

numbers of known Benedictine Oxbridge students 1500–40 are Bury St Edmunds (15), Canterbury Cathedral (43), Durham (30), Evesham (12), Glastonbury (15), Gloucester (13), St Albans (12), Westminster (28), Worcester (10): ibid., 182. 7. Knowles, *Religious Orders in England III*, 431–2. 8. Audley to Cromwell, 8 September [1538], SP 1/136 f. 86, *LP* 13 ii no. 306; on Great Malvern, Hugh Latimer to Cromwell, 13 December [1538], BL MS Cotton Cleopatra E/IV f. 320, *LP* 13 ii no. 1036, and on Hailes, see a remembrance of Cromwell's from September 1538, BL MS Cotton Caligula B/III f. 209, *LP* 13 ii no. 488. 9. For Walsingham, see Richard Vowell Prior of Walsingham to Cromwell, 12 August [1538], SP 1/135 f. 78, *LP* 13 ii no. 86; Robert Ferrar Prior of St Oswald's (Nostell) to Cromwell, 5 September [1538], SP 1/136 f. 76, *LP* 13 ii no. 285; for Thetford, Duke of Norfolk to Matthew Parker, 19 August 1538, Corpus Christi College Cambridge MS 114A 106. The Duke's proposals for Thetford dated to 1539 by *LP*, SP 1/156 ff. 95–102, *LP* 14 ii nos. 815–16, are actually probably near-contemporary with the letter to Parker. For a hint that Leicester Abbey might be turned into a collegiate church at exactly this time, see above, p. 466. 10. Richard Thornden to Cromwell, 30 September [1538], SP 1/137 f. 51, *LP* 13 ii no. 465. 11. John Freeman to Cromwell, 3 October [1538], SP 1/137 ff. 89–92r, *LP* 13 ii no. 528[1, 2]; John Uvedale to Cromwell, 4 October [1538], SP 1/137 f. 96, *LP* 13 ii no. 534, and on the Uvedales at Marrick, see Smith, 671. 12. Colvin (ed.), *History of the King's Works* 4, 367–83. 13. Ralph Sadler to Cromwell, 16 March [1539], SP 1/144 f. 116, *LP* 14 i no. 529. 14. Castillon to [Constable Montmorency], 26 January 1539, Ribier (ed.), *Lettres et mémoires d'estat*, 1, 364, *LP* 14 i no. 144. 15. On what follows, see the inspired reconstruction of events in A. J. Slavin, 'The Rochepot Affair', *SCJ* 10/1 (Spring 1979), 3–19. 16. Cromwell to the Privy Council, 24 July 1540, Merriman 2 no. 351, *LP* 15 no. 910. 17. M. D. Orth, 'The English Great Bible of 1539 and the French connection', in S. L'Engle and G. B. Guest (eds.), *Tributes to Jonathan J. G. Alexander* (London, 2006), 171–84, argues for a French artist, known only as the Master of François de Rohan. A French artist would seem logical, but a case for an English Court artist is pressed by T. C. String, *Art and Communication in the Reign of Henry VIII* (Abingdon, 2008), 96. Her argument that such a knowing portrait of the current English political and religious scene would have to come from someone resident in England is interesting but not conclusive. 18. T. C. String, 'Henry VIII's illuminated "Great Bible"', *Journal of the Warburg and Courtauld Institutes* 59 (1996), 315–24, at 323. 19. John Hutton to Cromwell, 4 December [1537], SP 1/127 f. 5, *LP* 12 ii no. 1172. 20. Chapuys and Mendoza to Charles V, 17 June 1538, *Spanish Calendar* V ii no. 225, at 531. 21. McEntegart, *Henry VIII, the League of Schmalkalden and the English Reformation*, 142, sees Cromwell taking an initiative in a Cleves marriage proposal earlier, in August 1538, on the basis of his reading of a report by Burchard to the Elector of Saxony that '[H]err Crumellus, welcher zum hochsten der Teutschen Nation genaigt ist, wolte am liebsten das sich seine Mait. mit den Teutschen fursten befreien det', which he translates as 'lord Cromwell, who is most favourably inclined to the German nation, wants most dearly that the king should wed himself with the German princes.' Reading 'befreundet' at the end of the sentence, I would suggest that this simply means 'Lord Cromwell, who is well disposed to the noblest of the German nation, would prefer that his Majesty develops friendship with the German princes.'   22. Ibid., 142–4: the main documents, dateable to January 1539, are the King's instructions in SP 1/142 f. 105, and Cromwell's in BL MS Cotton Vitellius B/XXI ff. 175–176r, *LP* 14 i no. 103[1, 2]; the quotation is from BL MS Vitellius B/XXI f. 175v.   23. This is attested in a slightly garbled sentence of the account of the argument by Thomas Wakefield's later reminiscence to Archbishop Cranmer in Bodl. MS Jesus College 74 f. 299v. See also above, p. 443.   24. McEntegart, *Henry VIII, the League of Schmalkalden and the English Reformation*, 149–53.   25. TNA, E 36/143 129, *LP* 14 i no. 655.   26. MacCulloch, *Thomas Cranmer*, 241–2.   27. Cromwell to Henry VIII, 17 March [1539], BL MS Cotton Titus B/I f. 265, *LP* 14 i no. 538.   28. Sowerby, *Renaissance and Reform*, 134–5, usefully clarifies the nature of the appointment.   29. For what follows on this Parliament where not otherwise referenced, see Lehmberg, *Later Parliaments of Henry VIII*, 40–84.   30. On Cheyney see *HC 1509–1558* 1, 634–8, on his religious conservatism, MacCulloch, *Thomas Cranmer*, 198–200, 207, 365, and on his appointment as Warden, John Husee to Lord Lisle, 13 May [1536], SP 1/103 f. 278, *Lisle Letters* 3 no. 695.   31. See the account in Lehmberg, *Later Parliaments of Henry VIII*, 43–4, as part of a generally sound survey of what we know about the elections nationwide.   32. For a piece of the evidence against the Countess of Salisbury's chaplain John Helyar delivered to Goring on 18 September 1538, see SP 1/136 f. 141, *LP* 13 ii no. 376. Cromwell was staying with Goring at Burton on 13 September 1538 as the White Rose conspiracy broke: see the letter cited in Elton, 'Two unpublished letters of Thomas Cromwell', 38, and discussed above, p. 686, n. 85. For Cromwell's involvement in the collusive sale of Hardham Priory to Goring in 1534, see above, p. 200.   33. Earl of Southampton and Lord St John to Cromwell, 20 March 1539, BL MS Cotton Otho E/IX f. 73, *LP* 14 i no. 573; Southampton to Cromwell, 14 March 1539, BL MS Cotton Cleopatra E/IV f. 209, *LP* 14 i no. 520.   34. John Kingsmill to Thomas Wriothesley, 31 March and 1 April [1539], SP 1/144 f. 197, *LP* 14 i no. 634, and SP 1/146 f. 237, *LP* 14 i no. 662. On Kingsmill, see R. Fritze, ' "A rare example of godlyness amongst gentlemen": the role of the Kingsmill and Gifford families in promoting the Reformation in Hampshire', in Lake and Dowling (eds.), *Protestantism and the National Church in Sixteenth Century England*, 144–61, especially 146–9.   35. John Kingsmill to Thomas Wriothesley, 1 April [1539], SP 1/146 f. 239r, *LP* 14 i no. 662.   36. William Earl of Southampton to [Cromwell], 14 March 1539, BL MS Cotton Cleopatra E/IV f. 209, *LP* 14 i no. 520.   37. Thomas Soulemont to Thomas Wriothesley, 16 April 1539, TNA, SP 7/1 f. 53, *LP* 14 i no. 783.   38. John Husee to Lord Lisle, 4 April [1539], SP 1/146 f. 258, *Lisle Letters* 5 no. 1372; Lehmberg, *Later Parliaments of Henry VIII*, 56.   39. For this and what follows where not otherwise referenced, MacCulloch, *Thomas Cranmer*, 242–5, and there is very useful comment and analysis in McEntegart, *Henry VIII, the League of Schmalkalden and the English Reformation*, 159–66.   40. McEntegart, *Henry VIII, the League of Schmalkalden and the English Reformation*, 162–3.   41. See my discussion in MacCulloch, *Thomas Cranmer*, 247–8.   42. This is cogently argued by

NOTES TO PP. 500–508 693

McEntegart, *Henry VIII, the League of Schmalkalden and the English Reformation*, 150, 159–62, although the wider domestic background does need to be taken into consideration. **43.** On the discovery of Damplip's links to Shaxton, Lord Lisle to Cromwell, 10 June [1539], SP 1/152 f. 52, *Lisle Letters* 5 no. 1447. On John Goodall of Salisbury, see *HC 1509–1558* 2, 228–30. **44.** Shaxton to Cromwell, 25 June [1539], SP 1/152 f. 82, *LP* 14 i no. 1157. **45.** Murray, *Enforcing the English Reformation in Ireland*, 141–5, 151–4. **46.** Shaxton to Cromwell, first week of July 1539, SP 1/152 f. 118, *LP* 14 i no. 1217. **47.** Thomas Key to Cromwell, 15 June [1539], SP 1/152 f. 59, *LP* 14 i no. 1114. **48.** MacCulloch, *Thomas Cranmer*, 252–3. **49.** Lehmberg, *Later Parliaments of Henry VIII*, 62–3. **50.** Ibid., 66–7. **51.** Ibid., 58–60; *Statutes of the Realm* 3 729 (31 Henry VIII, cap. 10). **52.** T. Lott, 'Account of the Muster of the Citizens of London in the 31st Year of the Reign of Henry VIII', *Archaeologia* 32 (1847), 30–37; John Husee to Lord Lisle, 8 May [1539], SP 3/4 f. 54, *Lisle Letters* 5 no. 1406, 466–7; Cromwell's accounts, *LP* 14 ii no. 782, at 341, 343. **53.** Foxe introduced Morice's material into his 1570 edition, and reprinted it thereafter, duplicating the main story, so the doublet in Foxe 1570, 1337 and 2075, becomes Foxe 1576, 1134–5, and 1781, and Foxe 1583, 1160 and 1886. The story of the row with the Duke of Norfolk is Foxe 1570, 1398–9, Foxe 1576, 1184, and Foxe 1583, 1213. In all cases, Foxe misdates the anecdote to 1540 while making it quite clear that the incident followed the 1539 Parliament. Morice's anecdote which he did not use is Nichols (ed.), *Narratives of the days of the Reformation*, 258–9. **54.** Foxe 1570, 1399; my italics.

Chapter 22: Downfall: 1539–1540

1. Paisey and Bartrum, 'Hans Holbein and Miles Coverdale'. **2.** The following paragraphs where not otherwise referenced are based on MacCulloch, *Thomas Cranmer*, 256–61, and McEntegart, *Henry VIII, the League of Schmalkalden and the English Reformation*, 167–84. I have to emphasize once more (as at p. 614, n. 44) that I am making no use in this account of summer 1539 of the material in [Collier, forger], 'Transcript of an original manuscript, containing a memorial from George Constantyne to Thomas Lord Cromwell', 'ed.' Amyot. **3.** Depositions of Christopher Chaitour made in further investigations of Tunstall, *c.* 16 December 1539, SP 1/155 ff. 154v, 157rv, *LP* 14 ii no. 750[i and ii]. Chaitour recorded that he heard these stories, some of them from servants of Southampton and Browne, on the progress at Woodstock, which dates them to 24–29 August 1539. **4.** SP 1/155 ff. 156r, 157v, *LP* 14 ii no. 750[i and ii]. **5.** See Bonner's letter to the King, in fact addressed to Cromwell, 1 October [1539], BL MS Cotton Caligula E/IV f. 4, *LP* 14 ii no. 270; see also the thorough round-up of leading members of Cromwell's household to be given compliments in Bonner to Thomas Wriothesley, 12 October [1539], SP 1/154 f. 14, *LP* 14 ii no. 318. For insightful discussion of Bonner's extraordinary religious turn, see A. Ryrie, *The Gospel and Henry VIII: evangelicals in the early English Reformation* (Cambridge, 2003), 82–4, 216–18. **6.** Nicholas Wotton to [Henry VIII], 11 August 1539, BL MS Cotton

Vitellius B/XXI f. 203, *LP* 14 ii no. 33.   7. Quotations (my translations) from the Saxon ambassadors' reports, McEntegart, *Henry VIII, the League of Schmalkalden and the English Reformation*, 180–81: 'Jdoch aber es bisherkeine execution erfolget Ehr achtet es auch genzlich darfur do es die Zeit nicht aussgangen es wurde nun nicht mehr geschen'; 'es were etzliche der selbige sindt der Zeit auss dem geheimsten rath aussgeschlossen und abgesundert'.   8. A good overview, and remarkably fair-minded to Cromwell, is Knowles, *Religious Orders in England III*, 376–82.   9. Richard Whiting Abbot of Glastonbury to Cromwell, 9 September [1535], SP 1/96 f. 106, *LP* 9 no. 313. The letter shows that Whiting had prudently refrained from sending More his Steward's fee after he had been sent to the Tower. Subsequent letters from the Abbot to Cromwell are not as easy to date to precise years as *LP* might suggest.   10. William Popley to Lord Lisle, 30 June [1539], SP 3/13 f. 63, *Lisle Letters* 5 no. 1461; William Lord Stourton to Lady Lisle, 29 June [1539], SP 3/13 f. 173, *Lisle Letters* 5 no. 1460b.   11. Richard Leighton to Cromwell, 16 September [1539], SP 1/153 f. 102, *LP* 14 ii no. 185.   12. Richard Munslow Abbot of Winchcombe to Cromwell, 17 August [1539], SP 1/153 f. 29, *LP* 14 ii no. 58; Richard Tracey to Cromwell, 24 August [1539], SP 1/153 f. 46, *LP* 14 ii no. 79.   13. Remembrance, BL MS Cotton Titus B/I f. 443, *LP* 14 ii no. 548; see also Smith, 83.   14. Petition of Evesham to Cromwell, ?summer 1539, SP 1/139 ff. 114v–115r, *LP* 13 ii no. 866. *LP* puzzlingly dated this as between 18 and 19 November 1538, but it is far more plausibly of summer 1539: the list of godly purposes is reminiscent of the Bishoprics Act of that summer, and also speaks of being near Warwickshire where there is no monastery standing: Coombe was dissolved in January 1539, Kenilworth on 14 April 1539, Polesworth nunnery in January 1539 and Nuneaton nunnery in November 1539. Evesham itself was dissolved on 30 January 1540.   15. Robert Southwell and seven other commissioners to [Cromwell], 4 January 1540, BL MS Cotton Cleopatra E/IV f. 307, *LP* 15 no. 19.   16. Deposition of Christopher Chaitour about the words of 'one Craye', c. 16 December 1539, SP 1/155 f. 157v, *LP* 14 ii no. 750[ii] 'it was a saying that Peterborough should be a college, but now it shall be clearly taken away.' For the gift, *LP* 16 no. 380, 179.   17. *LP* 16 no. 380, 179. The Abbot of Waltham was also one of the select elite group (and the only abbot) to give Edward a present that New Year: BL MS Royal appendix 89 f. 41, *LP* 14 i no. 5. For further discussion of the cathedral schemes, see N. Orme, *The History of England's Cathedrals* (Exeter, 2017), 101–7.   18. Dymond (ed.), *The Register of Thetford Priory II*, 735–6: two drafts of Prior Burden's letter to the Dowager Duchess, following her earlier letter of 16 July: these letters from the content can only be of 1539.   19. See the evidence of continuing uncertainty about the future of the priory in the will of ex-Prior Burden, made in July 1540: Norfolk and Norwich Record Office, NCC Reg. Anmer f. 530. The grant was on 9 July 1540, with a Crown rent reserved, and in exchange for lands in Oxfordshire, *LP* 15 no. 942[43].   20. The most recent attempt to elucidate this tangled story is N. Clark, 'The gendering of dynastic memory: burial choices of the Howards, 1485–1559', *JEH* 68 (2017), 747–65, which has not solved quite all the problems. I am dubious about the suggestion of a move of the tombs to Kenninghall presented in

P. Lindley, 'Materiality, movement and the historical moment', in Lindley (ed.), *The Howards and the Tudors: studies in science and heritage* (Stamford, 2015), 43–75. The statement repeated in *ODNB* that the Duchess died in May 1545 and was at first buried at Thetford seems mistaken: see G. Leveson-Gower, 'The Howards of Effingham', *Surrey Archaeological Collections* 9 (1888), 395–436, at 397–8. **21.** On what follows, the best summary account is still Scarisbrick, *Henry VIII*, 368–83. **22.** Depositions of Cray, SP 1/155 f. 162v, *LP* 14 ii no. 750[2]. **23.** T. C. String, 'A neglected Henrician decorative ceiling', *Antiquaries Journal* 76 (1996), 139–51. **24.** See the examples of Tunstall's marriage drafts in *LP* 14 ii no. 733. **25.** For the depositions, already frequently cited, see SP 1/155 ff. 153–66, *LP* 14 ii no. 750; for Parson Tunstall's arrest, and the search of his chamber in the Bishop's Palace at Auckland, John Uvedale to Cromwell, 27 December [1539], SP 1/155 f. 147, *LP* 14 ii no. 748. John Tunstall was parson of Tanfield in 1535, *VE* 5, 246, and probably corresponds to Cuthbert's brother John recorded in the family genealogy, C. B. Norcliffe (ed.), *The Visitation of Yorkshire in the years 1563 and 1564, made by William Flower* ... (Harleian Society 16, 1881), 327. **26.** There is an excellent summary account of this initiative in Edwards, *Mary I*, 61–2. **27.** Marillac to Montmorency, 27 December [1539], Kaulek (ed.), *Correspondance*, 148, *LP* 14 ii no. 744. **28.** Gregory Cromwell to Cromwell, 1 December 1539, SP 1/155 f. 75, *LP* 14 ii no. 622. **29.** Earl of Southampton and Nicholas Wotton to Henry VIII, 13 December [1539], SP 1/155 f. 111v, *LP* 14 ii no. 677. **30.** Cranmer to Cromwell, 29 December [1539], SP 1/156 f. 2, *LP* 14 ii no. 752; Cromwell's accounts, *LP* 14 ii no. 782, at 344. **31.** Deposition of Sir Anthony Browne, *LP* 15 no. 850[7], and what follows is from Southampton's own deposition, *LP* 15 no. 850[5]. The extensive depositions around the Cleves marriage debacle have ended up among the Cecil Papers at Hatfield (see [Hatfield House] *Calendar of the manuscripts ... preserved at Hatfield House, Hertfordshire* (24 vols., Historical Manuscripts Commission, series 9, 1883–1976), 1 nos. 61, 66–7). There are extremely accurate contemporary notarial transcriptions of those by the Registrar of York Diocese, William Glossop, in Borthwick Institute, York: Abp. Reg. 28 [Register of Archbishop Edward Lee], ff. 141Av–150r, with the depositions themselves beginning at f. 144v. Further depositions involving the King himself are to be found in BL MS Cotton Otho C/X ff. 241–2, *LP* 15 no. 822[2, 3], and BL MS Cotton Titus B/I f. 418, *LP* 15 no. 822[1]. **32.** Hume (trans. and ed.), *The Chronicle of King Henry VIII*, 91. **33.** Cromwell to Henry VIII, July 1540, Merriman 2 no. 349, at 268–73, *LP* 15 no. 823. **34.** Merriman 1, 279: 'er siehe unser maynunge den glauben betreffen aber wie die weldt iczt stehet wesz sich sin her der konnig halte desz wolle er sich auch halten und solte er darumb sterben ...' (my translation). **35.** Here I concur with the analysis of McEntegart, *Henry VIII, the League of Schmalkalden and the English Reformation*, 190–91. **36.** It is infuriating that *Statutes of the Realm* did not print the text of Cromwell's attainder. G. Burnet, *The History of the Reformation* ... (2 vols., London, 1679, Wing B5797), 1 ii 187–92, first put it into print, and subsequent editions still provide the most convenient way of seeing the text. All my subsequent citations of the Act of Attainder are from Burnet. This remark is said to have been made 'at the parish of St Martin in the Fields', which is likely to make its setting his lodgings in St James's Palace.   37. William Barlow Bishop of St David's to Cromwell, 31 August [1539], SP 1/153 f. 58, *LP* 14 ii no. 107, about a prebend in the cathedral; Shaxton had likewise collated Barnes to the Prebend of Netherbury in Salisbury Cathedral on 18 October 1538. Barnes was paid money owing for his embassy this same February: royal accounts, *LP* 16 no. 380, 182. Redworth, *In Defence of the Church Catholic*, 106–16, provides a generally accurate account of the Gardiner/Barnes clashes, though he makes an unnecessary effort to detach them from the political crisis.   38. Ostensibly Gregory had asked for the information, but its theological detail seems best suited to his father's interest. Interestingly, Dowes made two copies of the report to Gregory in his own hand, 29 March [1540], SP 1/158 ff. 95–6, and BL MS Cotton Cleopatra E/V ff. 405–6, *LP* 15 no. 414[1, 2]. That alone suggests that two readers are in mind.   39. McEntegart, *Henry VIII, the League of Schmalkalden and the English Reformation*, 192–3: 'er sei von seinen gelerten sovil, das die unsern in denen puncten die priesteree, die communion sub utraque specie und die privatmessen belangend ze weit gangen.'   40. Sir John Wallop to Lord Lisle, 31 March 1540, SP 3/8 f. 49, *Lisle Letters* 6 no. 1663, with useful editorial comment there on dating the dinner party in March.   41. The Act of Attainder misdates this incident to 30 Henry VIII, which would have been 31 March 1539, when Barnes was in high favour and a royal ambassador, not in prison. It is pinned to Austin Friars by the Act's specification that it took place in the parish of St Peter-le-Poer.   42. Marillac to Montmorency, 10 April [1540], Ribier (ed.), *Lettres et mémoires d'estat*, 1, 513, *LP* 15 no. 486.   43. On what follows in this paragraph, see MacCulloch, *Thomas Cranmer*, 267–8.   44. Lehmberg, *Later Parliaments of Henry VIII*, 66.   45. Ibid., 92–3.   46. BL MS Cotton Titus B/I ff. 109–17, *LP* 14 i no. 869, well discussed in G. R. Elton, 'Taxation for war and peace in early-Tudor England', in Elton, *Studies* 3, 216–33, at 224–8, and Sowerby, *Renaissance and Reform*, 140–41; they both rightly redate the text from 1539 to 1540.   47. Herbert, *Life and Raigne of King Henry the Eighth*, 456; on Fuller and Christ Church Aldgate, see above, p. 201.   48. Elton, *Reform and Renewal*, 96.   49. Lehmberg, *Later Parliaments of Henry VIII*, 97–9.   50. *LP* 15 no. 613[12] (24 April 1540).   51. SP 1/158 f. 122, *LP* 15 no. 437. Detailed discussion by Elton, *Tudor Revolution in Government*, 312–15, confirms the date of this measure as of April 1540, but curiously ignores the explicitly Parliamentary provisions of the warrant in favour of the bureaucratic implications, providing secretarial assistance separately for King and Lord Privy Seal. This sidesteps the realities of political crisis at the time of the creation.   52. For the creation and grant, see *LP* 15 nos. 611[37, 38]. For the ceremonies, see royal payments to the heralds, *LP* 16 no. 380, 186. For comment on the importance of the Lord Great Chamberlain, see Starkey, 'Intimacy and innovation', 115n.   53. The sale is revealed in the Act of Parliament setting up the Honour of Hampton Court, 31 Henry VIII c. 55, not printed in *Statutes of the Realm* but summarized in *LP* 15 no. 498[36], 213–14. It is specified that the estates had come to the King by purchase from Cromwell, not by attainder. Henry subsequently demolished Mortlake parish church as being too near the house and rebuilt it elsewhere (an action not quite as drastic as his sacrilegious action at Nonsuch): Colvin (ed.), *History of the King's Works* 4, 169–70. The transaction may already have been discussed in autumn 1539, to judge by a note in a remembrance of Cromwell's of late October 1539, BL MS Cotton Titus B/I f. 446, *LP* 14 ii no. 427: 'For mine exchange, and to procure a house to dwell in'. **54.** The alienation licence for the Duke and Duchess of Suffolk on 15 January 1539 is *LP* 14 i no. 191[17], and the sale came the following day, recorded in BL MS Harley Charters 47 A. 50, *LP* 14 i no. 71. **55.** Colvin (ed.), *History of the King's Works* 4, 179–80. The Honour was set up by an Act of the 1539 Parliament: 31 Henry VIII, cap. 5: *Statutes of the Realm* 3, 721–4. **56.** There is an account in BL MS Harley 69 f. 18, *LP* 15 no. 617. **57.** For a summary account of the increasing political, military and financial failure, Ellis, 'Thomas Cromwell and Ireland, 1532–1540', 515–16, and on the forward campaign in the Church, Murray, *Enforcing the English Reformation in Ireland*, 118–24. **58.** Bradshaw, *Irish Constitutional Revolution*, 177–85. On the other summonses, see John Allen, James Earl of Ormond, Archbishop Browne, William Brabazon and Robert Cowley to Cromwell, 30 April [1540], SP 60/9 f. 44, *LP* 15 no. 44, and Earl of Ormond to Cromwell, 1 May [1540], SP 60/9 f. 46, *LP* 15 no. 620. **59.** Archbishop of Dublin to Cromwell, 19 May [1540], SP 60/9 f. 61, *LP* 15 no. 692. **60.** Council of England to Sir William Brereton, the Archbishop of Dublin and John Allen, 12 June 1540, SP 60/9 f. 69, *LP* 15 no. 775. **61.** Where not otherwise referenced, the following paragraphs follow MacCulloch, *Thomas Cranmer*, 269, drawing heavily on the Marillac correspondence, and for a vivid and exhaustive account of the Calais events, see *Lisle Letters* 5, 53–158. **62.** Marillac to Constable Montmorency, 1 June 1540, Kaulek (ed.), *Correspondance*, 187–9, *LP* 15 no. 737. **63.** Ralph Sadler to Cromwell, *c.* 1 June 1540, SP 1/160 f. 87, *LP* 15 no. 719. **64.** Brigden, *London and the Reformation*, 313. **65.** Cromwell to Sir George Lawson, 4 June 1540, SP 1/160 f. 116, *LP* 15 no. 746: an unsigned file copy. **66.** Bodl. MS Jesus College 74 f. 299r: 'the Earl of Essex (who made this match) was sent to the Tower because he would not consent to the Divorce.' **67.** Deposition of Cromwell to Henry VIII, 12 June 1540, BL MS Cotton Titus B/I f. 273, *LP* 15 no. 776 (in which *LP* misidentifies the Admiral as Russell; it was Southampton); deposition of Sir Thomas Wriothesley, *LP* 15 no. 850[11]. **68.** For examples of this closeness, see Bonner to Wriothesley, 22 April [1539], SP 1/150 f. 165, *LP* 14 i no. 831; 12 October [1539], SP 1/154 f. 14, *LP* 14 ii no. 318. **69.** P. Janelle, 'An unpublished poem on Bishop Stephen Gardiner', *Bulletin of the Institute of Historical Research* 6 (1928–9), 12–25, 89–96, 167–74, quotation at 22. Janelle demonstrates that it was written by William Palmer, one of the first Gentlemen Pensioners in 1539, who took part in the reception for Anne of Cleves; he wrote in the reign of Edward VI. **70.** Marillac to Montmorency, 23 June 1540, Kaulek (ed.), *Correspondance*, 193–5, *LP* 15 no. 804. **71.** The draft Council letter of 10 June is SP 1/160 ff. 140–43, *LP* 15 no. 765. **72.** Richard Pate to the Privy Council, 16 June 1540, SP 1/160 f. 155, *LP* 15 no. 794. For his further bile against Cromwell in letters home of 27 June, see Pate to Henry VIII, SP 1/160 f. 165, *LP* 15 no. 811; Pate to the Duke of Norfolk, SP 1/160 f. 167, *LP* 15 no. 812. **73.** King of France to Marillac, 15 June 1540, Kaulek (ed.), *Correspondance*, 191–2, *LP* 15 no. 785. **74.** Sadler's very neat copy is BL MS Harley 288 ff. 47–8, *LP* 15 no. 792, and there is a further copy now much mutilated at BL MS Cotton Caligula E/IV ff. 42–3, *LP* 15 no. 792[2]; they must be a few days later than the date of 16 June given them in *LP*. See Henry VIII's reply to Sir John Wallop, 22 June 1540, SP 1/160 f. 161, *LP* 15 no. 801, in which he comments on having seen this material. **75.** Henry VIII to Sir John Wallop, 22 June 1540, SP 1/160 f. 161, *LP* 15 no. 801, and see Wallop's follow-up to the King in reply, 5 July 1540, SP 1/161 f. 25, *LP* 15 no. 842. On the German letters, Marillac to Montmorency, 23 June 1540, Kaulek (ed.), *Correspondance*, 194, *LP* 15 no. 804. **76.** Woking: Surrey History Centre, Loseley MSS, LM 59/150. I am very grateful to Steven Gunn for sharing his notes on the inventory with me. **77.** Cromwell to Henry VIII, 5 February [1539], BL MS Cotton Titus B/I f. 263, *LP* 14 i no. 227. **78.** A representative example is Thomas Lord De La Warr to Cromwell, 18 November [1539], SP 1/154 f. 146, *LP* 14 ii no. 455. **79.** Herbert, *Life and Raigne of King Henry the Eighth*, 457, 'from an original', *LP* 15 no. 770. Given the other unique material surviving only in Thomas Master's notes for Herbert in Bodl. MS Jesus 74, there is no good reason to doubt the authenticity of this letter. I date it to 12 June, since it is after a Council meeting 'yesterday', yet it seems implausible that Cranmer attended the tumultuous meeting of 10 June. If he did, then the date should be 11 June as *LP* tentatively suggests. **80.** Foxe 1563, 1547. The story does of course sound like the denouement of the Prebendaries' Plot in 1543 (see MacCulloch, *Thomas Cranmer*, 319–21), but it is likely not to be a doublet; quite apart from its exceptionally racy presentation, Foxe may have felt it would detract from the drama of his fuller account of the 1543 events, and hence dropped it in later editions than 1563. It is interesting to attempt to match the circumstantial detail of the narrative to the layout of Whitehall (cf. Thurley, *Houses of Power*, 134–5). Cranmer probably came in via the watergate from Lambeth and relied on his status to get access to the privy stair. **81.** *Lords Journals* 1, 144–6; Lehmberg, *Later Parliaments of Henry VIII*, 107–9; MacCulloch, *Thomas Cranmer*, 271–2. **82.** Herbert, *Life and Raigne of King Henry the Eighth*, 458. For discussion of the Act and its passage, see Lehmberg, *Later Parliaments of Henry VIII*, 107–12. **83.** MacCulloch, *Thomas Cranmer*, 271–4. **84.** The letter of 12 July 1540 in which Suffolk, Southampton and Wriothesley reported their negotiations with Anne to Henry VIII, BL MS Cotton Otho C/X ff. 254–5, *LP* 15 no. 874, suggests a lady who was rapidly learning how to get the best out of a set of men squirming with embarrassment at their task. **85.** BL MS Cotton Otho C/X f. 250v, *LP* 15 no. 824. **86.** BL MS Cotton Titus B/I f. 273v, *LP* 15 no. 776. **87.** BL MS Cotton Otho C/X f. 248r, *LP* 15 no. 824; this letter was much damaged in the Cotton fire of 1731. **88.** Borthwick Institute, York: Abp. Reg. 28 [Register of Archbishop Edward Lee], f. 147v; the transcript begins at f. 147r. Some of the letters were purloined from government papers by a former protégé of Cromwell's, William Cecil, as a souvenir of his great predecessor in government, and are now in the Cecil archive at Hatfield House; cf. the original there, printed at Merriman 1, 268–73. **89.** Lehmberg, *Later Parliaments of Henry VIII*, 118–19, though he did not understand that the whole list was directed against Anabaptist belief.   90. *ODNB*, s.v. Hungerford, Walter, sums up the perplexing evidence, but an important extra strand is Cromwell's vice-gerential commission to examine Hungerford's separation from his wife, 3 February 1540: P. Ayris, 'The public career of Thomas Cranmer', *Reformation and Renaissance Review* 4 (Dec. 2000), 75–125, at 116. We need a thorough examination of this episode.   91. Hall 2, 306–7, is the primary source for the text of his speech, repeated in Foxe 1563, 654, but the largely lost chronicle of Anthony Anthony has some interesting supplements, interleaved with a Bodleian copy of Herbert, *Life and Raigne of King Henry the Eighth*, Bodl. Folio Δ 624, facing 462.   92. Corpus Christi College Cambridge, Parker Society MS 168 f. 209rv: among the papers of Richard Cox, Elizabethan Bishop of Ely. Other enrichments of the text show that this version is not merely a copy from the version deriving from Hall; Hall would no doubt have thought it indiscreet to allude to Wyatt at the time of his publication.   93. Hume (trans. and ed.), *The Chronicle of King Henry VIII*, 104.

Chapter 23: Futures

1. The text is Foxe 1563, 666–8: for Barnes's continuing reputation, Maas, *Reformation and Robert Barnes*, pt III, and for immediate London controversy around his memory and that of Cromwell, Brigden, *London and the Reformation*, 322–4.   2. A. Ryrie, 'The strange death of Lutheran England', *JEH* 53 (2002), 64–92.   3. Marillac to the King of France, 6 August 1540, Kaulek (ed.), *Correspondance*, 210, *LP* 15 no. 953. The reference in Hall 2, 309–10, to Thomas Epsam, monk of Westminster, 'the last monk that was seen in his clothing in England', may in fact be a more accurate reference than Marillac's to an unnamed Carthusian who refused to relinquish his habit; the Carthusian and the monk of Westminster did die together, as is witnessed in Kingsford (ed.), 'Two London Chronicles', 16, though the punctuation there needs to be emended as it runs together the monk and Giles Heron, another victim.   4. File of London indictments, 17 July 1540, SP 1/243 ff. 45–64, *LP Addenda* 1 ii no. 1463, and see Brigden, *London and the Reformation*, 320–22; on Ferrar, Dickens, *Lollards and Protestants*, 150.   5. This includes Sir Richard Morison, who David Starkey asserted ('Intimacy and innovation', 114–15) was dismissed from the Privy Chamber at this time. Sowerby, *Renaissance and Reform*, pp. 143, 145, 150–51, gives good reasons for doubting this.   6. Brigden, *London and the Reformation*, 322–3, and see extended discussion in C. Boswell, 'The culture and rhetoric of the answer-poem, 1485–1625' (Leeds University PhD, 2003), 121–8; J. Hyde, 'Mid-Tudor ballads: music, words and context' (University of Manchester PhD, 2015).   7. H. Nicolas (ed.), *Proceedings and Ordinances of the Privy Council of England VII* (London, 1837), 3. Geoffrey Elton spent much of his career avoiding the obvious problems of this dating for his 'Revolution' thesis: see the initial statement of his argument in Elton, *Tudor Revolution in Government*, ch. 5.   8. The principal fragments are in Elizabethan transcripts by Robert Beale, now BL MS

Additional 48022 ff. 83–96; Ayris, 'Public career of Thomas Cranmer', 104–16, provides a calendar of the contents, likely a small fraction of the original. The Beale papers were in private hands until the 1950s and not properly catalogued in the BL when I first saw them in the late 1970s; many riches have emerged from them.   9. The grants are *LP* 15 no. 831[69] (23 June 1540) and *LP* 15 no. 831[83] (28 June 1540); cf. Lehmberg, *Later Parliaments of Henry VIII*, 107.   10. The advances of money for St Leger and Maltravers, respectively on 25 and 27 June, are in the King's payments at *LP* 16 no. 380, 188. For St Leger as prospective Deputy and Grey's anger, Thomas Allen to Cromwell, 20 October [1538], SP 60/7 f. 150, *LP* 13 ii no. 658.   11. Keepership of Leeds, 25 June 1540: *LP* 15 no. 942 [25], boosted with an extensive grant of Kentish lands the same day, *LP* 15 no. 942[36]. Clerkship of the Hanaper, 26 July 1540, *LP* 15 no. 942[111].   12. On Ryther, *LP* 15 no. 1027[41, 42], and on Henry Polstead, *LP* 15 no. 1027[43]; these three grants were all made on 28 August 1540. For the order to Ryther to give access to the archive, 23 January 1541, Nicolas (ed.), *Proceedings and Ordinances of the Privy Council of England VII*, 121.   13. Grant to Thomas Polstead, 3 August 1540, *LP* 15 no. 1027[15]; presentation of Bellasis, 29 August 1540, *LP* 15 no. 1027[46].   14. MacCulloch, *Thomas Cranmer*, 283.   15. String, 'Henry VIII's illuminated "Great Bible"'.   16. See payments to David Vincent, Edward Lloyd and Humphrey Orince, of the wardrobe of Beds, and Nicholas Bristowe, the King's clerk, *LP* 16 no. 380, 190.   17. Sir John Gostwick to the King, 9 July 1540, BL MS Cotton Appendix XXVIII ff. 127–31, *LP* 15 no. 862. For Gostwick's humiliation by the King in relation to Cranmer, see MacCulloch, *Thomas Cranmer*, 252, and for his activity against evangelicals in 1536, e.g. Francis Hall to Lord Lisle, 17 November 1536, SP 3/4 f. 4, *Lisle Letters* 3 no. 783, 515–16, and John London to Gostwick, November 1536, SP 1/112 f. 30, *LP* 11 no. 1183.   18. *LP* 21 i no. 970[18] (9 May 1546).   19. Challis, *Tudor Coinage*, especially 82–6, 118–28. His account gives no especial reason to associate Cromwell with the debasement which began in 1542, and good reasons to associate it with Thomas Wriothesley. For incisive comment on the effects of debasement, see R. W. Hoyle, 'Place and public finance', *TRHS* 6th series 7 (1997), 197–215.   20. *LP* 16 no. 305[80].   21. Marillac to Constable Montmorency, 3 March 1541, Kaulek (ed.), *Correspondance*, 274, *LP* 16 no. 590.   22. Elizabeth Cromwell to Henry VIII, [autumn 1540], BL MS Cotton Vespasian F/XIII f. 262, *LP* 15 no. 940.   23. For the grant itself and its sequence of stages on 5 and 18 December at respectively Woking and Westminster, *LP* 16 no. 379[34]. For Marillac's description of the King's holiday at Woking with a small company, Marillac to the King of France, 4 December 1540, Kaulek (ed.), *Correspondance*, 246, *LP* 16 no. 311. For the movements of the Privy Council, see Nicolas (ed.), *Proceedings and Ordinances of the Privy Council of England VII*, 89–93; no proceedings were noted between 15 December (Whitehall) and 19 December (Hampton Court).   24. *LP* 19 ii no. 812[113] (30 June 1544): a lease of the forfeited moiety for twenty-one years.   25. A remembrance of late October 1539, BL MS Cotton Titus B/I f. 446, *LP* 14 ii no. 427. Gregory's grant of Launde is *LP* 16 no. 580[49] (8 February 1540).   26. For the Cromwells and their household amid the epidemic, see B. Winchester, *Tudor*

Family Portrait (London, 1955), ch. 10.   **27.** See various references summed up in Winchester, *Tudor Family Portrait*.   **28.** *HC 1509–1558* 1, 728. The dismissal of Gregory in Lehmberg, *Later Parliaments of Henry VIII*, 138, is just silly.   **29.** The notice of Lord Cromwell is in the heralds' account of the funeral printed in J. Strype, *Ecclesiastical Memorials, relating chiefly to Religion . . .* (3 vols., London, 1721), 2 ii 9; on the strategy around these opening months of Edward VI's reign, D. MacCulloch, *Tudor Church Militant: Edward VI and the Protestant Reformation* (London, 1999), 62–3. For his knighting, see Shaw, *Knights of England*, 1, 150.   **30.** *Calendar of Patent Rolls . . . Edward VI . . .* (6 vols., London, 1924–9), 4, 198–9: grant of 25 May 1548.   **31.** MacCulloch, *Thomas Cranmer*, 351–60.   **32.** The best summary account of this is Starkey, *Reign of Henry VIII*, 158–67.   **33.** For an absorbing analysis of his part in Surrey's fall, see S. Brigden, 'Henry Howard, Earl of Surrey, and the "conjured league"', *HJ* 37 (1994), 507–37.   **34.** For my account of the whole Edwardian revolution, see MacCulloch, *Tudor Church Militant*, and for a microscopic examination of the Zürich link, MacCulloch, 'Heinrich Bullinger and the English-speaking world'.   **35.** Washington, DC, Folger Shakespeare Library, MS V.b.303, 183–6, quoted in P. Collinson, 'Puritans, men of business and Elizabethan Parliaments', *Parliamentary History* 7 (1988), 187–211, at 192.   **36.** See D. MacCulloch, 'The Church of England and international Protestantism, 1530–1570', in A. Milton (ed.), *The Oxford History of Anglicanism I: Reformation and Identity, c. 1520–1662* (Oxford, 2017), 316–32.   **37.** For a more extended consideration of this theme, see D. MacCulloch, 'The latitude of the Church of England', in K. Fincham and P. Lake (eds.), *Religious Politics in Post-Reformation England: essays in honour of Nicholas Tyacke* (Woodbridge, 2006), 41–59.   **38.** *Complete Peerage* 12 ii, 764n.   **39.** An excellent analyis of how Elton's thesis came into being, and its historiographical antecedents, is I. Harris, 'Some origins of a Tudor Revolution', *EHR* 126 (2011), 1355–85.   **40.** I. Cooper, 'The speed and efficiency of the Tudor south-west's royal post-stage service', *History* 99 (2014), 754–74, at 758.   **41.** A fine overview of the importance of John ap Rhys is provided by the introduction to J. Prise, *Historiae Britannicae Defensio / A Defence of the British History*, ed. and trans. C. Davies (Oxford, 2015).   **42.** Ellis, 'Thomas Cromwell and Ireland, 1532–1540', 517.   **43.** Bradshaw, *Irish Constitutional Revolution*, 130–32, 193–4.   **44.** S. G. Ellis, *Defending English Ground: war and peace in Meath and Northumberland 1460–1542* (Oxford, 2015), 130–33.   **45.** Browne's story is absorbingly laid out in Murray, *Enforcing the English Reformation in Ireland*, particularly ch. 4. For comparison on government concessions, see M. L. Bush, 'A progress report on the Pilgrimage of Grace', *History* 90 (2005), 566–78, particularly at 576.   **46.** Speight, 'The politics of good governance', 625; D. MacCulloch, 'The consolidation of England, 1485–1603', in J. Morrill (ed.), *The Oxford Illustrated History of Tudor and Stuart England* (Oxford and New York, 1996), 35–52, particularly 41–5.   **47.** C. S. L. Davies, 'The Cromwellian decade: authority and consent', *TRHS* 6th series 7 (1997), 177–95, at 186.   **48.** G. R. Elton, 'Tudor government: the points of contact', in Elton, *Studies* 3, 3–57, especially 4–21, though see some useful qualification from a medieval point of view in Cavill, *English Parliaments of*

Henry VII, 128–31.   **49.** Lehmberg, *Later Parliaments of Henry VIII*, 75–8; G. R. Elton, 'Henry VIII's Act of Proclamations', in Elton, *Studies* 1, 339–54.   **50.** Fletcher and MacCulloch, *Tudor Rebellions*, 54–5.   **51.** For what follows where not otherwise referenced, Fletcher and MacCulloch, *Tudor Rebellions*, 66–7.   **52.** William Cavendish to Cromwell, 5 September 1536, SP 1/106 f. 136, *LP* 11 no. 406.   **53.** A. H. Smith, *County and Court: government and politics in Norfolk, 1558–1603* (Oxford, 1974), 27, 247–53.   **54.** *HC 1558–1603* 3, 539–40, s.v. Ughtred, Henry; *Complete Peerage* 3, 557–9.   **55.** L. Busfield, 'Protestant epistolary counselling in early modern England, *c.* 1559–1660' (University of Oxford DPhil, 2016), 212, and see also R. Spalding, *Contemporaries of Bulstrode Whitelocke 1605–1675* (Records of Social and Economic History new series 14, 1990), 465.

Index